Modern
REAL ESTATE
Practice in North Carolina

EIGHTH EDITION UPDATE

Fillmore W. Galaty

Wellington J. Allaway

Robert C. Kyle

Deborah B. Carpenter, DREI, Contributing Author

This publication is designed to provide accurate and authoritative information in regard to the subject matter covered. It is sold with the understanding that the publisher is not engaged in rendering legal, accounting, or other professional advice. If legal advice or other expert assistance is required, the services of a competent professional should be sought.

President: Dr. Andrew Temte
Chief Learning Officer: Dr. Tim Smaby
Executive Director, Real Estate Education: Melissa Kleeman-Moy
Development Editor: Rosita Hernandez

MODERN REAL ESTATE PRACTICE IN NORTH CAROLINA EIGHTH EDITION UPDATE
©2014 Kaplan, Inc.
Published by DF Institute, Inc., d/b/a Dearborn Real Estate Education
332 Front St. S., Suite 501
La Crosse, WI 54601

All rights reserved. The text of this publication, or any part thereof, may not be reproduced in any manner whatsoever without written permission from the publisher.

Printed in the United States of America

ISBN: 978-1-4754-2182-8 / 1-4754-2182-6
PPN: 1510-669A

Contents

Preface   x
Acknowledgments   xii

CHAPTER 1
Basic Real Estate Concepts   1
Introduction   1
General Characteristics of Real Estate   2
General Concepts of Land Use and Investment   5
The Scope of the Real Estate Business   7
The Real Estate Market   10
Related Websites   13
Key Point Review   14
Questions   16

CHAPTER 2
Property Ownership and Interests   18
The Concept of Property   19
Estates in Real Property   26
Ownership of Real Property   32
Related Websites   39
Key Point Review   39
Questions   43

CHAPTER 3
Encumbrances on Real Property   46
Encumbrances on Real Property   46
Property Taxation   53
Key Point Review   58
Questions   60

CHAPTER 4
Property Description   63
Describing Land   63
Methods of Describing Real Estate   64
Related Website   73
Key Point Review   73
Questions   74

CHAPTER 5

Transfer of Title to Real Property 78

Methods of Transferring Title 78
Title Records 93
Public Records 94
Title Assurance 96
Related Website 101
Key Point Review 101
Questions 104

CHAPTER 6

Land-Use Controls 107

Public Land-Use Controls 108
Privately Imposed Land-Use Controls 119
Government Ownership 121
Related Websites 121
Key Point Review 121
Questions 123

CHAPTER 7

Real Estate Brokerage and the Law of Agency 126

Introduction to Brokerage and Agency 127
The Law of Agency 127
General Agency Definitions 128
Brokerage Defined 129
Agency Relationships 132
Agency Disclosure in North Carolina 139
Duties and Liabilities of Agents 145
Duties and Liabilities of Principals 153
Nature of the Brokerage Business 154
Related Websites 155
Key Point Review 156
Questions 159

CHAPTER 8

Basic Contract Law 163

Contracts 163
Performance of Contract 169
Broker's Authority to Prepare Documents 171
Key Point Review 173
Questions 175

CHAPTER 9

Agency Contracts 178

Agency Contracts and Practices for Working with Sellers 178
The North Carolina Residential Property Disclosure Act 197
Working with Buyers 199
Working as a Dual Agent 203
Related Websites 204
Key Point Review 204
Questions 208

CHAPTER 10
Sales Contracts and Practices 211
The Sales Contract 211
Installment Land Contract 226
Option to Purchase Real Estate 228
Related Websites 230
Key Point Review 230
Questions 232

CHAPTER 11
Landlord and Tenant 235
Leasing Real Estate 236
Leasehold (Nonfreehold) Estates 236
Types of Leases 238
Lease Provisions 240
North Carolina Residential Rental Agreements Act 244
Laws Protecting Tenants in Foreclosure Situations 247
Tenant Security Deposit Act 248
Constitutional Rights of Tenants in Public Housing 250
North Carolina Vacation Rental Act 250
Other Landlord/Tenant Rules 250
Related Websites 251
Key Point Review 251
Questions 254

CHAPTER 12
Property Management 257
Property Management 257
Functions of the Property Manager 259
Property Management Fee 261
Typical Property Management Duties 261
Risk Management for Property Managers 269
Related Websites 271
Key Point Review 271
Questions 273

CHAPTER 13
Real Estate Financing: Principles 275
Basis Mortgage Terms and Concepts 276
Security and Debt 276
The Promissory Note 278
Mortgage Loan Repayment Plans 285
The Mortgage (or Deed of Trust) Instrument 288
Related Websites 298
Key Point Review 298
Questions 301

CHAPTER 14
Real Estate Financing: Practices 304
Introduction to the Real Estate Financing Market 305
Types of Mortgage Loans 311
Residential Lending Practices and Procedures 321
Financing Legislation 327
Related Websites 330
Key Point Review 330
Questions 334

CHAPTER 15
Closing the Real Estate Transaction 338
Preclosing Procedures 338
Conducting the Closing 343
RESPA Requirements 345
Preparation of Settlement Statement 348
Prorations 354
Sample Settlement Statement 360
Related Websites 370
Key Point Review 370
Questions 372
Settlement Statement Problem 374

CHAPTER 16
Basic Residential Construction 375
Architectural Types and Styles 376
Foundations 376
Framing 378
Elements of Construction 378
HVAC 384
Government Regulation 385
Related Website 386
Key Point Review 386
Questions 387

CHAPTER 17
Real Property Valuation 388
Appraising 389
Value 390
The Appraisal Process 393
Approaches to Value (Appraisal Methods) 398
The Profession of Appraising 408
Related Websites 409
Key Point Review 409
Questions 411

CHAPTER 18
Property Insurance 415
Basic Insurance Concepts 415
Homeowners' Insurance 416
Related Websites 421
Key Point Review 421
Questions 423

CHAPTER 19
Federal Income Taxation of Real Property Ownership 425
Introduction 425
Tax Benefits for Homeowners 426
Tax Benefits of Selling Real Property 426
Tax Benefits of Real Estate Investment 430
Related Website 434
Key Point Review 434
Questions 436

CHAPTER 20
Fair Housing and Ethical Practices 439
Equal Opportunity in Housing 439
Federal Fair Housing Act 440
Equal Credit Opportunity Act 447
North Carolina Fair Housing Act of 1983 447
Sexual Harassment 448
Implications for Brokers 448
Americans with Disabilities Act 450
Fair Housing Prohibited Practices 451
Professional Ethics 454
Related Websites 455
Key Point Review 455
Questions 458

CHAPTER 21
Environmental Issues and the Real Estate Transaction 461
Environmental Issues 462
Hazardous Substances 462
CERCLA and Environmental Protection 473
North Carolina Environmental Issues 474
Liability of Real Estate Professionals 475
Related Websites 477
Key Point Review 477
Questions 480

CHAPTER 22
Basic Real Estate Investment 482
Investing in Real Estate 482
The Investment 484
Leverage 485
Calculating Profitability 486
Forms of Business Ownership (for Investment Purposes) 488
Related Websites 489
Key Point Review 490
Questions 492

APPENDIX A
Study Tips and Comprehensive Practice Examination 493
Preparing for the Exam 493
Comprehensive Practice Exam 496

APPENDIX B
Residential Square Footage Guidelines 509

APPENDIX C
Real Estate License Law and Commission Rules 534
Key Point Review 611
Questions 615

APPENDIX D
North Carolina Real Estate Forms 619

Math FAQs 705
Glossary 765
Answer Key 789
Index 802

Preface

Since its first printing in 1994, *Modern Real Estate Practice in North Carolina* has provided thousands of readers with valuable real estate information, presented in a logical and accessible manner. Specifically tailored to North Carolina law and practice, *Modern Real Estate Practice in North Carolina* sets the standard for real estate textbooks, whether it is used to prepare for the licensing examination, for a college or university program, or simply for personal knowledge.

FEATURES

Real estate students and instructors alike will appreciate the following features:

- Each chapter opens with **learning objectives** that list what concepts and information you should be able to identify, describe, explain, and distinguish when you have finished.
- **Key terms** are provided at the beginning of each chapter. This feature identifies terms to watch for as you read and helps you study and review as well.
- **Margin notes** serve as memory prompts for more efficient and effective studying of important concepts and vocabulary.
- **For example** scenarios help illustrate how issues like fair housing, agency, and brokerage affect real estate professionals and real estate transactions.
- **Chapter review** and **sample exam questions** feature many fact-patterned problems that encourage you to understand and apply information rather than just memorize it.
- **Math FAQs: Answers to Your Most Frequently Asked Real Estate Math Questions** helps you apply the basic math principles that real estate professionals use when working with clients or customers. In addition, **math rationales** are included in the answer key for the chapter quizzes.
- **Quick Math Reference** is a great time-saving reference tool. The most frequently used real estate math equations are printed inside the front and back covers of the book.

FEATURES OF THE EIGHTH EDITION UPDATE

- **Legislative updates.** Content throughout the chapters and questions and answers reflects the latest changes to North Carolina Real Estate License Law and Commission Rules.
- **Key Point Reviews** are chapter summaries organized into key point, bulleted reviews providing you with a quick review tool of the most essential content covered in each chapter.
- **Forms Appendix:** Important North Carolina forms subject to change are placed in a separate appendix in the order encountered in a basic residential sales transaction with other purpose forms following.

- **Questions and answers** in the chapter quizzes and the practice exam reflect the current economic climate.
- **Web links** are updated and placed at the end of each chapter for easy reference.
- **New topics** have been added including: Oil and Gas Rights Disclosure, North Carolina Broker Price Opinion Law, Commercial Real Estate Broker Lien Act, Consumer Financial Protection Bureau, and more.
- **Content updates** are incorporated throughout the book and include: expanded coverage of the revised forms, easements, condemnation process, standard practices of a listing agent and a buyer's agent, working with out-of-state brokers, property management including laws affecting tenants in foreclosure situations, specific performance, standard addenda to the sales contract, secondary market update, loan qualification, buyer's due diligence process, and broker price opinions.
- **Study and exam tips** to help students prepare for, take, and pass the real estate exam are contained in **Appendix A**, preceding the practice exam.

One thing, however, has stayed the same. As in the first seven editions, the goal of *Modern Real Estate Practice in North Carolina*, Eighth Edition Update, is to help you understand the dynamics of the real estate industry and prepare you for the licensing exam. In this edition, we have met that challenge, providing you with the critical information you need to pass the real estate examination, buy or sell property, or establish a real estate career.

Acknowledgments

■ CONTRIBUTING AUTHOR

The publishers would like to thank Deborah B. Carpenter of Raleigh, North Carolina, who served as contributing author for the Eighth Edition Update of *Modern Real Estate Practice in North Carolina*. From her first interaction as a reviewer on the Fifth Edition, Deb has developed an intimate acquaintance with and understanding of the material in this textbook. Deb worked as a Consulting Editor on the Sixth Edition and became a Contributing Author in the Seventh Edition and Seventh Edition Update of *Modern Real Estate Practices in North Carolina*.

As the owner and lead instructor of Real Estate Success Academy, Deb's passion for teaching has helped countless students prepare for a successful career in real estate. Deb is a two-time recipient of the North Carolina Educator of the Year Award and the NCREEA President's Award for Exceptional Service. She also holds the highly respected Distinguished Real Estate Educator (DREI) designation for excellence in classroom instruction. Deb has served with the Real Estate Educators Association (REEA) and the North Carolina Real Estate Educators Association (NCREEA) in many leadership positions, including past president of the NCREEA. In her position as broker-in-charge of a large Keller Williams Market Center in Cary, NC, Deb keeps on top of current market trends and concerns.

■ REVIEWERS

For their input in the development of the Eighth Edition Update, the authors wish to thank the following individuals:

- Deborah H. Long, DREI, EdD, Long Talks and Fonville Morisey Center for Real Estate Studies
- Sherry Steele, Kaplan Professional Schools, Colorado

Each new edition of *Modern Real Estate Practice in North Carolina* builds on earlier editions. For their input in the development of the Eighth Edition, the authors wish to thank the following individuals:

- Larry A. Outlaw, Director of Education and Licensing, North Carolina Real Estate Commission
- Tricia Moylan, Legal Education Officer, North Carolina Real Estate Commission
- Deborah H. Long, DREI, EdD, Long Talks and Fonville Morisey Center for Real Estate Studies

CHAPTER 1

Basic Real Estate Concepts

■ **LEARNING OBJECTIVES** *When you have finished reading this chapter, you should be able to*

- ■ **describe** the physical and economic characteristics of real property; the concept of land use and development, including highest and best use; and the advantages and disadvantages of real estate investments.

- ■ **identify** the various careers and areas of real estate specializations and the professional organizations that support them.

- ■ **explain** the operation of supply and demand in the real estate market.

- ■ **define** these *key terms:*

broker	highest and best use	provisional broker
business cycles	land	real estate
chattel	market	real property
demand	nonhomogeneity	situs
heterogeneity	personal property	supply
	personalty	

■ **INTRODUCTION**

It is important that real estate students understand the basic characteristics of real estate, how real estate is used, and the real estate market. This chapter presents those fundamental concepts and lays the foundation for the exciting and challenging study of real estate practice.

GENERAL CHARACTERISTICS OF REAL ESTATE

There are two major classifications of property: real property and personal property. The distinction between these two types of property is an important one. **Real property** is defined as the land, everything that is permanently attached to the land, and everything that is appurtenant to (or goes with) the land. **Personal property**, or **personalty**, is considered to be all property that does not fit the definition of real property. The primary characteristic of personal property is movability. Items of personal property, also referred to as **chattels**, include such tangibles as furniture, clothing, money, bonds, and bank accounts. In other words, a *chattel* is *an item of movable personal property*.

Land, Real Estate, and Real Property

The words *land*, *real estate*, and *real property* are often used interchangeably. However, for a full understanding of the nature of real estate and the laws that affect it, brokers need to be aware of subtle yet important differences in meaning.

Land. Land is defined as the earth's surface extending downward to the center of the earth and upward to infinity, including things permanently attached by nature, such as trees and water (see Figure 1.1).

FIGURE 1.1

Land, Real Estate, and Real Property

Land
Earth's surface to the center of the earth and the airspace above the land, including the trees and water

Real Estate
Land plus permanent human-made additions

Real Property
Real estate plus "bundle of legal rights"

Land includes the minerals and substances below the earth's surface together with the airspace above the land up to infinity. The surface, subsurface, and airspace can be owned separately as surface rights, subsurface rights, and air rights and can be severed by separate conveyance. A specific tract of land is commonly referred to as a *parcel*.

Real estate. Real estate, or realty, is defined as land at, above, and below the earth's surface, including all things permanently attached to it, whether natural or artificial (see Figure 1.1). The term *real estate* is therefore somewhat broader than the term *land* and includes not only the physical components of the land provided by nature but also all human-made permanent improvements on and to the land. Land is referred to as *improved* when streets, utilities, sewers, and other improvements are brought to the land, therefore making the land suitable for building.

Real property. Real property is defined as the land itself, the improvements thereon, and the interests, benefits, and rights inherent in the ownership of real estate (see Figure 1.1).

The broader term *real property* includes the physical surface of the land, what lies below it, what lies above it, and what is permanently attached to it, as well as all the rights of ownership that are usually referred to as the bundle of legal rights (including the right to possession and use, right to exclude others, the right to profit from the land, and the right to dispose of or encumber the land).

IN PRACTICE When people talk about buying or selling houses, office buildings, land, and the like, they usually call all of these things real estate. For all practical purposes, the term is synonymous with real property, as defined here. Therefore, in everyday usage, real estate, or realty, includes the legal rights of ownership specified in the definition of real property.

Physical and Economic Characteristics of Real Property

Seven characteristics define the nature of real property and affect its use. These characteristics fall into two broad categories: physical characteristics and economic characteristics (see Figure 1.2).

FIGURE 1.2

Characteristics of Real Estate

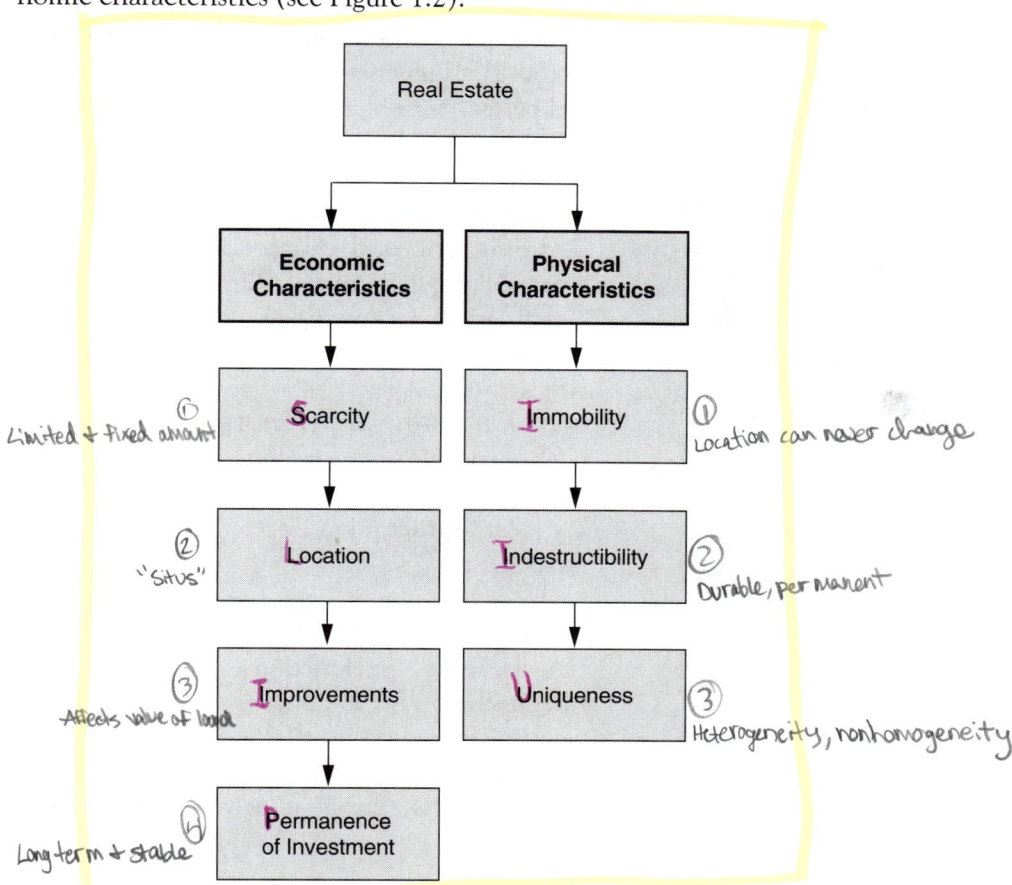

Physical characteristics. Land has three physical characteristics that set it apart from other commodities: immobility, indestructibility, and uniqueness.

Immobility. It is true that some of the substances of land are removable and that topography can be changed, but the geographic location of any given parcel of land can never be changed. Because land is immobile, the rights to use land are more easily regulated than are other forms of property use.

Indestructibility. Land is durable and indestructible (or permanent). The permanence of land, coupled with the long-term nature of the improvements placed on it, has tended to stabilize investments in land. However, while land is indestructible, the improvements on it depreciate and can become obsolete, thereby reducing values—perhaps drastically. (Depreciation should not be confused with the fact that a given location can become undesirable economically, therefore creating a decrease in market value.)

Uniqueness. No two parcels of land are ever exactly the same. Although they may share substantial similarity, all parcels differ geographically. The uniqueness of land is also referred to as its nonhomogeneity or heterogeneity. In fact, it is the uniqueness of each parcel of land that gives rise to the remedy of specific performance for the breach of a real estate contract. Under the doctrine of *specific performance*, the party harmed by the breach of a real estate contract can ask a judge to force the breaching party to carry out the terms of the contract rather than ordering the breaching party to pay monetary damages. Because each parcel of land is unique, monetary damages cannot compensate the damaged party for the loss of that particular parcel.

> **Three Physical Characteristics of Real Estate**
> 1. Immobility
> 2. Indestructibility
> 3. Uniqueness

Economic characteristics. The basic economic characteristics of land are the factors that influence its value as an investment: scarcity, location, improvements, and permanence of investment. (*SLIP* is the mnemonic.)

Scarcity. Although land is not thought of as a rare commodity, its total supply is fixed. Even though a considerable amount of land in the United States is still not used or inhabited, the supply of land in a given location (i.e., ocean front) or of a particular quality may be limited, therefore creating increased demand for that specific land. Because no more land can be produced, the increasing use of land has a positive impact on value.

Location (area preferences). Area preference, sometimes called *location*, refers to people's choices and tastes regarding a given area. Location is one of the most important economic characteristics of land. **Situs** is a related term regarding location that takes into consideration social factors in addition to economic factors.

Improvements. Any addition or change to land or a building that affects the property's value is referred to as an *improvement*. Improvements of a private nature, such as the house, fencing, et cetera, are referred to as *improvements* **on** *the land*, whereas improvements of a public nature, such as sidewalks, sewer systems, curbing, et cetera, are referred to as *improvements* **to** *the land*. Additions or alterations to the property that are merely repairs or replacements may not be considered to be improvements. Brokers should be aware that the term *improved land* has two meanings. If buildings are constructed on the land, the buildings can be considered *improvements*. If the land has been prepared for development, such as with grading, installation of utilities, et cetera, the land may be referred to as *improved land*.

Building an improvement on one parcel of land affects the value and utilization of neighboring tracts and can have a direct bearing on whole communities. For example, improving a parcel by constructing a shopping center or selecting it as the site for a nuclear power plant can directly influence a large area. Such land improvements can influence not only other parcels and other communities favorably or unfavorably, they may affect the use, value, and price of the land.

Permanence of investment. Once land is improved, the total capital and labor used to build the improvement represents a large fixed investment. Although even a well-built structure can be torn down to make way for a newer building or another use of the land, improvements to the land such as drainage, electricity, and water and sewer systems remain because they generally cannot be dismantled or removed economically. The owner has no way to transfer the investment to another parcel of land. The return on such investments, therefore, tends to be long-term and relatively stable. This permanence generally makes improved real estate unsuitable for short-term, rapid-turnover investing. A disadvantage of owning real estate is that it lacks liquidity.

> **Four Economic Characteristics of Real Estate**
> 1. Scarcity
> 2. Location
> 3. Improvements
> 4. Permanence of investment

GENERAL CONCEPTS OF LAND USE AND INVESTMENT

The various characteristics of a parcel of real estate affect its desirability for a specific use. For example, contour and elevation of the parcel, and availability of transportation and natural resources, such as water, all affect the use that can be made of a property, and the way in which a property is used has a dramatic impact on the value of that property.

Highest and Best Use

The **highest and best use** is the use that will give the owners the greatest actual return on their investment. Extensive studies are often prepared to determine whether a property is being properly utilized. For example, a highest-and-best-use study may show that a parking lot in a busy downtown area or a farm surrounded by urbanized land is not the current highest and best use of the property.

If a property can be put to its highest and best use, its value will be maximized. For example, if the highest and best use of a piece of property is as a high-rise office building rather than as a parking lot, changing its use accordingly will increase its value and also will give the owners the highest return on their investment.

Although a property can have only one highest and best use at any given time, the highest and best use can change. Because of changes in socioeconomic conditions, a property's highest and best use may be a retail shopping center today but a large apartment complex five years from now.

Land-Use Controls

The potential uses of real property are limited by various land-use controls. Property owners cannot simply decide to tear down their single-family home and replace it with a convenience store. Chances are they would be violating a land-use law. The regulation of land use is accomplished through both public and private land-use controls, discussed in Chapter 6.

Real Estate as an Investment

Real estate, no matter what its use, is virtually always considered an investment. Customers often expect a real estate broker to act as an investment counselor. Though brokers should possess a basic knowledge of real estate investment, they should always refer a potential real estate investor to a competent accountant, lawyer, or investment specialist who can give expert advice regarding the investor's specific interest or objective.

So real estate practitioners can deal with customers on a basic level, real estate brokers should possess a rudimentary knowledge of real estate investment. Such knowledge begins with a brief examination of the traditional advantages and disadvantages of investing in real estate, as discussed in Chapter 22.

Advantages of real estate investment. Historically, well-located and fairly-priced real estate investments have shown a good rate of return, often higher than the prevailing interest rate charged by mortgage lenders. Theoretically, this means that an investor can use the leverage of borrowed money to finance a real estate purchase and feel relatively sure that, if held long enough, the asset will yield more money than it costs to finance the purchase. It should be remembered that part of the return must make up for the value lost by a depreciating asset, such as a building.

Most real estate values tend to keep pace with the rate of inflation. Such an inflation hedge provides the prudent real estate investor with relative assurance that if the purchasing power of the dollar decreases, the value of the investor's assets will increase to offset the inflationary effects. In addition, real estate entrepreneurs may enjoy various tax advantages, which are discussed in more detail in Chapter 22.

Disadvantages of real estate investment. Unlike stocks and bonds, real estate is not a liquid asset. This means that an investor may not be able to sell real estate quickly without taking a loss. Contrast this with the investor in stocks listed on the New York Stock Exchange, who needs only call a stockbroker to liquidate assets when funds are needed quickly. Even though a real estate investor may raise a limited amount of cash by refinancing the property, that property is usually listed with a real estate broker, and the investor may have to sell at a substantially lower price than full market value to facilitate a quick sale.

In addition, it is difficult to invest in real estate without some degree of expert advice. Investment decisions must be based on a careful study of all the facts in a given situation, reinforced by a broad and thorough knowledge of real estate and the manner in which it affects and is affected by the marketplace—the human element. Unsophisticated investors should seek legal and tax counsel before making any real estate investments.

Rarely can a real estate investor sit idly by and watch the invested money grow. Management decisions must be made. For example, should the investor manage the property personally or would it be preferable to hire a professional property manager? How much rent should be charged? How should repairs and tenant grievances be handled? Is sweat equity (physical improvements accomplished by the investor personally) required to make the asset profitable?

Finally, and most important, a high degree of risk often is involved in real estate investment. There is always the possibility that an investor's property will decrease in value during the period it is held or that it will fail to generate sufficient income to make it profitable. External influences beyond the investor's control may come into play in negative or positive ways, affecting the value of the investment.

■ THE SCOPE OF THE REAL ESTATE BUSINESS

Billions of dollars' worth of real estate is sold each year in the United States. Adding to this great volume of sales are rental collections by real estate management firms, appraisals of properties ranging from vacant land to modern office and apartment buildings, and the lending of money through mortgage loans on real estate.

Millions of people depend on some aspect of the real estate business for their livelihood. As the technical aspects of real estate activities become more complex, real estate offices require an increasing number of people properly trained to handle such transactions. Many professionals and business organizations, such as lawyers, architects, surveyors, accountants and tax specialists, banks, trust companies, and abstract and title insurance companies also depend on the real estate specialist.

Real Estate: A Business of Many Specializations

Despite the size and complexity of the real estate business, many people think of it as being comprised only of brokers. Actually, today's real estate industry employs millions of knowledgeable individuals who are well trained in specialty areas such as appraisal, property management, financing, development, counseling, and education. Each of these areas is a business unto itself, but every real estate professional must have a basic knowledge of all of these specializations to be successful.

Real estate brokerage. The business of bringing together people interested in completing a real estate transaction is called *brokerage*. Usually, the **broker** acts as an agent who negotiates the sale, purchase, or rental of property on behalf of others for a fee or commission. The commission, generally a percentage of the amount of the transaction, is usually paid by the seller in a sales transaction or by the owner in a rental transaction (although it can be paid by any party). Brokerage is further discussed in Chapter 7.

In North Carolina

North Carolina's real estate license law (G.S. 93A-1 & 2) stipulates that a person must be licensed as a real estate broker if he or she lists or offers to list; sells or offers to sell; buys or offers to buy; auctions or offers to auction; negotiates the purchase, sale, or exchange of; leases or offers to lease; or rents or offers to rent any real estate for others for compensation or the promise of compensation. The license law also requires that a **provisional broker** that engages in any of these activities must be under the supervision of a real estate broker-in-charge.

Appraisal. The process of estimating the value of a parcel of real estate is *appraisal*. Although brokers must have some understanding of valuation as part of their training, qualified appraisers are generally employed when property is financed or is sold by court order. The appraiser must have sound judgment, experience, a detailed knowledge of the methods of valuation, and be licensed as an appraiser. Appraisal is covered in Chapter 17.

Property management. Someone who handles the operations of a property for its owner is involved in *property management*. The property manager may be responsible for soliciting tenants, collecting rents, altering or constructing new space for tenants, ordering repairs, and generally maintaining the property. The manager's basic responsibility is to protect the owner's investment and maximize the owner's return on the investment. Property management is discussed in Chapter 12.

Financing. The business of providing the funds necessary to complete real estate transactions is called *financing*. Most transactions are financed by means of a loan secured by a mortgage or deed of trust by which the property is pledged as security for the eventual payment of the loan. This and other methods of real estate financing are examined in Chapter 13 and Chapter 14.

Property development. This specialty includes the work of developers, or subdividers, who purchase raw land, divide it into lots, build roads, and install *sewer systems*. *Property development* also includes the skills of architects and builders, who improve the building lots with houses and other buildings and who sell the improved real estate, either themselves or through brokerage firms. Property development is discussed in Chapter 6. House construction is discussed in Chapter 16.

Counseling. Providing competent independent advice and guidance on a variety of real estate problems is known as *counseling*. A counselor attempts to furnish the client with direction in choosing alternative courses of action. Increasing the client's knowledge is every counselor's function in rendering services.

Education. *Education* is the provision of information to both the real estate practitioner and the consumer. Colleges, universities, private schools, and trade organizations conduct courses and seminars on all aspects of the business, from the principles of the prelicensing program to the technical aspects of tax and exchange law.

Other areas. Many other specialties and professionals also are part of the real estate business. Practitioners associated with mortgage banking firms and those who negotiate mortgages for banks and savings associations are examples of professionals associated with these other areas of specialty. Members of corporate real estate departments as well as officials and employees of government agencies such as zoning boards and assessing offices are further examples.

Professional organizations. The real estate business has many trade organizations, the largest being the National Association of REALTORS® (NAR). Organized in 1908, NAR sponsors various affiliated organizations that offer professional designations to brokers and others who complete required courses (see Figure 1.3). NAR, along with the state and local boards, serves the interests of its members by keeping them informed of developments in their fields, publicizing

FIGURE 1.3

National Association of REALTORS® Institutes and Sample Professional Designations

Institute	Designation(s)
National Association of REALTORS® (NAR)	Graduate REALTORS® Institute (GRI) Certified International Property Specialist (CIPS) Certified Property Manager® (CPM®) Accredited Buyer Representative® (ABR®)
American Society of Real Estate Counselors (ASREC)	Counselor of Real Estate (CRE)
Commercial Investment Real Estate Institute (CIREI)	Certified Commercial Investment Member (CCIM)
Institute of Real Estate Management (IREM)	Accredited Management Organization® (AMO®) Accredited Resident Manager® (ARM®)
REALTORS® Land Institute (RLI)	Accredited Land Consultant (ALC)
Society of Industrial and Office REALTORS® (SIOR)	Professional Real Estate Executive (PRE)
Women's Council of REALTORS® (WCR)	Leadership Training Graduate (LTG)

[Handwritten note: ★ If you're an agent (licensee), you CAN become a Realtor. To be a Realtor, you HAVE to be an agent (licensee).]

the services of its members, improving standards and practices, and recommending or taking positions on public legislation or regulations affecting the operations of members and member firms.

The majority of local real estate associations throughout the United States and Canada are affiliated with NAR. Members of the North Carolina Association of REALTORS® (NCAR) and affiliated local boards subscribe to the association's strict Code of Ethics and are entitled to be known as REALTORS® or REALTOR-Associates®. The term REALTORS® is a registered trademark. In North Carolina there are just under 90,000 licensed brokers, of whom approximately 41,000 are REALTORS®. All REALTORS® are brokers, but not all brokers are REALTORS®. Please do not confuse NCAR with the North Carolina Real Estate Commission (NCREC), which is the regulatory licensing agency of the state.

Among the many other professional associations is the National Association of Real Estate Brokers (NAREB), whose members also subscribe to a code of ethics. Members of NAREB are known as *Realtists*.

Five Categories of Real Property

1. Residential
2. Commercial
3. Industrial
4. Agricultural
5. Special-purpose

Uses of Real Property

Just as there are many areas of specialization within the real estate industry, there are many different types of property in which to specialize. According to its use, real estate can generally be classified into one of five categories:

1. *Residential*—all property used for housing, from acreage to small city lots, both single-family and multifamily, in urban, suburban, and rural areas
2. *Commercial*—business property, including offices, shopping centers, stores, theaters, hotels, and parking facilities
3. *Industrial*—warehouses, factories, land in industrial districts, and power plants
4. *Agricultural*—farms, timberland, ranches, and orchards
5. *Special-purpose*—churches, schools, cemeteries, and government-held lands

The market for each of these types of properties can be further subdivided into the *sales market*, which involves the transfer of title, and the *rental market*, which involves the transfer of space on a rental basis.

IN PRACTICE Although in theory a real estate broker or firm can perform all the services listed above and handle all five classes of property, this is rarely done except in small towns. Most real estate firms tend to specialize to some degree, especially in urban areas. In some cases, a real estate broker may perform only one service for one type of property. Residential property brokers and industrial property managers are two examples of such specialization.

■ THE REAL ESTATE MARKET

In literal terms, a **market** is a place where goods are bought and sold, where value for those goods is established, and where it is advantageous for buyers and sellers to trade. The function of the market is to facilitate this exchange by providing a setting in which the supply and demand forces of the economy can establish market value. The real estate market is a free market and is local in nature.

Supply and Demand

When supply increases and demand remains stable, prices go down.

When demand increases and supply remains stable, prices go up.

The economic forces of supply and demand continually interact in the market to establish and maintain price levels. Essentially, when **supply** increases, prices drop as more producers compete for buyers; when **demand** increases, prices rise as more buyers compete for the product.

Production slows or stops during a period of oversupply. When the market cannot meet the demand, production increases to take advantage of demand. Supply and demand are balanced at what is called the *point of equilibrium*.

■ **FOR EXAMPLE** Here's how one broker describes market forces: "In my 17 years in real estate, I've seen supply and demand in action many times. When a car maker relocated its factory to my region a few years back, hundreds of people wanted to buy the few higher-bracket houses for sale at the time. Those sellers were able to ask ridiculously high prices for their properties, and two houses actually sold for more than the asking prices! On the other hand, when the naval base closed and

2,000 civilian jobs were transferred to other parts of the country, it seemed like every other house in town was for sale. We were practically giving houses away to the few people who were buying."

Supply and demand in the real estate market. Characteristics of goods in the marketplace determine how quickly the forces of supply and demand will be able to achieve equilibrium. Such characteristics are the degree of standardization of the product, the mobility and financial stability of the product, and the mobility of the parties (buyer and seller).

Real estate is not a standardized product; no two parcels can ever be exactly alike. Each parcel of real estate is unique because it has its own geographic location.

Because real estate is fixed in nature (immobile), it cannot be moved from area to area to satisfy the pressures of supply and demand. Property buyers are also generally limited in their mobility—retirees are a major exception in regard to residences. For these reasons, the real estate business has tended toward local markets, where firms can maintain detailed familiarity with market conditions and available units. The increasing mobility of the population, the growing impact of new technologies in communication, and data handling have resulted in the geographic expansion of real estate firms.

Where standardization and mobility are relatively great, the forces of supply and demand balance relatively quickly. But because of real estate's characteristics of uniqueness and immobility, the real estate market is generally relatively slow to adjust. To a certain extent, the product can be removed from the market (as when a home offered for resale is withdrawn), yet an oversupply of product usually results in a lowering of price levels. Because development and construction of real estate take a considerable period of time from conception to completion, increases in demand also may not be met immediately. Building may occur in uneven spurts of activity owing to such factors.

Factors affecting supply. Factors that tend to affect supply in the real estate market include the labor force, construction costs, government controls, and monetary or financial policies.

Labor force and construction costs. A shortage of labor in the skilled building trades, an increase in the cost of building materials, or a scarcity of materials tends to decrease the amount of housing built or increase its cost. The impact of the labor force on price levels depends on the extent to which higher costs can be passed on to the buyer or renter in the form of higher purchase prices or rents. Technological advances that result in lower-priced materials and more efficient means of construction may tend to counteract some price increases.

Government controls and financial policies. The government's monetary policy can have a substantial impact on the real estate market. The Federal Reserve Board (the Fed) establishes a discount rate of interest for the money it lends to commercial banks. That discount rate has direct impact on the interest rates the banks charge to borrowers, which in turn plays a significant part in people's ability to buy homes. The Federal Housing Administration (FHA) and the Government National Mortgage Association (Ginnie Mae) can also affect the amount of money available to lenders for mortgage loans.

In 2008, America's greatest challenge became the uncertainty of the financial institutions. Until then, the Federal National Mortgage Association (Fannie Mae) and the Federal Home Loan Mortgage Corporation (Freddie Mac), which were private companies under congressional charter, had been the driving force of monies to provide loans to low-, moderate-, and middle-income families. Failed judgments in buying mortgages on the secondary market and irregular accounting practices contributed to the unpredictable and chaotic real estate market in 2009. This resulted in the federal government taking over Freddie Mac and Fannie Mae by placing them into conservatorship.

Virtually any government action has some effect on the real estate market. For instance, federal environmental regulations may increase or decrease the supply and value of land in a local market. Real estate taxation is one of the primary sources of revenue for local governments. Policies on taxation of real estate can have either positive or negative effects. High taxes may deter investors. On the other hand, tax incentives can attract new businesses and industries. Of course, along with these enterprises come increased employment and expanded residential real estate markets.

At the local level, real estate taxation is one of the primary sources of revenue for government. Policies on taxation of real estate can have either positive or negative effects. Tax incentives have been one way for communities to attract new businesses and industries to their areas. And, of course, along with these enterprises come increased employment and expanded residential real estate markets.

Local governments also can affect market operations and the development and construction of real estate by applying land-use controls. Building codes and zoning ordinances are used by communities to control the use of land. Real estate values and markets are thereby stabilized. Community amenities—for example, churches, schools, and parks—and efficient government policies are influential factors affecting the real estate market. Local governments can negatively influence development by imposing excessive fees or overly restrictive zoning and building codes.

Factors affecting demand. Factors that tend to affect demand in the real estate market include population, demographics, and employment and wage levels.

Population. Because shelter (whether in the form of owned or rented property) is a basic human need, the general need for housing grows as the population grows. Even though the total population of the country may continue to increase, growth is not uniform. Some areas grow faster than others, and some do not grow at all. Some places have become modern-day ghost towns, where the exhaustion of natural resources or the termination of an industrial operation has resulted in a mass exodus.

Demographics. Not only population but the makeup of that population—demographics—affects demand. Family size and the ratio of adults to children; the number of people moving into assisted care facilities and retirement communities;

the effect of doubling up, where two or more families use one housing unit; and the changing number of single-parent households all contribute to the amount and type of housing needed. Also pertinent are the number of young people who would prefer to rent or own their own residences, but for economic reasons, have roommates or remain in their parents' homes.

Employment and wage levels. Home ownership and rental decisions are closely related to the ability to pay. Employment opportunities and wage levels in a small community can be affected drastically by decisions made by major employers in the area. Individuals involved in the real estate market in such communities must keep well informed about the business plans of local employers.

To estimate how changes in wage levels will affect people's decisions concerning real estate, it is also important to look for trends in how individual income is likely to be used. General trends in the economy (availability of mortgage money, interest rates, rate of inflation, and the like) will influence an individual's spending decisions.

Business cycles. The upward and downward fluctuations in business activity are called **business cycles**. Although business cycles often seem to recur within a certain number of years, they are actually caused primarily by forces such as population growth, taxes, interest rates, wars, and oil embargoes. A business cycle can generally be characterized by four stages: expansion, recession, depression, and revival. The movements of a cycle are usually gradual and indistinct.

The real estate cycle. As stated earlier, the real estate market is slow in adjusting to variations in supply and demand. Because one factor of a real estate cycle is building activity, the time lag between the demand for units and the completion of those units causes real estate cycles to peak after the rest of the economy does and to take longer to recover from depressed periods than do other economic sectors. The local character of the real estate market creates many local conditions that may not correspond to the general movement of a real estate cycle.

Governmental anticyclical efforts. Ever since the Great Depression of the 1930s, the federal government has attempted to establish fiscal and monetary policies to prevent extreme fluctuations in the business cycle. By increasing government spending during times of recession and taking money out of circulation through taxation and control of lending institutions during times of inflation/expansion, the government attempts to promote steady, gradual economic growth.

■ RELATED WEBSITES

Building Owners and Managers Association International: www.boma.org
Commercial Investment Real Estate Institute: www.ccim.com
Counselors of Real Estate: www.cre.org
Institute of Real Estate Management: www.irem.org
National Association of Exclusive Buyers Agents: www.naeba.org
National Association of Independent Fee Appraisers: www.naifa.com
National Association of REALTORS®:   www.realtor.org
North Carolina Association of REALTORS®:   www.ncrealtors.org

North Carolina Real Estate Commission: www.ncrec.gov
Real Estate Buyer's Agent Council: www.rebac.net
Real Estate Educators Association: www.reea.org
REALTORS® Land Institute: www.rliland.com
Society of Industrial and Office REALTORS®: www.sior.com
Women's Council of REALTORS®: www.wcr.org

■ KEY POINT REVIEW

Land
- is the earth's surface,
- extends downward to the center of the earth with subsurface rights, and
- stretches upward to infinity with air rights.

Real estate includes
- land at, above, and below the earth's surface, plus
- all things permanently attached to the land, both natural and man-made.

Real property includes
- interests,
- benefits, and
- rights that are automatically included in the ownership of land and real estate.

The **characteristics of real estate** include the following:
- Physical
  — Immobility
  — Indestructibility
  — Nonhomogeneity, or uniqueness
- Economic
  — Scarcity
  — Location (most important)
  — Improvements
  — Permanence of investment

Real estate brokerage is the business of bringing people together in a real estate transaction conducted by
- a **broker** who is a person or company licensed to list, lease, buy, exchange, auction, negotiate, or sell real property for others for compensation and who may be the agent of buyer, seller, or both, or
- a **provisional broker** who conducts brokerage activities on behalf of the broker.

Appraisal is the process of estimating a property's value (typically, market value) that is based on established methods and an appraiser's professional judgment and is regulated by the following:
- Licensing or certification is required for many federally related transactions.
- North Carolina requires licensing or certification for local transactions.

Property management is conducted by a **property manager**, a person or company hired to maintain and manage property on behalf of its owner whose

- scope of work depends on a management agreement, and
- basic responsibility is to protect owner's investment while maximizing the owner's financial return.

Financing is the business of providing the funds that make real estate transactions possible through

- mortgage or deed of trust loans secured by the property, and
- commercial banks, savings associations, mortgage bankers, and mortgage brokerage companies.

Property development involves splitting a single property into smaller parcels (subdividing) and constructing improvements on the land (development).

Counseling involves independent advice based on sound professional judgment.

Education provides real estate information to practitioner and consumer alike.

Types of real property include the following:

- **Residential**—single-family and multifamily
- **Commercial**—office space, shopping centers, stores, theaters, hotels, parking facilities
- **Industrial**—warehouses, factories, land in industrial districts, power plants
- **Agricultural**—farms, timberland, ranches, orchards
- **Special-purpose**—schools, places of worship, cemeteries, government-held property

The **real estate market** reflects principles of supply and demand, influenced by the uniqueness and immobility of parcels of real estate so that

- when the supply increases and demand remains stable, prices go down; and
- when demand increases and supply remains stable, prices go up.

The factors affecting the supply of real estate include the following:

- Labor force availability
- Construction and material costs
- **Government controls**—environmental restrictions, land use, building codes, zoning
- **Government financial policies** that impact interest rates and the money supply

The factors affecting the demand for real estate include the following:

- **Population**—some areas grow faster than others; some decline
- **Demographics**—family size, lifestyles, niche marketing
- **Employment and wage levels**—influence housing affordability

QUESTIONS

1. Which of the following *best* defines real estate?
   a. Land and the air above it
   b. Land and the buildings permanently affixed to it
   c. Land and all things permanently affixed to it
   d. Land and the mineral rights in the land

2. Which of the following is NOT a physical characteristic of land?
   a. Indestructibility
   b. Scarcity
   c. Immobility
   d. Uniqueness

3. The term heterogeneity refers to which of the following?
   a. Scarcity
   b. Uniqueness
   c. Mobility
   d. Indestructibility

4. Situs refers to
   a. view from the property.
   b. improvements made to the building site.
   c. societal factors that are related to the location.
   d. immobility of real estate.

5. Which of the following is NOT an economic characteristic of real estate?
   a. Indestructibility
   b. Scarcity
   c. Permanence of improvement
   d. Location

6. Which of the following physical and economic factors would a land developer take into consideration when determining the optimum use of a parcel of land?
   a. Transportation
   b. Available natural resources
   c. Contour and elevation
   d. All of the above

7. A theater or a hotel would be classified under the real estate category of
   a. residential.
   b. commercial.
   c. agricultural.
   d. industrial.

8. The demand for real estate is influenced by the
   a. number of real estate brokers in the area.
   b. ethnic makeup of neighborhoods.
   c. wage levels and employment opportunities in the area.
   d. price of new homes being built in the area versus the price of existing homes.

9. The designation REALTOR® refers to
   I. any licensed real estate broker.
   II. an active member of the National Association of REALTORS®.
      a. I only
      b. II only
      c. Both I and II
      d. Neither I nor II

10. Which of the following statements is/are TRUE of business cycles?
    I. Business cycles involve periods of expansion, recession, depression, and revival.
    II. The real estate business cycle is quicker to recover from depressed times than other business sectors.
       a. I only
       b. II only
       c. Both I and II
       d. Neither I nor II

11. All of the following factors tend to affect supply EXCEPT
    a. the labor force.
    b. construction costs.
    c. government controls.
    d. demographics.

12. Real estate can be a poor investment if
    a. the inflation rate is high.
    b. the investor plans to hold the investment for a long time.
    c. the investor needs ready cash.
    d. land values are appreciating in the area.

13. In general, when the supply of a certain commodity increases, prices
    a. tend to rise.
    b. tend to drop.
    c. tend to stabilize.
    d. can no longer be established.

14. In general terms, a market refers to which of the following?
    a. Place where goods are standardized for sell
    b. Amount of goods available at a given price
    c. Quality of goods available to the public
    d. Place where the value of goods is established

15. The demand for real estate in a particular community is LEAST affected by
    a. population.
    b. wage levels.
    c. employment.
    d. international trade.

16. The real estate market is considered local in character for all the following reasons EXCEPT
    a. land is fixed or immobile.
    b. consumers generally invest in real estate that is near their home or work.
    c. local controls can have a significant impact on the market.
    d. most people eagerly visit and invest in real estate in distant areas.

17. Highest and best use of real estate will
    a. maximize the property's value.
    b. stay constant throughout time.
    c. always be the property's current use.
    d. not be affected by local economic trends.

18. A major manufacturer of automobiles announces that it will relocate one of its factories, along with 2,000 employees, to a small town. What effect will this announcement MOST likely have on the small town's housing market?
    a. Houses will likely become less expensive as a result of the announcement.
    b. Houses will likely become more expensive as a result of the announcement.
    c. Because the announcement involves an issue of demographics, not of supply and demand, housing prices will stay the same.
    d. The announcement involves an industrial property; residential housing will not be affected.

19. A buyer is interested in a house that fits most of her needs, but it is located in a busy area where she is not sure she wants to live. Her concern about the property's location is called
    a. physical deterioration.
    b. area preference.
    c. permanence of investment.
    d. immobility.

20. A professional estimate of a property's market value, based on established methods and using trained judgment, is performed by a
    a. real estate appraiser.
    b. real estate broker.
    c. real estate counselor.
    d. home inspector.

CHAPTER 2

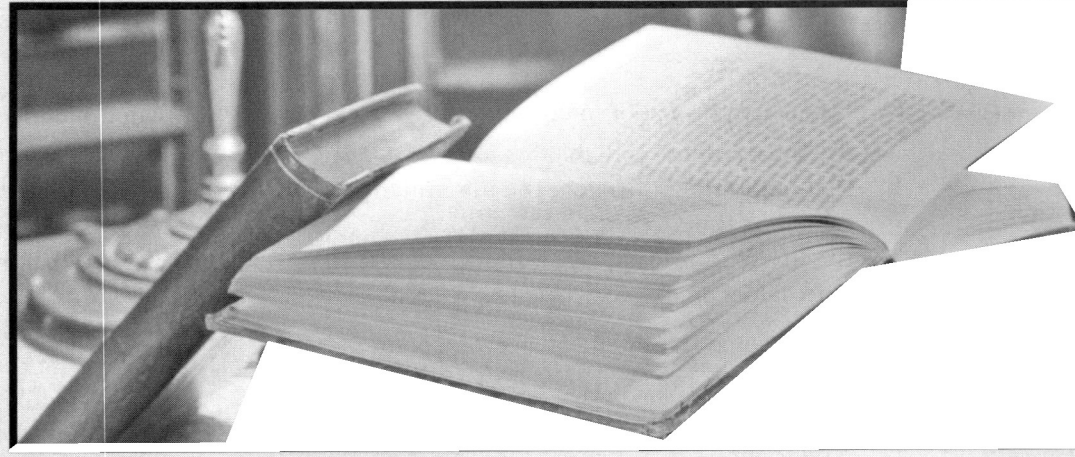

Property Ownership and Interests

■ **LEARNING OBJECTIVES** *When you have finished reading this chapter, you should be able to*

- ■ **explain** the concept of the *bundle of legal rights*; the characteristics of real estate; the types of freehold estates.

- ■ **describe** all types of fixtures and be able to identify items that may or may not be fixtures by applying all parts of the Total Circumstances Test.

- ■ **describe** the different types of real property ownership.

- ■ **define** these *key terms:*

accretion	fructus industriales	planned unit development (PUD)
agricultural fixtures	fructus naturales	proprietary lease
air rights	future interests	pur autre vie
appurtenance	homeowners association (HOA)	reliction
avulsion	homestead	remainder interest
bundle of legal rights	joint tenancy	remainderman
common elements	lateral support	reversionary interest
condominium ownership	life estate	right of survivorship
cooperative ownership	life tenant	riparian rights
emblements	limited common elements	severalty
erosion	littoral rights	subjacent support
estovers	manufactured home	subsurface rights
fee simple absolute	modular home	surface rights
fee simple defeasible	nonfreehold (leasehold) estates	tenancy by the entirety
fee simple determinable	North Carolina Condominium Act of 1986	tenancy in common
fee simple with condition subsequent	North Carolina Uniform Commercial Code (UCC)	time-share ownership
fixture		Total Circumstances Test
foreshore		town house ownership
freehold estates		trade fixture
		waste

THE CONCEPT OF PROPERTY

The unique nature of real estate has given rise to a distinctive set of laws and rights. Even the simplest of real estate transactions brings into play a complex body of laws, and brokers must understand not only the effect of these laws but also how the laws define real property.

The Bundle of Legal Rights

Real property is often described as a **bundle of legal rights.** This is a "legal relationship" between the owner and the property. In other words, a purchaser of real estate is actually buying the rights of ownership held by the seller. The rights of ownership (see Figure 2.1) include the

- right of *disposition* (to sell, will, transfer, or otherwise dispose of or encumber the property);
- right of *enjoyment* (to uninterrupted use of the property without interference of any third party claiming superior title);
- right of *exclusion* (to keep others from entering or using the property);
- right of *possession* (to use or occupy); and
- right of *control* (of the property and its profits within the framework of the law).

FIGURE 2.1

Bundle of Legal Rights

The concept of the bundle of rights comes from old English law and a population that, for the most part, could not read or write. Therefore, a seller transferred property by giving the purchaser a bundle of bound sticks from a tree on the property. This process was referred to as a *livery of seisin*. The purchaser who held the bundle also owned the tree from which the sticks came and the land to which the tree was attached. Because the rights of ownership can be separated and individually transferred, the sticks became symbolic of those rights.

Appurtenances

An **appurtenance** is defined as a right or privilege that goes with the ownership of land. These rights include subsurface rights (such as mineral rights), air rights, and water rights. A property owner is entitled to the right of lateral and/or subjacent support from adjacent landowners. The land may benefit from an appurtenant easement that will be discussed in Chapter 3. An improvement to the property, whether utility lines or a residential dwelling, is considered an appurtenance. The protective benefit of restrictive covenants also "runs with the land" like other appurtenant rights and will be covered in Chapter 6. An appurtenance is generally transferred with the property to the new owner.

Subsurface and Air Rights

Surface rights are simply the rights to use the surface of the earth. However, real property ownership also can include **subsurface rights**, which are the rights to use the space below ground level and to extract the natural resources lying below the earth's surface. Such natural resources might include minerals, coal, gas, oil, or water.

A transfer of surface rights may, however, be accomplished without the transfer of subsurface rights. For example, a landowner could sell the rights to any oil and gas found in the land to an oil company. The landowner then could sell his remaining interest. After the sale, the new buyer would own all the property except the oil and gas rights, which would be held by a third party: the oil company.

The rights to use the air above the land also may be sold or leased independently of the land. Such **air rights** are an increasingly important part of real estate, particularly in large cities, where air rights over railroads have been purchased to construct huge office buildings such as the Pan-Am Building in New York City and the Merchandise Mart in Chicago. To construct such a building, the developer must purchase not only the air rights but also numerous small portions of the land's surface for the building's foundation supports, called *caissons*.

Until the development of airplanes, a property's air rights were considered to be unlimited. Today, however, the courts permit reasonable interference with these rights, such as those necessary for aircraft, as long as the owner's right to use and occupy the land is not unduly lessened. Governments and airport authorities often purchase air rights adjacent to an airport to provide approach patterns for air traffic.

With the continuing development of solar power, air rights—more specifically, sun rights—have been redefined by the courts. They consider tall buildings that block sunlight from smaller solar-powered buildings to be interfering with the smaller buildings' sun rights.

In summary, one parcel of real property may be owned by many people, each holding a separate right to a different part of the real estate. These rights may be severed by separate conveyance. For example, while highly unlikely, there could exist at the same time

- an owner of the surface rights,
- an owner of the subsurface mineral rights,
- an owner of the subsurface gas and oil rights, and
- an owner of the air rights.

Water rights. One of the interests that may attach to the ownership of real estate is the right to use adjacent bodies of water.

In North Carolina

Riparian rights are granted to owners of land located along the course of a river, stream, or lake. Such an owner has the unrestricted right to use the water, provided such use does not harm owners upstream or downstream by interrupting or altering the flow of the water or by contaminating it. In addition, an owner of land that borders a nonnavigable waterway owns the land under the water to the exact center of the waterway. In North Carolina, the ownership of water and the land adjacent to it is determined by the doctrine of riparian rights. Land adjoining navigable rivers is owned only to the banks of the river in North Carolina (see Figure 2.2). Navigable waters are considered public highways on which the public has an easement or a right to travel.

FIGURE 2.2

Riparian Rights

Closely related to riparian rights are the **littoral rights** of owners whose land borders oceans and large, navigable lakes that have a tide. Owners with littoral rights enjoy unrestricted use of navigable waters but own the land adjacent to the water only up to the mean high-water mark (see Figure 2.3). All land below this point is owned by the government. (The strip of land between high and low tide lines, called the **foreshore,** belongs to the state of North Carolina. This makes all beaches in North Carolina publicly owned.)

In North Carolina

FIGURE 2.3

Littoral Rights

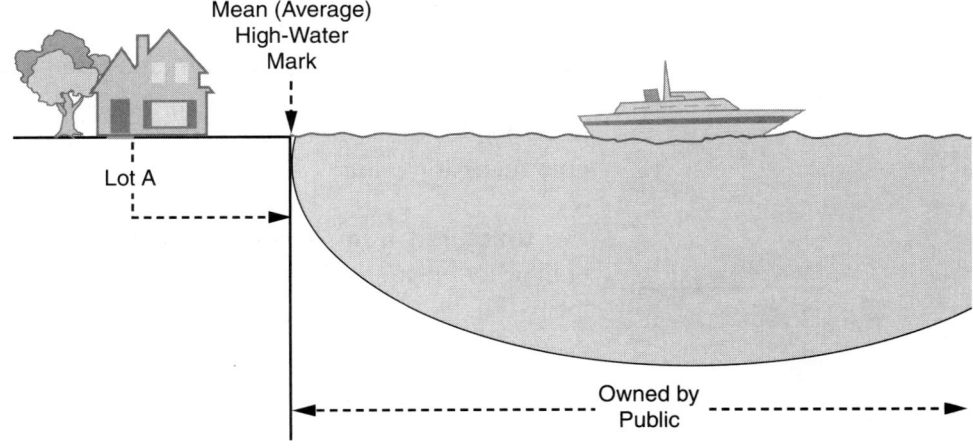

Riparian and littoral rights are *appurtenant* (attached) to the land and cannot be retained when the property is sold. This means that the right to use the water belongs to whoever owns the bordering land and cannot be retained by a former owner after the land is sold.

The boundaries of land can be affected by the natural action of the water. An owner is entitled to all land created by accretion, or a gradual increase in land resulting from the deposit of soil by the water. If water gradually recedes or disappears permanently, new land is acquired by reliction. Erosion, the gradual wearing away of land caused by flowing water or other natural forces, may cause an owner to lose land. When a sudden act of nature such as a flood or avalanche removes soil, this is known as avulsion. Loss of land by avulsion does not change the property boundaries, so the owner has the right to *reclaim* the lost land.

Support Rights

The owner of real property has the right to **lateral support,** or the right to have adjacent property support the natural boundaries of the land. Therefore, construction or excavation on a neighboring property should not cause the soil on the owner's property to subside.

As discussed above, occasionally the landowner severs the subsurface rights from the land and sells them. In such a situation, the property owner is entitled to **subjacent support** for the surface of the property from the owner of the subsurface rights. Therefore, any subterranean mining projects must assure continued support of the land's surface.

Real Property Versus Personal Property

As discussed in Chapter 1, *real property* is defined as the land, everything attached to the land, and everything appurtenant to the land. *Personal property* is defined as everything that is not real property. While the distinction between real and personal property is important to all real estate transactions, it is not always obvious. For instance, is a pile of lumber in the backyard of a house personal property or part of the real property? What about the drapes or an antique mirror attached to the wall of a home? If these items are considered personal property, they can be taken by the seller when he or she moves out of the house. On the other hand, if these items are considered real property, the buyer becomes their new owner and the seller cannot remove them. Real estate brokers must be careful to see that both parties to a real estate transaction understand clearly which items are real property and which items are personal property to prevent confusion and disappointment at closing.

> **In North Carolina**

Manufactured homes versus modular homes. A **manufactured home** is built according to the United States Department of Housing and Urban Development (HUD) construction standards and is defined by North Carolina General Statute §143-143.9(6) as:

> A structure, transportable in one or more sections, which, in the traveling mode, is eight feet or more in width or is 40 feet or more in length, or when erected on site, is 320 or more square feet, and which

is built on a permanent chassis and designed to be used as a dwelling with or without a permanent foundation when connected to the required utilities, and includes plumbing, heating, air conditioning, and electrical systems contained therein.

A manufactured home, sometimes referred to as a mobile home or house trailer, can be either personal property or real property. While the manufactured home is still mobile with its own wheels and chassis, it has a Vehicle Identification Number registered with the North Carolina Department of Motor Vehicles and is considered personal property. Manufactured housing is not considered real property just because the unit was placed on a residential lot. To convert the home into real property, the moving hitch, wheels and axles must be removed and the unit must be attached to a permanent foundation on land owned by the owner of the manufactured home. Once the owner files an affidavit confirming the aforementioned actions, the home is considered real property and an improvement to the lot.

Manufactured buildings, which include single-family **modular homes**, are governed by North Carolina General Statute §143-139.1. These units are constructed in factories off site according to state building codes and contain a label certifying compliance. Once the modular home is assembled on the home site, it is immediately considered to be real property.

Brokers should be able to differentiate between "manufactured homes" and "modular homes" when listing or selling such properties. The mandatory compliance labels from HUD for the manufactured housing and from the state for modular housing are usually found on the back exterior of the unit, under the kitchen sink, or near the electrical power box. Some older subdivisions have restrictive covenants that prohibit "house trailers," "mobile homes," or "manufactured homes" but do not strictly prohibit "modular homes."

> The legal term for plants that do not require annual cultivation (such as trees and shrubbery) is *fructus naturales* (fruits of nature); plant or crops that require annual cultivation are legally known as **emblements** or *fructus industriales* (fruits of industry).

Plants. Plants generally fall into one of two classes. Trees, perennial bushes, and grasses that do not require annual cultivation (*fructus naturales*—fruits of nature) are considered real property. Annual crops, such as wheat, corn, vegetables, and fruit, are known as **emblements** (*fructus industriales*—fruits of industry) and are generally considered personal property. In a lease situation, a tenant may re-enter the land after lease termination, if necessary, to harvest crops that result from the tenant's labor. But in a sales transaction, if an annual crop is growing, it will be transferred as part of the real property if no special provision is made in the sales contract.

It is possible to change an item of real property to personal property by *severance*. For example, a growing tree is real estate until the owner cuts down the tree and thereby severs it from the earth, or an apple becomes personal property once it is picked from a tree. Severance also may be the result of a contract. For example, if the owner of an apple orchard sells the apple crop while it is still ripening on the trees, the crop has been severed (and, therefore, turned into personal property) even though it is still physically attached to the trees.

It is also possible to change personal property into real property. If a landowner buys several azalea bushes, fertilizer, and mulch to landscape the front yard, the component parts, which were originally personal property, are converted into real property once planted and applied. They have become permanent improvements on the land. This process is called *annexation*.

Fixtures. In considering the differences between real property and personal property, it is important to be able to distinguish between a fixture and personal property.

An item that was once personal property but has been so affixed (or attached) to land or a building that the law construes it to be part of the real estate is a **fixture**. Examples of fixtures are heating plants, elevator equipment in highrise buildings, kitchen and bathroom cabinets, light fixtures, and plumbing fixtures. *If an item is a fixture, it automatically transfers with the property unless excluded by either party to the contract.* As a matter of fact, almost any item that has been added as a permanent part of a building is considered a fixture.

Legal tests of a fixture. The **Total Circumstances Test** is a legal test applied by the courts to determine whether an item is a fixture (and, therefore, part of the real property) or personal property. All four parts of the test must be applied, but intention is the major part of the test. These four tests are easy to remember by using the mnemonic IRMA:

1. **Intention of the annexor:** Did the person who installed the item intend it to remain permanently or to be removable? (The courts look at objective evidence of the party's intent, not the party's subjective intent. In other words, the courts look at the facts surrounding the situation and determine what a reasonable person would have intended by them.)
2. **Relationship of the annexor:** Is the person making the attachment an owner or a tenant? It is presumed that an owner intends a permanent attachment (the item becomes a fixture), while a tenant intends a temporary attachment (the item remains personal property). The greater the legal relationship the annexor has to the real property, the greater the likelihood the item will be declared a fixture.
3. **Method of annexation:** How permanently was the item attached? Can it be removed without causing damage?
4. **Adaptation to real estate:** Has either the item or the property been tailored to facilitate working together? Has it been customized or built in to the property?

Four Legal Tests of a Fixture
1. Intention
2. Relationship
3. Method of annexation
4. Adaptation to real estate

Although these tests seem simple, court decisions have not been consistent regarding what constitutes a fixture. Articles that appear to be permanently affixed have sometimes been held by the courts to be personal property, whereas items that do not appear to be permanently attached have been held to be fixtures.

In the sale of property, the one certain way to avoid confusion over the nature of an article is for the parties to enter into a written agreement that establishes which items are considered part of the real property. A real estate broker should ensure that a sales contract includes a list of all articles of personal property and fixtures that are being included in the sale, particularly if there is any doubt as to whether they are permanently attached fixtures. Articles that might cause confusion include freestanding appliances, invisible fencing and controls, light bulbs, above-ground pools, and swing sets.

IN PRACTICE The NCAR/NCBA Standard Form 2-T, "The Offer to Purchase and Contract," dated 2013, in paragraph 2, lists items that are normally fixtures and provides for items that may be exempted by the seller or buyer. "2. FIXTURES: The following items, if any, are deemed fixtures and are included in the purchase price free of liens: range/stove/oven, any built-in appliances, light fixtures, ceiling fans, attached floor coverings, blinds, shades, drapery rods and curtain rods, brackets and all related hardware, window and door screens, storm windows, combination doors, awnings, antennas, satellite dishes and receivers, burglar/fire/smoke/carbon monoxide alarms, pool and spa equipment, solar energy systems, attached fireplace screens, gas logs, fireplace inserts, electric garage door openers with controls, outdoor plants and trees (other than in movable containers), basketball goals, storage sheds, mailboxes, wall and/or door mirrors, fuel tank(s) whether attached or buried and including contents if any, as of Settlement, landscape and/or foundation lighting, invisible fencing including all related equipment, lawn irrigation systems and all related equipment, water softener/conditioner and filter equipment, and any other items attached or affixed to the Property, EXCEPT the following items which are leased or not owned by Seller or which Seller does not intend to convey: _____."

Trade fixtures. An article owned by a tenant and attached to a rented space or building for use in conducting a business is a **trade fixture**, or a chattel fixture. Examples of trade fixtures are bowling alleys, store shelves, bars, and restaurant equipment. Do not confuse trade fixtures, items a commercial tenant installs to further the tenant's business, with *up-fits*, such as walls or sinks installed by the landlord while preparing the property for the tenant's occupancy.

Trade fixtures differ from other types of fixtures in three ways:

1. Fixtures are part of the real property and belong to the owner of that property. Trade fixtures are usually owned and installed by a tenant for personal use and remain the tenant's personal property.
2. Fixtures are considered a permanent addition to a building, but trade fixtures are removable. Trade fixtures may be attached to a building in the same manner as other fixtures. However, due to the relationship of the parties (landlord and tenant), the law gives a tenant the right to remove trade fixtures, provided the removal is completed before the term of the lease expires and the rented space is restored to approximately its original condition.
3. Because fixtures are legally construed to be real property, they are included in any sale or mortgage of the real property. Trade fixtures are not included in the sale or mortgage of real property except by special agreement because they are considered to be personal property of the commercial tenant.

Trade fixtures that are not removed at the end of the lease become the real property of the landlord. Acquiring the items in this way is known as *accession*.

■ **FOR EXAMPLE** A pizza parlor leases space in a small shopping center. The restaurateur bolts a large iron oven to the floor of the unit. When the pizza parlor goes out of business or relocates, the restaurateur will be able to remove the pizza oven if the bolt holes in the floor can be repaired. The oven is a trade fixture. On the other hand, if the pizza oven was brought into the restaurant in pieces, welded together, then set in concrete, the restaurateur might not be able to remove it without causing structural damage. In that case, the oven might become a fixture.

26 Modern Real Estate Practice in North Carolina

| In North Carolina | **Agricultural fixtures.** There is a special class of fixtures in North Carolina: **agricultural fixtures**. While fixtures used in a farming operation would seem to fall into the category of trade fixtures, agricultural fixtures are considered real property rather than personal property. Therefore, in North Carolina, if a tenant farmer installed feeding troughs during the tenancy, they would be considered real property and could not be removed by the tenant at the end of the lease without special written agreement. |

| In North Carolina | **Effect of the North Carolina Uniform Commercial Code (UCC).** All brokers should be aware of the effect of the **North Carolina Uniform Commercial Code (UCC)** on fixtures. According to the UCC, if a homeowner purchases an item on credit (a dishwasher, for example) and gives the creditor a security agreement, that item remains personal property and may be removed by the creditor in the event of default. When the item has been paid for in full, it becomes real property. Suppose the homeowner decides to sell her home before the dishwasher has been paid for. She could remove the dishwasher when she moves out of the house because it is still her personal property. On the other hand, she may leave the dishwasher behind and the buyer might assume that it is real property that was included in the purchase price. The buyer may be surprised to learn that he must pay the secured creditor the outstanding balance or risk having the appliance repossessed. All home buyers should make sure there are no security agreements filed on items within the home. This is normally included in the title search, which the buyer's lawyer will perform. The filing of the security agreement in effect makes the potential fixture an item of personal property until it is paid for in full. |

■ ESTATES IN REAL PROPERTY

The amount and kind of interest that a person has in real property is called an *estate in land*. An *estate* may be defined as the degree, quantity, nature, and extent of interest one has in real property. Estates in land are divided into two major classifications: (1) nonfreehold estates or leasehold estates (those involving tenants' rights of possession) and (2) freehold estates (those involving rights of ownership) (see Figure 2.4). (Nonfreehold estates are discussed in detail in Chapter 11.)

FIGURE 2.4

Freehold Estates and Interests in North Carolina

```
                          Freehold Estates
                         /                \
            Estates of                    Estates Not of
            Inheritance                   Inheritance
           /     |      \                 /            \
    Fee Simple  Fee Simple  Estate for the   Conventional   Marital Life
    Absolute    Defeasible  Life of Another  Life Estate    Estate
                            (Pur Autre Vie)
                /        \
        Fee Simple    Fee Simple
        Determinable  Subject to a
                      Condition
                      Subsequent
```

Freehold estates are estates of indeterminable length of ownership, such as those existing for a lifetime or forever. Freehold estates are passed from grantor to grantee via the deed when title to real estate is conveyed. The types of freehold estates that can be transfered include

- fee simple estate (can pass by inheritance),
- defeasible fee estate (can pass by inheritance),
- *pur autre vie* estate (estate for the life of another) with remainder or reversion (can pass by inheritance), and
- ordinary conventional life estate with remainder or reversion (does not pass by inheritance).

The first three of these estates continue for an indefinite period and are inheritable by the heirs of the owner; they are called *estates of inheritance*. The fourth terminates on the death of the named person on whose life the estates are based, called the *measuring life*; they are called *estates not of inheritance*.

Nonfreehold, or **leasehold, estates,** which will be discussed thoroughly in Chapter 11, include any estate that is not a freehold estate. A leasehold estate exists on property in addition to a freehold estate when the property owner has rented the property to a tenant. The four types of leasehold estates are the

1. estate for years,
2. estate from year to year,
3. estate at will, and
4. estate at sufferance.

Fee Simple Estate

A holder of an estate in fee simple is entitled to all rights in the property. An estate in fee simple is the highest type of interest in real estate recognized by law. It is complete ownership. This estate is of potentially unlimited duration. When the owner dies, the estate passes to the owner's heirs or devisees (as provided in the owner's will). A fee simple estate is an estate of inheritance and is always legally transferable, but it is not always free of encumbrances. There are two major types of fee simple estates: *fee simple absolute* that basically has no ownership limitation and *fee simple defeasible* where the ownership can be terminated due to the actions of the current owner.

Fee simple absolute. A fee simple ownership on which there are no limitations (other than governmental restrictions) is a **fee simple absolute** estate. In common usage, the terms *fee* and *fee simple* are used interchangeably with fee simple absolute. Owners of a fee simple estate can do whatever they wish with the property as long as the use does not violate public land use regulations, deed restrictions, or the rights of others. This is the highest form of land ownership and is the type of estate conveyed via the deed in most real estate transactions.

> **Fee simple subject to a condition subsequent:**
> "on the condition that"
>
> **Fee simple determinable:**
> "so long as"
> "while"
> "during"

Fee simple defeasible. A **fee simple defeasible** (or *defeasible fee*) estate may be lost (or defeated) on the occurrence or nonoccurrence of a specified event. Also known as a *qualified fee estate*, the new owner must stay *qualified* to own the estate by obeying deed restrictions imposed on the estate by a previous owner. Whether the restriction prohibits an activity or requires a specified land use will dictate which type of defeasible fee estate has been granted. Two types of defeasible estates are *fee simple subject to a condition subsequent* and *fee simple determinable*.

(1) A **fee simple subject to a condition subsequent** estate dictates some action or activity that the new owner must not perform. The former owner retains a right of re-entry, called a *reversionary right*, so that if the condition is broken, the former owner can retake possession of the property through court proceedings. A fee simple estate with condition subsequent does not automatically revert to the original owner.

■ **FOR EXAMPLE** A grantor that deeds his land with the deed condition that there be no sale of alcohol on the premises is a fee simple subject to a condition subsequent. If alcohol is sold on the property, the former owner has the right to reacquire full ownership. It will be necessary for the grantor (or the grantor's heirs or successors) to go to court to assert that right. There is no automatic right of reversion.

(2) A **fee simple determinable** estate requires that a specified activity or land use continue. In a fee simple determinable estate, the ownership is held "so long as" or "during the period" the condition or limitation is maintained. The former owners, their heirs, or their successors retain the right of reversion that automatically reacquires full ownership if the special condition ceases to exist. No lawsuit is necessary for reversion. The use of the land has been pre-determined and the penalty for noncompliance has been predetermined.

■ **FOR EXAMPLE** When an owner grants land as a gift to a church, *so long as the land is used only for religious purposes*, it is known as a fee simple determinable. The church has the full bundle of rights in the property the grantor/owner had, including ownership, with the exception of one of the sticks in the bundle known as the *control "stick"* in this case. If the church ever decides to use the land for a nonreligious purpose, the property automatically reverts back to the original former owner or the heir without having to go to court.

It is important not to confuse the two estates. The difference between them is in the language used to create the estate and whether a court process is required for re-entry. A *fee simple estate subject to a condition subsequent* is conveyed *provided that*, or *on the condition that* some situation in the future does not happen. The language used for a *fee simple determinable estate* is based on time. It is conveyed *as long as*. Both of these defeasible estates are the same as far as possession and use are concerned. A real estate broker is strongly encouraged to have competent legal advice when encountering any qualified estate scenario, as only attorneys can create or interpret these types of estates.

Because they will take effect only at some time in the future (if at all), the right of re-entry and the possibility of reversion are called **future interests.**

Life Estate

A **life estate** is a freehold estate in land that is limited in duration to the life of the new owner or to the life or lives of some other designated person or persons. This form of ownership is occasionally called a partial estate because it does not last forever.

Conventional life estate. A conventional life estate is created by grant from the current owner of the fee simple estate. The current owner retains a reversionary interest in the property or names a *remainderman* that will ultimately receive fee simple absolute title (see Figure 2.5). A conventional life estate is limited to the lifetime of the new owner of the life estate (the **life tenant**). An ordinary life estate ends with the death of the person to whom it was granted (see Figure 2.6). It is possible to have successive life estates.

FIGURE 2.5

Remainder Interest

Grantor — Title → Life Tenant → Remainderman

FIGURE 2.6

Reversionary Interest

Grantor — Title → Life Tenant — Title → (back to Grantor)

■ **FOR EXAMPLE** A man wants his children ultimately to have ownership of a piece of property. But he wants his mother to be able to own it for as long as she lives. So he deeds the property to his mother for her life. The man's mother is the life tenant with her life being the measurement for how long she will own the estate; his children are the remaindermen. When she dies, the ownership of the property will automatically transfer to his children, who will then have a fee simple absolute estate.

Life estate *pur autre vie*. There is also an estate known as an *estate for the life of another*; the legal term being *life estate pur autre vie*. As with a conventional life estate, the life tenant owns the property. In this estate, it is owned for the lifetime of some named third party, called the *measuring life*. The measuring life has no present or future ownership in the property and only serves as the yardstick for the term of the life tenant's ownership. Upon the death of the measuring life, the estate would either revert to the original owner or become the property of the named remainderman. If the life tenant should die before the measuring life, the heirs of the deceased life tenant will inherit the life estate either by will or by descent.

■ **FOR EXAMPLE** Austin owns fee simple title to a property. He conveys a life estate to his brother Carl for the life of Carl's daughter. Carl has the right to enjoy the ownership of the property and is the life tenant, but the daughter is the measuring life. Should the daughter die, Carl's estate will terminate and revert to Austin or Austin's heirs. The daughter has no present or future ownership interest in the property.

While a conventional life estate is not considered an estate of inheritance, a life estate pur autre vie can be inherited by the life tenant's heirs, but only until the death of the measuring life. For example, if Carl died before his daughter, she and any other of Carl's heirs would inherit the life estate. However, the inherited life estate would terminate on the death of the daughter.

Remainder and reversion. A fee simple owner who creates a life estate must consider the future ownership of the property after the termination of the life estate. The future interest may take one of two forms:

1. **Remainder interest:** The grantor names someone other than the grantor to receive title to the property when the life estate terminates. This occurred in our example when a man provided that his children would receive title and a fee simple absolute estate once his mother's life estate terminated. The person(s) named (the children, in our example) is said to own a remainder interest and is called a **remainderman.** A **remainder interest** is a *nonpossessory estate*—a future interest. This interest can be sold. (See Figure 2.5)
2. **Reversionary interest:** If the grantor does not name a remainderman, then ownership returns to the grantor when the life estate terminates. This is called a **reversionary interest.** If the grantor is deceased when the life estate terminates, the property goes to the grantor's heirs or devisees. This interest or estate is called a *reversion* and is also a future interest. (See Figure 2.6)

When the life estate terminates, the holder of the future interest (the remainder or reversion) will be the owner of a fee simple absolute estate.

Rights of life tenants. A life tenant's interest in real property is a true ownership interest. In general, the life tenant is not answerable to the holder of the future interest as long as the property is maintained. A life tenant is entitled to all income and profits arising from the property during the life tenancy and, typically, is obligated to pay the property taxes and maintain homeowners insurance. A life tenant also may use some of the property's resources to maintain the property. For example, a life tenant may sell some of the timber growing on the property to pay for damages caused by a flood. This right to use property resources is referred to as **estovers**. A life tenant also can sell or mortgage a life tenancy, although there may be few parties willing to purchase or lend money that is secured by such a limited interest. Life tenants must pay real estate *ad valorem* taxes and special assessments that arise during the tenancy. They must also pay the interest, but not the principal, on any pre-existing debt secured by the property.

A life tenant's rights are not absolute, however. A life tenant can enjoy the rights of the land but cannot encroach on those of the reversioner or remainderman. In other words, the life tenant cannot perform any act that would permanently injure the land or property. For example, a life tenant would not be allowed to destroy an orchard on the property to avoid having to bother with it. This kind of injury to real estate is known in legal terms as **waste.** Those with a future interest in the property could bring legal action for damages or seek an injunction against the life tenant.

Legal life estate. A legal life estate is one created by statute rather than common law. It becomes effective automatically by operation of law on the occurrence of certain events. Homestead rights are an example of a legal life estate used in most states.

A **homestead** is a legal life estate in real estate occupied as the family home. In effect, the home (or at least some part of it) is protected from most creditors during the occupant's lifetime. In states that have homestead exemption laws, a portion of the acreage or value of the property occupied as the family home is exempt from certain judgments for debts, such as charge accounts and personal loans. The homestead is not protected from real estate taxes billed against the property or a mortgage for the purchase or cost of improvements; that is, if the debt is secured by the property, the property cannot be exempt from a judgment on that debt.

In some states, all that is required to establish a homestead is for the head of a household (which may be a single person) to own or lease the premises occupied as a primary residence. In other states, the owner is required by statute to file a notice of homestead rights. A family can have only one homestead at any given time.

In most states, the homestead exemption merely reserves a certain amount of money for the household in the event of a court sale. In a few states, however, the entire homestead is protected from sale altogether. Once the sale occurs, any debts secured by the home (a mortgage, unpaid taxes, or mechanics' liens, for instance) will be paid from the proceeds. Then the household will receive the amount reserved by the homestead exemption. Whatever remains will be applied to the household's unsecured debts.

In North Carolina North Carolina provides for a limited exemption for individuals from claims of creditors ($35,000; $60,000 for certain unmarried individuals age 65 or older) against a personal residence of the individual or his dependent (North Carolina Constitution, Article X, Section 2 and G.S.1C-1601). There is no exemption from a sale to pay taxes or from payment of an obligation contracted for the property's purchase (i.e., purchase money mortgage). Thus, this exemption applies basically to the enforcement of general judgment liens. Homestead exemptions in other states may be much more extensive than North Carolina's exemption.

OWNERSHIP OF REAL PROPERTY

Freehold estates define what rights are being conveyed with the real estate. Ownership of real estate defines who will hold the title and what form the ownership will take. Ownership may be held in (1) severalty, which means that title is held by one owner (sometimes referred to as *sole ownership*), or (2) co-ownership, cotenancy, or concurrent ownership, where title is held by two or more persons at the same time. The form of ownership will be noted in the purchase contract and then used in the deed to convey the property from the current owner to the new owner (in severalty) or owners (in one of the concurrent forms).

The manner in which the property title is held is important to the real estate broker for two reasons: (1) the form of ownership existing when a property is sold determines who must sign the various documents involved (listing contract, acceptance of offer to purchase or sales contract, and deed) and (2) the new purchaser must determine in what form to take title. For example, a sole purchaser generally takes title in the purchaser's name alone, and a tenancy in severalty is created. However, if there are two or more purchasers, they may take title in a tenancy in common, in joint tenancy, or in tenancy by the entirety. When questions about these forms of ownership are raised by the parties to a transaction, the real estate broker should recommend that the parties seek legal and tax advice.

Ownership in Severalty

When title to real estate is vested in (presently owned by) one person or a single entity, such as a corporation, or limited liability company (LLC), that person or entity is said to own the property in **severalty**. This person or entity is also referred to as the *sole owner*.

Concurrent Ownership

When title to one parcel of real estate is vested in two or more persons or entities, those parties are said to be *concurrent owners*, or *co-owners*, of the property. An important aspect to concurrent ownership is the unity of possession, which means no one tenant may possess a portion of the property and not allow access to the other tenants. For example, owner A cannot build a fence down the middle of the property and keep owners B and C from entering that side of the property. All owners have equal rights to all the property. There are several forms of co-ownership, each having unique legal characteristics. The three forms of concurrent ownership are

1. tenancy in common,
2. joint tenancy, and
3. tenancy by the entirety.

Tenancy in common. A parcel of real estate may be owned by two or more people/entities in what is known as a **tenancy in common**. An important characteristic of tenancy in common is that while co-owners have unity of possession, they may have unequal shares. This means that although a tenant in common may hold, for example, a one-half or one-third share in a property, it is impossible to distinguish physically which specific half or third of the property the tenant in common owns. The deed creating a tenancy in common may or may not state the fractional shares held by each co-owner; if no fractions are stated, the tenants are presumed to hold equal shares. For example, if five people hold title, each would own an undivided one-fifth share. Although ownership shares are frequently equal, it is not a requirement of this type of ownership.

The second important characteristic of a tenancy in common is that each owner holds an undivided interest in severalty and can sell, convey, mortgage, or transfer that interest through the right of partition. On the death of a co-owner, that tenant's undivided interest passes to the heirs through a probate proceeding. The interest of a deceased tenant in common does not pass to another co-owner tenant in common unless the surviving co-owner is an heir in the deceased owner's will or is purchasing the deceased owner's share (see Figure 2.7).

FIGURE 2.7

Tenancy in Common

A and B are tenants in common.

A ½ | B ½

B dies and wills his interest to C and D equally.

A ½ | C ¼ / D ¼

In states that do not recognize tenancy by the entirety (discussed later), when two or more people acquire title to a parcel of real estate and the deed does not stipulate the type of tenancy created, by operation of law, they acquire title as tenants in common. In states that recognize tenancy by the entirety, this would only apply if the parties taking title were unmarried.

Joint tenancy. Most states recognize some form of **joint tenancy** in property owned by two or more people. With joint tenancy, the ownership shares are usually required to be equal. The main feature that distinguishes joint tenancy from tenancy in common is the **right of survivorship**. With survivorship, the death of one of the joint tenants does not destroy the ownership unit; it only reduces by one the number of people who hold title to the property. As each successive joint tenant dies, the surviving joint tenant(s) will acquire the interest of the deceased joint tenant. The joint tenancy continues until there is only one owner, who then holds title in severalty. The last surviving joint tenant has the same rights to dispose of the property as any sole owner. This type of ownership also requires that the joint tenants have equal possession, equal interests (shares), and that title be taken at the same time. This means all owners have unity of possession, all ownership shares are equal, title to the property was taken together at the same time, and that the names of all joint tenants appear on the deed. If property is owned by three or more joint tenants and one conveys their interest to an outside party, the new owner will hold interest as a tenant in common with the remaining joint tenants. The original remaining joint tenants will still hold their undivided interests as joint tenants among themselves (see Figure 2.8).

FIGURE 2.8

Joint Tenancy with Right of Survivorship

1. A, B, and C are joint tenants.
2. When C dies, A and B remain as joint tenants.
3. When B dies, A holds title in severalty, which is inheritable.

In North Carolina

Unlike other states, North Carolina does not favor the right of survivorship for a joint tenancy. In 2009, the language in North Carolina General Statute 41-2(b) and (c) was changed to allow unequal ownership interests, if so desired. In North Carolina, joint tenancy interests will be presumed to be equal unless clearly marked as unequal. The right of survivorship can be created if the deed is worded in exact compliance with North Carolina court decisions, making it clear that the right of survivorship is intended. Otherwise, North Carolina statutes provide that on the death of a joint tenant, the decedent's estate does not pass to the surviving joint tenant but instead goes to the heirs in the same manner as estates held by tenancy in common. In other words, unless the deed is worded exactly right, a joint tenancy can be created, but the right of survivorship does not apply. Note that where a right of survivorship is created, if one joint tenant owner conveys an interest to another person, that right of survivorship will be destroyed. The new owner becomes a tenant in common with the other owners because title is conveyed at a separate time (see Figure 2.9).

FIGURE 2.9

Combination of Tenancies

A, B, and C are joint tenants.

A sells her interest to D.

D becomes a tenant in common with B and C as joint tenants.

A lawyer should always be consulted if the parties to a transaction insist on the right of survivorship. There are many technical requirements that must be met before a North Carolina court will recognize a joint tenancy with a right to survivorship.

Termination of tenants in common and joint tenancy co-ownership by partition suit. Each co-owner of real estate has an absolute right to force a partition of the land by voluntary action and agreement, which will divide their real estate according to their interests. When a division among co-owners cannot be agreed on voluntarily, the division can be ordered by a court in a suit for partition. The court may actually divide the land into pro rata parcels or, if this cannot be done, may order the property sold and the proceeds divided proportionately among the owners.

Three Forms of Concurrent Ownership in North Carolina

1. Tenancy in common
2. Joint tenancy
3. Tenancy by the entirety

Tenancy by the entirety. *Tenancy by the entirety* is a special form of tenancy used in many states in which the owners must be husband and wife. Each spouse has an equal, undivided interest in the property; each, in essence, owns the entire estate. On the death of one spouse, full title automatically passes to the surviving spouse through the right of survivorship without a probate hearing. The transfer of the interest of the deceased spouse may be recorded by filing a certificate of death, an affidavit, or a certificate of transfer, as provided by law.

The distinguishing characteristics of tenancy by the entirety are

- the owners must be husband and wife when title is received;
- the owners have rights of survivorship;
- during the owners' lives, title can be conveyed only by a deed signed by both parties (one party cannot convey a one-half interest); and
- there is generally no right to partition.

In North Carolina

In North Carolina, any conveyance to a husband and wife by deed or by will creates a tenancy by the entirety by default unless specifically stated otherwise. A tenancy by the entirety may be terminated by the death of either spouse, by divorce (leaving the parties as tenants in common), or by the mutual agreement of both spouses. Note that a husband and wife can choose another form of ownership for property that is owned during marriage—tenancy by the entirety is not the only available option; tenants in common or joint tenancy can be used. Furthermore, property that is jointly owned before marriage (or owned in severalty by one of the spouses) does not automatically become a tenancy by the entirety simply by virtue of the fact of marriage. If a couple owned property before marriage as tenants in common, they will continue to own the property as tenants in common unless the husband and wife choose to legally change the form of ownership.

Common Interest Community Ownership

Some forms of ownership are called *common interest community ownership* because they contain elements of both ownership in severalty and concurrent ownership. Owners of individual units may hold title to their unit in any legal way previously discussed (**severalty, tenants in common, joint tenancy,** or **tenancy by the entireties**). The owners of the individual units must also legally support the maintenance of the common areas through membership in a **homeowners association (HOA)** and payment of periodic dues. While many common interest communities are residential in use, this ownership model is increasing in popularity for commercial uses.

Condominium ownership. The **condominium** form of ownership started with apartment buildings in Europe before gaining wide acceptance in the United States. Condominium laws, often called common interest ownership acts or *horizontal property acts*, have been enacted in every state, including North Carolina. Under these laws, the occupant/owner of each unit holds a fee simple absolute title to the unit (which is often called *title to airspace*). Each unit owner also owns a share of the **common elements**, such as the pool, hallways, and other amenities. These elements are owned and held by the unit owner as a tenant in common with the other unit owners in the complex (see Figure 2.10). The individual unit owners in a condominium own and use these common elements together as tenants in common. The individual unit owners pay their own separate property taxes and mortgage payments and typically belong to an owners' association that manages the common elements of the condominium complex and determines the homeowners association dues or fees. These fees are used to maintain the common elements and establish reserves to pay for upkeep of the common elements. Condominiums are created by declarations that determine which spaces will be

FIGURE 2.10

Condominium Ownership

The owner of unit 4 owns his or her unit, plus an undivided one-fifth share of the elevator, lobby, grounds, and structure.

individual unit ownership and which are common elements as well as how the HOA will be structured and how dues and fees will be set.

The condominium form of ownership may be used in any type of real estate. The most typical type of real estate is residential, but office, warehouse, and mixed-use spaces may also use this form of ownership. It is usually used for apartment buildings. These may range from freestanding highrise buildings to town house-like arrangements. The common elements include such items as the land, exterior structure, hallways, elevators, stairways, and roof. In some instances, lawns and recreational facilities such as swimming pools, clubhouses, tennis courts, and golf courses also may be considered common areas. In addition, the condominium form of ownership is used for other types of properties such as commercial properties, office buildings, and multiuse buildings that contain offices and shops as well as residential units.

Some condominium projects offer a special type of common elements that is reserved for the use of only one or more units to the exclusion of the other units. Assigned storage areas or parking spaces would be examples of **limited common elements**.

In North Carolina

Creation of a condominium. The **North Carolina Condominium Act of 1986** specifies that a condominium is created and established when the developer of the property executes and records a declaration of its creation in the county where the property is located. The declaration must include any covenants, conditions, or restrictions on the use of the property. The developer must file a plat map or plan of the condominium property, buildings, and any other improvements. The developer also must prepare a set of bylaws. The bylaws usually provide for

- the creation of a unit owners' association giving a vote to each unit owner,
- the election of a board of managers from among the unit owners,
- the duties of the board of managers,
- the compensation of its members,
- their method of election and removal,
- whether a managing broker is to be engaged, and
- the method of collecting the unit owners' association monthly dues from each member to cover the costs of management and maintenance of the common areas.

In North Carolina

Consumer protection. The North Carolina law also requires disclosure and other consumer protection measures in connection with new residential condominium unit sales in the form of public offering statements. The developer must disclose all ownership and other appropriate documents to the purchaser before the purchase contract is signed. The purchaser then has a seven-day rescission period, which begins after the purchase contract is signed. At any time during that seven-day period, the purchaser can cancel the sale and receive a full refund of any monies paid. On a resale unit (a sale of a condominium other than the original sale from the developer), a resale certificate detailing the monthly dues assessment and any other fees payable by a unit owner must be given to a purchaser prior to conveyance. There is no right to cancel in resale transactions.

Cooperative ownership. Under the usual **cooperative** arrangement, title to land and building is held by a corporation (or partnership or land trust). The building management sets a price for stock shares for each unit in the building. Each tenant of a unit in the building purchases stock in the corporation when the tenant pays the agreed-on price for use of a specific apartment. The purchaser then becomes a shareholder of the corporation and, by virtue of that stock ownership, receives a **proprietary lease** to the unit for the life of the corporation; there is no deed because there is no ownership of the individual unit.

The cooperative building's real estate taxes are assessed against the corporation as owner. Generally, the mortgage is signed by the corporation, creating one lien on the entire parcel of real estate. Taxes, mortgage interest, and principal, plus operating and maintenance expenses are shared by the tenants/shareholders in the form of monthly assessments.

While the cooperative tenants/owners do not actually own an interest in real estate (they own stock, which is personal property), for all practical purposes they control the property through their stock ownership and their voice in the management of the corporation. The bylaws of the corporation generally provide that each prospective purchaser of an apartment lease must be approved by an administrative board. This hybrid form of ownership has not enjoyed much popularity in North Carolina to date.

Town house ownership. **Town house** projects are typically a group of two-story or three-story units that are horizontally attached to each other; that is, they share *party walls* and are sometimes called *row houses*. Each town house unit is individually owned; all unit owners have membership in the homeowner association that owns the common areas. The homeowners association will pay real property taxes on the common areas, while each individual unit owner will pay the real property taxes on the unit they own. Town house ownership is similar to condominium ownership with one fundamental difference: the owner of each town house unit also owns the land on which that unit is built.

Time-share ownership. A **time-share** is any right to occupy a unit of real property during five or more separated time periods (usually consisting of one or two weeks) over a period of at least five years. Time-sharing permits multiple purchasers to buy interests in real estate—usually a unit of a resort hotel, an apartment, or a condominium—with each purchaser having a right to use the facility for a specific time period. For instance, a time-share owner may have the right to use an oceanfront apartment for the first three weeks of June every calendar year.

In North Carolina

Due in large part to the historically high-pressure sales practices associated with the sale of time-shares, the North Carolina Time Share Act (G.S. 93A, Article 4) was passed to regulate the development and sale of time-shares. Despite the name given to a development project, if the format meets the definition in the Act, it will be classified a *time-share* and subject to its requirements. For example, all time-share projects must be registered with the state; developers must give prospective purchasers public offering statements prior to contract; and purchasers have a five-day cancellation or rescission period during which they can cancel the purchase without penalty. Time-share salespeople must be active real estate brokers operating under a project broker, who are subject to disciplinary action by the North Carolina Real Estate Commission. The Commission can also fine unlicensed time-share developers $500 for each violation of the Act or revoke the project's registration certificate. (See Appendix C.)

Planned unit development. A **planned unit development (PUD)** is really a method of real estate development, not ownership. The major feature of a PUD is flexible zoning. It differs from a normal subdivision in that buildings may be clustered together (rather than complying with normal lot size and setback requirements), leaving more room for open spaces and recreational areas. Sometimes PUDs include a variety of land uses as well. For example, instead of being solely single-family residential, a PUD also may include some multifamily complexes as well as some retail or commercial uses. Typically, residential owners receive title to their individual units, while the homeowners' association typically has title to the common areas of the development.

RELATED WEBSITES

Manufactured Housing Institute: www.manufacturedhousing.org
Modular Today: www.modulartoday.com
Water Law in North Carolina:
   www.bae.ncsu.edu/programs/extension/publicat/arep/waterlaw.html
North Carolina Department of the Secretary of the State/UCC laws:
   www.secretary.state.nc.us/ucc
North Carolina Condominium Act:
   www.ncga.state.nc.us/gascripts/statutes/StatutesTOC.pl?Chapter=0047C

KEY POINT REVIEW

Bundle of legal rights includes the

- right of disposition,
- right to enjoyment,
- right of exclusion,
- right of possession, and
- right of control the property.

Appurtenance is a right or privilege associated with real property that normally transfers along with the property to the new owner when the property is sold. An appurtenance could include such rights as an improvement to the property like a building or a parking space in a multiunit building, an easement, or water rights.

Real estate

- is the earth's surface, where water rights are held by owners of land adjacent to rivers, lakes, or oceans;
- extends downward to the center of the earth, where **subsurface rights** include mineral rights and other natural resources that can be transferred separately from **surface rights**;
- stretches upward to infinity, where **air rights** can be sold separately from surface rights with some limitations to enable air travel; and
- includes things naturally attached (**fructus naturales**) to the land, such as trees and crops that do not need cultivation and perennial crops, orchards, and vineyards (**fructus industriales**).

Water rights are determined by common law and statute:

- **Riparian rights** are common-law rights granted to owners of land along rivers, streams, or similar bodies of water.
- **Littoral rights** belong to owners of land that borders commercially navigable lakes, seas, and oceans.

Personal property (chattel or personalty) includes

- movable items, such as a chair or a sofa;
- **emblements** (fructus industriales), annual plantings or crops of grains, vegetables, and fruit;
- items of real property that can become personal property by severance;
- items of personal property that can become real property by attachment or annexation (construction materials); and
- **manufactured homes** are personal property until permanently affixed to land.

A **fixture** is personal property that has been affixed to the land or to a building so that by law it becomes part of the real property.

- **Modular homes** immediately become part of the real estate.
- Fructus naturales are considered real property.

Legal tests for a fixture **(Total Circumstances Test)** include the following:

- Intent of annexor—was it meant to go or stay
- Relationship of annexor—owner or tenant
- Method of annexation—not easily removable
- Adaptation to real estate—ordinarily considered a permanent addition

Trade fixtures include property attached to the structure but used in the course of business:

- personal property, if removed by tenant and the premises are returned to original condition before the lease expires; and
- real property if left behind by tenant. The landlord can acquire this type of property by accession.

Agricultural fixtures include improvements made to North Carolina farm by tenant farmer become real property.

Per the **Uniform Commercial Code (UCC)**

- an item bought on credit remains personal property until paid for, and
- a creditor can repossess the item in event of default.

A **freehold estate** lasts for an indeterminable length of time:

- **Fee simple** is the highest estate recognized by law.
- **Fee simple defeasible** is a qualified estate.
  - **Fee simple subject to a condition subsequent** is a nonoccurrence of some specified event.
  - **Fee simple determinable** is automatic ownership reversion if specified action stops.

- **Pur autre vie estate** is based on the lifetime of another person.
- **Life estate** is based on the lifetime of owner.

Ownership in severalty, title held by one individual/entity, has the following characteristics:

- Sole rights to ownership
- Sole discretion to transfer part or all ownership rights to another person
- May be a single individual or an artificial person, such as a corporation

Concurrent ownership, title held by two or more individuals, may be one of three forms: tenancy in common, joint tenancy, or tenancy by the entirety.

- **Tenancy in common**, where
  — each tenant holds an undivided fractional interest;
  — co-owners have unity of possession—right to occupy entire property;
  — each interest can be sold, conveyed, mortgaged, or transferred; and
  — interest passes by will when a co-owner dies; right of survivorship not possible.
- **Joint tenancy** is where tenants enjoy the four unities (PITT):
  — Unity of possession—all joint tenants have undivided right to possession.
  — Unity of interest—all joint tenants usually own an equal interest.
  — Unity of time—all joint tenants acquire their interest at the same time.
  — Unity of title—title is conveyed to all joint tenants by the same document.

Joint tenants usually enjoy the **right of survivorship**; upon the death of a joint tenant, interest passes to the other joint tenant or tenants. In North Carolina, joint tenancy ownership can have unequal interests and is created without right of survivorship, unless there is specific wording in the deed to include the right of survivorship.

Termination of joint tenancy is by

- death of all but one joint tenant, who then owns the property in severalty;
- conveyance of a joint tenant's interest, but only as to that interest; or
- partition, which can be brought to force division or sale of property.

Tenancy by the entirety, recognized by North Carolina, has the following characteristics:

- Only available to husband and wife;
- Title conveyed only by deed signed by both; and
- Carries right of survivorship; survivor becomes owner in severalty.

Common interest community ownerships include condominium, town house, cooperative, and time-share ownerships. **Condominium** laws of each state define the following:

- The condominium owner holds fee simple title to the airspace of a unit as well as an undivided share in the remainder of the building and land, known as the common elements.

- **Common elements** are owned by condominium unit owners as tenants in common.
- The condominium is administered by an owners' association of unit owners that may decide to hire an outside property management firm.
- Maintenance of common elements is funded by fees charged to each unit owner.
- Unit owners have no right to partition common elements.
- Condominium units may be mortgaged; default on payment does not affect other unit owners.
- **North Carolina Condominium Act of 1986** requires disclosures and allows 7-day rescission on purchase of new unit.

In a **cooperative**, title to the land and the building is held by a corporation, which sells shares of stock to prospective tenants.

- A purchaser of stock becomes a shareholder in the corporation and receives a **proprietary lease** to the apartment for the life of the corporation.
- Stock is owned as personal property and not real estate.
- The lender may accept stock as collateral for financing, which expands the pool of potential owners.
- The IRS treats a cooperative the same as houses or condominiums for tax purposes.

In a **town house**, a horizontal form of ownership in which houses share common vertical walls, titles to individual units include a fractional interest in common areas. Some land (e.g., directly under the individual unit) is owned by the individual unit owner and is not part of the common area.

A time-share permits the sale of a leasehold interest (time-share use) or deeded ownership (time-share estate) that allows occupancy during a specific period of time, typically weekly. Time-share transactions are governed by the North Carolina Time Share Act.

- **Time-share ownership** permits multiple purchasers to buy interests in real estate, a form of ownership most commonly found with resort property.

North Carolina Time Share Act (part of the North Carolina Real Estate License Law)

- There must be at least five separated periods of use over at least five years.
- Buyer has a five-day right of rescission (mailbox rule does apply).
- Any deposits must be held in trust for at least 10 days to allow for receipt of rescission notice.
- NCREC can fine a time-share developer $500 per violation of the act. There is no maximum fine.
- Time-share sales people must be actively licensed real estate brokers.

QUESTIONS

1. Real property is often referred to as a bundle of legal rights. Which of the following is NOT among these rights?
   a. Right of exclusion
   b. Right to override local zoning
   c. Right of enjoyment
   d. Right to sell or otherwise convey the property

2. A property is bordered by a small stream. The property ends
   a. at the stream edge.
   b. at the center of the stream.
   c. five feet before the stream edge.
   d. at the mean high-water mark of the stream.

3. Oceanfront property ends
   a. at the water's edge.
   b. at the edge of the dunes.
   c. at the low tide water mark.
   d. at the mean high-water mark.

4. A property owner has placed a manufactured home on his lakefront lot. In order to make the home a legal part of the real estate, he must do all of the following EXCEPT
   a. remove the trailer hitch, wheels, and axles.
   b. attach the home to a permanent foundation.
   c. remove the HUD label from the exterior of the home.
   d. cancel the motor vehicle title with an affidavit.

5. Which of the following would normally be considered a fixture?
   a. A portable basketball goal on the parking pad
   b. A custom-made mailbox attached to the house
   c. Curtains in the master bedroom that match the wallpaper
   d. A porch swing that is hanging from hooks on the front porch

6. Which of the following would NOT be considered in determining if an item is a fixture?
   a. Intent
   b. Adaptability
   c. Value
   d. Method of attachment

7. Which of the following items would normally convey as a fixture with the property?
   a. Refrigerator and countertop microwave
   b. Free-standing butcher block table in the kitchen
   c. Decorative lights draped around the enclosed patio
   d. The large mirror bolted over the fireplace mantel

8. A tenant is renting a single-family home under a one-year lease. With the landlord's approval, she installs awnings over the front windows to shade some delicate hanging plants. What is the status of the awnings at the end of the lease?
   a. The tenant can remove the awnings when she vacates.
   b. The awnings are considered real property of the landlord and must stay.
   c. It is at the discretion of the landlord whether the tenant can take the awnings.
   d. The awnings are considered trade fixtures and must stay.

9. A purchaser of real estate learns that her ownership rights will continue forever and that no other person has any ownership control over the property. This person owns a
   a. fee simple interest.
   b. life estate pur autre vie.
   c. determinable fee estate.
   d. fee simple subject to a condition subsequent.

10. A fee simple estate has all the following characteristics EXCEPT that it is
    a. of indefinite duration.
    b. free of encumbrances.
    c. transferable by deed or by will.
    d. transferable with or without valuable consideration.

11. A freehold estate in land that will automatically extinguish upon the cessation of a specified condition is called a
    a. fee simple subject to condition subsequent
    b. fee simple determinable.
    c. fee simple absolute.
    d. fee simple unmarketable title

12. A property owner wanted to donate a vacant lot she owned adjacent to a hospital to the hospital for expansion purposes. She wanted to make sure the land was used as she intended, so her attorney prepared the deed to convey ownership of the lot to the hospital "so long as it is used for hospital purposes." Upon receipt of the gift, the hospital owned a
    a. fee simple absolute estate.
    b. conventional life estate.
    c. fee simple determinable estate.
    d. leasehold estate.

13. A property owner has a freehold estate in a single-family home. He rents the home to a young couple.
    a. The man no longer has a freehold estate because a freehold estate and a leasehold estate cannot exist in the same property.
    b. The man must give up his freehold estate in order to rent the property to others.
    c. The tenants now hold the freehold estate in the property.
    d. The man has a freehold estate in the property, and the tenants have a leasehold estate in the property.

14. A life tenant can do all the following EXCEPT
    a. sell their lifetime rights.
    b. receive profits from the property.
    c. strip cut the timber on the property.
    d. use the resources of the property to maintain the property.

15. If property is held by two or more owners as tenants in common, the interest of a deceased co-owner will pass to the
    a. remaining owner or owners.
    b. heirs of the deceased owner.
    c. trust under which the property was owned.
    d. state by the law of escheat, regardless of whether the deceased has any heirs.

16. What form of concurrent ownership can only be held by husband and wife?
    a. Tenants by the entirety
    b. Joint tenants with survivorship
    c. Tenants in common
    d. Joint tenants without survivorship

17. William, Frank, and Jane are joint tenants without the right of survivorship. Jane sells her interest to Lloyd, and then Frank dies. As a result,
    a. Frank's heirs, Lloyd and William, are joint tenants.
    b. Frank's heirs and William are joint tenants.
    c. William and Lloyd are tenants in common and are the only remaining owners of the property.
    d. William, Lloyd, and Frank's heirs are tenants in common.

18. Concerning concurrent ownership, which of the following statements is/are TRUE?
    I. Tenancy in common is not available to a married couple holding title on a property.
    II. Joint tenants may hold title to the property with equal, undivided interests.
    a. I only
    b. II only
    c. Both I and II
    d. Neither I nor II

19. A buyer and a seller/developer executed a purchase contract for a new condominium on May 6 with the buyer giving $5,000 in earnest money. The buyer changed her mind and notified the seller on May 11 that she was rescinding the contract. Which of the following is *TRUE*?
    a. The buyer can legally cancel the contract and have all the earnest money refunded.
    b. The buyer cannot cancel the contract because the three-day right of rescission has passed.
    c. The buyer can cancel only if she forfeits the earnest money.
    d. The buyer cannot cancel the contract because there is no right of rescission.

20. Which of the following statements is/are *TRUE*?
    I. A condominium owner individually owns only the "airspace" in the unit and no land.
    II. A town house owner individually owns the ground under the unit.
    a. I only
    b. II only
    c. Both I and II
    d. Neither I nor II

CHAPTER 3

Encumbrances on Real Property

LEARNING OBJECTIVES *When you have finished reading this chapter, you should be able to*

- **identify** different types of encumbrances on real property.
- **describe** different types of liens, easements, and encroachments.
- **explain** property taxation laws and procedures; and how real property is assessed and taxed.
- **define** these *key terms*:

ad valorem taxes	encumbrance	mill
assessment	general lien	octennial reappraisal
deed restrictions	judgment	priority
dominant tenement	license	servient tenement
easement	lien	special assessments
easement appurtenant	lien agent	specific lien
easement by necessity	lis pendens	tax lien
easement by prescription	Machinery Act	writ of attachment
easement in gross	mass appraisal	writ of execution
encroachment	mechanic's lien	

ENCUMBRANCES ON REAL PROPERTY

A claim, charge, or liability that attaches to and is binding on real estate is called an **encumbrance**. An encumbrance is anything that affects title to real estate. It is a right or interest held by a party who is not the fee owner of the property. An encumbrance may affect the value or obstruct the use of the property, but it does not necessarily prevent a transfer of title.

Chapter 3 Encumbrances on Real Property   47

Liens

A nonpossessory charge against property that provides security for a debt or an obligation of the property owner is a **lien.** If the obligation is not repaid, the lienholder, or creditor, has the right to have it paid out of the debtor's property, usually from the proceeds of a court sale. Real estate taxes, mortgages and trust deeds, judgments, and mechanics' liens all represent possible liens against an owner's real estate. A lien does not constitute ownership; it is a type of encumbrance. Note, however, that whereas all liens are encumbrances, not all encumbrances are liens.

Liens fall into several categories, based on how they are created. A voluntary lien is contractual or consensual and is created by the debtor's action, as when someone takes out a mortgage loan to buy real estate. An involuntary lien is created by law, such as a **tax lien** imposed by a municipality. Liens may be further classified as general or specific, as illustrated in Figure 3.1.

FIGURE 3.1

Types of Liens

```
                    Liens
                   /     \
              Specific    General
              /      \         \
         Voluntary  Involuntary  Involuntary
         Mortgage   Real Property Taxes/Judgments
                    Taxes/Assessments/
                    Mechanic's Lien
```

Specific Liens

A **specific lien** is secured by a specific parcel of property and affects only that particular property. Examples would be mortgage or deed of trust liens, real property taxes or special assessments liens, and mechanics' liens.

Mortgage and deed of trust liens. In general, a *mortgage* or *deed of trust lien* is a voluntary specific lien on real estate given to a lender by a borrower as security for a real estate loan. It becomes a lien on real property when the lender records the mortgage or deed of trust in the office of the register of deeds in the county where the property is located. Mortgage and deed of trust liens are the most common form of lien or encumbrance. Mortgages and mortgage liens are discussed in detail in Chapter 14.

Real property tax and special assessment liens. If a property owner fails to pay the taxes levied by a city or county on the property, the unpaid tax becomes a specific, involuntary lien on that property. The lien attaches to the property on the date the property is listed (January 1 of each year) and, as a superior lien, takes priority over all other liens. Real property is taxed on an *ad valorem* basis, which means *according to value.*

In addition to the ad valorem real estate taxes, special assessment (improvement) taxes may be levied against specific real property. The purpose of these taxes is to pay for an improvement that has benefited the taxed property, such as street paving or the installation of a sewer system.

In North Carolina

In North Carolina, both ad valorem and special assessment tax liens are valid for 10 years and have priority over other types of liens. (Property taxes are discussed in more detail later in this chapter.)

Mechanic's lien. The purpose of the mechanic's lien is to give security to those who perform labor or furnish material in the improvement of real property. A **mechanic's lien** is a specific, involuntary lien and is available to contractors, subcontractors, architects, equipment lessors, surveyors, laborers, and others. This type of lien is filed when the property owner has not paid for the work or when the general contractor has been paid but has not paid the subcontractors or suppliers.

To be entitled to a mechanic's lien, the person who did the work must have had a contract (express or implied) with the owner or the owner's authorized representative. A person claiming a mechanic's lien must file the lien claim within 120 days after last furnishing the labor or materials; the lien takes effect from the date that person first furnished the labor or materials. The action to enforce a properly filed mechanic's lien must be brought within 180 days after a worker last furnished labor or materials. Major changes were made to North Carolina mechanic's lien rights in early 2013. A property owner that applies for a building permit for improvements totaling more than $30,000 must designate an approved **lien agent** for the project. This includes all private residential and commercial construction projects except improvement to owner-occupied single-family detached property (even if the project cost exceeds $30,000). Any potential lien claimant must serve notice to the lien agent within 15 days of beginning work on the project or lose the lien priority afforded mechanics' liens. Projects costing under $30,000 are exempt from requirement for a lien agent designation.

In North Carolina

North Carolina Commercial Real Estate Broker Lien. A 2011 North Carolina law allows a real estate broker with a written agency agreement to represent a property owner in a commercial transaction to place a lien on the property to be sold or leased to protect the broker's commission. The lien must be filed in a sales transaction after the broker has fully performed but before closing; in a lease transaction, the broker has up to 90 days after tenant possession to file the lien. The lien must be satisfied within 18 months and is inferior to all mechanics' liens.

General Liens

General liens affect all the property of a debtor, both real and personal, rather than a specific parcel of real property. Examples include judgments, personal property tax liens, and state and federal tax liens.

Judgments. A **judgment** is a decree issued by a court. When the decree provides for the awarding of money and sets forth the amount of money owed by the debtor to the creditor, the judgment is referred to as a *money judgment*.

When a judgment is properly docketed in a county (entered and indexed in a judgment book), that judgment becomes an involuntary, general lien on all of the current and future real estate and personal property owned by the judgment debtor in that county. Real estate of the judgment debtor in other counties is not affected unless the judgment is docketed in those counties as well. In North Carolina, a judgment lien is good for 10 years from the date of the judgment.

Personal property tax liens. A personal property tax is assessed on certain types of personal property. If unpaid, this tax becomes a general, involuntary lien against all the property owned by the taxpayer. Like real property tax liens, personal property tax liens have priority over other types of liens.

State tax liens. Both unpaid state inheritance taxes and unpaid state income taxes give rise to general, involuntary liens against all property owned by the individual taxpayer. In North Carolina, both types of liens last for 10 years.

Federal tax liens. An Internal Revenue Service (IRS) tax lien results from a person's failure to pay any portion of federal IRS taxes, such as income and withholding taxes. A federal tax lien is a general, involuntary lien on all real and personal property held by the delinquent taxpayer. Its priority is based on the date of filing or recording; it does not supersede previously recorded liens.

Effects of Liens

Effects of liens on title. Although the fee simple estate held by a typical real estate owner can be reduced in value by the lien rights of others, the owner is still free to convey title to a willing purchaser. The purchaser will, however, buy the property subject to any liens because liens run with the land; that is, they will bind successive owners if steps are not taken to clear the liens.

Remember, liens attach to the property, not to the property owner. Therefore, although a purchaser who buys real estate under a delinquent lien is not responsible for payment of the debt secured by the lien, the purchaser does face a possible loss of the property if the creditors take court action to enforce the payment of their liens.

Priority of Liens

Because property taxes and special assessments generally take **priority** over all other liens, they are called superior liens. Therefore, if the property is sold through a court-ordered sale to satisfy unpaid debts, outstanding real estate taxes, special assessments, and unpaid debts, will be paid from the proceeds first. The remainder of the proceeds will be used to pay other outstanding liens in the order of the date and time they were recorded. The first lien to be recorded is the first lien to be paid. (This is called a *pure race system* of determining lien priority.) One exception to this rule is the mechanic's lien: the priority of a mechanic's lien dates back to the date the labor began or materials were first provided rather than to the date the lien was filed. Remember, real property tax and special assessments can move in front of or take priority over any of these recorded liens.

Deed Restrictions

Deed restrictions are another type of encumbrance on real property. Deed restrictions (also referred to as *covenants, conditions,* and *restrictions* or CC&Rs) are private agreements placed in the public record that affect the use of land. They are usually imposed by the original developer of real estate when property is sold and are included in the deed to the buyer. Deed restrictions typically would be imposed by a developer or subdivider for the purpose of maintaining specific standards in a subdivision, and they would be listed in the original development plans for the subdivision filed in the public record. Deed restrictions are discussed further in Chapter 6.

Lis Pendens

A judgment or another decree affecting real estate is rendered at the conclusion of a lawsuit. Generally, there is a considerable time lag between the filing of a lawsuit and the rendering of a judgment. When any suit is filed that affects title to a specific parcel of real estate (such as a foreclosure suit), the person bringing the lawsuit may file a **lis pendens** (Latin for "litigation pending"). When a *lis pendens* is filed, anyone acquiring an interest in the property takes that interest subject to any judgment or decree the court may issue. *Lis pendens* is not a lien but rather a notice that there is an action or lawsuit pending that may adversely affect the title. The *lis pendens* acts more like an encumbrance against the title.

■ **FOR EXAMPLE** If a lender is filing a foreclosure suit against a property owner, it will file a *lis pendens* against the property. If the property owner should sell the property during the course of the legal action, the new purchaser would take title subject to the outcome of the foreclosure action.

Writ of Attachment

Another encumbrance against real property is a recorded **writ of attachment** for a debt other than a mortgage. A creditor can request the court to issue a writ of attachment against the debtor's unsecured property. By ordering a lien on the debtor's assets until the law suit is decided and a judgment is rendered, the unsecured real estate remains available to satisfy the judgment. Once a judgment is recorded, a **writ of execution** will be issued directing the county sheriff to sell the property to satisfy the judgment.

Easements

A *nonpossessory right* to use the land of another for a particular purpose is called an **easement**. An easement is not a form of ownership; it merely grants the use of the property.

Easement appurtenant. An easement that is annexed to the ownership of one parcel of land and used for the benefit of another parcel of land is an **easement appurtenant**. For an easement appurtenant to exist, two adjacent tracts of land must be owned by different parties. The tract over which the easement runs is known as the **servient tenement** or estate; the tract that benefits from the easement is known as the **dominant tenement** or estate (see Figure 3.2).

FIGURE 3.2

Easement Appurtenant and Easement in Gross

The owner of Lot B has an appurtenant easement across Lot A to gain access to his property from the public road. Lot B is dominant, and Lot A is servient.

The utility company has an easement in gross across both parcels of land for its power lines.

■ **FOR EXAMPLE** If Able and Baker own adjacent properties in a lake resort community and only Able's property borders the lake, Able may grant Baker an easement across Able's property so that Baker can have access to the lake. Able's property is the servient tenement; Baker's property is the dominant tenement. Baker's property benefits from the easement because it now has lake access, which did not exist before the easement was granted.

An easement appurtenant is considered part of both the dominant and the servient lands, and if either tract is conveyed to another party, the easement passes with the title. In legal terms, the easement *runs with the land*. In North Carolina, an easement must be recorded to be enforceable against the purchaser of the servient estate.

A *party wall* can be an exterior wall of a building that straddles the boundary line between two lots, or it can be a commonly shared partition wall between two connected properties. Each lot owner owns the half of the wall on their lot, and each has a cross easement in the other half of the wall. A written party-wall agreement should be used to create the easement rights. Expenses to build and maintain the wall are usually shared. A party driveway shared by adjoining owners and straddling the property boundary also should be created by written agreement, specifying responsibility for expenses.

Easement in gross. A personal interest in or right to use the land of another is an **easement in gross**. An easement in gross benefits a person or an entity, not a parcel of property, so *there is no dominant tenement or estate*. Examples of commercial easements in gross are the easement rights a railroad has in its right-of-way, billboards easements, or utilities easements. (See Figure 3.2.) The railroad company, the billboard owner or the utility company receive the use and benefit of someone else's land while the land subject to the easement receives little or no benefit. Commercial easements in gross, such as the ones mentioned, may last an indefinite period of time and may be assigned or conveyed. Because North Carolina treats an easement in gross as a personal right, personal easements in gross are irrevocable during the owner's life, usually are not assignable, and terminate on the death of the personal easement owner.

Creating an easement. An easement is created by a written agreement between the parties that establishes the easement right. The creation of an easement always involves two separate parties, one of whom is the owner of the land over which the easement runs.

The person who has the easement interest has a nonpossessory interest with the right to use the land. The owner of the land burdened by the easement has a possessory interest in the land (the owner can use and possess the land), but the owner cannot interfere with the easement holder's rights of use. Two other ways for an easement to be created are *easement by necessity* and *easement by prescription*.

Necessity. An **easement by necessity**, or easement by implication of law, arises because all owners must have rights of ingress to and egress from their land—they cannot be landlocked. If a grantor has conveyed property that is completely surrounded by the grantor's property (thus landlocking the grantee), an easement by necessity will be created.

Prescription. When a claimant has made use of another's land for a certain period of time, as defined by state law, an **easement by prescription** is acquired. This prescriptive period is 20 years in North Carolina. The claimant's use must have been continuous, exclusive, and without the owner's approval. Additionally, the use must have been visible, open, and notorious, so that the owner could have readily learned of it. A property owner can prevent an easement by prescription from being created by giving permission to the user.

Terminating an easement. An easement may be terminated

- when the purpose for which the easement was created no longer exists;

- if the easement holder becomes the owner of the land where the easement is located (e.g., land owner B buys lot A) (a situation called a *merger*);
- by release of the right of easement to the owner of the servient tenement;
- by abandonment of the easement (the intention of the parties is the determining factor); or
- by non-use of a prescriptive easement.

Licenses. A **license** is a personal non-transferable privilege to enter the land of another for a specific purpose, such a license for a friend to hunt on a farmer's land during the winter.

A license differs from an easement in that it can be terminated or revoked. Generally, if the right to use another's property is given orally or informally, it is considered to be a license rather than an easement. Because a license is not considered to be an interest in the land itself, it is not considered an encumbrance. A license automatically ends with the death of either party or with the sale of the land.

Encroachments

Unwanted intrusion

An **encroachment** arises when an improvement or any portion of an improvement, such as a building, a fence, or a driveway illegally extends beyond the land of its owner and covers some land of an adjoining owner, a street, or an alley. For instance, two landowners are neighbors. The garage of one landowner actually extends one foot onto the neighbor's property. This is an encroachment.

Encroachments are usually disclosed by either a physical inspection of the property or a location survey. A location survey shows the location of all improvements on a property and determines whether any improvements extend over the lot lines. If the building on a lot encroaches on neighboring land, the neighbor may be able either to recover damages or to secure removal of the portion of the building that encroaches. Encroachments of long standing (for the prescriptive period of 20 years in North Carolina) may give rise to easements by prescription. The primary reason for a property survey is to ensure no encroachments have occurred. The legal effect of an encroachment is to potentially make both titles unmarketable.

IN PRACTICE Because an undisclosed encroachment could render a title unmarketable, the existence of an encroachment should be noted in a listing agreement, and the sales contract governing the transaction should be made subject to the existence of the particular encroachment. Encroachments are not disclosed by the usual title evidence provided in a real estate sale unless a survey is submitted while the examination is being made. Mortgage lenders may resist loans on properties with encroachments.

■ PROPERTY TAXATION

The ownership of real estate is subject to certain government powers. One of these powers is the right of state and local governments to impose tax liens for the support of their governmental functions. Because the location of real estate is permanently fixed, the government can levy property taxes with a high degree of certainty that the taxes will be collected. Furthermore, because the lien for property

In North Carolina — taxes levied on real estate has priority over other previously recorded liens in most states, the property tax lien will almost always be the first lien to be paid from the proceeds of a court-ordered sale of the real estate. In North Carolina, a property tax lien will have priority over all previously recorded liens except a previously recorded state income tax lien.

Real estate property taxes fall into two categories: (1) general real estate, or ad valorem, property taxes and (2) special assessment, or improvement, property taxes. Both of these property taxes are levied against specific parcels of property and automatically become liens on those properties.

General Tax (Ad Valorem Tax)

General real estate property taxes are levied for the general support of the government agency authorized to impose the levy. Property taxes are known as **ad valorem taxes** because the amount of the tax varies in accordance with the value of the property being taxed.

In North Carolina — **North Carolina property subject to taxation.** All real property in North Carolina is subject to taxation. Although counties and municipalities determine real estate property tax rates within their jurisdictions, the **Machinery Act** regulates standards for real property taxation, standards for property tax assessment, standards for property tax appraisal, and requirements for tax-exempt status. Property generally considered tax-exempt or eligible for special tax treatment includes that owned by nonprofit religious, educational, and charitable organizations; property owned by the elderly and handicapped; agricultural, horticultural, and forest lands; and some properties with energy-efficient heating and cooling systems.

Assessment. Real estate is valued for property tax purposes by county or township assessors or appraisers. This official valuation process is called **assessment**. A property's **assessed value** is generally based on the sales prices of comparable properties, although practices may vary. Land values may be assessed separately from buildings or other improvements, and different valuation methods may be used for different types of property. In some states, assessed value may be less than market value, such as 80% of market value. The North Carolina Machinery Act mandates that assessed value is 100% of market value. State laws may provide for property to be periodically reassessed. *(In North Carolina)*

Sometimes, a property owner believes that an error was made in determining the assessed property value—usually that the assessment is too high in comparison with the assessments of neighboring properties. Such owners may present their objections to a local board of appeal or board of review. Protests or appeals with regard to tax assessments may ultimately be taken to court.

Tax rates. The process of arriving at a real estate property tax rate begins with the adoption of a budget by each taxing district. Each budget covers the financial requirements of the taxing body for the coming fiscal year. The fiscal year may be the January through December calendar year or some other 12-month period designated by statute. The budget must include an estimate of all expenditures for the year.

Chapter 3 Encumbrances on Real Property **55**

The next step is appropriation. *Appropriation* is the way a taxing body authorizes the expenditure of funds and provides for the sources of the funding. Appropriation generally involves the adoption of an ordinance or the passage of a law that states the specific terms of the proposed taxation.

The amount to be raised from the general real estate property tax is then imposed on property owners through a tax levy. A *tax levy* is the formal action taken to impose the tax, usually by a vote of the taxing district's governing body.

The property tax rate for each taxing body is computed separately. To arrive at a property tax rate, the total monies needed for the coming fiscal year are divided by the total assessments of all the real estate located within the taxing body's jurisdiction.

The property tax rate may be stated in a number of ways. In many areas, it is expressed in mills. ==A **mill** is 1/1,000 of a dollar, or $0.001.== The property tax rate may be expressed as a mill-per-dollar ratio—for instance, in dollars per hundred or in dollars per thousand. A property tax rate of 0.032, or 3.2%, could be expressed as 32 mills, or $3.20 per $100 of assessed value or $32 per $1,000 of assessed value.

A property owner's tax bill is computed by applying the property tax rate to the assessed valuation of the property.

■ **FOR EXAMPLE** If a property is assessed for tax purposes at $160,000, at a tax rate of 3%, or 30 mills, the tax will be $4,800 ($160,000 × 0.03).

If an equalization factor is used, the computation with an equalization factor of 120% will be $5,760 ($160,000 × 1.20 = $192,000, then $192,000 × 0.03 = $5,760).

In North Carolina

Taxation timetable. In North Carolina, in January of each tax year, all taxable real property must be listed in the county in which it is located. All listed property is assessed at its fair market value. ==Real property is appraised based on a statutory schedule and then is reappraised every eight years, a process referred to as **octennial reappraisal**.== Real property may be reassessed more frequently than every eight years. In addition, the county or city may choose to make horizontal adjustments in the fourth year after reappraisal. This means the values of certain types of property or of properties within certain areas may be uniformly adjusted to current value by applying an *across the board* percentage increase or decrease.

Each county or municipality determines the appropriate property tax rate every year as part of its budgeting process. The rate is calculated by dividing the total amount of revenue needed by the total assessed value of all the property in the county or city. A new property tax rate must be established by July 1 of each year or the property tax rate from the previous year will stand. Property tax rates are usually expressed as a certain dollar amount per $100 of assessed value. Per the Machinery Act (NCGS §105-271), assessed value must be equal to market value, at least at the time the assessment is established.

MATH CONCEPTS

PROPERTY TAXES

Owners of real property in North Carolina are required to pay annual property taxes based on an assessed value of the property and an annual tax rate.

Formulas:
Annual taxes = Tax rate × Assessed value
Assessed value = Annual taxes ÷ Tax rate
Tax rate = Annual taxes ÷ Assessed value

Note: The tax rate is expressed as a dollar amount per $100 of assessed value. If the tax rate is $1.67/$100, the property owner will pay $1.67 for each $100 of assessed value. The assessed value can be divided by 100, and the result multiplied by $1.67 to get the annual taxes. Or divide the $1.67 by 100 (1.67 ÷ 100 = 0.0167) and multiply by the assessed value (0.0167 × Assessed value).

Example 1: If the tax rate is $1.67/$100 and the assessed value is $120,000, what are the annual taxes?

$1.67 ÷ $100 = 0.0167 × $120,000 = $2,004 annual taxes, or
$120,000 ÷ 100 = $1,200 × $1.67 = $2,004.

Example 2: If the annual taxes are $1,800 and the assessed value is $110,000. What is the annual tax rate?

$1,800 ÷ $110,000 = 0.0163636, rounded to 0.0164 × 100 = $1.64/$100

Example 3: If the tax rate is $1.20/$100 and the annual taxes are $1,200, what is the assessed value?

$1,200 ÷ 0.012 (rate ÷ $100) = $100,000 assessed value.

■ **FOR EXAMPLE** If a city has an annual budget of $705,600 and has property within its jurisdiction with assessed value of $78,400,000, this year's tax rate would be

$705,600 ÷ $78,400,000 = $0.90 per $100 of valuation

If the tax rate were $0.90 per $100 of value, a $90,000 home would get a tax bill for $810.

$90,000 ÷ $100 × 0.90 = $810

If the tax rate were only $0.80 per $100 of value, the same $90,000 home would get a tax bill for $720.

$90,000 ÷ $100 × 0.80 = $720

In North Carolina

Each year's property taxes are legally due and payable on September 1. However, because interest does not begin accruing until early in January of the following year, most people pay their real property taxes in late December. The last day that current real property taxes can be paid without penalty is January 5 of the following year. It is worth noting that even though cities and counties operate under a fiscal year (beginning on July 1 and ending on June 30), taxes are prorated based on the calendar year (see Figure 3.3).

FIGURE 3.3

North Carolina Taxation Timetable

Jan 1	Jan 5	Jan 31	July 1	Aug	Sept 1
Tax lien filed	Last year's tax must be paid	Taxable property listed	New tax rate set	Tax bills mailed	Tax due & payable

In North Carolina

North Carolina property tax liens. As noted earlier, property taxes are liens that attach to real property as of the listing date. In other words, even though property taxes are not due until September 1 of any given year, the tax lien takes effect the previous January 1. Remember, this tax lien takes priority over all other liens.

Appraisal versus Assessment

The *appraisal* of real property may be defined as a process or an opinion as to value of property and how that value is communicated (see Chapter 17). The **assessment** is an official valuation of property for the purpose of establishing assessed value for tax purposes. Even though similar in concept, the techniques used in appraisal and assessment are quite different. Tax assessors do not have the time to assess individual properties like appraisers for reasons such as loan applications. In the assessment process one method routinely used is the **mass appraisal** technique that determines assessed value for all lands in a given area by applying an overall percentage increase or decrease. This method is often used in North Carolina in conjunction with a *horizontal adjustment*. Real property may be subject to reassessment if substantial improvements are added to the property.

Special Assessments

Special assessments, the second category of real estate taxes, are special taxes levied on real estate for public improvements made to that real estate. Typically, an assessment is levied for an entire neighborhood or area that has sought improvements from the government.

Property owners of properties that benefit directly from the improvements are required to pay for them. Special assessments are authorized for the installation of paved streets, curbs, gutters, sidewalks, storm sewers, street lighting, beach erosion drainage projects, and water control, to mention just a few. Because these improvements increase the value of the affected properties, the owners are, in effect, merely reimbursing the taxing entity for that increase. Either a county or a city may levy the special assessment, and statutes regulate how the assessment is to be prorated and levied. The assessment could be based on the cost per front foot or on the total area of the land that benefits. Large assessment bills may be prorated over several years.

Like ad valorem taxes, special assessment liens enjoy priority over other types of liens. (However, they do not take precedence over ad valorem property taxes.) Unlike property tax, special assessments are not tax deductible.

KEY POINT REVIEW

An **encumbrance** is a claim, charge, or liability that attaches to real estate and may be one of the following:

- **Lien** is a claim of a creditor or taxing authority against the real property of a debtor that is used as security to ensure repayment of the debt. Note the following: A lien is not an ownership interest in real estate; it is an encumbrance that transfers with it (runs with the land) and lessens its value or impairs its use because it binds all successive owners until paid and cleared. If a debtor defaults in payment of debt, a lienholder must bring legal action to
  — force the sale of the property, or
  — acquire title.
- **Deed restrictions** or **covenants, conditions, and restrictions (CC&Rs)** are private agreements that affect the use of land.
- **Lis pendens** is a lawsuit that may affect title.

A lien is either of the following:

- **General**—affects all of a debtor's property, both real and personal. General liens include judgments, estate and inheritance taxes, decedent's debts, corporate franchise taxes, and Internal Revenue Service taxes.
- **Specific**—affects only identified property. Specific liens include a vendor's lien, a mechanic's lien, a mortgage lien, a real estate tax lien, and a lien for special assessments and utilities.
- In North Carolina, private residential and commercial construction projects costing more than $30,000 must designate a lien agent. Vendors must give notice to lien agent within 15 days of starting work to retain mechanic's lien priority. Owner-occupied, detached, single-family projects are exempt.
- North Carolina Commercial Real Estate Broker Lien allows listing agent in a commercial transaction to secure commission with a lien.

Priority of liens determines the order in which claims will be satisfied (paid off):

- Generally, first to record is first in right.
- Real estate taxes and special assessments take priority over all other liens.
- A **subordination agreement** between lienholders can be used to change order of priority.

Easements are rights to use the land of another:

- An **easement appurtenant** is said to *run with the land* when title is transferred.
- An **easement in gross** is an individual or company interest in or right to use another's land.
- An easement is usually created by written agreement between the parties.
- An **easement by necessity** arises when land has no access to a street or public way.
- An **easement by prescription** is acquired when a claimant has used another's land for 7 to 20 years. The use must be open, continuous, exclusive, adverse and notorious.

An easement is terminated

- when the need no longer exists,
- when the owner of either the dominant or the servient tenement becomes the sole owner,
- by release of the right of easement to the owner of the servient tenement,
- if the easement is abandoned, or
- by the nonuse of prescriptive easement.

License is a personal privilege to enter the land of another for a specific purpose.

Encroachment occurs when all or part of a structure or improvement illegally intrudes on the land of another or beyond legal building lines.

Real estate taxes include the following:

- **Ad valorem** taxes, based on value of property taxed, are
  — specific, involuntary, statutory liens; and
  — levied by states, counties, municipalities, school districts, utility districts, parks and recreation districts, and others.
- Property **assessments** (valuations) are conducted by county or township tax assessors or appraisers.
  — Assessed value is generally based on sales prices of comparable properties. Land value may be assessed separately from building value and improvements, and different valuation methods may be used for different types of property.
- Tax rates for each taxing body are computed separately (and may be expressed in mills—1/1,000 of a dollar, or $0.001). **Mills** may be shown as dollars per hundred or thousand dollars of assessed value.
- Regulated by North Carolina **Machinery Act**
  — **Octennial reappraisal** is required by statute but property may experience horizontal adjustment in fourth year.

Levied on property that benefits from public improvements, **special assessments**

- are always specific and statutory,
- may be voluntary or involuntary,
- are not tax deductible, and
- are usually paid in annual installments over a period of years.

QUESTIONS

1. Which of the following is an example of a specific lien?
   a. Judgment lien
   b. Special assessment lien
   c. Personal property tax lien
   d. IRS income tax lien

2. Which of the following is an example of a general lien?
   a. Mortgage lien
   b. Real estate tax lien
   c. Mechanics' lien
   d. State income tax lien

3. A mechanics' lien
   a. must be filed within 180 days after last day of labor.
   b. is a general lien that is good for 10 years.
   c. is used to collect payment from the general contractor.
   d. gives security to persons that work on real property owned by others.

4. According to typical lien priority, which of the following would be paid first from proceeds from a court-ordered sale?
   a. Mortgage lien
   b. Judgment lien
   c. Real property tax lien
   d. Special assessment lien

5. Which of the following liens typically would be given higher priority?
   a. Mortgage dated last year
   b. Current real estate taxes
   c. Mechanics' liens for work started before the mortgage was made
   d. Judgments rendered yesterday

6. Under city contract, ABC Paving Company paved a dirt road that runs adjacent to your property. As property owner, you would pay for this in the form of
   a. ad valorem real property taxes.
   b. personal property taxes.
   c. an invoice from the contractor.
   d. a special assessment.

7. A property owner has the legal right to pass over the land owned by his neighbor. He holds an
   a. easement.
   b. emblement.
   c. estate in land.
   d. encroachment.

8. After moving into his new home, Marco discovers that his neighbor gets to his workshop by regular use of Marco's driveway. Marco's lawyer explains that the neighbor's lot owns an easement over Marco's driveway. Marco's property is called
   a. the servient estate.
   b. a leasehold estate.
   c. a pur autre vie estate.
   d. the dominant estate.

9. All of the following terms are related to easements EXCEPT
   a. appurtenant.
   b. assessment.
   c. by necessity.
   d. by prescription.

10. In North Carolina, all real property MUST be reassessed every
    a. four years.
    b. six years.
    c. eight years.
    d. 10 years.

11. The ad valorem property tax rates may be adjusted every
    a. year.
    b. two years.
    c. four years.
    d. five years.

12. What is the assessed value of a house located in the city limits if the city tax rate is $0.80 per $100, the county tax rate is $0.50 per $100, and the owner's annual taxes are $1,600?
    a. $123,077
    b. $200,000
    c. $208,000
    d. $320,000

13. What is the monthly tax liability on a property assessed at $133,000 if the published tax rate is $1.678 per $100 of assessed value?
    a. $66.05
    b. $185.98
    c. $792.61
    d. $2,231.74

14. If you recently paid $2,000 in annual property taxes and the assessed value of your house is $183,500, what is the tax rate?
    a. $.9175 per $100
    b. $1.09 per $100
    c. $9.12 per $100
    d. $10.90 per $100

15. Property is appraised at $129,000. If property is assessed at 75% of the appraised value, what is the assessed value of the property?
    a. $69,750
    b. $96,750
    c. $129,000
    d. $172,000

16. A house was appraised at $389,000 for tax purposes. It was assessed at 85% of the appraised value. The taxes were $1.10 per $100 of value. How much were the annual taxes?
    a. $281.35
    b. $356.58
    c. $3,637.15
    d. $4,279.00

17. Market value for a property outside the city limits of Greensboro is $295,000. Assessed value is calculated at 80% of market value. The city tax rate is $0.84 per $100 and the county tax rate is $0.63 per $100. What is the monthly tax liability for this property?
    a. $123.90
    b. $154.88
    c. $289.10
    d. $361.38

18. A city has an annual budget of $7,248,000. If the city has taxable property that has an assessed value of $1,135,500,000, what tax rate per $100 of assessed value must be levied to raise the necessary money to meet the budget?
    a. $0.64
    b. $1.56
    c. $6.40
    d. $15.63

19. What is the annual real estate tax on a property valued at $135,000 and assessed for tax purposes at $47,250, with an equalization factor of 125%, when the tax rate is 25 mills?
    a. $945
    b. $1181
    c. $1418
    d. $1477

20. A residential lot in Mecklenburg County is presently assessed by the county tax assessor's office at $75,000, and the tax rate is $1.678/$100 of assessed value. If the property owner constructs a house on the lot that is assessed at $250,000 upon completion, what is the property owner's new monthly tax liability?
    a. $454.46
    b. $2,261.20
    c. $4,195.33
    d. $5,453.50

21. All of the following statements about mechanics' liens in North Carolina are true EXCEPT
    a. a lien agent must be designated only for private residential construction projects that cost over $30,000.
    b. a vendor that does not serve notice to the named lien agent of a construction project within 15 days of first furnishing materials or labor will forfeit mechanic's lien priority.
    c. private construction projects on a single-family home do not need to designate a lien agent if the properties are owner-occupied.
    d. a vendor must file the mechanic's lien no later than 120 days after delivery of their last labor or materials.

22. Which of the following North Carolina brokers can file a lien to secure payment of brokerage fees?
    a. Listing agent for a $10 million mansion
    b. Tenant's representative for the 20-year lease of a manufacturing plant
    c. Listing agent for the sale of a shopping center
    d. Buyer's agent for the purchase of an office building

CHAPTER 4

Property Description

LEARNING OBJECTIVES *When you have finished reading this chapter, you should be able to*

- **explain** the importance of an accurate legal description and list those documents requiring legal descriptions.
- **discuss** the legally acceptable methods of property description used in North Carolina, give examples, and know the characteristics of each.
- **learn** the various land measurements used in real estate practices and the importance of a survey.
- **define** these *key terms*:

base lines	monuments	section
calls	plat map	survey
government (rectangular or geodetic) survey system	point of beginning (POB)	tier
	principal meridians	topographic survey
	ranges	township
legal description	reference to a recorded plat (lot-and-block or recorded plat system)	
metes-and-bounds (boundary) description		

DESCRIBING LAND

One of the essential elements of a valid deed is an accurate legal description of the land being conveyed. The real estate involved must be identifiable from the wording of the deed and with reference to only the documents named in the deed. The courts have usually held that a description of land is legally sufficient if a competent surveyor can locate the real estate in question. Legal descriptions describe the land but not the improvements that are appurtenant and automatically run with the land. This means all items attached to the land will convey in the deed with the legal description unless specifically excluded by contract such as fixtures.

A **legal description** is an exact way of describing real estate in a contract, a deed, a mortgage, or another document that will be accepted by a court of law. While street addresses are not sufficient legal descriptions, the legal description in a deed or mortgage may be followed by the words *commonly known as* and the street address. The street address standing alone is referred to as an *informal description or reference*.

A typical parcel of land has been conveyed and transferred many times in the past. The description of the land in a deed, a mortgage, or another instrument should be the same as that used in the previous instrument of conveyance. Discrepancies, errors, and legal problems can be avoided or reduced if this practice is followed in drawing up subsequent conveyances.

IN PRACTICE One of the most frequent causes of lawsuits against brokers is inaccurate monuments and lot lines. Buyers need to be confident that the property they are purchasing is in fact what they believe they are buying. Relying on old surveys is not a good idea; the property should be resurveyed by a competent land surveyor, whether or not the lender requires it. Brokers should be very careful when stating the location of boundary lines. Brokers should encourage prospective buyers to hire a registered land surveyor if they plan to install fences or add to the buildings on their property. Recent flooding in North Carolina points out the need to be sure that buyers are informed about whether their property is in a flood plain that can also be determined by an appropriate survey.

■ METHODS OF DESCRIBING REAL ESTATE

There are three basic methods of legally describing real estate used in the United States: (1) metes and bounds, (2) the rectangular (government) survey, and (3) reference to recorded plat (lot and block). North Carolina also uses reference to a publicly recorded document that contains a legal description.

Metes and Bounds

A **metes-and-bounds description** is the earliest form of legal description used in the United States and is still the primary method of describing property in the original 13 colonies. It makes use of the boundaries and measurements of the land in question. This description shows the boundaries of the parcel and where they meet. Such a description starts at a definitely designated place called the **point of beginning (POB)** and proceeds around the boundaries of the tract (clockwise or counterclockwise) by reference to linear measurements and compass directions, referred to as **calls**. Each call gives the distance (metes) and direction (bounds). Each call begins with either North or South (the cardinal directions), then the number of degrees East or West, using a surveyor's compass. A metes-and-bounds description always ends at the POB so that the tract being described has closure.

In a metes-and-bounds description, the actual distance between monuments takes precedence over any linear measurement set forth in the description if the two measurements differ. **Monuments** are fixed objects used to establish real estate boundaries. Natural objects such as stones, large trees, lakes, and streams, as well as streets, highways, and markers placed by surveyors, are commonly used as monuments. Measurements often include the words *more or less*; the location of the monuments is more important than the distance stated in the wording. Problems are created in some instances when a monument has shifted or disappeared over the years.

An example of a metes-and-bounds description of a parcel of land (pictured in Figure 4.1) follows:

> A tract of land located in _____, _____, described as follows: Beginning at the intersection of the east line of Jones Road and the south line of Skull Drive; thence north 90° east along the south line of Skull Drive 200 feet; thence south 15° east 216.5 feet, more or less, to the center thread of Red Skull Creek; thence north 4° west along the center line of said creek to its intersection with the east line of Jones Road; thence north 105 feet, more or less, along the east line of Jones Road to the place of beginning.

FIGURE 4.1

Metes-and-Bounds Tract

When used to describe property within a town or city, a metes-and-bounds description may begin as follows:

> Beginning at a point on the southerly side of Kent Street, 100 feet easterly from the corner formed by the intersection of the southerly side of Kent Street and the easterly side of Broadway; thence . . .

In this description, the POB is given by reference to the intersection. The description must close by returning to the POB.

Metes-and-bounds descriptions may be very complex and should be handled with extreme care. When they include compass directions of the various lines and concave or convex curved lines, they can be difficult to understand. In such cases, the advice and counsel of a professional surveyor should be sought.

Rectangular (Government) Survey System

The **rectangular survey system**, sometimes called the *government survey system*, was established by Congress in 1785 to standardize the description of land acquired by the newly formed federal government. By dividing the land into rectangles, the survey provided land descriptions by describing the rectangle(s) in which the land was located. The system is based on two sets of intersecting lines: principal meridians and base lines. (See Figure 4.2.) The **principal meridians** run north and south, and the **base lines** run east and west. Both are located by reference to degrees of longitude and latitude. Each principal meridian has a name or number and is crossed by a base line. Each principal meridian and its corresponding base line are used to survey a definite area of land, indicated on the map by boundary lines. There are 37 principal meridians in the United States.

FIGURE 4.2

Township Lines

The directions of township lines and range lines may be easily remembered by thinking of the words this way:

Township lines
Range lines

FIGURE 4.3

Range Lines

Each principal meridian describes only specific areas of land by boundaries. No parcel of land is described by reference to more than one principal meridian. The meridian used may not necessarily be the nearest one.

Ranges The land on either side of a principal meridian is divided into six-mile-wide strips by lines that run north and south, *parallel to the meridian*. These north-south strips of land are called **ranges**. (See Figure 4.3.) They are designated by consecutive numbers east or west of the principal meridian. For example, Range 3 East would be a strip of land between 12 and 18 miles east of its principal meridian.

Township tiers Lines running east and west, *parallel to the base line* and six miles apart, are referred to as **township lines**. (See Figure 4.2.) They form strips of land called **township tiers**. These township tiers are designated by consecutive numbers north or south of the base line. For instance, the strip of land between 6 and 12 miles north of a base line is Township 2 North.

Township squares When the horizontal township lines and the vertical range lines intersect, they form squares. These *township* squares are the basic units of the rectangular survey system. (See Figure 4.4.) **Townships** are 6 miles square and contain 36 square miles (23,040 acres).

FIGURE 4.4

Townships in the Rectangular Survey System

Each township is given a legal description. The township's description includes the following:

- Designation of the township tier in which the township is located
- Designation of the range strip
- Name or number of the principal meridian for that area

■ **FOR EXAMPLE** In Figure 4.4, the shaded township is described as Township 3 North, Range 4 East of the Principal Meridian. This township is the third strip, or tier, north of the base line, and it designates the township number and direction. The township is also located in the fourth range strip (those running north and south) east of the principal meridian. Finally, reference is made to the principal meridian because the land being described is within the boundary of land surveyed from that meridian. This description is abbreviated as T3N, R4E 4th Principal Meridian.

Sections Township squares are subdivided into sections and subsections called halves and quarters, which can be further divided. Each township contains 36 sections. Each section is one square mile or 640 acres, with 43,560 square feet in each acre. Sections are numbered 1 through 36, as shown in Figure 4.5. Section 1 is always in the northeast, or upper right-hand, corner. The numbering proceeds right to left to the upper left-hand corner. From there, the numbers drop down to the next tier and continue from left to right, then back from right to left. By law, each Section 16 was set aside for school purposes, and the sale or rental proceeds from this land were originally available for township school use. The schoolhouse was usually located in this section so it would be centrally located for all the students in the township. As a result, Section 16 is commonly referred to as a *school section*.

> Townships are numbered the same way a field is plowed. Remember: *right to left, left to right, right to left.*

FIGURE 4.5

Sections in a Township

Sections are divided into *halves* (320 acres) and *quarters* (160 acres). In turn, each of those parts is further divided into halves and quarters. The southeast quarter of a section, which is a 160-acre tract, is abbreviated SE¼. The SE¼ of SE¼ of SE¼ of Section 1 would be a 10-acre square in the lower right-hand corner of Section 1. (See Figure 4.6.)

FIGURE 4.6

A Section

	5,280 Feet		
1,320	1,320	2,640	
W½ of NW¼ (80 Acres)	E½ of NW¼ (80 Acres)	NE¼ (160 Acres)	2,640
NW¼ of SW¼ (40 Acres)	NE¼ of SW¼ (40 Acres)	N½ of NW¼ of SE¼ (20 Acres) / 20 Acres	W½ of NE¼ of SE¼ (20 Acres) / 1 Furlong / 20 Acres	1,320
SW¼ of SW¼ (40 Acres)	40 Acres / 440 Yards	(10 Acres) / 660 Feet / (10 Acres) / 660 Feet	5 Acres / 5 Acres / SE¼ of SE¼ of SE¼ 10 Acres / 5 Acs. / 5 Acs.	1,320

> **Math Shortcut**
>
> To calculate acres in a survey system description, multiply all the denominators and divide that number into 640 acres. For instance, the SE¼ of SE¼ of SE¼ of Section 1 = 4 × 4 × 4 = 64; 640 ÷ 64 = 10 acres.

The rectangular survey system sometimes uses a shorthand method in its descriptions. For instance, a comma may be used in place of the word *of*: SE¼, SE¼, SE¼, Section 1. It is possible to combine portions of a section, such as NE¼ of SW¼ and N½ of NW¼ of SE¼ of Section 1, which could also be written NE¼, SW¼; N½, NW¼, SE¼ of Section 1. A semicolon means *and*. Because of the semicolon in this description, the area is 60 acres.

Starting with township and range lines, Figure 4.7 illustrates how sections are created and subdivided.

FIGURE 4.7

Parts of a Township

Township Lines
(Six miles lines running east and west)

Range Lines
(Six miles lines running north and south)

Township
(The squares formed by the intersections of the lines to form the basic units of the rectangular systems)

Section in a Township
(Each township is divided into 36 sections)

A Section
(The various subdivisions into which a 640 acre sections may be divided)

Reading a rectangular survey description To determine the location and size of a property described in the rectangular or government survey style, *start at the end* and work backward to the beginning, *reading from right to left*. For example, consider the following description (see Figure 4.6):

> The S½ of the NW¼ of the SE¼ of Section 11, Township 8 North, Range 6 West of the Fourth Principal Meridian.

To locate this tract of land from the citation alone, first search for the fourth principal meridian on a map of the United States and note its base line. Then, on a regional map, find the township in which the property is located by counting six range strips west of the fourth principal meridian and eight townships north of its corresponding base line. After locating Section 11, divide the section into quarters. Then divide the SE¼ into quarters, and then the NW¼ of that into halves. The S½ of that NW¼ contains the property in question.

Legal descriptions should always include the name of the county and state in which the land is located because meridians often relate to more than one state and occasionally relate to two base lines. For example, the description "the southwest quarter of Section 10, Township 4 North, Range 1 West of the Fourth Principal Meridian" could refer to land in either Illinois or Wisconsin.

③ Reference to a Recorded Plat (Lot and Block)

[Handwritten margin note: survey recorded by Plat book # and Plat page #]

The third legal description commonly used is by **reference to a recorded plat (lot-and-block** or **recorded plat system).** It is a system that uses lot and block numbers—referred to as a *plat* or *subdivision*—placed in the Registry of Deeds of the county where the land is located. This is the most common and worry-free method of describing property in urban areas.

The first step in subdividing land is the preparation of a **plat map**—by a licensed surveyor or engineer—as illustrated in Figure 4.8.

FIGURE 4.8

Subdivision Plat Map

On this plat map, the land is divided into numbered or lettered blocks and lots, and streets or access roads for public use are indicated. Lot sizes and street details must be indicated completely and must comply with all local ordinances and requirements. When properly signed and approved, the subdivision plat must be recorded in the public records in the county where the land is located to be a legally acceptable property description. In describing a lot from a recorded subdivision plat, the lot and block number, name or number of the subdivision plat, and name of the county and state are used. For example:

> Being all of Lot Number Forty-one (41) as shown and designated on a certain map prepared by John Doe, C.E., dated May 16, 1980, entitled "Plan of Bradford Extension," which said map is duly recorded in Map Book 7 at Page 32, in the Office of the Register of Deeds of Craven County, to which map reference is hereby made for a further and better description. Less and except any existing road right of ways of record.

Reference to a Recorded Deed

The third method of land description used in North Carolina is by reference to a publicly recorded document, usually an earlier deed to the identical property. This deed typically contains a legal description of the property that is to be conveyed. For example, if a deed dated September 17, 1993, included the previous description by reference to a recorded plat, a deed prepared four years later that conveyed the same property could incorporate that same description by referring to the previous deed. Deeds do not make reference to buildings on the property.

IN PRACTICE When filling in the blanks of a sales contract, a broker should exercise great care to ensure that a proper and accurate legal description is used. Never list the legal description as N/A for "not applicable."

Because legal descriptions of newly subdivided land, once recorded, affect title to real estate, they should only be prepared by a professional land surveyor or a lawyer. Real estate brokers who attempt to draft legal descriptions create potential risks for themselves and their clients and customers. (See G.S. 93A-6 (a)(11), and Rule A.0111.) Furthermore, when entered on a document of conveyance such as a deed, legal descriptions should be copied with care. For example, an incorrectly worded legal description in a sales contract may obligate the seller to convey or the buyer to purchase more or less land than either one intended. Title problems can also arise for the buyer who seeks to convey the property at a future date.

Informal References

The use of informal references in describing property can often lead to legal problems, but informal references may be sufficient if they enable a surveyor to precisely locate the parcel of real estate. A street address is a good example of an informal reference and is often used in a listing contract and short-term rental agreements. Any contract to convey a real property interest and any type of deed should always contain a legally acceptable description.

Preparation and Use of a Survey

Legal descriptions should not be changed, altered, or combined without adequate information from a competent authority such as a surveyor or title lawyer. Legal descriptions should always include the name of the county and state in which the land is located.

A professional land surveyor is trained and licensed to locate a given parcel of land and to determine its legal description. The surveyor does this by preparing a **survey,** which sets forth the legal description of the property, and a *survey sketch,* which shows the location and dimensions of the parcel. When a survey also shows the location, size, and shape of buildings located on the lot, it is referred to as a *physical survey,* a *mortgage location survey,* or an *identification survey.* When a survey shows the *lay of the land,* such as where there are hills and valleys, it is called a **topographic survey** or *topo survey.* Surveys are required in many real estate transactions, such as when conveying a portion of a given tract of land, conveying real estate as security for a mortgage loan, showing the location of new construction, locating roads and highways, and determining the legal description of the land on which a particular building is located. When underwriting a real estate loan, the lender might require an up-to-date survey of the collateral property to make sure that there are no encroachments on the property because an encroachment could render the title to the property unmarketable. Encroachments could cross boundary lines, easements, or setbacks. Title insurance routinely excludes coverage of title defects that would have been discovered by a survey, if a survey was not conducted.

MATH CONCEPTS

LAND ACQUISITION COSTS

To calculate the cost of purchasing land, use the same unit in which the cost is given. Costs quoted per square foot must be multiplied by the proper number of square feet; costs quoted per acre must be multiplied by the proper number of acres; et cetera.

To calculate the cost of a parcel of land of three acres at $1.10 per square foot, convert the acreage to square feet before multiplying:

43,560 square feet per acre × 3 acres = 130,680 square feet

130,680 square feet × $1.10 per square foot = $143,748

To calculate the cost of a parcel of land of 17,500 square feet at $60,000 per acre, convert the cost per acre into the cost per square foot before multiplying by the number of square feet in the parcel:

$60,000 per acre ÷ 43,560 square feet per acre =
$1.38 (rounded) per square foot

17,500 square feet × $1.38 per square foot = $24,150

RELATED WEBSITE

North Carolina Society of Surveyors: www.ncsurveyors.com

KEY POINT REVIEW

The four methods of **legal description** of land are the following.

The **metes-and-bounds method**

- measures distances (metes);
- starts from a **point of beginning (POB)**;
- follows compass directions or angles (bounds);
- arrives at the point of ending (POE), which must be the same as the POB; and
- uses **monuments** (fixed objects or markers) to identify the POB and corners or places where boundary lines change direction.

The **government rectangular survey system**

- divides land into rectangles;
- is measured from the intersection of **principal meridians** and **base lines**;
- is referenced by degrees of longitude and latitude;
- uses **township lines**, which run east to west parallel to and counted from base lines that are
  — 6 miles apart,
  — in units called *townships* of 36 square miles each,
  — in rows of townships called *tiers*, and
- arranged so each township is divided into 36 sections of one mile square (640 acres), counted from northeast and running right to left, then left to right, et cetera; and
- uses **range lines**, which run north to south parallel to (and counted from) principal meridian, that are
  — 6 miles apart and
  — in rows called *ranges*.

The **reference to a recorded plat (lot-and-block)** is

- approved by the governing body, and
- filed in public records of the county where the land is located.

The **reference to a recorded deed** is identical property referenced in an earlier deed.

An **informal reference**, such as a street address, is not adequate to convey property but is acceptable in a lease.

A **survey** should be obtained to verify lot dimensions and identify easements and encroachments.

QUESTIONS

1. In a sales contract, which of the following is an acceptable legal description of property?
   a. MLS number of the listed property
   b. "Johnson property on Maple Street"
   c. Metes and bounds description
   d. Lot number

2. A monument is used in which of the following types of legal descriptions?
   a. Lot and block
   b. Metes and bounds
   c. Rectangular survey
   d. Government survey

3. In describing real estate, the system that uses feet, degrees, and natural markers is the
   a. rectangular survey.
   b. metes-and-bounds description.
   c. government survey.
   d. lot and block system.

4. If the property being transferred is residential property within an established subdivision, the most commonly used legal description would be
   a. street address.
   b. metes-and-bounds.
   c. reference to a recorded plat.
   d. reference to a recorded deed.

5. A street address would be adequate property description for a
   a. short-term lease.
   b. sales contract.
   c. special warranty deed.
   d. deed of trust.

Answer questions 6 through 9 according to the information given on the plat of Mountainside Manor in Figure 4.9.

6. Which of the following statements is true?
   a. Lot 9, Block A is larger than Lot 12 in the same block.
   b. The plat for the lots on the southerly side of Wolf Road between Goodrich Boulevard and Carney Street is found on Sheet 3.
   c. Lot 8, Block A has the longest road frontage.
   d. Lot 11, Block B has more frontage than Lot 2, Block A.

7. Which of the following lots has the most road frontage on Jasmine Lane?
   a. Lot 10, Block B
   b. Lot 11, Block B
   c. Lot 7, Block A
   d. Lot 2, Block A

8. On the plat, how many lots have easements?
   a. One
   b. Two
   c. Three
   d. Four

9. If the local market value of undeveloped land is $25,000 per acre, what is the value of a lot that has 21,780 square feet?
   a. $12,500
   b. $15,755
   c. $215,422
   d. $544,500

10. A rectangular parcel of land was purchased that contained 350 acres with 1,300 feet of road frontage. An investor wants to buy the neighboring rectangular tract that has the same depth but has 6,000 feet of road frontage. How many acres are in the tract of land that the investor wants to buy?
    a. 1,430 acres
    b. 1,615.4 acres
    c. 1,815.3 acres
    d. 1,840 acres

11. A parcel of land is 660 ft. by 660 ft., and a small stream equally divides the parcel into two lots. How many acres are contained in each lot?
    a. 0.5
    b. 2.5
    c. 5
    d. 10

12. Find the cost of building a house 29' × 34' × 17' with a gable roof 8' high at the highest point. The cost of construction is $2.25 per cubic foot.
    a. $55,462.50
    b. $46,588.50
    c. $37,714.50
    d. $27,731.25

13. If you purchase a lot that is 125' × 150' for $6,468.75, what price did you pay per front foot?
    a. $23.52
    b. $43.13
    c. $51.75
    d. $64.69

14. What is the proper description of this shaded area of a section using the rectangular government survey?

    a. SW¼ of the NE¼ and the N½ of the SE¼ of the SW¼
    b. N½ of the NE¼ of the SW¼ and the SE¼ of the NW¼
    c. SW¼ of the SE¼ of the NW¼ and the N½ of the NE¼ of the SW¼
    d. S½ of the SW¼ of the NE¼ and the NE¼ of the NW¼ of the SE¼

15. When surveying land, a surveyor refers to the principal meridian that is
    a. nearest the land being surveyed.
    b. in the same state as the land being surveyed.
    c. not more than 40 townships or 15 ranges distant from the land being surveyed.
    d. within the rectangular survey system area in which the land being surveyed is located.

16. The N½ of the SW¼ of a section contains how many acres?
    a. 20
    b. 40
    c. 60
    d. 80

17. In describing real estate, the system that may use a property's physical features to determine boundaries and measurements is
    a. rectangular survey.
    b. metes-and-bounds.
    c. government survey.
    d. lot-and-block.

Questions 18 through 21 refer to the following illustration of a whole township and parts of the adjacent townships.

18. The section marked A is which of the following?
    a. School section
    b. Section 31
    c. Section 36
    d. Government lot

19. Which of the following is Section 6?
    a. A
    b. B
    c. C
    d. D

20. The section directly below C is
    a. Section 7.
    b. Section 12.
    c. Section 25.
    d. Section 30.

21. Which of the following is Section D?
    a. Section 1
    b. Section 6
    c. Section 31
    d. Section 36

22. Which of these shaded areas of a section depicts the NE¼ of the SE¼ of the SW¼?

    a. Area 1
    b. Area 2
    c. Area 3
    d. Area 4

23. A buyer purchased a half-acre parcel for $2.15 per square foot. What was the selling price of the parcel?
    a. $774
    b. $46,827
    c. $1,376
    d. $93,654

24. How many acres are contained in the tract described as "beginning at the NW corner of the SW¼, then south along the west line to the SW corner of the section, then east along the south line of the section 2,640 feet, more or less, to the SE corner of the said SW¼, then in a straight line to the POB"?
    a. 80 acres
    b. 90 acres
    c. 100 acres
    d. 160 acres

FIGURE 4.9

Plat of Mountainside Manor Subdivision

CHAPTER 5

Transfer of Title to Real Property

■ **LEARNING OBJECTIVES** *When you have finished reading this chapter, you should be able to*

- **identify** and understand the methods of transferring title, and the essential and nonessential elements of a deed.
- **calculate** excise tax due when property is transferred.
- **describe** the three major types of deeds used in North Carolina.
- **explain** the processes of title examination and recordation.
- **define** these *key terms*:

abstract of title	covenant	marketable title
action to quiet title	deed	Marketable Title Act
adverse possession	delivery and acceptance	North Carolina Intestate
alienation	eminent domain	Succession Act
ALTA policy	escheat	quitclaim deed
bargain and sale deed	excise tax	recording
chain of title	general warranty deed	special warranty deed
cloud on the title	grantee	title
condemnation	granting clause	title insurance
Conner Act	grantor	title search
constructive notice	intestate	will

■ METHODS OF TRANSFERRING TITLE

Title to real estate means the right to or ownership of the land. The word *title* also is used to refer to the documentary evidence of the right of ownership, such as a deed. The word *title* refers to a summation of all the things property owners possess to prove and protect their ownership interest in property. The term *title* has two functions: (1) it represents the bundle of legal rights the owner possesses in the real estate, and (2) it denotes the facts that, if proven, enable a person to recover or retain ownership or possession of a parcel of real estate.

A parcel of real estate may be transferred voluntarily by sale or gift, or it may be taken involuntarily by operation of law. In addition, it may be transferred by will or descent after a person has died. Transfer of title is referred to as **alienation**, which means the act of transferring property to another.

Voluntary Alienation

Most transactions utilizing real estate brokers involve voluntary alienation. Voluntary alienation (transfer) of title may be made by either gift or sale with the wishes and consent of the property owner. To transfer title by voluntary alienation during an owner's lifetime, that owner must use some form of deed.

A **deed** is a written instrument by which an owner of real estate intentionally conveys right, title, or interest in the parcel of real estate to another. A deed is evidence of title. The owner is referred to as the **grantor**, and the person who receives title is called the **grantee** (see Figure 5.1). A deed is executed (signed) only by the grantor(s). The grantee(s) does not sign the deed.

FIGURE 5.1

Legal Terms for Parties in Real Estate Transactions

In reference to parties to a real estate instrument, such as a deed, the parties are referred to in legal terms such as *grantor* and *grantee*. The "OR" is the giver of the paper, and the "EE" is the receiver of the paper.

Type of Document	Giver	Receiver
Deed	Grantor (Seller)	Grantee (Buyer)
Offer	Offeror (Buyer)	Offeree (Seller)
Counteroffer	Offeror (Seller)	Offeree (Buyer)
Lease	Lessor (Landlord)	Lessee (Tenant)
Mortgage	Mortgagor (Buyer)	Mortgagee (Lender)
Option	Optionor (Seller)	Optionee (Buyer)
Installment Contract	Vendor (Seller)	Vendee (Buyer)
Will	Devisor (Deceased)	Devisee (Heir)
Contract	Vendor (Seller)	Vendee (Buyer)

In North Carolina

Requirements for a valid conveyance. A valid deed must contain certain essential elements, including the following:

- The deed must be in writing.
- The grantor must have the legal capacity to execute a deed.
- Grantee named with reasonable certainty to be identified.
- There must be adequate words of conveyance.
- There must be an accurate legal description of the property conveyed.
- The deed must be signed by the grantors.
- The deed must be delivered to and voluntarily accepted by the grantee.

Grantor. A grantor must have a legal existence, be of lawful age, and be legally competent in order to convey title to real estate.

> A **grantor** conveys property to a grantee.
>
> A **grantee** receives property from a grantor.
>
> A **deed** is the instrument that conveys property from a grantor to a grantee.

A grantor generally is held to have sufficient mental capacity to execute a deed if that grantor is capable of understanding the action. A deed executed by a person while mentally impaired (for example, by intoxication) is only voidable—it is not void. A deed executed by a person who has been judged legally incompetent is considered to be void. A minor (a person who has not reached the age of majority) does not have legal capacity to transfer title, so any attempted conveyance by a minor is voidable.

Identification of grantor and grantee. To be valid, a deed must name both the grantor and the grantee in such a way that they are readily identifiable. Furthermore, the grantee must be a real person, either a natural person or an artificial person, such as a corporation. A deed naming as the grantee a fictitious person, a company that does not exist, or a society or club that is not properly incorporated is considered void. The grantee cannot be a dead person but may be a minor. The minor may receive real property via deed but may not legally convey the property (sign a deed) until after turning 18.

Words of conveyance. A deed of conveyance transfers a present interest (freehold estate) in real estate, and it must contain words that state the grantor's intention to convey the property at this time. An expression of intent to convey at some future time is inadequate. Such words of conveyance are often called the **granting clause**. Depending on the type of deed and the obligations agreed to by the grantor, the wording is generally *convey and warrant*; *grant, bargain, and sell*; or *remise, release, and quitclaim*.

Legal description. To be valid, a deed must contain an acceptable, accurate, legal description of the real estate conveyed. Land has been described adequately if a competent surveyor could locate the property from the description used. The rules relative to describing real estate were discussed in Chapter 4.

Signature of grantor. To be valid, a deed must be signed by all the grantors (or their authorized agents) named in the deed. In North Carolina, if the grantor is married, both the grantor and the grantor's spouse must sign the deed even if only one spouse is named in the deed.

Delivery. Before a transfer of title by conveyance can take effect, there must be **delivery and acceptance**; that is, actual *delivery* of the deed by the grantor and either actual or implied *acceptance* by the grantee. Delivery may be made by the grantor to the grantee personally or to a third party who is authorized by the grantee to accept the deed (such as a lawyer). Title is said to *pass* when a deed is delivered and voluntarily accepted. In North Carolina, recordation of the deed by the buyers or their agent is recognized as acceptance. The effective date of the transfer of title from the grantor to the grantee is the date of delivery of the deed itself.

Elements that are not required. Nonessential elements often appear in deeds, but are not required for validity. Nonessential elements include the following:

- Deeds do not have to be *witnessed*.
- Deeds do not have to be *dated* (although, for practical matters, it may be wise to do so).

Chapter 5 Transfer of Title to Real Property 81

- Deeds do not have to include a statement as to the amount of *consideration* (the amount of money that was paid for the property).
- Deeds do not have to be *acknowledged* (i.e., *notarized*).
- Deeds do not have to be *recorded* to be valid but, under the Conner Act, the grantees must record the valid deed to protect their interest as to third parties under the law.

In North Carolina
- Effective in 1999, deeds do not have to be *sealed* in North Carolina to be valid. Standard deed forms may continue to have the word *seal* after the signature; however, it is no longer required to create a valid deed. Signing *under seal* does have certain legal advantages such as extending the statute of limitations protecting the parties' rights from three years to 10 years.

Note that acknowledgment (or notarization) is necessary before a deed can be recorded, and recording a deed is necessary to protect the grantee's interests in the property. Recording is discussed later in this chapter.

Types of Deeds

Three common forms of deeds—the general warranty deed, the special warranty deed, and the quitclaim deed—and in North Carolina several types of special-purpose deeds are used.

General warranty deed. For a purchaser of real estate, a **general warranty deed** provides greater protection than any other deed. It is the best deed for the grantee, but it gives the grantor the greatest degree of liability. It is referred to as a *general warranty deed*, a *full covenant and warranty deed*, or simply a *warranty deed* because the grantor is legally bound by certain basic **covenants** or warranties:

General Warranty Deed

Five covenants:
1. Covenant of seisin
2. Covenant against encumbrances
3. Covenant of quiet enjoyment
4. Covenant of further assurance
5. Covenant of warranty forever

- *Covenant of seisin and the right to convey:* The grantor warrants that he or she is the legal owner of the property and has the right to convey title to it. Delivery of seisin is the actual transfer of title.
- *Covenant against encumbrances:* The grantor warrants that the property is free from any liens or encumbrances except those of record. Encumbrances would generally include such items as mortgages, mechanics' liens, real estate tax liens, protective covenants, and easements.
- *Covenant of quiet enjoyment:* The grantor guarantees that the grantee's title will be good against third parties who might bring court actions to establish superior title to the property. If the grantee's title is found to be inferior, the grantor is liable for damages.
- *Covenant of further assurance:* The grantor promises to obtain and deliver any instrument needed to make the title good. For example, if an error in the deed is found, the grantor agrees to resign a new deed to correct the mistake.
- *Covenant of warranty forever:* The grantor guarantees that if at any time in the future the title fails, he or she will compensate the grantee for the loss sustained. However, it is in the best interest of the grantee to obtain title insurance because at the time of a later claim, the grantor may be dead or financially insolvent.

These covenants in a general warranty deed are not limited to matters that occurred during the time the grantor owned the property; they extend back to its origin. An example of a general warranty deed appears in Figure 5.2. Note that the first three covenants are most important.

FIGURE 5.2

General Warranty Deed

NORTH CAROLINA GENERAL WARRANTY DEED

Excise Tax: _____

Parcel Identifier No. _____ Verified by _____ County on the ____ day of _____, 20__
By:_____

Mail/Box to: _____

This instrument was prepared by:_____

Brief description for the Index: _____

THIS DEED made this _____ day of _____, 20___, by and between

| GRANTOR | GRANTEE |

Enter in appropriate block for each party: name, address, and, if appropriate, character of entity, e.g. corporation or partnership.

The designation Grantor and Grantee as used herein shall include said parties, their heirs, successors, and assigns, and shall include singular, plural, masculine, feminine or neuter as required by context.

WITNESSETH, that the Grantor, for a valuable consideration paid by the Grantee, the receipt of which is hereby acknowledged, has and by these presents does grant, bargain, sell and convey unto the Grantee in fee simple, all that certain lot or parcel of land situated in the City of _____, _____ Township, _____ County, North Carolina and more particularly described as follows:

The property hereinabove described was acquired by Grantor by instrument recorded in Book _____ page _____.

A map showing the above described property is recorded in Plat Book _____ page _____.

NC Bar Association Form No. 3 © 1976, Revised © 1977, 2002   + James Williams & Co., Inc.
Printed by Agreement with the NC Bar Association - 1981   www.JamesWilliams.com

Source: This form is copyrighted by the North Carolina Bar Association (NCBA) and may not be reproduced without the written permission of the NCBA.

FIGURE 5.2

General Warranty Deed (continued)

TO HAVE AND TO HOLD the aforesaid lot or parcel of land and all privileges and appurtenances thereto belonging to the Grantee in fee simple.

And the Grantor covenants with the Grantee, that Grantor is seized of the premises in fee simple, has the right to convey the same in fee simple, that title is marketable and free and clear of all encumbrances, and that Grantor will warrant and defend the title against the lawful claims of all persons whomsoever, other than the following exceptions:

IN WITNESS WHEREOF, the Grantor has duly executed the foregoing as of the day and year first above written.

_____ _____(SEAL)
(Entity Name)

By:_____ _____(SEAL)
   Title:_____

By:_____ _____(SEAL)
   Title:_____

By:_____ _____(SEAL)
   Title:_____

USE BLACK INK ONLY

SEAL-STAMP

State of North Carolina - County of _____

I, the undersigned Notary Public of the County and State aforesaid, certify that _____
_____ personally appeared before me this day and acknowledged the due execution of the foregoing instrument for the purposes therein expressed. Witness my hand and Notarial stamp or seal this _____ day of _____, 20__.

My Commission Expires:_____ _____
                                                Notary Public

SEAL-STAMP

State of North Carolina - County of _____

I, the undersigned Notary Public of the County and State aforesaid, certify that _____
_____ personally came before me this day and acknowledged that _he is the _____ of _____, a North Carolina or _____ corporation/limited liability company/general partnership/limited partnership (strike through the inapplicable), and that by authority duly given and as the act of each entity, _he signed the forgoing instrument in its name on its behalf as its act and deed. Witness my hand and Notarial stamp or seal this _____ day of _____, 20__.

My Commission Expires:_____ _____
                                                Notary Public

SEAL-STAMP

State of North Carolina - County of _____

I, the undersigned Notary Public of the County and State aforesaid, certify that _____
_____
_____
Witness my hand and Notarial stamp or seal this _____ day of _____, 20__.

My Commission Expires:_____ _____
                                                Notary Public

The foregoing Certificate(s) of _____ is/are certified to be correct.
This instrument and this certificate are duly registered at the date and time and in the Book and Page shown on the first page hereof.
_____ Register of Deeds for _____ County
By:_____ Deputy/Assistant - Register of Deeds

NC Bar Association Form No. 3 © 1976, Revised © 1977, 2002   * James Williams & Co., Inc.
Printed by Agreement with the NC Bar Association - 1981   www.JamesWilliams.com

> ① Grantor has deed
> ② No encumbrances while he held deed

Special Warranty Deed

Two warranties:
- ① Warranty that grantor received title
- ② Warranty that property was unencumbered by grantor

Special warranty deed (limited warranty deed). A conveyance that carries only two covenants is called a **special warranty deed** (also known as a *limited warranty deed*). The grantor warrants that he or she received title to the land and that the property was not encumbered during the time he or she held title except as noted in the deed. Special warranty deeds generally contain the words *remise, release, alienate,* and *convey* in the granting clause. Any additional warranties to be included must be specifically stated in the deed. An example of a special warranty deed appears in Figure 5.3.

Bargain and Sale Deed

No express warranties:
- Implication that grantor holds title and possession

Bargain and sale deed. A **bargain and sale deed** contains no express warranties against encumbrances. However, it does imply that the grantor holds title and possession of the property. The granting clause usually states a person's name or name of an entity and the words *grants and releases* or *grants, bargains, and sells*. Because the warranty is not specifically stated, the grantee has little legal recourse if title defects appear later. In some areas, this deed is used in foreclosures and tax sales. The buyer should purchase, or the seller provide, title insurance for protection.

A covenant against encumbrances initiated by the grantor may be added to a standard bargain and sale deed to create a bargain and sale deed with covenant against the grantor's acts. This deed is closely equivalent to a quitclaim deed. Warranties used in general warranty deeds may be inserted in a bargain and sale deed to give the grantee similar protection.

Quitclaim Deed

- No express or implied covenants or warranties
- Used primarily to convey less than fee simple or to cure a title defect

> Ex: use in divorce cases to take a name off the title

Quitclaim deed (non-warranty deed). A **quitclaim deed** (non-warranty deed) provides the grantee with the least protection of any deed. It carries no covenant or warranties and conveys only such interest, if any, that the grantor may have when the deed is delivered. By a quitclaim deed, the grantor only *remises, releases, and quitclaims* an interest in the property to the grantee. The deed might convey an easement; it might re-convey equitable title back to a seller; it might convey nothing at all. An example of a quitclaim deed appears in Figure 5.4.

If the grantor under a quitclaim deed has no interest in the property described, the grantee acquires nothing by virtue of the quitclaim deed; nor does the grantee acquire any right of warranty against the grantor. A quitclaim deed can convey title as effectively as a warranty deed if the grantor has good title when the deed is delivered, but it provides none of the guarantees of a warranty deed.

A quitclaim deed is frequently used to cure a defect, called a **cloud on the title**, in the recorded history of a real estate title. For example, if the name of the grantee is misspelled on a warranty deed placed in the public record, a quitclaim deed with the correct spelling may be executed to the grantee to perfect the title. A quitclaim deed is sometimes used to convey ownership rights from one spouse to the other in a divorce agreement. A quitclaim deed also is used when a grantor allegedly has inherited property but is not certain of the validity of the title of the decedent from whom the property was inherited. The use of a warranty deed in such an instance could carry with it obligations of warranty, while a quitclaim deed would convey only the grantor's interest.

FIGURE 5.3

Special Warranty Deed

NORTH CAROLINA SPECIAL WARRANTY DEED

Excise Tax: _____

Parcel Identifier No. _____ Verified by _____ County on the ____ day of _____, 20__
By: _____

Mail/Box to: _____

This instrument was prepared by: _____

Brief description for the Index: _____

THIS DEED made this _____ day of _____, 20___, by and between

GRANTOR	GRANTEE

Enter in appropriate block for each party: name, address, and, if appropriate, character of entity, e.g. corporation or partnership.

The designation Grantor and Grantee as used herein shall include said parties, their heirs, successors, and assigns, and shall include singular, plural, masculine, feminine or neuter as required by context.

WITNESSETH, that the Grantor, for a valuable consideration paid by the Grantee, the receipt of which is hereby acknowledged, has and by these presents does grant, bargain, sell and convey unto the Grantee in fee simple, all that certain lot or parcel of land situated in the City of _____, _____ Township, _____ County, North Carolina and more particularly described as follows:

The property hereinabove described was acquired by Grantor by instrument recorded in Book _____ page _____.

A map showing the above described property is recorded in Plat Book _____ page _____.

NC Bar Association Form No. 6 © 1977, 2002   + James Williams & Co., Inc.
Printed by Agreement with the NC Bar Association - 1981   www.JamesWilliams.com

Source: This form is copyrighted by the North Carolina Bar Association and may not be reproduced without the written permission of the NCBA.

FIGURE 5.3

Special Warranty Deed (continued)

TO HAVE AND TO HOLD the aforesaid lot or parcel of land and all privileges and appurtenances thereto belonging to the Grantee in fee simple.

And the Grantor covenants with the Grantee, that Grantor has nothing to impair such title as Grantor received, and Grantor will warrant and defend the title against the lawful claims of all persons claiming by, under or through Grantor, other than the following exceptions:

IN WITNESS WHEREOF, the Grantor has duly executed the foregoing as of the day and year first above written.

_____   _____(SEAL)
               (Entity Name)

By:_____   _____(SEAL)
        Title:_____

By:_____   _____(SEAL)
        Title:_____

By:_____   _____(SEAL)
        Title:_____

USE BLACK INK ONLY

SEAL-STAMP

State of North Carolina - County of _____
I, the undersigned Notary Public of the County and State aforesaid, certify that _____
_____ personally appeared before me this day and acknowledged the due execution of the foregoing instrument for the purposes therein expressed. Witness my hand and Notarial stamp or seal this _____ day of _____, 20__.
My Commission Expires:_____   _____
                                                   Notary Public

SEAL-STAMP

State of North Carolina - County of _____
I, the undersigned Notary Public of the County and State aforesaid, certify that _____
_____ personally came before me this day and acknowledged that _he is the _____ of _____,
a North Carolina or _____ corporation/limited liability company/general partnership/limited partnership (strike through the inapplicable), and that by authority duly given and as the act of each entity, _he signed the forgoing instrument in its name on its behalf as its act and deed. Witness my hand and Notarial stamp or seal this _____ day of _____, 20__.
My Commission Expires:_____   _____
                                                   Notary Public

SEAL-STAMP

State of North Carolina - County of _____
I, the undersigned Notary Public of the County and State aforesaid, certify that _____
_____ personally appeared before me this day and acknowledged the due execution of the foregoing instrument for the purposes therein expressed. Witness my hand and Notarial stamp or seal this _____ day of _____, 20__.
My Commission Expires:_____   _____
                                                   Notary Public

The foregoing Certificate(s) of _____ is/are certified to be correct.
This instrument and this certificate are duly registered at the date and time and in the Book and Page shown on the first page hereof.
_____ Register of Deeds for _____ County
By:_____ Deputy/Assistant - Register of Deeds

NC Bar Association Form No. 6 © 1977, 2002   + James Williams & Co., Inc.
Printed by Agreement with the NC Bar Association - 1981   www.JamesWilliams.com

FIGURE 5.4

Quitclaim Deed (Non-Warranty Deed)

NORTH CAROLINA NON-WARRANTY DEED

Excise Tax: _____

Parcel Identifier No. _____ Verified by _____ County on the ____ day of _____, 20__
By: _____

Mail/Box to: _____

This instrument was prepared by: _____

Brief description for the Index: _____

THIS DEED made this _____ day of _____, 20___, by and between

GRANTOR	GRANTEE

Enter in appropriate block for each party: name, address, and, if appropriate, character of entity, e.g. corporation or partnership.

The designation Grantor and Grantee as used herein shall include said parties, their heirs, successors, and assigns, and shall include singular, plural, masculine, feminine or neuter as required by context.

WITNESSETH, that the Grantor, for a valuable consideration paid by the Grantee, the receipt of which is hereby acknowledged, has and by these presents does grant, bargain, sell and convey unto the Grantee in fee simple, all that certain lot or parcel of land situated in the City of _____, _____ Township, _____ County, North Carolina and more particularly described as follows:

The property hereinabove described was acquired by Grantor by instrument recorded in Book _____ page _____.

A map showing the above described property is recorded in Plat Book _____ page _____.

NC Bar Association Form No. 7 © 1977, 2002
Printed by Agreement with the NC Bar Association - 1981

+ James Williams & Co., Inc.
www.JamesWilliams.com

Source: This form is copyrighted by the North Carolina Bar Association and may not be reproduced without the written permission of the NCBA.

FIGURE 5.4

Quitclaim Deed (Non-Warranty Deed) (continued)

TO HAVE AND TO HOLD the aforesaid lot or parcel of land and all privileges and appurtenances thereto belonging to the Grantee in fee simple.

The Grantor makes no warranty, express or implied, as to title to the property hereinabove described.

IN WITNESS WHEREOF, the Grantor has caused this instrument to be duly executed and delivered.

_____   _____(SEAL)
           (Entity Name)

By:_____   _____(SEAL)
      Title:_____

By:_____   _____(SEAL)
      Title:_____

By:_____   _____(SEAL)
      Title:_____

SEAL-STAMP

State of North Carolina - County of _____

I, the undersigned Notary Public of the County and State aforesaid, certify that _____ _____ personally appeared before me this day and acknowledged the due execution of the foregoing instrument for the purposes therein expressed. Witness my hand and Notarial stamp or seal this _____ day of _____, 20___.

My Commission Expires:_____   _____
                                                          Notary Public

---

SEAL-STAMP

State of North Carolina - County of _____

I, the undersigned Notary Public of the County and State aforesaid, certify that _____ _____ personally came before me this day and acknowledged that _he is the _____ of _____, a North Carolina or _____ corporation/limited liability company/general partnership/limited partnership (strike through the inapplicable), and that by authority duly given and as the act of each entity, _he signed the forgoing instrument in its name on its behalf as its act and deed. Witness my hand and Notarial stamp or seal this _____ day of _____, 20___.

My Commission Expires:_____   _____
                                                          Notary Public

---

SEAL-STAMP

State of North Carolina - County of _____

I, the undersigned Notary Public of the County and State aforesaid, certify that _____ _____ personally appeared before me this day and acknowledged the due execution of the foregoing instrument for the purposes therein expressed. Witness my hand and Notarial stamp or seal this _____ day of _____, 20___.

My Commission Expires:_____   _____
                                                          Notary Public

---

The foregoing Certificate(s) of _____ is/are certified to be correct.
This instrument and this certificate are duly registered at the date and time and in the Book and Page shown on the first page hereof.
_____ Register of Deeds for _____ County
By:_____ Deputy/Assistant - Register of Deeds

NC Bar Association Form No. 7 © 1977, 2002   + James Williams & Co., Inc.
Printed by Agreement with the NC Bar Association - 1981   www.JamesWilliams.com

Chapter 5 Transfer of Title to Real Property   **89**

IN PRACTICE A licensed real estate broker in North Carolina is prohibited from drafting a deed for others and is also prohibited from filling in the blanks of a deed form for others. While a licensed real estate broker may prepare a deed to convey the broker's own property, an attorney should be consulted for all deed preparations.

North Carolina Special-Purpose Deeds

There are many specialized forms of deeds used in North Carolina for various specific purposes. A few significant examples of these are discussed below.

Correction deed. A correction deed is used when there has been an error in a previous deed. For example, if the description of the property in the original deed was incorrect, a correction deed will be used to make the correction. Errors in names or dates would also be corrected by this deed.

Deed of gift. When a grantor conveys property as a gift (that is, no consideration or only token consideration has been accepted for the property), a deed of gift is used. A deed of gift must be recorded within two years or it becomes void. Because no consideration is exchanged, there is no need to pay excise tax.

Deed of release. A deed of release is used to release a parcel of property from a mortgage or deed of trust lien when the real estate loan has been paid in full.

[Handwritten note: Lender takes their name off the title, put yours on it]

Trustee's deed. A deed of conveyance executed by a trustee is a trustee's deed and is used when a trustee named in a will, trust agreement, or trust deed conveys the real estate to anyone other than the trustor. The trustee's deed sets forth the fact that the trustee executes the instrument in accordance with the powers and authority granted to him or her by the trust instrument. A trustee's deed is generally used to transfer title after a foreclosure auction.

Timber or mineral deed. As discussed in Chapter 2, some ownership rights can be severed from the land and transferred by deed, such as the harvesting of timber or minerals located on the property.

Deeds executed pursuant to court order. This classification covers deeds such as a sheriff's deed, a tax deed, a guardian's deed, and an executor's deed. These deeds are used to convey title to property that is transferred by court order or by will.

One characteristic of these special-purpose deeds is that the full consideration is usually stated in the deed. This is done because the deed is executed pursuant to a court order; because the court has authorized the sale of the property for a given amount of consideration, this amount should be exactly stated in the document.

North Carolina Excise Tax

[Handwritten note: Seller pays it, like a sales tax for the priviledge of selling your house]

All sellers of real property in North Carolina must pay an **excise tax** that is based on the sales price of the property. The statute states, "There is levied an excise tax on each deed, instrument, or writing by which any interest in real property is conveyed to another person." Prior to year 2000, actual *revenue stamps* were affixed to each deed as proof that this excise tax had been paid. Now, because the Registrar

[Margin label: In North Carolina]

of Deeds must mark the document to show the tax amount paid prior to recording the document, the term *revenue stamps* has been discontinued. The amount of the tax is $1 for every $500 of consideration or fraction thereof and always is expressed as a whole dollar amount. The type of financing used, if any, has no effect on the calculation of excise tax.

The statute establishing the payment of excise tax exempts certain types of conveyances, such as transfer by a government entity, transfer by will or intestate succession because of death, transfer by deed of gift when no consideration is paid, transfer by merger or consolidation, transfer by lease for a term of years, and transfer by instruments securing a debt, such as a mortgage and/or deed of trust.

MATH CONCEPTS

CALCULATE NORTH CAROLINA EXCISE TAX

To calculate the amount of the excise tax, if the sales price is not an even $500 amount, round the sales price up to the nearest $500, divide by 500, and multiply by $1. For example, suppose the purchase price is $89,250. Round up the price to $89,500, and divide by 500 which equals 179. Multiply 179 by $1 and you have determined that the seller will need to pay $179 in excise tax.

As another example, suppose the purchase price is $94,750. Round up the price to $95,000, and divide by 500 which equals 190. Multiply 190 by $1. The seller will need to pay $190 in excise tax.

Involuntary Alienation

Title to property also can be transferred by involuntary alienation—that is, without the owner's wishes or consent (see Figure 5.5). Such transfers are usually carried out by operation of law and range from government condemnation of land for public use to the sale of property to satisfy delinquent tax or mortgage liens.

Escheat. When a person dies **intestate** (without a will) and leaves no heirs, the title to that person's real estate passes to the state by the state's power of **escheat**.

Eminent domain. Federal, state, and local governments; school boards; some government agencies; and certain public and quasi-public corporations and utilities have the power of eminent domain. **Eminent domain** is the right of the government to acquire privately owned real estate for public use. **Condemnation** is the process by which the government exercises this right, by either judicial or administrative proceedings. In the taking of property, just compensation is to be paid to the owner, and the rights of the property owner are to be protected by due process of law. Ideally, the public agency and the owner of the property in question agree on compensation through direct negotiation, and the government purchases the property for a price considered fair by the owner. In some cases, the owner may simply dedicate the property to the government as a site for a school, park, or another beneficial use. Sometimes, however, in cases where the owner's consent cannot be obtained, the government agency can initiate condemnation proceedings to acquire the property. Even in the taking of the property through condemnation, the property owner must be paid just compensation. If the taken property

---

Eminent domain is the government's right to acquire private property for public use; **condemnation** is the actual process of taking property.

FIGURE 5.5

Involuntary Alienation

Action	Process	Property Taken By
Person dies intestate; no heirs	Escheat	State
Eminent domain (Land needed for public use)	Eminent domain (Condemnation)	Public or governmental agency
Nonpayment of a debt secured by real property	Foreclosure	Creditor
Adverse use of another's property for prescriptive period	Adverse possession through suit to quiet title	Adverse possessor

was leased, the tenant will be entitled to compensation for damages caused by the termination of the tenancy.

Generally, states delegate their power of eminent domain to cities and counties or public entities for public services. For instance, a public housing authority might take privately owned land to build low-income housing, or the state's land-clearance commission or redevelopment authority could use the power of eminent domain to make way for urban renewal. If there were no other feasible way to do so, a railway, utility company, or state highway department might acquire farmland to extend railroad tracks, bring electricity to a remote new development, or build a highway.

In the past, the proposed use for taking property was to be for the public good. However, in June 2005, the U.S. Supreme Court in *Kelo v. City of New London* significantly changed the definition of public use. The court held that local governments can condemn homes and businesses for private or economic development purposes.

In *Kelo v. City of New London*, a development agent, on behalf of the city, initiated condemnation proceedings on land owned by nine property owners who refused to have their property taken. The development plan involved land for commercial, residential, and recreational purposes. The court noted that the development plan was not going to benefit a particular class of identifiable individuals. Further, although the owners' properties were not blighted, the city determined that a program of economic rejuvenation was justified and entitled to deference. Economic development fit within the broad definition of the term *public purpose*. The court found that the city's proposed disposition of petitioners' properties qualified as a public use within the meaning of the Takings Clause of the Fifth Amendment of the U.S. Constitution.

In this case, the city had invoked a state statute that authorized the use of eminent domain to promote economic development. The court decision leaves it to the states to establish rules that cities must follow when exercising eminent domain powers. In response to this court decision, many state legislators have enacted legislation to impose a narrower definition of the term *public use* in eminent domain proceedings to stop condemnations justified on purely economic grounds.

In North Carolina Like many state legislatures, North Carolina's General Assembly reacted to the *Kelo* decision by clarifying state laws governing the power of eminent domain. In 2006, North Carolina clarified "that eminent domain may only be used to take a blighted parcel." Consequently, the *Kelo* decision is not currently applicable in North Carolina.

North Carolina also recognizes a *quick take* method of condemnation; when authorized by law, title and possession of private property can immediately be transferred to the public authority. Furthermore, a taking of a leased property terminates any existing lease on that property.

Lien foreclosure. Land also may be transferred without an owner's consent to satisfy debts contracted by the owner that have become liens against the real property. In such cases, the liens are foreclosed, the property is sold, and the proceeds of the sale are applied to pay off the debts. Debts that could be foreclosed include mortgage loans, real estate taxes, mechanics' liens, and general judgments against the property owner. Foreclosure will be discussed in more depth in Chapter 13.

Requirements for Adverse Possession
Open
Continuous
Exclusive
Adverse
Notorious

Adverse possession. Adverse possession is another means of involuntary transfer. For persons to make a claim of ownership under adverse possession they must have some reason to believe the land is theirs. Owners who do not use or inspect their land for a number of years may lose title to another person who makes a claim to the land, takes possession, and, most importantly, uses the land. The mnemonic *OCEAN* reminds us that the possession of the claimant must be

- **O**pen (well known to others),
- **C**ontinuous (uninterrupted for the required period),
- **E**xclusive (not shared with another),
- **A**dverse to the true owner's possession (the adverse possessor must intend to claim that the land occupied is his or her own), and
- **N**otorious/hostile (without the permission of the owner).

In North Carolina In North Carolina, the required period of continuous possession varies widely, depending on the circumstances. If the adverse possessor is trying to acquire privately owned property and has *color of title* (a faulty document that purports to give the adverse possessor title), the period of possession is seven years. If there is no color of title, the period of possession is 20 years. Property owned by the government is not subject to acquisition by adverse possession.

Even if the adverse possessor fulfills all the legal requirements for adverse possession, he or she must go to court to get clear title to the property. This is done with a lawsuit called an **action to quiet title**. It is difficult to prove title by adverse possession, and until a court decides that title has been acquired, the claimant's title is considered to be unmarketable.

Transfer of a Deceased Person's Property

By descent (intestate succession). Every state, including North Carolina, has a law known as a *statute of descent and distribution*. When a person dies intestate (without having left a will), the decedent's real estate and personal property pass to the decedent's heirs according to this statute. In effect, the state makes a will for anyone who did not do so. A court appoints a person to distribute the deceased's property according to the provisions of the **North Carolina Intestate Succession Act**. This person is called an *administrator* if a man or an *administratrix* if a woman. As noted previously, if the property owner dies intestate and leaves no heirs, the property will escheat to the state of North Carolina. North Carolina's provisions for intestate succession are quite complicated, and a lawyer should be consulted when intestate succession questions arise.

Transfer of title by will. A **will** is an instrument made by a mentally competent owner to convey title to real and personal property on the owner's death. A will takes effect only after death; until that time, any property covered by the will can be conveyed by the owner and thus removed from the owner's estate. An ownership interest, such as joint tenancy or tenancy by entirety, that contains survivorship rights cannot be affected by a will. In North Carolina, if a husband and wife own property as tenants by the entirety, that property cannot pass by will. Neither spouse can disinherit the other spouse by will.

The gift of real property by will is known as a *devise*, and a person who receives real property by will is known as a *devisee*. Technically, an heir is one who takes property by the law of descent, but the term is commonly used to include devisees as well. A legacy or *bequest* is a gift of personal property; the person receiving personal property is known as a *beneficiary*.

The North Carolina Intestate Succession Act provides for the distribution of the property of an intestate person (one who dies without a valid will). This statute allows for the equal division of property among eligible heirs, or, in the event of no heirs, having the property escheat to the North Carolina State Educational Assistance Authority. This statute does not override an active survivorship clause in a deed.

■ TITLE RECORDS

Public records are just that—records that are open to the public, which means that anyone interested in a particular property can review the records to learn about the documents, claims, and other details that affect its ownership. A prospective buyer, for example, needs to be sure that the seller can convey title to the property. If the property is subject to any liens or other encumbrances, a prospective buyer or lender needs to know. An attorney or title company typically performs a search of the public records to ensure that good title is being conveyed. Nonetheless, it is important for a real estate licensee to understand what is in the public record and what the searchers are likely to find.

PUBLIC RECORDS

Public records contain detailed information about each parcel of real estate in a city or a county. These records are crucial in establishing ownership, giving notice of encumbrances, and establishing priority of liens. They protect the interests of real estate owners, taxing bodies, creditors, and the general public. The real estate recording system includes written documents that affect title, such as deeds and mortgages. Public records regarding taxes, judgments, probate, and marriage also may offer important information about the title to a particular property.

Public records are maintained by

- recorders of deeds,
- county clerks,
- county treasurers,
- city clerks,
- collectors, and
- clerks of court.

For example, prospective buyers rarely search public records for evidence of title or encumbrances themselves. Instead, title companies, attorneys, and lenders conduct the searches.

Recording

Recording is the act of placing documents in the public record. The specific rules for recording documents are a matter of state law. Although the details may vary, all recording acts essentially provide that any written document that affects any estate, right, title, or interest in land *must be recorded in the county (or, in some states, the town) where the land is located* to serve as public notice. This way, anyone interested in the title to a parcel of property will know where to look to discover the various interests of all other parties. Recording acts also generally give legal priority to those interests recorded first—the *first in time, first in right*, or *first come, first served* principle. To be *eligible for recording*, a document must be drawn and executed according to the recording acts of the state in which the real estate is located. For instance, a state may require that the parties' names be typed below their signatures or that the document be acknowledged before a notary public. In some states, the document must be witnessed. Others require that the name of the person who prepared the document appear on it. States may have specific rules about the size of documents and the color and quality of paper they are printed on. Electronic recording—using computers or fax machines, for instance—is permitted in a growing number of localities. Some states require a certificate of real estate value and the payment of current property taxes due for recording.

Notice

Anyone with an interest in a parcel of real estate can take certain steps, called *giving notice*, to ensure that the interest is available to the public. The two basic types of notice are constructive notice and actual notice.

Constructive notice is the legal presumption that information may be obtained by an individual through due diligence. Properly recording documents in the public record serves as constructive notice to the world of an individual's rights or interest, as does the physical possession of a property. Because the information or evidence is readily available to the world, a prospective purchaser or lender is responsible for discovering the interest.

Actual notice means not only that the information available but also that someone has been given the information and actually knows it. An individual who has searched the public records and inspected the property has actual notice, also known as *direct knowledge*. If it can be proved that an individual has had actual notice of information, that person cannot use a lack of constructive notice (such as an unrecorded deed) to justify a claim.

Priority

Priority refers to the order of when documents or liens were recorded. Many complicated situations can affect the priority of rights in a parcel of real estate—who recorded first, which party was in possession first, or who had actual or constructive notice. How the courts rule in any situation depends, of course, on the specific facts of the case. These are strictly legal questions that should be referred to the parties' attorneys.

For example, buyer A purchased a property from seller B and received a deed. Buyer A did not record the deed but took possession of the property in June. In November, seller B sold the same property to buyer C who received a deed, which buyer C promptly recorded.

Buyer C never inspected the property to determine whether someone was in possession of it.

By taking possession of the property, buyer A has the superior right to the property even though buyer A did not record the deed.

Unrecorded Documents

Certain types of liens are not recorded. Real estate taxes and special assessments are liens on specific parcels of real estate and are not usually recorded until sometime after the taxes or assessments are past due. Inheritance taxes and franchise taxes are statutory liens and are placed against all real estate owned by a decedent at the time of death or by a corporation at the time the franchise taxes became a lien. Like real estate taxes, they are not recorded.

Notice of these liens must be gained from sources other than the recorder's office. Evidence of the payment of real estate taxes, special assessments, municipal utilities, and other taxes can be gathered from paid tax receipts and letters from municipalities. Creative measures are often required to get information about *off the record* liens.

Chain of Title

Chain of title is the record of a property's ownership. Beginning with the earliest owner, a title may pass to many individuals. Each owner is linked to the next so that a chain is formed.

An unbroken chain of title can be traced through linking conveyances from the present owner back to the earliest recorded owner. Chain of title does not include liens and encumbrances or any other document not directly related to ownership.

If ownership cannot be traced through an unbroken chain, a gap or cloud in the chain of title is said to exist. In these cases, the cloud on the title makes it necessary to establish ownership by a court action called a suit to quiet title. For instance, a suit might be required when a grantor acquired title under one name and conveyed it under another name. There may be a forged deed in the chain, after which no subsequent grantee acquired legal title.

■ TITLE ASSURANCE

Under the terms of a typical real estate sales contract, the seller is required to deliver **marketable title** to the buyer at the closing. To be marketable, a title must meet five criteria: (1) be free from any significant liens and encumbrances; (2) disclose no serious defects; (3) be free of doubtful questions of law or fact to prove its validity; (4) protect a purchaser from the hazard of litigation or any threat to quiet enjoyment of the property; and (5) convince a reasonably well-informed and prudent person, acting on business principles and willful knowledge of the facts and their legal significance, that the property could in turn be sold or mortgaged at a fair market value.

Most people spend more money on the purchase of real estate than on any other single item. Therefore, it is understandable that buyers want to be sure they get what they pay for—marketable title to the property. So while a deed might contain several warranties of title, the buyer should insist on a title search and a property survey to make sure he or she is getting marketable title.

Title Search

A **title search** is the examination of all public records that might affect a title. The title examiner tries to establish a **chain of title,** which shows the record of ownership of the property over a period of time, depending on the length of the title search. In the United States, chains of title in colonial states frequently date back to a grant from the king of England. In those states admitted to the Union after the formation of the United States, the deeds of conveyance in the chain of title generally stem from the patent issued by the U.S. government. A lawyer, a trained paralegal, or title company staff in some states can perform a title search, or title examination, but only attorneys may give an opinion of title. Real estate brokers are prohibited from giving an opinion on the condition of a title.

Through the chain of title, the ownership of the property can be traced backward from its present owner to its source; this thorough, condensed history of the title is called an **abstract of title**. Frequently, the title examination is conducted for a shorter period of time based on local custom or practical considerations. Most title defects are revealed in a search that traces back 30 to 60 years, especially if title insurance has been in place. Ownership is traced by means of searching the *grantee and grantor indices* that are kept in the Register of Deeds' offices. Under this system, all documents relating to a parcel of property are indexed under the names of the grantors and the grantees, not under the property itself.

If there is a period for which ownership is unaccounted, there is a gap in the chain. In such cases, it is usually necessary to establish ownership by a court action called a *suit to quiet title*. The court's judgment, following a proceeding in which all possible claimants are allowed to present evidence, can be filed. A suit to quiet title may be required when, for instance, a grantor has acquired title under one name and conveyed title under a different name. Title acquired by adverse possession also can be established of record by a quiet title action.

When a title examination is conducted, the title examiner lists each instrument in chronological order along with information relative to taxes, judgments, special assessments, surveys, easements, and the like. The title examiner concludes with an opinion of title indicating which records were examined and when, and stating the examiner's opinion of the quality of the title. The grantor and grantee index system is used in North Carolina to examine the title. Any defect of title will appear in the grantor index.

In North Carolina

Marketable Title Act. North Carolina's **Marketable Title Act** provides that if a chain of title can be traced back for 30 years and no other claim has been recorded during that time, the title becomes a marketable title. Any conflicting claims predating the 30-year chain of title may be extinguished. The practical effect of this act is to eliminate obsolete defects in the chain of title.

Title Insurance

A **title insurance** policy is a contract by which a title insurance company agrees, subject to the terms of its policy, to indemnify (to compensate or reimburse) the insured (the owner, the mortgagee, or another interest holder) against any losses sustained as a result of defects in a title that existed at the time the policy was issued, other than those exceptions listed in the policy.

Title companies issue various forms of title insurance policies; the most common are the owner's title insurance policy and the mortgagee's title insurance policy. As the names indicate, each type of policy is issued to insure specific interests. An owner's policy insures an owner's interest in property; a mortgagee's policy insures a lender's interest in property. The owner's coverage is usually the face amount of the purchase price and the owner is permanently protected. The lender's coverage is limited to the loan amount and is of a *diminishing liability*. Lender's coverage ends with the payoff of the mortgage loan.

A standard coverage policy usually insures against defects that may be found in the public records plus many defects not found there. The extended coverage provided by an **ALTA** (American Land Title Association) **policy** includes all the protection of a standard policy plus additional protection to cover risks that may be discovered only through inspection of the property (including rights of persons in actual possession of the land, even if unrecorded) or revealed by examination of an accurate survey. The company does not insure against any defects in or liens against the title that are found by the title examination and listed in the standard policy.

The ALTA owner's title insurance policy protects the owner against title defects not found in the public records, such as

- falsification of the records;
- misrepresentation of the true owner(s) of the land;
- old unsettled estates;
- forged deeds, releases, or wills;
- instruments executed under a fabricated or expired power of attorney;
- errors in copying and indexing;
- deeds delivered after the death of a grantor or grantee or without consent of the grantor;
- mistakes in recording legal documents;
- undisclosed or missing heirs;
- birth or adoption of children after the date of the will;
- deeds by persons of unsound mind;
- deeds by persons supposedly single but secretly married; and
- deeds by minors.

The consideration for the policy (the premium) is paid once at closing for the life of the policy. The maximum loss for which the company may be liable cannot exceed the face amount of the policy (unless the amount of coverage has been extended by use of an inflation rider). When a title company settles a claim covered by a policy, it can then step into the shoes of the insured party and seek compensation from anyone responsible for the settled claim.

With the owner's title insurance policy, if the insured owner were to lose title because of a covered claim, the title company would pay the owner the value of the property up to the face amount of the policy (plus the amount covered in the policy's available inflation clause). The title company also assumes any costs incurred in the defense of the title. ALTA coverage is summarized in Figure 5.6.

In North Carolina

North Carolina is considered an approved attorney state. That means that title searches are usually performed by an attorney rather than by a title insurance company. When the title search is completed, the attorney submits a preliminary opinion on title to the title insurance company, which, in essence, serves as an application for title insurance. Based on the preliminary opinion on title, the title insurance company issues a title commitment. The title commitment includes a description of the title insurance policy; the name of the insured party; the legal description of the real estate; the estate or interest covered; a schedule of all exceptions, consisting of encumbrances and defects found in the public records; and conditions and stipulations under which the commitment is issued.

FIGURE 5.6

Owner's Title Insurance Policy

Standard Coverage	Extended Coverage	Not Covered by Either Policy
1. Defects found in public records 2. Forged documents 3. Incompetent grantors 4. Incorrect marital statements 5. Improperly delivered deeds	Standard coverage plus defects discoverable through: 1. Property inspection, including unrecorded rights of persons in possession 2. Examination of survey 3. Unrecorded liens not known by policyholder	1. Defects and liens listed in policy 2. Defects known to buyer 3. Changes in land use brought about by zoning ordinances 4. Defects that would have been shown by an accurate survey, if a survey was not done

The title commitment is used at closing as assurance of a clear title to the property in question.

After closing, the attorney issues a final opinion on title, which includes recording information for the deed and deed of trust and so forth. The final opinion on title goes to the title insurance company, which issues the title insurance policy based on this information. Under the title insurance policy, the title insurance company promises to defend the title as insured, as well as to pay any claims against the property if the title proves to be defective. This coverage begins after closing and issuance of the policy and covers only title defects undiscovered before closing or title defects not exempted in the title commitment. The opinion issued by the attorney is just that, an *opinion* based on the search of public records. It is not a guarantee of good title.

IN PRACTICE Before a lender will forward money on a loan secured by real estate, it normally orders a title search at the expense of the borrower to assure itself that there are no recorded liens superior in priority to its mortgage on the property. The lender also typically requires the borrower to purchase a title insurance policy to protect the lender's interest. The owner-borrower may also purchase an "owner's policy." An owner's policy is highly recommended, but the owner-borrower must request this policy since it is not automatic.

Title Recordation

Both title insurance and title examinations depend on the fact that all conveyances of real property, as well as most other interests in real property, must be recorded to be enforceable. All owners or parties interested in real estate need to record, or file, all documents affecting their interests in the real estate to give public notice to the world of those interests. This public notice is called **constructive notice** or legal notice. Physically taking possession of the property is *actual notice*.

Necessity for recording. Through the process of **recording,** documents that affect property ownership are readily available as matters of public record. Therefore, a person can inspect the documents that affect a property before making a decision about purchasing it. A potential purchaser can verify that the seller can probably convey good title to the property as well as what liens and encumbrances affect that title.

> **FOR EXAMPLE** A purchaser offering cash for a property might want to be sure, before the settlement takes place, that the seller has paid in full all of the debts outstanding against the property. By inspecting the recorded documents, the purchaser could determine what debts encumber the property.

To serve as public notice, all instruments in writing affecting any estate, right, title, or interest in land must be recorded with the county recorder or, in North Carolina, the Register of Deeds in the county where the land is located. *Lien satisfactions*, such as a mortgage payoff, should also be recorded to clear the encumbrance from the title. Everyone interested in the title to a parcel of property can, with a thorough title search of recorded interests, therefore, receive notice of the various interests of all other parties. Because North Carolina is a pure race state (see below), recording gives legal priority to those interests that are recorded first.

In North Carolina

North Carolina Conner Act. The **Conner Act** is a state law that provides that many types of real estate documents are not valid as to third parties unless they are recorded. The documents covered include deeds, mortgages, installment land contracts, assignments, options, leases of more than three years, easements, and restrictive covenants. Under the Conner Act, if a purchaser fails to record a deed but a subsequent purchaser does, the subsequent purchaser's title takes precedence over the first purchaser's title. This kind of recording statute is called a *pure race statute*: whoever records first prevails, even if that purchaser had personal knowledge of a previous interest that was unrecorded.

> **FOR EXAMPLE** Suppose Zackermann sells her property to Sands. Sands fails to record his deed. Two weeks later, Zackermann sells the same property (even though it is no longer hers) to Hanson. Hanson suspects that Zackermann no longer owns the property but accepts the deed and quickly records it. Because Hanson recorded his deed, he now has marketable title to the property, and Sands is out of luck.

Torrens System of Land Registration. The Torrens title system is a legal registration system used to verify ownership and encumbrances similar to the registration of ship titles. Registration in the **Torrens System** provides evidence of title without the need for an additional search of the public records; the registering government basically guarantees that the named person is the owner of the registered title. Under the Torrens System, an owner of real property submits a written application to register a title. The application is submitted to the court clerk of the county in which the real estate is located. If the applicant proves ownership, the court enters an order to register the real estate. The registrar of titles is directed to issue a certificate of title. The original Torrens certificate of title in the registrar's office reveals the owner of the land and all mortgages, judgments, and similar liens. It does not, however, reveal federal or state taxes and some other items. The Torrens title system of registration relies on the physical title document itself; a person acquires title only when it is registered.

The Torrens System is governed by Chapter 43 of the North Carolina General Statutes and is rarely used in North Carolina. As noted in the 2011-2012 Edition of the North Carolina Real Estate Manual:

> Every owner of land registered under the Torrens System holds the land free from any and all adverse claims, rights, or encumbrances

not noted in the certificate of title. In addition, no title to nor right or interest in Torrens registered land contrary to the rights of the registered owner can be acquired by prescription or adverse possession.

■ RELATED WEBSITE

American Land Title Association: www.alta.org

■ KEY POINT REVIEW

Title is ownership, or the right to ownership, of land and evidence of that ownership.

Voluntary alienation is the voluntary transfer of title to real estate by gift or sale, using some form of deed.

- **Grantor** (person who transfers title) must be of legal age and legally competent to execute (sign) a deed. A deed executed by a minor is voidable.
    — Mental impairment at time of signing deed makes the deed voidable.
    — If the grantor has been declared incompetent by a judge, the deed is void.
    — All names the grantor has used should be provided.
- **Grantee** (person receiving the title) must be identifiable with sufficient certainty.
- Consideration (payment) of some form must be stated.
- Granting clause (words of conveyance) must be used.
- Habendum clause must define ownership interest taken by the grantee; it specifies limits on ownership, such as with a time-share.
- Legal description of the property conveyed is essential.
- Exceptions or reservations of any relevance must be included.
- Signature of the grantor(s) must be acknowledged by a notary public or other official authorized by the state in which the property is located.
- Delivery of the deed and acceptance by the grantee are necessary.

Nonessential elements of a deed include the following:

- Does not need to be dated
- Does not need to show amount of consideration
- Does not need to be acknowledged
- Does not have to be recorded, but highly recommended
- Does not have to be sealed

Types of deeds include the following:

- **General warranty deed** provides the greatest protection to the grantee and includes
    — covenant of seisin—warrants the grantor has the right to convey title;
    — covenant against encumbrances—warrants the property is free from liens or encumbrances, unless expressly stated;
    — covenant of quiet enjoyment—makes the grantor liable for damages if the grantee's title is found to be inferior;

- covenant of further assurance—the grantor's promise to obtain any other document necessary to convey good title; and
- covenant of warranty forever—the grantor's promise to compensate the grantee if title fails at any future time.
- **Special warranty deed** includes the warranties that the grantor received title and that the property was not encumbered during the time the grantor held title, except as otherwise noted.
- **Bargain and sale deed** implies that the grantor holds title and possession of the property, and there are no express warranties against encumbrances.
- **Quitclaim deed** provides the least protection of any deed, carries no covenants or warranties, and conveys only whatever interest the grantor may have when the deed is delivered.

Excise tax (transfer tax stamps) is required to be affixed to deeds and conveyances before being recorded, at the tax rate of $1.00 per $500 of value in North Carolina.

Involuntary alienation (transfer) of title to property is usually by operation of law.

- **Escheat** is property taken by state when deceased has no heirs.
- **Eminent domain** is property taken by public or government agency.
- Foreclosure is property taken by creditor for nonpayment of debt secured by real property.
- **Adverse possession** is property seizure occurring when someone who is not the lawful owner takes possession of property for the length of time specified by state law and usually in a way that is Open, Continuous, Exclusive, Adverse, and Notorious.

Transfer of title by will occurs when the deceased dies testate (leaving a will):

- Wills take effect only after death and can be changed by codicil or revoked while the testator is still alive.
- Devise is a gift of real property by will to the devisee.
- Bequest is a gift of personal property to a beneficiary.
- Legacy is a gift of money.
- To pass title to property on death, the will must be filed with the court and probated.
- Wills cannot supersede state laws protecting inheritance rights or survivorship clause in the titles.

Transfer of title under **North Carolina Intestate Succession Act** occurs when a person dies **intestate** (without a will). Probate proceedings must have an administrator appointed, and laws of the state where the real property is located govern property distribution.

Chain of title is a record of property ownership, but it does not include liens and other encumbrances:

- A gap in the chain or other dispute of ownership creates a **cloud on the title**.
- A cloud on title is resolved by **action to quiet title**.

An **abstract of title**, prepared by an abstractor or an attorney, is a summary report of what the title search reveals. It includes all recorded liens and encumbrances and lists records searched but does not indicate forgeries and interests that are unrecorded or could be discovered by property inspection.

A **marketable title** is one that must

- not have serious defects, nor rely on doubtful questions of law or fact to prove its validity;
- not expose the purchaser to litigation or threaten quiet enjoyment of property; and
- convince a reasonably well-informed and prudent purchaser that the property could be sold or mortgaged at a later time.

Proof of ownership may be established by certificate of title, but it will not reveal unrecorded liens or rights of parties in possession.

Unrecorded documents that may affect title, such as a tax lien, may not be recorded immediately, yet are still given priority by law and require a search of tax records and other sources.

To serve as **constructive notice**, and with priority over subsequent documents, a written document is needed that

- affects an estate, right, title, or interest in land (such as deeds; mortgages, tax liens, and judgments; and marriage, probate, and other proceedings that may affect title);
- must be drafted and executed (signed);
- is written according to state law (recording acts); and
- is recorded in the public records that are maintained by the designated official, such as the recorder of deeds, county clerk, or city clerk, and held in the county (or city) in which the property is located.

Public records are typically searched by closing attorneys and title companies that provide title insurance to prospective purchasers based on the findings of the **title search**.

Constructive notice of a document is assumed when due diligence (such as a search of public records and inspection of the property) would reveal its existence. *Actual notice* means that an individual has direct knowledge of documents in the public records and facts revealed by an inspection of the property.

North Carolina Marketable Title Act requires chain of title to be traced back only 30 years in most cases.

Title insurance, issued as an owner's policy or mortgagee's (lender) policy under which the insured is protected from losses arising from defects in title, insures against hidden defects and identifies exclusions that include readily apparent title defects, zoning, and others.

The **Conner Act** requires recordation of most real estate related documents to be enforceable against third parties.

QUESTIONS

1. In North Carolina, the statutory period for adverse possession (without color of title) is an uninterrupted period of how many years when trying to acquire privately owned property?
   a. 3
   b. 7
   c. 20
   d. 30

2. When property is sold for $75,000, the excise tax would be
   a. $75.
   b. $125.
   c. $135.
   d. $150.

3. A seller sold his property for $185,900 and let the buyer assume his loan balance of $125,000. How much excise tax will the seller pay at closing?
   a. $121.80
   b. $122.00
   c. $371.80
   d. $372.00

4. Title to real estate may be transferred during a person's lifetime by which of the following means?
   a. Escheat
   b. Descent
   c. Alienation
   d. Devise

5. What type of deed might an owner of real estate use to voluntarily transfer a right, a title, or an interest in real estate?
   a. Sheriff's deed
   b. Warranty deed
   c. Foreclosure deed
   d. Trustee's deed

6. A man owned property as a tenant in common with his two best friends. Years later, the man was adjudged legally incompetent and moved into a nursing home. During his stay at a nursing home, the man wrote a will leaving his entire estate to the nursing assistant assigned to his care. The man was survived by three children when he died. After his death, his real estate interests passed to
   a. his two best friends due to ownership rights.
   b. the nursing assistant named in his will.
   c. his children by the law of intestate succession.
   d. the state by escheat.

7. Which of the following is NOT a means of title transfer by involuntary alienation?
   a. Eminent domain
   b. Escheat
   c. Foreclosure
   d. Will

8. Which of the following BEST describes the covenant of quiet enjoyment?
   a. The grantor promises to obtain and deliver any instrument needed to make the title good.
   b. The grantor guarantees that if the title fails in the future, the grantor will compensate the grantee.
   c. The grantor warrants that the grantor is the owner of the property and has the right to convey title to it.
   d. The grantor ensures that the title will be good against the title claims of third parties.

9. A purchaser went to the Registry of Deeds to check the public records. She found that the seller was the grantee in the last recorded deed and that no mortgage was ever on record against the property. Therefore, the purchaser may assume which of the following?
    a. All taxes are paid, and no judgments are outstanding.
    b. The seller has good title.
    c. The seller probably did not mortgage the property.
    d. Probably no one else is occupying the property.

10. The person who examines the chain of title and prepares an opinion of title for a parcel of real estate
    a. writes a brief history of the record of ownership of the property.
    b. ensures the condition of the title.
    c. inspects the physical condition of the property.
    d. issues a guarantee as to the quality of the title.

11. Instruments affecting real estate are recorded in the public records of the county where the property is located because
    I. recording gives constructive notice to the world of the rights and interests in a particular parcel of real estate.
    II. the instruments must be recorded to comply with the terms of the county recording laws.
    a. I only
    b. II only
    c. Both I and II
    d. Neither I nor II

12. Chain of title refers to a
    a. summary of all instruments and legal proceedings affecting a specific parcel of land.
    b. series of links measuring 7.92 inches each.
    c. document that protects the insured parties against defects and hidden risks such as forgeries, undisclosed heirs, errors in the public records, and so forth.
    d. succession of conveyances from some starting point whereby the present owner derives title.

13. A title insurance policy with standard coverage generally covers all of the following EXCEPT
    a. forged documents.
    b. incorrect marital statements.
    c. rights of parties in possession.
    d. incompetent grantors.

14. Condemnation is
    a. the right of the government to take private property.
    b. rezoning of private property.
    c. the process by which eminent domain is exercised.
    d. adverse possession with just compensation.

15. Which of the following is NOT a necessary condition of eminent domain?
    a. Use benefits the public.
    b. Property is to be given to the owner of a quasi-public corporation.
    c. Property owner is protected by due process of law.
    d. Just compensation is paid to the property owner.

16. Which of the following real estate documents is LEAST likely to be recorded?
    a. Deed
    b. Month-to-month lease
    c. Option contract
    d. Land contract

17. Which of the following should be discoverable in a search of the public records?
    a. Encroachments
    b. Rights of any party in possession
    c. Inaccurate surveys
    d. Easements

18. In North Carolina, the statutory period of possession required to acquire title of privately owned property by adverse possession with color of title is how many years?
    a. 7
    b. 12
    c. 20
    d. 30

19. Which type of deed merely implies but does NOT specifically warrant that the grantor holds good title to the property?
    a. Special warranty
    b. Bargain and sale
    c. Quitclaim
    d. Trustee

CHAPTER 6

Land-Use Controls

LEARNING OBJECTIVES *When you have finished reading this chapter, you should be able to*

- **identify** different types of public and private land-use controls and their effect on property use.

- **understand** the development of the master (comprehensive) plan and how it affects the development, control, and use of property.

- **explain** the basic stages in developing a subdivision, including compliance with zoning, regulations, building codes, and the approval process.

- **understand** land-use controls and real estate brokers' disclosure responsibilities.

- **define** these *key terms*:

aesthetic zoning	Federal Emergency Management Agency (FEMA)	overlay district
buffer zones		plat map
building codes		police power
building permit	flood hazard area	property report
certificate of occupancy	historic preservation zoning	protective covenant
cluster zoning		restrictive covenant
conditional-use permit	Interstate Land Sales Full Disclosure Act	spot zoning
declaration of restrictive covenants		subdivision
	laches	variance
enabling act	master plan	zoning ordinances
extra-territorial jurisdictions (ETJs)	nonconforming use	

Historical overview. Since North Carolina was one of the original 13 English colonies, it is logical that English common law would serve as the bedrock of legal concepts embraced and adopted for use within the state. Consequently, the common law tended to favor a landowner's unfettered right to use his land without restriction. As the size of neighboring land parcels and the distance between residences continued to shrink, the land use of the adjoining parcel became more and more important. Privately regulated and enforced land use restrictions in the form of restrictive covenants began to surface in planned neighborhoods. Even when present, these private covenants seldom heeded the needs of the larger public good.

The need for more comprehensive land-use guidelines became obvious early in the 20th century. While highrise tenements and early skyscrapers were becoming popular products to maximize income for real estate investors in larger American cities, neighboring property owners were protesting the loss of sunlight and air circulation. The construction of the 42-story Equitable Building in the lower Manhattan area of New York City cast an alarming seven-acre shadow over the surrounding properties. This building proved to be the catalyst, in 1916, for the adoption of the first citywide comprehensive zoning resolution to restrict height and setbacks in the country.

The complexity of zoning regulations have developed over the years, not only in New York City, but around the country and world.

The regulation of land use is accomplished through public land-use controls, private land-use controls (deed restrictions), and public ownership of land—including parks, schools, and expressways—by federal, state, and local governments.

■ PUBLIC LAND-USE CONTROLS

The governmental right of **police power** of the states is their inherent authority to create and adopt regulations necessary to protect the public health, safety, and general welfare of the citizenry. The states, in turn, allow counties, cities, and towns to make regulations in keeping with general laws. The largely urban population and the increasing demands placed on our limited natural resources have made it necessary for cities, towns, and villages to increase limitations on the private use of real estate. There are now controls over noise, air, and water pollution, as well as population density.

Public land-use controls include

- planning,
- zoning,
- subdivision regulations,
- building codes, and
- environmental protection legislation.

The Master Plan

The primary method by which local governments recognize development goals is through the formulation of a comprehensive **master plan,** also commonly referred to as a *general plan*. Cities and counties develop long-term master plans for 20 years or longer to ensure that social and economic needs are balanced against environmental and aesthetic concerns.

The master plan is both a statement of policies and a presentation of how those policies can be realized. As created by the city, county, or regional *planning commission*, a typical master plan provides for

- *land use*, including standards of population density and economic development;
- *public facilities*, including schools, civic centers, and utilities;
- *circulation*, including public transportation and highways;
- *conservation* of energy and natural resources; and
- *noise abatement*.

Both economic and physical surveys are essential in preparing a master plan. Countywide plans also must include the coordination of numerous civic plans and developments to ensure orderly city growth with stabilized property values. City plans are put into effect by the enactment and enforcement of zoning ordinances.

Zoning

The provisions of the master plan are implemented by zoning ordinances. **Zoning ordinances** are laws imposed by local government authorities (such as cities and counties) that regulate and control the use of land and structures within designated districts or zones.

Zoning regulates and affects such things as

- permitted uses of each parcel of land,
- lot sizes,
- types of structures,
- building heights,
- setbacks (the minimum distance away from streets or sidewalks that structures may be built),
- style and appearance of structures,
- density (the ratio of land area to structure area), and
- protection of natural resources.

Zoning ordinances cannot be static; they must remain flexible to meet the changing needs of society.

■ **FOR EXAMPLE** In many large cities, factories and warehouses sit empty. Some cities have begun changing the zoning ordinances for such properties to permit new residential or commercial developments in areas once zoned strictly for heavy industrial use. Coupled with tax incentives, the changes lure developers back into the cities. The resulting housing is modern, conveniently located, and affordable. Simple zoning changes can help revitalize whole neighborhoods in big cities.

In North Carolina Zoning powers are conferred on municipal governments by North Carolina's **enabling act** through the General Assembly. There are no nationwide or statewide zoning ordinances; zoning is local in nature. (State and federal governments may, however, regulate land use through special legislation, such as scenic easement or coastal management laws.) Because there is no conformity of zoning codes or definitions, it is critical for brokers to check with local municipalities before answering any questions about zoning.

Zoning ordinances generally divide land use into general use classification such as: residential, commercial, industrial, and agricultural. There are usually many specific sub-classifications under each general use category. Many communities now include **cluster zoning** and *multiple-use zoning;* the first utilizes the clustering of residential lots in cul-de-sacs to increase open space while the latter permits planned unit developments (PUDs). In cluster zoning, a developer can provide the same number of housing units as traditional subdivision plans but with substantially increased tracts of open space. This is accomplished by slightly reducing the sizes of the individual lots and clustering the lots around varying street plans such as cul-de-sacs.

To ensure adequate control, land-use areas are further divided into subclasses. Resi-dential areas may be subdivided to provide for detached single-family dwellings, semi detached structures containing not more than four dwelling units, walkup apartments, or highrise apartments. Some communities require the use of **buffer zones**—such as landscaped parks and playgrounds—to separate and screen residential areas from nonresidential areas.

In North Carolina	**Zoning ordinances.** Today, almost all cities have enacted comprehensive zoning ordinances governing the use of land located within corporate limits. North Carolina General Assembly has enacted legislation that allows a municipality to regulate development in areas adjacent to, but not within, the corporate limits. These areas outside the incorporated limits, but subject to the zoning restrictions of a municipality, are called **extra-territorial jurisdictions (ETJs)**. Population of the municipality will determine if the regulatory power extends one mile or up to three miles from the corporate limits.

Zoning ordinances must not violate the rights of property owners (as provided under the due-process provisions of the Fourteenth Amendment to the U.S. Constitution) or the various provisions of the North Carolina State Constitution. If the means used to regulate the use of property are destructive, unreasonable, arbitrary, or confiscatory, the legislation is usually considered void. Tests commonly applied in determining the validity of ordinances require that

- the power be exercised in a reasonable manner;
- the provisions be clear and specific;
- the ordinance be free from discrimination;
- the ordinance promote public health, safety, and general welfare under the police power concept; and
- the ordinance apply to all property in a similar manner.

When land is taken for public use by the government's power of eminent domain, the owner must receive fair compensation. When *downzoning* occurs in an area—for instance, when land zoned for residential construction is rezoned for conservation or recreational purposes only—the state is ordinarily not responsible for compensating property owners for any resulting loss of value. However, if the courts find that a *taking* has occurred, the downzoning will be held to be an unconstitutional attempt to use the power of eminent domain without providing fair compensation to the property owner. (See Chapter 5 for a discussion of eminent domain.)

Zoning laws are generally enforced by requiring that building permits be obtained before property owners can build on their land. A permit will not be issued unless a proposed structure conforms to the permitted zoning, among other requirements.

Legal nonconforming use. It is not unusual to find real property uses that were legally established before the adoption of the current zoning plan. This *grandfathered* use is referred to as a legal **nonconforming use** (or simply "nonconforming use") of the property. Nonconforming use can apply to the way the land is used, the type of structure that is on the property, the way the structure is used, or even the lot size itself. For instance, a small factory building may be the last one left in a neighborhood that was once industrial but has since been zoned for residential use. The factory owner has a *matter of right* to continue this nonconforming pre-existing use.

Nonconforming uses are generally not permitted to continue indefinitely. Zoning statutes may prohibit the reconstruction of a building that is destroyed by fire or otherwise dismantled if it does not conform to current zoning requirements. Generally, nonconforming use property can only be maintained, not improved nor enlarged, since the zoning authority usually desires eventual conformity by all property. Compliance with current zoning requirements may also be required upon transfer of title. A real estate broker should never guarantee the continuance of a nonconforming use after a purchase; refer the buyer to the zoning power for verification.

Illegal use. An illegal nonconforming use (or simply "illegal use") is one that violates the zoning laws at the time it is put into place. For example, opening a gas station in a single-family residential zone would be an illegal use. The zoning body (city or county) can go to court to stop an illegal use at any time, even if the unpermitted use has been in place for an extensive period of time. To create an illegal nonconforming use is a misdemeanor.

Zoning variations. Each time a master plan is created or a zoning ordinance enacted, some owners are inconvenienced and want to change the use of their property. Zoning boards of adjustment have been established in most communities to hear complaints about the effects of zoning ordinances on specific parcels of property. Petitions may be presented to the board for variances or exceptions to the zoning law. Generally, such owners may appeal for either a conditional-use permit or a variance to allow a use that does not meet current zoning requirements.

A **conditional-use permit,** or *special-use permit,* is provided for in the zoning laws. It is granted to a property owner who wishes to use property in a special way that is in the public interest—such as a church or hospital in a residential district. A **variance** may also be sought to allow a deviation from an ordinance due to unique circumstances. As discussed in Chapter 1, under highest and best use, it is in the public interest to put land to use rather than have it lie fallow. To get a variance, the property owner must prove that there is no other reasonable use for the

Conditional-use permits allow nonconforming, but related land uses.

Variances permit prohibited land uses to avoid undue hardship.

property and the property owner will suffer a substantial hardship if the variance is not granted. The hardship also must not have been created by the property owner.

■ **FOR EXAMPLE** If an owner's lot is level next to a road but slopes steeply 30 feet away from the road, the zoning board may allow a variance so the owner can build closer to the road than the setback requirement allows. Otherwise, the lot could not be used.

A property owner can change the zoning classification of a parcel of real estate by obtaining an amendment to the official zoning map, which is part of the original zoning ordinance for the area. The proposed amendment must be brought before a public hearing on the matter and approved by the governing body of the community. When local officials fail to grant the desired relief from zoning regulations, the unhappy property owner can appeal to the courts, which may override the local officials and even the voters.

Overlay districts. An **overlay district** is a type of zoning that is superimposed over another type of zoning. The overlay zone can modify the use of the original zone. A common example is when an area that is zoned single-family residential is also designated as a flood zone. This means that additional restrictions and regulations are imposed on developments and improvements in that area. Two other examples of overlay districts are historic preservation and aesthetic zoning.

Historic preservation zoning. The purpose of **historic preservation zoning** is to preserve historic buildings and sites that are irreplaceable. An owner whose property falls within a historic preservation zone may have difficulty changing or upgrading the exterior of a structure on the property.

Before making material changes to a property located in a designated historic district or to individual property designated as a historic property, the owner must obtain a *certificate of appropriateness* from the appropriate regulatory entity. This certificate confirms that the local historic preservation commission, or other appropriate entity, has approved of the changes to be made to the property.

[In North Carolina] **Aesthetic zoning.** In North Carolina, an area can be zoned strictly for aesthetic or appearance considerations. Therefore, a property's value can be increased or decreased for the public good of an aesthetically-pleasing neighborhood. Exterior surfaces of structures being restricted to a particular color palette or construction material would be an example of **aesthetic zoning**.

[In North Carolina] **Spot zoning.** When a particular property or group of properties is rezoned to permit a use different from the neighboring properties' use, it is referred to as **spot zoning**. Whether spot zoning is legal or illegal in any particular case depends on whether the spot zoning is truly in the public interest rather than being for the benefit of a single property owner (or a few property owners) at the expense of neighboring property owners or the community at large. Some of the factors considered by North Carolina courts when determining the legality of spot zoning include: (1) the size of the rezoned area—rezoning a single lot is more questionable than rezoning multiple tracts; (2) the degree of compatibility of the different zoning with the government's adopted plans for the area; (3) the impact of the rezoning on the landowner(s), neighboring landowners and the surrounding community; and (4) the degree of difference between the zoning of the surrounding area and the new zoning for the tract(s) in question.

Broker's Duty to Disclose Zoning

Brokers' responsibilities concerning knowledge of land-use controls vary. Brokers working with urban properties—both commercial and residential—usually have more responsibilities and require more knowledge than brokers working in more rural areas. Residential brokers may require more knowledge of subdivision regulations, street disclosure laws, and protective covenants than commercial brokers, who may require more knowledge about rezoning, variances, and special-use permits.

Brokers should be able to recognize situations such as mixed use and property alterations where a closer check of zoning may be necessary. A broker should never make assumptions about the current or future zoning of a property on behalf of a client or customer. Purchasers are strongly encouraged to verify with the regulatory power any property use that is material to their desire for the property in question. Proper disclosure of zoning and protective covenants should be routinely made before the buyer signs an offer to purchase. A listing broker should acquire copies of any deed restrictions and protective covenants at the time of taking the listing.

Subdivision Regulations

There is *no uniform planning and land development legislation that affects the entire country.* Laws governing subdividing and land planning are controlled by the state and by local governing bodies of the county, city, town, or village where the land is located. Local regulations are by no means uniform but reflect customs and local climate, health, and hazardous conditions. Despite the local nature of land-use laws, rules and regulations developed by government agencies such as the Federal Housing Administration (FHA) have provided certain *minimum standards* that have served as usable guides. A large number of local governments have established higher standards for subdividers of land under their jurisdiction.

In North Carolina

In North Carolina, state law defines the term **subdivision** as "all divisions of a tract or parcel of land into two or more lots, building sites, or other divisions for the purpose of sale or building development (whether immediate or future) and includes all division of land involving the dedication of a new street or a change in existing streets." There are a few exceptions to this definition of subdivision. The following two types of parcels are not considered subdivisions: (1) a division of land if each parcel has more than 10 acres with no street right-of-way dedication and (2) a division of land no larger than two acres into no more than three lots with no street right-of-way dedication involved, when the parcel is owned by a single entity.

Although an approved preliminary plat of subdivision of land prior to public sale for residential or commercial use is required, land planning precedes the actual subdividing process. The land development plan must comply with the overall master plan adopted by the county, city, town, or village. The basic city plan and zoning requirements are not inflexible, but long, expensive (and frequently complicated) hearings are usually required before alterations can be authorized. Approval of the subdivision **plat map** by local authorities is, however, a necessary step before recording. Actual transfer of title cannot occur until the final plat has been recorded.

Most cities, villages, and other areas that are incorporated under state laws have *planning commissions*. Depending on how the particular group is organized, such a committee or commission may have only an advisory status to the council or trustees of the community. In other instances, the commission may have authority to approve or disapprove plans.

Communities establish strict criteria before approving new subdivisions. Frequent requirements are *dedication* of land for streets, schools, and parks; assurance by *bonding* that sewer and street costs will be paid or that such improvements will be completed before construction begins; and *compliance with zoning ordinances* governing use and lot size, along with fire and safety ordinances.

Because of the fear that they may pollute streams, rivers, lakes, and underground water sources, septic tank systems are no longer authorized in many areas, and an environmentally approved sewage-disposal arrangement must be included in a land development plan. The shortage of water has caused great concern, and local authorities usually require that land planners submit information on how they intend to satisfy sewage-disposal and water-supply requirements. Development and septic tank installation may first require a *soil evaluation test* of the soil's absorption and drainage capacities. Frequently, a planner will also have to submit an *environmental impact report*.

Subdivision process. The process of subdivision normally involves three distinct stages of development: (1) the initial planning stage, (2) the final planning stage, and (3) the disposition, or start-up.

During the *initial planning stage*, the subdivider seeks out raw land in a suitable area. Once the land is located, the property is analyzed for its highest and best use, and preliminary subdivision plans are drawn up accordingly. Close contact is initiated between the subdivider and local planning and zoning officials. If the project requires zoning variances, negotiations for these begin. The subdivider also locates financial backers and initiates marketing strategies.

The *final planning* stage is basically a follow-up of the initial stage. Final plans are prepared, approval is sought from local officials, permanent financing is obtained, the land is purchased, final budgets are prepared, and marketing programs are designed.

The *disposition*, or *start-up*, carries the subdividing process to a conclusion. Subdivision plans are recorded with local officials, and streets, sewers, and utilities are installed. Buildings, open parks, and recreational areas are constructed and landscaped if they are part of the subdivision plan. Marketing programs are then initiated, and title to the individual parcels of subdivided land is transferred as the lots are sold.

Subdivision Regulations

1. Land is divided into two or more lots.
2. Cities and counties implement subdivision regulations.
3. Planning boards have administrative responsibilities.
4. Subdividing must have preliminary plat approval before selling lots.
5. Final plat must be recorded prior to closing.
6. Subdivision must comply with street disclosure laws.
7. Protective covenants are enforceable.

Chapter 6　Land-Use Controls　**115**

In North Carolina

Subdivision Streets Disclosure Law. A developer of most new subdivisions must have streets approved, based on construction standards set by the North Carolina Department of Transportation, and must declare the streets to be for public or private use. Developers and their brokers must disclose to buyers whether new subdivision streets will be public or private prior to selling or conveying the lot, pursuant to North Carolina disclosure laws [G.S. 136-102.6, paragraph (f)]. This mandated written disclosure, which requires a signature from the buyer, must explain the consequences and responsibilities of a private street, disclose the party or parties responsible for construction and maintenance of the street, and disclose that the street will not be constructed to the minimum standard required of publicly maintained streets. Regardless of the age of the subdivision, real estate brokers should determine if the streets are public or private before making any statements to that effect.

It is worth noting that, just because streets have been dedicated for public use and approved by the North Carolina Department of Transportation (DOT), does not mean that the DOT has assumed responsibility for maintenance of the streets. There is usually a minimum population requirement prior to state adoption. Street maintenance issues are on the rise as many subdivisions with private streets that were built during the real estate boom of the 1990s and 2000s have begun to deteriorate to the point that maintenance is needed. An inquiry frequently reveals that the streets are actually private and the unsuspecting property owners are responsible for expensive street maintenance.

IN PRACTICE The question of the public or private status of the subdivision streets is very important to buyers, and it is very possible that the buyers do not even know to inquire about the status of the streets. If the property is in a new subdivision, the developer must voluntarily disclose the status of subdivision streets as mandated by state law. A subsequent property owner does not have to make such disclosure upon the resale of the property. Consequently, any prudent broker working with a buyer would be well advised to recommend that the buyer inquire about the status of the subdivision streets (or just make the inquiry directly on behalf of the buyer). If the inquiry reveals that the streets are public, further inquiry should be made to determine if the state (or municipality, if applicable) has assumed responsibility for street maintenance. If the inquiry reveals that the streets are private, further inquiry should be made to determine exactly who is responsible for maintenance. Of course, if any real estate broker involved in a house sale has actual knowledge that subdivision streets where the house is located are private, that broker absolutely must disclose this material fact to any prospective buyer.

Real estate brokers should be well aware of the needed verification of approved subdivisions, especially in regards to selling recently subdivided lots. Before selling or listing lots in newly subdivided land, a broker should check with the Register of Deeds Office in the county where the lot is located to ensure the plat has been properly recorded. Approval must be granted by the proper county agency (usually a planning board) before recordation can take place. North Carolina now allows the acceptance of monies and contracts on subdivision parcels once the preliminary plat has been approved. However, if there are any material changes from the preliminary to the final plat map, a buyer is allowed to cancel any existing contract and receive a refund of all monies. A broker who closes a sale on a lot before final approval of the subdivision is granted and recorded may be subject to a civil lawsuit or may be criminally prosecuted as well as face disciplinary action by the North Carolina Real Estate Commission.

Plat of subdivision. The subdivider's completed plat of subdivision, a map of the development indicating the location and boundaries of individual properties, must contain all necessary approvals of public officials and must be recorded in the county where the land is located. Once the plat is recorded, each lot then has a legal description that is used to convey the property.

The plat will be the basis for future conveyance, so the subdivided land should be measured carefully, with all lot sizes and streets noted by the surveyor and entered accurately on the document. Survey monuments should be established, and measurements should be made from these monuments, with the location of all lots carefully marked. As noted above, brokers engaged to sell subdivided land should be certain that the subdivision has been approved by the appropriate government body.

Covenants and restrictions. Deed restrictions, discussed in more detail later in this chapter, are usually originated and recorded by a subdivider as a means of controlling and maintaining the desirable quality and character of the subdivision. These restrictions can be included in the subdivision plat or they may be set forth in a separate recorded instrument, commonly referred to as a declaration of restrictions.

Deed restrictions may include the size of structures that can be built; the cost—often the minimum cost—of structures that can be built; the number of structures that can be built; or even architectural styles, fence heights, setbacks, or outbuildings that can be built on the land. Almost anything that is not illegal can be set forth in the restrictive covenants.

FHA standards. FHA minimum standards have been established for residential-area subdivisions that are to be submitted for approval for FHA loan insurance. The primary minimum standards established by the FHA deal with the actual development and infrastructure of the subdivision.

FHA standards also apply to building construction. Since 1986, in recognition of the more stringent local codes in effect, the FHA has allowed local building codes (where pre-approved by HUD—the Department of Housing and Urban Development) to serve as the standards. Exceptions generally include site condition standards, thermal (insulation) standards, and certain other material standards.

Interstate Land Sales Full Disclosure Act

To protect consumers from fraudulent and "overenthusiastic" sales promotions in interstate land sales, Congress passed the **Interstate Land Sales Full Disclosure Act** in 1968. The law requires those engaged in the interstate sale or leasing of subdivision lots (including condominiums, cooperative units, and campsites) to file a *statement of record* and register the details of the land with HUD. The Act exempts the sale of lots in a subdivision containing fewer than 25 lots. Interstate sales or leasing activities include out-of-state mailers, newspaper ads, television advertising directed to out-of-state buyers, and out-of-state telephone solicitation.

Brokers involved in interstate selling of lots across state lines that come under this Act should seek legal advice to ensure full compliance.

Prior to signing a purchase agreement or lease, the developer must furnish prospective buyers or lessees with a **property report** containing all essential information about the property, such as

- distance over paved roads to nearby communities,
- number of homes currently occupied,
- soil conditions affecting foundations and septic systems,
- type of title a buyer receives, and *(you want a General Warranty Deed)*
- existence of liens.

The Act provides a number of exemptions. For instance, it does not apply to subdivisions consisting of fewer than 25 lots or to those in which each lot is 20 acres or more. Lots offered for sale solely to developers also are exempt from the Act's requirements, as are lots on which buildings exist or where a seller is obligated to construct a building within two years.

Failure to provide the Property Report prior to contract formation may give the consumer grounds to void the contract.

If the seller misrepresents the property in any sales promotion, anyone induced to purchase a lot by the promotion can sue the seller for civil damages. Failure to comply with the law also may subject a seller to criminal penalties of fines and imprisonment.

Building Codes

In North Carolina

North Carolina has enacted a series of statewide **building codes** containing requirements as to construction standards, and the primary purpose is safety. Most cities, towns, and counties have enacted ordinances that enforce these *minimum construction standards* that must be met when repairing or erecting buildings. This enforcement is through the local building inspectors certified by the North Carolina Department of Insurance (NCDI). These building codes set the requirements for kinds of materials, sanitary equipment, electrical wiring, fire prevention standards, and the like.

> Unpermitted space is a material fact and can not be included in quoted heated living square footage, unless unpermitted status is fully disclosed.

C.O. needed before a buyer can close on a house

Most communities require the issuance of a **building permit** by the city clerk or another official before a person can build a new structure or alter or repair an existing building on property within the municipality. The permit requirement allows officials to verify compliance with building codes and zoning ordinances as they examine the plans and inspect the work. Once the completed structure has been inspected and found satisfactory, the building inspector issues a **certificate of occupancy (CO).** Not securing a building permit can make the property uninsurable for hazard insurance purposes until the oversight has been rectified. Some municipalities will allow retroactive approval of permits; some will require total removal of the improvement or repair. Unpermitted space may be included in heated living square footage quoted by real estate brokers, though the lack of a necessary permit must be disclosed as a material fact to all parties.

Unpermitted space is a material fact & must be disclosed, CANNOT be included in size (sq ft) of the house

If the construction violates a private deed restriction (discussed later in this chapter), the issuance of a building permit will not cure this violation. A building permit is merely evidence of the applicant's compliance with municipal regulations.

Flood Hazard Regulations and Insurance

The Federal Emergency Management Agency (FEMA) has designated many areas bordering on rivers and streams as **flood hazard areas**, which are subject to federal regulations concerning improvements and construction in those areas. FEMA produces maps that designate these flood hazard areas, and flood insurance is required under the National Flood Insurance Program (NFIP) if a federally related mortgage loan is to be used for properties within those areas. The lender will insist on appropriate flood insurance, which the buyer can purchase through most regular insurance companies that sell homeowners' policies. The standard homeowners' policies do not cover flood damage. Flood insurance is a separate policy from the federally operated NFIP but is brokered through local insurance companies. Land located in these flood hazard areas is subject to restrictions in terms of location, types of improvements, and elevations of the improvements. Real estate brokers should inform any potential buyers of possible flood areas and have them review the latest version of the flood maps compiled by the Army Corps of Engineers.

Highway Access Restrictions

Access to a public road or street is important to any buyer, and the broker should make sure that public road access is available. If any government entity takes away road access, the owner must be compensated under eminent domain. If there is any planned construction of new highways, freeways, loop roads, etc., real estate brokers are expected to be aware of this and make full disclosure to any potential customer or client. Changes in road access have a great impact on value and usability of the property. Failure of a real estate broker to properly disclose material

| In North Carolina | facts about road access could lead to disciplinary action by the North Carolina Real Estate Commission [see G.S. 93A-6(a)(1)].

IN PRACTICE The subject of city planning, zoning, and restriction of the use of real estate is extremely technical, and interpretation of the law is not altogether clear. Real estate brokers should never offer advice on whether a particular use will be allowed or whether a variance or special-use permit will be granted. Questions concerning any of these subjects in relation to real estate transactions should always be referred to the appropriate authority or legal counsel.

Environmental Protection Legislation

Federal and state legislators have passed a number of environmental protection laws in an attempt to respond to the growing public concern over the improvement and preservation of America's natural resources. (See Chapter 21 for further discussion on environmental issues.) The various states also have responded to the environmental issue by passing a variety of local environmental protection laws regarding all forms of pollution—air, water, noise, and solid-waste disposal. Many states have enacted laws that prevent builders or private individuals from considering septic tanks or other waste disposal systems in certain areas, particularly where streams, lakes, and rivers are affected. In addition to the state and federal governments, cities and counties frequently pass environmental legislation. A broker should stay informed of local environmental concerns so they may inform consumers.

Americans with Disabilities Act (ADA)

The federal government has recently mandated that new commercial buildings and older public buildings that undergo remodeling must meet the standards of the Americans with Disabilities Act (ADA). The purpose of this legislation is to facilitate accessibility and mobility by ramp construction, safety rails, wider doors, and other accommodations. (See Chapter 20 for further discussion on ADA.) ADA does not apply to residential housing.

PRIVATELY IMPOSED LAND-USE CONTROLS

Private land-use controls are put in place by individual developers or property owners, usually when they transfer property. When property is conveyed, a property owner can include restrictions in the deed that limit the new owner's use of the property. For example, the property may be conveyed on the condition that it is used only as a bird sanctuary. The most common examples of private land-use controls are the restrictions imposed by subdivision developers. All those who purchase lots in a subdivision promise to abide by the developer's restrictions, which usually include provisions requiring regular property maintenance and restrictions on parking, fences, architectural details, et cetera.

There is a distinction between restrictions on the grantee's right to *sell* and restrictions on the grantee's right to *use*. In general, provisions in a deed conveying a fee simple estate with restrictions on the grantee's right to sell, mortgage, or convey it are void. Such restrictions attempt to limit the basic principle of the *free alienation (transfer) of property*; the courts consider them against public policy and, therefore, unenforceable.

A developer may establish limitations on the right to use land through a covenant in a deed or by reference to a separate recorded declaration, called a **declaration of restrictive covenants**. When a lot in that subdivision is conveyed by an owner's deed, the deed refers to the plat and declaration of restrictions and incorporates these restrictions as limitations on the title conveyed by the deed. In this manner, the restrictive covenants are included in the deed by reference and become binding on all grantees. Such covenants or restrictions usually relate to type of building; use to which the land may be put; type of construction, height, setbacks, and square footage; and possibly cost. Private use restrictions are used primarily to protect property values and need not pass the test of promoting the public welfare, the test that public use restrictions must pass.

IN PRACTICE The term **restrictive covenant** is being replaced by the term **protective covenant**. Both have essentially the same meaning, which is defined by the North Carolina Real Estate Commission as follows: "Protective covenants are enforceable conditions that restrict the manner in which an owner may use his/her property" (1997-1998 Update Course). The term protective covenant is a more modern term and better implies the intended use, which is to protect owners from uses that may have an adverse effect on value or enjoyment.

> When public zoning and private covenants differ, the more restrictive of the two will prevail.

Use restrictions usually are considered valid if they are reasonable and are for the benefit of all property owners in the subdivision. However, if such restrictions are so broad in their terms that they prevent the free transfer of property, they may not be enforceable. If any restrictive covenant or condition is considered ineffective by a court, the property is freed from the invalid covenant or condition. Note that deed restrictions can be more restrictive on an owner's use than zoning ordinances. When zoning and covenants are in conflict, the more restrictive of the two takes precedence.

Generally, a subdivision developer will transfer the covenant enforcement rights to an established owners association at some predetermined time. Subdivision restrictions give the owners association and each lot owner the right to apply to the court for an injunction or legal action to prevent a neighboring lot owner from violating the recorded restrictions. If granted, the court injunction directs the violator to stop or remove the violation on penalty of being in contempt of court. The court retains the power to punish the violator for failure to obey the court order. If adjoining lot owners stand idle while a violation is being committed, they can *lose the right* to petition for injunctive relief by their inaction; the court might claim their right was lost through **laches**—that is, loss of a right through undue delay or failure to assert it.

Responsibilities of Real Estate Brokers

When a broker knows, or should have known, that the property in question is subject to protective covenants, there are certain obligations that the broker has to the prospective buyer. The broker should inform the buyer that since the property might be subject to private use restrictions, the buyer should obtain and carefully read a copy of the most recent version of the covenants before making an offer on the property.

In North Carolina

In North Carolina, a note under Provision 1 in the NCAR/NCBA Standard Form 2-T Offer to Purchase and Contract (see Appendix D, Form 11), the purchaser is cautioned to review Restrictive Covenants, if any, plus any governing documents for the subdivision or any established owners' association. The additional documents should clarify under what conditions the current covenants might be amended. Although a prudent broker should always volunteer general knowledge of the possible existence of land use restrictions, there are some situations that would require a broker to actively disclose and notify the buyer of possible problems. If the broker is aware of an intended use of the property by the buyer that is typically restricted in many residential communities, the broker should recognize this as a "red flag" situation, point out the potential for conflict with most residential subdivision covenants, assist the buyer in obtaining a copy of the covenants, and suggest that the buyer consult a competent attorney for clarification if necessary. A broker is strongly cautioned to refrain from stating whether or not a particular use of the property will be allowed or if a certain act will be in violation of the covenants. Also, making assumptions about allowed activities or uses based on what other property owners have done is a recipe for liability disaster! Some aberrant uses may have been legally grandfathered and some may be illegal violations of the current covenants. Always have the consumer consult an attorney if there is any uncertainty about a proposed land use.

■ GOVERNMENT OWNERSHIP

Over the years, the government's general policy has been to encourage private ownership of land. A certain amount of land is owned by the government for such uses as municipal buildings, state legislative houses, schools, and military stations. Such direct public ownership is a means of land control.

Publicly owned streets and highways serve a necessary function for the entire population. Public land is often used for recreational purposes as well. National and state parks and forest preserves create areas for public use and recreation and at the same time help to conserve our natural resources. At present, the federal government owns approximately 775 million acres of land, nearly one-third of the total area of the United States. At times, the federal government has held title to as much as 80% of the nation's total land area.

■ RELATED WEBSITES

Federal Emergency Management Authority: www.fema.gov
North Carolina Department of Insurance: www.ncdoi.com
North Carolina Department of Transportation projects:
    www.ncdot.org/projects
North Carolina Flood Mapping Program: www.ncfloodmaps.com

■ KEY POINT REVIEW

The **police power** of the state is its authority to create regulations to protect the public health, safety, and welfare. State **enabling acts** allow the power to enact laws authorized by the state's police power to be passed down to municipalities and other local governing authorities.

Public land use is controlled and regulated through

- public restrictions—planning, zoning, building codes, subdivision plans; and
- direct ownership of land by federal, state, and local governments.

A **master plan** (comprehensive plan) created by a local government usually covers land use, movement of people and goods, community facilities and utilities, energy and natural resource conservation, and noise abatement.

Zoning ordinances are local laws implementing the land uses designated in the comprehensive plan and typically cover items such as permitted uses, lot sizes, types of structures, building heights, setbacks, style and appearance of structures, density, and protection of natural resources. Such regulations must be

- exercised in a reasonable manner,
- clear and specific,
- nondiscriminatory, and
- applicable to all property in a similar manner.

Zoning classifies property by uses and types, such as commercial, industrial, residential, agricultural, and **extra-territorial jurisdictions (ETJs)**.

Zoning is enforced through the use of permits, and an individual case may be considered by a zoning hearing board (or zoning board of appeals), which may decide to

- allow a **nonconforming use** to continue,
- grant a **variance** from a zoning ordinance to permit a prohibited land use to avoid undue hardship,
- grant a **conditional-use permit** (special-use permit), or
- superimpose additional zoning requirements through the use of **overly districts** such as **historic preservation zoning**, or **aesthetic zoning**.

Spot zoning is usually illegal and must be discontinued once discovered.

Brokers have a duty to disclose zoning which is a material fact.

Building codes require permits for new construction and remodeling of or additions to existing construction.

A **certificate of occupancy** (occupancy permit) is issued upon satisfactory completion of work for which the **building permit** was issued.

Subdivision and land development ordinances may be created by the state or may be made part of a local government's comprehensive plan. These ordinances usually include the following:

- Subdividers, who buy undeveloped acreage and divide it into smaller lots for sale to individuals or developers
- Developers, who improve the land, construct homes or other buildings, and sell them
- **Plat map** (subdivision map), which shows geographic boundaries of separate land parcels, usually by showing blocks of land divided into individual lots
- Subdivision plan, which describes subdivision features and compliance with zoning and other laws, including utility easements, and density zoning
- Private land-use controls, such as restrictive covenants (deed restrictions), which are placed in deeds to all property owners in a subdivision and cannot impose an illegal covenant or condition and may be enforced by injunction against property owner in violation of covenant or restriction
  — If in conflict with local zoning, the more restrictive controls prevail.

Brokers are responsible for disclosing whether streets are public or privately maintained. Any restriction about highway accessibility should also be disclosed. Presence of the property in a FEMA flood hazard area or any known environmental concerns should be disclosed by a broker.

The **Federal Interstate Land Sales Full Disclosure Act** regulates the interstate sale of unimproved lots in subdivisions of 25 or more lots of less than 20 acres each. The law does not apply to subdivisions sold solely to developers.

QUESTIONS

1. A provision in a subdivision declaration used as a means of forcing the grantee to live up to the terms under which the grantee holds title to the land is a
   a. protective covenant.
   b. reversion clause.
   c. loss through laches.
   d. conditional-use permit.

2. Tests commonly applied in determining the validity of zoning ordinances require all of the following EXCEPT that the
   a. power be exercised in a reasonable manner.
   b. ordinance be free from discrimination.
   c. ordinance apply to all property in a similar manner.
   d. ordinance causes a loss of property value for the public good.

3. Public land-use controls include all of the following EXCEPT
   a. subdivision regulations.
   b. restrictive covenants.
   c. environmental protection laws.
   d. master plan specifications.

4. Zoning powers are conferred on municipal governments by
   I. state enabling acts.
   II. eminent domain.
      a. I only
      b. II only
      c. Both I and II
      d. Neither I nor II

5. Zoning laws are generally enforced by
   a. homeowner associations.
   b. nonissuance of building permits to properties that do not conform to zoning.
   c. restrictive covenants.
   d. the North Carolina Secretary of State.

6. Zoning boards of adjustment are established to hear complaints about
   a. protective covenants.
   b. the effects of a zoning ordinance.
   c. state building codes.
   d. the effects of public ownership.

7. The zoning allows regulation of all of the following EXCEPT
   a. number of buildings.
   b. size of buildings.
   c. building ownership.
   d. building occupancy.

8. The purpose of a building permit is to
   I. maintain municipal control over the volume of building.
   II. provide evidence of compliance with municipal building codes.
      a. I only
      b. II only
      c. Both I and II
      d. Neither I nor II

9. A local man owns a vacant lot in a residential neighborhood. His friends in the city government manage to change the zoning on his lot to commercial, so he can increase his profits on the property. This type of zoning is called
   a. spot zoning.
   b. a nonconforming use.
   c. an illegal use.
   d. a variance.

10. The grantor of a deed may place effective restrictions on the
    I. right to sell the land.
    II. use of the land.
       a. I only
       b. II only
       c. Both I and II
       d. Neither I nor II

11. A new zoning code is enacted. A building that is permitted to continue in its current use even though that use does not conform to the new zoning is an example of a(n)
    a. legal nonconforming use.
    b. hardship variance.
    c. conditional use.
    d. inverse condemnation.

12. To determine whether a location can be put to future use as a retail store, one would examine the
    a. building code.
    b. current use.
    c. housing code.
    d. zoning code.

13. A list of deed restrictions probably would NOT include
    a. types of buildings that may be constructed.
    b. allowable ethnic origins of purchasers.
    c. activities that are not to be conducted at the site.
    d. minimum size of buildings to be constructed.

14. A seller's deed restriction may be enforced by
    a. court injunction.
    b. zoning board of adjustment.
    c. city building commission.
    d. state legislature.

15. Two business partners just purchased a vacant lot next to their retail shop. They plan to expand their shop onto the newly acquired lot. The architectural plans extend the addition two feet into the setback requirements for that location. To construct the building legally, the owners must obtain a
    a. license.
    b. variance.
    c. nonconforming-use permit.
    d. permit issued by the state.

16. A residential neighborhood in Central City consists of homes built in the late 1800s. The neighborhood is subject to special zoning that prohibits property owners from tearing down a current home and replacing it with a modern one. This type of zoning is called
    a. historic preservation zoning.
    b. spot zoning.
    c. zoning amendments.
    d. eminent domain.

17. A drawing showing the sizes and locations of streets, utility easements, and lots in a subdivision is called a
    a. gridiron pattern.
    b. topographic survey.
    c. plat map.
    d. property report.

18. The property report required by the Interstate Land Sales Full Disclosure Act, would NOT need to include
    a. soil conditions affecting foundations.
    b. original purchase price paid by developer.
    c. number of homes currently occupied.
    d. existence of liens.

19. When other property owners in an established subdivision wish to remedy a violation of a restrictive covenant by a neighbor, they should
    a. appeal to the zoning commission.
    b. write the city council.
    c. complain to the developer.
    d. hire an attorney and sue the offender.

20. Due to the strange shape of the a lot, present zoning restrictions about parking space requirements will cause an undue hardship for the owner's planned use of the property as an office building. If there are no other reasonable uses for the property, the owner may be allowed to proceed with his plans under
    a. nonconforming use.
    b. a variance.
    c. spot zoning.
    d. a special-use permit.

21. A gas station has operated at the edge of town for 20 years. Pursuant to a new comprehensive plan, the city rezones the land as residential. Which of the following statements is TRUE?
    a. The gas station can probably continue to operate under a variance.
    b. If the station is sold, the new owner can continue to operate under the grandfather clause.
    c. The city can force the closure of the gas station immediately.
    d. The station can continue to operate as long as the building is not enlarged.

22. Which of the following statements is/are TRUE about subdivision regulations?
    I. A subdivision consists of at least five parcels of land for the purpose of sale or development now or in the future.
    II. A broker can create a sales contract on lots in a new subdivision only after the final subdivision plat has been recorded.
    a. I only
    b. II only
    c. Both I and II
    d. Neither I nor II

23. Flood insurance is
    a. part of most homeowner hazard insurance policies.
    b. required on all FHA loans if the property is located in a flood hazard area.
    c. sold only by agents of the Federal Emergency Management Agency.
    d. coverage for all property damage caused by any water source.

24. The type of residential subdivision zoning that would maximize open space would be
    a. cluster zoning.
    b. multi-use zoning.
    c. aesthetic zoning.
    d. spot zoning.

25. Which of the following statements about subdivision street disclosure in North Carolina is NOT true?
    a. A subdivision developer must disclose whether streets in a new subdivision are intended for public or private use.
    b. Buyers of new subdivision lots must receive and sign a written disclosure of street status.
    c. Real estate brokers are only responsible for determining and disclosing whether subdivision streets are privately or publicly maintained in new subdivisions.
    d. Subdivision streets built to the North Carolina Department of Transportation's standards for public road maintenance are not automatically adopted for state maintenance.

CHAPTER 7

Real Estate Brokerage and the Law of Agency

■ **LEARNING OBJECTIVES** *When you have finished reading this chapter, you should be able to*

- **identify** all types of agency relationships and characteristics of each (single, subagency, dual agency, and designated dual agency) and explain how fiduciary relationships are established and terminated.

- **differentiate** between client-level and customer-level responsibilities of the agent.

- **explain** agency disclosure requirements in North Carolina; how, when, and to whom proper agency disclosures must be made.

- **explain** the duties and liabilities of principals to their agents and third parties.

- **define** these *key terms:*

agency
agent
broker
brokerage
broker-in-charge (BIC)
caveat emptor
client
commingling
commission
cooperating broker
customer
designated dual agency
dual agency
employee
express agreement
fiduciary
first substantial contact
fraud
general agent
implied agreement
independent contractor
in-house sale
material facts
multiple listing service (MLS)
negligent misrepresentation
negligent omission
OLD CAR
oral buyer agency
principal
provisional broker
puffing
ratification
special agent
stigmatized properties
subagent
tort
universal agent
willful misrepresentation
willful omission
Working with Real Estate Agents

■ INTRODUCTION TO BROKERAGE AND AGENCY

The nature of real estate brokerage services, particularly those provided in residential sales transactions, has changed significantly over the years. Through the 1950s, real estate brokerage firms were primarily one-office, minimally staffed, family-run operations. The broker listed the owner's property for sale and found a buyer without assistance from other companies. Then the sale was negotiated and closed. It was relatively clear that the broker represented the seller's interests.

In the 1960s, however, the ways buyers and sellers were brought together in a transaction began to change. Brokers started to share information about properties they had listed, which resulted in two brokers/firms cooperating with one another to sell a property. Brokers formalized this exchange of information by creating **multiple-listing services (MLSs)**. By increasing exposure to potential buyers, the MLS expedited sales and, therefore, became a widely used industry service.

Unfortunately, confusion quickly arose over whom the broker represented in these cooperative co-brokered transactions. With two different brokers/firms involved in a sale, the natural assumption was that there was a clear division of responsibility. Consumers assumed that the broker who had the property listed for sale represented the seller; the broker who found the buyer represented the buyer. However, this was not the case. In these shared transactions, both brokerage firms and their brokers or salespersons represented the seller as agents and owed all loyalty to the seller and owed no duties other than honesty and fairness to the buyer. Generally, the MLSs provided for a *unilateral subagency*, which was created when a seller listed property with a listing broker or firm. The listing broker then submitted the listing to the MLS so the listing could be shared with other MLS members. These MLS members immediately became subagents of the seller; the seller became their client or principal. This common *traditional view* of agency began to erode when buyers became concerned about having their own representation.

| In North Carolina |

Such misunderstandings ultimately led buyers to question exactly how their interests were being protected. This helped spur a growing trend in which buyer consumers began to demand that their rights be protected so that they could make informed decisions. In many states, lawmakers have departed from the common-law doctrine of **caveat emptor**—let the buyer beware—toward greater consumer protection. Buyers seek not only accurate, factual information but also advice, particularly as real estate transactions have become much more complex. Buyers view the real estate broker as the expert on whom they can rely to guide them. Today, most buyers seek and obtain representation. However, North Carolina is still considered to be a *caveat emptor* state.

■ THE LAW OF AGENCY

The basic framework of the law that governs the legal responsibilities of the broker to the people the broker represents—known as the *law of agency*—has not changed. However, its *application* has. The law of agency is a common-law concept (law from the judgments and decrees of courts as opposed to the legislature); it is being widely replaced or modified by state statute in many jurisdictions but not in North Carolina. Brokers are re-evaluating their services. They are determining whether they will represent the seller, the buyer, or both (if permitted by state law) in the sale or rental of property. They also must decide how they will cooperate with other brokers in a transaction. In short, the brokerage business is undergoing many changes as brokers focus on ways to enhance their services to buyers and sellers.

In North Carolina The North Carolina Real Estate Commission (NCREC) strongly encourages the **broker-in-charge (BIC)** of a real estate firm to have a written office policy as to the type(s) of agency the firm will practice. The firm is technically the agent in a transaction. The company policy should cover whether the firm will practice seller single agency only, buyer single agency only, or dual and designated agency. Which party the firm will represent is a decision that is largely based on economics. For instance, a single-agency practice could result in a loss of income in certain areas of the state. Whichever form of representation the firm adopts, the written policy should clearly state how that type of agency representation will be exercised. The written policy also should explain how the firm will enter into cooperative relationships among other firms, how it will arrange commission splits, and how it will implement disclosure requirements.

■ GENERAL AGENCY DEFINITIONS

The job of being a real estate broker is commonly referred to as a real estate agent. Legally, however, the term *agent* refers to a strictly defined legal relationship. In the real estate industry, it is the relationship a licensee has with buyers and sellers. In the *law of agency*, the body of law that governs these relationships, the following terms have specific definitions:

> An *agent* is a person authorized to act on behalf of another.

Even the BIC is a subagent of the firm

- **Agent**—the individual who is authorized and consents to represent the interests of another person. In the real estate industry, principals are hiring an entire company and all the company's affiliated brokers to represent them. Even though *the firm* is the agent, the broker-in-charge would be personally accountable for agency law compliance.
- **Subagent**—one who is employed by a person already acting as an agent (such as a provisional broker licensed under a broker-in-charge who is employed under the terms of a listing agreement). Simply stated, a *subagent* is *an agent of an agent*.
- **Principal**—the person who hires and delegates to the agent through a brokerage contract the responsibility of representing that person's best interests. In the real estate business, the principal can be the buyer, seller, landlord, or tenant.
- **Agency**—the fiduciary relationship between the principal and the agent.
- **Subagency**—the fiduciary relationship between the subagent and the principal.
- **Fiduciary**—a relationship in which the agent is placed in the position of trust and confidence to the principal.
- **Client**—the principal.
- **Customer**—the third party for whom some level of service is provided by an agent of another party, but who is not represented by the agent.

services provided, but no signed agreement
represented by an agent of another party, but not by YOU
you work for the client & with the customer

The principal-agent relationship evolved from the master-servant relationship under English common law. The servant owed absolute loyalty to the master. This loyalty superseded the servant's personal interest as well as any loyalty the servant might owe to others. The agent owes the principal similar loyalty. As masters used the services of servants to accomplish what they could not or did not want to do for themselves, the principal uses the services of the agent. The agent is regarded as an expert on whom the principal can rely for specialized professional advice.

> An agent works **for** *the client* and **with** *the customer*.

There is a distinction between the level of services that agents provide to clients and the level they provide to customers. The client is the principal to whom the agent gives advice and counsel. The agent is entrusted with certain *confidential information* and has *fiduciary responsibilities* (discussed in greater detail later in this chapter) to the principal. In contrast, the customer is entitled to factual information and fair and honest dealings as a consumer but does not receive advice and counsel or confidential information about the principal. The agent works *for* the principal and *with* the customer. Essentially, the agent is an advocate for the principal, but not for the customer.

The relationship between the principal and agent must be consensual: the principal *delegates* authority; the agent *consents* to act. The parties must mutually agree to form the relationship. An agent may be authorized by the principal to use the assistance of others, called subagents of the principal.

■ BROKERAGE DEFINED

Before discussing the intricacies of agency, it is important to look more closely at the parties who provide the client and customer services in a real estate agency relationship.

> In North Carolina

Brokerage is the business of bringing buyers and sellers together in the marketplace. Buyers and sellers in many fields of business employ the services of brokers to facilitate complex business transactions. In the real estate business in North Carolina, a **broker** is defined as a person who is licensed to list, lease, buy, exchange, auction, negotiate, or sell interest in real property for others and to charge a fee for services. The **provisional broker** works under direct supervision of the broker-in-charge (see G.S. 93A-1, G.S. 93A-2).

The principal who employs the firm may be a seller, a prospective buyer, an owner (landlord) who wishes to lease out property, or a person (tenant) seeking property to rent. The real estate firm or broker-in-charge acts as the agent of the principal, and the brokers employed by the firm act as the subagents of the principal. The principal usually compensates the firm with a **commission,** contingent on the firm successfully performing the service for which it was employed. That service generally involves negotiating a transaction with a prospective purchaser, seller, landlord, or tenant who is ready, willing, and able to complete the contract. However, the source of compensation does not necessarily dictate the agency relationship.

In a typical real estate listing contract, the seller will authorize the firm to use brokers employed by the firm as well as other **cooperating brokers/***firms* (members of the MLS). Cooperating brokerages through agreement with the listing firm may act as subagents of the seller-principal and may in turn employ their own brokers. The relationship of a broker to an employing broker/firm is also an agency relationship. The individual broker is, therefore, the agent of his firm in addition to being the subagent of the consumer/principal.

REALTOR® Board/Association MLSs may not require that members make blanket offers of subagency to other members. Instead, MLS members must offer cooperation with compensation to other members. Thus, other members of the MLS may find a buyer for listed property while working as a subagent of the listing agent or as an agent of the buyer. The cooperating agent then will receive a portion of the commission when the sale closes. While all offers of cooperation to other MLS members must be accompanied by an offer of compensation, the listing broker may offer differing amounts to subagents and to buyer agents.

Classification of Agency Relationships

An agent may be classified as a universal agent, a general agent, or a special agent, based on the nature of the agent's authority.

A **universal agent** is a person who is empowered to do anything the principal could do personally. There are virtually no limits to the universal agent's authority to act on behalf of the principal. An unlimited power of attorney would be an example of universal agency. This type of agency is seldom practiced by a real estate broker in a typical real estate transaction.

A **general agent** may represent the principal in a broad range of matters *related to a particular business or activity*. The general agent may, for example, bind the principal to any contracts within the scope of the agent's authority. A real estate broker typically does not have this scope of authority as an agent for a consumer in a real estate sales transaction. A broker usually serves as a general agent of their real estate brokerage firm. A property manager may be hired to be a general agent for the landlord in the management of certain properties.

A **special agent** is authorized to represent the principal in only one specific act or business transaction, and under limited, detailed instructions with no power to bind the principal. A real estate broker is usually a special agent. If hired by a seller, the broker's duty is limited to finding a "ready, willing, and able buyer" for the property. A special agent for a buyer has the limited responsibility of finding a property that fits the buyer's criteria. As a special agent, the broker cannot bind the principal to any contract. It is important to remember that a special agency gives *limited authority.*

Creation of Agency

Brokers are employed for their expertise. However, provision of services does not in itself create an agency relationship. No agency exists without mutual consent between the principal and the agent. The agent consents to undertake certain duties on behalf of the principal, subject to the principal's control. The principal authorizes the agent to perform these acts when dealing with others.

Common-law agency relationships can be created in the following ways:

- With a written listing contract whereby a seller employs an agent to produce a buyer for the property; the seller is the principal, the firm/broker is the seller's agent
- With a buyer agency contract whereby a prospective buyer hires a firm/broker to locate properties for the buyer with buyer representation; the buyer is the principal, the firm/broker is the buyer's agent
- With a dual-agency contract whereby the agent legally represents both parties; both seller and buyer are principals, firm/broker is agent to both, but written informed consent from both parties is required
- With a property management contract whereby the owner of rental properties engages the services of an agent to rent and manage the property; the owner is the principal and the firm/broker is the property manager/agent
- With an in-house brokerage employment contract whereby a broker signs an employment agreement with a firm/broker that defines the legal and agency relationship between them; the firm/broker is the principal and the licensee is the agent
- By the conduct of the parties (implied agency)

(Examples of these agency agreements are fully discussed in Chapter 9.)

Scope of Authority

Under general agency law principles, an agency relationship can be created by either an oral or a written agency agreement between the principal and the agent. It also can be implied from conduct. To ensure that all parties have a clear understanding of the agency relationship, it is in everyone's best interest to create an agency relationship through an expression of agreement rather than through implication. Principal and agent should have an **express agreement** (written or oral), such as those reviewed in Chapter 9.

Agency also can be created by **implied agreement** when principal and agent, without formally agreeing to the agency, act as if one exists. However, an implied contract will not be established simply on trade custom and practice. There must be sufficient evidence to show that the principal authorized the agent to perform acts under circumstances in which a reasonable principal would be expected to compensate the agent for the services. The fact that a seller simply allows a broker to show the property is not sufficient to create an implied agency agreement. Implied agency agreements are illegal under North Carolina real estate license law, which requires all agency agreements be in writing.

In North Carolina

When someone claims to be an agent but there is no express agreement, the *principal* can establish an agency relationship by **ratification** (apparent authority)—in other words, by performing any act that accepts (ratifies) the conduct of the agent as that of an agent.

If someone has stated incorrectly that another person is acting as the person's agent and a third person has relied on that representation, an agency relationship may have been created by estoppel. In such an event, in dealing with the *agent*, the *principal* cannot later deny the existence of an agency.

Compensation. Creation of an agency relationship must include promise of compensation to the agent by the principal. An agent owes his loyalty to the party that *employs* him; that may not be the party that *pays* him. Because the source of an agent's compensation does not necessarily determine whether an agency relationship exists between two parties, an agent might not represent the party who pays the commission. In theory, an agency relationship can exist even if there is no fee involved (a gratuitous agency); however, such situations are rare, especially in real estate transactions. Buyers and sellers can make any agreement with a firm/broker they choose about compensating the firm/broker, regardless of which one is the agent's principal. For example, the seller could agree with the listing firm/broker to pay a commission to the broker who is the buyer's agent.

In North Carolina — North Carolina real estate license law mandates that an agency agreement must be in writing in order for a broker to be entitled to compensation. All agency agreements should state how the agent [FIRM] is being compensated.

Termination of Agency

When an agent completes an assignment, the agency relationship ends, as does all responsibility to that former principal. An agency agreement may be terminated at any time for any of the following reasons:

- Completion or fulfillment of the purpose for which the agency was created
- Expiration of the terms of the agency
- Mutual agreement to terminate the agency
- Breach by one of the parties, such as abandonment by the agent or revocation by the principal (The breaching party might be liable for damages.)
- By operation of law, as in a bankruptcy of the principal (because title to the property would be transferred to a court-appointed receiver)
- Destruction or condemnation of the property
- Death or incapacity of either party (Notice of death is not necessary. Note that if a property is listed with a brokerage firm, the firm must dissolve to "die." If the individual listing agent dies, the listing would not be terminated because the listing belongs to the brokerage firm rather than to the deceased listing agent.)

■ AGENCY RELATIONSHIPS

A variety of agency relationships may be created. The distinctions between them are not always clear. When consumers feel their individual interests have not been adequately protected, brokers may face legal and ethical problems. The broker-in-charge must decide the agency policies and procedures for the firm, determine who will be represented, disclose the agency alternatives to each party, and then act according to the agency relationship defined.

In North Carolina — In North Carolina every agreement for brokerage services in real estate transactions must be in writing [see Rule A.0104(a)]. Real estate agency relationships typically are created with a listing agreement, a property management agreement, a buyer-agency agreement, or a tenant-agency agreement. Listing agreements and buyer-agency agreements will be discussed in detail in Chapter 9.

Chapter 7 Real Estate Brokerage and the Law of Agency 133

Single Agency

In single agency, the agent represents only one party in any single transaction. The real estate agent must provide either fiduciary or statutory duties exclusively to one principal within the transaction (who may be either the buyer or the seller or the landlord or the tenant). The customer is the party not represented by the agent (see Figure 7.1).

FIGURE 7.1

Single Agency

```
          Agent
         /      \
     Client    Customer
```

A single agent represents either the buyer or the seller in a transaction.

While a single agency broker may represent both sellers and buyers, that broker cannot represent both the buyer and the seller in the same transaction and remain a single agent. This avoids conflicts and results in client-based service and loyalty to only one principal. On the other hand, it traditionally rules out the sale of in-house listings (where the brokerage works with both sides) to prospective buyers.

Buyer Agency

When a buyer contracts with a firm/broker to locate property and represent the buyer's interests in the transaction, the buyer is the principal—the broker's client. The broker as agent is strictly accountable to the buyer. The seller is the third party.

In the past, it was simple: brokers always represented sellers, and buyers were expected to look out for themselves. With the widespread use of MLSs and sub-agency, a buyer often had the mistaken impression that the subagent was the buyer's agent, although the reality was that both agent and subagent exclusively represented the seller's interest. Today, however, many residential brokers recognize the opportunities afforded by buyer representation. Some brokers have become specialists in the field of buyer brokerage, representing buyers exclusively. Real estate regulatory agencies (including the North Carolina Real Estate Commission) across the country have developed rules and procedures to regulate such buyers' brokers, and local real estate associations have developed agency representation forms and other materials for them to use. The buyer agency agreement forms are discussed in Chapter 9. Professional organizations offer assistance, certification, training, and networking opportunities for buyers' agents. The buyer's agent may receive a flat fee or a share of the listing commission or both, depending on the terms of the agency agreement.

In North Carolina

A buyer-agency or tenant-agency relationship is also established by *express* contract or agreement. Unlike agency agreements with a property owner, buyer agency may be oral initially, but must be reduced to writing no later than the time an offer is extended by any party to the transaction. If the agent seeks to restrict the buyer's right to work with other agents or independently or to bind the client to the agent for any specified period, then the buyer-agency agreement must be in writing from the formation of the restricted relationship.

Subagency

A subagency is created when one broker/firm, usually the seller's agent, appoints other brokers/firms (with the authority of the seller) to assist in performing client-based functions on the principal's behalf. These cooperating brokers/firms have the same fiduciary obligations to the seller-principal as the listing broker, assisting in producing a ready, willing, and able buyer for the property. The listing broker and the seller now become potentially liable for the conduct of all of the cooperating brokers/firms and their affiliated brokers. *Vicarious liability* is a legal concept that might allow a consumer to successfully sue the seller and/or the listing firm for illegal or inept actions performed by the subagent firm and/or its brokers (see Figure 7.2). It is also important to note that when a real estate broker/firm becomes an agent under an agency agreement with a principal, all individual real estate brokers affiliated with the broker/firm automatically become subagents of the principal, unless there is a specific agreement to the contrary.

> A *subagent* is the agent of an agent. The person designated by an agent to assist in performing client-based functions on behalf of the principal.

FIGURE 7.2

Subagency

```
              Client
                │
                ▼
           Agent ──────────▶ Subagent
```

Dual Agency

In a **dual agency** situation, the broker/firm represents the buyer and the seller in the same transaction. Dual agency requires that the agent be equally loyal to two separate principals at the same time. The challenge is to fulfill the fiduciary obligations to each principal without compromising fiduciary obligations to the other. Under the strict terms of the law of agency, dual agency seems to be a logical impossibility. How can one person serve two masters, especially when their interests are not only separate but may also be opposite? Because agency originates with the broker/firm, dual agency arises when the broker/firm is the agent of both parties in the same transaction. The firm brokers, as agents of the brokerage firm, have fiduciary responsibilities to the same principals as well. A real estate firm/broker representing one party in a transaction shall not undertake to represent another party in the same transaction without the express approval of both parties.

> A *dual agent* represents two principals with opposing interests in the same transaction.

■ **FOR EXAMPLE** A real estate broker is the agent for the owner of Roomy Manor, a large mansion. A prospective buyer comes into the real estate broker's office and asks for representation in a search for a modest home. After several weeks of activity, including two offers unsuccessfully negotiated by the broker, the prospective buyer spots the For Sale sign in front of Roomy Manor and wants to make an offer and asks for his advice on a likely price range. The real estate broker is now in the difficult position of being a dual agent by representing the seller (who naturally is interested in receiving the highest possible price) and the prospective buyer (who is interested in making a successful low offer).

Undisclosed dual agency. A broker/firm may not intend to create a dual agency situation. However, by a broker associate's words and actions, it can occur *unintentionally* or *inadvertently*. Sometimes the cause is carelessness. Other times the subagent does not fully understand the fiduciary responsibilities. Some brokers lose sight of other responsibilities when they focus intensely on bringing buyers and sellers together. For example, a broker representing a seller might tell a buyer that the seller will accept less than the listing price, which is a breach of the duty of loyalty (discussed later in this chapter). Giving a buyer any specific advice on how much to offer can lead the buyer-customer to believe that the broker is their agent or advocate. This would create an *implied agency* with the buyer and violate the duties of loyalty and confidentiality to the principal/seller. Because neither party has been informed of the situation or given the opportunity to seek separate representation, the interests of both are jeopardized. This undisclosed dual agency violates license laws [see G.S. 93A-6(a)(4)] and the law of agency. It can result in rescission of the sales contract, forfeiture of the commission, or the filing of a suit for damages.

■ **FOR EXAMPLE** Using the previous Roomy Manor example, the real estate broker must tell the prospective buyer that he represents the seller of the property, or he will be an illegal undisclosed dual agent. Knowing the buyer's comfortable financial situation and intense desire for the property, the broker might choose not to tell about the dual-agency situation. If the broker told her that Roomy Manor's owner will accept nothing less than the full asking price, this will ensure that the broker receives the maximum possible commission, but it will also subject him to severe penalties for violating the state's license laws. Alternatively, the broker should disclose his relationship with the seller and work out a dual-agency agreement with both parties in which he legally and impartially represents both parties' interests.

A more common example of dual agency would be if the real estate brokerage firm employed two brokers. One broker is the listing agent for Roomy Manor, and the other broker is the buyer's agent. Because both brokers are associated with the same real estate brokerage, the broker-in-charge and his affiliated brokers will still be acting as dual agents and have to enter into a legal disclosed dual-agency agreement with the parties.

Disclosed dual agency. Although the possibility of conflict of interest still exists, disclosure is intended to minimize the risk *for the broker*. The disclosure alerts the principals that they might have to assume greater responsibility for protecting their interests than they would if they had independent representation. Because the duties of disclosure and confidentiality are often limited by the express terms of the dual agency agreement, the effect of these limitations, as well as any other reduction in the services the broker may provide, they must be carefully explained to the parties in order to establish *informed consent*.

In North Carolina

Dual agency should be purposely created. In North Carolina, the key to *lawful* dual agency is that *all parties (seller/buyer, lessor/lessee)* must be *informed* and must *consent* to the broker representing both of them in the same transaction. In North Carolina, a firm that represents more than one party in the same real estate transaction is a dual agent and must disclose its dual agency status to the parties. The written authority for dual agency must be *obtained upon the formation of the relationship, except when an agent is working with a buyer or tenant under an oral agency* agreement pursuant to A.0104(a), in which event the express oral authority for dual agency must be reduced to writing not later than the time that one of the parties represented by the agent makes an offer to purchase, sell, rent, lease, or exchange real estate to another party. Though the possibility of conflict of interest still exists, the disclosure is intended to minimize the risk for the broker and ensure that both principals are aware of its effect on their respective interests. Written authorization to practice dual agency within a North Carolina transaction is typically obtained in the original agency agreement which will be discussed further in Chapter 9.

Throughout any discussion of agency duties, it is important to remember that an agent's duties to the principal are greater than the agent's duties to the customer (third person). However, a dual agent represents both parties equally. Therefore, the agent and subagents are generally restricted by the dual agency agreement from disclosing to either client the following types of information about the other party without that party's written permission:

- Willingness to accept any terms of sale other than those offered
- Motivation for participating in the transaction (unless required by statute)
- Any confidential information unless disclosure is mandated by statute

Consequently, a dual agent is *required by law* to disclose all material facts about the property to both principals but is absolved from disclosing confidential information about either principal by the terms of the dual agency agreement.

The appropriate paragraphs of North Carolina Real Estate Commission Rule A.0104 are quoted below.

> (d) A real estate broker representing one party in a transaction shall not undertake to represent another party in the transaction without the written authority of each party. Such written authority must be obtained upon the formation of the relationship except when a buyer or tenant is represented by a broker without a written agreement in conformity with the requirements of paragraph (a) of this rule. Under such circumstances, the written authority for dual agency must be reduced to writing not later than the time that one of the parties represented by the broker makes an offer to purchase, sell, rent, lease, or exchange real estate to another party.
>
> (i) A firm which represents more than one party in the same real estate transaction is a dual agent and, through the brokers associated with the firm, shall disclose its dual agency to the parties.
>
> (j) When a firm represents both the buyer and seller in the same real estate transaction, the firm may, with the prior express approval of its buyer and seller clients, designate one or more individual agents associated with the firm to represent only the interest of the seller and one or more other individual brokers associated with the firm to represent only the interests of the buyer in the transaction. The authority for designated agency must be reduced to writing not later than the time that the parties are required to reduce their dual agency agreement to writing in accordance with subsection (d) of this rule. An individual broker shall not be so designated and shall not undertake to represent only the interest of one party if the broker has actually

received confidential information concerning the other party in connection with the transaction. A broker-in-charge shall not act as a designated agent for a party in a real estate sales transaction when a provisional broker under his supervision will act as a designated agent for another party with a competing interest.

(k) When a firm acting as a dual agent designates an individual broker to represent the seller, the broker so designated shall represent only the interest of the seller and shall not, without the seller's permission, disclose to the buyer or a broker designated to represent the buyer:

    (1) that the seller may agree to a price, terms, or any conditions of sale other than those established by the seller;

    (2) the seller's motivation for engaging in the transaction unless disclosure is otherwise required by statute or rule; and

    (3) any information about the seller which the seller has identified as confidential unless disclosure of the information is otherwise required by statute or rule.

(l) When a firm acting as a dual agent designates an individual broker to represent the buyer, the broker so designated shall represent only the interest of the buyer and shall not, without the buyer's permission, disclose to the seller or a broker designated to represent the seller:

    (1) that the buyer may agree to a price, terms, or any conditions of sale other than those offered by the buyer;

    (2) the buyer's motivation for engaging in the transaction unless disclosure is otherwise required by statute or rule; and

    (3) any information about the buyer which the buyer has identified as confidential unless disclosure of the information is otherwise required by statute or rule.

(m) A broker designated to represent a buyer or seller in accordance with Section (j) of this Rule shall disclose the identity of all of the brokers so designated to both the buyer and the seller. The disclosure shall take place no later than the presentation of the first offer to purchase or sell.

(n) When an individual broker represents both the buyer and seller in the same real estate sales transaction pursuant to a written agreement authorizing dual agency, the parties may provide in the written agreement that the broker shall not disclose the following information about one party to the other without written permission from the party about whom the information pertains:

    (1) that a party may agree to a price, terms, or any conditions of sale other than those offered;

    (2) the motivation of a party for engaging in the transaction, unless disclosure is otherwise required by statute or rule; and

    (3) any information about a party which that party has identified as confidential, unless disclosure is otherwise required by statute or rule.

Designated dual agency occurs in an in-house transaction when the firm appoints one broker to exclusively represent the seller and appoints another broker to exclusively represent the buyer. The firm stays in dual agency providing impartial representation to both principals.

In North Carolina

Designated dual agency. Designated dual agency, sometimes called *designated agency*, might be used when a transaction is an **in-house sale**. It involves appointing one or more brokers of a firm to exclusively represent the seller as an agent and appointing another broker of the same firm to exclusively represent the buyer as an agent in the same real estate transaction. However, it must be done with prior express approval of both the seller and the buyer. The firm continues to act as a dual agent; the individually designated brokers do not. The major advantage of designated dual agency is that both of the firm's clients (the seller and the buyer) receive a fuller and direct representation from their respective designated agent.

If a firm wants to practice the designated dual agency option, the broker-in-charge (BIC) must establish a comprehensive written company policy on designated agency, and this policy must comply with North Carolina Real Estate Commission (NCREC) Rules. Firms electing to practice designated dual agency must specify who within the firm is authorized to appoint designated agents. This person is normally the BIC.

If a firm practices dual agency and designated dual agency, full written disclosure of this practice should be given to clients and customers at the earliest opportunity. When a firm enters into an agency contract with the seller/client or buyer/client, the client must be given an opportunity to indicate in writing which agency relationship he or she is authorizing. *The authority for designated agency must be reduced to writing not later than the time that the parties are required by NCREC rule to reduce their dual agency agreement to writing.*

The BIC must follow current NCREC rules when appointing the designated dual agents. *If the BIC represents one of the parties as a designated dual agent, the BIC can appoint only a licensed nonprovisional broker as the designated dual agent for the other party.* The BIC cannot appoint a provisional broker as a designated dual agent if the BIC represents the other party [see Rule A.0104(j)]. The BIC may, however, appoint a licensed nonprovisional broker to represent one party and appoint a licensed provisional broker to represent the other party; or the BIC could be designated opposite a nonprovisional broker.

NCREC rules impose another major restriction on the appointment of a designated dual agent. Namely, if an agent has received *confidential information* about one party to the transaction, that agent has an obligation to refuse an appointment as the designated dual agent of the other party to the transaction. After a broker has been appointed as a designated agent for one of the firm's clients, the designated agent exclusively represents that principal in the transaction. Therefore, if the agent learns any confidential information about the other principal in the transaction after being designated, the designated agent must disclose that information to the client that they exclusively represent. This is a major reason that firms should protect the transfer of information within the firm. An agent who illegally becomes a designated dual agent when already in possession of confidential information about the opposite principal in the transaction creates potential legal liability for the firm as well as becoming subject to possible disciplinary action by the NCREC. Further, the company may have legal exposure if the post-designation receipt of confidential information occurs in-house. Note that while a client's confidential information must be kept confidential, agents must always disclose any information required by law to be disclosed, such as material facts about the property.

Some important points about dual and designated dual agency include the following:

- To become a dual agent, the same firm must have a client relationship with both the seller and the buyer.
- There cannot be designated dual agency unless dual agency exists first.
- The firm owes the same fiduciary duties to both parties which has the effect of neutralizing the firm and its agents when acting as dual agents, but designated dual agents owe their fiduciary duties exclusively to the party they are designated to represent, even though the firm has an equal obligation to both parties.
- Designated dual agency is a form of dual agency that is optional, but it has the potential to result in both of the firm's clients receiving better representation.
- To practice dual or designated dual agency, the firm's policy must authorize it and both parties must give their written consent.

Agency relationships in real estate rentals. Another type of brokerage contract that creates an agency relationship is the Property Management Agreement, which is entered into by a management firm/broker and a property owner who wishes to hire someone to manage rental properties. *As with all agency agreements involving a property owner, the property management agreement must be in writing from the formation of the relationship.* The property manager/broker becomes the agent and the property owner becomes the principal. The fiduciary—agency—relationship between the property manager/broker and the property owner is the same as that between the broker and the property seller or buyer. Any licensed employees of the property manager/broker become subagents of the property owner. Prospective tenants *are* customers (or third parties) of the property manager, who owes certain duties *to the tenants* imposed by North Carolina Real Estate Law (N.C.G.S. Chapter 93A), fair housing laws (discussed in Chapter 20), and landlord/tenant laws (discussed in Chapter 11). *A property manager of residential property usually will represent only the property owner and will not seek to represent the tenant as well, which would cause the agent to become a dual agent.* However, whenever an agent seeks to establish an agency relationship with a tenant thereby making the tenant a client, the agreement for brokerage services between the broker and the tenant shall be express and shall be reduced to writing not later than the time any party makes an offer to rent or lease property.

■ AGENCY DISCLOSURE IN NORTH CAROLINA

To resolve some of the potential confusion surrounding agency relationships, North Carolina requires that real estate agents disclose their agency status to both buyers and sellers in every real estate sales transaction. No later than first substantial contact with a buyer or seller, an agent must provide the buyer or seller with a copy of the mandatory NCREC-published brochure entitled **Working with Real Estate Agents** [see Rule A.0104(c)]. The text of this brochure is shown in Figure 7.3. While the *Working with Real Estate Agents* brochure is not required in lease transactions, an optional version of the brochure is available for use by agents of landlords and tenants.

In every real estate *sales* transaction (residential and commercial) the broker shall review available agency options to any prospective buyer or seller no later than **first substantial contact**. First substantial contact occurs when conversation between a broker and a consumer shifts from facts about the property to possible confidential information about the consumer's needs, wishes, and abilities or when the consumer or broker begins to act as if there is a fiduciary relationship. The broker must review the brochure with the buyer or seller and make a determination if the broker will act as the agent of the seller or the agent of the buyer. An agency relationship cannot be formed without this review. The nature and obligations of an agency relationship must be clearly explained to the consumer so that the consumer understands that an agent owes all client-level fiduciary duties only to the client/principal. The purpose of the agency disclosure brochure is informed consent by the consumer as to the best agency relationship for them. A broker should always make agency disclosure prior to showing property to a buyer consumer; first substantial contact with a prospective buyer occurs no later than the time information is gathered to use in the selection of properties for viewing.

The *Working with Real Estate Agents* brochure contains information on the various agency relationships available such as (1) seller's agent, (2) dual agent, (3) buyer's agent, and (4) seller's agent working with a buyer. If the first substantial contact does not occur *face-to-face*, then the brochure must be mailed, faxed, or e-mailed to the prospective buyer or seller as soon as possible, but in no event later than three calendar days from the date of first substantial contact. Then, the broker must review the contents of the brochure with the prospective seller or buyer at the earliest opportunity thereafter. The brochure can be reformatted to allow for various means of communication, but the text cannot be changed. It must be exactly as written by the NCREC. The brochure is not designed to replace the review and explanation of agency by the broker, but rather to facilitate this explanation. The brochure contains a *tear-off* panel for the buyer or seller to sign, acknowledging receipt and review of the contents by the broker. Because the consumer cannot be forced to sign the panel, the broker shall note on the panel if the consumer refuses to sign the acknowledgment panel. The broker must keep this panel on file as proof of compliance with Rule A.0104 for three years. (See Rule A.0108.)

Rule A.0104(e) also requires a seller's agent or subagent working with a prospective buyer to disclose, *in writing* at first substantial contact, the agency status of representing the seller. If first substantial contact occurs other than a face-to-face meeting where it is not practical to provide written disclosure, the broker shall immediately disclose by similar means whom he or she represents and shall immediately, but in no event later than three calendar days from the first substantial contact, mail or otherwise transmit a copy of the written disclosure to the buyer. Note that this written disclosure of seller agency or subagency to the prospective buyer may be accomplished merely by the buyer initialing the box at the bottom of the acknowledgment panel of the *Working with Real Estate Agents* brochure (see Figure 7.3).

FIGURE 7.3

Text from the *Working with Real Estate Agents* Brochure

WORKING WITH REAL ESTATE AGENTS

When buying or selling real estate, you may find it helpful to have a real estate agent assist you. Real estate agents can provide many useful services and work with you in different ways. In some real estate transactions, the agents work for the seller. In others, the seller and buyer may each have agents. And sometimes the same agents work for both the buyer and the seller. It is important for you to know whether an agent is working for you as **your** agent or simply working **with** you while acting as an agent of the other party.

This brochure addresses the various types of working relationships that may be available to you. It should help you decide which relationship you want to have with a real estate agent. It will also give you useful information about the various services real estate agents can provide buyers and sellers, and it will help explain how real estate agents are paid.

SELLERS

Seller's Agent

If you are selling real estate, you may want to "list" your property for sale with a real estate firm. If so, you will sign a "listing agreement" authorizing the firm and its agents to represent you in your dealings with buyers as your *seller's agent*. You may also be asked to allow agents from other firms to help find a buyer for your property.

Be sure to read and understand the listing agreement before you sign it. Your agent must give you a copy of the listing agreement after you sign it.

Duties to Seller: The listing firm and its agents must • promote your best interests • be loyal to you • follow your lawful instructions • provide you with all material facts that could influence your decisions • use reasonable skill, care and diligence, and • account for all monies they handle for you. Once you have signed the listing agreement, the firm and its agents may not give any confidential information about you to prospective buyers or their agents without your permission so long as they represent you. **But until you sign the listing agreement, you should avoid telling the listing agent anything you would not want a buyer to know.**

Services and Compensation: To help you sell your property, the listing firm and its agents will offer to perform a number of services for you. These may include • helping you price your property • advertising and marketing your property • giving you all required property disclosure forms for you to complete • negotiating for you the best possible price and terms • reviewing all written offers with you and otherwise promoting your interests.

For representing you and helping you sell your property, you will pay the listing firm a sales commission or fee. The listing agreement must state the amount or method for determining the commission or fee and whether you will allow the firm to share its commission with agents representing the buyer.

Dual Agent

You may even permit the listing firm and its agents to represent you and a buyer at the same time. This "dual agency relationship" is most likely to happen if an agent with your listing firm is working as a buyer's agent with someone who wants to purchase your property. If this occurs and you have not already agreed to a dual agency relationship in your listing agreement, your listing agent will ask you to amend your listing agreement to permit the agent to act as agent for both you and the buyer.

It may be difficult for a *dual agent* to advance the interests of both the buyer and seller. Nevertheless, a *dual agent* must treat buyers and sellers fairly and equally. Although the *dual agent* owes them the same duties, buyers and sellers can prohibit *dual agents* from divulging **certain** confidential information about them to the other party.

Some firms also offer a form of dual agency called "designated agency" where one agent in the firm represents the seller and another agent represents the buyer. This option (when available) may allow each "designated agent" to more fully represent each party.

If you choose the "dual agency" option, remember that since a dual agent's loyalty is divided between parties with competing interests, it is especially important that you have a clear understanding of • what your relationship is with the *dual agent* and • what the agent will be doing for you in the transaction.

BUYERS

When buying real estate, you may have several choices as to how you want a real estate firm and its agents to work with you. For example, you may want them to represent only you (as a **buyer's agent**). You may be willing for them to represent both you and the seller at the same time (as a **dual agent**). Or you may agree to let them represent only the seller (**seller's agent** or **subagent**). Some agents will offer you a choice of these services. Others may not.

Buyer's Agent

Duties to Buyer: If the real estate firm and its agents represent you, they must • promote your best interests • be loyal to you • follow your lawful instructions • provide you with all material facts that could influence your decisions • use reasonable skill, care and diligence, and • account for all monies they handle for you. Once you have agreed (either orally or in writing) for the firm and its agents to be your buyer's agent, they may not give any

Continued on the back

FOR BUYER/SELLER

_____
Date

_____
Firm Name

_____   _____
Agent Name   License Number

Disclosure of Seller Subagency
(Complete, if applicable)
☐ When showing you property and assisting you in the purchase of a property, the above agent and firm will represent the SELLER. For more information, see "Seller's Agent Working with a Buyer" in the brochure.

Agent's Initials Acknowledging Disclosure: _____

WORKING WITH REAL ESTATE AGENTS

Agents must retain this acknowledgment for their files.

This is not a contract

By signing, I acknowledge that the agent named below furnished a copy of this brochure and reviewed it with me.

_____
Buyer or Seller Name (Print or Type)

_____
Buyer or Seller Signature

_____
Buyer or Seller Name (Print or Type)

_____
Buyer or Seller Signature

_____
Date

_____
Firm Name

_____   _____
Agent Name   License Number

Disclosure of Seller Subagency
(Complete, if applicable)
☐ When showing you property and assisting you in the purchase of a property, the above agent and firm will represent the SELLER. For more information, see "Seller's Agent Working with a Buyer" in the brochure.

Buyer's Initials Acknowledging Disclosure: _____

Source: Reproduced with permission of the North Carolina Real Estate Commission.

FIGURE 7.3

Text from the *Working with Real Estate Agents* Brochure (continued)

confidential information about you to sellers or their agents without your permission so long as they represent you. But **until you make this agreement with your buyer's agent, you should avoid telling the agent anything you would *not* want a seller to know.**

Unwritten Agreements: To make sure that you and the real estate firm have a clear understanding of what your relationship will be and what the firm will do for you, you may want to have a written agreement. However, some firms may be willing to represent and assist you for a time as a *buyer's agent* without a written agreement. But if you decide to make an offer to purchase a particular property, the agent must obtain a written agency agreement before writing the offer. If you do not sign it, the agent can no longer represent and assist you and is no longer required to keep information about you confidential.

Be sure to read and understand any agency agreement before you sign it. Once you sign it, the agent must give you a copy of it.

Services and Compensation: Whether you have a written or unwritten agreement, a *buyer's agent* will perform a number of services for you. These may include helping you • find a suitable property • arrange financing • learn more about the property and • other-wise promote your best interests. If you have a **written** agency agreement, the agent can also help you prepare and submit a written offer to the seller.

A *buyer's agent* can be compensated in different ways. For example, you can pay the agent out of your own pocket. Or the agent may seek compensation from the seller or listing agent first, but require you to pay if the listing agent refuses. Whatever the case, be sure your compensation arrangement with your *buyer's agent* is spelled out in a buyer agency agreement before you make an offer to purchase property and that you carefully read and understand the compensation provision.

Dual Agent

You may permit an agent or firm to represent you **and** the seller at the same time. This "dual agency relationship" is most likely to happen if you become interested in a property listed with your *buyer's agent* or the agent's firm. If this occurs and you have not already agreed to a dual agency relationship in your (written or oral) buyer agency agreement, your *buyer's agent* will ask you to amend the buyer agency agreement or sign a separate agreement or document permitting him or her to act as agent for both you and the seller. It may be difficult for a *dual agent* to advance the interests of both the buyer and seller. Nevertheless, a *dual agent* must treat buyers and sellers fairly and equally. Although the *dual agent* owes them the same duties, buyers and sellers can prohibit *dual agents* from divulging **certain** confidential information about them to the other party.

Some firms also offer a form of dual agency called "designated agency" where one agent in the firm represents the seller and another agent represents the buyer. This option (when available) may allow each "designated agent" to more fully represent each party.

If you choose the "dual agency" option, remember that since a *dual agent's* loyalty is divided between parties with competing interests, it is especially important that you have a clear understanding of • what your relationship is with the *dual agent* and • what the agent will be doing for you in the transaction. This can best be accomplished by putting the agreement in writing at the earliest possible time.

Seller's Agent Working With a Buyer

If the real estate agent or firm that you contact does not offer *buyer agency* or you do not want them to act as your *buyer agent*, you can still work with the firm and its agents. However, they will be acting as the *seller's agent* (or "subagent"). The agent can still help you find and purchase property and provide many of the same services as a *buyer's agent*. The agent must be fair with you and provide you with any "material facts" (such as a leaky roof) about properties.

But remember, the agent represents the seller—not you—and therefore must try to obtain for the seller the best possible price and terms for the seller's property. Furthermore, a *seller's agent* is required to give the seller any information about you (even personal, financial or confidential information) that would help the seller in the sale of his or her property.

Agents must tell you *in writing* if they are *sellers' agents* before you say anything that can help the seller. But **until you are sure that an agent is not a *seller's agent*, you should avoid saying anything you do *not* want a seller to know.**

Sellers' agents are compensated by the sellers.

(Note: This brochure is for informational purposes only and does not constitute a contract for service.)

The North Carolina Real Estate Commission
P.O. Box 17100 • Raleigh, North Carolina 27619-7100
919/875-3700 • Web Site: www.ncrec.gov
REC 3.45 3/1/11

00,000 copies of this public document were printed at a cost of $.000 per copy.

Source: Reproduced with permission of the North Carolina Real Estate Commission.

■ **FOR EXAMPLE** A broker is holding an open house for a seller-client of his firm. Many prospective buyers tour the listed property during the afternoon. Does the broker have to provide and review the **Working with Real Estate Agents** brochure with the prospective buyers? If so, at what point must the agency disclosure occur? Most prospective buyers will tour the open house without requesting or disclosing any confidential information; if all conversation between the consumer and the broker is strictly facts about the property, first substantial contact has not been reached and agency disclosure is not mandated. However, if the consumer begins asking more specific or personal questions, the brochure must be reviewed and the broker and prospective buyer must determine and agree in what capacity the broker will work with the buyer—whether as a seller's subagent or as a dual agent (since his firm already has an agency relationship with the seller). If the buyer consumer is not ready or willing to enter into an agency relationship with the broker and his firm, the prospective buyer must initial the "Disclosure of Seller Subagency" at the bottom of the brochure panel before the broker continuing to provide assistance. If the buyer-consumer is ready and willing to enter some form of buyer agency with the broker and his firm, they must determine whether the buyer and dual agency agreement will be written or oral, and whether designated agency is authorized. Full disclosure of agency options to consumers as soon as possible should always be the preferred action.

Oral buyer agency is an agency option a firm may use when the consumer is unwilling to commit to a written buyer agency relationship. A real estate broker may enter into an oral buyer agency agreement at first substantial contact with a prospective buyer [Rule A.0104(a)]. A broker who works with and represents a buyer initially under an oral agreement must do so in a *nonexclusive capacity*. All oral buyer agency agreements must be nonexclusive. Any buyer agency agreement that seeks to bind the buyer to the broker or firm for a particular time period or that prohibits the buyer from working with other brokers or firms must be in writing from the start. Under the oral buyer agency agreement, a buyer is free to enter into similar agreements with other firms and brokers. An oral agreement is considered to be of indefinite duration and can be terminated at the will of either party at any time.

■ **FOR EXAMPLE** A broker is contacted by a prospective buyer to look at properties for sale. During the initial interview, the broker merely hands the brochure to the buyer without any explanation or review and tells the buyer he will represent the buyer as her agent during this transaction. Has a buyer agency been formed? The answer is no. The brochure must be reviewed and the broker and prospective buyer must mutually agree in what capacity the broker will work with the buyer—whether as a seller's subagent or as a buyer's agent, and if the latter, whether under an oral or written buyer agency agreement.

Rule A.0104(a) also states, "A broker shall not continue to represent a buyer or tenant without a written agreement when such agreement is required by this rule." A broker must enter into a written buyer agency agreement no later than the time the first offer to purchase is presented. A buyer's agent working under oral agency *cannot* actually present the offer to the seller's agent unless the buyer/client first has signed a *written* buyer agency agreement. Although a broker may enter into an oral buyer agency agreement at first substantial contact, the rule does not prohibit the broker from getting an agency agreement in writing at first substantial contact. The written agency agreement does not have to be exclusive, but the broker should attempt to get the agency agreement in writing as soon as possible.

■ **FOR EXAMPLE** Broker has given the prospective buyer the brochure at first substantial contact, has reviewed it with the buyer, and has entered into an oral buyer agency agreement with the buyer. The buyer finds a home and wants to make an offer. After the offer has been prepared and before presentation to the seller or seller's agent, Broker attempts to get the buyer agency agreement in writing and signed by the buyer as required by Rule A.0104(a). The buyer refuses to sign the buyer agency agreement. At this time, Broker can no longer represent the buyer, but can present the offer acting as the seller's subagent with the buyer's and seller's permission. Of course, as the seller's subagent, Broker must share information about the buyer/customer with the seller/client and is no longer required to keep information about the buyer confidential.

In the above example the broker must follow very specific conditions in order to present the offer as a seller's agent or subagent:

- The broker must clearly explain to the buyer that the broker will now represent the seller and will have a duty to the now *seller/client* to convey any information, confidential or not, about the now *buyer/customer* that the broker learned during their relationship as buyer agent under the previous oral agreement.
- The broker must officially terminate the oral buyer agency agreement in writing, which should include the former buyer/client's consent to do so, and an understanding that confidential information must be revealed.
- The broker must have the consent from the listing firm to act as a seller's subagent and must provide written disclosure of his seller subagency status to the buyer.

Note: Prior to switching to seller subagency, the oral buyer agent should consider entering into a written buyer agency agreement limited solely to that property, which few reasonable buyers should refuse.

Because a broker may work with a buyer under an oral buyer agency agreement, the rule of necessity also allows an agent to enter into an oral dual agency agreement that must also be put in writing no later than the time an offer is presented. In order to work under oral dual agency, the dual agency arrangement must have been discussed and the prospective buyer must orally agree for the agent to be a dual agent at the time the oral buyer agency is established. The same applies to oral designated dual agency.

The following may be used as a five-point checklist to properly follow disclosure rules:

1. The agency disclosure brochure must be given to prospective sellers and buyers no later than first substantial contact in all real estate sales transactions.
2. The broker must review the brochure and a determination of agency status must take place. The buyer/seller can acknowledge receipt by signing the tear-off panel to be retained by the broker.
3. Listing agreements are *required to* be in writing from the start of the agency relationship.
4. The rule *allows* for an agent to act as a buyer's agent, a dual agent, or a designated dual agent under an oral agreement, until such time as the agreements

must be put in writing, which is not later than the time the first offer is going to be presented.

5. Any buyer agency agreement that sets forth agency exclusivity or a definite period of time must be in writing from the start of the agency relationship.

■ DUTIES AND LIABILITIES OF AGENTS

Agent's Responsibilities to Principal

As mentioned earlier, an agency relationship is a **fiduciary** relationship, one of trust and confidence between the broker and the principal. In a fiduciary relationship, the broker, by law, owes the principal specific duties—the duties of loyalty, obedience, accounting, disclosure of information, and skill, care, and diligence, easily remembered by the acronym **OLD CAR** (see Figure 7.4). These duties are described below. Note that such duties are not simply moral or ethical obligations; they are the law of agency.

FIGURE 7.4

Agent's Responsibilities to Principal

Agent —
- **O**bedience
- **L**oyalty
- **D**isclosure
- **C**onfidentiality
- **A**ccounting
- **R**easonable skill and care

— Principal

Obedience. The fiduciary relationship obligates the broker to act in good faith at all times, obeying the principal's instructions in accordance with the contract. That obedience is not absolute, however. The broker may not obey any instructions that are unlawful or unethical. For example, the broker may not follow instructions to make the property unavailable to members of a minority group or to conceal a defect in the property. Because illegal acts do not serve the principal's best interest, obeying such instructions violates the broker's duty of loyalty, not to mention other laws making the conduct illegal. On the other hand, a broker who exceeds the authority assigned in the contract is liable for any losses that the principal suffers as a result.

Loyalty. The broker/firm owes the principal the utmost loyalty. That means placing the principal's interests above those of all others, including the broker's own. The agent must be particularly sensitive to any possible conflicts of interest. *Confidentiality* about the principal's personal affairs is a key element of loyalty. An agent may not, for example, disclose the principal's financial condition. When the principal is the seller, the agent may not reveal such things as the principal's willingness to accept less than the listing price or any anxiousness to sell unless the principal has authorized the disclosure. If the principal is the buyer, the agent may not disclose, for instance, that the buyer will pay more than the offered price if necessary, or that the buyer is under a tight moving schedule or any other fact that might harm the principal's bargaining position. (These are several reasons why undisclosed dual agency could result in rescission, monetary damages, forfeiture of commission, and disciplinary action by the NCREC.)

Real estate transactions are ideally arm's-length transactions where all parties are dealing from equal footing without bias. Because the agent may not act out of self-interest, the negotiation of a sales contract must be conducted without regard to how much the agent will earn in commission. All states forbid brokers to buy property listed with them for their own use or in which they have a personal interest without first disclosing that interest and receiving the principal's consent. An agent must disclose to a client any personal or business relationship the agent may have with another party to the transaction, even if it is a former relationship to avoid claims of "self-dealing." North Carolina Real Estate License Law and agency law require a buyer's agent to disclose to the buyer/client any personal interest that agent may have in the property. If the broker is a seller's listing agent, there is no duty to disclose to the buyer the broker's personal interest.

In North Carolina

Disclosure of information. Another very important duty of an agent to his/her principal is the duty of disclosure of information. It is the firm/broker's duty to keep the principal fully informed at all times of all facts or information the broker obtains that could affect the principal's decision in the transaction. A broker who fails to disclose such information may be held liable for any damages that result. A broker must also disclose any personal benefit from the transaction because making a secret profit out of a transaction is prohibited.

The real estate agent also may be liable for facts he or she *should have known* and revealed to the principal but did not. This duty of *discovery* includes facts favorable or unfavorable to the principal's position, even if the disclosure of those facts would end the transaction.

Examples of facts an agent for the seller has a duty to disclose to the seller include:

- all offers (See NCREC Rule A.0106);
- the identity of the prospective purchasers, including the agent's relationship, if any, to them (such as a relative of the broker being a participating purchaser);
- the ability of the purchaser to complete the sale or offer a higher price;
- any relationship the broker has with the buyer (such as an agreement for the broker to manage the buyer's property after it is purchased); and
- the buyer's intention to resell the property for a profit.

An agent for the buyer must disclose deficiencies of a property as well as factors that may adversely affect a property's value or desirability. The agent should disclose information that could affect the buyer's ability to negotiate the lowest purchase price, such as how long a property has been listed or why the seller is selling, if known by the agent.

In North Carolina

North Carolina requires that sellers of most residential properties give the buyer a completed mandatory residential property disclosure statement. While the real estate agent cannot fill out the form, the agent is required to inform the seller of the agent's responsibilities in regard to the property disclosure. Property disclosure is discussed in more detail in Chapter 9.

Confidentiality. Confidentiality is a key element of fiduciary duties. An agent shall not disclose the principal's financial condition, motivation, or acceptable contract terms without the client's permission. If the principal is the seller, the agent may not reveal such things as willingness to accept less than the listing price or urgency to sell, unless the principal has authorized the disclosure. If the principal is the buyer, the agent shall not disclose that the buyer is willing to pay a higher price, is under a tight moving schedule, or other facts that might affect the principal's bargaining position.

Under the laws of most states, the agent must disclose material facts about the condition of the property. Some states, however, permit a seller disclaimer—essentially a statement that the property is sold as is, with no promises regarding its quality. Note, however, that even with this disclaimer, most sellers are still required to disclose known problems with the property if they affect the health and well-being of the occupants.

It is important to remember that anything a real estate agent learns about a client must remain confidential. In most states, confidentiality terminates upon completion, expiration, or termination of the agency relationship.

Accounting. The broker must be able to account for all funds received from, or on behalf of, the principal. It is illegal for the broker to commingle such monies with personal funds. **Commingling** is a term used to describe when trust funds and the firm/broker's personal/business funds are placed in the same account. All states have laws that require accounting for trust funds and the maintenance of transaction files and records. North Carolina real estate license laws require that brokers give accurate copies of all documents to all parties affected by them and keep copies of such documents on file for three years (see Rule A.0108). In addition, the license laws generally require that the broker deposit immediately all trust funds entrusted to the broker in a special trust account (see Rule A.0107).

In North Carolina

■ **FOR EXAMPLE** A broker has accepted an earnest money deposit in connection with an offer to purchase and deposits that money into his business account. The broker receives an earned commission check from another firm and deposits that check into the trust account. Both are examples of commingling, a mixing of trust funds with non-trust funds. Licensing law in North Carolina prohibits commingling.

Reasonable skill and care. The broker must exercise a reasonable degree of skill, care, and diligence while transacting the business entrusted by the principal. The principal is entitled to expect the agent's skill and expertise in real estate matters to be superior to that of the average person.

The most fundamental way in which the broker meets this standard is to use the broker's skill and knowledge on the principal's behalf. Whether acting as a buyer's agent or as a seller's agent, the broker has an affirmative duty to try to discover and disclose to the principal all facts that are pertinent to the principal's decision-making process in the transaction. If the broker represents the seller, the broker's duties include helping the seller arrive at an appropriate and realistic listing price, discovering and disclosing facts that affect the seller, and properly presenting the contracts that the seller signs. Skill, care, and diligence also means making reasonable efforts to market the property, such as advertising and holding open houses, as well as helping the seller evaluate the terms and conditions of all offers to purchase.

A broker who represents the buyer will be expected to help the buyer locate suitable property and evaluate property values, neighborhood and property conditions, and financing alternatives, as well as to prepare offers and counteroffers with the buyer's best interest in mind.

A broker who does not make a reasonable effort to properly represent the interests of the principal could be found negligent. The firm/broker is liable to the principal for any loss resulting from negligence or carelessness.

Agent's Responsibilities to Third Parties

Even though an agent's primary responsibility is to the principal, the agent also has duties to third parties. The duties of an agent to a third party come from three sources: (1) North Carolina license law, (2) the North Carolina Unfair or Deceptive Trade Practices Act, and (3) common law of agency as interpreted by court opinions. These duties include

- being honest and fair, and
- complying with North Carolina Real Estate License Law and NCREC rules, including disclosure of material facts relating to a property or transaction about which the agent has knowledge or should reasonably have acquired knowledge.

When working with a buyer, a broker (as an agent of the seller) must exercise extreme caution and have knowledge of the laws and ethical considerations that affect this relationship. For example, brokers must be careful about the statements they or their brokers make about a parcel of real estate. General statements of opinion are permissible as long as they are offered as opinions and without any intent to deceive.

Statements of fact, however, must be accurate. Opinion statements that exaggerate a property's benefits are called **puffing**. Although puffing is legal and a common practice, it must not constitute a misrepresentation of the property. Brokers must ensure that none of their statements can be interpreted as involving **fraud**. Fraud is the *intentional* misrepresentation of a material fact in such a way as to harm or take advantage of another person. In addition to false statements about a property, the concept of fraud covers intentional concealment or nondisclosure of important facts. If a contract to purchase real estate is obtained as a result of fraudulent misstatements made by a seller's agent, the contract is voidable and may be disaffirmed or renounced by the purchaser. In such a case, the client loses a contract and the broker will lose a commission. If either party suffers loss because of a broker's misrepresentations, the broker can be held liable for damages. If the broker's misstatements are based on the owner's own inaccurate statements to the broker, however, and the broker had no independent duty to investigate their accuracy, the broker may be entitled to a commission even if the buyer rescinds the sales contract.

Brokers must also be careful not to make any misrepresentations or omissions where **material facts** are concerned. As noted previously, the common law of agency requires an agent to disclose to the principal *any facts that might affect the principal's decision in a transaction*. To determine an agent's duty to disclose material

Chapter 7 Real Estate Brokerage and the Law of Agency **149**

In North Carolina

facts to a third party, one must look to the North Carolina Real Estate License Law, which requires disclosure of material facts to all parties to the transaction regardless of whom the broker represents in the transaction. Per the *North Carolina Real Estate Manual*, the NCREC has historically interpreted *material facts to be disclosed to any party* under the Real Estate License Law to include at least

Material facts are
- about the property itself,
- relating directly to the property,
- relating to ability of principals to act, and
- of specific importance.

- *facts about the property itself* (i.e., significant physical characteristics such as unpermitted space, a structural defect, or defective mechanical systems);
- *facts relating directly to the property* (usually factors outside the property that may directly affect value, use, or desirability of the property, such as a pending zoning change or planned highway construction in the immediate vicinity);
- *facts relating directly to the ability of the agent's principal to complete the transaction* (such as a pending foreclosure sale or buyer's inability to qualify for financing); and
- *facts known to be of specific importance to a party* (most likely to be items of special interest to a purchaser's intended use of the property, such as zoning allowing home businesses or covenants allowing multiple pets).

Some issues have been declared to be material facts by the North Carolina Real Estate Commission. For example if a residence has ever been clad in an exterior insulating and finishing system commonly called "EIFS" or "synthetic stucco," that will remain a material fact for that property forever. Also, if a residence has ever had leaking polybutylene pipes, this must be disclosed. Finally, if a property was the site of a meth lab, this also must be disclosed.

Prohibited Conduct

In North Carolina

North Carolina real estate license law specifically prohibits the following types of acts in the broker's relationship with any party to the transaction [G.S. 93A-6(a)(1)]:

- ① *Willful misrepresentation:* intentionally misinforming any party involved in a transaction about a material fact
- ② *Negligent misrepresentation:* unintentionally misinforming any party involved in a transaction about a material fact
- ③ *Willful omission:* intentionally failing to disclose a material fact to any party involved in a transaction
- ④ *Negligent omission:* unintentionally failing to disclose a material fact to any party involved in a transaction

① Willful Misrepresentation

More examples = pg. 597

Willful misrepresentation takes place when brokers who have *actual knowledge* of a material fact deliberately misinform a buyer, seller, tenant, or landlord concerning such fact. Willful misrepresentation also takes place when a broker who does *not* have actual knowledge of a matter material to the transaction intentionally provides information concerning such matter to a buyer, seller, tenant, or landlord without regard for the truthfulness of the information. (See the examples that follow.) This is an act that is intentional on the part of the broker. A broker could also be involved in *indirect misrepresentation*, which occurs when an agent misrepresents a material fact to a subagent who in turn passes it on to a third party. If a material fact is misrepresented, courts could provide relief to the injured party in the form of damages or rescission of the contract. A broker guilty of misrepresentation could also face disciplinary action by the NCREC.

■ FOR EXAMPLE

- A broker tells a buyer the cost of utilities is very reasonable without verification from the owner. If the costs are very high, the broker could be guilty of willful misrepresentation.
- A broker tells a buyer the foundation of a house is sound and has been properly built, when the broker knows the foundation is substandard and improperly constructed.
- A builder explains to an agent that the poor exterior wall insulation resulted from the developer's overall goal of containing cost. When this agent's buyer/client asks about the insulation, the agent replies that the builder was highly reputable and he was certain the insulation met the necessary standards.
- A buyer signs a buyer agency agreement with an agent. The buyer wants to purchase property with low taxes. The agent informs the buyer that a particular property has annual taxes of $600 when in fact the agent knows the new assessed value will increase taxes to $1,200.

Negligent Misrepresentation

Negligent misrepresentation takes place when brokers *unintentionally* misinform a buyer, seller, tenant, or landlord concerning a material fact because they do not have actual knowledge of the fact, because they have incorrect information, or because of a mistake by the agent. If the broker *should reasonably have known* the truth of the matter that was misrepresented, then the broker may be guilty of *negligent misrepresentation* even though acting in good faith. The fact that the broker was ignorant about the issue is no excuse. If a buyer relies on the agent's statement, the agent is liable for any damages that may result. If a buyer's agent relies on incorrect information provided by a listing (seller's) agent through the MLS property data, even with disclaimers, the buyer's agent may be held liable if the agent should reasonably have known the information was incorrect.

■ FOR EXAMPLE

- A listing agent relies on a recent appraiser's report that a house has 2,500 square feet of heated living floor space and enters that information into the MLS property data. However, the house actually has 2,000 square feet. Although the **Residential Square Footage Guidelines** written by the NCREC (see Appendix B) allows a broker to "reasonably rely" on a recent report from a qualified appraiser, a prudent and knowledgeable broker in this case should have recognized a 500-square-foot error (i.e., 25% error). If the agent unreasonably relied on the appraiser's report and informed a buyer the house has 2,500 square feet, she has made a negligent misrepresentation. A buyer's agent also should recommend that a buyer measure a property if square footage is important to the buyer.
- An agent tells a buyer/client that the home being shown has Levelor blinds throughout, without actually checking the brand name. The blinds are actually cheap, imported imitations of Levelor blinds.

③ Willful Omission

(handwritten note: Must be disclosed to everyone, not just client ↓)

Willful omission takes place when brokers have *actual knowledge* of a material fact and a duty to disclose such fact to a buyer, seller, tenant, or landlord, but deliberately fail to disclose such fact.

■ **FOR EXAMPLE**

- A broker knows that a highway relocation is pending that would adversely affect value and use of a property a buyer wants to purchase but does not reveal this to the buyer.

- A broker lists a property in midwinter knowing that the air-conditioning system does not operate properly but does not reveal that fact to a prospective buyer.

④ Negligent Omission

Negligent omission takes place when brokers do *not* have actual knowledge of a material fact but *should reasonably have known* of such fact. If they fail to disclose this fact to a buyer, seller, tenant, or landlord, they may be guilty of *negligent omission*, even though they acted in good faith in the transaction.

Agents have an obligation to *discover and disclose* material facts about the property that any prudent agent would reasonably have discovered during the transaction. A listing agent would be held more accountable than would a buyer's agent in discovery and disclosure of defects in the property because of the listing agent's direct fiduciary relationship with the seller and the fact that the listing agent inspected the property and should be more familiar with the property than the selling agent.

■ **FOR EXAMPLE** A broker has listed a property in a neighborhood where a vacant lot is being considered by the city for installation of a garbage recycling system. The plan has been well publicized in the news media, which also has given much publicity to the fact that the neighbors have filed legal action against the city. The agent does not reveal this information to a buyer and, when questioned, states that he was not aware of these plans.

Frequently, the buyer or the buyer's mortgage lender will request inspections or tests to determine the presence or level of environmental risks. If environmental risk questions arise in a transaction, brokers should recommend that their client/customer obtain advice from state and local authorities responsible for environmental regulation or other appropriate experts, whenever toxic waste dumping, contaminated soil or water, nearby chemical or nuclear facilities, or health hazards such as radon, asbestos, and lead paint may be present.

IN PRACTICE NCREC has published other examples of these prohibited acts in the License Law and Rule Comments section of *North Carolina Real Estate License Law and Commission Rules* (Appendix C), to which the student is referred. Students should be thoroughly familiar with these topics.

Stigmatized Properties

Over the years, brokers have encountered what are called **stigmatized properties**, those properties branded by society as undesirable because of events that occurred there. Some properties are typically marked by a criminal event: a homicide, suicide, or other violence; illegal drug or gang-related activity; or other events that render the property socially unmarketable in the community's view. Another psychologically impacted property would be a purported haunted house, which is not a material fact.

In North Carolina Under current North Carolina law (G.S. 39–50 and G.S. 42–14.2), the death—even the violent death—or serious illness of a previous owner or resident of a residential property is not a material fact. Therefore, it need not be voluntarily disclosed to a prospective buyer or tenant by the listing agent. If the prospective buyer specifically asks the listing agent about the death or illness, the agent can refuse to answer. Any answer the agent chooses to give, however, must be truthful. The one exception to this rule is if the death or illness is AIDS-related. Because persons with AIDS (or HIV infection) are considered legally handicapped under fair housing laws, an agent cannot disclose this condition, even if asked. Instead, the agent should tell the person who asked the question that the agent is prohibited by law from answering the question.

Sex Offender Disclosure

The above-mentioned General Statutes, also provide that the fact that a registered sex offender (or any other person convicted of a crime requiring registration by the Sex Offender and Public Protection Registration Programs) resides in or near a property for sale or lease is not a material fact requiring disclosure by brokers. The real estate broker's agency status in the transaction will have no effect on the requirement to disclose either the presence of the sex offender in the area or the existence of the state sex offender registry. It does not matter if the broker is a seller's agent, a landlord's agent, a buyer's agent, a tenant's agent, or a dual agent. If a broker chooses to *voluntarily* disclose the presence of the registered sex offender, or to advise a prospective buyer or tenant to visit the sex offender registry, it will not be a violation of the Real Estate License Law. Providing false or misleading information when asked about the presence of sex offenders in a given area will be construed by NCREC as a violation of the Real Estate License Law.

IN PRACTICE Because real estate brokers have, under the law, enormous exposure to liability, some brokers purchase errors and omissions insurance policies for their firms. Similar to malpractice insurance in the medical field, such policies generally cover liability for errors, mistakes, and negligence in the usual listing and selling activities of a real estate office. Individual agents, likewise, should be insured. Note that no insurance will protect a broker from litigation arising from criminal acts such as fraud. Also, insurance companies normally exclude coverage for violation of civil rights laws. Nor will errors and omission insurance relieve a licensed agent from disciplinary action by the NCREC.

Liabilities and Consequences of Breach of Duty

Any agent who breaches an agent's duties to either the principal or a third party must bear the consequences of that breach. These consequences may include any (or all) of the following:

In North Carolina

- **Disciplinary action by NCREC.** Any violation of a duty owed to the principal or third parties is grounds for disciplinary action by NCREC. If the Commission finds that the agent did in fact violate the license law, that agent's license may be revoked or suspended.
- **A civil action in court brought by the injured party.** If the breach of duty harms either the principal or a third party, the agent may be sued and found liable for the damages caused by the breach. Note that if the agent's improper behavior is deemed to be within the scope of the agent's duties, the agent's principal also may be held liable for the damages caused by the agent. The principal can in turn sue the agent for reimbursement for those damages.
- **Criminal prosecution brought by the district attorney.** A violation of a provision of the real estate license law is also a misdemeanor (see G.S. 93A-8). If the agent's breach of duty also is a criminal act, such as fraud or embezzlement, the district attorney may bring a criminal action against the agent.

■ DUTIES AND LIABILITIES OF PRINCIPALS

Duties to Agent

The principal has two basic duties to the agent:

1. **To act in good faith** (to cooperate with the agent and refrain from hindering the agent's efforts). For example, if the seller-client refuses to let the agent show the property, this is a breach of good faith.
2. **To pay the agent the agreed-on compensation when the agent finds a ready, willing, and able buyer.** Once the agent brings the seller a buyer who is ready, willing, and able to purchase the property on the seller's terms, the agent has earned a commission, whether or not the seller decides to sell the home.

Duties to Third Parties

Historically, real estate transactions were governed by the doctrine of caveat emptor, or let the buyer beware. The principal was liable to a buyer only if the principal willfully misrepresented the property. It was up to the buyer to thoroughly examine and research the property, and the buyer was, for all intents and purposes, expected to purchase the property *as is*. Property owners had no affirmative duty to reveal defects about the property. This is still true in North Carolina. However, this principle has been gradually eroded by both court decisions and consumer protection laws. Sellers are always liable for fraudulent misrepresentations.

Liabilities and Consequences of Breach of Duty

The principal who violates the principal's duties either to the agent or to a third party is liable for the damage caused. The principal may be subject to both a civil lawsuit and criminal prosecution (if so warranted). The principal also may be held liable and accountable for the agent's misconduct, referred to as a **tort,** which is a wrongful act by an agent while representing the principal and *acting within the scope of the employment agreement that created the agency.*

■ NATURE OF THE BROKERAGE BUSINESS

Even if affiliated with a national franchise or marketing organization, a real estate broker is an independent businessperson who sets the policies of the broker's office. A broker-in-charge may engage employees and other brokers, determine their compensation, and direct their activities. A broker is free to accept or reject agency relationships with principals. This is an important characteristic of the brokerage business: *a broker has the right to reject agency contracts that, in the broker's judgment, violate the ethics or high standards of the office.* However, once a brokerage relationship has been established, the broker represents the principal and owes that person the duty to exercise care, skill, and integrity in carrying out instructions.

Broker-in-Charge–Licensed Associate Relationship

Although brokerage firms vary widely in size, few brokers today perform their agency duties without the assistance of other brokers. Consequently, much of the business's success hinges on the *broker-in-charge–licensed associate relationship.*

In North Carolina A provisional broker is any person licensed to perform real estate activities on behalf of a licensed real estate brokerage firm. The broker-in-charge is fully responsible for the actions performed in the course of the real estate business by all persons affiliated with the brokerage firm. In turn, *all of a provisional broker's activities must be performed in the name of the supervising broker* (see NCREC Rule A.0506). A nonprovisional broker associate has more autonomy in brokerage activities but generally will still operate under the supervision of a broker-in-charge.

The provisional broker can carry out only those responsibilities assigned by the broker-in-charge under whom the provisional broker is actively licensed and can receive compensation only from that broker-in-charge [see G.S. 93A-6(a)(5)]. As an agent of the broker, the provisional broker has no authority to make contracts with or receive compensation directly from any other party, whether the principal, another broker, a buyer, or a seller.

Independent contractor versus employee. The employment agreement between a broker-in-charge and a licensed associate preferably should be in writing and should define the obligations and responsibilities each has in the relationship. The broker-in-charge is responsible for supervising all provisional brokers in any brokerage activity and may be answerable to the Real Estate Commission for the conduct of those provisional brokers. A broker-in-charge has fewer supervisory responsibilities for the associated nonprovisional brokers, who are held more accountable for their own acts, thereby reducing the broker-in-charge's exposure to disciplinary action by the Real Estate Commission for the conduct of the associated nonprovisional brokers. The real estate *company* remains civilly liable for the acts of all of its associated brokers, whether provisional or nonprovisional.

Associated brokers with an active license may be paid for tax purposes either as a Form W-2 **employee** or as a Form 1099 **independent contractor**. This distinction is relevant primarily for tax purposes and is determined by tests set forth by the Internal Revenue Service (IRS) as to the degree of control exercised by the employer/principal over its employees/agents. The real estate broker may reimburse marketing expenses or require an employee to follow rules such as those governing working hours, office routine, assignment of sales quotas, and adherence to dress codes.

A broker's relationship with a broker associate who is an independent contractor is different. As the name implies, an independent contractor operates more independently than an employee, and a broker may not exercise the same degree of control over an independent salesperson's activities. Although the broker may control *what* the independent contractor does, the broker cannot dictate *how* to do it. The broker cannot require the independent contractor to keep specific office hours or attend sales meetings. The primary distinction for the employer/principal is that the employer is liable for withholding and paying Social Security and income taxes to the IRS for persons who are paid as Form W-2 employees, whereas Form 1099 independent contractors are responsible for reporting their income and paying estimated taxes with no contribution from the employer/principal. An employer may pay certain benefits on behalf of its employees, but not its independent contractors, and generally will be required to pay unemployment compensation tax on the wages of its employees, but not its independent contractors.

Regardless of whether associated brokers are paid as employees or independent contractors, the real estate company has the right to determine company policy and to dictate certain procedures or rules governing how its associated brokers will conduct their brokerage business, as they are engaging in brokerage as agents of the company which remains liable for its brokers' conduct.

IN PRACTICE The Internal Revenue Service (IRS) often investigates the independent-contractor-versus-employee situation in real estate offices. Under the *qualified real estate agent* category in the Internal Revenue Code, three requirements can establish independent contractor status: (1) The individual must have a current real estate license. (2) The individual must have a written contract with the broker containing the following clause: "The salesperson will not be treated as an employee with respect to the services performed by such salesperson as a real estate agent for federal tax purposes." (3) Ninety percent or more of the individual's income as a broker must be based on sales production and not on the number of hours worked. The broker should have a standardized agreement drawn up or reviewed by a lawyer to ensure its compliance with these federal dictates. The broker should also be aware that written agreements mean little to an IRS auditor if the actions of the parties are contrary to the document's provisions.

■ RELATED WEBSITES

Association of Real Estate License Law Officials: www.arello.org
National Do Not Call Registry: www.donotcall.gov
North Carolina Department of Justice: Do Not Call:
   http://ncdoj.gov/Protect-yourself/Stop-Telemarketers.aspx

North Carolina Real Estate Commission: www.ncrec.gov
North Carolina Sexual Offender Registry: http://ncfindoffender.com
US Department of Internal Revenue: www.irs.gov
US Department of Justice, Antitrust Division: www.justice.gov/atr

■ KEY POINT REVIEW

An **agent** is hired by principals to act on their behalf.

Agency is the **fiduciary** relationship in which the agent is held in a position of special trust and confidence by the principal.

A **client** is the **principal**.

A **customer** is the nonrepresented party for whom some level of service is provided and who is entitled to fairness and honesty.

Real estate agency relationships are governed by common law, which is established by tradition and court decisions, and statutory law enacted by the General Assembly, and rules promulgated by regulatory agencies such as the North Carolina Real Estate Commission.

A **universal agent** is empowered to do anything the principal could do personally.

A **general agent** represents the principal in a broad range of matters.

A **special agent** represents the principal in one specific act or business transaction only, under detailed instruction.

Creation of agency may be accomplished by a written listing or property management agreement with a property owner; a written or oral buyer agency agreement; or a dual agency agreement.

Agency relationships encompass the following:

- **Express agency** is based on a formal agreement between the parties.
- **Implied agency** results from the behavior of the parties.
- The compensation source does not determine agency because the agent may be compensated by someone other than agent's client, and agency can exist even if no compensation is involved gratuitous agency.

Termination of agency may be accomplished by the

- completion, performance, or fulfillment of purpose of agency;
- destruction or condemnation of the property;
- expiration of the terms of the agency;
- mutual agreement of all parties to the contract;
- breach by one of the parties, who may be liable for damages; and
- operation of law, as in the bankruptcy of the principal.

A single agency is one in which an agent/firm represents only one party in a transaction.

A buyer's broker represents a buyer as an agent to find property that meets the buyer's specifications, as set out in the buyer agency agreement.

A **subagent** is the agent of an agent.

A **dual agency** is one in which an agent/firm represents two principals in the same transaction.

A **designated agent** is authorized by the broker to act as the exclusive agent of a specific principal in a dual agency situation.

Disclosure by real estate brokers of agency relationship is required in every state.

NCREC's *Working with Real Estate Agents* brochure

- Reviewed with consumer no later than first substantial contact
- Broker must review all agency options
- Request signature of consumer on acknowledgment panel
- Does not create agency; only proof of disclosure

An agent has a fiduciary relationship of trust and confidence with the principal. Transactions should be arm's length with no self-dealing by the agents. The six common-law fiduciary duties can be remembered as **OLD CAR**, which is an acronym for the following:

- **Obedience**—An agent must act in good faith at all times, with obedience toward the principal's instructions that are legal and ethical.
- **Loyalty**—An agent must place the principal's interests above those of all others, including the agent's own interests.
- **Disclosure**—An agent is duty-bound to inform the principal of any information concerning the transaction that might reasonably influence the principal's decision, particularly those mandated by state law.
- **Confidentiality**—An agent must keep the principal's price, terms, and motivation confidential at all times.
- **Accounting**—An agent must be able to report the status of all funds received from or on behalf of the principal.
- **Reasonable skill and care**—An agent must exercise a reasonable degree of care.

Duty to third parties: comply with license law and NCREC's rules and to be fair and honest including disclosure of **material facts**, which include

- facts about the property itself,
- facts relating directly to the property,
- fact relating directly to ability of parties to complete the transaction,
- facts of special importance to the party.

Statements to clients and customers should be clearly identified as opinion or fact. Note the following distinctions:

- **Puffing** is legal exaggeration of a property's benefits.
- **Fraud** is the intentional or willful misrepresentation or omission of a material fact to harm or take advantage of another person.
- **Negligent misrepresentation** occurs when a broker should have known that a statement about a material fact was false.
- **Negligent omission** occurs when a broker did not disclose a material fact that the broker should have known.

Stigmatized properties are seen as undesirable due to events not the condition of the property.

Death or serious illness of an owner or occupant of a property or the presence of a sexual offender in the area does *not* constitute a material fact that must be disclosed by brokers in North Carolina.

A broker-employer is liable for the actions of the **provisional broker** within the scope of the employment agreement.

An **independent contractor** is a real estate broker who

- usually receives a commission, with no withholding for Social Security, income tax, and other purposes;
- has the freedom to set hours and accomplish goals;
- does not relieve the broker of liability for related work activities of the broker; and
- must comply with Internal Revenue Service (IRS) requirements for a qualified real estate agent.

An **employee** is a broker

- who may receive salary in lieu of or in addition to commission;
- who may receive benefits, such as health insurance, profit-sharing, and workers' compensation;
- whose broker is required to withhold Social Security, income taxes, and other applicable federal and state taxes from earnings of the broker;
- whose broker-in-charge sets hours, duties, and other specifics of day-to-day work; and
- whose broker-in-charge has liability for related work activities of the broker.

QUESTIONS

1. A real estate broker acting as the agent of the seller
   a. is obligated to render faithful service to the seller.
   b. has a fiduciary duty to the buyer.
   c. can agree to a change in price without the seller's approval.
   d. can accept a bonus from the buyer without the seller's approval.

2. Fiduciary refers to
   a. the independent contractor status of a broker.
   b. the relationship of trust between the agent and the principal.
   c. the seller's subagent that is working with the buyer.
   d. the principal in an exclusive agency relationship.

3. While in the employ of a real estate broker, a provisional broker has the authority to
   a. act as an agent for the seller.
   b. assume responsibilities assigned by the broker.
   c. accept a commission from another broker.
   d. advertise a property on his or her own behalf.

4. The legal relationship between broker and seller is usually a
   a. universal agent.
   b. special agent.
   c. dual agent.
   d. general agent.

5. A real estate broker learns that her neighbor wishes to sell his house. The broker knows the property well and is able to persuade a buyer to make an offer for the property. No listing agreement has been made. The broker then asks the seller if she can present an offer to him, and the seller agrees. At this point,
   a. the seller is not obligated to pay the broker a commission.
   b. the buyer is obligated to pay the broker for locating the property.
   c. the seller must pay the broker a commission.
   d. the broker has become a subagent of the buyer.

6. A real estate firm who engages brokers as independent contractors must
   a. withhold income tax from all commissions they earn.
   b. provide insurance plans offered to firm employees.
   c. withhold Social Security from all commissions they earn.
   d. still supervise the brokers and remain civilly liable for the brokerage activities of the brokers.

7. Single agency occurs when a real estate agent
   a. represents only one party in a transaction.
   b. represents both the buyer and the seller in a transaction.
   c. chooses to be a designated dual agent.
   d. has both the listing and the sales sides of a transaction.

8. An agent who breaches the fiduciary duties may be subject to all of the following EXCEPT
   a. a civil lawsuit.
   b. disciplinary action by the state Real Estate Commission.
   c. suspension of licensure by the Board of REALTORS®.
   d. criminal prosecution.

9. The principal owes the agent
   I. the duty of acting in good faith.
   II. payment of compensation.
      a. I only
      b. II only
      c. Both I and II
      d. Neither I nor II

10. In North Carolina, the doctrine of caveat emptor
    a. has been completely replaced by case law and consumer protection laws.
    b. is still intact for property owners in real estate transactions.
    c. is applicable only if the agent acts as a dual agent.
    d. is overridden by agents' disclosure laws.

11. Under the common law of agency, a real estate broker owes all of the following duties to the principal EXCEPT
    a. care.
    b. obedience.
    c. disclosure.
    d. novation.

12. An agency relationship may be legally terminated by all of the following means EXCEPT
    a. the owner decides not to sell the house.
    b. the broker discovers that list price will not yield an adequate commission.
    c. the owner dies.
    d. the broker secures a ready, willing, and able buyer for the seller's property.

13. A broker represents the seller at an open house. When should she disclose her agency relationship to a potential buyer at the open house?
    a. After answering questions for the buyer about the house
    b. As soon as the buyer enters the open house
    c. When preparing an offer for the buyer
    d. At first substantial contact

14. A disclosure of agency status should be made by a buyer's agent to the seller
    I. with a written confirmation in the offer to purchase and contract.
    II. at the initial contact with the seller or seller's agent, orally or in writing.
       a. I only
       b. II only
       c. Both I and II
       d. Neither I nor II

15. A broker is representing the property seller. She is showing the property to a prospective buyer customer. The buyer likes the house but does not want to pay as much as the seller wants. He asks the broker if the seller would take less than the listing price. The broker knows that the seller is very anxious to sell and would probably agree to $7,000 less than his asking price. The broker suggests that the buyer make an offer at $5,000 less than the listing price. In this situation, the broker
    a. has done a good job securing an acceptable offer for the seller.
    b. has violated her fiduciary duties to the seller.
    c. will now be considered a designated dual agent.
    d. is making a secret profit from the transaction.

16. An agent is representing the seller. The agent shows the house to his cousin and she is very interested in buying it. The agent presents his cousin's full price offer to the seller, who eagerly accepts it. Both the seller and the buyer are very happy with the transaction. Which statement is TRUE?
    a. Because both parties are happy with the transaction, it doesn't matter whether the agent disclosed his relationship with the buyer to the seller.
    b. The seller cannot complain about the agent's actions because the offer was for the full listing price.
    c. The agent has violated his fiduciary duties to the seller by failing to disclose his relationship with the buyer and could be subject to disciplinary action.
    d. The agent has done nothing wrong; he was not required to disclose his relationship with the buyer.

17. The seller tells the listing agent about a latent defect in the property. The listing agent tells the buyer's agent about the defect, but the buyer's agent does not inform the buyer. Who would most likely be held responsible for the omission in North Carolina?
    a. The seller because he made no representation on the Residential Property Disclosure form regarding the defect
    b. The listing agent because he has the duty to inform the buyer personally of any latent defects
    c. The listing firm because the listing firm is liable for all disclosures in a sale transaction
    d. The buyer's agent because he should not withhold information from his client

18. If a broker's misrepresentation causes loss or financial injury to a buyer customer, which of the following could be found liable?
    I. Principal
    II. Broker
        a. I only
        b. II only
        c. Both I and II
        d. Neither I nor II

19. Which of the following statements about dual agency is/are correct?
    I. Dual agency can occur within one firm if a broker shows his buyer-client his or her own listing.
    II. Dual agency can occur within one firm if a broker has become a buyer's agent and is showing a property listed by the broker-in-charge.
        a. I only
        b. II only
        c. Both I and II
        d. Neither I nor II

20. Under North Carolina License Law and Commission Rules, which of the following is/are TRUE concerning designated agency?
    I. The broker-in-charge cannot be a designated agent.
    II. An agent cannot be appointed as a designated agent if she has prior confidential knowledge about the other party to the transaction.
        a. I only
        b. II only
        c. Both I and II
        d. Neither I nor II

21. It is discovered after a sale that the land parcel is 10% smaller than the owner represented it to be. The broker who passed the erroneous information on to the buyer is
    a. not liable as long as she only repeated the seller's data.
    b. not liable if the misrepresentation was unintentional.
    c. not liable if the buyer actually inspected what she was getting.
    d. liable if the broker knew or should have known of the discrepancy.

22. A broker is representing the property seller. An agent at the same firm is representing a buyer. The two agents confer during a sales meeting and discover the compatible needs of the clients. All of the following are true EXCEPT
    a. the listing agent is being diligent in trying to find a buyer for the seller.
    b. the second agent has performed his fiduciary duties to the buyer.
    c. the broker-in-charge must designate two other brokers who did not attend the meeting to represent the clients.
    d. if the parties have consented to dual agency, the broker-in-charge can allow the two agents to continue their representation in brokering this transaction.

23. Which of the following situations would be considered a material fact that would require disclosure by a North Carolina listing agent?
    a. Owner's son committed suicide in the basement of the property
    b. An upstairs bedroom is believed to be haunted
    c. A group home for unwed mothers is located down the street
    d. The house was totally replumbed after a polybutylene pipe broke in the master bathroom.

24. A provisional broker is acting as an exclusive buyer agent. In accordance with NCREC Rules, the broker has a written agency agreement with the buyer. When co-brokering a transaction with a listing agent at a different firm, the provisional broker is NOT allowed to
    a. be compensated from the commission paid by the seller to the listing firm.
    b. require the buyer to compensate the provisional broker's firm.
    c. be compensated directly by the buyer.
    d. negotiate compensation with the buyer because the seller has already negotiated commission with the listing agent.

25. A North Carolina listing agent has the seller's permission to practice dual agency. A different agent with the listing firm holds an open house over the weekend. A prospective buyer attends the open house, but never shows an interest in open house property. The buyer begins to discuss his specific needs for property with the agent hosting the open house. The agent must
    a. disclose that the firm is a dual agent since the buyer is sharing his needs.
    b. refuse to represent the buyer since the agent already works for the seller.
    c. stop the buyer's information sharing until they have reviewed the *Working with Real Estate Agents* brochure and decided their agency relationship.
    d. require the buyer to initial the acknowledgement panel on the *Working with Real Estate Agents* brochure.

CHAPTER 8

Basic Contract Law

LEARNING OBJECTIVES *When you have finished reading this chapter, you should be able to*

- **define** all types of contracts and give the requirements for a valid contract.
- **identify** the essential elements of contracts and their legal effect if absent.
- **define** statutes that apply to contract law and the legal remedies on breach of a contract.
- **define** these *key terms:*

assignment	express contract	rescission
auction	implied contract	specific performance
bilateral contract	legality of object	statute of frauds
breach of contract	legally competent parties	statute of limitations
compensatory damages	liquidated damages	time is of the essence
consequential damages	"meeting of the minds"	unenforceable contract
consideration	mutual assent	unilateral contract
contract	novation	valid contract
counteroffer	offer	voidable contract
earnest money deposit	offer and acceptance	void contract
executed contract	parol evidence rule	
executory contract	reality of consent	

CONTRACTS

In the course of their business, brokers use many types of contracts and agreements to carry out their responsibilities to sellers, buyers, landlords, tenants, and the

164 Modern Real Estate Practice in North Carolina

general public. Among these are listing contracts, buyer agency contracts, sales contracts, option contracts, land installment contracts, and leases. The general body of law that governs the operation of such contracts is known as *contract law*. This chapter discusses basic contract law that applies to all types of contracts.

A **contract** is a *legally enforceable promise or set of promises between legally competent parties, supported by legal consideration, to do (or refrain from doing) a legal act that must be performed and for which the law provides a remedy if a breach of promise occurs.* A contract must be

- ① *voluntary*—no one may be forced into a contract,
- ② *an agreement or a promise*—a contract is essentially a legally enforceable promise,
- ③ *made by legally competent parties*—the parties must be viewed by the law as capable of making a legally binding promise,
- ④ *supported by legal consideration*—a contract must be supported by some valuable thing that induces a party to enter into a contract and that must be legally sufficient to support a contract, and
- ⑤ *about a legal act*—no one may make a legal contract to do something illegal.

Depending on the situation and the nature or language of the agreement, a contract may be express or implied, unilateral or bilateral, executory or executed, valid, unenforceable, voidable, or void.

Express and Implied Contracts

Depending on how a contract is created, it may be *express* or *implied*. In an **express contract,** the parties state the terms and show their intentions in words to that effect. An express contract may be either oral or written. The Statute of Frauds (discussed later) requires all contracts for the transfer of an interest in real estate to be in writing. Therefore, all real estate contracts should be expressed written contracts. In an **implied contract,** the agreement of the parties is demonstrated by their actions or conduct. In a seller-agency relationship, a listing agreement is a written, express contract between the seller and the broker/firm, naming the broker/firm as the fiduciary representative of the seller.

■ **FOR EXAMPLE**

- Hugh approaches his neighbor, Bob, and says, "I will paint your house today for $500." Bob replies, "If you paint my house today, I will pay you $500." Hugh and Bob have entered into an express oral contract.
- Betty writes, signs, and delivers an offer, which Sam then signs. Betty and Sam have an express written contract.
- Ken goes into a restaurant and orders a meal. Ken has entered into an *implied contract* with the restaurant to pay for the meal, even though payment was not mentioned before the meal was ordered.

Bilateral and Unilateral Contracts

Contracts may also be classified as either *bilateral* or *unilateral*. In a **bilateral contract,** both parties promise to do or refrain from doing something; one promise is exchanged for another. ("I will do this, and you will do that.") A real estate sales contract is a bilateral contract because the seller promises to sell a parcel of real estate and deliver title to the property to the buyer, who promises to pay a certain sum of money for the property. Most real estate-related contracts are bilateral in nature.

In a **unilateral contract,** one party makes a promise to induce a second party to do something. The second party is not legally obligated to act; however, if the second party does comply, the first party is obligated to keep the promise. ("I will do this if you do that.") For example, a seller who agrees to give the buyer four months to decide whether to buy a property is giving the buyer an option, which is considered a unilateral contract.

Executed and Executory Contracts

A contract may be classified as either *executory* or *executed*, depending on whether the agreement has been performed completely. An **executory contract** exists when something remains to be done by one or both parties. A sales contract, signed by all parties, pending closing, is an example of an executory contract. An **executed contract** is one in which all parties have fulfilled their promises and, therefore, fully performed the contract, such as a sales contract that has closed. (Do not be confused by the fact that the word *execute* is also used to refer to the signing of a contract.)

Validity of Contracts

A contract can be described as *valid, void, voidable,* or *unenforceable* (see Figure 8.1), depending on the circumstances.

FIGURE 8.1

Legal Effects of Contracts

Classification of Contract	Legal Effect	Example
Valid	Binding and enforceable on both parties	Agreement complies with essentials of a valid contract
Void	No legal effect	Contract for an illegal purpose
Voidable	Valid but may be disaffirmed by one party	Contract with a minor
Unenforceable	Valid between the parties, but neither party may force performance	Certain oral agreements

A **valid contract** complies with all the essential elements of a contract, which will be discussed later in this chapter, and is binding and enforceable on both parties.

A **void contract** is one that has no legal force or effect. It is unenforceable in a court of law because it does not meet the essential elements of a contract. However, a void contract may be fully executed unless one of the parties disaffirms it.

FOR EXAMPLE A seller enters into a purchase agreement with a buyer who has been adjudicated incompetent by a court. The contract is void because both parties must be competent to create a valid contract.

A **voidable contract** is one that seems, on the surface, to be valid but may be rescinded, or disaffirmed, by one of the parties, based on some legal principle.

If someone makes a contract while drugged or intoxicated, the contract is voidable by that person. A voidable contract will be considered by the courts to be valid if the party who has the option to disaffirm the agreement does not do so within a prescribed period of time. A contract with a minor is voidable by the minor. A contract entered into with a person who is known to be mentally ill is usually voidable during the mental illness. On the other hand a contract entered into with a person who is insane is void.

An **unenforceable contract** has all the elements of a valid contract; however, neither party can sue the other to force performance. Unenforceable contracts are said to be *valid as between the parties* because once the agreement is fully executed and both parties are satisfied, neither has reason to initiate a lawsuit to force performance. For example, an oral agreement for the sale of a parcel of real estate would be unenforceable, because the Statute of Frauds (discussed later) requires that real estate sales contracts be in writing to be enforceable. However, if both the seller and the buyer perform their obligations under the oral agreement, a valid transfer can occur, but if one of the parties refuses to perform, there is nothing the other party can do to compel performance.

> A contract may be
> - **valid**—has all legal elements; is fully enforceable;
> - **void**—lacks one or all elements; has no legal force or effect;
> - **voidable**—has all legal elements; may be rescinded or disaffirmed; or
> - **unenforceable**—has all legal elements; is enforceable only between the parties.

Essential elements of a valid contract. In general, the four essentials of a valid contract are as follows:

> **Four Elements of a Valid Contract**
> 1. Legally competent parties
> 2. Mutual assent or deliberate agreement
> 3. Legality of object
> 4. Consideration

1. **Legally competent parties:** Both parties to the contract must be of legal age and have sufficient mental capacity. In North Carolina, 18 is the age of contractual capacity. Persons younger than 18 years of age are deemed *infants* or minors. Generally, minors' contracts are voidable by the minor or may be canceled before or within a reasonable time after the minor reaches age 18. (In other words, an adult cannot hold a minor to a contract, but a minor can hold an adult to a contract.) A broker should inquire carefully into the ages of both the purchaser and the seller of real estate. Advanced age, in contrast, may be an indication of a person's incapacity to contract as a result of senility. In questions of legal competency, it may be desirable to consult with the client's lawyer. A party who understands the nature and effect of the contract has sufficient mental capacity. Mental capacity is not the same as medical sanity.

2. **Mutual assent or deliberate agreement:** An offer by one party that is accepted by the other party. **Offer and acceptance** means that there must be a **meeting of the minds**. Courts look to the objective intent of the parties to determine whether they intended to enter into a binding agreement. The terms of the agreement must be fairly definite and understood by both parties. Furthermore, the acceptance must be actually communicated to the offeror. (The methods of making and receiving offers, the counteroffer, the acceptance, and communication will be discussed in detail in Chapter 10.)

3. **Legality of object**: To be valid, a contract must not contemplate a purpose that is illegal or against public policy. If a contract calls for immoral performance, discrimination, or a criminal act to take place, the contract is void.
4. **Consideration**: Courts will not enforce gratuitous (free) promises. Consideration is something of legal value, bargained for and given in exchange for a promise or an act. Any return promise to perform that has been bargained for and exchanged is legally sufficient to satisfy the consideration element; for example, the purchase price is the consideration in exchange for the transfer of the property in a real estate contract. A binder or an earnest money deposit is merely an expression of good faith and is not required to create a valid contract.

Requirement for reality of consent. Contracts signed by a person under duress or undue influence are voidable by that person or by a court. Extreme care should be taken when one or more of the parties to a contract are elderly, sick, in great distress, or under the influence of alcohol or drugs, both legal and illegal. To be valid, every contract must be signed as the free and voluntary act of each party. Misrepresentation, fraud, or mistake of fact could render a contract voidable by the injured party. In the absence of these factors, **reality of consent** has been reached.

Revocation of an offer. An offer may be *revoked* or withdrawn by the offeror (the party making the offer, usually the buyer) at any time prior to acceptance if the revocation is communicated directly to the offeree (the party in receipt of the offer, usually the seller) by the offeror. It also can be revoked if the parties are notified through their agents.

Any attempt by the offeree to change any of the terms proposed by the offeror creates a **counteroffer**. The offeror is relieved of the original offer because the offeree has, in effect, rejected it by making changes. The offeror can accept the offeree's counteroffer, reject it, or, if the offeror wishes, make another counteroffer. Any change in the most recent offer results in another counteroffer, until one party agrees to the other party's counteroffer and both parties sign the final contract. Counteroffers may be made by *pen and ink* changes as long as each individual change within the offer is initialed and dated by all parties in addition to the signatures and dates necessary at the bottom of the contract. To avoid confusion and mistakes, signing a new offer to purchase and contract form that incorporates all the changes is the preferred practice.

An offer or a counteroffer *may be revoked at any time before it has been accepted* (even if the person making the offer or counteroffer agreed to keep the offer open for a set period of time). The offeree, or the offeree's agent, must receive notification of the revocation. The contract should stipulate the manner of acceptance; generally, an offer is not considered accepted until the person making the offer has been *notified of the other party's acceptance* (signature).

When the parties communicate through an agent or at a distance, questions may arise regarding whether an acceptance, a rejection, or a counteroffer has effectively taken place. The real estate broker should transmit all offers, acceptances, or other responses as soon as possible to avoid such problems. In North Carolina, these notifications should be delivered as soon as possible, but in no event later

In North Carolina

than five days after execution [see G.S. 93A-6(a)(13) and Rule A.0106]. Remember that as an agent, a real estate broker stands in the shoes of the principal. Communication of acceptance or revocation to an agent is the same as communication directly to the principal.

■ **FOR EXAMPLE** A buyer who is represented by an agent has presented an offer to the seller on Monday. On Tuesday, the seller decides to accept the offer. The seller signs the offer to purchase, and on Tuesday night, the seller's agent tells the buyer's agent that the seller has accepted the buyer's offer. Because it is so late, the buyer's agent decides to wait until Wednesday to tell the buyer that the seller has accepted the offer. Early Wednesday morning, the buyer changes his mind and decides to revoke the offer. It is too late. The communication of the seller's acceptance to the buyer's agent is deemed to be communication to the buyer. Because the offer has been accepted (signed) and communicated, the buyer can no longer revoke his offer. They are under contract.

Agreement in writing and signed. Not all contracts must be in writing to be enforceable; however, every state has adopted the common-law doctrine known as the **statute of frauds**, which requires that certain types of contracts be in writing to be enforceable in a court of law. Most notably, all contracts for the transfer of an interest in real estate must be in writing, with the only exception being leases of a certain period.

In North Carolina

The North Carolina Statute of Frauds requires that to be enforceable in a court of law, conveyances of interests in real property—such as deeds, contracts for sale, mortgages, options, easements, and certain leases (those that are for longer than three years from their making)—must be in writing and signed by the party to be bound or by the party's legally authorized agent. A listing agreement or a buyer representation agreement is an employment contract and is not covered by the North Carolina Statute of Frauds; however, North Carolina Real Estate Commission rules require that agency agreements be in writing (Rule A.0104). The purpose of the North Carolina Statute of Frauds is to prevent fraudulent proof of an oral contract.

The **parol evidence rule**, another heritage of the common law, is a rule of evidence that dictates that no oral agreements that contradict the terms of a written contract may be considered in a lawsuit based on the written agreement. The written contract is assumed to be the complete manifestation of the agreement of the parties. The many exceptions to the rule include evidence that a contract was entered into illegally or evidence intended to clarify ambiguous contract terms. The party who drafted the ambiguous terms would most likely be ruled against in a court hearing.

IN PRACTICE If there is any ambiguity in a contract, the courts generally will interpret the agreement against the party who prepared it. For example, if the seller prepares the offer to purchase and contract, and one of the terms is ambiguous, the court will interpret that term in favor of the buyer.

PERFORMANCE OF CONTRACT

Under any contract, each party has certain rights and duties to fulfill. The question of when a contract duty must be performed is an important factor. Many contracts call for a specific time at or by which the agreed-on acts must be completely performed. In addition, many contracts state that **time is of the essence**. This means that the contract must be performed within the time limit specified, and any party who has not performed on time is liable for breach of contract. If an offeror includes *time is of the essence* in the offer, the offeror can still revoke the offer at any time prior to acceptance.

When a date is noted in a contract but is not followed by the phrase, "time is of the essence," the date is a general target date that all parties should attempt to meet. If the promised action is not completed by the *target date*, the contract is not automatically terminated or made voidable. As long as the action is completed within a reasonable time, the contract will probably still be binding on all parties. The definition of *a reasonable time* would necessitate a court ruling. When a contract does not specify a date for performance, the acts it requires should be performed within a reasonable time (as determined by the court, if a conflict arises). The interpretation of what constitutes a reasonable time will depend on the situation. Generally, if the act can be done immediately—such as a payment of money—it should be performed immediately unless the parties agree otherwise.

IN PRACTICE Despite the best efforts of buyer and seller, it may be impossible to close a transaction on the date stipulated. The seller may not be able to complete necessary repairs before that date. The buyer's lender may be swamped with loan applications and unable to provide funding on the date requested. Buyer and seller can adjust the closing date (or any other contract term) by a modification of the contract—a written amendment signed by all parties. The broker may negotiate the new term(s) but may not sign the modification on behalf of any of the parties. Contingencies must be anticipated to allow sufficient time for completion when contracts are executed.

Assignment and Novation

Occasionally, after a contract has been entered into, one party wants to withdraw without actually terminating the agreement. This may be accomplished through either assignment or novation.

Assignment = substitution of *parties*

Novation = substitution of *new contract*

In North Carolina

Assignment refers to a transfer of rights or duties but not the liabilities under a contract to a third party. Rights in a contract may be assigned to a third party unless the agreement forbids such an assignment. Duties may also be assigned (delegated), but the original obligor remains secondarily liable for them (after the new obligor). The exception to this rule is a contract for personal services, which may not be assigned. Most contracts include a clause that either permits or forbids assignment. The North Carolina Association of REALTORS®/North Carolina Bar Association Standard Offer to Purchase and Contract is not assignable without mutual written consent. An assignment does not terminate the contract or change the terms of the contract.

■ **FOR EXAMPLE** Joe signs a 12-month lease but is getting transferred in 6 months. Joe's landlord agrees to allow Joe to sublet or assign the lease obligations to his friend, Ben. Ben has primary responsibility, but Joe is also liable to meet all lease terms.

Novation is another way to avoid the terms of an existing contract without breaching that contract. *Nova* means new, and *novation* is the substitution of a new contract for an existing agreement with the intent of extinguishing the old contract. The new agreement may be between the same parties, or a new party may be substituted for either (*novation of the parties*). The parties' intent must be to discharge (cancel) the old obligation; therefore, it does terminate the original contract. The new agreement must be supported by consideration and must conform to all the essential elements of a valid contract. In the previous example, if Joe's landlord agreed to rescind Joe's lease and sign a new lease with Ben, this would be a novation. Joe would have no further liability for the lease.

Discharge of Contract

A contract may be performed completely, with all terms carried out, or it may be breached (broken) if one of the parties defaults. A contract also may be discharged (canceled) by various other methods. These include the following:

- *Partial performance* of the terms of the contract. This is sometimes referred to as *accord and satisfaction*. When one party accepts something less than agreed on as complete performance, the contract is considered discharged.
- *Substantial performance*, in which one party has substantially performed the contract but does not complete all the details exactly as the contract requires. Such performance—for example, under construction contracts—may be sufficient to force payment, with certain adjustments for any damages suffered by the other party.
- *Impossibility of performance*, in which an act required by the contract cannot be accomplished.
- *Mutual agreement* of the parties to cancel.
- *Operation of law*, as in the voiding of a contract by a minor, as a result of fraud or the expiration of the statute of limitations (discussed later in this chapter), or as a result of the alteration of a contract without the written consent of all parties involved. Bankruptcy can also discharge a contractual obligation.

Default—Breach of Contract

A **breach of contract** is a violation, without legal excuse, of any of the terms or conditions of a contract, as when a seller breaches a sales contract by not delivering title to the buyer under the conditions stated in the agreement. The nondefaulting party has certain rights.

If a party to a contract defaults, the nondefaulting party has the following alternatives:

- The injured party may *sue the breaching party for money damages* or **compensatory damages**. Money damages are awarded to the injured party to compensate him or her for the breach of the contract, not to punish the party who breached the contract. The amount of the money damages should be only what is necessary to *make the party whole*—that is, put the party in the position he or she would have been in if the contract had been performed as agreed. Thus, in many jurisdictions (but not North Carolina), the buyer can be sued for compensatory damages if the earnest money is not adequate to cover the seller's losses.

- The injured party may be entitled to collect **liquidated damages.** *Liquidated damages* are defined as *the amount of money that will compensate the injured party for breach, which the parties agree to at the time they enter into the contract.* For example, in North Carolina, the **earnest money deposit** is considered liquidated damages in the event the buyer breaches the contract. The seller is entitled to keep the amount of the deposit as compensation for any injuries caused by the buyer's breach of contract.
- **Consequential damages** are special damages that might be obtained if the damages upon breach were reasonably foreseeable to the breaching party at the time of making the contract. It also allows the injured party to sue for lost profits.
- The injured party may file a court action, known as a suit for **specific performance,** to force the other party to perform the contract as agreed. Specific performance is ordered only when the subject matter of the contract is not readily available from another source and when each party has the ability to perform the contractual obligations. Because every parcel of real estate is considered unique, a suit for specific performance brought by the buyer against the seller under a purchase and sales contract may be successful if the buyer can demonstrate that the property is unique and/or rare. Sellers are seldom successful with this remedy against the buyer; acceptance of liquidated damages is a more likely remedy against a buyer that has breached.
- The injured party may *rescind the contract*, which means the contract is declared invalid and both parties return to the position they were in before they entered into the contract. **Rescission** may be appropriate when facts were misrepresented or one party entered the contract under duress. A right of rescission may be written into the contract or may be stipulated by law, such as the five-day right of rescission for a time-share purchase or the seven-day right of rescission for a new condominium purchase.

[In North Carolina]

Statute of Limitations

All states have laws that allow a specific time limit during which parties to a contract may bring legal suit to enforce their rights. The **statute of limitations** varies for different legal actions, and any rights not enforced within the applicable time period are lost.

■ BROKER'S AUTHORITY TO PREPARE DOCUMENTS

[In North Carolina]

A licensed real estate broker is not authorized to practice law and may be disciplined under G.S. 93A-6(a)(11) for attempting to perform any legal service. Because drafting (preparing) legal documents for others is considered to be a legal service, Rule A.0111 of the North Carolina Real Estate Commission states that an agent "in a real estate transaction shall not draft offers, sales contracts, options, leases, promissory notes, deeds, deeds of trust or other legal instruments by which rights of others are secured." A broker is, however, permitted to fill in the blanks on certain approved preprinted documents (such as sales contracts and leases) when authorized to do so by the parties, provided the broker does not charge a separate fee for completing such forms.

IN PRACTICE Brokers are permitted to use electronic, computer, or word processing equipment to store preprinted approved forms; however, the form may not be altered in any way before the form is presented to the parties to the contract. Brokers may, however, make written notes, memoranda, or correspondence recording negotiations of the parties to the transaction as long as they do not constitute binding agreements. The parties to the instruments may delete or change provisions, but the change or deletion must be marked to so indicate.

Contract forms. States vary as to what real estate contract forms brokers are authorized to use. *Preprinted forms* are used for many kinds of contracts because most transactions are consistently similar in nature. The use of preprinted forms raises three issues: (1) how to *fill in the blanks*, (2) what printed matter is not applicable to a particular sale and is to be *ruled out* by drawing a line through the unwanted words, and (3) what additional clauses or agreements (called *riders* or *addenda*) are to be included. All changes and additions should be dated and must be initialed in the margin or on the rider by both parties when the contract is executed.

Auction Sales

In North Carolina

The familiar procedure of a buyer making an offer to purchase, which the real estate agent then presents to the seller for acceptance or rejection, is avoided with an **auction**. Instead of merely presenting the offer to the seller, an auctioneer actually accepts the offer on behalf of the seller. (The typical real estate agent virtually never has the authority to accept an offer on behalf of the seller.) After the auctioneer accepts the offer, or bid, the buyer and seller formalize their oral agreement with a written document (to satisfy the Statute of Frauds) [see Rule A.0104(h)]. A real estate auctioneer must have two licenses: (1) a real estate license and (2) an auctioneer's license. The mere crier of sales is exempt from real estate licensure [see G.S. 93A-2(a)].

There are two types of auctions:

- *Auctions with reserve:* The seller reserves the right to stop the bidding if it becomes apparent that the high bid will be unacceptable to the seller. The seller must reject all bids before the auction is concluded and the auctioneer accepts a bid.
- *Auctions without reserve:* The seller agrees to accept the high bid, no matter what the terms of that bid. This is also called an *absolute auction* in North Carolina.

Note that when the seller accepts any bid at any auction, no matter what type, the property is sold. A seller should fully understand that once the auctioneer declares a bid accepted, the property is sold on those terms because the auctioneer can bind the seller.

KEY POINT REVIEW

Following are characteristics of a **valid contract**:

- A voluntary agreement (**reality of consent**) based on consent
  — If a mistake, misrepresentation, fraud, undue influence, or duress occurs, it is voidable by the injured party.
- The agreement or promise is based on an offer by one party (offeror) that is accepted by the other (offeree).
  — **Mutual assent** or *meeting of the minds* exists.
  — Acceptance (signed by all parties) must be communicated by last offeree to last offeror.
  — Revocation must be communicated by offeror to offeree prior to notification of the offeree's acceptance of the offer.
  — A counteroffer terminates the original offer and initiates a new offer.
- Made by legally competent parties between parties of legal age who are able to understand the nature or consequences of their actions
  — A contract with a minor is voidable.
- Supported by legal consideration,
  — something of legal value, which could be love and affection, and
  — free of undue influence or fraud
- Concerned with a legal act

A **contract** may be

- **express** or **implied** by conduct of parties;
- in some instances, required to be in writing to be enforceable in a court of law;
- **bilateral** (having obligations on both sides) or **unilateral** (a promise by one side that can be accepted or rejected by the other side);
- **executed** (all parties have fulfilled their promises) or **executory** (one or both parties still have an act to perform);
- **void** if one of the essential elements is missing; or
- **voidable**, if it may be rescinded or disaffirmed by one of the parties because one of the essential contract elements is missing, such as legal age or capacity of a party.

Offers may be terminated by the following:

- Revocation, a withdrawal by any acceptable method
- **Counteroffer**, any change to the original offer is a rejection that creates a new offer

The **parol evidence rule** dictates that verbal agreements cannot override the written contract terms.

Contracts may be discharged (completed) by the following:

- Performance, which completes the contract terms
- Partial performance, if agreeable to both parties
- Substantial performance, depending on circumstances
- Impossibility of performance (required acts cannot be legally accomplished)

- **Assignment** (transfer of rights, but not the liabilities, to assignee or delegation of duties)
- **Novation** (substitutes a new contract or party for the original with a release of liability)
- Breach by one of the parties without legal cause
- Failure to enforce contract within **statute of limitations**
- Mutual agreement of parties
- Operation of law, as when a contract is void from inception
- **Rescission** (cancellation) by one or both parties

Remedies for **breach of contract** include the following.

- **Compensatory damages** is the amount necessary to make the injured party whole.
- **Liquidated damages** is the amount the seller will receive if the buyer defaults, such as earnest money or tenant security deposit.
- **Consequential damages** are obtained if the breach was foreseeable.
- **Specific performance** is a lawsuit that requires the party to perform contract obligations.
- Rescission is due to nonperformance of some specific action.

QUESTIONS

1. To be enforceable, contracts for the purchase and sale of real estate would need all of the following EXCEPT
   a. mentally capable parties that understand the terms of the contract.
   b. earnest money deposit must accompany the contract.
   c. mutually acceptable terms of the agreement.
   d. in writing and signed by all parties to be charged.

2. A real estate license gives the broker the right to
   a. draft offers to purchase for a client.
   b. fill in the blanks on pre-printed standard forms.
   c. act as a principal to the contract.
   d. perform as a notary public.

3. The injured party in a real estate transaction with the right to a suit for specific performance is the
   a. broker.
   b. buyer.
   c. title company.
   d. lender.

4. To be enforceable, a contract must be entered into by a person who is at least
   a. 16 years old.
   b. 18 years old.
   c. 21 years old.
   d. 25 years old.

5. A contract is said to be bilateral if
   a. one of the parties is a real estate broker.
   b. the contract has yet to be fully performed.
   c. only one party to the agreement is bound to act.
   d. all parties to the contract are bound to act.

6. During the period of time after a valid real estate sales contract is created, but before title actually passes, the status of the contract is
   a. void.
   b. executory.
   c. executed.
   d. unilateral.

7. A buyer is under contract but would rather let her friend buy it. Unless the contract prohibits it, the friend can take over the buyer's obligation by the process known as
   a. assignment.
   b. substantial performance.
   c. subordination.
   d. mutual consent.

8. All of the following persons would have the potential of creating a voidable contract EXCEPT
   a. a seller that was taking strong pain medication after surgery.
   b. a seller that drank a bottle of champagne prior to signing the contract.
   c. a buyer that does not read well.
   d. a buyer that will turn 18 after closing the transaction.

9. A traveler drives into a gas station and fills her gas tank. She is obligated to pay for the fuel through what kind of contract?
   a. Express
   b. Implied
   c. Voluntary
   d. Executed

10. A seller is under contract to convey ownership of a property to a buyer. The seller changes his mind, and the buyer sues for specific performance. What is the buyer seeking in the lawsuit?
    a. Money damages
    b. New contract
    c. Deficiency judgment
    d. Conveyance of the property

11. In which of the following situations has reality of consent been reached?
    a. Seller signed sales contract at gunpoint.
    b. Buyer's spouse threatened divorce if buyer did not buy property.
    c. Listing agent lied about completion dates of recreational amenities.
    d. Seller lied about her motivation for selling.

12. A buyer submits an offer to purchase property through the use of his exclusive buyer's agent. After the buyer's agent has delivered the offer to the listing agent at the other firm, the buyer calls and asks the buyer's agent to cancel the offer since he has located a different property that he likes better. The buyer's agent cannot revoke the offer if the
    a. listing agent has already presented the offer to the seller.
    b. seller has already signed the offer but has not told anyone.
    c. listing agent has sent an email to the buyer's agent saying that the seller signed the offer.
    d. seller signed the offer after making one change about removing a ceiling fan.

13. A contract states that closing will take place on or before June 22 of this year, *time is of the essence*. If the buyer cannot close until June 26,
    I. the buyer has breached the contract.
    II. the seller has the potential of terminating the contract.
        a. I only
        b. II only
        c. Both I and II
        d. Neither I nor II

14. A builder/seller advertising a selling bonus to any selling agent is an example of a(n)
    a. voidable contract.
    b. unilateral contract.
    c. bilateral contract.
    d. open listing contract.

15. A buyer and a seller sign a contract to purchase. The seller backs out, and the buyer sues for specific performance. What is the buyer seeking in this lawsuit?
    a. Money damages
    b. New contract
    c. Deficiency judgment
    d. Transfer of the property

16. In a standard sales contract, several words were crossed out or inserted by the parties. To eliminate future controversy as to whether the changes were made before or after the contract was signed, the usual procedure is to
    a. write a letter to each party listing the changes.
    b. have each party write a letter to the other approving the changes.
    c. redraw the entire contract.
    d. have both parties initial or sign in the margin near each change.

17. The sales contract says the buyer will purchase only if an attorney approves the sale by the following Saturday. The attorney's approval is a
    a. contingency.
    b. reservation.
    c. warranty.
    d. consideration.

18. Under the statute of frauds, all contracts for the sale of real estate must be
    a. originated by a real estate broker.
    b. on preprinted forms.
    c. in writing to be enforceable.
    d. accompanied by earnest money deposits.

19. If, upon the receipt of an offer to purchase a property subject to certain conditions, the seller makes a counteroffer, the prospective buyer is
    a. bound by the original offer.
    b. bound to accept the counteroffer.
    c. bound by whichever offer is lower.
    d. relieved of the original offer.

20. A broker has found a buyer for a seller's home. The buyer has indicated in writing a willingness to buy the property for $1,000 less than the asking price and has deposited $5,000 in earnest money with the broker. The seller is out of town for the weekend, and the broker has been unable to inform the seller of the signed document. At this point, the buyer has signed a(n)
    a. voidable contract.
    b. offer.
    c. executory agreement.
    d. implied contract.

CHAPTER 9

Agency Contracts

LEARNING OBJECTIVES *When you have finished reading this chapter, you should be able to*

- **describe** the different types of agency contracts and the procedures for using agency contracts.
- **identify** different types of compensation and disclosure requirements.
- **understand** how to be entitled to and calculate compensation.
- **describe** the typical listing process including calculations for seller net and minimum sales price.
- **understand** the requirements of the North Carolina Residential Property Disclosure Act.
- **define** these *key terms:*

  antitrust laws
  buyer-agency agreement
  comparative market analysis (CMA)
  employment contract
  exclusive-agency listing
  exclusive right-to-sell listing
  extender clause
  fee-for-service agreement

  frontage
  listing agreement
  multiple listing service (MLS)
  National Do Not Call Registry
  net listing
  North Carolina Residential Property Disclosure Act
  open listing

  override clause
  price fixing
  procuring cause
  protection agreement
  puffing
  ready, willing, and able buyer
  retainer fee
  success fee

AGENCY CONTRACTS AND PRACTICES FOR WORKING WITH SELLERS

As mentioned in Chapter 7, an agency agreement for brokerage services creates a special agency relationship between the principal (seller, buyer, landlord, or tenant) and the agent (broker/firm), wherein the agent is authorized to represent

In North Carolina

the principal and the principal's property to third parties, including submitting or receiving offers for the property. Per NCREC Rule A.0104(a & b), all written agency agreements must (1) be signed by all parties; (2) include the broker's real estate license number; (3) have a definite termination date; and (4) contain the prescribed nondiscrimination provision. This chapter will review in depth the different standardized agency agreements used in sales transactions and closely examine a typical listing process. Entering into an agency agreement follows the agency disclosure discussed in Chapter 7. *Note:* Forms referenced in this and other chapters are located in Appendix D, North Carolina Real Estate Forms.

[handwritten annotation: Fair Housing clause → points to "prescribed nondiscrimination provision"]

Why Use a Listing Agreement?

Just as a supermarket without inventory will have no customers, the real estate industry without inventory will have no business. To acquire inventory, most brokers obtain listings of properties for sale (although some work with properties for lease, rent, exchange, or option). Under the provisions of North Carolina's real estate license laws, only a broker/firm having an active license can act as an agent to list, sell, or rent another person's real estate.

In North Carolina

The first type of contract an agent is likely to encounter is the **listing agreement.** As with most agency agreements, the listing agreement is an **employment contract** rather than a real estate contract. With a listing agreement, the broker/firm is hired to represent the seller-principal, but real property is not transferred. An agreement for brokerage services between a broker and an owner of real property must be in writing from the outset of the relationship [see Rule A.0104(a)]. Under NCREC rules, *an oral agency agreement with a property owner—whether a listing contract with a seller or property management agreement with an owner— is not permitted.* The agreement must be in writing before any brokerage services are provided. There is only one exception to this rule: if a seller did not originally give permission for dual or designated dual agency in the listing agreement and the buyer agency agreement has not been reduced to writing, the seller can orally amend their written listing agreement to authorize either type of dual agency at a later date. This oral consent to dual agency must be reduced to writing prior to submission of the first offer on the property.

Note: Throughout this chapter, unless otherwise stated, the terms *broker* and *agent* are intended to include both a nonprovisional broker and a provisional broker working under the broker-in-charge. However, only the broker/firm has the direct authority to provide services to a principal; the individual brokers will usually provide services as a subagent (i.e., as an affiliated agent of the company serving as agent).

Laws Affecting Solicitation of Clients/Customers

The obvious first step to securing a listing agreement is to identify possible seller-clients. The exploration of various methods to locate and solicit clients is beyond the scope this text. Despite that point, it is imperative that several important legal and ethical issues be addressed that might modify the method utilized.

Soliciting active clients of other firms/brokers. Article 16 of the REALTOR® Code of Ethics prohibits members of the National Association of REALTORS® from the solicitation of business from a consumer that is party to an active exclusive agency agreement with another REALTOR®. Regardless of one's trade affiliation, it is ill advised to solicit a property owner subject to a current listing agreement. Not only will such unethical behavior create controversy among fellow real estate brokers, it could be the foundation for a lawsuit for *tortious interference with contractual relations*. Even the appearance of encouraging a party to breach their contractual duties should be avoided at all costs.

Do-not-call laws/rules. In 2003, federal do-not-call legislation was signed into law, and real estate professionals must comply with the provisions of the **National Do Not Call Registry**. The registry is managed by the Federal Trade Commission; it is a list of telephone numbers from consumers who have indicated their preference to limit the telemarketing calls they receive. The registry applies to any plan, program, or campaign to sell goods or services through interstate phone calls. The registry does not limit calls by political organizations, charities, or telephone surveyors.

A real estate broker may call a consumer with whom they have an established business relationship for up to 18 months after the consumer's last purchase, delivery, or payment, even if the consumer is listed on the National Do Not Call Registry. A broker also may call a consumer for up to three months after the consumer makes an inquiry or submits an application. Note that if a consumer asks a company not to call, even if there is an established business relationship, the company must abide by the consumer's wishes. Real estate brokers are prohibited from calling registered owners of for-sale-by-owner properties or owners of expired listings with another firm since these solicitation scenarios are subject to the Act. On the other hand, a buyer's agent may call for sale by owners that are on the Registry if the buyer-client is interested in the property.

In North Carolina

On the National Do Not Call Registry, the only information accessible (for a fee) from the registry is a registrant's telephone number. Telemarketers and sellers are now required to search the registry at least once every 31 days and drop registered consumer phone numbers from their call lists. North Carolina's do-not-call statute mirrors the federal rules and piggybacks on the federal registry. Penalties on the federal level are up to $11,000 per call and North Carolina fines range from $500 to $5,000 depending on the violation.

Junk fax laws/rules. In 2005, the Junk Fax Prevention Act amended the Telephone Consumer Protection Act that had been in effect since the early 1990s. Unsolicited advertisements by fax are banned without prior invitation or permission of the recipient. A prominent opt-out notice must appear on the cover sheet. A prior existing relationship that has not been terminated by either party is an exemption to the Act; there is no time limit on this relationship. Real estate brokers/firms are encouraged to secure written permission to fax consumers.

MATH CONCEPTS

SHARING COMMISSIONS

Two brokerage firms and their brokers might share a single commission: the listing brokerage firm, the listing agent, the selling brokerage firm, and the selling agent. Drawing a diagram can help you determine which person is entitled to receive what amount of the total commission.

Agent Eve, while working for ABC Realty, took a listing on a $189,000 house at a 6% commission rate. Agent Ted, while working for Homes Realty, found the buyer for the property. The property sold for the listed price, and the listing firm and the selling firm shared the commission equally. If the selling firm kept 45% of what it received, how much did agent Ted receive? (If the selling firm retained 45% of the commission split that it received, its broker would receive the balance of the split: 100% − 45% = 55%.)

$189,000 × 6% (.06 as a decimal) = $11,340

↙ ↘ ← Co-op firm/Selling firm

ABC Realty
$11,340 × 50% (.50) = $5,670
to be split between ABC Realty and Agent Eve

Homes Realty
$11,340 × 50% (.50) = $5,670
to be split between Homes Realty and Agent Ted

↙ ↘

$5,670 × 45% (.45) = $2,551.50
(Homes Realty's share)

$5,670 × 55% (.55) = $3,118.50
(Agent Ted's share)

CAN-SPAM Act. The Controlling the Assault of Non-Solicited Pornography and Marketing Act (CAN-SPAM) of 2003 restricts *spamming* by email. Like the Junk Fax laws, any mass marketing by email should include a prominent opt-out instruction. This Act is not seen to have much impact on the real estate industry.

Broker's Entitlement to a Commission

The listing broker's/firm's compensation is specified in the listing agreement. The most widely-used type of compensation is a commission, or brokerage fee, computed as a *percentage of the final accepted gross sales price*. A flat-fee commission is another way to receive compensation. The commission payment, usually considered earned when the broker has accomplished the work for which the broker was hired, is due at the closing of the transaction. Most sales commissions are paid when all terms of the purchase contract have been fulfilled.

To be entitled to collect a commission, a broker must be actively licensed, must be employed by the principal under a valid written agency agreement, or be the procuring cause of the sale, and must produce a **ready, willing, and able buyer**. North Carolina provisional brokers can only be paid directly by their employing brokers, not directly by a principal. Commission Rule A.0109 further stipulates that a broker in a sales transaction cannot receive any compensation, incentive, bonus, or other consideration from any party or person without full and timely disclosure of the compensation to the broker's principal. Timely disclosure must be confirmed in writing prior to making or accepting any offer. (See Confirmation of Compensation, Appendix D, Form 12.)

==Once a broker obtains an offer from a ready, willing, and able buyer that meets the seller's terms, the seller is technically liable for the listing broker's commission.== A ready, willing, and able buyer is one who is *financially qualified, prepared to buy on the seller's terms, and ready to take positive steps toward consummation of the transaction by showing willingness to enter into an enforceable contract.* But even if the transaction is not consummated, the broker still may be entitled to a commission when the seller

- has a change of mind and refuses to sell,
- has a spouse who refuses to sign the deed,
- has a title with uncorrected defects,
- commits fraud with respect to the transaction,
- is unable to deliver possession within a reasonable time,
- insists on terms not in the listing (for example, the right to restrict the use of the property), or
- has a mutual agreement with the buyer to cancel the transaction.

In other words, *a listing broker generally is due a commission if a sale is not consummated because of the principal's unjustified default.* Even if the buyer backs out without legal cause after the seller has accepted the offer, the broker may be entitled to a commission, but collecting it may be difficult. To be considered the **procuring cause** of sale, the broker must have taken action to start (or cause) an unbroken chain of events that resulted in the sale. In North Carolina, a broker who causes or completes such action without a written agency contract that promises compensation is deemed a *volunteer* and has no legal claim to compensation.

In North Carolina

A broker's compensation is negotiable in every case. For members of the profession to attempt, however subtly, to impose uniform commission rates is a clear violation of federal antitrust laws. The important point is for broker and client to agree on a rate before the agency relationship is established. If no amount or percentage rate of commission is stated in the listing contract and a legal action results, the court may determine a reasonable commission by evidence of the custom in a particular community. NCREC is prohibited by law from regulating the amount of commission charged by licensees [see G.S. 93A-3(c)].

In North Carolina

Naturally, to earn any compensation, the buyer's broker must have an active real estate license and have a valid written buyer-agency contract. The terms of that buyer-agency agreement will control how much compensation is to be paid to the buyer's agent and which party will pay that compensation. (There are currently no points of law or court cases in North Carolina to provide legal guidance on the question of how to pay a buyer agent.)

Buyers' agents may also be compensated by the buyer paying *retainer fees* and/or *success fees.* The **retainer fee** is typically a small amount of compensation, usually paid up front by the buyer/client when the buyer-agency agreement is established. This fee is advanced partial compensation for services. The **success fee** is due and payable by the buyer/principal on the signing and acceptance of an offer to purchase property found by the buyer's agent. Typically, however, it is actually paid at closing. The buyer-agency agreement normally states that the buyer's agent will first try to recover the success fee from the listing firm via the cooperative agreement, and if unsuccessful, then from the buyer. (see Appendix D, Form 9, Provision 4).

In North Carolina **Working with broker licensed in another state (foreign broker).** A North Carolina broker can share a brokerage fee with a broker from another state if that broker is actively licensed in the state from which he is making the referral *and* does not physically enter North Carolina to engage in real estate brokerage activity that would require a North Carolina real estate license. Generally, such a situation would result in a referral fee being paid to the out-of-state broker for referring a buyer or seller client to the North Carolina broker. (Most states require all referral fees to be paid to the brokerage firm who then pays the referring broker or salesperson.) The reverse holds true in that the North Carolina broker can receive compensation for referring brokerage business to an active broker in another state . . . as long as the North Carolina broker physically stays out of the state of the broker that received the referral. A North Carolina broker should secure a written compensation agreement and not assume that the out-of-state broker can or will be able to pay them. These fees must usually be paid to the out-of-state broker's brokerage firm and not directly to the out-of-state broker.

Antitrust Laws

The real estate industry is subject to federal and state **antitrust laws.** Generally, these laws prohibit monopolies and contracts, combinations, and conspiracies that unreasonably restrain trade. The most common antitrust violations are **price fixing,** group boycotting, and allocation of customers or markets.

Price fixing is the practice of setting prices for products or services rather than letting competition in the open market establish those prices. In real estate it occurs when brokers agree to set sales commissions, fees, or management rates, and it is illegal. Brokers must independently determine commission rates or fees only for their own firms. These decisions must be based on the broker's business judgment and revenue requirements without input from other brokers.

Multiple-listing organizations, Boards of REALTORS®, and other professional organizations may not set fees or commission splits. Nor are they allowed to deny membership to brokers based on the fees the brokers charge. Either practice could lead the public to believe that the industry sanctions not only the unethical practice of withholding cooperation from certain brokers but also the illegal practice of restricting open-market competition.

The broker's challenge is to avoid any impression of attempts at price-fixing as well as the actual practice. Hinting in any way to prospective clients that there is a *going rate* of compensation implies that rates are, in fact, standardized. A broker must clarify to clients that the rate stated is only what the firm charges. Likewise, discussions of rates among brokers from different firms could be construed as a price-fixing activity and should be avoided scrupulously.

In North Carolina — NCREC is specifically prohibited by law (G.S. 93A-3) from making rules and regulations that regulate or dictate commissions, salaries, or fees to be charged by licensees. Commission Rule A.0109(f) states: "The Commission shall not act as a board of arbitration and shall not compel parties to settle disputes concerning such matters as the rate of commissions, the division of commissions, pay of brokers, and similar matters." All commission arrangements between an agent and a principal must be made in a way that shows they have been negotiated between the principal and agent.

Group boycotting occurs when two or more businesses conspire against other businesses or agree to withhold their patronage to reduce competition. Group boycotting is illegal under the antitrust laws.

Allocating markets or customers involves an agreement between brokers to divide their markets and refrain from competing with each other for business. Allocations have been made on a geographic basis, with brokers agreeing to specific territories within which they will operate exclusively. The division might occur by markets, such as by price range. These agreements conspire to eliminate competition and are illegal.

The penalties for such acts are severe. For example, under the federal Sherman Antitrust Act people who are found guilty of fixing prices or allocating markets may be punishable by a maximum $100,000 fine and three years in prison. For corporations, the penalty may be as high as $1 million. In a civil suit, a person who has suffered a loss because of the antitrust activities of a guilty party may recover triple the value of the actual damages plus attorney's fees and costs.

Types of Listing Agreements

The forms of full-service listing agreements generally used are (1) open listing, (2) exclusive-agency listing, and (3) exclusive right-to-sell listing.

Open Listing
- There are multiple agents.
- Only selling agent is entitled to a commission.
- Seller retains the right to sell independently without obligation.

① Open listing. In an **open listing**, the seller retains the right to employ any number of brokers as agents; it is a nonexclusive-type of listing. The brokers can act simultaneously, and the seller is obligated to pay a commission only to that broker who successfully procures a ready, willing, and able buyer. If the seller personally sells the property *without the aid of any of the brokers*, the seller is not obligated to pay any broker a commission; the seller can compete with the agents for the commission. If the owner or any of the brokers sells the property, all other open listing agreements on that property will terminate the authority given to those brokers. A broker who was in any way a procuring cause of the transaction, however, may be entitled to a commission if the procuring cause of sale can be proved.

Exclusive-Agency Listing
- There is one authorized agent.
- Broker receives a commission if any broker is procuring cause.
- Seller retains the right to sell without obligation to listing broker.

② Exclusive-agency listing. In an **exclusive-agency listing**, one broker is specifically authorized to act as the exclusive agent of the principal. The seller under this form of agreement *retains the right to personally sell the property, without obligation to the broker*; the seller can compete with the agent to save the commission. If the seller sells through his or her own efforts, the exclusive agency of the broker is automatically terminated. The seller is obligated to pay a commission to the broker if the broker has been the procuring cause of a sale. The listing brokerage

Chapter 9   Agency Contracts   **185**

can also offer and pay a co-op fee to another brokerage to bring a buyer. In which case, both firms would be paid.

Exclusive right-to-sell Listing
- There is one authorized agent.
- Broker receives a commission regardless of who sells the property.

Exclusive right-to-sell listing. In an *exclusive right-to-sell listing*, one brokerage firm is appointed as sole exclusive agent of the seller and is given the exclusive right, or *authorization*, to represent the property in question. Under this form of listing contract, the seller must pay the broker a *commission regardless of who sells the property* if it is sold while the listing agreement is in effect. In other words, if the seller gives a broker an exclusive right-to-sell listing but finds a buyer without the broker's assistance, the seller still must pay the broker a commission. In real estate, this is the most common form of listing agreement. Please note that the listing agreement contains specific language stating that the broker is entitled to the commission regardless of who actually sells the property. Claiming a commission as the procuring cause of the sale has no legal effect. The term *exclusive right to sell* does not imply that the broker has the authority to enter into a *sales contract* on behalf of the property owner. The listing agreement is not an offer to sell the property; it is an *employment* agreement. The seller cannot be forced to sell the property even if the offer matches the terms of the listing agreement exactly; the seller is only required to pay the earned commission to the broker.

In North Carolina

North Carolina protection agreement. When a particular property is not currently listed with any real estate brokerage firm, a **protection agreement** is used to guarantee a broker a commission if that particular property is sold to a specific buyer. The agreement does not create a general listing. When the broker is an exclusive buyer agent, the broker may use the protection agreement to guarantee the seller's payment of the sales commission without creating any agency relationship with the seller. The North Carolina Association of REALTORS® created the Unrepresented Seller Disclosure and Fee Agreement (Std. Form 150) to address required agency disclosure to a property owner selling their own property, and compensation by that property owner to a buyer's agent. (See Appendix D, Form 11.)

■ **FOR EXAMPLE** A broker may use a protection agreement when she has a client who is interested in a specific type of property. The broker knows this buyer would be interested in a particular house that is "For Sale by Owner." However, the broker does not want to suggest that the buyer view the house because the broker could lose the opportunity to earn a commission. Instead, the broker might first approach the homeowner/seller and ask whether he would agree to pay her a commission if her client decided to purchase the home.

Fee-for-services, or limited services, agreement. The internet has revolutionized the real estate profession in many ways. One of the more notable impacts of the internet is that it has allowed buyers and sellers to have tremendous access to information about real estate, housing, financing, and law. The internet has caused a radical shift in that the average consumer is now much more knowledgeable about real estate matters. With knowledge and information, a consumer is more innovative and independent. The advent of the internet also has meant that the consumer is privy to information immediately. Consumers now want instant access to real estate information.

Successful brokers will understand and encourage consumers' innovation. In the process, it is critical for brokers to identify what services can be provided and to underscore the value of those services. While emphasizing the services that brokers provide, it may be important for brokers to think of themselves as consultants. While consumers are more independent, real estate expertise is almost always needed.

It may be more important for brokers to be more flexible and open to seeing their occupation as a *bundle of services* that can be unbundled. **Fee-for-services agreement**, or limited service agreements, is the arrangement where the consumer decides which services are needed and then works with and pays the broker solely for those services.

Unbundling services means offering services in a piecemeal fashion. For example, a consultant may want to offer a seller the following services:

- Helping the seller prepare the property for sale
- Performing a comparative market analysis (CMA) and pricing the property
- Assisting with marketing the property using the MLS and any other websites
- Locating and screening a buyer
- Completing an offer to purchase agreement and helping with negotiations
- Assisting with closing a transaction

Other services include those for a buyer. For example, a consultant may offer a buyer the following services:

- Consulting on renting versus owning
- Helping a buyer with a mortgage preapproval
- Consulting on a buyer's desired location
- Visiting properties with a buyer and checking property information
- Completing an offer to purchase agreement and helping with negotiations
- Assisting with closing a transaction

Note the discussion below regarding minimum level of services and the problems that can occur when providing a limited service.

While brokers want to encourage consumers to use all of their services (full-service) for a commission rate, when it becomes apparent that a consumer wants help with one or several services only, then it would be helpful for the broker to have in mind the best compensation model. Many brokers use either an hourly rate or a flat fee for particular services. In determining a flat fee, brokers consider the amount of hours it would take to do a particular task and multiply that by an hourly rate. In order to avoid a price-fixing claim, it is important that brokers independently establish their fees and do not develop their fees based on a "norm" in the industry.

Brokers may also want to develop their own lists of services for sellers and buyers, as well as a list of specific services to help those consumers selling their home on their own (FSBOs).

Communicating with consumers and identifying their real estate needs are important factors. Brokers provide an array of valuable services from which consumers can pick and choose. Knowledgeable and independent consumers can seem threatening to a broker; however, the broker has the opportunity to emphasize the value and variety of real estate services offered, for varying fees. Remember that it is ultimately the broker who decides whether an unbundling of services is good for the company.

■ **FOR EXAMPLE** Chris wants to buy a house without contracting with a brokerage firm for a full range of brokerage services but needs help writing an offer. Chris asks Sally, a broker friend of hers, to write an offer to purchase. Sally enters into a written buyer agency agreement with Chris for this limited service, writes the offer to purchase, and charges Chris a set fee for her service.

Minimum Level of Service Problems have emerged with the growing number of brokerages offering limited-service listing agreements. These agreements may stipulate that a listing broker offers no services other than that of placing a listing in the MLS. When sellers enter into this kind of agreement, the sellers are essentially representing themselves. The seller may well be aware of this; however, when questions emerge involving the transaction, the seller sometimes turns to the buyer's agent for answers. Seller questions and broker answers of this type should be handled carefully or they could lead to a claim of undisclosed dual agency. In response to this problem, some states have enacted legislation defining an exclusive brokerage agreement. Other states have proposed regulations that define the minimum level of services a consumer should expect from a broker and brokerage firm.

> In North Carolina

North Carolina has no laws or rules on this issue; however, the NCREC has shared some insight in the 2011-2012 Edition of the *North Carolina Real Estate Manual*. While there is currently no standard limited services listing contract form, a carefully worded limited services listing agreement drafted by an attorney is perfectly legal in North Carolina. Although a broker may limit by contract the services that will be provided to a client, the broker may not limit or waive duties under North Carolina License Law. The major duties of a listing agent that may not be waived or limited include: disclosure of any material fact to any party; avoidance of false promises; avoidance of undisclosed conflict of interest; proper accounting for trust funds; competence in performance of duties; prompt delivery of all offers and contracts; and compliance with the Residential Property Disclosure Act. Consequently, a limited service firm that contracts with the seller to only enter the property information into the local MLS will still be held liable for the accuracy of the property information.

Multiple Listing Services

A *multiple-listing clause* is usually included in an exclusive listing. Brokers who are members of a **multiple listing service (MLS)** agree to pool their listings. The multiple-listing provision gives additional authority to the listing broker to *distribute the listing to other brokers who belong to the MLS*. The contractual obligations among the member brokers of a multiple listing organization vary widely. Most listing agreements include what is called *an offer of compensation and cooperation*. Under this provision, the commission is divided between the listing broker and the selling broker, regardless of which party the selling broker represents.

Under most MLS contracts, the broker who secures a listing is not only authorized but *obligated* to submit the listing to the MLS within a definite period of time so that it can be distributed to the other member brokers. The length of time during which the listing broker can offer the property exclusively without notifying the other member brokers varies by REALTOR® board.

A multiple listing provision offers advantages to both the broker and the seller. Brokers develop a sizable inventory of properties to be sold and are ensured a portion of the commission if they list a property or participate in its sale. Sellers also gain under this form of listing agreement because all members of the multiple listing organization are eligible to sell their property and are made aware of its availability. Many MLS agreements now allow all members to upload all the MLS entries onto their firm websites for even more exposure to the properties.

Information needed when listing properties in MLS. It is important to obtain as much information as possible concerning a parcel of real estate when taking a listing. It is wise to complete a physical inspection of the property in the presence of the seller and collect all the physical data necessary to submit to the MLS for inclusion in its property data block. It is prudent to ask the seller to provide information on current property liens such as mortgages and copies of any property documentation they possess [their deed or survey (if available) and protective covenants or homeowners association information (if applicable)]. Of course, it is important to make sure all data is accurate. (**Puffing**, which is the use of exaggerated comments or opinions, is not permitted.) The agent should point out any defects to the seller that may need correcting before the property can be shown. The broker should also ask the seller to verify that any improvements or major repairs made to the property were adequately permitted through the appropriate municipality. Septic system capacity needs to also be confirmed by the broker to avoid misrepresentation of occupancy limits. Also, during this phase of the listing procedure, the agent should identify all items of personal property the seller may wish to leave behind and identify any fixtures the seller may wish to remove. This process ensures that all possible contingencies are anticipated and provided for, particularly when the listing will be shared with other brokers in a multiple-listing agreement.

As part of the MLS agreement, listing brokers generally use a separate information form, known as a profile or data sheet, for recording many of the property's features. This information generally includes the following (where appropriate):

- Names, addresses, and relationship, if any, of the owners
- Legal description of the property
- Size of the improvements (square footage)
- Age of the improvements and their type of construction
- Number and general dimensions of rooms
- Lot size (**frontage** and depth) as well as information concerning the facilities, services, and institutions (e.g., schools, parks and recreational areas, churches, public transportation) available in the neighborhood where the property is located (frontage is defined in Math FAQs on page 713)
- Information on any existing loans, including name and address of each lender; type of loan; loan number; loan balance; interest rate; monthly payment and what it includes (principal, interest, real estate tax impounds,

hazard insurance impounds, mortgage insurance premiums); whether the loan may be assumed by the buyer and, if so, under what circumstances; whether the loan may be prepaid without penalty; and so forth
- Possibility of seller financing
- Amount of any outstanding special assessments and whether they will be paid by the seller or assumed by the buyer
- Zoning classification of the property
- Current (or most recent year's) property taxes
- Any real property to be removed from the premises by the seller and any personal property to be included in the sale for the buyer (both the listing contract and the subsequent purchase contract should be explicit on these points)
- Any additional information that would make the property appealing and marketable
- Any required disclosures concerning agency representation, property condition, known defects in the property, and the like

Termination of Listings

A listing agreement may be terminated for any of the following reasons:

- Completion or fulfillment of the purpose for which the agency was created (the best way to terminate a listing)
- Expiration of the terms of the agency
- Mutual agreement to terminate the agency
- Breach by one of the parties, such as abandonment by the agent or revocation by the principal (The breaching party might be liable for damages.)
- By operation of law, as in bankruptcy of the principal (because title to the property would be transferred to a court-appointed receiver)
- Destruction or condemnation of the property
- Death or incapacity of either party (Notice of death is not necessary. Note that if a property is listed with a brokerage firm and the listing agent dies, the listing would not be terminated because the listing belongs to the firm.)

A listing agreement is a *personal service contract* with the brokerage firm (not the individual broker), and its success depends on the personal efforts of the broker who is party to the agreement. The broker cannot turn over the listing to another broker. If the broker abandons the listing by failing to work toward its fulfillment or if he or she revokes the agreement, the property owner cannot force the broker to comply with it. The property owner can, however, sue the broker for damages.

The property owner could fail to fulfill the terms of the agreement by refusing to cooperate with reasonable requests of the broker (such as allowing tours of the property by prospective buyers) or by refusing to proceed with a sales contract. A property owner who cancels the listing agreement could be liable for damages to the broker.

In North Carolina

North Carolina Listing Contract Forms

A wide variety of listing contract forms is available today. Some brokers have attorneys draft contracts for their firm's use; some use forms prepared by their MLS;

some use forms produced by the North Carolina Association of REALTORS®. No matter which form is used, most listing contracts require similar information because the same considerations arise in almost all real estate sales transactions. A copy of the North Carolina Association of REALTORS® Exclusive Right to Sell Listing Agreement, Form 101, (provisions of which will be referenced in this section) is contained in Appendix D, Form 1.

All listing agents should make sure the listing contract form is filled in properly and approved by the firm and/or the broker-in-charge. Note that a broker/firm can draft the listing form because broker/firm is a party to that agreement; a listing form is an employment agreement between the broker and the seller, not a contract between the buyer and the seller. However, the broker-in-charge should have an attorney approve the form. The listing agreement also must comply with NCREC rules.

Agency disclosure. As previously discussed in Chapter 7, the real estate broker at first substantial contact with a prospective buyer or seller in all real estate sales transactions must give and review the agency disclosure brochure, *Working with Real Estate Agents*, and determine agency status. The tear-out panel on the brochure must be completed appropriately, hopefully signed by the buyer/seller, and a copy retained by the broker for three years. Review of this mandatory brochure will facilitate understanding of the need for agency-related decisions within the listing agreement, such as cooperation with and compensation to other firms or possible authorization of dual agency. Agency disclosure must happen before a broker begins to gather information to complete a listing agreement. In Provision 1, the seller is asked to confirm that he is not a party to another listing agreement on the property and that he has received the *Working with Real Estate Agents* brochure that was reviewed by the broker.

The names of all parties to the contract. Anyone who has an ownership interest in the property must be identified and should sign the listing to validate it. If the property is owned under some form of co-ownership, that fact should be clearly established. (See Chapter 2.) If one or more of the owners is married, the spouse's consent and signature on the contract to release any marital rights is required. If the property is in the possession of a tenant, that should be disclosed (along with the terms of the tenancy), and instructions should be included on how the property is to be shown to prospective buyers.

Term of listing agreement. In North Carolina, *all written agency agreements must specify a definite termination date* of the agency relationship [NCREC Rule A.0104(a)]. The listing form must provide for a definite period of time with an automatic termination date (Provision 1). If the property has not been sold by midnight of the termination date, the listing agreement is automatically terminated without notification being required of either party. If mutually acceptable, the listing can be either extended or renewed in writing. Automatic extension or renewal clauses are prohibited in all agency agreements except for property management agreements that allow the landlord to terminate with notice at the end of any contract period.

Description of the property. All listing agreements should include a clear and precise description of the real estate to be sold. While the legal description does not have to be included for the listing agreement to be valid, it is always wise to do so to avoid confusion and ambiguity (Provision 2).

Note that in addition to the real property, all items of personal property that are to be included in the sale should be adequately described. Most listing agreements include a section (Provision 4) that lists the items of personal property that will be left with the real estate when it is sold and the items of real property (fixtures) the seller expects to remove at the time of sale (Provision 3). Each item should be explicitly identified (brand name, serial number, color), even though some items may become points of negotiation should a ready, willing, and able buyer be found. Examples of items to address in these provisions are major appliances, pool and spa equipment, fireplace accessories, storage sheds, stacked firewood, stored heating fuel, leased equipment, window hardware and treatments, et cetera.

Listing price. A listing agreement always should state the price the seller wants for the listed property (Provision 6). The other terms of the sale also should be included. For example, whether the price is to be paid in cash or financed is an important term. If the seller's mortgage cannot be assumed or if the seller refuses to offer any type of seller financing, then the seller must be paid in cash. Most buyers must get a mortgage loan in order to pay the seller cash, so the type of loan might be important to the seller because of loan requirements for the financed property. Remember, if the broker procures a buyer who is ready, willing, and able to purchase on the terms stated in the listing agreement, the broker will be deemed to have earned the commission whether or not the seller accepts the offer. For this reason, it is critical to clarify all terms of the listing, including acceptable sales price and how it will be paid.

Note that the listing price is the proposed gross sales price. The seller should understand that any outstanding obligations, such as unpaid real estate taxes, special assessments, and mortgage and trust deed debts, remain the seller's responsibility and must be paid from the proceeds of the sale unless otherwise contractually agreed to by the buyer.

Brokerage fee. The listing agreement must specify the compensation to be paid to the broker (Provision 7). The brokerage fee must be freely negotiable between the parties (therefore, it cannot be preprinted on a standard form). To comply with federal antitrust laws, real estate brokers cannot state or imply that the brokerage fee is set by law, by an MLS, or a Board of REALTORS®, nor can they state that it is the standard or customary fee. The agreement should also address the possibility of and the permission for additional compensation to the firm. As noted earlier, NCREC Rule A.0109 requires written notification to the client prior to making or receiving any offer if such a fortuitous situation arises. The NCAR Confirmation of Compensation form (see Appendix D, Form 12) has been created to satisfy this Rule requirement and is referenced in the listing agreement.

Brokerage fees can be calculated as a commission (a percentage of the gross sales price), a flat fee (a specific sum of money to be paid at some specified time), or a net amount. If the listing calls for a net fee, the agreement is referred to as a **net listing**. A net listing provision refers to the amount of money the seller will receive if the property is sold. The seller's property is listed for this net amount, and the broker is free to offer the property for sale at any price higher than the listing price. If the property is sold, the broker receives from the seller any proceeds exceeding the stipulated net amount to be retained by the seller. Although not illegal in North Carolina, *this type of listing is not recommended* because of an obvious conflict of interest. The question of fraud frequently is raised because of uncertainty over the sales price set or compensation received by the broker. The term *net amount* is often misunderstood and disputed. This type of listing is strongly discouraged.

> In North Carolina

Protection period clause. Some listing contracts contain an **override** or **extender clause** [Provision 7(b)(iii)], which provides that the property owner will pay the listing broker a commission if, within a specified number of days after the listing expires, the owner sells, rents, leases, or options the property to or exchanges the property with someone the owner originally met or made contact with through the broker. This clause protects the broker who introduces two parties and is the procuring cause of a sale, only to have the parties intentionally delay entering into a contract and complete the transaction after the listing expires. The override clause usually parallels the terms of the listing agreement; for example, a six-month listing might carry a broker protection clause of six months after the listing's expiration. To enforce this clause, the listing broker must provide the seller, within a specified time, the names of potential buyers who looked at the property during the listing period. However, to protect the owner and prevent owner liability for two separate commissions, most of these clauses stipulate that they cannot be enforced if the property is listed under a new listing agreement, either with the original listing broker or with another broker.

Authority to cooperate with other firms. Since the major advantages of belonging to a multiple listing service are the sharing of listed property information and the offer of shared agent compensation, it is critical that the seller-client understands and authorizes how other firms will be paid if they sell the listed property (Provision 8). Seller is cautioned about sharing confidential information with other brokers that might have to disclose that information to the buyer.

The listing agreement should also establish the listing firm's authority from the seller to cooperate with other real estate firms in the procurement of a buyer for the seller's property (Provision 8). The seller-client must also grant permission for the listing firm to compensate other firms through the sharing or splitting of the brokerage fee. Whether or not the listing firm and/or the seller-client will agree to cooperate with and compensate only other firms that represent the buyer or whether they will extend seller sub-agency to other firms is a very important issue. Since a principal may be held liable for the actions of their agent under the law of tort (mentioned in Chapter 7), there is potential for vicarious liability for the listing firm and seller-client due to the actions of the cooperating firm's brokers when they are acting as a subagent of the seller.

Firm's duties. The agreement should state the obligations the broker promises to fulfill (Provision 9). These include but are not limited to advertising, showing the property, submitting the listing information to an MLS, presenting all offers, and accounting for funds received on behalf of the seller. The broker should comply with the principles of the agency's fiduciary duties discussed in Chapter 7.

All brokerage services must be delivered without discriminatory practices or intentions. Brokers should always be conscious of performing brokerage activities in compliance with federal, state, and local fair housing laws, which will be covered in detail in Chapter 20. Inclusion of the following prescribed nondiscriminatory language is required in all agency agreements in North Carolina: "The agent shall conduct all brokerage activities in regard to this agreement without respect to the race, color, religion, sex, national origin, handicap or familial status of any party or prospective party." (Provision 9) All REALTOR®-approved agency contracts must also contain an additional sentence in the anti-discrimination statement: "Further, REALTORS® have an ethical duty to conduct such activities without respect to the sexual orientation of any party or prospective party to this agreement."

Broker also needs permission from the seller for certain marketing activities (Provision 10). For example, according to the terms of the agreement, will the broker be able to place a sign on the property? Advertise and market the property using the broker's best efforts? Submit the listing to an MLS? Show the property at reasonable times and on reasonable notice to the seller? Place a lockbox on the property? Advertise the property on the internet? Conduct an open house? Without written consent of the seller, the broker cannot undertake any such activities. If the seller does not wish to have the property advertised via the internet, which has become a prime advertising tool, they must opt-out of this service by signing an Internet Advertising Addendum (Appendix D, Form 4) and attaching it to the listing agreement.

Seller's representations and duties. Since the listing agreement is a bilateral contract, it should also state the obligations the seller promises to fulfill (Provision 12). These include completing the Residential Property and Owners' Association Disclosure Statement, unless the property is exempt from the Act (Appendix D, Form 5); complying with the Lead-Based Paint Hazard Reduction Act if the property was built prior to 1978 (Appendix D, Form 6); making the property available for showing; and cooperating with the firm in good faith. The seller is asked to disclose information concerning flood hazard potential, previous use of synthetic stucco, if the property is subject to an owner's association, existence of a termite bond, ownership and residency questions, and status of any liens against the property. The seller also is responsible for providing good, marketable title to convey the property and promises there are no circumstances to prevent that transfer. The seller should disclose any situation that might prevent conveyance of a clear title; and, if the property is subject to participation in a short sale, seller should complete the Short Sale Addendum (Appendix D, Form 3) as part of the listing agreement. Seller acknowledges receipt of sample copies of the Offer to Purchase and Contract and the Professional Services Disclosure and Election form (Appendix D, Form 8) for review purposes.

Handling of earnest money. The firm's policies for holding and crediting of any earnest money needs to be disclosed as well as the disbursement of any forfeited earnest money (Provision 11). Traditionally, the listing firm deposits any

In North Carolina earnest money offered with a sales contract into its trust account in accordance with NCREC rules. Any forfeited earnest money may be given in its entirety to the seller or split between the seller and the listing firm. This provision also addresses state statute regarding disposition of earnest money that is disputed between the seller and the buyer.

Dual agency. Seller should acknowledge receipt and review of the *Working with Real Estate Agents* brochure and address whether or not to authorize the practice of dual agency in any form (Provision 16). A concise review of the treatment of information and availability of advice from the listing agent during dual agency is noted. Authorization for the practice of dual agency or use of the designated agent option requires the seller's initials.

Miscellaneous provisions. Other provisions of the listing agreement address whether the seller authorizes a home inspection; and agreement for mediation in the event of a dispute between the firm and the seller. There also is a provision for customized terms or conditions to be included in the agreement. The seller can acknowledge receipt of several standardized informational brochures on various topics. At the end of the agreement, both the seller(s) and the agent of the firm must sign and share contact information. The broker also must include the broker's individual license number and agency status for NCREC Rule compliance.

In North Carolina

Due diligence by agent. Since the real estate broker is responsible for the disclosure of any material information regarding the property, it is important to get as much initial information from the seller as possible. It is important to discover what fixtures the seller plans to sever and keep as personal property and what personal property items the seller may be willing to leave. It is sometimes necessary to ask penetrating and possibly embarrassing questions to save both principal and agent from potential legal difficulties. It has become more crucial for brokers to determine the existence of liens due to the rising number of short sales and foreclosures in recent years. That a transaction will, or is likely to, involve lienholder approval is a material fact that must be disclosed. Identifying all parties with ownership interests can be challenging if there are deaths, divorces, and/or remarriages, so preliminary title searches are becoming more popular. If applicable, the seller must be informed of the seller's duty to give the buyer a property disclosure statement under the North Carolina Residential Property Disclosure Act, which is discussed later in this chapter. If the property is a residential structure built prior to 1978, the agent must also explain the requirement for lead-based paint disclosure. The agent should also gather such pertinent information as legal descriptions.

In North Carolina

The agent's duty to *discover and disclose* material facts, including defects in the property, begins with a thorough personal inspection of the property. Preliminary home inspections to determine the condition of the property and initiate needed repairs or improvements are becoming commonplace. It is also good business practice to use other sources to verify information provided by the seller, such as verifying land-use restrictions. In the listing of industrial, commercial, and agricultural properties, pertinent information may be extensive and detailed. A broker experienced in these areas would be best qualified to gather the information in a complete and accurate manner.

The agent should also collect copies of all of the seller's legal documents concerning the property, such as the deed and survey, and verify the following: (1) the seller's interest in the property, (2) any land-use restrictions that may apply, (3) the size (acreage or square feet) of the land, and (4) the square footage of all the buildings.

Determining Square Footage in North Carolina

In North Carolina, square footage is not considered a material fact that must be disclosed. However, the listing agent is traditionally expected to report the square footage of all buildings located on the listed property. Of primary importance is the residential dwelling. The square footage is normally reported as the *heated living area*, that is, the living area heated by the primary heating system. Measurements for heated living area are derived from exterior measurement to the extent possible. If interior measurements must be utilized, a broker should add six inches to include the exterior wall width. When measuring attached housing such as town houses, duplexes, and condominiums, additional measuring challenges may be encountered. Per the NCREC "Residential Square Footage Guidelines," a broker should add six inches for the common walls in town houses or duplexes, but add nothing for exterior walls in condos, since the unit does not include the exterior walls. Any deviations, alterations, or changes should be given special mention.

North Carolina Real Estate License Law does not require that brokers advertise or report the square footage, but if brokers do communicate square footage, the NCREC expects the information to be verifiable and accurate. There are several guidelines for measuring properties available that brokers may use. See Appendix B of this text for the North Carolina Real Estate Commission's "Residential Square Footage Guidelines." These guidelines or comparable guidelines should be used when calculating square footage. Such guidelines will assist a broker if a party to the transaction challenges their reported square footage. These guidelines contain specific procedures for measuring and reporting square footage, for which a broker would be held accountable by the NCREC.

Pricing the Property

Once a listing decision is secured and all necessary information obtained, the pricing of the real estate is of primary importance. It is the responsibility of the broker to advise and assist, but ultimately it is the *seller* who must determine the listing price for the property. Because the average seller does not usually have the background to make an informed decision about a fair market value, real estate brokers must be prepared to offer their knowledge, information, and expertise in this area.

A broker can help the seller determine a listing price for the property by means of a **comparative market analysis (CMA)**. Essentially, a CMA compares the prices of recently sold and/or listed properties that are similar in location, style, and amenities to the subject property. If no such comparisons can be made, or if the seller feels the property is unique in some way, a full-scale real estate appraisal—a detailed estimate of a property's value by a professional certified appraiser—may be warranted.

> A real estate broker performs a CMA to estimate probable sales price, whereas an appraiser would prepare a detailed full appraisal report.

> **MATH CONCEPTS**
>
> **CALCULATING SALES PRICES, COMMISSIONS, AND NETS TO SELLER**
>
> When a property sells, the sales price equals 100% of the money being transferred. Therefore, if a broker is to receive a 6% commission, 94% will remain for the seller's other expenses and equity. To calculate a commission using a sales price of $80,000 and a commission rate of 6%, multiply the sales price by the commission rate:
>
> $$\$80,000 \times 6\% = \$80,000 \times 0.06 = \$4,800 \text{ commission}$$
>
> To calculate a sales price using a commission of $4,550 and a commission rate of 7% (0.07 as a decimal), divide the commission by the commission rate:
>
> $$\$4,550 \div 7\% = \$4,550 \div 0.07 = \$65,000 \text{ sales price}$$
>
> To calculate a commission rate using a commission of $3,200 and a sales price of $64,000, divide the commission by the sales price:
>
> $$\$3,200 \div \$64,000 = 0.05 \text{ as a decimal} = 5\% \text{ commission rate}$$
>
> To calculate the net to the seller using a sales price of $85,000 and a commission rate of 8% (0.08 as a decimal), multiply the sales price by 100% minus the commission rate:
>
> $$\$85,000 \times (100\% - 8\%) = \$85,000 \times 92\% = \$78,200 \text{ net to seller}$$
>
> The same result could be achieved by calculating the commission ($85,000 × 0.08 = $6,800) and deducting it from the sales price ($85,000 − $6,800 = $78,200). However, this involves unnecessary extra calculations.
>
> Sales price × commission rate = commission
> Commission ÷ commission rate = sales price
> Commission ÷ sales price = commission rate
> Sales price × (100% − commission rate) = net to seller

Whether a CMA or formal appraisal is used, the figure sought is the subject property's market value. *Market value*, as will become clear in Chapter 17, is the most probable price the property will bring in an arm's-length transaction under normal conditions on the open market. A broker performing a CMA (sometimes called a *broker price opinion* or *BPO*) will estimate probable sales price as likely to fall within a range (for example, $135,000 to $140,000).

At this point, the agent should also prepare and give the seller an estimate of closing costs, which might help the seller establish the listing price. Although it is the property owner's privilege to set the asking price, a broker may reject any listing in which the price is substantially exaggerated. Once the listing price has been established, only this price can be quoted to a prospective buyer unless seller gives permission to share another price.

Chapter 9　Agency Contracts　**197**

■ THE NORTH CAROLINA RESIDENTIAL PROPERTY DISCLOSURE ACT

Property Disclosure Statement

> In North Carolina

The **North Carolina Residential Property Disclosure Act** requires that the sellers of most residential properties containing one to four units give the buyer a Residential Property and Owners' Association Disclosure Statement, if required (see Appendix D, Form 5). There are properties that are excluded from compliance with this Act. The most common exclusions that real estate brokers will encounter are new construction that has never been inhabited, foreclosure sales, and any rent-to-own scenarios. The statement must be given to the buyer *no later than the time the buyer makes an offer on the property.* The property disclosure statement may be included in the sales contract, in an addendum to the contract, or in a separate document. The form is a state-mandated form and must be used when required. No other form can be substituted. Additional forms may be used, however, such as a copy of a home inspection.

The statement includes disclosures about items relative to the condition of the property about which the owner has actual knowledge. In addition to existing questions about property condition, the property owner is asked if the property to be conveyed is subject to any *owners' associations and governing documents that impose various mandatory covenants, conditions, and restrictions upon the lot, including, but not limited to, obligations to pay regular assessments or dues and special assessments.* If the property owner answers "yes" to the existence of owners' associations or governing documents, the owner must answer the four remaining questions on the disclosure statement. The addition of these questions on the disclosure statement serve to address the majority of the information previously gathered on the Owners' Association Disclosure and Addendum (Appendix D, Form 7) to the standard NCAR/NCBA Offer to Purchase and Contract. This addendum has been revised to be used only for properties that are exempt from the Residential Property Disclosure Act. The Residential Property Disclosure Act also allows the owner to make no representations as to the condition of the property except as otherwise provided in the purchase and sale agreement. As befits a *caveat emptor* state, an owner who decides to make *no representation* as to the condition of the property has no duty to disclose those defects, whether or not the owner knows about them.

An amendment to the Residential Property Disclosure Act became effective on October 1, 2012. It requires mandatory seller disclosure language verbatim from the North Carolina statute about the status of oil and gas rights in sales contracts of all transactions subject to the act. (See Provision 7(f) of the NCBA/NCAR Standard Offer to Purchase and Contract.) Oil and gas rights disclosure is also required in two scenarios that are normally exempt under the act: (1) first sale of a dwelling that has never been inhabited and (2) transfers where parties have agreed to no property disclosure or owners' association disclosure. Despite *caveat emptor*, sellers are required to disclose whether they have severed or retained, or intend to sever or retain, any oil and gas rights from the interests transferred to buyers in the transaction. This disclosure information is requested from the sellers in the listing agreement to facilitate the sharing of the oil and gas rights status in the MLS.

If the property owner does not deliver the disclosure statement to the buyer prior to or at the time the purchaser makes an offer, the purchaser may cancel, or rescind, any resulting real estate contract. North Carolina G.S. 47E-5(b) addresses the buyer's right of rescission as follows:

> The purchaser's right to cancel shall expire if not exercised prior to the following, whichever occurs first:
> (1) The end of the third calendar day following the purchaser's receipt of the disclosure statement
> (2) The end of the third calendar day following the date the contract was made
> (3) Settlement or occupancy by the purchaser in the case of a sale or exchange
> (4) Settlement in the case of a purchase pursuant to a lease with option to purchase

If the buyer decides to rescind the sales contract, the buyer must give the seller written notice of the withdrawal within the three-day period. The buyer who exercises this rescission right is entitled to a full refund of any deposit monies given to the seller. The 2012 version of the standard Offer to Purchase and Contract (Appendix D, Form 13) clarifies that this refund of monies does include any paid due diligence fee.

■ **FOR EXAMPLE** A completed Residential Property and Owners' Association Disclosure Statement was *not* provided to the buyer prior to contract formation on the 15th. The seller provides the buyer with a completed disclosure statement on the 17th. If the buyer wishes to exercise the right to rescind the contract based solely on the seller's failure to timely provide the disclosure statement, the buyer must give written notice of rescission before midnight on the 18th. Contract formation on the 15th would be the starting point of the three-calendar-day deadline since it occurred prior to the late delivery of the statement on the 17th.

The disclosure statement should be kept accurate throughout the listing period. If, after the seller delivers the disclosure statement to the buyer, the disclosure statement is rendered inaccurate (or discovered to be inaccurate) in a material way, the seller must promptly deliver a corrected disclosure statement to the buyer. If the seller fails to deliver the corrected disclosure statement or fails to make any repairs necessary to make the original disclosure statement correct, the buyer may have a legal action for damages.

| In North Carolina |

Review of agent's responsibilities. Nondisclosure by the seller in no way relieves brokers from their *statutory duty to discover and disclose all material facts to all parties in the transaction.* As noted previously, the listing agent is responsible for informing the seller that it is the seller's responsibility to complete and provide the mandatory disclosure form to all prospective buyers. Although brokers are prohibited from actually completing the form, they can provide insight and advice to the seller. The broker should also assist the seller in providing a complete and up-to-date form to the buyer or their agent. It is common practice around the state for this disclosure form to be available in the listed property and/or as an additional page of information on the MLS listing. All brokers in the transaction,

Broker cannot complete the North Carolina Residential Property Disclosure Report for the seller.

■ WORKING WITH BUYERS

Like a listing agreement, a **buyer agency agreement** is an employment contract. In this case, the broker is employed as the *buyer's* agent—the buyer, rather than the seller, is the principal. The purpose of the agreement is to find a suitable property. An agency agreement gives the buyer a degree of representation possible only in a fiduciary relationship. A buyer's broker must protect the buyer's interests at all points in the transaction.

A number of issues must be discussed by a broker and a buyer before signing a buyer agency agreement. For instance, the broker should make the same disclosures to the buyer that the broker would make to a seller in a listing agreement. The licensee should explain the forms of agency available and the parties' rights and responsibilities under each type. The specific services provided to a buyer-client should be clearly explained. Compensation issues need to be addressed as well. Buyer's agents may be compensated in the form of a flat fee for services, an hourly rate, or a percentage of the purchase price. The agent may require a *retainer fee* at the time the agreement is signed to cover initial expenses. The retainer may be applied as a credit toward any fees due at the closing. A buyer's agent may be compensated by sharing the commission paid by the seller.

As in any agency agreement, the source of compensation does not determine the relationship. A buyer's agent may be compensated by either the buyer or the seller. Issues of compensation are always negotiable.

In North Carolina All buyer scenarios in North Carolina must start with a thorough explanation of agency relationship options no later than first substantial contact. Prospective buyers must receive a copy of the NCREC's *Working with Real Estate Agents* brochure and a review of agency options available with the broker's firm. A decision must be made as to what agency relationship will exist between the buyer consumer and the broker before the agent can provide *any* brokerage services to the buyer. Let us explore the different ways a broker can legally work with a buyer-consumer.

Working as a Seller's Subagent

In North Carolina If the buyer-consumer chooses not to be represented by any type of buyer agency, after proper review by the broker of all agency choices in the *Working with Real Estate Agents* brochure, the buyer must initial the "Disclosure of Seller Subagency" statement at the bottom of the brochure panel authorizing the broker to work as a seller's subagent. Assuming the seller will allow seller subagency in this situation, the broker is in a fiduciary relationship with the seller, not the buyer; therefore, the buyer should be very careful what information is shared with the broker who must communicate everything to the seller-client. The buyer-consumer should fully grasp the fact that while a broker acting as a seller's subagent must deal fairly and honestly with the buyer, this interaction falls far short of a buyer's agent's fiduciary relationship that must promote the buyer's best interest. If the buyer will not authorize buyer agency or seller subagency, the broker cannot continue to work with the buyer; there is no legal alternative.

In today's real estate practice, a listing firm and seller may refuse to offer seller subagency to other firms and only co-broker transactions with firms acting as a buyer's agent. The listings of such firms cannot be shown by a broker acting as a seller's subagent. The buyer-consumer would have to enter into a buyer agency agreement with the broker, at least for that property.

Switching from a seller's subagent to a buyer's agent. Sometimes a buyer-consumer may decide after working for a while with a broker as a seller's subagent that the buyer-consumer would like to switch to a buyer's agency relationship with the broker. Any confidential information about the seller-client learned by the agent while acting as a seller's subagent must be disclosed to the seller when asking for permission to change the agency relationship. Although this shift in agency allegiances can be done with the fully informed consent of the seller, it is strongly discouraged.

Working as a Buyer's Agent

Nonexclusive buyer-agency agreement. Under this type of buyer-agency contract (Appendix D, Form 10), the buyer does not have exclusive representation from one particular agent. The potential buyer is free to enter into other buyer-agency contracts with other brokers/firms. This also frees the buyer to view and purchase property through a seller's subagent or to purchase property directly from a property owner. Buyer will only be obligated to compensate the broker if the buyer's broker is the procuring cause of the purchase Buyer agent compensation under this type of contract may involve a retainer fee or success fee, as previously discussed.

[In North Carolina] **Oral buyer agency.** NCREC Rule A.0104(a) permits licensees to work initially as a buyer or tenant agent under an express *oral* buyer agency agreement. After proper review of agency options in the *Working with Real Estate Agents* brochure, a buyer/tenant consumer may wish representation but elect to postpone the execution of a written agency agreement. (Reminder: All agency agreements with property owners must be in writing from inception.) Minimally, the oral agreement should address issues of compensation and whether the client authorizes dual agency, if the situation arises. All oral buyer/tenant agency agreements must be *nonexclusive,* which means the client may work with other agents or independently and the relationship may be terminated by the agent or the client with notice at any time. Any oral agency agreement must, by NCREC Rule, be open-ended with no definite termination date. If the agent seeks to restrict the buyer/tenant's ability to work with other agents or to bind the client for a specified period, then the agreement must be in writing from the outset of the restricted relationship. Despite the legality of limited oral buyer/tenant agency use, written agency agreements are strongly preferred and should be secured as soon as possible. *At the latest,* an oral buyer/tenant agency agreement must be reduced to writing not later than the time any party to the transaction makes an offer to buy, sell, rent, lease, or exchange property to another. Virtually any written agency agreement will satisfy the Rule's requirement for written agency, whether the agreement is nonexclusive or limited to one particular property.

An agent shall *not* continue to act as a buyer or tenant agent if the client refuses to enter into a written agency agreement when required by the rule. If the client refuses to reduce the oral agency to writing, the only way the agent can go forward in the transaction is if the client will allow the agent to switch to acting as a seller's subagent. This change must be agreeable to the seller as well as the buyer. Such a shift in agency affiliation is strongly discouraged by the NCREC because the oral buyer agent is quite likely to have gathered confidential information about the buyer client while showing property. If the client will neither reduce agency to a written agreement nor authorize the agency switch to seller's subagent, a broker is forbidden to present any offers on behalf of the unrepresented buyer/tenant; despite Rule 58A.0106(a) that mandates timely presentation of all offers. Brokers cannot be forced to comply with a rule that will cause them to violate another rule or law. Brokers are strongly advised to refrain from drafting any offer until agency has been ratified.

All terms of the oral buyer/tenant agency agreement must be clearly understood by the broker and the client despite its verbal nature. The NCREC strongly recommends that the broker send the client a letter that confirms the terms of the verbal agreement, including dual agency authorization if approved. Termination of oral agency may be tendered verbally although follow-up written communication is recommended. Firms do not have to allow oral buyer/tenant agency; it is only an agency option.

Exclusive buyer-agency agreement. Under this type of buyer-agency contract, one broker/firm is selected by a potential buyer to represent him or her in the purchase of a property on an exclusive basis. The buyer agrees not to work with any other broker/firm in the purchase of a property. The employed broker is the *only real estate firm* with whom the buyer can work to locate and purchase property. When the buyer has signed an exclusive buyer-agency contract, all agents working for that firm become subagents of that buyer. The buyer, however, may not be restricted from buying directly from a property owner, but language in the contract can still require the buyer to pay the broker a success fee. Some buyers who are resistant to an exclusive agency agreement may be more willing to sign if the agreement is short in time duration (i.e., a day, two weeks, or a month) or limited to named properties. An exclusive buyer-agency agreement must be in writing from the formation of the exclusive agency. A buyer-agency agreement terminates automatically on the date stated in the agreement, unless renewed by that expiration date. It also terminates upon the closing of a purchase obtained by the buyer's agent. The Exclusive Buyer Agency Agreement (Appendix D, Form 9) is an example of an exclusive buyer-agency agreement.

In North Carolina

Buyer agent's responsibilities. A buyer's agent must

- give and review the *Working with Real Estate Agents* brochure with the buyer;
- explain agency duties and responsibilities;
- ensure that a proper agency contract is executed;
- properly qualify the prospective buyer/client;

- obtain and verify information about the property, including, if applicable, the Residential Property and Owners' Association Disclosure Statement, the Lead-based Paint Addendum, and the Owner Association Disclosure and Addendum...;
- disclose agency status to all parties to the transaction;
- discover and disclose material facts about the property;
- assist in the preparation, presentation, and negotiation of offers submitted by and on behalf of the buyer/client; and
- assist the buyer/client with preparation for closing the transaction.

Working With Sellers as a Buyer's Agent

Occasionally, a buyer-client is interested in a property that is not listed with a full service real estate firm. There are two scenarios that would necessitate a buyer's agent to contact the property owner directly: a for sale by owner (FSBO) or a property listed with a limited service real estate firm that directs all property inquiries to the property owner.

Working with an unrepresented seller. Commonly referred to in the real estate industry as a *FSBO*, an unrepresented seller might be willing to allow a buyer's agent to preview and/or show the property to the agent's buyer-client. As with most contacts with the public, the buyer's agent should provide the FSBO with a copy of the *Working with Real Estate Agents* brochure, discuss agency options, and disclose the agent's status as a buyer's agent. Brokers should be careful not to accidentally engage in undisclosed dual agency by providing service that could be construed as being on behalf of the seller. Even if buyer's agent will be compensated by the seller, the seller will not automatically be represented by the broker. Although unusual for the seller to want representation by the buyer's agent, dual agency could be created with written consent of both the seller and the buyer-client.

Working with seller listed with a limited service broker. Some sellers see the advantage of engaging a real estate firm to provide limited brokerage services, such as entry of the property for sale in the local multiple listing service (MLS). Some, but not all, limited service brokers will offer no buyer's agent compensation and direct all property inquiries to the property owner. Buyer's agents should not avoid showing such listings to their clients if the property represents a possible match for their clients' search parameters. Such avoidance could be viewed as a breach of fiduciary duties to buyer-client or as a antitrust boycott. Sellers, buyer's agents, and buyers would be wise to be very clear about compensation agreements before entering a transaction.

The Buyer Agency Agreement

> In North Carolina

Since all agency agreements must comply with NCREC Rules, there are many similarities between a seller's listing agreement and a **buyer agency agreement**. There are provisions dealing with similar issues such as duration of the agreement, broker's compensation, descriptions of the duties of the firm and the client, nondiscrimination clause, acknowledgement of receipt of agency disclosure brochure, and the possible practice of dual agency. There are, of course, several unique issues with buyer agency that need to be addressed in the agency agreement. The provisions that are substantially different from the listing agreement will be reviewed using the North Carolina Association of REALTORS® Exclusive Buyer Agency Agreement form (Appendix D, Form 9).

Type of property. Since the primary purpose of the buyer's agent is to help the buyer locate and purchase an acceptable property, it seems obvious that general property requirement parameters need to be established (Provision 1). These parameters may be very general, such as residential property within a specific county, or very specific, such as residential property that allows multiple horses within five miles of a major interstate road. The agreement may even be restricted to one specific property.

Other professional advice. Buyer is advised to seek professional advice as needed about different matters involved in a real estate purchase from subject matter experts, such as attorneys, surveyors, engineers, etc (Provision 10). Although the broker may provide suggestions of available subject matter experts, the buyer agrees not to hold the broker/firm responsible for the buyer's selection of advisors or the actions of the advisors. Buyer acknowledges receipt of multiple standard publications for review and educational purposes.

Confidentiality issues. Unless otherwise noted in the agency agreement, the buyer authorizes the broker to disclose the buyer's name(s) as necessary (Provision 7). The buyer also is advised that although brokers are prohibited from disclosing terms of any offer without the express permission of the offering party, the seller is under no such restriction (Provision 12).

■ WORKING AS A DUAL AGENT

Dual Agency

Dual agency involves serving as the agent for two or more parties with adverse interests in the same transaction. A real estate brokerage firm whose policy allows dual agency, electing to represent both the buyer(s) and the seller(s) in the same transaction, must use a written dual agency agreement—no later than the making of the first offer—to modify existing relationships that were created when entering into either a listing contract or a buyer-agency contract. The most recent versions of the listing and buyer-agency agreements have the dual agency agreement incorporated into the form.

IN PRACTICE Firms practicing dual agency will normally require that their brokers, when entering into either a listing agreement or a buyer's agreement, have the client (buyer or seller) authorize dual agency in the agency agreement. This meets the requirement for written informed consent and ideally should be obtained when the agency relationship is established. The dual agency provision basically gives a blanket authorization for dual agency, if needed later in the transaction.

The dual agency authorization in the standard agency agreements contains:

- Provisions for agreeing to dual agency;
- The Broker's role as a dual agent;
- The Seller's and the Buyer's roles; and
- Provisions for the option of designated dual agency.

As discussed in Chapter 7, if the listing firm also represents the buyer in the purchase transaction, a dual agency situation exists that requires fair and balanced treatment of both clients. Dual agency exists whether only one or multiple firm brokers are involved because the firm is the agent of record. The dual agency provisions on all North Carolina Association of REALTORS® agency agreements seek to modify and limit the duties of the agent to the principals. Both of the firm's clients are responsible for making their own decisions during the transaction. When acting as a traditional dual agent, the firm's brokers typically are absolved by the language in the dual agency agreement from sharing confidential information about either party with the other as would be required under common law agency fiduciary duties. Dual agents must still discover and disclose all material facts but not personal information, which does not affect contract performance by either client.

A dual agency agreement can be drafted by an attorney to create dual agency and provide written informed consent if written agency has not been previously entered into by the respective parties to be represented by the broker. Such an agreement is required when a broker brings together a potential buyer and a potential seller in hopes of negotiating a successful transaction, but neither party has signed any agency agreement with the broker.

■ RELATED WEBSITES

National Do Not Call Registry: www.donotcall.gov
North Carolina Department of Justice: No Calls NC: www.nocallsnc.com

■ KEY POINT REVIEW

A **listing agreement** is an **employment contract** between a broker and a seller that clarifies the obligations of each party. In North Carolina, the listing agreement

- must be in writing pursuant to rule,
- must be signed by all parties,
- must include the broker's license number,
- must have a definite termination date,
- must contain the non-discrimination clause, and
- may be terminated when
  — the agreement's purpose is fulfilled,
  — the agreement's term expires,
  — the property is destroyed,
  — title to the property is transferred by operation of law (e.g., bankruptcy),
  — the broker and the seller mutually agree to end the listing,
  — either party dies or becomes mentally incapacitated, or
  — either the broker or the seller breaches the contract.

As an agent, the broker is authorized to represent the principal and the principal's real estate to consumers. A provisional broker is a general agent of the broker and can carry out listing services only in the name of and under the supervision of the broker-in-charge.

Do-not-call legislation is found at federal and state levels:

- The **National Do Not Call Registry** (regulated by the Federal Trade Commission)
    — lists telephone numbers of consumers who have asked to be registered and
    — prohibits interstate calls to those numbers to sell goods or services.
- Many states, including North Carolina, provide their own do-not-call legislation for in-state calls.

Broker's entitlement to commission (once a ready, willing, and able buyer is procured) survives if the seller

- has a change of mind and refuses to sell,
- has a spouse who refuses to sign the deed,
- has a title with uncorrected defects,
- commits fraud with respect to the transaction,
- is unable to deliver possession within a reasonable time,
- insists on terms not in the listing (for example, the right to restrict the use of the property), or
- has a mutual agreement with the buyer to cancel the transaction.

In an **open listing**,

- the seller retains the right to employ any number of brokers;
- the seller is obligated to pay a commission only to the broker who successfully produces a **ready, willing, and able buyer**; and
- the seller is not obligated to pay a commission if the seller personally sells the property without the aid of any broker.

An **exclusive-agency listing**

- authorizes one broker to act as the sole agent of the seller, but
- allows the seller to retain the right to sell the property without obligation of payment to the broker.

In an **exclusive right-to-sell listing**:

- One broker is appointed as the seller's sole agent.
- If the property is sold while the listing is in effect, the broker is entitled to a commission, no matter who sells the property.

A **net listing** has the following characteristics:

- The excess over the net from the sale will go to the listing broker as commission.
- The broker is free to offer the property at any price greater than the net amount.
- Net listings are strongly discouraged as a matter of policy in North Carolina.

A **protection agreement** guarantees compensation if a particular property is sold to a specific buyer.

Broker's compensation with a principal must be agreed upon before an agency relationship is established and can be a commission based on sales price, flat fee, or hourly rate:

Fee-for-services agreement, or limited services agreement, is based on charges for separate broker activities that the client desires (unbundling of services). Some states (not North Carolina) now require minimum services to be offered by the broker.

Entitled to compensation means that an individual must be

- an actively licensed real estate broker,
- employed by a client under a valid written agency contract, and
- the **procuring cause** of the sale by starting or causing a chain of events that resulted in the sale.

The commission is earned when the seller accepts an offer from ready, willing, and able buyer prepared to buy on the seller's terms and ready to take positive steps toward consummation of the transaction.

Antitrust laws are both state and federal (Sherman Antitrust Act) that prohibit

- monopolies; and
- contracts, combinations, and conspiracies that unreasonably restrain trade, including
  — **price fixing**;
  — group boycotting;
  — allocation of customers or markets; and
  — tie-in agreements (tying agreements) forcing customers to purchase a product when only another was wanted.

A **multiple-listing clause** permits cooperation with other brokers in the multiple listing service (MLS).

Due diligence by agent should discover and voluntarily disclose material facts about the property to all parties to the transaction.

Square footage is not a material fact in North Carolina but if represented, it must be correct. Heated living area is calculated using exterior measurements.

North Carolina Residential Property Disclosure Act requirements include

- most residential sellers (including for-sale-by-owners) to provide a completed Disclosure Statement to prospective buyers prior to presentation of first offer;
- exempted properties include new construction, bank-owned foreclosures, and lease options;
- seller may choose to mark no representation because of *caveat emptor* doctrine;
- statement must be accurate at all times;
- possible three-calendar-day rescission period from contract formation or late delivery of the statement, whichever occurs first, for noncompliance;

- broker not allowed to complete statement, but to facilitate delivery; and
- broker must discover and disclose material facts regardless of seller's representation on the statement.

When working with buyers as a seller's subagent,

- the buyer must initial the disclosure of seller subagency on acknowledgment panel of *Working with Real Estate Agents*, and
- the seller and listing firm must be willing to allow subagency.

When working with buyers as a buyer's agent,

- the buyer agency agreement (the employment contracts between a broker and a buyer) must be in writing prior to presentation of first offer,
- in a nonexclusive buyer agency (as an oral or written agreement), the agent is in competition for compensation with other agents and the buyer-client,
- in an exclusive buyer agency, compensation is owed regardless of how property is found, and
- the buyer's agent is working directly with the seller in a FSBO or a limited service listing firm scenario requires agency disclosure and confirmation prior to showing property.

When working with buyers as a dual agent,

- the agent/firm represents the buyer and seller in the same transaction with permission, and
- all standard dual agency agreements modify the exclusive agent's duties.

North Carolina Oil and Gas Rights Disclosure

- is required in all sales contracts of transactions subject to the Residential Property Disclosure Act, plus first sale of a dwelling that has never been inhabited and transfers where parties have agreed to no property disclosure or owners' association disclosure,
- is mandatory disclosure language verbatim from North Carolina statute, and
- requires sellers to disclose the status of oil and gas rights being transferred to buyers.

QUESTIONS

1. In North Carolina, a listing agreement
   a. can allow automatic renewal until either party gives notice.
   b. with an override clause protects the listing firm's commission in all situations for the prescribed time period.
   c. is allowed to be oral prior to presentation of an offer.
   d. is required by North Carolina License Law to be written from formation.

2. How are an exclusive-agency listing and an exclusive right-to-sell listing alike?
   a. The seller retains the right to sell the real estate without the broker's help and without paying the broker a commission.
   b. The seller authorizes only one particular agent to show the property.
   c. The responsibility of representing the seller is given to one broker only.
   d. There is no similarity between the two listing types.

3. All of the following would terminate a listing EXCEPT
   a. expiration of the contract period.
   b. death or incapacity of the seller.
   c. nonpayment of the commission by the seller.
   d. destruction of the improvements on the property.

4. The parties to the listing contract are the
   a. seller and the buyer.
   b. seller and the broker.
   c. buyer and the broker.
   d. broker and the MLS.

5. A listing taken by a real estate broker belongs to the
   a. firm.
   b. seller.
   c. agent.
   d. agent and firm equally.

6. A seller's residence is listed with a broker, and the seller stipulates that she wants to receive $85,000 from the sale, but the broker can sell the property for as much as possible and keep the difference as the commission. The broker agrees. This is what type of listing?
   a. Exclusive right to sell
   b. Exclusive agency
   c. Open listing
   d. Net listing

7. A real estate commission rate is set by the
   a. local real estate board.
   b. North Carolina Real Estate Commission.
   c. principal and the agent.
   d. local multiple listing service.

8. In a sales transaction, which of the following statements is/are *TRUE* of a listing agreement?
   I. It must be in writing to be legal and enforceable.
   II. It requires the seller to sell the property if terms of an offer match the terms in the listing.
   a. I only
   b. II only
   c. Both I and II
   d. Neither I nor II

9. A listing contract contains a clause that gives the broker the right to collect a commission after the listing contract terminates if the owner sells the property to someone the broker introduced to the property. This is what type of clause?
   a. Extender
   b. Subordination
   c. Exclusivity
   d. Procurement

10. A broker listed a property at an 8% commission rate. After the sale closed, the seller discovered that the broker had been listing similar properties at a 7% commission rate. Based on this information, which of the following statements is/are TRUE?
    I. The broker has violated antitrust laws.
    II. The seller can cancel the listing agreement without penalty.
    a. I only
    b. II only
    c. Both I and II
    d. Neither I nor II

11. A broker gets a commission if her listed property is sold, no matter who sells it, if she used what type of listing agreement?
    a. Net
    b. Open
    c. Exclusive agency
    d. Exclusive right to sell

12. Under the North Carolina Residential Property Disclosure Act, the seller must
    I. provide a completed property disclosure form to the buyer before the buyer makes an offer.
    II. disclose all known property defects on the mandatory form.
    a. I only
    b. II only
    c. Both I and II
    d. Neither I nor II

13. Which of the following statements is NOT true about the North Carolina Residential Property Disclosure Act?
    a. If the form is not provided per the statute, the buyer may be able to cancel any resulting contract.
    b. If the seller marks *No Representation* on the form, the agent is relieved of their duty to discover and disclose material facts.
    c. If the buyer rescinds the contract within the allowed time period, all deposit monies will be refunded to the buyer.
    d. Act compliance is required of the seller even if there is no real estate broker involved in the transaction.

14. The seller has signed a listing agreement with a listing firm that authorizes the listing firm to collect a 6% commission. According to company policy, the firm offers 40% of the total commission to any cooperating broker that sells the listing. If another firm sells the listing for $125,000, what commission amount will the listing firm retain?
    a. $3,000
    b. $4,500
    c. $5,000
    d. $7,500

15. A listing agent received $4,287.50 as her portion of the commission earned on the sale of her listing. She received 70% of the commission retained by the listing firm. The firm split the 5% listing commission equally with the selling firm. What was the sales price of the property?
    a. $245,000
    b. $171,500
    c. $122,500
    d. $120,000

16. Two firms split a 6 percent commission equally on a $73,000 home. The selling agent was paid 70 percent of his broker's share. The listing agent was paid 30 percent of her broker's share. How much did the listing agent receive?
    a. $657
    b. $1,314
    c. $1,533
    d. $4,380

17. A house recently sold for $135,000 at a commission rate of 6.5 percent. The MLS service got 5 percent of the commission as a listing fee. The listing broker got 40 percent of the commission with 55 percent going to the selling broker. You, the selling agent, have an in-house split of 60 percent to you, 40 percent to your broker. What was your earned commission?
    a. $1,930.50
    b. $2,106.00
    c. $2,750.96
    d. $2,895.75

18. A recent in-house sale generated a gross commission of $2,000. The listing agent received 2 percent of the sales price, the listing firm received 5 percent of the sales price, and the selling agent received 3 percent of the sales price. How much in dollars did the listing agent, the firm, and selling agent, respectively, receive for this transaction?
    a. $200, $800, $1,000
    b. $400, $1,000, $600
    c. $500, $1,000, $500
    d. None of the above

19. A seller needs $120,000 to pay off their mortgage loan and $1,000 for other closing expenses, plus he would like to net $50,000 to use to purchase his next home. If the listing firm charges a 5% listing fee, what is the minimum sales price that will meet these requirements?
    a. $162,450
    b. $171,000
    c. $179,550
    d. $180,000

20. The seller wants to net $85,000 cash from the sales transaction. The sales commission is 7%, the seller's closing costs are $1,000, and the seller's loan payoff figure is $65,000. What must the sales price be to accomplish the seller's goal?
    a. $151,000
    b. $155,000
    c. $161,750
    d. $162,366

21. In North Carolina, the transferability of the oil and gas rights to the buyer in a residential transaction is
    a. the sole responsibility of the buyer to determine during the due diligence period of the contract.
    b. a required seller disclosure that must be included in most residential sales contracts.
    c. not a required disclosure for new construction sales.
    d. included in the seller-completed Residential Property Disclosure Report.

CHAPTER 10

Sales Contracts and Practices

■ **LEARNING OBJECTIVES** *When you have finished reading this chapter, you should be able to*

- ■ **determine** when a contract has been formed and explain how to handle modifications and counteroffers.
- ■ **identify** the purpose of the Uniform Electronic Transactions Act.
- ■ **describe** all required provisions of a sales contract and be able to determine when certain addenda are required.
- ■ **explain** the features and uses of the installment land contract.
- ■ **define** the following *key terms:*

acceptance	offer	preemptive right
backup offer	offeree	right of first opportunity to purchase
contingency	offeror	
due diligence	option	right of first refusal
installment land contract	optionee	Uniform Electronic Transaction Act (UETA)
mailbox rule	optionor	

■ THE SALES CONTRACT

A *real estate sales contract* sets forth *all* details of the agreement between a buyer and a seller for the purchase and sale of a parcel of real estate. Depending on the state or locality, this agreement may be known as *an offer to purchase, a contract of purchase and sale, a purchase agreement, an earnest money agreement, a deposit receipt,* or another variation of these titles. In North Carolina the most common title is Offer to Purchase and Contract.

In North Carolina

Whatever the form is called, when it has been prepared and signed by the purchaser, it is an offer to purchase the subject real estate. Later, if the document is accepted and signed by the seller, it becomes, or *ripens into*, a contract of sale. The most commonly used sales contract in North Carolina is the Standard Form 2-T Offer to Purchase and Contract (Appendix D, Form 13) approved jointly by the North Carolina Association of REALTORS® (NCAR) and the North Carolina Bar Association (NCBA). There are several additional sales contract forms that have been promulgated by the NCAR/NCBA Joint Forms Task Force: one for the sale of vacant lot or land (Appendix D, Form 14), one for new construction sales, and one for commercial sales transactions. Brokers are expected to know which standard form is appropriate for a given scenario and when it is appropriate to refer a consumer to an attorney to have a suitable contract drafted. Remember that North Carolina real estate brokers are legally allowed to fill in the blanks on a standard contract form but are prohibited from drafting contract provisions because that would constitute the unlawful practice of law. The standard NCAR forms and guidelines for completion are accessible as sample forms to the general public on NCAR's website, www.ncliving.net. The provisions in the Standard 2-T Offer to Purchase and Contract (OPC) and some of the most used standard addenda will be discussed in depth later in this chapter.

Any preprinted offer-to-purchase form offered for use by a real estate broker in North Carolina must meet the provisions and standards of Rule A.0112 of the North Carolina Real Estate Commission (NCREC) (see Figure 10.1). In addition to the 19 mandated entries of information, two informational provisions are prohibited in any preprinted offer to purchase: (1) any discussion of brokerage compensation and (2) any attempt to disclaim brokerage liability in connection with the transaction. The inclusion of either provision has no place in a contract between the buyer and the seller.

IN PRACTICE NCREC Rule A.0112 outlines the provisions that must appear in any preprinted offer to purchase and contract form suggested for use in North Carolina by real estate brokers. License law strictly prohibits real estate brokers from drafting sales contracts that bind other people. The NCREC does not create or approve contract forms. The contract forms used in this textbook are NCAR standard forms that have been jointly approved by NCBA and NCAR and are utilized in most residential sales transactions in North Carolina.

The contract of sale is the most important document in the sale of real estate because it sets the terms of the agreement between buyer and seller and establishes each party's legal rights and obligations.

Every sales contract requires at least two parties—a seller (the vendor) and a buyer (the vendee). The same person cannot be both buyer and seller because a person cannot legally contract with himself or herself. *The contract of sale is the most important document in the sale of real estate* because it sets the parameters of the agreement between the buyer and the seller and establishes their legal rights and obligations. It is more important than the deed itself because *the contract*, in effect, *dictates the contents of the deed.*

Issues to be addressed in a real estate sales contract are price, terms, legal description of the property, kind and condition of the title, form of deed the seller will deliver, kind of title evidence required, who will provide title evidence, and how defects in the title, if any, are to be eliminated. The contract must state all the terms of the agreement and spell out all **contingencies** and/or conditions.

FIGURE 10.1   **Rule A.0112**

A.0112 Offers and Sales Contracts

(a) A broker acting as an agent in a real estate transaction shall not use a preprinted offer or sales contract form unless the form describes or specifically requires the entry of the following information:

   (1) the names of the buyer and seller;

   (2) a legal description of the real property sufficient to identify and distinguish it from all other property;

   (3) an itemization of any personal property to be included in the transaction;

   (4) the purchase price and manner of payment;

   (5) any portion of the purchase price that is to be paid by a promissory note, including the amount, interest rate, payment terms, whether or not the note is to be secured, and other material terms;

   (6) any portion of the purchase price that is to be paid by the assumption of an existing loan, including the amount of such loan, costs to be paid by the buyer or seller, the interest rate and number of discount points and a condition that the buyer must be able to qualify for the assumption of the loan and must make every reasonable effort to qualify for the assumption of the loan;

   (7) the amount of earnest money, if any, the method of payment, the name of the broker or firm that will serve as escrow agent, an acknowledgment of earnest money receipt by the escrow agent, and the criteria for determining disposition of the earnest money, including disputed earnest money, consistent with Commission Rule .0107 of this Subchapter;

   (8) any loan that must be obtained by the buyer as a condition of the contract, including the amount and type of loan, interest rate and number of discount points, loan term, and who shall pay loan closing costs; and a condition that the buyer shall make every reasonable effort to obtain the loan;

   (9) a general statement of the buyer's intended use of the property and a condition that such use must not be prohibited by private restriction or governmental regulation;

   (10) the amount and purpose of any special assessment to which the property is subject and the responsibility of the parties for any unpaid charges;

   (11) the date for closing and transfer of possession;

   (12) the signatures of the buyer and seller;

   (13) the date of offer and acceptance;

   (14) a provision that title to the property must be delivered at closing by general warranty deed and must be fee simple marketable title, free of all encumbrances except ad valorem taxes for the current year, utility easements, and any other encumbrances specifically approved by the buyer, or a provision otherwise describing the estate to be conveyed, and encumbrances, and the form of conveyance;

   (15) the items to be prorated or adjusted at closing;

   (16) who shall pay closing expenses;

   (17) the buyer's right to inspect the property prior to closing and who shall pay for repairs and improvements, if any;

   (18) a provision that the property shall at closing be in substantially the same condition as on the date of the offer (reasonable wear and tear excepted), or a description of the required property condition at closing, and

   (19) a provision setting forth the identity of each real estate agent and firm involved in the transaction and disclosing the party each agent and firm represents.

(b) A broker acting as an agent in a real estate transaction shall not use a preprinted offer or sales contract form containing the provisions or terms listed in Subparagraphs (b)(1) and (2) of this Rule. A broker or anyone acting for or at the direction of the broker shall not insert or cause such provisions or terms to be inserted into any such preprinted form, even at the direction of the parties or their attorneys:

   (1) any provision concerning the payment of a commission or compensation, including the forfeiture of earnest money, to any broker or firm, or

   (2) any provision that attempts to disclaim the liability of a broker for his representations in connection with the transaction.

(c) The provisions of this Rule shall apply only to preprinted offer and sales contract forms which a broker acting as an agent in a real estate transaction proposes for use by the buyer and seller. Nothing contained in this Rule shall be construed to prohibit the buyer and seller in a real estate transaction from altering, amending or deleting any provision in a form offer to purchase or contract; nor shall this Rule be construed to limit the rights of the buyer and seller to draft their own offers or contracts or to have the same drafted by an attorney at law.

Source: Reproduced with permission of the North Carolina Real Estate Commission.

In situations where a contract is vague or ambiguous in its terms and one party sues the other based on one of these terms, the courts may refuse to enforce a contract for the parties. The real estate broker must be aware that the responsibilities and legal rights of the parties to a sale are governed by the terms of the contract that must be adequately prepared.

Contracts in Writing

In North Carolina

The statute of frauds provides that no action may be brought on any contract for the sale of real estate unless the contract is in writing and signed by the parties to be bound by the agreement. The offer to purchase and contract, therefore, must be in writing to be enforceable. The written requirement has encountered some new interpretations in recent years. In the year 2000, the General Assembly enacted North Carolina's version of the federal *E-sign* legislation, **Uniform Electronic Transactions Act (UETA)**, that addresses electronic commerce which clearly includes real estate transactions. Under the scope of this Act, contracts can be created by electronic means such as email and faxes. Also of major importance for the real estate industry is that under the legislation, an electronic signature is binding. The statute defines an electronic signature as "an electronic sound, symbol, or process attached to, or logically associated with, a record and executed or adopted by a person with the intent to sign the record." Therefore, a faxed signature on an offer or contract will probably be just as effective as ink on paper.

The Offer and Acceptance

One of the essential elements of a contract being formed (discussed in Chapter 8) was that of *mutual assent* or *deliberate agreement*. To form a valid real estate sales contract there must be an *offer* made, an *acceptance* of that offer, and communication of the acceptance to the other party (the offeror).

The offer.   Anyone who makes an **offer** to purchase property is known as the **offeror**—the person making the offer. Anyone who receives an offer is known as the **offeree**.

■ **FOR EXAMPLE** Betty signs an offer on Sam's house. Her buyer agent presents the offer to the listing agent. At this point Betty is the offeror, and Sam is the offeree.

In the previous example, a contract is not yet formed; there is merely an offer to buy that has been made by an offeror to an offeree. Those preparing an offer must make certain there are no ambiguities with respect to the language or construction of the offer because the intent of the offer is to bind the parties when it is accepted. An offer must be definite and precise in its terms; it cannot be of an illusory or deceptive nature. Mere advertisements of a property for sale do not constitute an offer, nor does the typical listing contract constitute an offer. Preliminary negotiations also do not constitute an offer.

Many times an offer may contain conditions and/or contingencies. In other words, the offeror is saying to the offeree, "This is my offer, if the following conditions or contingencies can be met."

■ **FOR EXAMPLE** Betty, in the previous example, made her offer contingent on her ability to obtain a permit to install an in-ground pool. If zoning prohibits an in-ground pool on the property under contract, even after contract formation, Betty is relieved from the terms of the contract.

The acceptance. For an offer to become a binding contract, it must be communicated to and accepted by the offeree according to the exact terms and conditions of the offer. An **acceptance** occurs when the offeree signs the offer without making any changes to it, thereby evidencing his acceptance and willingness to be bound by and perform all terms of the offer. If an acceptance of exact terms and conditions takes place (mirror-image) and that acceptance is properly communicated back to the offeror, a binding contract is formed. If the offeree changes *any* terms or conditions of the offer, no matter how slight or small, an acceptance does not take place; instead a counteroffer has been made. Any earnest money that was presented with the offer to purchase must be handled in accordance with NCREC Rule A.0107. If no contract is ever formed, the full earnest money is returned to the offeror.

> In North Carolina

> A counteroffer rejects the original offer and constitutes a new offer, not a revision of the original offer.

The counteroffer. As discussed in Chapter 8, when the offeree receives the offer and makes any change to that offer, it constitutes a counteroffer, which is a rejection of the first offer. When the counteroffer takes place, the original offer cannot be revived. The offeree also cannot later reconsider and *accept* the original offer. *It has been rejected; it no longer exists.*

■ **FOR EXAMPLE** When Betty made her offer, she entered $100,000 as the purchase price. Sam changed the purchase price to $105,000 with a pen and ink change, dated and initialed the change and signed the form as the seller. At this time, Sam becomes the offeror, making a new offer back to Betty, who is now the offeree. Once this new offer is communicated to Betty, if she accepts it by initialing and dating the change to the form, she has accepted the offer from Sam. When her acceptance is properly communicated to Sam, a contract has been formed.

If Betty changes the $105,000 to $103,000 and initials and dates the change, a counter-counteroffer has taken place. Betty is once again the offeror and Sam is once again the offeree. This process of countering the previous offer can continue for an indefinite period until total agreement between parties has been reached.

Methods of Communicating Offers and Acceptance

There are various ways that offers and acceptance may be communicated. Probably the most common and the most acceptable way is to communicate in writing; the offeror signs the written offer and communicates it to the offeree, and the offeree signs the written offer, denoting acceptance. When the acceptance is properly communicated back to the offeror, a contract is formed.

Communication of the acceptance to the offeror may be either oral—by telephone, voice mail, or in person—or by personal delivery of the written acceptance by the offeree or by another person on behalf of the offeree. Communication to either party's agent is deemed communication to that party.

Traditional, special, or electronic mail are acceptable ways to communicate an offer or an acceptance. If an acceptance is placed into the mail service to the other party or that party's agent, it is considered as having been delivered when mailed, not necessarily when actually received; this is known as the **mailbox rule.** The parties cannot revoke the offer once the acceptance is mailed because it is now a contract. The telegraph and telegram are other means of communicating an acceptance, although they are seldom used today in the real estate business. Facsimiles (fax machine, email, telecopier, etc.) are acceptable means of communicating offer and acceptance. Acceptance of an offer becomes complete, and a contract is formed, when communication of acceptance is received by the offeror's communication device. This form of communicating the offer and acceptance is commonplace in the real estate business. Mailbox rule is only effective to create a contract.

Termination of Offers

There are several ways to terminate an offer (remember that an offer is not a contract, which is terminated in other ways). Termination of offers can take place

- if the offeree rejects the offer and/or creates a counteroffer;
- if the offeree fails to accept within the prescribed time stipulated in the offer;
- within a reasonable time, if a time of acceptance is not prescribed;
- prior to acceptance, if the offeror communicates a revocation of the offer; or
- by the death of the offeror or offeree.

In North Carolina — Major Contract Provisions of NCAR/NCBA Standard Form 2-T

All real estate sales contracts can address the vast array of issues related to a typical real estate sales transaction. The major contract provisions of the NCBA/NCAR Standard Form 2-T (OPC) should be well understood by all North Carolina real estate brokers since it is used in the majority of all residential sales transactions in the state. The form is located in Appendix D as Form 13.

Terms and definitions. Paragraph 1 of the OPC is basically a two-page dictionary of most of the major terms utilized in the contract. With rare exception, any capitalized term found later in the contract will be a defined term that first appeared in Paragraph 1.

Names. (Para. 1a and b) It is essential to identify *all* the parties to the contract by their full individual names, which includes a full first and last name plus a middle initial if available and any suffix, such as Sr. or Jr. Spouses should be identified by individual legal names, not as Mr. and Mrs. The NCREC has little patience with a broker that uses the term *owner of record* to identify the property owners because the seller's name can be easily ascertained by various sources including the listing agent or tax records. If a party to the contract is a business entity, be sure to use the complete *legal* name versus a trade name. If the property to be sold is part of an estate sale, all heirs and spouses must be named individually as sellers unless one individual has the power to sell through an executed power of attorney. Although ill-advised due to potential legal liability, a buyer's agent can be named as *agent for an undisclosed principal* if the buyer wishes to remain anonymous.

Property. (Para. 1c) A legal description of the property that would distinguish it from all other property is necessary to create an enforceable contract for sale. Street address is helpful but usually not adequate for a binding legal description. Brokers should complete all possible blanks in this section to maximize the ability to identify the property without question. Although used alone by many veteran brokers, the parcel identifier number (PIN or PID) and the tax map reference number seldom provide an adequate description. Arguably the most reliable source for the best legal description is the seller's deed that is public record.

Purchase price. (Para. 1d) The amount to be paid for the property may be only slightly more material to the parties than when the amount is due and how it will be paid. The total purchase price may be comprised of several smaller amounts paid prior to settlement, such as due diligence fee, initial or additional earnest money, assumption of seller's loan, seller financing, or building deposit. Any outstanding balance is to be paid in *cash* at settlement. If any of the funds paid by the buyer are dishonored, the buyer will have one banking day after written request from the seller to provide cash or immediately available funds or the seller has the unilateral right to terminate the contract. Brokers are cautioned to make sure that the total of the amounts entered on lines 2 through 8 equal the amount on the first line.

Earnest money. (Para. 1e) While earnest money is not an essential element of a valid contract, it is unusual for a seller to accept an offer to purchase that does not require an earnest money deposit as an indication of the buyer's good faith. An argument for a substantial deposit is that earnest money will be credited toward the purchase price if the buyer goes forward with the purchase, and it is the seller's *sole and exclusive remedy* for a breach by the buyer after the expiration of the due diligence period. Earnest money deposit is defined as including both initial and any additional earnest money. While initial earnest money may be paid in several ways including personal bank check, earnest money that comes at a later date must be *immediately available funds such as official bank check or wire transfer* by a *time is of the essence* date. If the parties insist on suing each other for the earnest money, the party that loses the lawsuit will have to pay the attorney fees and legal costs of the winning party as well as the party's own expense of the suit.

[margin note: aka "Liquidated Damages"]

Escrow agent. (Para. 1f) The escrow agent identified by name to hold the earnest money in trust is usually a real estate firm, a title company, or an attorney. It is tradition that the listing firm act as escrow agent, but other arrangements are not unusual. The real estate firm's name should be entered as escrow agent, not the name of the individual broker within the firm. If earnest money is paid by check, the check should be made payable to firm serving as escrow agent with a note on the check's memo line as to the purpose of the funds. Escrow agent can sign for receipt of initial earnest money on page 10 of the OPC.

The handling of trust money, such as earnest money, is strictly regulated by North Carolina License Law and NCREC Rule 58A.0107. Earnest money must be deposited in a trust account held in an insured bank or savings and loan association legally conducting business in North Carolina within three banking days of contract formation. The funds can be deposited sooner if the escrow agent so chooses. The account can be interest-bearing according to the language in this paragraph. If the offer never matures into a contract, earnest money must be returned to the buyer. Once a contract is achieved, the disbursement of the earnest money is clearly determined by the terms of the OPC. If parties dispute how the funds should be disbursed, the escrow agent is prohibited from making an independent decision on who is to receive the funds. The only ways to resolve the disputed funds issues are parties agree in writing on how to disburse funds, court rules in lawsuit, or with written 90-day notice to the parties by the escrow agent, funds can be transferred to Clerk of Superior Court of the county in which the property is located.

Effective date. (Para. 1g) The effective date, the date that contract was formed, is defined as when the last offeree to sign the offer or initial the last change communicates this action to the last offeror. A signed offer is still not a contract until notice of acceptance by the last party is communicated to the opposite party. Oral negotiations and/or agreements are not binding because the statute of fraud requires written contracts for the enforceable transfer of any interest in real property. Because the effective date frequently serves as the initiation of certain time periods in the contract, it is critical that all brokers can identify effective date accurately.

Due diligence, due diligence fee, and due diligence period. (Para. 1h–j) In exchange for a negotiated due diligence fee paid directly to the seller, the buyer has the unlimited right to fully investigate the condition and allowed uses of the property to determine if the buyer wishes to consummate the purchase contract on the negotiated terms. The buyer has the unilateral right described in Paragraph 4g to terminate the OPC for *any reason or no reason* by delivering written notice of termination to the seller no later than 5:00 pm of the expiration date of the due diligence period, *time being of the essence*. If the buyer proceeds to settlement, the due diligence fee will be credited toward the purchase price. If the buyer exercises the right to terminate within the due diligence period, the buyer will receive a refund of any paid earnest money deposit. The due diligence fee is generally nonrefundable regardless of the outcome of the transaction with two exceptions: (1) a material breach by the seller as noted in Paragraph 8m or (2) material damage or destruction of the property improvements prior to closing as noted in Paragraph 12. The due diligence fee should not be confused with the earnest money deposit that serves as the liquidated damages.

The length of the due diligence period or the amount of the fee is negotiable by the parties prior to contract formation. Language in this section states that the contract is not illusory even if no fee is required or paid. Caution should be used to allow adequate time for the completion of possible term renegotiations after the receipt of all necessary inspections and reports. The due diligence period is significantly different from the conventional option to purchase contract discussed later in this chapter. Whereas a conventional option is the right to purchase by a certain date, the due diligence option is a right not to purchase by a certain date. Instead of exercising a right to opt in and create a purchase contract, the buyer under the NCAR/NCBA Standard Form 2-T is opting out of a contract to purchase. During the period, the buyer is encouraged to secure financing and negotiate any repairs or changes in contract terms the buyer deems necessary. If the buyer and the seller cannot reach an agreement regarding repairs or terms, the buyer can give written notice to the seller that the buyer is exercising the right to terminate the contract prior to the end of the period (Form 350-T, Appendix D, Form 15). If the buyer does not exercise the right to terminate before the end of the period, the buyer must proceed with the purchase of the property in its current condition unless an agreement has been signed, such as the Due Diligence Request and Agreement (Form 310-T, Appendix D, Form 14).

Settlement, settlement date, and closing. (Para. 1k–m) Although closing is still identified as the recording of the deed, settlement is the process of the settlement agent gathering all the documents and funds necessary to complete the sales transaction. While both parties may still meet together on the settlement date to bring funds and verify that the terms of the contract have been met, it is becoming more likely that some actions are completed electronically or by express mail. A settlement agent will not disburse funds until after the recordation of the deed.

Special assessments. (Para. 1n) Special assessments are charges that may become a lien against the property by a governmental authority for something other than taxes or by an owners' association for something other than dues. In Paragraph 6b, the buyer agrees to take the property subject to proposed special assessments which are under formal consideration but not approved by settlement. In Paragraph 8i, the seller agrees to pay all confirmed special assessments that the amount can be determined by settlement.

Fixtures. (Para. 2) Items identified as fixtures in an ever-growing list automatically convey with the property if present on the property and owned by the seller unless they are exempted in this paragraph. It is not necessary to cross out any listed item that is not present on the property. Any item that is exempted should be clearly identified. The seller is responsible for repairing any damage to the property caused by the removal of an exempted item.

Personal property. (Para. 3) No personal property, even if advertised with the property, should ever be presumed to convey as part of the sales contract unless clearly identified in this paragraph. Even though this paragraph states that any personal property will convey *at no value*, most lenders will not finance a contract with any entry in this paragraph. The buyer is strongly encouraged to consult his lender before including any personal property in the OPC.

Buyer's due diligence process. (Para. 4) An extensive, but not necessarily exhaustive, list of activities that should be performed during the due diligence period is outlined to guide the buyer in their investigation of the property. Contract conditions that appeared in previous versions of the OPC, such as financing and appraisal conditions, should be explored and satisfied during the due diligence period. If the buyer cannot satisfy all his questions or concerns about the property during the due diligence period, the buyer can request an extension of the expiration date of the period, but there is no obligation for the seller to comply. Enough time should be allowed during the period to negotiate any repair or remediation work. Any repair agreement should be in writing and be considered an addition to the contract.

If the buyer decides to terminate the contract during the due diligence period, a written notice of termination must be delivered to the seller prior to the expiration of the period. The buyer should heed the approved notice information in Paragraph 21 that specifies what is considered an acceptable method of communication of notice. The mailbox rule does not apply for the delivery of termination of contract; the mailbox rule is only applicable to the creation of a contract. Although not required by the contract, a prudent real estate broker would obtain and retain proof of delivery of the notice.

Buyer representations. (Para. 5) In this section, the buyer discloses his transactional plans and needs to the seller. The seller should be able to rely on these representations when making decisions about the offer. These representations, such as the buyer needs to sell a currently held property prior to settlement, do not automatically become conditions of the contract unless appropriate addenda, such as the Contingent Sale Addendum, are made part of the OPC in Paragraph 15.

Buyer obligations. (Para. 6) The expenses and fees for which the buyer is obligated to pay are enumerated here: owners' association fees/charges, proposed special assessments, and certain closing costs.

Seller representations. (Para. 7) Seller disclosures, other than the Residential Property and Owners' Association Disclosure Statement, that are required by law or are needed to satisfy buyer financing guidelines are shared in this paragraph. The Oil and Gas Rights Disclosure language mandated by North Carolina law requires buyer initials on all three statements.

Seller obligations. (Para. 8) This section consolidates in one place all the duties of the seller. The seller is to provide the buyer with title information, access to the property with working utilities, premises free of garbage, lien waivers, a general warranty deed, a completed Owners' Association Disclosure and Addendum... (Form 2A12-T, Appendix D, Form 7), negotiated seller concessions, and paid confirmed assessments. If the seller commits a material breach to the contract and the buyer decides to terminate the contract, the seller must refund all earnest money and the due diligence fee and reimburse the buyer for *reasonable costs* incurred in good faith during the due diligence period. If the possibility exists that the contract terms will result in a short sale situation, the seller is strongly encouraged to make the lienholder's approval a condition of the contract by attaching a completed Short Sale Addendum (Form 2A14-T, Appendix D, Form 18).

Prorations and adjustments. (Para. 9) Proration of listed items are established unless there is written agreement for different treatment.

Home warranty. (Para. 10) If the seller is providing a home warranty, the parameters are addressed.

Condition of the property at closing/risk of loss. (Para. 11 and 12) These two paragraphs work together to ensure that the buyer receives the property in the same or better condition as when the contract was created. Both paragraphs survive the expiration of the due diligence period and remain binding through closing.

Delay in settlement/closing. (Para. 13) Although the settlement date is set in Paragraph 1(l), there are many things that conspire to delay the actual completion of settlement. The use of *time is of the essence* in regard to the settlement date is discouraged because it might have an unanticipated adverse effect on the parties. Consequently, the OPC has limited the time parameters for a *reasonable time* after the stated Settlement Date to a 14-day grace period that the non-delaying party agrees to wait for the delaying party to close the transaction. On the 15th day after the stated contract settlement date, the nondelaying party has the unilateral right to terminate the contract and enforce any legal remedies for the breach of the contract by the delaying party.

Possession. (Para. 14) Possession of the property is to be delivered at closing (after recordation of the deed) due to reasons that include insurability issues. If the buyer will take possession prior to closing or the seller will retain possession after closing, the execution and attachment of the appropriate named addendum to the OPC is strongly recommended.

Other provisions and conditions. (Para. 15) Because brokers are prohibited from drafting legal contract clauses or addenda, the use of the 13 NCBA/NCAR standard addenda is highly recommended. With the two possession addenda noted in Paragraph 14, this paragraph lists all the standard addenda to be indicated as attachments to the OPC. All checked addenda and subsequently ratified ancillary agreements between the parties, such as a repair agreement, are part of the contract and must be provided to both parties plus the lender and settlement attorney.

Concluding standard provisions. (Para. 16–23) The remaining paragraphs address the need for written mutual consent for assignment of the contract except in the case of a tax-deferred exchange, the agreement to cooperate in a tax-deferred exchange, the parties to the contract, survival of contract provisions after closing, the non-existence of agreements outside the contract, the definitions of notice and execution, plus the computation of days.

NCBA/NCAR Standard Addenda

Several standard NCBA/NCAR addenda have been approved for use with the NCBA/NCAR Standard Form 2-T Offer to Purchase and Contract (Appendix D, Form 13) when appropriate (see Figure 10.2). These addenda address specific issues that may be too complicated to include in the space allowed for *other provisions*. The broker should use approved addenda when dealing with these issues because they increase the chances of proper preparation and negate any suspicion that the broker may be illegally practicing law by drafting a contract.

In North Carolina

FIGURE 10.2

Addenda Forms Approved by NCAR and NCBA

2A1-T	Backup Contract Addendum
2A2-T	Contingent Sale Addendum
2A3-T	New Construction Addendum
2A4-T	FHA/VA Financing Addendum
2A5-T	Seller Financing Addendum
2A6-T	Loan Assumption Addendum
2A7-T	Buyer Possession Before Closing Agreement Addendum
2A8-T	Seller Possession After Closing Agreement Addendum
2A9-T	Lead-Based Paint or Lead-Based Paint Hazard Addendum
2A11-T	Additional Provisions Addendum
2A12-T	Owners' Association Disclosure and Addendum for Properties Exempt from Residential Property Disclosure Statement
2A13-T	Vacation Rental Addendum
2A14-T	Short Sale Addendum

FHA/VA financing addendum (2A4-T). If the buyer will be using either FHA-insured or VA-guaranteed mortgage loans to purchase the property, this addendum is required. The addendum allows the borrower to terminate the OPC without forfeiture of any monies if the property does not appraise for at least the purchase price specified in the OPC.

Buyer possession before closing agreement (2A7-T). If the buyer will be allowed to take possession of the property prior to closing, this addendum will address many issues that might arise. Among other things, the provisions of this agreement address rent, pets, insurance, and responsibility for payment of expenses, utilities, repairs, and maintenance. This agreement is not to be used for possession for longer than 14 days nor in connection with a lease purchase or lease option contract. The agreement wisely suggests that possession not be granted until the due diligence period has expired.

Seller possession after closing agreement (2A8-T). If the seller wishes to retain possession of the property after closing, this agreement will serve in a similar manner to the addendum above for buyer possession.

Lead-based paint or lead-based paint hazard addendum (2A9-T, Appendix D, Form 6). Under the federal disclosure requirements of the Residential Lead-Based Paint Hazard Reduction Act of 1992, a residential seller must disclose what he/she knows about the presence of lead-based paint in the property and must provide any known reports about lead-based paint hazards in the property. When coupled with delivery of the EPA pamphlet about the hazards of lead poisoning, this addendum meets the disclosure requirements of the federal act and should be completed and signed by the seller as part of the listing process. The listing agent must initial on the second page that the seller has been advised of her obligations to comply with the act. The buyer may utilize or waiver a 10-day risk assessment period to determine the buyer's willingness to proceed with the purchase of the property.

Additional provisions addendum (2A11-T, Appendix D, Form 17). Probably one of the most-used addenda, this form addresses five separate contract concerns. The first provision allows the offeror to implement an automatic expiration date and time for the attached Offer to Purchase and Contract. In the second provision, the buyer secures the seller's assistance in testing the property to determine if an adequate septic system can be installed or modified for the buyer's specific needs. If the property is currently subject to leases, the third provision requires all lease-related documentation to be given to the buyer for review during the due diligence period. The fourth provision would request repair or improvement projects that are known prior to contract formation. The fifth provision asks for the identifying information for any manufactured housing that will be included in the transaction.

Owners' association disclosure and addendum for properties exempt from residential property disclosure statement (2A12-T, Appendix D, Form 7). The seller is mandated to provide this completed addendum in transactions where the property to be conveyed is subject to an owners' association but is exempt from compliance with the North Carolina Residential Property Disclosure Act. The most common exempt transactions would include unimproved real estate, first sale of a dwelling never inhabited, lease purchase, and bank-owned foreclosures. This form discloses what services the association dues provide, the contact person for the association, and any known pending litigation that involves the association.

Vacation rental addendum (2A13-T). This addendum should be used with any property that is subject to the North Carolina Vacation Rental Act.

Short sale addendum (2A14-T, Appendix D, Form 18). If the transaction is subject to a short sale approval by the seller's lienholder, this very informative addendum should be used. This form allows both parties to terminate the OPC under certain circumstances. The due diligence period and settlement dates are automatically tied to the seller's notice of the lienholder's approval for the transaction. The form also addresses whether the property owner has known bankruptcy or foreclosure issues.

A review of the most commonly used standard addenda found in Appendix D will familiarize brokers with proper legal language for many of the recurring issues in a real estate sales transaction.

Backup contract addendum (2A1-T, Appendix D, Form 15). Although a property is under contract, there is frequently a chance that the transaction will not close due to any of multiple reasons. The primary buyer could exercise the right to terminate the contract during the due diligence period, the buyer financing might fall through, or the seller and the buyer cannot agree to repair negotiations. Consequently, the seller may wish to continue to market the property and encourage backup offers until the primary contract actually closes. A subsequent buyer may be interested waiting in a secondary contract position to see what transpires during the due diligence period in the primary contract. The Back-Up Contract Addendum language automatically makes the secondary contract null and void if the primary contract closes or upon reaching a named date, whichever occurs first. The secondary contract moves to primary position upon notification to the secondary buyer that the primary contract is terminated; written proof of primary contract termination is required. The back-up buyer must close on the property within a specified number of days after notification of primary position or the settlement date noted in the back-up contract, whichever is later. Any time prior to being notified of being in primary position, the secondary buyer may terminate the back-up contract by delivering written notice to the seller.

Contingent sale addendum (2A2-T, Appendix D, Form 16). If the buyer has indicated in Paragraph 5(b) of the OPC that he needs to sell other property to consummate the purchase of the subject property, it is highly recommended that the buyer consider using the contingent sale addendum. If the buyer's other property is under contract, the buyer must provide a copy of said contract to the seller. The buyer's right to terminate this contract without forfeiture of earnest money will survive the expiration of the due diligence period. The addendum allows the buyer to terminate this contract and receive a refund of earnest money within three days after the settlement date of this contract if buyer does not believe the contract on the other property will close in a timely manner. If the contract on the buyer's other property is terminated for any reason after the expiration of the due diligence period in this contract, either party may terminate this contract and the buyer will receive a refund of all earnest money.

Submitting Offers to Seller

In North Carolina

Real estate brokers are obligated by License Law [93A-6(a)(13)] and Commission Rule A.0106 to disclose all offers to sellers immediately, but no later than five days from the date of the offer. Simply telephoning the offeree with the terms of an offer is not sufficient delivery, according to the NCREC 2008-9 Update material. Furthermore, listing agents must disclose any additional information they know that may affect a seller's decision to accept an offer. This includes information about the offeror's financial ability to close the transaction, as well as the possibility of other offers that may be presented shortly.

A listing agent can neither reject nor accept an offer on behalf of a seller, nor can a listing agent screen offers presenting only those offers that the agent feels have merit. All offers, written or verbal, must be communicated to the seller. It is up to the seller to accept or reject any offer that is made, however unreasonable that offer is. Brokers also must present those offers that may be at a disadvantage to them.

■ **FOR EXAMPLE** One buyer may offer the seller $90,000 in cash for the seller's home, while another buyer offers the seller $95,000, contingent on obtaining financing. The listing agent must present both offers as soon as possible, even though if the seller accepts the first offer (because it is in cash), it will mean a smaller commission for the agent.

Handling Offer to Purchase Modifications and Counteroffers

Frequently, a seller wants certain changes to be made to an offer before accepting it. For example, instead of a $1,000 earnest money deposit, the seller may demand a $5,000 earnest money deposit. As discussed earlier, once the offeree makes any material change in the offer, the offeree has *rejected* that offer and created a *counteroffer*. No contract has been formed at this stage. It is up to the original offeror to accept or reject the counteroffer. If the original offeror accepts the counteroffer *with a few changes*, another counteroffer has been created and the process begins again.

Negotiations between a buyer and seller may consist of a series of counteroffers before final terms are agreed on. Any changes to the original offer must be made in writing and initialed by both parties. Unfortunately, if all the changes are written into the initial offer form, the contract can become virtually unreadable. It is a good idea for the broker to fill in a new standard form with the final terms and have both parties sign and date it. This avoids later confusion over which terms were changed and how.

In North Carolina

Response to buyer's offer (Form 340-T). An alternative to making *pen and ink* changes to the original offer is for the seller to utilize the NCAR Response to Buyer's Offer (Appendix D, Form 19). The form allows the seller to list terms that would be more acceptable and suggest the buyer (offeror) consider them when revising the original offer. The response form rejects the original offer but does not create a counteroffer; this allows the seller to remain free to accept any new offers while the original offeror is deciding how to proceed with negotiations. This form is also an excellent way to respond to multiple offers simultaneously without binding the seller to any one offer.

The fact that there are multiple offers on a property is not considered a material fact that must be disclosed. However, if one of the offering parties is notified of the existence of a competing offer, then all offering parties must receive the same notification. This maintains a *level playing field* for all offerors. NCREC Rule A.0115 prohibits any broker from disclosing the price or any other material term in any offer to purchase, sell, lease, rent, or option real property to a competing party without the express authority of the offeror. *Shopping the offer* by brokers has long been considered unethical and is now also illegal in North Carolina. Of course, unlicensed principals in the transaction are not bound by this NCREC rule.

Furnishing Copies of Offers and Contracts to Buyer and Seller

In North Carolina

According to Commission Rule A.0106, real estate brokers must provide all parties with a copy of any instrument they sign at the time of execution, or no later than five days after execution. It is important to remember that a contract may have been created long before the offeror receives a written copy of the signed contract.

■ **FOR EXAMPLE** When a buyer signs an offer to purchase, the broker must immediately provide the buyer with a copy of that offer. Then if the seller signs the offer, the broker must immediately provide the seller with a copy of that signed offer. And of course, the broker also must give a copy of the offer to purchase and contract—with both signatures—to the buyer. Per the Rule, *immediately* has its common meaning, with the outside limit being no later than five days from execution.

It used to be standard practice to create six copies of the forms, sometimes called *counterparts*. (Note that a *signed copy becomes an original*.) One copy went to each of the following: the buyer, the seller, the listing real estate office, the selling real estate office, the closing attorney, and the lender. Only one signed original was necessary to create a contract. This process is no longer standard practice.

INSTALLMENT LAND CONTRACT

A real estate sale can be made under an **installment land contract,** sometimes called a *land contract, land sales contract,* or *contract for deed.* An installment land contract is not only a sales contract but also a financing instrument. The seller agrees to owner financing with some type of installment payment method for the buyer. Under an installment land contract, the seller, also known as the *vendor,* retains legal title, while the buyer, known as the *vendee,* secures possession of and an equitable interest in the property. The buyer holds equitable title, and the contract is a cloud on the seller's title.

The buyer usually agrees to give the seller a down payment and pay regular monthly installments of principal and interest over a number of years. The buyer also agrees to pay real estate taxes, assessments, homeowner dues, insurance premiums, repairs, and upkeep on the property. While the buyer obtains possession when the contract is signed by both parties, the seller does not execute and deliver a deed to the buyer until the final payment has been made and all the terms of the contract have been satisfied.

Advantages and Disadvantages

For the seller. The typical installment land contract is advantageous to the seller for a number of reasons. There is an income tax benefit that comes from receiving the sales price in installments over several years instead of in a lump sum. The seller gets to retain legal title, which makes the seller feel more secure. If the buyer defaults, many land contracts provide forfeiture as a remedy. Forfeiture means that all the monthly payments the buyer has made are forfeited as well as all rights in the property. Finally, the land contract may be the only way to make property desirable and/or attainable to buyers when interest rates are high or institutional loans are hard to obtain.

On the other hand, sellers often receive small down payments under a land contract, and a seller may prefer to be *cashed out*—that is, to get immediate cash for the equity. For example, the seller may need cash to make a down payment on a new home.

For the buyer. If the buyer has a poor credit rating, a history of foreclosures or bankruptcies, or marginal income, a land contract may be the only way to finance a transaction. The down payment and the closing costs are usually lower than in institutional financing arrangements. The purchaser also has the tax advantages that come with ownership of real estate. If the property being purchased is income-producing property, profit from the property itself can help finance the purchase, such as rent collected from a financed apartment building providing the monthly loan payment. All these are obvious advantages for the buyer.

However, if the buyer defaults under a land contract, the forfeiture remedy available to the seller is extremely harsh for the buyer. The buyer can lose all the payments made under the land contract in addition to the property itself. Also, because the buyer does not get legal title to the property until the end of the contract term, the buyer will find it virtually impossible to use the property as collateral for interim financing needs. It is also possible that the seller may have encumbered the title during the term of the contract.

In North Carolina There is no standard approved form for an installment land contract and it is never appropriate to use the Standard Form 2T for an installment land contract; therefore, all interested parties should consult an attorney for advice and drafting expertise. All installment land contracts must be in writing to be valid and enforceable, as required by the statute of frauds, and must be recorded, as required by the Conner Act (see page 100).

As of October, 2011, North Carolina state law (NCGS 47H) governs any installment land contract that will convey property that will be used as the primary residence of the buyer. This application would include a one- to four-family dwelling structure or if the buyer's principal residence manufactured home will be placed on the property. The minimum contents of a North Carolina contract for deed are enumerated in the section below. As noted in the 2011–2012 NCREC's BICAR course, the buyer has three business days to cancel the contract following execution or receipt of the contract, whichever is later. The statute requires the seller to record the contract for deed or a memorandum of the contract within five business days of execution. The seller must allow the buyer at least 30 days to cure any default.

Required Provisions

Per NCGS 47H-2, installment land contracts must contain the following 17 provisions:

- The full names and addresses of all the parties to the contract
- The date the contract is signed by each party
- A legal description and the physical address of the property conveyed
- The sales price of the property conveyed (a)
- Any charges or fees for services included in the contract separate from the sale price (b)
- The amount of the purchaser's down payment (c)
- The principal balance owed by the purchaser, which is the sum of the amounts stated in subdivisions
- Provisions (a) and (b) of this subsection, less the amount stated in subdivision (c) of this subsection
- The amount and due date of each installment payment and the total number of installment payments
- The interest rate on the unpaid balance, if any, and the method of determining the interest rate
- A conspicuous statement of any pending order of any public agency or other matters of public record adversely affecting the property, provided the seller has actual knowledge of the pending order or matter
- A statement of the rights of the purchaser to cure a default
- A statement setting forth the obligation of each party who is responsible for making repairs to the property or paying of taxes, hazard insurance premiums, flood insurance premiums, homeowner association dues, and other charges against the property from the date of the contract

- A provision that the purchaser has the right to accelerate or prepay any installment payments without penalty; unless the property is encumbered by a deed of trust as permitted by G.S. 47H-6 and the loan secured by the property contains a prepayment penalty, in which case the contract may specify that the purchaser will compensate the seller for the prepayment penalty
- A description of conditions of the property that includes whether the property, including any structures thereon, has water, sewer, septic, and electricity service, whether the property is in a floodplain, whether anyone else has a legal interest in the property, and whether restrictive covenants prevent building or installing a dwelling; if restrictive covenants are in place that affect the property, a copy of the restrictive covenants shall be made available to the purchaser at or before the execution of the contract
- A statement indicating the current amount of any real estate taxes and/or homeowner association dues or special assessments required to be paid on the property and the amount of such taxes, dues, or assessments that are delinquent; to the extent these amounts are not known at the time the contract is executed, a reasonable estimate shall be given
- If the property being sold is encumbered by a deed of trust, mortgage, or other encumbrance evidencing or securing a monetary obligation that constitutes a lien on the property, and the seller is not a licensed general contractor within the meaning of Chapter 87 of the General Statutes, or a licensed manufactured home dealer within the meaning of Article 9A of Chapter 143 of the General Statutes, a statement of the amount of the lien, and the amount and due date, if any, of any periodic payments
- A conspicuous statement, in 14-point boldface type or larger, immediately above the purchaser's signature, that the purchaser has the right to cancel the contract at any time until midnight of the third business day following execution of the contract or delivery of the contract, whichever occurs later

OPTION TO PURCHASE REAL ESTATE

A conventional **option** is a *contract by which an* **optionor** *(generally an owner) gives an* **optionee** *(a prospective purchaser or lessee) the irrevocable right to buy or lease the owner's property at a fixed price within a stated period of time.* An option to purchase has two considerations: (1) the option fee when the option is given and (2) the agreed-on sales price when the option is exercised. The option fee is normally nonrefundable if the option is not exercised. The optionee must decide, within the specified time, either to exercise the option right (to buy or lease the property) or to allow the option right to expire. At the time the option is signed by the parties, the optionor does not sell, nor does the optionee buy. They merely agree that the optionee will have the right to buy and the owner will be obligated to sell *if* the optionee decides to exercise the option. An option is enforceable by only one party—the optionee, making it a unilateral contract. Because the seller is prohibited from selling the property to anyone else during the option period, it would probably be in the optionor's best interest to clearly terminate the optionee's rights by using the term *time is of the essence* regarding the option date. A common application of an option is a lease that includes an option for the tenant to purchase the property. Options on commercial real estate frequently depend on the fulfillment of specific conditions, such as obtaining a zoning change or a building permit. The optionee is usually obligated to exercise the option if the conditions are met.

In North Carolina

Requirements of North Carolina Options

All options for real property are required to be in writing under the statute of frauds. Under the Conner Act, an option must be recorded to be enforceable against the claims of third parties.

There is currently no standard approved Option to Purchase Contract. If a broker has parties that desire a conventional option to purchase agreement, an attorney should be contacted to draft the appropriate contract. A broker should never attempt to create an option contract.

The option should describe the manner in which the optionee will notify the optionor of the decision to exercise the option. Not only should the option spell out the terms under which the optionee can buy the property, it also should describe the major terms of the sale itself, such as the purchase price, financing terms, and type of deed that will be used to convey title. The consideration for the option (the option fee) also must be stated clearly. Furthermore, the option should explain whether the option fee will be applied toward the purchase price.

Agreements for Preemptive Rights

A **preemptive right** gives a party the first right to purchase real property. The major difference between an option and a preemptive right is which party has the power to initiate the sale or lease: the buyer/tenant initiates an option, while the seller/landlord initiates an agreement for a preemptive right. There are several forms of preemptive rights but the two most common versions are the right of first refusal and the right of first opportunity to purchase.

Right of first refusal. A **right of first refusal** is created when a property owner promises to give the contracting party the first chance to buy the property or to match the bona fide offer of a third party, should the owner decide to sell sometime in the future. Rights of first refusal are commonly found in leases. In a lease situation, a right of first refusal might give the tenant the right either to purchase the property, if offered for sale, or to renew the lease or lease adjoining space. In some condominiums, the association of unit owners retains the right of first refusal on any sale of a unit.

Note that with a right of first refusal, the property owner does not promise to sell the property at all—merely promises that *should* the decision be made to sell, the other party will get the first opportunity to buy. This is different from the option, where the owner promises to sell should the optionee choose to buy.

Right of first opportunity to purchase. The **right of first opportunity to purchase** is a preemptive right agreement that endeavors to avoid some of the vague legalities of the right of first refusal. If the property owner decides to sell the property, the seller must offer to sell the property to the party with the right of first opportunity to purchase for a designated price. The holder of the right may opt to purchase for that price or decline the offer. If the offer is declined, the seller may now sell the property for a specified period of time to a third party for the designated price. The agreement may allow the owner to sell for a percentage of the designated price (e.g., 90% or higher of the designated price). If the owner does not sell to a third party during the specified time, the process begins anew with owner offering to sell the property to the right holder for a designated price.

■ RELATED WEBSITES

Electronic Signatures in Global and National Commerce Act (E-SIGN):
    www.ftc.gov/os/2001/06/esign7.htm
Uniform Electronic Transactions Act:
    http://definitions.uslegal.com/u/uniform-electronic-transactions-act/

■ KEY POINT REVIEW

Real estate brokers in North Carolina can legally *fill in the blanks* on preprinted, standard contract forms. Real estate brokers who are not licensed attorneys may not draft legal contract language for others for compensation (unlawful practice of law).

- If North Carolina brokers offer preprinted contract forms, they must contain the mandated 19 items enumerated in NCREC Rule A.0012.
- Brokers' compensation and liability disclaimer are prohibited from inclusion in North Carolina sales contracts.

A real estate sales contract

- is usually accompanied by an earnest money deposit held in trust or escrow account to avoid commingling with broker's own funds,
- contains **contingencies** or conditions to the sale (such as property sale contingencies or seller's lienholder's approval for a short sale) that must be stated in the contract,
- may provide for the purchaser's right to inspect the property during a due diligence period, and
- includes disclosure forms required by state law or contract terms that must be given, such as the residential property and owners' association disclosure statement.

Electronic contracting includes the **Uniform Electronic Transactions Act (UETA)**, which has been adopted in most states and does not require electronic communication, but if it is used, the contract cannot be denied legal effect just because electronic method was used, and the signature cannot be denied legal effect just because it is in electronic format.

Communication of offers and acceptance can be

- oral: includes phone, voice mail, or in person;
- written: includes traditional, special and electronic mail;
- **mailbox rule:** where placement of signed offer in mail to other party constitutes acceptance; or
- directed to the party's agent, which is the same as communicating with the principal.

Termination of offers occurs

- if the offeree rejects the offer or creates a counteroffer;
- if the offer is not accepted by specified time or within reasonable time;
- if the offeror revokes prior to acceptance; or
- by death of either party.

The North Carolina Association of REALTORS® Response to Buyer's Offer form rejects the offer and lists desirable contract terms; it does not create a counteroffer; it is created primarily for use with multiple-offer scenarios.

In North Carolina, all parties must receive a copy of any legal instrument they sign immediately, but no later than five days from execution.

Installment land contract (contract for deed or land contract) is a sales contract and a financing document for owner-financed purchases.

- The seller's advantages include a tax benefit, earned interest, and selling feature.
- The buyer can overcome poor credit, and income-producing property can help pay for itself.

Option to purchase is when the **optionee** pays an option fee to purchase time to make a decision to purchase on terms in option or renegotiate terms before the option period expires. The seller (**optionor**) cannot sell property to anyone else during the option period.

Agreements for preemptive rights include **right of first refusal** and **right of first opportunity to purchase**.

QUESTIONS

1. To sell his property the seller has entered into a contract. While the sale is pending, the listing agent receives another offer to purchase the property from a different firm. Which of the following statements is *TRUE*?
   a. The listing agent does not have to present this offer to the seller.
   b. The listing agent must present this offer to the seller.
   c. The listing agent has to present this offer only if its terms are better than the terms of the pending sale.
   d. The listing agent must tell the offeror that offers are prohibited while a sale is pending.

2. Which of the following statements is *TRUE* of a conventional option to purchase contract?
   a. It need not recite a set amount of consideration for purchase of the property.
   b. It must be exercised within a specified time period by the optionee.
   c. It does not allow negotiation on changes to contract terms during the option period.
   d. It is enforceable by both the optionor and the optionee.

3. At 1:30 pm, a broker faxed an offer to purchase to her seller client. At 2:00 pm, after considering the offer, the seller called and informed his agent that he wanted to increase the earnest money deposit by $1,000. To make the seller's requested change for additional earnest money, the seller's agent need only
   I. change the term in the original offer, initial, and date the one change on behalf of the seller.
   II. prepare a new offer and, with the seller's permission, sign on behalf of the seller.
      a. I only
      b. II only
      c. Both I and II
      d. Neither I nor II

4. The buyer's offer is made on the condition that the buyer's present home sells in the next 30 days. This condition is called a(n)
   a. first right of refusal.
   b. contingency.
   c. unilateral offer.
   d. option.

5. The buyer's offer is made on the condition that the buyer is able to obtain an 80% institutional loan at a specified interest rate by a specified date. If the buyer notifies the seller in writing of the inability to obtain such a loan, the buyer will
   a. have to go ahead with the purchase anyway.
   b. not have to purchase the home, but will forfeit the whole earnest money deposit.
   c. not have to purchase the home, but will forfeit half of the earnest money deposit.
   d. not have to purchase the home and will be entitled to a full refund of the earnest money deposit.

6. An offer to purchase is submitted on a listing while the property owner is out of town on business. The offer is faxed to the owner and the owner signs the faxed copy of the offer with no changes in terms. If the signed offer is then faxed to the listing agent who calls the buyer's agent with this information, which of the following statements is *TRUE*?
   a. The seller is under contract to sell his property since faxed signatures are binding.
   b. The original signatures of both buyer and seller must appear on the same copy of the offer; therefore, a contract does not exist.
   c. No contract exists yet since the buyer has not been personally told of the contract acceptance.
   d. No contract exists since no one on the buyer's side of the transaction has seen the seller's signature.

7. Which of the following statements is/are TRUE when an offer to purchase has been signed by the buyer and then given to the seller's broker with an earnest money deposit check for the seller to consider?
   I. The earnest money check must be deposited immediately into the listing firm's trust account.
   II. If the buyer withdraws the offer before it is accepted by the seller, the earnest money will be forfeited.
   a. I only
   b. II only
   c. Both I and II
   d. Neither I nor II

8. An offer to purchase real estate can be terminated by all of the following reasons EXCEPT
   a. failure to accept the offer within a prescribed period.
   b. revocation by the offeror communicated to the offeree after acceptance.
   c. acceptance of the offer by the offeree after making one change in terms.
   d. death of the offeror or offeree.

9. Which of the following statements is TRUE of the due diligence fee in of the NCAR/NCBA 2-T Offer to Purchase and Contract?
   a. The due diligence fee is applied to the purchase price at closing.
   b. It requires all the systems of the property to be functioning adequately.
   c. The earnest money check is paid directly to the seller.
   d. Within three business days after the due diligence period expires, the buyer must notify the seller of the buyer's decision to proceed with the contract.

10. When a buyer and seller have entered into an installment land contract,
    I. the seller retains an interest called legal title.
    II. the buyer acquires an immediate interest in the property known as equitable title.
    a. I only
    b. II only
    c. Both I and II
    d. Neither I nor II

11. Under contract terms, one party will pay the property owner $500 a month for 10 years. The property owner will continue to hold legal title to the property. That party will live on the property and pay all real estate taxes, insurance premiums, and regular upkeep costs. What kind of contract is in place?
    a. Option to purchase contract
    b. Contract for mortgage
    c. Unilateral contract
    d. Installment land contract

12. A married couple offers in writing to purchase a house for $120,000, including the draperies, with the offer to expire on Saturday at noon. The owners reply in writing on Thursday, accepting the $120,000 offer, but excluding the draperies. On Friday, while the couple considers this response, the owners reconsider the original offer, and decide to accept the original offer in writing, including the draperies. Since it is before Saturday noon, the couple
    a. is legally bound to buy the house including the draperies.
    b. is not bound to buy because they are not under contract.
    c. must buy the house and is not entitled to the draperies.
    d. must buy the house, but may deduct the value of the draperies from the $120,000.

13. A man signs a contract under which he may purchase a house for $80,000 any time within the next three months. The man pays the current owner $500 at the time the contract is signed. Which of the following best describes this contract?
    a. Contingency
    b. Option to purchase
    c. Installment land contract
    d. Contract for deed

14. A for-sale-by-owner signs a written offer to purchase without making any changes to the offer. The seller then mails the signed offer to the buyer by express mail without any further contact with the buyer. Before receipt of the envelope from the seller, the buyer changes her mind about purchasing the property and calls the seller to withdraw the offer. Which of the following statements is *TRUE*?
    a. Buyer cannot withdraw offer, because she is already under contract.
    b. Buyer can withdraw offer since she has not received the signed contract yet.
    c. Buyer was under contract as soon as the seller signed the offer to purchase.
    d. Contract has been formed but is unenforceable since real estate brokers were not involved.

15. A seller receives two offers to purchase her North Carolina property at the same time. One offer is for full listing price but wants a delayed closing that is not in the seller's best interest. The second offer has terms that are very agreeable to the seller but offers less than full price for the property. Without any knowledge or consent of the first offeror, the listing agent contacts only the second offeror and tells them that there is a full price offer on the table and asks if they would like to increase the purchase price in their offer. Listing agent is
    a. honoring his fiduciary duty to the seller by soliciting a higher offer.
    b. in violation of Commission Rules because he must also respond to the first offeror.
    c. in violation of Commission Rules because he revealed offer terms.
    d. working within Commission Rules as long as his actions were at the direction of his seller client.

16. Which of the following is *TRUE* of a right of first refusal given to the tenant of a rental house?
    a. The landlord must sell the property if the tenant decides to buy.
    b. The landlord cannot sell the property to anyone but this tenant.
    c. The tenant must buy the property if the landlord decides to sell.
    d. The landlord must offer to sell the property to the tenant first, if the landlord decides to sell the house.

17. A preprinted North Carolina sales contract provided for use by a real estate broker may *NOT* contain a provision about
    a. negotiated repair issues.
    b. payment terms of purchase price.
    c. broker compensation.
    d. items to be prorated at settlement.

18. The effective date of a sales contract is defined as the date that
    a. the last party to the transaction signs the offer.
    b. the buyer takes possession of the property.
    c. the contract parties meet to transfer title.
    d. notification of acceptance is given to the other party.

19. Per the NCAR/NCBA 2-T Offer to Purchase and Contract, if the seller commits a material breach and the buyer elects to terminate the contract, the buyer is entitled to
    a. a refund of paid earnest money, due diligence fee, and all reasonable costs of the buyer's due diligence.
    b. a refund of any earnest money and due diligence fee.
    c. a refund of any earnest money only.
    d. nothing more than contract termination.

20. During the buyer's due diligence period in the NCAR/NCBA 2-T Offer to Purchase and Contract, the buyer is entitled to
    a. renegotiate any term in the contract.
    b. only request repair of broken items.
    c. a return of any paid due diligence fee if written termination is given.
    d. verbally terminate the contract prior to the period's expiration date.

CHAPTER 11

Landlord and Tenant

LEARNING OBJECTIVES *When you have finished reading this chapter, you should be able to*

- **identify** and explain the characteristics of the four types of nonfreehold estates.

- **explain** the concepts of the Residential Rental Agreements Act, the Tenant Security Deposit Act, the Doctrine of Retaliatory Eviction, and the North Carolina Vacation Rental Act.

- **describe** the various types of leases and their purposes; the requirements and general conditions of a valid lease; and how a lease may be terminated.

- **explain** the general provisions of leases as they relate to possession, recording, improvements, maintenance, assignment and subleasing, and breach.

- **understand** the major provisions of NCAR's Standard Residential Rental Contract form.

- **define** these *key terms:*

constructive eviction	holdover tenant	percentage lease
covenant of quiet enjoyment	implied warranty of habitability	periodic tenancy
estate at sufferance	index lease	Residential Rental Agreements Act
estate at will	law of negligence	retaliatory eviction
estate for years	lease	sandwich lease
estate from period to period	leasehold estate	security deposit
fixed lease	lessee	self-help eviction
full-service lease	lessor	subleases
graduated lease	net lease	summary ejectment
gross lease	North Carolina Vacation Rental Act	Tenant Security Deposit Act
ground lease	novation	

LEASING REAL ESTATE

A lease covers the conditions upon which a tenant may possess, occupy, and use the property.

A **lease** is a contract between a landlord, an owner of real estate (known as the **lessor**), and a tenant (the **lessee**) that transfers the right of possession and use of the owner's property to the tenant for a specified period of time. A *lease* is also a contract that generally sets forth the length of time the contract is to run, the amount to be paid by the lessee for the right to use the property, and other rights and obligations of the parties.

Since a lease is a bilateral agreement, both parties have rights and obligations under the lease. The landlord grants the tenant the right to occupy the premises and use them for purposes stated in the lease. In return, the landlord retains the right to receive payment for the use of the premises as well as a reversionary right to retake possession after the lease term has expired. The lessor's interest in leased property is called a *leased fee estate plus reversionary right*.

LEASEHOLD (NONFREEHOLD) ESTATES

When a landowner leases real estate to a tenant, the tenant's right to occupy the land for the duration of the lease is called a **leasehold estate**. A leasehold estate is a possessionary estate in land that is generally considered personal property, because no ownership of the real property has changed hands.

In the discussion of interests and estates in Chapter 2, freehold estates were differentiated from leasehold estates. Just as there are several types of freehold (ownership) estates, there are also various leasehold estates. The four most important are *estate for years, estate from period to period, estate at will,* and *estate at sufferance* (see Figure 11.1). The major difference between the various leasehold estates is the way each is terminated. One parcel of property can be held in both a nonfreehold by a tenant and freehold estate by the landlord at the same time.

FIGURE 11.1

Leasehold Estates

Type of Estate	Distinguishing Characteristics
Estate for years	Automatic termination after a definite period; no notice to terminate required unless written into the lease.
Estate from period to period	Automatic renewal after a definite initial period, until terminated by either party with required notice
Estate at will	Terminated by either party at any time with no required notice
Estate at sufferance	Landlord must evict illegal holdover tenant

Estate for Years (Tenancy for Years)

Estate for years = Any definite period.

A leasehold estate that continues for a *definite period of time*, whether for years, months, weeks, or even days, is an **estate for years.** An estate for years always has a specific starting and ending time, and it may be for a term of less than one year. It automatically terminates at the end of the lease period. No notice is required to terminate the lease at the end of the lease period. When the lease period expires, the lessee is required to vacate the premises and surrender possession to the lessor. A lease for years may be terminated prior to the expiration date by the mutual consent of both parties, but otherwise neither party may terminate without showing that the lease agreement has been breached. As is characteristic of all leases, an estate for years gives the lessee the right to occupy and use the leased property—subject, of course, to the terms and covenants contained in the lease agreement itself.

Estate from Period to Period (Periodic Tenancy)

Estate from period to period = Indefinite term; automatically renews.

An **estate from period to period,** or a **periodic tenancy**, is created when the landlord and tenant enter into an agreement that continues for a specific period, *being automatically renewed for an indefinite time without a specific ending date.* Rent is payable at definite intervals. Such a tenancy is generally created by agreement or operation of law to run for a certain amount of time, such as week-to-week, month-to-month, or year-to-year. Often a residential lease starts as an estate for years and, at the end of the lease period, automatically rolls over into a periodic tenancy until a lease extension is signed or the lease is terminated. The agreement is automatically renewed for similar succeeding periods until one of the parties gives notice to terminate. In effect, the payment and acceptance of rent extend the lease for another period. In North Carolina, the minimum notice-of-termination periods are as follows:

In North Carolina

- For a week-to-week tenancy, the notice period is two days.
- For a month-to-month tenancy, the notice period is seven days.
- For a year-to-year tenancy, the notice period is one month.

A month-to-month tenancy generally is created when a tenant takes possession with no definite termination date and pays rent monthly. This is usually a valid agreement.

IN PRACTICE A common residential apartment lease is originally for the period of one year and then converts to a month-to-month lease creating a periodic tenancy. As long as the tenant makes the rent payment on time and the landlord accepts the payment, the lease is extended for another monthly period. With a thirty-day notice, either the landlord or the tenant can terminate this lease.

Estate at Will

An estate that gives the tenant *the right to possess property with the consent of the landlord for a term of unspecified or uncertain duration* is an **estate at will,** or a tenancy at will. It may be created by express agreement or by operation of law, and during its existence the tenant has all the rights and obligations of a lessor/lessee relationship.

Estate at will = Indefinite term; possession with landlord's consent.

■ **FOR EXAMPLE** At the end of a lease period, a landlord informs a tenant that in a few months the city is going to demolish the apartment building to make way for an expressway. The landlord gives the tenant the option to occupy the premises until demolition begins. If the tenant agrees to stay, a tenancy at will is created.

An estate at will can be terminated at any time, *at the will* of either party. All that is required is for one party to declare that the tenancy is over. No prior notice is required.

Estate at Sufferance

Estate at sufferance = Tenant's previously lawful possession continued without landlord's consent.

An **estate at sufferance,** or a *tenancy at sufferance*, arises when a tenant who lawfully came into possession of real property continues, after the tenant's rights have expired, to hold possession of the premises *without the consent of the landlord.* An example of an estate at sufferance is when a tenant for years *fails to surrender possession at the expiration of the lease.* The **holdover tenant** has no rights in the property, and the landowner can have him or her evicted at any time, without advance notice. This is not a trespass situation because the tenant originally took possession with the consent of the lessor. This is the lowest estate in real estate.

If a tenant has an estate at will or an estate at sufferance and pays the landlord rent monies that the landlord accepts, a periodic tenancy is created. If the landlord wishes to end the tenant's estate, rent cannot be accepted under either the estate at will or the estate at sufferance.

■ TYPES OF LEASES

The manner in which rent is determined indicates the type of lease that is in force (see Figure 11.2).

Fixed or Gross Lease

In a **fixed or gross lease,** the tenant's obligation is to pay a *fixed amount*, and the landlord pays all taxes, insurance premiums, mortgage payments, repair costs, and the like connected with the property (usually called *property charges*). This type of lease is most often used for residential rentals but could be used in any type of property.

Percentage Lease (Retail Lease)

A **percentage lease** provides for rental based on a *percentage of the gross or net income* received by a tenant doing business on the leased property. This type of lease is usually used in the rental of retail business locations. The percentage lease usually provides for a smaller than normal fixed rental fee (base rent) plus a percentage of that portion of the tenant's gross or net business income that exceeds a stated minimum.

FIGURE 11.2

Characteristics of Lease Types

Lease Type	Generally Used for	Lease Characteristics
Fixed rental lease	Residential leases	Tenant pays a fixed amount of rent but none of the property charges
Percentage lease	Commercial leases	Tenant pays a percentage of the gross or net income as rent
Net lease	Commercial leases	Tenant pays rent plus all or some of the property charges
Graduated lease	Commercial leases	Tenant pays rent, which increases at predetermined dates
Ground lease	Commercial leases	Tenant typically pays rent on land and builds on it

■ **FOR EXAMPLE** A lease might provide for a fixed base monthly rental of $1,500, with a further agreement that the tenant pays an additional amount each month equivalent to 4% of all gross sales in excess of $30,000. The percentage charged in such leases varies widely with the nature of the business and is negotiable between landlord and tenant. A tenant's bargaining power is determined by the volume of business. Percentages also vary with the location of the property and general economic conditions.

> **MATH CONCEPTS**
>
> **CALCULATING PERCENTAGE LEASE RENTS**
> Percentage leases usually call for a fixed base monthly rent plus a percentage of gross sales income exceeding a stated monthly or annual amount. For example, a lease might require minimum rent of $1,300 per month plus 5% of the annual sales of the business that exceed $160,000. On an annual sales volume of $250,000, the annual rent would be calculated as follows:
>
> $1,300 base rent per month × 12 months = $15,600
> $250,000 − $160,000 = $90,000 subject to percentage rent
> $90,000 × .05 (5%) = $4,500
> $15,600 base rent + $4,500 percentage rent = $20,100 total annual rent

Net Lease

A **net lease** provides that, in addition to the base rent, *the tenant pays all or some of the property charges such as maintenance, property taxes, and insurance*. This type of lease is called a net lease and, based upon how many of the property expenses the tenant pays, it would be a single net, double net, or triple net et cetera. Commercial brokers frequently referred to these charges as TICAM (**t**axes, **i**nsurance, and **c**ommon **a**rea **m**aintenance). The monthly rental paid to the landlord is in addition to these charges and is net income for the landlord after operating costs have been paid. Leases for entire commercial or industrial buildings and the land on which they are located, ground leases, and long-term leases are frequently net leases.

Graduated Lease

A **graduated lease** provides for *increases in rent to occur at set future dates*. Graduated leases are often used in the rental of office space for multiple-year terms. Sometimes called a step-up lease.

■ **FOR EXAMPLE** A three-year office lease may provide for the rent to be $1,000 a month for the first year, $1,200 a month for the second year, and $1,400 a month for the third year.

Index Lease

An **index lease** allows *rent to be increased or decreased periodically*, based on changes in a stipulated index, such as the government cost-of-living index or some other named index.

Ground Lease

When a landowner leases land to a tenant who agrees to *erect a building* on the land, the lease is usually referred to as a **ground lease**. Ground leases usually involve separate ownership of land and building. Such a lease must be for a long enough term to make the transaction desirable to the tenant investing in the building. These leases are generally net leases that require the lessee to pay rent as well as real estate taxes, insurance, upkeep, and repairs. Ground leases often run for terms of 99 years or longer. Such leases should be very clear about ownership of the improvements on the land at the end of the lease.

Oil and Mineral Lease

When oil companies lease land to explore for oil, gas, and other minerals, a special lease agreement must be negotiated. Usually, the landowner receives a cash payment for executing the lease. If minerals are found, the property owner usually receives a portion of the value of the minerals as a royalty. The North Carolina Statute of Frauds states that any mineral lease, regardless of duration, must be in writing to be enforceable.

Full-Service Lease

Full-service leases are commercial leases that are often used in large office or multi-tenant buildings such as shopping centers where the tenants share in overall operating expenses for the common areas and the building(s). Under a full-service lease, the landlord will provide most or all services related to the lease, such as utilities, cleaning services, grounds maintenance, etc. Usually rent is paid as a base amount plus a prorated share of the complex's operating expenses.

■ LEASE PROVISIONS

Most leases are complex documents that should be carefully prepared, and both landlords and tenants should not hesitate to seek legal advice if they have questions about the application of certain provisions. Real estate brokers are allowed only to fill in the blanks in preprinted forms and it is critically important that a real estate broker use a form appropriate to the specific rental situation. Only a form drafted specifically by an attorney and/or approved forms promulgated by reputable trade organizations should be utilized plus a lawyer should prepare any additional clauses inserted into a standard lease.

Essential Provisions for a Valid Lease

The requirements for a valid lease are basically the same as those for any other contract. Generally, the four essentials of a valid lease are as follows:

Four Essentials of a Valid Lease
1. Mutual agreement
2. Consideration
3. Capacity to contract
4. Legal objectives

1. *Mutual agreement.* The parties must reach a mutual agreement on all material terms of the contract (i.e., time of possession, amount of rent, due date for rent, etc.), usually accomplished by means of offer and acceptance.
2. *Consideration.* All leases, being contracts, must be supported by valid consideration. In the leasing of real estate, rent is the normal consideration granted for the right to occupy the leased premises.

3. *Capacity to contract.* The parties must have the legal capacity to contract. That is, they must be of sound mind, sober, and of legal age.
4. *Legal objectives.* The objectives of the lease must be legal.

When the statute of frauds applies (lease over three years from the making thereof), an oral lease is considered to be unenforceable. A description of the leased premises should be stated clearly. If the lease covers land, the legal description of the real estate should be used. If the lease is for part of a building, such as office space or an apartment, that part of the property should be described clearly and carefully. If supplemental space is to be included, the lease should clearly identify it.

Common Major Provisions

Many other provisions are commonly found in lease agreements. Although the attorneys of the landlord and/or the tenant usually draft commercial leases to satisfy the unique requirements of the individual leasing situation, many of the following provisions will still be included. A copy of North Carolina's Association of REALTORS® Residential Rental Contract (Form 410-T) is shown in Appendix D, Form 23.

Tenant's use of premises. A lessor may restrict a lessee's use of the premises through provisions included in the lease. This is especially important in leases for stores or commercial space. For example, a lease may provide that the leased premises are to be used *only* for the purpose of a real estate office *and for no other purpose.* Tenant uses that could result in environmental concerns are addressed below. In the absence of such limitations, a lessee may use the premises for any lawful purpose. The tenant may also impose use restrictions in the lease, such as the lease being subject to rezoning approval for specific tenant use. The tenant may request use exclusivity, such as being the only restaurant in a small shopping center.

Environmental concerns. Industrial leases will frequently restrict or forbid the production, use, discharge, and/or storage of hazardous materials on the property due to environmental concerns. Since some state and federal regulations will hold the landowner liable for environmental contamination even if they did not create the problem, it is vital to contractually agree to the handling or disposal of any allowed contaminants. Lease provisions for periodic inspection of compliance with governmental regulations for the handling of hazardous materials would be appropriate. Lessee should conduct a thorough environmental evaluation of the site before signing any lease that would make them liable for all environmental clean-up expenses upon termination of the lease since contamination from a previous use might already exist.

Fixtures. Neither the landlord nor the tenant is required to make any improvements to the leased property. In the absence of an agreement to the contrary, the tenant may make improvements with the landlord's express permission. Any such alterations generally become the property of the landlord; that is, they become fixtures. However, as discussed in Chapter 2, a tenant may be given the right by the terms of the lease to install trade fixtures. It is customary to stipulate that such trade fixtures may be removed by the tenant before the lease expires, provided the tenant restores the premises to pre-lease condition, normal wear and tear excluded.

Repairs (nonresidential property). Unlike the landlord obligations under the Residential Rental Agreement Act, if the leased property is nonresidential and no lease provision exists to the contrary, landlords are generally not obligated to make any repairs to leased premises. Nonresidential tenants are generally deemed to have accepted the property with no implied promise that the premises are safe or suitable for the use intended. Landlords may be responsible for repairing *hidden*, or *latent*, *defects*, since a diligent inspection by the prospective tenant would not have revealed the defect. Tenants typically are required to make ordinary repairs or be held liable for *waste* of the property. Generally the tenant is required to return the premises in the same condition in which they were received, with allowance for ordinary use.

Upfitting improvements (commercial leases). A commercial landlord will usually provide for the initial customization of leased space for a new tenant. The tenant is frequently allowed, within cost parameters, to specify customizing preferences, such as wall and floor covering selection, location of interior walls, and placement of doors. If the tenant wants improvements that exceed the *upfit allowance*, the tenant usually negotiates their inclusion in the rent or pays for the excess expense. Occasionally, in an effort to retain a desirable tenant, the landlord may offer upfitting improvements to renovate the tenant's current space.

Assignment and subleases. The lessee may assign or sublease the lease if the lease terms do not prohibit it. Most leases prohibit the lessee from assigning or subletting without the lessor's written consent. The lessor, therefore, retains control over the occupancy of the leased premises but must not unreasonably withhold consent. With an *assignment*, a tenant transfers all leasehold interests, which include both the entire term of the lease and all premiums. One who transfers less than all of the leasehold interests by leasing them to a new tenant **subleases** and retains a reversionary interest to re-enter the property prior to the end of the original lease period. In effect, a sublease is the making of a new lease, wherein the original lessee (tenant) becomes a sublessor and the new tenant becomes a sublessee.

In most cases, the sublease or assignment, of a lease does not relieve the original lessee of the obligation to make rental payments. When a lease is assigned, the original tenant retains *secondary liability* for paying the rent. When a lease is sublet, the original tenant retains *primary liability* for paying the rent. The sublessor's (original lessee's) interest in the real estate is known as a **sandwich lease**. The landlord may offer the original tenant a **novation** where the landlord signs a new lease with the new tenant thereby releasing the original tenant from further liability.

Term of the lease and lease renewal. The term of a lease is the period for which the lease will be in effect, and it should be set out precisely in the lease contract. The date of the beginning of the term and the date of its ending should be noted, together with a statement of the total period of the lease; for example, *for a term of three years beginning December 1, 2011, and ending November 30, 2014.*

Unless specifically provided for in the lease, a lessee typically has no right to renew a lease. A renewal clause should stipulate when the lessee must notify the lessor that the lease will be renewed, how the lessor must be notified, and the length of the new lease period. A provision permitting automatic renewals should address timely termination notification requirements by either party.

Default. As with all well-written contracts, a provision should address legal remedies in the case of default by either party. The most common examples of default are by the lessee through nonpayment of rent, damage to the property, or abandonment of the property. Although the landlord can be in default, it is less likely. The remedies for default are limited to the conditions of the lease or applicable statutes.

Options to purchase or first right of refusal. Many leases contain an option that grants the lessee the right to purchase the leased premises at the end of the lease; this provision is particularly likely in a ground lease where the tenant has significantly improved the landlord's property. Usually, the price of the property is agreed to in advance, but sometimes the parties agree to abide by an estimate of value compiled by a selected group of appraisers done at the time of the purchase. Every option should state the purchase price or the exact method used to determine the purchase price. Instead of an option to purchase, a lease may contain a *right of first refusal* (see Chapter 10).

Landlord's right to enter and the covenant of quiet enjoyment. Once a valid lease has been executed, the lessor, as the owner of the real estate, is usually bound by the **covenant of quiet enjoyment** that is implied by law. Under this covenant, the lessor guarantees that the lessee may take possession of the leased premises and that no one, including the landlord, will interfere with the tenant's possession or use of the property. This covenant also means that the tenant will not be affected by any defects in the landlord's title.

The landlord has no right to enter the leased premises during the lease term unless the lease specifically gives the landlord or their agent this right. Usually, the landlord retains the right to enter to inspect the property, to make necessary repairs, to show the property to potential tenants, and in case of an emergency. Most leases provide that the landlord or their agent must give the tenant a certain amount of notice before entering the premises.

Termination of Leases

As with any contract, a lease is discharged when the contract terminates. Termination can occur when all parties have fully performed their obligations under the agreement. The landlord and tenant may mutually agree to cancel the lease, but if the tenant simply abandons the property, the tenant remains liable for the terms of the lease—including the payment of rent. Leases may be terminated in the following ways:

- The parties to a lease may mutually agree to cancel the lease.
- When the lease term expires, the lease is terminated automatically.

- A tenancy may be terminated by operation of law, as in a bankruptcy or condemnation proceeding.
- If one of the parties fails to perform a material obligation, such as the tenant fails to pay rent or the landlord fails to maintain habitable condition, the other party can terminate the lease.

If the tenant fails to pay rent, the landlord can evict the tenant. If the tenant refuses to leave the premises voluntarily, the landlord must bring an eviction action in court (summary ejectment) to have the tenant removed. If the landlord fails to maintain the premises in habitable condition, the tenant is considered *constructively evicted* and may move out and stop paying future rent.

Note that when the owner of leased property dies or the property is sold, *the lease does not terminate*. The heirs of a deceased landlord are bound by the terms of existing valid leases. In addition, if a landlord conveys leased real estate, the new landlord takes the property subject to the rights of the tenants.

North Carolina Statute of Frauds and Recordation

In North Carolina

Any North Carolina lease that lasts for *more than three years from the date of execution* must be in writing and signed by the landlord and the tenant to comply with the North Carolina Statute of Frauds. For instance, a lease signed on January 1, 2012, and terminating on December 31, 2012, does not have to be in writing. Generally, oral leases for three years or less are enforceable. But a lease signed on January 1, 2012, and terminating on January 31, 2015, does have to be in writing to be enforceable.

Under the Conner Act, leases required to be in writing under the North Carolina Statute of Frauds must be recorded to be enforceable against third parties. If the lease is not recorded and a third party buys the property, that person is not required to honor the terms of the lease. Failure to observe the statutory requirements in recording a lease does not in any way affect its validity between the parties, just third parties.

IN PRACTICE Even though an oral lease may be enforceable, such as a lease for one year commencing the day of agreement, it is always better practice to put lease agreements in writing and to have the writing signed by all parties to the agreement. The lease document should be as inclusive as possible, for reasons that will become apparent from reading this chapter.

■ NORTH CAROLINA RESIDENTIAL RENTAL AGREEMENTS ACT

In North Carolina

In North Carolina, residential leases and the landlord-tenant relationship are governed by the **Residential Rental Agreements Act** (NCGS §42-38 et. seq.). The primary purpose of this Act is to ensure that only habitable residential units are rented. A failure to comply with the terms of this Act has potentially serious consequences. The Act does not apply to transient quarters such as hotels or motels, nor does it apply to commercial or rent-free properties.

Obligations of Landlord and Tenant Are Mutually Dependent

The North Carolina Residential Rental Agreements Act makes *the obligations of the landlord and the tenant mutually dependent.* That is, if either the landlord or the tenant fails to fulfill a duty, the other party is no longer responsible for fulfilling an equivalent duty. For example, if the landlord fails to provide the tenant with habitable premises, the tenant does not have to remain in the premises for the full lease term. Furthermore, the statutory duties of the landlord according to this Act cannot be waived or altered by lease provision or other agreement between landlord and tenant. For example, the landlord is not allowed to lease the property for reduced rent in exchange for the tenant accepting the property in an "as is" condition. If a real estate broker is acting as an agent for a landlord, the court sees the broker as a *landlord* under the Act.

Landlord's Statutory Duties

In North Carolina

The Act provides that the landlord's primary duty is **implied warranty of habitability**—to supply *fit* and *habitable* premises to the tenant. This means the premises must be fit for human occupancy. The Act (NCGS §42-42 and 42-43) sets forth standards for *habitability* and instructs the landlord to *do whatever is necessary to put and keep the premises in a fit and habitable condition.* The landlord must comply with current building and housing codes; make all necessary repairs to keep the premises in a habitable condition; keep all common areas safe; and maintain all electrical, plumbing, sanitary, heating, ventilating, and other facilities.

A 2009 amendment to the Act added the requirement that the landlord remediate any *imminently dangerous condition* within a reasonable period of time (which is dependent on the nature of the problem). The statute further defined the following as *imminently dangerous conditions*: unsafe wiring, flooring or steps, ceilings or roofs, chimneys or flues; lack of potable water; lack of operable locks on all outside doors or windows on ground level; lack of operable heating facilities capable of heating to 65°F when it is 20°F outside from November 1 through March 31; lack of operable toilet, bathtub, or shower; rat infestation due to structural defect; and excessive standing water, sewage, or flooding due to plumbing leaks or inadequate drainage that lead to mosquito infestation or mold. The landlord must also provide operable smoke and carbon monoxide detectors installed and maintained in accordance with established standards. The landlord must repair detectors within 15 days of receiving notice of necessary repairs. The tenant shall replace batteries as needed during the occupancy.

If a material failure by the landlord to provide fit and habitable units occurs, the tenant can bring legal action against the landlord for damages, including recovery of some or all of the rent paid while the unit was unfit. The court can require that the landlord correct all material property defects.

Common law of constructive eviction. In addition to remedies under the North Carolina Residential Rental Agreement Act, the tenant can invoke the protection of the common-law doctrine of **constructive eviction**. This doctrine gives the tenant the right, in effect, to cancel the remainder of the lease and vacate the premises without penalties if the landlord repeatedly fails to satisfy habitability requirements. The tenant gives the landlord notice that the premises are uninhabitable. If the situation is not corrected within a reasonable time, the tenant can leave the premises and is no longer responsible for paying future rent. In effect, the tenant evicts himself or herself by building a case to prove the landlord's breach of the bilateral lease agreement. Of course, the tenant is responsible for paying rent up to and including the last day of occupancy. Tenant is forbidden to withhold rent while in possession of the unit. The tenant security deposit, if any, is to be returned to the tenant.

Common law of negligence. Tenants, or their guests, are sometimes injured on leased property, and the question arises as to whether the landlord can be held accountable for those injuries. The common law of negligence holds that the landlord is liable for injuries that occur in common areas—hallways, stairways, elevators, sidewalks, and parking lots—when the landlord has negligently failed to maintain safe conditions in those areas. Therefore, if a tenant or guest has the right to be on the premises and is injured because of the landlord's failure to maintain the common areas, the injured party may be able to recover damages from the landlord.

However, if the injury occurs in the area exclusively occupied by the tenant—such as an apartment or office space—the results are different. Generally, the landlord is not liable for injuries that occur within the leased premises. The only exception to this rule is if the landlord failed to keep the premises in a habitable condition. Under the North Carolina Residential Rental Agreements Act, the fact that the landlord failed to maintain the leased premises in a fit and habitable condition can be presented in court as evidence of the landlord's negligence. The negligence could mean that the landlord would be held liable for the injury.

With the increase in crime, the landlord's liability for criminal acts that occur on leased premises or the common areas of rental property has become an issue. In North Carolina, a landlord is not generally liable for criminal acts committed against tenants unless the landlord knew or should have known of a dangerous situation and did nothing to protect the tenants. For instance, if a rental property is in a high crime area and the landlord knows that the security system is grossly inadequate, the landlord may be liable if a tenant is injured in a mugging in a building hallway.

Tenant's Statutory Duties

The Act states that the tenant's primary duty is to *maintain the dwelling unit*. This means the tenant must keep the occupied premises clean and safe, dispose of all garbage and other waste, keep the plumbing fixtures clean, comply with the obligations imposed on tenants by current housing and building codes, replace batteries in smoke detectors as needed during the tenancy, refrain from deliberately or negligently damaging the premises, and take responsibility for any damage that does occur.

Tenant prohibited from unilaterally withholding rent. Under the Residential Rental Agreements Act, tenants do not have the right to withhold rent before they obtain a court order giving them that right. Thus, even when the tenant has a legitimate complaint against the landlord, the tenant cannot decide to withhold all or a portion of the rent as a remedy. Note that this provision does not alter the tenant's right to vacate the premises and stop paying future rent on the basis of constructive eviction. A tenant who withholds the rent but retains possession of the property has violated the rental agreement, giving the landlord the right to evict.

IN PRACTICE Despite several written requests from the tenant, the landlord has not had the heating system in the tenant's unit repaired. Tired of waiting on the landlord, the tenant hires a HVAC repairperson to fix the unit and pays for the service call himself. The tenant then deducts the cost of the repair from the rent check for that month. This might be considered *withholding rent* because the entire rent payment was not submitted. Furthermore, a tenant does not have the right to make changes or repairs to the landlord's property without the landlord's permission (preferably in writing).

Residential Eviction Laws/Procedures

The only possible legal eviction remedy is through the court system; in other words, a landlord cannot use self-help eviction remedies, no matter how peaceful. For example, the landlord cannot change the locks on the doors to prevent the tenant from entering the premises, cut off the tenant's utilities, or seize the tenant's possessions. Instead, the landlord must bring an eviction action in court before a magistrate in district court. A state statute (NCGS §42-21.1) sets forth public policy against the **self-help eviction** procedure and replaces it with a procedure called **summary ejectment.** This hearing before a magistrate in small claims court is the only legal way a landlord can evict a tenant. The law (NCGS §42-25.7) also provides direction on the appropriate disposal of an evicted tenant's abandoned personal property. Expedited eviction is possible when the tenant, their family member, or guest has engaged in criminal activity in the leased unit; landlord should seek legal assistance before filing for expedited eviction.

[In North Carolina]

Retaliatory eviction prohibited An important provision of this Act is known as the *doctrine of retaliatory eviction*. Under the **retaliatory eviction** provision (NCGS §42-37), a tenant cannot be evicted because the tenant has asserted a legal right against the landlord. Therefore, a landlord cannot evict a tenant who, in good faith, requests that the landlord make required repairs, exercises legal rights against the landlord, becomes involved in a tenants' rights association, or complains to a government entity about a landlord's violation of landlord-tenant law. If the landlord tries to evict a tenant within 12 months after the tenant tried to assert a protected legal right, the tenant can use this doctrine as a defense in the eviction action. The doctrine does not require the landlord to renew the lease.

■ LAWS PROTECTING TENANTS IN FORECLOSURE SITUATIONS

Protecting Tenants at Foreclosure Act of 2009

Tenants living in a foreclosed residential property are protected under the sweeping coverage of the federal Protecting Tenants at Foreclosure Act of 2009. This Act applies to *any foreclosure on any federally related mortgage loan or any dwelling* or *residential real property*. The new owner of the property must comply with the protective provisions of the act. If the residential tenant has a bona fide lease that was in place prior to the foreclosure notice, the tenant may occupy the property for the remainder of the lease period, with one exception. If the new owner wishes to occupy this property as a primary residence, the tenant is entitled to a 90-day notice to vacate the premises. If the tenant does not have a lease, a 90-day notice to vacate can be given to the tenant; this notice preempts any shorter notice allowed by state law.

A *bona fide lease* must meet the following three requirements: (1) the tenant is not the mortgagor or the child, spouse, or parent of the mortgagor; (2) the lease is an arm's-length transaction; and (3) the rent cannot be substantially less than fair market value unless it is subsidized by a government subsidy.

In North Carolina — State Law Allowing Early Termination by Tenant

While the previous federal law prohibits the new owner's immediate termination of a tenant's occupancy of a foreclosed residential dwelling, a North Carolina law (NCGS 42-25.2) allows a tenant to terminate a rental agreement early in some foreclosure situations. In North Carolina, a residential tenant must receive notice of an imminent foreclosure sale on the leased property under provisions of NCGS 42-21. If the leased unit is part of residential real property that contains less than 15 rental units and the tenant has received the required notice of foreclosure, the tenant has a statutory right to terminate the rental agreement subject to a 10-day notice to the landlord.

■ TENANT SECURITY DEPOSIT ACT

In North Carolina

In North Carolina, the **Tenant Security Deposit Act** (NCGS §42-50 et. seq.) regulates the amount of money that can be required as a **security deposit** and what the landlord can do with that deposit. The amount of the security deposit depends on the term of the tenancy. The maximum amount of security deposit is the equivalent of

- two weeks' rent if the tenancy is from week to week,
- one and one-half months' rent if the tenancy is from month to month, and
- two months' rent if the tenancy is longer than month to month.

The landlord may do one of two things with the security deposit: (1) the security deposit can be placed in a trust account with an insured North Carolina bank or savings institution or (2) the landlord can obtain a bond as a guarantee for the deposit. The landlord must tell the tenant either the name of the bank or savings institution or the name of the bonding company. (*If a real estate agent is handling the deposit, the agent has only one option: the security deposit must be deposited into a trust account* [see NCREC Rule A.0107].)

The Tenant Security Deposit Act provides that a security deposit on a residential unit may be used only to reimburse the landlord for nonpayment of rent, damage to the premises (other than *ordinary wear and tear*), nonfulfillment of the rental period, unpaid bills that may create a lien on the property due to the tenant's occupancy, cost of removing and storing tenant's property, costs of re-renting after a breach, or court costs in connection with an eviction action. If a tenant breaches the lease and abandons the property, the landlord is obligated to diligently attempt to find a new tenant as soon as possible. If the property is re-rented, the landlord can withhold only the part of the security deposit that covers the *lost* rent plus costs of re-renting. The remainder of the deposit must be returned to the breaching tenant. If the security deposit does not entirely cover the rent lost due to breach, the landlord may retain the entire deposit and employ other legal methods to recoup the loss of rent.

Upon the termination of the lease, the landlord or his agent must account for the tenant security deposit to the tenant in writing within 30 days. An itemized account of any permitted deductions from the deposit with the return of any unused money must be sent to the last known address of the tenant. If the landlord's claim against the tenant security deposit cannot be determined within 30 days, tenant must be provided an interim accounting with a final accounting no later than 60 days from termination of tenancy and delivery of possession of the premises to the landlord or his agent.

If pets are allowed on the premises, the landlord is allowed to charge a separate, reasonable pet fee that can be nonrefundable. If the animal is a service animal, such as a Seeing Eye dog, it would not be regarded as a *pet* and a pet fee would *not* be allowed because a service animal is considered to be an extension of the handicapped person.

Damages to the Premises

Even though the tenant security deposit may be retained in whole or in part to pay for damages to the premises, the landlord cannot use the deposit to pay for damages that may be classified under the broad term *ordinary wear and tear*. Real estate law in North Carolina does not define what may constitute ordinary wear and tear versus what may constitute actual damages to the premises. NCREC has published consumer information on tenant security deposits that provides excellent guidance to landlords, property managers, and tenants. Common examples of *ordinary wear and tear* are

- dirty carpet or carpet worn from long use;
- peeling, faded, and cracked paint;
- dirty walls and windows;
- leaking plumbing and worn plumbing fixtures; and
- frayed curtains and broken blind strings.

Examples of other damages for which use of the deposit is permitted are

- large holes in the walls;
- crayon marks;
- broken plumbing fixtures, windows, and counter tops;
- burned places and stains on carpeting;
- bizarre or unauthorized paint colors;
- appliances requiring extraordinary cleaning due to excessive filth; and
- extraordinary cleaning of the unit due to excessive filth.

CONSTITUTIONAL RIGHTS OF TENANTS IN PUBLIC HOUSING

The tenants of government-subsidized low-income housing (sometimes called *Section 8 Housing*) have some additional rights. These tenants have an entitlement to continued occupancy and cannot be evicted unless there is *good cause*. There must be a finding of fault on the tenant's part, not merely circumstances that are beyond the tenant's control such as loss of a job. Tenants are entitled to *procedural due process* before they can be evicted. The landlord must maintain property in habitable condition or risk being suspended from future program participation.

NORTH CAROLINA VACATION RENTAL ACT

In North Carolina

The **North Carolina Vacation Rental Act** (NCGS §42A) went into effect January 1, 2000, and is modeled after the Residential Rental Agreement Act. The statute establishes uniform rules for landlords, tenants, and their agents involved in the handling of short-term rentals under 90 days in length where the tenant has a primary residence elsewhere. The Act applies to all landlords (using an agent or not) who rent residential property for the purposes of vacation, recreation, or leisure. It is important to note that a vacation rental property manager, like other types of property managers for others, must be a licensed real estate broker. A broker may pay a *referral fee* to an unlicensed travel agent *(defined in the statute)* for procuring a tenant *only for vacation rentals, according to certain guidelines found in NCREC Rule A.0109(e), and* provided that no other acts of real estate brokerage requiring a license are performed by the travel agent (motels, hotels, etc., are exempt). The Vacation Rental Act authorizes

- all rental agreements to be in writing;
- the landlord to collect payments in advance of the tenancy, but monies must be placed in an escrow account (no later than three banking days after receipt of these payments);
- the landlord to refund tenant's payments if fit and habitable premises cannot be provided;
- regulations for the use of monies collected as security deposits;
- the new owner to take title subject to rentals for the next 180 days, if the property is sold;
- an expedited eviction procedure;
- the landlord to provide tenants with fit premises and keep property repaired and safe;
- the tenants to maintain the property and not damage the premises; and
- upon compliance, the tenants to be given a refund of their rent if tenants are ordered by authorities to evacuate, unless the tenants had been offered evacuation insurance to cover the potential risk.

OTHER LANDLORD/TENANT RULES

Landlords must comply with federal and state fair housing laws and must not discriminate unlawfully. (Fair housing rights are discussed in Chapter 20.) Violation of the Residential Rental Agreements Act may also constitute a violation of the Unfair and Deceptive Business or Trade Practices Act that can result in the

> **In North Carolina** payment of treble damages if found guilty. NCREC also can discipline a licensee for violation of these laws. Landlords must comply with *sexual harassment statutes*, which prohibit unsolicited overt demands for sexual favors when negotiating a lease or determining rights under a lease. Landlords also must comply with the Americans with Disabilities Act (see Chapter 20).

■ RELATED WEBSITES

National Association of Independent Landlords: www.landlordassociation.com
National Landlord Tenant Guide: www.rentlaw.com
North Carolina General Assembly (search by name of Act):
 www.ncga.state.nc.us/gascripts/statutes/Statutes.asp

■ KEY POINT REVIEW

A **lease** is a contract between the **lessor** (the owner of real estate) and the **lessee** (the tenant) that transfers possession and use of the property, lasts for a specified period, and is made in return for consideration (possession and payment).

The statute of frauds in North Carolina requires that leases for more than three years be in writing to be enforceable.

The lessor (landlord) has a reversionary right to possession of property when a lease expires.

North Carolina Residential Rental Agreements Act: mutually dependent obligations cannot be waived even by lease terms.

- A landlord's duties include: **implied warranty of habitability** of the premises; building code compliance; timely repairs; safety of common areas (common **law of negligence**); and installation of smoke and carbon monoxide detectors. A landlord may use
  — a **summary ejectment** (eviction) if tenant breaches lease, and
  — no **retaliatory eviction** or **self-help eviction** practices.
- A tenant's duties include: maintaining the unit; disposing of all garbage and waste; keeping plumbing fixtures clean; replacing smoke detector batteries, and repairing any damage. The tenant can
  — never withhold rent while in possession of the unit, and
  — invoke doctrine of **constructive eviction** if the landlord breaches the lease.

North Carolina Tenant Security Deposit Act regulates the following:

- Amount of deposit: dependent on length of tenancy
- Where deposit is held: insured bank or savings and loan lawfully doing business in North Carolina
- Allowed uses of the deposit by landlord
- Landlord must account for and/or return unused deposit within 30 days of termination of tenancy; can have up to 60 days for final accounting
- Reasonable, nonrefundable pet fees are allowed (no fees for service animals)

Tenants in public housing are entitled to *due process* prior to eviction.

North Carolina Vacation Rental Act applies to all short-term rentals for less than 90 days for the purpose of leisure or recreation. It is modeled after the Residential Rental Agreement Act and allows for statutory warrant of habitability, expedited eviction, and buyers honoring any rental for the next 180 days after purchase.

The lessee (tenant) has a **leasehold** (nonfreehold) **estate** that can be one of the following:

- **Estate for years** (tenancy for years)—continues for a definite period
- **Estate from period to period (periodic tenancy)**—has no specific expiration date, but rent is payable at definite intervals
  — Has continuity because it automatically renews
  — Month-to-month tenancy—most common form of residential lease
- **Estate at will** (tenancy at will)—has no specified initial term, is created by express agreement or operation of law, and can be terminated by the landlord or the tenant at any time on proper notice
- **Estate at sufferance** (tenancy at sufferance)—created when the tenant stays on without the landlord's consent after termination; **holdover tenancy**.
  — The landlord can begin eviction proceedings and action for damages under state laws.

Types of leases include the following:

- A **fixed lease (gross lease)** requires the tenant to pay basic rent and the landlord to pay expenses of ownership.
- In a **percentage lease**, the retail tenant pays basic rent plus a percentage of gross sales and may pay property expenses.
- A **net lease** requires the tenant to pay basic rent plus all or most property expenses and the landlord to pay some property expenses.
- A variable lease allows an increase in rent during the lease period.
  — A **graduated lease** states specific rent increases.
  — An **index lease** allows rent changes (up or down) based on the Consumer Price Index (CPI) or other indicator.
- A **ground lease** involves separate ownership of the land and the buildings.

A **valid lease** includes the following:

- Description of leased premises
- Implied **covenant of quiet enjoyment**
- Limitations on tenant's use of the property and the term (length) of the lease
- Security deposit, which must comply with state law
- Whether improvements may be made by the tenant
  — Fixtures generally become the landlord's property.
  — Federal fair housing law requires that the landlord allow a tenant with a physical disability to make reasonable modifications.
  — **Americans with Disabilities Act (ADA)** requires that commercial nonresidential property be free of barriers or that reasonable accommodations be provided.
- Maintenance of premises by landlord in compliance with state law
- Assignment of lease that relieves tenant of further obligation

- **Sublease** provisions
- Recording of lease that may be required by state law
- Nondisturbance clause
- Option that may give the tenant the right to renew the lease, right to purchase property, or right of first refusal before landlord can sell the property

QUESTIONS

1. A landlord may enter leased premises to make repairs if the landlord
   a. knocks first to give notice of intent to enter.
   b. is given this right in the lease.
   c. gives 48 hours notice of intent to enter.
   d. gives written notice of intent to enter 24 hours in advance.

2. For the tenant to terminate a tenancy from month to month, according to standard protocol, the tenant
   a. must give notice to the landlord prior to termination.
   b. need not give notice to the landlord about vacating the leased premises.
   c. must give 45 days' notice to the landlord prior to termination.
   d. must ask for the security deposit before vacating the leased premises.

3. A lease calls for a base rent of $1,200 per month plus 4% of the annual gross business exceeding $150,000. This is what type of lease?
   a. Gross
   b. Graduated
   c. Percentage
   d. Net

4. An agreement in which the tenant pays a fixed rent and the landlord pays all taxes, insurance, and maintenance on the property is a
   a. net lease.
   b. gross lease.
   c. index lease.
   d. ground lease.

5. A percentage lease provides for a
   a. long-term rental of a certain percentage of the space in a building.
   b. definite monthly rent not to exceed a stated percentage of the building's value.
   c. definite monthly rent plus a percentage of the tenant's gross receipts in excess of a certain amount.
   d. monthly graduated rent amount not to exceed a stated percentage of the original rent.

6. A tenant who transfers the remaining term of a lease to a third party is
   a. a sublessee in a sandwich lease.
   b. assigning the lease.
   c. relieved of any further obligation under the lease.
   d. giving the third party a gross lease.

7. If a tenant complains to the authorities about a housing code violation in the apartment building that affects her health, the landlord may
   I. reduce the rent as the remedy.
   II. evict the tenant for filing a compliant.
      a. I only
      b. II only
      c. Both I and II
      d. Neither I nor II

8. A property owner sells his North Carolina mountain chalet that he has been renting to vacationing ski fanatics for years. At the time of the sale, there are already 20 different week-long reservations in place for the upcoming ski season that starts in a couple of months. The purchaser of the chalet
   a. must honor any of the reservations that occur within the next six months.
   b. does not have to honor any of the reservations since they are with the old owner.
   c. must honor all reservations in place at the time of closing regardless of when they occur.
   d. does not have to honor any reservations as long as a 30-day advance written notice is given to the tenant.

9. If a landlord fails to repair the broken heating system in a timely manner, the tenant may
   a. stay in the premises and withhold rent until the repair is complete.
   b. personally pay for the repair and deduct the expense from the monthly rent.
   c. withhold rent and deposit it in an escrow account at a bank until the repair is complete.
   d. leave the premises and stop paying rent.

10. The Residential Rental Agreement Act requires the landlord to keep the
    I. apartment building in habitable condition.
    II. common areas in the rental property in safe condition.
    a. I only
    b. II only
    c. Both I and II
    d. Neither I nor II

11. A ground lease is usually
    a. short term.
    b. for 5 to 10 years.
    c. for 99 years.
    d. automatically renewable.

12. If a lessor sells the leased premises, the new owner
    a. can negotiate new rental payments with the tenants if the leases were recorded.
    b. takes the property subject to the terms of the tenants' leases.
    c. must wait to take title until all the leases expire.
    d. can change any of the lease terms after a two-month waiting period.

13. With a month-to-month tenancy, the landlord can require a maximum security deposit equal to
    a. seven days' rent.
    b. two weeks' rent.
    c. one and one-half months' rent.
    d. two months' rent.

14. If a residential tenant breaches the lease by not paying rent, the landlord may
    a. change the locks and prevent the tenant from entering the premises.
    b. turn off the tenant's utilities until rent is paid.
    c. file a summary ejectment with the courts.
    d. seize and sell the tenant's possessions to raise the rent money.

15. Constructive eviction occurs when the
    a. landlord forcibly removes the tenant from the premises after obtaining a court order.
    b. tenant moves out because the landlord fails to keep the premises in habitable condition.
    c. tenant fails to pay rent on time and the landlord changes the locks.
    d. landlord retaliates against the tenant for complaining to a state authority.

16. An estate for years
    a. renews itself automatically unless notice to terminate is given.
    b. terminates automatically at the expiration of the lease term.
    c. requires 45 days' notice to terminate.
    d. cannot be renewed.

17. An estate at sufferance usually terminates
    a. only with prior notice.
    b. on its second automatic renewal.
    c. through a summary ejectment.
    d. automatically on its expiration date.

18. A landlord has sold his building to the state so that a freeway can be built. The tenant's lease has expired, but the landlord is letting him remain until the time the building will be torn down. The tenant is part of a
    a. holdover tenancy.
    b. first right of refusal.
    c. tenancy at sufferance.
    d. tenancy at will.

19. If the landlord of an apartment building breaches her lease with one of the tenants and the tenant's unit becomes uninhabitable, which of the following would probably result?
    a. Suit for possession
    b. Constructive eviction
    c. Tenancy at sufferance
    d. Covenant of quiet enjoyment

20. Which of the following statements about the Tenant Security Deposit Act is NOT true?
    a. A property manager may be bonded for security deposits if the bonding company is located in North Carolina.
    b. The landlord has 60 days after the end of the lease to account for the use of the deposit money and/or return the funds to the tenant.
    c. The deposit money may be used to repair holes in the walls and stains in the carpet.
    d. A landlord can charge a deposit that is the equivalent of two months' rent for a one-year lease.

21. A tenant has a one-year leasehold interest in a property. The interest automatically renews itself at the end of each year. The tenant's interest is referred to as a tenancy
    a. for years.
    b. from period to period.
    c. at will.
    d. at sufferance.

22. A tenant has assigned her apartment lease to a friend, and the landlord has agreed to the assignment. If the friend fails to pay the rent, who is liable?
    a. The friend is primarily liable; the original tenant is secondarily liable.
    b. The original tenant is primarily liable; the friend is secondarily liable.
    c. The original tenant is solely liable.
    d. The friend is solely liable.

23. Which event would automatically terminate a residential lease?
    a. Destruction of the property
    b. Sale of the property
    c. Failure of the tenant to pay rent
    d. Death of the lessor

24. Which transaction would best be described as involving a ground lease?
    a. A landowner agrees to let a tenant search and drill for oil on a property for 99 years.
    b. With the landowner's permission, a tenant builds a shopping center on a rented property at the tenant's own expense.
    c. A landlord charges a commercial tenant separate rent amounts for the land and buildings under a lease.
    d. A tenant pays a base amount for the property, plus a percentage of business generated income.

25. The landlord is charging a monthly base rent of $900 plus 4% of the tenant's annual gross sales that exceed $150,000. If the tenant's business has annual gross sales of $275,000, the total annual rent would be
    a. $5,000.
    b. $11,000.
    c. $15,800.
    d. $21,800.

CHAPTER 12

Property Management

■ **LEARNING OBJECTIVES**   *When you have finished reading this chapter, you should be able to*

■ **explain** the need for property management as an industry specialization, and the functions and responsibilities of property managers.

■ **identify** the basic elements of a property management agreement.

■ **calculate** earned property management fees.

■ **explain** how to budget for operating expenses.

■ **define** these *key terms*:

budget comparison statement	operating expenses	property manager
cash flow	potential gross income	rental schedule
effective gross income	profit and loss statement	vacancy and collection losses
net operating income	property management agreement	

■ PROPERTY MANAGEMENT

The need for specialized property managers became apparent during the 1930s as lending institutions took possession of numerous foreclosed income properties. Lacking the expertise to administer these properties, they looked to the real estate industry for expert management assistance. In recent years the increased size of buildings; the technical complexities of construction, maintenance, and repair; and the trend toward absentee ownership by individual investors and investment groups have led to the expanded use of professional property managers for both residential and commercial properties. Property management has become so important that many brokerage firms maintain separate management departments staffed by carefully selected, well-trained people. A number of corporate and institutional owners of real estate have also established property management departments. Despite this trend, some real estate investors still manage their own property and therefore must acquire the knowledge and skills of a property manager. Although property owners have always had the privilege of managing their own property without the need of licensure, they cannot compensate any unlicensed friend, relative, or neighbor for assistance in the management. This includes showing the units and collecting rents.

In North Carolina In North Carolina, a property manager who is the owner's agent must have an active nonprovisional real estate broker's license. A property manager who is the employee of the owner is still required to have a real estate license unless the owner of the property is a Chapter C or Subchapter S corporation. If there is a corporate owner and the property is titled in the corporation's name, then a W-2 employee without a real estate license will be allowed to manage the property. Only title-holding owners can manage their property without an active North Carolina real estate license.

The property manager broker can utilize the services of other brokers and/or unlicensed salaried employees with limited authority. Onsite leasing agents that show available units and collect rent payments are frequently unlicensed employees of the property manager. G.S. 93A-2(c)(6), quoted below, grants licensing exemptions if the employee does not negotiate any lease terms.

> Any salaried person employed by a licensed real estate broker, for and on behalf of the owner of any real estate or the improvements thereon, which the licensed broker has contracted to manage for the owner, if the salaried employee is limited in his employment to: exhibiting units on the real estate to prospective tenants; providing the prospective tenants with information about the lease of the units; accepting applications for lease of the units; completing and executing preprinted form leases; and accepting security deposits and rental payments for the units only when the deposits and rental payments are made payable to the owner or the broker employed by the owner. The salaried employee shall not negotiate the amount of security deposits or rental payments and shall not negotiate leases or any rental agreements on behalf of the owner or broker.

With the huge increase in the number of homeowner and property owner associations in recent years, there has been a commensurate increase in the demand for association management services. Although licensed property management firms manage some communities, there is currently no real estate license requirement to provide association management. Of course, if a broker is involved in association management, they will be held to the higher level of conduct than an unlicensed manager and subject to license law.

■ FUNCTIONS OF THE PROPERTY MANAGER

In the simplest terms, a **property manager** is someone who *preserves the value of an investment property while generating income as an agent for the owner*. The agency relationship is created by the *property management contract*. The fiduciary relationship that exists between the property manager and the property owner based on the same relationship of trust that exists between a real estate broker and a seller or buyer, which was discussed in Chapter 7. A property manager usually serves the property owner as a general agent.

> A property manager's primary function is to preserve the value of an owner's investment property while generating income for the owner.

The property manager is expected to merchandise the property and control operating expenses in order to maximize income. With this expectation in mind, the property manager chooses the best possible means to carry out an agent's responsibilities and has more authority and discretion than an employee. The manager should maintain and modernize the property to preserve and enhance the owner's capital investment. The manager carries out these objectives by securing suitable tenants, collecting the rents, caring for the premises, budgeting and controlling expenses, hiring and supervising employees, keeping proper accounts, and making periodic reports to the owner. Property managers do not perform functions such as making capital improvements, reinvesting profits, paying the owner's income tax, or establishing a depreciation schedule.

Securing Management Business

In today's market, property managers may look to corporate owners, apartment and condominium associations, homeowners' associations, investment syndicates, trusts, and absentee owners as possible sources of management business. In securing business from any of these sources, word of mouth is often the best advertising. A manager who consistently demonstrates the ability to increase property income over previous levels should have no difficulty finding new business.

The Property Management Agreement

The first step in taking over the management of any property is to enter into a **property management agreement** with the owner. This agreement creates an agency relationship between the owner and the property manager. A property manager is usually considered to be a *general agent*, whereas a residential real estate broker is usually considered to be a *special agent*. As an agent, the property manager is charged with the same agency responsibilities as the listing broker—*loy*alty, *obedience, accounting, disclosure,* and *skill, care,* and *diligence* (LOADS). (Agency responsibilities are discussed at length in Chapter 7.)

> In North Carolina

Per Commission Rule A.0104, all property management agreements must be in writing from its inception. Unlike other agency agreements, the Commission rule allows property management agreements to contain an automatic renewal clause if the property owner can terminate with notice at the end of any contract period. The NCAR Exclusive Property Management Agreement (Form 401, Appendix D, Form 22) will be referenced to show provisions that a good agreement should include.

■ *Description* of the property (Provision 1).

- *Contract period* (Provision 2) should have definite beginning and ending dates but can allow for automatic term renewal if parties have the opportunity to terminate the agreement at the end of any term period.
- *Management fee* (Provision 3). The fee can be based on a percentage of gross income or net operating income, a commission on new rentals, a fixed fee, or a combination of these. For example, the manager may get 3% of all monthly rentals collected. Both the owner and manager must ensure that the agreement is very specific as to how the management fee will be determined. If the manager will collect additional fees, such as application fees or late payment fees, the ownership of those monies must be clarified in the agreement (Provision 4).
- *Definition of management's responsibilities* (Provision 5). All of the manager's duties should be stated in the contract; exceptions should be noted. Important inclusions are to whom the rent and security deposit are paid; the method used in returning security deposits; and the method of paying mortgages, utility costs, and other bills. Adherence to all fair housing laws required.
- *Extent of the manager's authority as an agent* (Provision 5). This provision should state what authority the manager is to have in such matters as hiring, firing, and supervising employees; establishing rental rates; making expenditures; and authorizing repairs within the limits set previously with the owner. (Repairs that exceed a certain expense limit may require the owner's written approval.) Authorization for marketing and/or cooperating with or compensating other brokers also would be necessary (Provisions 6 & 7). Making capital improvements would be the owner's responsibility.
- *Reporting* [Provision 5(e, f)]. Agreement should be reached on the frequency and detail of the manager's periodic reports on operations and financial position. These reports enable the owner to monitor the manager's work and serve as a basis for both the owner and the manager to assess trends that can be used in shaping future management policy.
- *Responsibilities of owner* (Provision 8). This provision should clarify the duties that the property owner retains including proper insurance coverage, adherence to fair housing laws, adequate provision of funds for management and maintenance of the property. Allocation of the property management expenses, such as fees for custodial help, advertising, supplies, and repairs, should state which are to be charged to the property's expenses versus which are to be paid by the owner.
- *Duties upon termination* (Provision 13). Both parties agree to act promptly to settle financial and recordkeeping accounts, some of which might include the transfer of funds and notifications of tenants.
- *Miscellaneous provisions*. Additional provisions should address tenant security deposits and trust-account management (Provision 9 &10); entry of the leased unit by owner or agent during the lease period (Provision 11); and Lead-Based Paint Hazard Reduction Act disclosure compliance (Provision 12). Agent should receive notification of sale of property (Provision 14) and owner should receive notification if the agent assigns or sells ownership right in the property management firm (Provision 24). Owner needs to acknowledge that the manager is only a real estate professional and other service experts might be indicated (Provision 26).

After entering into an agreement with a property owner, a manager handles the property as the owner would. In all activities, the manager's first responsibility is *to realize the highest return on the property that is consistent with the owner's instructions.* Before contracting to manage any property, the professional property manager should be certain that the owner has realistic income expectations and is willing to spend money on necessary maintenance. Attempting to meet impossible owner demands by dubious methods can endanger the manager's reputation and make it difficult to obtain future business.

PROPERTY MANAGEMENT FEE

As mentioned earlier, the property management fee can be based on a percentage of gross or net income, a commission on new rentals, a fixed fee, or a combination of these.

■ **FOR EXAMPLE** Assume a property management agreement provides that the property manager gets 9% of all rents collected from a 10-unit apartment building. Two of the units are studio apartments that each rent for $250 a month. Six of the units are one-bedroom apartments that each rent for $325 a month. The remaining two units are two-bedroom apartments that each rent for $400 a month. Because of vacancies and collection losses, the property manager collects the rent for both studio apartments but for only five of the one-bedroom apartments and only one of the two-bedroom units. The property manager's fee is calculated as follows (Note: the fee is based only on money actually collected):

$250 × 2 units = $ 500
$325 × 5 units = $1,625
$400 × 1 unit = $ 400
$2,525 total rents collected × 0.09 percentage of rents collected = $227.25 manager's fee for this month

As with real estate sales commission rates, all management fees must be negotiable between the parties. It is a violation of federal antitrust laws for property managers to conspire to set standard rates for their local areas. It is recommended that brokers should have a clear understanding with the owner of all the services to be rendered and who will pay for particular advertising and operating expenses prior to negotiating a property management fee.

TYPICAL PROPERTY MANAGEMENT DUTIES

A property manager must live up to both the letter and the spirit of the property management agreement. The owner must be kept well informed on all matters of policy, as well as on the financial condition of the property and its operation. A manager must stay in contact with others in the field, therefore becoming increasingly knowledgeable and keeping informed on current policies pertaining to the profession.

Preparing a Management Plan

Property management begins with a management plan prepared by the property manager. A management plan outlines the details of the owner's objectives with the property, as well as what the property manager expects to accomplish and how, including all financial objectives. In preparing a management plan, a property manager should take into consideration three factors: (1) the owner's objectives, (2) the regional and neighborhood market analysis, and (3) the specific property analysis. A regional market analysis should include the general economic trend, population trends, employment data, and transportation resources. The neighborhood market analysis should explore many of the same things on a more localized level that include neighborhood amenities and resources. Occupancy, absorption rates, and new starts are critical indicators. The property analysis should evaluate the number and size of the rental units, the physical condition of the property, the occupancy and rental history, plus what makes the property desirable to prospective tenants. The plan also includes a budgetary section on sources of revenue and anticipated expenses. While the management plan is a document for the present, it is forward-looking in determining the feasibility of a property owner's long-term goals for a specific property.

One of the primary responsibilities of a property manager is maintaining financial reports, including an operating budget, cash flow report, profit and loss statement, and budget comparison statement. While there are no standard formats for these reports, there is some similarity among the reports, and it is important for the property manager to adapt a report to meet an owner's needs.

Operating budget. An *operating budget* is the projection of income and expense for the operation of a property over a one-year period. This budget, developed before attempting to rent property, is based on anticipated revenues and expenses and provides the owner the amount of anticipated profit. The property uses the operating budget as a guide for the property's financial performance in the present and future.

After time a property manager can develop an operating budget based on the results of the profit and loss statement in comparison to the original budget (actual versus projected). After making the comparison, a new operating budget is prepared for a new time period in the future. See a sample annual operating budget in Figure 22.1.

The manager should also establish a cash reserve fund for variable expenses such as repairs, decorating, and supplies. The amount allocated for the reserve fund can be estimated from previous yearly totals of variable expenses.

Capital expenditures. If an owner and a property manager decide that modernization or renovation would enhance the property's value, the manager should budget money to cover the costs of remodeling. The property manager should be thoroughly familiar with the *principle of contribution* (discussed in Chapter 17) or should seek expert advice when estimating any increase in value expected by an improvement. In the case of large-scale construction, the expenses charged against the property's income should be spread over several years. The property owner decides to make capital improvements based on projections and advice from the property manager.

Cash flow report. A *cash flow report* is a monthly statement that details the financial status of the property. Sources of income and expenses are noted, as well as net operating income and net cash flow. The cash flow report is the most important financial report because it provides a picture of the current financial status of a property.

Income. **Potential gross income** includes potential gross rentals if 100% occupied and collected, delinquent rental payments, utilities, vending, contracts, late fees, and storage charges. Any losses from **vacancy and collection losses** or bad debt expenses (e.g., fees for bad checks) are deducted from the total potential gross income to arrive at the **effective gross income**.

In some properties, there is space that is not income-producing, such as the property manager's office. The rental value of the property that is not producing income is subtracted from the gross rental income to equal the gross collectible, or billable, rental income.

Expenses. Fixed and variable expenses include administrative costs (including building personnel), **operating expenses**, and maintenance costs. Fixed expenses that remain constant and do not change include employee wages, utilities, and other basic operating costs. Variable expenses may be recurring or nonrecurring and can include items such as building repairs and landscaping.

The formula for arriving at **cash flow** is as follows:

> Potential gross rental income + Other income − Losses incurred = Effective gross income

> Effective gross income − Operating expenses = Net operating income before debt service (e.g., mortgage payments)

> Net operating income before debt service − Debt service − Capital expenditures − Reserves = Cash flow

A **profit and loss statement** is a financial picture of the revenues and expenses used to determine whether the business has made money or suffered a loss. It may be prepared monthly, quarterly, semiannually, or annually. The statement is created from the monthly cash flow reports and does not include itemized information.

A formula for profit and loss statement looks like this:

> Gross receipts − Operating expenses − Total mortgage payment + Mortgage loan principal = Net profit

Budget comparison statement. The **budget comparison statement** compares the actual results with the original budget, often giving either percentages or a numerical variance of actual versus projected income and expenses. Budget comparisons are especially helpful in identifying trends in order to help with future budget planning.

Renting the Property

The role of the property manager should not be confused with that of a broker acting as a leasing agent. The property manager may use the services of a leasing agent, but that agent does not undertake the full responsibility of maintaining and managing the property. The manager must be concerned with the long-term financial health of the property; the leasing broker is concerned solely with renting space. Note that in North Carolina renting residential properties and dealing with residential tenants, property managers must be sure to follow the requirements of the North Carolina Residential Rental Agreements Act and Tenant Security Deposit Act (discussed in Chapter 11).

> In North Carolina

Establishing a rental schedule. In establishing a **rental schedule** for a property, a manager must be concerned that, in the long term, the income from the rentable space will cover the property's fixed charges and operating expenses, plus provide a fair return on the investment. Consideration must be given to the prevailing rates in comparable buildings and the current level of vacancy in the property to be rented—supply and demand. Once the manager makes a detailed survey of the competitive space available in the neighborhood, rental prices should be adjusted for differences between these neighboring properties and the subject property. Annual rent adjustments are usually warranted. Note that although residential apartment rental rates are stated in monthly amounts per unit, office and commercial space rentals may be stated according to the annual or the monthly rate per square foot of space.

In establishing rental rates, the property manager has four long-term considerations:

1. The rental income must be sufficient to cover the property's fixed charges, such as taxes and insurance, and operating expenses, such as maintenance. (Note that debt service [principal and interest payment] on a mortgage loan is not an operating expense.)
2. The rental income must provide a fair return on the owner's investment.
3. The rental rate should be in line with prevailing rates in comparable properties. It may be slightly higher or slightly lower, depending on the strength of the property.
4. The current vacancy rate in the property is a good indicator of how large a rent increase is advisable. A building with a low vacancy rate (that is, few vacant units) is a better candidate for an increase than one with a high vacancy rate.

If a high level of vacancy exists, an immediate effort should be made to determine why. *A high level of vacancy does not necessarily indicate that rents are too high.* The trouble may be inept management or defects in the property. The manager first should attempt to identify the problem (if any) and correct it, rather than automatically lowering rents. Conversely, *even though a high percentage of occupancy may appear to indicate an effective rental program, it could also mean that rental rates are too low.* With an apartment or office building, any time the occupancy level exceeds 95%, an analysis should be made to be certain that the building rates are not below market.

> **MATH CONCEPTS**
>
> **RENTAL COMMISSIONS**
> Rental commissions are usually based on the annual rent from a property. For example, if an office unit rents for $475 per month and the commission rate is 8%, the commission is calculated as follows
>
> $475 per month x 12 months = $5,700
>
> $5,700 x 0.08 (8%) = $456 annual commission

Marketing the property. One of the property manager's duties is to market the property to potential suitable tenants. The property management agreement generally authorizes the placement of signs on the property in compliance with any zoning or restrictive covenants. Advertising on the internet as well as print media also will expose the property to the general public. It should be noted that any advertising and/or marketing activities must comply with all federal, state, and local fair housing laws.

A cost-benefit analysis helps a property manager assess whether a particular advertising method worked to attract new tenants. Property marketing expenses are usually figured on a cost-per-prospect-per-lease basis. For example, if a three-bedroom apartment rents for $1,500 and is typically viewed by 10 prospects before it is leased, an $800 newspaper advertisement would cost $80 per prospect.

Selecting tenants. Generally, the highest rents can be secured from satisfied tenants. A residential broker dealing only with sales may sell a property and then have no further dealings with the purchaser, but much of a property manager broker's success depends on retaining sound, long-term relationships. The first and most important step is selection. In selecting a prospective commercial or industrial tenant, a manager should be certain that (1) *the size of the space* meets the tenant's requirements (each business *fits the space*), (2) the tenant has the *ability to pay* for the space, (3) the *tenant's business is compatible* with the building and the other tenants' businesses, and (4) if the tenant is likely to expand in the future, *expansion space will be available*. Once a prospect becomes a tenant, the manager must be certain that the tenant remains satisfied in all respects commensurate with fair business dealings.

Note that in selecting *residential* tenants, the property manager must comply with all federal, state, and local fair housing laws (discussed in Chapter 20). Lease application requirements and rental policies that are uniformly applied to all lease applicants are not discriminatory in nature and constitute good business practices. Requiring all applicants to pay an application fee that will purchase a criminal records background check and a credit report can reduce the likelihood of renting to an "unqualified" tenant. A property manager's desire for a high level of occupancy should not override good judgment in accepting only those tenants who can be expected to meet their financial obligations to the property owner. The property manager should uniformly investigate financial references given by the prospect, by local credit bureaus, and, when possible, by the prospective tenant's former landlords.

Collecting rents. The best way to minimize problems with rent collection is to make certain that the property manager has *qualified* all prospective tenants in the first place. The terms of rental payment should be spelled out in detail in the lease agreement. The property manager should establish a consistent, enforced collection plan with a sufficient system of notices and records. In cases of delinquency, every attempt must be made to make collections without resorting to legal action. For those cases in which legal recourse is required (i.e., summary ejectment), the property manager must be prepared to promptly initiate and follow through in conjunction with legal counsel.

In North Carolina It is important that property managers scrupulously follow all state laws, rules, and regulations when it comes to collecting and accounting for rents. The North Carolina Real Estate License Law and NCREC's Rules require that property managers deposit funds into trust accounts by mandated deadlines and maintain detailed and accurate trust account records (see NCREC Rule A.0107). The Tenant Security Deposit Act limits the amount of security deposits for residential property that can be required and mandates how they must be handled (discussed in Chapter 11). The property manager can collect tenant security deposits only if authorized in the property management agreement.

Performing landlord's duties under the lease. The property manager broker is considered by many leases to *be* the landlord as pertains to conducting actions or providing services to the tenants. The establishment and implementation of rules and regulations dealing with a multitude of issues within multi-tenant properties will help ensure satisfied tenants and landlords. The manager would be expected to coordinate and provide negotiated tenant services on behalf of the landlord, such as janitorial services, required repairs and grounds maintenance. Instituting legal actions, such as eviction proceedings, would also fall to the capable hands of the property manager.

Accountability and recordkeeping. It is crucial that property managers maintain accurate records of all monies received and handled on behalf of the landlord. Records of leases and compliance with various laws, such as the Lead-Based Paint Hazard Reduction Act, must also be maintained for a minimum of three years from the date of last activity. Unless otherwise negotiated in the property management agreement, the manager should render monthly accounting to the landlord. The property manager broker will be held responsible for compliance with all trust account maintenance laws even if daily trust fund activities were delegated to another person, such as a bookkeeper.

Maintaining the Property

One of the most important functions of a property manager is the supervision of property maintenance. The manager must learn to balance the services provided with the costs they entail in order to satisfy the tenants' needs while minimizing operating expenses. Assuring that tenants are being charged for repairs needed to correct damage occurring during tenancy helps minimize out-of-pocket expense for the property owner. Completion of a *property condition checklist* prior to possession by a new tenant can be compared to a newly-completed checklist immediately before tenant is due to vacate the premises. This will aid in the proper and accurate damage assessment in the leased property.

Efficient property maintenance demands accurate assessment of the needs of the building and the number and kinds of personnel that will meet these needs. Because staffing and scheduling requirements will vary with the type, size, and regional location of the property, the owner and the manager usually agree in advance on maintenance objectives for the property. For one property, the most viable plan may be to operate with a low occupancy level and minimal expenditures for services and maintenance. Another property may be more lucrative if kept in top condition and operated with all possible tenant services because it can then command premium rental rates.

The manager first must protect the physical integrity of the property to ensure that the condition of the building and its grounds is kept at present levels over the long term. For example, preserving the property by repainting the exterior or replacing the heating system will help keep the building functional and decrease routine maintenance costs.

Property maintenance encompasses four areas: (1) preventive maintenance, (2) repair or corrective maintenance, (3) routine maintenance and cleaning, and (4) construction.

Preventive maintenance includes regularly scheduled activities—such as regular painting and periodic lubrication of gears and motors—that will maintain the structure so that the long-range value and physical integrity of the building are preserved. Most authorities agree that preventive upkeep is the most critical, but most neglected maintenance responsibility.

> *Preventive maintenance* helps prevent problems and expenses.

Repair or corrective maintenance involves the actual repairs that keep the building's equipment, utilities, and amenities functioning as contracted for by the tenants. Repairing a boiler, fixing a leaky faucet, and mending a broken air-conditioning unit are acts of repair maintenance.

> *Corrective maintenance* corrects problems after they've occurred.

The property manager must also *supervise routine maintenance and cleaning* throughout the building, including such day-to-day duties as cleaning common areas; performing minor carpentry and plumbing tasks; and providing regularly scheduled upkeep of heating, air-conditioning, and landscaping.

Finally, property maintenance requires new or renovative *construction*. Especially when handling commercial or industrial space, the property manager often is called on to make tenant improvements—alterations to the interior of the building to meet the functional demands of the tenants. These alterations may range from repainting to completely gutting the interior and redefining the space. Tenant improvements are especially important when renting new buildings because the interior is usually left as an unfinished shell so that it can be customized for individual tenants.

Supervision of modernization or renovation of buildings that have become functionally obsolete (discussed in Chapter 17) and unsuited to today's building needs also is important. The renovation of a building often increases the building's marketability and therefore its income potential.

Hiring employees versus contracting for services. One of the major decisions a property manager faces is whether to contract for maintenance services from an outside firm (outsourcing) or to hire on-site employees to perform such tasks. This decision should be based on a number of factors, including size of the building and land area, complexity of tenants' requirements, and availability of suitable, affordable labor.

Handling Environmental Concerns

With the proliferation of federal and state laws and the increase in local regulation, environmental concerns have become a major responsibility of the property manager and will require increased management time and attention in the future. Although property managers are not expected to be experts in all of the disciplines necessary to operate a modern building, they are expected to be knowledgeable in many diverse subjects, most of which are technical in nature. Environmental concerns awareness is one such subject that will be discussed further in Chapter 21.

The property manager must be able to respond to a variety of environmental problems. She may manage structures containing asbestos, mold, or radon, or be asked to arrange an environmental audit of a property. Note that lead-based paint disclosures (discussed in Chapter 21) are required for residential tenant-occupied property built prior to 1978. The manager must see that hazardous wastes produced by her employer or a building's tenants receive proper disposal. Even the normally nonhazardous waste of an office building must be controlled to avoid violation of laws requiring segregation of types of wastes. In areas where recycling is practiced, the property manager must provide the facilities and see that tenants sort their trash properly.

The Americans with Disabilities Act

The Americans with Disabilities Act (ADA) has had a significant impact on the responsibilities of the property manager, both in building amenities and in employment issues.

Title I of the ADA provides for the employment of qualified job applicants regardless of their disability. Any employer with 15 or more employees must adopt nondiscriminatory employment procedures. In addition, employers must make reasonable accommodations to enable individuals with disabilities to perform essential job functions.

Property managers must also be familiar with Title III of the ADA, which prohibits discrimination in commercial properties and public accommodations. The ADA requires that managers ensure that people with disabilities have full and equal access to facilities and services. The property manager typically is responsible for determining whether a building meets the ADA's accessibility requirements. The property manager must also prepare a plan for retrofitting a building that is not in compliance when removal of existing barriers is *readily achievable*—that is, can be performed without much difficulty or expense. There are some tax advantages available to help offset the expense of complying with ADA requirements. ADA experts may be consulted, as may architectural designers who specialize in accessibility issues.

To protect owners of existing structures from the massive expense of extensive remodeling, the ADA recommends *reasonably achievable accommodations* to provide access to the facilities and services. New construction and remodeling, however, must meet higher standards of accessibility and usability because it costs less to incorporate accessible features in the design than to retrofit. Though the law intends to provide for people with disabilities, many of the accessible design features and accommodations benefit everyone.

IN PRACTICE The U.S. Department of Justice has ADA specialists available to answer general information questions about compliance issues. The ADA Information Line is at 800-514-0301 (TTY 800-514-0383). The ADA website is noted at the end of the chapter.

Existing barriers must be removed when this can be accomplished in a *readily achievable* manner—that is, with little difficulty and at low cost. The following are typical examples of readily achievable modifications:

- Ramping or removing an obstacle from an otherwise accessible entrance
- Lowering wall-mounted public telephones
- Adding raised letters and Braille markings on elevator buttons
- Installing auditory signals in elevators
- Reversing the direction in which doors open

Alternative methods can be used to provide reasonable accommodations if extensive restructuring is impractical or if retrofitting is unduly expensive. For instance, installing a cup dispenser at a water fountain that is too high for an individual in a wheelchair may be more practical than installing a lower unit.

IN PRACTICE Federal, state, and local laws may provide additional requirements for accommodating people with disabilities. Brokers should be aware of the full range of laws to ensure that their practices are in compliance.

RISK MANAGEMENT FOR PROPERTY MANAGERS

Homeowners are not the only ones who should be concerned about property insurance. Because enormous dollar losses can result from certain occurrences, one of the most critical areas of responsibility for a property manager is the field of insurance. Knowing the purposes of insurance coverage and how to make best use of the many types of insurance available is part of *risk management*.

Handling Risk
- Avoid it
- Retain it
- Control it
- Transfer it

Risk management involves answering the question, "What will happen if something goes wrong?" The perils of any risk must be evaluated in terms of options. In considering the possibility of a loss, the property manager must decide whether it is better to

- *avoid it* by removing the source of risk, such as a swimming pool;
- *retain it* to a certain extent by insuring it with a large *deductible* (loss not covered by the insurer);
- *control it* by installing sprinklers, fire doors, and other preventive measures; or
- *transfer it* by taking out an insurance policy.

When insurance is considered, a competent, reliable insurance agent should be selected to survey the property and make recommendations. Additional insurance surveys should be obtained if any questions remain. Final decisions, however, must be made by the property owner. A proper decision as to how much and what type of insurance to purchase and where to focus the insurance could save many thousands of dollars, especially in large buildings. The addition of lease requirements could contribute to risk management. Requiring tenants to purchase renter's insurance as a condition of the lease is possibly a way to minimize risk. Also, by refusing to allow certain types or breeds as pets, such as pit bull or Doberman dogs, the insurance premiums may be lowered due to the reduction in liability. Property managers often are responsible for large sums of funds held in escrow for owners and tenants. Often these funds are administered by the managers or their bookkeepers. *Bonding* should be seriously considered for employees who have such financial responsibilities. Bonding provides a form of *honesty* insurance so that any money lost or embezzled by an employee will be reimbursed by the insurance company.

Types of Insurance Coverage

Many kinds of insurance coverage are available to income-property owners and managers. Listed below are some of the more common types.

- *Fire and hazard.* Fire insurance policies provide coverage against direct loss or damage to property from a fire on the premises. Standard fire coverage can be extended to cover hazards such as windstorm, hail, smoke damage, or civil insurrection (like a typical homeowners' policy).
- *Consequential loss, use, and occupancy.* Consequential loss insurance, which can include rent loss, covers the loss of revenue to a business if the business's property cannot be used.
- *Contents and personal property.* This type of insurance covers building contents and personal property during periods when neither is actually located on the business premises, such as stolen from the company van while traveling.
- *Liability.* Public liability insurance covers the risks an owner assumes when the public enters the building. Payments under this coverage are used to settle claims for medical expenses for a person injured in the building as a result of the owner's negligence. Another liability risk is that of medical or hospital payments for injuries sustained by building employees in the course of their employment. These claims are covered by state laws known as workers' compensation acts. These laws require that a building owner who is an employer obtain a workers' compensation policy from a private insurance company.
- *Casualty.* Casualty insurance policies include coverage against theft, burglary, vandalism, and machinery damage as well as health and accident insurance. Casualty policies are usually written on specific risks, such as theft, rather than being all-inclusive.
- *Surety bonds.* Surety bonds cover an owner against financial losses resulting from an employee's criminal acts or negligence while performing assigned duties.

Today, many insurance companies offer multi-peril policies for apartment and business buildings. These policies offer the property manager an insurance package that includes such standard types of commercial coverage as fire, hazard, public liability, and casualty.

Claims

When a claim is made under a policy insuring a building or another physical object, the amount of the claim can be determined using one of two methods: the *depreciated actual value* or *cash value* of the damaged property or the *current replacement cost*. When purchasing insurance, a manager must assess whether the property should be insured at full replacement cost or at depreciated cost. As with the homeowners' policies discussed earlier, commercial policies include *coinsurance clauses* that require that the insured carry fire coverage, usually in an amount equal to 80% of the building's replacement value.

IN PRACTICE Brokers must be sure that homebuyers acquire a homeowners' insurance policy on or before the day of closing. This is required if there will be a mortgage, but it is still strongly advised if it is a cash purchase. Buyers should be reminded that the typical homeowners' insurance policies do not provide coverage for termite damage, breakdown of appliances, flood damage, loss of trees, or losses incurred over an extended period of time (such as a leaking roof). Assuming the seller's policy could mean that the buyer does not have a policy that fits the buyer's needs.

RELATED WEBSITES

American With Disabilities Act: www.ada.gov
Building Owners and Managers Association: www.boma.org
Institute of Real Estate Management: www.irem.org
National Association of Residential Property Managers: www.narpm.org
Online apartment vacancy listing sites: www.apartmentfinder.com, www.apartmentguide.com, www.craigslist.com, www.forrent.com

KEY POINT REVIEW

A **property manager**, whether an individual or a company, acts as the general agent of the investment property owner and has fiduciary duties to the owner of loyalty, obedience, accounting, disclosure and care in administering the property to accomplish the following:

- Achieve the objectives of the owner
- Generate income for the owner
- Preserve and increase the property's value

In North Carolina, a property manager must be a nonprovisional broker that can employ other brokers, or unlicensed persons for activities that do not require a license. A leasing agent does not have to be licensed as long as they do not negotiate any lease terms. A property manager for corporate-owned properties is usually an unlicensed employee of the corporation.

A **property management agreement** should include the following:

- Description of the property
- Time period of the agreement
- Method of termination of the agreement

- Definition of the management's responsibilities, including limitations and restrictions
- Statement of the owner's purpose—long-term goals
- Owner's responsibilities for management expenses
- Extent of the manager's authority
- Reporting requirements of the owner and the state
- Compensation to the manager
- Compliance with applicable federal, state, and local laws
- Financial reports
- Periodic profit and loss statement providing general financial information
- Budget comparison statement, comparing actual results with original budget

Typical property manager duties include the following:

- Preparing a management plan
- Preparing an operating budget
- Renting the property
- Establishing a rental schedule
- Marketing the property
- Tenant selection within certain parameters, while complying with all applicable federal, state, and local fair housing, antidiscrimination, and equal opportunity laws.
- Collecting rent
- Performing the landlord's duties
- Accounting and recordkeeping
- Maintaining the property
- Handling environmental concerns

Property managers are affected by Americans with Disabilities Act (ADA), which includes

- Title I: applies to employers with 15 or more employees and provides for employment of qualified job applicants, regardless of disability, with reasonable accommodations; and
- Title III: prohibits discrimination in commercial properties and public accommodations and requires that access to facilities and services be provided when reasonably achievable in existing buildings, with a higher standard for new construction or remodeling.

Risk management includes treatment of risk by deciding whether to avoid it, control it, transfer it, or retain it (ACTOR) and focuses on tenant security and types of insurance available.

QUESTIONS

1. Apartment rental rates are usually expressed
   a. in monthly amounts.
   b. on a per-room basis.
   c. in square feet per month.
   d. in square feet per year.

2. In preparing for variable expenses in a budget, the property manager should set up a(n)
   a. control account.
   b. floating allocation.
   c. cash reserve fund.
   d. asset account.

3. An important concern in setting rents is
   I. prevailing rates in the area.
   II. current vacancy rates.
      a. I only
      b. II only
      c. Both I and II
      d. Neither I nor II

4. Which of the following might suggest that rents are too low?
   a. Poorly maintained building
   b. Many For Lease signs in the area
   c. High occupancy rate
   d. High vacancy level

5. Repairing a boiler is classified as which type of maintenance?
   a. Preventative
   b. Corrective
   c. Routine
   d. Construction

6. In renting units in an apartment building, a property manager must comply with all of the following EXCEPT
   a. the terms of the management agreement.
   b. the lawful instructions of the owner.
   c. fair housing laws.
   d. the AMA Code of Ethics.

7. If the leasing agent gets an 8% commission on rents collected, what would his annual commission be if he leases 20 offices at $750 a month?
   a. $ 1,200
   b. $ 9,000
   c. $14,400
   d. $15,000

8. Generally, the provisions of the management agreement should include all of the following EXCEPT
   a. a definition of the manager's responsibilities.
   b. a listing of previous owners of the property.
   c. the extent of the manager's authority as an agent.
   d. the calculation of management fees.

9. When selecting a tenant, consideration should be given to all of the following EXCEPT
   a. size of the space versus the tenant's requirements.
   b. tenant's ability to pay.
   c. racial and ethnic background of the tenant.
   d. compatibility of the tenant's business with other tenants' businesses.

10. A property manager is usually responsible for
    I. developing a budget and controlling expenses.
    II. communicating with the owner about physical problems with a building.
       a. I only
       b. II only
       c. Both I and II
       d. Neither I nor II

11. Last year your firm managed a 48-unit apartment building. Two units were four-bedroom, penthouse units renting for $1,000 per month with no vacancies. Twenty-five units with three bedrooms rented for $850 per month and carried a 5% vacancy factor. Ten two-bedroom units rented for $750 per month and carried a 5% vacancy factor. Eleven one-bedroom apartments with balconies rented for $650 per month and carried a 10% vacancy factor. The management fee is 12%. How much commission did your firm gross last year managing this building?
    a. $45,480
    b. $50,036
    c. $51,476
    d. $53,136

12. When a property manager is establishing a budget for the building, all of the following should be included as an operating expense EXCEPT
    a. cleaning supplies.
    b. management fees.
    c. debt service payments.
    d. routine repairs.

13. An active real estate license will be needed if the property manager is
    a. an employee of a partnership that owns the property to be managed.
    b. part owner of the property.
    c. an employee of a corporation that owns the property to be managed.
    d. a general partner of the partnership that owns the property to be managed.

14. A property manager who enters into a management agreement with an owner is usually a
    a. special agent.
    b. general agent.
    c. universal agent.
    d. designated agent.

15. Avoid, control, transfer, or retain are the four alternative techniques of
    a. tenant relations.
    b. acquiring insurance.
    c. risk management.
    d. property management.

16. Removing existing barriers when readily achievable in public buildings, such as adding Braille markings to elevator buttons, is a requirement of which law?
    a. Regulation Z
    b. Fair Housing Act
    c. Equal Credit Opportunity Act
    d. Americans with Disabilities Act

17. A semiannual statement sent to an owner that does NOT reflect the entire debt service as an expense is called a(n)
    a. cash flow report.
    b. profit and loss statement.
    c. budget comparison statement.
    d. operating budget statement.

18. Which of the following would be considered a variable expense when a manager develops an operating budget?
    a. Employee wages
    b. Utilities
    c. Building repairs
    d. Basic operating costs

19. A guest slips on an icy apartment building stair and is hospitalized. A claim against the building owner for medical expenses may be paid under which of the following policies held by the owner?
    a. Workers' compensation
    b. Casualty
    c. Liability
    d. Fire and hazard

20. Title III of the Americans with Disabilities Act (ADA) impacts which type of property?
    a. Residential
    b. Industrial
    c. Privately owned
    d. Commercial and public accommodations

CHAPTER 13

Real Estate Financing: Principles

LEARNING OBJECTIVES When you have finished reading this chapter, you should be able to

- **distinguish** between title theory and lien theory states.
- **identify** the basic provisions of security and debt instruments and rights and duties of lenders and borrowers.
- **explain** the characteristics of various types of loan repayment plans.
- **define** the effect of discount points on yield and calculate mathematically how to determine the number of points and the dollar amount of points to be paid by the borrower.
- **define** these *key terms*:

acceleration clause	equitable title	negotiable instrument
adjustable-rate mortgages (ARMs)	equity	power of sale foreclosure
	equity of redemption	prepayment penalty
alienation clause	foreclosure	principal
amortized loans	graduated payment mortgage (GPM)	promissory note
balloon payment		satisfaction of mortgage
beneficiary	grantor/trustor	short sale
debt service	hypothecation	statutory redemption period
deed in lieu of foreclosure	interest	
deed of trust	judicial foreclosure	statutory right of redemption
default	lien theory	
deficiency judgment	loan origination fee	term loan
direct reduction loans	mortgage	title theory
discount points	mortgagee/mortgagor	usury
due-on-sale clause	negative amortization	yield

BASIS MORTGAGE TERMS AND CONCEPTS

There are two different legal theories about the effect of mortgaging property—the title theory and the lien theory. Under the **lien theory**, which is the older, more traditional approach, a two-party mortgage instrument is used as security for the debt. The borrower (**mortgagor**) retains both legal and equitable title to the property. The lender (**mortgagee**) is given the right to have the property sold through the **judicial foreclosure** process and the proceeds applied to the debt, should the borrower **default** under the terms of the mortgage loan.

> In a lien theory state, the borrower retains both legal and equitable title.
>
> In a title theory state, the borrower retains equitable title and conveys legal title to a trustee until the debt has been satisfied.

In North Carolina

Title theory uses the three-party deed of trust instrument (a form of mortgage) as security for the debt. The borrower (**grantor** or **trustor**) actually conveys legal title to the **trustee** (third party) to hold for the lender (**beneficiary**) until the debt is satisfied. The borrower retains **equitable title** to the property. This means that the borrower has the right to use and possess the property as if he or she owned it and to demand the return of the legal title when the debt is repaid. Upon request of the lender, the trustee can initiate the **power of sale foreclosure** to sell the property if the debt is not paid per the terms of the promissory note. The lender's legal ownership is subject to termination on full payment of the debt or performance of the obligation. North Carolina follows the title theory.

The legal differences between title theory and lien theory are of little significance today. Under both theories, if a borrower defaults, the lender may foreclose the lien, offer the property for sale, and apply the funds received from the sale to reduce or extinguish the borrower's obligation. As protection to the borrower, most states allow a statutory redemption period during which the borrower in default can redeem the property.

SECURITY AND DEBT

Generally, any interest in real estate that may be sold may also be pledged as security or collateral for a debt. A basic principle of property law—that a person cannot convey greater rights in property than the person actually has—applies equally to the right to mortgage. In reality, the differences between the parties' rights in a lien theory state and those in a title theory state are more technical than actual. Regardless of the theory practiced in any particular state, all borrowers and lenders observe the same general requirements to protect themselves in a loan transaction. As with any contract, the parties must be legally competent, their signatures valid and attested, and adequate consideration exchanged.

Mortgage Loan Instruments

Two parts to a mortgage loan exist—the debt itself and the security for the debt. When a property is to be mortgaged, the owner must execute, or sign, two separate instruments:

1. The **promissory note**, or financing instrument, is the written promise or agreement to repay a debt in definite installments with interest. The mortgagor executes one or more promissory notes to reflect the amount of the debt. In some states, a bond is used as evidence of a debt secured by a mortgage.

2. The **mortgage** or **deed of trust**, that is, the security instrument, is the document that pledges the property to the lender as security or collateral for a debt.

A mortgagor is a borrower who gives a mortgage to a lender, the mortgagee, in return for the money. The relationship between mortgagor and mortgagee is shown in Figure 13.1.

FIGURE 13.1

Mortgages

Mortgage —Two Parties

When the Money Is Borrowed

Mortgagor (Borrower) → Note and Mortgage → Mortgagee (Lender) → Loan $ → Mortgagor (Borrower)

When the Money Is Repaid

Mortgagor (Borrower) → Pays the Loan $ → Mortgagee (Lender) → Satisfaction of Mortgage → Mortgagor (Borrower)

Hypothecation is the act of pledging real property as security for payment of a loan without giving up possession of the property. A pledge of security—a mortgage—cannot be effective legally unless there is a debt to secure. Both the note and the mortgage must be executed (signed) to create an enforceable mortgage loan.

In North Carolina

Deeds of trust. In some areas of the country, including North Carolina, lenders prefer to use a three-party security instrument known as a deed of trust, or trust deed (see Figure 13.2), rather than a mortgage document. In a deed of trust, the borrower conveys naked title or bare legal title (title without the right of possession) to the real estate as security for the loan from the borrower to a third party, called the trustee. The trustee then holds title on behalf of the lender, known as the beneficiary, who is the legal owner and holder of the promissory note. The wording of the conveyance sets forth actions that the trustee may take if the borrower, known as the grantor or trustor, defaults under any of the deed of trust terms. The procedure for foreclosing a deed of trust is simpler and faster than the procedure used to foreclose a mortgage, because the deed of trust contains an automatic power-of-sale clause that, in case of the borrower's default, gives the trustee the power to sell the property in a nonjudicial foreclosure. Note that the term mortgage loan is commonly used to refer to a loan secured by either a mortgage or deed of trust.

FIGURE 13.2

Deed of Trust

Deed of Trust—Three Parties

When the Money Is Borrowed

Grantor (Borrower) → Loan $ ← Beneficiary (Lender)
Grantor (Borrower) → Note → Beneficiary (Lender)
Grantor (Borrower) → Deed of Trust → Trustee (Holds Naked Title)

When the Money Is Repaid

Grantor (Borrower) → Pays the Loan $ → Beneficiary (Lender)
Trustee → Release Deed or Deed of Reconveyance → Grantor (Borrower)

■ THE PROMISSORY NOTE

When a real estate purchase is financed with a mortgage loan, the borrower must sign a promissory note. The promissory, or mortgage, note is legal evidence of the debt between the borrower and lender.

Essential Elements of a Valid Note

The essential elements of a note are (1) term, (2) promise to pay, and (3) signature of the borrower(s). A promissory note is a simple document that states the amount of the debt, the time and method of payment, and the rate of interest. The note may also refer to or repeat several of the clauses, such as acceleration, that appear in the mortgage document. The borrower is called the maker, or payor, or obligor, and the lender is called the payee. The note, like the mortgage, should be signed by all parties who have an interest in the property (for example, both spouses should sign the note). Remember that (1) only the borrowers (makers) of the note sign it, (2) it is not recorded (only the security instrument is recorded), and (3) there is only one original that is signed at the closing (although there may be copies given to the various parties).

A promissory note is usually a **negotiable instrument**—that is, a written promise or order to pay a specific sum of money. An instrument is said to be negotiable when its holder, the payee, may transfer the right to receive payment to a third party. This may be accomplished by signing the instrument over to the third party or, in some cases, merely by delivering the instrument to that person. Other examples of negotiable instruments include checks and bank drafts. It is important for the promissory note to be negotiable because lenders often sell their mortgage loans in the secondary mortgage market.

To be negotiable, or freely transferable, an instrument must meet certain requirements of the law. The instrument must be in writing, made by one person to another, and signed by the maker. It must contain an unconditional promise to pay a sum of money on demand or at a set date in the future. In addition, the instrument must be payable to the order of a specifically named person or to the bearer (whoever has possession of the note). Instruments that are payable to order must be transferred by endorsement; those payable to bearer may be transferred by delivery. A nonnegotiable note does not contain *to order* or *to bearer* but is payable to a named person. It is neither transferable nor assignable. The vast majority of real estate notes are negotiable, and therefore transferable.

It is important to understand the difference between the negotiability of a note—that is, whether a note is transferable from one lender to another—and the negotiability of the terms (such as the interest rate) of a note. The original parties to the note may negotiate the terms of the loan, but once those terms are determined, they are binding on the parties to the note, whether or not the note itself is transferred to another party.

Special Note Provisions

Virtually all promissory notes used by institutional lenders contain three additional provisions, which also appear in the mortgage or deed of trust.

1. **Acceleration clause.** The **acceleration clause** provides that if a borrower defaults, the lender has the right to accelerate the maturity of the debt—to declare the entire debt (plus accrued interest and costs) due and payable immediately—even though the terms of the mortgage originally allow the borrower to amortize the debt in regular payments over a period of years. Without the acceleration clause, the lender would have to sue the borrower every time a payment became due and in default (late).

2. **Prepayment penalty clause.** When a loan is paid in installments over a long term, the total interest paid by the borrower can exceed the principal of the loan. If such a loan is paid off before its full term, the lender collects less interest from the borrower. For this reason, some lenders include a prepayment penalty clause in the promissory note, requiring that the borrower pay a **prepayment penalty** against the unearned portion of the interest for any payments made ahead of schedule. A loan that does not have a prepayment penalty clause will include a prepayment privilege clause, which allows the borrower to prepay a portion or all of the outstanding balance without penalty. [In North Carolina] Lenders in North Carolina are not permitted to charge a prepayment penalty on any residential loan with an original balance of $150,000 or less that is the first lien on the borrower's primary residence. Also, federal law prohibits lenders from charging a prepayment penalty on any FHA-insured VA-guaranteed loan.

3. **Due-on-sale clause.** Frequently, when a conventional real estate loan is made, the lender wishes to prevent some future purchaser of the property from being able to assume that loan without the lender's permission, particularly at its original rate of interest. For this reason, some lenders include a **due-on-sale clause**, also known as an **alienation clause**, in the note. A due-on-sale clause provides that on sale of the property by the borrower to a buyer who wants to assume the loan, the lender has the choice of either declaring the entire debt to be due and payable immediately or permitting the buyer to assume the loan at current market interest rates. Use of this clause triggers the acceleration clause. The absence of a due-on-sale clause would permit a loan assumption without the lender's prior consent.

Principal and Interest (Debt Service)

A charge for the use of money borrowed (the **principal**) is called **interest**. Loan payments are usually described as principal and interest payments (P&I) or **debt service** payments. Interest may be due either at the end of each payment period (known as *payment in arrears*) or at the beginning of each payment period (*payment in advance*). Whether interest is charged in arrears or in advance is specified in the note, but the interest on the vast majority of mortgage loans is payable in arrears. In practice, the distinction becomes important if the property is sold before the debt is repaid in full, as will become evident in Chapter 15. Note that the interest charged on real estate loans is simple interest, and it is charged only on the outstanding loan balance.

Most mortgage loans are **amortized loans**. That is, as regular level payments are made, each payment is broken down and applied first to the interest owed, with the rest of the payment applied to the principal amount—over a term of perhaps 15 years or 30 years. At the end of the term, the full amount of the principal and all interest due is reduced to zero. Some mortgage loans require a fixed amount of principal to be paid in each payment with the amount applied to interest varying as the balance is reduced. Such loans are called **direct reduction loans**.

Each month, in addition to paying P&I, the borrower is normally required by the lender to pay one-twelfth of the annual real property taxes and one-twelfth of various annual insurance premiums, such as for homeowners', flood, or mortgage insurance policies. **P**rincipal, **i**nterest, **t**axes, and **i**nsurance is referred to as PITI. The taxes and insurance portion (TI) of the monthly payment is placed into the lender's escrow account and held until those bills are due. The lender receives the tax and insurance bills and pays those items from its escrow account on behalf of the borrower.

Most amortized mortgage loans are paid in monthly installments; some, however, are payable biweekly, quarterly, or semiannually. These payments may be computed based on a number of payment plans, which tend alternately to gain and lose favor with lenders and borrowers as the cost and availability of mortgage money fluctuates. Some of these basic payment plans are described in the following subsections.

Fully amortized fixed-rate mortgage. The fully amortized fixed-rate mortgage requires that the mortgagor pay a constant amount, usually monthly, that will completely pay off the loan amount with the last equal payment. The mortgagee first credits each payment to the interest due and then applies the balance to reduce the principal of the loan. Therefore, while each debt service payment remains the same, the portion applied toward repayment of the principal grows and the interest due declines as the unpaid balance of the loan is reduced (Figure 13.3).

FIGURE 13.3

Level-Payment Amortized Loan

Principal and Interest on 30-Year Mortgage

☐ Principal   ■ Interest

Partially amortized fixed-rate mortgage. With a partially amortized loan, the monthly principal and interest payments are a constant amount, but that payment amount is not sufficient to completely pay off the loan within the loan term. At maturity, a balloon payment will be due to pay the remaining principal. A *balloon payment* is a payment of an amount that is larger than the previous regular payments.

Simple interest and principal credited from amortized payment. Lenders charge borrowers a certain percentage of the principal as interest for each year a debt is outstanding. This is known as simple interest. The amount of interest due in a particular payment is calculated by computing the total yearly interest based on the unpaid balance and dividing that figure by the number of payments made each year. There are numerous software programs that will generate an amortization schedule showing the payment split between the principal and interest portions.

MATH CONCEPTS

CALCULATING SIMPLE INTEREST

To compute simple interest, use the formula I = P × R × T, where

$$I = \text{interest}$$
$$P = \text{principal}$$
$$R = \text{rate}$$
$$T = \text{time}$$

Apply this formula to a $30,000 loan (P) at 7% interest (R) to be repaid over 15 years (T). To calculate the interest owing for the first month, perform the following calculations:

$$I = \$30,000 \times 0.07 \times 15$$
$$I = \$31,500$$

$31,500 total interest ÷ 15 years = $2,100 yearly interest payment

(Note: After the borrower makes the first principal payment, the loan total will be reduced and therefore the interest payment also will be reduced.)

$2,100 ÷ 12 months = $175 first monthly interest payment

■ **FOR EXAMPLE** Assume the current outstanding balance of a loan is $70,000. The interest rate is 6¾% per year, and the monthly P&I payment is $454.30. Based on these facts, the interest and principal due on the next payment would be computed as shown:

$70,000 loan balance × 0.0675 annual interest rate = $4,725 annual interest
$4,725 annual interest ÷ 12 months = $393.75 monthly interest
$454.30 monthly P&I payment − $393.75 monthly interest =
$60.55 monthly principal
$70,000 beginning loan balance − $60.55 monthly principal =
$69,939.45 remaining loan balance after payment

This process is followed with each payment over the term of the loan. The same calculations are made each month, starting with the declining new loan balance figure from the previous month.

Usury. The maximum rate of interest legally charged on loans may be set by state usury laws. Charging interest in excess of this rate is called **usury** and is illegal. Lenders are penalized for making usurious loans. Usury laws were enacted primarily to protect consumers from unscrupulous lenders that charge unreasonably high interest rates. In some states, a lender that makes a usurious loan is permitted to collect the borrowed money, but only at the legal rate of interest. In other states, a usurious lender may lose the right to collect any interest or may lose the entire amount of the loan in addition to the interest. Loans made to corporations are generally exempt from usury laws.

Usury laws are state laws, but federal law preempted state law in this situation when the Depository Institutions Deregulation and Monetary Control Act of 1980 specifically exempted from state interest limitations all federally-related residential first mortgage loans made after March 31, 1980. This Act was passed to continue the availability of mortgage loans in the early 1980s when interest rates hit 18% while most state usury limits were below that rate. Federally related loans are those made by federally chartered institutions or those insured or guaranteed by a federal agency. The exemption includes loans used to finance manufactured housing (the federal term for mobile homes) and the acquisition of stock in a cooperative housing corporation. North Carolina exempts all residential first deeds of trust from state usury laws.

In North Carolina

Usury laws are complicated, and any broker who has questions about state or federal usury laws should consult a lawyer.

Discount points. The return or profit on a loan is sometimes called the **yield**. A large part of the yield comes from the interest rate the lender charges on the loan. However, the rate of interest that a lender charges for a mortgage loan might be less than the rate of return required by the lender or by an investor who might purchase that loan from the lender. For this reason, the lender can charge **discount points** to make up the difference between the mortgage interest rate and the required investor yield.

> One discount point equals 1% of the original loan amount and increases the yield of a loan by approximately one-eighth percent.

The number of points charged varies, depending on the difference between the interest rate and the required yield and on the average time the lender expects the loan to be outstanding. While most loans have an average term of 30 years, the average life of all loans is actually 11 years to 12 years because loans are usually paid off much sooner, when the borrower sells the property or refinances the loan. Lenders calculate that it takes an average of six to eight discount points to increase the yield 1%, with eight points being the rule of thumb; therefore, it is said that one point will increase the yield about one-eighth percent. Points can be charged on FHA-insured, VA-guaranteed, and conventional loans.

■ **FOR EXAMPLE** Suppose a lender wants to increase its yield on a $100,000 loan by one-half percentage point. If eight points equals a yield increase of one percentage point, to increase the yield by one-half percentage point, the lender would have to charge four points.

The cost to the borrower of a point equals 1% of the loan amount and is charged as prepaid interest at the closing. Thus, points charged on the $100,000 loan would be $4,000 ($100,000 × 4%). In this situation, the lender would actually fund $96,000 (the $100,000 principal amount of the loan minus the $4,000 for points), but $100,000 would have to be repaid by the borrower, thereby increasing the investor's yield (a $96,000 loan receiving interest calculated on $100,000).

MATH CONCEPTS

DISCOUNT POINTS: INVESTOR YIELD

From the standpoint of the investor, one discount point received increases the yield on the loan by one-eighth percent. Two points would increase the yield by one-fourth percent, four points by one-half percent, six points by three-quarter percent, and eight points by 1%. For example, if a loan carried an interest rate of 9½% and a discount of 6 points, the yield to the investor would be calculated as follows:

6 discount points = ¾% increase in yield
9½% interest per the contract + ¾% increase from the discount =
10¼% yield to the investor

If an investor requires a 10½% yield on a loan with a 10¼% interest rate, the number of discount points needed would be calculated as follows:

10½% = 10⁴⁄₈%; 10⁴⁄₈% required yield − 10²⁄₈% interest rate = ²⁄₈% difference;
²⁄₈% = 2 discount points

Discount points should not be confused with the **loan origination fee** charged by most lenders, which is an administrative expense for generating the loan. Unlike points, loan origination fees are not prepaid interest; they are an expense that must be paid to the lender, typically 1% of the loan amount regardless of any discount points that might also be charged.

■ **IN PRACTICE** Interest payments made under a mortgage loan secured by a first or second home are deductible for federal income tax purposes if the combined loan amounts do not exceed $1 million. This deduction, in effect, reduces the borrower's total cost of housing for the year. Interest deductions are limited, however, to the interest paid on an initial loan amount or refinancing no greater than the purchase price of the home plus capital improvements, unless the loan proceeds are used for qualified medical or educational purposes. Points (prepaid interest) paid at the time of financing a home purchase are fully deductible for the year paid by the buyer. Points on a loan to finance property improvements also are fully deductible for the year paid. Points paid on a loan refinancing may be deductible. If advance payments of loan principal are made, there is no increase in the deduction. If the entire loan is prepaid, however, any undeducted points may be deducted for that year. A tax expert should be consulted to accurately determine all tax liability and advantage.

Financing Calculations

Brokers must be familiar with calculations involving principal and interest, computation of monthly payments (PITI), mortgage debt reduction (amortization), total interest paid over the life of the loan, loan origination fees, discount points, loan-to-value ratios, and computation of total loan fees. Brokers also must be able to give buyers a general idea of about how much they will be able to borrow based on standard qualifying ratios.

Amortization (debt liquidation). Amortization is the process of paying off a home loan by making periodic (usually monthly) payments of principal (P) and interest (I), called debt service. *Amortization* literally means to *kill the debt*. A monthly PI payment can be easily computed by using a mortgage payment constant chart (amortization chart). The chart is based on a $1,000 loan. The interest rate and the term dictate the loan factor, which is the monthly P&I amount in dollars needed to amortize a $1,000 loan. Looking at the chart (see Table 14.2), if a person borrowed $1,000 for 30 years at 7% annual interest rate, the monthly payment would be $6.65. To compute a monthly PI payment: You want to borrow $75,000 at 7% for 30 years: $75,000 ÷ $1,000 = 75 thousand × $6.65 payment per thousand = $498.75 monthly PI.

Principal, interest, taxes, insurance (PITI). The borrower will probably be required by the lender to place into escrow ¹⁄₁₂ of the annual property taxes and one-twelfth of the homeowners' annual insurance premium each month. The PITI can be computed by adding monthly debt service (principal and interest) to the tax and insurance monthly escrow payments.

■ **FOR EXAMPLE** The borrower wants to borrow $130,000 at 7.5% for 30 years. The loan factor is 6.99 per thousand borrowed. The estimated annual taxes are $1,200, and the estimated annual insurance premium is $360. What is the monthly PITI payment?

$130,000 ÷ 1,000 = 130 thousands borrowed × 6.99 factor = $908.70 monthly PI

$1,200 annual tax ÷ 12 months = $100 monthly T

$360 annual insurance ÷ 12 months = $30.00 monthly I

$908.70 PI + $100 T + $30 I = $1,038.70 PITI

Total interest paid over the life of the loan. On a fixed-rate mortgage loan the monthly PI payment remains constant. Multiply the monthly PI payment by the number of payments made over the life of the loan and subtract the original principal to find the total interest paid. If the monthly PI is $498.75 on the 30-year $75,500 loan, total interest paid over the life of the loan is $104,050; ($498.75 PI × 360 payments = $179,550 total PI − $75,500 original P = $104,050 total I).

Mortgage debt reduction (amortization). The monthly PI payment will do two things. The principal portion will reduce the debt by the amount of monthly principal paid, and the interest portion will supply the lender's yield on the loan.

■ **FOR EXAMPLE** The monthly PI payment is $498.75 with the loan amount of $75,500 at 7%. After the first month's payment, what is the new loan balance?

$75,500 loan balance × 0.07 annual interest rate = $5,285 annual interest ÷ 12 months = $440.42 monthly I

$498.75 PI − $440.42 I = $58.33 P

$75,500 beginning loan balance − $58.33 P payment = $75,441.67 loan balance after one month's payment

Loan origination fees, discount points, and assumption fees. Lenders charge various fees to the borrower when processing a loan application. The origination fee is normally 1% of the loan amount, and discount points (previously discussed) may be charged to increase the yield. In the event of a loan assumption, the lender normally will charge an assumption fee, quoted as a percentage of the amount to be assumed.

■ **FOR EXAMPLE** The loan amount is $90,500. The lender will charge a 1% loan origination fee. Market interest rates are 6.5%, but the buyer wants to get a rate of 6%, which the lender has approved with payment of appropriate discount points. What is the total amount of fees to be paid by the buyer?

$90,500 loan amount × 0.01 = $905 origination fee; 6.5% − 6.0% = 0.5% = 4/8% = 4 points

$90,500 × 0.04 = $3,620 discount points

$905 origination fee + $3,620 points = $4,525 total loan fees

■ MORTGAGE LOAN REPAYMENT PLANS

Fixed rate-level payment mortgage (fully amortized). The most popular repayment plan, the fixed rate-level payment mortgage, was discussed earlier under fully amortized fixed-rate mortgage. This may also be referred to as a level-payment, simple interest loan. Mortgagors tend to prefer this repayment plan since there are no payment surprises during the course of the loan. Both the interest rate and the debt service amount are set for the duration of the loan.

Interest-only mortgage (term or straight loan). A mortgagor may choose an interest-only payment plan that calls for periodic payments of interest only, with the *principal to be paid in full at the end of the loan term in a balloon payment.* This is known as a **term loan**, or a *straight loan*. Historically, such plans were used for construction loans and second mortgages, but consumers occasionally used them for residential first mortgage loans. Prior to the 1930s, the only form of mortgage loan available was the straight-payment loan, payable in full after a relatively short term, such as three years to five years. The high rate of foreclosure on such loans in the depression years prompted the introduction and use of the more manageable long-term amortized loans that are now the norm. The popularity of term loans in recent years as first mortgages for primary residences in combination with very low or no down payment requirements is thought to have contributed to the huge number of foreclosures currently being experienced.

Adjustable-rate mortgage (ARM). Adjustable-rate mortgages (ARMs) generally originate at one rate of interest, with the rate fluctuating up or down during the loan term based on the movement of a *published index.* Because the interest may change, so may the mortgagor's loan payments. Details of how and when the rate of interest on the loan might change are included in the provisions of the mortgage note.

Generally, interest rate adjustments are limited to one per period, and a maximum amount of increase or decrease may be made over the life of the loan. Certain regulations may enable a lender to adjust the interest rate on a monthly basis. The borrower is usually given the right to repay the loan in full without penalty whenever the interest rate changes. (See the discussion of prepayment penalties earlier in this chapter.)

Common components of an ARM include the following:

- **Note rate (contract rate).** The original rate charged, which is stated in the closing documents, is called the note rate.
- **Index.** The interest rate on the outstanding balance of the loan is increased or decreased according to the movements of a named publicly published index. A very popular index used by lending institutions is the short-term U.S. Treasury bill rate, but many other indices are available and used.
- **Margin.** The amount of interest a lender charges over and above the index rate is called the margin. For example, if the most recent one-year Treasury bill rate was 3.25%, the lender could add a 2% margin and charge the borrower a 5.25% interest rate on the outstanding loan balance. The amount of the margin remains fixed for the entire life of the loan; it is the movement of the index rate that causes the ARM interest rate to fluctuate.
- **Interest rate caps.** Rate caps limit the amount the interest rate may increase or decrease in any one adjustment period, called the *anniversary* or *periodic interest rate cap*. They also limit the amount the interest rate can increase over the entire life of the loan, which is called the *lifetime* or *life of loan cap*.
- **Payment cap.** The payment cap, which sets a maximum amount for payment changes, protects the mortgagor against the possibility of individual payments that the mortgagor cannot afford. With a payment cap, a rate increase can result in **negative amortization**—an increase in the loan balance. For instance, suppose a borrower's rate increases a full 1%. For this borrower a

1% rate increase translates into a payment increase of $65 a month. However, the payment cap limits the increase to $45 a month. During that adjustment period, the borrower will be paying $20 a month less than the amount required to pay the full principal and interest payment. So, each month, $20 is added to the principal balance. This is negative amortization.

- **Adjustment period.** This establishes how often the loan rate may change. Common adjustment periods are every year (a 1-year ARM), every three years (a 3-year ARM), and every five years (a 5-year ARM), or some combination.
- **Conversion option.** Lenders may offer a conversion option, which permits the mortgage to be converted from an adjustable-rate to a fixed-rate loan at certain intervals during the life of the mortgage. The option is subject to certain terms and conditions for the conversion.

Figure 13.4 illustrates the effect interest rate fluctuations and periodic caps have on an adjustable-rate mortgage. Obviously, without rate caps and payment caps, a mortgage's interest rate could fluctuate wildly over several adjustment periods, depending on the behavior of the index to which it is tied. In Figure 13.4, the borrower's rate ranges from a low of 5.9% to a high of 9.5%. Such unpredictability makes personal financial planning difficult. On the other hand, if the loan had a lifetime rate cap of 7.5%, the borrower's rate would never go above that level, regardless of the index's behavior. Similarly, a lender would want a floor to keep the rate from falling below a certain rate (here, 6.5%). The shaded area in the figure shows how caps and floors protect against dramatic changes in interest rates.

Graduated payment mortgage (GPM). A flexible payment plan, such as a **graduated payment mortgage (GPM)**, allows a mortgagor to make lower monthly payments for the first few years of the loan (typically the first five years) and larger payments for the remainder of the term, when the mortgagor's income is expected to have increased. The interest on a GPM is fixed throughout the life of the loan. However, in the early years of the loan, the monthly payments are lower than the

FIGURE 13.4

Adjustable-Rate Mortgage

Interest Rate: 6.9%, 9%, 8.2%, 9.5%, 8.5%, 7.6%, 5.9%

Adjustment Periods

payments required to fully amortize the loan. This results in *negative amortization*. As each payment is made, the unpaid interest is added to the principal balance, resulting in an increasing loan balance for the first few years. The monthly payments then increase at stated intervals throughout the loan term, eventually making up for the negative amortization and paying off the loan in full by the end of the loan term. Generally, this type of loan is used to enable first-time buyers and buyers in times of high interest rates to purchase real estate.

Balloon payment loan. When a mortgage loan requires periodic payments that will not fully amortize the amount of the loan by the end of the loan term, the final payment is an amount that is larger than the previous payments—a balloon payment. Examples would be a partially amortized loan and a term loan.

■ **FOR EXAMPLE** A loan for $80,000 at 10% interest may be computed on a 30-year amortization schedule but paid over a 20-year term, with a final balloon payment due at the end of the 20th year. In this case, each monthly payment would be $792.24 (the amount taken from a 30-year amortization schedule), with a final balloon payment of $56,340 (the amount of principal still owing after 20 years).

MATH CONCEPTS | **INTEREST-ONLY BALLOON PAYMENT LOAN**

Consider a loan with the following terms: $80,000 at 8% interest, with only interest payable monthly and the loan fully repayable in 15 years. To calculate the amount of the final balloon payment:

$$\$80{,}000 \times 0.08 = \$6{,}400 \text{ annual interest}$$
$$\$6{,}400 \text{ annual interest} \div 12 \text{ months} = \$533.33 \text{ monthly interest payment}$$
$$\$80{,}000 \text{ principal payment} + \$533.33 \text{ monthly interest} =$$
$$\$80{,}533.33 \text{ final balloon payment}$$

It is frequently assumed that if payments are made promptly, the lender will extend the balloon payment for another limited term. The lender, however, is in no way legally obligated to grant this extension and can require payment in full when the note is due. The borrower may have to refinance the loan with another lender.

A loan that requires a balloon payment is called a *partially amortized* loan and is quite common in seller-financing situations. When sellers finance part or all of the purchase price, they often want to be *cashed out*—that is, have the seller financing paid off—within three to five years of the sale.

Growing-equity mortgage (GEM). The *growing-equity mortgage*, or rapid-payoff mortgage, makes use of a fixed interest rate, but payments of principal are increased according to an index or a schedule. The total payment, therefore, increases, but the borrower's income is expected to keep pace, and the loan is paid off more quickly. (*Note:* **equity is the borrower's financial interest in the property; that is, the value of the property minus all outstanding mortgages and other liens.**)

■ THE MORTGAGE (OR DEED OF TRUST) INSTRUMENT

A mortgage or deed-of-trust document is typically a little more complicated than a promissory note. The mortgage or deed of trust must refer to the terms of the promissory note and clearly establish through the use of a mortgaging clause that the property is intended to be security for a valid debt. It must identify the lender and the borrower (who must have the capacity to contract) and must include an accurate, adequate legal description of the property. It must be in writing and signed by all parties who have an interest in the real estate. If a property will be owned by a married couple as tenants by the entirety or as joint tenants, both spouses will be required to sign the mortgage or deed of trust even if only one spouse signed the mortgage note. (The lender does not sign the mortgage or deed of trust.) Finally, the mortgage or deed of trust must be recorded and delivered to and accepted by the lender or trustee (see Figure 13.5).

Rights and Duties of the Borrower

The borrower (mortgagor or grantor) is required to fulfill many obligations. These usually include

- payment of the debt in accordance with the terms of the note;
- payment of all real estate taxes on the property given as security;
- maintenance of adequate insurance to protect the lender if the property is destroyed or damaged by fire, windstorm, or another hazard;
- maintenance of the property in good repair at all times to not allow waste; and
- lender authorization before making any major alterations or demolishing any building on the mortgaged property.

Failure to meet any of these obligations can result in a borrower's default on the note. When this happens, the acceleration clause allows the lender to call the note and mortgage or deed of trust due and payable. The loan documents may provide for a grace period (e.g., 30 days) for the borrower to correct the default, after which the lender has the right to foreclose the mortgage or deed of trust and collect on the note. The most frequent cause of default is the borrower's failure to meet monthly payment installments.

The borrower has the right to possess and enjoy the property during the loan term, with no interference from the lender. The borrower also has the right (*right of defeasance*) to have legal title to the property transferred back to him or her when the loan is paid in full. Under the provisions of the mortgage or deed of trust, when the note has been fully paid, the trustee is required to execute a **satisfaction of mortgage**, also known as a deed of release, reconveyance deed, release of mortgage, or mortgage discharge. This document reconveys to the borrower all interest in the real estate that was conveyed to the lender by the original recorded mortgage or deed of trust document. By having this release entered in the public record, the owner shows that the mortgage lien has been removed from the property.

Rights of the Lender

A lender has the right to assign the mortgage debt as well as the right to foreclose the mortgage or deed of trust if the borrower defaults.

As mentioned earlier, because a note is a negotiable instrument, it may be sold to a third party without the consent of the borrower. The lender endorses the note to the third party and also executes an assignment of mortgage. The assignee becomes the new owner of the debt and security instrument with all the rights and obligations of the original lender. This assignment must be recorded. On payment in full, or satisfaction of the debt, the assignee is required to execute the

FIGURE 13.5

North Carolina Deed of Trust

North Carolina Deed of Trust

Do NOT write above this line.   Recording: Time, Book and Page

This instrument prepared by: _____
Brief description for the Index _____
This Deed of Trust made this _____ day of _____, 20___, by and between Grantor, Trustee, and Beneficiary:
Enter in appropriate block for each party: Name, address, county, state and if appropriate entity (i.e. corporation, partnership). The designation Grantor, Trustee, and Beneficiary as used herein shall include all parties, their heirs, successors and assigns and shall include singular, plural, masculine, feminine or neuter as required by context.

Grantor:

Trustee:

Beneficiary:

Debt: Grantor is indebted to the Beneficiary in the principal sum of _____
_____ Dollars ($ _____)
as described in the Promissory Note of this date whose terms are incorporated by reference. The final Due Date for payment of the Promissory Note is, (if not paid sooner) _____.
As security for the Note, advancements and other sums expended by the Beneficiary, as detailed in this Deed of Trust, and the costs of collection (including attorneys fees as listed in the Promissory Note) the receipt of which is hereby acknowledged, Grantor conveys to Trustee the Property described below:

Property: City of _____ ,
Township of _____ County of _____ , North Carolina.
This property was acquired by Grantor by an instrument recorded in Book_____, Page_____, _____ County.
A map showing the property is recorded in Plat Book _____, Page_____, _____ County.
The legal description of the Property is:

Continued on Page 2

Satisfaction: The debt secured by this Deed of Trust and the Promissory Note referenced has been satisfied in full.
Signed: _____   Date _____

After recording mail to: Tax Lot No. _____
_____   Parcel Identifier No. _____
_____   Verified By _____ County,
_____   on the _____ day of _____, 20___.
                                                By _____

Form 55-301 © 2007 by James Williams & Co., Inc. www.JamesWilliams.com   Page 1 of 3 Initial _____

Source: This form is reproduced with permission from James Williams & Co., Inc.

FIGURE 13.5

North Carolina Deed of Trust (continued)

Continued from Page 1

TO HAVE AND TO HOLD Property and all privileges and appurtenances (rights) belonging to Trustee, upon the trusts, terms and conditions and for the uses listed below:

If Grantor pays Promissory Note in accordance with its terms, together with the interest due, and any renewals or extensions thereof in whole or in part and all other sums secured hereby and shall comply with all of the covenants, terms and conditions of this Deed of Trust, then this conveyance shall be null and void and may be cancelled of record at the request and the expense of Grantor.

If, however, there shall be any default (a) in the payment of any sums due under Note, this Deed of Trust or any other instrument securing the Note and such default is not cured within ten (10) days from the due date, or (b) if there shall be default in any of the other covenants, terms or conditions of Note secured hereby, or any failure or neglect to comply with the covenants, terms or conditions contained in this Deed of Trust or any other instrument securing Note and such default is not cured within fifteen (15) days after written notice, then and in any of such events, without further notice, it shall be lawful for and the duty of Trustee, upon request of Beneficiary, to sell the land herein conveyed at public auction for cash, after having first giving such notice of hearing as to commencement of foreclosure proceedings and obtained such findings or leave of court as may then be required by law and giving such notice and advertising the time and place of such sale in such manner as may then be provided by law, and upon such and any resales and upon compliance with the law then relating to foreclosure proceedings under power of sale to convey title to the purchaser in as full and ample manner as Trustee is empowered. Trustee shall be authorized to retain an attorney to represent him in such proceedings.

The proceeds of Sale shall, after Trustee retains his commission, together with reasonable attorneys fees incurred by Trustee in such proceedings, be applied to the costs of sale, including, but not limited to, costs of collection, taxes, assessments, costs of recording, service fees and incidental expenditures, the amount due on Note hereby secured and advancements and other sums expended by Beneficiary according to the provisions hereof and otherwise as required by the then existing law relating to foreclosures. Trustee's commission shall be five percent (5%) of the gross proceeds of the sale or the minimum sum of $_____ whichever is greater, for a completed foreclosure. In the event foreclosure is commenced, but not completed, Grantor shall pay all expenses incurred by Trustee, including reasonable attorneys fees, and a partial commission computed on five percent (5%) of the outstanding indebtedness or the above stated minimum sum, whichever is greater, in accordance with the following schedule, to-wit: one-fourth (¼) thereof before Trustee issues a notice of hearing on the right to foreclosure; one-half (½) thereof after issuance of said notice, three-fourths (¾) thereof after such hearing; and the greater of the full commission or minimum sum after the initial sale.

And the said Grantor does hereby covenant and agree with Trustee as follows:

1. INSURANCE. Grantor shall keep all improvements on Property, now or hereafter erected, constantly insured for the benefit of Beneficiary against loss by fire, windstorm and such other casualties and contingencies, in such manner and in such companies and for such amounts, not less than that amount necessary to pay the sum secured by this Deed of Trust, and as may be satisfactory to Beneficiary. Grantor shall purchase such insurance, pay all premiums therefor, and shall deliver to Beneficiary such policies along with evidence of premium payments as long as Note secured hereby remains unpaid. If Grantor fails to purchase such insurance, pay premiums therefor or deliver said policies along with evidence of payment of premiums thereon, then Beneficiary, at his option, may purchase such insurance. Such amounts paid by Beneficiary shall be added to the principal of Note secured by this Deed of Trust, and shall be due and payable upon demand of Beneficiary. All proceeds from any insurance so maintained shall at the option of Beneficiary be applied to the debt secured hereby and if payable in installments, applied in the inverse order of maturity of such installments or to the repair or reconstruction of any improvements located upon Property.

2. TAXES, ASSESSMENTS, CHARGES. Grantor shall pay all taxes, assessments and charges as may be lawfully levied against Property within thirty (30) days after they become due. In the event that Grantor fails to so pay all taxes, assessments and charges as required, then Beneficiary, at his option, may pay them and the amounts he paid shall be added to the principal of Note secured by this Deed of Trust, and shall be due and payable upon demand of Beneficiary.

3. ASSIGNMENTS OF RENTS AND PROFITS. In the event of default, Grantor assigns to Beneficiary, all rents and profits from the land and any improvements, and authorizes Beneficiary to enter and take possession of the Property and improvements, to rent them, at any reasonable rate of rent determined by Beneficiary, and after deducting from any rents the cost of reletting and collection, to apply the remainder to the debt secured hereby.

4. PARTIAL RELEASE. Grantor shall not be entitled to the partial release of any of the Property unless a specific provision is included in this Deed of Trust. In the event a partial release provision is included in this Deed of Trust, Grantor must strictly comply with the terms thereof. Notwithstanding anything herein contained, Grantor shall not be entitled to any release of property unless Grantor is not in default and is in full compliance with all of the terms and provisions of the Note, this Deed of Trust, and any other instrument that may be securing said Note.

5. WASTE. Grantor promises that he will keep Property in as good order, repair and condition as they are now, reasonable wear and tear excepted, and will comply with all governmental requirements respecting Property or their use, and that he will not commit or permit any waste.

6. CONDEMNATION. In the event that any or all of Property shall be condemned and taken under the power of eminent domain, Grantor shall give immediate written notice to Beneficiary and Beneficiary shall have the right to receive and collect all damages awarded by reason of such taking, and the right to such damages hereby is assigned to Beneficiary who shall have the discretion to apply the amount so received, or any part thereof, to the Debt due and if payable in installments, applied in the inverse order of maturity of such installments, or to any alteration, repair or restoration of the Property by Grantor.

7. WARRANTIES. Grantor covenants with Trustee and Beneficiary that he is seized of Property in fee simple, has the right to convey Property in fee simple, that title is marketable and free and clear of all encumbrances, and that he will warrant and defend the title against the lawful claims of all persons whomsoever, except for the exceptions hereinafter stated. Title to property hereinabove described is subject to the following exceptions:

8. SUBSTITUTION OF TRUSTEE. Grantor and Trustee covenant and agree to and with Beneficiary that in case the said Trustee, or any successor trustee, shall die, become incapable of acting, renounce his trust, or for any reason the holder of Note desires to replace said Trustee, then the holder may appoint, in writing, a trustee to take the place of Trustee; and upon the probate and registration of the same, trustee thus appointed shall succeed to all rights, powers and duties of Trustee.

_____ **The Following Paragraph 9. Sale of Property shall NOT apply unless the line to the left is initialed** by Grantor.

9. SALE OF PROPERTY. Grantor agrees that if the Property or any part or interest in is sold, assigned, transferred, conveyed or otherwise alienated by Grantor, whether voluntarily or involuntarily or by operation of law [other than: (i) the creation of a lien or other encumbrance subordinate to this Deed of Trust which does not relate to a transfer of rights of occupancy in Property; (ii) the creation of a purchase money security interest for household appliances; (iii) a transfer by devise, descent, or operation of law on the death of a joint tenant or tenant by the entirety; (iv) the grant of a leasehold interest of three (3) years or less not containing an option to purchase; (v) a transfer to a relative resulting from the death of a Grantor; (vi) a transfer where the spouse or children of Grantor become the owner of Property; (vii) a transfer resulting from a decree of a dissolution of marriage, legal separation agreement, or from an incidental property settlement agreement, by which the spouse of Grantor becomes an owner of Property; (viii) a transfer into an inter vivos trust in which Grantor is and remains a beneficiary and which does not relate to a transfer of rights of occupancy in the Property, without the prior written consent of Beneficiary. Beneficiary, at its own option, may declare Note secured hereby and all other obligations hereunder to be forthwith due and payable. Any change in the legal or equitable title of Propertys or in the beneficial ownership of Property, including the sale, conveyance or disposition of a majority interest in Grantor if a corporation or partnership, whether or not of record and whether or not for consideration, shall be deemed to be the transfer of an interest in Property.

Continued on Page 3

Form 55-301 © 2007 by James Williams & Co., Inc. www.JamesWilliams.com   Page 2 of 3 Initial _____

Source: This form is reproduced with permission from James Williams & Co., Inc.

FIGURE 13.5

North Carolina Deed of Trust (continued)

Continued from Page 2

10. ADVANCEMENTS. If Grantor shall fail to perform any of the covenants or obligations contained herein or in any other instrument given as additional security for Note secured hereby, Beneficiary may, but without obligation, make advances to perform such covenants or obligations, and all such sums so advanced shall be added to the principal sum, shall bear interest at the rate provided in Note secured hereby for sums due after default and shall be due from Grantor on demand of Beneficiary. No advancement or anything contained in this paragraph shall constitute a waiver by Beneficiary or prevent such failure to perform from constituting an event of default.

11. INDEMNITY. If any suit or proceeding be brought against Trustee or Beneficiary or if any suit or proceeding be brought which may affect the value or title of the Premises, Grantor shall defend, indemnify and hold harmless and on demand reimburse Trustee or Beneficiary from any loss, cost, damage or expense and any sums expended by Trustee or Beneficiary shall bear interest as provided in Note secured hereby for sums due after default and shall be due and payable on demand.

12. WAIVERS. Grantor waives all rights to require marshaling of assets by Trustee or Beneficiary. No delay or omission of Trustee or Beneficiary in the exercise of any right, power or remedy arising under Note or this Deed of Trust shall be deemed a waiver of any default or acquiescence therein or shall impair or waive the exercise of such right, power or remedy by Trustee or Beneficiary at any other time.

13. CIVIL ACTION. In the event that Trustee is named as a party to any civil action as Trustee in this Deed of Trust, Trustee shall be entitled to employ an attorney at law, including himself if he is a licensed attorney, to represent him in said action and the reasonable attorney's fee of Trustee in such action shall be paid by Beneficiary and added to principal of Note secured by this Deed of Trust and bear interest at the rate provided in Note for sums due after default.

14. PRIOR LIENS. Default under the terms of any instrument secured by a lien to which this Deed of Trust is subordinate shall constitute default hereunder.

15. OTHER TERMS.

Signatures: Grantor has duly executed the foregoing instrument, as of the day and year first written above.

Entity — Individual

[Signature blocks with Name, By, Title fields and (Seal) notations]

SEAL-STAMP

INDIVIDUAL

STATE OF _____ COUNTY OF _____
I, the undersigned Notary Public of the County and State aforesaid, certify that _____
personally came before me this day and acknowledged the due execution of the foregoing instrument.
Witness my hand and Notarial stamp or seal, this ____ day of _____, 20____.
My Commission Expires: _____ Notary Public

SEAL-STAMP

INDIVIDUAL

STATE OF _____ COUNTY OF _____
I, the undersigned Notary Public of the County and State aforesaid, certify that _____
personally came before me this day and acknowledged the due execution of the foregoing instrument.
Witness my hand and Notarial stamp or seal, this ____ day of _____, 20____.
My Commission Expires: _____ Notary Public

SEAL-STAMP

ENTITY: Corporation, Limited Liability Company, General Partnership, or Limited Partnership

STATE OF _____ COUNTY OF _____
I, the undersigned Notary Public of the County and State aforesaid, certify that _____ personally came before me this day and acknowledged that he is _____ of _____ a North Carolina or _____ corporation / limited liability company / general partnership / limited partnership (*strike through the inapplicable*) and that by authority duly given and as an act of the Entity, has signed the foregoing instrument in its name and on its behalf as its act and deed.
Witness my hand and Notarial stamp or seal, this ____ day of _____, 20____.
My Commission Expires: _____ Notary Public

The foregoing Certificate(s) of _____
is/are certified to be correct. This instrument and this certificate are duly registered at the date and time and in the Book and Page shown on the first page hereof.

_____ – REGISTER OF DEEDS FOR _____ COUNTY
By _____ Deputy/Assistant - Register of Deeds

Form 55-301 © 4-07 by James Williams & Co., Inc. www.JamesWilliams.com

Source: This form is reproduced with permission from James Williams & Co., Inc.

satisfaction, or release, of the security instrument (discussed earlier). In the event of a foreclosure, the assignee is required to file the suit. The note and mortgage cannot be assigned if the loan is in default.

When a borrower defaults in making payments or fulfilling any of the obligations set forth in the mortgage or deed of trust, the lender can enforce its rights through a **foreclosure**. Such a default may include failure to make payments, destruction of all or part of the property, or failure to pay current insurance premiums or real property taxes. Foreclosure is the process of selling the mortgaged real estate to repay the debt from the proceeds of the sale. The foreclosure procedure brings the rights of the parties and all junior lienholders to a conclusion and passes title in the subject property to the highest acceptable bidder at a foreclosure sale. Property thus sold is free of the mortgage and all junior liens, but it still may have other encumbrances. Note that the purpose of foreclosure is to cut off the borrower's equity of redemption rights (discussed below).

Methods of foreclosure. Three general types of foreclosure proceedings exist—judicial, nonjudicial, and strict. The specific provisions of each method vary from state to state.

1. **Judicial foreclosure.** Mortgages are foreclosed through a court process called judicial foreclosure. A judicial foreclosure proceeding provides that the property pledged as security may be sold by court order after the mortgagee has given sufficient public notice. On a borrower's default, the lender may accelerate the due date of all remaining monthly payments. The lender's lawyer can then file a suit to foreclose the lien. On presentation of the facts in court, the property is ordered sold. A public sale is advertised and held, and the real estate is sold to the highest acceptable bidder. The new owner receives title to the property by means of a *sheriff's deed*.

   [In North Carolina]
2. **Nonjudicial foreclosure.** A deed of trust does not have to be foreclosed through a court action, so this type of foreclosure is called a *nonjudicial foreclosure* or **power of sale foreclosure**. Nonjudicial foreclosure is made possible by the power-of-sale clause in the deed of trust. The power-of-sale clause gives the trustee the power to sell the property and use the proceeds to repay the debt. (Note that a mini-hearing is required before the clerk of the court; otherwise, the property cannot be sold.)

   To institute a nonjudicial foreclosure, the trustee or lender must record a notice of default at the county courthouse in the Clerk of Court's office within a designated time period to give notice to the public of the intended auction. Generally, this official notice is accompanied by advertisements published in local newspapers that state the total amount due and the date of the public sale. The trustee then conducts the sale and transfers title to the high bidder by means of a *trustee's deed*. North Carolina deeds of trust allow for the power of sale foreclosure.
3. **Strict foreclosure.** Although the judicial and nonjudicial foreclosure procedures are the prevalent practices today, in a few states it is still possible for a lender to acquire the mortgaged property by a strict foreclosure process. After appropriate notice has been given to the delinquent borrower and the proper papers have been prepared and filed, the court establishes a specific

In North Carolina time period during which the balance of the defaulted debt must be paid in full. If this is not done, the court usually awards full legal title to the lender. Strict foreclosure is not used in North Carolina.

Distribution of proceeds. After the property is sold at the foreclosure sale, the proceeds are distributed in the following five-step order:

1. To pay all costs of the sale, including court costs or trustee fees, legal fees, advertising fees, et cetera
2. To pay any outstanding real and personal property taxes or assessments
3. To pay the mortgage(s) or deed(s) of trust debt (assuming this debt has first priority over any other liens) in order of recordation
4. To pay off any other liens in order of priority
5. To pay any surplus (equity) to the borrower

Redemption. Defaulting borrowers usually have a chance to redeem their property. In most cases, redemption has two parts—equity right of redemption or **statutory right of redemption**.

Historically, the **equity of redemption** (also called the *equity right of redemption*) is inherited from the old common-law proceedings in which the foreclosure process extinguished the borrower's right to regain the property. Adopted by statutory law, this concept provides that if, during the course of a foreclosure proceeding but before the confirmation of the foreclosure sale, the borrower pays the lender the total amount of back payments due, plus interest and costs, the foreclosure is stopped and the borrower retains the property. In some cases, the borrower who redeems will be required to repay the accelerated loan in full (see Figure 13.6).

FIGURE 13.6

Redemption

```
|──────────────────────────────|──────────────────────────────|
        Equity of Redemption              Statutory Redemption
          (before the sale)                  (after the sale)

Date of Default                   Date of Sale              End of
                                                     Redemption Rights
```

Certain states also allow defaulted borrowers a period in which to redeem their real estate after the sale. During this period (which may be as long as one year), the borrower has a statutory right of redemption. The mortgagor who can raise the necessary funds to redeem the property within the statutory period pays the redemption money to the court. Because the debt was paid from the proceeds of the sale, the borrower can take possession free and clear of the former defaulted loan. The court may appoint a receiver to take charge of the property, collect rents, and pay operating expenses during the redemption period.

In North Carolina During the North Carolina 10-day **statutory redemption period** after the auction (the *upset bid period*), a North Carolina mortgagor (borrower) can try to raise the necessary funds to redeem the property. During the upset bid period, any qualified bidder can submit an upset bid, a bid to purchase the property for an amount that exceeds the foreclosure sale price by a specific margin. Each upset bid triggers a new 10-day period. If the defaulted borrower can pay all that is owed to the lender (including accrued interest and penalties plus cost of foreclosure sale) anytime prior to confirmation of sale, the borrower redeems the property, receives legal title, and eliminates the previous winning bid. The foreclosure sale becomes final at the end of any 10-day period when no new bid is filed and the borrower's right to redeem the property is terminated.

Deficiency judgment. If the foreclosure sale of the real estate secured by a mortgage or trust deed does not produce sufficient proceeds to pay the loan balance and accrued unpaid interest plus costs of sale, the lender may be entitled to a personal judgment against the maker of the note for the unpaid balance. Such a judgment is called a **deficiency judgment**. It also may be obtained against any endorsers or guarantors of the note and any owners of the mortgaged property who may have assumed the debt by written agreement.

If any surplus proceeds exist from the foreclosure sale after real estate taxes, the mortgage debt and all junior liens (second mortgage, mechanics' liens, et cetera) are paid off and expenses and interest are deducted. These proceeds (equity) are paid to the borrower.

| In North Carolina | In North Carolina, deficiency judgments are prohibited in certain cases, such as when a purchase money deed of trust (seller financing) is used. If the seller is holding a purchase money mortgage/deed of trust, the seller has a special priority in lien payoffs in the foreclosure.

Deed in lieu of foreclosure. A **deed in lieu of foreclosure** is used when a borrower has defaulted on the mortgage loan and wants to avoid a foreclosure action. With the lender's agreement, the debtor simply gives the lender a deed in lieu of (title to the property instead of) foreclosure and, therefore, is spared both the foreclosure procedure and the possibility of a deficiency judgment. This is sometimes known as a *friendly foreclosure* because it is accomplished by agreement rather than by civil action. The major disadvantage to this manner of default settlement is that the mortgagee takes the real estate subject to all junior liens; foreclosure eliminates all such liens. Significant tax issues can arise when a deed in lieu of foreclosure is used. Competent legal or tax advice always should be obtained.

Short sales. A **short sale** is a transaction where the proceeds from the sale are not sufficient to fully satisfy the outstanding balance on the seller's existing mortgage(s), and the borrower lacks sufficient funds to make up the shortfall. A short sale is similar to a deed in lieu of foreclosure and occurs when a lender agrees to discount the remaining loan balance in the following manner: subject to the lender's approval, the borrower sells the mortgaged property for less than the outstanding balance of the loan and cedes all of the proceeds to the lender in full satisfaction of any mortgage debt. If the lienholder does not authorize the short sale, the seller cannot convey marketable title to a purchaser unless the seller can bring funds from another source to cover the shortfall.

As a practical matter, a lender will agree to a short sale only when convinced it will result in a smaller financial loss after factoring the cost and time of proceeding with a formal foreclosure. This may happen when the real estate market is a strong buyers' market, when housing prices are on a steep decline, or when a lender for legal or practical reasons lacks the ability or desire to obtain a deficiency judgment. However, keep in mind it is often possible for junior lienholders (such as second mortgages, tax liens, or mechanics liens) to prevent a short sale unless they receive guarantees that their interest will also be protected with the short sale.

If there is evidence that the sellers are in a possible short sale situation, a listing agent should recommend that the sellers discuss the situation with their lender or loan servicing company to determine if a short sale workout arrangement is possible. The listing agent should also encourage the property owner to seek expert legal and tax counsel to determine what the legal and tax ramifications of foreclosure, deed in lieu of foreclosure, short sale, and/or bankruptcy may be for the owner. Owners are oftentimes embarrassed to admit their circumstances. When a broker is late discovering that sellers are *upside down* or *underwater* in the property—that is, the borrowers owe more on the property than it is worth—the broker is unable to effectively serve their clients. Sellers may or may not be behind in their mortgage payments and still be confronting a possible short sale or foreclosure. There have been incidents of sellers intentionally overstating the amount of financial problems and understating their resources in order to encourage a lender to participate in a short sale. A broker does not want to participate in any form of lender fraud.

In North Carolina

Frequently, a request for a workout arrangement will not be considered until a signed sales contract has been obtained on the property. Because there is no guarantee that the lienholder(s) will approve the terms of the sales contract, it is highly advisable that a short sale approval contingency be inserted into the contract to allow the seller to cancel the contract if the lienholders' approval is not obtained, such as the NCAR Short Sale Addendum (Form 2A14-T, Appendix D, Form 18).

A workout arrangement will typically review factors that include the following:
- Loan status: in default or default is imminent
- Hardship: seller is facing hardship that is beyond his control that will adversely affect ability to make mortgage payments
- Seller's financial status: income documentation is generally required to determine if seller's resources are insufficient to make up any shortage
- Brokerage fee: any brokerage fee owed by the seller is considered
- Possibility of loan fraud: workout request is reviewed for fraud especially if default occurs in the first 12 months of the loan term
- Property value: loan servicer or lender will typically obtain an appraisal to evaluate the feasibility of the workout request; sometimes a broker price opinion (BPO) is requested instead of an appraisal

The lienholder that participates in a short sale typically reserves the right to file suit against the borrower to acquire the shortfall, called a *deficiency*. Although few lenders actually sue to recover the missing amount, they can. Because the borrower has received the money and has not repaid it, the borrower will generally receive an IRS Form 1099 because he/she owes income tax on the deficient amount that was *forgiven* in the short sale. Under the federal Mortgage Debt Relief Act of 2007, taxpayers are permitted to exclude from taxable income, the amount of debt reduced through mortgage restructuring, as well as mortgage debt forgiven through foreclosure or short sale. The Act currently applies to debt forgiven in the years 2007 through 2012. A competent tax advisor should be consulted for more details.

Buying Subject to or Assuming a Seller's Mortgage

When a person purchases real estate that is subject to an outstanding mortgage or deed of trust, the buyer may take the property in one of two ways. The property may be purchased subject to the mortgage, or the buyer may assume the mortgage and agree to pay the debt. This technical distinction becomes important if the buyer defaults and the mortgage or deed of trust is foreclosed.

When the property is sold *subject to the mortgage,* the buyer will not be personally obligated to pay the debt in full. The buyer takes title to the real estate knowing that he or she must make payments on the existing loan. On default, the lender forecloses and the property is sold by court order to pay the debt. If the sale does not pay off the entire debt, the purchaser is not liable for the difference. The practice of buying a property *subject to an existing mortgage* is extremely rare because the seller generally remains liable to the lender after the sale—even if the buyer has agreed to make the mortgage payments. In addition to the probability of extended seller liability for the loan, the pervasive use of due-on-sale clauses in mortgage lending has made this assumption options almost obsolete.

In contrast, a buyer who purchases the property and assumes the seller's debt becomes personally obligated for the payment of the entire debt. After the assumption by the buyer, the seller is not automatically released from liability for the loan repayment. If the mortgage is foreclosed and the court sale does not bring enough money to pay the debt in full, a deficiency judgment against the assumptor and the original borrower may be obtained for the unpaid balance of the note. If the original borrower received a release from liability by the lender, only the assumptor is liable.

■ **FOR EXAMPLE** When Jennifer bought her house a short time ago, interest rates were very low. Now Jennifer has been unexpectedly transferred out of the country and needs to sell the house quickly. Because interest rates have risen dramatically since the time of Jennifer's loan, buyers may be attracted by the prospect of assuming her low-interest mortgage. Clearly, if a buyer were to take out a new mortgage now, the rate would be higher and the cost of home ownership would be increased. By assuming an existing loan with a more favorable interest rate, a buyer can save money.

■ **FOR EXAMPLE** Dylan purchased his house when interest rates were high. In the short time since then, rates have fallen precipitously. If Dylan must sell quickly, he may find that buyers are not interested in assuming a high-interest mortgage. A buyer might purchase Dylan's property subject to the existing mortgage. That is, the buyer would purchase Dylan's equity; Dylan still would be liable for the mortgage; and the bank could foreclose on the property to recover a default. If the foreclosure sale failed to satisfy the debt, Dylan would be liable for the shortfall.

In most cases, a mortgage loan may not be assumed without lender approval. The lending institution requires the assumptor to qualify financially, and many lending institutions charge a transfer fee to cover the costs of changing the records. The purchaser usually pays any loan assumption charge. It is possible that the lender will issue to the original borrower/seller a release of liability for the loan. The widespread usage in recent years of due-on-sale clauses has made loan assumptions a rare event.

■ RELATED WEBSITES

Fannie Mae: www.fanniemae.com
Federal Deposit Insurance Corporation: www.FDIC.gov
Federal Housing Administration: www.fha.gov
Federal Reserve Board: www.federalreserve.gov
Freddie Mac: www.freddiemac.com
Housing and Urban Development: www.HUD.gov
Mortgage Bankers Association: www.mbaa.org
Mortgage Bankers Association of the Carolinas: www.mbac.org
Mortgage Debt Relief Act of 2007:   www.irs.gov/pub/irs-pdf/p4705.pdf
North Carolina Association of Mortgage Professionals: www.ncmortgage.org
North Carolina Commission of Banks: www.nccob.org
North Carolina Department of Justice: www.ncdoj.com
U.S. Department of Agriculture: www.usda.gov
U.S. Department of Justice, Civil Division: www.USDOJ.gov
U.S. Department of Veteran Affairs: www.homeloans.va.gov

■ KEY POINT REVIEW

A **mortgage** is any financing instrument by which real estate is used as security for a debt. The mortgage can take the form of either a mortgage lien or a deed of trust. **Hypothecation** is the act of pledging property as security without relinquishing possession of the property.

In a **mortgage**, the **mortgagor** (owner) borrows money from the **mortgagee** (lender), and the real estate is used as security for the debt.

Lien theory states have specific requirements that must be met.

- A mortgage document is executed by the borrower and recorded in the county in which the property is located.
- When a loan is paid in full, a defeasance clause requires the lender to execute a satisfaction (release or discharge) that is recorded to clear title.
- If the borrower defaults, the lender can accelerate the due date of the remaining principal balance and all other payments and costs.
- If the borrower continues in **default**, the lender can bring court action called **judicial foreclosure** where
  — the judge orders the property sold;
  — the public sale is advertised and the real estate is sold to the highest bidder;

- the borrower has **equitable right of redemption** within a time period (before and/or after sale) allowed by state law; and
- the mortgagee may have the right to a **deficiency judgment** against the borrower for an unpaid balance, if the sale proceeds are less than the amount owed.

■ The lender may accept a **deed in lieu of foreclosure** from a defaulting borrower, but title is subject to junior liens that are eliminated in a foreclosure.

A **deed of trust** transfers title from the **grantor/trustor** (property owner) to a trustee, who holds it on behalf of a **beneficiary** (lender). Note the following:

Title-theory states have specific requirements that must be met.

■ A deed of trust executed by the borrower is recorded in the county in which property is located.
■ The mortgagor transfers legal title to the mortgagee but retains **equitable title** and has the right to possession and use of the mortgaged property.
■ When the loan is paid in full, a defeasance clause requires the beneficiary to request the trustee to execute and deliver to the trustor a release deed (deed of reconveyance) to return legal title to the trustor.
■ If the borrower defaults, the lender can accelerate the due date of the remaining principal balance and all overdue costs.
■ If the borrower continues in default, a deed of trust with **power of sale** allows the beneficiary (lender) to ask the trustee to conduct the trustee's sale without court action.

Priority of mortgages and other liens is determined by the order in which they were recorded. Priority may be changed by subordination agreement.

The essential elements of a **promissory note** are: term, promise to pay, and borrower's signature. It is a **negotiable** note. Special note provisions include

■ **acceleration clause**,
■ **prepayment penalty** clause, and
■ **due-on-sale clause** (or **alienation clause**), which will prevent future purchasers from assuming the loan.

The loan payment can be remembered as PITI: Principal, Interest, Taxes, and Insurance.

An escrow (impound) account may be required to create a reserve fund to ensure that future tax, property insurance, and other payments are made. If a loan has an escrow account, the loan servicer or the lender makes tax, insurance, and other payments on the borrower's behalf.

The National Flood Insurance Reform Act of 1994 imposes obligations on lenders and loan servicers to set aside escrow funds for flood insurance on new loans for property in flood-prone areas.

A **fully amortized fixed-rate mortgage** requires a constant payment amount that will completely pay off the loan with the last equal payment.

Usury is the charging of interest in excess of the legal rate.

The return or profit on a loan is called the **yield**. **Discount points** are charged to make up the difference between the interest rate and the lender's desired yield.

Mortgage loan repayment plans include

- fixed rate-level payment;
- interest-only (**term loan**);
- **adjustable-rate (ARM)**;
- **graduated payment (GPM)**;
- **balloon payment** (partially amortized);
- growing-equity (GEM); and
- buydown.

When property with an outstanding mortgage or deed of trust is conveyed, the new owner may take title in one of two ways, if allowed by the loan document:

1. *Subject to*—the new owner makes payments on existing loans but is not personally liable if the property is sold upon default and proceeds of the sale do not satisfy debt.
2. Assuming the existing mortgage or deed of trust and agreeing to pay the debt, where the new owner takes personal responsibility for existing loans and is subject to a **deficiency judgment** if the property is sold on default and proceeds of the sale do not satisfy the debt.

QUESTIONS

1. North Carolina is characterized as a(n)
   a. lien theory state.
   b. title theory state.
   c. mortgage theory state.
   d. escrow theory state.

2. Which of the following statements is *TRUE* of a prepayment penalty in a mortgage instrument?
   a. It usually penalizes early payment of the mortgage loan.
   b. It is prohibited in all residential and commercial mortgage loans in North Carolina.
   c. It can never be waived, even if the buyer's mortgage is with the same lender as the seller's.
   d. It penalizes the lender when the mortgagor pays off the loan early.

3. A deed of trust
   a. is evidence of a debt.
   b. uses real estate as security for the repayment of a debt.
   c. is sometimes called a promissory note.
   d. is evidence of both legal and equitable title.

4. A charge to a borrower of three discount points on a $120,000 loan is
   a. $450
   b. $3,600
   c. $4,500
   d. $116,400

5. The person who obtains a real estate loan by signing a deed of trust is called the
   a. grantee.
   b. grantor.
   c. trustee.
   d. beneficiary.

6. All of the following components are common in an adjustable rate mortgage *EXCEPT*
   a. a payment cap.
   b. a life of the loan cap.
   c. an escrow cap.
   d. an anniversary cap.

7. Laws that limit the amount of interest that can be charged to the borrower are called
   a. truth-in-lending laws.
   b. usury laws.
   c. equal credit opportunity laws.
   d. RESPA legislation.

8. If a borrower pays $2,700 for points on a $90,000 loan, how many points is the lender charging for this loan?
   a. Two
   b. Three
   c. Five
   d. Six

9. Before the foreclosure sale, the borrower who has defaulted on the loan seeks to pay off the debt plus any accrued interest and costs under the right of
   a. redemption.
   b. defeasance.
   c. reentry.
   d. survivorship.

10. The clause in a promissory note that gives the lender the right to demand that all future installment payments become due on default is the
    a. escalation clause.
    b. defeasance clause.
    c. alienation clause.
    d. acceleration clause.

11. Which of the following statements is/are *TRUE* about a deed of trust?
    I. Foreclosure is conducted through the power of sale clause.
    II. It pledges the property as collateral for securing the loan.
       a. I only
       b. II only
       c. Both I and II
       d. Neither I nor II

12. Pledging property for a loan without giving up possession is best described as
    a. hypothecation.
    b. defeasance.
    c. alienation.
    d. novation.

13. Discount points on a mortgage are computed as a percentage of the
    a. selling price.
    b. amount borrowed.
    c. closing costs.
    d. down payment.

14. The clause in a deed of trust that allows the lender to call in the loan when the property is transferred is called the
    a. acceleration clause.
    b. prepayment penalty clause.
    c. alienation clause.
    d. defeasance clause.

15. Proceeds from a foreclosure sale first pay
    a. mortgages in the order of recordation.
    b. outstanding property taxes.
    c. junior liens in the order of recordation.
    d. the cost of the foreclosure sale.

16. In a deed in lieu of foreclosure situation,
    a. the lender is obligated to accept the deed.
    b. the lender takes the real estate subject to all junior liens.
    c. a civil action is required.
    d. all encumbrances on the property are extinguished.

17. A deficiency judgment on a promissory note may be granted to a
    a. holder of a purchase money mortgage.
    b. creditor whose loan was satisfied by the foreclosure sale.
    c. lender whose note was not fully satisfied by the foreclosure sale.
    d. mortgagor of the note.

18. Which of the following statements is/are TRUE if a buyer purchases property subject to the seller's loan and then defaults on the loan?
    I. The buyer is personally liable for the underlying debt.
    II. The seller remains personally liable for the underlying debt.
    a. I only
    b. II only
    c. Both I and II
    d. Neither I nor II

19. A term loan requires that the borrower pay
    a. only the interest during the loan term.
    b. both principal and interest during the loan term.
    c. an interest rate that adjusts during the loan term.
    d. increasing amounts of principal during the loan term.

20. A mortgage loan that calls for a substantially larger than normal payment at the end of the loan term is a(n)
    a. index loan.
    b. graduated payment loan.
    c. balloon payment loan.
    d. adjustable rate loan.

21. Interest charges by the lender on a fixed-rate conventional level payment loan are
    a. subject to periodic changes.
    b. almost always simple interest.
    c. usually paid in advance.
    d. all of the above.

22. A deficiency judgment is
    a. a court decision declaring that a debt is excused if a foreclosure sale does not satisfy the debt.
    b. a court decision for the balance owed on a debt after the security has been sold to apply toward the debt.
    c. a specific lien.
    d. a general lien with a life of five years.

23. Which of the following mortgages features increasing payments with the increases applied directly to the principal?
    a. Shared appreciation
    b. Growing equity
    c. Adjustable rate
    d. Graduated payment

24. A promissory note must be signed by the
    I. borrower.
    II. lender.
        a. I only
        b. II only
        c. Both I and II
        d. Neither I nor II

25. A deed of trust is a
    a. two-party instrument.
    b. three-party instrument.
    c. promissory note.
    d. security instrument that requires a judicial foreclosure.

26. A buyer has purchased a home under an agreement that made the buyer personally obligated to continue making payments under the seller's existing mortgage. If the buyer defaults and the court sale does not satisfy the debt, the buyer will be liable for making up the deficiency. The buyer has
    a. purchased the home subject to the seller's mortgage.
    b. assumed the seller's mortgage.
    c. adjusted the alienation clause in the seller's mortgage.
    d. benefited from the defeasance clause in the seller's mortgage.

27. A couple is in the process of buying a new home for $185,500 with an 80% LTV ratio. The lender is charging a 1% loan origination fee and is lending the money with 2 discount points. The buyers must pay an attorney $400 to handle the closing. How much money will the lender be paid in fees?
    a. $1,484
    b. $2,226
    c. $3,710
    d. $4,452

Based on the following scenario, answer questions 28 through 30.

A house is being bought for a purchase price of $180,000 with an 85% LTV ratio. The term of the loan is 30 years at a 7% rate of interest. It will take a loan factor of 6.65 to amortize the loan. The annual real property taxes are estimated to be $996. The annual premium for the homeowners' policy is estimated at $480.

28. What is the monthly PITI?
    a. $1,017.45
    b. $1,100.45
    c. $1,140.45
    d. $1,320.00

29. What will be the total amount of interest paid over the life of the loan if payments are made for the full 30-year term?
    a. $153,000
    b. $213,282
    c. $321,300
    d. $366,282

30. What will be the principal amount owed after the first monthly payment has been made?
    a. $152,775.05
    b. $152,875.05
    c. $153,000.00
    d. $152,323.33

303

CHAPTER 14

Real Estate Financing: Practices

■ **LEARNING OBJECTIVES** *When you have finished reading this chapter, you should be able to*

■ **understand** some of the components of the recent financial crisis.

■ **define** the prevailing criteria for (1) conventional, (2) FHA-insured, and (3) VA-guaranteed mortgage loans.

■ **identify** other types of financing techniques and special purpose loans.

■ **describe** how the secondary mortgage market operates, including the three major agencies, and federal legislation that affects mortgage lending practices.

■ **explain** residential lending practices and procedures.

■ **define** these *key terms*:

annual percentage rate (APR)
blanket mortgage
buydown
certificate of reasonable value (CRV)
conforming loan
construction loan
Consumer Financial Protection Bureau (CFPB)
conventional loan
Department of Housing and Urban Development (HUD)
Equal Credit Opportunity Act (ECOA)
Fair Credit Reporting Act
Fannie Mae
Federal Reserve System
FHA-insured loan
Freddie Mac
Ginnie Mae
home equity loans
jumbo loan
loan-to-value ratio (LTV)
open-end mortgages
package loan
Predatory Lending Act
primary mortgage market
private mortgage insurance (PMI)
purchase money mortgage
Real Estate Settlement Procedures Act (RESPA)
Regulation Z
reverse mortgage
sale and leaseback
secondary mortgage market
subordination agreement
subprime mortgage
trigger terms
Truth in Lending Act
VA-guaranteed loan

■ INTRODUCTION TO THE REAL ESTATE FINANCING MARKET

The real estate financing market has historically had the following three basic components:

1. Government influences, primarily the Federal Reserve System, but also the Home Loan Bank System and the Office of Thrift Supervision,
2. The primary mortgage market, and
3. The secondary mortgage market.

Under the umbrella of the financial policies set by the Federal Reserve System, the primary mortgage market originates loans that are bought, sold, and traded in the secondary mortgage market. It is important to have a clear understanding of the market in which mortgage loans exist.

Due to the severe financial situations experienced since 2007, the U.S. Congress passed sweeping legislation to prevent future abusive and deceptive lending practices. The most notable and far-reaching legislative action affecting the real estate industry and real estate financing is the Dodd-Frank Wall Street Reform and Consumer Protection Act, commonly referred to as the Dodd-Frank Act. This act was tasked with the most comprehensive overhaul of financial regulation since the 1930s. The Dodd-Frank Act created the **Consumer Financial Protection Bureau (CFPB)** as the oversight agency for consumer protection within seven federal agencies including the Fed, HUD, and the Federal Trade Commission. CFPB enforces regulations for banks, most credit unions, and mortgage-related businesses. CFPB is also tasked with administrating all the major laws and regulations that touch mortgage lending and will be discussed in detail elsewhere in this text: Truth in Lending Act, Equal Credit Opportunity Act, Fair Credit Reporting Act, Real Estate Settlement Procedures Act, Secure and Fair Enforcement for Mortgage Licensing Act, and the Interstate Land Sales Full Disclosure Act.

The Federal Reserve System

The role of the **Federal Reserve System** (the Fed) is to maintain sound credit conditions, help counteract inflationary and deflationary trends, and create a favorable economic climate. It does this by regulating the supply of money and interest rates. The Federal Reserve System divides the country into 12 Federal Reserve Districts, each served by a Federal Reserve Bank. All nationally chartered banks must join the Fed and purchase stock in its district reserve banks.

Open market operation. The Fed regulates the flow of money and interest rates in the marketplace through its member banks by controlling their reserve requirements and discount rates. The Fed also can regulate the money supply through the Federal Open Market Committee, which buys and sells U.S. government securities on the open market. The sale of securities removes the money paid by buyers from circulation. When it buys them, it infuses its own reserves back into the general supply.

Reserve requirements. The Federal Reserve System requires that each member bank keep a certain amount of assets on hand as reserve funds. These reserves are unavailable for loans or any other use. This requirement not only protects customer deposits, but it also provides a means of manipulation for the flow of cash in the money market.

By increasing its reserve requirements, the Fed in effect limits the amount of money that member banks can use to make loans. When the amount of money available for lending decreases, interest rates rise. By causing interest rates to rise, the government can slow down an overactive economy by limiting the number of loans that would have been directed toward major purchases of goods and services. The opposite is also true—by decreasing the reserve requirements, the Fed can encourage more lending. Increased lending causes the amount of money circulated in the marketplace to rise, while simultaneously causing interest rates to drop.

Discount rates. Federal Reserve member banks are permitted to borrow money from the district reserve banks to expand their lending operations. The discount rate is the rate charged by the Fed when it lends to its member banks. The federal funds rate is the rate recommended by the Fed for the member banks to charge each other on short-term loans. These rates form the basis on which the banks determine the percentage rate of interest they will charge their loan customers. The prime rate, the short-term interest charged to a bank's largest, most creditworthy customers, is strongly influenced by the Fed's discount rate. In turn, the prime rate is often the basis for determining a bank's interest rate on other loans, including mortgages. These rates are usually higher than the prime rate. In theory, when the Fed's discount rate is high, bank interest rates are high. When bank interest rates are high, fewer loans are made and less money circulates in the marketplace. On the other hand, a lower discount rate results in lower overall interest rates, more bank loans, and more money in circulation.

The Primary Mortgage Market

The **primary mortgage market** is made up of the lenders that originate mortgage loans. These lenders make money available directly to borrowers. From a borrower's point of view, a loan is a means of financing an expenditure; from a lender's point of view, a loan is an investment. All investors look for profitable returns on their investments. For a lender, a loan must generate enough income to be attractive as an investment. Income on the loan is realized from the following two sources:

1. Finance charges collected at closing, such as loan origination fees and discount points
2. Recurring income, that is, the interest collected during the term of the loan

An increasing number of lenders look at the income generated from the fees charged in originating loans as their primary investment objective. Once the loans are made, they are sold to investors. By selling loans to investors in the secondary mortgage market, lenders generate funds with which to originate additional loans. In addition to the income directly related to loans, some lenders derive income from servicing loans for other mortgage lenders or investors who have purchased the loans. Servicing involves such activities as

- collecting payments (including insurance and taxes),
- accounting,

- bookkeeping,
- preparing insurance and tax records,
- processing payments of taxes and insurance, and
- following up on loan payment and delinquency.

The terms of the servicing agreement stipulate the responsibilities and fees for the service.

Some of the major lenders in the primary market include the following:

- *Savings associations, or thrifts, and commercial banks.* These institutions are known as fiduciary lenders because of their fiduciary obligations to protect and preserve their depositors' funds. Mortgage loans are perceived as secure investments for generating income and enable these institutions to pay interest to their depositors. Fiduciary lenders are subject to standards and regulations established by government agencies such as the Federal Deposit Insurance Corporation (FDIC) and the Office of Thrift Supervision (OTS). These agencies govern the practice of fiduciary lenders. The various government regulations are intended to protect depositors against the reckless lending that characterized the savings and loan industry in the 1980s.
- *Insurance companies.* Insurance companies amass large sums of money from the premiums paid by their policyholders. While a certain portion of this money is held in reserve to satisfy claims and cover operating expenses, much of it is invested in profit-earning enterprises, such as long-term real estate loans. Although insurance companies are not considered primary lenders, they tend to invest their money in large, long-term loans that finance commercial, industrial, and larger multifamily properties rather than single-family home mortgages.
- *Credit unions.* Credit unions are cooperative organizations in which members place money in savings accounts, usually at higher interest rates than other savings institutions offer. In the past, most credit unions made only short-term consumer and home improvement loans, but in recent years they have been branching out to longer-term first and second mortgages and trust deed loans.
- *Pension funds.* Pension funds usually have large amounts of money available for investment. Because of the comparatively high yields and low risks offered by mortgages, pension funds have begun to participate actively in financing real estate projects. Most real estate activity for pension funds is handled through mortgage bankers and mortgage brokers.
- *Endowment funds.* Many commercial banks and mortgage bankers handle investments from endowment funds. The endowments of hospitals, universities, colleges, charitable foundations, and other institutions provide a good source of financing for low-risk commercial and industrial properties.
- *Investment group financing.* Large real estate projects, including highrise apartment buildings, office complexes, and shopping centers, are often financed as joint ventures through group financing arrangements such as syndicates, limited partnerships, and real estate investment trusts (REITs).
- *Mortgage banking companies.* Mortgage banking companies originate mortgage loans with money belonging to insurance companies, pension funds, and individuals, and with funds of their own. They make real estate loans with the intention of selling them to investors and receiving a fee for servicing the

loans. Mortgage banking companies are generally organized as stock companies. As a source of real estate financing, they are subject to fewer lending restrictions than are commercial banks or savings associations. Mortgage banking companies often are involved in all types of real estate loan activities and often serve as intermediaries between investors and borrowers. They are NOT mortgage brokers.

- *Mortgage brokers.* Mortgage brokers are NOT lenders. They are intermediaries who bring borrowers and lenders together. Mortgage brokers locate potential borrowers, process preliminary loan applications, and submit the applications to lenders for final approval. Frequently, they work with or for mortgage banking companies. They do not service loans once the loans are made. Mortgage brokers also may be real estate brokers who offer these financing services in addition to their regular real estate brokerage activities. Many state governments are establishing separate licensure requirements for mortgage brokers to regulate their activities.

IN PRACTICE A growing number of consumers apply for mortgage loans via the internet. Many major lenders have websites that offer information to potential borrowers regarding their current loan programs and requirements. In addition, online brokerage or matchmaking organizations link lenders with potential borrowers. Some borrowers prefer the internet for its convenience in shopping for the best rates and terms, accessing a wide variety of loan programs, and speeding up the loan approval process.

The Secondary Mortgage Market

The **secondary mortgage market** purchases, services, and sometimes re-sells existing mortgages and mortgage-backed securities created by the primary market lenders. This process replenishes funds to the primary mortgage market so they can originate more mortgage loans for the house-buying public, thereby helping homeownership become more affordable for all Americans. There are three major institutions in the secondary market: Fannie Mae, Ginnie Mae, and Freddie Mac. In September 2008, **Fannie Mae**, originally named the Federal National Mortgage Association (FNMA), became a federally owned enterprise that provides a secondary market for mortgage loans—conventional loans as well as FHA and VA loans. Until that time, Fannie Mae was a privately owned corporation that issued its own stock. Fannie Mae buys a *block* or *pool* of mortgages from a lender in exchange for *mortgage-backed securities* that the lender may keep or sell. Fannie Mae was instrumental in developing the uniform underwriting guidelines that helped assure investors of the quality of the mortgage-backed securities. As the oldest and largest of the secondary mortgage market institutions, a visit to the Fannie Mae website will yield a wealth of information.

Ginnie Mae, originally called the Government National Mortgage Association (GNMA), exists as a corporation without capital stock and has always been a division of HUD. Ginnie Mae is designed to administer special-assistance programs and work with Fannie Mae in secondary market activities. Fannie Mae and Ginnie Mae can join forces in times of tight money and high interest rates through their tandem plan. Basically, the *tandem plan* provides that Fannie Mae can purchase high-risk, low-yield (usually FHA) loans at full market rates, with

Ginnie Mae guaranteeing payment and absorbing the difference between the low yield and current market prices.

Ginnie Mae also guarantees investment securities issued by private offerors (such as banks, mortgage companies, and savings associations) and is backed by pools of FHA and VA mortgage loans. The Ginnie Mae pass-through certificate lets small investors buy shares in a pool of mortgages that provides for a monthly *pass through* of principal and interest payments directly to certificate holders. Ginnie Mae guarantees such certificates.

Freddie Mac, originally the Federal Home Loan Mortgage Corporation (FHLMC), functioning as a government-owned enterprise similar to Fannie Mae, provides a secondary market for mortgage loans, primarily conventional loans originated by savings associations. Freddie Mac has the authority to purchase mortgages, pool them, and sell bonds in the open market with the mortgages as security.

Many lenders use the standardized forms and follow the guidelines issued by Fannie Mae and Freddie Mac because use of these forms is mandatory for lenders that wish to sell mortgages in the agency's secondary mortgage market. The standardized documents include loan applications, credit reports, and appraisal forms.

The recent financial crisis. On September 6, 2008, due to the financial crisis in the mortgage lending industry and overwhelming concern for the continued stability of the secondary market, the federal government placed both Fannie Mae and Freddie Mac into a governmental conservatorship under the newly formed Federal Housing Finance Agency. At that time, the two mortgage giants together owned or guaranteed over $5.3 trillion-worth of mortgages—nearly half of the American mortgage market. In addition to placing Fannie and Freddie back into governmental control, the U.S. Department of the Treasury agreed to provide up to $100 billion of capital to ensure continued liquidity to the housing and mortgage markets. The ultimate stated goal of the conservatorship was to begin reducing the size of the mortgage portfolios of both Fannie and Freddie by 10% per year beginning in 2010 when the housing market is projected to be recovering. Federal officials sanctioned these actions as necessary to strengthen the housing market and stabilize the financial market. The governmental programs to help stabilize and strengthen the housing and lending industries will be found on a newly posted website: www.financialstability.gov.

Much speculation abounded and many fingers were pointed to locate the exact cause of the lending industry crisis. Was it the lack of oversight on the part of the federal government; predatory lending practices and low qualifying requirements by the lenders; borrowers overextending themselves financially; appraisers overvaluing collateral properties; Wall Street strongly backing subprime mortgage securities; or real estate brokers pushing up the high costs of housing? Perhaps the best explanation is a mixture of all the possible answers.

One major component of what has been termed a *financial meltdown* must be the huge surge and rapid decline in the popularity of the **subprime mortgage** market. As Fannie Mae and Freddie Mac were pressured to serve more of the consumer market, the qualifying standards became more and more liberal for borrowers and financing products became more flexible and creative. The secondary market created, endorsed, and purchased products such as 100% LTV loans, interest-only loans, hybrid (or exploding) ARMs, pay-option ARMs, and 40-year term loans. Lenders targeting subprime borrowers with relatively low credit scores flourished due to *stated income loans* (a loan where borrowers are asked to state their income and the lender believes them without verification) and/or *no documentation loans* (a loan with few to no documentation requirements, though easier to qualify for, generally carried a significantly higher interest rate); the number of subprime loans increased by over 300% from early 2000 to 2005. During the early years of the new century, escalating property values in many housing markets around the country offset the high risk of the subprime loans. If the rapidly increasing payments became burdensome, the borrower refinanced to access the newly acquired equity in the property or sold at a profit and financed a more expensive property.

Early 2005 saw the beginning of the housing market slowdown in some parts of the country. From the spring of 2005 to the fall of 2006, subprime mortgaged properties experienced a huge downward spiral in value with an increase in payment amounts that could not be corrected by refinancing. In early 2007, Freddie and Fannie stopped purchasing hybrid ARM loans and greatly reduced the number of no-doc or stated income loans (nicknamed *liar loans*) that they purchased.

By the summer of 2007, the subprime crisis exploded when several of the largest subprime lenders went bankrupt, leaving remaining subprime lenders suffering with huge drops in stock value. Banks absorbed millions of dollars in bad loans and began seriously restricting the money flow. According to RealtyTrac, which conducts and reports foreclosure statistics nationally, August 2007 saw an all-time record high number of foreclosures with one in every 557 households filing for foreclosure. Perhaps the final blow was at the end of 2008 when billions of dollars in subprime loans reset at greatly increased repayment terms causing even more widespread foreclosures. According to RealtyTrac, almost 3.2 million foreclosure filings were reported nationally in 2008 which is an 81% increase over 2007 and a 225% increase over 2006. The five states posting the highest foreclosure rates in 2008 were Nevada, Florida, Arizona, California and Colorado; North Carolina ranked 27th in foreclosure rates with a total of 41,750 filings in 2008.

In North Carolina

The end of 2011 did not bring the predicted real estate industry recovery. It is estimated that the major banks and loan servicers, including Fannie Mae and Freddie Mac, own over 700,000 foreclosed properties (REOs). After a few months of moderate declines in foreclosure numbers, the number of REOs is projected to increase because default notices, the first step in the foreclosure process, jumped 14% (almost 200,000 notices) in the third quarter of 2011. The number of foreclosures are increasing again now that the controversy over sloppy loan documentation and compliance has about run its course. Lenders have been intentionally holding REOs off the market to keep from crushing a fragile real estate market with 600,000 to one million additional distressed properties. Many lenders also appear to have delayed the filing of default notices as a financial strategy; this *shadow inventory* of delinquent homeowners is likely to become the next crop of REOs. Statistics from late 2011 project 4.5 million of the 55 million home loans are nonperforming. One in every 563 residential units in the United States received a foreclosure filing in October 2011. North Carolina ranks as the 38th state in level

In North Carolina

Chapter 14 Real Estate Financing: Practices **311**

of foreclosure activity with 2939 recorded foreclosure filings in October 2011, or one in every 1,449 residential units. The top five states in foreclosure activity in October 2011 were California, Florida, Michigan, Illinois, and Arizona.

■ TYPES OF MORTGAGE LOANS

The various types of mortgage loans that are available today can be divided roughly into private conventional loans and government-sponsored loans.

Conventional Loans *No govt. guarantee or insurance*

A **conventional loan** is a loan that is not *backed*—that is, made, insured, or guaranteed—by any government agency. In other words, the lender bears all the risk of borrower default when making a conventional loan. A conventional loan is viewed as the most secure loan because its *loan-to-value ratio* is lowest. A mortgage loan is generally classified based on its **loan-to-value ratio (LTV), which is the ratio of debt to value of the property.** *Value* is the sales price or the appraised value, whichever is less. The *lower* the ratio of debt to value, the *higher* the down payment by the borrower will be. For the lender, the higher down payment means a more secure loan, which minimizes the lender's risk. For instance, if a property is worth $100,000, an 80% loan would equal $80,000, and the borrower would make a $20,000 down payment.

MATH CONCEPTS

DETERMINING LTV

If a property has an appraised value of $100,000, secured by a $90,000 loan, the LTV is 90% (*Note:* if appraised value and sales price differ, the lender will use the lesser of the two to determine LTV.):

$90,000 loan ÷ $100,000 value = 0.90, or 90% LTV

Lenders that originate conventional loans usually intend to sell those loans to the secondary mortgage market once the transaction closes. Fannie Mae and other secondary market institutions will only purchase mortgage loans that conform to their lending guidelines to ensure that loans that are packaged together for purchase have similar characteristics.

Conforming loan guidelines for first mortgages secured by one to four family unit residences include a maximum loan amount; a minimum down payment; limits on seller contributions; and borrower qualifying ratios. The maximum loan amounts are set annually based on a formula utilizing average house prices. Loan limits have historically been uniform for the contiguous states with higher limits for Alaska, Guam, Hawaii, and the U.S. Virgin Islands. The Housing and Economic Recovery Act of 2008 has expanded the definition of *conforming loan* to allow higher loan limits in *high cost areas* as determined by the Federal Housing Finance Agency. Due to this change, maximum loan limits should be verified for specific areas. Most guidelines require a 5% minimum down payment (although some have required less) that necessitates the purchase of private mortgage insurance (PMI).

Generally, the borrower must personally provide at least 5% of the purchase price even if family members contribute additional down payment. Maximum contributions by the seller (or any third party) vary with different loan conditions, but are capped at 6% of the sales price. Borrower qualification requirements will be discussed later in the chapter.

Mortgage loans that do not meet all these guidelines are called *nonconforming loans*. Subprime loans made to borrowers who cannot meet the qualification requirements for a *conforming loan* are a good example of nonconforming loans. In addition, nonconforming loans include loans that exceed the maximum loan limits for conforming loans and are called **jumbo loans**.

Private mortgage insurance. One way a borrower can obtain a conventional mortgage loan with a smaller down payment is under a **private mortgage insurance (PMI) program**. When the LTV ratio is higher than a specified percentage, typically 80%, the lender requires additional security to minimize its risk. The borrower purchases insurance from a PMI company as additional security to insure the lender against borrower default. LTVs of up to 95% of the appraised value of the property are possible with PMI. PMI protects a certain percentage of a loan, usually 20% to 30%, against borrower default. Normally, the borrower is charged a fee for the first year's premium at closing and a monthly renewal fee while the insurance is in force. The premium may be financed or the fee at closing may be waived in exchange for slightly higher monthly payments. When a borrower has limited funds for investment, these alternative methods of reducing closing costs are very important. Because only a portion of the loan is insured, once the loan is repaid to a certain level (usually 75% or 70% of the value of the property), the lender may agree to allow the borrower to terminate the coverage. Practices for termination vary from lender to lender. In order to avoid purchasing private mortgage insurance during recent years, some borrowers would utilize *piggyback loans*. By taking out a first and second mortgage simultaneously, the PMI requirement could be avoided. The most common arrangements were either 80/10/10 or 80/15/5; both used a first mortgage LTV of 80%, a second mortgage LTV of either 10% or 15%, and then down payment in the amount of 10% or 5%.

IN PRACTICE Effective in July 1999, a federal law required that PMI automatically terminate if a borrower

- has accumulated at least 22% equity in the home; and
- is current on mortgage payments.

Under the Homeowners Protection Act, a borrower with a good payment history will have PMI canceled when he or she has built up equity equal to 20% of the purchase price or the appraised value. Lenders are required by the law to inform borrowers of their right to cancel PMI. Before this law was enacted, lenders could (and often did) continue to require monthly PMI payments long after borrowers had built up substantial equity in their homes and the lender no longer risked a loss from the borrower's default.

Chapter 14   Real Estate Financing: Practices   313

Mortgage Loan Types

② FHA-Insured Loans   *Insures*

The Federal Housing Administration (FHA) was created in 1934 under the National Housing Act to encourage improvement in housing standards and conditions, provide an adequate home-financing system through insurance of housing credit, and exert a stabilizing influence on the mortgage market. The FHA was the government's response to the lack of housing, the excessive foreclosures, and the collapsed building industry that occurred during the Great Depression.

The FHA, which operates under the **Department of Housing and Urban Development (HUD)**, neither builds homes nor lends money to purchase single-family housing. Rather, *it insures loans on real property made by approved lending institutions*. The FHA does not insure property; it insures lenders against loss in case of borrower default. An **FHA-insured loan**, then, refers not to a loan that is made by the agency but to a loan that is insured by it. FHA-insured loans are made by FHA-approved lenders, which are free to set the interest rates on the loans.

The most popular FHA program is Title II, Section 203(b), fixed-interest-rate loans for 10 years to 30 years on one-family to four-family residences. The FHA does not fix interest rates on these loans. These rates can be lower than those on conventional loans because the protection of FHA mortgage insurance makes them of less risk to lenders. Technical requirements established under congressional authority must be met before the FHA will issue the insurance. Three of these requirements are as follows:

1. In addition to paying interest, the borrower pays a *one-time mortgage insurance premium for the FHA insurance*. This amount (currently 1.5 to 3.0% of the loan amount depending on loan requirements, but subject to change) may be paid at closing by the borrower or someone else, or it may be added to the loan amount. (For example, on a $100,000 loan, the one-time premium would equal $1,500, to be either paid in cash at closing or added to the loan amount.) Also, the borrower is charged an annual renewal premium of one-half of 1% of the loan amount.
2. The mortgaged real estate must be appraised by an *approved FHA appraiser*. The loan amount generally cannot exceed either of the following: (1) 98.75% for loans over $50,000 (for loans less than $50,000, the buyer must contribute 3% of the sales price to the down payment and closing costs) or (2) 97.75% of the sales price or appraised value, whichever is less. Note that if the purchase price exceeds the FHA-appraised value, the buyer may pay the difference in cash as part of the down payment. In addition, the FHA has set maximum loan amounts for various regions of the country. (Contact your regional HUD office for such amounts in your area.) FHA regulations require that both buyer and seller sign a statement indicating that they have examined the FHA appraisal.
3. The FHA regulations set standards for type and construction of buildings, quality of neighborhood, and credit requirements for borrowers.

For a more thorough review of the FHA-insured loan requirements, limits, and options, visit the HUD website.

Prepayment privileges. When a mortgage loan is insured by the FHA and the real estate given as security is a single-family dwelling or an apartment building with no more than four units, the borrower has the privilege of prepaying the debt without penalty. On the first day of any month before the loan matures, the borrower may pay the entire debt or an amount equal to one or more monthly payments on the principal. The borrower must give the lender written notice of intention to exercise this privilege at least 30 days beforehand; otherwise, the lender has the option of charging up to 30 days' interest in lieu of such notification. This is also known as having no prepayment penalty.

Assumption rules. All FHA assumptions require the assuming buyer to qualify, and the borrower must occupy the property. All FHA loans made under the 203(b) program are for owner-occupied properties only.

Other FHA loan programs. In addition to loans made under Title II, Section 203(b), FHA-insured loans are granted under the following programs:

- *Title I:* Home improvement loans are covered under this title. Such loans are for relatively low amounts and have repayment terms of no longer than 7 years and 32 days.
- *Title II, Section 234:* Loans made to purchase condominiums are covered under this program, which in most respects is similar to the basic 203(b) program.
- *Title II, Section 245:* Graduated payment mortgages, as discussed in Chapter 13, are allowed under this program. Depending on interest rates, the LTV ratio of such loans might range from 87% to 93%.
- *Title II, Section 251:* Adjustable-rate mortgages (ARMs) are allowed under this program. The interest rate cannot change more than 1% per year or more than 5% over the life of the loan.

Points. The lender of an FHA-insured loan can charge discount points in addition to a 1% loan origination fee. The payment of points is a matter of negotiation between the seller and the buyer. However, if the seller pays more than the maximum percent allowed of the costs normally paid by the buyer—such as discount points, the loan origination fee, the mortgage insurance premium, buydown fees, prepaid items, impound or escrow amounts, and the like—the lender is to treat such payments as sales concessions, and the price of the property for purposes of the loan must be reduced.

Interest rates. Neither HUD nor the FHA regulates the interest rates paid on FHA-insured loans. The rates fluctuate from lender to lender, and the buyer is responsible for obtaining the lowest interest rate possible.

Lead paint notification. HUD now requires that a lead paint notification form be given to residential buyers to sign on or before the date the purchaser executes (signs) the sales contract. The FHA requires that the lender be provided with a copy of the notification form at the time of the loan application (Appendix D, Form 6). In the event the purchaser does not receive and sign the form on or before the date the sales contract is executed, the contract must be re-executed. This HUD guideline is required for FHA-insured loans on homes built prior to 1978.

Chapter 14 Real Estate Financing: Practices 315

Mortgage Loan Types

② VA-Guaranteed (GI) Loans — Guarantees

Under the Servicemen's Readjustment Act of 1944 and subsequent federal legislation, the Department of Veterans Affairs (VA) is authorized to guarantee loans to purchase or construct homes for eligible veterans. Eligibility status varies and is determined by length of service during peace or war times. Nonactive veterans wishing to use their entitlement cannot have received a dishonorable discharge from the military. The VA also guarantees loans to purchase mobile homes and plots on which to place them. GI loans assist veterans in financing the purchase of homes with little or no down payment at comparatively low interest rates. From time to time, the VA issues rules and regulations setting forth the qualifications, limitations, and conditions under which a loan may be guaranteed. (Figure 14.1 compares VA and FHA loan programs.)

FIGURE 14.1

Comparison of FHA and VA Loan Programs

FHA	VA
1. Financing is available to veterans and nonveterans.	1. Financing available only to veterans and certain unremarried widows and widowers.
2. Financing programs are for owner-occupied (1-family to 4-family), residential dwellings.	2. Financing is limited to owner-occupied residential (1-family to 4-family) dwellings; must sign occupancy certificate on two separate occasions.
3. Requires a larger down payment than VA.	3. Normally does not require down payment.
4. Different valuation methods; like VA, there are prescribed valuation procedures for the approved appraisers to follow.	4. Methods of valuation differ. VA issues a certificate of reasonable value (CRV).
5. FHA valuation sets the maximum loan FHA will insure but does not limit the sales price.	5. With regard to home loans, the law requires that the VA loan not exceed the appraised value of the home.
6. No prepayment penalty.	6. No prepayment penalty.
7. On default foreclosure and claim, the FHA lender usually gets U.S. debentures.	7. Following default, foreclosure, and claim, the lender usually receives cash (if VA elects to take the house).
8. Insures the loan by way of mutual mortgage insurance; premiums paid by buyer or seller. If by buyer, may be paid in cash or added to note.	8. Guarantees loans according to a sliding scale.
9. No secondary financing is permitted until after closing.	9. Secondary financing is permitted in exceptional cases.
10. Buyer pays a 1% loan origination fee.	10. Buyer may pay discount points but cannot finance them in the loan; he or she can pay a 1% loan origination fee.
11. Loans made prior to 12/1/86 are fully assumable; seller remains liable until the loan is paid off. Loans made between 12/1/86 and 12/15/89 are fully assumable after 12 months on owner-occupied loans; seller remains liable for 5 years. Loans made since 12/15/89 require prior approval of assumptor; seller is released from liability.	11. A funding fee from 0.05 to 3.33% must be paid to VA in addition to other fees. It may be paid by the seller or buyer. If paid by the buyer, it may be paid in cash or added to the note.
	12. VA loan can be assumed by nonveteran without VA approval for loans made prior to 3/1/88; otherwise, approval is required.
	13. For loans originated after 3/1/88, release of liability is automatic if VA approves the assumption.

Like the term *FHA loan*, *VA loan* is something of a misnomer. Normally, the VA does not lend money itself; it guarantees loans made by lending institutions approved by the agency. The term **VA-guaranteed loan**, then, refers not to a loan that is made by the agency, but to one that is guaranteed by it. The guarantee works to protect the lender in case of default much like private mortgage insurance or FHA's MIP. The regional VA office for North Carolina is located in Winston-Salem and can be reached at 800-827-1000. Extensive information about VA loan benefits and requirements is available at the VA website.

In North Carolina

To determine what portion of a mortgage loan the VA will guarantee, the veteran must apply for a *certificate of eligibility*. This certificate does not mean that the veteran will automatically receive a mortgage. It merely sets forth the maximum guarantee the veteran is entitled to, which is frequently called the *entitlement* or *eligibility*. Note that the maximum amount of the guarantee refers to the amount the lender would receive from the VA in case of default and foreclosure if the sale did not bring enough to cover the outstanding balance.

Ordinarily, a veteran obtains a loan from a VA-approved lending institution; only in locations where financing is not reasonably available, such as in isolated rural areas, does the VA actually lend money. Although there is no maximum VA loan amount, lenders will generally loan up to four times a veteran's available entitlement without a down payment. Although an eligible veteran's basic entitlement is currently $36,000, the guaranty in loans over $144,000 can be increased to a maximum of $89,912 thereby allowing a 100% loan of up to $359,650 ($89,912 max. guaranty × 4 = $359,648). The loan amount can be larger if the veteran is willing and able to make a down payment.

Maximum loan terms are 30 years for one-family to four-family dwellings and 40 years for farms. Residential property (up to a four-family unit) purchased with a VA loan must be owner-occupied. Interest rates are freely negotiable between the lender and the borrower. The VA also will issue a **certificate of reasonable value (CRV)** for the property being purchased, stating its current market value based on a VA-approved appraisal. The CRV places a ceiling on the amount of a VA loan allowed for the property; if the purchase price is greater than the amount cited in the CRV, the veteran may either pay the difference in cash or terminate the purchase agreement without penalty. Also, the seller may agree to lower the purchase price to the amount named in the CRV, or both the buyer and the seller may renegotiate the sale and each make a concession on the price.

Assumption rules. VA loans require lender approval of the buyer and an assumption agreement. Even when a VA loan is assumed, the original veteran borrower remains personally liable for the repayment of the loan unless the lender approves a release of liability.

To obtain a release of liability, the veteran must meet three requirements. First, the loan must be up-to-date (there are no past-due payments). Second, the assumptor must have sufficient income and a good enough credit history to qualify for the loan. Third, the assumptor must agree to assume the veteran's obligation for the loan. Note that any release of economic liability issued by the lender does not release or restore the veteran's entitlement that is tied to the loan. This must be obtained separately from the VA.

Restoration of entitlement. Even though a veteran has used a veteran's entitlement to purchase a home once, the veteran still may be eligible for another VA loan. If the veteran is selling a current VA-financed home, entitlement can be restored. For instance, if the first house is sold and the original VA loan is paid off, the veteran's entitlement will be restored and the veteran will be eligible for another VA home loan that can be used to purchase a replacement home. A veteran's entitlement also can be restored if the veteran sells the home to another veteran who is willing to assume the existing loan and if the buyer's entitlement is substituted for the entitlement of the selling veteran. The basic rule, with little exception, is that veterans can only have one property in their name at a time that is or was financed by a VA-guaranteed loan.

Prepayment. As with an FHA-insured loan, the borrower under a VA-guaranteed loan can prepay the debt at any time without penalty.

Points. Points are payable by either the veteran borrower or the seller. There also is a funding fee, which the veteran pays the VA at closing. The funding fee is a sliding fee, ranging from 0.5% to 3.33%. The funding fee can be added to the note.

IN PRACTICE Regulations and requirements regarding FHA and VA loans change frequently. Before making an offer based on FHA and/or VA financing, brokers working with buyers as clients or customers should always first check with local FHA-approved and VA-approved lenders as well as with local FHA and VA offices from time to time for current information regarding these government-backed loan programs. Sellers' agents should further check on hidden fees that sellers may be required to pay if they accept an offer based on FHA and/or VA financing.

Rural Economic and Community Development Services (USDA)

The Rural Economic and Community Development Services is a federal agency of the Department of Agriculture. This agency offers programs to help purchase or operate family farms. It also provides loans to help purchase or improve single-family homes in rural areas—generally areas with a population of fewer than 10,000 that are not suburbs of urban areas. Loans are made to low-income and moderate-income families, and the interest rate charged can be as low as 1%, depending on the borrower's income. The loan programs fall into two categories—*guaranteed loans*, made and serviced by a private lender and guaranteed by the agency, and *direct loans* from the agency.

The Farm Service Agency (FSA) has farm loan programs designed to help family farmers who are unable to obtain commercial private credit. These farmers may be beginning farmers, those who suffered financial setbacks such as natural disasters, or those with limited resources to maintain a profitable operation. Some farmers can satisfy their credit needs through the use of loan guarantees. The money is borrowed from a local agricultural lender that makes and services the loan, and FSA guarantees the lender against default loss up to a maximum of 90%. If a farmer cannot qualify for a guaranteed loan, FSA also makes direct loans, which are serviced by FSA. Eligible applicants may obtain a direct loan up to a $200,000 maximum, whereas a guaranteed loan may be as high as $300,000. Both have a maximum repayment period of 40 years.

The Rural Housing Service Agency, a branch of FSA, administers housing programs for low- to moderate-income rural residents. These types of loans include Direct Single Family Housing Loans, Guaranteed Single Family Housing Loans, and Repair Loans and Grants.

The Direct Single Family Housing Loan is designed for families with low to very low income—80% or less of county median income. These loans can be used to buy, build, improve, or repair rural homes. Eligibility requirements include (1) a rural area with a population of less than 10,000, (2) families who are without safe and decent housing, and (3) families to whom financing is not otherwise available. Availability of funds is based on annual appropriations. Loans may be made up to 100% of the appraised value. Interest rates are normally set at market rate, and the term of the loan is typically 33 years, but may be as long as 38 years. Applicants pay some costs, such as the credit report fee, appraisal fee, and closing costs, and the applicant must have good credit.

The Guaranteed Single Family Housing Loan is designed for moderate-income families who have limited down payment capability. Loans are processed by approved lenders and guaranteed by the U.S. government. Eligibility requirements are similar to the direct loan as discussed above. Maximum loan amounts range from $78,660 to $116,850, depending on the county in which the property is located. Interest rates are negotiable and fixed, with a 30-year loan term.

Repair Loans and Grants are designed for very-low-income individuals—those who earn 50% or less of the county median income. Funds can be used for repairs, installation of essential features, or to remove health and safety hazards. To qualify, the applicant must (1) live in a rural area of less than 10,000 population, (2) meet the income standards, and (3) be unable to get financing elsewhere. Grants are available only if the applicant is at least 62 years old. The interest rate is 1% annual percentage rate (APR), terms are up to 20 years, and there are no fees. The applicant must have a reasonable credit history.

Other Types of Loans

By altering the terms of the basic mortgage and note, a borrower and a lender can tailor financing instruments to best suit the type of transaction and the financial needs of both parties.

Purchase money mortgages. A **purchase money mortgage** is owner-financing given at the time of purchase to facilitate the sale and refers to the instrument *given by the purchaser to a seller who takes back a note and mortgage for part or all of the purchase price.* Takes back refers to the fact that the seller has taken back some interest in the property in exchange for financing. It may be a first or second deed of trust, and it becomes a lien on the property when the title passes. The borrower holds title under a purchase money mortgage. In the event of foreclosure on a purchase money mortgage, this lien takes priority over judgment liens against the borrower and over mechanics' liens. In North Carolina, a seller-lender is not entitled to a deficiency judgment.

Package loans. A package loan includes not only the real estate, but also all fixtures and appliances installed on the premises. In recent years, this type of loan has been used extensively in financing furnished condominium units. Such loans usually include the kitchen range, refrigerator, dishwasher, garbage disposal, washer and dryer, freezer, and other appliances, as well as furniture, drapes, and carpets. In other words, the lender has *packaged* both real and personal property in the same loan.

Blanket mortgages. A blanket mortgage covers *more than one parcel of land* and usually is used to finance subdivision developments, though it can be used to finance the purchase of improved properties as well. These loans usually include a provision, known as a *partial release clause,* so that the borrower may obtain the release of any one lot or parcel from the lien by repaying a definite amount of the loan at closing without triggering a due-on-sale clause for the rest of the financed property.

Open-end mortgages. Open-end mortgages act as a *line of credit* or *equity line*, allowing the mortgagee to make additional future advances of funds to the mortgagor, and are generally set up as home equity loans (discussed on next page). The mortgagee may have a prior lien for the amount of additional future advances if the mortgagee is obligated to make advances, as in construction loans. For unobligated future advances, the lien may be subordinate to other liens that may be created before the additional advancements are made.

Construction loans. A construction loan is made to *finance the construction of improvements* on real estate—homes, apartments, office buildings, and so forth. Under a construction loan, the lender commits the full amount of the loan but makes *partial installment payments* or *draws* as the building is being constructed.

Installment payments are made to the *general contractor* for that part of the construction work that has been completed since the previous payment. Prior to each payment, the lender inspects the construction site. The general contractor must provide the lender with adequate waivers of lien releasing all mechanic's lien rights (see Chapter 2) for the work covered by the payment. This kind of loan generally bears a higher interest rate because of the risks assumed by the lender. These risks include the inadequate releasing of mechanics' liens just referred to, possible delays in completing the building, and the financial failure of the contractor or subcontractors. The lender always runs the risk that the loan funds will run out before the construction has been completed. Construction financing is generally *short-term*, or *interim, financing*. The borrower is expected to arrange for a *permanent loan*—also known as an *end loan* or a *take-out loan*—that will repay, or *take out*, the construction financing lender when the work is completed. Construction loans normally pose a greater degree of risk to lenders than any other types of loans.

Sale and leaseback. Sale-and-leaseback arrangements are used rather extensively as a means of financing large commercial or industrial plants. The land and building, usually used by the seller for business purposes, are sold to an investor such as an insurance company. The real estate is then leased back by the investor to the seller, who continues to conduct business on the property as a tenant. The buyer becomes the lessor, and the original owner becomes the lessee. This enables a business firm that has money invested in real property to free that money so it can be used as working capital.

Sale-and-leaseback arrangements are very complex. They involve complicated legal procedures, and their success is usually related to the effects the transaction has on a firm's tax situation. A real estate broker should advise the parties to a sale-and-leaseback arrangement to consult with legal and tax experts when involved in this type of transaction.

Buydowns. A **buydown** is a way to lower the initial interest rate on a mortgage or deed of trust loan. Perhaps a homebuilder wishes to stimulate sales by offering a lower-than-market interest rate. Or, a first-time residential buyer may have trouble qualifying for a loan at the prevailing rates; relatives or the sellers might want to help the buyer qualify. In any case, a lump sum is paid in cash to the lender at closing. The payment offsets (and so reduces) the interest rate and monthly payments during the mortgage's first few years. Typical buydown arrangements reduce the interest rate by 1% to 3% over the first year to third year of the loan term. After that, the rate rises. The assumption is that the borrower's income also will increase and that the borrower will be more able to absorb the increased monthly payments. A common type of buydown is called the *3-2-1 buydown*. The interest rate is bought down by 3% in the first year, 2% in the second year, and 1% in the third year. For the fourth and succeeding years, the interest rate is the fixed note rate.

Home equity loans. **Home equity loans** are a source of funds for homeowners who wish to finance the purchase of expensive items; consolidate existing installment loans on credit card debt; or pay for medical, educational, home improvement, or other expenses. This type of financing has been used increasingly, partly because tax laws no longer allow deductibility of interest on debts not secured by real estate (*consumer interest*). Home equity loans are secured by the borrower's residence, and some or all of the interest charged may be deductible.

A home equity loan can be taken out as a fixed loan amount or as an equity line of credit. With the home equity line of credit (HELOC), the lender extends a line of credit that the borrowers can use whenever they want. The borrowers receive their money through checks sent to them, deposits made in a checking or savings account, or a book of drafts the borrowers can use, up to their credit limit.

Reverse mortgages. A **reverse mortgage** is one in which regular monthly payments are made *to the borrower*, based on the equity the homeowner has invested in the property given as security for the loan. A reverse mortgage allows senior citizens on fixed incomes to utilize the equity buildup in their homes without having to sell the property. The borrower is charged a fixed rate of interest, and the loan is eventually repaid from the sale of the property or from the borrower's estate on the borrower's death.

Mortgage Priorities

Mortgages and other liens normally have priority in the order in which they have been recorded. A mortgage on land that has no prior mortgage lien on it is a *first mortgage*. When the owner of this land executes another loan for additional funds, the new loan becomes a *second mortgage*, or a *junior mortgage*, when recorded. The second lien is subject to the first lien; the first has prior claim to the value of the land pledged as security. Because second loans represent greater risk to lenders, they are usually issued at higher interest rates and for shorter terms.

The normal recordation priority of mortgage liens may be changed by the execution of a **subordination agreement**, in which the first lender subordinates its lien to that of the second lender. To be valid, such an agreement must be signed by both lenders. Subordination agreements may be contained in the mortgage itself or they may be separate agreements filed for recordation.

■ RESIDENTIAL LENDING PRACTICES AND PROCEDURES

All mortgage lenders require that prospective borrowers file an application for credit that provides the lender with the basic information needed to evaluate the acceptability of the proposed loan. The application includes information regarding the purpose, the amount, the rate of interest, and the proposed terms of repayment of the loan. This is considered a preliminary offer of a loan agreement; final terms may require lengthy negotiations.

Application for Credit

A prospective borrower must submit personal information to the lender, including employment, earnings, assets, and financial obligations. Details of the real estate that will be the security for the loan must generally be provided, including legal description, improvements, title, survey, and taxes. For loans on income property or those made to corporations, additional information is required, such as financial and operating statements, schedules of leases and tenants, and balance sheets.

The lender carefully investigates the application information—studying credit reports and scores and an appraisal of the property—before deciding whether to grant the loan. The lender's acceptance of the application is written in the form of a loan commitment, which creates a contract to make a loan and sets forth the details.

Importance of credit scores. The creditworthiness of buyers is a key element in qualifying for a mortgage loan today. Underwriters consider several factors known about the applicant before determining whether or not to make the loan (e.g., credit scores and payment history). Today, with the exception of FHA loans and a few nonconforming loans, the interest rates available to borrowers are largely based on credit scores, which can range from 300 to 850. The higher the credit score, the lower the risk to the lender. Lenders offer these borrowers lower interest rates and may permit smaller down payments. Lenders almost always require a higher interest rate and/or a larger down payment for those with lower scores. Today, the FHA-insured loan is the best type of mortgage for a borrower with a lower credit score.

Importance of credit history. In addition to credit scores, underwriters consider two years in detail and up to seven years of repayment history. Particular attention is paid to whether the applicant made timely payments for rent and/or mortgage loans. A payments is considered late if more than 30 days past due. Underwriters especially look for bankruptcies, judgments, and foreclosures. Underwriters may make exceptions if the applicant can show specific reasons for the late payments (e.g., death, divorce, medical issues). Applicants who are consistently more than 30 days late with rent or mortgage payments will most likely be ineligible for VA and FHA loans and loans that are sold to the secondary market.

All the applicant's judgments must be paid in full, ideally more than two years prior to application, for approval on a FHA, VA, or conforming loan. Nonconforming loan requirements may allow judgments to remain unpaid if the title is not impacted. Normally, bankruptcies or foreclosures in an applicant's credit history must be older than three to four years. The long-term negative impact of participation in a short sale or deed in lieu of foreclosure on creditworthiness is still vague. Generally, the lender wants to see that the applicant has reestablished a strong credit history since the financial breakdown.

IN PRACTICE Because interest rates and loan terms change frequently, check with local sources of real estate financing on a regular basis to learn of specific loan rates and terms. As a broker, you can better serve your customers and clients if you can knowledgeably refer buyers to local lenders offering the most favorable terms.

Prequalifying Buyers

Every real estate broker should have a basic understanding of the loan standards lenders use as they decide whether or not to approve a loan. These loan standards, called *underwriting guidelines* or *qualifying standards*, can then be used by the broker to prequalify the agent's buyers. By prequalifying a buyer, the broker is more likely to avoid the disappointment of a rejected loan application. Note that broker prequalification is not the same as a lender's loan approval.

Qualifying standards are fairly complex; however, the basics are easy to understand and remember. The major element of any prequalification procedure is measuring the adequacy of a buyer's income. A lender will never approve a loan if the applicant does not have enough income to meet the monthly loan payments. Until a broker knows how large a loan payment the buyer can afford, the broker will not be able to effectively assist the buyer in selecting an affordable home.

MATH CONCEPTS

DETERMINING MAXIMUM AFFORDABILITY

You can use loan qualifying ratios to determine the price range of housing a prospective buyer can afford. Let's look at the Harrisons, whose gross monthly income is $3,900. To determine what kind of house they can afford, multiply their monthly income by a given standard debt ratio, 36%, for example.

$$\$3,900 \times 0.36 = \$1,404$$

Now subtract their recurring expenses, which total $475.

$$\$1,404 - \$475 = \$929$$

The maximum housing payment they can afford under this ratio is $929, including principal, interest, taxes, and insurance (PITI). Tax and insurance costs will vary according to location, but for purposes of this example, we will assume that 10% of the maximum payment is devoted to taxes and insurance. Deduct this 10% from the maximum payment.

$$\$929 \times 0.10 = \$92.90$$
$$\$929 - \$93 \text{ (rounded up)} = \$836$$

The Harrisons can afford to pay $836 a month in principal and interest. If current interest rates are 7%, they would qualify for a loan amount of $125,714. (You can use a financial calculator to determine this loan amount, or use a loan factor of 6.65. (See Figure 14.2.) To use a loan factor, divide the principal and interest payment by the rate factor and multiply by 1,000.) Assuming that the Harrisons have $12,650 for a down payment, they could afford to purchase a home for $138,364.

$$\$125,714 \text{ maximum loan amount} + \$12,650 \text{ down payment} = \$138,364$$

Computerized Loan Origination and Automated Underwriting

A computerized loan origination (CLO) system is an electronic network for handling loan applications through remote computer terminals linked to several lenders' computers. With a CLO system, a buyer can select a lender and apply for a loan right from the brokerage office.

On the lender's side, new automated underwriting procedures can shorten loan approvals from weeks to minutes. Automated underwriting also tends to lower the cost of loan application and approval by reducing lender's time spent on the process by as much as 60%. Complex or difficult mortgages can be processed in less than 72 hours. Such speed in the loan approval process can allow a buyer to submit proof of loan approval with offers to purchase; therefore, strengthening their negotiating position.

Scoring and automated underwriting. Lenders have been using credit scoring systems to predict prospective borrowers' likelihood of default for many years. When used in automated underwriting systems, the application of credit scores can become somewhat controversial. Critics of scoring are concerned that without human discretion the scores may result in more difficulty for low-income borrowers to qualify. Human judgment should be consulted especially when the loan application in a higher risk.

FIGURE 14.2

Mortgage Factor Chart

Equal Monthly Debt Service (PI) Payment to Amortize a Loan of $1,000

Rate	Term 10 Years	Term 15 Years	Term 20 Years	Term 25 Years	Term 30 Years
4	10.13	7.40	6.06	5.28	4.78
4 1/8	10.19	7.46	6.13	5.35	4.85
4 1/4	10.25	7.53	6.20	5.42	4.92
4 3/8	10.31	7.59	6.26	5.49	5.00
4 1/2	10.37	7.65	6.33	5.56	5.07
4 5/8	10.43	7.72	6.40	5.63	5.15
4 3/4	10.49	7.78	6.47	5.71	5.22
4 7/8	10.55	7.85	6.54	5.78	5.30
5	10.61	7.91	6.60	5.85	5.37
5 1/8	10.67	7.98	6.67	5.92	5.45
5 1/4	10.73	8.04	6.74	6.00	5.53
5 3/8	10.80	8.11	6.81	6.07	5.60
5 1/2	10.86	8.18	6.88	6.15	5.68
5 5/8	10.92	8.24	6.95	6.22	5.76
5 3/4	10.98	8.31	7.03	6.30	5.84
5 7/8	11.04	8.38	7.10	6.37	5.92
6	11.10	8.44	7.16	6.44	6.00
6 1/8	11.16	8.51	7.24	6.52	6.08
6 1/4	11.23	8.57	7.31	6.60	6.16
6 3/8	11.29	8.64	7.38	6.67	6.24
6 1/2	11.35	8.71	7.46	6.75	6.32
6 5/8	11.42	8.78	7.53	6.83	6.40
6 3/4	11.48	8.85	7.60	6.91	6.49
6 7/8	11.55	8.92	7.68	6.99	6.57
7	11.61	8.98	7.75	7.06	6.65
7 1/8	11.68	9.06	7.83	7.15	6.74
7 1/4	11.74	9.12	7.90	7.22	6.82
7 3/8	11.81	9.20	7.98	7.31	6.91
7 1/2	11.87	9.27	8.05	7.38	6.99
7 5/8	11.94	9.34	8.13	7.47	7.08
7 3/4	12.00	9.41	8.20	7.55	7.16
7 7/8	12.07	9.48	8.29	7.64	7.25
8	12.14	9.56	8.37	7.72	7.34
8 1/8	12.20	9.63	8.45	7.81	7.43
8 1/4	12.27	9.71	8.53	7.89	7.52
8 3/8	12.34	9.78	8.60	7.97	7.61
8 1/2	12.40	9.85	8.68	8.06	7.69
8 5/8	12.47	9.93	8.76	8.14	7.78
8 3/4	12.54	10.00	8.84	8.23	7.87
8 7/8	12.61	10.07	8.92	8.31	7.96
9	12.67	10.15	9.00	8.40	8.05
9 1/8	12.74	10.22	9.08	8.48	8.14
9 1/4	12.81	10.30	9.16	8.57	8.23
9 3/8	12.88	10.37	9.24	8.66	8.32
9 1/2	12.94	10.45	9.33	8.74	8.41
9 5/8	13.01	10.52	9.41	8.83	8.50
9 3/4	13.08	10.60	9.49	8.92	8.60
9 7/8	13.15	10.67	9.57	9.00	8.69
10	13.22	10.75	9.66	9.09	8.78
10 1/8	13.29	10.83	9.74	9.18	8.87
10 1/4	13.36	10.90	9.82	9.27	8.97
10 3/8	13.43	10.98	9.90	9.36	9.06
10 1/2	13.50	11.06	9.99	9.45	9.15
10 5/8	13.57	11.14	10.07	9.54	9.25
10 3/4	13.64	11.21	10.16	9.63	9.34

How To Use This Chart

To use this chart, find the appropriate interest rate. Then follow that row over to the column for the appropriate loan term. This number is the interest rate factor required each month to amortize a $1,000 loan. To calculate the principal and interest (PI) payment, multiply the interest rate factor by the number of 1,000s in the total loan.

For example, if the interest rate is 10% for a term of 30 years, the interest rate factor is 8.78. If the total loan is $100,000, the loan contains 100 1,000s. Therefore,

100 × 8.78 = $878 PI

To estimate a mortgage loan amount using the amortization chart, divide the PI payment by the appropriate interest rate factor. Using the same facts as in the first example:

$878 ÷ 8.78 = $100 1,000s, or $100,000 LV

Each of the three major types of loan programs has a different way of measuring the adequacy of a buyer's income.

Conventional conforming loans. Conventional lenders usually apply two ratios (income ratio and debt ratio) to the buyer's income to measure adequacy. First, the proposed monthly housing expense can usually be no more than 28% of the borrower's monthly gross income. Note that the proposed monthly housing expense includes principal and interest payments, plus monthly property taxes, insurance payments, and homeowner association dues, if applicable. Second, the proposed monthly housing expense plus the buyer's other long-term recurring monthly debts can usually total no more than 36% of the buyer's monthly gross income. Recurring monthly debts include items such as charge card payments, child support payments, personal loan payments, and car payments. These qualifying ratios can change, depending on the LTV ratio of the loan. The borrower must qualify on both ratios or they do not qualify for the loan. The larger the down payment the borrower makes, the easier it will be to qualify.

■ **FOR EXAMPLE** The Harrisons are seeking an 80% loan. They make $3,900 a month. Their recurring monthly payments include a $300 car payment, a $75 charge card payment, and a $100 college loan payment. They want to qualify for an $850 monthly loan payment, including principal, interest, taxes, and insurance (PITI).

First, add the three recurring monthly expenses, which total $475, to the $850 proposed housing expense to determine the total monthly expenses of $1,325.

If you divide $1,325 (total monthly expenses) by $3,900 (monthly income), you discover that the Harrisons' total monthly expenses equal about 34% of their monthly income. Therefore, they would qualify for the proposed loan under the second ratio because 34% is less than the debt ratio maximum of 36%. If you divide $850 (monthly PITI) by $3,900 (monthly income), you discover that the Harrisons' proposed housing expense is about 22% of their monthly income. This is well within the 28% income ratio maximum. Because both income standards are met, the Harrisons have a good chance of qualifying for the loan.

Let's assume the Harrisons want a more expensive home that would require a loan of $250,000. How much annual income would the Harrisons need to qualify using the 28:36 ratios if the estimated monthly PITI will be $1,665 and they have other monthly recurring obligations of $2,000? The first step would be to add up all monthly debts, then divide by the 36% debt ratio to get monthly income required; then multiply by 12 months.

$1,665 + $2,000 = $3,665 ÷ 0.36 = $10,180.56 monthly income × 12 months = $122,166.72 annual income

Let's take an example of determining maximum housing expenses that another couple could have with an annual income of $36,000 and recurring obligations (not including housing expenses) of $400 per month, using the 28:36% ratios to qualify.

$36,000 annual income ÷ 12 months = $3,000 monthly income × 0.36 = $1,080 maximum recurring obligation, not including housing. Their actual other monthly recurring obligations are $400. Their maximum monthly housing expenses would be $680 ($1,080 − $400 = $680).

FHA loans. The FHA also uses the same two ratios (income and debt) as in conventional loans to qualify its borrowers; however, the maximum proposed-housing-expense-to-income ratio is 31%, and the maximum proposed-total-monthly-debt-to-income ratio is 43%. These ratios are calculated in the same manner as the conventional ratios discussed above. The FHA ratios are not dependent on the loan's LTV ratio, unlike conventional ratios. FHA ratios remain constant, regardless of the amount of the down payment. Note that FHA standards are somewhat easier to meet than conventional standards.

VA loans. The VA uses a slightly different method to qualify its borrowers. The VA uses only the total-monthly-debt-to-income ratio, which the VA has set at 41% of the borrower's monthly income. Instead of a second ratio, the VA uses the *residual-income method*. With this qualifying method, buyers must have a certain amount of cash left over after paying their monthly housing expenses and other recurring debts. The VA publishes a table of how much residual income is required for buyers. The amount varies, depending on the number of dependents the buyer has and the geographic region in which the buyer lives. As with the two ratios used by conventional and FHA lenders, VA borrowers must qualify under both the total-monthly-debt-to-income ratio and the residual-income method before the loan will be approved.

■ **FOR EXAMPLE** A married couple with two children living in Raleigh with a combined annual gross income of $43,200 wants to apply for a $100,000 loan. The VA Cost of Living Table shows their required residual income is $964 for loan amounts above $70,000 for a family of four. Monthly withholding taxes and Social Security taxes are estimated to be $900 per month. Shelter expenses, which include principal, interest, taxes, and insurance (PITI), along with maintenance and utilities, are estimated to be $920. Other monthly obligations with six or more monthly payments left total $600.

$3,600	Monthly gross income
− 900	Taxes and Social Security
− 920	Shelter costs
− 600	Other debt obligations
$1,180	Residual income

The actual residual income exceeds the table amount, so the couple qualifies under this method.

Now let's take a look at whether the applicant couple from the previous example meets the 41% income ratio test. First add the total monthly obligations together.

$920	Shelter expense
+600	Other debt obligations
$1,520	Total monthly obligations

Then divide the total monthly obligations by the gross monthly income.

$$\$1,520 \div \$3,600 = 0.42 = 42\%$$

Because this ratio is more than the 41% maximum, the applicant does not qualify under this ratio.

If the applicant's residual income exceeds the required amount by more than 20%, the applicant may qualify for the loan, even if the applicant's total-monthly-debt-to-income ratio exceeds the 41% maximum.

■ **FOR EXAMPLE** The applicant couple's residual income in the previous example was $1,180. They were required to have only $964 in residual income.

$1,180 residual income − $964 required residual income =
$216 excess residual income

To find the percentage of excess residual income, divide the excess residual income by the required amount.

$216 excess residual income ÷ $964 required residual income =
0.224 or 22% of excess residual income

So even if the applicant couple's income ratio had been higher than 41%, they still might have qualified because they had a substantial amount of residual income.

■ FINANCING LEGISLATION

In North Carolina

The federal government regulates the lending practices of mortgage lenders through the Truth in Lending Act, the Equal Credit Opportunity Act, and the Real Estate Settlement Procedures Act. North Carolina legislation adds regulation through the Predatory Lending Act, the Residential Mortgage Fraud Act, and the North Carolina Secure and Fair Enforcement Mortgage Licensing Act.

Truth in Lending Act and Regulation Z

Regulation Z, which was promulgated pursuant to the Truth in Lending Act, requires that credit institutions inform borrowers of the true cost of obtaining credit so that the borrowers can compare the costs of various lenders and avoid the uninformed use of credit. Regulation Z applies when credit is extended to individuals for personal, family, or household uses and when the amount of credit is $25,000 or less. Regardless of the amount, Regulation Z always applies when a credit transaction is secured by a residence.

Regulation Z requires that the consumer be fully informed of all finance charges as well as the true annual interest rate before a transaction is consummated. The finance charges must include any loan fees, finder's fees, service charges, and points, as well as interest. In the case of a mortgage loan made to finance the purchase of a dwelling, the lender also must compute and disclose the **annual percentage rate (APR)** but does not have to indicate the total interest payable during the term of the loan. APR is frequently thought to be the interest rate because both are expressed as percentages. APR is the relationship of all finance charges to the loan amount and will always be higher than the interest rate. Also, the lender does not have to include as part of the finance charge such actual costs as title fees, legal fees, appraisal fees, credit report fees, survey fees, and closing expenses.

In total, the lender must disclose to the borrower (1) the loan's APR, (2) all finance charges associated with the loan, (3) the total number and amount of all payments, and (4) the total amount financed. These are called the *four chief disclosures* that must appear in a heavily outlined section, called the *Federal Box*, of the financing disclosure paperwork.

Advertising. Regulation Z provides strict regulation of real estate advertisements that include mortgage financing terms. General phrases like *liberal terms available* may be used, but if specifics, called **trigger terms**, are given, the advertiser must comply with this regulation. Generally, if any numbers related to the loan are disclosed, a trigger term has been hit and total financing term disclosure is mandatory. Under the provisions of Regulation Z, the APR—which includes all finance charges—rather than the interest rate alone must be stated. The total finance charge must be specified as well.

Specific credit terms, such as *down payment, monthly payment, dollar amount of the finance charge*, or *term of the loan*, may not be advertised unless the following information is set forth as well: cash price; required down payment; number, amounts, and due dates of all payments; and APR. The total of all payments to be made over the term of the mortgage must also be specified unless the advertised credit refers to a first mortgage or deed of trust to finance the acquisition of a dwelling.

Penalties. Regulation Z sets the penalties for noncompliance. The penalty for violation of an administrative order enforcing Regulation Z is $10,000 for each day the violation continues. A fine of up to $10,000 may be imposed for engaging in an unfair or a deceptive trade practice. In addition, a creditor may be liable to a consumer for twice the amount of the finance charge, for a minimum of $100 and a maximum of $1,000, plus court costs, lawyer's fees, and any actual damages. Willful violation is a misdemeanor punishable by a fine of up to $5,000 or one year's imprisonment or both.

Federal Equal Credit Opportunity Act (Regulation V)

The federal **Equal Credit Opportunity Act (ECOA),** in effect since 1975, prohibits lenders and others who grant or arrange credit to consumers from discriminating against credit applicants on the basis of race, color, religion, national origin, sex, marital status, age (provided the applicant is of legal age), dependence on public assistance, or exercise of the consumer's rights under this Act. In addition, lenders and other creditors must inform all rejected credit applicants, in writing, within 30 days, of the principal reasons why credit was denied or terminated.

Fair Credit Reporting Act (Regulation B)

The federal **Fair Credit Reporting Act,** effective since 1970, gives individuals the right to check their own credit reports and demand that mistakes be corrected. Credit bureaus are required to limit the credit information they provide to the previous seven years (except for bankruptcies, which can stay on credit records for 10 years). Individuals who have been denied credit based on information found in a credit report can examine their credit report at no charge. Under the Fair and Accurate Credit Transaction Act (FACT Act), individuals who have not been denied credit but want to examine their credit report may now receive one free credit report per year from each of the national credit bureaus. At this time, here are the three major credit bureaus where consumers can access their credit report and learn about protecting their credit identity: Equifax, Experian, and TransUnion. There is also a joint website for ordering the free annual report.

Loan Fraud Legislation

Loan fraud involves making any false representations in order to obtain a loan for a larger amount of money than the borrower is entitled to under the lender's guidelines. Misrepresentations may involve value of the collateral land, amount of down payment, personal information about the borrower, amount of closing expenses, undisclosed rebates or credits to a party, or occupancy. In almost every loan fraud, some false documentation was submitted to lenders, closing attorneys, real estate brokers, or other involved parties. Federal loan fraud statutes apply to all residential and commercial real estate transactions. *Any false statement to a lender is a federal felony crime punishable by fines up to $1,000,000 and/or imprisonment for up to 30 years.*

Residential Mortgage Fraud Act. In December 2007, North Carolina passed state-specific mortgage fraud legislation that made violation on one mortgage loan a felony. The penalty for commission of a felony includes incarceration, forfeiture of the property, or restitution. A real estate broker should report suspected mortgage fraud to the appropriate regulatory authority.

North Carolina Predatory Lending Act

With the passage of the **Predatory Lending Act** in 1999, North Carolina became the first state to enact comprehensive predatory lending laws. This North Carolina law that applies to lenders and addresses permissible fees that may be charged in connection with home loans secured by the first mortgage or first deed of trust. The Act's main provisions include the following:

- To impose restrictions and limitations on high-cost loans
- To revise the permissible fees and charges on certain loans
- To prohibit unfair or deceptive practices by mortgage brokers and lenders
- To provide for public education and counseling about predatory lenders

Real Estate Settlement Procedures Act

The federal **Real Estate Settlement Procedures Act (RESPA)** was created to ensure that the buyer and seller in a residential real estate transaction involving a new first mortgage loan have knowledge of all settlement costs. This important federal law experienced major revisions in 2010 and will be discussed in detail in Chapter 15.

RESPA requires that all transaction charges to the parties be clearly itemized on the HUD-1 closing statement that makes loan fraud harder to conceal.

■ RELATED WEBSITES

AARP; reverse mortgage info: www.aarp.org/money/revmort/
Center for Responsible Lending: www.responsiblelending.org
Equifax Credit Bureau: www.equifax.com
Experian Credit Bureau: www.experian.com
Fair Isaac: www.myfico.com
Fannie Mae: www.fanniemae.com and www.efanniemae.com
Federal Reserve Board: www.federalreserve.gov
Freddie Mac: www.freddiemac.com
Ginnie Mae: www.ginniemae.gov
HUD on Reverse Mortgages: http://portal.hud.gov/hudportal/HUD?src=/
    program_offices/housing/sfh/hecm/rmtopten
Making Home Affordable Program: www.makinghomeaffordable.gov
National Reverse Mortgage Lenders Association: www.reversemortgage.org
Realty Trac: www.realtytrac.com
Source for free annual credit report: www.annualcreditreport.com
Transunion Credit Bureau: www.tuc.com
U.S. Department of Agriculture; RECD loans: www.rurdev.usda.gov
U.S. Department of Housing and Urban Development (HUD):   www.hud.gov
U.S. Department of Veterans Affairs: www.homeloans.va.gov
U.S. Treasury Department: www.financialstability.gov

■ KEY POINT REVIEW

The **Consumer Financial Protection Bureau (CFPB)** oversees consumer protection within seven federal agencies that deal with consumer financing.

The **Federal Reserve System (Fed)** consists of 12 federal reserve district banks.

The **primary mortgage market** consists of lenders that originate mortgage loans based on

- finance charges collected at loan closing, including
    — loan origination fees, and
    — discount points;
- recurring income—interest collected during the term of loan, if kept;
- funds generated by sale of loans on the secondary mortgage market; and
- fees for loan servicing for other mortgage lenders or investors who have purchased the loans.

The **primary mortgage market lenders** include the following:

- Fiduciary lenders—thrifts, savings associations, commercial banks—subject to the Federal Deposit Insurance Corporation (FDIC)
- Insurance companies—generally investing in long-term commercial, industrial, and large multifamily properties
- Credit unions
- Pension funds
- Endowment funds of universities, colleges, and other institutions

- Investment group financing—joint ventures, syndicates, limited partnerships, and real estate investment trusts (REITs)
- Mortgage banking companies
- Mortgage brokers

The **secondary mortgage market**, where loans are bought and sold after being funded, does the following:

- Provides additional income to lenders and frees up funds to make more loans, with lenders often retaining servicing functions for a fee
- Purchases mortgage loans through agencies, assembles them into packages called pools, and sells them as shares (securitized) to investors or other agencies

Fannie Mae (Federal National Mortgage Association) is

- government-owned;
- creates mortgage-backed securities using pool of mortgages as collateral; and
- deals in conventional, FHA, and VA loans.

Freddie Mac (Federal Home Loan Mortgage Corporation) is

- government–owned, and
- has authority to purchase mortgages, pool them, and use them as security for bonds sold on the open market but does not guarantee payment of mortgages.

Ginnie Mae (Government National Mortgage Association) is entirely a government agency, a division of the Department of Housing and Urban Development (HUD), organized as a corporation but without corporate stock, that

- administers special-assistance programs, and
- guarantees mortgage-backed securities using FHA and VA loans as collateral.

Conventional loans are the most secure loans. Note the following:

- The **loan-to-value ratio (LTV)** is often lowest for these loans—traditionally 80%—meaning the down payment is 20%, but the LTV may be as high as 100%.
- Conventional loans are not government-insured or guaranteed.
- Conventional loans meet all the requirements of the secondary market, set by Fannie Mae and Freddie Mac, for **conforming loans**, including the following:
  — The borrower's monthly housing expenses, including PITI, should be no more than 28% of total monthly gross income.
  — The borrower's total monthly obligations, including housing costs and other regular monthly payments, must not exceed 36% of the total monthly gross income.
- Nonconforming loans must be retained in the lender's investment portfolio.

- **Private mortgage insurance (PMI)** may be required for LTVs higher than 80% (i.e., down payments of less than 20%). Note the following PMI conditions:
  — Federal law requires PMI to automatically terminate if the borrower has accumulated 22% equity in the home (based on purchase price) and is current on mortgage payments.
  — Fannie Mae and Freddie Mac have extended the automatic termination option to all loans that are in good standing and have had no additional financing added to the original loan.

FHA-insured loans are backed by the Federal Housing Administration (FHA), which is part of HUD. FHA does not make loans but insures loans made by an FHA-approved lending institution.

Mortgage insurance premium (MIP) has an up-front fee along with monthly installments. The premium can be financed within the FHA-insured loan.

VA-guaranteed loans are backed by the Department of Veterans Affairs and are available to eligible veterans and spouses. A veteran's entitlement can be restored by paying off the VA loan or letting an eligible veteran substitute their entitlement for the original borrower's.

Other types of loans include the following:

- A **purchase money mortgage** is a note and mortgage created at the time of purchase.
- The **package loan** includes all personal property and appliances as well as real estate.
- A **blanket loan** covers more than one parcel or lot, and a partial release clause allows a borrower to pay off part of a loan to remove the liens from one parcel or lot at a time.

Following are types of financing:

- A **straight loan (term loan** or interest-only loan) uses periodic payments of interest only for the life of the loan, with payment of principal in full at the end of the loan term.
- A **growing equity** (rapid-payoff) **mortgage** has a fixed interest rate but payments of principal increased according to an index or schedule so that the loan is paid off more quickly.
- An **open-end loan** secures the current loan to the borrower and future advances made by the lender to the borrower.
- **Construction loans** finance construction of property improvements.
- A **buydown** is a payment made at closing to reduce the interest rate on the loan.
- A **home equity loan** (home equity line of credit or HELOC) is junior to the original lien.

A **credit score** may be used as part of a loan application evaluation process.

The **Truth in Lending Act**, **Regulation Z** of the Federal Trade Commission (FTC), requires that when a loan is secured by a residence, lenders inform borrowers of the true cost of obtaining credit, advertising can not discriminate.

The **Equal Credit Opportunity Act (ECOA)** (Regulation V) prohibits discrimination in granting or arranging credit on the basis of race, color, religion, national origin, sex, marital status, age (as long as the applicant is not a minor), or dependence on public assistance.

The **Fair Credit Reporting Act** (Regulation B) gives consumers the right to check personal credit reports and demand that mistakes be corrected.

QUESTIONS

1. Which of the following defines the secondary mortgage market?
   a. Markets in which loans are bought and sold after they have been originated
   b. Lenders that deal exclusively in second mortgages
   c. Markets in which loans are originated
   d. Lenders that offer VA and FHA financing

2. The buyers purchased a residence for $95,000. They made a down payment of $15,000. The buyers financed the remaining $80,000 of the purchase price by executing a mortgage and note to the seller. This type of loan is called a
   a. purchase money mortgage.
   b. package mortgage.
   c. balloon mortgage.
   d. term mortgage.

3. Which of the following statement(s) is/are true about private mortgage insurance?
   I. Conventional lenders will usually require it on any loan over 80% LTV.
   II. It can be discontinued when the borrower's equity in the home exceeds 22% if he or she is current on the loan payments.
   a. I only
   b. II only
   c. Both I and II
   d. Neither I nor II

4. A borrower obtains a mortgage loan to make repairs on her home. The loan is not insured or guaranteed by a government agency, and the mortgage document secures the maximum amount of funds to be used for the current home repairs as well as any future funds to be advanced to the borrower by the lender. This borrower has obtained a(n)
   a. open-end mortgage.
   b. conventional open-end loan.
   c. installment contract.
   d. shared equity mortgage.

5. Regulation Z requires that lenders
   a. properly inform buyers and sellers of commercial property of all settlement costs in a real estate transaction.
   b. inform prospective borrowers of all charges, fees, and interest involved in making a home mortgage loan.
   c. not discriminate in the lending of credit based on protected class.
   d. study the economic market before they decide what interest rate to charge on residential mortgages.

6. A veteran's VA entitlement can be restored
   a. by letting a non-veteran assume the current VA home loan.
   b. once the equity in the property exceeds 25% of the market value.
   c. selling the property to a qualified veteran.
   d. by paying off the original VA loan that was secured by the entitlement.

7. An elderly woman continues to live in the home she purchased 40 years ago, but she now receives monthly loan installment checks from her mortgage lender thanks to her
   a. shared-appreciation mortgage.
   b. adjustable-rate mortgage.
   c. reverse mortgage.
   d. sale-leaseback agreement.

8. The buyers are purchasing an ocean-front summer home in a new resort development. The house is completely furnished, and the buyers have obtained a mortgage loan that covers the purchase price of the residence, including furnishings and appliances. This kind of financing is called a
   a. construction loan.
   b. package loan.
   c. blanket loan.
   d. home equity loan.

9. All of the following are true about the Rural Economic and Community Development loans EXCEPT
   a. Loans are insured by the federal government through Ginnie Mae. *(circled)*
   b. Loans are for low- to moderate-income homebuyers.
   c. The financed properties must be located in sparsely populated areas.
   d. Loans may be made for up to 100% of appraised value.

10. A developer received a loan that covers five parcels of real estate and provides for the release of the mortgage lien on each parcel when certain payments are made on the loan. This type of loan arrangement is called a(n)
    a. construction loan.
    b. blanket loan. *(circled)*
    c. package loan.
    d. open-end loan.

11. Funds for Federal Housing Administration (FHA) loans are usually provided by
    a. the FHA.
    b. the FDIC.
    c. qualified lenders. *(circled)*
    d. FNMA.

12. Under the provisions of the Truth in Lending Act (Regulation Z), the annual percentage rate (APR) of a finance charge does NOT include
    a. discount points.
    b. title preparation fees. *(circled)*
    c. loan origination fee.
    d. loan interest rate.

13. Which of the following is NOT a participant in the secondary market?
    a. FHLMC
    b. GNMA
    c. FNMA
    d. RESPA *(circled)*

14. All the following statements about junior mortgages are true EXCEPT
    a. "Their interest rates are usually higher than rates charged on first mortgages."
    b. "They are always purchase money mortgages." *(circled)*
    c. "They are more subject to default than first mortgages."
    d. "They are usually for a shorter term than first mortgages."

15. The buyers are applying for a home loan that will have a monthly loan payment of $750 (including taxes and insurance). Their recurring monthly expenses equal $500. How much monthly income do they need to qualify for a conventional loan using ratios of 28/36?
    a. $2,083
    b. $2,679
    c. $3,472 *(circled)*
    d. $4,464

16. All of the following financing information statements are trigger terms under Regulation Z of the Truth in Lending Act EXCEPT
    a. "Great assumable low interest rate loan" *(circled)*
    b. "Only $500 down and $750 a month"
    c. "FHA loan at 5% annual interest"
    d. "Easy qualifying on this 30-year loan"

17. The interest rate on FHA loans is set by the
    a. FHA.
    b. FNMA.
    c. lender. *(circled)*
    d. Federal Reserve.

18. All the following statements about Fannie Mae are true EXCEPT
    a. "She was originally a HUD agency."
    b. "She helped to standardize loan underwriting guidelines."
    c. "She was the first secondary market institution."
    d. "She makes mortgage loans directly to the consumer." *(circled)*

19. Mortgage bankers (companies) play an important role as a source of real estate financing. Their primary functions include all of the following EXCEPT
    a. servicing mortgage loans they sell to investors.
    b. originating all types of loans.
    c. charging service fees to investors and origination fees to loan applicants.
    d. using just their own funds from deposit assets to originate mortgage loans.

20. Which of the following loans exposes the lender to the greatest degree of risk?
    a. FHA
    b. Conventional, with 95% LTV ratios
    c. Construction
    d. VA, with no down payment

21. The main purpose of the Truth in Lending Act is to
    a. give a full disclosure of credit charges.
    b. regulate the practice of redlining.
    c. ensure that lenders give good-faith estimates of closing costs.
    d. establish legal usury limits.

22. For which type of loan would the buyer have to produce a CRV?
    a. FHA
    b. Conventional
    c. VA
    d. Reverse annuity

23. The major difference between a purchase money mortgage and an installment land contract is
    a. only one can be used for seller financing.
    b. the time at which the buyer gets possession and use of the property.
    c. the time at which delivery of the deed is made.
    d. there is no difference.

24. A buyer purchased a new home for $175,000. The buyer made a down payment of $15,000 and obtained a $160,000 mortgage loan. The builder-seller of the house paid the lender 2% of the loan balance for the first year and 1% of the loan balance for the second year. This represented total savings for the buyer of $4,800. What type of arrangement does this represent?
    a. Reverse mortgage
    b. Purchase money mortgage
    c. Blanket mortgage
    d. Buydown mortgage

25. The federal Equal Credit Opportunity Act prohibits lenders from discriminating against potential borrowers on the basis of all of the following EXCEPT
    a. marital status.
    b. gender.
    c. dependence on public assistance.
    d. amount of income.

26. If a lender agrees to make a loan based on an 80% LTV, what is the amount of the loan if the property appraises for $114,500 and the sales price is $116,900?
    a. $80,000
    b. $91,600
    c. $92,560
    d. $93,520

27. In determining LTV, value is
    a. 80% of the sales price or less.
    b. 95% of the appraised value.
    c. appraisal value or price, whichever is less.
    d. price or appraisal value, whichever is more.

28. Using the 28:36 qualifying ratios, what is the minimum annual income needed to qualify for a $120,000 loan at 6% annual interest rate for 30 years if the proposed PITI will be $847 and the borrower has other monthly recurring debts of $745?
    a. $28,233
    b. $36,300
    c. $53,067
    d. $68,229

336

29. What is the maximum loan a borrower can qualify for using the 28:36 ratios if her annual income is $60,000, the mortgage loan factor is 6.67, the estimated monthly taxes and insurance (TI) is $160, and her monthly nonhousing recurring debts total $700?
   a. $140,929.53
   b. $144,072.00
   c. $164,917.54
   d. $185,907.04

30. If a borrower has an annual gross income of $42,000 and will have monthly recurring debts of $500, not including housing expenses, what will be the maximum monthly housing expenses using the 28:36 ratios?
   a. $760
   b. $920
   c. $980
   d. $1,260

31. A husband and wife apply for an $80,000 conventional mortgage loan on a house valued at $85,000. The lender estimates that the couple's housing expenses will be $895 per month, and they have other recurring debts of $425 per month. The couple's combined annual gross income is $40,800. Under which of the following expense-to-income ratios will the lender find the couple to be qualified, based on the 28:36 ratio?
   a. Housing-expense-to-gross-income ratio
   b. Recurring-obligations-to-gross-income ratio
   c. Both a and b
   d. Neither a nor b

32. Using the 28:36 ratios, how much annual income must the borrower have to qualify for a $98,000 loan at 8% for 30 years if the proposed PI payment will be $719.32, taxes and insurance will be $135 per month, and the borrower's other monthly recurring debts total $500?
   a. $28,478.32
   b. $36,613.71
   c. $45,144.00
   d. $58,042.00

33. What is the maximum amount a buyer can borrow using the 28:36 ratio if her annual income is $53,000, her monthly taxes and insurance are estimated to be $150 per month, the mortgage factor is 8.0462, and her non-housing recurring debts total $650?
   a. $54,270.04
   b. $98,182.99
   c. $153,695.85
   d. $197,608.95

34. A man is buying a house for $123,000. His

CHAPTER 15

Closing the Real Estate Transaction

■ **LEARNING OBJECTIVES** *When you have finished reading this chapter, you should be able to*

- ■ **describe** closing, the preliminaries that must take place before actual closing, and the settlement meeting.
- ■ **describe** the steps involved in preparing a settlement statement and the steps involved in the transfer of title and funds.
- ■ **list** RESPA requirements.
- ■ **calculate** all types of prorations and prepare a detailed settlement statement worksheet.
- ■ **define** these *key terms*:

accrued items
closing
credit
debit
due diligence
Good Faith Estimate (GFE)

prepaid items
prorations
Real Estate Settlement Procedures Act (RESPA)
settlement
settlement agent

Settlement Statement (HUD-1)
soil suitability test
survey
walk-through
yield spread premium

■ PRECLOSING PROCEDURES

Everything a broker does in the course of a real estate transaction, from securing clients to presenting offers and coordinating inspections, leads to one final event: closing. **Closing**, or **settlement**, is the consummation of the real estate transaction. Closing actually involves three events: (1) the promises made in the sales contract are fulfilled, (2) the mortgage loan funds (if any) are distributed to the buyer for use, and (3) other settlement costs or funds are disbursed. It is the time when the title to the real estate is transferred via the deed in exchange for payment of the purchase price. Closing marks the end of any successful real estate sales transaction. Before the property changes hands, however, there are important issues that must be resolved.

North Carolina Buyer's Due Diligence Process

The buyer's **Due Diligence Period** (DDP) as described in Paragraph 1(h) of the NCAR/NCBA Standard Form 2-T Offer to Purchase and Contract (OPC) (Appendix D, Form 13) is the *Buyer's opportunity . . . to investigate the Property and the transaction contemplated by this Contract, including but not necessarily limited to the matters described in Paragraph 4 . . . , to decide whether Buyer, in Buyer's sole discretion, will proceed with or terminate the transaction.* There are no restrictions on what or how the buyer investigates the property under contract. The buyer is urged to utilize appropriate experts to facilitate the exploration of the property's condition and whether it will serve the buyer's need. The rather extensive list of issues in Paragraph 4 of the OPC should answer most standard questions and concerns that a buyer might have about purchasing a property.

Buyer's loan. There is no longer a separate loan financing condition in the OPC. The buyer is strongly advised to have a DDP that will allow time to assure that the buyer's lender will approve the requested financing. If the buyer is not comfortable that the loan will be approved, the buyer should exercise the right to terminate the contract before the expiration of the due diligence period. If the financing request is denied after the DDP has expired, the buyer will be in breach of the contract. This is an excellent reason why the buyer should begin the loan process before beginning the property search.

Property investigation. The buyer is given encouragement to conduct any desired inspection including some very standard items. A thorough inspection of all improvements on the property, ideally by experts, is a practice that should not be waived. Home inspectors can identify needed repairs and items of concern that might require more specialized scrutiny. Structural engineers, pest-infestation experts, environmental hazard specialists, and HVAC-licensed professionals are just a few of the advisors a buyer might use.

If the property is subject to subdivision protective covenants, a thorough review of what can and cannot be done on or to the property is critical to determine if the buyer is willing to proceed with the purchase. A title search should also be conducted by the closing attorney to assure that the seller's title is marketable and insurable as promised. Current or proposed zoning regulations could affect the intended use of the property by the buyer.

Insurance. The availability and affordability of homeowners' insurance on the property needs to be verified. If the property is in a FEMA flood hazard area, the cost of flood insurance may be prohibitive.

If possession of the property will not be given at closing, insurance becomes a very important issue. If the buyer will take possession prior to settlement or the seller will retain possession after closing, it is possible for the property to be uninsured for a period of time if careful attention is not paid to this issue. The seller's original homeowners' insurance will generally cover the property only if it is *owner-occupied*; after closing, the seller is no longer the owner, so insurance would have be changed to renter's insurance and the new owner would need to have landlord insurance on the property. The situation is just reversed if the buyer wishes early possession.

Appraisal. If the buyer is applying for a mortgage loan to purchase the property, the lender will order an appraisal to help evaluate the market value of the collateral property. Due to intensive audits caused by extensive mortgage fraud in recent years, appraisers tend to be very conservative in their appraisal values that can prompt an appraisal value below contract price. Consequently, a buyer is strongly advised to obtain the appraisal prior to the end of the DDP.

Survey. Any title defects discovered by a survey would survive the DDP because the seller is tasked with providing clear marketable title free of encumbrances. The **survey** is known for verifying property lines and possible encroachments, but it also identifies easements and setbacks that might impact the buyer's intended use for the property. For this reason, the survey should be obtained in the DDP also.

Septic system, if applicable. If property is unimproved and does not have access to a central sewage disposal system, the buyer should order a **soil suitability test**, sometimes called a *percolation test*. This test measures the soil's ability to absorb and drain water. Soil must percolate (i.e., perk) properly before approval will be given to install a septic system for on-site sewage disposal.

The septic permit will be usually issued by the county health department for a certain number of bedrooms, which indicates approved occupancy for the residence. The occupancy standard is two persons per bedroom count; hence, a permit for a three-bedroom residence has nothing to do with the number of rooms utilized for sleeping but everything to do with three bedrooms multiplied by two occupants equals a maximum occupancy of six people. Brokers should be careful not to advertise more bedrooms than is indicated in the septic permit. Septic permit records are maintained by the county health departments.

Repair/improvements negotiations. Although there are no mandatory repairs required by the OPC, the buyer and seller can negotiate anything during the DDP. The actual repairs/improvements do not need to be completed prior to the expiration of the DDP, but the negotiations need to be ratified during the DDP or the buyer may purchase the property in its current condition. The Due Diligence Request and Agreement (Form 310-T, Appendix D, Form 20) provides a standard form to solidify any repair agreement as part of the contract.

> In North Carolina

Right to terminate. If buyer is not satisfied with the property condition, terms of the contract, the loan application, repair negotiations, or anything else, the buyer may terminate the contract in writing by 5:00 pm of the DDP.

> In North Carolina

Physical inspection. After contract formation, the buyer and his representatives will need access to the property for initial and subsequent inspection of the property. The buyer is strongly advised to conduct a final **walk-through** inspection to verify completion of all negotiated repairs plus ascertain that no fixtures were removed prior to settlement. Mandated building permits should be obtained for any addition or major repair.

IN PRACTICE Brokers should avoid recommending one individual or one specific source for any inspections or testing services. If the buyer suffers any injury as a result of a provider's negligence, the broker also may be liable. At least three sources of each type of professional service provider should be recommended to give the parties free choice. Brokers should recommend a full set of inspections even if the purchase is made with no financing contingency involved.

Seller's Issues

Obviously, the seller's main interest is receiving payment for the property. The seller needs to be sure that the buyer has obtained the necessary financing and has sufficient funds to complete the sale. The seller also needs to be certain that all the requirements of the sales contract are met so the transaction can be completed.

Both parties will want to inspect the settlement statement to ensure that all monies involved in the transaction have been accounted for properly. Both parties may be accompanied to settlement by their attorneys although it is uncommon in North Carolina for the seller to have an attorney present at settlement.

IN PRACTICE Depending on local custom, the broker's role at settlement can vary from simply being present to conducting the proceedings. A broker's service generally continues after the sales contract is signed—the broker advises the parties in practical matters and makes sure all details are taken care of so that the closing can proceed smoothly. (Remember, a real estate broker is not authorized to give legal advice or otherwise engage in the practice of law.) The broker might make arrangements for such items as title evidence, surveys, appraisals, termite inspections, and repairs, or the broker might recommend sources of these services to the parties. The broker also is held responsible by the North Carolina Real Estate Commission (NCREC) for the accuracy and delivery of the settlement statement either at closing or within five days after closing [see G.S. 93A-6(a)(14)].

In North Carolina

Document Preparations

Preparation for settlement involves ordering and reviewing an array of documents. The closing attorney has the responsibility for ensuring that all legal documents are prepared and properly delivered. Legal documents required to close a residential transaction include items listed below.

Documents sellers are responsible for providing (either directly or through their attorney) include the following:

- The deed (usually prepared by the settlement agent)
- Affidavit as to mechanics' liens
- Bill of sale of personal property (If any of the seller's personal property is being transferred to the buyer, ownership can be shown by a bill of sale.)

- Leases and related documents (if the property being transferred is currently leased)
- Statement from the seller's lender (A current loan balance payoff figure must be available as of the day of closing.)
- Proof of repairs or services (If any repairs were necessary, the seller must bring proof to the closing that the repairs have been done.)

Documents buyer is responsible for providing (either directly or through the closing attorney) include the following:

- Financing documents (The settlement agent receives a closing package from the lender with instructions on how to prepare the financing documents, including the deed of trust and the promissory note.)
- Title insurance policy (issued after the attorney's opinion of good title)
- Property insurance policy (The buyer is required to bring a current policy to settlement.)
- Wood-destroying insect inspection report (The buyer normally pays for this unless the transaction is financed with a VA loan, in which case the seller normally pays.)
- Property survey

Title Procedures

Both the buyer and the buyer's lender want assurance that the seller's title complies with the requirements of the sales contract. After a thorough title search, the closing attorney usually submits a preliminary opinion on title to the title insurance company. Based on this opinion, the title insurance company will issue a title commitment. This is a commitment to issue a title insurance policy if the final title search confirms that the seller's title is marketable.

On the date of the settlement meeting (the date of delivery of the deed), the buyer has a title commitment that was probably issued several days or weeks before the closing. For this reason, the final opinion on title and the title insurance policy are issued after closing (see Chapter 5).

Unless the buyer is assuming the seller's mortgage loan, the seller's existing loan is paid in full and a mortgage release should be recorded. The exact amount required to pay off the existing loan is provided in a current *payoff statement* from the lender, effective on the date of closing. This payoff statement states the unpaid amount of principal, interest due through the date of payment, the fee for issuing the certificate of satisfaction or release, credits (if any) for tax and insurance reserves, and the amount of any prepayment penalties. The same procedure is followed for any other liens that must be released before the buyer takes title. If there is an escrow account for the mortgage loan, it could be applied to the balance owed or it may be refunded after closing.

For transactions in which the buyer assumes the seller's existing mortgage loan, the settlement agent needs to know the exact balance of the loan as of the closing date. It is customary for the settlement agent to obtain information from the lender that includes the terms of the mortgage loan being assumed. The settlement agent will have the buyer sign the assumption documents accepting the terms of the loan and the responsibility to repay the loan. The seller may also be required to execute an *affidavit of lien waiver* (*affidavit of title*). This is a sworn statement in which the seller assures the title insurance company and the buyer that there have been no judgments, bankruptcies, or divorces involving the seller since the date of the title examination. The affidavit promises that no unrecorded deeds or contracts were made, no repairs or improvements were made that have not been paid for, and the seller knows of no defects in the title. If the seller is the builder, the affidavit should address the payment of any subcontractors used in the construction process. The seller also affirms that he or she is in possession of the premises. This form is normally required before the title insurance company will issue an owner's policy to the buyer. The affidavit gives the title insurance company the right to sue the seller if the seller's statements in the affidavit are incorrect.

CONDUCTING THE CLOSING

In North Carolina

In North Carolina, closings are conducted by gathering the parties together and exchanging copies of the documents. This kind of closing is called the *settlement meeting* (or a *face-to-face closing*). Current practice in North Carolina is that a lawyer frequently represents the buyer although the settlement agent does not have to be an attorney. The seller also may be represented by a different lawyer but usually is not. The attorney/settlement agent, normally selected and paid by the buyer, also represents the lender's interest.

A closing involves the resolution of two issues. First, the promises made in the sales contract are fulfilled. Second, the buyer's loan is finalized and the mortgage lender or settlement attorney/agent disburses the loan funds. Settlement meetings are most often held in the attorney's office; however, they may be held at any number of locations, including the office of the lending institution or the broker. Those persons attending a typical residential settlement may include

- the buyer;
- the seller;
- the real estate brokers (both the buyer's and the seller's agents);
- the seller's and the buyer's attorneys;
- representatives of the lending institutions involved with the buyer's new mortgage loan, the buyer's assumption of the seller's existing loan, or the seller's payoff of an existing loan; and
- the representative of the title insurance company (although this seldom happens in North Carolina).

Escrow Type Settlement

The settlement agent may use the escrow-type closing if the parties cannot attend the settlement meeting. The parties can agree in advance who will act as escrow/settlement agent, and all funds and paperwork are delivered *into escrow*. The designated escrow agent is an impartial third party who conducts the settlement. When the deed has been prepared and delivered to the escrow agent, it is considered to have been legally delivered to the buyer under what is called the *relation back doctrine*. This type of closing is seldom used in North Carolina. In other states that practice this type of closing, title insurance companies and lending institutions often act as escrow agents.

North Carolina Settlement Agent

In North Carolina

One person called the **settlement agent** or officer usually conducts the proceedings at a closing and calculates the division of income and expenses between the parties (called settlement). In North Carolina, the settlement agent has historically been the buyer's attorney because so many of the functions performed at settlement are of a legal nature. In 2003, the North Carolina State Bar ruled in an ethics opinion that an attorney does not have to physically preside over the settlement meeting. A nonlawyer assistant under the direct supervision of an active member of the Bar may conduct the settlement meeting (identify documents to be signed, indicate the correct place to sign, and disburse proceeds) as long as that person does not engage in the unauthorized practice of law. The supervising attorney must be available to answer any legal concerns that may arise such as the need for legal advice on how to take title or the legal status of the title. NCREC strongly cautions that any real estate broker who conducts a settlement meeting under the above situation will be held fully responsible for all aspects of the closing.

Finalizing the Closing

Following the settlement meeting, the settlement agent will update the title search to verify that no recent recordings have occurred that would affect the title to the property. All pertinent documents then are recorded *in the correct order* to ensure continuity of title. For instance, if the seller is paying off an existing loan and the buyer is obtaining a new loan, the seller's satisfaction of mortgage should be recorded before the seller's deed to the buyer is recorded. The buyer's new mortgage or deed of trust must be recorded *after* the deed because the buyers cannot pledge the property as security for the loan until they own it. The transaction is *closed* when all documents have been recorded.

In North Carolina

The settlement agent can only disburse funds to the appropriate parties (including the real estate brokers) after recordation of the deed and the deed of trust. This delay in the disbursement of the proceeds is mandated by the North Carolina Good Funds Settlement Act (G.S. 45A).

IRS Reporting Requirements

Every real estate transaction must be reported to the IRS by the settlement agent on Form 1099-S. Information includes the sales price, the amount of property tax reimbursement credited to the seller, and the seller's Social Security number. If the closing agent does not notify the IRS, the responsibility for filing the form falls on the mortgage lender, although the brokers or the parties to the transaction ultimately could be held liable.

Lender's Interest in Closing

Whether a buyer is obtaining new financing or assuming the seller's existing loan, the lender wants to protect its security interest in the property. The lender has

Chapter 15 Closing the Real Estate Transaction

an interest in making sure that the buyer receives good, marketable title and that tax and insurance payments are maintained. Lenders want their mortgage liens to have priority over other liens. They also want to ensure that the insurance will be current if the property is damaged or destroyed. For this reason, a lender generally requires proof that the buyer has purchased both a title insurance policy for the benefit of the lender and a hazard insurance policy. In addition, a lender may require that the borrower provide additional information: a survey, a termite or other inspection report, or a certificate of occupancy (for newly constructed buildings). The lender also may request that a reserve or escrow account be established for tax and insurance payments. Lenders sometimes even require representation by their own attorney(s) at closings.

■ RESPA REQUIREMENTS

RESPA's Consumer Protections
- CLO regulation
- CBA disclosure
- Settlement cost booklet
- Good-faith estimate of settlement costs
- Uniform Settlement Statement
- Prohibition of kickbacks and unearned fees

The federal **Real Estate Settlement Procedures Act (RESPA)** was enacted to protect consumers from abusive lending practices. [covers almost every loan you will see] RESPA also aids consumers during the residential mortgage loan settlement process. It ensures that consumers are provided with important, accurate, and timely information about the actual costs of settling or closing the transaction. It also eliminates *kickbacks* and other referral fees that tend to inflate the costs of settlement unnecessarily. RESPA prohibits lenders from requiring excessive escrow account deposits.

RESPA requirements apply when the residential purchase is financed by a federally related mortgage loan. *Federally related loans* are loans made by banks, savings associations, or other lenders whose deposits are insured by federal agencies. The term also covers loans insured by the FHA or guaranteed by the VA; loans administered by HUD; or loans intended to be sold by the lender to Fannie Mae, Ginnie Mae, or Freddie Mac. RESPA, commonly referred to as *Regulation X*, is administered by HUD.

RESPA regulations apply to residential mortgage loans made to finance the purchase of one-family to four-family homes, cooperatives, and condominiums or property where such a dwelling will be constructed or placed within 2 years of settlement. RESPA also governs second or subordinate liens for home equity loans. RESPA does not normally cover a transaction financed solely by a purchase money mortgage taken back by the seller, an installment contract (contract for deed), or the buyer's assumption of the seller's existing loan. Loans for business, commercial, or agricultural purposes, or for property of 25 acres or more are also exempted.

IN PRACTICE While RESPA's requirements are aimed primarily at lenders, some of its provisions affect real estate brokers as well. Real estate brokers fall under RESPA when they refer buyers to particular lenders, title companies, attorneys, or other providers of settlement services. Brokers who offer computerized loan origination (CLO) services also are subject to regulation. Remember: buyers have the right to select their own providers of settlement services; therefore, the required use of a specific service provider is prohibited.

Controlled Business Arrangements

For the real estate consumer, a service that continues to increase in popularity is one-stop shopping. A real estate firm, title insurance company, mortgage broker, home inspection company, and even a moving company may agree to offer a package of services to consumers. RESPA permits such a controlled business arrangement (CBA) *as long as the consumer is clearly informed of the relationship among the service providers and that other providers are available.* Required use of a particular service provider is prohibited by RESPA. Fees may not be exchanged among the affiliated companies simply for referring business to one another. This may be a particularly important issue for brokers who offer *computerized loan origination (CLO)* services to their clients and customers. While a borrower's ability to comparison shop for a loan may be enhanced by a CLO system, the range of choices must not be limited. Consumers must be informed of the availability of other lenders.

Disclosure Requirements

RESPA mandates that lenders and settlement agents have the following disclosure obligations at the time of loan application and loan closing or within three business days of receiving the loan application. If the lender denies the loan within three days, then RESPA does not require that the lender provide the following documents:

- *Special information booklet:* Lenders must provide a copy of a special informational HUD booklet, *Shopping for Your Home Loan*, to every person from whom they receive or for whom they prepare a loan application. The booklet must be given at the time the application is received or within three days afterward. The booklet provides the borrower with general information about shopping for a house and a loan, plus information about the closing process. It also explains the various provisions of RESPA, including a line-by-line explanation of the Uniform Settlement Statement.
- *Good-faith estimate (GFE) of settlement costs:* The new three-page **Good Faith Estimate (GFE)** must contain the exact language specified by HUD, making it easier for borrowers to compare loan conditions from one lender to another.

The only fee that the lender may collect before the applicant receives the GFE is for a credit report. Once the GFE is issued, lenders are committed and may only modify the GFE in certain specific instances. If certain information or circumstances change after the original GFE is issued, then a new GFE must be issued. Issuing a new GFE triggers a new three-day waiting period; in which case, closing may not occur until after three days have passed.

The new GFE indicates which settlement costs may or may not change prior to settlement and, if they do, by how much. The fees are divided into three categories:
— *No tolerance*—fees that may not increase before closing: lender charges for taking, underwriting, and processing the loan application, including points, origination fees, and yield spread premiums
— *10% tolerance*—fees that cannot increase by more than 10% in any given category: settlement services for which the lender selects the provider or for which the borrower selects the provider from the lender's list, title

services and title insurance if the lender selects the provider, and recording fees
— *Unlimited tolerance*—fees for services that are out of the lender's control: services for which the borrower chooses the provider (such as escrow and title insurance), escrows for taxes, mortgage interest, and the cost of homeowners' insurance
- The last page of the GFE is a worksheet consumers can use to compare different loans and terms to aid in price shopping. The lender is responsible for the accuracy of the GFE and the actual costs that the lender charges on the HUD-1.
- *Uniform Settlement Statement (HUD-1)*: RESPA requires that the Uniform Settlement Statement itemize all charges that are normally paid by a borrower and a seller in connection with the settlement, whether required by the lender or another party, or paid by the lender or any other person. Charges required by the lender that are paid before settlement are indicated as paid outside of closing (POC). Many line items on page 2 of the HUD-1 reference a corresponding line item on the GFE form. The third page of the new HUD-1 form provides for a comparison of the original GFE estimates to the actual charges appearing on the HUD-1. Lenders are permitted to *correct* any violation of the tolerances by reimbursing the borrower within 30 days of settlement. If the tolerance violation is not cured at settlement, the settlement attorney must issue a corrected HUD-1 after the lender reimburses the borrower for the overcharge(s).

Borrower Credit for Yield Spread Premiums

During the 1990s and early 2000s, to encourage mortgage brokers to make the numerous types of low or no closing costs loans, lenders needed to find a way to compensate the mortgage brokers that sold these loans to marginal borrowers. A substantial fee, known as a **yield spread premium**, was paid to the mortgage brokers for making loans to subprime borrowers at *above-market* interest rates. Due to abuses of the yield spread premiums in the lending industry, RESPA now requires that the loan originator give the borrower a credit against the loan origination fees for the full amount of any yield spread premium. This credit must appear in the loan origination section of the GFE.

Escrow Account Restrictions

RESPA prohibits lenders from requiring borrowers to deposit amounts in escrow accounts for taxes and insurance that exceed certain limits, thus preventing the lenders from taking advantage of the borrowers. While RESPA does not require that escrow accounts be set up, certain government loan programs and some lenders require escrow accounts as a condition of the loan. RESPA places limits on the amounts that a lender may require: on a monthly basis, the lender may require only one-twelfth of the total of the disbursements for the year, plus an amount necessary to cover a shortage in the account. No more than one-sixth of the year's total disbursements may be held as a cushion (a cushion is not required). Once a year, the lender must perform an escrow account analysis and return any amount over $50 to the borrower.

In North Carolina By law, borrowers have the right to inspect a completed HUD-1 form, to the extent that the figures are available, one business day before settlement. (Sellers are not entitled to this privilege.) Lenders must retain these statements for two years after the closing date. In addition, North Carolina license law requires that real estate brokers retain all records of a transaction for a three-year period (see Rule A.0108).

Loan Servicing Disclosure Requirements

Servicers of all federally related mortgage loans must disclose at the time of loan application if the servicing of the loan can be sold, transferred or assigned to another servicer during the term of the loan. If the servicing is ever transferred, the borrower must be notified in writing from both the original and subsequent servicing entity. The notice must include the date of transfer, new payment address, and phone numbers for both servicing entities so the borrower can call for clarification. These requirements are in place each time the loan servicing is transferred during the term of the loan.

Kickbacks and Referral Fees

RESPA *prohibits the payment of kickbacks*, or *unearned fees*, incident to or as part of a real estate settlement service. It prohibits referral fees *when no services are actually rendered*. The payment or receipt of a fee, kickback, or anything of value for referrals for settlement services is prohibited for activities such as mortgage loans, title searches, title insurance, or services rendered by attorneys, surveyors, home inspectors, or appraisers.

Penalties for Violating RESPA

Violations of RESPA can elicit civil and criminal penalties, which include

- criminal fines up to $10,000 per violation;
- imprisonment up to one year;
- injunctions against illegal activity and orders to compensate victims for illegal profits; and
- civil lawsuits that may award treble damages plus legal fee reimbursement.

■ PREPARATION OF SETTLEMENT STATEMENT

A typical real estate transaction involves expenses for both parties in addition to the purchase price. These may include items prepaid by the seller for which he or she must be reimbursed (such as taxes) and items of expense the seller has incurred but for which the buyer will be billed (such as assumed mortgage interest paid in arrears). The financial responsibility for these items must be *prorated*, or divided equitably, between the buyer and the seller. All expense items and prorated items are accounted for on the settlement statement. This is how the exact amount of cash required from the buyer and the net proceeds to the seller are determined (see Figure 15.1). The closing statement worksheet and/or the HUD-1 form are not considered to be legal documents and may be prepared by a licensed real estate broker.

FIGURE 15.1

Allocation of Expenses

Item	Paid by Seller	Paid by Buyer
Broker's Commission	✗ by agreement	✗ by agreement
Attorney's fees	✗ by agreement	✗ by agreement
Recording expenses	✗ to clear title	✗ transfer charges
Excise tax	✗ state deed transfer tax	
Title expenses	✗ quitclaim deed if necessary to clear title defect	✗ attorney title examination and title insurance
Loan fees	✗ prepayment penalty (seller's loan)	✗ origination fee/assumption fee
Tax and insurance reserves (escrow or impound accounts)		✗ if required by lender
Appraisal fees		✗ if requested
Survey fees		✗ if requested

In North Carolina

North Carolina Broker's Responsibility for Settlement Statements

Reprinted from the 2013–2014 edition of the North Carolina Real Estate Manual with permission of the NCREC:

> In virtually all residential transactions, the settlement statement is prepared by the closing attorney prior to the settlement meeting using the HUD-1 Settlement Statement Form. Each broker involved in a transaction is expected to review the completed HUD-1 statement and to verify its accuracy and completion in accordance with the provisions of the sales contract. The broker is expected to confirm the accuracy of those entries about which he or she has direct knowledge. These would include items from the sales contract like the sales price, earnest money an due diligence fee, if any, as well as items such as the brokerage commission.
>
> With regard to entries on the HUD-1 representing amounts due to or from third parties, the broker may generally assume that the amounts for the charges an credits cited in the settlement statement are correct unless there is some reason that would lead a reasonably prudent broker to believe they are incorrect. However, the broker is expected to assure that
>
> - all relevant charges and credits are appropriately charge or credited (i.e., entered in the proper column) to the borrower-buyer and seller; and
> - all calculations for prorated items, escrow reserves interim interest, excise tax and "bottom line" figures (i.e., total settlement charges for borrower-buyer and seller, cash from borrower-buyer and cash to seller) are correct.
>
> The closing attorney should be immediately advised of any noted suspected errors or omissions. The broker must also be especially careful to take appropriate action in the event he or she becomes aware

of a misrepresentation of facts on the settlement that is potentially harmful to any party with an interest in the transaction. For example, an incorrectly reported sales price or a reported earnest money deposit that is in fact non-existent may be part of a scheme to defraud the lender as to the buyer's qualifications for a loan. A broker who fails to report a known misstatement of fact to a party who may be harmed by the misstatement (such as the buyer's lender) may be guilty of a willful misrepresentation under the Real Estate License Law, and, if the harmed party is a lender, may be implicated as a participant in a loan fraud scheme in violation of federal law.

How the Settlement Statement Works

The completion of a **settlement statement** involves an accounting of all the parties' debits and credits as of the time of settlement. A **debit** is a charge; an amount that a party owes and must pay at settlement. A **credit** is an amount entered in a person's favor—an amount that has already been paid, an amount being reimbursed, or an amount the buyer promises to pay in the form of a loan.

The settlement statement only reflects the accounting of the two parties to the transaction (the buyer and the seller). If both parties are involved with a bill or expense, it will be posted as a double entry. If an expense is between one of the principals and a third party (such as the surveyor), it will appear as a single entry.

> A *debit* is an amount to be paid by the buyer or seller; a *credit* is an amount payable to the buyer or seller.

To determine the amount of funds the buyer needs to bring to settlement, the buyer's debits are totaled. Any expenses and prorated amounts for items prepaid by the seller are added to the purchase price. Then the buyer's credits are totaled. These include the earnest money (already paid), the balance of the loan the buyer is obtaining or assuming, and the seller's share of any prorated items that the buyer will pay in the future (see Figure 15.2). Finally, the total of the buyer's credits is subtracted from the total debits to arrive at the actual amount of certified funds the buyer must bring to settlement. Usually the buyer brings a certified or official bank check or has the funds wired to the settlement attorney's escrow account. Although cash is definitely *certified funds*, the buyer who brings a bag of money to pay the bills at settlement may encounter resistance from the settlement agent because large amounts of cash (typically over $10,000) will trigger paperwork requirements by either banking regulations and/or the USA PATRIOT Act.

A similar procedure is followed to determine how much money the seller actually will receive. The seller's debits and credits are totaled separately. The credits include the purchase price plus the buyer's share of any prorated items that the seller has prepaid. The seller's debits include expenses, the seller's share of prorated items to be paid later by the buyer, and the balance of any mortgage loan or other lien that the seller is paying off. Finally the total of the seller's debits is subtracted from the total credits to arrive at the amount the seller will receive.

Broker's compensation. The responsibility for paying the broker's compensation is determined by signed agency agreement. If the broker is the agent for the seller, the seller is usually responsible for paying the compensation. If the listing firm entered the property into a multiple listing service (MLS), the compensation

FIGURE 15.2

Credits and Debits

Item	Credit to Buyer	Debit to Buyer	Credit to Seller	Debit to Seller	Prorated
Principal amount of new mortgage	X				
Payoff of existing mortgage				X	
Unpaid principal balance if assumed mortgage	X			X	
Accrued interest on existing assumed mortgage	X			X	X
Tenants' security deposits	X			X	
Purchase money mortgage	X			X	
Due diligence fee	X			X	
Seller concessions	X			X	
Unpaid real estate tax or utility bills	X			X	X
Buyer's earnest money	X				
Selling price of property		X	X		
Prepaid insurance and tax escrow for mortgage assumed by buyer		X	X		
Refund to seller of prepaid water charges and similar utility expenses		X	X		X
Prepaid real estate taxes		X	X		X
Excise tax (revenue stamps)				X	

of the selling agent (whether a buyer's agent or a seller's subagent) is generally disclosed in the MLS entry. Most of the time, the listing firm will split the compensation earned from the seller with a cooperating firm that brings the buyer to the transaction. If the listing firm or seller refuses to pay the buyer's agent, most buyer agency agreements state that the buyer is then responsible for the agent's compensation at a preset rate or figure.

Attorney's fees. If either of the parties' attorneys is to be paid from the closing proceeds, that party is charged with the expenses on the settlement statement. The attorney's fee may include preparation or review of documents, title search and opinion, or representation of the parties at settlement.

Recording expenses. The *seller* usually pays for recording charges (filing fees) necessary to clear all defects in order to furnish the purchaser with a marketable title. Items customarily charged to the seller include the recording of release deeds or satisfaction of mortgages, quitclaim deeds, affidavits, and satisfaction of mechanic's lien claims. The *purchaser* pays for recording charges that arise from the actual transfer of title.

Usually such items include recording the deed that conveys title to the purchaser and the mortgage or deed of trust executed by the purchaser. If the NCAR/NCBA Standard Form 2-T Offer to Purchase and Contract is used, recordation of the deed is required by contract to complete the closing process.

In North Carolina

Excise tax. North Carolina requires an excise tax (formerly known as revenue stamps) on the gross revenue generated by the sale of real estate. This tax, sometimes called a *deed transfer tax*, is levied at a rate of $1 per $500 of value, or portion thereof. The excise tax will always round up to the next whole dollar amount if the calculation includes cents. This expense is borne by the seller.

Title expenses. Custom usually requires that the buyer obtain and pay the title examination. Most of the time, this charge will be included in the attorney's fee.

Evidence of title relied on in the purchase of a parcel of real estate includes a title guaranty or a fee policy of title insurance. The title guaranty and fee policy of title insurance are one-time premium charges for insurance that insures the purchaser's title during the period of ownership of real estate. Some lenders request an American Land Title Association (ALTA) policy that insures the mortgagee for the amount of the mortgage loan, called a *lender's policy*. A buyer may also purchase an owner's policy to protect the entire purchase price; this higher level of coverage is always a good investment.

Loan fees. When the buyer secures a new loan to finance the purchase, the lender ordinarily charges an administrative fee called a loan origination fee of about 1% of the loan value. The borrower usually pays the fee at the time the transaction closes. The lender also may charge discount points to permanently buydown the interest rate. In order to prove creditworthiness, the buyer will pay for a credit report at the time of loan application that will show up as *paid outside of closing (POC)* on the HUD-1. If the buyer assumes the seller's existing financing, there will usually be an assumption fee. Also, under the terms of some mortgage loans, the seller may be required to pay a prepayment charge or penalty for paying off the mortgage loan in advance of its due date. Overnight mailing expenses to the lenders of both parties is very common because it saves additional days of interest for both parties.

Tax reserves and insurance reserves (escrow or impound accounts). Most mortgage lenders require that borrowers provide a reserve fund or escrow account to pay future real estate taxes and insurance premiums, especially when the loan-to-value ratio exceeds specified percentages. These payments are often referred to as *prepaids*. The borrower usually starts the account at settlement by depositing funds to cover at least two months of taxes and hazard insurance. The borrower's monthly loan payment includes the loan principal and interest plus one-twelfth of the estimated taxes and insurance (PITI) for the escrow account. The taxes and insurance are held by the lender in the escrow or impound account until the bills are due. Some lenders also use the escrow account for collecting private mortgage insurance premium and maintenance fees that are payable on a recurring basis to an owner's association. Although sellers occasionally agree to pay all or some of the buyer's settlement expenses, the lender will almost always require the borrower to pay for prepaids.

Appraisal fees. Generally, the purchaser pays the appraisal fees because it is customary for the lender to require an appraisal as a condition of the loan. If the fee is paid at the time of the loan application, it is reflected on the HUD-1 settlement statement as having been *paid outside closing (POC)*.

Survey fees. The purchaser who benefits from the information shown on a survey will customarily pay the survey fees. Clearing up any title defects that arise from the survey, such as eliminating an encroachment, would be the seller's responsibility. As discussed previously, some lenders will require a new survey as a condition of financing.

> In North Carolina

Due diligence fee. If the parties to the NCAR/NCBA Standard Form 2-T Offer to Purchase and Contract agree to any due diligence fee, the buyer will pay the fee directly to the seller for the right to terminate the contract for any or no reason. Per the contract, the due diligence fee will be credited to the buyer at settlement and will be debited from the seller's side because the seller already received it outside of settlement. This fee is not to be confused with earnest money that serves as liquidated damages.

Additional fees. Because each real estate transaction is unique, it is not uncommon to have additional fees or expenses charged to either party dependent on the sales contract. An FHA borrower owes a lump sum for payment of the mortgage insurance premium (MIP) if it is not being financed as part of the loan. A VA borrower pays a funding fee directly to the VA at closing. If a conventional loan carries private mortgage insurance, the buyer prepays one year's insurance premium at settlement. Charges for specialized inspections such as home inspections, radon tests, structural inspections, or environmental evaluations are becoming more commonplace. Because some service providers require payment at the time of service, those charges often appear on the settlement statement as POC (paid outside of closing). Any charge that seems unusual should be questioned by the broker or principal to verify its purpose.

Accounting for Expenses

Expenses paid out of the settlement proceeds are debited, or charged, only to the party making the payment. Occasionally the buyer and the seller may share an unpaid expense item such as current real estate taxes. In that case, the parties are debited for their share of the expense.

PRORATIONS

Most settlements involve a division of financial responsibility between the buyer and seller for such items as loan interest, taxes, rents, and fuel or utility bills. These allowances are called **prorations.** Settlement computations typically mean that each party pays for what they used or for the time they occupied the property during the appropriate period (month or year). Prorations are necessary to ensure that expenses are divided fairly between the seller and the buyer. For example, the seller may owe current taxes that have not yet been billed; the buyer will want this resolved at settlement. If real property taxes have been paid in advance, the seller is entitled to a rebate at settlement. If the buyer assumes the seller's existing mortgage or deed of trust, the seller usually owes the buyer an allowance for accrued interest through the date of closing. The seller is normally responsible for prorated expenses owed on the day of closing, except for the buyer's daily interim interest on a new loan that would be a single entry debit to the buyer.

Accrued items are unpaid items to be prorated (such as unpaid current real estate taxes or interest on an assumed mortgage) that are owed by the seller but will be paid later by the buyer. The seller therefore pays for the seller's portion of the bill by giving the buyer credit for it at settlement. The seller receives a debit for that prorated share, and the buyer is given an equal amount as a credit.

Prepaid items are expenses that have already been paid by the seller prior to settlement and the buyer needs to rebate that portion to the seller. Examples would be real estate taxes already paid by the seller for the current year prior to settlement or prepaid homeowner association dues. The item is prorated and the buyer's allocated portion is reflected as a credit to the seller and as a debit to the buyer.

The Arithmetic of Prorating

Accurate prorating involves four considerations:

1. The nature of the item being prorated (i.e., annual versus monthly expense, calendar versus fiscal year)
2. Whether it is an accrued item (unpaid) that requires the determination of an earned amount (i.e., an advance payment to the buyer)
3. Whether it is a prepaid item (overpaid) that requires that the unearned amount (i.e., a refund to the seller) be determined
4. What arithmetic processes must be used (see different methods below)

There are several different ways to prorate items that require a division of funds among the parties (the buyer and the seller). Those listed below are the most common ways to prorate, but the buyer and seller may agree to any other method.

360-day year/30-day month method. This method is referred to as the *banker's year/banker's month method* (sometimes as the *statutory method*) and is, perhaps, the easiest to use, but probably not the most accurate. (This is the method used for all prorations in the textbook and on the North Carolina Real Estate State License Examinations.) The year is treated as having 360 days with each month having 30 days.

365-day year method/Actual-days-in-the-month method. This method is the most accurate and normally will be used in actual real estate settlements. If the settlement takes place in a leap year, then a 366-day year is used. Using this method, the actual days in the month are used. For instance, January would have 31 days and November would have 30 days.

> **In North Carolina**

The final proration figure will vary slightly, depending on which computation method is used. (Note that whichever method is used, in North Carolina the seller is responsible for the day of closing on all prorations involving the seller unless otherwise agreed.) The final figure also will vary according to the number of decimal places to which the division is carried. *All of the computations in this textbook and on the North Carolina Real Estate License Examinations are computed by carrying the division to three decimal places.* The third decimal place is rounded off to cents only after the final proration figure is determined.

Accrued Items

When the real estate tax is levied for the calendar year (from January to December) and is payable either during that year or in the following year, the accrued portion is for the period from January 1 through and including the day of closing. If the current tax bill has not yet been issued, the parties must agree on an estimated amount based on the previous year's bill and any known changes in assessment or tax levy for the current year, referred to as the *best estimate* method.

Sample proration calculation (30-day month/360-day year method). For example, assume a sale is to be closed on April 17 and current real estate taxes of $1,200 are to be prorated accordingly. The accrued period, then, is 107 days (from January 1 through April 17).

January	30
February	30
March	30
April	17
Total	107 days

First determine the prorated cost of the real estate tax per day:

$$\$1{,}200 \div 360 = \$3.333 \text{ per day}$$

Next, multiply this figure by the accrued period to determine the prorated real estate tax:

$$\begin{array}{rl} \$3.333 & \text{per day} \\ \times\ 107 & \text{days} \\ \hline \$356.63 & \text{real estate tax} \end{array}$$

Therefore, the accrued real estate tax for 107 days is $356.63. This amount represents the seller's accrued earned tax. It is a *credit to the buyer* and a *debit to the seller* on the settlement statement because the seller must give his portion of the tax bill to the buyer who will eventually pay the entire bill when it becomes due and payable.

IN PRACTICE Many title insurance companies provide proration charts that detail tax factors for each day in the year. To determine a tax proration using one of these charts, multiply the factor given for the closing date by the annual real estate tax.

Prepaid Items

A tax proration could be a *prepaid item*. Because the real estate tax is due and payable on September 1, it may be paid before a settlement takes place. Tax prorations calculated for settlements taking place later in the year may reflect the fact that the seller has already paid the tax. The buyer then has to reimburse the seller for the buyer's portion of the taxes; the proration would be *credited to the seller* and *debited to the buyer*.

Sample prepaid item calculation (30-day month/360-day year method).

Assume that settlement is to take place on November 13 and the seller received the annual real estate tax bill of $1,850 in August and has paid the entire bill. Because the seller's liability for taxes is only for the period of January 1 through and including the day of closing, the seller should get back the taxes for the remainder of the year (buyer's portion).

$1,850 annual tax bill ÷ 360 = $5.139 per day
January 1 – November 13 = 313 days × $5.139 = $1,608.507
$1,850.00 total bill – $1,608.51 seller's portion = $241.49 credit seller/debit buyer

General Rules for Prorating

The following are some general prorating guidelines for preparing the settlement statement:

In North Carolina
- In North Carolina, the seller owns the property on the day of settlement (regardless of what time of day the settlement meeting is scheduled), and prorations or apportionments are usually made *through and including the day of settlement*.
- Always prorate for the seller first. If prorating an accrued item, once the seller's portion is computed, the buyer's amount will be the same, but an opposite entry: if a debit to the seller, it is a credit to buyer, and it is the same amount of money. (Think of the entries as if they represented a personal check from one party payable to the other party . . . the check amount is the same when it is written and when it is received.)
- If prorating a prepaid item, subtract the seller's portion from the total bill to determine the buyer's portion. The buyer's portion will be the same amount on the seller's entry: a credit to the seller and a debit to the buyer.
- Accrued or prepaid *real estate taxes* are usually prorated at settlement. When the amount of the current real estate tax cannot be determined definitely, the proration is usually based on the last obtainable tax bill.

- *Special assessments* for municipal improvements such as sewers, water mains, or streets are usually paid in annual installments over several years, with annual interest charged on the outstanding balance of future installments. The seller normally pays the entire balance due, unless the buyer and seller have agreed otherwise in the sales contract. *The special assessment generally is not prorated at settlement.* The contract of sale must address the manner in which special assessments are to be handled at settlement.
- *Rents* are usually adjusted on the basis of the *actual* number of days in the month of settlement in real life situations. It is customary for the seller to receive the rents for the day of settlement and to pay all expenses for that day. If any rents for the current month are uncollected when the sale is closed, the buyer often will agree by a separate letter to collect the rents if possible and remit the pro rata share to the seller. If the seller is holding a tenant security deposit, it can be transferred to the buyer by a double-entry (debit seller/credit buyer). The tenant security deposit is not prorated because it is the tenant's money . . . not the seller's.

Sample rent prorations (30-day month/360-day year method). Assume the monthly rent is $600, settlement takes place on June 21, and the seller has received the rent for the month of June (paid in advance).

$600 monthly rent ÷ 30 days	= $20 per day
21 days (when property owned by seller) × $20	= $420 seller's share
$600 − $420	= $180 buyer's share (debit seller/credit buyer)

Now assume that the monthly rent is $675, settlement takes place on June 5, and the seller has not collected the rent prior to settlement (paid in arrears). The buyer will collect the entire month's rent of $675.

$675 monthly rent ÷ 30 days	= 22.50 per day
5 days (when property owned by seller) × $22.50	= $112.50 seller's share (debit buyer/credit seller)

Mortgage loan interest. Interest paid on almost all mortgage loans is simple interest. On almost every mortgage loan, because the interest is paid *in arrears*, buyers and sellers must understand that the mortgage payment due on June 1, for example, includes interest due for the month of May. Thus, if the buyer is getting a new loan, the lender will start charging interest on the day of settlement and will normally collect interim interest for the day of settlement through the last day of the settlement month from the buyer (single entry debit to buyer) at settlement. The buyer will usually have at least one day of interim interest but never more than one month's worth. The buyer will not make a monthly payment until the first of the second month. Furthermore, the buyer who assumes a mortgage on May 18 and makes the June payment will be paying for the time the seller occupied the property and should be credited with the seller's part of the month's interest.

Sample interest on a new loan (interim interest) (30-day month/360-day year method). Pretend that settlement is April 12, and the buyer's first mortgage payment will be due on June 1. The buyer will owe for the day of settlement through the remainder of the month: 19 days. The loan amount is $95,600 and the interest rate is 6%. This is a simple interest example.

$95,600 × 0.06 interest rate = $5,736 annual interest
$5,736 ÷ 360 days = $15.933 daily interest
19 days × $15.933 = $302.73 interest owed by buyer (debit buyer)

Note that this is not a prorated item. It is a cost to be paid only by the buyer to the buyer's lender; therefore, the day of settlement belongs to the buyer. *Interim interest adjustment is the only time the buyer will pay for the closing day.*

Sample assumed loan interest proration (30-day month/360-day year method). The loan amount to be assumed is $105,555 at 7% interest. The day of settlement is May 18. The first step is to calculate the daily amount of interest, then multiply that by the number of days the seller owned the property during that month. This is a simple interest example.

$105,555 × 0.07 interest rate = $7,388.85 annual interest
$7,388.85 ÷ 360 days = $20.525 daily interest
18 days × $20.525 = $369.45 seller's share of interest (debit seller/credit buyer)

Security deposits. Security deposits made by tenants to cover the last month's rent of the lease or to cover the cost of repairing damage caused by the tenant are generally transferred in their entirety by the seller to the buyer (debit seller/credit buyer), not prorated.

Summary of Items to Be Prorated

Real estate taxes, unpaid	Debit seller/credit buyer
Real estate taxes, prepaid	Credit seller/debit buyer
Rents collected by seller	Debit seller/credit buyer
Rents to be collected by buyer	Credit seller/debit buyer
Interest on assumed loan	Debit seller/credit buyer
Owner's association dues, unpaid	Debit seller/credit buyer
Owner's association dues, prepaid	Credit seller/debit buyer

Note: A homeowners' insurance policy premium may be prorated if the policy is to be assigned to the buyer, which is extremely rare. Entries would be credit seller/debit buyer for the buyer's prorated share of the premium because insurance premiums are usually paid in advance.

Summary of Other Double-Entry Items

Sales price	Credit seller/debit buyer
Assumption of seller's loan	Debit seller/credit buyer
Purchase money mortgage	Debit seller/credit buyer
Transfer of seller's escrow account	Credit seller/debit buyer
Due diligence fee	Debit seller/credit buyer
Tenant security deposit, assigned	Debit seller/credit buyer
Cost of separately sold personal property	Credit seller/debit buyer

Normal Single-Entry Items to Seller

Seller's personal property taxes to be paid at closing	Debit seller
Pay off seller's existing loan	Debit seller
Deed preparation fee	Debit seller
Excise tax (revenue stamps)	Debit seller
Recordation fee, satisfaction of seller's mortgage	Debit seller
Broker's commission	Debit seller
Delinquent real/personal property taxes	Debit seller
IRS tax liens	Debit seller

Normal Single-Entry Items to Buyer

Homeowner's policy, if new	Debit buyer
Loan origination fee	Debit buyer
Financing documents preparation fee	Debit buyer
Deed/mortgage recording fees	Debit buyer
Title insurance premium	Debit buyer
Property survey fee	Debit buyer
Title examination/attorney fee	Debit buyer
Advanced escrow deposits	Debit buyer
Interim interest on buyer's new loan	Debit buyer
Loan discount points	Debit buyer
Earnest money deposit	Credit buyer
New first mortgage loan	Credit buyer
New second/third mortgage loan	Credit buyer

Note: If taxable personal property (such as a farm tractor) is to be conveyed to the buyer along with real property, the personal property taxes on the item would be prorated per the terms of the NCAR/NCBA Standard Form 2-T Offer to Purchase and Contract form.

Note: Real property taxes may be handled as a *double-debit* under certain circumstances: (1) agreement of the buyer and seller, (2) seller has received the tax bill, (3) the taxes have not been paid, and (4) the taxes are to be paid at settlement to satisfy the tax lien.

Example: The settlement date is December 15, annual taxes are $1,260, and the double-debit method will be used.

$1,260 annual tax ÷ 360 days = $3.50 daily taxes
January 1 – December 15 = 345 days
345 days × $3.50 = $1,207.50 debit seller
$1,260 – $1,207.50 = $52.50 debit buyer

SAMPLE SETTLEMENT STATEMENT

In North Carolina

There are many possible formats for settlement computations. The remaining portion of this chapter illustrates a sample transaction using the North Carolina Real Estate Commission Closing Exercise Worksheet in Figure 15.4. This worksheet will be used on the North Carolina license exam. This closing information is also reflected on the Good Faith Estimate (GFE) in Figure 15.3 and the HUD-1 Settlement Statement in Figure 15.5.

Basic Information of Offer and Sale

John and Joanne Iuro listed their home at 3045 North Racine Avenue in Riverdale, North Carolina, with the Open Door Real Estate Company. The listing price was $118,500, and possession could be given within two weeks after all parties had signed the contract. Under the terms of the listing agreement, the sellers agreed to pay the broker a commission of 6% of the gross sales price.

On April 18 the Open Door Real Estate Company submitted an offer to the Iuros from Brook Redeman, a bachelor, presently residing at 22 King Court, Riverdale. Redeman offered $115,000, with earnest money/down payment of $23,000 and the remaining $92,000 of the purchase price to be obtained through a new conventional loan. No private mortgage insurance will be necessary because the loan-to-value ratio will not exceed 80%. A check for the $100 due diligence fee was made payable to the Iuros. The Iuros signed the contract on April 29. Settlement was set for June 15 at the office of the Open Door Real Estate Company, 720 Main Street, Riverdale.

The unpaid balance of the Iuros' mortgage as of June 1 will be $78,200. Debt service payments are $540 per month with interest at 6% per annum on the unpaid balance.

The title insurance policy paid for by the buyer at the time of settlement cost $290, including $210 for lender's coverage and $80 for homeowners' coverage. Recording charges of $20 were paid for the recording of two instruments to clear defects in the sellers' title. State excise tax in the amount of $230 ($1 per $500 of sales price or fraction thereof) was paid by the sellers. In addition, the sellers must pay an attorney's fee of $75 for preparation of the deed and a $25 courier fee to send the sellers' mortgage payoff to their lender. This amount will be paid from the settlement proceeds.

FIGURE 15.3

Good Faith Estimate (GFE)

OMB Approval No. 2502-0265

Good Faith Estimate (GFE)

Name of Originator: Thrift Federal Savings	Borrower: Brook Redeman
Originator Address: 1100 Fountain Plaza, Riverdale, NC	Property Address: 3045 Racine Avenue, Riverdale, NC
Originator Phone Number: 910-333-XXXX	
Originator Email: yourlender@thriftsavings.com	Date of GFE: May 20, 20XX

Purpose — This GFE gives you an estimate of your settlement charges and loan terms if you are approved for this loan. For more information, see HUD's *Special Information Booklet* on settlement charges, your *Truth-in-Lending Disclosures*, and other consumer information at www.hud.gov/respa. If you decide you would like to proceed with this loan, contact us.

Shopping for your loan — Only you can shop for the best loan for you. Compare this GFE with other loan offers, so you can find the best loan. Use the shopping chart on page 3 to compare all the offers you receive.

Important dates
1. The interest rate for this GFE is available through **5:00 pm May 20, 20XX**. After this time, the interest rate, some of your loan Origination Charges, and the monthly payment shown below can change until you lock your interest rate.
2. This estimate for all other settlement charges is available through **June 30, 20XX**
3. After you lock your interest rate, you must go to settlement within **45** days (your rate lock period) to receive the locked interest rate.
4. You must lock the interest rate at least **30** days before settlement.

Summary of your loan

Your initial loan amount is	$ 92,000.00	
Your loan term is	30	years
Your initial interest rate is	7.25	%
Your initial monthly amount owed for principal, interest, and any mortgage insurance is	$ 627.44	per month
Can your interest rate rise?	☒ No ☐ Yes, it can rise to a maximum of ___ %. The first change will be in ___
Even if you make payments on time, can your loan balance rise?	☒ No ☐ Yes, it can rise to a maximum of $ ___
Even if you make payments on time, can your monthly amount owed for principal, interest, and any mortgage insurance rise?	☒ No ☐ Yes, the first increase can be in ___ and the monthly amount owed can rise to $ ___. The maximum it can ever rise to is $ ___
Does your loan have a prepayment penalty?	☒ No ☐ Yes, your maximum prepayment penalty is $ ___
Does your loan have a balloon payment?	☒ No ☐ Yes, you have a balloon payment of $ ___ due in ___ years.

Escrow account information — Some lenders require an escrow account to hold funds for paying property taxes or other property-related charges in addition to your monthly amount owed of $ **627.44**.
Do we require you to have an escrow account for your loan?
☐ No, you do not have an escrow account. You must pay these charges directly when due.
☒ Yes, you have an escrow account. It may or may not cover all of these charges. Ask us.

Summary of your settlement charges

A	Your Adjusted Origination Charges (See page 2.)	$2,760.00
B	Your Charges for All Other Settlement Services (See page 2.)	$2,830.95
A + B	Total Estimated Settlement Charges	$ 5,590.95

Good Faith Estimate (HUD-GFE) 1

FIGURE 15.3

Good Faith Estimate (GFE) (cont.)

Understanding your estimated settlement charges

	Your Adjusted Origination Charges	
1.	**Our origination charge** This charge is for getting this loan for you.	$920.00
2.	**Your credit or charge (points) for the specific interest rate chosen** ☐ The credit or charge for the interest rate of _____ % is included in "Our origination charge." (See item 1 above.) ☐ You receive a credit of $ _____ for this interest rate of _____ %. This credit **reduces** your settlement charges. ☒ You pay a charge of $ 1,840.00 for this interest rate of 7.25 %. This charge (points) **increases** your total settlement charges. The tradeoff table on page 3 shows that you can change your total settlement charges by choosing a different interest rate for this loan.	$1,840.00
A	Your Adjusted Origination Charges	**$ 2,760.00**

Some of these charges can change at settlement. See the top of page 3 for more information.

	Your Charges for All Other Settlement Services	
3.	**Required services that we select** These charges are for services we require to complete your settlement. We will choose the providers of these services. Service — Charge Appraisal — 300.00 Credit Report — 60.00	$360.00
4.	**Title services and lender's title insurance** This charge includes the services of a title or settlement agent, for example, and title insurance to protect the lender, if required.	$550.00
5.	**Owner's title insurance** You may purchase an owner's title insurance policy to protect your interest in the property.	$75.00
6.	**Required services that you can shop for** These charges are for other services that are required to complete your settlement. We can identify providers of these services or you can shop for them yourself. Our estimates for providing these services are below. Service — Charge Pest inspection — 85.00	$85.00
7.	**Government recording charges** These charges are for state and local fees to record your loan and title documents.	$45.00
8.	**Transfer taxes** These charges are for state and local fees on mortgages and home sales.	$0.00
9.	**Initial deposit for your escrow account** This charge is held in an escrow account to pay future recurring charges on your property and includes ☒ all property taxes, ☒ all insurance, and ☐ other _____.	$1,069.50
10.	**Daily interest charges** This charge is for the daily interest on your loan from the day of your settlement until the first day of the next month or the first day of your normal mortgage payment cycle. This amount is $ 18.528 per day for 16 days (if your settlement is June 15).	$296.45
11.	**Homeowner's insurance** This charge is for the insurance you must buy for the property to protect from a loss, such as fire. Policy — Charge HO3 policy premium — 350.00	$350.00
B	Your Charges for All Other Settlement Services	**$ 2,830.95**
A + B	**Total Estimated Settlement Charges**	**$ 5,590.95**

Good Faith Estimate (HUD-GFE) 2

FIGURE 15.3

Good Faith Estimate (GFE) (cont.)

Instructions

Understanding which charges can change at settlement

This GFE estimates your settlement charges. At your settlement, you will receive a HUD-1, a form that lists your actual costs. Compare the charges on the HUD-1 with the charges on this GFE. Charges can change if you select your own provider and do not use the companies we identify. (See below for details.)

These charges **cannot increase** at settlement:	The total of these charges **can increase up to 10%** at settlement:	These charges **can change** at settlement:
• Our origination charge • Your credit or charge (points) for the specific interest rate chosen *(after you lock in your interest rate)* • Your adjusted origination charges *(after you lock in your interest rate)* • Transfer taxes	• Required services that we select • Title services and lender's title insurance *(if we select them or you use companies we identify)* • Owner's title insurance *(if you use companies we identify)* • Required services that you can shop for *(if you use companies we identify)* • Government recording charges	• Required services that you can shop for *(if you do not use companies we identify)* • Title services and lender's title insurance *(if you do not use companies we identify)* • Owner's title insurance *(if you do not use companies we identify)* • Initial deposit for your escrow account • Daily interest charges • Homeowner's insurance

Using the tradeoff table

In this GFE, we offered you this loan with a particular interest rate and estimated settlement charges. However:

- If you want to choose this same loan with **lower settlement charges,** then you will have a **higher interest rate.**
- If you want to choose this same loan with a **lower interest rate,** then you will have **higher settlement charges.**

If you would like to choose an available option, you must ask us for a new GFE.

Loan originators have the option to complete this table. Please ask for additional information if the table is not completed.

	The loan in this GFE	The same loan with lower settlement charges	The same loan with a lower interest rate
Your initial loan amount	$ 92,000.00	$	$
Your initial interest rate[1]	7.25 %	%	%
Your initial monthly amount owed	$ 627.44	$	$
Change in the monthly amount owed from this GFE	No change	You will pay $ **more** every month	You will pay $ **less** every month
Change in the amount you will pay at settlement with this interest rate	No change	Your settlement charges will be **reduced** by $	Your settlement charges will **increase** by $
How much your total estimated settlement charges will be	$ 5,590.95	$	$

[1]*For an adjustable rate loan, the comparisons above are for the initial interest rate before adjustments are made.*

Using the shopping chart

Use this chart to compare GFEs from different loan originators. Fill in the information by using a different column for each GFE you receive. By comparing loan offers, you can shop for the best loan.

	This loan	Loan 2	Loan 3	Loan 4
Loan originator name	John Jones			
Initial loan amount	$92,000.00			
Loan term	360 months			
Initial interest rate	7.25%			
Initial monthly amount owed	$627.44			
Rate lock period	45 days			
Can interest rate rise?	no			
Can loan balance rise?	no			
Can monthly amount owed rise?	no			
Prepayment penalty?	no			
Balloon payment?	no			
Total Estimated Settlement Charges	$5,590.95			

If your loan is sold in the future

Some lenders may sell your loan after settlement. Any fees lenders receive in the future cannot change the loan you receive or the charges you paid at settlement.

Good Faith Estimate (HUD-GFE) 3

FIGURE 15.4

North Carolina Real Estate Commission Closing Exercise Worksheet

NORTH CAROLINA REAL ESTATE COMMISSION

Closing Exercise Worksheet - Part A

Settlement Charges	Paid from Borrower's Funds at Settlement *Charges to Borrower*	Paid from Seller's Funds at Settlement *Charges to Seller*
Real Estate Broker Fees		
Commission paid at settlement		6900.00
Items Payable in Connection with Loan		
Loan origination fee/charge	920.00	
Loan discount points for specific interest rate chosen	1840.00	
Appraisal fee $300 to Swift Appraisal	POC	
Credit report fee $60 to Acme Credit	POC	
Items Required by Lender to be Paid in Advance		
Daily interest charges from 6/15 to 6/30 @ $18.528 per day	296.45	
Mortgage insurance premium for ____ months		
Homeowner's insurance premium for _1_ years	345.00	
Reserves Deposited with Lender (for Escrow Account)		
Homeowner's insurance _2_ months @ $_28.75_ per month	57.50	
Mortgage insurance ____ months @ $____ per month		
Property taxes _7_ months @ $126.50 per month	885.50	
Title Charges		
Closing attorney's fee	350.00	
Title insurance premium (lender's and/or owner's policy)	290.00	
Deed preparation fee		75.00
Government Recording and Transfer Charges		
Recording fees: Deed $ 20 Mortgage $ 25	45.00	
Excise tax (state tax stamps)		230.00
Recording Fees to Clear Title		20.00
Additional Settlement Charges		
Survey	175.00	
Pest Inspection	85.00	
Courier Fees	25.00	25.00
Homeowner's Warranty		
Other: Home Inspection	400.00	
Total Settlement Charges *(Enter here and on the lines where indicated on **Part B** of the Worksheet)*	5714.45	7250.00

12/02/09

FIGURE 15.4

North Carolina Real Estate Commission Closing Exercise Worksheet (cont.)

NORTH CAROLINA REAL ESTATE COMMISSION
Closing Exercise Worksheet - Part B

Summary of Borrower's Transaction

Charges to Borrower

Gross Amount Due From Borrower	
Contract sales price	115,000.00
Personal property	
Settlement charges to borrower *(from bottom line of borrower's column on Part A of Worksheet)*	5714.45
Adjustments for items paid by seller in advance	
Real property taxes	
Assessments	
Gross Amount Due from Borrower *(Total Charges to Borrower)*	120,714.45

Credits to Borrower

Amounts Paid By or In Behalf of Borrower	
Deposit or earnest money	23,000.00
Principal amount of new mortgage loan(s)	92,000.00
Due Diligence Fee	100.00
Adjustments for items unpaid by seller	
Real property taxes 1/1 to 6/15	695.81
Assessments	
Total Paid By/For Borrower *(Total Credits to Borrower)*	115,795.81

Summary of Seller's Transaction

Credits to Seller

Gross Amount Due to Seller	
Contract sales price	115,000.00
Personal property	
Adjustments for items paid by seller in advance	
Real property taxes	
Assessments	
Gross Amount Due to Seller *(Total Credits to Seller)*	115,000.00

Charges to Seller

Reductions in Amount Due to Seller	
Settlement charges to seller *(from bottom line of seller's column on Part A of Worksheet)*	7250.00
Payoff of seller's mortgage loan(s)	78,395.50
Due Diligence Fee	100.00
Adjustments for items unpaid by seller	
Real property taxes	695.81
Assessments	
Total Reduction In Amount Due to Seller *(Total Charges to Seller)*	86,441.31

Cash at Settlement
(Reconciliation of Total Charges and Credits)

Cash At Settlement From/To Borrower

Gross amount due from borrower *(Total Charges to Borrower)*	120,714.45
Less amounts paid by/for Borrower *(Total Credits to Borrower)*	115,795.81
Cash **X** From ☐ To Borrower	4,918.64

Cash at Settlement To/From Seller

Gross amount due to seller *(Total Credits to Seller)*	115,000.00
Less reductions in amount due to seller *(Total Charges to Seller)*	86,441.31
Cash **X** To ☐ From Seller	28,558.69

12/02/09

366 Modern Real Estate Practice in North Carolina

FIGURE 15.5

Completed Form HUD-1

OMB Approval No. 2502-0265

A. Settlement Statement (HUD-1)

B. Type of Loan

| 1. ☐ FHA | 2. ☐ RHS | 3. ☐ Conv. Unins. | 6. File Number: | 7. Loan Number: | 8. Mortgage Insurance Case Number: |
| 4. ☐ VA | 5. ☒ Conv. Ins. | | | | |

C. Note: This form is furnished to give you a statement of actual settlement costs. Amounts paid to and by the settlement agent are shown. Items marked "(p.o.c.)" were paid outside the closing; they are shown here for informational purposes and are not included in the totals.

D. Name & Address of Borrower:	E. Name & Address of Seller:	F. Name & Address of Lender:
Brook Redeman 22 King Court Riverdale, NC	John & Joanne Iuro 3045 Racine Avenue Riverdale, NC	Thrift Federal Savings 1100 Fountain Plaza Riverdale, NC

G. Property Location:	H. Settlement Agent:	I. Settlement Date:
3045 Racine Avenue Riverdale, NC		June 15, 20XX
	Place of Settlement: Open Door Real Estate Company	

J. Summary of Borrower's Transaction

100. Gross Amount Due from Borrower	
101. Contract sales price	$115,000.00
102. Personal property	
103. Settlement charges to borrower (line 1400)	$5,714.45
104.	
105.	
Adjustment for items paid by seller in advance	
106. City/town taxes to	
107. County taxes to	
108. Assessments to	
109.	
110.	
111.	
112.	
120. Gross Amount Due from Borrower	**$120,714.45**
200. Amount Paid by or in Behalf of Borrower	
201. Deposit or earnest money	$23,000.00
202. Principal amount of new loan(s)	$92,000.00
203. Existing loan(s) taken subject to	
204. Due Diligence Fee	$100.00
205.	
206.	
207.	
208.	
209.	
Adjustments for items unpaid by seller	
210. City/town taxes to	
211. County taxes 1/1 to 6/15	$695.81
212. Assessments to	
213.	
214.	
215.	
216.	
217.	
218.	
219.	
220. Total Paid by/for Borrower	**$115,795.81**
300. Cash at Settlement from/to Borrower	
301. Gross amount due from borrower (line 120)	$120,714.45
302. Less amounts paid by/for borrower (line 220)	($115,795.81)
303. Cash ☒ From ☐ To Borrower	**$4,918.64**

K. Summary of Seller's Transaction

400. Gross Amount Due to Seller	
401. Contract sales price	$115,000.00
402. Personal property	
403.	
404.	
405.	
Adjustment for items paid by seller in advance	
406. City/town taxes to	
407. County taxes to	
408. Assessments to	
409.	
410.	
411.	
412.	
420. Gross Amount Due to Seller	**$115,000.00**
500. Reductions In Amount Due to seller	
501. Excess deposit (see instructions)	
502. Settlement charges to seller (line 1400)	$7,250.00
503. Existing loan(s) taken subject to	
504. Payoff of first mortgage loan	$78,395.50
505. Payoff of second mortgage loan	
506. Due Diligence Fee	$100.00
507.	
508.	
509.	
Adjustments for items unpaid by seller	
510. City/town taxes to	
511. County taxes 1/1 to 6/15	$695.81
512. Assessments to	
513.	
514.	
515.	
516.	
517.	
518.	
519.	
520. Total Reduction Amount Due Seller	**$86,441.31**
600. Cash at Settlement to/from Seller	
601. Gross amount due to seller (line 420)	$115,000.00
602. Less reductions in amounts due seller (line 520)	($86,441.31)
603. Cash ☒ To ☐ From Seller	**$28,558.69**

The Public Reporting Burden for this collection of information is estimated at 35 minutes per response for collecting, reviewing, and reporting the data. This agency may not collect this information, and you are not required to complete this form, unless it displays a currently valid OMB control number. No confidentiality is assured; this disclosure is mandatory. This is designed to provide the parties to a RESPA covered transaction with information during the settlement process.

Previous edition are obsolete   Page 1 of 3   HUD-1

FIGURE 15.5

Completed Form HUD-1 (cont.)

L. Settlement Charges		
700. Total Real Estate Broker Fees	Paid From Borrower's Funds at Settlement	Paid From Seller's Funds at Settlement
Division of commission (line 700) as follows:		
701. $ 6,900.00 to Open Door Real Estate Company		
702. $ to		
703. Commission paid at settlement		$6,900.00
704.		
800. Items Payable in Connection with Loan		
801. Our origination charge $ 920.00 (from GFE #1)		
802. Your credit or charge (points) for the specific interest rate chosen $ 1,840.00 (from GFE #2)		
803. Your adjusted origination charges (from GFE #A)	$2,760.00	
804. Appraisal fee to $300 POC to Swift Appraisal (from GFE #3)		
805. Credit report to $60 POC to Acme Credit (from GFE #3)		
806. Tax service to (from GFE #3)		
807. Flood certification to (from GFE #3)		
808.		
809.		
810.		
811.		
900. Items Required by Lender to be Paid in Advance		
901. Daily interest charges from June 15 to June 30 @ $ 18.518 /day (from GFE #10)	$296.29	
902. Mortgage insurance premium for months to (from GFE #3)		
903. Homeowner's insurance for 1 years to (from GFE #11)	$345.00	
904.		
1000. Reserves Deposited with Lender		
1001. Initial deposit for your escrow account (from GFE #9)	$943.00	
1002. Homeowner's insurance 2 months @ $ 28.75 per month $ 57.50		
1003. Mortgage insurance months @ $ per month $		
1004. Property Taxes 7 months @ $ 126.50 per month $ 885.50		
1005. months @ $ per month $		
1006. months @ $ per month $		
1007. Aggregate Adjustment -$		
1100. Title Charges		
1101. Title services and lender's title insurance (from GFE #4)	$585.00	
1102. Settlement or closing fee $ 350.00		
1103. Owner's title insurance Hite Insurance Company (from GFE #5)	$80.00	
1104. Lender's title insurance Hite Insurance Company $ 210.00		
1105. Lender's title policy limit $		
1106. Owner's title policy limit $		
1107. Agent's portion of the total title insurance premium to $		
1108. Underwriter's portion of the total title insurance premium to $		
1109. Courier fees of $25 included in Line 1101		
1110. General warranty deed prep		$75.00
1111.		
1200. Government Recording and Transfer Charges		
1201. Government recording charges (from GFE #7)	$45.00	
1202. Deed $ 20.00 Mortgage $ 25.00 Release $		
1203. Transfer taxes (from GFE #8)		
1204. City/County tax/stamps Deed $ Mortgage $		
1205. State tax/stamps Deed $ 230.00 Mortgage $		$230.00
1206. Recording fees to clear title		$20.00
1300. Additional Settlement Charges		
1301. Required services that you can shop for (from GFE #6)	$260.00	
1302. Survey $ 175.00		
1303. Pest Inspection $ 85.00		
1304. Home Inspection	$400.00	
1305. Courier fees		$25.00
1400. Total Settlement Charges (enter on lines 103, Section J and 502, Section K)	$5,714.29	$7,250.00

FIGURE 15.5

Completed Form HUD-1 (cont.)

Comparison of Good Faith Estimate (GFE) and HUD-1 Charges		Good Faith Estimate	HUD-1
Charges That Cannot Increase	**HUD-1 Line Number**		
Our origination charge	# 801	$920.00	$920.00
Your credit or charge (points) for the specific interest rate chosen	# 802	$1,840.00	$1,840.00
Your adjusted origination charges	# 803	$2,760.00	$2,760.00
Transfer taxes	# 1203		

Charges That In Total Cannot Increase More Than 10%		Good Faith Estimate	HUD-1
Government recording charges	# 1201	$45.00	$45.00
	#		
	#		
	#		
	#		
	#		
	#		
	#		
	Total		
Increase between GFE and HUD-1 Charges		$ or %	

Charges That Can Change		Good Faith Estimate	HUD-1
Initial deposit for your escrow account	# 1001		$943.00
Daily interest charges $ 10.03 /day	# 901		$296.45
Homeowner's insurance	# 903		$345.00
	#		
	#		
	#		

Loan Terms

Your initial loan amount is	$ 92,000.00
Your loan term is	30 years
Your initial interest rate is	7.25 %
Your initial monthly amount owed for principal, interest, and any mortgage insurance is	$ includes [X] Principal [X] Interest [ ] Mortgage Insurance
Can your interest rate rise?	[X] No [ ] Yes, it can rise to a maximum of %. The first change will be on and can change again every after . Every change date, your interest rate can increase or decrease by %. Over the life of the loan, your interest rate is guaranteed to never be **lower** than % or **higher** than %.
Even if you make payments on time, can your loan balance rise?	[X] No [ ] Yes, it can rise to a maximum of $
Even if you make payments on time, can your monthly amount owed for principal, interest, and mortgage insurance rise?	[X] No [ ] Yes, the first increase can be on and the monthly amount owed can rise to $. The maximum it can ever rise to is $
Does your loan have a prepayment penalty?	[X] No [ ] Yes, your maximum prepayment penalty is $
Does your loan have a balloon payment?	[X] No [ ] Yes, you have a balloon payment of $ due in years on .
Total monthly amount owed including escrow account payments	[ ] You do not have a monthly escrow payment for items, such as property taxes and homeowner's insurance. You must pay these items directly yourself. [X] You have an additional monthly escrow payment of $ that results in a total initial monthly amount owed of $. This includes principal, interest, any mortgage insurance and any items checked below: [X] Property taxes [X] Homeowner's insurance [ ] Flood insurance [ ] [ ]

Note: If you have any questions about the Settlement Charges and Loan Terms listed on this form, please contact your lender.

Previous edition are obsolete   Page 3 of 3   HUD-1

The buyer must pay an attorney's fee of $350 for examination of the title evidence and legal representation. There is also a $20 fee to record the deed and a $25 courier fee to return loan documents to the lender. These amounts also will be paid from the settlement proceeds.

Real estate taxes in Riverdale are paid in arrears. Taxes for this year, estimated at last year's figure of $1,518, have not been paid. According to the contract, prorations are to be made on the basis of the 360-day year/30-day month method.

Computing the Prorations and Charges

The following list illustrates the various steps in computing the prorations and other amounts to be included in the settlement to this point.

1. *Settlement date:* June 15
2. *Commission:* 6% × $115,000 (sales price) = $6,900
3. *Sellers' mortgage interest:*
   6% × $78,200 (principal after June 1 payment) = $4,692 interest per year
   $4,692 ÷ 360 days = $13.033 interest per day
   15 days of accrued interest to be paid by the sellers
   15 × $13.033 = $195.495, or $195.50 interest owed by the sellers
   $78,200 + $195.50 = $78,395.50 payoff of sellers' mortgage
4. *Real estate taxes* (estimated at $1,518):
   $1,518 ÷ 360 days = $4.217 per day
   January 1 through June 15 equals 165 days
   165 days × $4.217 = $695.81 debit seller/credit buyer
5. *Excise tax* ($1 per $500 of consideration or fraction thereof):
   $115,000 ÷ $500 = 230
   230 × $1 = $230 excise tax, debit seller

The buyer's new loan is from Thrift Federal Savings, 1100 Fountain Plaza, Riverdale, in the amount of $92,000 at 7¼% interest. In connection with this loan, Redeman will be charged $300 to have the property appraised by Swift Appraisal. The Acme Credit Bureau will charge $60 for a credit report. (Because appraisal and credit reports are performed prior to loan approval, they are paid at the time of loan application, whether or not the transaction eventually closes. These items will be noted as *POC* on the settlement statement.) In addition, Redeman will pay for interim interest on his loan for the remainder of the month of settlement: 16 days at $18.528 per day, or $296.45. His first full payment (including July's interest) will be due August 1. He must deposit $885.50 into a tax escrow account with the lender. That is seven-twelfths of the anticipated county real estate tax of $1,518. A one-year hazard insurance premium at $3 per $1,000 of appraised value ($115,000 ÷ $1,000 × 3 = $345) paid at settlement to Hite Insurance Company. An insurance reserve to cover the premium for two months is also deposited in an escrow account with the lender. Redeman will have to pay an additional $25 to record the deed of trust and $175 for a survey. He will also pay a loan origination fee of $920 and two discount points, plus $85 for a pest inspection. Buyer also owes $400 to A-1 Inspectors for a home inspection.

The Settlement Statement (HUD-1)

The **Settlement Statement (HUD-1)** used for most residential settlements consists of three pages (see Figure 15.3, the Sample Settlement Statement, completed with example problem information); Sections J and K on the first page are a summary of the borrower's and the seller's transactions. At the bottom of the first page, line 303 indicates the total amount of cash due from (or to) the borrower. Line 603 indicates the cash to (or from) the seller.

The second page itemizes the settlement charges to be paid from the borrower's funds or from the seller's funds at settlement. A number of the costs to the buyer must correlate to the GFE that the buyer received within three business days of loan application. All items in the borrower's column are added up and transferred to line 103 on the first page. All items in the seller's column are added up and transferred to line 502 on the first page.

RELATED WEBSITES

HUD site for HUD-1 and GFE forms:
 http://www.hud.gov/offices/adm/hudclips/forms/hud1.cfm
Dept. of Housing and Urban Development: RESPA:
 www.hud.gov/offices/hsg/sfh/res/respa_hm.cfm

KEY POINT REVIEW

Closing (settlement) is the point at which ownership of a property is transferred in exchange for the selling price.

The buyer's **due diligence** process investigates the following:

- Title evidence—a current abstract of title with opinion of title from the buyer's attorney or title commitment from the title insurance company
- Seller's deed
- Affidavit of title by the seller and documents showing the removal of prior encumbrances
- **Soil suitability test** (percolation test)
- Survey and the results of required inspections
- Leases, if tenants reside on the premises
- Successful final property inspection (**walk-through**)
- Settlement statement showing the amount and distribution of funds

To complete the transaction, the seller requires the following:

- Payoff statement from the seller's lender noting the amount owed
- Evidence that the buyer has the necessary funds
- Settlement statement showing the distribution of funds

Depending on state law and local custom, settlement may be conducted by a

- licensed escrow company, in which case the parties may execute documents separately and never meet, or
- face-to-face meeting of the parties at the escrow company, title company, lender's office, or attorney's office.

An **escrow** or settlement **agent** is a disinterested third party authorized to coordinate the closing activities usually an attorney in North Carolina.

The **Internal Revenue Service (IRS)** may require completion and submission of the Form 1099-S statement of income to the seller showing the seller's Social Security number. Form 1099-S is filed by a settlement agent or the mortgage lender, with the brokers or the parties being ultimately liable for the filing.

The **Real Estate Settlement Procedures Act (RESPA)** is a federal law enacted to protect consumers in the settlement process as follows:

- Requires accurate and timely information about the actual costs of a transaction
- Eliminates kickbacks and other referral fees
- Prohibits lenders from requiring excessive escrow account deposits

RESPA does not apply to a transaction financed solely by a purchase money mortgage taken back by a seller, installment contracts (contract for deed), or a buyer's assumption of a seller's existing loan.

RESPA requires that lenders and settlement agents provide a

- special information booklet produced by HUD to every person from whom they receive or for whom they prepare a loan application (except for refinancing),
- **good-faith estimate (GFE)** of settlement costs to the borrower no later than three business days after receiving a loan application, and
- Uniform Settlement Statement (HUD-1) to the borrower and the seller that itemizes all charges to be paid in connection with closing.

A **closing (settlement) statement (HUD-1)** involves an accounting of the amounts paid by or received by the parties, as follows:

- **Debit** (give) is a charge that must be paid by the buyer or the seller at settlement.
- **Credit** (receive) is the amount entered in favor of the buyer or the seller.
- In most instances, a debit to one party is a credit to the other party.
- Certain charges are **prorated**, divided between the buyer and the seller, in one of two ways:
  — Yearly charge is divided by a 360-day year (banking year), or 12 months of 30 days each.
  — Yearly charge is divided by a 365-day year (366 days in leap year) to determine the daily charge, the actual number of days in the proration period is determined, and the number of days is multiplied by the daily charge.
- In North Carolina, the charges are prorated as of the date of closing, with the seller being responsible for the date of closing.

QUESTIONS

1. Which of the following statements is TRUE of real estate closings in North Carolina?
   a. Closings are usually conducted by real estate brokers.
   b. The seller usually pays the expenses for the day of settlement.
   c. The buyer usually reimburses the seller for accrued but unpaid expenses.
   d. The seller usually pays the attorney for the preparation of the deed of trust.

2. Which of the following does NOT normally occur at closing?
   a. Seller transfers ownership to the buyer via general warranty deed.
   b. Buyer delivers certified funds for the purchase of the property.
   c. Settlement agent assures that all paperwork required by the lender have been properly signed and dated.
   d. Buyer pays for the appraisal and the credit report required by the lender.

3. The RESPA Uniform Settlement Statement must be used to illustrate all settlement charges for
   a. every real estate sales transaction.
   b. only real estate transactions financed by VA and FHA loans.
   c. all residential real estate transactions financed by federally related mortgage loans.
   d. all commercial real estate transactions.

4. If annual real estate taxes of $1,800 have been paid in advance of settlement, what would the HUD-1 entry for the current taxes be if closing is set for September 15?
   a. Credit seller $525; debit buyer $1,275
   b. Credit seller $1,275; debit buyer $525
   c. Credit buyer $1,275; debit seller $1,275
   d. Credit seller $525; debit buyer $525

5. A seller collected rent of $450 on June 1, payable in advance, from the tenant of the property being sold. How will the rent appear on the HUD-1 if settlement is scheduled for June 23?
   a. Credit seller $345; debit buyer $105
   b. Credit buyer $105; debit seller $105
   c. Credit seller $345; debit buyer $345
   d. Rent will not appear on the HUD-1 in this situation.

6. A building was purchased for $150,000, with 10% down and a loan for the balance. If the lender charged the buyer two discount points and a 1% loan origination fee, how much cash did the buyer need to pay the down payment and loan fees?
   a. $15,450
   b. $16,620
   c. $19,050
   d. $19,500

Questions 7 through 11 should be answered as to how certain items would normally appear on a settlement statement if the standard NCAR/NCBA Offer to Purchase and Contract is used.

7. The sales price of the property is a
   a. credit to the buyer.
   b. debit to the seller.
   c. credit to the buyer; debit to the seller.
   d. credit to the seller; debit to the buyer.

8. The earnest money held in escrow by the listing broker is a
   a. credit to the buyer.
   b. debit to the seller.
   c. credit to the buyer; debit to the seller.
   d. credit to the seller; debit to the buyer.

9. The cost of conducting a survey on the property is a
   a. debit to the buyer.
   b. debit to the seller.
   c. credit to the buyer; debit to the seller.
   d. credit to the seller; debit to the buyer.

10. The principal amount of the purchaser's new mortgage loan is a
    a. debit to the buyer.
    b. credit to the buyer.
    c. credit to the buyer; debit to the seller.
    d. credit to the seller; debit to the buyer.

11. Unpaid homeowners' association fees, water service charges, and waste disposal service fees are
    a. credits to the buyer.
    b. debits to the seller.
    c. credits to the buyer; debits to the seller.
    d. credits to the seller; debits to the buyer.

12. The Real Estate Settlement Procedures Act applies to the activities of
    a. brokers selling commercial and office buildings.
    b. security salespeople selling limited partnerships.
    c. Ginnie Mae or Fannie Mae when purchasing mortgages.
    d. lenders financing the purchase of a borrower's residence.

13. RESPA requires that
    I. a good faith estimate of settlement costs be given to the borrower within 7 business days of loan application.
    II. a standardized settlement statement be used to reflect all charges in connection with the transaction.
        a. I only
        b. II only
        c. Both I and II
        d. Neither I nor II

14. Which of the following settlement expenses is *NOT* typically paid by the seller?
    a. Excise tax
    b. Attorney's fee
    c. Deed preparation fee
    d. Brokers' commission

15. Which of the following closing expenses is *NOT* generally prorated between the buyer and the seller at settlement?
    a. Current ad valorem real estate taxes
    b. Homeowner association dues
    c. Rent
    d. Interim interest on new loan

16. Under RESPA, the settlement agent must
    I. allow the borrower to examine the settlement statement one business day before settlement.
    II. keep the settlement statement for two years after closing.
        a. I only
        b. II only
        c. Both I and II
        d. Neither I nor II

17. On the HUD-1, the prorations for unpaid real estate taxes at a March 24th settlement would be shown as a
    a. credit to the seller; debit to the buyer.
    b. debit to the seller; credit to the buyer.
    c. credit to both the seller and the buyer.
    d. debit to both the seller and the buyer.

18. On the HUD-1, the due diligence fee in the NCAR/NCBA Standard Offer to Purchase and contract will always be a
    I. credit to the buyer.
    II. debit to the seller.
        a. I only
        b. II only
        c. Both I and II
        d. Neither I nor II

19. You are purchasing a four-unit apartment building and will close on November 14. Each apartment rents for $575 per month. On November 1, one apartment is vacant and the other tenants have paid the November rent. Compute the rent proration through the day of settlement, and indicate proper entries on a settlement statement.
    a. $805 credit seller; debit buyer
    b. $805 debit seller; credit buyer
    c. $920 credit seller; debit buyer
    d. $920 debit seller; credit buyer

20. The buyer is going to assume the seller's 7% loan with a loan balance of $82,000 as of the day of settlement, which will be August 11. Which would be the correct settlement statement entries for the interest proration?
    a. $175.38 debit seller; credit buyer
    b. $175.38 credit seller; debit buyer
    c. $302.94 credit seller; debit buyer
    d. $302.91 debit seller; credit buyer

21. Settlement will take place on November 15. Annual real estate taxes are $1,260 and have been paid by the seller. Which would be the appropriate settlement statement entries for the taxes?
    a. $157.50 debit seller; credit buyer
    b. $157.50 credit seller; debit buyer
    c. $1,102.50 credit seller; debit buyer
    d. $1,102.50 debit seller; credit buyer

■ SETTLEMENT STATEMENT PROBLEM

Answer Questions 22–25 using the following information.

Julie and Vern Marenatha are selling their home to Martha and Joe White for $110,000. The parties have agreed to $50 due diligence fee payable to the Marenathas. The Whites made a $5,000 earnest money deposit, which is being held by the Marenathas' real estate broker in escrow until settlement. The Whites are to obtain an 80% conventional loan at 10% interest and make a 20% down payment. The settlement date is October 15. The Marenathas agreed to pay their broker a 6% commission.

The Marenathas' existing mortgage loan (at 10% interest) will have a balance of $82,750 after their October 1 payment. The sellers must also pay accrued interest on their loan payoff at settlement. The loan must be paid off at settlement. The property taxes for the current year are $1,100 and are unpaid; parties agreed to the double-debit method of proration.

The Whites will pay their mortgage company a $50 credit report fee and a $150 appraisal report fee at settlement. The mortgage company is charging a 1% loan origination fee and a 1.5% loan discount fee. Interim interest on the new loan is to be paid by the Whites at settlement. The first loan payment will be due on December 1. The Whites must pay a $345 homeowners' insurance premium, and must deposit an additional $500 into escrow at settlement for property taxes and homeowners' insurance premiums.

Other closing expenses (listed here) will be paid in accordance with custom.

   Property survey: $200
   Pest inspection report: $75
   Lender's title insurance premium: $250
   Excise tax at the current rate
   Fee to prepare deed: $50
   Fee to record deed: $7
   Fee to record buyers' deed of trust: $7
   Buyers' lawyer's fee: $500

Use a 360-day year and 30-day month to calculate prorations. As to prorations between the buyers and sellers, the seller is responsible for the day of settlement. Perform proration calculations without rounding. Final entries on the North Carolina Real Estate Commission Closing Exercise Worksheet for the buyers and sellers should be rounded to the nearest penny.

22. What are the Closing Exercise Worksheet Part A total settlement charges to the buyers?
    a. $4,675.10
    b. $4,904.14
    c. $5,546.06
    d. $7,747.96

23. What are the Closing Exercise Worksheet Part A total settlement charges to the sellers?
    a. $6,876.04
    b. $7,527.04
    c. $7,740.96
    d. $7,977.00

24. How much cash will come at settlement from the buyers?
    a. $19,157.25
    b. $21,675.10
    c. $21,854.14
    d. $22,775.10

25. How much cash will go at settlement to the sellers?
    a. $19,114.25
    b. $19,386.29
    c. $21,675.10
    d. $21,904.14

CHAPTER 16

Basic Residential Construction

■ **LEARNING OBJECTIVES** *When you have finished reading this chapter, you should be able to*

- **describe** basic architectural types and styles of residential construction.
- **identify** the components of a house foundation and the house framing.
- **describe** all components of residential construction.
- **explain** provisions of North Carolina Building Codes, HUD minimum standards, and contractor licensing.
- **define** these *key terms*:

baseboards	foundation wall	R-value
basement	frame	sheathing
BTU	frieze board	shingles
building code	girder	siding
ceiling joists	header	sill
certificate of occupancy	HVAC	soffit
concrete slab	insulation	sole plate
crawl space	pier	stud
eave	pitch	subfloor
fascia board	rafter	top plate
floor joists	ridge board	
footings	roofing felt	

Only need to know these vocab words for this chapter, pg 379

It is important for real estate brokers to have a basic knowledge of residential construction. As brokers show homes to prospective buyers, they need to be able to point out basic features and answer basic construction questions. This chapter offers a rudimentary introduction to wood-frame residential construction. Wood-frame construction is most popular because it (1) has flexibility of design, (2) costs less, (3) is easy to insulate, and (4) takes less time to build.

ARCHITECTURAL TYPES AND STYLES

A few basic architectural styles maintain high levels of popularity, including the one-story, or ranch-style, home; the split-level home; and several types of two-story homes, such as the Cape Cod, colonial, and French provincial.

Ranch-style homes offer easy accessibility and maintenance because everything is on one floor. Owners have no need to make frequent trips upstairs or to use high ladders to paint second-story exterior surfaces. Although ranch houses are usually moderate-sized and affordable, they are the most expensive to build per square foot because the two most expensive elements of a house, the roof and the foundation, must cover the same amount of space as the living area of the house.

The split-level home, sometimes called a tri-level, takes advantage of uneven terrain with a minimum of grading to prepare the lot. Two-story homes are the most economical to build on a cost per square foot basis because they offer twice the living area for the cost of only one foundation and roof. A story and a half (1½ story) house functions much like a two-story residence except that the upper level's ceiling is the underside of the roofline and there is no attic space above that living area. Just due to height of the construction alone, maintenance and access of multilevel homes is more difficult than a single-story home. Contemporary designs usually combine elements of one-story, two-story, or split-level homes with a lot of open space, multilevel rooflines, and skylights or windows. Contemporary designs are particularly popular in scenic areas due to the generous use of large windows.

No one design is inherently superior to another. Whether a buyer prefers a contemporary ranch-style to a colonial two-story is simply a matter of individual taste and style and how the architectural style fits in with the topography of the property.

FOUNDATIONS

The foundation of a home must be built on firm soil with materials that are capable of supporting the weight of the house and resisting damage caused by wood-eating pests.

Basic Components

The basic components of a foundation include the following:

- *Footings.* The foundation rests on **footings,** which are usually made of concrete that is poured into trenches or forms that have been dug or placed beneath the soil line. Footings must be wider than the structure being supported and are typically 16 inches wide and 6 inches to 8 inches deep. The bottom of each footing must be located below the frost line to avoid the shifting that can be caused when the ground freezes. Footings are the lowest part of construction and serve to spread the weight of the structure over the ground.

- *Foundation walls*. **Foundation walls** rest on top of the footings and provide a surface upon which the flooring is built. Foundation walls are usually made out of poured concrete, masonry block, or brick and are typically 8 inches to 12 inches thick.
- *Piers*. **Piers** (columns), usually made of masonry block, may be required to support the flooring between the foundation walls when a crawlspace or basement construction is used.

These basic components of a house, as well as those of a foundation, are illustrated in Figure 16.3.

Major Types

The three major types of foundations found in North Carolina include the following:

In North Carolina

- **Crawl space**. Foundation walls with a crawl space are very popular in North Carolina residential construction. Lifting the living space above the ground aids with ventilation, moisture control, and prevention of pest infestation. Proper ventilation of the crawl space through the adequate use of *foundation vents* works in conjunction with proper grading of the soil to drain moisture away from under the building. Additional moisture control may be accomplished by waterproofing the foundation walls and/or installing a *vapor barrier* in the crawl space.
- **Basement**. Basements are basically story-high crawl spaces that may be used for storage or living space, depending on the quality of finish used. While basement space is popular, it is also expensive to construct, especially in the central and eastern parts of North Carolina due to the high water table and the additional excavation below the frost line.
- **Concrete slab**. A flat, horizontal, reinforced with steel bars, concrete slab poured directly on the level ground to create the foundation without use of a crawlspace or basement. The two types of slab foundations are: (1) a *monolithic slab* that is poured in one large section with the thicker edges serving as the footings for the building, and (2) *a floating slab* that poured inside the outline of the footings and foundation walls.

Termite Protection

In North Carolina

Because North Carolina is home to many wood-destroying insects, builders must be very careful to protect structures from damage from such pests. All firewood or wood materials must be removed from around the foundation construction site and the decking of the residence to discourage termites and other wood-destroying insects.

In new construction, the soil near the foundation walls and piers must be chemically treated. Any lumber used in the construction that comes in contact with the ground must be pressure-treated. Frequently, the company that treats the soil will offer a termite bond that is renewable and transferable to provide infestation protection warranty.

FRAMING

Various dimensions of lumber are used to build the **frame** of a house, which is similar to the skeleton of a body. The elements of the framing consist of the floors, the walls, the ceiling, and the roof. See Figure 16.1 and Figure 16.2 for examples of various framing cross-sections.

- *Floor framing.* The floor framing consists of the **sill** (the lowest horizontal wooden part of framing), pieces of treated lumber that are placed on top of the foundation walls. **Floor joists** are then attached to the sills at 16-inch or 24-inch intervals. Because the floor joists must support the entire weight of the floor, they typically cannot span the entire width of the structure. Instead, **girders,** which rest on top of piers, are used to support the joists between sills. The **subfloor** is then attached to this system of joists and girders. The subfloor is usually made of sheets of plywood or pressboard, which are laid on top of the joists and girders. Finally, the subfloor is covered with the floor covering, such as vinyl, carpeting, tile, or hardwood strips.
- *Wall framing.* Wall framing consists of **studs,** vertical lumber spaced about 16 inches apart. The **sole plate** connects the studs to the flooring; the **top plate** connects the studs to the ceiling framing. **Headers,** two pieces of lumber joined together to form a beam, are used to give extra support to wall framing where a window or door will be positioned. This type of framing is called *platform* framing.

    Two other less typical types of framing include *balloon* framing and *post and beam* framing. With balloon framing, a single system of lengthy wall studs is used. The studs run from the foundation up to the ceiling (through both the first and second stories). With post and beam framing, extra-large framing members are used—either 4 x 4 inch or 6 x 6 inch. These large posts can be placed farther apart than the traditional 16-inch distance between wall studs.
- *Roof framing.* Ceiling joists are attached to the top plate of the wall and carry the weight of the roof. **Rafters**, the sloping members of the roof frame, connect the ceiling joists and the **ridge boards** (the highest part of the construction). The rafters support the decking or other roofing materials. An alternative method to using ceiling joists, rafters, and ridge boards is *truss framing.* The roof truss is a prefabricated triangular structure that serves the same functions as the ceiling joists, rafters, and ridge boards but is easier and quicker to install. The overhang of the roof is called the **eave,** which is made up of the **fascia board**, the **soffit**, and the **frieze board**. Gutters are usually attached to the fascia board. Ventilation for the attic is usually located in the soffit of the eaves. The frieze board is a sometimes decorative board at the top of the exterior wall directly under the soffit that prevents penetration of the elements through the joint between the exterior wall and roof.

ELEMENTS OF CONSTRUCTION

Refer to Figure 16.3 for a complete illustration of home construction.

Chapter 16   Basic Residential Construction   **379**

FIGURE 16.1

Roof Framing Systems

In a truss roof the upper and lower chords are joined together by either a gusset plate or a split ring and bolt.

FIGURE 16.2

Exterior Structure Walls and Framing

Exterior Walls

To build the exterior walls, **sheathing** is added to the wall framing to insulate the house from the elements. Several types of materials are used for sheathing, including particleboard, foam sheathing, and plywood. Exterior siding is then added to the sheathing. Exterior siding may be wood-manufactured hardboard (e.g., Masonite®), brick veneer, fiber cement board, vinyl, aluminum, stucco, or synthetic stucco (e.g., EIFS). In older existing homes, wood is the most common siding material; however, in recent years most homes built in North Carolina use one of the other types of siding. **Siding** protects the home from the elements and provides a pleasing look.

> In North Carolina

Windows and Exterior Doors

Windows allow for ventilation, light, a view, and style. Today, windows are made of wood, aluminum, and some composite materials, plus they normally use multi-pane insulated glass for energy efficiency. There are three basic types of window: (1) the sliding windows that have sash units that slide either vertically (sometimes called double-hung) or horizontally past each other to open or close the window opening; (2) the swinging windows that include the casement (a sash unit is hinged on one side to fully swing outward), jalousie (glass louvers), hopper (hinged on the bottom), and awning (hinged on the top) styles; and (3) the fixed windows that do not open include bay, bow, picture, and Palladian styles.

In addition to providing access, exterior doors add to the style of a home. Exterior doors are usually made of wood, steel, or a combination of wood and glass (such as French doors) with a solid core for maximum insulation value. The major types of exterior doors include: (1) the *flush door* that is of smooth finish construction and appearance; (2) the *panel door* that has multiple raised or indented panels; (3) the *sliding glass door* that is frequently used as access to patios or decks; and (4) the *French door* that provides a more upscale decorative door with glass panels.

The major components of window and door framework are the same: the *sill* is the bottom, the *jamb* is the side, and the *header* is the top of the framing. In a window, the glass panel that moves is the *sash*. The sash used to be composed of several small rectangular windowpanes that were joined together by pieces of wood. The cross hatch of dividing wood is comprised of the *muntins* (horizontal pieces) and the *mullions* (vertical pieces).

Roofing

Roofing materials must be able to withstand the elements and provide water protection to the structure. Of course, roofing materials also add to the home's style and character. The most common types of roofing materials are composition **shingles** (made of asphalt and fiberglass), wood shingles or shakes, and layers of **roofing felt** interspersed with tar or asphalt (called a *built-up roof*). Sometimes, the same sheathing that is attached to the exterior walls for insulation purposes also is attached to the rafters and is called decking.

FIGURE 16.3

Home Construction

1. FOOTING
2. FOUNDATION DRAIN TILE
3. CRUSHED/WASHED STONE
4. FOUNDATION WALL
5. DAMPPROOFING OR WEATHERPROOFING
6. BACKFILL
7. ANCHOR BOLT
8. SILL PLATE
9. TERMITE SHIELD
10. FLOOR JOIST
11. BAND OR BOX BEAM
12. SOLE PLATE
13. SUBFLOORING
14. BUILDING PAPER
15. WALL STUD
16. CORNER STUDS
17. INSULATION
18. HOUSE WRAP
19. WALL SHEATHING
20. SIDING
21. MULLION
22. MUNTIN
23. WINDOW SASH
24. EAVE (ROOF PROJECTION)
25. WINDOW JAMB TRIM
26. WINDOW HEADER
27. CEILING JOIST
28. TOP AND TIE PLATES
29. GABLE STUD
30. RAFTERS
31. COLLAR TIES
32. GABLE END OF ROOF
33. RIDGE BEAM
34. CHIMNEY FLUES
35. CHIMNEY CAP
36. CHIMNEY
37. CHIMNEY FLASHING
38. ROOFING SHINGLES
39. ROOFING FELT/ICE AND WATER MEMBRANE
40. ROOF SHEATHING
41. EVE TROUGH OR GUTTER
42. FRIEZE BOARD
43. FIRESTOP
44. DOWNSPOUT
45. LATHS
46. PLASTER BOARD
47. PLASTER FINISH
48. MANTEL
49. ASH DUMP
50. BASE TOP MOLDING
51. BASEBOARD
52. SHOE MOLDING
53. FINISH MOLDING
54. CROSS BRIDGING
55. PIER
56. GIRDER
57. FOOTING
58. RISER
59. TREAD
60. STRINGER
61. CLEANOUT DOOR
62. CONCRETE BASEMENT FLOOR
63. CRUSHED/WASHED STONE

The gable roof is the most common roof design. Refer to Figure 16.4 for examples of popular roof designs. The slope of the roof is measured by the **pitch**, which is the number of inches of rise per foot of horizontal distance. The larger the rise per foot, the steeper the slope will be.

FIGURE 16.4

Roof Designs

Gable

Hip

Gable with Dormers
— Shed Dormer
Single Dormer

Saltbox

Shed

Flat

Gambrel

Mansard

Insulation

Insulation is an important factor in any building. Today's energy-conscious consumers are anxious to buy homes that take little energy to heat and cool. Materials used to insulate homes include batts or blankets of insulating materials (which come in rolls) or loose fill insulation (which is blown into open spaces). In addition to this interior insulation, the sheathing or house wrapping materials used under the exterior covering of the building would add extra insulating value. Of course, any materials containing asbestos are prohibited.

The insulation value of materials is expressed as an **R-value.** The higher the R-value, the more resistant the material is to the transfer of heat. Building codes require different elements of each home to have different minimum R-values. For example, North Carolina building codes require R-19 insulation in floors, R-13 in walls, and R-30 in ceilings. Higher R-values are required in the colder, mountainous sections of the state.

> In North Carolina

In addition to installing the appropriate insulation throughout the building, property owners are wise to weatherstrip around exterior doors and windows. *Weatherstrips* of felt, metal, or other substance are used to block drafts between the door or window sash and the casing. *Caulking* around openings can also reduce energy loss.

Interior Finishes

Interior finishes are mostly a matter of cost and taste. There is a wide variety of interior finishes—one suited for every budget.

Drywall or gypsum board that has been textured and painted is a typical finish for interior walls, as is wood paneling. Ceilings may be finished with Sheetrock™, acoustical tiles, or tongue-and-groove boards. Floors are usually finished with hardwood strips, ceramic tiles, carpeting, or vinyl. Moldings, such as **baseboards** and casings, are used to finish the seams between the walls and the floors and the areas around doors and windows. Crown molding is used to cover the joint between the walls and the ceiling and can be quite elaborate.

■ HVAC

Several types of *heating, ventilation, and air-conditioning* (**HVAC**) systems exist. The most common forms include central heating units fueled by gas, oil, or electricity; heat pumps; and forced warm air systems (which use a central blower). Some less common power sources are coal, wood, steam, and electric wire. The most efficient type of heating system is warm forced air, even though other systems can still be found, especially in older homes. Electric baseboard heating system, wood stoves, electric heaters, and kerosene heaters have all had periods of popularity that have waned. Fireplaces, while aesthetically appealing, can be a drain on the pocketbook since they usually act as an exhaust vent for the home's air. Modern air conditioning systems, much like the heating systems, are generally forced air systems powered by electricity, gas or oil. Occasionally, room-sized heating and air units are installed for small areas that may be separated from the rest of the living area, such as an office over the garage.

Solar panels, which provide energy on a year-round basis, have gained in popularity over the last few years but are still not as common as gas, oil, or electric heating systems. Solar heating systems can be either passive or active. Passive solar systems utilize the natural heating power of direct sunlight captured through the use of southern exposure windows and brick interior walls that radiate heat back into the room at night. Active systems require a system of collection, storage, and distribution throughout the house. Generally, a solar heating system will require an auxiliary system to supplement the solar power.

Chapter 16 Basic Residential Construction **385**

In North Carolina A very popular HVAC system in most of North Carolina, the heat pump provides a combination of heating and air conditioning. The heat pump *pulls* heat from the outside winter air and pumps it into the house and then reverses the process to remove heat from the residence during the summer months. This system functions best in temperate climates and usually has an auxiliary system to supplement when nature is too hot or too cold for efficiency.

The **BTU,** or British Thermal Unit, is a measure of heat and is used in rating the capacity of air-conditioning and heating equipment. While R-values are stated as smaller numbers, BTU numbers are in the thousands. A 4,000 BTU furnace might be called a *two-ton* unit. Many larger homes utilize a dual system (one system for the first floor and a second system for the upper floor) while some incorporate zoned heating for different *zones* of the residence.

■ GOVERNMENT REGULATION

North Carolina Uniform Building Code

North Carolina has adopted a statewide uniform **building code** that sets minimum construction standards for public safety. The state building code is under the supervision of the North Carolina Department of Insurance.

In North Carolina The code consists of hundreds of pages of requirements on the structure of buildings and their electrical and plumbing systems. Local municipalities may adopt more stringent building codes to raise the quality of construction in their jurisdiction. Each municipality has a building department that issues building permits and enforces the building code by inspecting buildings during construction. Before a structure can be occupied, the building department must issue a **certificate of occupancy**, which means that the construction has been completed in a safe, satisfactory manner. There appears to be a significant misunderstanding in the general population about the need for building permits. Even though a property owner does not need a general contractor's license to build or renovate their personal property, they will usually need to apply for the appropriate building permits. Although there is significant variance about what activities require a permit among county and city inspectors, there appears to be a fairly consistent agreement about three types of work that prompt the need for a permit: any electrical, plumbing, or structural work. The definition of structural work seems to be the type of work that is the most subject to interpretation. A broker listing a property that has had additions or major improvements should verify that the work was permitted. Unapproved space is a material fact since unpermitted space may have to be taken down or pass inspection retroactively, and may not be insurable.

HUD Minimum Standards

Homes that are financed with government-backed loans (such as FHA or VA loans) must meet minimum construction standards set by HUD. Some of these standards may be stricter than the state building codes.

IN PRACTICE North Carolina uniform building codes are subject to change periodically as are HUD minimum standards. A broker working with a buyer who wants to obtain FHA and/or VA financing should always check to ensure that the property meets both standards before an offer to purchase containing provisions for FHA or VA financing is presented to a seller.

Contractor Licensing

In North Carolina

In North Carolina, anyone who contracts to construct a building for others that costs more than $30,000 must obtain a general contractor's license from the state. Different classifications of licenses exist for different types of construction. For example, single-family home construction requires a residential building classification.

■ RELATED WEBSITE

North Carolina Department of Insurance: www.ncdoi.com

■ KEY POINT REVIEW

Most economical house style to build is a two-story house.

The lowest member of the house is the **footing** or the footprint of the house. **Foundation wall** and **piers** support the flooring system.

Three foundation types in North Carolina include **crawl space, basement,** or **concrete slab**.

Framing is the skeleton of the building:

- Floor framing includes the **sill** (lowest horizontal wooden member of framing), **floor joists, girders,** and **subfloor**
- Wall framing includes **studs** (usually 16 or 24 inches apart), **sole plate, top plate,** and **headers**
- Roof framing includes **ceiling joists, rafters, ridge boards** (the highest part of construction), **eaves, fascia board, soffit,** and **frieze board**

Exterior walls have **sheathing** and **siding**. Doors and windows provide ventilation and light. Window components include the sill, the jamb, the header, the sash, and the muntins and mullions.

Roofing materials include decking, roofing felt and **shingles. Pitch** tells the slope or steepness of the roof. The most popular roof style in North Carolina is the gable roof.

Insulation's **R-value** indicates the level of heat resistance. Many homes use a dual system for **HVAC**.

State-wide **building codes** set minimum safety standards for construction. A **certificate of occupancy** must be issued before any structure can be occupied. Unpermitted construction or remodeling is a material fact due to safety and insurability issues.

A general contractor's license is required in North Carolina for building a structure for others that costs more than $30,000.

QUESTIONS

1. R-value refers to
   a. resistance to the transfer of heat. ✓
   b. resistance to termite infestation.
   c. reduction in construction costs.
   d. high-end residential zoning.

2. Pressure-treated lumber is used
   a. to improve the appearance of a home.
   b. to help prevent termite infestation. ✓
   c. to increase the R-value.
   d. for moisture resistance in bathrooms.

3. The vertical framing member of a wall is a
   a. sole plate.
   b. girder.
   c. joist.
   d. stud. ✓

4. Based on the cost per square foot of living space, which of the following is the most economical house design?
   a. Split-level
   b. One-story
   c. Two-story ✓
   d. Tri-level

5. The most common roof style in North Carolina is
   a. hip.
   b. gambrel.
   c. gable. ✓
   d. mansard.

6. The foundation wall rests on top of the
   a. footing. ✓
   b. sill.
   c. girder.
   d. floor joist.

7. A certificate of occupancy is required
   I. from the local building department.
   II. before anyone can move into a home.
   a. I only
   b. II only
   c. Both I and II ✓
   d. Neither I nor II

8. The lowest wooden part of residential construction is the
   a. sill. ✓
   b. foundation wall.
   c. footing.
   d. ridge board.

9. The highest part of the frame construction is the
   a. soffit.
   b. rafter.
   c. ridge board. ✓
   d. ceiling joist.

10. The following are components of an eave EXCEPT the
    a. soffit.
    b. fascia board.
    c. header. ✓
    d. frieze board.

CHAPTER 17

Real Property Valuation

■ **LEARNING OBJECTIVES** *When you have finished reading this chapter, you should be able to*

- ■ **explain** the concepts and types of value, how value may be used, value-in-exchange and value-in-use.
- ■ **give** examples of the basic economic principles of value.
- ■ **explain** the steps in the appraisal process and the three basic valuation approaches used by appraisers.
- ■ **describe** the three types of depreciation and the concepts of effective age and economic life.
- ■ **define** these *key terms*:

age-life method
appraisal
arm's-length transaction
broker price opinion (BPO)
capitalization rate
comparable (comp)
comparative market analysis (CMA)
cost approach
depreciation
economic life

economic obsolescence
effective age
functional obsolescence
gross rent multiplier (GRM)
highest and best use
income capitalization approach
net operating income (NOI)
physical deterioration
quantity-survey method

reconciliation
replacement cost
reproduction cost
sales comparison approach
square-foot method
straight-line method
substitution
unit-in-place method
value

Chapter 17   Real Property Valuation   **389**

■ APPRAISING

[Handwritten margin note: As agents, we cannot perform an "appraisal", we generate a probable sales price after doing a Competitive market analysis]

An **appraisal** is an estimate or opinion of value, completed by a licensed appraiser, of a specific property as of a specific date. Appraisal reports are relied on in important decisions made by mortgage lenders, investors, public utilities, government agencies, businesses, and individuals.

The highest level of appraisal activity is conducted by skilled professionals. However, everyone engaged in the real estate business, even those who are not experts in appraisal, must possess at least a fundamental knowledge of real estate valuation. In the appraisal of residential real estate, a person familiar with the market in a given neighborhood could try to make a quick judgment of market values, but this is not an appraisal and should not be considered particularly reliable and useful.

To conduct a formal appraisal that can be used in federally related transactions, appraisers must be licensed by the state. *Certified residential appraisers* usually appraise residential properties; *certified general appraisers* typically appraise commercial properties. Note that appraisers are paid a fee, not a commission. The fee is based on the complexity of the appraisal and the length of time necessary to complete it. The fee never should be based on a percentage of the appraised value of the property.

In North Carolina

The Financial Institutions Reform, Recovery and Enforcement Act of 1989 (FIRREA) was passed by Congress for the primary purpose of overhauling regulations of the thrift industry. However, a major portion of this Act was for the regulation of appraisers performing appraisals for federally related loan transactions. This Act established many federal agencies charged with the task of setting appraisal standards and minimum qualification requirements. The Appraisal Qualifications Board sets qualification standards and requirements for state-certified appraisers. The Appraisal Standards Board sets minimum standards of practice. In North Carolina, appraisers are licensed and certified through the North Carolina Appraisal Board after meeting minimum education and experience requirements and passing state examinations. The licensed appraiser need not have a real estate license to perform a real estate appraisal.

In North Carolina

Informal estimate of value by real estate brokers. As an exception to the North Carolina Appraisers Act, NCGS 93E, licensed real estate brokers are allowed to perform a comparative market analysis (which will be discussed later in this chapter) as long as they do not in any way represent themselves as a real estate appraiser. Brokers have historically been compensated only for completing a comparative market analysis (CMA) for prospective or current brokerage clients. The Act defines a CMA as "… the analysis of sales of similar recently sold properties in order to derive an indication of the *probable sales price* of a particular property *by a licensed real estate broker.*" In the North Carolina Real Estate Manual, brokers are cautioned to never refer to their estimate of value as an *appraisal* and to consider making some clarifying statement about it being an informal estimate of probable sales price and not to be confused with an appraisal.

Due to the increased need for opinions of value by lienholders of distressed properties in the aftermath of the real estate industry crisis in 2007, many real estate brokers were enticed to perform **broker price opinions (BPOs)** for entities that had no potential of becoming legitimate real estate brokerage clients, which were illegal at that time. Despite strong resistance from the NCREC and the North Carolina Appraisal Board, the 2012 North Carolina General Assembly enacted amendments to both the North Carolina Real Estate License Law and the North Carolina Appraisal Act that now allows North Carolina real estate brokers to provide BPOs for a fee to nonbrokerage clients. The authorization in the license law and the NCREC rules for such activity must be read together to fully understand the stipulations for full compliance with the law. Only full brokers (nonprovisional) may perform a BPO or CMA (terms are synonymous per statute) for a fee as long as the BPO is not intended to determine value of a property for the purpose of originating a mortgage loan or any purpose where an appraisal is required by law. A BPO must be in writing and must contain all the contents required by law. Please note that the NCREC does not consider a CMA performed for general brokerage services by full or provisional brokers to constitute a "fee" as defined by the statute.

VALUE

Value is an abstract word with many acceptable definitions. In a broad sense, **value** may be defined as the relationship between an object desired and a potential purchaser. It is the power of a good or service to command other goods or services in exchange. In terms of real estate appraisal, value may be described as *the present worth of future benefits arising from the ownership of real property.*

> The four characteristics of value may be remembered by the acronym *DUST*: **D**emand, **U**tility, **S**carcity, and **T**ransferability.

For a property to have value in the real estate market, it must have four characteristics, which can be remembered by the acronym DUST:

1. *Demand*—the need or desire for possession or ownership backed by the financial means to satisfy that need
2. *Utility*—the capacity to satisfy future owners' needs and desires; how future owners can make good use of the property
3. *Scarcity*—a finite supply
4. *Transferability*—the relative ease of transfer of ownership rights from one person to another; often relates to clear title and satisfactory physical condition

Market Value

Even though a given parcel of real estate may have many different kinds of value at the same time, such as insurance value, assessed value, et cetera, generally the goal of an appraiser is to estimate *market value*. The market value of real estate is the most probable price that a property will bring in a competitive and open market, allowing a reasonable time to find a purchaser who buys the property with knowledge of all the uses to which it is adapted and for which it is capable of being used. Included in this definition are the following key points:

- Market value is the *most probable* price a property will bring.
- Payment must be made in *cash* or its equivalent.
- Buyer and seller must act without *undue pressure*.

- A *reasonable length of time* must be allowed for the property to be exposed in the open market.
- Both buyer and seller must be *well informed* of the property's use and potential, including its assets and defects.

> *Market value* is a reasonable opinion of a property's value; *market price* is the actual selling price of a property; *cost* may not equal either market value or market price.

Market value versus market price. Market value is an opinion of value based on an analysis of data that may include not only an analysis of comparable sales but also an analysis of potential income, expenses, and replacement costs (less depreciation). *Market price*, on the other hand, is what a property *actually* sells for—its sales price. Theoretically, the market price should be the same as the market value. Market price can be taken as accurate evidence of current market value, but only if the conditions essential to market value exist. However, the market price may not be indicative of market value. There are circumstances under which a property may be sold below market value, as when the seller is forced to sell quickly or when a sale is arranged between relatives.

Market value versus cost. An important distinction exists between market value and cost. Cost represents past expenditures on the property: what the owner has spent on the property. One of the most common misconceptions about valuing property is that cost represents market value. Cost and market value may be equal and often are when the improvements on a property are new. But more often, cost does not equal market value.

■ **FOR EXAMPLE** Two homes are identical in every respect, except that one is located on a street with heavy traffic and the other is on a quiet residential street. The value of the former may be less than that of the latter, although the cost of each may be exactly the same. Another example is a homeowner who installs a swimming pool at a cost of $15,000; however, the cost of the improvement may not add $15,000 to the value of the property.

Forces and Factors Influencing Property Value

Four forces affect property values:

1. *Social forces.* Social forces that affect property values include trends in marriage and divorce rates, family size and longevity, and desirability of social activities.
2. *Economic forces.* Economic forces include income and employment levels, the rate of property taxation, current interest rates, and general economic growth.
3. *Political forces.* Political forces include government activities such as zoning and building codes, growth management, environmental legislation, and tax structures.
4. *Physical forces.* Physical forces that affect property values include topography, location, climate, size, shape, proximity to major arterials, jobs, and public transportation.

Basic Economic Principles of Value

A number of economic principles affect the value of real estate. The most important of these principles are defined in the following paragraphs.

Highest and best use. The most profitable single use to which a property is adapted and for which it is needed, or the use that is likely to be in demand in the reasonably near future, is its **highest and best use**. Highest and best use is noted in every appraisal but also may be the object of a more extensive analysis. For example, a highest-and-best-use study may show that a parking lot in a busy downtown area or a farm surrounded by urbanized land is not the highest and best use of the property. Note that there can be only one highest and best use at any given time. Highest and best use is subject to change—the highest and best use of a property today may not be the highest and best use of the same property five years from now.

Substitution. The principle of **substitution** states when several items with essentially the same amenities and utilities are available, the item with the lowest price will attract the most demand. In other words, a consumer will purchase what is perceived to be the best buy for the money. This principle is the cornerstone of the sales comparison approach to value (discussed in detail later). For example, if house A and house B are equally desirable properties with similar assets and house A is selling for $160,000 and house B is selling for $170,000, virtually every buyer will choose house A.

Supply and demand. This principle states that the value of a property will change if the supply decreases and the demand either increases or remains constant—and vice versa. For example, the last lot to be sold in a residential area where the demand for homes is high would probably be worth more than the first lot sold in that area, assuming normal economic conditions exist. Supply and demand in real estate is sometimes referenced as being in a *buyer's market* or a *seller's market*.

Conformity. *Conformity* means that maximum value is realized if the use of land conforms to existing neighborhood standards. In residential areas of single-family houses, for example, buildings should be similar in design, construction, size, and age. Subdivision protective covenants rely on the principle of conformity to ensure maximum future value. Building a home that is significantly bigger than surrounding houses violates the principle of conformity. This mistake is commonly referred to as *overbuilding the neighborhood*.

Anticipation. This principle holds that value can increase or decrease *in anticipation* of some future benefit or detriment affecting the property. For example, the value of a house could be affected by rumors that an adjacent parcel may be converted to some different use in the near future. In other words, current value is being affected by future possibilities whether based on fact or rumor.

Contribution. This principle affirms that the value of any component of a property is defined by what its addition *contributes* to the value of the whole or what its absence detracts from that value. For example, the cost of installing an air-conditioning system and remodeling an older office building may be greater than is justified by the increase in market value (a function of expected net increases) that may result from the improvement to the property. In residential properties an owner sometimes will make a super-improvement such as installing solid mahogany kitchen cabinets. While these cabinets may be quite attractive, the average buyer will not pay for the added cost of this *overimprovement*.

Competition. This principle states that profits tend to attract competition. For example, the success of a retail store may motivate investors to open similar stores in the area. This tends to mean less profit for all stores concerned unless the purchasing power in the area increases substantially. Note that excess profit tends to attract ruinous competition.

Change. No physical or economic condition remains constant. Real estate is subject to natural phenomena, such as tornadoes, fires, and routine wear and tear of the elements. The real estate business also is subject to the changing demands of its market, as is any business. It is an appraiser's job to study the past to be better able to predict the effects of natural phenomena and the behavior of the marketplace in the future. Appraisers must also be sensitive to the stage of progression within the *neighborhood life cycle*. Most residential neighborhoods go through four phases of the cycle of change: growth, stability, decline, and renewal. The area's position within the *life cycle* will affect value.

■ THE APPRAISAL PROCESS

The key to an accurate appraisal lies in the methodical collection of data. The appraisal process is an orderly set of procedures used to collect and analyze data to arrive at an ultimate value conclusion. The data are divided into two basic classes:

1. *Specific data*, covering details of the subject property (the property that is being appraised) and including comparative data relating to costs, sales, and income and expenses of properties similar to and competitive with the subject property.
2. *General data*, covering the nation, region, city, and neighborhood. Of particular importance is the neighborhood, where an appraiser finds the physical, economic, social, and political influences that directly affect the value and potential of the subject property.

The steps an appraiser takes in carrying out an appraisal assignment are as follows:

1. *State the problem.* The kind of value to be estimated must be specified, and the valuation approach(es) most valid and reliable for the kind of property under appraisal must be selected.
2. *List the data needed and the sources.* Based on the approach(es) the appraiser will be using, the types of data needed, and the sources to be consulted are listed.
3. *Gather, record, and verify the necessary data.* Specific data about the subject site and improvements must be collected and verified. Depending on the appraisal approach(es) used, comparative information relating to sales, income, expenses, and construction costs of comparable properties must be collected.
4. *Determine the highest and best use.* The appraiser analyzes market forces such as competition and current versus potential uses to determine the reasonableness of the property's present use in terms of its profitability.
5. *Estimate the land value.* The features and sales prices of comparable sites are compared with the subject property to determine the value of the land alone. Neither the cost nor the income approach can be used to estimate land value.

6. *Estimate the value by each of the three approaches.* The sales comparison, cost, and income capitalization approaches are used to estimate the value of the subject property.
7. *Reconcile the estimated values for the final value estimate.* The appraiser makes a definite statement of conclusions reached, usually in the form of a value estimate of the property. Note that the three approaches are never simply averaged.
8. *Report the final value estimate.* After the three approaches have been reconciled and an opinion of value has been reached, the appraiser prepares a formal written report for the client. All information used to estimate the value of a property should be included in this report. A complete appraisal report should

- identify the real estate and real property interest being appraised;
- state the purpose and intended use of the appraisal;
- define the value to be estimated;
- state the effective date of the value and the date of the report;
- describe the process of collecting, confirming, and reporting the data;
- list all assumptions and limiting conditions that affect the analysis, opinion, and conclusions of value;
- describe the information considered, the appraisal procedures followed, and the reasoning that supports the report's conclusions (if an approach was excluded, the report should explain why);
- describe (if necessary or appropriate) the appraiser's opinion of the highest and best use of the real estate;
- describe any additional information that may be appropriate in order to show compliance with specific guidelines established in the Uniform Standards of Professional Appraisal Practice (USPAP) or to clearly identify and explain any departures from these guidelines; and
- include a signed certification, as required by the Uniform Standards.

IN PRACTICE The role of the appraiser is not to determine value. Rather, an appraiser develops a supportable and objective report about the value of the subject property. The appraiser relies on experience and expertise in valuation theories to evaluate market data. The appraiser does not establish the property's worth but instead verifies what the market indicates. This is important to remember, particularly when dealing with a property owner who may lack objectivity about the realistic value of the property. The lack of objectivity also can complicate a broker's ability to list the property within the most probable range of market value. Brokers are cautioned against listing property at a price that is so unreasonably high that it is unlikely the property will be shown or sold.

Many lenders and federal agencies have their own form reports. One of the most frequently used is the Fannie Mae Form 1004, Uniform Residential Appraisal Report; only the first three pages are shown in Figure 17.1, since the rest of the form is just instructions for the form's use. This form is required by many government agencies. The major sections of this form are as follows:

- *Subject:* identification of the property being appraised
- *Neighborhood:* information showing boundaries, characteristics, and market conditions
- *Site:* information on lot dimensions, utilities, topography, off-site improvements, easements, flood conditions, etc.

FIGURE 17.1

Uniform Residential Appraisal Report

Uniform Residential Appraisal Report   File

The purpose of this summary appraisal report is to provide the lender/client with an accurate, and adequately supported, opinion of the market value of the subject property.

SUBJECT

Field	Value
Property Address	4807 Catalpa Road
City	Woodview
State	IL
Zip Code	60000
Borrower	
Owner of Public Record	
County	Dakota
Legal Description	attached to this report
Assessor's Parcel #	
Tax Year	
R.E. Taxes $	2,278
Neighborhood Name	
Map Reference	
Census Tract	
Occupant	[X] Owner [ ] Tenant [ ] Vacant
Special Assessments $	
[ ] PUD	HOA $ [ ] per year [ ] per month
Property Rights Appraised	[X] Fee Simple [ ] Leasehold [ ] Other (describe)
Assignment Type	[ ] Purchase Transaction [ ] Refinance Transaction [ ] Other (describe)
Lender/Client	Address

Is the subject property currently offered for sale or has it been offered for sale in the twelve months prior to the effective date of this appraisal? [X] Yes [ ] No
Report data source(s) used, offering price(s), and date(s).

CONTRACT

I [ ] did [ ] did not analyze the contract for sale for the subject purchase transaction. Explain the results of the analysis of the contract for sale or why the analysis was not performed.

Contract Price $ ___ Date of Contract ___ Is the property seller the owner of public record? [ ] Yes [ ] No Data Source(s)
Is there any financial assistance (loan charges, sale concessions, gift or downpayment assistance, etc.) to be paid by any party on behalf of the borrower? [ ] Yes [ ] No
If Yes, report the total dollar amount and describe the items to be paid.

NEIGHBORHOOD

Note: Race and the racial composition of the neighborhood are not appraisal factors.

Neighborhood Characteristics	One-Unit Housing Trends	One-Unit Housing	Present Land Use %
Location [ ] Urban [X] Suburban [ ] Rural	Property Values [X] Increasing [ ] Stable [ ] Declining	PRICE / AGE	One-Unit 100 %
Built-Up [X] Over 75% [ ] 25–75% [ ] Under 25%	Demand/Supply [ ] Shortage [X] In Balance [ ] Over Supply	$ (000) (yrs)	2-4 Unit %
Growth [ ] Rapid [X] Stable [ ] Slow	Marketing Time [X] Under 3 mths [ ] 3–6 mths [ ] Over 6 mths	Low	Multi-Family %
Neighborhood Boundaries Boundaries are shown on attached map		High	Commercial %
		Pred.	Other %

Neighborhood Description   Subject property is located in a desirable subdivision in the Central Eastern section of the Village of Woodview. Schools, shopping, and other necessary facilities and services are within a reasonable distance.

Market Conditions (including support for the above conclusions)   Steady demand for housing with a gradual uptrend in values reflects a relatively healthy local economy. Conventional financing readily available with interest rates at 6% to 8%. The desirability of this neighborhood is reflected by the fact that most homes are sold within 2 months of being put on the market.

SITE

Field	Value
Dimensions	65' × 130'
Area	8,450 squre feet
Shape	rectangular
View	tree-lined st/typical
Specific Zoning Classification	R-2
Zoning Description	Single-family residence

Zoning Compliance [X] Legal [ ] Legal Nonconforming (Grandfathered Use) [ ] No Zoning [ ] Illegal (describe)
Is the highest and best use of the subject property as improved (or as proposed per plans and specifications) the present use? [X] Yes [ ] No If No, describe

Utilities	Public	Other (describe)		Public	Other (describe)	Off-site Improvements—Type	Public	Private
Electricity	[X]	[ ]	Water	[X]	[ ]	Street	[X]	[ ]
Gas	[X]	[ ]	Sanitary Sewer	[X]	[ ]	Alley	[ ]	[ ]

FEMA Special Flood Hazard Area [ ] Yes [X] No   FEMA Flood Zone   FEMA Map #   FEMA Map Date
Are the utilities and off-site improvements typical for the market area? [X] Yes [ ] No If No, describe
Are there any adverse site conditions or external factors (easements, encroachments, environmental conditions, land uses, etc.)? [ ] Yes [X] No If Yes, describe
Underground electric and telephone lines; no easements or encroachments

IMPROVEMENTS

General Description	Foundation	Exterior Description materials/condition	Interior materials/condition
Units [X] One [ ] One with Accessory Unit	[ ] Concrete Slab [X] Crawl Space	Foundation Walls Concrete/gd	Floors Vinyl/cpt/oak/gd
# of Stories 1	[ ] Full Basement [ ] Partial Basement	Exterior Walls Brick veneer/gd	Walls Drywall/paint/gd
Type [ ] Det. [ ] Att. [ ] S-Det/End Unit	Basement Area sq. ft.	Roof Surface Asphlt.shingle/gd	Trim/Finish Wood/Avg
[X] Existing [ ] Proposed [ ] Under Const.	Basement Finish %	Gutters & Downspouts Galv./paint/gd	Bath Floor Ceram/gd
Design (Style) Ranch	[ ] Outside Entry/Exit [ ] Sump Pump	Window Type Wood double-hung/gd	Bath Wainscot Ceram/gd
Year Built 25 years ago	Evidence of [ ] Infestation	Storm Sash/Insulated Comb.alum/gd	Car Storage [ ] None
Effective Age (Yrs) 15	[ ] Dampness [ ] Settlement	Screens Comb.alum/gd	[X] Driveway # of Cars 2
Attic [ ] None	Heating [X] FWA [ ] HWBB [ ] Radiant	Amenities [ ] Woodstove(s) #	Driveway Surface Asphalt
[X] Drop Stair [ ] Stairs	[ ] Other Fuel	[ ] Fireplace(s) # [ ] Fence	[X] Garage # of Cars
[ ] Floor [ ] Scuttle	Cooling [X] Central Air Conditioning	[ ] Patio/Deck [ ] Porch	[ ] Carport # of Cars
[ ] Finished [ ] Heated	[ ] Individual [ ] Other	[ ] Pool [ ] Other	[ ] Att. [X] Det. [ ] Built-in

Appliances [X] Refrigerator [X] Range/Oven [X] Dishwasher [X] Disposal [ ] Microwave [ ] Washer/Dryer [X] Other (describe) Oven fan/hood
Finished area **above** grade contains: 7 Rooms   3 Bedrooms   2.00 Bath(s)   1,950 Square Feet of Gross Living Area Above Grade
Additional features (special energy efficient items, etc.)   6" insulation above ceiling and behind drywall; 6' redwood fence around rear yard.

Describe the condition of the property (including needed repairs, deterioration, renovations, remodeling, etc.).   Overall, house and garage are in good shape with normal wear and tear indicating 25% depreciation. There is no evidence of functional or external obsolescence.

Are there any physical deficiencies or adverse conditions that affect the livability, soundness, or structural integrity of the property? [ ] Yes [X] No If Yes, describe
No detrimental influences.

Does the property generally conform to the neighborhood (functional utility, style, condition, use, construction, etc.)? [X] Yes [ ] No If No, describe

Freddie Mac Form 70   March 2005   Fannie Mae Form 1004   March 2005

FIGURE 17.1

Uniform Residential Appraisal Report (cont.)

Uniform Residential Appraisal Report

File #

There are 2 comparable properties currently offered for sale in the subject neighborhood ranging in price from $ 178,90.00 to $ 184,500.00.
There are 5 comparable sales in the subject neighborhood within the past twelve months ranging in sale price from $ 152,000.00 to $ 186,240.00.

FEATURE	SUBJECT	COMPARABLE SALE #1	COMPARABLE SALE #2	COMPARABLE SALE #3
Address	4807 Catalpa Road	4310 W. Gladys	3840 W. Monroe	316 Iowa
Proximity to Subject				
Sale Price	$	$ 177,750	$ 180,000	$ 186,240
Sale Price/Gross Liv. Area	$ sq. ft.	$ 90.00 sq. ft.	$ 92.31 sq. ft.	$ 96.00 sq. ft.
Data Source(s)				
Verification Source(s)				
VALUE ADJUSTMENTS	DESCRIPTION	DESCRIPTION / +(-) $ Adjustment	DESCRIPTION / +(-) $ Adjustment	DESCRIPTION / +(-) $ Adjustment
Sale or Financing Concessions		conventional	conventional	conventional
Date of Sale/Time		6 wks. ago	3 wks. ago	6 wks. ago
Location	Suburban	quiet res.	quiet res.	quiet res.
Leasehold/Fee Simple	fee simple	fee simple	fee simple	fee simple
Site	8,450 sq. ft.	65' × 130'	65' × 130'	65' × 130'
View	good/street	good/street	good/street	good/street
Design (Style)	ranch	ranch	ranch	ranch
Quality of Construction	good	good	good	good
Actual Age	25 yrs.	25 yrs.	25 yrs.	25 yrs.
Condition	good	good	good	good
Above Grade Room Count	Total 7 / Bdrms. 3 / Baths 2	Total 7 / Bdrms. 3 / Baths 2	Total 7 / Bdrms. 3 / Baths 2	Total 7 / Bdrms. 3 / Baths 2
Gross Living Area	1,950 sq. ft.	1,975 sq. ft.	1,950 sq. ft.	1,940 sq. ft.
Basement & Finished Rooms Below Grade	crawlspace	crawlspace	crawlspace	finished basement / −10,000
Functional Utility	adequate	adequate	adequate	adequate
Heating/Cooling	central h/a	central h/a	central h/a	central h/a
Energy Efficient Items	extra insulation	equal	equal	equal
Garage/Carport	2-car detached	2-car detached	2-car detached	2-car detached
Porch/Patio/Deck				
Fireplace	masonry	none / +5,000	masonry	masonry
Fence	fence	fence	fence	fence
Net Adjustment (Total)		☒ + ☐ − $ 5,000	☐ + ☐ − $	☐ + ☒ − $ −10,000
Adjusted Sale Price of Comparables		Net Adj. 2.80 % / Gross Adj. 2.80 % $ 182,750	Net Adj. % / Gross Adj. % $ 180,000	Net Adj. −5.40 % / Gross Adj. 5.40 % $ 176,240

☒ did ☐ did not research the sale or transfer history of the subject property and comparable sales. If not, explain

My research ☐ did ☒ did not reveal any prior sales or transfers of the subject property for the three years prior to the effective date of this appraisal.
Data source(s)   County tax assessor
My research ☐ did ☒ did not reveal any prior sales or transfers of the comparable sales for the year prior to the date of sale of the comparable sale.
Data source(s)   County tax assessor
Report the results of the research and analysis of the prior sale or transfer history of the subject property and comparable sales (report additional prior sales on page 3).

ITEM	SUBJECT	COMPARABLE SALE #1	COMPARABLE SALE #2	COMPARABLE SALE #3
Date of Prior Sale/Transfer				
Price of Prior Sale/Transfer				
Data Source(s)				
Effective Date of Data Source(s)				

Analysis of prior sale or transfer history of the subject property and comparable sales

Summary of Sales Comparison Approach

Indicated Value by Sales Comparison Approach $ 180,000
Indicated Value by: Sales Comparison Approach $ 180,000   Cost Approach (if developed) $ Income Approach (if developed) $ 169,000

This appraisal is made ☒ "as is", ☐ subject to completion per plans and specifications on the basis of a hypothetical condition that the improvements have been completed, ☐ subject to the following repairs or alterations on the basis of a hypothetical condition that the repairs or alterations have been completed, or ☐ subject to the following required inspection based on the extraordinary assumption that the condition or deficiency does not require alteration or repair:

Based on a complete visual inspection of the interior and exterior areas of the subject property, defined scope of work, statement of assumptions and limiting conditions, and appraiser's certification, my (our) opinion of the market value, as defined, of the real property that is the subject of this report is
$, as of   , which is the date of inspection and the effective date of this appraisal.

Freddie Mac Form 70   March 2005   Fannie Mae Form 1004   March 2005

FIGURE 17.1

Uniform Residential Appraisal Report (cont.)

Uniform Residential Appraisal Report   File

ADDITIONAL COMMENTS

COST APPROACH TO VALUE (not required by Fannie Mae)

Provide adequate information for the lender/client to replicate the below cost figures and calculations.
Support for the opinion of site value (summary of comparable land sales or other methods for estimating site value)

ESTIMATED [X] REPRODUCTION OR [ ] REPLACEMENT COST NEW	OPINION OF SITE VALUE .... =$ 45,000
Source of cost data	Dwelling 1,950 Sq. Ft. @ $ 90 ......=$ 175,500
Quality rating from cost service Effective date of cost data	Sq. Ft. @ $ ......=$
Comments on Cost Approach (gross living area calculations, depreciation, etc.)	Extra insulation 1,200
Depreciation based on normal wear and tear for well-maintained	Garage/Carport 500 Sq. Ft. @ $ 30 ......=$ 15,000
property with effective age of 15 years.	Total Estimate of Cost-New ......=$ 191,700
	Less Physical Functional External
	Depreciation 47,925 =$(47,925)
	Depreciated Cost of Improvements................=$ 143,775
	"As-is" Value of Site Improvements................=$ 8,400
Estimated Remaining Economic Life (HUD and VA only) Years	Indicated Value By Cost Approach ....=$ 197,175

INCOME APPROACH TO VALUE (not required by Fannie Mae)

Estimated Monthly Market Rent $ 1,300   X Gross Rent Multiplier   130 = $ 169,000   Indicated Value by Income Approach
Summary of Income Approach (including support for market rent and GRM)   Comparable home sales prices/monthly rental income:
$160,000/$1,200; $166,500/$1,275; $173,500/$1,300.

PROJECT INFORMATION FOR PUDs (if applicable)

Is the developer/builder in control of the Homeowners' Association (HOA)? [ ] Yes [ ] No   Unit type(s) [ ] Detached [ ] Attached
Provide the following information for PUDs ONLY if the developer/builder is in control of the HOA and the subject property is an attached dwelling unit.
Legal name of project
Total number of phases   Total number of units   Total number of units sold
Total number of units rented   Total number of units for sale   Data source(s)
Was the project created by the conversion of an existing building(s) into a PUD? [ ] Yes [ ] No   If Yes, date of conversion
Does the project contain any multi-dwelling units? [ ] Yes [ ] No Data source(s)
Are the units, common elements, and recreation facilities complete? [ ] Yes [ ] No   If No, describe the status of completion.

Are the common elements leased to or by the Homeowners' Association? [ ] Yes [ ] No   If Yes, describe the rental terms and options.

Describe common elements and recreational facilities

Freddie Mac Form 70   March 2005   Fannie Mae Form 1004   March 2005

- *Description of improvements:* general descriptions, exterior, interior, foundation, effective age, etc.
- *Comments:* additional features, condition of improvements, and adverse environmental conditions
- *Cost approach:* showing applicable estimates derived from the cost approach
- *Sales comparison analysis:* showing three comparables and adjustments and estimated value derived from the sales comparison approach
- *Indicated value by the income approach*
- *Reconciliation:* showing the final estimate of value, the date of the estimate, signatures, and license numbers of the appraisers

■ APPROACHES TO VALUE (APPRAISAL METHODS)

To arrive at an accurate estimate of value, three basic approaches, or techniques, are traditionally used by appraisers:

1. The sales comparison approach
2. The cost approach
3. The income capitalization approach

Each method, when completed independently, serves as a check against the others and narrows the range within which the final estimate of value will fall. Generally, each method is considered most reliable for specific types of property.

The Sales Comparison Approach

The Sales Comparison Approach
1. Date of sale
2. Location
3. Physical features
4. Terms and conditions of sale

In the **sales comparison approach,** also known as the *market data approach*, an estimate of value is obtained by comparing the subject property (the property under appraisal) with recently sold comparable properties (properties similar to the subject). This approach is most often used in valuing single-family homes and land. Because no two parcels of real estate are exactly alike, each comparable property must be compared with the subject property, and the sales prices of the comparables must be adjusted for any dissimilar features. The principal factors for which adjustments must be made fall into four basic categories:

1. *Date of sale.* An adjustment must be made if economic changes occur between the date of sale of a comparable property and the date of the appraisal.
2. *Location.* An adjustment may be necessary to compensate for location differences. For example, similar properties might differ in price from neighborhood to neighborhood or even within the same neighborhood.
3. *Physical features.* Physical features that may require adjustment include age of building, size of lot, landscaping, construction, number of rooms, square feet of living space, interior and exterior condition, presence or absence of a garage, a fireplace or an air conditioner, and so forth.
4. *Terms and conditions of sale.* This consideration becomes important if a sale is not financed with a standard mortgage. Be sure that the sale was an **arm's-length transaction**, which means that the property did not sell for an unusually high or low price because of a special relationship between the buyer and seller. An example would be a low-price sale between a parent and child.

Selecting Comparables

First and foremost, the **comparables**, sometimes called *comps*, selected should be as similar to the subject property as possible, and should have been recently sold (preferably within the past 120 days) in an open and competitive market, under typical market conditions, when the seller and buyer are well informed and are not acting under undue pressure. Please note that the acceptable age of comps is greatly dependent upon the degree of change in the market condition within a particular local area. For example, in markets where prices have been very stable for a long period of time, a comparable that has closed within 12–15 months may be acceptable. However, in markets where there have been drastic increases or decreases in market conditions, a more recent comp no older than six months may be more appropriate. Nontypical conditions may involve seller financing; an estate sale; a buyer under pressure to buy quickly because of school, business, or family pressure; and so forth. An important point to remember is this: *the more similar the comparable is, the more recently sold, and the fewer adjustments that are required, the more reliable the estimate of value will be*. To have a reliable estimate of value, at least three similar comparable properties should be located.

Historically when searching for closed properties to use as comparables for an appraisal or CMA, any transaction under duress (e.g., short sale, pre-foreclosure, or foreclosure) was immediately discarded. Due to the pervasive presence of such transactions in the real estate market during the last few years, such distressed transactions can no longer be ignored as value indicators. In many subdivisions, the sales of foreclosed, bank-owned (REO) properties or short-sale transactions are the only comparables. In numerous scenarios, appraisers are being instructed that they must use at least one foreclosure or short-sale comparable to yield a true indication of the market value. For many transactions in the last few years, distressed properties truly are the competition that vies for every buyer's attention. Obviously if there are very few or no distressed sales in the area around a subject property, there is no mandate to import the value of a noncomparable property.

After a careful analysis of the differences between comparable properties and the subject property, the appraiser assigns a dollar value to each of the major differences. On the basis of the appraiser's knowledge and experience, the appraiser estimates dollar adjustments that reflect actual values assigned in the marketplace. The value of a feature present in the subject property but not in a comparable property is *added to the comparable property's total sales price*. This presumes that, all other features being equal, a property having a feature (such as a fireplace or wet bar) not present in a comparable property would tend to have a higher market value solely because of this feature. (The feature need not be a physical amenity; it may be locational or aesthetic.) Likewise, the value of a feature present in a comparable but not in the subject property *is subtracted from the comparable property's total sales price*. Remember, *all adjustments are made to the sales prices of the comparables, not to that of the subject property*. It must be stressed that a variable is adjusted by value in the marketplace and not by cost. For example, a fireplace may add less value to a dwelling than the actual cost of creating it. If the comparable property has a feature that is *inferior* to the subject, the appraiser will make a *positive* adjustment to the value of the comparable. Conversely, if the comparable property has a feature that is *superior* to the subject a *negative* adjustment will be made to the value of the comparable. Remember to *never* adjust the value of the subject.

==The adjusted sales prices of the comparables represent the probable value range of the subject property.== The appraiser then *correlates* the adjusted sales prices of the comparables to determine a single market value estimate for the subject property. The correlation is the result of a *weighted averaging process*; never use simple averaging of the adjusted sales prices. The comparable that is most similar to the subject property is given more weight than the other comparables when calculating the single estimate of value.

The sales comparison approach is essential in almost every appraisal of real estate. It is considered the most reliable of the three approaches in appraising residential property, where the amenities (intangible benefits) may be difficult to measure. The most difficult time to employ the sales comparison approach occurs when there are no comparable sales. Brokers may want to use the services of a licensed appraiser for any property for which it is difficult to establish an asking price. An example of the sales comparison approach is shown in Figure 17.2.

FIGURE 17.2

Sales Comparison Approach to Value

	Subject Property: 155 Potter Dr.	A	B	C	D	E
Sales price		$118,000	$112,000	$121,000	$116,500	$110,000
Financing concessions	none	none	none	none	none	none
Date of sale		current	current	current	current	current
Location	good	same	poorer + 6,500	same	same	same
Age	6 years	same	same	same	same	same
Size of lot	60' × 135'	same	same	larger – 5,000	same	larger – 5,000
Landscaping	good	same	same	same	same	same
Construction	brick	same	same	same	same	same
Style	ranch	same	same	same	same	same
No. of rooms	6	same	same	same	same	same
No. of bedrooms	3	same	same	same	same	same
No. of baths	1½	same	same	same	same	same
Sq. ft. of living space	1,500	same	same	same	same	same
Other space (basement)	full basement	same	same	same	same	same
Condition—exterior	average	better – 1,500	poorer + 1,000	better – 1,500	same	poorer + 2,000
Condition—interior	good	same	same	better – 500	same	same
Garage	2-car attached	same	same	same	same	none + 5,000
Other improvements	none	none	none	none	none	none
Net Adjustments		– 1,500	+ 7,500	– 7,000	-0-	+ 2,000
Adjusted Value		$116,500	$119,500	$114,000	$116,500	$112,000

Note: The value of a feature that is present in the subject but not in the comparable property is added to the sales price of the comparable. Likewise, the value of a feature that is present in the comparable but not in the subject property is subtracted. The adjusted sales prices of the comparables represent the probable range of value of the subject property. From this range, a single market value estimate can be selected. Because the value range of the properties in the comparison chart (excluding comparables B and E) is close, and comparable D required no adjustment, an appraiser might conclude that the indicated market value of the subject is $116,500. However, appraisers use a complex process of evaluating adjustment percentages and may consider other objective factors or subjective judgments based on research.

Comparative market analysis (CMA). An informal version of the sales comparison approach is used by real estate brokers to help a seller-client set a realistic asking price for residential real estate or to help a buyer-client determine a reasonable purchase price in an active market. This informal version is called a **comparative market analysis**, or CMA. While the CMA is a form of appraisal, the licensed real estate broker need not hold an appraiser's license to perform this function while serving a client. However, the North Carolina Real Estate Commission (NCREC) will hold brokers accountable for not performing a CMA in a competent manner, and it can take appropriate disciplinary action against the broker. One major difference between an appraisal and a CMA is that while an appraiser must declare a specific appraised value, a real estate broker usually determines a range for probable sales price. It is common for brokers preparing a CMA to reference listed properties and properties whose listings have expired as well as recently sold properties. Listed properties that have not sold generally represent the upper ceiling of value because sales prices tend to be lower than listing prices. Expired listings are useful in showing the seller how unreasonable prices affect sales (generally, listings that have expired were priced too high to sell within the listing period). Once you have listed a property, it is a good idea to update the CMA on at least a monthly basis. Make the sellers aware of the changes in listing and sales prices in their area. Have the CMA on hand when presenting an offer to purchase from any prospective buyer.

> In North Carolina

Information about these three types of properties (active listings, expired listings, and closed sales) is very helpful when putting together a CMA to help a client establish an appropriate amount to use as either a list or offer price. However, bear in mind that an appraiser is allowed to use only actual closed sales when preparing a sales comparison appraisal. Do not count a listing that is under contract as a *sold* property because the contract sales price is subject to change until the transaction is closed.

Remember that a CMA is a client-level service that requires brokers to use their opinion about market values to manipulate the data to project a reasonable sales price. A broker acting as a dual agent must perform a CMA for both clients as part of fiduciary duties owed. The two clients of the dual agent do not have to receive the same CMA; a buyer client may require the CMA months after the listing CMA was completed for the seller-client. A broker cannot perform a CMA for a third party/customer, but the broker can provide a customer with a factual list of properties that are currently listed or recently sold, withdrawn, or expired. Bottom line, a nonclient is owed market data but not interpretation of market data.

The Cost Approach

The **cost approach** to value is also based on the principle of substitution, which states that the maximum value of a property tends to be set by the cost of acquiring an equally desirable and valuable substitute property. The cost approach consists of five steps:

1. Estimate the value of the land as if it were vacant and available to be put to its highest and best use, based on the sales comparison approach, because land cannot be depreciated.

2. Separate the land from the improvements, and estimate the current cost of constructing the building(s) and site improvements based, in general, on cost data and experience.
3. Estimate the amount of accrued depreciation of the improvements resulting from physical deterioration, functional obsolescence, or economic obsolescence.
4. Deduct the accrued depreciation from the estimated construction cost of the new building(s) and the contributory depreciated value of site improvements.
5. Add the estimated value of the land to the depreciated cost of the building(s) and site improvements to determine the total property value.

Land is always valued as if vacant, and land value is estimated by using the sales comparison approach (step 1); that is, the location and improvements of the subject site are compared with those of similar nearby vacant sites, and adjustments are made for significant differences in size, shape, topography, utilities available, assessments, et cetera.

There are two ways to look at the construction cost of a building for appraisal purposes (step 2): reproduction cost versus replacement cost. **Reproduction cost** is the dollar amount required to construct an exact duplicate of the subject building at current prices. Reproduction cost is mainly used when appraising historical property. **Replacement cost** is the construction cost, at current prices and using modern materials and methodology, of a property that is not necessarily an exact duplicate but serves the same purpose or function as the original property. Replacement cost is most often used in appraising because it eliminates obsolete features and takes advantage of current construction materials and techniques.

An example of the cost approach to value is shown in Figure 17.3.

FIGURE 17.3

Cost Approach to Value

Subject Property: 155 Potter Dr.

Land Valuation: Size 60' × 135' @ $450 per front foot =		$27,000
Plus site improvements: driveway, walks, landscaping, etc. =		8,000
Total		$35,000

Building Valuation: Replacement Cost
1,500 sq. ft. @ $65 per sq. ft. = $97,500

Less Depreciation:
Physical depreciation
  Curable
    (items of deferred maintenance)
      exterior painting $4,000
  Incurable (structural deterioration)   9,750
Functional obsolescence   2,000
External depreciation   -0-
Total   −15,750

Depreciated Value of Building $ 81,750
Indicated Value by Cost Approach $116,750

Determining reproduction or replacement cost. An appraiser using the cost approach computes the reproduction or replacement cost of a building using one of the following methods:

- **Square-foot method.** The cost per square foot of a recently built comparable structure is multiplied by the number of square feet in the subject building. The **square-foot method** is the most common method of cost estimation. The example in Figure 17.2 uses the square-foot method. For some property, the cost per cubic foot of a recently built comparable structure is multiplied by the number of cubic feet in the subject structure.
- **Unit-in-place method.** The replacement cost of a structure is estimated based on the construction cost per unit of measure of individual building components, including material, labor, overhead, and builder's profit. In the **unit-in-place method**, most components are measured in square feet, although items like plumbing fixtures are estimated by unit cost.
- **Quantity-survey method.** An estimate is made of the quantities of raw materials needed to replace the subject structure (lumber, plaster, brick, et cetera) as well as of the current price of such materials and their installation costs. These factors are added to indirect costs (building permit, survey, payroll taxes, builder's profit) to arrive at the total replacement cost of the structure. The **quantity-survey method** is similar to the approach a building contractor takes when preparing a bill for the construction of a building.

Depreciation. In a real estate appraisal, **depreciation** (a loss in value for any reason) refers to any condition that adversely affects the value of an *improvement* to real property. Land does not depreciate because it is here forever and can always be put to its highest and best use when economically and legally feasible to do so. For appraisal purposes (as opposed to depreciation for tax purposes, which will be discussed in Chapter 19), depreciation is divided into three classes according to its cause:

1. **Physical deterioration**—*curable*: Repairs that are physically possible and economically feasible and will result in an increase in appraised value equal to or exceeding their cost fall into this category. Routine maintenance, such as painting and roof replacement, is an example of curable **physical deterioration**.

    Physical deterioration—*incurable*: Repairs to major structural components of a building, which deteriorate at different rates, may not be economically feasible and therefore fall into this category. Examples are load-bearing walls and foundations.

2. **Functional obsolescence**—*curable*: Physical or design features that are no longer considered desirable by property buyers but can be replaced or redesigned at low cost constitute this class of depreciation. For example, outmoded fixtures, such as plumbing, are usually easily replaced. Room function might be redefined at no cost if the basic room layout allows it. A bedroom adjacent to a kitchen, for instance, may be converted to a family room.

    Functional obsolescence—*incurable*: Currently undesirable physical or design features that cannot be remedied easily are considered functionally obsolete. Many older multistory industrial buildings are considered less suitable than one-story buildings, for example. An office building that cannot be air-conditioned because of the cost of duct installation also suffers from functional obsolescence. A residential example might be a home with five bedrooms but only one bath.

3. **Economic (environmental or external) obsolescence**—*incurable only:* Caused by factors outside the subject property, **economic (environmental or external) obsolescence** cannot be considered curable. For instance, proximity to a nuisance, such as a polluting factory, is an unchangeable factor that cannot be cured by the owner of the subject property. Economic obsolescence also may be referred to as *locational obsolescence*.

In determining a property's depreciation, most appraisers use the *breakdown method*, in which depreciation is broken down into the three classes, with separate estimates for curable and incurable factors in each class. Depreciation is difficult to measure, and the older the building, the more difficult it is to estimate. The easiest but least precise way to determine depreciation is the **age-life method**, which uses the effective age of a building and its economic (useful) life. When the cost of an asset is depreciated evenly over its useful life, this is called **straight-line method** of depreciation, as illustrated in the example below. Depreciation is assumed to occur at an even rate over a structure's **economic life, the period during which it is expected to remain useful for its original intended purpose**. (Compare this with a property's *actual life*, the period during which the improvements are expected to remain standing.) To derive the amount of annual depreciation, the property's cost is divided by the number of years of its expected economic life.

■ **FOR EXAMPLE** A $120,000 property may have a land value of $30,000 and an improvement value of $90,000. If the improvements are expected to last 60 years, the annual straight-line depreciation would be $1,500 ($90,000 ÷ 60 years). Such depreciation can be calculated as an annual dollar amount or as a percentage of the property's replacement cost.

Likewise, you can determine a building's **effective age** by multiplying its economic life by the amount of depreciation the building has already suffered.

■ **FOR EXAMPLE** If a building has suffered 25% depreciation and it has an economic life of 25 years, its effective age is 6.25 years (25 years × 0.25 = 6.25 years). Regardless of this building's actual age, its effective age would be considered to be about 6 years. Thus it could be considered to have a remaining economic life of 18.75 years.

Much functional obsolescence and all economic obsolescence, however, can be evaluated only by considering the actions of buyers in the marketplace.

Special-purpose properties. The cost approach is most helpful in the appraisal of special-purpose buildings such as schools, churches, and public buildings. Such properties are difficult to appraise using other methods because there are seldom any local sales to use as comparables and these properties ordinarily do not generate income.

In the appraisal of special-purpose properties, an inexperienced appraiser may complete only a cost approach analysis and may estimate market value based on the results of that approach alone. But just because a structure was originally constructed for a certain purpose does not mean that it is necessarily the highest and best use for the property. This being the case, a market analysis of other properties having the same projected highest and best use is very important in this type of appraisal. Adjustments must be made for such variables as modification costs, location, time of sale, lot sizes, and the like, to make valid comparisons between the comparables and the subject property.

The Income Capitalization Approach

The **income capitalization approach** to value, also known as the *income approach*, is based on the present worth of the future rights to income. It assumes that the income derived from a property will control the value of that property. The income approach is used for valuation of income-producing properties—apartment buildings, office buildings, shopping centers, and the like. Many properties have potential for producing income but do not because they are owner-occupied. In such cases, the appraiser projects income and expenses based on market studies of similar income-producing properties. In using the income approach to estimate value, an appraiser must work through the following steps:

1. Estimate the annual potential *gross income* using rents from comparable properties, as well as income from other sources such as concessions, laundry facilities, and vending machines.
2. Based on market experience, deduct an appropriate allowance for vacancy and rent collection losses to arrive at the *effective gross income*.
3. Based on appropriate operating standards, deduct the annual *operating expenses* of the real estate from the effective gross income to arrive at the annual **net operating income (NOI)**. Operating expenses include taxes, insurance, maintenance, repairs, and reserves for replacement. Management costs are always included as operating expenses, even if the current owner manages the property and does not show a cost for this item. Mortgage payments of principal and interest, are debt service and are not considered operating expenses. For example, if a property owner spends $35,000 a year on operating expenses and $25,000 a year on mortgage payments, the $35,000 would be subtracted from effective gross income to determine the property's net income; the $25,000 of mortgage payments (debt service) would not.
4. Estimate the price a typical investor would pay for the income produced by this particular type and class of property. This is done by estimating the rate of return (or yield) that an investor will demand for the investment of capital in this type of building. This rate of return is called the **capitalization (or *cap*) rate** and is determined by comparing the relationship of NOI to the sales prices of similar properties that have sold in the current market. For example, a comparable property that produces an annual NOI of $15,000 is sold for $187,500. The capitalization rate is $15,000 ÷ $187,500, or 8%. If other comparable properties sell at prices that yield substantially the same rate, it may be assumed that 8% is the rate that the appraiser should apply to the subject property. Note that the cap rate is inversely related to the market value of the property; as one goes up, the other goes down.
5. Finally, the capitalization rate is applied to the property's annual NOI, resulting in the appraiser's estimate of the property value.

Memory Tip
Income Approach (GIVEN)

Gross Income
− Vacancy
− Expenses
= Net Operating Income

With the appropriate capitalization rate and the projected annual net operating income, the appraiser can estimate value by the income approach in the following manner (and as shown in Figure 17.4):

FIGURE 17.4

Income Approach Formula for Value

[Circle diagram divided into three sections labeled I (top), R (bottom left), V (bottom right)]

Net Operating Income ÷ Capitalization Rate = Value
Example: $18,000 NOI ÷ 9% cap rate = $200,000 value

This formula and its variations are important in estimating the value of income-producing property.

$$\frac{\text{Income}}{\text{Rate}} = \text{Value} \qquad \frac{\text{Income}}{\text{Value}} = \text{Rate} \qquad \text{Value} \times \text{Rate} = \text{Income}$$

A very simplified version of the computations used in applying the income capitalization approach is illustrated in Figure 17.5.

FIGURE 17.5

Income Capitalization Approach to Value

Potential Gross Annual Income Market rent (100% capacity)		$60,000
Income from other sources (vending machines and pay phones)		+ 600
		$60,600
Less vacancy and collection losses (estimated) @4%		− 2,424
Effective Gross Income		$58,176
Expenses:		
Real estate taxes	$9,000	
Insurance	1,000	
Heat	2,800	
Maintenance	6,400	
Utilities, electricity, water, gas	800	
Repairs	1,200	
Decorating	1,400	
Replacement of equipment	800	
Legal and accounting	600	
Advertising	300	
Management	3,000	
Total		$ − 27,300
Annual Net Operating Income		$ 30,876

Capitalization rate = 10% (overall rate)

Capitalization of annual net income: $\frac{\$30,876}{0.10}$

Indicated Value by Income Approach = $308,760

IN PRACTICE The most difficult step in the income approach to value is determining the appropriate capitalization rate for the property. This rate must be selected to recapture the original investment over the building's economic life, must give the owner an acceptable rate of return on investment, and must provide for the repayment of borrowed capital. An income property that carries with it a great deal of risk as an investment generally requires a higher rate of return than does a property considered a safe investment. Capitalization rates for similar properties may be different from block to block within a city owing to varying neighborhood influences.

Gross rent multipliers or gross income multipliers. Certain properties, such as one-family or two-family homes, are not generally purchased as income properties. As a substitute for a more elaborate income analysis, the **gross rent multiplier (GRM)** method may be used in appraising such properties. The GRM relates the sales price of a property to its expected rental income. (Gross *monthly* income is used for residential property; gross *annual* income is used for commercial and industrial property.) The formula is as follows:

$$\frac{\text{Sales Price}}{\text{Rental Income}} = \text{Gross Rent Multiplier}$$

■ **FOR EXAMPLE** If a property recently sold for $82,000 and its monthly rental income was $650, the GRM for the property would be computed thus:

$$\frac{\$82,000}{\$650} = 126.2 \text{ GRM}$$

To establish an accurate GRM, an appraiser should have recent sales and rental data from at least three properties similar to the subject property. The most appropriate GRM can then be applied to the estimated fair market rental of the subject property to arrive at its market value. The formula would then be

$$\text{Rental Income} \times \text{GRM} = \text{Estimated Market Value}$$

Figure 17.6 shows some examples of GRM comparisons.

FIGURE 17.6

Gross Rent Multiplier

Comparable No.	Sales Price	Monthly Rent	GRM
1	$93,600	$650	144
2	78,500	450	174
3	95,500	675	141
4	82,000	565	145
Subject	?	625	?

Note: Based on an analysis of these comparisons, a GRM of 145 seems reasonable for homes in this area. In the opinion of an appraiser, then, the estimated value of the subject property would be $625 × 145, or $90,625.

If a property's income also comes from nonrental sources (such as sales concessions), a *gross income multiplier (GIM)* is used similarly.

Much skill is required to use multipliers accurately because no fixed multiplier exists for all areas or all types of properties. Therefore, many appraisers view the technique simply as a quick, informal way to check the validity of a property value obtained by one of the other appraisal methods. Because the gross multiplier methods are based on gross income rather than net income (they do not take into account operating expenses), the results may not be very accurate.

Reconciliation

If more than one of the three approaches to value are applied to the same property (and appraisers should apply all three methods whenever possible), they will normally produce different indications of value. **Reconciliation** (sometimes called *final reconciliation*) is the art of analyzing and effectively weighing the findings from the different approaches used. To come up with a valid estimate, the appraiser must give more weight to the most appropriate appraisal method for that particular type of property.

Although each approach may serve as an independent guide to value, whenever possible all three approaches should be used as a check on the final estimate of value. The process of reconciliation is more complicated than simply taking the average of the derived value estimates. An average implies that the data and logic applied in each of the approaches are equally valid and reliable and should therefore be given equal weight. In fact, certain approaches are more valid and reliable with some kinds of properties than with others.

Simple averaging is considered an improper methodology. In fact, reconciliation never simply entails averaging the three value estimates. For example, in appraising a home, the income capitalization approach is rarely used, and the cost approach is of limited value unless the home is relatively new; therefore, the sales comparison approach is usually given greatest weight in valuing single-family residences. In the appraisal of income or investment property, the income capitalization approach is normally given the greatest weight. In the appraisal of churches, libraries, museums, schools, and other special-use properties that produce little or no income or sales revenue, the cost approach is usually assigned the greatest weight. From this analysis, or reconciliation, a single estimate of market value is produced.

■ THE PROFESSION OF APPRAISING

In 1932, the American Institute of Real Estate Appraisers was founded. A few years later, another organization, now known as the Society of Real Estate Appraisers, was formed. These two organizations have recently merged. Through the years, a number of other professional appraisal organizations have come into existence; they include the American Society of Appraisers, the National Association of Review Appraisers, the National Association of Independent Fee Appraisers, and the American Society of Farm Managers and Rural Appraisers. These organizations have professional designations and strict codes of ethics.

The Appraisal Institute offers two professional designations: RM (Residential Member) and MAI (Member of the Appraisal Institute). The National Association of Independent Fee Appraisers offers the designations IFA (member) and IFAS (senior member). The American Society of Appraisers designation is ASA (senior member).

Through these groups, courses have been established in universities and colleges, plus books, journals, and other publications devoted to various aspects of appraising have been published. Appraising has become the most specialized branch of real estate. Before awarding their designations, the major recognized appraisal associations require a four-year college degree or the equivalent, plus five years of full-time appraisal experience, in addition to passing an examination and writing acceptable appraisals.

Federally related appraisals must follow the guidelines stated in Uniform Standards of Professional Appraisal Practice (USPAP). To become state-licensed, appraisers must meet educational, experiential, and examination requirements. An application and information book on becoming an appraiser can be obtained by writing to the North Carolina Appraisal Board at PO Box 20500, Raleigh, NC 27619-0500 or by visiting their website.

In North Carolina

■ RELATED WEBSITES

American Society of Appraisers: www.appraisers.org
American Society of Farm Managers and Rural Appraisers: www.asfmra.org
Appraisal Foundation: www.appraisalfoundation.org
Appraisal Institute: www.appraisalinstitute.org
National Association of Master Appraisers: www.masterappraisers.org
North Carolina Appraisal Board: www.ncappraisalboard.org

■ KEY POINT REVIEW

Appraisal is an estimate or opinion of value based on supportable evidence and appraisal methods, defined by the Uniform Standards of Appraisal Practice (USPAP) and set by the Appraisal Foundation's Appraisal Standards Board.

An **appraiser** must be state licensed or certified for an appraisal performed as part of a federally related transaction.

A **comparative market analysis (CMA)** is a report by a real estate broker of market statistics, but it is not an appraisal. It is used to guide probable sales price decisions by seller and buyer clients; it is a client-level service. A CMA should declare a range for probable sales price whereas an appraisal delivers a specific appraised value.

In North Carolina, a full (nonprovisional) broker can perform a **broker's price opinion (BPO)** for a nonbrokerage client for a fee as long as the BPO is in writing and contains all contents required by law.

Value is created by demand, utility, scarcity, and transferability of property (DUST). Market value is the most probable price that property should bring in an open market with the parties acting knowledgeably and prudently without undue influence but not necessarily the same as price paid or cost to construct.

Forces influencing value are social, economic, political, and physical.

Economic principles of value include the following:

- **Highest and best use**
- **Substitution** (basis for sales comparison approach)
- Supply and demand
- Conformity
- Anticipation
- Contribution
- Competition
- Change

A **sales comparison approach** (market data approach) makes use of sales of properties comparable to the property that is the subject of the appraisal by adding or subtracting the value of a feature present or absent in the subject property versus the comparable.

- If the comparable property is *inferior* to the subject, make a *positive* adjustment to the value of the comparable.
- If the comparable property is *superior* to the subject, make a *negative* adjustment to the value of the comparable.
- Remember to *never* adjust the value of the subject.

Comparable properties (referred to as **comps**) should be as similar to the subject property as possible. For a good indication of value, at least three comps should be used. Sales should have occurred within the last 12 months under typical market conditions. The adjusted sales prices of the comps should never be averaged without giving weight to the better comps.

The **cost approach** estimates current **reproduction or replacement cost** of constructing building and other property improvements using the **square-foot method, the unit-in-place method, the quantity-survey method,** and

- estimates accrued **depreciation** using the **straight-line method** (economic age-life method), or
- by estimating items of **physical deterioration, functional obsolescence,** or **economic obsolescence.**

The **income approach** is based on the present value of the right to future income and uses the following five steps:

1. Estimate annual potential gross income.
2. Deduct allowance for vacancy and rent loss to find effective gross income.
3. Deduct annual operating expenses to find **net operating income (NOI).**
4. Estimate rate of return (**capitalization rate or cap rate**) for subject by analyzing cap rates of similar properties.
5. Derive estimate of subject's market value by applying cap rate to annual NOI using this formula: Net operating income ÷ Capitalization rate = Value.

Reconciliation is the process by which the validity and reliability of the results of the approaches to value are weighed objectively to determine the appraiser's final opinion of value.

QUESTIONS

1. Reconciliation refers to
   a. averaging the results of the sales comparison approach.
   b. separating the value of land from the total value of property to compute depreciation.
   c. analyzing the results obtained by the three different approaches to value to determine a final estimate of value.
   d. the process by which an appraiser determines the highest and best use for a parcel of land.

2. One method to determine a building's replacement cost uses the estimated cost of the raw materials needed to build the structure, plus labor and indirect costs. This is called the
   a. square-foot method.
   b. quantity-survey method.
   c. cubic-foot method.
   d. unit-in-place method.

3. If a property's annual net income is $24,000 and it is valued at $300,000, what is its capitalization rate?
   a. 8%
   b. 10.5%
   c. 12.5%
   d. 15%

4. An appraiser needs certain financial figures in order to determine value by the income approach. Which one of the following numbers is NOT required for the income approach to value?
   a. Annual net operating income
   b. Capitalization rate
   c. Accrued depreciation
   d. Annual gross income

5. The highest and best use of a property is the
   a. sales price paid for a similar property.
   b. most return the owner can receive for the use of the property.
   c. cost of buying a lot and erecting a similar building on it.
   d. use of the land for a long-term lease.

6. The income capitalization approach is given the most weight in the valuation of a(n)
   a. single-family residence.
   b. one-bedroom condominium.
   c. office building.
   d. school.

7. Capitalization is the process by which annual net operating income is used as the basis to
   a. determine cost.
   b. estimate value.
   c. establish depreciation.
   d. determine potential tax value.

8. The depreciation that an appraiser uses in the cost approach to value represents the
   a. remaining economic life of the building.
   b. remodeling costs to increase rentals.
   c. loss of value due to any cause.
   d. costs to modernize the building.

9. The appraised value of a residence with four bedrooms and one bathroom would probably be reduced because of
   a. external obsolescence.
   b. functional obsolescence.
   c. physical deterioration—curable.
   d. physical deterioration—incurable.

10. The reason for loss of value that is always incurable is
    a. functional obsolescence.
    b. physical deterioration.
    c. replacement obsolescence.
    d. economic obsolescence.

11. Which appraisal approach makes use of a rate of investment return?
    a. Sales comparison
    b. Cost
    c. Income capitalization
    d. Market data

12. Which of the following is NOT true about market value?
    a. It is the highest price a property could bring in an open market.
    b. Buyer and seller must be knowledgeable and acting without undue pressure.
    c. It should be an arm's length transaction.
    d. A reasonable amount of time should be allowed for full exposure to the market.

13. Developers have just announced a new championship golf course community. Property values in the area will tend to increase due to this announcement. This is an example of the principle of
    a. supply and demand.
    b. anticipation.
    c. substitution.
    d. conformity.

14. Which of the following statements is TRUE of the income approach to value?
    a. The reproduction or replacement cost of the building must be computed.
    b. The capitalization rate must be estimated.
    c. Depreciation must be determined.
    d. Sales of similar properties must be considered.

15. In the cost approach to value, it is necessary to
    a. determine a dollar value for depreciation.
    b. estimate future expenses and operating costs.
    c. check sales prices of recently sold comparable properties in the area.
    d. reconcile differing value estimates.

16. The subject property has two bedrooms and the comparable property has three bedrooms. The estimated value of the third bedroom is $2,500. According to the sales comparison method, the appraiser should
    a. deduct $2,500 from the value of the subject property.
    b. add $2,500 to the value of the subject property.
    c. deduct $2,500 from the value of the comparable property.
    d. add $2,500 to the value of the comparable property.

17. All of the following items should be deducted from gross income to compute net operating income EXCEPT
    a. utility bills.
    b. mortgage payments.
    c. maintenance expenses.
    d. repair costs.

18. If the appraiser decides to increase the capitalization rate, the market value of the property will
    a. increase.
    b. decrease.
    c. stay the same.
    d. be equal to the capitalization rate.

19. The number of years a property is expected to remain useful for its original purpose is called its
    a. actual life.
    b. economic life.
    c. progressive life.
    d. depreciated life.

20. The formula for estimating value based on the gross rent multiplier is
    a. rental income × gross rent multiplier = estimated market value.
    b. rental income ÷ gross rent multiplier = estimated market value.
    c. estimated market value × rental income = gross rent multiplier.
    d. net operating income × gross rent multiplier = estimated market value.

21. In estimating the value of real estate using the cost approach, the appraiser should
    a. estimate the replacement cost of the improvements.
    b. deduct for depreciation of the land.
    c. determine the original cost and adjust for changes in capitalization rates.
    d. review the sales prices of comparable properties.

22. Under the income approach to estimating the value of real estate, the capitalization rate is the
    a. rate at which the property will increase in value.
    b. rate of return the property will earn as an investment.
    c. rate of capital required to keep the property operating efficiently.
    d. maximum rate of return allowed by usury limits.

23. An example of economic obsolescence is
    a. numerous pillars supporting the ceiling in a store.
    b. roof leaks making the premises unusable and therefore unrentable.
    c. massive cornices in an older structure.
    d. abandoned buildings in the area.

24. A house is located in a suburban community. A new expressway is being built a few blocks away that will reduce the commute time to the urban employment center by 30 minutes. The house is expected to increase in value based on the principle of
    a. anticipation.
    b. competition.
    c. contribution.
    d. highest and best use.

25. An apartment building generates a monthly gross income of $6,000. Monthly managerial expenses total $1,000. Monthly taxes total $300. Monthly debt service totals $2,675. Monthly repairs and maintenance total $1,100. What is the building's monthly net income?
    a. $925
    b. $1,225
    c. $3,600
    d. $3,900

26. The subject property is a two-story home with three bedrooms, three baths, a family room, a dining room, and an attached two-car garage. Which of the following would be a legitimate comparable sale?
    I. Two-story home with 3 bedrooms and 2.5 baths in the same neighborhood that sold 18 months ago
    II. One-story home in a different neighborhood with 3 bedrooms and 2 baths, a detached one-car garage, and no family or dining room
    a. I only
    b. II only
    c. Both I and II
    d. Neither I nor II

27. The subject property has 2,100 square feet, 4 bedrooms, a 2-car garage, no patio, no pool, 2.5 baths, and sits on 1 acre. The comparable recently sold for $140,000 and has 1,900 square feet, 3 bedrooms, a 1-car garage, a patio, a pool, 2 baths, and sits on 1.5 acres. Market cost data shows the following values: Square foot = $72, 1 bedroom = $2,000, 1-car garage = $1,500, patio = $2,000, pool = $14,000, ½ bath = $800, and 1 acre = $30,000. Using this cost data, what is the estimated value of the subject property?
    a. $113,700
    b. $125,700
    c. $127,700
    d. $129,200

28. A broker is asked to estimate the value of a property. She finds four recently sold comparables, A, B, C, and D. Comparables A, B, and D have positive features worth $3,000, $2,000, and $5,000, respectively, which are not common to the subject property. Comparable C has negative features worth $3,500 that are not common to the subject property. The comparables sold for the following prices: A, $73,000; B, $74,000; C, $62,000; and D, $71,000. What is the range of indicated values for the subject property?
    a. $58,500 to $76,000
    b. $65,500 to $66,000
    c. $65,500 to $72,000
    d. $66,000 to $72,000

29. Which of the following statements is TRUE of a comparative market analysis?
    a. It is another term for an appraisal.
    b. It can help the seller price the property.
    c. By law, it must be completed for each listing taken.
    d. Per Commission Rule, it must be retained by the broker for at least five years.

30. The subject property to be appraised is a three-bedroom brick ranch with 3,000 square feet. It does not have a garage but does have a patio. Comparable 1 is a three-bedroom brick ranch that recently sold for $100,000. It has 2,800 square feet, a garage, and a patio. Comparable 2, a three-bedroom brick ranch, recently sold for $110,000. It also has a garage and a patio and 3,000 square feet. Comparable 3, a three-bedroom brick ranch, recently sold for $86,000, has 2,600 square feet and no garage, but it does have a patio. Using the sales comparison approach, estimate the value of the subject property.
    a. $94,000
    b. $106,000
    c. $109,000
    d. $114,000

CHAPTER 18

Property Insurance

LEARNING OBJECTIVES

When you have finished reading this chapter, you should be able to

- **describe** the protection afforded by insurance and the characteristics of various types of standard policies.
- **identify** insurance policy terms such as condition, exclusion, and endorsement.
- **explain** the following legal issues: (1) insurable interest, (2) coinsurance clause, and (3) unoccupied building exclusion.
- **explain** the purpose of the Federal Emergency Management Agency.
- **define** these *key terms*:

broad form (HO-2)	endorsement	package insurance
casualty insurance	exclusion	premium
coinsurance clause	homeowners' insurance policy	property insurance
condition		subrogation clause
deductible	liability insurance	

BASIC INSURANCE CONCEPTS

Because home ownership represents a large financial investment for most purchasers, homeowners usually protect their investment by taking out insurance on the property. If the property is mortgaged, homeowners' insurance is usually mandatory because the lender wishes to protect the collateral.

An insurance policy is an agreement between two parties: the insurer and the insured. Insurance represents the transfer of risk from the individual homeowner to the group of policyholders affiliated with the insurance company. The insurer is the insurance company, which agrees to reimburse the insured, the property owner, for losses caused by a covered event. For example, if a homeowner buys an insurance policy that protects against fire loss and the insured property burns down, the insurer must reimburse the homeowner for the loss, within the limitations of the insurance policy. Insurance companies and insurance policies are regulated by government agencies.

However, the insurance policy is also a contract, subject to all the normal rules of contract law. For example, consideration in the form of **premiums** is required for the insurance contract to be valid. Premiums are considered to be the consumer's cost of coverage. Insurance policies have definite beginning and ending dates.

A **property insurance** or **casualty insurance** policy protects the insured from losses caused by damage to the property and the improvements on that property. A **liability insurance** policy protects the insured from losses caused to third persons or their property. A **package insurance** policy protects the insured from both types of losses.

HOMEOWNERS' INSURANCE

Although it is possible for a homeowner to obtain an individual policy for each type of risk, most residential property owners take out insurance in the form of a packaged **homeowners' insurance policy** (also called hazard insurance) on their residence. These policies insure holders against the destruction of their property by named perils, injury to others that occurs on the property, and theft from the premises of any personal property that is owned by the insured or members of the insured's immediate family.

Coverage and Claims

The basis for most homeowners' policies is called a basic form (HO-1), and it usually provides property coverage against:

- fire and lightning,
- glass breakage,
- windstorm and hail,
- explosion,
- riot and civil commotion,
- damage by aircraft,
- damage from vehicles,
- damage from smoke,
- vandalism and malicious mischief,
- theft, and
- loss of property removed from the premises when it is endangered by fire or other perils.

The packaged homeowners' policy also includes *liability coverage* for (1) personal injuries to others resulting from the insured's acts of negligence, (2) voluntary medical payments and funeral expenses for accidents sustained by guests or resident employees on the insured's property, and (3) physical damage to the property of others caused by the insured. Voluntary medical payments cover injuries to a resident employee but do not cover benefits due under any workers' compensation or occupational disease law.

Characteristics of Homeowners' Policies

Although coverage provided may vary among policies, all homeowners' policies have three common characteristics. First, they all have *fixed ratios of coverage*. That is, each type of coverage in a policy must be maintained at a certain level. The amount of coverage on household contents and other items must be a fixed percentage of the amount of insurance on the building itself. Although the amount of contents coverage may be increased, it cannot be reduced below the standard percentage. In addition, theft coverage may be contingent on the full amount of the contents coverage.

Second, homeowners' policies have an *indivisible premium*, which means the insured receives coverage for all the perils included in the policy for a single rate and may not exclude certain perils from coverage.

Finally, *first-party and third-party insurance* is the liability coverage discussed above. It covers not only damage or loss to the insured's property or its contents but also the insured's legal liability for losses or damages to another's property as well as for injuries suffered by another party while on the insured's property.

The following basic types of insurance policies are identified by number.

- *HO-2*. This Homeowners' **Broad Form** insurance policy is a *named peril policy*, which means that if a specific peril or hazard is not named in the policy, it is not covered. HO-2 covers more perils than the basic form (including falling objects; weight of ice, snow, or sleet; collapse of buildings; malfunctioning heating systems; accidental discharge of water or steam, and electrical currents).
- *HO-3*. This Homeowners' Special Form is an *all-risk form* insurance policy that provides even greater coverage than HO-2 because loss and damage to real property caused by all perils is covered without having to be named. HO-3 remains a named peril policy regarding damage or loss to personal property. Because it provides the insured with a greater amount of protection, it is the most commonly used residential policy today.
- *HO-4*. This Homeowners' Contents Broad Form is a *tenant's policy* (renter's policy) that covers the same perils as HO-2 regarding the insured's personal property. It cannot cover the building in which the tenant lives because the tenant does not hold the required financial interest in the property. HO-4 will frequently include liability insurance for any damage that the tenant might cause to the rented property.
- *HO-6*. This Homeowners' Unit-Owners Form policy is designed for the special needs of *condominium owners*. Because condo ownership is limited to *air space*, fixture coverage is the main area of real property concern.

- *HE-7.* An extended all-risk form providing broad coverage of both real and personal property. The HE-7 is designed for and primarily sold to owners of very expensive property.
- *HO-8.* This Homeowners' Modified Coverage Form is generally used when properties have less market value than the cost to replace them. It may be used to insure older homes.

Contents of Standard HO-3 Policy

Agreement to insure. As with all enforceable bilateral contracts, both parties promise some action in exchange for the other party's promised action. The insurer promises to financially reimburse the insured in the event of a covered loss while the insured promises to make timely payment of premiums.

Declaration page. This section clearly states the terms of the insurance policy. The actual dates of coverage are specified; and the insurance rating is determined by the property description. The basic details of the real and personal property coverage includes the limits of liability coverage and any **deductibles** that the insured might have to personally pay before coverage can be applied. Any endorsements, or perils that have been added to the general policy, will be noted here. The declaration page will also contain the name of any mortgagee, signature of an authorized agent, and other administrative matters.

Standardized policy provisions. All the details of coverage are contained in the various policy provisions. If it is a named peril policy, those perils that are covered will be clearly stated; whereas, if it is an all risk policy, all the exclusions will be clarified. Any conditions or added endorsements to the policy will be specified.

Insurance definitions. A **condition** is a limitation on the coverage of a specific insured property. For example, damage to a vehicle will only be covered if the vehicle was inside the garage at the time of the damage.

An **endorsement** is coverage for specific property or perils that are not covered in the original policy and is sometimes called a rider. For example, if the homeowner owns a collection of rare books, an endorsement would probably be needed to fully insure the collection against loss.

An **exclusion** is some item, or loss due to a specific event, that is not covered by the policy. For example, most policies exclude the coverage of loss due to acts of war or terrorism.

Selected Legal Issues

Insurable interest. The insured party must have some type of financial interest in the property to recover any losses. The insured person may be the homeowner, the lender, or even a property manager. Sometimes the conditions of the policy will limit a concurrent owner to the amount of their financial interest. The insured will, however, *never recover more than the actual loss.*

Unoccupied building exclusion. Most policies contain provisions that state that *if the insured building is unoccupied for more than a certain length of time, the owner may not be able to recover any losses that may occur.* According to the courts in North Carolina, insurance companies may use 60 days as the vacancy time period. A property owner should make sure the building is not vacant for a longer period than that stated in the insurance policy (e.g., 60 days). The contract definition of *vacant* can vary widely from policy to policy. For example, in one policy if there is no human occupancy for the prescribed time, vacancy has occurred. A similar policy may specify that as long as one piece of furniture is present in each room of the residence, despite presence or absence of humans, the property is still classified as *occupied*. Awareness of this insurance policy exclusion is important for brokers because sellers occasionally move from their listed or under-contract property and expect their broker to look after the property in their absence.

[In North Carolina]

Interpretation of Policies

The insurance policy is a contract. Most insurance policy contracts are standard forms approved by the North Carolina Department of Insurance. These standard forms have been drafted mostly in favor of the insurer, not the insured. The owner may have to ask a court to interpret any ambiguous clauses. To obtain a clear interpretation of the policies, it is necessary to read and interpret the policy as a whole in order to understand what is and is not covered.

Coinsurance. Most homeowners' insurance policies contain a **coinsurance clause**, which penalizes the policyholder for underinsuring the property. This provision usually requires that the insured maintain insurance on the property in an amount equal to at least 80% of the replacement cost of the dwelling (not including the price of the land). If the owner carries such a policy, a claim may be made for the cost of the repair or replacement of the damaged property without deduction for depreciation.

The formula for calculating the amount of recovery for a fully insured claim is as follows:

$$\frac{\text{Amount of insurance carried}}{80\% \text{ replacement value}} \times \text{Claim} = \text{Recovery}$$

For example, assume a homeowner's dwelling has a replacement cost of $100,000 and is damaged by fire. The estimated cost to repair the damaged portion of the dwelling is $71,000. Thus, if the homeowner carries at least $80,000 (equivalent of 80% replacement value) worth of insurance on the dwelling, the claim against the insurance company can be for the full $71,000.

If the homeowner carries coverage of less than 80% of the full replacement cost of the dwelling, the loss will be either settled for the actual cash value (replacement cost less depreciation) or prorated by dividing the percentage of replacement cost actually covered by the policy by the minimum coverage requirement (usually 80%). For example, if the building is insured for only 60% of its value and suffers a $71,000 loss, the insurance company will pay only $53,250 ($60,000 ÷ $80,000, or 75% of $71,000 = $53,250).

In any event, the *total settlement cannot exceed the face value of the policy*. Because of coinsurance clauses, it is important that homeowners periodically review all policies to be certain that the coverage equals at least 80% of the current replacement (new) cost of their home.

Most policies also have a **subrogation clause**, which provides that if the insured collects for damage from the insurance company, any rights the insured may have to sue the person who caused the damage are assigned to the insurance company. A subrogation clause allows the insurance company to pursue legal action to collect the amount paid out from the party at fault and prevents the insured from collecting twice for the same damage.

Insurability Issues

At least partially due to the excessive numbers of natural disasters and class action suits, insurance companies are reluctant to fully insure properties or policyholders that have an active history of claims. In recent years, noninsurability of a particular property or property owner due to large or multiple claims has become an issue because providing adequate homeowner insurance on the collateral property is generally a condition of financing. Insurance companies are relying more and more on policy purchasers' credit reports and property loss history reports to decide insurability issues. Insurers and property buyers are accessing the Comprehensive Loss Underwriting Exchange (CLUE) report on property addresses and on property owners to determine insurability. CLUE manages a loss history exchange primarily where insurers exchange and store claim information by address and owner. The claim/loss history stays with the property *and* goes with the property owner who filed the claim(s).

IN PRACTICE In recent years, builders used a synthetic stucco exterior finish on some residential properties. This exterior insulating finishing system (EIFS) is a highly effective moisture barrier that also tends to seal in moisture, trapping water in the home's walls and resulting in massive wood rot. Frequently, the effects of the rotting cannot be seen until the damage is extensive and sometimes irreparable. Some insurance companies are now refusing to insure homes with EIFS exteriors, and class action lawsuits have been brought against builders by distressed homeowners.

Federal Flood Insurance Program

The National Flood Insurance Act of 1968 was authorized by Congress to help owners of property located in flood-prone areas by subsidizing flood insurance. As of 1975, such property owners must obtain flood damage insurance on properties financed by mortgages or other loans, grants, or guarantees obtained from federal agencies and federally insured or regulated lending institutions. The program also seeks to improve future management of floodplain areas through land-use and land-control measures.

The Federal Emergency Management Agency (FEMA), which administers the flood insurance program, has maps prepared by the Army Corps of Engineers that identify specific flood-prone areas throughout the country. Property owners in the designated areas who do not obtain flood insurance are unable to obtain federal and federally related financial assistance.

IN PRACTICE Brokers must be sure that homebuyers acquire a homeowners' insurance policy on or before the day of closing. This is required if there will be a mortgage, but it is still strongly advised if it is a cash purchase. Buyers should be reminded that the typical homeowners' insurance policies do not provide coverage for termite damage, breakdown of appliances, flood damage, loss of trees, or losses incurred over an extended period of time (such as a leaking roof). Assuming the seller's policy could mean that the buyer does not have a policy that fits the buyer's needs.

RELATED WEBSITES

LexisNexis Insurance Report: www.consumerdisclosure.com
Federal Emergency Management Authority: www.fema.gov

KEY POINT REVIEW

A **homeowners' insurance policy** usually covers the following:

- Fire and lightning, windstorm and hail, and glass breakage
- Explosion, riot, and civil commotion
- Damage by aircraft, vehicles, and smoke
- Vandalism, malicious mischief, and theft
- Loss of property removed from the premises when it is endangered by fire or other perils

The homeowners' insurance **broad-form policy** covers

- falling objects and damage due to weight of ice, snow, or sleet;
- collapse of all or part of the building;
- bursting, cracking, burning, or bulging of steam or water heating system or appliances used to heat water;
- accidental discharge, leakage, or overflow of water or steam from within a plumbing, heating, or air-conditioning system;
- freezing of plumbing, heating, and air-conditioning systems and domestic appliances; and
- damage to electrical appliances, devices, fixtures, and wiring from short circuits or other accidentally generated currents.

Contents of Standard HO-3 Policy
- Agreement to insure
- Declaration page: This section clearly states the terms of the insurance policy; dates of coverage, insurance rating, liability coverage, **deductibles**, endorsements, conditions, exclusions or added perils
- Standardized policy provisions
- Insurance definitions:
    — A **condition** is a limitation on the coverage of a specific insured property.
    — An **endorsement** is coverage for specific property or perils that are not covered in the original policy and is sometimes called a rider.
    — An **exclusion** is some item, or loss due to a specific event, that is not covered by the policy.

A coinsurance clause

- requires the homeowner to maintain insurance equal to at least 80% of replacement cost of the dwelling for full replacement on loss; or
- if not, the loss will be settled for actual cash value or a prorated amount.

Comprehensive Loss Underwriting Exchange (CLUE) is a database of consumer insurance claim history.

The National Flood Insurance Act of 1968

- subsidizes flood insurance, and
- is administered by the Federal Emergency Management Agency (FEMA).

QUESTIONS

1. A typical homeowners' insurance policy covers all of the following EXCEPT
   a. personal injury claims due to property owner's negligence.
   b. theft of property.
   c. vandalism and malicious mischief.
   d. flood damage.

2. In homeowners' insurance, coinsurance refers to the
   a. specific form of policy which allows the premium to be split equitably between multiple owners.
   b. stipulation that the homeowner must purchase insurance coverage equal to at least 80% of the replacement cost of the structure to be able to collect the full insured amount in the event of a loss.
   c. stipulation that the homeowner must purchase insurance coverage equal to at least 75% of the replacement cost of the structure to be able to collect the full insured amount in the event of a loss.
   d. specific form of policy purchased when a property is owned by co-owners.

3. Federal flood insurance is
   a. required in certain areas to insure properties financed by federally backed mortgage loans against flood damage.
   b. only required on real estate purchases located on the North Carolina coast.
   c. only required in North Carolina on federally-owned lands.
   d. paid for by the federal government.

4. A subrogation clause in an insurance policy enables the
   a. insurer to sue the party responsible for damage to the insured's property.
   b. insured to receive 100% of replacement cost less depreciation.
   c. insurer to receive full cost of the repair or replacement of the damaged property.
   d. insured to protect the property in case of a flood.

5. When a property manager chooses an insurance policy with a $150 deductible, the risk management technique being employed is risk
   a. avoidance.
   b. abatement.
   c. control.
   d. transfer.

6. Which of the following statements is NOT true about homeowner insurance?
   a. Most policies exclude coverage for property that is unoccupied longer than a set time period.
   b. Most homeowners purchase an HO-3 policy for their residence.
   c. A homeowner policy can be purchased on a residence by any interested party.
   d. A property owner with an extensive history of filing insurance claims may be denied insurance.

7. Although the insurance company requires 80% coverage on an insured dwelling, the owner only purchased 50% coverage on the $175,000 dwelling. If a fire causes $82,000 of damage, how much will the insurance cover?
   a. $41,000
   b. $51,250
   c. $65,600
   d. $82,000

8. Which type of insurance coverage protects the property owner against the claims of employees injured on the job?
   a. Consequential loss
   b. Workers' compensation
   c. Casualty
   d. Surety bond

9. A tenant slips on an icy apartment building stair and is hospitalized. A claim for medical expenses may be paid under which of the following policies held by the owner?
   a. Workers' compensation
   b. Casualty
   c. Liability
   d. Fire and hazard

10. Which clause in a standard homeowners' insurance policy literally makes the insured share in the loss?
    a. Exclusion clause
    b. Coinsurance clause
    c. Conditions clause
    d. Casualty clause

CHAPTER 19

Federal Income Taxation of Real Property Ownership

LEARNING OBJECTIVES *When you have finished reading this chapter, you should be able to*

- **identify** the tax benefits of home ownership, including itemized deductions and adjustments that reduce gain.
- **explain** basic tax concepts as they relate to home ownership and when gains may or may not be taxable.
- **explain** the differences in taxation on personal residences and on investment property.
- **calculate** the basis, adjusted basis, amount realized, and gains on factual situations.
- **define** these *key terms*:

adjusted basis	cost basis	long-term capital gain
basis	depreciation	short-term capital gain
boot	gain	tax-deferred exchange
capital gain	installment sale	
capital loss	like-kind properties	

INTRODUCTION

All real estate brokers should have a general understanding of the tax implications of owning a home. The tax advantages available to homeowners can significantly reduce the out-of-pocket cost of owning a home, and this should be explained to homebuyers, especially first-time homebuyers. However, the discussion and examples used in this chapter are designed to introduce the reader to only general tax concepts—a tax lawyer or certified public accountant (CPA) should be consulted for further details on specific regulations. Real estate brokers should never try to give their clients or customers tax advice. Instead, they should indicate that all real estate transactions have tax implications that should be discussed with a competent adviser.

■ TAX BENEFITS FOR HOMEOWNERS

To encourage home ownership, the federal government allows homeowners certain income tax advantages. Even though the Tax Reform Act of 1986 greatly restricted or eliminated tax deductions in other areas, benefits for homeowners were kept largely intact.

Tax-Deductible Loan Expenses

Homeowners may be able to deduct from their taxable income

- *mortgage interest payments* on first and second homes. For a principal residence, a second residence, or both, the total amount of acquisition debt for which interest can be deducted cannot exceed a total of $1 million. *Acquisition indebtedness* is defined as the debt incurred in acquiring, constructing, or substantially improving a principal residence or second residence (or both) of the taxpayer, where the debt is secured by such property. Home equity loans—loans secured by the property and in amounts less than the difference between fair market value and outstanding mortgage loan balance—cannot exceed $100,000. *Home equity indebtedness* is defined as the debt secured by the taxpayer's residence(s) that does not exceed the fair market value of such a residence(s) less the amount of acquisition indebtedness.
- *loan discount points* (those that are prepaid interest to reduce the loan interest rate when acquiring a residence, not a refinance, are deductible in the year of purchase).
- *mortgage prepayment penalties* (rare in North Carolina).
- *some loan origination fees,* if they are quoted as a percent of the loan amount and if paid to obtain the loan. (Brokers and buyers should check with their tax advisers before stating that such fees may or may not be deductible.)

Real Property Taxes

Real property taxes paid by a homeowner also are deductible in the year paid. Note that the interest paid on overdue taxes is not deductible. The mortgage interest deduction combined with the real property tax deduction can mean a substantial annual tax savings for the homeowner.

■ TAX BENEFITS OF SELLING REAL PROPERTY

While the two tax benefits discussed above are available to those who currently own real estate, other tax benefits are available to those selling their property. However, before discussing these tax advantages, some basic tax concepts must be explained.

Basic Tax Concepts

Tax benefits of owning a home:
- Tax-deductible interest payments
- Tax-deductible property taxes
- Adjustments to reduce capital gain liability

Because the government taxes income, it is worth quickly noting the definition of income. Obviously, income includes wages from employment, interest on savings, dividends on stock, pension payments, and other commonly accepted forms of income. However, income also includes the gain that a person recognizes when he or she sells a capital asset. If a person sells a painting for $10,000 that was acquired for $6,000, that person has recognized a **gain**, that is, income, of $4,000, and that income is taxable (unless specifically excluded by the tax code). So it is with the buying and selling of real property.

When a person sells real property for more than its cost, that person has received a **capital gain.** Capital gains, the profits realized from the sale or exchange of property, are taxed as ordinary income if it is a **short-term capital gain** (held 12 months or less). However, the maximum tax rate that applies to **long-term capital gain** (held longer than 12 months) is currently 15% (not the ordinary 39.6%). Because capital gain laws change often, check with a tax specialist before quoting any rates.

The amount of the gain realized from a sale of real property depends on that property's **basis**. The **cost basis** of property is the owner's initial cost for the real estate (purchase price plus allowable closing expenses). The owner of a property can add to the cost basis the cost of any physical capital improvements that add value to the property or prolong its life. This is the property's **adjusted basis**. (Note that the cost of ordinary repairs or maintenance does not increase the adjusted basis.) When the owner sells the property, the amount by which the amount realized (sales price minus allowable closing expenses) exceeds the property's adjusted basis is the capital gain subject to taxation. If the amount realized is less than the adjusted basis, a **capital loss** has occurred. Capital loss is not currently recognized on the sale of a personal residence, but can frequently be used to off-set capital gain in other situations. As noted before, a tax specialist should be consulted on this matter.

Essentially, a property owner determines the adjusted basis by adding:

          Purchase price
          Allowable closing costs
         + Capital improvements
          Adjusted basis

■ **FOR EXAMPLE** Suppose Johnson buys a home for $85,000. The closing costs that can be allocated to purchasing the property (but not to obtaining financing) include the lawyer's fees and recording fee, which equal $250. One year later, Johnson spends $2,000 pressure washing and treating her roof. Two years later, Johnson spends $10,000 on a room addition to the house. Johnson will calculate her adjusted basis as follows:

$85,000	purchase price
250	allowable closing costs
+10,000	capital improvements
$95,250	adjusted basis

Notice that the $2,000 spent maintaining the roof is not added to the basis. This is a normal maintenance expense whereas roof replacement might be an acceptable capital expense.

To determine the gain that is realized from the sale of a property, the property owner takes the sales price and deducts the allowable closing costs from that.

$$\frac{\text{Sales price} - \text{Allowable closing costs}}{\text{Amount realized}}$$

■ **FOR EXAMPLE** Let's continue our previous example. Johnson sells the house for $110,000. Her selling expenses are $5,300. To calculate the amount she realized on the sale, subtract her allowable closing costs from the sales price.

$110,000	sales price
− $5,300	allowable closing costs
$104,700	amount realized

To calculate an owner's gain on the sale of a property, simply subtract the adjusted basis from the amount realized on the sale.

$$\frac{\text{Amount realized} - \text{Adjusted basis}}{\text{Capital gain (or loss)}}$$

■ **FOR EXAMPLE** Once again, let's return to Johnson's situation. To calculate her gain on the sale, take the amount realized and subtract her adjusted basis.

$104,700	amount realized
− 95,250	adjusted basis
$ 9,450	capital gain

Johnson's taxable capital gain on the sale of her house is $9,450.

Tax-Free Gains from Sale of Principal Residence

Taxpayers who sell their principal residences can take advantage of tax laws that took effect in May 1997. Under current tax law, capital gains—up to $500,000 for a married couple filing jointly and up to $250,000 for a single person or a married person filing singly—from the sale of a principal residence are excluded from taxation.

There are a few restrictions on this tax benefit: (1) the seller must have occupied the property as a primary residence for two of the previous five years (residency does not have to be continuous) and (2) the exclusion is available only once every two years. Because of the first restriction, this exclusion of gain does not apply to vacation properties or second homes.

Under these tax provisions, homeowners with substantial capital gains can downsize into smaller, less-expensive homes without a tax penalty (in most cases). If a seller has gains that exceed the $500,000 or $250,000 limit, those gains will be currently taxed at the maximum 15% long-term capital gains rate.

■ **FOR EXAMPLE** Suppose the Bowers sold their principal residence, where they have lived for the previous 20 years. They originally purchased the house for $98,000, paying $550 in closing costs. They sold it for $879,000, having $54,600 in selling expenses. The gain on the sale can be calculated as follows:

```
  $98,000   purchase price
+    550    original closing costs
  $98,550   adjusted basis


  $879,000  sales price
-  54,600   allowable closing costs
  $824,400  amount realized


  $824,400  amount realized
-  98,550   adjusted basis
  $725,850  capital gain
```

Because the Bowers are married/filing jointly and have occupied the primary residence far in excess of the two-year minimum requirement, they will be able to take the full $500,000 tax exemption. The amount of capital gain in excess of the exemption is taxable at the long-term capital gains rate of 15% (owned longer than 12 months). The Bowers will only owe capital gains tax in the amount of $33,877.50 on a total gain of over $700,000.

```
  $725,850  capital gain
- 500,000   tax exemption
  $225,850  taxable capital gain
```

$225,850 (taxable capital gain) × 15% (tax rate) = $33,877.50 (tax bill)

Office in the Home

To qualify for tax deductions for an office in the home, that portion of the home must be used *exclusively* for business purposes; it must be the taxpayer's principal place of business; it must be where clients, customers, or patients are met in the normal course of business; or it must be a separate structure not attached to the dwelling. Consult with a tax expert for more details.

■ TAX BENEFITS OF REAL ESTATE INVESTMENT

One of the main reasons real estate investments were popular—and profitable—in the past was that federal law allowed investors to use losses generated by the investments to shelter income from other sources. The Tax Reform Act of 1986 eliminated some important tax advantages of owning investment real estate, but with professional tax advice investors still may be able to make wise real estate investment purchases.

Adjusted Basis

As discussed earlier, the adjusted basis in a property is roughly equivalent to the owner's investment in the property. The adjusted basis affects the amount of gain that is realized from the sale of real property. The owner of an investment property calculates the owner's basis in that property a little differently from the homeowner. The owner of income property can also add to the cost basis the cost of any physical capital improvements (as opposed to repairs that may be expensed annually) subsequently made to the property. He must subtract from the basis any payment received for the sale of an easement on the property and/or the amount of any depreciation claimed as a tax deduction (discussed later) to arrive at the property's adjusted basis.

Installment Sales

When a seller finances the sale of the seller's property, or when the seller is to receive all or some portion of the sales price in a year or years other than the year of sale, the sale qualifies as an **installment sale**. For instance, a seller may agree to personally finance the sale of the property, receiving a 5% down payment, with the balance of the purchase price to be received in monthly payments over a 10-year term. The seller benefits tax-wise from this type of sale by being able to spread taxation of any gain over the term of the loan.

With an installment sale, the taxpayer is taxed on a pro rata portion of the total gain as each installment actually is received. For example, if a taxpayer received a gain of $10,000 on a $100,000 contract price, her profit percentage would be 10%. If during the tax year she received $5,000 in principal payments, 10% of those payments would be taxable that year. Ten percent of $5,000 is $500. She would have to report a taxable gain of $500 in that tax year.

Note that if a homeowner sells a principal residence and the gain will exceed the statutory limits of exclusion discussed previously, the homeowner may also benefit by selling the principal residence on an installment basis.

Vacation Homes

If a property owner has a vacation home and if it is in full use by others, certain expenses may be deductible for tax purposes. But if the owner personally uses the property for more than 14 days per year, or for more than 10% of the number of days for which the property is rented, whichever is greater, certain deductions will be disallowed.

Tax-Deferred Exchanges

Real estate investors can *defer* taxation of capital gains by exchanging property versus selling it and receiving taxable profit. A **tax-deferred exchange** offers significant tax advantages because no matter how much a property has appreciated since its initial purchase, it may be exchanged for another property and the taxpayer may be able to defer taxes on the entire gain. Note that the tax is deferred, not eliminated, so whenever the investor actually sells the newly acquired property without the use of an exchange, the capital gain will be taxable.

The requirements for a tax-deferred exchange, sometimes called a Section 1031 Exchange based on the federal tax code, are fairly straightforward. First of all, there must be a property transferred (*the relinquished property*) and a property received (*the replacement property*). These properties must be *exchanged*—they cannot be sold. Both the property transferred and the property received must be held for productive use in a trade or business or for investment. (An exchange of principal residences will not qualify for tax-deferral.) Finally, the properties must be **like-kind properties**. Essentially, the like-kind requirement is met when real estate is exchanged for real estate. An apartment building can be exchanged for an office building or gas station, and the exchange will still qualify as like-kind. The apartment building real estate does not have to be exchanged for an apartment building to qualify.

Sometimes, a property is exchanged for another property that is worth substantially more or less money. When this happens, cash or personal property may be included in the transaction to even out the value of the exchange. This cash or personal property is called **boot**. The party receiving boot is taxed on the value of the boot at the time of the exchange. Direct, equal-value property swaps are very rare, so most Section 1031 exchanges are *delayed exchanges* where the relinquished property and the replacement property are disposed of and acquired at different times. The rules for a delayed exchange are very clear and strict with deadlines that cannot be missed (time is of the essence).

| In North Carolina | The North Carolina Real Estate Commission (NCREC) cautions brokers not to give advice about tax-deferred exchanges or the eligibility of property for such an exchange. Clients should be counseled to consult a tax adviser or attorney who has experience with such exchanges.

Depreciation

Depreciation, or *cost recovery*, allows an investor to recover the cost of an income-producing asset by taking tax deductions over the period of the asset's useful life. Even though investors usually expect the value of the property to appreciate over time, according to the tax laws all physical structures deteriorate and lose value over time. Cost recovery deductions may be taken only on personal property and improvements to land and only if they are used in a trade or business or for the production of income. Cost recovery deductions cannot be claimed on a principal residence or on land (technically, land never wears out or becomes obsolete).

When depreciation is taken in equal amounts over an asset's useful life, the method used is called *straight-line depreciation*. For certain property purchased before 1987, it was also possible to use an *accelerated cost recovery* system to claim greater deductions in the early years of ownership, gradually reducing the amount deducted in each year of the useful life.

For residential rental property placed in service as of January 1, 1987, the recovery period is set at 27.5 years; for nonresidential property placed in service after May 12, 1993, the recovery period is set at 39 years, using only the straight-line depreciation method. The accelerated depreciation schedule is not allowed on property purchased after 1987.

Deducting Losses

In addition to tax deductions for depreciation, investors may be able to deduct losses from their real estate investments. The tax laws are very complex, particularly as a result of the Tax Reform Act of 1986. The amount of loss that may be deducted depends on the following factors:

- Whether an investor actively participates in the day-to-day management of the rental property or makes management decisions
- The amount of the loss
- The source of the income against which the loss is to be deducted

Investors who do not actively participate in the management or operation of the real estate are considered *passive investors*, which prevents them from using a loss to offset *active income*. Active income is considered to be wages, income generated from active participation in real estate management, or income from stocks, bonds, and the like. The tax code cites specific rules for active and passive income and losses and is subject to changes in the law.

Profit and loss. When real property is sold, a profit or a loss may occur. Many times sellers are concerned about the profit they may earn or, if a low price is accepted, a loss they may incur. The broker must understand the concepts of profit and loss math and how it applies to real estate transactions.

If the problem gives the value (present or original) and asks for a percent of loss or a percent of profit, the math is quite simple. Divide the amount of profit (or loss) by the original value, and that gives the percent of profit or loss.

Example 1: A house recently sold for $120,000 and was originally purchased for $100,000. The profit is 20% ($120,000 present value − $100,000 original value = $20,000 amount of profit ÷ original value of $100,000 = 0.20, or 20%).

Example 2: A house was purchased for $100,000 a few years ago and just sold at $90,000. The loss of 10% ($100,000 present value − $90,000 original value = $10,000 loss ÷ original value of $100,000 = 0.10, or 10%).

If a problem gives the original or present value, gives the percentage of profit or loss in the problem, then asks for the present or original value, the math becomes a bit more complicated. Following are three rules to remember:

1. When a problem gives the *original value* and asks for *present value*, you *multiply* by the percentage of profit or loss.
2. When the problem gives the *present value* and asks for the *original value*, you *divide* by the percentage of profit or loss.
3. If a profit occurs, add; if a loss occurs, subtract. Treat the original value given in the problem as the 100% figure.

Example 1: A house recently sold for $120,000 at a 13% profit. What was the original value?

$120,000 present value = 100% original value + 13% gain = 113% =
1.13 ratio between present and original value
$120,000 ÷ 1.13 = $106,194.69 original value

Example 2: A house recently sold for $96,000 at a 10% loss. What was the original value?

$96,000 present value = 100% original value − 10% loss = 90% =
0.90 ratio between present and original value
$96,000 ÷ 0.90 = $106,666.66 original value

Example 3: A house cost $230,000 four years ago and just sold at a 9% profit. What was the sales price?

$230,000 original value = 100% original value + 9% profit = 109% =
1.09 ratio between present and original value
$230,000 × 1.09 = $250,700 sales price (present value)

Example 4: A house cost $180,000 four years ago and just sold at an 11% loss. What did it sell for?

$180,000 original value = 100% original value − 11% loss = 89% =
0.89 ratio between present and original value
$180,000 × 0.89 = $160,200 sales price (present value)

Gross profit versus net profit. *Gross profit* is nothing more than the present value less the original value, and the difference equals the amount of gross profit. The amount of gross profit divided by the original value equals the percent of gross profit.

Example: The original value of a house was $80,000, and it recently sold for $100,000. The gross profit is 25% ($100,000 present value − $80,000 original value = $20,000 gross profit ÷ $80,000 original value = 0.25 = 25%).

To find *net profit,* take into consideration the closing costs the buyer had to pay when the house was purchased and the selling expenses that had to be paid when it was sold.

Example: (using the figures in the preceding example) When the owners bought the house for $80,000, they had to pay $1,000 in closing costs, making the original cost $81,000. When they later sold for $100,000, they had to pay $7,000 in selling expenses. Their net profit is 14.8% ($80,000 + $1,000 = $81,000 original net value; $100,000 − $7,000 = $93,000 present net value; $93,000 − $81,000 = $12,000 net profit; $12,000 net profit ÷ $81,000 original value = 0.148 = 14.8% net profit).

■ RELATED WEBSITE

Internal Revenue Service: www.irs.gov

■ KEY POINT REVIEW

Homeownership has tax-deductible expenses: loan expenses includes mortgage interest payments, loan discount points, mortgage prepayment penalties, and some loan origination fees plus real property tax.

Capital gain or loss is the difference between the **adjusted cost basis** of a property and its net selling price, and gain may be taxed at a more favorable rate than a taxpayer's earned income.

Short-term capital gain (held less than 12 months) is taxed as ordinary income; but **long-term capital gain** (held more than 12 months) is usually taxed at a reduced rate.

```
  Purchase price
+ Allowable closing costs
+ Capital improvements
  Adjusted basis

  Sales price
− Allowable closing costs
  Amount realized

  Amount realized
− Adjusted basis
  Capital gain (or loss)
```

Capital gains taxation exclusion of up to $250,000 (if single or married filing separately) or $500,000 (married, filing jointly) profit on sale of principal residence, if owned and occupied at least two of the past five years.

The tax benefits of owning investment real estate depend on current tax law; the following are issues to consider:

- **Installment sales**
- Vacation homes
- **Tax-deferred exchanges**
- **Depreciation**

QUESTIONS

1. In June of 2012, a couple sold their principal residence that they have lived in since they purchased it in February, 2011. They received capital gains of $22,000. The gain will most probably be
   a. tax exempt since it is their principal residence.
   b. taxed at the couple's regular tax rate.
   c. taxed as ordinary income, but at a lower rate.
   d. subject to the purchase price rule.

2. For tax purposes, the initial cost of an investment property plus the cost of any subsequent improvements to the property less depreciation represents the investment's
   a. adjusted basis.
   b. capital gain.
   c. basis.
   d. market value.

3. Which of the following statements is TRUE of capital gains?
   a. They may be realized only from the sale of improvements to real estate, not from the sale of the land itself.
   b. They may be realized only from the sale of the land itself, not from the sale of improvements to the real estate.
   c. They will be taxed at the taxpayer's regular tax rate if the property was owned for one year or less.
   d. They must be paid only by property owners under the age of 65.

4. Federal income tax law allows for
   I. a tax on all capital gains over $250,000.
   II. a possible exclusion of gain up to $500,000 from the sale of a personal residence by a married couple filing jointly.
      a. I only
      b. II only
      c. Both I and II
      d. Neither I nor II

5. Federal income tax laws do NOT currently allow a homeowner to deduct which of the following expenses from taxable income?
   a. Mortgage interest
   b. Real estate taxes
   c. Discount points
   d. Repairs or maintenance

6. The profit a homeowner receives from the sale of their principal residence may be
   a. rolled over into the purchase of a more expensive property without any tax liability, once every 24 months.
   b. subject to long-term federal income tax if the profit exceeds the excluded limits.
   c. excluded from taxation every year up to a statutory limit of $500,000 per married couple filing jointly.
   d. taxed at a lower rate because depreciation is deductible from each annual income tax return.

7. An unmarried man, age 38, sells his home of eight years and realizes a $25,000 gain from the sale. Income tax on this gain may be
   a. excluded from taxation.
   b. excluded from taxation if the man purchases a property with a value equal to or exceeding the adjusted basis of the previous residence.
   c. reduced by subtracting the depreciation of the property when compared to the reproduction cost of a like-kind improvement.
   d. reduced by the amount of mortgage interest paid over the life of the property's owner.

8. A woman, age 62, sells the home she has occupied for 18 months of the previous five years and realizes a $52,000 gain from the sale. Income tax on the profit from this sale may be
   a. taxed as long-term capital gains.
   b. postponed by purchasing another residence of equal or greater value within 12 months before or after the sale.
   c. eliminated if she donates at least 50% of the profit to a charity.
   d. reduced by the amount of mortgage interest paid over the property's economic life.

9. A homeowner sold his principal residence for $127,500. Selling expenses were $750. The house had been purchased new three years earlier for $75,000. What is the homeowner's gain on this transaction?
   a. $51,750
   b. $52,500
   c. $53,250
   d. $75,000

10. In question 9, if the property were an investment property, how much of the gain would be subject to income tax?
    a. $21,000
    b. $42,300
    c. $51,750
    d. $52,500

11. A homeowner bought her house for $72,000. She spent $15,000 on an addition, $3,000 on a new deck, $5,000 on repairs, and $2,000 on interior painting. Her adjusted basis is
    a. $87,000.
    b. $90,000.
    c. $95,000.
    d. $97,000.

12. Which of the following statements is true about tax-deferred exchanges?
    a. The properties being exchanged must be of equal value.
    b. A taxpayer's personal home can be used as an exchange property.
    c. A retail property must be exchanged for another retail property.
    d. Any boot that is received will be taxable.

13. Which of the following statements is/are TRUE?
    I. Some of the expenses of a vacation home, that is also a rental property, may be tax deductible if the taxpayer/owner limits their private use of the home.
    II. An installment sales contract may provide tax benefits to the seller by spreading the sales income over several tax years.
       a. I only
       b. II only
       c. Both I and II
       d. Neither I nor II

Use the following information to answer questions 14 through 17.

When you bought your home, you paid $120,000 for it plus $2,600 in closing costs. You added $16,000 worth of capital improvements. When you sold the home for $165,000, you paid a 7% commission and other closing costs of $1,300. Answer the following questions.

14. What was your cost basis?
    a. $120,000
    b. $122,600
    c. $138,600
    d. $152,150

15. What was your adjusted basis?
    a. $120,000
    b. $122,600
    c. $138,600
    d. $152,150

16. What was your amount realized?
    a. $120,000
    b. $122,600
    c. $138,600
    d. $152,150

17. What was your capital gain?
    a. $13,550
    b. $29,000
    c. $45,000
    d. $165,000

18. A man bought a cabin in the mountains five years ago for $20,000. Today he sold it for $25,000. What percent profit did he make on his investment?
    a. 20%
    b. 25%
    c. 33%
    d. 80%

19. Five lots were bought several months ago for $20,000 each. During the next few months, the lots were surveyed and redivided into nine lots that sold for $17,000 each. What was the percent profit?
    a. 33%
    b. 47%
    c. 53%
    d. 65%

20. A woman bought a home five years ago for $105,000 with a 90% LTV ratio. She is now selling the home for 20% more than it cost. Her loan balance has been reduced by 8 percent. What is her percent of equity increase?
    a. 2.72%
    b. 27.2%
    c. 272%
    d. 372%

CHAPTER 20

Fair Housing and Ethical Practices

LEARNING OBJECTIVES When you have finished reading this chapter, you should be able to

- **describe** the purpose of federal and state fair housing laws, how they are enforced, and their impact on real estate brokers.
- **list** and define the classes of people who are protected against discrimination by various federal and state laws.
- **explain** the purposes of the Americans with Disabilities Act.
- **define** what constitutes sexual harassment.
- **define** these *key terms*:

    Americans with
      Disabilities Act (ADA)
    blockbusting
    channeling
    Civil Rights Act of 1866
    code of ethics
    Department of Housing
      and Urban Develop-
      ment (HUD)
    Equal Credit Opportunity
      Act (ECOA)
    Federal Fair Housing Act
    North Carolina Fair
      Housing Act of 1983
    North Carolina Human
      Relations Commission
    Office of Fair Housing
      and Equal Opportunity
      (OFHEO)
    panic peddling
    protected classes
    redlining
    steering

EQUAL OPPORTUNITY IN HOUSING

The purpose of civil rights laws that affect the real estate industry is to create a marketplace in which all persons of similar financial means have a similar range of housing choices. The goal is to ensure that everyone has the opportunity to live where he or she chooses. Owners, real estate brokers, apartment management companies, real estate organizations, lending agencies, builders, and developers must all take a part in creating this single housing market. Federal, state, and local fair housing or equal opportunity laws affect every phase of a real estate transaction, from listing to closing.

The U.S. Congress and the Supreme Court have created a legal framework that preserves the Constitutional rights of all citizens. However, while the passage of laws may establish a code for public conduct, centuries of discriminatory practices and attitudes are not so easily changed. Real estate brokers cannot allow their own prejudices to interfere with the ethical and legal conduct of their profession. Similarly, the discriminatory attitudes of property owners or property seekers must not be allowed to affect compliance with the fair housing laws. This is not always easy, and the pressure to avoid offending the person who pays the commission can be intense. However, just remember: *Failure to comply with fair housing laws is both a civil and criminal violation, and it is grounds for disciplinary action against a broker* (see Rule A.1601).

> "All citizens of the United States shall have the same right in every state and territory as is enjoyed by white citizens thereof to inherit, purchase, lease, sell, hold, and convey real and personal property."
> —Civil Rights Act of 1866

The federal government's effort to guarantee equal housing opportunities to all U.S. citizens began with the passage of the **Civil Rights Act of 1866**. This law prohibited any type of discrimination based on race. Unlike many laws, there are no exceptions to the Civil Rights Act of 1866.

The U.S. Supreme Court's 1896 decision in *Plessy v. Ferguson* established the *separate but equal* doctrine of legalized racial segregation. A series of court decisions and federal laws in the 20 years between 1948 and 1968 attempted to address the inequities in housing that were results of *Plessy*. Those efforts, however, tended to address only certain aspects of the housing market (such as federally funded housing programs). As a result, their impact was limited.

■ FEDERAL FAIR HOUSING ACT

In 1968, the federal government began to address specific discriminatory practices throughout the real estate industry. Title VIII of the Civil Rights Act of 1968 (called the *Federal Fair Housing Act*) prohibited discrimination in housing based on race, color, religion, or national origin. In 1974, the Housing and Community Development Act added sex to the list of **protected classes.** In 1988, the Fair Housing Amendments Act included handicapping condition and familial status. Today, these laws are known as the **Federal Fair Housing Act** (see Figure 20.1). The Federal Fair Housing Act, as amended, prohibits discrimination on the basis of the following protected classes:

- *Race:* a group of people that an individual was born into or has affiliated with all of their lives;
- *Color:* the actual color of the skin's pigmentation including the degree of darkness;
- *Religion:* the spiritual beliefs of an individual;
- *National origin:* the country in which an individual was born or from which they derive their direct ancestry (not related to citizenship);
- *Sex:* strictly male or female gender (does not include sexual orientation);

- *Handicapping condition:* defined by HUD as *any physical or mental impairment that substantially limits one or more major life activities, or being regarded as having such an impairment;* which includes persons with AIDS and HIV; and
- *Familial status:* any type of family unit with at least one dependent child (under the age of 18), includes pregnant women.

FIGURE 20.1

Federal Fair Housing Laws

Legislation	Race	Color	Religion	National Origin	Sex	Age	Marital Status	Disability	Familial Status	Public Assistance Income
Civil Rights Act of 1866	✔	✔								
Federal Fair Housing Act of 1968 (Title VIII)	✔	✔	✔	✔						
Housing and Community Development Act of 1974					✔					
Fair Housing Amendments Act of 1988								✔	✔	
Equal Credit Opportunity Act of 1974 (lending)	✔	✔	✔	✔	✔	✔	✔			✔

The Act also prohibits discrimination against individuals because of their *association* with persons in the protected classes. This law is administered by the **Department of Housing and Urban Development (HUD).** HUD has established rules and regulations that further interpret the practices affected by the law. In addition, HUD distributes an *equal housing opportunity poster* (see Figure 20.2). The poster declares that the office in which it is displayed promises to adhere to the Federal Fair Housing Act and pledges support for affirmative marketing and advertising programs.

FIGURE 20.2

Equal Housing Opportunity Poster

U. S. Department of Housing and Urban Development

EQUAL HOUSING OPPORTUNITY

We Do Business in Accordance With the Federal Fair Housing Law

(The Fair Housing Amendments Act of 1988)

It is illegal to Discriminate Against Any Person Because of Race, Color, Religion, Sex, Handicap, Familial Status, or National Origin

- In the sale or rental of housing or residential lots
- In advertising the sale or rental of housing
- In the financing of housing
- In the provision of real estate brokerage services
- In the appraisal of housing
- Blockbusting is also illegal

Anyone who feels he or she has been discriminated against may file a complaint of housing discrimination:
1-800-669-9777 (Toll Free)
1-800-927-9275 (TTY)

U.S. Department of Housing and Urban Development
Assistant Secretary for Fair Housing and Equal Opportunity
Washington, D.C. 20410

Previous editions are obsolete   form HUD-928.1 (2/2003)

IN PRACTICE When HUD investigates a broker for discriminatory practices, it may consider failure to prominently display the equal housing opportunity poster in the broker's place of business as evidence of discrimination.

Figure 20.3 describes the activities prohibited by the Federal Fair Housing Act.

FIGURE 20.3

Federal Fair Housing Act Restrictions

Prohibited by Federal Fair Housing Act	Example
Refusing to sell, rent, or negotiate the sale or rental of housing	Kate owns an apartment building with several vacant units. When an Asian family asks to see one of the units, she tells them to go away.
Changing terms, conditions, or services for different individuals as a means of discriminating	Sarah, a Roman Catholic, calls on a duplex, and the landlord tells her the rent is $400 per month. When she talks to the other tenants, she learns that all the Lutherans in the complex pay only $325 per month.
Advertising any discriminatory preference or limitation in housing or making any inquiry or reference that is discriminatory in nature	A real estate broker places the following advertisement in a newspaper: "Just Listed! Perfect home for white family, near excellent parochial school!" A developer places this ad in an urban newspaper: "Sunset River Hollow—Dream Homes Just for You!" The ad is accompanied by a photo of several African American families.
Representing that a property is not available for sale or rent when in fact it is	Jason, who uses a wheelchair, is told that the house he wants to rent is no longer available. The next day, however, the For Rent sign is still in the window.
Profiting by inducing property owners to sell or rent on the basis of the prospective entry into the neighborhood of persons of a protected class	Nancy, a real estate broker, sends brochures to homeowners in the predominantly white Ridgewood neighborhood. The brochures, which feature her past success selling homes, include photos of racial minorities, population statistics, and the caption, "The Changing Face of Ridgewood."
Altering the terms or conditions of a home loan, or denying a loan, as a means of discrimination	A lender requires Maria, a divorced mother of two young children, to pay for a credit report. In addition, her father must cosign her application. After talking to a single male friend, Maria learns that he was not required to do either of those things, despite his lower income and poor credit history.
Denying membership or participation in a multiple listing service, a real estate organization, or another facility related to the sale or rental of housing as a means of discrimination	The Topper County Real Estate Practitioners' Association meets every week to discuss available properties and buyers. None of Topper County's African American or female brokers are allowed to be members of the association.

Expanded Definitions

HUD's regulations provide specific definitions that clarify the scope and application of the Federal Fair Housing Act.

Housing. The regulations define *housing* as a *dwelling*, which includes any building or part of a building designed for occupancy as a residence by one or more families. This includes any residence, such as a single-family house, a condominium, a cooperative, or manufactured housing, as well as vacant land on which any of these structures will be built.

Familial status. *Familial status* refers to the presence of one or more individuals who have not reached the age of 18 and who live with either a parent or legal guardian. The term also includes a woman who is pregnant. Unless a property qualifies as housing for older persons, all properties must be made available to families with children under the same terms and conditions as to anyone else. It is illegal to advertise properties as being for adults only or to indicate a preference for a certain number of children. The number of persons permitted to reside in a property (the occupancy standards) must be based on objective factors such as sanitation or safety. HUD's general standard of occupancy is *two heartbeats per bedroom*. Landlords cannot restrict the number of occupants to eliminate families with children. Complaints about discrimination based on familial status account for a major portion of fair housing violations. Consistency and documentation of applied standards are crucial to compliance with the laws.

■ **FOR EXAMPLE** Greg owned an apartment building. One of his elderly tenants, Paul, was terminally ill. Paul requested that no children be allowed in the vacant apartment next door because the noise would be difficult for him to bear. Greg agreed and refused to rent to families with children. Even though Greg only wanted to make things easier for a dying tenant, he was nonetheless found to have violated the Federal Fair Housing Act by discriminating on the basis of familial status. Intentions, whether good or bad, are irrelevant in determining the violation of the Act.

Handicapping condition. It is unlawful to discriminate against prospective buyers or tenants on the basis of a handicapping condition. Landlords must make reasonable accommodations to existing policies, practices, or services to permit persons with disabilities to have equal enjoyment of the premises. For instance, it would be reasonable for a landlord to permit service animals (such as guide dogs) in a normally no-pets building or to provide a designated handicapped parking space in a generally unreserved lot.

> A *handicapping condition* is an impairment that substantially limits one or more of a person's major life activities.

IN PRACTICE The Federal Fair Housing Act's protection of disabled persons does not include those who are current users of illegal or controlled substances. Nor are individuals who have been convicted of the illegal manufacture or distribution of a controlled substance protected under this law. However, the law does prohibit discrimination against those who are participating in addiction recovery programs. For instance, a landlord could lawfully discriminate against a cocaine user but not against a rehabilitated member of Narcotics Anonymous.

People with disabilities must be permitted to make reasonable modifications to the premises at their own expense. Such modifications might include lowering countertops or installing bath rails to accommodate a person in a wheelchair. Failure to permit reasonable modification constitutes discrimination. However, the law recognizes that some reasonable modifications might make a rental property undesirable to the general population. In such a case, the landlord is allowed to require that the property be restored to its previous condition by the tenant when the lease period ends.

The law does not prohibit restricting occupancy exclusively to persons with handicaps in dwellings that are designed specifically for their accommodation.

For new construction of certain multifamily properties, a number of accessibility and usability requirements must be met under the **Americans with Disabilities Act (ADA)**. Access is specified for public and common-use portions of the buildings, and adaptive and accessible design must be implemented for the interior of the dwelling units. Some states have their own accessibility laws as well.

Exemptions to the Federal Fair Housing Act

The Federal Fair Housing Act provides for certain exemptions. It is important for brokers to know in what situations the exemptions apply. However, brokers should be aware that *no exceptions apply when a real estate broker is involved in a transaction.*

The sale or rental of a single-family home is exempt when

- the home is owned by an individual who does not own more than three such homes at one time (and who does not sell more than one every two years);
- a real estate broker is *not* involved in the transaction; and
- discriminatory advertising is not used.

The rental of rooms or units is exempt in an *owner-occupied* one-family to four-family dwelling.

Dwelling units owned by religious organizations may be restricted to people of the same religion if membership in the organization is not restricted on the basis of protected class. A private club that is not open to the public may restrict the rental or occupancy of lodgings that it owns to its members as long as the lodgings are not operated commercially.

The Federal Fair Housing Act does not require that housing be made available to any individual whose tenancy would constitute a direct threat to the health or safety of other individuals or that would result in substantial physical damage to the property of others.

Housing for older persons. While the Federal Fair Housing Act protects families with children, certain properties can be restricted to occupancy by elderly persons. The Housing for Older Persons Act of 1995 (HOPA) allows certain exemptions from the familial status protection. Housing intended solely for occupancy by persons age 62 or older or housing occupied by at least one person 55 years of age or older per unit (where 80% of the units are occupied by individuals 55 or older) is exempt.

Jones v. Mayer

In 1968, the Supreme Court heard the case of *Jones v. Alfred H. Mayer Company*, 392 U.S. 409 (1968). In its decision, the Court upheld the Civil Rights Act of 1866. This decision is important because although the federal law exempts individual homeowners and certain groups, the 1866 law *prohibits all racial discrimination without exception.* A person who is discriminated against on the basis of race may still recover damages under the 1866 law. *Where race is involved, no exceptions apply.*

The U.S. Supreme Court has expanded the definition of the term *race* to include ancestral and ethnic characteristics, including certain physical, cultural, or linguistic characteristics that are commonly shared by a national origin group. These rulings are significant because discrimination on the basis of race, as it is now defined, affords due process of complaints under the provisions of the Civil Rights Act of 1866.

Enforcement of the Federal Fair Housing Act

The Federal Fair Housing Act is administered by the **Office of Fair Housing and Equal Opportunity (OFHEO)** under the direction of the Secretary of HUD. Any aggrieved person who believes illegal discrimination has occurred may file a complaint with HUD within one year of the alleged act. HUD may also initiate its own complaint. Complaints may be reported to the Office of Fair Housing and Equal Opportunity, Department of Housing and Urban Development, Washington, DC 20410, or to the Office of Fair Housing and Equal Opportunity in care of the nearest HUD regional office. Complaints also may be submitted directly to HUD using an online form.

Upon receiving a complaint, HUD initiates an investigation. Within 100 days of the filing of the complaint, HUD either determines that reasonable cause exists to bring a charge of illegal discriminaton or dismisses the complaint. During this investigation period, HUD can attempt to resolve the dispute informally through conciliation. *Conciliation* is the resolution of a complaint by obtaining assurance that the person against whom the complaint was filed (the respondent) will remedy any violation that may have occurred. The respondent further agrees to take steps to eliminate or prevent discriminatory practices in the future. If necessary, these agreements can be enforced through civil action.

The aggrieved person has the right to seek relief through administrative proceedings. Administrative proceedings are hearings held before *administrative law judges (ALJs)*. An ALJ has the authority to award actual damages to the aggrieved person or persons and, if it is believed the public interest will be served, to impose monetary penalties. The penalties range can be up to $10,000 for the first offense, up to $25,000 for a second violation within five years, and up to $50,000 for further violations within seven years. The ALJ also has the authority to issue an injunction to order the offender to either do something (such as rent an apartment to the complaining party) or refrain from doing something (such as acting in a discriminatory manner).

The parties may elect civil action in federal court at any time within two years of the discriminatory act. For cases heard in federal court, unlimited punitive damages can be awarded in addition to actual damages. The court can also issue injunctions. As noted in Chapter 7, errors and omissions insurance carried by brokers normally does not cover losses caused by violations of the fair housing laws.

Whenever the attorney general has reasonable cause to believe that any person or group is engaged in a pattern or practice of resistance to the full enjoyment of any of the rights granted by the federal fair housing laws, the attorney general may file a civil action in any federal district court. Civil penalties may result in an amount not to exceed $50,000 for a first violation and an amount not to exceed $100,000 for second and subsequent violations.

Complaints brought under the Civil Rights Act of 1866 are taken directly to federal courts. The only time limit for bringing legal action is a state's statute of limitations for *torts*—injuries one individual inflicts on another.

EQUAL CREDIT OPPORTUNITY ACT

> The Equal Credit Opportunity Act prohibits discrimination in granting credit based on
> - race,
> - color,
> - religion,
> - national origin,
> - sex,
> - marital status,
> - age, and
> - receipt of public assistance.

The federal **Equal Credit Opportunity Act (ECOA)** guarantees nondiscrimination in the granting of credit by protecting classes of persons similar to the Federal Fair Housing Act. It prohibits discrimination based on race, color, religion, national origin, sex, marital status, or age in the granting of credit. Marital status and age are classes that are unique to ECOA. It also prevents lenders from discriminating against recipients of public assistance programs such as food stamps and Social Security. As in the Federal Fair Housing Act, the ECOA requires that credit applications be considered only on the basis of income, net worth, job stability, and credit rating. More information about the ECOA is available at the Federal Trade Commission's website.

NORTH CAROLINA FAIR HOUSING ACT OF 1983

In 1983, North Carolina passed a fair housing law that is almost identical to the Federal Fair Housing Act of 1968. The North Carolina list of protected classes is the same as the list used under the federal Act. The major difference between the state and federal discrimination laws is the differences in exemptions.

Prohibited Acts

The **North Carolina Fair Housing Act of 1983** prohibits the same activities as the federal law (refer to the list of prohibited activities discussed under the Federal Fair Housing Act). Thus, one discriminatory act violates both federal and state laws and subjects the violator to both federal and state penalties.

Exemptions

> There are substantial differences in exemptions under federal and state laws; the stricter law rules.
>
> In North Carolina

While the state law's prohibited activities are identical to those of the federal law, the exemptions to the state Act contain substantial differences.

- The Federal Fair Housing Act exempts private owners who sell their own homes without the use of a real estate broker. There is no similar exemption to the state Fair Housing Act. *Note that when there is a conflict between state and federal law, the most restrictive law applies:* persons selling their own homes must not resort to discriminatory practices even though they are exempted by federal law. The state does, however, exempt the rental of rooms in a private home occupied by the owner.
- The state Act exempts the rental of a unit in a one- to four-unit residential building if the owner or one of the owner's family members lives in one of the units. The federal law exempts such a unit only if the owner lives in one of the units.
- The state Act exempts the rental of rooms in a single-sex dormitory. The federal law does not include this exemption (although it is doubtful that such a practice would be prosecuted as a violation of the federal law).

The other exemptions in the federal Act are mirrored in the state Act. Again, if there is disagreement between the state and federal fair housing legislation, the stricter of the two will rule.

Enforcement of North Carolina Fair Housing Act

The first place to file a complaint by those who have been injured by discriminatory housing acts is the **North Carolina Human Relations Commission.** The Commission then begins investigating the complaint and simultaneously tries to resolve the conflict through conference, conciliation, or persuasion. If the Commission finds there are no reasonable grounds for the complaint, it is dismissed, but the injured party may still bring a discrimination suit in state court. However, if there are reasonable grounds to believe unlawful discrimination took place and the Commission's informal negotiation process does not work, the Commission must then

- dismiss the complaint and issue a right-to-sue letter to the injured party (which entitles the party to bring a court case against the accused at the complainant's own expense), or
- file a lawsuit in state court against the accused.

SEXUAL HARASSMENT

In North Carolina   North Carolina has a law (G.S. 14-395) pertaining to sexual harassment of a prospective tenant by a landlord (lessor) or a lessor's agent. This statute defines sexual harassment as *unsolicited overt requests or demands for sexual acts* when (1) submission to such conduct is made a term of the execution or continuation of the lease agreement or (2) submission to or rejection of such conduct by an individual is used to determine whether rights under the lease are accorded.

Sexual harassment has been further defined as any type of sexual behavior that creates an intimidating, hostile, or offensive environment. Examples of sexual harassment include

- *verbal harassment*—sexual innuendo, suggestive comments, insults, jokes about sex or gender, sexual propositions, and threats;
- *nonverbal harassment*—suggestive or insulting sounds, leering, whistling, and obscene gestures; and
- *physical harassment*—inappropriate touching, pinching, brushing the body, fondling the body, coerced sexual intercourse, and sexual assault.

IN PRACTICE   The North Carolina Real Estate Commission can take disciplinary measures against licensees for violating state fair housing laws. Rule A.1601 Fair Housing states: "Conduct by a licensee which violates the provisions of the State Fair Housing Act constitutes improper conduct in violation of G.S. 93A-6(a)(10)."

IMPLICATIONS FOR BROKERS

To a large extent, the laws place the burden of responsibility for effecting and maintaining fair housing on real estate brokers. Brokers must comply with the laws, which are clear and widely known. The complainant does not have to prove that the accused was guilty of actual knowledge or specific intent—only the fact that discrimination occurred. In other words, if a broker violated a fair housing law, that broker could be found guilty of discrimination even if there was no intent to discriminate.

How does a broker go about complying with the laws and making that policy known? HUD offers guidelines for nondiscriminatory language and illustrations for use in real estate advertising. The agency further requires that every broker take affirmative marketing action in the choice of advertising media and in individual canvassing to ensure that all interested individuals have the same range of housing options.

In addition, the National Association of REALTORS® affirms that a broker's position can be emphasized and problems avoided by the prominent display of a sign stating that it is against company policy as well as state and federal laws to offer any information on the protected class composition of a neighborhood or to place restrictions on listing, showing, or providing information on the availability of homes for any of these reasons. If a prospect still expresses a locational preference for housing based on presence or absence of a protected class, the NAR's guidelines suggest the following response: "I cannot give you that kind of advice. I will show you several homes that meet your specifications. You will have to decide which one you want."

There is more to fair housing practices than just following the letter of the law, however. Discrimination involves a sensitive area of human emotions—specifically, fear and the drive for self-preservation based on considerable prejudice and misconception. The broker who complies with the law still must interact, in many cases, with a general public whose attitudes cannot be altered by legislation alone. Therefore, a broker who wishes to comply with the fair housing laws and also succeed in the real estate business must work to educate the public.

In North Carolina

To further understanding of and adherence to the fair housing laws, all agency agreements in North Carolina must contain the following non-discrimination clause that is printed in a font that will attract attention. Note that the National Association of REALTORS® membership has added the protected class of sexual orientation to the seven state and national classes.

> THE AGENT (FIRM) SHALL CONDUCT ALL BROKERAGE ACTIVITIES IN REGARD TO THIS AGREEMENT WITHOUT RESPECT TO THE RACE, COLOR, RELIGION, SEX, NATIONAL ORIGIN, HANDICAP OR FAMILIAL STATUS OF ANY PARTY OR PROSPECTIVE PARTY TO THE AGREEMENT. FURTHER, REALTORS® HAVE AN ETHICAL DUTY TO CONDUCT SUCH ACTIVITIES WITHOUT RESPECT TO THE SEXUAL ORIENTATION OF ANY PARTY OR PROSPECTIVE PARTY TO THIS AGREEMENT.

For every broker, a sincere, positive attitude toward fair housing laws is a good start in dealing with this sensitive issue. It provides an effective model for all who come in contact with the broker. Active cooperation with local real estate board programs and community committees is also an excellent idea. This shows the broker's willingness to serve the community and observe the laws, and it helps to change public attitudes. Both factors can result in good public relations and, ultimately, more business for the broker.

IN PRACTICE Brokers encounter clients and customers who may want to discriminate on purpose or who may not realize their intentions are actually forms of discrimination. Following are some typical situations with suggested responses.

Situation: A seller-client wants their agent to discriminate against a protected class.

Response: The agent should advise the seller that the federal Act prohibits sellers, when using a broker, to discriminate. Suggested response: "Under the North Carolina Fair Housing Act, you have a right to sell to anyone as long as you do not discriminate on the basis of race, color, religion, sex, handicap, national origin, or familial status."

Situation: A buyer (client or customer) does not want to be shown dwellings in a neighborhood occupied by persons in a protected class.

Response: Collect all information on all properties in all areas that meet the buyer's needs. Have the information available and allow the buyer to choose which properties to see.

Situation: A buyer wants information about the racial and/or ethnic makeup of a neighborhood in which the buyer is interested.

Response: "We do not keep records or statistics on racial or ethnic population in particular areas since distribution of that information would be a violation of state and federal fair housing laws."

■ AMERICANS WITH DISABILITIES ACT

Although the Americans with Disabilities Act (ADA) is not a housing or credit law, it has a significant effect on the real estate industry. The ADA is important to brokers because it addresses the rights of individuals with disabilities in employment and public accommodations. Real estate brokers are often employers, and real estate brokerage offices are public spaces. The ADA's goal is to enable individuals with disabilities to become part of the economic and social mainstream of society.

> The Americans with Disabilities Act requires reasonable accommodations in employment and access to goods, services, and public buildings.

Title I of the ADA requires that employers (including real estate brokers) make *reasonable accommodations* that enable an individual with a disability to perform essential job functions. Reasonable accommodations include making the work site accessible, restructuring a job, providing part-time or flexible work schedules, and modifying equipment that is used on the job. The provisions of the ADA apply to any employer with 15 or more employees.

Title III of the ADA provides for accessibility to goods and services for individuals with disabilities. While the federal civil rights laws have traditionally been viewed in the real estate industry as housing-related, the practices of brokers who deal with nonresidential property are significantly affected by the ADA. Because people with disabilities have the right to full and equal access to businesses and public services under the ADA, building owners and managers must ensure that any obstacle restricting this right is eliminated. The Americans with Disabilities Act

Accessibility Guidelines (ADAAG) contain detailed specifications for designing parking spaces, curb ramps, elevators, drinking fountains, toilet facilities, and directional signs to ensure maximum accessibility.

ADA and the Federal Fair Housing Act

The ADA exempts two types of property from its requirements:

1. Property that is covered by the Federal Fair Housing Act
2. Property that is exempt from coverage by the Federal Fair Housing Act

Some properties, however, are subject to both laws. For example, in an apartment complex, the rental office is a *place of public accommodation*. As such, the rental office is covered by the ADA, and must be accessible to persons with disabilities at the owner's expense. The Federal Fair Housing Act would cover individual rental units. A tenant who wishes to modify the unit to make it accessible would be responsible for the cost.

IN PRACTICE Real estate brokers need a general knowledge of the ADA's provisions. It is necessary that a broker's workplace and employment policies comply with the law. Also, brokers who are building managers must ensure that the properties are legally accessible. However, ADA compliance questions may arise with regard to a client's property too. Unless the broker is a qualified ADA expert, it is best to advise commercial clients to seek the services of an attorney, an architect, or a consultant who specializes in ADA issues. It is possible that an appraiser may be liable for failing to identify and account for a property's noncompliance.

■ FAIR HOUSING PROHIBITED PRACTICES

For the civil rights laws to accomplish their goal of eliminating discrimination, brokers must apply them routinely. Of course, compliance also means that brokers avoid violating both the laws and the ethical standards of the profession. The following discussion examines the ethical and legal issues that confront real estate brokers.

Blockbusting

Blockbusting: Encouraging the sale or renting of property by claiming that the entry of a protected class into the neighborhood will negatively affect property values.

Blockbusting (also known as **panic peddling**) is the act of encouraging people to sell or rent their homes by claiming that the entry of a protected class into the neighborhood will have some negative impact on property values. Blockbusting was a common practice during the 1950s and 1960s, as unscrupulous real estate brokers profited by fueling *white flight* from cities to suburbs. Any message, however subtle, that property should be sold or rented because the neighborhood is *undergoing changes* is considered blockbusting. It is illegal to assert that the presence of members of a certain protected class will cause property values to decline, crime or antisocial behavior to increase, and the quality of schools to suffer.

A critical element in blockbusting, according to HUD, is the profit motive. A property owner may be intimidated into selling a property at a depressed price to the blockbuster, who in turn sells the property to another person at a higher price. Another term for this activity is *panic selling*. To avoid accusations of blockbusting,

Steering

> *Steering:* Channeling home seekers toward or away from particular neighborhoods based on presence or absence of a protected class.

Steering is the **channeling** of home seekers to particular neighborhoods based on the presence or absence of a protected class. It also includes discouraging potential buyers from considering some areas. In either case, it is an illegal limitation of a purchaser's options.

The intent of steering may be either to preserve the character of a neighborhood or to change its character intentionally. Many cases of steering are subtle, motivated by assumptions or perceptions about a home seeker's preferences, based on some stereotype. Assumptions are not only dangerous—they are often *wrong*. The broker cannot *assume* that a prospective home seeker expects to be directed to certain neighborhoods or properties. Steering anyone is illegal. Brokers should always allow the client to select which properties or neighborhoods are viewed.

■ **FOR EXAMPLE**

- A broker lists a home in a predominantly Hispanic neighborhood. He places an ad in a publication primarily aimed at Hispanic readers and does not advertise the property in any other publications.
- A broker showing property to a black couple in a predominantly white neighborhood does not use his best efforts to present the offer and get it accepted.
- A broker is marketing homes in a new subdivision and in pictorial ads shows only adults enjoying the amenities.

Advertising

No advertisement of property for sale or rent may include language indicating a preference or limitation for the protected class status of the prospective buyer or tenant. No exception to this rule exists, regardless of how subtle the choice of words. HUD's regulations cite examples that are considered discriminatory (see Figure 20.4).

The media used for promoting property or real estate services cannot target one protected class population to the exclusion of others. The selective use of media, whether by language or geography, may have discriminatory impact. For instance, advertising property only in a Korean-language newspaper tends to discriminate against non-Koreans. Similarly, limiting advertising to a magazine targeted to female subscribers may be construed as a discriminatory act. However, if an advertisement also appears in general-circulation media, it may be legal.

Appraising

Those who prepare appraisals or any statements of valuation, whether they are formal or informal, oral or written (including a competitive market analysis), may consider any factors that affect value. However, race, color, religion, national origin, sex, handicap, and familial status are not factors that may be considered.

FIGURE 20.4

HUD's Advertising Guidelines

Category	Rule	Permitted	Not Permitted
Race Color National Origin	No discriminatory limitation or preference may be expressed	"master bedroom" "good neighborhood"	"white neighborhood" "no French"
Religion	No religious preference or limitation	"chapel on premises" "kosher meals available" "Merry Christmas"	"no Muslims" "nice Christian family" "near great Catholic school"
Sex	No explicit preference based on gender	"mother-in-law suite" "master bedroom" "bachelor apartment"	"great house for a man" "wife's dream kitchen" "only female tenants allowed"
Handicap	No exclusions or limitations based on disability	"wheelchair ramp" "walk to shopping" "walk-in closet"	"no wheelchairs" "able-bodied tenants only"
Familial Status	No preference or limitation based on family size or composition	"two-bedroom" "family room" "quiet neighborhood"	"no more than two children" "adults only"
Photographs Illustrations of People	People should be clearly representative and nonexclusive	Illustrations showing ethnic races, family groups, singles, etc.	Illustrations showing groups of all-adult people, people of a single ethnicity, elderly white adults, etc.

Redlining

Redlining is an illegal practice by lending institutions to deny or discourage loan applications in an area based on its racial composition or deterioration.

The practice of refusing to make mortgage loans or issue insurance policies in specific areas for reasons other than the economic qualifications of the applicants or the collateral value of the property offered is known as **redlining**. Redlining refers to literally drawing a line around particular areas. This practice is often a major contributor to the deterioration of older neighborhoods. Redlining is frequently based on racial or ethnic grounds rather than on any real objection to an applicant's creditworthiness. For example, the lender makes a policy decision that no property in a certain area is qualified for a loan, no matter who wants to buy it, because of the neighborhood's ethnic character. The Federal Fair Housing Act prohibits discrimination in mortgage lending and covers not only the actions of primary lenders but also activities in the secondary mortgage market. A lending institution can refuse a loan, but solely on *sound* economic grounds. Charging different loan fees or interest rates based on protected class membership by the proposed borrower also would constitute redlining.

The Home Mortgage Disclosure Act requires that all institutional mortgage lenders with assets in excess of $10 million and one or more offices in a given geographic area make annual reports. The reports must detail all mortgage loans the institution has made or purchased, broken down by census tract. This law enables the government to detect patterns of lending behavior that might constitute redlining.

Intent and Effect

If a property owner or real estate broker *purposely* sets out to engage in blockbusting, steering, or other unfair activities, the intent to discriminate is obvious. However, owners and brokers must examine their activities and policies carefully to determine whether they have *unintentional discriminatory effects*. Whenever policies or practices result in unequal treatment of persons in the protected classes, they are considered discriminatory regardless of any innocent intent. This *effects* test is applied by regulatory agencies to determine whether an individual has been subjected to discrimination.

Threats or Acts of Violence

Being a real estate broker is not generally considered a dangerous occupation. However, some brokers may find themselves the targets of threats or violence merely for complying with fair housing laws. The Federal Fair Housing Act of 1968 protects the rights of those who seek the benefits of the open housing law. It also protects property owners and brokers who aid or encourage the enjoyment of open housing rights. Threats, coercion, and intimidation are punishable by criminal action. In such a case, the victim should report the incident immediately to the local police and to the nearest office of the Federal Bureau of Investigation.

■ PROFESSIONAL ETHICS

Professional conduct involves more than just complying with the law. In real estate, state licensing laws establish those activities that are illegal and therefore prohibited. However, merely complying with the letter of the law may not be enough: brokers may perform *legally*, yet not *ethically*. Ethics refers to a system of *moral* principles, rules, and standards of conduct. The ethical system of a profession establishes conduct that goes beyond merely complying with the law. These moral principles address two sides of a profession:

1. They establish standards for integrity and competence in dealing with consumers of an industry's services.
2. They define a code of conduct for relations within the industry, among its professionals.

Code of Ethics

One way that many organizations address ethics among their members or in their respective businesses is by adopting codes of professional conduct. A **code of ethics** is a written system of standards for ethical conduct. The code contains statements designed to advise, guide, and regulate job behavior. To be effective, a code of ethics must be specific by dictating rules that either prohibit or demand certain behavior. Lofty statements of positive goals are not especially helpful. By including sanctions for violators, a code of ethics becomes more effective.

The National Association of REALTORS® (NAR), the largest trade association in the country, adopted a Code of Ethics for its members in 1913. REALTORS® are expected to subscribe to this strict code of conduct. NAR has established procedures for professional standards committees at the local, state, and national levels of the organization to administer compliance. Interpretations of the code are known as *Standards of Practice*. NAR has instituted a quadrennial ethics refresher course requirement for all REALTORS®. The NAR Code of Ethics has proved helpful because it contains practical applications of business ethics. Many other professional organizations in the real estate industry have codes of ethics as well. In addition, many state real estate regulatory commissions are required by law to establish codes or canons of ethical behavior for their states' brokers.

■ RELATED WEBSITES

Federal Trade Commission: www.ftc.gov
National Association of REALTORS®:   www.realtor.org
National Fair Housing Advocate Online: www.fairhousing.com
Office of Fair Housing and Equal Opportunity:
   www.hud.gov/offices/fheo/index.cfm

■ KEY POINT REVIEW

Equal opportunity in housing is intended to create a marketplace in which all persons of similar financial means have a similar range of housing choices. Equal opportunity laws apply to owners, real estate brokers, apartment management companies, real estate organizations, lending agencies, builders, and developers.

The **Civil Rights Act of 1866**

- guaranteed equal housing opportunities to all U.S. citizens,
- was upheld in *Jones v. Mayer, 1968*, and
- prohibits all racial discrimination with no exceptions.
- Complaints under the Civil Rights Act of 1866 go directly to federal court.

Race was defined by the U.S. Supreme Court to include ancestral and ethnic characteristics, including certain physical, cultural, or linguistic traits that are shared by a group with a common national origin.

The **Federal Fair Housing Act** is Title VIII of the Civil Rights Act of 1968 and

- prohibits discrimination in housing based on race, color, religion, or national origin;
- does not prohibit discrimination based solely on a person's citizenship status; and
- prohibits illegal activities that include **steering, blockbusting**, and **redlining**.

The Housing and Community Development Act of 1974 added sex to list of protected classes.

The **Fair Housing Amendments Act of 1988**, which added handicapping condition and familial status (families with children) to protected classes,

- prohibits discrimination against individuals because of their association with people in the protected classes; and

- is administered by HUD, which
  — establishes rules and regulations to further clarify the law, and
  — created the equal housing opportunity poster.

The Housing for Older Persons Act of 1995 repealed facilities and services requirements designed for older persons and prohibited an award of monetary damages against those who reasonably rely in good faith on property designated as housing for older persons as being exempt from familial status provisions of the Fair Housing Act.

Housing is exempt from familial status protection if it is restricted to persons age 62 or older, or if 80% of the units are occupied by persons over age 55.

Exemptions from the Federal Fair Housing Act (but not the Civil Rights Act of 1866) include

- rentals in owner-occupied buildings with no more than four units;
- housing operated by organizations and private clubs that limit occupancy to members; and
- the sale or rental of a single-family home when fewer than three homes are owned by an individual, discriminatory advertising is not used, and a real estate broker is not involved in the transaction.

The **Equal Credit Opportunity Act of 1974** prohibits discrimination in lending on the basis of race, color, religion, national origin, sex, age, marital status, and public assistance.

Familial status extends fair housing protections to families with children, meaning a family in which one or more individuals under the age of 18 live with either a parent or a guardian, or a woman who is pregnant, including the following:

- Families with children must be considered under the same terms and conditions as anyone else.
- The property cannot be advertised as adults only, and the ads cannot indicate limitation on the number of children accepted.
- Limitations on the number of people permitted to reside in a house or apartment must be based on objective factors such as sanitation or safety.

A *handicapping condition* is a physical or mental impairment that substantially limits one or more of an individual's major life activities.

- Persons with AIDS or that are HIV-positive are included under the handicapping condition protected class.
- The law does not protect individuals who are current users of illegal or controlled substances or who have been convicted of the illegal manufacture or distribution of a controlled substance. However, the law does protect individuals who are participating in addiction recovery programs.
- Reasonable modifications to property to make it usable by an individual with a disability must be allowed, but the individual must return the property to its former condition on vacating it.

The **Americans with Disabilities Act (ADA)** prohibits discrimination in employment and public accommodations; access to facilities and services in commercial properties must be provided when reasonably achievable in existing buildings, with higher standards for new construction/remodeling. Exempt properties include those covered by federal fair housing laws.

North Carolina Fair Housing Act of 1983 mirrors the federal act with the only difference being the exemptions under state law:

- Exemptions from the North Carolina Fair Housing Act:
    — owner can discriminate in the rental of a 1-4 unit residential dwelling if the owner or their family member resides in one of the units
    — a college or university can discriminate in the rental of rooms in a single sex dormitory
    — a seller can NOT discriminate in the sale of residence, even if selling it without a real estate broker
- Complaints are filed with the North Carolina Human Relations Commission.

North Carolina law prohibits sexual harassment of a tenant by landlords or their agents.

QUESTIONS

1. Which of the following actions is permitted under the Federal Fair Housing Act?
   a. Advertising property for sale only to a particular ethnic group
   b. Altering the terms of a loan for a member of a minority group
   c. Refusing to sell a home to an individual because of a poor credit history
   d. Telling a wheelchair-bound individual that an available apartment has been rented because the property owner does not want to allow reasonable accommodations by the applicant

2. What will happen if there is conflict between the federal and state fair housing legislation?
   a. The federal law will prevail over the state law.
   b. The state law will prevail over the federal law.
   c. The more recent law will prevail.
   d. The stricter law will prevail.

3. The Civil Rights Act of 1866 is unique because it
   a. has been broadened to protect the aged.
   b. adds welfare recipients as a protected class.
   c. contains *choose your neighbor* provisions.
   d. provides no exceptions to racial discrimination.

4. "They are the first of their kind to move into the neighborhood. Better list with me today before the property values start to drop!" is an example of
   a. steering.
   b. blockbusting.
   c. redlining.
   d. testing.

5. The act of channeling home seekers to a particular area either to maintain or to change the character of the neighborhood is
   a. blockbusting.
   b. redlining.
   c. steering.
   d. permitted under the Federal Fair Housing Act of 1968.

6. Under the provisions of the Federal Fair Housing Act, if a lender refuses to make loans in certain areas because the population is made up of more than 25% African-Americans, the lender is probably practicing
   a. redlining.
   b. blockbusting.
   c. steering.
   d. borrower qualifying.

7. Which practice is NOT permitted under the Federal Fair Housing Act as amended?
   I. Preference in the rental of rooms by a private club to its members
   II. An owner of a 20-unit apartment building renting exclusively to females
   a. I only
   b. II only
   c. Both I and II
   d. Neither I nor II

8. Under federal law, families with children may be refused rental or purchase in buildings where strict conditions are met and occupancy is reserved exclusively for those at least how many years old?
   a. 55
   b. 60
   c. 62
   d. 65

9. A newspaper ad reads: "For sale: 4 BR brick home; Redwood School District; excellent location; short walk to St. John's Catholic Church; and right on the bus line. Move-in conditions. Priced to sell." Which of the following statements is *TRUE*?
   a. The ad describes the property for sale and is very appropriate.
   b. The fair housing laws do not apply to newspaper advertising.
   c. The ad should state that the property is available to families with children.
   d. The ad should not mention St. John's Catholic Church.

10. An African American real estate broker's practice of offering a special discount to African American clients is
    a. legally acceptable.
    b. illegal.
    c. legal but ill-advised.
    d. of no consequence.

11. Protection from discrimination against a single father with a child under 18 in the sale or rental of real estate is provided by the
    a. Fair Housing Amendments Act of 1988.
    b. Civil Rights Act of 1866.
    c. Americans with Disabilities Act.
    d. Equal Credit Opportunity Act of 1974.

12. The Federal Fair Housing Amendments Act of 1988 added which of the following as protected classes?
    a. Occupation and source of income
    b. Handicap and familial status
    c. Political affiliation and country of origin
    d. Age and marital status

13. A real estate broker told a single man with two small children that units for sale in a condominium complex are available only to married couples with no children. Which of the following statements is *TRUE*?
    a. The condominium complex is permitted to restrict buyers in any way as long as it is uniform in applying the restrictions.
    b. Multi-family complexes are exempt from the fair housing laws.
    c. The man may file a fair housing complaint alleging discrimination on the basis of familial status.
    d. The man may file a fair housing complaint alleging discrimination on the basis of marital status.

14. The seller requests that showings be restricted to buyers of a particular race and national origin. The listing agent
    a. must obey the seller-client regardless of the agent's personal beliefs.
    b. should terminate the listing if the seller will not reconsider the instructions.
    c. may obey the client as long as the agent is not obvious in the restriction.
    d. should ignore the seller's instructions and show to all buyers.

15. In North Carolina, a person who feels she has been discriminated against in housing by a property owner should file a complaint with the
    a. local sheriff.
    b. North Carolina Human Relations Commission.
    c. North Carolina Board of REALTORS®.
    d. North Carolina Real Estate Commission.

16. After a broker takes a residential listing, the owner states that he does not want his home shown or sold to a Mexican buyer. The broker should
    a. advertise the property exclusively in Spanish-language newspapers.
    b. explain that the broker cannot knowingly comply with any instruction that violates federal law.
    c. abide by the client's directions since the agency's duty of obedience overrides fair housing laws.
    d. require that the owner sign a separate legal document stating the additional instruction as an amendment to the listing agreements.

17. All of the following are in violation of the Federal Fair Housing Act of 1968 EXCEPT the
    a. refusal of a property manager to rent an apartment to a Catholic couple who are otherwise qualified.
    b. general policy of a loan company to avoid granting home loans in an ethnically transitional neighborhoods.
    c. intentional neglect of a broker to show an Asian family property listings in all-white neighborhoods.
    d. insistence of a widowed woman on renting her spare bedroom only to another widow.

18. A real estate broker wants to end racial segregation. As an office policy, the broker requires that affiliated brokers show prospective buyers from racial or ethnic minority groups only properties that are in certain areas of town in order to create more diversity in residential areas. The broker has prepared a map illustrating the appropriate neighborhoods for each racial or ethnic group. Which of the following statements is true regarding this broker's policy?
    a. The broker's policy constitutes blockbusting only because of the use of the prepared area map.
    b. It constitutes illegal steering, regardless of the broker's intentions.
    c. The broker's policy clearly shows the intent to improve community diversity and is therefore legal.
    d. The broker's policy constitutes steering because the broker requires policy compliance by his affiliated brokers.

19. All of the following are protected classes under the Equal Credit Opportunity Act EXCEPT
    a. national origin.
    b. familial status.
    c. religion.
    d. age.

20. The provisions of the Fair Housing Act apply
    a. in all states.
    b. only in those states that have ratified the act.
    c. only in those states that do not have substantially equivalent laws.
    d. only in those states that do not have specific state fair housing laws.

CHAPTER 21

Environmental Issues and the Real Estate Transaction

■ **LEARNING OBJECTIVES** *When you have finished reading this chapter, you should be able to*

- ■ **identify** the basic environmental hazards of which a broker should be aware in order to protect the interests of clients.
- ■ **describe** the warning signs, characteristics, causes, and solutions of the most common environmental hazards found in real estate transactions.
- ■ **understand** the disclosure requirements of the Lead-Based Paint Hazard Reduction Act.
- ■ **recognize** North Carolina environmental laws and their relevance to specific transactions.
- ■ **explain** the liability issues arising under environmental protection laws.
- ■ **name** the agencies that administer and enforce environmental laws.
- ■ **define** these *key terms*:

asbestos	Lead-Based Paint Hazard Reduction Act	North Carolina Sediment Pollution Control Act
carbon monoxide	lead poisoning	radon
Comprehensive Environmental Response, Compensation, and Liability Act (CERCLA)	mitigation	underground storage tank (UST)
	North Carolina Coastal Area Management Act (CAMA)	urea-formaldehyde foam insulation (UFFI)
electromagnetic fields (EMFs)	North Carolina Dredge and Fill Act	water table
encapsulation	North Carolina Leaking Petroleum Underground Storage Tank Cleanup Act	
groundwater		
landfill		

■ ENVIRONMENTAL ISSUES

Most states have recognized the need to balance the legitimate commercial use of land with the needs to preserve vital resources and protect the quality of their air, water, and soil. A growing number of homebuyers base their decisions in part on the desire for fresh air, clean water, and outdoor recreational opportunities. Preservation of a state's environment both enhances the quality of life and helps strengthen property values. The prevention and cleanup of pollutants and toxic wastes not only revitalize the land but also create greater opportunities for responsible development.

Environmental issues have become an important factor in the practice of real estate. Consumers are becoming more health-conscious and safety-concerned and are enforcing their rights to make informed decisions. Scientists are learning more about our environment, and consumers are reacting by demanding that their surroundings be free of chemical hazards. These developments affect not only participants in sales transactions, but also appraisers, developers, lending institutions, and property managers.

Real estate brokers must be alert to the existence of environmental hazards. Although it is important to ensure the health and safety of property users, the burden of disclosure or elimination of hazards is heaviest at the time ownership of property transfers. This creates added liability for real estate practitioners if the presence of a toxic substance causes a health problem. If a property buyer suffers physical harm because of the substance, the broker can be vulnerable to a personal injury suit in addition to other legal liability. Environmental issues are health issues, and health issues based on environmental hazards have become real estate issues. For this reason, it is extremely important that brokers not only make property disclosures but also see that prospective purchasers get authoritative information about and inspections for hazardous substances so that they can make informed decisions.

Brokers should be familiar with state and federal environmental laws and the regulatory agencies that enforce them. Brokers are not expected to have the technical expertise necessary to determine whether a hazardous substance is present. However, they must be aware of environmental issues and take steps to ensure that the interests of all parties involved in real estate transactions are protected.

■ HAZARDOUS SUBSTANCES

Pollution and hazardous substances in the environment are of interest to real estate brokers because they affect the attractiveness, desirability, and market value of cities, neighborhoods, and backyards. A toxic environment is not a place where anyone would want to live (see Figure 21.1).

Chapter 21 Environmental Issues and the Real Estate Transaction   **463**

FIGURE 21.1

Environmental Hazards

[Diagram of a house with labels: Urea-Formaldehyde Insulation, Asbestos Ceiling Tiles, Mold in the House, Electromagnetic Radiation, Dripping PCBs, Lead-Based Paint, Carbon Monoxide, Contaminated Well Water, Contaminated Groundwater from Nearby Landfill, Radon Gas, Underground Storage Tanks]

Asbestos

Asbestos is a mineral that was once used as insulation because it is resistant to fire and contains heat effectively. Until the use of asbestos insulation was banned in 1978, asbestos was found in most residential construction. It was a component of more than 3,000 types of building materials, including appliances, ceiling and floor tiles, exterior siding, and roofing. The Environmental Protection Agency (EPA) estimates that about 20% of the nation's commercial and public buildings contain asbestos.

Today, we know that inhaling microscopic asbestos fibers may result in a variety of respiratory diseases as well as lung and stomach cancer. The mere presence of asbestos insulation is not necessarily a health hazard if the asbestos-laden item is intact. Asbestos is harmful only if it is disturbed or exposed, as often occurs during renovation or remodeling. Asbestos is highly *friable*; that is, as it ages, asbestos fibers break down easily into tiny filaments and particles. When these particles become airborne, they pose a health risk to humans. Airborne asbestos contamination is most prevalent in public and commercial buildings, including schools. If the asbestos fibers in the indoor air of a building reach a dangerous level, the building becomes almost impossible to lease, finance, or insure since no safe level of asbestos exposure has been determined.

> Asbestos insulation can create airborne contaminants that may result in respiratory diseases and cancer.

Asbestos contamination also can be found in residential properties. Asbestos was used to cover pipes, ducts, plus heating and hot water units. Its fire-resistant properties made it a popular material for use in floor tile, exterior siding, and roofing products. Though it may be easy to identify asbestos when it is visible (for instance, when it is wrapped around heating units and water pipes), identification may be more difficult when it is behind walls or under floors.

Asbestos is costly to remove because the process requires state-licensed asbestos abatement contractors and specially sealed environments. In addition, removal itself may be dangerous: improper removal procedures may further contaminate the air within the structure. The waste generated should be disposed of at a licensed facility, which further adds to the expense of removal. **Encapsulation, or the sealing off of disintegrating asbestos, is an alternate method of asbestos control that may be preferable to removal in certain circumstances.** However, an owner must periodically monitor the condition of the encapsulated asbestos to make sure it is not disintegrating.

Tests can be conducted to determine the level of airborne asbestos to provide an accurate disclosure in a sales transaction. An engineer skilled in identifying the presence of materials that contain asbestos can perform a thorough analysis of a building. An asbestos report is now required in North Carolina before a permit will be issued for the reconstruction, renovation, or demolition of any residential or commercial structure. Either of these approaches can satisfy the concerns of a consumer. Appraisers also should be aware of the possible presence of asbestos.

More information on asbestos-related issues is available from the EPA (telephone: 202-554-1404). In addition, the EPA has numerous publications that provide guidance, information, and assistance with asbestos issues.

Lead-Based Paint and Other Lead Hazards

Lead was used as a pigment and drying agent in alkyd oil-based paint prior to 1978. Lead-based paint may be on any interior or exterior surface, but it is particularly common on doors, windows, and other woodwork. The federal government estimates that lead is present in about 75% of all private housing built before 1978; that involves approximately 57 million homes, ranging from low-income apartments to million-dollar mansions.

Lead poisoning from paint or other sources can result in damage to the brain, nervous system, kidneys, and blood.

An elevated level of lead in the human body causes **lead poisoning** that can lead to serious damage to the brain, kidneys, nervous system, and red blood cells. The degree of harm is related to the amount of exposure and the age at which a person is exposed. Children are most at risk, and it is estimated that as many as one in every six children may have dangerously high amounts of lead in the blood that may first manifest as learning disabilities. Lead dust can be ingested from the hands by a crawling infant, inhaled by any occupant of a structure, or ingested from the water supply because of lead pipes or lead solder. In fact, lead particles can be present elsewhere, too. Soil and groundwater may be contaminated by everything from lead plumbing in leaking landfills to discarded skeet and bullets from an old shooting range. High levels of lead have been found in the soil near waste-to-energy incinerators.

The residential use of lead-based paint was banned in 1978. Brokers who are involved in the sale, management, financing, or appraisal of properties constructed before 1978 face potential liability for any personal injury that might be suffered by an occupant. Numerous legislative efforts affect brokers, sellers, and landlords. There is considerable controversy about practical approaches for handling the presence of lead-based paint. Some suggest that it should be removed; others argue that it should be encapsulated; still others advocate testing to determine the amount of lead present, which then would be disclosed to a prospective owner or resident. In many states, only licensed lead inspectors, abatement contractors, risk assessors, abatement project designers, and abatement workers may deal with the removal or encapsulation of lead in a structure.

No federal law requires that homeowners test for the presence of lead-based paint. However, known lead-based paint hazards must be disclosed. In 1996, the EPA and the Department of Housing and Urban Development (HUD) issued final regulations requiring disclosure of the presence of any known lead-based paint hazards to potential buyers or renters. Under the **Residential Lead-Based Paint Hazard Reduction Act**, persons selling or leasing residential housing constructed before 1978 must disclose the presence of known lead-based paint and provide purchasers or lessees with any relevant records or reports. A lead-based paint disclosure statement must be attached to all sales contracts and leases regarding residential properties built before 1978, and a lead hazard informational pamphlet must be distributed to all prospective buyers and tenants. Purchasers and tenants must be given 10 days in which to conduct risk assessments or inspections for lead-based paint or lead-based paint hazards. Purchasers are not bound by any real estate contract until the 10-day period has expired. A tenant's right to rescind a lease under this Act terminate when the tenant begins occupancy of the rental unit. The regulations specifically require that real estate brokers ensure that all parties comply with the law. The purpose of the rule is to ensure that buyers and renters of housing built prior to 1978 receive proper disclosures. The North Carolina law, the Lead-Based Paint Poisoning Act of 1971 (NCGS §130A-131.5), is a statute that targets the elimination of lead-based paint in houses connected with HUD-assisted projects. Note that lead poisoning may also result from plumbing systems that contain lead pipes. Systems that use lead pipes should be tested frequently. EPA guidance pamphlets and other information about lead-based hazards are available from the National Lead Information Center, 800-424-5323, or online.

In North Carolina

Beginning April 2010, federal law requires anyone who is paid to perform work that disturbs paint in housing and child-occupied facilities to be trained and certified in the EPA's new lead-based work practices. This includes residential rental property owners/managers, general contractors, and special trade contractors (e.g., painters, plumbers, carpenters, electricians). Do-it-yourself property owners are exempted. The Renovation, Repair, and Painting (RR&P) program involves pre-renovation education. This education includes distribution of the pamphlet "Renovate Right" to the property owners before work commences. Sellers, lessors, and renovators are required to disclose any prior test results or any knowledge of lead-based paint hazards. With only a very narrow exception, all real estate licensees (subagent, buyer's agent, dual agent) are required to advise sellers to make the required disclosures. Only buyer's agents who are paid entirely by the buyer are exempt. The North Carolina Real Estate Commission has advised that if a broker

In North Carolina

knows for a fact that renovations were completed in violation of the new EPA rule after April 2010, this will be a material fact which must be disclosed.

Radon

In North Carolina

Radon is a radioactive gas produced as a by-product of the natural decay of other radioactive substances. Although radon can occur anywhere, some areas are known to have abnormally high amounts. Radon is found in every state, with the highest concentrations in the plains states, the upper Midwest, and northeastern United States (see Figure 21.2). Radon has been found in every county in North Carolina, with the heaviest concentration in the mountainous areas of the state. If radon dissipates into the atmosphere, it is not likely to cause harm. However, when radon enters buildings and is trapped in high concentrations (usually in basements with inadequate ventilation), it can cause health problems.

FIGURE 21.2

Radon Concentration in the United States

GENERALIZED GEOLOGIC RADON POTENTIAL OF THE UNITED STATES
by the U.S. Geological Survey

Geologic Radon Potential
(Predicted Average Screening Measurement)

- LOW (<2 pCi/L)
- MODERATE/VARIABLE (2-4 pCi/L)
- HIGH (>4 pCi/L)

Scale
Continental United States and Hawaii
0 100 200 300 400 500
Miles

Opinions differ as to minimum safe levels, but the EPA has established guidelines that concentrations of 4.0 picocuries or higher are undesirable. Exposure to radon does not usually cause immediate symptoms, but prolonged contact with elevated levels has been linked to increased risk of lung cancer. Growing evidence suggests that radon may be the most underestimated cause of lung cancer, particularly for children, individuals who smoke, and those who spend considerable time indoors.

Because radon is clear, odorless and tasteless, it is impossible to detect without testing. Care should be exercised in the manner in which tests are conducted to ensure that the results are accurate. Radon levels vary, depending on the amount of fresh air that circulates through a house, the weather conditions, and the time of year. It is relatively easy to reduce levels of radon by installing a **mitigation** system using ventilation systems or exhaust fans.

Chapter 21 Environmental Issues and the Real Estate Transaction

> *Radon* is a naturally occurring radioactive gas that causes lung cancer.

Interestingly, the modern practice of creating energy-efficient homes and buildings with practically airtight walls and windows may increase the potential for radon gas accumulation. Once radon enters a building through tiny openings in the foundation or around openings for pipes or drains and accumulates in a low area like a basement, efficient heating and ventilation systems can rapidly spread the gas throughout the building.

In North Carolina

Home radon-detection kits are available, although radon-detection professionals can conduct more accurate testing. It is estimated that about one-third of all radon testing is done in connection with a real estate transaction. The EPA's pamphlet "A Citizen's Guide to Radon" is available from your local EPA office or on the EPA website. North Carolina also has a radon-specific website listed at the end of the chapter.

Urea-Formaldehyde

Urea-formaldehyde was first used in building materials, particularly insulation, in the 1970s. Gases leak out of the **urea-formaldehyde foam insulation (UFFI),** as it hardens, and they become trapped in the interior of a building. In 1982, the Consumer Product Safety Commission originally banned the use of UFFI; but the ban was reduced to a warning after courts determined that there was insufficient evidence to support a ban. Urea-formaldehyde is known to cause cancer in animals, though the evidence of its effect on humans is inconclusive.

Formaldehyde does cause some individuals to suffer respiratory problems or asthma attacks as well as eye and skin irritations. Consumers are becoming increasingly wary of the presence of formaldehyde, particularly if they are sensitive to it.

> *UFFI* is an insulating foam that can release harmful formaldehyde gases.

Tests can be conducted to determine the level of formaldehyde gas in a house. Again, however, care should be exercised to ensure that the results of the tests are accurate and that the source of the gases is properly identified. Elevated levels could be due to a source other than the insulation such as glues or bonding agents found in furniture or other home furnishings. Brokers should be careful that any conditions in an agreement of sale that require tests for formaldehyde are worded properly to identify the purpose for which the tests are being conducted, such as to determine the presence of the insulation or some other source. Appraisers should also be aware of the presence of UFFI.

Carbon Monoxide

> *Carbon monoxide* is a by-product of incomplete fuel combustion that may result in deathly concentrations in poorly ventilated areas.

Carbon monoxide (CO) is a colorless, odorless gas that occurs as a by-product of burning such fuels as wood, oil, and natural gas if combustion is incomplete. Furnaces, water heaters, space heaters, fireplaces, and wood stoves all produce CO as a natural result of their combustion of fuel. When these appliances function properly and are properly ventilated, their CO emissions are not a problem. When improper ventilation or equipment malfunctions permit large quantities of CO to be released into a residence or commercial structure, it poses a significant health hazard. Its effects are compounded by the fact that CO is so difficult to detect. Carbon monoxide is quickly absorbed by the human body where it inhibits the blood's ability to transport oxygen, resulting in dizziness and nausea. As the concentrations of CO increase, the symptoms become more severe. More than 200 deaths from CO poisoning occur each year.

Carbon monoxide detectors are available, and their use is mandatory in some areas. Annual maintenance of heating systems also helps avoid CO exposure. Buyers should have an inspection of the HVAC system that includes CO monitoring prior to purchase.

Electromagnetic Fields

> *EMFs are produced by electrical currents and may be related to a variety of health complaints.*

Electromagnetic fields (EMFs) are generated by the movement of electrical currents. The use of any electrical appliance creates a small field of electromagnetic radiation: clock radios, blow dryers, televisions, and computers all produce EMFs. The major concern regarding electromagnetic fields involves high-tension power lines. The EMFs produced by these high-voltage lines, as well as by secondary distribution lines and transformers, are suspected of causing cancer, hormonal changes, and behavioral abnormalities. There is considerable controversy (and much conflicting evidence) about whether EMFs pose a health hazard. In a May 1999 report to the U.S. Congress, the National Institute of Environmental Health Science reported that there is no evidence of a correlation between EMFs and adverse health effects. Buyers who are aware of the controversy may, however, be unwilling to purchase property near power lines or transformers. As research into EMFs continues, real estate brokers should stay informed about current findings. At the time of this publication, Progress Energy's website states that they will address questions about EMFs through their customer service number (800-700-8744).

Groundwater Contamination

Groundwater is the water that exists under the earth's surface within the tiny spaces or crevices in geological formations. Groundwater forms the **water table,** the natural level at which the ground is saturated. This may be near the surface in areas where the water table is very high or several hundred feet underground. Surface water also can be absorbed into the groundwater.

Any contamination of the underground water can threaten the supply of pure, clean water for private wells or public water systems. If groundwater is not protected from contamination, the earth's natural filtering systems may be inadequate to ensure the availability of pure water. Numerous state and federal laws have been enacted to preserve and protect the water supply including the amended Safe Drinking Water Act of 1974.

Water can be contaminated from a number of sources. Runoff from waste disposal sites, leaking underground storage tanks, improperly discarded commercial byproducts, and pesticides and herbicides are some of the main culprits. Because water flows quickly from one place to another, contamination can spread far from its source. As an example of the far reaching effects of leakage, it is estimated that one gallon of gasoline can contaminate one million gallons of drinking water. Once contamination has been identified, its source can be eliminated and the water may eventually become clean. However, the process can be time consuming and extremely expensive.

IN PRACTICE Real estate brokers need to be on the alert for potential groundwater contamination sources both on and off a property. These include underground storage tanks, septic systems, holding ponds, dry wells, buried materials, and surface spills. Remember, because groundwater flows over wide areas, the source of contamination may not be nearby.

Underground Storage Tanks

Approximately 3 million to 5 million **underground storage tanks (USTs)** exist in the United States. According to the EPA, an underground storage tank system is a tank and any underground piping connected to the tank that has at least 10% of its combined volume underground. As of the end of the EPA September 2008 reporting period, almost a half million of those USTs have experienced confirmed leaks. The increase in reports of leaks can be partially attributed to the fact that until the mid-1980s, most USTs were made of bare steel, which will corrode over time. Underground storage tanks are commonly found on sites where petroleum products are used or where gas stations and auto repair shops are located. They also may be found in a number of other commercial and industrial establishments—including printing and chemical plants, wood treatment plants, paper mills, paint manufacturers, dry cleaners, and food processing plants—for storing chemical or other process waste. Military bases and airports also are common sites for underground tanks. Many, if not most, of the residential UST tanks that were used to store heating oil have been abandoned when newer heating systems were installed.

Some tanks are currently in use, but many are long forgotten. It is an unfortunate fact that it was once common to dispose of toxic wastes by simple burial: *out of sight, out of mind.* Over time, however, neglected tanks may leak hazardous substances into the environment. This permits contaminants to pollute not only the soil around the tank but also adjacent parcels and groundwater. Brokers should be particularly alert to the presence of fill pipes, vent lines, stained soil, oil sheens in wet areas, and fumes or odors, any of which may indicate the presence of a UST. Detection, removal, and cleanup of surrounding contaminated soil can be an expensive operation.

■ **FOR EXAMPLE** In the 1940s, a gas station in a rural town went out of business. The building fell into disrepair and was torn down. The site was vacant for several years, and its former use was forgotten. A series of commercial ventures were built on the land: a grocery store, a drive-in restaurant, and a convenience store. In the late 1980s, residents of the town began noticing strong gasoline fumes in their basements, particularly after a rainstorm. Government investigators concluded that the gasoline tanks buried beneath the former gas station had broken down with age and leaked their contents into the soil. Because the town was located over a large subsurface rock slab, the gasoline could not leach down into the soil, but rather it was forced to spread out under the entire town and surrounding farmland. Because the water table floated on the rock slab and the gasoline floated on the water, rains that raised the water table forced the gasoline into the soil near the residents' basements and crawlspaces, resulting in the unpleasant and potentially unhealthy fumes. When the gasoline fumes ignited and destroyed a local manufacturing plant, the residents learned that the problem was not only unpleasant but dangerous, as well.

State and federal laws impose very strict requirements on landowners on which underground storage tanks are located to detect and correct leaks in an effort to protect the groundwater. The EPA under the Resource Conservation and Recovery Act of CERCLA created the Office of Underground Storage Tanks in 1985 to regulate the federal UST program. The federal UST regulations apply to only underground tanks and piping storing either petroleum or certain hazardous substances. Commercial UST owners are required to register their tanks and adhere to strict technical and administrative requirements that govern installation, maintenance, corrosion prevention, overspill prevention, monitoring, and recordkeeping. Owners also are required to demonstrate that they have sufficient financial resources to cover any damage that might result from leaks.

The following types of tanks are among those that are exempt from federal regulations:

- Tanks that hold less than 110 gallons
- Farm and residential tanks that hold 1,100 gallons or less of motor fuel used for noncommercial purposes
- Tanks that store heating oil burned on the premises
- Tanks on or above the floor of underground areas, such as basements or tunnels
- Septic tanks and systems for collecting stormwater and wastewater

In North Carolina

North Carolina, like many states, has adopted laws regulating underground storage tanks that are sometimes more stringent than the federal laws. North Carolina has maintained an EPA-approved UST program since 1999 under the North Carolina Department of Environment and Natural Resources (DENR). According to the 2007-2008 DENR report to the EPA, North Carolina has over 28,000 active regulated tanks that accounted for just over 200 confirmed releases plus over 500 confirmed leaks from non-regulated USTs, primarily for heating oil.

In addition to being aware of possible noncompliance with state and federal regulations, the parties to a real estate transaction should be aware that many older tanks have never been registered or fall into the exempt category. There may be no visible sign of their presence. If a leaking UST cannot be removed and the contamination totally remediated, the leak will become a cloud on the title of the property.

Waste Disposal Sites

Americans produce vast quantities of garbage every day. Despite public and private recycling and composting efforts, huge piles of waste materials—from beer cans, junk mail, and diapers to food, paint, and toxic chemicals—require disposal. Landfill operations have become the main receptacles for garbage and refuse. Special hazardous-waste disposal sites have been established to contain radioactive waste from nuclear power plants, toxic chemicals, and waste materials produced by medical, scientific, and industrial processes.

Perhaps the most prevalent method of common waste disposal is simply to bury it. A **landfill** is an enormous hole, either excavated for the purpose of waste disposal or left over from surface mining operations. The hole is lined with clay or a synthetic liner to prevent leakage of waste material into the water supply. A system of underground drainage pipes permits monitoring of leaks and leaching. Waste is laid on the liner at the bottom of the excavation, and a layer of topsoil is then compacted onto the waste. The layering procedure is repeated again and again until the landfill is full, the layers mounded up sometimes as high as several hundred feet over the surrounding landscape. *Capping* is the process of laying two to four feet of soil over the top of the site and then planting grass or some other vegetation to enhance the landfill's aesthetic value and to prevent erosion. A ventilation pipe runs from the landfill's base through the cap to vent off accumulated natural gases created by the decomposing waste.

Federal, state, and local regulations govern the location, construction, content, and maintenance of landfill sites. Test wells around landfill operations are installed to constantly monitor the groundwater in the surrounding area, and soil analyses can be used to test for contamination. Completed landfills have been used for such purposes as parks and golf courses. Rapid suburban growth has resulted in many housing developments and office campuses being built on landfill sites. However, buildings constructed on landfills may have problems caused by settling.

■ **FOR EXAMPLE** A suburban office building constructed on an old landfill site was very popular until its parking lot began to sink. While the structure itself was supported by pylons driven deep into the ground, the parking lot was unsupported. As the landfill beneath it compacted, the wide concrete lot sank lower and lower around the building. Each year, the building's management had to re-landscape to cover the exposed foundations. The sinking parking lot eventually severed underground phone and power lines and water mains, causing the tenants considerable inconvenience. Computers were offline for hours, and flooding was frequent on the ground floor. Finally, leaking gases from the landfill began causing unpleasant odors. The tenants moved out, and the building was left vacant, a victim of a poorly conceived landfill design.

Hazardous and radioactive waste disposal sites are subject to strict state and federal regulation to prevent the escape of toxic substances into the surrounding environment. Some materials, such as radioactive waste, are sealed in containers and placed in *tombs* buried deep underground. The tombs are designed to last thousands of years and are built according to strict federal and state regulations.

IN PRACTICE Environmental issues have a significant impact on the real estate industry. In 1995, a jury awarded $6.7 million to homeowners whose property values had been lowered because of the defendant tire company's negligent operation and maintenance of a hazardous waste dumpsite. The 1,713 plaintiffs relied on testimony from economists and a real estate appraiser to demonstrate how news stories about the site had lowered the market values of their homes. Nationwide, some landfill operators now offer price guarantees to purchasers of homes near waste disposal sites. A recent university study found that a home's value increases by more than $6,000 for each mile of its distance from a garbage incinerator.

Mold

Mold is the latest environmental issue of concern in the last decade due in large part to massive exposure in the media to extraordinary situations of excessive amounts of *toxic* mold in some homes around the country. Perhaps the major real estate industry issue related to mold is how the surge in insurance claims has affected the insurability of properties with previous water claims. Mold can be found almost anywhere and can grow on almost any organic substance, so long as moisture, oxygen, and an organic food source are present. Moisture feeds mold growth. If a moisture problem is not discovered or addressed, mold growth can gradually destroy the surface on which it grows.

In addition, some molds can cause serious health problems. They can trigger allergic reactions and asthma attacks. Some molds are known to produce potent toxins and/or irritants.

Some moisture problems in homes and buildings have been directly linked to recent changes in construction practices. Some of these practices have resulted in buildings that are too tightly sealed, preventing adequate ventilation. Building materials, such as drywall, may not allow moisture to escape easily. The material used in drywall wicks moisture to the nutrition source of glue and paper. Vinyl wallpaper and exterior insulation finish systems (EIFS), also known as *synthetic stucco*, also do not allow moisture to escape. Other moisture problems include roof leaks, unvented combustion appliances, and landscaping or gutters that direct water to the building.

The EPA has published guidelines for the remediation and/or cleanup of mold and moisture problems in schools and commercial buildings. See the list of EPA websites at the end of this chapter for these guidelines.

Mold is an important issue for brokers. Initially, lawsuits were brought against construction and insurance companies until the insurance companies started amending their homeowners' insurance policies to exclude mold from coverage. Now, plaintiffs name sellers, landlords, property management companies, and real estate brokers as defendants, in addition to construction and insurance companies.

■ **FOR EXAMPLE** In a 2005 case, *Eddy v. B.S.T.V., Inc.*, a couple sued a real estate company for failing to disclose mold contamination in the home they purchased. The real estate company's insurers refused to provide coverage, stating that the insurance policies had specific exclusion clauses that would not cover property damage arising out of a real estate broker's failure to render professional services. The issue in the case was whether the professional-services exclusion clause in the insurance policy issued to the real estate company applied to the couple's claims. The couple alleged that the real estate brokers breached the real estate company's professional-service responsibilities and that, therefore, the exclusions applied. The real estate company tried to argue that because its real estate brokers were trained in identifying mold-related hazards, the claim did not fit the exclusion clause. The court did not agree, and the real estate company was held liable. The court held that the exclusion clauses in the policies prevented insurance coverage for the injuries.

In light of this case and other court decisions on this topic, real estate companies and brokers will find it difficult to know what to do when mold is suspected or found on a property. There are no federal requirements to disclose mold contamination at this time, and only a few states require disclosure. The mere presence of mold in a residence is not a material fact according to NCREC unless there is an

In North Carolina

excessive amount of mold in unusual locations. Numerous websites can be visited to garner information about mold and its treatment. Brokers should remind buyers that sellers cannot disclose what they do not know. Also, brokers should advise buyers that they have not only the right but also the burden to discover.

Brokers may need to take extra steps to protect themselves from liability. Brokers who suspect that mold is present in a home should ask many questions about leaks, floods, and prior damage and remind the sellers to honestly and truthfully disclose any insurance claims regarding mold and other water issues.

CERCLA AND ENVIRONMENTAL PROTECTION

The majority of legislation dealing with environmental problems has been instituted within the past two decades. Although the EPA was created at the federal level to oversee such problems, several other federal agencies' areas of concern generally overlap. The federal laws were created to encourage state and local governments to enact their own legislation.

Comprehensive Environmental Response, Compensation, and Liability Act

The **Comprehensive Environmental Response, Compensation, and Liability Act (CERCLA)** was created in 1980. It established a fund of $9 billion, called the *Superfund*, to clean up uncontrolled hazardous waste sites and to respond to spills. It created a process for identifying potentially responsible parties (PRPs) and ordering them to take responsibility for the cleanup action. CERCLA is administered and enforced by the EPA.

Liability. A landowner is liable under CERCLA when a release or a threat of release of a hazardous substance has occurred on the landowner's property. Regardless of whether the contamination is the result of the landowner's actions or those of others, the owner can be held responsible for the cleanup. This liability includes the cleanup not only of the landowner's property but also of any neighboring property that has been contaminated. A landowner who is not responsible for the contamination can seek reimbursement for the cleanup cost from previous landowners, any other responsible party, or the Superfund. However, if other parties are not available, even a landowner who did not cause the problem could be solely responsible for the cleanup costs.

Once the EPA determines that hazardous material has been released into the environment, it is authorized to begin remedial action. First, it attempts to identify the PRPs. If the PRPs agree to cooperate in the cleanup, they must agree about how to divide the cost. If the PRPs do not voluntarily undertake the cleanup, the EPA may hire its own contractors to do the necessary work. The EPA then bills the PRPs for the cost. If the PRPs refuse to pay, the EPA can seek damages in court for up to three times the actual cost of the cleanup.

Liability under the Superfund is considered to be strict, joint and several, and retroactive. *Strict liability* means that the owner is responsible to the injured party without excuse. *Joint and several liability* means that each of the individual owners is personally responsible for the total damages. If only one of the owners is financially able to handle the total damages, that owner must pay the total and collect the proportionate shares from the other owners whenever possible. *Retroactive liability* means that the liability is not limited to the current owner but includes people who have owned the site in the past.

Superfund Amendments and Reauthorization Act. In 1986, the U.S. Congress reauthorized the Superfund. The amended statute contains stronger cleanup standards for contaminated sites and five times the funding of the original Superfund, which expired in September 1985.

The amended Act also sought to clarify the obligations of lenders. As mentioned, liability under the Superfund extends to both the present and all previous owners of the contaminated site. Real estate lenders found themselves either as present owners or somewhere in the chain of ownership through foreclosure proceedings.

The amendments created a concept called *innocent landowner immunity*. It was recognized that in certain cases, a landowner in the chain of ownership was completely innocent of all wrongdoing and therefore should not be held liable. The innocent landowner immunity clause established the criteria by which to judge whether a person or business could be exempted from liability. The criteria included the following:

- The pollution was caused by a third party.
- The property was acquired after the fact.
- The landowner had no knowledge of the damage.
- Due care was exercised when the property was purchased (the landowner made a reasonable search, called an *environmental site assessment*) to determine that no damage to the property existed.
- Reasonable precautions were taken in the exercise of ownership rights.

NORTH CAROLINA ENVIRONMENTAL ISSUES

North Carolina Leaking Petroleum Underground Storage Tank Cleanup Act

The purpose of the **Leaking Petroleum Underground Storage Tank Cleanup Act** (NCGS §143-215.94A) is to regulate underground storage tanks' discharge of any hazardous substance, including gas and oil. Owners of properties with tanks that may be leaking face the heavy financial burden of cleanup costs, *even though they themselves did not install the tanks or cause the leak*. This Act covers both residential and commercial properties.

North Carolina Coastal Area Management Act

The **North Carolina Coastal Area Management Act (CAMA)** (NCGS §113A-100) is designed to protect, preserve, and give management guidelines in coastal areas of the state. It places a severe limitation on developments in the coastal estuarine system. A majority of coastal areas in North Carolina, such as wetlands and marshes, have been declared *areas of environmental concern*. Any proposed development or changes in these areas, such as building, dredging, filling or digging, clearing or bulkheading, must first be approved through a permit process. Property owners in violation of CAMA will face serious legal problems including the probability of a court order mandating that they finance the repair of any damage done to the estuarine system. Brokers practicing in the eastern third of the state should consider CAMA compliance a material fact in transactions that might involve land development.

Mountain Ridge Protection Act

The Mountain Ridge Protection Act (NCGS §113A-208) was the first comprehensive law in the nation passed by a state to regulate construction on protected mountain ridges. The construction of a 10-story condominium project on Little Sugar Mountain in Avery County sparked public outrage locally at what was perceived as a *blight* upon the scenic views of the Blue Ridge Mountains. The Act allows a municipality to adopt and enforce ...*any ordinance that regulates the construction of tall buildings or structures on protected mountain ridges...*

North Carolina Dredge and Fill Act

Under the **North Carolina Dredge and Fill Act** (NCGS §113-229), a property owner must obtain a permit from the Coastal Resources Commission before participating in any dredging or filling that may affect vegetation or aquatic conditions in North Carolina waters or marshlands. This Act is part of compliance with the federal Clean Water Acts that protect wetlands and other waters of the United States. The federal government defines *wetlands* as *areas periodically inundated or saturated to the extent that they can or do support vegetation adapted to aquatic conditions*.

North Carolina Sediment Pollution Control Act

The **North Carolina Sediment Pollution Control Act** (NCGS §113A-50) was enacted to handle problems that occur as a result of sedimentation in state waters. Sedimentation may have natural causes, such as erosion, or human-made causes that result in a deposit of soil or other materials into water. Such deposits may have an adverse effect on the aquatic life in the area. Any type of development, construction, or any other activity that may disturb vegetation or topography in a way that may cause sedimentation is illegal and subject to the Act. The Act calls for erosion control devices, the development of sedimentation plans, and the creation of natural buffer zones. The law is enforced by the North Carolina Department of Environment, Natural Resources.

■ LIABILITY OF REAL ESTATE PROFESSIONALS

Environmental law is a relatively new phenomenon. Although federal and state laws have defined many of the liabilities involved, common law is being used for further interpretation. The real estate professional and all others involved in a real estate transaction must be aware of both actual and potential liability.

Sellers, as mentioned earlier, often carry the most legal exposure. Innocent landowners might be held responsible, even though they did not know about the presence of environmental hazards. Purchasers may be held liable, even if they did not cause the contamination. Lenders may end up owning worthless assets if owners default on the loans rather than undertake expensive cleanup efforts. Real estate brokers could be held liable for improper disclosure; therefore, it is necessary to be aware of the potential environmental risks from neighboring properties such as gas stations, manufacturing plants, or even funeral homes.

Additional exposure is created for individuals involved in other aspects of real estate transactions. For example, real estate appraisers must identify and adjust for environmental problems. Adjustments to market value typically reflect the cleanup cost plus an adjustment for the degree of panic and suspicion that exist in the current market. Although the sales price can be affected dramatically, it is possible that the underlying market value would remain relatively equal to others in the neighborhood. The real estate appraiser's greatest responsibility is to the lender, who depends on the appraiser to identify environmental hazards. Although the lender may be protected under certain conditions through the 1986 amendments to the Superfund Act, the lender must be aware of any potential problems and may require additional environmental reports.

Insurance carriers also might be affected in the transactions. Mortgage insurance companies protect lenders' mortgage investments and might be required to carry part of the ultimate responsibility in cases of loss. More importantly, hazard insurance carriers might be directly responsible for damages if such coverage was included in the initial policy.

Discovery of Environmental Hazards

Real estate brokers are not expected to have the technical expertise necessary to discover the presence of environmental hazards. However, because they are presumed by the public to have special knowledge about real estate, brokers must be aware both of possible hazards and of where to seek professional help.

Obviously, the first step for a licensee is to ask the owner. The owner already may have conducted tests for carbon monoxide or radon. He or she also may be aware of a potentially hazardous condition. A previous environmental hazard can actually be turned into a marketing plus if the owner has already completed the detection and abatement work. The most appropriate people on whom a licensee can rely for sound environmental information are scientific or technical experts. Environmental auditors can provide the most comprehensive studies; frequently beginning with a *Phase I Environmental Site Assessment* which may prompt further testing. Developers and purchasers of commercial and industrial properties usually rely on these expert services. An environmental audit includes the property's history of use and the results of extensive and complex tests of the soil, water, air, and structures. Trained inspectors conduct air-sampling tests to detect radon, asbestos, or EMFs. They can test soil and water quality and can inspect for lead-based paints. While environmental auditors may be called at any stage in a transaction, they are most frequently brought in as a condition of closing. Not only can such experts detect environmental problems, they can usually offer guidance about how best to resolve the conditions.

Disclosure of Environmental Hazards

State laws address the issue of disclosure of known material facts regarding a property's condition. These same rules apply to the known presence of environmental hazards. A real estate licensee may be liable if he or she should have known of a condition, even if the seller neglected to disclose it. Property condition disclosures are discussed in Chapter 9.

■ RELATED WEBSITES

Environmental Protection Agency (EPA):   www.epa.gov
Mold Help Organization: www.mold-help.com
National Institute of Environmental Health Sciences: Electromagnetic Fields:
 www.niehs.nih.gov/health/topics/agents/emf/
NC Dept. of Coastal Management: CAMA:
 www.nccoastalmanagement.net/index.htm
NC Dept. of Environment and Natural Resources: Radon Program:
 www.ncradon.org
NC Dept. of Environment and Natural Resources: Underground storage tanks:
 http://ust.ehnr.state.nc.us/web/wm/ust
Safe Drinking Water Act: www.epa.gov/safewater/sdwa/index.html

■ KEY POINT REVIEW

Asbestos is a mineral composed of fibers that have fireproofing and insulating qualities.

- Asbestos is a health hazard when fibers break down (become *friable*) and are inhaled.
- Asbestos has been banned for use in insulation since 1978.
- **Encapsulation** can prevent asbestos fibers from becoming airborne.

Lead can be found in pipes, pipe solder, paints, air, and soil.

- Lead-based paint is found in many of the housing units built before 1978.
- Lead accumulates in the body and can damage the brain, nervous system, kidneys, and blood.
- The **Lead-Based Paint Hazard Reduction Act of 1992** (LBPHRA) requires disclosure of known lead-based paint hazards to potential buyers or renters.
  — Real estate brokers provide buyers and lessees with a pamphlet created by EPA, HUD, and the U.S. Consumer Product Safety Commission.
  — Since 2010, renovation and repair that disturbs lead-based paint must be done by certified vendor.

Radon is an odorless, tasteless, radioactive gas produced by the natural decay of radioactive substances in the ground and is found throughout the United States. Radon gas may cause lung cancer. Testing for radon in buildings is not a federal requirement.

Formaldehyde, described as a hazardous air pollutant in the Clean Air Act Amendments of 1990, is used for building and household products, such as urea-formaldehyde foam insulation (UFFI), and may cause respiratory problems, eye and skin irritations, and possibly cancer. Since 1985, it has been regulated by HUD for use in wood products.

Carbon monoxide (CO), a colorless, odorless gas that is by-product of fuel burning,

- is produced by furnaces, water heaters, space heaters (including kerosene heaters), fireplaces, and wood stoves;
- may cause carbon monoxide poisoning, which can result in death unless the gas is properly vented; and
- is detectable with available carbon monoxide detectors, which may be required by state law.

Electromagnetic fields (EMFs) are produced by all electrical appliances. High-voltage electrical lines producing EMFs are under investigation for health risks.

Groundwater is found under the earth's surface and forms the water table. The Safe Drinking Water Act (SDWA) of 1974 regulates the public drinking water supply. On property transfers, any water source other than a municipal supply should be tested, as should any septic system.

Underground storage tanks (USTs), which contain petroleum products, industrial chemicals, and other substances, are a concern because the leakage may imperil both public and private water sources.

- USTs are subject to federal law and state law.
- The EPA regulates the federal UST program.
- When a property purchase is being considered, a careful inspection of any property on which USTs are suspected should be conducted.

Waste disposal sites can be owned by municipalities, be part of commercial enterprises, or be found on farms and other rural properties.

- A **landfill** disposal site, whether excavated or making use of previously mined property, is
  — lined to prevent seepage,
  — capped with soil for aesthetic reasons, and
  — vented to release gases created by decomposing waste.

Mold is present in the air everywhere and grows in the presence of moisture, oxygen, and a cellulosic (organic) food source.

- Some molds can cause serious health problems.
- The EPA has guidelines for remediation and/or cleanup of mold and moisture problems in schools and commercial buildings.
- Real estate brokers should recommend a mold inspection if mold is evident or suspected because of water problems.

The **Comprehensive Environmental Response, Compensation, and Liability Act (CERCLA)** is administered and enforced by the EPA. CERCLA

- established a Superfund to clean up uncontrolled hazardous waste sites;
- identifies potential responsible parties (PRPs);
- established liability as follows:
  — Strict liability where the landowner has no defense to the responsibility for cleanup
  — Joint and several liability in which each of several landowners is responsible for the entire cleanup
  — Retroactive liability where the present owner and previous owners are responsible
- defined when *innocent landowner* immunity applies.

Environmental liability issues for real estate professionals include the following:

- Discovery of environmental hazards that includes
  — questioning the owner,
  — recommending an environmental audit (environmental site assessment), and
  — an environmental impact statement (EIS), as required for federally funded projects and by the state or locality, if required.
- **Disclosure of environmental hazards** is a material fact regarding property condition.

North Carolina-specific environmental legislation includes: **North Carolina Leaking Petroleum Underground Storage Tanks Cleanup Act, North Carolina Coastal Area Management Act, Mountain Ridge Protection Act, North Carolina Dredge and Fill Act,** and **North Carolina Sediment Pollution Control Act.**

QUESTIONS

1. Asbestos is most dangerous when it
   a. is used as insulation.
   b. becomes airborne.
   c. gets wet.
   d. is around water pipes.

2. Encapsulation refers to the
   a. process of sealing a landfill with three to four feet of topsoil.
   b. way to apply asbestos insulation to pipes and wiring systems.
   c. method of sealing disintegrating asbestos.
   d. way in which asbestos becomes friable.

3. A broker shows a pre-World War I house to a prospective buyer. The buyer has two toddlers and is worried about potential health hazards. Which of the following is TRUE?
   a. There is a risk that urea-foam insulation was used in the original construction.
   b. The licensed real estate broker can offer to inspect for and remove any environmental hazards.
   c. There is a good likelihood of the presence of lead-based paint.
   d. Radon should not be a concern due to the age of the property.

4. Which of the following is TRUE regarding asbestos?
   a. The improper removal of asbestos can cause further contamination of a building.
   b. Asbestos causes health problems only when it is eaten.
   c. Asbestos was only used in various types of insulation.
   d. HUD requires asbestos to be removed from all residential buildings prior to transfer of title.

5. Underground storage tanks
   a. are found only on commercial properties.
   b. that leak and can not be removed may create a cloud on the title of the property.
   c. are currently regulated only by local laws.
   d. are easily detected by a vent pipe.

6. All of the following are true of electromagnetic fields EXCEPT that electromagnetic fields are
   a. a suspected but unproven cause of cancer, hormonal abnormalities, and behavioral disorders.
   b. generated by all electrical appliances.
   c. present only near high-tension wires or large electrical transformers.
   d. caused by the movement of electricity.

7. Which of the following describes the process of creating a landfill site?
   a. Waste is liquefied, treated, and pumped through pipes to *tombs* under the water table.
   b. Waste and topsoil are layered in a pit, mounded up, then covered with dirt and plants.
   c. Waste is compacted and sealed into a container, then placed in a *tomb* designed to last several thousand years.
   d. Waste is buried in an underground concrete vault.

8. Liability under the Superfund is
   a. limited to the current owner of record.
   b. joint and several, retroactive, but not strict.
   c. voluntary.
   d. strict, joint and several, and retroactive.

9. All of the following have been proven to pose health hazards EXCEPT
   a. asbestos fibers.
   b. carbon monoxide.
   c. electromagnetic fields.
   d. urea-formaldehyde.

10. Which of the following is/are TRUE about radon?
    I. Radon is easily detected by its strong fruity odor.
    II. Radon can be remediated by encapsulation.
       a. I only
       b. II only
       c. Both I and II
       d. Neither I nor II

11. Under the Federal Lead-Based Paint Hazard and Reduction Act, which of the following statements is *TRUE*?
    a. All residential housing built prior to 1978 must be tested for the presence of lead-based paint before being listed for sale or rent.
    b. A disclosure statement must be provided to all purchasers and lessees involving residential properties built prior to 1978.
    c. A lead hazard pamphlet must be distributed to all prospective buyers but not to tenants.
    d. Purchasers of housing built before 1978 must be given five days to test the property for the presence of lead-based paint.

12. Radon poses the greatest potential health risk to humans when it is
    a. contained in insulation material used during the 1970s.
    b. found in high concentrations of unimproved land.
    c. trapped and concentrated in inadequately ventilated areas.
    d. emitted by malfunctioning or inadequately ventilated appliances.

13. Radon is
    a. only found in the eastern United States
    b. easy to detect because of its odor.
    c. a known human carcinogen.
    d. not found in older homes.

14. The *MOST* common source of harmful lead in older residences is in
    a. asbestos.
    b. basements.
    c. appliances.
    d. alkyd oil-based paint.

15. Urea-formaldehyde is found in residential properties in
    a. lead-based paints
    b. insulating foam.
    c. home appliances.
    d. electromagnetic fields.

CHAPTER 22

Basic Real Estate Investment

LEARNING OBJECTIVES *When you have finished reading this chapter, you should be able to*

- **identify** the advantages and disadvantages of property investing; and
- **define** these *key terms*:

after-tax cash flow	equity buildup	operating statement
appreciation	equity dividend rate	partnerships
before-tax cash flow	general partnership	real estate investment
cash flow	inflation	real estate investment trust (REIT)
cash-on-cash rate of return	leverage	return on investment (ROI)
cash throw-off	limited liability company (LLC)	scheduled gross income (SGI)
corporation	limited partnership	syndicate
effective gross income (EGI)	liquidity	

INVESTING IN REAL ESTATE

Real estate brokers should have a basic understanding of real estate investment terms and concepts. Whether consumers are investing in their own homes or in non-owner occupied properties, they want assurance that their purchases are going to provide an acceptable return on investment. While brokers should never provide tax or legal advice, they should be able to provide a basic analysis of a property's income and value potential to interested consumers.

Advantages of real estate investment. In recent years, real estate values nationwide have significantly changed. Some investments have failed to produce returns greater than the rate of inflation; some investments have even suffered significant depreciation; but some real estate investments have shown above-average rates of return. Some real estate investment experts suggest that with real estate prices at a 10-year low in many parts of the United States and interest rates below 4%, real estate is poised for significant appreciation potential.

Another advantage of real estate investment is that buyers can **leverage** their purchase. In theory, this means that investors should be able to borrow money to finance a real estate purchase and feel relatively sure that an asset, if held long enough, will return more money than the cost to finance the purchase.

Unlike other investments such as stocks, bonds, and collectibles, investors can exert some measure of control over the performance of their investments. Knowledgeable landlords can choose tenants wisely, make repairs and improvements in a timely manner, and maintain effective rent policies. When landlords do not personally have this expertise, they can choose good property management firms to guide them.

Many investors put their occupational skills to good use in real estate investments. Handy individuals, carpenters, and electricians can add significant value to their properties by applying their building skills. Teachers and psychologists can use their gifts in dealing with people to choose well-qualified tenants. Accountants and attorneys have experience effectively negotiating lease and/or handling income streams. Just being a primary residential property owner gives a beginning investor an edge since property owners encounter maintenance issues in taking care of their own homes.

Real estate professionals may use their knowledge of the market to enter into transactions on their own behalf as well. However, because of license laws and fiduciary obligations to clients, brokers either must and/or should disclose their license status when they are acting as principles in a transaction. Providing that brokers make these disclosures, there is nothing unlawful or unethical about real estate brokers investing in real estate themselves. In fact, real estate professionals who own real estate investments can offer the benefit of their experience to their clients, making them more valuable to consumers when they do.

Real estate investors also receive certain tax benefits. Tax laws can have a positive impact on the investment performance of real estate. Most real estate investment properties can shelter not only the income the property generates but other income earned by the owners. Furthermore, current tax laws allow investors to pay a relatively low capital gains tax on profit from a sale or to avoid taxes by participating in a tax-deferred exchange.

Disadvantages of real estate investment. Unlike stocks and bonds, real estate is not highly liquid over the short term. **Liquidity** is how quickly an asset may be converted into cash. For instance, an investor who holds stocks can easily direct a stockbroker to sell stocks when funds are needed. The stockbroker sells the stock, and the investor receives the cash. In contrast, a real estate investor may have to sell the property at a substantially lower price than desired to ensure a quick sale or to refinance the property. Thus, real estate is a relatively illiquid investment.

Real estate investments are expensive and potentially complex. Large amounts of capital are usually required. Many lenders require a down payment of 25% or more on investment property. Investing in real estate can be difficult without expert advice. Investment decisions must be based on careful studies of all the facts, reinforced by a thorough knowledge of local and national real estate market trends.

Real estate requires active management. A real estate investor can rarely just sit and watch the money grow. Management decisions must be made. How much rent should be charged? How should repairs and tenant grievances be handled? The investor may choose to personally manage the property or hire a professional property manager.

Finally, despite its popularity, real estate investment does not guarantee profit or an adequate return on investment. It involves a high degree of risk. The possibility that an investment property will decrease in value or not generate enough income are among the risk factors for the investor to consider.

■ THE INVESTMENT

The most prevalent form of real estate investment is direct ownership. Both individuals and corporations may own real estate directly and manage it for appreciation and/or cash flow (income).

Real estate is an avenue of investment open to those interested in holding property primarily for increasing value, which is known as **appreciation**. Two main factors affect appreciation: inflation and intrinsic value. **Inflation** is the increase in the amount of money in circulation. When more money is available, its value declines. When the value of money declines, wholesale and retail prices rise. This is essentially an operation of supply and demand, as discussed in Chapter 1. An intrinsic value of real estate is the result of a person's individual choices and preferences for a given geographic area. For example, property located in a desirable neighborhood near attractive business and shopping areas has a greater intrinsic value to most people than similar property in a more isolated location. As a rule, the greater the intrinsic value, the more money a property commands on its sale.

Unimproved land. Often, investors speculate in purchases of either agricultural land or undeveloped land located in what they expect to be a major path of growth. In these cases, however, the property's intrinsic value and potential for appreciation are not easy to determine. This type of investment carries many inherent risks. How fast will the area develop? Will it grow sufficiently for the investor to make a good profit? Will the expected growth occur? Most important, will the profits eventually realized from the property be great enough to offset the costs of holding it, such as property taxes? Because these questions often cannot be answered with any degree of certainty, lending institutions may be reluctant to lend money for the purchase of raw land.

Income tax laws does not favor investment in land since it does not allow for the depreciation of land. Land is also one of the most illiquid types of real estate investment because few investors will purchase raw or agricultural land on short notice. Despite its risks, land has historically been a good inflation hedge if it is held for the long term.

Income. A person who wishes to buy and personally manage real estate may find that property that generates income can be a solid investment. The objective of directing funds into income property is to generate spendable income, called **cash flow**. Cash flow is the total amount of money remaining after all expenditures have been paid. These expenses generally include taxes, operating costs, and maintenance. Investment analysis can also take into account mortgage payments (debt service) and income taxes in the calculation of cash flow.

Generally, the amount of rent (income) that a property may command depends on a number of factors, including the property's location, physical appearance, and amenities. If the cash flow from rents is not enough to cover all expenses, negative cash flow will result. Negative cash flow is not unusual in the early years of owning an investment property, but a prolonged period of negative cash flow could make it a questionable investment. Landlord-investors must also balance the need to receive high rents with the desire to keep operating expenses low. An unhealthy balance of the two could turn an investment into dilapidated property. Investors should anticipate that operating expenses will include regular building maintenance, repairs, utilities, and tenant services.

An investor often stands to make more money by investing with borrowed money, usually obtained through a mortgage loan or deed of trust loan. Low mortgage payments spread over a long period result in a higher cash flow because they allow the investor to retain more income. In turn, high mortgage payments contribute to a lower cash flow. A more detailed discussion of income property considerations is found in Chapter 12. The tax benefits of investing in real estate are addressed in Chapter 19.

LEVERAGE

Leverage is the use of borrowed money to finance an investment. As a rule, an investor can receive a maximum return from the initial investment by making a small down payment, paying a low interest rate, and spreading mortgage payments over as long a period as possible.

The effect of leveraging is to provide a return that reflects the result of market forces on the entire original purchase price but that is measured only against the actual cash invested. For example, if an investor purchases a $100,000 rental property, makes a $20,000 down payment, and then sells the property five years later for $125,000, the return over five years is $25,000. (The sales price of $125,000 minus the purchase price of $100,000 equals $25,000 profit or return.) Disregarding ownership expenses, the return is not 25% ($25,000 return compared with $100,000 sales price), but 125% of the original amount invested ($25,000 return compared with $20,000 down payment).

Borrowing money can have a positive, negative, or neutral impact on an investor's return. For example, if an investor purchases a $100,000 condominium that appreciates 10% in one year, he makes a $10,000 profit. If he purchases it with all cash, his return will be 10% (profit of $10,000 divided by investment of $100,000). However, if he uses leverage and invests only $10,000 of cash and borrows the balance, the leverage could increase his return. Leverage could also decrease his return, depending on the cost of financing. Leverage can be classified as follows:

- *Positive leverage* occurs when the rate of return from the investment exceeds the interest rate paid on borrowed funds.
- *Negative leverage* occurs when the rate of return from the investment is lower than the interest rate paid on borrowed funds.
- *Neutral leverage* occurs when the rate of return from the investment is equal to the interest rate paid on borrowed funds.

MATH CONCEPTS

CALCULATING RATE OF RETURN

For example, a warehouse is available for $150,000. A purchaser who pays cash would have a return of $15,000. If the purchaser arranges an interest-only loan for $100,000 at 12%, which statement regarding the rate of return would be true?

a. The true rate of return would be 10% and would reflect negative leverage.
b. The true rate of return would be higher if the loan had been $120,000.
c. The true rate of return is 12% reflecting positive leverage.
d. The true rate of return is 6% and would reflect negative leverage.

The correct answer is d. If the purchase is cash, then the return is 10% ($15,000 Cash Throw Off (CTO) divided by $150,000 equity = 10%). If the purchase is leveraged, then the return is 6% ($100,000 loan × 12% interest = $12,000 in Debt Service). $15,000 NOI – $12,000 DS = $3,000 CTO. $3,000 CTO divided by $50,000 down payment/equity ($150,000 purchase price – $100,000 loan = $50,000 equity) = 6% rate of return. Since leveraging returns a lower rate than a cash purchase, the effect of leveraging is negative.

Risks are *directly proportionate to leverage*. A high degree of leverage translates into greater risk for the investor and the lender because of the high ratio of borrowed money to the value of the real estate. Lower leverage results in less risk. When property values drop in an area or vacancy rates rise, the highly leveraged investor may be unable to pay even the financing costs of the property.

Equity buildup. Equity buildup is a result of a loan payment directed toward the principal rather than the interest, plus any gain in property value due to appreciation. In a sense, equity buildup is like money in the investor's bank account. This accumulated equity is not realized as cash unless the property is sold, refinanced, or exchanged.

■ CALCULATING PROFITABILITY

An investment's value can be estimated based on the projected rental income over a specific period of time. Investors and lenders both want to know that an investment property can pay the annual debt service and leave enough before-tax cash flow to provide a cushion. These calculations of value will help the investor evaluate the economic soundness of the potential investment purchase.

Capitalization. Using a capitalization rate (or cap rate) to evaluate a potential investment involves the same calculations discussed in Chapter 17 under the income capitalization approach to value. The capitalization approach determines an estimate of value based on the present worth of future income generated by the subject property. The rates used to determine a property's net operating income (NOI) are abstracted from the rates of return of similar properties. (See Chapter 17 for more information on NOI.) The following steps must be followed to determine first the net operating income, and then, the before and after tax cash flow amounts for an investment property.

First, the **scheduled** (or *potential*) **gross income (SGI)** is estimated for the following 12 months. This is the maximum income the property would produce in a year if there were no vacancies and a prevailing market rental rate was charged. Actual contract rents or lease amounts should be used to calculate SGI on investment units which are under contract for the following 12-month period. If investment units will be available, then market rent figures should be used in the calculation of SGI.

Because it is unusual for any property to actually produce the SGI, a reduction in projected income must be taken to allow for typical vacancy and collection losses. The costs of carrying out an eviction or other legal costs would be examples of collection losses. The subtraction of the vacancy and collection loss from the SGI will produce the **effective gross income (EGI)**, the more realistic amount of income to actually be collected. Net operating income (NOI) is determined by subtracting annual operating expenses from the EGI. Operating expenses would include *fixed expenses*, which are not dependent on occupancy, such as real property tax and insurance; *variable expenses* vacillate based on occupancy, such as utilities, property management fees, maintenance and repairs; and replacement reserves for the periodic replacement of short-lived components, such as the roof or heating system. The net operating income is what the investor is buying and what the lender is willing to finance.

To determine the **before-tax cash flow**, or **cash throw-off**, the debt service on the mortgage loan would be subtracted from the property's NOI. See Figure 22.1 for an example of an **operating statement**, which is also referred to as a *profit and loss statement*. For the sake of our example, the investor is wanting a 9% cap rate on an office building that has a SGI of $125,696 a year. The investor is making a $250,000 down payment and financing the balance with a fully amortized 20-year mortgage loan with an annual interest rate of 5%. The monthly debt service payment is $5,118.00. The other expenses are noted in Figure 22.1. (The calculation of **after-tax cash flow** is more complicated and requires an understanding of tax laws and rules. Real estate brokers interested in the impact of after-tax cash flow on an investor's return on investment should consider taking courses or reading texts on advanced investment concepts.)

To project a good price to pay for the property, the property's NOI in Figure 22.1 is divided by the market appropriate capitalization rate. Unlike the cap rate used by appraisers that is based on market-derived rates, the cap rates used by investors is subjective and relative to the investors' desired rate of return. For example, the annual NOI in Figure 22.1 is $92,306 and the investor's desired cap rate is

Modern Real Estate Practice in North Carolina

9 percent, then $92,306 divided by 0.09 equals $1,025,622 as the maximum purchase price that could yield the desired 9% return. The larger the desired yield, the less the investor would pay for the property.

FIGURE 22.1

Sample Operating Statement

Scheduled gross income		$125,696.00
− Vacancy and collection loss (5%)		− 6,285.00
= EFFECTIVE GROSS INCOME		$119,411.00
Fixed operating expenses:		
Real estate tax	$9,115	
Insurance	3,125	
Landscaping	2,260	
Variable operating expenses:		
Property management (5% EGI)	5,970	
Electricity	2,060	
Water and sewer	1,075	
Maintenance	1,800	
Reserves:		
Roof replacement	800	
Resurface parking lot	900	
− TOTAL OPERATING EXPENSES		− 27,105.00
= NET OPERATING INCOME		$92,306.00
− Debt service		− 61,416.00
= BEFORE-TAX CASH FLOW		$30,890.00
(Cash Throwoff)		

Equity dividend rate (cash-on-cash rate of return). To fully appreciate the impact of leveraging borrowed money to purchase an investment property, consider the investment purchase noted above that was generating a 9% annual **return of investment (ROI)**. If the property was purchased with $250,000 cash down payment and the rest of the purchase price financed, the ROI based on the actual cash invested by the purchaser is substantially higher. After deducting the Annual Debt Service from the NOI, the resulting Before-Tax Cash Flow ($30,890) divided by the Cash Down Payment ($250,000) equals 12.4% **equity dividend rate** or **cash-on-cash rate of return**.

FORMS OF BUSINESS OWNERSHIP (FOR INVESTMENT PURPOSES)

Sometimes it may be more advantageous for investors to join together with other investors in the purchase and ownership of a real estate investment versus maintaining total independence as a sole proprietorship. Investors could organize in various business entities, such as a corporation, a limited liability company (LLC), or some type of partnership. Ownership of investments through real estate syndicate or real estate investment trust also has advantages.

The main advantages of investment ownership by entities rather than by individuals would include limited liability; the enhanced potential of the investment by individual strengths and talents; business entities enjoyment of more favorable tax regulations; and the consolidation of financial resources for sounder financial footing.

A **corporation** is separate legal entity that can own and sell real estate in its own name. Ownership in the corporation is achieved through the purchase of stock certificates. This entity probably offers the best insulation from personal liability since the corporation owns the property. However, corporations with many shareholders experience double taxation—the corporation must pay tax on its income and any monies after taxes are paid are then distributed to shareholders who must pay tax on them again. Corporations with fewer shareholders can avoid double taxation. The smaller corporation, called a Chapter S corporation in IRS terminology, must report its income but does not pay tax on it. Income is distributed to the shareholders who pay tax on the income only once.

A **limited liability company (LLC)** offers the legal insulation of the corporation and the flexibility of the partnership in a relatively simple business entity. Unless stated otherwise in the LLC's articles of organization, every owner is a manager with the power to execute documents on behalf of the LLC. An LLC's income tax is similar to that of a partnership where the entity reports tax but distributes income to the members where tax is then levied and paid.

Partnerships are usually classified as general or limited. In a **general partnership**, the co-owners share everything equally and operate as agents of the partnership. In a **limited partnership**, there are general partners that control and operate the business while the limited partners are silent and only provide capital for investment.

A real estate investment **syndicate** is a business venture in which people pool their resources to own or develop a particular piece of property. This structure permits people with only modest capital to invest in large-scale operations. Syndicate members realize some profit from rents collected on the investment. The main return usually comes with the sale of the property. Any pooling of individuals' funds raises questions of securities registration under federal and state securities laws, known as *blue-sky laws*.

By directing their funds into a **real estate investment trust (REIT)**, real estate investors take advantage of the same tax benefits as do mutual fund investors. A REIT does not have to pay corporate income tax as long as 95% of its income is distributed to its shareholders. Certain other conditions also must be met. To qualify as a REIT, at least 75% of the trust's income must come from real estate. Investors purchase certificates in the trust, which in turn invests in real estate or mortgages (or both). Profits are distributed to investors.

■ RELATED WEBSITES

American Investors in Real Estate Online: www.aireo.com
National Association of Real Estate Investment Trusts: www.nariet.com
National Real Estate Investors Association: www.nationalreia.com

■ KEY POINT REVIEW

Investment in real estate offers advantages of

- **leverage**, which is offered by the use of borrowed money;
- above-average rate of return, generally;
- greater control than ownership of securities;
- tax benefits in certain situations;
- income (**cash flow**) production; and
- possibility of property **appreciation** (increase in value over time).

Disadvantages of investment in real estate include

- lack of **liquidity** (ready conversion into cash);
- high cost to acquire;
- active management or cost of hiring a professional property manager; and
- high degree of risk, although an investor's ability to hold onto property long term tends to reduce risk.

Cash flow of income property, the amount remaining after all ownership expenses have been paid, tends to make it the safest form of real estate investment:

- Rent paid by tenants is a major source of property income and depends on the property's location, physical appearance, and available amenities.
- When rent does not cover property expenses, negative cash flow results.

Leverage is the use of borrowed money to finance an investment.

- Risk is directly proportional to degree of leverage.
- **Equity buildup** will not be realized until the sale of the property.

Profitability will be determined by **return on investment (ROI)** which will use net operating income and operating expenses to calculate the **before-tax cash flow** (or cash throw-off) and the **cash-on-cash rate of return** or **equity dividend rate**.

Advantages of investment ownership by entities include

- separate legal identity from individual members to limit liability,
- investment enhanced by individual strengths and talents,
- favorable tax regulations for entities, and
- consolidation of financial resources.

Types of business ownership for investments could include

- **sole proprietorship**—individually owned and managed but may not have as many tax advantages as other business entities
- a **corporation**
- a **limited liability company (LLC)** offers its members the following benefits:
  — Limited liability offered by a corporate form of ownership
  — Tax advantages of a partnership (no double taxation)
  — Flexible management structure without corporation requirements or restrictions on limited partnership

- a **partnership** is an association of two or more persons who carry on a business for profit as co-owners in general or a limited partnership.
  — In a **general partnership**,
    - all partners participate in operation and management, and
    - partners share full liability for business losses and obligations.
  — A **limited partnership** has both general partners and limited partners.
    - **General partners** run the business.
    - **Limited partners** do not participate in running the business and are liable for business losses only up to the amount of the individual's investment.
- a **syndicate** is a business venture in which participants pool resources to own or develop property. Pooling of funds may involve securities registration under federal and state securities laws.
- a **real estate investment trust (REIT)** does not pay corporate income tax as long as 95% of its income is distributed to its shareholders and other conditions are met. Restrictions and regulations on the formation and operation of REITs are complex.

QUESTIONS

1. A small multifamily property generates $50,000 in rental income, $10,000 in expenses, and $35,000 in debt service. The property appreciates about $25,000 each year. What is the cash flow on this property?
   a. $5,000
   b. $15,000
   c. $25,000
   d. $30,000

2. Cash flow is
   a. equivalent to operating expense.
   b. the total amount of spendable income left after expenses.
   c. the use of borrowed money to finance an investment.
   d. selling costs plus depreciation.

3. A property is sold for $500,000 with a $100,000 down payment and a $400,000 mortgage with debt service payments of $54,000 per year. The potential gross income is $110,000, effective gross income is $104,500, and operating expenses are $36,500 including reserves of $3,000. The equity dividend rate is
   a. 17%.
   b. 14%.
   c. 12%.
   d. 10%.

4. An investor can purchase a property for $150,000 cash. The property has a net operating income of $18,000 producing a before-tax equity dividend rate of 12%. If the investor bought the property using a mortgage of $120,000 with annual payments of $13,500, what would be the before-tax equity dividend rate?
   a. 3.75%
   b. 18.00%
   c. 15.00%
   d. 12.50%

5. A tax entity created by the Tax Reform Act of 1986 that issues securities backed by a pool of mortgages is a
   a. REIT.
   b. REMIC.
   c. limited partnership.
   d. pyramid.

6. Advantages of an investment in real estate include all of the following EXCEPT
   a. the possibility of more personal control of asset.
   b. high liquidity.
   c. the use of leverage to increase rates of return.
   d. tax deductions.

7. Which situation would result in the highest degree of leverage?
   a. Using your own funds entirely
   b. Using more of your own funds than those you borrow
   c. Using more of the funds you borrow than your own funds
   d. Using borrowed funds entirely

8. Someone looking for a tax-advantaged investment similar to a mutual fund would probably invest in a
   a. real estate investment trust.
   b. general partnership.
   c. limited partnership.
   d. corporation.

9. When considering an investment in real estate, the prospective investor should consider all of the following EXCEPT
   a. anticipated appreciation of the property.
   b. possible effects of inflation on the property.
   c. assessed valuation of the property.
   d. intrinsic value of the property.

10. Cash flow refers to the
    a. amount of money flowing into and out of a property.
    b. bookkeeping function that accounts for the cash each day.
    c. taxes, operating expenses, and loan payments on the property.
    d. total amount of income left after all expenses have been paid.

Appendix A: Study Tips and Comprehensive Practice Examination

■ PREPARING FOR THE EXAM

Mental and Physical Preparation. An excellent method of preparing for an exam is to take practice tests prior to the actual exam. You can gain important points simply by being an experienced test taker. That is the strategy behind the end of chapter quizzes and the practice exam that follows this discussion. It is also critical to know your vocabulary; it is very difficult to answer a question when you do not understand the word used in the question!

You will also earn a better score if you are in top physical and mental shape the day of the exam. Get your normal amount of sleep the night before the exam; it is *NOT* wise to pull an *all-nighter* in a panic-stricken attempt to cram. Eat normally, but do not have a heavy meal before taking the test. If you tend to be easily distracted, you might consider bringing and using ear plugs during the exam to tune out random noise in the testing site.

Your attitude is at least as important as your metabolic state. A small amount of anxiety is natural and can even help you do your best; too much anxiety is a handicap. You should be prepared, determined, and positive. That positive attitude is much easier to possess if you feel prepared; that requires a game plan to maximize your study benefits. Short regular study sessions are usually better than lengthy cram sessions. Schedule your study periods in a quiet place during a time of the day when you function best. Utilize acronyms to help with memorization. Consider making flashcards of difficult terms to increase your retention. Coordinate a study group . . . but only after you have done some studying on your own.

Taking the Exam. Most of the computer-administered exam software programs provide a tutorial on how to effectively use the testing program. Take the time to review this tutorial because it will show how to utilize all the features during the exam, such as marking items for later review. The time to use the tutorial does not count toward your four hours for the exam. When you actually begin taking the exam, read directions and questions carefully, not quickly. Be sure you understand each question before answering. Read each question twice to make sure of the question being asked. A major cause of test errors is carelessness. Always try to choose the *BEST* answer to a question; more than one answer alternative may be partially correct. Do not look for trick questions; choose the most logical answer to the premise of each question. Statistically, your first answer is likely to be the correct answer, so do not change it unless you are absolutely sure you have marked an incorrect answer.

Work through the exam at a comfortable rate. You are allowed ample time to finish the exam; however, you should work as rapidly as you can without sacrificing accuracy. Budget your time before you begin the exam. Plan on having more than half the questions answered before half the exam time has elapsed. You may want to take a short break halfway through the exam. You can at least stretch your legs and relax in your seat for a minute or two; even though the clock continues to run, this breaks the tension and helps prevent mistakes.

As you work through the exam, consider answering the easy questions first—they are worth as much as the hard questions and they build your confidence! On the exam, you can mark and return to difficult or time-consuming calculations later. Do not give hurried answers just because you are intimidated by the number of questions.

All North Carolina license exams use the multiple-choice format exclusively; no fill-in-the-blank or essay questions ever appear. One of the most important things to remember about multiple-choice test questions: the correct answer is always one of the choices provided. You do not have to remember how to spell words, you have only to decide which of the choices best answers the question. Most objective questions are not very time consuming. Do not become discouraged if the exam seems difficult. No one is expected to get a perfect score. If you do not know the correct answer immediately, rule out the answer choices that you know are wrong and see if you can narrow your choice down to two . . . then may a reasonable guess. The only sure way to increase your odds of a correct answer is to *study and learn the material*.

In the multiple-choice test format, the question is in the last line of the stem before the answer choices. Exam questions frequently have superfluous information to distract you, so you must determine which information is necessary to answer the question. It is still very important to read every single word in the question. If the terms used in the question are very legalistic, translate to everyday language . . . and the question becomes clearer and easier; *seller* is a lot clearer than *grantor*. Reading the questions too quickly might cause you to skim over an important clue in the wording; slow down! Make sure that the right person is performing the action in the answer choice or the correct number of days is noted.

On multiple-choice exams, the math problems are word problems in paragraph format that intimidate some people. Take the facts out of the paragraph format and just write the facts as a list. Use a reliable, easy to read calculator that you are comfortable using. Arithmetic problems frequently require multi-step calculations. The incorrect answer options are often numbers created on the way to the right answer. Re-read the question to make sure you answered the actual question and did not stop with the first number that showed up in the answer options. Math problems also tend to have units that need to be converted or standardized, such as converting square feet to acres or making sure everything is standardized to a monthly amount. Sometimes, you can work a math problem backwards using the answer options. If you do have to guess blindly on an arithmetic problem, the odds favor the discard of the two extreme answers and picking one of the remaining choices.

On the North Carolina licensing exam, there is no separate arithmetic section. Math questions are sprinkled throughout the exam. If you are confident about the math calculations, consider looking for those questions first while your mind is fresh. If your are not comfortable with arithmetic, work the math questions as you come across them. If you get overwhelmed or stumped by a math question, make an educated guess at the best answer, mark the question for later review, and move to the next question. Keep working through the exam at a steady pace. Once you have answered all the questions, go back to the questions you marked for review. Unless you are very competent with settlement statements (HUD-1s), you may prefer to leave the settlement problem until last because it is so time-consuming and only counts for four answers.

Test-taking summary:

1. Read the items carefully to determine the general subject that the question is testing and exactly what is being asked.
2. Reread the question for essential facts and qualifiers.
3. Eliminate answers that you know are incorrect.
4. Rephrase the problem (often helpful).
5. Determine what principles or formulas are necessary and how to solve the problem.
6. Apply relevant information to arrive at a solution.
7. Reread the question and check the answer.

Good luck and successful testing!

COMPREHENSIVE PRACTICE EXAM

The following comprehensive practice exam contains questions on topics examinees might find on the North Carolina license examination. These questions are meant to provide prospective licensees with additional practice in preparing for the examination. Note that proration calculations are based on a 30-day month/360-day year unless otherwise stated.

■ REAL ESTATE LAW AND BROKERAGE PRACTICE

1. Which method of describing land is NOT used in North Carolina?
   a. Metes and bounds
   b. Government rectangular survey
   c. Lot and block
   d. Reference to a recorded deed

2. In North Carolina, the last day that real estate taxes for the current year may be paid without penalty is
   a. at any time.
   b. by September 1 of the current tax year.
   c. by January 5th of the next year.
   d. by December 31st of the current tax year.

3. A description of property that reads "Beginning at the large oak tree on the northern line of State Road 18, approximately one mile west to the intersection of State Road and the Great Southern Railroad right-of-way, north approximately 15′ along the old drainage ditch . . ." is
   I. a legal description that could be used in North Carolina.
   II. a metes-and-bounds description.
   a. I only
   b. II only
   c. Both I and II
   d. Neither I nor II

4. To be valid in North Carolina, a deed must include
   a. the grantor's seal.
   b. the grantee's signature.
   c. total consideration amount.
   d. words of conveyance.

5. All these freehold estates can pass by inheritance EXCEPT a(n)
   a. fee simple estate.
   b. defeasible fee estate.
   c. estate for the life of another.
   d. conventional life estate.

6. Which of the following contains no warranties at all and may convey no title at all, depending on the grantor's interest in the property when the deed is executed?
   a. Sheriff's deed
   b. Quitclaim deed
   c. Trustee's deed
   d. Deed of trust

7. Which of the following statements is TRUE about manufactured homes in North Carolina?
   I. It is regulated by North Carolina building codes.
   II. Permanently attaching the unit to a permanent foundation is all that is required to convert the unit from personal property to real property for legal and tax purposes.
   a. I only
   b. II only
   c. Both I and II
   d. Neither I nor II

8. The North Carolina law that provides that a contract to sell land is not protected against a third party unless recorded is called the
   a. Statute of Frauds.
   b. Conner Act.
   c. Machinery Act.
   d. Marketable Title Act.

9. The deed that contains covenants against all encumbrances that would affect the title conveyed and assures quiet enjoyment is the
   a. general warranty deed.
   b. quitclaim deed.
   c. special warranty deed.
   d. grant deed.

496

10. A woman grants a life estate to her grandson and stipulates that on the grandson's death, the title to the property will pass to her son-in-law. This second estate is known as an estate
    a. in remainder.
    b. in reversion.
    c. pur autrie vie.
    d. at sufferance.

11. A tenancy for years is a tenancy that
    a. renews automatically.
    b. expires on a specific date.
    c. requires notice to terminate.
    d. is only used to lease land.

12. A builder built a structure with six stories. Several years later, an ordinance was passed in that area banning any building higher than four stories. The building should be allowed to continue in its existing state because of a
    a. nonconforming use.
    b. conditional use.
    c. variance.
    d. zoning amendment.

13. Under the North Carolina Statute of Frauds, an oral lease for longer than three years is
    a. not assignable.
    b. renewable.
    c. illegal.
    d. unenforceable.

14. Police power does NOT include
    a. zoning.
    b. deed restrictions.
    c. building codes.
    d. subdivision statutes and regulations.

15. A cloud on title to a property may be cured by
    a. obtaining quitclaim deeds from the party or parties with possible interests in the property.
    b. recording the new owner's title as per the Conner Act.
    c. paying cash for the property at closing to avoid RESPA compliance.
    d. bringing an action to repudiate the title.

16. Which of the following is/are true regarding liens in North Carolina?
    I. A specific lien is enforceable for three years, while a general lien good for five years.
    II. A specific lien is a lien against a particular parcel of real estate, while a general lien may apply to all of the debtor's property.
    a. I only
    b. II only
    c. Both I and II
    d. Neither I nor II

17. Someone seeking to be excused from the dictates of a zoning ordinance because of hardship should request a
    a. building permit.
    b. certificate of alternative usage.
    c. variance.
    d. certificate of nonconforming use.

18. Under the concept of riparian rights, North Carolina owners of property adjacent to navigable rivers or streams have the right to use the water and
    a. may erect a dam across the navigable river or stream.
    b. are considered to own the submerged land to the center point of the waterway.
    c. are considered owners of the water adjacent to the land.
    d. are considered to own the land to the edge of the water.

19. A leasehold estate that automatically renews itself at each expiration is a
    a. tenancy for years.
    b. periodic tenancy.
    c. tenancy at will.
    d. tenancy at sufferance.

20. In the typical real estate sales transaction in North Carolina, the buyer is responsible for the cost of
    a. title insurance.
    b. deed preparation.
    c. excise tax.
    d. clearing a title defect.

21. Which of the following does NOT terminate an offer?
    a. Revocation of the offer before its acceptance
    b. The death of the offeror before acceptance
    c. A counteroffer by the offeree
    d. An offer from a third party

22. A buyer is under contract to purchase a vacation lot for $50,000. Shortly after going under contract, the buyer changes her mind. A friend of the buyer would like to buy the lot on the same terms as the original buyer. The lot owner agrees and enters into a new contract with the friend. The lot owner and the original buyer tear up their original contract. This is known as a(n)
    a. assignment.
    b. novation.
    c. substitution.
    d. rescission.

23. An offer to purchase real estate is a binding contract after it has been signed, communicated, and accepted by whom?
    a. Buyer
    b. Seller
    c. Both a and b
    d. Lender

24. A broker enters into a listing agreement with a seller wherein the seller will receive $120,000 from the sale of a vacant lot and the broker will receive any sales proceeds exceeding that amount as commission. This type of agreement is called a(n)
    a. exclusive-agency listing.
    b. exclusive right-to-sell listing.
    c. net listing.
    d. illegal listing.

25. While using the NCAR/NCBA Standard 2-T Offer to Purchase and Contract Form, buyer and seller agree upon a 45-day due diligence period. Which of the following is TRUE?
    a. Buyer must purchase the property but may do so only during the due diligence period.
    b. Buyer is entitled to a refund of all monies if buyer notifies seller of cancellation within 10 days of entering into the contract.
    c. Buyer can cancel the contract and receive all monies back until after the due diligence period has expired.
    d. Buyer has no obligation to purchase the property during the due diligence period and may be entitled to a full refund of any earnest money deposit paid.

26. On Monday, an offer was written to buy a seller's vacant lot for $32,000. On Tuesday, the seller counteroffers by raising the purchase price to $33,500. The prospective buyer does not reply, so on Friday, the seller changes his mind and accepts the original price of $32,000. Under these circumstances, there is
    a. a valid agreement because the seller accepted the original offer exactly as it was made.
    b. a valid agreement because the seller accepted before the prospective buyer withdrew his original offer.
    c. no valid agreement because the original offer was not accepted within 72 hours of its having been made.
    d. no valid agreement because the seller's counteroffer was a rejection of the original offer.

27. Which of the following situations present at signing would result in a void contract?
    a. The seller has been declared incompetent by a court.
    b. The buyer is 17 years old.
    c. The buyer is very drunk.
    d. The seller was under anesthesia for surgery less than 24 hours earlier.

28. Which of the following items are NOT usually prorated between the seller and buyer at closing?
    a. Tenant security deposits
    b. Real estate taxes
    c. Prepaid rents
    d. Owner association dues

29. The sellers agree to an open listing for their house with only ABC Realty and Homes Realty. Open listings are not allowed to be entered into the local multiple listing service. The house is sold by a licensee with XYZ Realty. Which statement is TRUE regarding the sellers' obligation to pay commission?
    a. ABC Realty and Homes Realty will share the commission.
    b. Only XYZ Realty is entitled to the commission.
    c. ABC Realty, Homes Realty, and XYZ Realty are all entitled to share the commission.
    d. The sellers are not obligated to pay the commission to anyone.

30. A broker found a buyer for a seller's house. The buyer put down an earnest money deposit with the broker, and the parties signed a sales contract. Before the sale was closed, a title search revealed a defect in the seller's title, making it impossible for the seller to deliver good title. Which statement is TRUE?
    a. The buyer was entitled to cancel the sale without penalty.
    b. The seller was entitled to keep the buyer's deposit if the buyer canceled the sale.
    c. The buyer must accept a non-warranty deed at closing.
    d. The buyer must complete the transaction if the seller reduces the sales price appropriately.

31. Which type of listing provides the strongest protection of the broker's interests?
    a. Net
    b. Exclusive agency
    c. Exclusive right to sell
    d. Open

32. Which contract does NOT have to be in writing to be enforceable in North Carolina?
    a. Contract to sell real estate
    b. Listing agreement
    c. Three-year lease
    d. Agreement creating an easement

33. On the settlement statement, the earnest money deposit appears as a
    a. credit to the seller and a debit to the buyer.
    b. debit to the seller and a credit to the buyer.
    c. credit to the seller.
    d. credit to the buyer.

34. In North Carolina, a seller's agent must disclose the agency status to a prospective buyer no later than
    a. before closing the transaction.
    b. before presenting the buyer's offer to the seller.
    c. at first substantial contact.
    d. before the seller accepts the buyer's offer.

35. A property manager should make efforts to do all the following EXCEPT
    a. maximize the property owner's net profit.
    b. maintain or increase the value of the property.
    c. perform the landlord's duties under the lease.
    d. reinvest the profits by making capital improvements on the property.

36. A broker receives an earnest money deposit with a written offer that indicates that the buyer will leave the offer open for the seller's acceptance for 10 days. On the fifth day, and prior to acceptance by the seller, the buyer notifies the broker that he is withdrawing his offer and demands the return of the deposit. In this situation, which statement is TRUE?
    a. The offeror cannot withdraw the offer; it must be held open for the full 10-day period.
    b. The offeror has the right to withdraw the offer and have the deposit returned any time before contract acceptance.
    c. The offeror can withdraw the offer, but the seller and the broker will each retain one-half of the forfeited deposit.
    d. The offeror can withdraw the offer, but the broker will declare the deposit forfeited and retain all of it in lieu of a commission.

37. Which of the following items would normally be considered to be a fixture that would transfer to the buyer with the purchase of a residential property?
    a. A basketball goal that is cemented into the driveway extension
    b. Curtains in the master bedroom that match the wallpaper
    c. A dining room chandelier that is a family heirloom
    d. A security system that is leased by the seller

38. When the subdivision developer built the roads and installed the utilities throughout the neighborhood, what type of easement was given to the utility providers?
    a. Implied easement
    b. Easement in gross
    c. Appurtenant easement
    d. Prescriptive easement

39. Which of the following statements about subdivisions in North Carolina is/are TRUE?
    I. There must be at least five separate parcels or lots to be called a subdivision.
    II. No sales contracts can be accepted on subdivision lots until the final plat has been recorded.
    a. I only
    b. II only
    c. Both I and II
    d. Neither I nor II

40. Which of the following statements is/are correct about the North Carolina Real Estate Commission's *Working with Real Estate Agents* brochure?
    I. The licensee must provide and review the publication with consumers in all real estate transactions upon initial contact.
    II. The consumer must sign the acknowledgment panel to create an agency relationship with the broker.
    a. I only
    b. II only
    c. Both I and II
    d. Neither I nor II

41. The buyer agent has found a property that meets his client's detailed list of required features. The listing firm is offering the selling agent a $1500 bonus for a signed contract by the end of the month. In North Carolina, does the buyer agent have to disclose the bonus to his buyer-client before writing an offer?
    a. No, because the buyer will want to share part of the bonus.
    b. Yes, because all compensation must be disclosed to a broker's client is a timely manner.
    c. No, because disclosure of the bonus on the closing statement will be adequate.
    d. Yes, because the buyer will find out about the bonus eventually anyway.

42. The legal practice of oral buyer agency in North Carolina requires
    a. the relationship be put in writing before presenting an offer.
    b. that the consumer go under contract to buy a property within 30 days.
    c. a definite time period for the agency relationship.
    d. the buyer to agree to oral dual agency as well.

MISCELLANEOUS TOPICS

43. Which tax advantage is NOT associated with owner-occupied personal dwellings?
    a. Ability to depreciate the property
    b. Capital gains treatment of resale profits
    c. Possibility of tax-free capital gains
    d. Deductibility of mortgage interest

44. Which of the following statements is/are TRUE about the sale of property that has been the owner's principal residence for the last 10 years?
    I. If the seller is single, capital gains up to $500,000 is tax-free.
    II. Any capital gain in excess of the tax-exempt amount will be subject to long-term capital gains tax.
        a. I only
        b. II only
        c. Both I and II
        d. Neither I nor II

45. Steering is the practice of
    a. leading prospective buyers to or away from certain areas based on protected class.
    b. refusing to make loans to people of a protected class.
    c. requiring brokers to join a multiple-listing service.
    d. illegally setting standard commission rates in an area.

46. A Chinese buyer-client has instructed his buyer agent to show him properties that are in predominantly Chinese neighborhoods. If the agent were to comply with this client's instructions, the agent would
    a. violate the Civil Rights Act of 1866.
    b. be in compliance with the North Carolina Fair Housing Act.
    c. violate the Federal Fair Housing Act of 1968.
    d. be in compliance with the North Carolina Real Estate License Law because he must obey his client.

47. A broker calls several property owners in a neighborhood. He states that several minority homebuyers are moving into the area and that this will decrease property values. The broker tries to solicit listings from these owners. Under the Federal Fair Housing Act of 1968, this would be considered
    a. blockbusting.
    b. redlining.
    c. steering.
    d. channeling.

48. All the following are parts of the flooring system EXCEPT
    a. sill.
    b. girders.
    c. joists.
    d. header.

49. Which of the following statements is/are TRUE?
    I. The sale of a house built prior to 1978 will require the seller to disclose what the seller knows about the presence of lead-based paint in the property.
    II. Radon gas is easily detected by its sickly sweet smell.
        a. I only
        b. II only
        c. Both I and II
        d. Neither I nor II

50. Which of the following statements is/are TRUE about the North Carolina Residential Property Disclosure Act?
    I. Seller must disclose property condition in the mandatory form to the buyer prior to first offer unless the property is exempted from the Act.
    II. If the buyer does not receive the information required by the Act in a timely manner, the buyer will have a 10-day rescission period after contract.
    a. I only
    b. II only
    c. Both I and II
    d. Neither I nor II

51. The Lead-Based Paint Hazard Reduction Act requires that in residential transactions subject to the Act, a
    a. seller test the property to discover any lead-based paint in the living areas prior to offering the property for sale.
    b. prospective buyer be given the EPA lead hazard informational pamphlet and a disclosure statement about the presence of lead in the property.
    c. seller remove all lead-based paint from the property prior to closing.
    d. prospective buyer test the property to discover any lead-based paint in the living areas within 10 days of contract execution.

NORTH CAROLINA REAL ESTATE LAW

52. The North Carolina Real Estate Commission has the power to
    a. regulate the brokerage activities of licensees.
    b. determine the maximum commission a broker may charge on any one transaction.
    c. fine licensees that do not comply with licensing law and/or Commission Rules.
    d. interpret the legality of a real estate contract between consumers.

53. If a person is being compensated, which of the following activities does NOT require an active North Carolina real estate license?
    a. Managing apartments in several different complexes for family members
    b. Negotiating exchanges of property
    c. Listing property for sale
    d. Negotiating the sale of personally owned real estate

54. Which statement is TRUE of advertising regulations in North Carolina?
    a. A broker must have the owner's permission before placing a For Sale sign on any property.
    b. A provisional broker may advertise another person's property so long as the firm's office phone number is given in the ad.
    c. A provisional broker can place ads on her own initiative as long as she personally pays for the advertising.
    d. Advertising cannot include any financing information.

55. Which statement is TRUE regarding North Carolina trust account records?
    a. The North Carolina Real Estate Commission requires that records be kept for a period of three years.
    b. Office records are considered trade secrets and not subject to inspection by the North Carolina Real Estate Commission.
    c. A broker-in-charge is responsible for trust funds and cannot delegate daily trust account activities to anyone else.
    d. Trust funds cannot be held in interest-bearing accounts.

56. Rental payments received by a broker must be deposited into a trust or an escrow account
    a. no later than three banking days following receipt of the money.
    b. no later than five calendar days following receipt.
    c. no later than 24 hours after receipt.
    d. per landlord's instructions regardless of other time limits.

57. A broker-in-charge in North Carolina is responsible for all the following EXCEPT
    a. all advertising done in the name of the firm.
    b. supervision of all provisional brokers in the firm even if there are multiple office locations.
    c. retention of current pocket cards by all brokers affiliated with the firm.
    d. proper maintenance and record retention of trust funds.

58. In North Carolina, the annual license pocket renewal card
    a. must be carried by the licensee at all times when conducting real estate activities.
    b. expires on June 30th unless the licensee has met all continuing education requirements.
    c. shows whether the license status is active or inactive.
    d. expires on June 10th unless the licensee has paid the renewal fee.

59. A North Carolina real estate firm may establish one or more branch offices, provided that
    a. each office has a broker-in-charge.
    b. each office has at least five brokers.
    c. the qualifying broker personally supervises the provisional brokers at each office.
    d. the firm uses a different trade name for each branch office.

60. The license status of a North Carolina licensee who completed all continuing education and post licensing education in a timely manner but forgot to pay the license renewal fee on time is
    a. active.
    b. canceled.
    c. expired.
    d. inactive.

61. The license status of a North Carolina provisional broker who paid the license renewal fee on time and completed all continuing education in a timely manner but did not complete at least one of the postlicensing courses by the first required deadline is
    a. active.
    b. canceled.
    c. expired.
    d. inactive.

62. The license status of a North Carolina provisional broker who paid the license renewal fee on time and completed all continuing education in a timely manner but did not complete all three of the postlicensing courses by the required deadline is
    a. active.
    b. canceled.
    c. expired.
    d. inactive.

63. A provisional broker must successfully complete all three of the postlicensing courses
    I. to remove the provisional status on the license.
    II. prior to the second renewal of the license.
       a. I only
       b. II only
       c. Both I and II
       d. Neither I nor II

64. Which of the following statements about the North Carolina Time Share Act is/are TRUE?
    I. An active real estate license is required to sell time shares in North Carolina.
    II. If a public offering statement is not given to the buyer prior to contract, the buyer has a seven-day contract rescission period.
       a. I only
       b. II only
       c. Both I and II
       d. Neither I nor II

REAL ESTATE FINANCE

65. A mortgage requires monthly payments of $875.70 for 20 years and a final payment of $24,095. The final payment is known as what type of payment?
    a. Wraparound
    b. Variable
    c. Balloon
    d. Accelerated

66. In North Carolina, a trustee is the conditional holder of title to mortgaged real estate. North Carolina is considered what type of state?
    a. Title theory
    b. Lien theory
    c. Statutory share
    d. Strict forfeiture

67. A woman purchased a condominium unit and obtained financing from a local savings association. In this situation, which best identifies the buyer's role under a deed of trust?
    a. Mortgagee
    b. Grantor
    c. Trustee
    d. Beneficiary

68. A typical promissory note for an FHA-insured loan may contain all the following EXCEPT a(n)
    a. acceleration clause.
    b. alienation clause.
    c. prepayment penalty.
    d. mortgage insurance requirement.

69. Which statement is TRUE of an adjustable rate mortgage loan?
    a. The monthly payment is usually fixed for the life of the loan.
    b. The interest rate always adjusts to the prevalent market interest rate on the date of adjustment.
    c. Negative amortization is possible if there is a payment cap.
    d. The original interest rate is usually slightly higher than comparable fixed rate loans.

70. The effect of discount points is
    a. an increase in the lender's yield.
    b. a decrease in the borrower's interest rate.
    c. both a and b.
    d. neither a nor b.

71. A home is purchased under a land contract. Until the contract is paid in full, the buyer has
    a. legal title to the premises.
    b. no interest in the property.
    c. a legal life estate in the premises.
    d. equitable title to the property.

72. A buyer has just made the final payment on his mortgage loan to his bank. The buyer will regain his full legal title once what is recorded?
    a. Satisfaction of mortgage
    b. Mortgage novation
    c. Deed of trust
    d. Promissory note

73. Discount points on a real estate loan are usually an expense to the buyer. The value of points is
    a. set by the FHA and VA for their loan programs.
    b. charged only on conventional loans.
    c. limited by government regulations.
    d. determined by the market.

74. Acceleration is a loan provision that says
    a. the borrower can make extra payments at any time.
    b. the lender can call the loan due and payable in full if the borrower defaults.
    c. the trustee can speed up the foreclosure procedure due to the amount of the loan.
    d. the lender can charge additional interest if the payment is late.

75. A real estate loan indicates that if the title transfers to the property, the lender must be paid in full immediately. This is known as
    a. acceleration.
    b. alienation.
    c. subordination.
    d. satisfaction.

76. A borrower defaulted on his mortgage loan payments, and the lender foreclosed. At the foreclosure sale, the property sold for $64,000; the unpaid loan balance at the time of foreclosure was $78,000. What must the lender do in an attempt to recover the $14,000 that is still owed?
    a. Sue for specific performance
    b. Sue for damages
    c. Seek a deficiency judgment
    d. Seek a judgment by default

77. Which is TRUE of a term mortgage loan?
    a. All of the interest is paid at the end of the term.
    b. The debt is partially amortized over the life of the loan.
    c. The length of the term is limited by state statutes.
    d. The entire principal amount is due at the end of the term.

78. A real estate loan that uses both real estate and personal property as collateral is known as a
    a. blanket mortgage.
    b. package mortgage.
    c. growing-equity mortgage.
    d. graduated payment mortgage.

79. Which of the following loan terms will NOT be considered a trigger term under the Truth in Lending Act?
    a. Annual percentage rate
    b. Monthly payment amount
    c. Annual interest rate
    d. Number of payments

80. In funding a loan that is secured by a residence, the lender is required to disclose all costs involved in obtaining the financing. This consumer protection is provided by the
    a. Fair Credit Reporting Act.
    b. Truth in Lending Act.
    c. Sherman Anti-trust Act.
    d. Equal Credit Opportunity Act.

■ REAL ESTATE VALUATION

81. A residence with leaky plumbing is suffering from
    a. functional obsolescence.
    b. curable physical deterioration.
    c. incurable physical deterioration.
    d. external obsolescence.

82. The market value of a parcel of land is
    a. an estimate of the present worth of future benefits.
    b. a measure of past expenditures.
    c. the price the seller wants for the property.
    d. equal to assessed value.

83. Each legitimate comparable should be as similar as possible in all the following EXCEPT
    a. location.
    b. sale price.
    c. date of sale.
    d. square footage.

84. If the annual net income of a commercial property remains constant and the capitalization rate increases, the value of the property will
    a. be unaffected.
    b. increase.
    c. increase the tax basis only.
    d. decrease.

85. A property is being appraised for loan purposes. The property is an elegant old mansion that has been converted into three apartments. Which approach to value is the appraiser most likely to use?
    a. Reproduction cost approach
    b. Sales comparison approach
    c. Replacement cost approach
    d. Income capitalization approach

86. A $125,000 home is being built in a residential neighborhood. The block next to it is going to be rezoned to allow a mix of residential and retail uses. Because of this future zoning change, the value of the home dropped to $100,000. This is due to the principle of
    a. substitution.
    b. competition.
    c. anticipation.
    d. supply and demand.

87. An appraiser is using the cost approach to value. After determining the replacement cost of the building, she will
    a. estimate depreciation on the building.
    b. add the land value that was determined by the sales comparison approach.
    c. do both a and b.
    d. do neither a nor b.

88. All the following are elements of value EXCEPT
    a. scarcity.
    b. demand.
    c. utility.
    d. uniqueness.

89. The principle that is the basis for the sales comparison approach is the principle of
    a. replacement.
    b. competition.
    c. substitution.
    d. highest and best use.

90. The method that is the most reliable in estimating the value of an owner-occupied, single-family residence is the
    a. sales comparison approach.
    b. cost approach.
    c. income capitalization approach.
    d. gross rent multiplier method.

91. A house is three blocks away from an international airport. This is an example of
    a. functional obsolescence.
    b. economic obsolescence.
    c. physical deterioration.
    d. deferred maintenance.

92. The art of analyzing and effectively weighing the findings from the different appraisal methods is called
    a. averaging.
    b. capitalization.
    c. final estimating.
    d. reconciliation.

93. When determining net income, which of the following are NOT deducted from gross income?
    a. Mortgage payments
    b. Management costs
    c. Utility costs
    d. Insurance expenses

REAL ESTATE MATHEMATICS

Use a 30-day month/360-day year for all calculations.

94. The principal balance on a loan is $98,763 and the monthly debt service payment is $584.00. The interest rate on the loan is 5.75%. What is the balance of the principal after the next monthly payment has been made?
    a. $98,179.00
    b. $98,289.76
    c. $98,652.24
    d. $98,729.42

95. A purchaser buys a home for $143,900 and assumes the seller's loan balance of $109,700. How much excise tax will be paid at closing?
    a. $69.00
    b. $220.00
    c. $287.80
    d. $288.00

96. A property owner is selling a rectangular lot that has 150' of road frontage and is 375' deep. If the owner sells the lot for $50,000 per acre, what would be the sales price per front foot?
    a. $333.33
    b. $430.43
    c. $50,000
    d. $64,565

97. A borrower computed the interest he was charged for the previous month on his $60,000 loan balance as $412.50. What is his annual interest rate?
    a. 6.875%
    b. 7.75%
    c. 8.25%
    d. 8.5%

98. Assuming that the listing broker and the selling broker in a transaction split the commission equally, what was the sales price of the property if the commission rate was 6.5% and the listing broker received $2,593.50?
    a. $39,900
    b. $56,200
    c. $79,800
    d. $88,400

99. A seller wants to net $65,000 from the sale of her house after paying the broker's 6% fee based on gross sales price. Her gross sales price needs to be
   a. $61,100.
   b. $61,321.
   c. $68,900.
   d. $69,149.

100. The commission rate is 7¾% on a sale of $50,000. What is the dollar amount of the commission?
   a. $3,500
   b. $3,875
   c. $4,085
   d. $6,452

101. A buyer is purchasing a $107,000 home with an 80% loan. The lender is charging two and one-half discount points. The loan discount expense will total
   a. $1,980.
   b. $2,140.
   c. $2,575.
   d. $2,675.

102. The assessed value of a parcel of land is $64,000 and the local ad valorem tax rate is $.72 per $100. Which of the following is the correct tax proration in accordance with customary practice if the closing is April 28?
   a. Seller will be debited $151.04 and buyer will be credited $151.04.
   b. Seller will be credited $151.04 and buyer will be debited $151.04.
   c. Seller will be debited $151.04 and buyer will be debited $309.76.
   d. Seller will be debited $309.76 and buyer will be credited $309.76.

103. Assume a house is sold for $84,500 and the commission rate is 7%. The commission is split so that 60% goes to the selling broker and 40% goes to the listing broker. Each broker splits her share of the commission evenly with the provisional broker responsible for procuring the sale. How much will the provisional broker who personally listed the property receive from this sale?
   a. $1,183
   b. $1,775
   c. $2,366
   d. $3,549

104. A borrower has been approved for a 6.5% fixed rate 30-year mortgage loan for $138,000. He will be closing on September 27. What will be the HUD-1 interim interest entry?
   a. $847.17
   b. $672.75
   c. $99.67
   d. $74.75

105. A subject property is a 1,800 square foot house with 3 bedrooms, 1½ baths, a 2-car garage and a deck that is listed for $163,500. A great comparable for the subject property sold for $166,200 and has 1850 square feet, 3 bedrooms, 2 baths, a 1-car garage and a deck. The comparable property closed 2 months ago and appreciation in the area has averaged 6% per year. Estimate a market value for the subject property, using the following market values: full bathroom = $2000; 2-car garage = $5000; additional square footage = $55 per square foot.
   a. $164,750
   b. $163,500
   c. $166,612
   d. $166,549

106. A seller wants to net $72,000 on the sale of his home. He has agreed to pay a brokerage commission of 6%. What is the minimum sales price that will ensure that the seller will net his $72,000?
   a. $75,935
   b. $76,320
   c. $76,596
   d. $77,890

107. The buyers enter into a purchase contract with the sellers to buy the sellers' house for $84,500. The buyers deposit $2,000 as earnest money and obtain a new mortgage loan for $67,600. The purchase contract provides for a March 15 settlement. The buyers and sellers prorate the year's estimated real estate taxes (using the 360-day method) of $880.96. The taxes are unpaid and will be paid later in the year by the buyers. The buyers have additional closing costs of $1,250, and the sellers have other closing costs of $850. How much cash must the buyers bring to the settlement?
   a. $15,966
   b. $16,238
   c. $16,338
   d. $16,638

108. A man sold his house for $105,000. He owned the house for five years and made a profit of 25% on the sale over his previous purchase price. How much was originally paid for the house?
   a. $78,750
   b. $80,000
   c. $84,000
   d. $95,000

109. A buyer wants to purchase a house for $185,000 and applies to a lender for a $166,500 conventional mortgage loan to finance the purchase. The buyer's mortgage PITI payment on this loan would be $1386 per month. Recurring monthly obligations for a car payment and a school loan payment total $725 per month. What is the minimum monthly income, rounded to the nearest dollar, needed by the buyer to qualify for this loan if the qualifying ratios are 28:36?
   a. $7,539
   b. $5,864
   c. $4,950
   d. $3,850

110. A buyer is financing her new house with a fixed rate mortgage for $394,000 for 30 years at a 6% interest rate. Her monthly principal and interest payment will be $2,364.00. If the buyer takes all 30 years to pay off this loan, what will be the total interest paid over the life of her loan?
   a. $425,520
   b. $457,040
   c. $709,200
   d. $851,040

APPENDIX B: Residential Square Footage Guidelines

INTRODUCTION

It is often said that the three most important factors in making a homebuying decision are "location," "location," and "location." Other than "location," the single most-important factor is probably the size or "square footage" of the home. Not only is it an indicator of whether a particular home will meet a homebuyer's space needs, but it also affords a convenient (though not always accurate) method for the buyer to estimate the value of the home and compare it with other properties.

Although real estate agents are not required by the Real Estate License Law or Real Estate Commission rules to report the square footage of properties offered for sale (or rent), when they do report square footage, it is essential that the information they give prospective purchasers be accurate. At a minimum, information concerning square footage should include the amount of *living area* in the dwelling. The following guidelines and accompanying illustrations are designed to assist real estate brokers and salespersons in measuring, calculating and reporting (both orally and in writing) the *living area* contained in detached and attached single-family residential buildings. When reporting square footage, real estate agents should carefully follow these *Guidelines* or any other standards that are comparable to them, including those approved by the American National Standards Institute, Inc. (ANSI) which are recognized by the North Carolina Real Estate Commission as comparable standards.* Agents should be prepared to identify, when requested, the standard used.

LIVING AREA CRITERIA

Living area (sometimes referred to as "heated living area" or "heated square footage") is space that is intended for human occupancy and is:

1. *Heated* by a conventional heating system or systems (forced air, radiant, solar, etc.) that are permanently installed in the dwelling—not a portable heater—which generates heat sufficient to make the space suitable for year-round occupancy;

2. *Finished*, with walls, floors and ceilings of materials generally accepted for interior construction (e.g., painted drywall/sheet rock or panelled walls, carpeted or hardwood flooring, etc.) and with a ceiling height of at least seven feet, except under beams, ducts, etc. where the height must be at least six feet four inches *[Note: In rooms with sloped ceilings (e.g., finished attics, bonus rooms, etc.) you may also include as living area the portion of the room with a ceiling height of at least five feet if at least one-half of the finished area of the room has a ceiling height of at least seven feet.]*; and

3. *Directly accessible from other living area* (through a door or by a heated hallway or stairway).

---

*The following materials were consulted in the development of these *Guidelines*:
The *American National Standard for Single-Family Residential Buildings:
Square Footage-Method for Calculating* approved by the American National Standards Institute, Inc.;
House Measuring & Square Footage published by the Carolina Multiple Listing Services, Inc.; and
materials compiled by Bart T. Bryson, MAI, SRA, and Mary L. D'Angelo.

Source: Reprinted with permission of the North Carolina Real Estate Commission.

Real estate appraisers and lenders generally adhere to more detailed criteria in arriving at the *living area* or "gross living area" of residential dwellings. This normally includes distinguishing "above-grade" from "below-grade" area, which is also required by many multiple listing services. "Above-Grade" is defined as space on any level of a dwelling which has *living area* and no earth adjacent to any exterior wall on that level. "Below-Grade" is space on any level which has *living area*, is accessible by interior stairs, and has earth adjacent to any exterior wall on that level. If earth is adjacent to any portion of a wall, the entire level is considered "below-grade." Space that is "at" or "on grade" is considered "above-grade."

While real estate agents are encouraged to provide the most complete information available about properties offered for sale, the *Guidelines* recognize that the separate reporting of "above-grade" and "below-grade" area can be impractical in the advertising and marketing of homes. For this reason, *real estate agents are permitted under these Guidelines to report square footage of the dwelling as the total "living area"* without a separate distinction between "above-grade" and "below-grade" areas. However, to help avoid confusion and concern, agents should alert purchasers and sellers that the appraisal report may reflect differences in the way *living area* is defined and described by the lender, appraiser, and the *North Carolina Building Code* which could affect the amount of *living area* reported.

Determining whether an area is considered *living area* can sometimes be confusing. Finished rooms used for general living (living room, dining room, kitchen, den, bedrooms, etc.) are normally included in *living area*. For other areas in the dwelling, the determination may not be so easy. *For example, the following areas are considered* **living area** *if they meet the criteria (i.e., heated, finished, directly accessible from living area):*

- *Attic*, but note in the listing data that the space is located in an attic (Fig. 2). *[Note: If the ceiling is sloped, remember to apply the "ceiling height" criteria.]*

- *Basement (or "Below-Grade")*, but note in the listing data that the space is located in a basement or "below-grade" (Fig. 1). *[Note: For reporting purposes, a "basement" is defined as an area below the entry level of the dwelling which is accessible by a **full** flight of stairs and has earth adjacent to some portion of at least one wall above the floor level.]*

- *Bay Window*, if it has a floor, a ceiling height of at least seven feet, and otherwise meets the criteria for living area (Fig. 2).

- *Bonus Room (e.g., Finished Room over Garage)* (Fig. 3). *[Note: If the ceiling is sloped, remember to apply the "ceiling height" criteria.]*

- *Breezeway* (enclosed).

- *Chimney*, if the chimney base is inside *living area*. If the chimney base is outside the *living area* but the hearth is in the *living area*, include the hearth in the *living area* but not the chimney base (Fig. 1).

- *Closets*, if they are a functional part of the *living area*.

- *Dormers* (Fig. 6).

- *Furnace (Mechanical) Room* Also, in order to avoid excessive detail, if the furnace, water heater, etc. is located in a small closet in the *living area*, include it in *living area* even if it does not meet other *living area* criteria (Fig. 4).

- *Hallways*, if they are a functional part of the *living area*.

- *Laundry Room/Area* (Fig. 6).

- *Office* (Fig. 1).

- *Stairs*, if they meet the criteria and connect to *living area* (Fig. 1, 2, 3, 4, 5, 6). Include the stairway with the area from which it descends, **not to exceed the area of the opening in the floor.** If the opening for the stairway exceeds the length and width of the stairway, deduct the excess open space from the upper level area. Include as part of the lower level area the space beneath the stairway, regardless of its ceiling height.

- *Storage Room* (Fig. 6).

OTHER AREA

Note in the listing data and advise purchasers of any space that does not meet the criteria for *living area* but which contributes to the value of the dwelling; for example, unfinished basements, unfinished attics (with permanent stairs), unfinished bonus rooms, shops, decks, balconies, porches, garages and carports.

HELPFUL HINTS

Concealed in the walls of nearly all residential construction are pipes, ducts, chases, returns, etc. necessary to support the structure's mechanical systems. Although they may occupy *living area*, to avoid excessive detail, do **not** deduct the space from the *living area*.

When measuring and reporting the *living area* of homes, be alert to any remodeling, room additions (e.g., an enclosed porch) or other structural modifications to assure that the space meets all the criteria for *living area*. **Pay particular attention to the heating criteria, because the heating system for the original structure may not be adequate for the increased square footage.** Although agents are not required to determine the adequacy of heating systems, they should at least note whether there are heat vents, radiators or other heat outlets in the room before deciding whether to include space as *living area*.

When an area that is not part of the *living area* (e.g., a garage) shares a common wall with the *living area*, treat the common wall as the exterior wall for the *living area*; therefore, the measurements for the *living area* will include the thickness of the common wall, and the measurements for the other area will not.

Interior space that is open from the floor of one level to the ceiling of the next higher level is included in the square footage for the lower level only. However, any area occupied by interior balconies, lofts, etc. on the upper level or stairs that extend to the upper level is included in the square footage for the upper level.

MEASURING

The amount of *living area* and "other area" in dwellings is based upon **exterior measurements**. A one-hundred-foot-long tape measure is recommended for use in measuring the exterior of dwellings, and a thirty-foot retractable tape for measuring interior and hard-to-reach spaces. A tape measure that indicates linear footage in "tenths of a foot" will greatly simplify your calculations. For best results, take a partner to assist you in measuring. But if you do not have someone to assist you, a screwdriver or other sharp tool can be used to secure the tape measure to the ground.

Begin at one corner of the dwelling and proceed with measuring each exterior wall. **Round off your measurements to the nearest inch** (or tenth-of-a-foot if your tape indicates footage in that manner). Make a sketch of the structure. Write down each measurement as you go, and record it on your sketch. A clipboard and graph paper are helpful in sketching the dwelling and recording the measurements. Measure *living area* and "other area," but identify them separately on your sketch. Look for offsets (portions of walls that "jut out"), and adjust for any "overlap" of exterior walls (Fig. 3) or "overhang" in upper levels (Fig. 5).

When you cannot measure an exterior surface (such as in the case of attics and below-grade areas), measure the perimeter walls of the area from the inside of the dwelling. Remember to add **six inches** for each exterior wall and interior wall that you encounter in order to arrive at the exterior dimensions (Fig. 2, 3, 4, 6).

Measure all sides of the dwelling, making sure that the overall lengths of the front and rear sides are equal, as well as the ends. Then inspect the interior of the dwelling to identify spaces which cannot be included in *living area*. You may also find it helpful to take several photographs of the dwelling for later use when you return to your office.

CALCULATING SQUARE FOOTAGE

From your sketch of the dwelling, identify and separate *living area* from "other area." If your measurements are in inches (rather than tenths-of-a-foot), convert your figures to a decimal as follows:

1" = .10 ft.	7" = .60 ft.
2" = .20 ft.	8" = .70 ft.
3" = .25 ft.	9" = .75 ft.
4" = .30 ft	10" = .80 ft.
5" = .40 ft.	11" = .90 ft.
6" = .50 ft.	12" = 1.00 ft.

Calculate the *living area* (and other area) by multiplying the length times the width of each rectangular space. Then add your subtotals and round off your figure for total square footage to the nearest **square foot**. Double-check your calculations. When in doubt, re-check them and, if necessary, re-measure the house.

ATTACHED DWELLINGS

When measuring an "attached" single-family home (e.g., townhouse, duplex, condominium, etc.), use the same techniques just described. If there is a common wall, measure to the inside surface of the wall and add **six inches**. [*Note: In the case of condominiums, do not include the thickness of exterior or common walls.*] Do not include any "common areas" (exterior hallways, stairways, etc.) in your calculations.

PROPOSED CONSTRUCTION

For proposed construction, your square footage calculations will be based upon dimensions described in blueprints and building plans. When reporting the projected square footage, be careful to disclose that you have calculated the square footage based upon plan dimensions. Therefore, the square footage may differ in the completed structure. Do not rely on any calculations printed on the plans.

AGENTS' RESPONSIBILITIES
(Effective May 9, 2001)

Real estate agents are expected to be able to accurately calculate the square footage of most dwellings. When reporting square footage, whether to a party to a real estate transaction, another real estate agent, or others, a real estate agent is expected to provide accurate square footage information that was compiled using these *Guidelines* or comparable standards. While an agent is expected to use reasonable skill, care and diligence when calculating square footage, it should be noted that the Commission does not expect absolute perfection. Because all properties are unique and no guidelines can anticipate every possibility, minor discrepancies in deriving square footage are not considered by the Commission to constitute negligence on the part of the agent. Minor variations in tape readings and small differences in rounding off or conversion from inches to decimals, when multiplied over distances, will cause reasonable discrepancies between two competent measurements of the same dwelling. In addition to differences due to minor variations in measurement and calculation, discrepancies between measurements may also be attributable to reasonable differences in interpretation. For instance, two agents might reasonably differ about whether an addition to a dwelling is sufficiently finished under these *Guidelines* to be included within the measured living area. Differences which are based upon an agent's thoughtful judgment reasonably founded on these or other similar guidelines will not be considered by the Commission to constitute error on the agent's part. Deviations in calculated square footage of less than five percent will seldom be cause for concern.

As a general rule, the most reliable way for an agent to obtain accurate square footage data is by personally measuring the dwelling unit and calculating the square footage. It is especially recommended that *listing agents* use this approach for dwellings that are not particularly unusual or complex in their design.

As an alternative to personally measuring a dwelling and calculating its square footage, an agent may rely on the square footage reported by other persons when it is reasonable under the circumstances to do so. Generally speaking, an agent working with a buyer (either as a buyer's agent or as a seller's agent) may rely on the listing agent's square footage representations except in those unusual instances when there is an error in the reported square footage that should be obvious to a reasonably prudent agent. For example, a buyer's agent would not be expected to notice that a house advertised as containing 2200 square feet of living area in fact contained only 2000 square feet. On the other hand, that same agent, under most circumstances, would be expected to realize that a house described as containing 3200 square feet really contained only 2300 square feet of living area. If there is such a "red flag" regarding the reported square footage, the agent working with the buyer should promptly point out the suspected error to the buyer and the listing agent. The listing agent should then verify the square footage and correct any error in the information reported.

It is also appropriate for an agent to rely upon measurements and calculations performed by other professionals with greater expertise in determining square footage. A new agent who may be unsure of his or her own calculations should seek guidance from a more experienced agent. As the new agent gains experience and confidence, he or she will become less reliant on the assistance of others. In order to ensure accuracy of the square footage they report, even experienced agents may wish to rely upon a competent state-licensed or state-certified appraiser or another agent with greater expertise in determining square footage. For example, an agent might be confronted with an unusual measurement problem or a dwelling of complex design. The house described in Figure 8 in these *Guidelines* is such a property. When an agent relies upon measurements and calculations personally performed by a competent appraiser or a more expert agent, the appraiser or agent must use these *Guidelines* or other comparable standards and the square footage reported must be specifically determined in connection with the current transaction. An agent who relies on another's measurement would still be expected to recognize an obvious error in the reported square footage and to alert any interested parties.

Some sources of square footage information are by their very nature unreliable. For example, an agent should **not** rely on square footage information determined by the property owner or included in property tax records. An agent should also **not** rely on square footage information included in a listing, appraisal report or survey prepared in connection with an earlier transaction.

In areas where the prevailing practice is to report square footage in the advertising and marketing of homes, agents whose policy is **not** to calculate and report square footage must disclose this fact to prospective buyer and seller clients before entering into agency agreements with them.

ILLUSTRATIONS

For assistance in calculating and reporting the area of homes, refer to the following illustrations showing the *living area* shaded. To test your knowledge, an illustration and blank "Worksheet" for a home with a more challenging floor plan has also been included. (A completed "Worksheet" for the Practice Floor Plan can be found on page 23.) In reviewing the illustrations, assume that for those homes with basements, attics, etc., the exterior measurements shown have been derived from interior measurements taking into account walls and partitions. (*see page 4*). Where there is a common wall between *living area* and other area (*see page 3*) the measurements shown in the illustrations include the thickness of the common wall in *living area* except in the condominium example where wall thickness is not included.

One Story With Basement and Carport

(Figure 1)

Chimney
Do not include in living area the portion of chimney which is outside the living area.

Hearth
Include in living area.

Carport
22 × 25

Breezeway
(Not enclosed)

First Floor
50 × 33, with 28 and 22 (with 3 offset)

Stairs
Include with area from which they descend. Include space beneath stairway in lower level area regardless of ceiling height beneath stairs.

Basement
(Heated/Finished)
33

Office
(Heated/Finished)

One Story With Basement and Carport Worksheet

LIVING AREA			
AREA	DIMENSIONS	SUBTOTAL	TOTAL
1st Floor	50 x 30	1,500	
	3 x 22	+ 66	1,566
Basement	22 x 33		<u>726</u>
Total			2,292

OTHER AREA			
AREA	DIMENSIONS	SUBTOTAL	TOTAL
Carport	22 x 25		550

REPORT: ONE-STORY DETACHED HOUSE WITH 2,292 SQUARE FEET OF LIVING AREA OF WHICH 726 SQUARE FEET ARE IN A FINISHED BASEMENT, PLUS A 550-SQUARE-FOOT CARPORT.

Two Story With Open Foyer and Finished Attic

(Figure 2)

Attic
Add 1 ft. (6" for each exterior side wall) to inside measurements. Thus, 19' inside measurement equals 20' exterior measurement. In this example, do NOT add for front and rear walls since the allowable square footage (5' ceiling height) does not extend to the kneewalls.

Stairway with Open Area
1. Calculate area of open space (10' x 12' = 120 sf).
2. Subtract from second floor area (1,200−120=1,080 sf).
3. Add stairway (6' x 4' = 24 + 1,080 = 1,104 sf).

3RD Floor Attic (Heated/Finished)

3 Ft. Kneewall In rooms with sloped ceilings, do not include any area with a ceiling height of less than 5 ft.

Bay Window
(Floored)
Include in living area if it is floored and has ceiling height of at least 7 ft.
1. Calculate area of triangles (3' x 4' ÷ 2 = 6 sf x 2 = 12 sf).
2. Add area of triangles (12 sf) to remaining area of bay window (6' x 4' = 24 sf) = 36 sf.

Two Story With Open Foyer and Finished Attic Worksheet

LIVING AREA				
AREA	DIMENSIONS	SUBTOTAL	TOTAL
1st Floor	40 x 30	1,200	
Bay Window		36	1,236
2nd Floor	40 x 30	1,200	
	10 x 12	– 120	
	4 x 6	+ 24	1,104
Fin. Attic	20 x 15		300
Total			2,640
OTHER AREA				
AREA	DIMENSIONS	SUBTOTAL	TOTAL
Garage	25 x 24		600

Report: Two-story detached house with 2,640 square feet of living area of which 300 square feet are in a finished attic, plus a 600-square-foot garage.

Two Story With "Bonus Room" Over Garage

(Figure 3)

Bonus Room
If the "Bonus Room" is accessible from living area through a door, hallway or stairway, include in living area; otherwise, report as other area.

In rooms with sloped ceilings, add 6" for each knee wall at least 5' in height.

Bonus Room (14) (Heated/Finished) (23.5) — 15 × 24	**Second Floor** with Stairway with No Excess Open Space. Do not deduct from living area for either floor. — 40 wide
Garage — 32 × 24. Overlap: Remember to add 1 ft. to front measurement. 25 across bottom.	**First Floor** — 30 × 40 (39 across bottom, 2 overlap)

Two Story With "Bonus Room" Over Garage Worksheet

LIVING AREA			
AREA	DIMENSIONS	SUBTOTAL	TOTAL
1st Floor	40 x 30		1,200
2nd Floor	40 x 30		1,200
Bonus Room	15 x 24		<u>360</u>
Total			2,760
OTHER AREA			
AREA	DIMENSIONS	SUBTOTAL	TOTAL
Garage	24 x 32	768	
	1 x 2	+ 2	770

REPORT: Two-story detached house with 2,760 square feet of living area of which 360 square feet are in a "Bonus Room" over the garage, plus a 770-square-foot Garage.

Split Foyer

(Figure 4)

Upper Level Floor Plan (42 wide)

Entry — Include mid-level entry in living area for upper level (as if it were a stairway landing).

Upper Level

6, 2

Lower Level Floor Plan (27 deep)

Garage — Do not include in living area even if it is heated, finished and accessible from other living areas

14 / 13

Furn. 10, 9

Lower Level (Heated/Finished)

2, 2

22 + 6 + 14

Furnace Room (Unfinished) — Do not include in living area unless it is heated, finished and accessible from living area. If furnace is located in a closet in living area, include in living area.

Split Foyer Worksheet

LIVING AREA			
AREA	DIMENSIONS	SUBTOTAL	TOTAL
Upper Level	27 x 42	1,134	
	6 x 2	– 12	1,122
Lower Level	22 x 27	594	
	6 x 2	– 12	
	13 x 2	– 26	
	9 x 10	– 90	<u>466</u>
Total			1,588
OTHER AREA			
AREA	DIMENSIONS	SUBTOTAL	TOTAL
Garage	27 x 20	540	
	2 x 13	+ 26	566
Furnace Room	9 x 10		90

REPORT: Split-foyer detached house with 1,588 square feet of living area, plus a 566-sqaure-foot garage and 90-square-foot furnace room.

524 Appendix B

SPLIT (TRI-) LEVEL WITH OVERHANG

(Figure S)

OVERHANG
Measure or estimate as accurately as possible any overhang on upper level, and include in upper level dimensions.

LOWER LEVEL
Report this as "lower level" rather than "basement" because it is not accessible by a full flight of stairs.

Upper Level: 20 × 27
Main Level: 23 × 22 (with 2 offset), Deck 8 × 10
Lower Level (Heated/Finished): 25 × 18
Overhang: 2

Split (Tri-) Level With Overhang Worksheet

LIVING AREA			
AREA	DIMENSIONS	SUBTOTAL	TOTAL
Main Level	22 x 23		506
Lower Level	18 x 25		450
Upper Level	27 x 20		<u>540</u>
Total			1,496

OTHER AREA			
AREA	DIMENSIONS	SUBTOTAL	TOTAL
Deck	8 x 10		80

REPORT: Split-level detached house with 1,496 square feet of living area, plus an 80-square-foot deck.

526 Appendix B

ONE AND ONE-HALF STORY

(Figure 6)

Exterior measurements shown include 6" for each wall.

- 12
- 28
- 16
- 12
- 4
- 4
- 4

SECOND STORY (Heated/Finished)

DORMERS — Include in living area if they are part of living area.

- 73
- 22
- 5
- 6
- 2
- 25
- 20
- 16
- 12

GARAGE

LAUNDRY (Heated/Finished)

FIRST FLOOR

STORAGE — Include in living area only if it is heated, finished and directly accessible from living area.

One and One-Half Story Worksheet

\multicolumn{4}{c	}{Living Area}
Area	Dimensions	Subtotal	Total
1st Floor	48 x 22	1,056	
	16 x 2	+ 32	
	5 x 6	− 30	1,058
2nd Floor	16 x 28	448	
	4 x 4	+ 16	
	4 x 4	+ 16	
	12 x 12	+ 144	<u>624</u>
Total			1,682
\multicolumn{4}{c	}{Other Area}
Area	Dimensions	Subtotal	Total
Garage	22 x 25		550
Storage	5 x 6		30

REPORT: One and one-half Story detached house with 1,682 square feet of living area, plus a 550-square-foot garage.

528 Appendix B

CONDOMINIUM

(Figure 7)

For condominiums, do not include thickness of exterior or common walls in living area.

First Floor (19'2") × (34'7")
Bay Window Floored, 7' ceiling height

Second Floor (19'2") × (34'7")

13.4 — 6.8
2.6
7.4
Deck
Storage
3 — 6 — 3
4

Inside measurements

Condominium Worksheet

Living Area			
Area	Dimensions	Subtotal	Total
1st Floor	34.6 x 19.2	664.3	
Bay Window		36.0	700
2nd Floor	34.6 x 19.2	664.3	664
Total			1,364

Other Area			
Area	Dimensions	Subtotal	Total
Deck	13.4 x 7.4	99.2	99
Storage	10 x 6.8		68

Report: Two-story condominium with 1,364 square feet of living area, plus a 99 square foot deck.

530 Appendix B

Practice Floor Plan

(Figure 8)

Second Floor exterior measurements shown include 6" for each wall.

Bay Window

Practice Floor Plan Worksheet

Living Area			
Area	Dimensions	Subtotal	Total

Other Area			
Area	Dimensions	Subtotal	Total

Report:

532 Appendix B

PRACTICE FLOOR PLAN
(Zoned to facilitate calculations)

Practice Floor Plan Worksheet

Living Area			
Area	Dimensions	Subtotal	Total
1st Floor A	22 x 33	726	
1st Floor B	2 x 10	20	
1st Floor C	4 x 15	60	
1st Floor D	19 x 33	627	
1st Floor E	3 x 12	36	
1st Floor F	8 x 25	200	
1st Floor G	4 x 3	12	
1st Floor H	15 x 13	195	
1st Floor I	7 x 5	35	
Bay Window J		12	
Oct. Window K		82	2,005
2nd Floor L	24 x 12	288	
2nd Floor M	3 x 6	18	
2nd Floor N	17 x 35	595	
2nd Floor O	15 x 6	90	
2nd Floor P	15 x 15	225	
2nd Floor Q	3 x 7	21	1,237
Total			3,242

Other Area			
Area	Dimensions	Subtotal	Total
Garage	24 x 23		552

Report: One and one-half story detached house with 3,242 square feet of living area, plus a 552-square-foot garage.

Appendix C: Real Estate License Law and Commission Rules

In 1957, the North Carolina General Assembly enacted into law, to be effective July 1, 1957, the Real Estate Licensing Act, codified as Chapter 93A of the General Statutes of North Carolina. This law created the North Carolina Real Estate Commission (NCREC) and empowered it to write and enforce reasonable rules and regulations concerning the business activities of real estate licensees. The Commission has the authority to approve real estate prelicensing schools and also publishes prelicensing course syllabi. The Real Estate Commission also publishes and updates as required a booklet entitled *Real Estate Licensing in North Carolina*. The real estate licensing applicant is required to be knowledgeable about the portions of General Statute 93A and Commission Rules, which are contained in this appendix. The study of this material should take place directly from the materials in this appendix. The NCREC has provided clarifying comments and examples for some of the more complex sections of the law and rules in the *License Law and Rule Comments* beginning on page 594. In an effort to further clarify some of the remaining sections of the law and rules, the publisher has added a *Key Point Review* at the end of the appendix.

CHAPTER 93A – REAL ESTATE LICENSE LAW

ARTICLE 1 - REAL ESTATE BROKERS AND SALESPERSONS

§ 93A-1	License required of real estate brokers
§ 93A-2	Definitions and exceptions
§ 93A-3	Commission created; compensation; organization
§ 93A-4	Applications for licenses; fees; qualifications; examinations; privilege licenses; renewal or reinstatement of license; power to enforce provisions
§ 93A-4.1	Continuing education
§ 93A-4.2	Broker-in-charge qualification
§ 93A-4.3	Elimination of salesperson license; conversion of salesperson licenses to broker licenses (SECTION OMITTED)
§ 93A-4A	Recodified as G.S. 93A-4.1 by Session Laws 2005-395, s. 6
§ 93A-5	Register of applicants and roster of brokers (SECTION OMITTED)
§ 93A-6	Disciplinary action by Commission
§ 93A-6.1	Commission may subpoena witnesses, records, documents, or other materials
§ 93A-7	Power of courts to revoke
§ 93A-8	Penalty for violation of Chapter
§ 93A-9	Licensing foreign brokers
§ 93A-10	Nonresident licensees; filing of consent as to service of process and pleadings (SECTION OMITTED)
§ 93A-11	Reimbursement by real estate independent contractor of brokers' workers' compensation (SECTION OMITTED)
§ 93A-12	Disputed monies
§ 93A-13	Contracts for broker services
§ 93A-14	Reserved for future codification purposes
§ 93A-15	Reserved for future codification purposes

ARTICLE 2 - REAL ESTATE EDUCATION AND RECOVERY FUND
(SECTION OMITTED)

ARTICLE 3 - PRIVATE REAL ESTATE SCHOOLS
(SECTION OMITTED)

ARTICLE 4 - TIME SHARES

§ 93A-39	Title (SECTION OMITTED)
§ 93A-40	Registration required of time share projects; real estate license required (SECTION OMITTED)
§ 93A-41	Definitions (SECTION OMITTED)
§ 93A-42	Time shares deemed real estate (SECTION OMITTED)
§ 93A-43	Partition (SECTION OMITTED)
§ 93A-44	Public offering statement (SECTION OMITTED)
§ 93A-45	Purchaser's right to cancel; escrow; violation (SECTION OMITTED)
§ 93A-46	Prizes (SECTION OMITTED)
§ 93A-47	Time shares proxies (SECTION OMITTED)
§ 93A-48	Exchange programs (SECTION OMITTED)
§ 93A-49	Service of process on exchange company (SECTION OMITTED)
§ 93A-50	Securities laws apply (SECTION OMITTED)
§ 93A-51	Rule-making authority
§ 93A-52	Application for registration of time share project; denial of registration; renewal; reinstatement; and termination of developer's interest
§ 93A-53	Register of applicants; roster of registrants; registered projects; financial report to Secretary of State
§ 93A-54	Disciplinary action by Commission
§ 93A-55	Private enforcement
§ 93A-56	Penalty for violation of Article
§ 93A-57	Release of liens
§ 93A-58	Registrar required; criminal penalties; project broker
§ 93A-59	Preservation of time share purchaser's claims and defenses
§§ 93A-60	through 93A-69 Reserved for future codification purposes

ARTICLE 5 - REAL ESTATE APPRAISERS
(SECTION OMITTED)

ARTICLE 6 - BROKER PRICE OPINIONS AND COMPARATIVE MARKET ANALYSES

§ 93A-82	Definitions
§ 93A-83	Broker price opinions and comparative market analyses for a fee

CHAPTER 93A – REAL ESTATE LICENSE LAW

ARTICLE 1 – REAL ESTATE BROKERS AND SALESPERSONS

§ 93A-1 LICENSE REQUIRED OF REAL ESTATE BROKERS

From and after July 1, 1957, it shall be unlawful for any person, partnership, corporation, limited liability company, association, or other business entity in this State to act as a real estate broker, or directly or indirectly to engage or assume to engage in the business of real estate broker or to advertise or hold himself or herself or themselves out as engaging in or conducting such business without first obtaining a license issued by the North Carolina Real Estate Commission (hereinafter referred to as the Commission), under the provisions of this Chapter. A license shall be obtained from the Commission even if the person, partnership, corporation, limited liability company, association, or business entity is licensed in another state and is affiliated or otherwise associated with a licensed real estate broker in this State.

§ 93A-2 DEFINITIONS AND EXCEPTIONS

(a) A real estate broker within the meaning of this Chapter is any person, partnership, corporation, limited liability company, association, or other business entity who for a compensation or valuable consideration or promise thereof lists or offers to list, sells or offers to sell, buys or offers to buy, auctions or offers to auction (specifically not including a mere crier of sales), or negotiates the purchase or sale or exchange of real estate, or who leases or offers to lease, or who sells or offers to sell leases of whatever character, or rents or offers to rent any real estate or the improvement thereon, for others.

(a1) The term broker-in-charge within the meaning of this Chapter means a real estate broker who has been designated as the broker having responsibility for the supervision of brokers on provisional status engaged in real estate brokerage at a particular real estate office and for other administrative and supervisory duties as the Commission shall prescribe by rule.

(a2) The term provisional broker within the meaning of this Chapter means a real estate broker who, pending acquisition and documentation to the Commission of the education or experience prescribed by either G.S. 93A-4(a1) or G.S. 93A-4.3, must be supervised by a broker-in-charge when performing any act for which a real estate license is required.

(b) The term real estate salesperson within the meaning of this Chapter shall mean and include any person who was formerly licensed by the Commission as a real estate salesperson before April 1, 2006.

(c) The provisions of G.S. 93A-1 and G.S. 93A-2 do not apply to and do not include:

(1) Any partnership, corporation, limited liability company, association, or other business entity that, as owner or lessor, shall perform any of the acts aforesaid with reference to property owned or leased by them, where the acts are performed in the regular course of or as incident to the management of that property and the investment therein. The exemption from licensure under this subsection shall extend to officers and employees of an exempt corporation, the general partners of an exempt partnership, and the managers of an exempt limited liability company when said persons are engaged in acts or services for which the corporation, partnership, or limited liability company would be exempt hereunder.

(2) Any person acting as an attorney-in-fact under a duly executed power of attorney from the owner authorizing the final consummation of performance of any contract for the sale, lease or exchange of real estate.

(3) Acts or services performed by an attorney who is an active member of the North Carolina State Bar if the acts and services constitute the practice of law under Chapter 84 of the General Statutes.

(4) Any person, while acting as a receiver, trustee in bankruptcy, guardian, administrator or executor or any person acting under order of any court.

(5) Any person, while acting as a trustee under a written trust agreement, deed of trust or will, or that person's regular salaried employees. The trust agreement, deed of trust, or will must specifically identify the trustee, the beneficiary, the corpus of trust, and the trustee's authority over the corpus.

(6) Any salaried person employed by a licensed real estate broker, for and on behalf of the owner of any real estate or the improvements thereon, which the licensed broker has contracted to manage for the owner, if the salaried employee's employment is limited to: exhibiting units on the real estate to prospective tenants; providing the prospective tenants with information about the lease of the units; accepting applications for lease of the units; completing and executing preprinted form leases; and accepting security deposits and rental payments for the units only when the deposits and rental payments are made payable to the owner or the broker employed by the owner. The salaried employee shall not negotiate the amount of security deposits or rental payments and shall not negotiate leases or any rental agreements on behalf of the owner or

broker. However, in a vacation rental transaction as defined by G.S. 42A-4(3), the employee may offer a prospective tenant a rental price and term from a schedule setting forth prices and terms and the conditions and limitations under which they may be offered. The schedule shall be written and provided by the employee's employing broker with the written authority of the landlord.

(7) Any individual owner who personally leases or sells the owner's own property.

(8) Any housing authority organized in accordance with the provisions of Chapter 157 of the General Statutes and any regular salaried employees of the housing authority when performing acts authorized in this Chapter with regard to the sale or lease of property owned by the housing authority or the subletting of property which the housing authority holds as tenant. This exception shall not apply to any person, partnership, corporation, limited liability company, association, or other business entity that contracts with a housing authority to sell or manage property owned or leased by the housing authority.

§ 93A-3 COMMISSION CREATED; COMPENSATION; ORGANIZATION

(a) There is hereby created the North Carolina Real Estate Commission, hereinafter called the Commission. The Commission shall consist of nine members, seven members to be appointed by the Governor, one member to be appointed by the General Assembly upon the recommendation of the President Pro Tempore of the Senate in accordance with G.S. 120-121, and one member to be appointed by the General Assembly upon the recommendation of the Speaker of the House of Representatives in accordance with G.S. 120-121. At least three members of the Commission shall be licensed real estate brokers. At least two members of the Commission shall be persons who are not involved directly or indirectly in the real estate or real estate appraisal business. Members of the Commission shall serve three-year terms, so staggered that the terms of three members expire in one year, the terms of three members expire in the next year, and the terms of three members expire in the third year of each three-year period. The members of the Commission shall elect one of their members to serve as chairman of the Commission for a term of one year. The Governor may remove any member of the Commission for misconduct, incompetency, or willful neglect of duty. The Governor shall have the power to fill all vacancies occurring on the Commission, except vacancies in legislative appointments shall be filled under G.S. 120-122.

(b) The provisions of G.S. 93B-5 notwithstanding, members of the Commission shall receive as compensation for each day spent on work for the Commission a per diem in an amount established by the Commission by rule, and mileage reimbursement for transportation by privately owned automobile at the business standard mileage rate set by the Internal Revenue Service per mile of travel along with actual cost of tolls paid. The total expense of the administration of this Chapter shall not exceed the total income therefrom; and none of the expenses of said Commission or the compensation or expenses of any office thereof or any employee shall ever be paid or payable out of the treasury of the State of North Carolina; and neither the Commission nor any officer or employee thereof shall have any power or authority to make or incur any expense, debt or other financial obligation binding upon the State of North Carolina. After all expenses of operation, the Commission may set aside an expense reserve each year. The Commission may deposit moneys in accounts, certificates of deposit, or time deposits as the Commission may approve, in any bank, savings and loan association, or trust company. Moneys also may be invested in the same classes of securities referenced in G.S. 159-30(c).

(c) The Commission shall have power to make reasonable bylaws, rules and regulations that are not inconsistent with the provisions of this Chapter and the General Statutes; provided, however, the Commission shall not make rules or regulations regulating commissions, salaries, or fees to be charged by licensees under this Chapter.

(c1) The provisions of G.S. 93A-1 and G.S. 93A-2 notwithstanding, the Commission may adopt rules to permit a real estate broker to pay a fee or other valuable consideration to a travel agent for the introduction or procurement of tenants or potential tenants in vacation rentals as defined in G.S. 42A-4. Rules adopted pursuant to this subsection may include a definition of the term "travel agent", may regulate the conduct of permitted transactions, and may limit the amount of the fee or the value of the consideration that may be paid to the travel agent. However, the Commission may not authorize a person or entity not licensed as a broker to negotiate any real estate transaction on behalf of another.

(c2) The Commission shall adopt a seal for its use, which shall bear thereon the words "North Carolina Real Estate Commission." Copies of all records and papers in the office of the Commission duly certified and authenticated by the seal of the Commission shall be received in evidence in all courts and with like effect as the originals.

(d) The Commission may employ an Executive Director and professional and clerical staff as may be necessary to carry out the provisions of this Chapter and to put into effect the rules and regulations that the Commission may promulgate. The Commission shall fix salaries and shall require employees to make good and sufficient surety bond for the faithful performance of their duties. The Commission shall reimburse its employees for travel on official business. Mileage expenses for transportation by privately owned automobile shall be reimbursed at the business standard mileage set by the Internal Revenue Service per mile of travel along with the actual tolls paid. Other travel expenses shall be reimbursed in accordance with G.S. 138-6. The Commission may, when it deems it necessary or convenient, delegate to the Executive Director, legal counsel for the Commission, or other

Commission staff, professional or clerical, the Commission's authority and duties under this Chapter, but the Commission may not delegate its authority to make rules or its duty to act as a hearing panel in accordance with the provisions of G.S. 150B-40(b).

(e) The Commission shall be entitled to the services of the Attorney General of North Carolina, in connection with the affairs of the Commission, and may, with the approval of the Attorney General, employ attorneys to represent the Commission or assist it in the enforcement of this Chapter. The Commission may prefer a complaint for violation of this Chapter before any court of competent jurisdiction, and it may take the necessary legal steps through the proper legal offices of the State to enforce the provisions of this Chapter and collect the penalties provided therein.

(f) The Commission is authorized to acquire, hold, convey, rent, encumber, alienate, and otherwise deal with real property in the same manner as a private person or corporation, subject only to the approval of the Governor and Council of State. The rents, proceeds, and other revenues and benefits of the ownership of real property shall inure to the Commission. Collateral pledged by the Commission for any encumbrance of real property shall be limited to the assets, income, and revenues of the Commission. Leases, deeds, and other instruments relating to the Commission's interest in real property shall be valid when executed by the executive director of the Commission. The Commission may create and conduct education and information programs relating to the real estate business for the information, education, guidance and protection of the general public, licensees, and applicants for license. The education and information programs may include preparation, printing and distribution of publications and articles and the conduct of conferences, seminars, and lectures. The Commission may claim the copyright to written materials it creates and may charge fees for publications and programs.

§ 93A-4   APPLICATIONS FOR LICENSES; FEES; QUALIFICATIONS; EXAMINATIONS; PRIVILEGE LICENSES; RENEWAL OR REINSTATEMENT OF LICENSE; POWER TO ENFORCE PROVISIONS

(a) Any person, partnership, corporation, limited liability company, association, or other business entity hereafter desiring to enter into business of and obtain a license as a real estate broker shall make written application for such license to the Commission in the form and manner prescribed by the Commission. Each applicant for a license as a real estate broker shall be at least 18 years of age. Each applicant for a license as a real estate broker shall, within three years preceding the date the application is made, have satisfactorily completed, at a school approved by the Commission, an education program consisting of at least 75 hours of classroom instruction in subjects determined by the Commission, or shall possess real estate education or experience in real estate transactions which the Commission shall find equivalent to the education program. Each applicant for a license as a real estate broker shall be required to pay a fee, fixed by the Commission but not to exceed thirty dollars ($30.00).

(a1) Each person who is issued a real estate broker license on or after April 1, 2006, shall initially be classified as a provisional broker and shall, within three years following initial licensure, satisfactorily complete, at a school approved by the Commission, a postlicensing education program consisting of 90 hours of classroom instruction in subjects determined by the Commission or shall possess real estate education or experience in real estate transactions which the Commission shall find equivalent to the education program. The Commission may, by rule, establish a schedule for completion of the prescribed postlicensing education that requires provisional brokers to complete portions of the 90-hour postlicensing education program in less than three years, and provisional brokers must comply with this schedule in order to be entitled to actively engage in real estate brokerage. Upon completion of the postlicensing education program, the provisional status of the broker's license shall be terminated. When a provisional broker fails to complete all 90 hours of required postlicensing education within three years following initial licensure, the broker's license shall be placed on inactive status. The broker's license shall not be returned to active status until he or she has satisfied such requirements as the Commission may by rule require. Every license cancelled after April 1, 2009, because the licensee failed to complete postlicensing education shall be reinstated on inactive status until such time as the licensee satisfies the requirements for returning to active status as the Commission may by rule require.

(a2) An approved school shall pay a fee of ten dollars ($10.00) per licensee to the Commission for each licensee completing a postlicensing education course conducted by the school, provided that these fees shall not be charged to a community college, junior college, college, or university located in this State and accredited by the Southern Association of Colleges and Schools.

(b) Except as otherwise provided in this Chapter, any person who submits an application to the Commission in proper manner for a license as real estate broker shall be required to take an examination. The examination may be administered orally, by computer, or by any other method the Commission deems appropriate. The Commission may require the applicant to pay the Commission or a provider contracted by the Commission the actual cost of the examination and its administration. The cost of the examination and its administration shall be in addition to any other fees the applicant is required to pay under subsection (a) of this section. The examination shall determine the applicant's qualifications with due regard to the paramount interests of the public as to the applicant's competency. A person who fails the license examination shall be entitled to know the result and score. A person who passes the exam shall be notified only that the person passed the examination. Whether a person passed or failed the examination shall be a matter of public record; however, the scores for license examinations shall not be considered public records. Nothing in this subsection shall limit the rights granted to any person under G.S. 93B-8. An applicant for licensure under this Chapter shall satisfy the Commission that he or she possesses the competency, honesty, truthfulness, integrity, good moral character, and general fitness, including mental and emotional fitness, necessary to protect the public interest and promote public confidence in the real estate brokerage business. The Commission may investigate the moral character and fitness, including the mental and emotional fitness, of each applicant for licensure as the applicant's character and fitness may generally relate to the real estate brokerage business, the public interest, and the public's confidence in the real estate brokerage business. The Commission may also require an applicant to provide the Commission with a criminal record report. All applicants shall obtain criminal record reports from one or more reporting services designated by the Commission to provide criminal record reports. Applicants are required to pay the designated reporting service for the cost of these reports. Criminal record reports, credit reports, and reports relating to an applicant's mental and emotional fitness obtained in connection with the application process shall not be considered public records under Chapter 132 of the General Statutes. If the results of any required competency examination and investigation of the applicant's moral character and fitness shall be satisfactory to the Commission, then the Commission shall issue to the applicant a license, authorizing the applicant to act as a real estate broker in the State of North Carolina, upon the payment of any privilege taxes required by law.

Notwithstanding G.S. 150B-38(c), in a contested case commenced upon the request of a party applying for licensure regarding the question of the moral character or fitness of the applicant, if notice has been reasonably attempted, but cannot be given to the applicant personally or by certified mail in accordance with G.S. 150B-38(c), the notice of hearing shall be deemed given to the applicant when a copy of the notice is deposited in an official depository of the United States Postal Service addressed to the applicant at the latest mailing address provided by the applicant to the Commission or by any other means reasonably designed to achieve actual notice to the applicant.

(b1) The Department of Justice may provide a criminal record check to the Commission for a person who has applied for a license through the Commission. The Commission shall provide to the Department of Justice, along with the request, the fingerprints of the applicant, any additional information required by the Department of Justice, and a form signed by the applicant consenting to the check of the criminal record and to the use of the fingerprints and other identifying information required by the State or national repositories. The applicant's fingerprints shall be forwarded to the State Bureau of Investigation for a search of the State's criminal history record file, and the State Bureau of Investigation shall forward a set of the fingerprints to the Federal Bureau of Investigation for a national criminal history check. The Commission shall keep all information pursuant to this subsection privileged, in accordance with applicable State law and federal guidelines, and the information shall be confidential and shall not be a public record under Chapter 132 of the General Statutes.

The Department of Justice may charge each applicant a fee for conducting the checks of criminal history records authorized by this subsection.

(b2) Records, papers, and other documentation containing personal information collected or compiled by the Commission in connection with an application for examination, licensure, certification, or renewal or reinstatement, or the subsequent update of information shall not be considered public records within the meaning of Chapter 132 of the General Statutes unless admitted into evidence in a hearing held by the Commission.

(c) All licenses issued by the Commission under the provisions of this Chapter shall expire on the 30th day of June following issuance or on any other date that the Commission may determine and shall become invalid after that date unless reinstated. A license may be renewed 45 days prior to the expiration date by filing an application with and paying to the Executive Director of the Commission the license renewal fee. The license renewal fee is thirty dollars ($30.00) unless the Commission sets the fee at a higher amount. The Commission may set the license renewal fee at an amount that does not exceed fifty dollars ($50.00). The license renewal fee may not increase by more than five dollars ($5.00) during a 12-month period. The Commission may adopt rules establishing a system of license renewal in which the licenses expire annually with varying expiration dates. These rules shall provide for prorating the annual fee to cover the initial renewal period so that no licensee shall be charged an amount greater than the annual fee for any 12-month period. The fee for reinstatement of an expired license shall be fifty-five dollars ($55.00). In the event a licensee fails to obtain a reinstatement of such license within six months after the expiration date thereof, the Commission may, in its discretion, consider such person as not having been previously licensed, and thereby subject to the provisions of this Chapter relating to the issuance of an original license, including the examination requirements set forth herein. Duplicate licenses may be issued by the Commission upon payment of a fee of five dollars ($5.00) by the licensee. Commission certification of a licensee's license history shall be made only after the payment of a fee of ten dollars ($10.00).

(d) The Commission is expressly vested with the power and authority to make and enforce any and all reasonable rules and regulations connected with license application, examination, renewal, and reinstatement as shall be deemed necessary to administer and enforce the provisions of this Chapter. The Commission is further authorized to adopt reasonable rules and regulations necessary for the approval of real estate schools, instructors, and textbooks and rules that prescribe specific requirements pertaining to instruction, administration, and content of required education courses and programs.

(e) Nothing contained in this Chapter shall be construed as giving any authority to the Commission nor any licensee of the Commission as authorizing any licensee to engage in the practice of law or to render any legal service as specifically set out in G.S. 84-2.1 or any other legal service not specifically referred to in said section.

§ 93A-4.1 CONTINUING EDUCATION

(a) The Commission shall establish a program of continuing education for real estate brokers. An individual licensed as a real estate broker is required to complete continuing education requirements in an amount not to exceed eight classroom hours of instruction a year during any license renewal period in subjects and at times the Commission deems appropriate. Any licensee who fails to complete continuing education requirements pursuant to this section shall not actively engage in the business of real estate broker.

(a1) The Commission may, as part of the broker continuing education requirements, require real estate brokers-in-charge to complete during each annual license period a special continuing education course consisting of not more than four classroom hours of instruction in subjects prescribed by the Commission.

(b) The Commission shall establish procedures allowing for a deferral of continuing education for brokers while they are not actively engaged in real estate brokerage.

(c) The Commission may adopt rules not inconsistent with this Chapter to give purpose and effect to the continuing education requirement, including rules that govern:

    (1) The content and subject matter of continuing education courses.
    (2) The curriculum of courses required.
    (3) The criteria, standards, and procedures for the approval of courses, course sponsors, and course instructors.
    (4) The methods of instruction.
    (5) The computation of course credit.
    (6) The ability to carry forward course credit from one year to another.
    (7) The deferral of continuing education for brokers not engaged in brokerage.
    (8) The waiver of or variance from the continuing education requirement for hardship or other reasons.
    (9) The procedures for compliance and sanctions for noncompliance.

(d) The Commission may establish a nonrefundable course application fee to be charged to a course sponsor for the review and approval of a proposed continuing education course. The fee shall not exceed one hundred twenty-five dollars ($125.00) per course. The Commission may charge the sponsor of an approved course a nonrefundable fee not to exceed seventy-five dollars ($75.00) for the annual renewal of course approval.

An approved course sponsor shall pay a fee of ten dollars ($10.00) per licensee to the Commission for each licensee completing an approved continuing education course conducted by the sponsor.

The Commission shall not charge a course application fee, a course renewal fee, or any other fee for a continuing education course sponsored by a community college, junior college, college, or university located in this State and accredited by the Southern Association of Colleges and Schools.

(e) The Commission may award continuing education credit for an unapproved course or related educational activity. The Commission may prescribe procedures for a licensee to submit information on an unapproved course or related educational activity for continuing education credit. The Commission may charge a fee to the licensee for each course or activity submitted. The fee shall not exceed fifty dollars ($50.00).

§ 93A-4.2 BROKER-IN-CHARGE QUALIFICATION

To be qualified to serve as a broker-in-charge of a real estate office, a real estate broker shall possess at least two years of full-time real estate brokerage experience or equivalent part-time real estate brokerage experience within the previous five years or real estate education or experience in real estate transactions that the Commission finds equivalent to such experience and shall complete, within a time prescribed by the Commission, a course of study prescribed by the Commission for brokers-in-charge not to exceed 12 classroom hours of instruction. A provisional broker may not be designated as a broker-in-charge.

§ 93A-4.3 ELIMINATION OF SALESPERSON LICENSE; CONVERSION OF SALESPERSON LICENSES TO BROKER LICENSES (SECTION OMITTED)

§ 93A-4A RECODIFIED AS G.S. 93A-4.1 BY SESSION LAWS 2005-395, S. 6

§ 93A-5 REGISTER OF APPLICANTS AND ROSTER OF BROKERS (SECTION OMITTED)

§ 93A-6 DISCIPLINARY ACTION BY COMMISSION

(a) The Commission has power to take disciplinary action. Upon its own initiative, or on the complaint of any person, the Commission may investigate the actions of any person or entity licensed under this Chapter, or any other person or entity who shall assume to act in such capacity. If the Commission finds probable cause that a licensee has violated any of the provisions of this Chapter, the Commission may hold a hearing on the allegations of misconduct.

The Commission has power to suspend or revoke at any time a license issued under the provisions of this Chapter, or to reprimand or censure any licensee, if, following a hearing, the Commission adjudges the licensee to be guilty of:

(1) Making any willful or negligent misrepresentation or any willful or negligent omission of material fact.

(2) Making any false promises of a character likely to influence, persuade, or induce.

(3) Pursuing a course of misrepresentation or making of false promises through agents, advertising or otherwise.

(4) Acting for more than one party in a transaction without the knowledge of all parties for whom he or she acts.

(5) Accepting a commission or valuable consideration as a real estate broker on provisional status for the performance of any of the acts specified in this Article or Article 4 of this Chapter, from any person except his or her broker-in-charge or licensed broker by whom he or she is employed.

(6) Representing or attempting to represent a real estate broker other than the broker by whom he or she is engaged or associated, without the express knowledge and consent of the broker with whom he or she is associated.

(7) Failing, within a reasonable time, to account for or to remit any monies coming into his or her possession which belong to others.

(8) Being unworthy or incompetent to act as a real estate broker in a manner as to endanger the interest of the public.

(9) Paying a commission or valuable consideration to any person for acts or services performed in violation of this Chapter.

(10) Any other conduct which constitutes improper, fraudulent or dishonest dealing.

(11) Performing or undertaking to perform any legal service, as set forth in G.S. 84-2.1, or any other acts constituting the practice of law.

(12) Commingling the money or other property of his or her principals with his or her own or failure to maintain and deposit in a trust or escrow account in a bank as provided by subsection (g) of this section all money received by him or her as a real estate licensee acting in that capacity, or an escrow agent, or the custodian or manager of the funds of another person or entity which relate to or concern that person's or entity's interest or investment in real property, provided, these accounts shall not bear interest unless the principals authorize in writing the deposit be made in an interest bearing account and also provide for the disbursement of the interest accrued.

(13) Failing to deliver, within a reasonable time, a completed copy of any purchase agreement or offer to buy and sell real estate to the buyer and to the seller.

(14) Failing, at the time a sales transaction is consummated, to deliver to the broker's client a detailed and accurate closing statement showing the receipt and disbursement of all monies relating to the transaction about which the broker knows or reasonably should know. If a closing statement is prepared by an attorney or lawful settlement agent, a broker may rely on the delivery of that statement, but the broker must review the statement for accuracy and notify all parties to the closing of any errors.

(15) Violating any rule adopted by the Commission.

(b) The Commission may suspend or revoke any license issued under the provisions of this Chapter or reprimand or censure any licensee when:

(1) The licensee has obtained a license by false or fraudulent representation;

(2) The licensee has been convicted or has entered a plea of guilty or no contest upon which final judgment is entered by a court of competent jurisdiction in this State, or any other state, of any misdemeanor or felony that involves false swearing, misrepresentation, deceit, extortion, theft, bribery, embezzlement, false pretenses, fraud, forgery, larceny, misappropriation of funds or property, perjury, or any other offense showing professional unfitness or involving moral turpitude which would reasonably affect the licensee's performance in the real estate business;

(3) The licensee has violated any of the provisions of G.S. 93A-6(a) when selling, leasing, or buying the licensee's own property;

(4) The broker's unlicensed employee, who is exempt from the provisions of this Chapter under G.S. 93A-2(c)(6), has committed, in the regular course of business, any act which, if committed by

the broker, would constitute a violation of G.S. 93A-6(a) for which the broker could be disciplined; or

(5) The licensee, who is also licensed as an appraiser, attorney, home inspector, mortgage broker, general contractor, or member of another licensed profession or occupation, has been disciplined for an offense under any law involving fraud, theft, misrepresentation, breach of trust or fiduciary responsibility, or willful or negligent malpractice.

(c) The Commission may appear in its own name in superior court in actions for injunctive relief to prevent any person from violating the provisions of this Chapter or rules adopted by the Commission. The superior court shall have the power to grant these injunctions even if criminal prosecution has been or may be instituted as a result of the violations, or whether the person is a licensee of the Commission.

(d) Each broker shall maintain complete records showing the deposit, maintenance, and withdrawal of money or other property owned by the broker's principals or held in escrow or in trust for the broker's principals. The Commission may inspect these records periodically, without prior notice and may also inspect these records whenever the Commission determines that they are pertinent to an investigation of any specific complaint against a licensee.

(e) When a person or entity licensed under this Chapter is accused of any act, omission, or misconduct which would subject the licensee to disciplinary action, the licensee, with the consent and approval of the Commission, may surrender the license and all the rights and privileges pertaining to it for a period of time established by the Commission. A person or entity who surrenders a license shall not thereafter be eligible for or submit any application for licensure as a real estate broker during the period of license surrender.

(f) In any contested case in which the Commission takes disciplinary action authorized by any provision of this Chapter, the Commission may also impose reasonable conditions, restrictions, and limitations upon the license, registration, or approval issued to the disciplined person or entity. In any contested case concerning an application for licensure, time share project registration, or school, sponsor, instructor, or course approval, the Commission may impose reasonable conditions, restrictions, and limitations on any license, registration, or approval it may issue as a part of its final decision.

(g) A broker's trust or escrow account shall be a demand deposit account in a federally insured depository institution lawfully doing business in this State which agrees to make its records of the broker's account available for inspection by the Commission's representatives.

(h) The Executive Director shall transmit a certified copy of all final orders of the Commission suspending or revoking licenses issued under this Chapter to the clerk of superior court of the county in which the licensee maintains his or her principal place of business. The clerk shall enter the order upon the judgment docket of the county.

§ 93A-6.1 COMMISSION MAY SUBPOENA WITNESSES, RECORDS, DOCUMENTS, OR OTHER MATERIALS

(a) The Commission, Executive Director, or other representative designated by the Commission may issue a subpoena for the appearance of witnesses deemed necessary to testify concerning any matter to be heard before or investigated by the Commission. The Commission may issue a subpoena ordering any person in possession of records, documents, or other materials, however maintained, that concern any matter to be heard before or investigated by the Commission to produce the records, documents, or other materials for inspection or deliver the same into the custody of the Commission's authorized representatives. Upon written request, the Commission shall revoke a subpoena if it finds that the evidence, the production of which is required, does not relate to a matter in issue, or if the subpoena does not describe with sufficient particularity the evidence, the production of which is required, or if for any other reason in law the subpoena is invalid. If any person shall fail to fully and promptly comply with a subpoena issued under this section, the Commission may apply to any judge of the superior court resident in any county where the person to whom the subpoena is issued maintains a residence or place of business for an order compelling the person to show cause why he or she should not be held in contempt of the Commission and its processes. The court shall have the power to impose punishment for acts that would constitute direct or indirect contempt if the acts occurred in an action pending in superior court.

(b) The Commission shall be exempt from the requirements of Chapter 53B of the General Statutes with regard to subpoenas issued to compel the production of a licensee's trust account records held by any financial institution. Notwithstanding the exemption, whenever the Commission issues a subpoena under this subsection, the Commission shall send a copy to the licensee at his or her address of record by regular mail.

§ 93A-7 POWER OF COURTS TO REVOKE

Whenever any person, partnership, association or corporation claiming to have been injured or damaged by the gross negligence, incompetency, fraud, dishonesty or misconduct on the part of any licensee following the calling or engaging in the business herein described and shall file suit upon such claim against such licensee in any court of record in this State and shall recover judgment thereon, such court may as part of its judgment or decree in such case, if it deem it a proper case in which so to do, order a written copy of the transcript of record in said case to be forwarded by the clerk of court to the chairman of the said Commission with a recommendation that the licensee's certificate of license be revoked.

§ 93A-8 PENALTY FOR VIOLATION OF CHAPTER
Any person violating the provisions of this Chapter shall upon conviction thereof be deemed guilty of a Class 1 misdemeanor.

§ 93A-9 LICENSING FOREIGN BROKERS
(a) The Commission may issue a broker license to an applicant licensed in a foreign jurisdiction who has satisfied the requirements for licensure set out in G.S. 93A-4 or such other requirements as the Commission in its discretion may by rule require.
(b) The Commission may issue a limited broker's license to a person or an entity from another state or territory of the United States without regard to whether that state or territory offers similar licensing privileges to residents in North Carolina if the person or entity satisfies all of the following:
- (1) Is of good moral character and licensed as a real estate broker or salesperson in good standing in another state or territory of the United States.
- (2) Only engages in business as a real estate broker in North Carolina in transactions involving commercial real estate and while the person or entity is affiliated with a resident North Carolina real estate broker.
- (3) Complies with the laws of this State regulating real estate brokers and rules adopted by the Commission.

The Commission may require an applicant for licensure under this subsection to pay a fee not to exceed three hundred dollars ($300.00). All licenses issued under this subsection shall expire on June 30 of each year following issuance or on a date that the Commission deems appropriate unless the license is renewed pursuant to the requirements of G.S. 93A-4. A person or entity licensed under this subsection may be disciplined by the Commission for violations of this Chapter as provided in G.S. 93A-6 and G.S. 93A-54.

Any person or entity licensed under this subsection shall be affiliated with a resident North Carolina real estate broker, and the resident North Carolina real estate broker shall actively and personally supervise the licensee in a manner that reasonably assures that the licensee complies with the requirements of this Chapter and rules adopted by the Commission. A person or entity licensed under this subsection shall not, however, be affiliated with a resident North Carolina real estate provisional broker. The Commission may exempt applicants for licensure under this subsection from examination and the other licensing requirements under G.S. 93A-4. The Commission may adopt rules as it deems necessary to give effect to this subsection, including rules establishing: (i) qualifications for licensure; (ii) licensure and renewal procedures; (iii) requirements for continuing education; (iv) conduct of persons and entities licensed under this subsection and their affiliated resident real estate brokers; (v) a definition of commercial real estate; and (vi) any requirements or limitations on affiliation between resident real estate brokers and persons or entities seeking licensure under this subsection.

§ 93A-10 NONRESIDENT LICENSEES; FILING OF CONSENT AS TO SERVICE OF PROCESS AND PLEADINGS (SECTION OMITTED)

§ 93A-11 REIMBURSEMENT BY REAL ESTATE INDEPENDENT CONTRACTOR OF BROKERS' WORKERS' COMPENSATION (SECTION OMITTED)

§ 93A-12 DISPUTED MONIES
(a) A real estate broker licensed under this Chapter or an attorney licensed to practice law in this State may deposit with the clerk of court in accordance with this section monies, other than a residential security deposit, the ownership of which are in dispute and that the real estate broker or attorney received while acting in a fiduciary capacity.
(b) The disputed monies shall be deposited with the clerk of court in the county in which the property for which the disputed monies are being held is located. At the time of depositing the disputed monies, the real estate broker or attorney shall certify to the clerk of court that the persons who are claiming ownership of the disputed monies have been notified in accordance with subsection (c) of this section that the disputed monies are to be deposited with the clerk of court and that the persons may initiate a special proceeding with the clerk of court to recover the disputed monies.
(c) Notice to the persons who are claiming ownership to the disputed monies required under subsection (b) of this section shall be provided by delivering a copy of the notice to the person or by mailing it to the person by first-class mail, postpaid, properly addressed to the person at the person's last known address.
(d) A real estate broker or attorney shall not deposit disputed monies with the clerk of court until 90 days following notification of the persons claiming ownership of the disputed monies.

(e) Upon the filing of a special proceeding to recover the disputed monies, the clerk shall determine the rightful ownership of the monies and distribute the disputed monies accordingly. If no special proceeding is filed with the clerk of court within one year of the disputed monies being deposited with the clerk of court, the disputed monies shall be deemed unclaimed and shall be delivered by the clerk of court to the State Treasurer in accordance with the provisions of Article 4 of Chapter 116B of the General Statutes.

§ 93A-13 CONTRACTS FOR BROKER SERVICES
No action between a broker and the broker's client for recovery under an agreement for broker services is valid unless the contract is reduced to writing and signed by the party to be charged or by some other person lawfully authorized by the party to sign.

§ 93A-14 RESERVED FOR FUTURE CODIFICATION PURPOSES

§ 93A-15 RESERVED FOR FUTURE CODIFICATION PURPOSES

ARTICLE 2 - REAL ESTATE EDUCATION AND RECOVERY FUND
(SECTION OMITTED)

ARTICLE 3 - PRIVATE REAL ESTATE SCHOOLS
(SECTION OMITTED)

ARTICLE 4 – TIME SHARES

§ 93A-39 TITLE (SECTION OMITTED)

§ 93A-40 REGISTRATION REQUIRED OF TIME SHARE PROJECTS; REAL ESTATE LICENSE REQUIRED (SECTION OMITTED)

§ 93A-41 DEFINITIONS (SECTION OMITTED)

§ 93A-42 TIME SHARES DEEMED REAL ESTATE (SECTION OMITTED)

§ 93A-43 PARTITION (SECTION OMITTED)

§ 93A-44 PUBLIC OFFERING STATEMENT (SECTION OMITTED)

§ 93A-45 PURCHASER'S RIGHT TO CANCEL; ESCROW; VIOLATION (SECTION OMITTED)

§ 93A-46 PRIZES (SECTION OMITTED)

§ 93A-47 TIME SHARES PROXIES (SECTION OMITTED)

§ 93A-48 EXCHANGE PROGRAMS (SECTION OMITTED)

§ 93A-49 SERVICE OF PROCESS ON EXCHANGE COMPANY (SECTION OMITTED)

§ 93A-50 SECURITIES LAWS APPLY (SECTION OMITTED)

§ 93A-51 RULE-MAKING AUTHORITY
The Commission shall have the authority to adopt rules and regulations that are not inconsistent with the provisions of this Article and the General Statutes of North Carolina. The Commission may prescribe forms and procedures for submitting information to the Commission.

§ 93A-52 APPLICATION FOR REGISTRATION OF TIME SHARE PROJECT; DENIAL OF REGISTRATION; RENEWAL; REINSTATEMENT; AND TERMINATION OF DEVELOPER'S INTEREST
(a) Prior to the offering in this State of any time share located in this State, the developer of the time share project shall make written application to the Commission for the registration of the project. The application shall be accompanied by a fee in an amount fixed by the Commission but not to exceed one thousand five hundred dollars ($1,500), and shall include a description of the project, copies of proposed time share instruments including public offering statements, sale contracts, deeds, and other documents referred to therein, information pertaining to any

marketing or managing entity to be employed by the developer for the sale of time shares in a time share project or the management of the project, information regarding any exchange program available to the purchaser, an irrevocable appointment of the Commission to receive service of any lawful process in any proceeding against the developer or the developer's time share salespersons arising under this Article, and such other information as the Commission may by rule require.

Upon receipt of a properly completed application and fee and upon a determination by the Commission that the sale and management of the time shares in the time share project will be directed and conducted by persons of good moral character, the Commission shall issue to the developer a certificate of registration authorizing the developer to offer time shares in the project for sale. The Commission shall within 15 days after receipt of an incomplete application, notify the developer by mail that the Commission has found specified deficiencies, and shall, within 45 days after the receipt of a properly completed application, either issue the certificate of registration or notify the developer by mail of any specific objections to the registration of the project. The certificate shall be prominently displayed in the office of the developer on the site of the project.

The developer shall promptly report to the Commission any and all changes in the information required to be submitted for the purpose of the registration. The developer shall also immediately furnish the Commission complete information regarding any change in its interest in a registered time share project. In the event a developer disposes of, or otherwise terminates its interest in a time share project, the developer shall certify to the Commission in writing that its interest in the time share project is terminated and shall return to the Commission for cancellation the certificate of registration.

(b) In the event the Commission finds that there is substantial reason to deny the application for registration as a time share project, the Commission shall notify the applicant that such application has been denied and shall afford the applicant an opportunity for a hearing before the Commission to show cause why the application should not be denied. In all proceedings to deny a certificate of registration, the provisions of Chapter 150B of the General Statutes shall be applicable.

(c) The acceptance by the Commission of an application for registration shall not constitute the approval of its contents or waive the authority of the Commission to take disciplinary action as provided by this Article.

(d) All certificates of registration granted and issued by the Commission under the provisions of this Article shall expire on the 30th day of June following issuance thereof, and shall become invalid after such date unless reinstated. Renewal of such certificate may be effected at any time during the month of June preceding the date of expiration of such registration upon proper application to the Commission and by the payment of a renewal fee fixed by the Commission but not to exceed one thousand five hundred dollars ($1,500) for each time share project. The developer shall, when making application for renewal, also provide a copy of the report required in G.S. 93A-48. Each certificate reinstated after the expiration date thereof shall be subject to a fee of fifty dollars ($50.00) in addition to the required renewal fee. In the event a time share developer fails to reinstate the registration within 12 months after the expiration date thereof, the Commission may, in its discretion, consider the time share project as not having been previously registered, and thereby subject to the provisions of this Article relating to the issuance of an original certificate. Duplicate certificates may be issued by the Commission upon payment of a fee of one dollar ($1.00) by the registrant developer. Except as prescribed by Commission rules, all fees paid pursuant to this Article shall be nonrefundable.

§ 93A-53 REGISTER OF APPLICANTS; ROSTER OF REGISTRANTS; REGISTERED PROJECTS; FINANCIAL REPORT TO SECRETARY OF STATE

(a) The Executive Director of the Commission shall keep a register of all applicants for certificates of registration, showing for each the date of application, name, business address, and whether the certificate was granted or refused.

(b) The Executive Director of the Commission shall also keep a current roster showing the name and address of all time share projects registered with the Commission. The roster shall be kept on file in the office of the Commission and be open to public inspection.

(c) The Commission shall include a copy of the roster of time share projects current on the preceding June 30 and a statement of the income received by the Commission in connection with the registration of time share projects during the fiscal year ending on June 30 with the report required by G.S. 93B-2.

§ 93A-54 DISCIPLINARY ACTION BY COMMISSION

(a) The Commission has power to take disciplinary action. Upon its own motion, or on the verified complaint of any person, the Commission may investigate the actions of any time share salesperson, developer, or project broker of a time share project registered under this Article, or any other person or entity who shall assume to act in such capacity. If the Commission finds probable cause that a time share salesperson, developer, or project broker has violated any of the provisions of this Article, the Commission may hold a hearing on the allegations of misconduct.

The Commission has the power to suspend or revoke at any time a real estate license issued to a time share salesperson or project broker, or a certificate of registration of a time share project issued to a developer; or to reprimand or censure such salesperson, developer, or project broker; or to fine such developer in the amount of five hundred dollars ($500.00) for each violation of this Article, if, after a hearing, the Commission adjudges either the salesperson, developer, or project broker to be guilty of:

(1) Making any willful or negligent misrepresentation or any willful or negligent omission of material fact about any time share or time share project;

(2) Making any false promises of a character likely to influence, persuade, or induce;

(3) Pursuing a course of misrepresentation or making of false promises through agents, salespersons, advertising or otherwise;

(4) Failing, within a reasonable time, to account for all money received from others in a time share transaction, and failing to remit such monies as may be required in G.S. 93A-45 of this Article;

(5) Acting as a time share salesperson or time share developer in a manner as to endanger the interest of the public;

(6) Paying a commission, salary, or other valuable consideration to any person for acts or services performed in violation of this Article;

(7) Any other conduct which constitutes improper, fraudulent, or dishonest dealing;

(8) Performing or undertaking to perform any legal service as set forth in G.S. 84-2.1, or any other acts not specifically set forth in that section;

(9) Failing to deposit and maintain in a broker's trust or escrow account as defined by G.S. 93A-6(g) all money received from others in a time share transaction as may be required in G.S. 93A-45 of this Article or failing to place with an independent escrow agent the funds of a time share purchaser when required by G.S. 93A-42(c);

(10) Failing to deliver to a purchaser a public offering statement containing the information required by G.S. 93A-44 and any other disclosures that the Commission may by regulation require;

(11) Failing to comply with the provisions of Chapter 75 of the General Statutes in the advertising or promotion of time shares for sale, or failing to assure such compliance by persons engaged on behalf of a developer;

(12) Failing to comply with the provisions of G.S. 93A-48 in furnishing complete and accurate information to purchasers concerning any exchange program which may be offered to such purchaser;

(13) Making any false or fraudulent representation on an application for registration;

(14) Violating any rule or regulation promulgated by the Commission;

(15) Failing to record or cause to be recorded a time share instrument as required by G.S. 93A-42(c), or failing to provide a purchaser the protection against liens required by G.S. 93A-57(a); or

(16) Failing as a time share project broker to exercise reasonable and adequate supervision of the conduct of sales at a project or location by the brokers and salespersons under the time share project broker's control.

(a1) The clear proceeds of fines collected pursuant to subsection (a) of this section shall be remitted to the Civil Penalty and Forfeiture Fund in accordance with G.S. 115C-457.2.

(b) Following a hearing, the Commission shall also have power to suspend or revoke any certificate of registration issued under the provisions of this Article or to reprimand or censure any developer when the registrant has been convicted or has entered a plea of guilty or no contest upon which final judgment is entered by a court of competent jurisdiction in this State, or any other state, of the criminal offenses of: embezzlement, obtaining money under false pretense, fraud, forgery, conspiracy to defraud, or any other offense involving moral turpitude which would reasonably affect the developer's performance in the time share business.

(c) The Commission may appear in its own name in superior court in actions for injunctive relief to prevent any person or entity from violating the provisions of this Article or rules promulgated by the Commission. The superior court shall have the power to grant these injunctions even if criminal prosecution has been or may be instituted as a result of the violations, or regardless of whether the person or entity has been registered by the Commission.

(d) Each developer shall maintain or cause to be maintained complete records of every time share transaction including records pertaining to the deposit, maintenance, and withdrawal of money required to be held in a trust or escrow account, or as otherwise required by the Commission, under G.S. 93A-45 of this Article. The Commission may inspect these records periodically without prior notice and may also inspect these records whenever the Commission determines that they are pertinent to an investigation of any specific complaint against a registrant.

(e) When a licensee is accused of any act, omission, or misconduct under this Article which would subject the licensee to disciplinary action, the licensee may, with the consent and approval of the Commission, surrender the licensee's license and all the rights and privileges pertaining to it for a period of time to be established by the Commission. A licensee who surrenders a license shall not be eligible for, or submit any application for, licensure as a real estate broker or registration of a time share project during the period of license surrender. For the purposes of this section, the term licensee shall include a time share developer.

§ 93A-55 PRIVATE ENFORCEMENT

The provisions of the Article shall not be construed to limit in any manner the right of a purchaser or other person injured by a violation of this Article to bring a private action.

§ 93A-56 PENALTY FOR VIOLATION OF ARTICLE

Except as provided in G.S. 93A-40(b) and G.S. 93A-58, any person violating the provisions of this Article shall be guilty of a Class 1 misdemeanor.

§ 93A-57 RELEASE OF LIENS

(a) Prior to any recordation of the instrument transferring a time share, the developer shall record and furnish notice to the purchaser of a release or subordination of all liens affecting that time share, or shall provide a surety bond or insurance against the lien from a company acceptable to the Commission as provided for liens on real estate in this State, or such underlying lien document shall contain a provision wherein the lienholder subordinates its rights to that of a time share purchaser who fully complies with all of the provisions and terms of the contract of sale.

(b) Unless a time share owner or a time share owner who is his predecessor in title agree otherwise with the lienor, if a lien other than a mortgage or deed of trust becomes effective against more than one time share in a time share project, any time share owner is entitled to a release of his time share from a lien upon payment of the amount of the lien attributable to his time share. The amount of the payment must be proportionate to the ratio that the time share owner's liability bears to the liabilities of all time share owners whose interests are subject to the lien. Upon receipt of payment, the lien holder shall promptly deliver to the time share owner a release of the lien covering that time share. After payment, the managing agent may not assess or have a lien against that time share for any portion of the expenses incurred in connection with that lien.

§ 93A-58 REGISTRAR REQUIRED; CRIMINAL PENALTIES; PROJECT BROKER

(a) Every developer of a registered project shall, by affidavit filed with the Commission, designate a natural person to serve as time share registrar for its registered projects. The registrar shall be responsible for the recordation of time share instruments and the release of liens required by G.S. 93A-42(c) and G.S. 93A-57(a). A developer may, from time to time, change the designated time share registrar by proper filing with the Commission and by otherwise complying with this subsection. No sales or offers to sell shall be made until the registrar is designated for a time share project.

The registrar has the duty to ensure that the provisions of this Article are complied with in a time share project for which the person is registrar. No registrar shall record a time share instrument except as provided by this Article.

(b) A time share registrar is guilty of a Class I felony if he or she knowingly or recklessly fails to record or cause to be recorded a time share instrument as required by this Article.

A person responsible as general partner, corporate officer, joint venturer or sole proprietor of the developer of a time share project is guilty of a Class I felony if the person intentionally allows the offering for sale or the sale of time share to purchasers without first designating a time share registrar.

(c) The developer shall designate for each project and other locations where time shares are sold or offered for sale a project broker. The project broker shall act as supervising broker for all time share salespersons at the project or other location and shall directly, personally, and actively supervise all such persons at the project or other location in a manner to reasonably ensure that the sale of time shares will be conducted in accordance with the provisions of this Chapter.

§ 93A-59 PRESERVATION OF TIME SHARE PURCHASER'S CLAIMS AND DEFENSES

(a) For one year following the execution of an instrument of indebtedness for the purchase of a time share, the purchaser of a time share may assert against the seller, assignee of the seller, or other holder of the instrument of indebtedness, any claims or defenses available against the developer or the original seller, and the purchaser may not waive the right to assert these claims or defenses in connection with a time share purchase. Any recovery by the purchaser on a claim asserted against an assignee of the seller or other holder of the instrument of indebtedness shall not exceed the amount paid by the purchaser under the instrument. A holder shall be the person or entity with the rights of a holder as set forth in G.S. 25-3-301.

(b) Every instrument of indebtedness for the purchase of a time share shall set forth the following provision in a clear and conspicuous manner:

"NOTICE

FOR A PERIOD OF ONE YEAR FOLLOWING THE EXECUTION OF THIS INSTRUMENT OF INDEBTEDNESS, ANY HOLDER OF THIS INSTRUMENT OF INDEBTEDNESS IS SUBJECT TO ALL CLAIMS AND DEFENSES WHICH THE PURCHASER COULD ASSERT AGAINST THE

SELLER OF THE TIME SHARE. RECOVERY BY THE PURCHASER SHALL NOT EXCEED AMOUNTS PAID BY THE PURCHASER UNDER THIS INSTRUMENT."

§§ 93A-60 THROUGH 93A-69. RESERVED FOR FUTURE CODIFICATION PURPOSES

ARTICLE 5 - REAL ESTATE APPRAISERS.
(SECTION OMITTED)

ARTICLE 6 – BROKER PRICE OPINIONS AND COMPARATIVE MARKET ANALYSES

§ 93A-82   DEFINITIONS

As used in this Article, the terms "broker price opinion" and "comparative market analysis" mean an estimate prepared by a licensed real estate broker that details the probable selling price or leasing price of a particular parcel of or interest in property and provides a varying level of detail about the property's condition, market, and neighborhood, and information on comparable properties, but does not include an automated valuation model.

§ 93A-83   BROKER PRICE OPINIONS AND COMPARATIVE MARKET ANALYSES FOR A FEE

(a) Authorized. – A person licensed under this Chapter, other than a provisional broker, may prepare a broker price opinion or comparative market analysis and charge and collect a fee for the opinion if:

(1) The license of that licensee is active and in good standing; and
(2) The broker price opinion or comparative market analysis meets the requirements of subsection (c) of this section.
(3) The requirements of this Article shall not apply to any broker price opinion or comparative market analysis performed by a licensee for no fee or consideration.

(b) For Whom Opinion May Be Prepared. – Notwithstanding any provision to the contrary, a person licensed under this Chapter may prepare a broker price opinion or comparative market analysis for any of the following:

(1) An existing or potential seller of a parcel of real property.
(2) An existing or potential buyer of a parcel of real property.
(3) An existing or potential lessor of a parcel of or interest in real property.
(4) An existing or potential lessee of a parcel of or interest in real property.
(5) A third party making decisions or performing due diligence related to the potential listing, offering, sale, option, lease, or acquisition price of a parcel of or interest in real property.
(6) An existing or potential lienholder or other third party for any purpose other than as the basis to determine the value of a parcel of or interest in property, for a mortgage loan origination, including first and second mortgages, refinances, or equity lines of credit.
(7) The provisions of this subsection do not preclude the preparation of a broker price opinion or comparative market analysis to be used in conjunction with or in addition to an appraisal.

(c) Required Contents of a Broker Price Opinion or Comparative Market Analysis. – A broker price opinion or comparative market analysis shall be in writing and conform to the standards provided in this Article that shall include, but are not limited to, the following:

(1) A statement of the intended purpose of the broker price opinion or comparative market analysis.
(2) A brief description of the subject property and property interest to be priced.
(3) The basis of reasoning used to reach the conclusion of the price, including the applicable market data or capitalization computation.
(4) Any assumptions or limiting conditions.
(5) A disclosure of any existing or contemplated interest of the broker issuing the broker price opinion, including the possibility of representing the landlord/tenant or seller/buyer.
(6) The effective date of the broker price opinion.
(7) The name and signature of the broker issuing the broker price opinion and broker license number.
(8) The name of the real estate brokerage firm for which the broker is acting.
(9) The signature date.
(10) A disclaimer stating that "This opinion is not an appraisal of the market value of the property, and may not be used in lieu of an appraisal. If an appraisal is desired, the services of a licensed or certified appraiser shall be obtained. This opinion may not be used by any party as the primary basis to determine the value of a parcel of or interest in real property for a mortgage loan origination, including first and second mortgages, refinances, or equity lines of credit."
(11) A copy of the assignment request for the broker price opinion or comparative market analysis.

(d) Rules. – The North Carolina Real Estate Commission shall have the power to adopt rules that are not inconsistent with the provisions in this Article.

(e) Additional Requirements for Electronic or Form Submission. – In addition to the requirement of subsection (c) of this section, if a broker price opinion is submitted electronically or on a form supplied by the requesting party, the following provisions apply:
  (1) A signature required by subdivision (7) of subsection (c) of this section may be an electronic signature, as defined in G.S. 47-16.2.
  (2) A signature required by subdivision (7) of subsection (c) of this section and the disclaimer required by subdivision (10) of subsection (c) of this section may be transmitted in a separate attachment if the electronic format or form supplied by the requesting party does not allow additional comments to be written by the licensee. The electronic format or form supplied by the requesting party shall do the following:
    a. Reference the existence of a separate attachment.
    b. Include a statement that the broker price opinion or comparative market analysis is not complete without the attachment.

(f) Restrictions. – Notwithstanding any provisions to the contrary, a person licensed pursuant to this Chapter may not knowingly prepare a broker price opinion or comparative market analysis for any purpose in lieu of an appraisal when an appraisal is required by federal or State law. A broker price opinion or comparative market analysis that estimates the value of or worth a parcel of or interest in real estate rather than sales or leasing price shall be deemed to be an appraisal and may not be prepared by a licensed broker under the authority of this Article, but may only be prepared by a duly licensed or certified appraiser, and shall meet the regulations adopted by the North Carolina Appraisal Board. A broker price opinion or comparative market analysis shall not under any circumstances be referred to as a valuation or appraisal.

(g) No Report of Predetermined Result. – A broker price opinion or comparative market analysis shall not include the reporting of a predetermined result.

CHAPTER 58 - REAL ESTATE COMMISSION

SUBCHAPTER 58A - REAL ESTATE BROKERS

21 NCAC 58A .0101	Proof of licensure	
21 NCAC 58A .0102	Branch office (REPEALED)	
21 NCAC 58A .0103	Broker name and address	
21 NCAC 58A .0104	Agency agreements and disclosure	
21 NCAC 58A .0105	Advertising	
21 NCAC 58A .0106	Delivery of instruments	
21 NCAC 58A .0107	Handling and accounting of funds (REPEALED)	
21 NCAC 58A .0108	retention of records	
21 NCAC 58A .0109	brokerage fees and compensation	
21 NCAC 58A .0110	Broker-in-charge	
21 NCAC 58A .0111	Drafting legal instruments	
21 NCAC 58A .0112	Offers and sales contracts	
21 NCAC 58A .0113	Reporting criminal convictions and disciplinary actions	
21 NCAC 58A .0114	Residential property and owners' association disclosure statement	
21 NCAC 58A .0115	Disclosure of offers prohibited	
21 NCAC 58A .0116	Handling of trust money	
21 NCAC 58A .0117	Accounting for trust money	
21 NCAC 58A .0118	Trust money belonging to property owners' associations	
21 NCAC 58A .0200	General provisions (REPEALED)	
21 NCAC 58A .0300	Application for License (SECTION OMITTED)	
21 NCAC 58A .0400	Examinations (SECTION OMITTED)	
21 NCAC 58A .0501	Character (REPEALED)	
21 NCAC 58A .0502	Business entities	
21 NCAC 58A .0503	License renewal; penalty for operating while license expired	
21 NCAC 58A .0504	Active and inactive license status	
21 NCAC 58A .0505	Reinstatement of expired license, revoked, surrendered or suspended license	
21 NCAC 58A .0506	Provisional broker to be supervised by broker	
21 NCAC 58A .0507	Payment of fees	
21 NCAC 58A .0508	Duplicate license fee (REPEALED)	
21 NCAC 58A .0509	Duplicate license fee	
21 NCAC 58A .0510	Cancellation of salesperson license upon broker licensure	
21 NCAC 58A .0511	Licensing of persons licensed in another jurisdiction	
21 NCAC 58A .0600	Real Estate Commission Hearings (SECTION OMITTED)	
21 NCAC 58A .0700	Petitions for rules	
21 NCAC 58A .0800	Rule making	
21 NCAC 58A .0900	Declaratory rulings	
21 NCAC 58A .1000	Schools (TRANSFERRED TO c.0100)	
21 NCAC 58A .1101	Real estate pre-licensing courses (TRANSFERRED/REPEALED. TRANSFERS ARE AT c.0300)	
21 NCAC 58A .1200	Certification of real estate instructors (REPEALED)	
21 NCAC 58A .1300	Private real estate schools (TRANSFERRED/REPEALED. TRANSFERS ARE AT c.0200)	
21 NCAC 58A .1401	Real estate education and recovery fund	
21 NCAC 58A .1500	Forms (REPEALED)	
21 NCAC 58A .1601	Fair housing	
21 NCAC 58A .1701	Purpose and applicability	
21 NCAC 58A .1702	continuing education requirement	
21 NCAC 58A .1703	Continuing education for license activation	
21 NCAC 58A .1704	No credit for prelicensing or postlicensing courses	
21 NCAC 58A .1705	Attendance and participation requirements	
21 NCAC 58A .1706	Repetition of courses	
21 NCAC 58A .1707	elective course carry-over credit	
21 NCAC 58A .1708	Equivalent credit	
21 NCAC 58A .1709	Extensions of time to complete continuing education	
21 NCAC 58A .1710	Denial or withdrawal of continuing education credit	
21 NCAC 58A .1711	Continuing education required of nonresident licensees	
21 NCAC 58A .1801	General provisions	
21 NCAC 58A .1802	Definitions	
21 NCAC 58A .1803	requirements for licensure; application and fee	
21 NCAC 58A .1804	Active status	
21 NCAC 58A .1805	Renewal	
21 NCAC 58A .1806	Limitations	
21 NCAC 58A .1807	Affiliation with resident broker	
21 NCAC 58A .1808	Trust monies	
21 NCAC 58A .1809	Advertising	
21 NCAC 58A .1810	Payment of fees	
21 NCAC 58A .1901	Purpose and applicability	
21 NCAC 58A .1902	Postlicensing education requirement	
21 NCAC 58A .1903	Extensions of time to complete postlicensing education	
21 NCAC 58A .1904	Denial or withdrawal of postlicensing education credit	
21 NCAC 58A .2000	Annual Reports (SECTION OMITTED)	
21 NCAC 58A .2103	Postponement of continuing education	
21 NCAC 58A .2104	Postponement of postlicensing education	
21 NCAC 58A .2105	Proof of eligibility	
21 NCAC 58A .2201	Applicability	
21 NCAC 58A .2202	Standards	

SUBCHAPTER 58B – TIME SHARES

21 NCAC 58B .0101	Application for registration
21 NCAC 58B .0102	Registration fee
21 NCAC 58B .0103	Renewal of time share project registration
21 NCAC 58B .0104	Amendments to time share project registration
21 NCAC 58B .0105	Notice of termination
21 NCAC 58B .0201	General provisions
21 NCAC 58B .0202	Public offering statement summary
21 NCAC 58B .0203	Receipt for public offering statement
21 NCAC 58B .0301	Proof of cancellation
21 NCAC 58B .0401	Retention of time share records
21 NCAC 58B .0402	Time share agency agreements and disclosure
21 NCAC 58B .0501	Time share trust funds
21 NCAC 58B .0601	Designation of project broker
21 NCAC 58B .0602	Duties of the project broker
21 NCAC 58B .0701	Forms for time share projects

SUBCHAPTER 58C – REAL ESTATE PRELICENSING EDUCATION

SUBCHAPTER 58D – REAL ESTATE APPRAISERS (REPEALED)

SUBCHAPTER 58E – REAL ESTATE CONTINUING EDUCATION

SUBCHAPTER 58F – BROKER TRANSITION COURSE (REPEALED)

SUBCHAPTER 58G – NORTH CAROLINA REAL ESTATE COMMISSION ADMINISTRATION

21 NCAC 58G .0101	Per diem

CHAPTER 58 – REAL ESTATE COMMISSION

SUBCHAPTER 58A - REAL ESTATE BROKERS

SECTION .0100 - GENERAL BROKERAGE

21 NCAC 58A .0101   PROOF OF LICENSURE
(a) The annual license renewal pocket card issued by the Commission to each licensee shall be retained by the licensee as evidence of licensure. Each licensee shall carry his or her pocket card on his or her person at all times while engaging in real estate brokerage and shall produce the card as proof of licensure whenever requested.
(b) The qualifying broker of a firm shall retain the firm's renewal pocket card at the firm and shall produce it upon request as proof of firm licensure as required by Rule .0502.
(c) Every licensed real estate business entity or firm shall prominently display its license certificate or facsimile thereof in each office maintained by the entity or firm. A broker-in-charge shall also prominently display his or her license certificate in the office where he or she is broker-in-charge.
(d) Every licensee shall include his or her license number in agency contracts and disclosures as provided in Rule .0104 of this Subchapter.

21 NCAC 58A .0102   BRANCH OFFICE (REPEALED)

21 NCAC 58A .0103   BROKER NAME AND ADDRESS
(a) Upon initial licensure and at all times thereafter, every broker shall assure that the Commission has on record the broker's current personal name, firm name, trade name, residence address and firm address. Every broker shall notify the Commission in writing of each change of personal name, firm name, trade name, residence address and firm address within 10 days of said change. All addresses shall be sufficiently descriptive to enable the Commission to correspond with and locate the broker.
(b) Registration of Assumed Name. In the event that any broker shall advertise in any manner using a firm name or an assumed name which does not set forth the surname of the broker, the broker shall first file the appropriate certificate with the office of the county register of deeds in each county in which the broker intends to engage in brokerage activities in compliance with G.S. 66-68 and notify the Commission in writing of the use of such a firm name or assumed name.
(c) Business names. A broker shall not include the name of a provisional broker or an unlicensed person in the name of a sole proprietorship, partnership or business entity other than a corporation or limited liability company. No broker shall use a business name that includes the name of any active, inactive, or cancelled broker without the permission of that broker or that broker's authorized representative.

21 NCAC 58A .0104   AGENCY AGREEMENTS AND DISCLOSURE
(a) Every agreement for brokerage services in a real estate transaction and every agreement for services connected with the management of a property owners association shall be in writing and signed by the parties thereto. Every agreement for brokerage services between a broker and an owner of the property to be the subject of a transaction must be in writing and signed by the parties from the time of its formation. Every agreement for brokerage services between a broker and a buyer or tenant shall be express and shall be reduced to writing and signed by the parties thereto not later than the time one of the parties makes an offer to purchase, sell, rent, lease, or exchange real estate to another. However, every agreement between a broker and a buyer or tenant which seeks to bind the buyer or tenant for a period of time or to restrict the buyer's or tenant's right to work with other agents or without an agent shall be in writing and signed by the parties thereto from its formation. A broker shall not continue to represent a buyer or tenant without a written, signed agreement when such agreement is required by this Rule. Every written agreement for brokerage services of any kind in a real estate transaction shall provide for its existence for a definite period of time, shall include the licensee's license number, and shall provide for its termination without prior notice at the expiration of that period, except that an agency agreement between a landlord and broker to procure tenants or receive rents for the landlord's property may allow for automatic renewal so long as the landlord may terminate with notice at the end of any contract period and any subsequent renewals. For the purposes of this rule, an agreement between licensees to cooperate or share compensation shall not be considered an agreement for brokerage services and, except as required by Rule .1807 of this Subchapter, need not be memorialized in writing.
(b) Every listing agreement, written buyer agency agreement or other written agreement for brokerage services in a real estate transaction shall contain the following provision: The broker shall conduct all brokerage activities in regard to this

agreement without respect to the race, color, religion, sex, national origin, handicap or familial status of any party or prospective party. The provision shall be set forth in a clear and conspicuous manner which shall distinguish it from other provisions of the agreement. For the purposes of this Rule, the term, familial status, shall be defined as it is in G.S. 41A-3(1b).

(c) In every real estate sales transaction, a broker shall, at first substantial contact directly with a prospective buyer or seller, provide the prospective buyer or seller with a copy of the publication "Working with Real Estate Agents," set forth the broker's name and license number thereon, review the publication with the buyer or seller, and determine whether the agent will act as the agent of the buyer or seller in the transaction. If the first substantial contact with a prospective buyer or seller occurs by telephone or other electronic means of communication where it is not practical to provide the "Working with Real Estate Agents" publication, the broker shall at the earliest opportunity thereafter, but in no event later than three days from the date of first substantial contact, mail or otherwise transmit a copy of the publication to the prospective buyer or seller and review it with him or her at the earliest practicable opportunity thereafter. For the purposes of this Rule, "first substantial contact" shall include contacts between a broker and a consumer where the consumer or broker begins to act as though an agency relationship exists and the consumer begins to disclose to the broker personal or confidential information.

(d) A real estate broker representing one party in a transaction shall not undertake to represent another party in the transaction without the written authority of each party. The written authority must be obtained upon the formation of the relationship except when a buyer or tenant is represented by a broker without a written agreement in conformity with the requirements of Paragraph (a) of this Rule. Under such circumstances, the written authority for dual agency must be reduced to writing not later than the time that one of the parties represented by the broker makes an offer to purchase, sell, rent, lease, or exchange real estate to another party.

(e) In every real estate sales transaction, a broker working directly with a prospective buyer as a seller's agent or subagent shall disclose in writing to the prospective buyer at the first substantial contact with the prospective buyer that the broker represents the interests of the seller. The written disclosure shall include the broker's license number. If the first substantial contact occurs by telephone or by means of other electronic communication where it is not practical to provide written disclosure, the broker shall immediately disclose by similar means whom he represents and shall immediately mail or otherwise transmit a copy of the written disclosure to the buyer. In no event shall the broker mail or transmit a copy of the written disclosure to the buyer later than three days from the date of first substantial contact with the buyer.

(f) In every real estate sales transaction, a broker representing a buyer shall, at the initial contact with the seller or seller's agent, disclose to the seller or seller's agent that the broker represents the buyer's interests. In addition, in every real estate sales transaction other than auctions, the broker shall, no later than the time of delivery of an offer to the seller or seller's agent, provide the seller or seller's agent with a written confirmation disclosing that he represents the interests of the buyer. The written confirmation may be made in the buyer's offer to purchase and shall include the broker's license number.

(g) The provisions of Paragraphs (c), (d) and (e) of this Rule do not apply to real estate licensees representing sellers in auction sales transactions.

(h) A broker representing a buyer in an auction sale transaction shall, no later than the time of execution of a written agreement memorializing the buyer's contract to purchase, provide the seller or seller's agent with a written confirmation disclosing that he represents the interests of the buyer. The written confirmation may be made in the written agreement.

(i) A firm which represents more than one party in the same real estate transaction is a dual agent and, through the brokers associated with the firm, shall disclose its dual agency to the parties.

(j) When a firm represents both the buyer and seller in the same real estate transaction, the firm may, with the prior express approval of its buyer and seller clients, designate one or more individual brokers associated with the firm to represent only the interests of the seller and one or more other individual brokers associated with the firm to represent only the interests of the buyer in the transaction. The authority for designated agency must be reduced to writing not later than the time that the parties are required to reduce their dual agency agreement to writing in accordance with Paragraph (d) of this Rule. An individual broker shall not be so designated and shall not undertake to represent only the interests of one party if the broker has actually received confidential information concerning the other party in connection with the transaction. A broker-in-charge shall not act as a designated broker for a party in a real estate sales transaction when a provisional broker under his or her supervision will act as a designated broker for another party with a competing interest.

(k) When a firm acting as a dual agent designates an individual broker to represent the seller, the broker so designated shall represent only the interest of the seller and shall not, without the seller's permission, disclose to the buyer or a broker designated to represent the buyer:

(1) that the seller may agree to a price, terms, or any conditions of sale other than those established by the seller;
(2) the seller's motivation for engaging in the transaction unless disclosure is otherwise required by statute or rule; and
(3) any information about the seller which the seller has identified as confidential unless disclosure of the information is otherwise required by statute or rule.

(l) When a firm acting as a dual agent designates an individual broker to represent the buyer, the broker so designated shall represent only the interest of the buyer and shall not, without the buyer's permission, disclose to the seller or a broker designated to represent the seller:
(1) that the buyer may agree to a price, terms, or any conditions of sale other than those established by the seller;
(2) the buyer's motivation for engaging in the transaction unless disclosure is otherwise required by statute or rule; and
(3) any information about the buyer which the buyer has identified as confidential unless disclosure of the information is otherwise required by statute or rule.

(m) A broker designated to represent a buyer or seller in accordance with Paragraph (j) of this Rule shall disclose the identity of all of the brokers so designated to both the buyer and the seller. The disclosure shall take place no later than the presentation of the first offer to purchase or sell.

(n) When an individual broker represents both the buyer and seller in the same real estate sales transaction pursuant to a written agreement authorizing dual agency, the parties may provide in the written agreement that the broker shall not disclose the following information about one party to the other without permission from the party about whom the information pertains:
(1) that a party may agree to a price, terms or any conditions of sale other than those offered;
(2) the motivation of a party for engaging in the transaction, unless disclosure is otherwise required by statute or rule; and
(3) any information about a party which that party has identified as confidential, unless disclosure is otherwise required by statute or rule.

21 NCAC 58A .0105   ADVERTISING
(a) Authority to Advertise.
(1) A provisional broker shall not advertise any brokerage service or the sale, purchase, exchange, rent or lease of real estate for another or others without the consent of his or her broker-in-charge and without including in the advertisement the name of the broker or firm with whom the provisional broker is associated.
(2) A broker shall not advertise or display a "for sale" or "for rent" sign on any real estate without the written consent of the owner or the owner's authorized agent.

(b) Blind Ads. A broker shall not advertise the sale, purchase, exchange, rent or lease of real estate, for another or others, in a manner indicating the offer to sell, purchase, exchange, rent, or lease is being made by the broker's principal only. Every such advertisement shall conspicuously indicate that it is the advertisement of a broker or brokerage firm and shall not be confined to publication of only a post office box number, telephone number, street address, internet web address, or e-mail address.

(c) A person licensed as a limited nonresident commercial broker shall comply with the provisions of Rule .1809 of this Subchapter in connection with all advertising concerning or relating to his or her status as a North Carolina broker.

21 NCAC 58A .0106   DELIVERY OF INSTRUMENTS
(a) Except as provided in Paragraph (b) of this Rule, every broker shall immediately, but in no event later than five days from the date of execution, deliver to the parties thereto copies of any required written agency agreement, contract, offer, lease, or option affecting real property.

(b) A broker may be relieved of his or her duty under Paragraph (a) of this Rule to deliver copies of leases or rental agreements to the property owner, if the broker:
(1) obtains the express written authority of the property owner to enter into and retain copies of leases or rental agreements on behalf of the property owner;
(2) executes the lease or rental agreement on a pre-printed form, the material terms of which may not be changed by the broker without prior approval by the property owner except as may be required by law;

(3) promptly provides a copy of the lease or rental agreement to the property owner upon reasonable request; and
(4) delivers to the property owner within 45 days following the date of execution of the lease or rental agreement, an accounting which identifies the leased property and which sets forth the names of the tenants, the rental rates and rents collected.

21 NCAC 58A .0107   HANDLING AND ACCOUNTING OF FUNDS (REPEALED)

21 NCAC 58A .0108   RETENTION OF RECORDS
(a) Brokers shall retain records of all sales, rental, and other transactions conducted in such capacity, whether the transaction is pending, completed or terminated prior to its successful conclusion. The broker shall retain such records for three years after all funds held by the broker in connection with the transaction have been disbursed to the proper party or parties or the successful or unsuccessful conclusion of the transaction, whichever occurs later. However, if the broker's agency agreement is terminated prior to the conclusion of the transaction, the broker shall retain such records for three years after the termination of the agency agreement or the disbursement of all funds held by or paid to the broker in connection with the transaction, whichever occurs later.
(b) Such records shall include the following:
(1) contracts of sale,
(2) written leases,
(3) agency contracts,
(4) options,
(5) offers to purchase,
(6) trust or escrow records,
(7) earnest money receipts,
(8) disclosure documents,
(9) closing statements,
(10) brokerage cooperation agreements,
(11) declarations of affiliation,
(12) broker price opinions and comparative market analyses prepared pursuant to G.S. 93A, Article 6, including any notes and supporting documentation, and
(13) any other records pertaining to real estate transactions.
(c) All such records shall be made available for inspection and reproduction by the Commission or its authorized representatives without prior notice.

21 NCAC 58A .0109   BROKERAGE FEES AND COMPENSATION
(a) A licensee shall not receive, either directly or indirectly, any commission, rebate or other valuable consideration of more than nominal value from a vendor or a supplier of goods and services for an expenditure made on behalf of the licensee's principal in a real estate transaction without the written consent of the licensee's principal.
(b) A licensee shall not receive, either directly or indirectly, any commission, rebate, or other valuable consideration of more than nominal value for services which the licensee recommends, procures, or arranges relating to a real estate transaction for a party, without full and timely disclosure to such party.
(c) In a real estate sales transaction, a broker shall not receive any compensation, incentive, bonus, rebate, or other consideration of more than nominal value:
(1) from his principal unless the compensation, incentive, bonus, rebate, or other consideration is provided for in a written agency contract prepared in conformity with the requirements of 21 NCAC 58A .0104.
(2) from any other party or person unless the broker provides full and timely disclosure of the incentive, bonus, rebate, or other consideration, or the promise or expectation thereof to the broker's principal. The disclosure may be made orally, but must be confirmed in writing before the principal makes or accepts an offer to buy or sell.
(d) Full disclosure shall include a description of the compensation, incentive, bonus, rebate, or other consideration including its value and the identity of the person or party by whom it will or may be paid. A disclosure is timely when it is made in sufficient time to aid a reasonable person's decision-making.
(e) Nothing in this rule shall be construed to require a broker to disclose to a person not his principal the compensation the broker expects to receive from his principal or to disclose to his principal the compensation the broker expects to

receive from the broker's employing broker. For the purpose of this Rule, nominal value means of insignificant, token, or merely symbolic worth.

(f) The Commission shall not act as a board of arbitration and shall not compel parties to settle disputes concerning such matters as the rate of commissions, the division of commissions, pay of brokers, and similar matters.

(g) Except as provided in (h) of this rule, a licensee shall not undertake in any manner, any arrangement, contract, plan or other course of conduct, to compensate or share compensation with unlicensed persons or entities for any acts performed in North Carolina for which licensure by the Commission is required.

(h) A broker may pay or promise to pay consideration to a travel agent in return for procuring a tenant for a vacation rental as defined by the Vacation Rental Act if:
- (1) the travel agent only introduces the tenant to the broker, but does not otherwise engage in any activity which would require a real estate license;
- (2) the introduction by the travel agent is made in the regular course of the travel agent's business; and
- (3) the travel agent has not solicited, handled or received any monies in connection with the vacation rental.

For the purpose of this Rule, a travel agent is any person or entity who is primarily engaged in the business of acting as an intermediary between persons who purchase air, land, and ocean travel services and the providers of such services. A travel agent is also any other person or entity who is permitted to handle and sell tickets for air travel by the Airlines Reporting Corporation (ARC). Payments authorized hereunder shall be made only after the conclusion of the vacation rental tenancy. Prior to the creation of a binding vacation rental agreement, the broker shall provide a tenant introduced by a travel agent a written statement advising him or her to rely only upon the agreement and the broker's representations about the transaction. The broker shall keep for a period of three years records of a payment made to a travel agent including records identifying the tenant, the travel agent and their addresses, the property and dates of the tenancy, and the amount paid.

(i) Nothing in this Rule shall be construed to permit a licensee to accept any fee, kickback or other valuable consideration that is prohibited by the Real Estate Settlement Procedures Act (12 USC 2601 et. seq.) or any rules and regulations promulgated by the United States Department of Housing and Urban Development pursuant to said Act or to fail to make any disclosure required by said Act or rules.

21 NCAC 58A .0110   BROKER-IN-CHARGE

(a) When used in this Rule, the term:
- (1) "Office" means any place of business where acts are performed for which a real estate license is required or where monies received by a broker acting in a fiduciary capacity are handled or records for such trust monies are maintained;
- (2) "Principal Office" means the office so designated in the Commission's records by the qualifying broker of a licensed firm or the broker-in-charge of a sole proprietorship; and
- (3) "Branch Office" means any office in addition to the principal office of a broker which is operated in connection with the broker's real estate business.

(b) Except as provided in Paragraphs (d) and (e) of this Rule, every real estate firm, including a sole proprietorship, shall have a broker designated by the Commission as provided in Paragraph (f) of this Rule to serve as the broker-in-charge at its principal office and a broker to serve as broker-in-charge at any branch office. No broker shall be broker-in-charge of more than one office at a time. No office of a firm shall have more than one designated broker-in-charge.

(c) If a firm shares office space with one or more other firms, the same broker may serve as broker-in-charge of multiple firms at that location. All firms at that location having the same designated broker-in-charge shall maintain with the Commission as a delivery address the same delivery address as that of the single designated broker-in-charge.

(d) A licensed real estate firm is not required to have a broker-in-charge if it:
- (1) has been organized for the sole purpose of receiving compensation for brokerage services furnished by its qualifying broker through another firm or broker;
- (2) is treated for tax purposes as a Subchapter S corporation by the United States Internal Revenue Service;
- (3) has no principal or branch office; and
- (4) has no licensed or unlicensed person associated with it other than its qualifying broker.

(e) A broker who is a sole proprietor shall obtain the Commission's designation of himself or herself as a broker-in-charge if the broker engages in any transaction where the broker is required to deposit and maintain monies belonging to others in a trust account, engages in advertising or promoting his or her services as a broker in any manner, or has one or more other brokers affiliated with him or her in the real estate business. Maintenance of a trust or escrow account by a broker solely for holding residential tenant security deposits received by the broker on properties owned by the broker in compliance with G.S. 42-50 shall not, standing alone, subject the broker to the requirement to designate himself or herself as a broker-in-charge.

(f) A broker desiring to be a broker-in-charge shall request in writing his or her designation as broker-in-charge by the Commission on a form provided by the Commission. Upon receipt of notice from the Commission that the broker has been designated as broker-in-charge, the broker shall assume the duties of broker-in-charge.

(g) To qualify to become a broker-in-charge, a broker shall:

    (1)   have a license on active status but not on provisional status;

    (2)   possess at least two years of full-time real estate brokerage experience or equivalent part-time real estate brokerage experience within the previous five years or real estate education or experience in real estate transactions that the Commission finds equivalent to such experience; and

    (3)   complete the Commission's 12 classroom hour broker-in-charge course either within three years prior to designation as a broker-in-charge or within 120 days following designation as a broker-in-charge.

Upon the request of the Commission, a broker shall provide to the Commission evidence that he or she possesses the requisite experience. A broker-in-charge designation shall be immediately terminated if a broker-in-charge fails to complete the broker-in-charge course during the required time period or if the Commission finds the broker-in-charge does not possess the required experience. A broker who is removed as broker-in-charge for failure to timely complete the Commission's 12 hour broker-in-charge course must first complete the 12 hour broker-in-charge course before he or she may again be designated as broker-in-charge.

(h) By submission of a broker-in-charge designation request to the Commission, a broker certifies that he or she possesses the experience required to become a broker-in-charge and upon designation by the Commission, the broker shall be authorized to act as a broker-in-charge. Upon his or her designation as broker-in-charge and completion of the broker-in-charge course within the time period prescribed in Subparagraph (g)(3) of this Rule, the designated broker-in-charge acquires the eligibility to be re-designated as a broker-in-charge at any time in the future after a period of not actively serving as a broker-in-charge without having to again satisfy the qualification requirements for initial designation stated in this Paragraph so long as the broker continuously satisfies the requirements to retain such eligibility described in Paragraph (k) of this Rule.

(i) The broker-in-charge shall, in accordance with the requirements of G.S. 93A and the rules adopted by the Commission, assume the responsibility at his or her office for:

    (1)   the retention of current license renewal pocket cards by all brokers employed at the office for which he or she is broker-in-charge; the proper display of licenses at such office in accordance with Rule .0101 of this Section; and assuring that each broker employed at the office has complied with Rules .0503, .0504, and .0506 of this Subchapter;

    (2)   the proper notification to the Commission of any change of business address or trade name of the firm and the registration of any assumed business name adopted by the firm for its use;

    (3)   the proper conduct of advertising by or in the name of the firm at such office;

    (4)   the proper maintenance at such office of the trust or escrow account of the firm and the records pertaining thereto;

    (5)   the proper retention and maintenance of records relating to transactions conducted by or on behalf of the firm at such office, including those required to be retained pursuant to Rule .0108 of this Section;

    (6)   the proper supervision of provisional brokers associated with or engaged on behalf of the firm at such office in accordance with the requirements of Rule .0506 of this Subchapter;

    (7)   the proper supervision of all brokers employed at the office for which he or she is broker-in-charge with respect to adherence to agency agreement and disclosure requirements.

(j) A broker who was the broker-in-charge of a real estate office on April 1, 2006, whose broker-in-charge declaration was received by the Commission prior to that date, and who completed the Commission's broker-in-charge course prior to April 1, 2006 or within 120 days following designation as a broker-in-charge, may continue to serve as a broker-in-charge thereafter until his or her eligibility to serve as a broker-in-charge is terminated as provided in Paragraph (l) of this Rule.

(k) Once a broker has been designated as a broker-in-charge and completed the 12 hour broker-in-charge course as prescribed by Paragraph (g) of this Rule, the broker may maintain broker-in-charge eligibility by timely annual renewal of his or her broker license, completion each license year of the four hour mandatory continuing education update course prescribed for all brokers and known as the "Real Estate Update Course," and completion each license year of the four hour special continuing education course prescribed by the Commission only for brokers-in-charge and known as the "Broker-In-Charge Annual Review Course." The Broker-In-Charge Annual Review Course must be taken initially by a broker-in-charge during the first full license year following the license year in which the broker was designated as a broker-in-charge and must be taken each license year thereafter in order for the broker to maintain broker-in-charge eligibility. The Broker-In-Charge Annual Review Course shall satisfy the broker's general continuing education elective course requirement, but the broker must also take the mandatory continuing education Real Estate Update Course each license year. The Broker-In-Charge Annual Review Course is reserved exclusively for current brokers-in-charge, and brokers who are not currently acting as a broker-in-charge but who desire to retain their broker-in-charge eligibility. Only these brokers shall receive continuing education elective credit for taking the course.

(l) A broker's broker-in-charge eligibility and, if currently designated as a broker-in-charge, his or her broker-in-charge designation shall be terminated upon the occurrence of any of the following events:

(1) the broker's license expires or the broker's license is suspended, revoked or surrendered;
(2) the broker's license is made inactive for any reason, including failure to satisfy the continuing education requirements described in Rule .1702 of this Subchapter;
(3) the broker fails to complete the Broker-In-Charge Annual Review Course described in Paragraph (k) of this Rule; or
(4) the broker is found by the Commission to have not possessed the experience required in Paragraph (g) of this Rule at the time of either initial designation as a broker-in-charge or re-designation as a broker-in-charge.

(m) When a broker who is a former broker-in-charge desires to be re-designated as a broker-in-charge following termination of his or her broker-in-charge designation or eligibility, he or she must first have a license on active status. The broker then must satisfy the experience requirements for initial designation set forth in Paragraph (g) of this Rule, and the broker must complete the 12 hour broker-in-charge course prior to re-designation as broker-in charge.

(n) A broker-in-charge shall notify the Commission in writing that he or she no longer is serving as broker-in-charge of a particular office within 10 days following any such change.

(o) A non-resident broker who has been designated by the Commission as the broker-in-charge of an office not located in North Carolina is not required to complete the broker-in-charge course or the Broker-In-Charge Annual Review Course prescribed for brokers-in-charge under Paragraph (k) of this Rule. However, if such broker-in-charge either becomes a resident of North Carolina or becomes broker-in-charge of an office located within North Carolina, then he or she must take the 12 hour broker-in-charge course within 120 days of such change, unless he or she has taken the 12 hour course within the preceding three years. Such broker-in-charge shall take the Broker-In-Charge Annual Review Course prescribed in Paragraph (k) of this Rule during the first full license year following the change and each license year thereafter so long as the broker-in-charge remains a resident of North Carolina or continues to manage an office located in North Carolina.

(p) A nonresident commercial real estate broker licensed under the provisions of Section .1800 of this Subchapter shall not act as or serve in the capacity of a broker-in-charge of a firm or office in North Carolina.

21 NCAC 58A .0111   DRAFTING LEGAL INSTRUMENTS

(a) A broker acting as an agent in a real estate transaction shall not draft offers, sales contracts, options, leases, promissory notes, deeds, deeds of trust or other legal instruments by which the rights of others are secured; however, a broker may complete preprinted offers, option contracts, sales contracts or lease forms in a real estate transaction when authorized or directed to do so by the parties.

(b) A broker may use electronic, computer, or word processing equipment to store preprinted offer and sales contract forms which comply with Rule .0112, as well as preprinted option and lease forms, and may use such equipment to complete and print offer, contract and lease documents. Provided, however, a broker shall not alter the preprinted form before it is presented to the parties. If the parties propose to delete or change any word or provision in the form, the form must be marked to indicate the change or deletion made. The language of the form shall not be modified, rewritten, or changed by the broker or their clerical employees unless directed to do so by the parties.

(c) Nothing contained in this Rule shall be construed to prohibit a broker from making written notes, memoranda or correspondence recording the negotiations of the parties to a real estate transaction when such notes, memoranda or correspondence do not themselves constitute binding agreements or other legal instruments.

21 NCAC 58A .0112   OFFERS AND SALES CONTRACTS

(a) A broker acting as an agent in a real estate transaction shall not use a preprinted offer or sales contract form unless the form describes or specifically requires the entry of the following information:

(1) the names of the buyer and seller;
(2) a legal description of the real property sufficient to identify and distinguish it from all other property;

(3) an itemization of any personal property to be included in the transaction;
(4) the purchase price and manner of payment;
(5) any portion of the purchase price that is to be paid by a promissory note, including the amount, interest rate, payment terms, whether or not the note is to be secured, and other material terms;
(6) any portion of the purchase price that is to be paid by the assumption of an existing loan, including the amount of such loan, costs to be paid by the buyer or seller, the interest rate and number of discount points and a condition that the buyer must be able to qualify for the assumption of the loan and must make every reasonable effort to quality for the assumption of the loan;
(7) the amount of earnest money, if any, the method of payment, the name of the broker or firm that will serve as escrow agent, an acknowledgment of earnest money receipt by the escrow agent, and the criteria for determining disposition of the earnest money, including disputed earnest money, consistent with Commission Rule .0107 of this Subchapter;
(8) any loan that must be obtained by the buyer as a condition of the contract, including the amount and type of loan, interest rate and number of discount points, loan term, and who shall pay loan closing costs, and a condition that the buyer shall make every reasonable effort to obtain the loan;
(9) a general statement of the buyer's intended use of the property and a condition that such use must not be prohibited by private restriction or governmental regulation;
(10) the amount and purpose of any special assessment to which the property is subject and the responsibility of the parties for any unpaid charges;
(11) the date for closing and transfer of possession;
(12) the signatures of the buyer and seller;
(13) the date of offer and acceptance;
(14) a provision that title to the property must be delivered at closing by general warranty deed and must be fee simple marketable title, free of all encumbrances except ad valorem taxes for the current year, utility easements, and any other encumbrances specifically approved by the buyer or a provision otherwise describing the estate to be conveyed with encumbrances, and the form of conveyance;
(15) the items to be prorated or adjusted at closing;
(16) who shall pay closing expenses;
(17) the buyer's right to inspect the property prior to closing and who shall pay for repairs and improvements, if any;
(18) a provision that the property shall at closing be in substantially the same condition as on the date of the offer (reasonable wear and tear excepted), or a description of the required property condition at closing; and
(19) a provision setting forth the identity of each real estate agent and firm involved in the transaction and disclosing the party each agent and firm represents.

(b) A broker acting as an agent in a real estate transaction shall not use a preprinted offer or sales contract form containing:
(1) any provision concerning the payment of a commission or compensation, including the forfeiture of earnest money, to any broker or firm; or
(2) any provision that attempts to disclaim the liability of a broker for his or her representations in connection with the transaction.

A broker or anyone acting for or at the direction of the broker shall not insert or cause such provisions or terms to be inserted into any such preprinted form, even at the direction of the parties or their attorneys.

(c) The provisions of this Rule shall apply only to preprinted offer and sales contract forms which a broker acting as an agent in a real estate transaction proposes for use by the buyer and seller. Nothing contained in this Rule shall be construed to prohibit the buyer and seller in a real estate transaction from altering, amending or deleting any provision in a form offer to purchase or contract nor shall this Rule be construed to limit the rights of the buyer and seller to draft their own offers or contracts or to have the same drafted by an attorney at law.

21 NCAC 58A .0113 REPORTING CRIMINAL CONVICTIONS AND DISCIPLINARY ACTIONS

Any broker who is convicted of any felony or misdemeanor, or who is disciplined by any governmental agency in connection with any other occupational license, or whose notarial commission is restricted, suspended, or revoked, shall file with the Commission a written report of such conviction or action within 60 days of the final judgment, order, or disposition in the case. A form for this report is available from the Commission.

21 NCAC 58A .0114   RESIDENTIAL PROPERTY AND OWNERS' ASSOCIATION DISCLOSURE STATEMENT

(a) Every owner of real property subject to a transfer of the type contemplated by Chapter 47E of the General Statutes shall complete the following Residential Property and Owners' Association Disclosure Statement and furnish a copy of the complete statement to a purchaser in accordance with the requirements of G.S. 47E-4. The form shall bear the seal of the North Carolina Real Estate Commission and shall read as follows:

(b) The form described in Paragraph (a) of this Rule may be reproduced, but the form shall not be altered or amended in any way.

(c) The form described in Paragraph (a) of this Rule as amended effective January 1, 2013, applies to all properties placed on the market on or after January 1, 2013. The form described in Paragraph (a) of this Rule as amended effective January 1, 2012, applies to all properties placed on the market prior to January 1, 2013. If a corrected disclosure statement required by G.S. 47E-7 is prepared on or after January 1, 2013, for a property placed on the market prior to January 1, 2013, the form described in Paragraph (a) of this Rule as amended effective January 1, 2013, shall be used.

[N.C. REAL ESTATE COMMISSION SEAL]

STATE OF NORTH CAROLINA
RESIDENTIAL PROPERTY AND OWNERS' ASSOCIATION DISCLOSURE STATEMENT

Instructions to Property Owners

1. The Residential Property Disclosure Act (G.S. 47E) ("Disclosure Act") requires owners of residential real estate (single-family homes, individual condominiums, townhouses, and the like, and buildings with up to four dwelling units) to furnish purchasers a Residential Property and Owners' Association Disclosure Statement ("Disclosure Statement"). This form is the only one approved for this purpose. A disclosure statement must be furnished in connection with the sale, exchange, option and sale under a lease with option to purchase where the tenant does not occupy or intend to occupy the dwelling. A disclosure statement is not required for some transactions, including the first sale of a dwelling which has never been inhabited and transactions of residential property made pursuant to a lease with option to purchase where the lessee occupies or intends to occupy the dwelling. For a complete list of exemptions, see G.S. 47E-2.

2. You must respond to each of the questions on the following pages of this form by filling in the requested information or by placing a check √ in the appropriate box. In responding to questions, you are only obligated to disclose information about which you have actual knowledge.

   a. If you check "Yes" for any question, you must explain your answer and either describe any problem or attach a report from an attorney, engineer, contractor, pest control operator or other expert or public agency describing it. If you attach a report, you will not be liable for any inaccurate or incomplete information contained in it so long as you were not grossly negligent in obtaining or transmitting the information.

   b. If you check "No," you are stating that you have no actual knowledge of any problem. If you check "No" and you know there is a problem, you may be liable for making an intentional misstatement.

   c. If you check "No Representation," you are choosing not to disclose the conditions or characteristics of the property, even if you have actual knowledge of them or should have known of them.

   d. If you check "Yes" or "No" and something happens to the property to make your Disclosure Statement incorrect or inaccurate (for example, the roof begins to leak), you must promptly give the purchaser a corrected Disclosure Statement or correct the problem.

3. If you are assisted in the sale of your property by a licensed real estate broker, you are still responsible for completing and delivering the Disclosure Statement to the purchasers; and the broker must disclose any material facts about your property which he or she knows or reasonably should know, regardless of your responses on the Statement.

4. You must give the completed Disclosure Statement to the purchaser no later than the time the purchaser makes an offer to purchase your property. If you do not, the purchaser can, under certain conditions, cancel any resulting contract (See **"Note to Purchasers"** below). You should give the purchaser a copy of the Disclosure Statement containing your signature and keep a copy signed by the purchaser for your records.

Note to Purchasers

If the owner does not give you a Residential Property and Owners' Association Disclosure Statement by the time you make your offer to purchase the property, you may under certain conditions cancel any resulting contract without penalty to you as the purchaser. To cancel the contract, you must personally deliver or mail written notice of your decision to cancel to the owner or the owner's agent within three calendar days following your receipt of the Disclosure Statement, or three calendar days following the date of the contract, whichever occurs first. However, in no event does the Disclosure Act permit you to cancel a contract after settlement of the transaction or (in the case of a sale or exchange) after you have occupied the property, whichever occurs first.

5. In the space below, type or print in ink the address of the property (sufficient to identify it) and your name. Then sign and date.

> Property Address: _____
> Owner's Name(s): _____
> *Owner(s) acknowledge having examined this Disclosure Statement before signing and that all information is true and correct as of the date signed.*
>
> Owner Signature: _____ Date _____ , ____
> Owner Signature: _____ Date _____ , ____
> *Purchasers acknowledge receipt of a copy of this Disclosure Statement; that they have examined it before signing; that they understand that this is not a warranty by owners or owners' agents; that it is not a substitute for any inspections they may wish to obtain; and that the representations are made by the owners and not the owners' agents or subagents. Purchasers are strongly encouraged to obtain their own inspections from a licensed home inspector or other professional. As used herein, words in the plural include the singular, as appropriate.*
>
> Purchaser Signature: _____ Date _____ , ____
> Purchaser Signature: _____ Date _____ , ____

Property Address/Description: _____

The following questions address the characteristics and condition of the property identified above about which the owner has *actual knowledge*. Where the question refers to "dwelling," it is intended to refer to the dwelling unit, or units if more than one, to be conveyed with the property. The term "dwelling unit" refers to any structure intended for human habitation.

		Yes	No	No Representation
1.	In what year was the dwelling constructed? _____ Explain if necessary: _____			☐
2.	Is there any problem, malfunction or defect with the dwelling's foundation, slab, fireplaces/chimneys, floors, windows (including storm windows and screens), doors, ceilings, interior and exterior walls, attached garage, patio, deck or other structural components including any modifications to them?	☐	☐	☐
3.	The dwelling's exterior walls are made of what type of material? ☐ Brick Veneer ☐ Wood ☐ Stone ☐ Vinyl ☐ Synthetic Stucco ☐ Composition/Hardboard ☐ Concrete ☐ Fiber Cement ☐ Aluminum ☐ Asbestos ☐ Other _____ (Check all that apply)			☐
4.	In what year was the dwelling's roof covering installed? _____ (Approximate if no records are available.) Explain if necessary: _____			☐
5.	Is there any leakage or other problem with the dwelling's roof?	☐	☐	☐
6.	Is there any water seepage, leakage, dampness or standing water in the dwelling's basement, crawl space, or slab?	☐	☐	☐
7.	Is there any problem, malfunction or defect with the dwelling's electrical system (outlets, wiring, panel, switches, fixtures, generator, etc.)?	☐	☐	☐

8. Is there any problem, malfunction or defect with the dwelling's plumbing system (pipes, fixtures, water heater, etc.)? ☐ ☐ ☐

9. Is there any problem, malfunction or defect with the dwelling's heating and/or air conditioning? ☐ ☐ ☐

10. What is the dwelling's heat source? ☐ Furnace ☐ Heat Pump ☐ Baseboard ☐
    ☐ Other_____ (Check all that apply)
    Age of system: _____

11. What is the dwelling's cooling source? ☐ Central Forced Air ☐ Wall/Window Unit(s) ☐
    ☐ Other_____ (Check all that apply)
    Age of system: _____

12. What is the dwelling's fuel sources? ☐ Electricity ☐ Natural Gas ☐ Propane ☐ Oil ☐
    ☐ Other_____ (Check all that apply)
    If the fuel source is stored in a tank, identify whether the tank is ☐ above ground or ☐ below ground, and whether the tank is ☐ leased by seller or ☐ owned by seller.
    (Check all that apply)

13. What is the dwelling's water supply source? ☐ City/County ☐ Community System ☐
    ☐ Private Well ☐ Shared Well ☐ Other_____(Check all that apply)

14. The dwelling's water pipes are made of what type of material? ☐ Copper ☐ Galvanized ☐
    ☐ Plastic ☐ Polybutylene ☐ Other_____(Check all that apply)

15. Is there any problem, malfunction or defect with the dwelling's water supply (including water quality, quantity or water pressure)? ☐ ☐ ☐

16. What is the dwelling's sewage disposal system? ☐ Septic Tank ☐ Septic Tank with Pump ☐
    ☐ Community System ☐ Connected to City/County System ☐ City/County System available ☐ Straight pipe (wastewater does not go into a septic or other sewer system [note: use of this type of system violates State law])
    ☐ Other_____(Check all that apply)

17. If the dwelling is serviced by a septic system, do you know how many bedrooms are allowed by the septic system permit? If your answer is "Yes," how many bedrooms are allowed? _____ ☐ ☐ ☐
    ☐ No records available.

18. Is there any problem, malfunction or defect with the dwelling's sewer and/or septic system? ☐ ☐ ☐

19. Is there any problem, malfunction or defect with the dwelling's central vacuum, pool, hot tub, spa, attic fan, exhaust fan, ceiling fans, sump pump, irrigation system, TV cable wiring or satellite dish, garage door openers, gas logs, or other systems? ☐ ☐ ☐

20. Is there any problem, malfunction or defect with any appliances that may be included in the conveyance (range/oven, attached microwave, hood/fan, dishwasher, disposal, etc.)? ☐ ☐ ☐

21. Is there any problem with present infestation of the dwelling, or damage from past infestation of wood destroying insects or organisms which has not been repaired? ☐ ☐ ☐

22. Is there any problem, malfunction or defect with the drainage, grading or soil stability of the property? ☐ ☐ ☐

23. Are there any structural additions or other structural or mechanical changes to the dwelling(s) to be conveyed with the property? ☐ ☐ ☐

24. Have you been notified by a governmental agency that the property is in violation of any local zoning ordinances, restrictive covenants, or other land-use restrictions, or building codes (including the failure to obtain proper permits for room additions or other changes/improvements)? ☐ ☐ ☐

25. Are there any hazardous or toxic substances, materials, or products (such as asbestos, formaldehyde, radon gas, methane gas, lead-based paint) which exceed government safety standards, any debris (whether buried or covered) or underground storage tanks, or any environmentally hazardous conditions (such as contaminated soil or water, or other environmental contamination) which affect the property? ☐ ☐ ☐

26. Is there any noise, odor, smoke, etc. from commercial, industrial or military sources which affects the property? ☐ ☐ ☐

27. Is the property subject to any utility or other easements, shared driveways, party walls or encroachments from or on adjacent property? ☐ ☐ ☐

28. Is the property subject to any lawsuits, foreclosures, bankruptcy, leases or rental agreements, judgments, tax liens, proposed assessments, mechanics' liens, materialmens' liens, or notices from any governmental agency that could affect title to the property? ☐ ☐ ☐

29. Is the property subject to a flood hazard or is the property located in a federally-designated flood hazard area? ☐ ☐ ☐

30. Does the property abut or adjoin any private road(s) or street(s)? ☐ ☐ ☐

31. If there is a private road or street adjoining the property, is there in existence any owners' association or maintenance agreements dealing with the maintenance of the road or street? ☐ ☐ ☐

If you answered "yes" to any of the questions listed above (1-31) please explain (attach additional sheets if necessary):
_____
_____
_____

In lieu of providing a written explanation, you may attach a written report to this Disclosure Statement by a public agency, or by an attorney, engineer, land surveyor, geologist, pest control operator, contractor, home inspector, or other expert, dealing with matters within the scope of that public agency's functions or the expert's license or expertise.

The following questions pertain to the property identified above, including the lot to be conveyed and any dwelling unit(s), sheds, detached garages, or other buildings located thereon.

| | Yes | No | No Representation |

32. To your knowledge, is the property subject to regulation by one or more owners' association(s) or governing documents which impose various mandatory covenants, conditions, and restrictions upon the lot, including, but not limited to obligations to pay regular assessment or dues and special assessments? If your answer is "yes," please provide the information requested below as to each owners' association to which the property is subject [insert N/A into any blank that does not apply]:
(specify name) _____ whose regular

assessments ("dues") are $ _____ per _____. The name, address and telephone number of the president of the owners' association or the association manager are

_____
_____

_____
(specify name) _____ whose regular assessments ("dues") are $ _____ per _____. The name, address and telephone number of the president of the owners' association or the association manager are

_____
_____
_____

* If you answered "Yes" to question 32 above, you must complete the remainder of this Disclosure Statement. If you answered "No" or "No Representation" to question 32 above, you do not need to answer the remaining questions on this Disclosure Statement. Skip to the bottom of the last page and initial and date the page.

	Yes	No	No Representation

33. Are any fees charged by the association or by the association's management company in connection with the conveyance or transfer of the lot or property to a new owner? If your answer is "yes," please state the amount of the fees: ☐ ☐ ☐
_____
_____

34. As of the date this Disclosure Statement is signed, are there any dues, fees or special assessment which have been duly approved as required by the applicable declaration or by-laws, and that are payable to an association to which the lot is subject? If your answer is "yes," please state the nature and amount of the dues, fees or special assessments to which the property is subject: ☐ ☐ ☐
_____
_____
_____

35. As of the date this Disclosure Statement is signed, are there any unsatisfied judgments against or pending lawsuits *involving the property or lot to be conveyed*? If your answer is "yes," please state the nature of each pending lawsuit and the amount of each unsatisfied judgment: ☐ ☐ ☐
_____
_____
_____

36. As of the date this Disclosure Statement is signed, are there any unsatisfied judgments against or pending lawsuits *involving the planned community or the association to which the property and lot are subject*, with the exception of any action filed by the association for the collection of delinquent assessments on lots other than the property and lot to be conveyed? If your answer is "yes," please state the nature of each pending lawsuit and the amount of each unsatisfied judgment: ☐ ☐ ☐
_____
_____
_____

37. Which of the following services and amenities are paid for by the owners' association(s) identified above out of the association's regular assessments ("dues")? (Check all that apply.)

	Yes	No	No Representation
Management Fees	☐	☐	☐
Exterior Building Maintenance of Property to be Conveyed	☐	☐	☐
Exterior Yard/Landscaping Maintenance of Lot to be Conveyed	☐	☐	☐
Common Areas Maintenance	☐	☐	☐
Trash Removal	☐	☐	☐
Recreational Amenity Maintenance (specify amenities covered)_____	☐	☐	☐
Pest Treatment/Extermination	☐	☐	☐
Street Lights	☐	☐	☐
Water	☐	☐	☐
Sewer	☐	☐	☐
Storm Water Management/Drainage/Ponds	☐	☐	☐
Internet Service	☐	☐	☐
Cable	☐	☐	☐
Private Road Maintenance	☐	☐	☐
Parking Area Maintenance	☐	☐	☐
Gate and/or Security	☐	☐	☐
Other: (specify)_____	☐	☐	☐

Owner Initials and Date _____   Owner Initials and Date _____

Purchaser Initials and Date _____   Purchaser Initials and Date _____

21 NCAC 58A .0115   DISCLOSURE OF OFFERS PROHIBITED
A broker shall not disclose the price or other material terms contained in a party's offer to purchase, sell, lease, rent, or to option real property to a competing party without the express authority of the offering party.

21 NCAC 58A .0116   HANDLING OF TRUST MONEY
(a) Except as provided in Paragraph (b) of this Rule, all monies received by a broker acting in his or her fiduciary capacity (hereinafter "trust money") shall be deposited in a trust or escrow account as defined in Rule .0117(b) of this Section no later than three banking days following the broker's receipt of such monies.
(b) Exceptions to the requirements of Paragraph (a):
- (1) All monies received by a provisional broker shall be delivered upon receipt to the broker with whom he or she is affiliated.
- (2) All monies received by a non-resident commercial broker shall be delivered as required by Rule .1808 of this Subchapter.
- (3) Earnest money or tenant security deposits paid by means other than currency and received by a broker in connection with a pending offer to purchase or lease shall be deposited in a trust or escrow account no later than three days following acceptance of such offer to purchase or lease; the date of such acceptance of such offer or lease shall be set forth in the purchase or lease agreement.
- (4) A broker may accept custody of a check or other negotiable instrument made payable to the seller of real property as payment for an option or due diligence fee, but only for the purpose of delivering the instrument to the seller. While the instrument is in the custody of the broker, the broker shall, according to the instructions of the buyer, either deliver it to the seller or return it to the buyer. The broker shall safeguard the instrument and be responsible to the parties on the instrument for its safe delivery as required by this Rule. A broker shall not retain such an instrument for more than three business days after the acceptance of the option or other sales contract.

(c) Prior to depositing trust money into a trust or escrow account that bears interest, the broker having custody over such money shall first secure written authorization from all parties having an interest in the money. Such authorization shall specify and set forth in a conspicuous manner how and to whom the interest shall be disbursed.
(d) In the event of a dispute between buyer and seller or landlord and tenant over the return or forfeiture of any deposit other than a residential tenant security deposit held by the broker, the broker shall retain the deposit in a trust or escrow account until the broker has obtained a written release from the parties consenting to its disposition or until disbursement is ordered by a court of competent jurisdiction. Alternatively, the broker may deposit the disputed monies with the appropriate Clerk of Superior Court in accordance with the provisions of G.S. 93A-12. If it appears that one of the parties has abandoned his or her claim to the funds, the broker may disburse the money to the other claimant according to the written agreement. Before doing so, however, the broker must first make a reasonable effort to notify the absent party and provide that party with an opportunity to renew his or her claim to the funds. Tenant security deposits shall be disposed of in accordance with G.S. 42-50 through 56 and G.S. 42A-18.
(e) A broker may transfer an earnest money deposit from his or her trust or escrow account to the closing attorney or other settlement agent no more than 10 days prior to the anticipated settlement date. A broker shall not disburse prior to settlement any earnest money in his or her possession for any other purpose without the written consent of the parties.
(f) A broker shall not disburse trust money to or on behalf of a client in an amount exceeding the balance of trust money belonging to the client and held in the trust account.
(g) Every broker shall safeguard any money or property of others which comes into the broker's possession in a manner consistent with the Real Estate License Law and Commission Rules. A broker shall not convert the money or property of others to his or her own use, apply such money or property to a purpose other than for which it was intended or permit or assist any other person in the conversion or misapplication of such money or property.

21 NCAC 58A .0117   ACCOUNTING FOR TRUST MONEY
(a) A broker shall create, maintain and retain records sufficient to identify the ownership of all funds belonging to others. Such records shall be sufficient to show proper deposit and disbursement of such funds into and from a trust or escrow account and to verify the accuracy and proper use of the trust or escrow account.
(b) A trust or escrow account shall satisfy the requirements of G.S. 93A-6(g) and shall be designated as a "Trust Account" or "Escrow Account." All bank statements, deposit tickets and checks drawn on said account shall bear the words "Trust Account" or "Escrow Account." A trust account shall provide for the full withdrawal of funds on demand without prior notice and without penalty or deduction to the funds.
(c) A broker shall create, maintain or retain the following records:

(1) bank statements;

(2) canceled checks and other evidence or memoranda of payments from the trust or escrow account, whether by transfer between accounts, wire payments, or payments by electronic means, which shall be referenced to the corresponding journal entry or check stub entries and to the corresponding sales transaction ledgers or for rental transactions, the corresponding property or owner ledgers. Checks and other evidence or memoranda of payments from the account shall identify the payee by name and shall bear a notation identifying the purpose of the disbursement. When a payment is used to disburse funds for more than one sales transaction, owner, or property, the check or other evidence or memoranda of payment shall bear a notation identifying each sales transaction, owner, or property for which disbursement is made, including the amount disbursed for each, and the corresponding sales transaction, property, or owner ledger entries. When necessary, the check notation may refer to the required information recorded on a supplemental disbursement worksheet which shall be cross-referenced to the corresponding check or payment. In lieu of retaining canceled checks, a broker may retain digitally imaged copies of the canceled checks or substitute checks provided that such images are legible reproductions of the front and back of such instruments with no smaller images than 1.1875 x 3.0 inches and provided that the broker's bank retains for a period of at least five years the original checks, "substitute checks" as described in 12 C.F.R. 229.51 or the capacity to provide substitute checks as described in 12 C.F.R. 229.51 and makes the original or substitute checks available to the broker and the Commission upon request;

(3) deposit tickets or other evidence or memoranda of deposits or payments into the account, whether by transfer between accounts, wire payments, or payments by electronic means:

    (A) for a sales transaction, the deposit ticket or other evidence or memoranda of deposits or payments into the account shall identify the purpose and remitter of the funds deposited, the property, the parties involved, and a reference to the corresponding sales transaction ledger;

    (B) for a rental transaction, the deposit ticket or other evidence or memoranda of deposits or payments into the account shall identify the purpose and remitter of the funds deposited, the tenant, and the corresponding property or owner ledger;

    (C) for deposits of funds belonging to or collected on behalf of a property owner association, the deposit ticket or other evidence or memoranda of deposits or payments into the account shall identify the property or property interest for which the payment is made, the property or interest owner, the remitter, and the purpose of the payment;

    (D) when a single deposit ticket or payment is used to deposit funds collected for more than one sales transaction, property owner, or property, the required information shall be recorded on the ticket or other evidence or memoranda of deposits or payments into the account for each sales transaction, owner, or property, or it may refer to the same information recorded on a supplemental deposit worksheet which shall be cross-referenced to the corresponding deposit ticket;

(4) a separate ledger for each sales transaction, for each property or owner of property managed by the broker and for company funds held in the trust account:

    (A) the ledger for a sales transaction shall identify the property, the parties to the transaction, the amount, date, and purpose of the deposits and from whom received, the amount, date, check number, and purpose of disbursements and to whom paid, and the running balance of funds on deposit for each deposit and disbursement entry;

    (B) the ledger for a rental transaction shall identify the particular property or owner of property, the tenant, the amount, date, and purpose of the deposits and from whom received, the amount, date, check number, and purpose of disbursements and to whom paid, and the running balance of funds on deposit for each deposit and disbursement entry. Monies held as tenant security deposits in connection with rental transactions may be accounted for on a separate tenant security deposit ledger for each property or owner of property managed by the broker. For each security deposit the tenant security deposit ledger shall identify the remitter, the date the deposit was paid, the amount, the tenant, landlord, and subject property as well as the check number, amount, date, payee, purpose and a running balance for each disbursement. When tenant security deposit monies are accounted for on a separate ledger as provided in this Rule, deposit tickets, canceled checks and supplemental worksheets shall reference the corresponding tenant security deposit ledger entries;

- (C) a broker may maintain a maximum of one hundred dollars ($100.00) in company funds in a trust account for the purpose of paying service charges incurred by the account. In the event that the services charges exceed one hundred dollars ($100.00) monthly, the broker may deposit an amount each month sufficient to cover the service charges. A broker shall maintain a separate ledger for company funds held in the trust account identifying the date, amount and running balance for each deposit and disbursement;
- (5) a general journal, check register or check stubs identifying in chronological order each bank deposit and disbursement of monies to and from the trust or escrow account, including the amount and date of each deposit and a reference to the corresponding deposit ticket and any supplemental deposit worksheet, and the amount, date, check number, and purpose of disbursements and to whom paid. The journal or check stubs shall also show a running balance for each entry into the account;
- (6) a payment record for each property or interest for which funds are collected and deposited into a property owner association trust account as required by Rule .0118 of this Section. Payment record(s) shall identify the amount, date, remitter, and purpose of payments received, the amount and nature of the obligation for which payments are made, and the amount of any balance due or delinquency;
- (7) copies of earnest money checks, due diligence fee checks, receipts for cash payments, contracts, and closing statements in sales transactions;
- (8) copies of leases, security deposit checks, property management agreements, property management statements, and receipts for cash payments in leasing transactions;
- (9) copies of covenants, bylaws, minutes, management agreements and periodic statements relating to the management of property owner associations;
- (10) copies of invoices, bills, and contracts paid from the trust account; and
- (11) copies of any documents not otherwise described in this Rule necessary and sufficient to verify and explain record entries.

(d) Records of all receipts and disbursements of trust or escrow monies shall be maintained in such a manner as to create an audit trail from deposit tickets and canceled checks to check stubs or journals and to the ledger sheets.

(e) Brokers shall reconcile their trust or escrow accounts monthly. The trust account reconciliation shall be performed in the following manner as of a specific cutoff date selected by the broker:
- (1) a trial balance shall be prepared showing a list of the property or owner ledgers, their balances, and the total of all of the property or owner ledger balances as of the cutoff date;
- (2) a bank statement shall be reconciled by deducting from the statement's ending balance the amount of any outstanding checks and then adding to the balance the amount of any deposits-in-transit as of the cutoff date; and
- (3) the trial balance, reconciled bank statement balance, and the journal balance shall be compared as of the cutoff date. If the amounts on the trial balance, journal balance and reconciled bank balance do not agree, the broker shall investigate the reason for any variation between the balances and make the necessary corrections to bring the balances into agreement.

A broker shall maintain and retain a worksheet for each monthly trust account reconciliation showing the balance of the journal or check stubs, the trial balance and the reconciled bank statement balance to be in agreement as of the cutoff date.

(f) In addition to the records required by Paragraph (d) of this Rule, a broker acting as agent for the landlord of a residential property used for vacation rentals shall create and maintain a subsidiary ledger sheet for each property or owner of such properties on which all funds collected and disbursed are identified in categories by purpose. On a monthly basis, the broker shall reconcile the subsidiary ledgers to the corresponding property or property owner ledger. In lieu of maintaining a subsidiary ledger, the broker may maintain an accounts payable ledger for each owner or property and each vendor to whom trust monies are due for monies collected on behalf of the owner or property identifying the date of receipt of the trust monies, from whom the monies were received, rental dates, and the corresponding property or owner ledger entry including the amount to be disbursed for each and the purpose of the disbursement. The broker may also maintain an accounts payable ledger in the format described above for vacation rental tenant security deposit monies and vacation rental advance payments.

(g) Upon the written request of a client, a broker shall promptly, but in no event later than ten days after receipt of the request, furnish the client with copies of any records retained as required by Rule 21 NCAC 58A .0108 that pertain to the transaction to which the client was a party.

(h) All trust or escrow account records shall be made available for inspection by the Commission or its authorized representatives in accordance with Rule 21 NCAC 58A .0108.

21 NCAC 58A .0118   TRUST MONEY BELONGING TO PROPERTY OWNERS' ASSOCIATIONS
(a) The funds of a property owners' association, when collected, maintained, disbursed or otherwise controlled by a broker, are trust money and shall be treated as such in the manner required by this Rule. Such trust money must be deposited into and maintained in a trust or escrow account dedicated exclusively for trust money belonging to a single property owners' association and may not be commingled with funds belonging to other property owners' associations or other persons or parties. A broker who undertakes to act as manager of a property owners' association or as the custodian of trust money belonging to a property owners' association shall provide the association with periodic statements which report the balance of association trust money in the broker's possession or control and which account for the trust money the broker has received and disbursed on behalf of the association. Such statements must be made in accordance with the broker's agreement with the association, but not less frequently than every 90 days.
(b) A broker who receives trust money belonging to a property owners' association in his or her capacity as an officer of the association in a residential development in which the broker is a property owner and for which the broker receives no compensation is exempt from the requirements of Rule .0116 of this Section except that said broker shall not convert trust money belonging to the association to his or her own use, apply such money or property to a purpose other than that for which it was intended or permit or assist any other person in the conversion or misapplication of such money or property.

SECTION .0200 - GENERAL PROVISIONS (REPEALED)

SECTION .0300 – APPLICATION FOR LICENSE (SECTION OMITTED)

SECTION .0400 - EXAMINATIONS

SECTION .0500 - LICENSING

21 NCAC 58A .0501   CHARACTER (REPEALED)

21 NCAC 58A .0502   BUSINESS ENTITIES
(a) Every business entity other than a sole proprietorship shall apply for and obtain from the Commission a firm license prior to engaging in business as a real estate broker. An entity that changes its business form other than by conversion shall submit a new license application immediately upon making the change and obtain a new firm license. An entity which converts to a different business entity in conformity with and pursuant to applicable North Carolina General Statutes is not required to apply for a new license. However, such converted entity shall provide the information required by this Paragraph in writing to the Commission within 10 days of said conversion and shall include the applicable fee to have the firm license reissued in the legal name of the converted entity. Incomplete applications shall not be acted upon by the Commission. Application forms for partnerships, corporations, limited liability companies, associations and other business entities required to be licensed as brokers shall be available upon request to the Commission and shall require the applicant to set forth:
    (1)   the name of the entity;
    (2)   the name under which the entity will do business;
    (3)   the type of business entity;
    (4)   the address of its principal office;
    (5)   the entity's NC Secretary of State Identification Number if required to be registered with the Office of the NC Secretary of State;
    (6)   the name, real estate license number and signature of the proposed qualifying broker for the proposed firm;
    (7)   the address of and name of the proposed broker-in-charge for each office as defined in Rule .0110(b) of this Subchapter, along with a completed broker-in-charge declaration form for each proposed broker-in-charge;
    (8)   any past criminal conviction of and any pending criminal charge against any principal in the company or any proposed broker-in-charge;
    (9)   any past revocation, suspension or denial of a business or professional license of any principal in the company or any proposed broker-in-charge;

(10) if a general partnership, a full description of the applicant entity, including a copy of its written partnership agreement or if no written agreement exists, a written description of the rights and duties of the several partners;

(11) if a business entity other than a corporation, limited liability company or partnership, a full description of the organization of the applicant entity, including a copy of its organizational documents evidencing its authority to engage in real estate brokerage;

(12) if a foreign business entity, a certificate of authority to transact business in North Carolina and an executed consent to service of process and pleadings; and

(13) any other information required by this Rule.

When the authority of a business entity to engage in the real estate business is unclear in the application or in law, the Commission shall require the applicant to declare in the license application that the applicant's organizational documents authorize the firm to engage in the real estate business and to submit organizational documents, addresses of affiliated persons and similar information. For purposes of this Rule, the term principal, when it refers to a person or entity, means any person or entity owning 10 percent or more of the business entity, or who is an officer, director, manager, member, partner or who holds any other comparable position.

(b) After filing a written application with the Commission and upon a showing that at least one principal of the business entity holds a broker license on active status and in good standing and will serve as qualifying broker of the entity, the entity shall be licensed provided it appears that the applicant entity employs and is directed by personnel possessed of the requisite truthfulness, honesty, and integrity. The qualifying broker of a partnership of any kind must be a general partner of the partnership; the qualifying broker of a limited liability company must be a manager of the company; and the qualifying broker of a corporation must be an officer of the corporation. A licensed business entity may serve as the qualifying broker of another licensed business entity if the qualifying broker-entity has as its qualifying broker a natural person who is licensed as a broker. The natural person who is qualifying broker shall assure the performance of the qualifying broker's duties with regard to both entities. A provisional broker may not serve as a qualifying broker.

(c) The licensing of a business entity shall not be construed to extend to the licensing of its partners, managers, members, directors, officers, employees or other persons acting for the entity in their individual capacities regardless of whether they are engaged in furthering the business of the licensed entity.

(d) The qualifying broker of a business entity shall assume responsibility for:

(1) designating and assuring that there is at all times a broker-in-charge for each office and branch office of the entity as office and branch office are defined in Rule .0110(b) of this Subchapter;

(2) renewing the real estate broker license of the entity;

(3) retaining the firm's renewal pocket card at the firm and producing it as proof of firm licensure upon request and maintaining a photocopy of the firm license certificate and pocket card at each branch office thereof;

(4) notifying the Commission of any change of business address or trade name of the entity and the registration of any assumed business name adopted by the entity for its use;

(5) notifying the Commission in writing of any change of his or her status as qualifying broker within ten days following the change;

(6) securing and preserving the transaction and trust account records of the firm whenever there is a change of broker-in-charge at the firm or any office thereof and notifying the Commission if the trust account records are out of balance or have not been reconciled as required by Rule .0107 of this Subchapter;

(7) retaining and preserving the transaction and trust account records of the firm upon termination of his or her status as qualifying broker until a new qualifying broker has been designated with the Commission or, if no new qualifying broker is designated, for the period of time for which said records are required to be retained by Rule .0108 of this Subchapter; and

(8) notifying the Commission if, upon the termination of his or her status as qualifying broker, the firm's transaction and trust account records cannot be retained or preserved or if the trust account records are out of balance or have not been reconciled as required by Rule .0107(e) of this Subchapter.

(e) Every licensed business entity and every entity applying for licensure shall conform to all the requirements imposed upon it by the North Carolina General Statutes for its continued existence and authority to do business in North Carolina. Failure to conform to such requirements is grounds for disciplinary action or denial of the entity's application for licensure. Upon receipt of notice from an entity or agency of this state that a licensed entity has ceased to exist or that its authority to engage in business in this state has been terminated by operation of law, the Commission shall cancel the license of the entity.

21 NCAC 58A .0503   LICENSE RENEWAL; PENALTY FOR OPERATING WHILE LICENSE EXPIRED

(a) All real estate licenses issued by the Commission under G.S. 93A, Article 1 shall expire on the 30th day of June following issuance. Any broker desiring renewal of a license shall apply for renewal within 45 days prior to license expiration by submitting a renewal application on a form prescribed by the Commission and submitting with the application the required renewal fee of forty-five dollars ($45.00).

(b) Any person desiring to renew his or her license on active status shall, upon the second renewal of such license following initial licensure, and upon each subsequent renewal, have obtained all continuing education required by G.S. 93A-4.1 and Rule .1702 of this Subchapter.

(c) A person renewing a license on inactive status shall not be required to have obtained any continuing education in order to renew such license; however, in order to subsequently change his or her license from inactive status to active status, the broker must satisfy the continuing education requirement prescribed in Rule .1703 or .1711 of this Subchapter.

(d) Any person or firm that engages in the business of a real estate broker while his, her, or its license is expired is subject to the penalties prescribed in G.S. 93A-6.

21 NCAC 58A .0504   ACTIVE AND INACTIVE LICENSE STATUS

(a) Except for licenses that have expired or that have been revoked, suspended or surrendered, all licenses issued by the Commission shall be designated as being either on active status or inactive status. Subject to compliance with Rule .0110 of this Subchapter, the holder of a license on active status may engage in any activity requiring a real estate license and may be compensated for the provision of any lawful real estate brokerage service. The holder of a license on inactive status shall not engage in any activity requiring a real estate license, including the referral for compensation of a prospective seller, buyer, landlord or tenant to another real estate broker or any other party. A broker holding a license on inactive status must renew the license and pay the prescribed license renewal fee in order to continue to hold the license. The Commission may take disciplinary action against a broker holding a license on inactive status for any violation of G.S. 93A or any rule adopted by the Commission, including the offense of engaging in an activity for which a license is required.

(b) A license issued to a provisional broker shall, upon initial licensure, be assigned to inactive status. A license issued to a firm or a broker other than a provisional broker shall be assigned to active status. Except for persons licensed under the provisions of Section .1800 of this Subchapter, a broker may change the status of his or her license from active to inactive status by submitting a written request to the Commission. A provisional broker's license shall be assigned by the Commission to inactive status when the provisional broker is not under the active, direct supervision of a broker-in-charge. A firm's license shall be assigned by the Commission to inactive status when the firm does not have a qualifying broker with an active license. Except for persons licensed under the provisions of Section .1800 of this Subchapter, a broker shall also be assigned to inactive status if, upon the second renewal of his or her license following initial licensure, or upon any subsequent renewal, he or she has not satisfied the continuing education requirement described in Rule .1702 of this Subchapter.

(c) A provisional broker with an inactive license who desires to have the license placed on active status must comply with the procedures prescribed in Rule .0506 of this Section.

(d) A broker, other than a provisional broker, with an inactive license who desires to have the license placed on active status shall file with the Commission a request for license activation on a form provided by the Commission containing identifying information about the broker, a statement that the broker has satisfied the continuing education requirements prescribed by Rule .1703 of this Subchapter, the name and address of any broker-in-charge, the date of the request, and the signature of the broker. Upon the mailing or delivery of this form, the broker's status will be considered to be active. If the broker is eligible for license activation, the Commission shall send a written acknowledgement of the license activation to the broker and his or her affiliated broker-in-charge, if any. If neither the broker nor his or her affiliated broker-in-charge receive from the Commission a written acknowledgment of the license activation within 30 days of the date shown on the form, the broker shall immediately terminate his or her real estate brokerage activities pending receipt of the written acknowledgment from the Commission. If either the broker or his or her affiliated broker-in-charge, if any, is notified that he or she is not eligible for license activation due to a continuing education deficiency, the broker shall terminate all real estate brokerage activities until such time as the continuing education deficiency is satisfied and a new request for license activation is submitted to the Commission.

(e) Upon an active, non-provisional broker's affiliation with a firm and broker-in-charge, the broker-in-charge of the office where the broker will be engaged in the real estate business shall notify the Commission of the affiliation on a form provided by the Commission containing identifying information about the affiliating broker and the broker-in-charge, and the signature of the broker-in-charge. If neither the broker nor the broker-in-charge receive from the Commission a written acknowledgment of the license affiliation within 30 days of the date shown on the form, the broker and his or her broker-in-charge shall cease representing the broker as being affiliated with such broker-in-charge pending receipt of the written acknowledgment from the Commission.

(f) A firm with an inactive license which desires to have its license placed on active status shall file with the Commission a request for license activation containing identifying information about the firm and its qualifying broker and satisfy the requirements of Rule .0110 of this Subchapter. If the qualifying broker has an inactive license, he or she must satisfy the requirements of Paragraph (d) of this Rule. Upon the mailing or delivery of the completed form by the qualifying broker, the firm may engage in real estate brokerage activities requiring a license; however, if the firm's qualifying broker does not receive from the Commission a written acknowledgment of the license activation within 30 days of the date shown on the form, the firm shall immediately terminate its real estate brokerage activities pending receipt of the written acknowledgment from the Commission. If the qualifying broker is notified that the firm is not eligible for license activation due to a continuing education deficiency on the part of the qualifying broker, the firm must terminate all real estate brokerage activities until such time as the continuing education deficiency is satisfied and a new request for license activation is submitted to the Commission.

(g) A person licensed as a broker under Section .1800 of this Subchapter shall maintain his or her license on active status at all times as required by Rule .1804 of this Subchapter.

21 NCAC 58A .0505   REINSTATEMENT OF EXPIRED LICENSE, REVOKED, SURRENDERED OR SUSPENDED LICENSE

(a) Licenses expired for not more than six months may be reinstated upon the submission of payment of a fifty-five dollar ($55.00) reinstatement fee. In order to reinstate the license on active status, the person requesting reinstatement shall have obtained the continuing education as is required by Rule .1703 of this Subchapter to change an inactive license to active status. A person reinstating a license on inactive status is not required to have obtained any continuing education in order to reinstate the license; however, in order to subsequently change his or her reinstated license from inactive status to active status, the licensee must satisfy the continuing education requirement prescribed in Rule .1703 of this Subchapter, and be supervised by a broker-in-charge in compliance with the requirements of Rule .0506 of this Section.

(b) Reinstatement of licenses expired for more than six months shall be considered upon the submission of a complete and accurate application and payment of a fifty-five dollar ($55.00) reinstatement fee. Applicants must satisfy the Commission that they possess the current knowledge, skills and competence, as well as the truthfulness, honesty and integrity, necessary to function in the real estate business in a manner that protects and serves the public interest. To demonstrate knowledge, skills and competence, the Commission may require the applicants to complete real estate education or pass the license examination or both.

(c) Reinstatement of a revoked license shall be considered upon the submission of a complete and accurate application and payment of a thirty dollar ($30.00) fee. Applicants must satisfy the same requirements as those prescribed in Paragraph (b) of this Rule for reinstatement of licenses expired for more than six months.

(d) Reinstatement of a license surrendered under the provisions of G.S. 93A-6(e) shall be considered upon termination of the period of surrender specified in the order approving the surrender and upon the submission of a complete and accurate application and payment of a thirty dollar ($30.00) fee. Applicants must satisfy the same requirements as those prescribed in Paragraph (b) of this Rule for reinstatement of licenses expired for more than six months.

(e) When a license is suspended by the Commission, the suspended license shall be restored at the end of the period of active suspension provided that any applicable license renewal fees that accrued during the time of the suspension are paid by the licensee within 60 days from the end of the period of license suspension. In order for the license to be restored on active status, the licensee shall demonstrate that the licensee has satisfied the continuing education requirement for license activation prescribed by Rule .1703 of this Subchapter and that the licensee is supervised by a broker-in-charge in compliance with the requirements of Rule .0506 of this Section, if applicable. Failure to pay the accrued license renewal fees within the time set forth in this Paragraph shall result in expiration of the license effective the last day of the suspension period. A former licensee whose license expires under this Paragraph and who thereafter seeks reinstatement must satisfy the same requirements as those prescribed in Paragraph (b) of this Rule for reinstatement of licenses expired for more than six months.

(f) Whenever a license is reinstated by the Commission following expiration for more than six months, revocation, or voluntary surrender, the date of licensure for the licensee shall be the date of reinstatement and not the date of original licensure.

21 NCAC 58A .0506   PROVISIONAL BROKER TO BE SUPERVISED BY BROKER
(a) This Rule shall apply to all real estate provisional brokers.
(b) A provisional broker may engage in or hold himself or herself out as engaging in activities requiring a real estate license only while his or her license is on active status and he or she is supervised by the broker-in-charge of the real estate firm or office with which the provisional broker is affiliated. A provisional broker may be supervised by only one broker-in-charge at a time.
(c) Upon a provisional broker's affiliation with a real estate broker or brokerage firm, the broker-in-charge of the office where the provisional broker will be engaged in the real estate business shall immediately file with the Commission a provisional broker supervision notification on a form provided by the Commission containing identifying information about the provisional broker and the broker-in-charge, a statement from the broker-in-charge certifying that he or she will supervise the provisional broker in the performance of all acts for which a license is required, the date that the broker-in-charge assumes responsibility for such supervision, and the signature of the broker-in-charge. If the provisional broker is on inactive status at the time of associating with a broker or brokerage firm, the broker-in-charge shall also file, along with the provisional broker supervision notification, a request for license activation on a form provided by the Commission containing identifying information about the provisional broker, the statement of the broker-in-charge that he or she has verified that the provisional broker has satisfied the continuing education requirements prescribed by Rule .1703 of this Subchapter, and the postlicensing education requirements, if applicable, prescribed by Rule .1902 of this Subchapter, the date of the request, and the signature of the proposed broker-in-charge. Upon the mailing or delivery of the required form(s), the provisional broker may engage in real estate brokerage activities requiring a license under the supervision of the broker-in-charge; however, if the provisional broker and broker-in-charge do not receive from the Commission a written acknowledgment of the provisional broker supervision notification and, if appropriate, the request for license activation, within 30 days of the date shown on the form, the broker-in-charge shall immediately terminate the provisional broker's real estate brokerage activities pending receipt of the written acknowledgment from the Commission. If the provisional broker and broker-in-charge are notified that the provisional broker is not eligible for license activation due to a continuing education or postlicensing education deficiency, the broker-in-charge shall cause the provisional broker to immediately cease all activities requiring a real estate license until such time as the continuing education or postlicensing education deficiency is satisfied and a new provisional broker supervision notification and request for license activation is submitted to the Commission.
(d) A broker-in-charge who certifies to the Commission that he or she will supervise a provisional broker shall actively and directly supervise the provisional broker in a manner that reasonably assures that the provisional broker performs all acts for which a real estate license is required in accordance with the Real Estate License Law and Commission rules. A supervising broker who fails to supervise a provisional broker as prescribed in this Rule may be subject to disciplinary action by the Commission.
(e) Upon the termination of the supervisory relationship between a provisional broker and his or her broker-in-charge, the provisional broker and the broker-in-charge shall provide written notification of the date of termination to the Commission not later than 10 days following said termination.

21 NCAC 58A .0507   PAYMENT OF FEES
Checks, credit cards, and other forms of payment given the Commission for fees due which are returned unpaid shall be considered cause for license denial, suspension, or revocation.

21 NCAC 58A .0508   DUPLICATE LICENSE FEE (REPEALED)

21 NCAC 58A .0509   DUPLICATE LICENSE FEE
A licensee may, by filing a prescribed form and paying a five dollar ($5.00) fee to the Commission, obtain a duplicate real estate license or pocket card to replace an original license or pocket card which has been lost, damaged or destroyed or if the name of the licensee has been lawfully changed.

21 NCAC 58A .0510   CANCELLATION OF SALESPERSON LICENSE UPON BROKER LICENSURE (REPEALED)

21 NCAC 58A .0511   LICENSING OF PERSONS LICENSED IN ANOTHER JURISDICTION
(a) Persons applying for a North Carolina broker license who hold a current real estate license that has been on active status within the previous three years in another state of the United States, a United States territory or possession or a Canadian jurisdiction shall meet the licensing requirements prescribed in G.S. 93A-4 except that such persons shall be

exempt from the "national" section of the North Carolina real estate license examination, but shall pass the "state" section of that examination. A person qualifying for licensure under this provision shall be issued a North Carolina broker license on a status comparable to the category of license held by the person in the jurisdiction where the qualifying license is held.

(b) Brokers who were licensed in North Carolina by reciprocity shall be entitled to retain such license indefinitely, unless suspended, revoked or surrendered pursuant to G.S. 93A-6, so long as the license is continuously renewed or is reinstated within six months of expiration. A person who was previously licensed in North Carolina by reciprocity and who seeks reinstatement of that license after the license has been expired for more than six months, suspended, revoked or surrendered shall satisfy the requirements described in Rule .0505 of this Section.

SECTION .0600 – REAL ESTATE COMMISSION HEARINGS (SECTION OMITTED)

SECTION .0700 - PETITIONS FOR RULES

SECTION .0800 - RULE MAKING

SECTION .0900 - DECLARATORY RULINGS

SECTION .1000 – SCHOOLS (TRANSFERRED TO C.0100)

SECTION .1100 - REAL ESTATE PRE-LICENSING COURSES (TRANSFERRED/REPEALED. TRANSFERS ARE AT C.0300)

SECTION .1200 - CERTIFICATION OF REAL ESTATE INSTRUCTORS (REPEALED)

SECTION .1300 - PRIVATE REAL ESTATE SCHOOLS (TRANSFERRED/REPEALED. TRANSFERS ARE AT C.0200)

SECTION .1400 – REAL ESTATE EDUCATION AND RECOVERY FUND

SECTION .1500 – FORMS (REPEALED)

SECTION .1600 - DISCRIMINATORY PRACTICES PROHIBITED

21 NCAC 58A .1601   FAIR HOUSING
Conduct by a licensee which violates the provisions of the State Fair Housing Act constitutes improper conduct in violation of G.S. 93A-6(a)(10).

SECTION .1700 – MANDATORY CONTINUING EDUCATION

21 NCAC 58A .1701   PURPOSE AND APPLICABILITY
This Section describes the continuing education requirement for real estate brokers authorized by G.S. 93A-4.1, establishes the continuing education requirement to change a license from inactive status to active status, establishes attendance requirements for continuing education courses, establishes the criteria and procedures relating to obtaining an extension of time to complete the continuing education requirement, establishes the criteria for obtaining continuing education credit for an unapproved course or related educational activity, and addresses other similar matters.

21 NCAC 58A .1702   CONTINUING EDUCATION REQUIREMENT
(a) Except as provided in 21 NCAC 58A .1708 and .1711, in order to renew a broker license on active status, the person requesting renewal of a license shall, upon the second renewal of such license following initial licensure, and upon each subsequent annual renewal, have completed, within one year preceding license expiration, eight classroom hours of real estate continuing education in courses approved by the Commission as provided in Subchapter 58E. Four of the required eight classroom hours must be obtained each license period by completing a mandatory update course developed annually by the Commission. The remaining four hours must be obtained by completing one or more Commission-approved

elective courses described in Rule .0305 of Subchapter 58E. The licensee shall provide upon request of the Commission, evidence of continuing education course completion satisfactory to the Commission.
(b) No continuing education shall be required to renew a broker license on inactive status; however, to change a license from inactive status to active status, the licensee must satisfy the continuing education requirement described in Rule .1703 of this Section.
(c) No continuing education shall be required for a licensee who is a member of the U.S. Congress or the North Carolina General Assembly in order to renew his or her license on active status.
(d) The terms "active status" and "inactive status" are defined in Rule .0504 of this Subchapter. For continuing education purposes, the term "initial licensure" shall include the first time that a license of a particular type is issued to a person, the reinstatement of a canceled, revoked or surrendered license, and any license expired for more than six months. The issuance, pursuant to G.S. 93A-4.3, of a broker license on provisional status on April 1, 2006 to licensees who held a salesperson license as of that date shall not be considered to constitute initial licensure for continuing education purposes.

21 NCAC 58A .1703   CONTINUING EDUCATION FOR LICENSE ACTIVATION
(a) A broker requesting to change an inactive license to active status on or after the licensee's second license renewal following his or her initial licensure shall demonstrate completion of continuing education as described in Paragraph (b) or (c) of this Rule, whichever is appropriate.
(b) If the inactive licensee's license has properly been on active status at any time since the preceding July 1, the licensee is considered to be current with regard to continuing education and no additional continuing education is required to activate the license.
(c) If the inactive licensee's license has not properly been on active status since the preceding July 1 and the licensee has a deficiency in his or her continuing education record for the previous license period, the licensee must make up the deficiency and fully satisfy the continuing education requirement for the current license period in order to activate the license. Any deficiency may be made up by completing, during the current license period or previous license period, approved continuing education elective courses; however, such courses shall not be credited toward the continuing education requirement for the current license period. When crediting elective courses for purposes of making up a continuing education deficiency, the maximum number of credit hours that will be awarded for any course is four hours. When evaluating the continuing education record of a licensee with a deficiency for the previous license period to determine the licensee's eligibility for active status, the licensee shall be deemed eligible for active status if the licensee has fully satisfied the continuing education requirement for the current license period and has taken any two additional continuing education courses since the beginning of the previous license period, even if the licensee had a continuing education deficiency prior to the beginning of the previous license period.

21 NCAC 58A .1704   NO CREDIT FOR PRELICENSING OR POSTLICENSING COURSES
No credit toward the continuing education requirement shall be awarded for completing a real estate prelicensing or postlicensing course.

21 NCAC 58A .1705   ATTENDANCE AND PARTICIPATION REQUIREMENTS
In order to receive any credit for satisfactorily completing an approved continuing education course, a licensee must attend at least 90 percent of the scheduled classroom hours for the course, regardless of the length of the course, and must comply with student participation standards described in Rule .0511 of Subchapter 58E. No credit shall be awarded for attending less than 90 percent of the scheduled classroom hours. The 10 percent absence allowance is permitted for any reason at any time during the course except that it may not be used to skip the last 10 percent of the course unless the absence is for circumstances beyond the licensee's control that could not have been reasonably foreseen by the licensee and is approved by the instructor. With regard to the Commission's 12-hour Broker-In-Charge Course that is taught over two days, a licensee must attend at least 90 percent of the scheduled classroom hours on each day of the course and the 10 percent absence allowance cited above shall apply to each day of the course.

21 NCAC 58A .1706   REPETITION OF COURSES
A continuing education course may be taken only once for continuing education credit within a single license period.

21 NCAC 58A .1707   ELECTIVE COURSE CARRY-OVER CREDIT
A maximum of four hours of continuing education credit for an approved elective course taken during the current license period may be carried over to satisfy the continuing education elective requirement for the next following license period

if the licensee receives no continuing education elective credit for the course toward the elective requirement for the current license period or the previous license period. However, if a continuing education elective course is used to wholly or partially satisfy the elective requirement for the current or previous license period, then any excess hours completed in such course which are not needed to satisfy the four-hour elective requirement for that license period may not be carried forward and applied toward the elective requirement for the next following license period.

21 NCAC 58A .1708   EQUIVALENT CREDIT

(a) A licensee may request that the Commission award continuing education credit for a course taken by the licensee that is not approved by the Commission, or for some other real estate education activity, by making such request on a form prescribed by the Commission and submitting a nonrefundable evaluation fee of thirty dollars ($30.00) for each request for evaluation of a course or real estate education activity. In order for requests for equivalent credit to be considered and credits to be entered into a licensee's continuing education record prior to the June 30 license expiration date, such requests and all supporting documents must be received by the Commission on or before June 10 preceding expiration of the licensee's current license, with the exception that requests from instructors desiring equivalent credit for teaching Commission-approved continuing education courses must be received by June 30. Any equivalent continuing education credit awarded under this Rule shall be applied first to make up any continuing education deficiency for the previous license period and then to satisfy the continuing education requirement for the current license period; however, credit for an unapproved course or educational activity, other than teaching an approved elective course, that was completed during a previous license period shall not be applied to a subsequent license period.

(b) The Commission may award continuing education elective credit for completion of an unapproved course which the Commission finds equivalent to the elective course component of the continuing education requirement set forth in Section .0300 of Subchapter 58E. Completion of an unapproved course may serve only to satisfy the elective requirement and shall not be substituted for completion of the mandatory update course.

(c) Real estate education activities, other than teaching a Commission-approved course, which may be eligible for credit include: developing a Commission-approved elective continuing education course; authorship of a published real estate textbook; and authorship of a scholarly article, on a topic acceptable for continuing education purposes, which has been published in a professional journal such as a law journal or professional college or university journal or periodical. The Commission shall award continuing education elective credit for activities which the Commission finds equivalent to the elective course component of the continuing education requirement set forth in Section .0300 of Subchapter 58E. No activity other than teaching a Commission-developed mandatory update course shall be considered equivalent to completing the mandatory update course.

(d) The Commission shall award credit for teaching the Commission-developed mandatory update course and for teaching an approved elective course. Credit for teaching an approved elective course shall be awarded only for teaching a course for the first time. Credit for teaching a Commission-developed mandatory update course shall be awarded for each licensing period in which the instructor teaches the course. The amount of credit awarded to the instructor of an approved continuing education course shall be the same as the amount of credit earned by a licensee who completes the course. Licensees who are instructors of continuing education courses approved by the Commission shall not be subject to the thirty dollars ($30.00) evaluation fee when applying for continuing education credit for teaching an approved course. No credit toward the continuing education requirement shall be awarded for teaching a real estate prelicensing or postlicensing course.

(e) A licensee completing a real estate appraisal prelicensing, precertification or continuing education course approved by the North Carolina Appraisal Board may obtain real estate continuing education elective credit for such course by submitting to the Commission a written request for equivalent continuing education elective credit accompanied by a nonrefundable processing fee of twenty dollars ($20.00) and a copy of the certificate of course completion issued by the course sponsor for submission to the North Carolina Appraisal Board.

21 NCAC 58A .1709   EXTENSIONS OF TIME TO COMPLETE CONTINUING EDUCATION

A licensee on active status may request and be granted an extension of time to satisfy the continuing education requirement for a particular license period if the licensee provides evidence satisfactory to the Commission that he or she was unable to obtain the necessary education due to an incapacitating illness or other circumstance which existed for a substantial portion of the license period and which constituted a severe and verifiable hardship such that to comply with the continuing education requirement would have been impossible or unreasonably burdensome. The Commission shall in no case grant an extension of time to satisfy the continuing education requirement for reasons of business or personal conflicts. The Commission also shall not grant such an extension of time when, in the opinion of the Commission, the principal reason for the licensee's inability to obtain the required education in a timely manner was unreasonable delay on the part of the licensee in obtaining such education. If an extension of time is granted, the licensee shall be permitted to renew his or her license on active status but the license shall be automatically changed to inactive status at the end of the extension period unless the licensee satisfies the continuing education requirement prior to that time. If an extension of time is not granted, the licensee may either satisfy the continuing education requirement prior to expiration of the license period or renew his or her license on inactive status. The length of any extension of time granted and the determination of the specific courses which shall be accepted by the Commission as equivalent to the continuing education the licensee would have been required to have completed had the licensee not been granted the extension is wholly discretionary on the part of the Commission. The licensee's request for an extension of time must be submitted on a form prescribed by the Commission.

21 NCAC 58A .1710 DENIAL OR WITHDRAWAL OF CONTINUING EDUCATION CREDIT
(a) The Commission may deny continuing education credit claimed by a licensee or reported by a course sponsor for a licensee, and may withdraw continuing education credit previously awarded by the Commission to a licensee upon finding that:
- (1) The licensee or course sponsor provided incorrect or incomplete information to the Commission concerning continuing education completed by the licensee;
- (2) The licensee failed to comply with either the attendance requirement established by Rule .1705 of this Section or the student participation standards set forth in Rule .0511 of Subchapter 58E; or
- (3) The licensee was mistakenly awarded continuing education credit due to an administrative error.

(b) When continuing education credit is denied or withdrawn by the Commission under Paragraph (a) of this Rule, the licensee remains responsible for satisfying the continuing education requirement. However, when an administrative error or an incorrect report by a course sponsor results in the denial or withdrawal of continuing education credit for a licensee, the Commission may, upon request of the licensee, grant the licensee an extension of time to satisfy the continuing education requirement.
(c) A licensee who obtains or attempts to obtain continuing education credit through misrepresentation of fact, dishonesty or other improper conduct shall be subject to disciplinary action pursuant to G.S. 93A-6.

21 NCAC 58A .1711 CONTINUING EDUCATION REQUIRED OF NONRESIDENT LICENSEES
(a) To be considered a nonresident for continuing education purposes, a real estate broker licensed in North Carolina shall not have a North Carolina business address, mailing address or residence address at the time he or she applies for license renewal if he or she seeks to renew his or her license on active status. A nonresident North Carolina broker who wishes to renew his or her license on active status may fully satisfy the continuing education requirement by any one of the following means:
- (1) A nonresident licensee may, at the time of license renewal, hold a real estate license on active status in another state and certify on a form prescribed by the Commission that the licensee holds such license.
- (2) A nonresident licensee may, within one year preceding license expiration, complete the Commission-prescribed Update course plus one Commission-approved continuing education elective course, or complete two Commission-approved continuing education elective courses.
- (3) A nonresident licensee may, within one year preceding license expiration, complete eight classroom hours in courses approved for continuing education credit by the real estate licensing agency in the licensee's state of residence or in the state where the course was taken. To obtain credit for a continuing education course completed in another state and not approved by the Commission, the licensee must submit a written request for continuing education credit accompanied by a nonrefundable processing fee of twenty dollars ($20.00) per request and evidence satisfactory to the Commission that the course was completed and that the course was approved for continuing education credit by the real estate licensing agency in the licensee's state of residence or in the state where the course was taken.
- (4) A nonresident licensee may obtain eight hours equivalent credit for a course or courses not approved by the Commission or for related educational activities as provided in Rule .1708 of this Section. The maximum amount of continuing education credit the Commission will award a nonresident licensee for an unapproved course or educational activity is eight hours.

(b) When requesting to change an inactive license to active status, or when applying for reinstatement of a license expired for not more than six months, a nonresident broker may fully satisfy the continuing education requirements described in Rules .0505 and .1703 of this Subchapter by complying with any of the options described in Paragraph (a) of this Rule, except that the requirements in Subparagraphs (a)(2) and (a)(3) of this Rule restricting the taking of courses to one year preceding license expiration shall not be applicable.

(c) No carry-over credit to a subsequent license period shall be awarded for a course taken in another state that has not been approved by the North Carolina Real Estate Commission as an elective course.

SECTION .1800 - LIMITED NONRESIDENT COMMERCIAL LICENSING

21 NCAC 58A .1801   GENERAL PROVISIONS
(a) Any person resident in a state or territory of the United States other than North Carolina may perform the acts or services of a real estate broker in North Carolina in transactions involving commercial real estate if said person first applies for and obtains a limited nonresident commercial real estate broker license as provided in this Section.
(b) Corporations, business associations and entities shall be ineligible for licensure under this Section.
(c) Nothing in this Section shall be construed to limit the rights of any person duly licensed as a real estate broker in North Carolina under the provisions of G.S. 93A-4 or 93A-9(a).

21 NCAC 58A .1802   DEFINITIONS
For the purposes of this Section:
- (1) "Commercial Real Estate" means any real property or interest therein, whether freehold or non-freehold, which at the time the property or interest is made the subject of an agreement for brokerage services:
    - (a) is lawfully used primarily for sales, office, research, institutional, warehouse, manufacturing, industrial or mining purposes or for multifamily residential purposes involving five or more dwelling units;
    - (b) may lawfully be used for any of the purposes listed in Subitem (1)(a) of this Rule by a zoning ordinance adopted pursuant to the provisions of G.S. 153A, Article 18 or G.S. 160A, Article 19 or which is the subject of an official application or petition to amend the applicable zoning ordinance to permit any of the uses listed in Subitem (1)(a) of this Rule which is under consideration by the government agency with authority to approve the amendment; or
    - (c) is in good faith intended to be immediately used for any of the purposes listed in Subitem (1)(a) of this Rule by the parties to any contract, lease, option, or offer to make any contract, lease, or option.
- (2) "Qualifying state" means the state or territory of the United States where an applicant for, and the holder of, a limited nonresident commercial license issued under this Section is licensed in good standing as a real estate broker or salesperson. The qualifying state must be the state or territory where the applicant or limited nonresident commercial licensee maintains his or her primary place of business as a real estate broker or salesperson. Under no circumstances may North Carolina be a qualifying state.

21 NCAC 58A .1803   REQUIREMENTS FOR LICENSURE; APPLICATION AND FEE
(a) A person desiring to obtain a broker license under this Section shall demonstrate to the Real Estate Commission that:
- (1) he or she is a resident of a state or territory of the United States other than North Carolina;
- (2) he or she is licensed as a real estate broker or salesperson in a qualifying state and that said license is on active status and not in abeyance for any reason. If licensed as a salesperson, he or she shall also demonstrate that he or she is acting under the supervision of a broker in accordance with the applicable governing statutes or regulations in the qualifying state; and
- (3) he or she possesses the requisite honesty, truthfulness, integrity, and moral character for licensure as a broker in North Carolina.

A person applying for licensure under this Section shall not be required to show that the state or territory where he or she is currently licensed offers reciprocal licensing privileges to North Carolina brokers.

(b) A person desiring to be licensed under this Section shall submit an application on a form prescribed by the Commission and shall show the Commission that he or she has satisfied the requirements set forth in Paragraph (a) of this Rule. In connection with his or her application a person applying for licensure under this Rule shall provide the Commission with a certification of license history from the qualifying state where he or she is licensed. He or she shall also provide the Commission with a report of his or her criminal history from the service designated by the Commission.

An applicant for licensure under this Section shall be required to update his or her application as required by Rule .0302(c) of this Subchapter.
(c) The fee for persons applying for licensure under this Section shall be one hundred dollars ($100.00) and shall be paid in the form of a certified check, bank check, cashier's check, money order, or by credit card. Once paid, the application fee shall be non-refundable.
(d) If the Commission has received a complete application and the required application fee and if the Commission is satisfied that the applicant possesses the moral character necessary for licensure, the Commission shall issue to the applicant a limited nonresident commercial real estate broker license.

21 NCAC 58A .1804   ACTIVE STATUS
Broker licenses issued under this Section shall be issued on active status and shall remain valid only so long as the licensee's license in the qualifying state remains valid and on active status. In addition, a license issued to a salesperson under this Section shall remain valid only while the salesperson is acting under the supervision of a real estate broker in accordance with the applicable laws and rules in the qualifying state. Individuals licensed under this Section shall immediately notify the Commission if his or her license in the qualifying state lapses or expires, is suspended or revoked, made inactive, or is placed in abeyance for any reason.

21 NCAC 58A .1805   RENEWAL
(a) A license issued under this Section shall expire on June 30 following issuance unless it is renewed in accordance with the provisions of Rule .0503 and .1711 of this Subchapter.
(b) The Commission shall not renew a license issued under this Section unless the licensee has demonstrated that he or she has complied with the requirements of Paragraph (a) of this Rule and that his or her license in the qualifying state is on active status in good standing and is not lapsed, expired, suspended, revoked, or in abeyance for any reason.

21 NCAC 58A .1806   LIMITATIONS
(a) A person licensed under this Section may act as a real estate broker in this state only if:
    (1)   he or she does not reside in North Carolina;
    (2)   the real property interest which is the subject of any transaction in connection with which he or she acts as a broker in this state is commercial real estate as that term is defined in Rule .1802 of this Section; and
    (3)   he or she is affiliated with a resident North Carolina real estate broker as required in Rule .1807 of this Section.
(b) A nonresident commercial real estate broker licensed under the provisions of Section .1800 of this Subchapter shall not act as or serve in the capacity of a broker-in-charge of a firm or office in North Carolina.

21 NCAC 58A .1807   AFFILIATION WITH RESIDENT BROKER
(a) No person licensed under G.S. 93A-9(b) shall enter North Carolina to perform any act or service for which licensure as a real broker is required unless he or she has first entered into a brokerage cooperation agreement and declaration of affiliation with an individual who is a resident in North Carolina licensed as a North Carolina real estate broker.
(b) A brokerage cooperation agreement as contemplated by this Rule shall be in writing and signed by the resident North Carolina broker and the non-resident commercial licensee. It shall contain:
    (1)   the material terms of the agreement between the signatory licenses;
    (2)   a description of the agency relationships, if any, which are created by the agreement among the nonresident commercial licensee, the resident North Carolina broker, and the parties each represents;
    (3)   a description of the property or the identity of the parties and other information sufficient to identify the transaction which is the subject of the affiliation agreement; and
    (4)   a definite expiration date.
(c) A declaration of affiliation shall be written and on the form provided by the Commission and shall identify the nonresident commercial licensee and the affiliated resident North Carolina licensee. It shall also contain a description of the duties and obligations of each as required by the North Carolina Real Estate License Law and rules adopted by the Commission. The declaration of affiliation may be a part of the brokerage cooperation agreement or separate from it.
(d) A nonresident commercial licensee may affiliate with more than one resident North Carolina broker at any time. However, a nonresident commercial licensee may be affiliated with only one resident North Carolina broker in a single transaction.

(e) A resident North Carolina broker who enters into a brokerage cooperation agreement and declaration of affiliation with a nonresident commercial licensee shall:
- (1) verify that the nonresident commercial licensee is licensed in North Carolina;
- (2) actively and directly supervise the nonresident commercial licensee in a manner which reasonably insures that the nonresident commercial licensee complies with the North Carolina Real Estate License Law and rules adopted by the Commission;
- (3) promptly notify the Commission if the nonresident commercial licensee violates the Real Estate License Law or rules adopted by the Commission;
- (4) insure that records are retained in accordance with the requirements of the Real Estate License Law and rules adopted by the Commission; and
- (5) maintain his or her license on active status continuously for the duration of the brokerage cooperation agreement and the declaration of affiliation.

(f) The nonresident commercial licensee and the affiliated resident North Carolina broker shall each retain in his or her records a copy of brokerage cooperation agreements and declarations of affiliation from the time of their creation and for at least three years following their expiration. Such records shall be made available for inspection and reproduction by the Commission or its authorized representatives without prior notice.

21 NCAC 58A .1808 TRUST MONIES

A nonresident commercial licensee acting as real estate broker in North Carolina shall immediately deliver to the North Carolina resident broker with whom he or she is affiliated all money belonging to others received in connection with the nonresident commercial licensee's acts or services as a broker. Upon receipt of said money, the resident North Carolina broker shall cause said money to be deposited in a trust account in accordance with the provisions of Rule .0107 of this Subchapter.

21 NCAC 58A .1809 ADVERTISING

In all advertising involving a nonresident commercial licensee's conduct as a North Carolina real estate broker and in any representation of such person's licensure in North Carolina, the advertising or representation shall conspicuously identify the nonresident commercial licensee as a "Limited Nonresident Commercial Real Estate Broker".

21 NCAC 58A .1810 PAYMENT OF FEES

Commissions, fees, or other compensation earned by a nonresident commercial licensee shall not be paid directly to the licensee if said licensee is employed by or working for a real estate broker or firm. Instead, such fees or compensation shall be paid to the licensee's employing broker or firm.

SECTION .1900 – POST-LICENSING EDUCATION

21 NCAC 58A .1901 PURPOSE AND APPLICABILITY

This Section prescribes specific procedures relating to the postlicensing education requirement for real estate brokers as prescribed by G.S. 93A-4(a1).

21 NCAC 58A .1902 POSTLICENSING EDUCATION REQUIREMENT

(a) The 90 classroom hour postlicensing education program shall consist of three 30 classroom hour courses prescribed by the Commission which may be taken in any sequence. A provisional broker as described in G.S. 93A-4(a1) or G.S. 93A-4.3(d) must satisfactorily complete at least one of the 30-hour courses during each of the first three years following the date of his or her initial licensure as a broker in order to retain his or her eligibility to actively engage in real estate brokerage. Upon completion of all three courses by a provisional broker, the provisional status of the broker's license shall be terminated by the Commission. The three courses shall be devoted to:
- (1) real estate brokerage relationships and responsibilities;
- (2) real estate contracts and transactions; and
- (3) specialized topics, including commercial real estate, rental management, real estate finance, real estate appraisal, real estate development, and real estate regulation.

(b) If a provisional broker as describe in G.S. 93A-4(a1) or G.S. 93A-4.3(d) fails to complete the required postlicensing education described in Paragraph (a) of this Rule by the end of either the first or second year following the date of his or her initial licensure as a broker, his or her license shall be placed on inactive status. Between the end of the first year after initial licensure and the end of the third year after initial licensure, a provisional broker who is subject of the postlicensing education requirement and who desires to activate a license that is on inactive status shall make up any postlicensing education deficiency as well as satisfy the continuing education requirements for license activation described in Rule .1703 of this Subchapter, satisfy the requirement for supervision by a broker-in-charge described in Rule .0506 of this Subchapter and file with the Commission a request for license activation as described in Rule .0504 of this Subchapter.

(c) If a provisional broker as described in G.S. 93A-4(a1) or G.S. 93A-4.3(d) fails to complete all three postlicensing courses within three years following the date of his or her initial licensure, his or her license shall be placed on inactive status. In order to activate the license, the provisional broker shall demonstrate completion of all three postlicensing courses within the previous three years, which will terminate the provisional status of the broker's license, and shall satisfy the continuing education requirements for license activation described in Rule .1703 of this Subchapter.

21 NCAC 58A .1903   EXTENSIONS OF TIME TO COMPLETE POSTLICENSING EDUCATION
A provisional broker as described in G.S. 93A-4(a1) or G.S. 93A-4.3(d) may request and be granted an extension of time to satisfy the postlicensing education requirement for any of the first three years following the date of his or her initial licensure as a broker if the licensee provides evidence satisfactory to the Commission that he or she was unable to obtain the necessary education due to an incapacitating illness or other circumstance which existed for a substantial portion of the year in question and which constituted a severe and verifiable hardship such that to comply with the education requirement would have been impossible or unreasonably burdensome. The Commission shall not grant an extension of time when the reason for the request is a business or personal conflict or when, in the opinion of the Commission, the principal reason for the provisional broker's failure to obtain the required education in a timely manner was unreasonable delay on the part of the provisional broker in obtaining such education. If an extension of time is granted, the provisional broker may retain his or her license on active status until expiration of the extension period, but the license shall be automatically changed to inactive status at the end of the extension period unless the licensee obtains the required postlicensing education prior to that time. If an extension of time is not granted, the provisional broker's license shall be treated as described in Rule .1902(b) or (c) of this Section. A request for an extension of time must be submitted on a form provided by the Commission.

21 NCAC 58A .1904   DENIAL OR WITHDRAWAL OF POSTLICENSING EDUCATION CREDIT
(a) The Commission may deny postlicensing education credit claimed by a provisional broker or reported by a school for a provisional broker, and may withdraw postlicensing education credit previously awarded by the Commission to a provisional broker and make appropriate license status changes for that licensee upon finding that:
- (1) the provisional broker or school provided incorrect or incomplete information to the Commission concerning postlicensing education completed by the provisional broker;
- (2) the provisional broker was mistakenly awarded postlicensing education credit due to an administrative error; or
- (3) the provisional broker attended a postlicensing course while concurrently attending a different postlicensing course at the same school or a different school if such concurrent attendance in the two courses resulted in the provisional broker participating in postlicensing course sessions for more than 21 classroom hours in any given seven-day period.

(b) When postlicensing education credit is denied or withdrawn by the Commission under Paragraph (a) of this Rule, the provisional broker remains responsible for satisfying the postlicensing education requirement in a timely manner.

(c) A licensee who obtains or attempts to obtain postlicensing education credit through misrepresentation of fact, dishonesty or other improper conduct is subject to disciplinary action pursuant to G.S. 93A-6.

SECTION .2000 - ANNUAL REPORTS

SECTION .2100 - BROKERS IN MILITARY SERVICE

21 NCAC 58A .2101   APPLICABILITY
This Section shall apply to every broker whose license is not revoked, suspended, or surrendered, or who is otherwise the subject of a disciplinary order, and who is eligible for an extension of time to file a tax return under the provisions of G.S. 150-249.2 and 26 U.S.C. 7508.

21 NCAC 58A .2102   POSTPONEMENT OF FEES

(a) A Broker described in 21 NCAC 58A .2101 shall not be required to pay renewal fees accrued during the time to be disregarded described in 26 U.S.C. 7508 until the June 30 immediately following the end of such time. The provisions of 21 NCAC 58A .0504 notwithstanding, during such time and until the June 30 immediately thereafter, the license of a broker other than a provisional broker shall remain on active status. During such time, the license of a provisional broker shall not expire, but shall remain on active status only if the provisional broker remains under the supervision of a broker-in-charge.
(b) All fees postponed by operation of this subsection shall be due and payable on June 30 immediately following the time to be disregarded as described in 26 U.S.C. 7508.

21 NCAC 58A .2103   POSTPONEMENT OF CONTINUING EDUCATION
(a) A broker described by 21 NCAC 58A .2101 shall not be required to complete the continuing education required as a condition of license renewal for any June 30 license expiration date if that date falls during the time to be disregarded described in 26 U.S.C. 7508 until the June 10 immediately following the end of such time to be disregarded. If such time ends on or after May 1, the broker shall have until September 1 of the same year to complete the required continuing education.
(b) If a broker entitled to a postponement of continuing education under this Rule accumulates a deficiency in his or her continuing education of 16 or more hours because of the length of the time to be disregarded under 26 U.S.C. 7508, the broker may satisfy the deficiency by satisfying the requirements of 21 NCAC 58A .1703(c) established for an inactive broker returning to active status.
(c) The license of a broker entitled to postponement of continuing education under this Rule shall not be placed on inactive status for failure to complete continuing education until the deadline for completion set out in Paragraph (a) of this Rule has passed.

21 NCAC 58A .2104   POSTPONEMENT OF POSTLICENSING EDUCATION
A broker described by 21 NCAC 58A .2101 who is a provisional broker shall not be required to complete any post-licensing education required to be completed during the period to be disregarded under 26 U.S.C. 5708 until the 180th day following the ending of such period. The broker's license shall not be placed on inactive status or cancelled for his or failure to complete the required post-licensing education prior to the deadline established in this Rule.

21 NCAC 58A .2105   PROOF OF ELIGIBILITY
It shall be the responsibility of every broker eligible for the postponement of fees and education requirements established by this section to demonstrate his or her eligibility and the beginning and ending of the time to be disregarded as described in 26 U.S.C. 5708.

SECTION .2200 - BROKER PRICE OPINIONS AND COMPARATIVE MARKET ANALYSES

21 NCAC 58A .2201   APPLICABILITY
This Section applies to broker price opinions and comparative market analyses provided for a fee by a real estate broker whose license is not on provisional status pursuant to Article 6, Chapter 93A of the General Statutes.

21 NCAC 58A .2202   STANDARDS
(a) A broker performing a broker price opinion or comparative market analysis for a fee shall comply with all the requirements in G.S. 93A-83 and in this Rule.
(b) A broker shall only accept an assignment to provide a broker price opinion or comparative market analysis for a property if the broker has knowledge of the real estate market, direct access to real estate market sales or leasing data, and brokerage or appraisal experience in the subject property's geographic location.
(c) A broker shall not provide a broker price opinion or comparative market analysis for a property unless the broker can exercise objective, independent judgment free of any influence from any interested party in the performance of his or her analysis of the facts relevant to determination of a probable selling or leasing price.
(d) A broker shall not provide a broker price opinion or comparative market analysis for a property unless the broker has personally inspected the exterior and interior of that property, provided, however, that an inspection of the exterior or interior is not required if this is waived in writing by the party for whom the opinion or analysis is being performed.
(e) When developing a broker price opinion or comparative market analysis for a property or interest therein, a broker shall utilize methodology such as analysis of sales or income of sold or leased properties comparable to the subject property or capitalization as is appropriate for the assignment and type of subject property.

(f) When analyzing sales or income of properties comparable to the property that is the subject of a broker price opinion or comparative market analysis assignment, a broker shall comply with the following standards:
- (1) The broker shall select from reliable information sources a minimum of three sold or leased comparable properties for use in his or her analysis that are similar to the subject property with regard to characteristics such as property type, use, location, age, size, design, physical features, amenities, utility, property condition and conditions of sale. The comparable properties selected shall reflect the prevailing factors or market conditions influencing the sale or lease prices of similar properties in the subject property's local market; and
- (2) The broker shall make adjustments to the selling or leasing price of selected comparable properties for differences between the characteristics of the comparable properties and the subject property as necessary to produce a credible estimate of the probable selling or leasing price. Adjustments shall be considered for differences in property characteristics such as location, age, size, design, physical features, amenities, utility, condition, economic or functional obsolescence and conditions of sale. The amounts of adjustments shall reflect the values that the local real estate market places on the differences in the characteristics in question.

(g) A broker price opinion or comparative market analysis provided to the party for whom the opinion or analysis is being performed shall address, in addition to matters required to be addressed by G.S. 93A-83 and other provisions of this Rule, the following items:
- (1) a description of the comparable properties used in the analysis (including any unsold properties listed for sale or rent that were used as comparable properties);
- (2) the adjustments made to the selling or leasing prices of comparable properties;
- (3) local real estate market conditions;
- (4) if the date on which the sale or lease of a comparable property became final is more than six months prior to the effective date of the broker price opinion or comparative market analysis, an explanation of why the comparable property was used in the analysis and a description of the market conditions affecting the comparable property at the time the sale or lease became final; and
- (5) each method used in deriving the estimate of probable selling or leasing price.

(h) In connection with a broker price opinion or comparative market analysis, an estimated probable leasing price may be reported by a broker as a lease rate and an estimated probable selling or leasing price may be reported by a broker either as a single figure or as a price range. When the estimated probable selling or leasing price is stated as a price range and the higher figure exceeds the lower figure by more than 10 percent, the broker shall include an explanation of why the higher figure exceeds the lower figure by more than 10 percent.

SUBCHAPTER 58B – TIME SHARES

SECTION .0100 – TIME SHARE PROJECT REGISTRATION

21 NCAC 58B .0101   APPLICATION FOR REGISTRATION
(a) Every application for time share project registration shall be filed at the Commission's office upon a form prescribed by the Commission. Every such application shall contain or have appended thereto:
- (1) information concerning the developer's title or right to use the real property on which the project is located, including a title opinion provided by an independent attorney performed within 30 days preceding the date of application;
- (2) information concerning owners of time shares at the project other than the developer;
- (3) a description of the improvements and amenities located at the project, including a description of the number and type of time share units;
- (4) a description of the time share estate to be sold or conveyed to purchasers;
- (5) information concerning the developer and his or her financial ability to develop the project (including the developer's most recent audited financial statement, any loan commitments for completion of the proposed time share project, a projected budget for the construction, marketing and operation of the time share project until control by purchasers is asserted, and details of any source of funding for the time share project other than consumer sales proceeds), and information concerning the marketing and managing entities and their relationship to the developer;
- (6) the developer's name and address, past real estate development experience and such other information necessary to determine the moral character of those selling and managing the project;
- (7) copies of all documents to be distributed to time share purchasers at the point of sale or immediately thereafter; and
- (8) such information as may be required by G.S. 93A-52.

The form shall also describe the standards for its proper completion and submission.

(b) In accordance with G.S. 93A-52, an application for time share registration shall be considered to be properly completed when it is wholly and accurately filled out and when all required documents are appended to it and appear to be in compliance with the provisions of the Time Share Act, and, where the project is a condominium, the Condominium Act or Unit Ownership Act.

(c) An entity which owns time shares at a time share project where there are one or more existing registered developers may also apply to the Commission for registration of its time shares, provided that the entity does not control a registered developer, is not controlled by a registered developer, and is not in common control of the project with a registered developer.

21 NCAC 58B .0102   REGISTRATION FEE
(a) Every application for time share project registration must be accompanied by a certified check made payable to the North Carolina Real Estate Commission. For the initial registration or subsequent registration of a time share project by a developer proposing to sell or develop 16 or more time shares, the fee is one thousand dollars ($1,000). For an initial or subsequent registration of a time share project in which the developer proposes to sell 15 or fewer time shares, the fee is seven hundred dollars ($700.00). For any time share registration by a homeowner association for the purpose of re-selling time shares in its own project which it has acquired in satisfaction of unpaid assessments by prior owners, the fee is four hundred fifty dollars ($450.00).

(b) Applications for registration not accompanied by the appropriate fee shall not be considered by the Commission.

(c) In the event a properly completed application filed with the Commission is denied for any reason, or if an incomplete application is denied by the Commission or abandoned by the developer prior to a final decision by the Commission, the amount of two hundred fifty dollars ($250.00) shall be retained by the Commission from the application fee and the balance refunded to the applicant developer.

21 NCAC 58B .0103   RENEWAL OF TIME SHARE PROJECT REGISTRATION
(a) Every developer desiring the renewal of a time share project registration shall apply for the same in writing upon a form provided by the Commission during the month of June. Every such renewal application shall be accompanied by a certified check made payable to the North Carolina Real Estate Commission in the amount of   eight hundred dollars ($800.00). To renew the time share project registration, the properly completed renewal application accompanied by the prescribed fee must be received at the Commission's office prior to the expiration of the certificate of registration.

(b) Applications for the renewal of a time share project registration shall be signed by the developer, by two executive officers of the developer, or by the developer's attorney at law and shall certify that the information contained in the registration filed with the Commission is accurate and current on the date of the renewal application. Making a false certification on a time share project registration renewal application shall be grounds for disciplinary action by the Commission.

21 NCAC 58B .0104   AMENDMENTS TO TIME SHARE PROJECT REGISTRATION
(a) A developer shall notify the Commission immediately, but in no event later than 15 days, after any material change in the information contained in the time share project registration.
(b) A material change shall be any change which reflects a difference in:
- (1) the nature, quality or availability of the purchaser's ownership or right to use the time share;
- (2) the nature, quality or availability of any amenity at the project;
- (3) the developer's title, control or right to use the real property on which the project is located;
- (4) the information concerning the developer, the managing or marketing entities, or persons connected therewith, previously filed with the Commission;
- (5) the purchaser's right to exchange his or her unit; however, a change in the information required to be disclosed to a purchaser by G.S. 93A-48 shall not be a material change; or
- (6) the project or time share as originally registered which would be significant to a reasonable purchaser.

(c) Amendments to time share project registrations shall be submitted in the form of substitute pages for material previously filed with the Commission. New or changed information shall be conspicuously indicated by underlining in red ink. Every amendment submitted shall be accompanied by a cover letter signed by the developer or the developer's attorney containing a summary of the amendment and a statement of reasons for which the amendment has been made. The cover letter shall state:
- (1) the name and address of the project and its registration number;
- (2) the name and address of the developer;
- (3) the document or documents to which the amendment applies;
- (4) whether or not the changes represented by the amendment required the assent of the time share owners and, if so, how the assent of the time share owners was obtained; and
- (5) the recording reference in the office of the register of deeds for the changes, if applicable.

Developers of multiple projects must submit separate amendments and cover letters for each project for which amendments are submitted.
(d) The Commission may, in its discretion, require the developer to file a new time share project registration application in the place of an amendment form. Such refiling shall be without fee.

21 NCAC 58B .0105   NOTICE OF TERMINATION
(a) A developer of a registered time share project which, for any reason, terminates its interest, rights, ownership or control of the project or any significant part thereof shall immediately notify the Commission in writing on a form prescribed by the Commission for that purpose. Notice of termination to the Commission shall include the date of termination, the reasons therefor, the identity of the developer's successor, if any, and a report on the status of time share sales to purchasers on the date of termination.
(b) Upon receipt of a properly executed notice of termination of the developer's interest in a time share project, the Commission shall enter a notation of cancellation of registration in the file of the project, and shall notify the developer of cancellation. A developer's failure to give notice of termination as provided herein shall not prevent cancellation of the project's registration under G.S. 93A-52.

SECTION .0200 - PUBLIC OFFERING STATEMENT

21 NCAC 58B .0201   GENERAL PROVISIONS
(a) Information contained in a public offering statement shall be accurate on the day it is supplied to a purchaser. Before any public offering statement is supplied to a purchaser, the developer shall file a copy of the statement with the Commission.
(b) In addition to the information required to be contained in a public offering statement by G.S. 93A-44, every public offering statement shall disclose to the purchaser of a time share complete and accurate information concerning:

(1) the real property type of the time share program, whether tenancy-in-common, condominium or other, and a description of the estate the purchaser will own, the term of that estate and the remainder interest, if any, once the term has expired;
(2) the document creating the time share program, a statement that it is the document which governs the program and a reference to the location where the purchaser may obtain or examine a copy of the document;
(3) whether or not the property is being converted to a time share from some other use and, if so, a statement to that effect and disclosure of the prior use of the property;
(4) the maximum number of time shares in the project, each recreational and other commonly used facility offered, and who or what will own each facility, if the project is to be completed in one development or construction phase;
(5) if the project is planned in phased construction or development, the complete plan of phased offerings, including the maximum number of time shares which may be in the project, each recreational and other commonly used facility, who or what will own each facility, and the developer's representations regarding his or her commitment to build out the project;
(6) the association of owners or other entity which will ultimately be responsible for managing the time share program, the first date or event when the entity will convene or commence to conduct business, each owner's voting right, if any, and whether and for how long the developer, as time share owner, will control the entity;
(7) the location where owners may inspect the articles and bylaws of the owners association, or other organizational documents of the entity and the books and records it produces;
(8) whether the entity has lien rights against time share owners for failure to pay assessments;
(9) whether or not the developer has entered into a management contract on behalf of the managing entity, the extent to which the managing entity's powers are delegated to the manager and the location where a copy of the management contract may be examined;
(10) whether or not the developer will pay assessments for time shares which it owns and a statement that the amount of assessments due the managing entity from owners will change over time, as circumstances may change;
(11) whether or not the developer sponsors or will sponsor a rental or resale program and, if so, a summary of the program or programs; and
(12) the developer's role at the project, if the developer is a separate entity from any other registered developer of the time share project.

(c) The inclusion of false or misleading statements in a public offering statement shall be grounds for disciplinary action by the Commission.

21 NCAC 58B .0202   PUBLIC OFFERING STATEMENT SUMMARY

Every public offering statement shall contain a one page cover prescribed by the Commission and completed by the developer entitled Public Offering Statement Summary. The Public Offering Statement Summary shall read as follows:

PUBLIC OFFERING STATEMENT

SUMMARY

NAME OF PROJECT:

NAME AND REAL ESTATE LICENSE NUMBER OF BROKER:

This Public Offering Statement contains information which deserves your careful study, as you decide whether or not to purchase a time share.

The Public Offering Statement includes general information about the real estate type, the term, and the size of this time share project. It also includes a general description of the recreational and other facilities existing now, or to be provided in the future. The Public Offering Statement will tell you how maintenance and management of the project will be provided and how the costs of these services will be charged to purchasers. From the Public Offering Statement, you will also learn how the project will be governed and whether purchasers will have a voice in that government. You will also learn that a time share instrument will be recorded to protect your real estate interest in your time share.

The Public Offering Statement contains important information, but is not a substitute for the detailed information contained in the contract of purchase and the legal documents which create and affect the time share program at this project.

Please study this Public Offering Statement carefully. Satisfy yourself that any questions you may have are answered before you decide to purchase. If a salesperson or other representative of the developer has made a representation which concerns you, and you cannot find that representation in writing, ask that it be pointed out to you.

NOTICE

UNDER NORTH CAROLINA LAW, YOU MAY CANCEL YOUR TIME SHARE PURCHASE WITHOUT PENALTY WITHIN FIVE DAYS AFTER SIGNING YOUR CONTRACT. TO CANCEL YOUR TIME SHARE PURCHASE, YOU MUST MAIL OR HAND DELIVER WRITTEN NOTICE OF YOUR DESIRE TO CANCEL YOUR PURCHASE TO (name and address of project). IF YOU CHOOSE TO MAIL YOUR CANCELLATION NOTICE, THE NORTH CAROLINA REAL ESTATE COMMISSION RECOMMENDS THAT YOU USE REGISTERED OR CERTIFIED MAIL AND THAT YOU RETAIN YOUR POSTAL RECEIPT AS PROOF OF THE DATE YOUR NOTICE WAS MAILED. UPON CANCELLATION, ALL PAYMENTS WILL BE REFUNDED TO YOU.

21 NCAC 58B .0203   RECEIPT FOR PUBLIC OFFERING STATEMENT
(a) Prior to the execution of any contract to purchase a time share, a time share developer or a time share salesperson shall obtain from the purchaser a written receipt for the public offering statement, which shall display, directly over the buyer signature line in type in all capital letters, no smaller than the largest type on the page on which it appears, the following statement: DO NOT SIGN THIS RECEIPT UNLESS YOU HAVE RECEIVED A COMPLETE COPY OF THE PUBLIC OFFERING STATEMENT TO TAKE WITH YOU.
(b) Receipts for public offering statements shall be maintained as part of the records of the sales transaction.

SECTION .0300 - CANCELLATION

21 NCAC 58B .0301   PROOF OF CANCELLATION
(a) The postmark date affixed to any written notice of a purchaser's intent to cancel his or her time share purchase shall be presumed by the Commission to be the date the notice was mailed to the developer. Evidence tending to rebut this presumption shall be admissible at a hearing before the Commission.
(b) Upon receipt of a purchaser's written notice of his or her intent to cancel his or her time share purchase, the developer, or his or her agent or representative, shall retain the notice and any enclosure, envelope or other cover in the developer's files at the project, and shall produce the file upon the Commission's request.
(c) When there is more than one registered developer at a time share project and a purchaser gives written notice of his or her intent to cancel his or her time share purchase that is received by a developer or sales staff other than the one from whom his or her time share was purchased, the developer or sales staff receiving such notice shall promptly deliver it to the proper developer who shall then honor the notice if it was timely sent by the purchaser.

SECTION .0400 - TIME SHARE SALES OPERATION

21 NCAC 58B .0401   RETENTION OF TIME SHARE RECORDS
A time share developer and a time share salesperson shall retain or cause to be retained for a period of three years complete records of every time share sale, rental, or exchange transaction made by or on behalf of the developer. Records required to be retained shall include but not be limited to offers, applications and contracts to purchase, rent or exchange time shares; records of the deposit, maintenance and disbursement of funds required to be held in trust; receipts; notices of cancellation and their covers if mailed; records regarding compensation of salespersons; public offering statements; and any other records pertaining to time share transactions. Such records shall be made available to the Commission and its representatives upon request.

21 NCAC 58B .0402   TIME SHARE AGENCY AGREEMENTS AND DISCLOSURE
Time share sales transactions conducted by licensees on behalf of a time share developer are subject to 21 NCAC 58A .0104.

SECTION .0500 – HANDLING AND ACCOUNTING OF FUNDS

21 NCAC 58B .0501   TIME SHARE TRUST FUNDS
(a) Except as otherwise permitted by G.S. 93A-45(c), all monies received by a time share developer or a time share salesperson in connection with a time share sales transaction shall be deposited into a trust or escrow account not later than three banking days following receipt and shall remain in such account for ten days from the date of sale or until cancellation by the purchaser, whichever first occurs.
(b) All monies received by a person licensed as a broker in connection with a time share transaction shall be delivered immediately to his or her project broker.
(c) When a time share purchaser timely cancels his or her time share purchase, the developer shall refund to the purchaser all monies paid by the purchaser in connection with the purchase. The refund shall be made no later than 30 days following the date of execution of the contract. Amounts paid by the purchaser with a bankcard or a credit card shall be refunded by a cash payment or by issuing a credit voucher to the purchaser within the 30-day period.
(d) Every project broker shall obtain and keep a written representation from the developer as to whether or not lien-free or lien-subordinated time share instruments can be recorded within 45 days of the purchaser's execution of the time share purchase agreement. When a lien-free or lien-subordinated instrument cannot be recorded within said time period, on the business day following the expiration of the ten day time share payment escrow period, a project broker shall transfer from his or her trust account all purchase deposit funds or other payments received from a purchaser who has not cancelled his or her purchase agreement, to the independent escrow agent in a check made payable to the independent escrow agent. Alternatively, the check may be made payable to the developer with a restrictive endorsement placed on the back of the check providing "For deposit to the account of the independent escrow agent for the (name of time share project) only."

SECTION .0600 - PROJECT BROKER

21 NCAC 58B .0601   DESIGNATION OF PROJECT BROKER
The developer of a registered timeshare project shall designate for each project subject to the developer's control a project broker by filing with the Commission an affidavit on the form prescribed. The developer may from time to time change the designated project broker by filing a new designation form with the Commission within 10 days following the change. A broker licensed under the provisions of Section .1800 of Subchapter 58A shall not be designated as a project broker. Provisional brokers shall not be designated as a project broker.

21 NCAC 58B .0602   DUTIES OF THE PROJECT BROKER
(a) The broker designated by the developer of a time share project to be project broker shall assume responsibility for:
(1) The display of the time share project certificate registration and the license certificates of the real estate brokers associated with or engaged on behalf of the developer at the project;
(2) The determination of whether each licensee employed has complied with Rules .0503 and .0506 of Subchapter 58A;
(3) The notification to the commission of any change in the identity or address of the project or in the identity or address of the developer or marketing or managing entities at the project;
(4) The deposit and maintenance of time share purchase or rental monies in a trust or escrow account until proper disbursement is made; and
(5) The proper maintenance of accurate records at the project including all records relating to the handling of trust monies at the project, records relating to time share sales and rental transactions and the project registration and renewal.
(b) The project broker shall review all contracts, public offering statements and other documents distributed to the purchasers of time shares at the project to ensure that the documents comport with the requirements of the Time Share Act and the rules adopted by the commission, and to ensure that true and accurate documents have been given to the purchasers.
(c) The project broker shall not permit time share sales to be conducted by any person not licensed as a broker and shall not delegate or assign his or her supervisory responsibilities to any other person, nor accept control of his or her supervisory responsibilities by any other person.
(d) The project broker shall notify the commission in writing of any change in his or her status as project broker within ten days following the change.

SECTION .0700 - TIME SHARE FORMS

21 NCAC 58B .0701   FORMS FOR TIME SHARE PROJECTS

The following forms are required by the Commission for use in filing and submitting information with respect to applications for time share project registration, renewal and termination:

(1) Application for Time Share Project Registration;
(2) Affidavit of Time Share Project Broker;
(3) Affidavit of Time Share Registrar;
(4) Affidavit of Independent Escrow Agent;
(5) Developer Designation of Time Share Project Broker, Registrar and Independent Escrow Agent;
(6) Application for Time Share Project Renewal;
(7) Notice of Developer Termination of Time Share Project Registration;
(8) Consent to Service of Process and Pleadings.

SUBCHAPTER 58C – REAL ESTATE PRELICENSING EDUCATION

Rules for Subchapter 58C are not reprinted in this book but are available upon written request to the North Carolina Real Estate Commission.

SUBCHAPTER 58D – REAL ESTATE APPRAISERS (REPEALED)

SUBCHAPTER 58E – REAL ESTATE CONTINUING EDUCATION

Rules for Subchapter 58E are not reprinted in this book but are available upon written request to the North Carolina Real Estate Commission.

SUBCHAPTER 58F – BROKER TRANSITION COURSE (REPEALED)

SUBCHAPTER 58G – NORTH CAROLINA REAL ESTATE COMMISSION ADMINISTRATION

SECTION .0100 – REAL ESTATE COMMISSION SERVICE

21 NCAC 58G .0101   PER DIEM

A member of the Real Estate Commission shall receive a per diem payment of two hundred dollars ($200.00) for each day during which the member is engaged in business for or on behalf of the Real Estate Commission.

LICENSE LAW AND RULE COMMENTS

**Comments on Selected Provisions of the
North Carolina Real Estate License Law
and Real Estate Commission Rules**

INTRODUCTION

These comments on selected North Carolina Real Estate License Law and Real Estate Commission Rules provisions are intended to assist real estate licensees, prelicensing course students and others in understanding the License Law and Commission rules. The comments are organized in a topic format that often differs from the sequence in which the topics are addressed in the License Law and Commission rules. The topics selected for comment here are not only of particular importance in real estate brokerage practice but also are likely to be tested on the real estate license examination. The appropriate references to the License Law and Commission rules are provided beside each listed topic.

REQUIREMENT FOR A LICENSE
General [G.S. 93A-1 and 93A-2]

Any person or business entity who directly or indirectly engages in the business of a real estate broker for compensation or the promise thereof while physically in the state of North Carolina must have a North Carolina real estate broker license. In North Carolina, a real estate licensee may only engage in brokerage as an "agent" for a party to a transaction. Thus, a real estate licensee is commonly and appropriately referred to as a real estate "agent" even though the latter term does not actually appear in the License Law. Note that a real estate "licensee" is NOT automatically a "REALTOR®." A licensed real estate agent is a REALTOR® **only** if he/she belongs to the National Association of REALTORS®, a private trade association. Thus, the term REALTOR® should not be used to generally refer to all real estate licensees.

License Categories [G.S. 93A-2]

There is only one "type" of license, a **broker** license; however, there are several license status categories as described below:

Provisional Broker – This is the "entry level" license status category. A person who has met all the license qualification requirements (including a *75-hour prelicensing course and passing the Commission's license examination*) is initially issued **a broker license on "provisional" status** and is referred to as a **"provisional broker."** A provisional broker generally may perform the same acts as a broker whose license is NOT on provisional status so long as he or she is supervised by a broker who is a designated **broker-in-charge**. A provisional broker may not operate independently in any way. G.S. 93A-2(a2) defines a **"provisional broker"** as "...*a real estate broker who, pending acquisition and documentation to the Commission of the education or experience prescribed by either G.S. 93A-4(a1) or G. S. 93A-4.3, must be supervised by a broker-in-charge when performing any act for which a real estate license is required."* This license status category is comparable to a "salesperson" license in most other states except that it is a **temporary license status category**. Provisional brokers may not retain this status indefinitely – they must complete required **postlicensing education** (one 30-hour course each year for the three years following initial licensure – total of 90 hours) to remove the "provisional" status of their licenses and to remain eligible for "active" license status.

Broker – A "provisional broker" who satisfies all postlicensing education requirements to terminate the "provisional" status of such license becomes simply a **"broker"** and is NOT required to be supervised by a broker-in-charge in order to hold an "active" license. Applicants qualifying for licensure in NC based on **broker** licensure in another state (both applicants who qualify for direct licensure by reciprocity and applicants from non-reciprocal states who qualify by taking the NC license examination) may be licensed directly as a **broker NOT on provisional status**. All others must first be licensed in NC as a **provisional broker** and then satisfy the postlicensing education requirement to become a non-provisional broker.

Most frequently, brokers elect to work for another broker or brokerage firm. Brokers may also elect to operate independently as a sole proprietor; however, with limited exceptions, such broker will have to qualify for and designate himself or herself as a **broker-in-charge** in order to operate independently and perform most brokerage activities (discussed further below under "broker-in-charge" and also in a subsequent section on brokers-in-charge that appears near the end of this appendix).

Broker-In-Charge – G.S. 93A-2(a1) defines a **"broker-in-charge"** as "...*a real estate broker who has been designated as the broker having responsibility for the supervision of real estate provisional brokers engaged in real estate brokerage at a particular real estate office and for other administrative and supervisory duties as the Commission shall prescribe by rule."* Commission Rule A.0110 requires that each real estate office must have a broker who meets the qualification requirements to serve as "broker-in-charge" of the office and who has designated himself or herself as the broker-in-charge of that office. As is the case with "provisional broker," *broker-in-charge" is not a separate license, but only a **separate license status category**. A broker who is to serve as the broker-in-charge (BIC) of an office (including working independently) must be designated as a BIC with the Commission.

North Carolina Real Estate License Law and Commission Rules

To qualify for designation as a broker-in-charge, a broker's license must be on "active" status but NOT on "provisional" status, the broker must have **two years full-time or part-time equivalent ACTUAL brokerage experience within the previous five years** (or education/experience the Commission finds equivalent to such experience), and the broker must complete a 12-hour **Broker-In-Charge Course** within 120 days after designation. Broker-in-charge requirements are addressed in detail in a separate subsequent section titled "Broker-In-Charge."

Limited Nonresident Commercial Broker – A broker or salesperson residing in a state other than North Carolina who holds an active broker or salesperson license in the state where his or her primary place of real estate business is located may apply for and obtain a North Carolina **"limited nonresident commercial broker license"** that entitles such licensee to engage in transactions for compensation involving "commercial real estate" in North Carolina, but the licensee must enter into a "declaration of affiliation" and a "brokerage cooperation agreement" with a resident North Carolina broker and the licensee must be supervised by the North Carolina broker while performing commercial real estate brokerage in North Carolina. Like a "firm" license, a limited nonresident commercial broker license is a separate license.

Licensing of Business Entities [G.S. 93A-1 and 2; Rule A.0502]

In addition to individuals (persons), "business entities" also must be licensed in order to engage in the real estate business. Any corporation, partnership, limited liability company, association or other business entity (other than a sole proprietorship) must obtain a separate real estate **firm** broker license.

Activities Requiring a License [G.S. 93A-2]

Persons and business entities who for compensation or the promise thereof perform the activities listed below as an agent for others are considered to be performing brokerage activities and must have a real estate license unless specifically exempted by the statute (see subsequent section on "Exemptions"). There is no exemption for engaging in a limited number of transactions. A person or entity who performs a brokerage service in even one transaction must be licensed. Similarly, no fee or other compensation is so small as to exempt one from the application of the statute when acting for another in a real estate transaction. *Brokerage activities include*:

1. **Listing (or offering to list) real estate for sale or rent**, including any act performed by a real estate licensee in connection with obtaining and servicing a listing agreement. Examples of such acts include, but are not limited to, soliciting listings, providing information to the property owner, and preparing listing agreements or property management agreements.
2. **Selling or buying (or offering to sell or buy) real estate**, including any act performed by a real estate licensee in connection with assisting others in selling or buying real estate. Examples of such acts include, but are not limited to, advertising listed property for sale, "showing" listed property to prospective buyers, providing information about listed property to prospective buyers (other than basic property facts that might commonly appear in an advertisement in a newspaper, real estate publication or internet website), negotiating a sale or purchase of real estate, and assisting with the completion of contract offers and counteroffers using preprinted forms and communication of offers and acceptances.
3. **Leasing or renting (or offering to lease or rent) real estate**, including any act performed by real estate licensees in connection with assisting others in leasing or renting real estate. Examples of such acts include, but are not limited to, advertising listed property for rent, "showing" listed rental property to prospective tenants, providing information about listed rental property to prospective tenants (other than basic property facts that might commonly appear in an advertisement in a newspaper, real estate publication or internet website), negotiating lease terms, and assisting with the completion of lease offers and counteroffers using preprinted forms and communication of offers and acceptances.
4. **Conducting (or offering to conduct) a real estate auction.** (Mere criers of sale are excluded.) NOTE: An auctioneer's license is also required to auction real estate.
5. **Selling, buying, leasing, assigning or exchanging any interest in real estate, including a leasehold interest, in connection with the sale or purchase of a business.**
6. **Referring a party to a real estate licensee, if done for compensation.** Any arrangement or agreement between a licensee and an unlicensed person that calls for the licensee to compensate the unlicensed person in any way for finding, introducing or referring a party to the licensee has been determined by North Carolina's courts to be prohibited under the License Law. Therefore, *no licensee may pay a finder's fee, referral fee, "bird dog" fee or similar compensation to an unlicensed person.*

Unlicensed Employees — Permitted Activities

The use of unlicensed assistants and other unlicensed office personnel in the real estate industry is very widespread and the Commission is frequently asked by licensees what acts such persons may lawfully perform. To provide guidance to licensees regarding this matter, the Commission has prepared the following list of acts that an unlicensed assistant or employee may lawfully perform so long as the assistant or employee is salaried or hourly paid and is not paid on a per-transaction basis.

An unlicensed, salaried employee MAY:
1. Receive and forward phone calls and electronic messages to licensees.

2. Submit listings and changes to a multiple listing service, but only if the listing data or changes are compiled and provided by a licensee.
3. Secure copies of public records from public repositories (i.e., register of deeds office, county tax office, etc.).
4. Place "for sale" or "for rent" signs and lock boxes on property at the direction of a licensee.
5. Order and supervise routine and minor repairs to listed property at the direction of a licensee.
6. Act as a courier to deliver or pick up documents.
7. Provide to prospects basic factual information on listed property that might commonly appear in advertisements in a newspaper, real estate publication or internet website.
8. Schedule appointments for showing property listed for sale or rent.
9. Communicate with licensees, property owners, prospects, inspectors, etc. to coordinate or confirm appointments.
10. Show rental properties managed by the employee's employing broker to prospective tenants and complete and execute preprinted form leases for the rental of such properties.
11. Type offers, contracts and leases from drafts of preprinted forms completed by a licensee.
12. Record and deposit earnest money deposits, tenant security deposits and other trust monies, and otherwise maintain records of trust account receipts and disbursements, under the close supervision of the office broker-in-charge, who is legally responsible for handling trust funds and maintaining trust accounts.
13. Assist a licensee in assembling documents for closing.
14. Compute commission checks for licensees affiliated with a broker or firm and act as bookkeeper for the firm's bank operating accounts.

Exemptions [G.S. 93A-2]

The following persons and organizations are specifically exempted from the requirement for real estate licensure:

1. A **business entity** selling or leasing real estate owned by the business entity when the acts performed are in the regular course of or are incident to the management of that real estate and the investment therein. This exemption extends to officers and employees of an exempt corporation, the general partners of an exempt partnership, and the managers of an exempt limited liability company when engaging in acts or services for which the corporation, partnership or limited liability company would be exempt.
2. A person acting as an **attorney-in-fact** under a power of attorney from the owner authorizing the final consummation of performance of any contract for the sale, lease or exchange of real estate. (Note: This limited exemption applies only to the final completion of a transaction already commenced. The licensing requirement may not be circumvented by obtaining a power of attorney.)
3. An **attorney-at-law** who is an active member of the North Carolina State Bar only when performing an act or service that constitutes the practice of law under Chapter 84 of the General Statutes. Thus, the attorney exemption is strictly limited and attorneys may NOT generally engage in real estate brokerage practice without a real estate license.
4. A person acting as a receiver, trustee in bankruptcy, guardian, administrator or executor or any person acting under a court order.
5. A **trustee** acting under a written trust agreement, deed of trust or will.
6. **Certain salaried employees of broker-property managers.** (See G.S. 93A-2(c)(6) for details.)
7. An individual owner selling or leasing the owner's own property.
8. A **housing authority** organized under Chapter 157 of the General Statutes and any regular salaried employee with regard to the sale or lease of property owned by the housing authority or to the subletting of property which the housing authority holds as tenant.

THE REAL ESTATE COMMISSION
Composition [G.S. 93A-3(a)]

The Real Estate Commission consists of nine (9) members who serve three-year terms. Seven members are appointed by the Governor and two are appointed by the General Assembly upon the recommendations of the Speaker of the House of Representatives and the President Pro Tempore of the Senate. At least three (3) members must be licensed brokers. At least two (2) members must be "public members" who are NOT involved directly or indirectly in the real estate brokerage or appraisal businesses.

Purpose and Powers [G.S. 93A-3(a), (c) and (f); G.S. 93A-6(a) and (b); G.S. 93A-4(d) and 93A-4A]

The principal purpose of the Real Estate Commission is to protect the interests of members of the general public in their dealings with real estate brokers. This is accomplished through the exercise of the following statutory powers granted to the Commission:

1. Licensing real estate brokers and brokerage firms, and registering time share projects.
2. Establishing and administering prelicensing and postlicensing education programs for prospective licensees and a continuing education program for licensees.
3. Providing education and information relating to the real estate brokerage business for licensees and the general public.
4. Regulating the business activities of brokers and brokerage firms, including disciplining licensees who

violate the License Law or Commission rules.

It should be noted that the Commission is specifically prohibited, however, from regulating commissions, salaries or fees charged by real estate licensees and from arbitrating disputes between parties regarding matters of contract such as the rate and/or division of commissions or similar matters. [See G.S. 93A-3(c) and Rule A.0109.]

Disciplinary Authority [G.S. 93A-6(a)-(c)]

The Real Estate Commission is authorized to take a variety of disciplinary actions against licensees who the Commission finds guilty of violating the License Law or Commission rules while acting as real estate licensees. These are: **reprimand, censure, license suspension** and **license revocation**. The License Law also permits a licensee under certain circumstances to surrender his/her license with the consent of the Commission. Disciplinary actions taken against licensees are regularly reported in the Commission's quarterly newsletter which is distributed to all licensees and also may be reported in local and regional newspapers.

It should be noted that licensees may be disciplined by the Commission for committing acts prohibited by the License Law when selling, leasing, or buying real estate for themselves, as well as for committing such acts in transactions handled as agents for others. [G.S. 93A-6(b)(3)]

The Commission also has the power to seek in its own name **injunctive relief** in superior court to prevent any person (licensees and others) from violating the License Law or Commission rules. A typical example of where the Commission might pursue injunctive relief in the courts is where a person engages in real estate activity without a license or during a period when the person's license is suspended, revoked or expired. [G.S. 93A-6(c)]

Any violation of the License Law or Commission rules is a criminal offense (misdemeanor) and may be prosecuted in a court of law. However, a finding by the Commission that a licensee has violated the License Law or Commission rules does not constitute a criminal conviction. [G.S. 93-8]

PROHIBITED ACTS BY LICENSEES

G.S. 93A-6 provides a list of prohibited acts which may result in disciplinary action against licensees. Discussed below are the various prohibited acts, except for those related to handling and accounting for trust funds, broker's responsibility for closing statements, and the failure to deliver certain instruments to parties in a transaction, which are discussed in the subsequent sections on "General Brokerage Provisions" and "Handling Trust Funds."

Important Note

The provisions of the License Law relating to misrepresentation or omission of a material fact, conflict of interest, licensee competence, handling of trust funds, and improper, fraudulent or dishonest dealing generally apply independently of other statutory law or case law such as the law of agency. Nevertheless, another law may have an effect on the application of a License Law provision. For example, the requirements of the N.C. Tenant Security Deposit Act relating to the accounting to a tenant for a residential security deposit within 30 days after termination of a tenancy amplify the general License Law provisions (and Commission rules) requiring licensees to account for such funds within a reasonable time. Thus, in this instance, a violation of the Tenant Security Deposit Act's provisions would also be considered by the Commission to be a violation of the License Law.

Similarly, the law of agency and the law of contracts, which are derived from case law, may be taken into consideration when applying the provisions of the License Law. Thus, a licensee's agency status and role in a transaction might affect the licensee's duties under the license law. Examples of how an agent's duties under the License Law may be affected by the application of other laws are included at various points in this section on "Prohibited Acts by Licensees."

Misrepresentation or Omission [G.S. 93A-6(a)(1)]

Misrepresentation or omission of a material fact by brokers or salespersons is prohibited, and this prohibition includes both "willful" and "negligent" acts. A "willful" act is one that is done intentionally and deliberately, while a "negligent" act is one that is done unintentionally. A **"misrepresentation"** is communicating false information, while an **"omission"** is failing to provide or disclose information where there is a duty to provide or disclose such information.

For purposes of applying G.S. 93A-6(a)(1), whether a fact is "material" depends on the facts and circumstances of a particular transaction and the application of statutory and/or case law. The Commission has historically interpreted **"material facts"** under the Real Estate License Law to at least include:

Facts about the property itself (such as a structural defect or defective mechanical systems);

Facts relating directly to the property (such as a pending zoning change or planned highway construction in the immediate vicinity); and

Facts relating directly to the ability of the agent's principal to complete the transaction (such as a pending foreclosure sale).

Regardless of which party in a transaction a real estate agent represents, the facts described above must be disclosed to both the agent's principal and to third parties the agent deals with on the principal's behalf. In addition, an agent has a duty to disclose to his or her principal any information that may affect the principal's rights and interests or influence the principal's decision in the transaction.

Note, however, that G.S. 39-50 and 42-14.2 specifically provide that the fact that a property was occupied by a person who died or had a serious illness while occupying the property is NOT a material fact. Thus, agents do not need to voluntarily disclose such a fact. If a prospective buyer or tenant specifically asks about such a matter, the agent may either decline to answer or respond honestly. If, however, a prospective buyer or tenant inquires as to whether a previous owner or occupant had AIDS, the agent is prohibited by fair housing laws from answering such an inquiry because persons with AIDS are considered to be "handicapped" under such laws and disclosure of the information may have the effect of discriminating against the property owner based on the handicapping condition.

This introductory information should assist in understanding G.S. 93A-6(a)(1), which establishes four separate (although closely related) categories of conduct which are prohibited. These are discussed below, and a few examples of prohibited conduct are provided for each category.

Willful Misrepresentation — *This occurs when a licensee who has "actual knowledge" of a material fact deliberately misinforms a buyer, seller, tenant or landlord concerning such fact.* A misrepresentation is also considered to be "willful" when a licensee who does NOT have actual knowledge of a matter material to the transaction provides incorrect information concerning such matter to a buyer, seller, tenant or landlord *without regard for the actual truth of the matter* (i.e., when a licensee intentionally provides information without knowing whether or not it is true and the information provided is in fact not true).

Note: The following examples of willful misrepresentation apply regardless of the licensee's status (seller's agent or buyer's agent) or role (listing agent or selling agent).

- **Example:** An agent knows that a listed house has a severe problem with water intrusion in the crawl space during heavy rains. In response to a question from a prospective buyer who is being shown the house during dry weather, the agent states that there is no water drainage problem.
- **Example**: An agent knows that the heat pump at a listed house does not function properly, but tells a prospective buyer that all mechanical systems and appliances are in good condition.
- **Example:** An agent knows that the approximate market value of a house is $225,000, but tells the property owner that the house is worth $250,000 in order to obtain a listing.
- **Example:** An agent is completely unfamiliar with the features or condition of a listed property; however, the agent informs a prospective buyer that the plumbing is in good working order without first checking with the owner. (The agent in such instance is acting without regard for the truth of the matter being represented. If the plumbing in fact needs significant repair, then the agent may be guilty of willful misrepresentation.)
- **Example:** Without checking with the owner, an agent tells a prospective buyer of a listed house that heating and cooling costs are "very reasonable." (Because the agent acted without regard for the truth of the matter, he may be guilty of willful misrepresentation if heating and cooling costs are in fact extraordinarily high.)

Negligent Misrepresentation — *This occurs when a licensee unintentionally misinforms a buyer, seller, tenant or landlord concerning a material fact either because the licensee does not have actual knowledge of the fact, because the licensee has incorrect information, or because of a mistake by the licensee.* If a reasonably prudent licensee *"should reasonably have known"* the truth of the matter that was misrepresented, then the licensee may be guilty of "negligent misrepresentation" even though the licensee was acting in good faith.

Negligent misrepresentation by real estate licensees occurs frequently in real estate transactions. A very common situation is the recording of incorrect information about a property in an MLS® listing due to the negligence of the listing agent. When a prospective buyer is subsequently provided the incorrect information from the MLS® by the agent working with the buyer, a negligent misrepresentation by the listing agent occurs.

A listing agent is generally held to a higher standard with regard to negligent misrepresentation of material facts about a listed property to a buyer than is a selling agent who is acting as a seller's subagent. This is because (1) The listing agent is in the best position to ascertain facts about the property, (2) the listing agent is expected to take reasonable steps to assure that property data included with the listing is correct and (3) it is generally considered reasonable for a selling agent to rely on the accuracy of the listing data except in those situations where it should be obvious to a reasonably prudent agent that the listing information is incorrect. However, *a buyer's agent may in some cases be held to a higher standard than a seller's subagent because of the buyer's agent's duties to the buyer under the law of agency and the buyer's agent's special knowledge of the buyer's particular situation and needs.*

- **Example:** An agent has previously sold several lots in a subdivision under development and all those lots passed a soil suitability test for an on-site septic system. The agent then sells Lot 35 without checking as to whether this lot satisfies the soil test; however, the agent informs the buyer that Lot 35 will support an on-site septic system when in fact the contrary is true. (While the agent's conduct may not rise to the level of willful disregard for the truth of the matter, the agent was at least negligent in not checking the soil test result on Lot 35 and is therefore guilty of negligent misrepresentation. This result is not affected by the agent's agency status or role in the transaction.)
- **Example:** An owner tells a listing agent with ABC Realty that his house has 1850 heated square feet. Without verifying the square footage, the agent records 1850 square feet on the listing form and in the listing information published in the local MLS. The house is subsequently sold by a sales agent with XYZ Realty who tells the buyer that according to the MLS data, the house has 1850 square feet. The buyer later discovers that the house actually has only 1750

North Carolina Real Estate License Law and Commission Rules

square feet. (In this situation, the listing agent did not make a direct misrepresentation to the buyer; however, he/she initiated the chain of communication which led to the buyer being misinformed, and thus indirectly misrepresented a material fact. Further, the listing agent's failure to verify the square footage constituted negligence. Therefore, the listing agent is guilty of a negligent misrepresentation. Although the selling agent directly communicated the incorrect information to the buyer, he/she probably acted reasonably in relying on the data in the MLS book. In this case, if the selling agent had no reason to doubt the MLS data, the selling agent is not guilty of a negligent misrepresentation. Note, however, that if the square footage discrepancy had been sufficiently large that a reasonably prudent selling agent should have known the listed data was incorrect, then the selling agent would also have been guilty of negligent misrepresentation. The result in this particular example is not affected by the selling agent's agency status (seller's subagent or buyer's agent), although this might be a factor in other situations.

Willful Omission — *This occurs when a licensee has "actual knowledge" of a material fact and a duty to disclose such fact to a buyer, seller, tenant, or landlord, but deliberately fails to disclose such fact.*

- **Example:** An agent knows that a zoning change is pending which would adversely affect the value of a listed property, but fails to disclose such information to a prospective buyer. The agent has committed a willful omission and this result is not affected by the agent's agency status or role in the transaction.

[**Note:** Information about a zoning change, planned highway or similar matter that would enhance the value of a seller's property must also be disclosed to the seller, even if the licensee is a buyer's agent.]

- **Example:** An agent knows that the city has just decided to extend water and sewer lines to a subdivision that has been plagued for years by serious water quality and sewage disposal problems. This will result in a substantial increase in the value of homes in the subdivision. The agent, who is working with a buyer to purchase a house in the subdivision, does not inform the seller of the city's recent decision. The agent has committed a willful omission and this result is not affected by the agent's agency status or role in the transaction.
- **Example:** An agent knows that a listed house has a major defect (e.g., crumbling foundation, no insulation, malfunctioning septic tank, leaking roof, termite infestation, or some other problem) but fails to disclose such information to a prospective buyer. The agent has committed a willful omission and this result is not affected by the agent's agency status or role in the transaction.
- **Example:** A selling agent working with a buyer as a subagent of the seller learns that the buyer is willing to pay more than the price in the buyer's offer, but fails to disclose this information to the seller (or listing agent) when presenting the offer. The selling agent has committed a willful omission. If, however, the selling agent were acting as a buyer's agent, then the result would be different because the agent does not represent the seller.
- **Example**: A buyer's agent becomes aware that the seller with whom his buyer is negotiating is under pressure to sell quickly and may accept much less than the listing price. Believing such information should always be kept confidential, the buyer's agent does not provide the buyer with this information. The buyer's agent is guilty of a willful omission. An agent must disclose to his/her principal any information that might affect the principal's decision in the transaction.
- **Example**: Suppose in the immediately preceding example that the seller's property is listed with the firm of the buyer's agent and the firm's policy is to practice dual agency in in-house sales situations where it represents both the seller and the buyer. In this situation, the buyer's agent would not be considered to have committed a willful omission under the License Law by not disclosing the information about the seller's personal situation to the buyer. NOTE: This assumes however that the buyer's agent properly disclosed his/her status as a buyer's agent to the seller or seller's agent upon "initial contact," that dual agency was properly authorized in writing by both the seller and buyer prior to showing the seller's property to the buyer and that the agency agreements provided for this limitation on disclosure of information in dual agency situations (as is the case with the agency agreement forms provided by the North Carolina Association of REALTORS® for use by its members).

Negligent Omission — *This occurs when a licensee does NOT have actual knowledge of a material fact and consequently does not disclose the fact, but a reasonably prudent licensee "should reasonably have known" of such fact.* In this case, the licensee may be guilty of "negligent omission" if he/she fails to disclose this fact to a buyer, seller, tenant or landlord, even though the licensee acted in good faith in the transaction.

The prohibition against negligent omission creates a *"duty to discover and disclose" material facts* which a reasonably prudent licensee would typically have discovered in the course of the transaction. *A listing agent is typically in a much better position than a selling agent to discover material facts relating to a listed property and thus, will be held to a higher standard than will a selling agent acting as a seller's subagent.*

On the other hand, a buyer's agent in some circumstances may be held to a higher standard than a seller's subagent because of the buyer's agent's duties to the buyer under the law of agency, particularly if the buyer's agent is aware of a buyer's special needs with regard to a property. Again we see how the agency relationships between agents and principals to a transaction and the licensee's role in the transaction can affect a licensee's duties and responsibilities under the License Law.

Instances of negligent omission occur much less frequently than instances of negligent misrepresentation. This is because most facts about a listed property are recorded on a detailed property data sheet from which information is taken for inclusion in MLS computer files/books. If incorrect information taken from an MLS computer file/book is passed on to a prospective purchaser, then a "misrepresentation," rather than an "omission," has occurred. Nevertheless, there are examples of negligent omission which can be cited.

> **Example:** A listing agent lists for sale a house located adjacent to a street that is about to be widened into a major thoroughfare. The thoroughfare project has been very controversial and highly publicized. The city recently finalized its decision to proceed with the project and the plans for the street widening are recorded in the city planner's office. A buyer, working with a selling agent, makes an offer to buy the house. The listing agent does not disclose the street widening plans to the buyer or selling agent and claims later that he/she was not aware of the plans. In this situation, both the listing and selling agents are probably guilty of a negligent omission because each "should reasonably have known" of the street widening plans, clearly a material fact, and should have disclosed this fact to the buyer. This result is not affected by whether the selling agent is a buyer agent or seller's subagent.

> **Example:** A seller has a 30,000 square foot commercial property for sale which cannot be expanded under local zoning laws. The buyer is looking for property in the 25,000 - 30,000 square foot range, but has told his buyer's agent that he needs a property where he can expand to 50,000 square feet or more in the future. The seller does not think to advise the buyer's agent that the property cannot be expanded, and the buyer's agent makes no inquiry about it although he is aware of the buyer's special needs. If the buyer purchases the property without knowing about the restriction on expansion, the buyer's agent is guilty of a negligent omission for failing to discover and disclose a special circumstance that the agent knew was especially important to his/her client.

> **Example:** When listing a house, a listing agent is told by the seller that one area of the roof leaks badly when it rains, but the moisture so far is being contained in the attic. The listing agent forgets to note this on the MLS data sheet and forgets to disclose the leaking roof problem to prospective buyers and selling agents. The listing agent is guilty of a negligent omission. Because the agent's failure to disclose the leaking roof problem was unintentional, the listing agent is not guilty of a willful omission; however, his/her forgetfulness resulting in his/her failure to disclose the defect constitutes a negligent omission.

Making False Promises [G.S. 93A-6(a)(2)]

Real estate brokers are prohibited from "making any false promises of a character likely to influence, persuade or induce." It is unimportant whether or not the broker originally intended to honor his/her promise – failure to honor a promise is sufficient to constitute a violation of this provision. The promise may relate to any matter which might influence, persuade or induce a person to perform some act which he/she might not otherwise perform.

> **Example:** An agent promises a prospective apartment tenant that the apartment the prospect is considering renting will be repainted before the tenant moves in. The agent then fails to have the work done after the lease is signed.

> **Example:** An agent promises a property owner that if he/she lists his/her house for sale with the agent's firm, then the firm will steam-clean all the carpets and wash all the windows. The firm then fails to have the work done after the listing contract is signed.

Other Misrepresentations [G.S. 93A-6(a)(3)]

Real estate brokers are prohibited from pursuing a course of misrepresentation (or making of false promises) through other agents or salespersons or through advertising or other means.

> **Example:** In marketing subdivision lots for a developer, a broker regularly advertises that the lots for sale are suitable for residential use when in fact the lots will not pass a soil suitability test for on-site sewage systems.

> **Example:** A broker is marketing a new condominium complex which is under construction. Acting with the full knowledge and consent of the broker, the broker's agents regularly inform prospective buyers that units will be available for occupancy on June 1, when in fact the units won't be available until at least September 1.

Conflict of Interest [G.S. 93A-6(a)(4) and (6); Rule A.0104(d)]

Undisclosed Dual Agency. G.S. 93A-6(a)(4) prohibits a real estate agent from *"acting for more than one party in a transaction without the knowledge of all parties for whom he or she acts."* Commission Rule A.0104(d) takes this a step further by providing that a broker or brokerage firm representing one party in a transaction shall not undertake to represent another party in the transaction without the express written authority (i.e., authorization of dual agency) of each party (subject to one exception, explained as part of the dual agency discussion in the "General Brokerage Provisions" section). A typical violation of this provision occurs when the agent has only one principal in a transaction but acts in a manner which benefits another party without the principal's knowledge. In such a situation, the agent violates the duty of loyalty and consent owed to his principal.

> **Example:** A house is listed with Firm X. When showing the house to a prospective buyer not represented by Firm X, an agent of Firm X advises the buyer to offer substantially less than the listing price because the seller must move soon and is very anxious to sell the property fast. The agent and Firm X are contractually obligated to represent only the seller. By advising the prospective buyer as indicated in this example, the agent is acting to benefit the buyer without the seller's knowledge and consent. This act violates both the License Law and the Law of Agency.
>
> **Example:** An agent with Firm Y assists her sister in purchasing a house listed with Firm X without advising Firm X or the seller of her relationship with the buyer. The agent is "officially" acting as a subagent of the seller in the transaction. In this situation, there is an inherent conflict of interest on the part of the agent. If the agent does not disclose her relationships to both parties, then the agent violates both the License Law and Law of Agency. In fact, since her allegiance lies with her sister, the agent should instead act as a buyer's agent from the outset. The same would be true if the buyer were a close friend or business associate of the agent, or in any way enjoyed a special relationship to the agent which would clearly influence the agent to act in behalf of the buyer rather than the seller.

Self-dealing. G.S. 93A-6(a)(4) also prohibits any **"self-dealing"** on the part of an agent. For example, if an agent attempts to make a secret profit in a transaction where he is supposed to be representing a principal, then the agent violates this "conflict of interest" provision.

> **Example:** An agent lists a parcel of undeveloped property which is zoned for single-family residential use. The agent knows that this property is about to be rezoned for multi-family residential use, which will greatly increase the property's value. Rather than informing the seller of this fact, the agent offers to buy the property at the listed price, telling the seller that he wants to acquire the property as a long-term investment. The deal closes. Several months later, after the rezoning has been accomplished, the agent sells the property at a substantial profit.

Representing Another Broker without Consent. G.S. 93A-6(a)(6) prohibits a licensee from "representing or attempting to represent a real estate broker other than the broker by whom he or she is engaged or associated, without the express knowledge and consent of the broker with whom he or she is associated." While brokers may work for or be associated with more than one real estate company, so long as they have the express consent of all brokers-in-charge, provisional brokers may never engage in brokerage activities for more than one company at a time.

Improper Brokerage Commission [G.S. 93A-6(a)(5) and (9)]

A broker may NOT pay a commission or valuable consideration to any person for acts or services performed in violation of the License Law. [G.S. 93A-6(a)(9)] *This provision flatly prohibits a broker or salesperson from paying an unlicensed person for acts which require a real estate license.* Following are examples of prohibited payments:

> **Example:** The payment by brokers of commissions to previously licensed sales associates who failed to properly renew their licenses for any acts performed after their licenses had expired. [Note that payment could properly be made for commissions earned while the license was on active status, even if the license is inactive or expired at time of payment. The determining factor is whether the license was on active status at the time all services were rendered which generated the commission?]
>
> **Example:** The payment of a commission, salary or fee by brokers to unlicensed employees or independent contractors (e.g., secretaries, "trainees" who haven't passed the license examination, etc.) for performing acts or services requiring a real estate license.
>
> **Example:** The payment by licensees of a "finder's fee," "referral fee," "bird dog fee," or any other valuable consideration to unlicensed persons who find, introduce, or bring together parties to a real estate transaction. This is true even if the ultimate consummation of the transaction is accomplished by a licensee and even if the act is performed without expectation of compensation. Thus, a licensee may NOT compensate a friend, relative, former client or any other unlicensed person for "referring" a prospective buyer, seller, landlord or tenant to such licensee. This prohibition extends to "owner referral" programs at condominium or time share complexes and "tenant referral" programs at apartment complexes.

In addition, a *provisional* broker may NOT accept any compensation for brokerage services from anyone other than his employing broker or brokerage firm. Consequently, *a broker may not pay a commission or fee directly to a provisional broker of another broker or firm. Any such payment must be made through the provisional broker's employing broker or firm.* [G.S. 93A-6(a)(5)]

Note: *See also the discussion of Rule A.0109 on "Brokerage Fees and Compensation" under the subsequent section titled "General Brokerage Provisions."*

Unworthiness and Incompetence [G.S. 93A-6(a)(8)]

This broad provision authorizes the Real Estate Commission to discipline any licensee who, based on his or her conduct and consideration of the public interest, is found to be unworthy or incompetent to work in the real estate business. A wide range of conduct may serve as the basis for a finding of unworthiness or incompetence, including conduct which violates other specific provisions of the License Law or Commission rules. Here are a few examples of improper conduct which do not specifically violate another License Law provision but which might support a finding of unworthiness or incompetence.

1. Failure to properly complete (fill in) real estate contracts or to use contract forms which are legally adequate.
2. Failure to diligently perform the services required under listing contracts or property management contracts.
3. Failure to provide accurate closing statements to sellers and buyers or accurate income/expense reports to property owners.

Improper Dealing [G.S. 93A-6(a)(10)]

This broad provision prohibits a real estate licensee from engaging in "any other conduct [not specifically prohibited elsewhere in the License Law] which constitutes **improper, fraudulent or dishonest dealing**." The determination as to whether particular conduct constitutes "improper, fraudulent or dishonest dealing" is made by the Real Estate Commission on a case-by-case basis. Therefore, a broad range of conduct might be found objectionable under this provision, depending on the facts in a case.

One category of conduct which violates this provision is any breach of the duty to exercise skill, care, and diligence in behalf of a client under the Law of Agency. (Note that other breaches of Agency Law duties constituting either a "misrepresentation or omission," a "conflict of interest" or a "failure to properly account for trust funds" are covered by other specific statutory provisions.)

Another category of conduct which violates this provision is any violation of the State Fair Housing Act. This is mentioned separately under the "Discriminatory Practices" heading.

Example: A broker is personally conducting the closing of a real estate sale he has negotiated. The seller does not show up for the closing. In order to avoid a delay in closing the transaction, the broker forges the seller's signature on a deed to the property and proceeds with the closing in the seller's absence.

Example: An agent assists a prospective buyer in perpetrating a fraud in connection with a mortgage loan application by preparing two contracts — one with false information for submission to the lending institution, and another which represents the actual agreement between seller and buyer. (This practice is commonly referred to as "dual contracting" or "contract kiting.")

Example: A broker lists a property for sale and agrees in the listing contract to place the listing in the local MLS, to advertise the property for sale, and to use his best efforts in good faith to find a buyer. The broker places a "For Sale" sign on the property, but fails to place the property in the MLS for more than 30 days and fails to otherwise advertise the property during the listing period. (The broker has failed to exercise reasonable skill, care and diligence in behalf of his client as required by the listing contract and the Law of Agency.)

Example: An agent is aware that the owners of a house listed with his company are out of town for the weekend, yet the agent gives a prospective buyer the house keys and allows such prospect to look at the listed house without accompanying the prospect. (The agent has failed to exercise reasonable skill, care and diligence in behalf of his client.)

Discriminatory Practices [G.S. 93A-6(a)(10); Rule A.1601]

Any conduct by a licensee which violates the provisions of the State Fair Housing Act is considered by the Commission to constitute "improper conduct" and to be a violation of the License Law.

Practice of Law [G.S. 93A-4(e); G.S. 93A-6(a)(11); Rule A.0111]

Real estate licensees may not perform for others any legal service described in G.S. 84-2.1 or any other legal service. Following are several examples of real estate-related legal services which licensees may NOT provide.

1. Drafting legal documents such as deeds, deeds of trust, leases and real estate sales contracts for others. Although licensees may "fill in" or "complete" pre-printed real estate contract forms which have been drafted by an attorney, they may NOT under any circumstances complete or fill in deed or deed of trust forms.
2. Abstracting or rendering an opinion on legal title to real property.
3. Providing "legal advice" of any nature to clients and customers, including advice concerning the nature of any interest in real estate or the means of holding title to real estate. (Note: Although providing advice concerning the legal ramifications of a real estate sales contract is prohibited, merely "explaining" the provisions of such a contract is not only acceptable, but highly recommended.)

Violating any Commission Rule [G.S. 93A-6-(a)(15)]

The law also has a "catch-all" provision that subjects a licensee to disciplinary action for violating any rule adopted by the Commission.

Note: The provisions of G.S. 93A-6(a)(12)-(14) are addressed elsewhere in these "Comments" under the "General Brokerage Provisions" section.

Other Prohibited Acts [G.S. 93A-6(b)]

In addition to those prohibited acts previously discussed, G.S. 93A-6(b) prescribes several other specific grounds for disciplinary action by the Commission, including:

1. Where a licensee has obtained a license by false or

fraudulent representation (e.g., falsifying documentation of prelicensing education, failing to disclose prior criminal convictions, etc.).
2. Where a licensee has been convicted of, or pled guilty or no contest to, a number of listed misdemeanors or felonies plus any other offense that shows professional unfitness or involves moral turpitude that would reasonably affect the licensee's performance in the real estate business.
3. Where a broker's unlicensed employee, who is exempt from licensing under G.S. 93A-2(c)(6) (property management exception), has committed an act which, if committed by the broker, would have constituted a violation of G.S. 93A-6(a) for which the broker could be disciplined.
4. Where a licensee who is also licensed as an appraiser, attorney, home inspector, mortgage broker, general contractor, or another licensed profession or occupation has been disciplined for an offense under any law involving fraud, theft, misrepresentation, breach of trust or fiduciary responsibility, or willful or negligent malpractice..

Lastly, be aware that under (b)(3), licensees may be disciplined for violating any of the 15 provisions under subsection (a) when selling, buying, or leasing their own property.

GENERAL BROKERAGE PROVISIONS

Discussed below are selected Commission rules related to general brokerage.

Agency Agreements and Disclosure [Rule A.0104]

Provided below is a brief summary of the various provisions of the Commission's rule regarding agency agreements and disclosure. For a much more in-depth discussion of this rule and its application, the reader is referred to the Commission's *North Carolina Real Estate Manual*.

Agency Agreements. Rule A.0104(a) requires all agency agreements for brokerage services (in both sales and lease transactions) to be in writing and signed by the parties thereto. Paragraph (a):

- Requires agency agreements with **property owners** (both sellers and lessors) of any type of property to be in writing from the time the agreement is initially made;
- Allows an express **oral buyer/tenant agency agreement** from the outset of the relationship, *but the agreement must be reduced to writing no later than the time any party to the transaction wants to extend an offer.* As a practical matter, this oral agreement needs to address all key aspects of the relationship, including agent compensation, authorization for dual agency, etc.

(Note: A buyer/tenant agency agreement must be in writing from the outset if it seeks to limit the buyer/tenant's right to work with other agents or binds the client to the agent for any definite time period. In other words, *an oral buyer/tenant agency agreement must be "non-exclusive" and must be for an indefinite period and terminable by the client at any time.***)**

Further, every **written** agency agreement of any kind must also:

- *Provide for its existence for a definite period of time* and terminate without prior notice at the expiration of that period. [Exception: an agency agreement between a broker and a landlord to procure tenants for the landlord's property may allow for automatic renewal so long as the landlord may terminate with notice at the end of any contract or renewal period.]
- *Contain the Rule A.0104(b) non-discrimination (fair housing) provision*, namely: "The broker shall conduct all his brokerage activities in regard to this agreement without respect to the race, color, religion, sex, national origin, handicap or familial status of any party or prospective party to the agreement." (This provision must be set forth in a clear and conspicuous manner which shall distinguish it from other provisions of the agency agreement.)
- *Include the license number of the individual licensee* who signs the agreement.

Allowing an agent to work with a buyer under an express *oral* buyer agency agreement is intended to address the problem of buyers being reluctant to sign a written buyer agency agreement at the outset of their relationship with a buyer agent. The idea underlying this approach is to allow an agent to work temporarily with a prospective buyer as a buyer's agent under an oral agreement while the agent establishes a rapport with the buyer that makes the buyer feel more comfortable with signing a written buyer agency agreement.

Although the rule allows oral buyer/tenant agency agreements until the point in time when any party is ready to make an offer, it nevertheless is highly advisable that agents have such agreements reduced to writing and signed by the buyer/tenant at the earliest possible time in order to avoid misunderstanding and conflict between the buyer/tenant and agent. Recall also that the agent must obtain a written buyer agency agreement from the buyer not later than the time either party to the transaction extends an offer to the other.

If the buyer will not sign a written buyer agency agreement prior to making or receiving an offer, then the agent may not continue to work with the buyer as a buyer's agent. Moreover, the agent may not begin at this point to work with the buyer as a seller's subagent unless the agent (1) fully advises the buyer of the consequences of the agent switching from buyer's agent to seller's agent (including the fact that the agent would have to disclose to the seller any information, including "confidential" information about the buyer, that might influence the seller's decision in the transaction), (2) obtains the buyer's consent, and (3) obtains the consent of the seller and listing firm, which is the seller's agent.

Agency Disclosure Requirement. While Rule A.0104(a) requires all agency agreements, whether for lease or sales transactions, to be in writing, the *Rule A.0104(c) agency disclosure requirement applies only to sales transactions.* It requires licensees to provide prospective buyers and sellers, at **"first substantial contact,"** with a copy of the **Working with Real Estate Agents** brochure, to review the brochure with them and then reach an agreement regarding their agency relationship. The licensee providing the brochure should also include his/her name and license number on the brochure. Note that the obligation under this rule is not satisfied merely by handing the prospective seller or buyer the brochure to read. The agent is required to review the contents of the brochure with the prospective buyer or seller and then reach agreement with the prospective buyer or seller as to whether the agent will work with the buyer or seller as his/her agent or as the agent of the other party.

In the case of a prospective **seller**, the agent may either (1) act as the seller's agent, which is the typical situation and which requires a written agreement from the outset of their relationship, or (2) work with the seller as a buyer's agent if the agent already represents a prospective buyer.

In the case of a prospective **buyer**, the agent may either (1) act as the buyer's agent under either an oral or written agreement as addressed in Rule A.0104(a), or (2) work with the buyer as a seller's agent, disclosure of which must be in writing from the outset.

Disclosure of Agency Status by Sellers' Agents and Subagents to Prospective Buyers: Paragraph (e) of Rule A.0104, like paragraph (c), requires a seller's agent or subagent in sales transactions to disclose his/her agency status in writing to a prospective buyer at the "first substantial contact" with the buyer. It is recommended that sellers' agents make this required written disclosure using the form provided for this purpose in the *Working with Real Estate Agents* brochure that must be provided to buyers (as well as to sellers) at first substantial contact. This form has a place for the buyer to acknowledge receipt of the brochure and disclosure of agency status, thereby providing the agent with written evidence of having provided the brochure and disclosure. The disclosure may, however, be made using a different form — *the most important point is that the disclosure be made in writing in a timely manner.* The reason for this requirement is that buyers tend to assume that an agent they contact to work with them in locating a property for purchase is "their" agent and working primarily in their interest. This may or may not be the case in reality. *The purpose of the disclosure requirement is to place prospective buyers on notice that the agent they are dealing with is NOT "their" agent before the prospective buyer discloses to the agent information which the buyer would not want a seller to know because it might compromise the buyer's bargaining position.*

Most frequently, **"first substantial contact"** will occur at the first "face-to-face" meeting with a prospective buyer. However, the point in time that "first substantial contact" with a prospective buyer occurs will vary depending on the particular situation and may or may not be at the time of the first or initial contact with the prospective buyer. Many first contacts are by telephone and do not involve discussions which reach the level that would require disclosure, although some initial phone contacts, especially those with out-of-town buyers, could reach this level.

"First substantial contact" occurs at the point in time when a discussion with a prospective buyer begins to focus on the buyer's specific property needs and desires or on the buyer's financial situation. Typically, that point in time is reached when the agent is ready to solicit information from the prospective buyer that is needed to identify prospective properties to show the buyer. Therefore, *an agent planning to work with a prospective buyer as a seller's agent or subagent should assure that disclosure of his/her agency status is made in writing to the prospective buyer prior to obtaining from the prospective buyer any personal or confidential information that the buyer would not want a seller to know.*

A few **examples of such personal or confidential information include**: *The maximum price a buyer is willing to pay for a property; the buyer's ability to pay more than the price offered by the buyer; or the fact that a buyer has a special interest in purchasing the seller's property rather than some other similar property.* In any event, the disclosure must be made prior to discussing with the prospective buyer his/her specific needs or desires regarding the purchase of a property. As a practical matter, this means the *disclosure will always need to be made prior to showing a property to a prospective buyer.* The best policy is to simply make the disclosure at the earliest possible time.

If first substantial contact occurs by telephone or by means of other electronic communication where it is not practical to provide written disclosure, the agent shall immediately disclose by similar means whom he/she represents and shall immediately, but in no event later than three days from the date of first substantial contact, mail or otherwise transmit a copy of the written disclosure to the buyer.

Disclosure of Agency Status by Buyers' Agents to Sellers or Sellers' Agents. Paragraph (f) of Rule A.0104 *requires a buyer's agent to disclose his/her agency status to a seller or seller's agent at the* **"initial contact"** *with the seller or seller's agent.* "Initial contact" will typically occur when a buyer's agent telephones or otherwise contacts the listing firm to schedule a showing. The initial disclosure may be oral, but a written confirmation of the previous oral disclosure must be made (except in auction sale transactions) no later than the time of delivery of an offer to purchase. The written confirmation may be (and usually is) included in the offer to purchase. In fact, Commission Rule A.0112(a)(19) requires that any preprinted offer to purchase and contract form used by an agent include a provision providing for confirmation of agency status by each real estate agent (and firm) involved in the transaction.

Consent to Dual Agency. Paragraph (d) of Rule A.0104 requires generally that an agent must obtain the written authority of all parties prior to undertaking to represent those parties as a dual agent. It is important to note that this requirement applies to all real estate transactions (sales and lease/rentals), not just sales transactions. [In sales transactions, this written authority to act as a dual agent is usually limited to "in-house" sales transactions and is usually included in the listing and buyer agency contracts. If those contracts do not grant such authority, then the agent must have both the seller and buyer consent to the dual agency prior to beginning to act as a dual agent for both parties.]

Paragraph (d) of Rule A.0104 currently *requires written authority for dual agency from the formation of the relationship except situations where a buyer/tenant is represented by an agent working under an oral agency agreement as permitted by A.0104(a), in which case written authority for dual agency must be obtained no later than the time one of the parties represented by the agent working as a dual agent makes an offer to purchase, sell, rent, lease, or exchange real estate to the other party.* Thus, it is permissible for the agent to operate for a limited period of time under an oral dual agency agreement. It is very important to remember that G.S. 93A-6(a)(4) still requires.agents to obtain the consent of all parties prior to beginning to act as a dual agent for those parties. Therefore, it is essential that agents electing to operate as a dual agent for a limited period of time without obtaining this authority in writing still explain fully the consequences of their acting as a dual agent and obtain the parties' oral consent.

As a practical matter in sales transactions, agents will frequently have already obtained written authority to act as a dual agent for in-house sales transactions at the time the initial written listing or buyer agency agreement is executed. However, under Paragraph (a) of Rule A.0104, many buyer's agents may elect to work with their buyer clients for a period of time under an oral buyer agency agreement. Paragraph (d) permits such buyer's agents to also operate for a limited period of time as a dual agent under an oral agreement in order to deal with situations where a buyer client is interested in a property listed with the agent's firm. Note that, *although an oral dual agency agreement for a limited period of time is permitted by Commission rules, it is strongly recommended that agents have any dual agency agreement in writing from the outset of the dual agency arrangement.* This will provide the agent with some evidence that the matter of dual agency was discussed with the parties and that they consented to it. Such evidence could prove quite useful if a party later asserts that the agent did not obtain their consent for dual agency in a timely manner.

Auction Sales Exemption. Paragraph (g) of Rule A.0104 provides that the provisions of Paragraphs (c), (d) and (e) of the Rule shall not apply to real estate licensees representing sellers in auction sales transactions. Note that in auction sales, the real estate agents involved almost invariably work only as seller's agents and this fact is considered to be self-evident. Thus, there is no need for agents to distribute and review the *Working with Real Estate Agents* brochure, no need for disclosure of agency status by the seller's agents, and no dual agency. For the unusual situation where a buyer may be represented by an agent in an auction sale transaction, Paragraph (h) of Rule A.0104 provides that such a buyer's agent shall, no later than the time of execution of a written agreement memorializing the buyer's contract to purchase, provide the seller or seller's agent with a written confirmation that he/she represents the buyer.

Dual Agency Status of Firm. Paragraph (i) of Rule A.0104 codifies in the Commission's rules the common law rule that *a firm which represents more than one party in the same real estate sales transaction is a dual agent, and further states that the firm, through the brokers and salespersons affiliated with the firm, shall disclose its dual agency to the parties.* This rule provision does not establish any additional requirement for licensees and is intended merely to clarify that the Commission follows the common law rule. In other words, dual agency is not limited to those situations where an individual agent is working with both a buyer client and seller client (or lessor and commercial tenant) in the same transaction. If one agent of a firm is working with a buyer client of the firm and another agent of the same firm is working with a seller client of the firm in a transaction involving the sale of the seller client's property to the buyer client, then the firm is a dual agent (as it also holds the agency agreements). However, a firm functions through its employees, namely, its associated agents; thus, under the common law, whenever the firm is a dual agent of certain parties in a transaction, all licensees affiliated with that firm are also dual agents of those parties in that transaction.

Designated Agency. Paragraphs (j) - (m) of Rule A.0104 authorize real estate firms to engage in a form of dual agency practice referred to in the rule as "designated agency" in certain sales transactions involving in-house dual agency. *"Designated agency" is an optional method of practicing dual agency that may be adopted by a real estate firm if the firm establishes a policy consistent with the Commission's designated agency rules. Designated agency involves appointing or "designating" an individual agent(s) in a firm to represent only the interests of the seller and another individual agent(s) to represent only the interests of the buyer when a firm has an in-house dual agency situation.*

The principal advantage of the designated agency approach over the "standard" dual agency approach is that each of a firm's clients (seller and buyer) receive fuller representation by their designated agent. In the typical dual agency situation, client advocacy is essentially lost because the dual agent may not seek an advantage for (i.e, "advocate" for) one client to the detriment of the other client. The dual agent must remain completely neutral and impartial at all times. Designated agency returns "advocacy" to the services provided by the respective designated agents and allows them to more fully represent their respective clients.

Authority to practice designated agency must be in writing no later than the time a written dual agency agreement is required under A.0104(d). Additional required procedures for practicing designated agency are clearly spelled out in

Paragraphs (j) - (m) and are not discussed further here. For more detailed coverage of dual and designated agency, the reader is once again referred to the Commission's *North Carolina Real Estate Manual.*

Dual Agency by Individual Agent. Paragraph (n) of Rule A.0104 authorizes individual agents representing both the buyer and seller in the same real estate sales transaction pursuant to a written dual agency agreement to include in the agreement a provision authorizing the agent not to disclose certain "confidential" information about one party to the other party without permission from the party about whom the information pertains. This provision is intended to allow individual dual agents to treat confidential information about their clients in a manner similar to that allowed for firms practicing designated agency.

Advertising [Rule A.0105]

The rule prohibits any advertisement by a licensee that indicates an offer to sell, buy, exchange, rent or lease real property is being made by the licensee's principal without the involvement of a broker – i.e., a **"blind ad."** All advertising by a licensee must indicate that it is the advertisement of a broker or brokerage firm. The rule prohibits a provisional broker from advertising "without the consent of his or her broker-in-charge" and requires that any such advertisement include the name of the broker or firm with which the provisional broker is associated. The rule further requires that brokers obtain the consent of a property owner to display a "for sale" or "for rent" sign on the owner's property.

Licensees may not advertise under an **assumed name** without registering the assumed name with the applicable County Register of Deeds office in accordance with the requirements of G.S. 66-68 and notifying the Commission of such assumed name. For individuals and partnerships, a name is "assumed" when it does not include the surname of the licensee(s). For a firm required to be registered with the Secretary of State and licensed by the Commission, a name is "assumed" when it is different from the firm's registered and licensed name.

A licensee operating as a sole proprietorship, partnership or non-corporate business entity may NOT include in its name the name of an unlicensed person or a provisional broker.

Delivery of Instruments [G.S. 93A-6(a)(13); Rule A.0106]

Among other things, this rule, which implements G.S. 93A-6(a)(13), *requires agents to "immediately, but in no event later than five days from the date of execution, deliver to the parties thereto copies of any required written agency agreement, contract, offer, lease, or option affecting real property."* Regarding offers, this does NOT mean that agents may in every case wait up to five days to present an offer to a seller. Rather, it means that an agent must immediately, as soon as possible, present to the seller any offer received by the agent. If the agent is the "selling agent," then the offer should be immediately presented to the "listing agent" who should, in turn, immediately present the offer to the seller. The "five day" provision is included only to allow for situations where the seller is not immediately available (e.g., seller is out of town), and represents an outside time limit within which offers must always be presented. In all cases where the seller is available, the offer should be presented as soon as possible.

The same rule also means that a prospective buyer who signs an offer must immediately be provided a copy of such offer. (A photocopy is acceptable for this purpose.) Do NOT wait until after the offer is accepted (or rejected) by the seller.

In addition, this rule means that an offer must be immediately presented to a seller even if there is a contract pending on the property. Of course, in this instance, it is essential that the agent also advise the seller that serious legal problems could result from the seller's acceptance of such offer and that the seller should contact an attorney if he is interested in treating the offer as a "back-up" offer or in attempting to be released from the previously signed contract.

Copies of any signed sales contract or lease must also be promptly delivered to the parties within the five-day period.

Finally, G.S. 93A-6(a)(14) requires a broker to provide his/her client a detailed and accurate closing statement showing the receipt and disbursement of all monies relating to the transaction about which the broker knows or reasonably should know.

Retention of Records [Rule A.0108]

Licensees are required to retain documents pertaining to their brokerage transactions for three years from the successful or unsuccessful conclusion of the transaction or the disbursement of all trust monies pertaining to that transaction, whichever occurs later. Documents that must be retained include sale contracts, leases, offers (even those not accepted), agency contracts, earnest money receipts, trust account records, disclosure documents, closing statements, broker cooperation agreements, and any other records relating to a transaction.

Brokerage Fees and Compensation [Rule A.0109]

This rule addresses various issues associated with the disclosure of and sharing of compensation received by a real estate licensee.

Disclosure to principal of compensation from a vendor or supplier of goods or services. Paragraph (a) prohibits a licensee from receiving any form of valuable consideration from a vendor or supplier of goods or services in connection with an expenditure made on behalf of the licensee's principal in a real estate transaction without first obtaining the written consent of the principal.

Example: A broker manages several rental units for various owners and routinely employs Ajax Cleaning Service to clean the units after the tenants leave. The broker pays Ajax a $50 per unit fee for its services out of rental proceeds received and deposited in his trust account. Ajax then "refunds" to the broker $10 for each $50 fee it receives, but the property owners are not aware that the broker receives this payment from Ajax in addition to his regular brokerage fee. The broker in this situation is making a secret profit without the property owners' knowledge and is violating the rule.

Disclosure to a party of compensation for recommending, procuring or arranging services for the party. Paragraph (b) prohibits a licensee from receiving any form of valuable consideration for recommending, procuring, or arranging services for a party to a real estate transaction without full and timely disclosure to such party. The party for whom the services are recommended, procured, or arranged does not have to be the agent's principal.

Example: An agent sells a listed lot to a buyer who wants to build a house on the lot. Without the buyer's knowledge, the agent arranges with ABC Homebuilders for ABC to pay the agent a 3% referral fee if the agent recommends ABC to the buyer and the buyer employs ABC to build his house. The agent then recommends ABC to the buyer, ABC builds the buyer's house for $100,000 and ABC secretly pays the agent $3,000 for his referral of the buyer. The agent has violated this rule. (Note that the buyer in this situation likely paid $3,000 more for his house than was necessary because it is very likely the builder added the agent's referral fee to the price he charged the buyer for building the house. The main point here is that the buyer had the right to know that the agent was not providing disinterested advice when recommending the builder.)

Example: A selling agent in a real estate transaction, while acting as a subagent of the seller, recommends to a buyer who has submitted an offer that the buyer apply to Ready Cash Mortgage Company for his mortgage loan. The agent knows that Ready Cash will pay him a "referral fee" of $100 for sending him the buyer's business if the loan is made to the buyer, but the agent does not disclose this fact to the buyer. If the agent subsequently accepts the referral fee from the lender, he will have violated this rule. (The buyer has the right to know that the agent's recommendation is not a disinterested one.)

Disclosure to principal of compensation for brokerage services in sales transactions. Paragraphs (c) and (d) deal with disclosure to a licensee's principal of the licensee's compensation in a **sales** transaction from various sources other than in situations addressed in paragraphs (a) and (b). A broker may not receive any compensation, incentive, bonus, rebate or other consideration of more than nominal value (1) from his or her principal unless the compensation, etc. is provided for in a written agency contract or (2) from any other party or person unless the broker provides a full and timely disclosure of the compensation, etc., including any promise or expectation of compensation, to the broker's principal. The disclosure is "timely" when it is made in sufficient time to aid a reasonable person's decision-making. The disclosure may by made orally, but must be confirmed in writing before the principal makes or accepts an offer to buy or sell.

Example: ABC Homebuilders offers to pay any broker who procures a buyer for one of ABC's inventory homes a **bonus** of $1,000 that is in addition to any brokerage commission the broker earns under any agency contract and/or commission split agreements. Any broker working with a buyer-client who is considering the purchase of one of ABC's homes must comply with the disclosure requirement and disclose the bonus to the buyer in a timely manner. **Note:** If ABC Homebuilders also offers a bonus of $2,000 on a second sale of one of its homes and $3,000 on a third sale, and if a buyer's broker has already sold one of ABC's homes, then the broker must disclose to his or her buyer principal the entire bonus program and that his or her bonus will be at least $2,000 if the buyer purchases an ABC home.

Compensation is considered to be "nominal" if it is of insignificant, token or merely symbolic worth. The Commission has cited gifts of a $25 bottle of wine or a $50 dinner gift certificate as being examples of "nominal" compensation.

Restrictions on compensation disclosure requirement. Paragraph (e) clarifies that a broker does NOT have to disclose to a person who is not his or her principal the compensation the broker expects to receive from his or her principal, and further clarifies that a broker does NOT have to disclose to his principal the compensation the broker expects to receive from the broker's employing broker.

Commission will not arbitrate commission disputes. G.S 93A-3(c) provides that the Commission shall not make rules or regulations regulating commission, salaries, or fees to be charged by licensees. Paragraph (f) of Rule A.0109 augments that statutory provision by providing that the Commission will not act as a board of arbitration regarding such matters as the rate of commissions, the division of commissions, pay of brokers and similar matters.

Compensation of unlicensed persons by brokers prohibited. G.S. 93A-6(a)(9) authorizes the Commission to take disciplinary action against a licensee for paying any person for acts performed in violation of the License Law. Paragraph (g) of Rule A.0109 simply augments this statutory provision by providing an affirmative statement that a licensee shall not in any manner compensate or share compensation with unlicensed persons or entities for acts performed in North Carolina for which a license is required. [Note that NC brokers may split commissions or pay referral fees to licensees of another state so long as the out-of-state licensee does not provide any brokerage services while physically in North Carolina.] One narrow, limited exception to this restriction is provided in Paragraph (h) – licensees may pay referral fees to travel agents who contact them

North Carolina Real Estate License Law and Commission Rules

to book vacation rentals only, so long as well-defined procedures are followed.

RESPA prohibitions control. Finally, Paragraph (i) of Rule A.0109 provides that nothing in this rule permits a licensee to accept any fee, kickback, etc. that is prohibited by the federal Real Estate Settlement Procedures Act (RESPA) or implementing rules, or to fail to make any disclosure required by that act or rules.

Broker-In-Charge [Rule A.0110].

Requirement for a Broker-In-Charge. Paragraph (a) of Rule A.0110 requires that each real estate firm designate a broker who meets the qualification requirements to serve as **"broker-in-charge"** of the firm's principal office and a different broker to serve in the same capacity at each branch office. It is important to note, as discussed previously under "License Requirement," that **"broker-in-charge"** *is not a separate license, but only a separate license status category.*

This rule specifies that the "qualifying broker" of each real estate firm is responsible for assuring that a qualified broker is designated as broker-in-charge for the firm's principal office and each branch office where the firm conducts brokerage business. The broker who is to serve as broker-in-charge of an office is responsible for officially designating himself or herself with the Commission as the broker-in-charge of that office.

Sole Proprietors. In addition to each firm having to have a broker-in-charge for each office, *most broker-sole proprietors (including sole practitioners) also must be a broker-in-charge.*

Commission Rule A.0110 (a) provides that a broker who is a **sole proprietor** shall designate himself or herself as a broker-in-charge if the broker: (1) engages in any transaction where the broker is required to deposit and maintain monies belonging to others in a trust account; (2) engages in advertising or promoting his or her services as a broker in any manner; OR (3) has one or more other brokers affiliated with him or her in the real estate business. A 2009 rule revision provided that maintenance of a trust account by a broker solely for holding residential tenant security deposits received by the broker on properties owned by the broker in compliance with G.S. 42-50 shall not, standing alone, subject the broker to the requirement to designate himself or herself as a broker-in-charge.

The most misunderstood of the three broker-in-charge triggering requirements for sole proprietors cited above is # (2): *"...engages in advertising or promoting his or her services as a broker **in any manner**."* Acts of a sole proprietor that trigger the BIC requirement under # (2) include, but are not limited to: Placing an advertisement for his or her services as a broker in any form or any medium; distributing business cards indicating he or she is a real estate broker; orally soliciting the real estate business of others; or listing a property for sale (which inherently involves holding oneself out as a broker and advertising).

Therefore, *a broker-sole proprietor may lawfully provide only limited brokerage services without designating himself or herself as a BIC.* A couple of examples of *permissible* brokerage activities by a broker-sole proprietor who is NOT a designated BIC include receiving a referral fee from another broker or brokerage firm for referring business to the broker or firm or representing a relative or friend as a buyer's broker in a sales transaction provided the broker has not solicited the business, has not advertised or promoted his or her services, and does not hold earnest money beyond the time it is required to be deposited in a trust account.

The practical effect of these requirements is that a broker who will be operating independently in most cases must also designate himself or herself as a BIC. The real significance of these requirements for a sole proprietor will be better understood when the qualification requirements to serve as a BIC are subsequently discussed.

Broker-In-Charge Duties. The broker-in-charge is the person the Commission will hold responsible for the supervision and management of an office. The specific responsibilities of a broker-in-charge are enumerated in Paragraph (a) of Rule A.0110 and are not repeated here.

Requirements to Serve as Broker-In-Charge (BIC). Paragraph (c) of this rule provides that the qualifying requirements to serve as a broker-in-charge are:

- Broker license must be on "active" status but NOT on "provisional" status. A "provisional broker" is ineligible to serve as a broker-in-charge, as is an "inactive" broker.
- Broker must have at least *two (2) years full-time (or part-time equivalent) real estate brokerage experience within the preceding five (5) years, or qualifications the Commission finds equivalent to such experience.* The requirement is for *actual brokerage experience, not just having a license on "active" status.* Note that by submission of a broker-in-charge declaration to the Commission, a broker certifies that he or she possesses the required experience. The Commission may at its discretion require the broker to provide evidence of possessing the required experience. It is possible for some brokers with exceptional "equivalent" qualifications other than brokerage experience (for example, several years of experience as a real estate attorney or new homes sales representative) to obtain a full waiver of the qualifying experience requirement. Others may be able to obtain a **partial** waiver based on *substantial* non-brokerage direct experience in real estate transactions or substantial brokerage experience that is more than five years old. Experience waivers must be specially requested in accordance with guidelines available upon request from the Commission.
- After designation as a broker-in-charge, a broker must complete the Commission's 12-hour **Broker-In-Charge Course** within 120 days of designation (unless the 12-hour course has been taken within the previous three years). Failure to complete this course within 120 days will result in the BIC being removed as BIC. The broker

must then take the course before he or she may again be designated as a BIC.

Retaining Broker-In-Charge Eligibility. A newly designated broker-in-charge who completes the Broker-In-Charge Course within the prescribed time period acquires the eligibility to be re-designated as a broker-in-charge at any time in the future after a period of not actively serving as a broker-in-charge without having to again satisfy the qualification requirements for initial designation so long as the broker continuously satisfies the requirements to retain such eligibility. To retain eligibility to serve as a broker-in-charge, Paragraph (e) of Rule A.0110 provides that a BIC must:

- Renew his or her broker license in a timely manner each license year and keep the license on active status at all times.
- Complete each license year the four-hour mandatory CE update course known as the *Real Estate Update Course* and also the four-hour special mandatory CE course for brokers-in-charge known as the *Broker-In-Charge Annual Review (BICAR) Course*. The BICAR Course must be taken initially during the first full license year following designation as a broker-in-charge and each license period thereafter. The *BICAR Course* satisfies the broker's general CE elective course requirement. Note that this special CE requirement for BICs means that a BIC does not have a CE elective option after the first renewal of his or her license following BIC designation. If a broker-in-charge fails to take the BICAR Course in any given year in which it is required, then the broker will be removed as broker-in-charge the following July 1.

Termination of Broker-In-Charge Eligibility. Paragraph (f) of Rule A.0110 provides that a broker's BIC eligibility and, if currently designated as a BIC, his or her BIC designation, shall be terminated upon the occurrence of any of the following events:

License **expiration** (licensee fails to renew license annually by June 30), suspension, revocation or surrender.

License made **inactive** for any reason, *including the failure to complete all CE required for BICs.*

Broker is found by the Commission to have not possessed the required qualifying experience at the time of either initial designation or re-designation as a BIC.

The reader is referred to Paragraph (f) for the requirements to regain BIC eligibility and be redesignated as a BIC after losing BIC eligibility for any of the above reasons.

Notice to Commission. A BIC must notify the Commission in writing within 10 days upon ceasing to serve as BIC of a particular office. [See Paragraph (g).]

Exception for certain Subchapter S corporations. See Paragraph (h).

Nonresidents. Nonresident individuals and firms holding a NC broker and/or firm license and *engaging in brokerage activity in NC* are subject to the same requirements as NC resident brokers/firms with regard to when they must designate themselves as a NC broker-in-charge. Thus, a nonresident firm engaging in brokerage in NC must designate a NC broker as broker-in-charge of the firm for purposes of its NC business. Similarly, a nonresident NC broker sole practitioner engaging in activity that triggers broker-in-charge designation for a resident NC broker sole practitioner (see previous discussion on this subject) also must designate himself or herself as a NC broker-in-charge.

Education Exception for Certain Nonresident NC Brokers-In-Charge: A nonresident NC broker who has designated himself or herself as the broker-in-charge of an office NOT located in NC (and who does not operate an office in NC) is NOT required to complete the 12-hour Broker-In-Charge Course and is NOT required to complete the Broker-In-Charge Annual Review Course. [See Paragraph (i).]

Drafting Legal Instruments [Rule A.0111]

This rule prohibits licensees from drafting legal instruments, e.g., contracts, deeds, deeds of trust, etc., but does allow them to fill in the blanks on preprinted sales contract forms, which is not construed to be the unauthorized practice of law.

Offers and Sales Contracts [Rule A.0112]

This rule specifies what minimum terms must be contained in any preprinted offer or sales contract form a licensee, acting as an agent, proposes for use by a party in a real estate transaction.

Reporting Criminal Convictions [Rule A.0113]

Licensees are required to report to the Commission any criminal convictions for a felony or misdemeanor, any disciplinary action taken against them by any other occupational licensing board, or any restriction, suspension or revocation of a notarial commission within sixty (60) days of the final judgment or order in the case. This reporting requirement is ongoing in nature. *Note that Driving While Impaired (DWI) is a misdemeanor!*

Residential Property Disclosure Statement [Rule A.0114]

State law (Chapter 47E of the General Statutes) requires that most residential property owners complete a disclosure form to give to prospective purchasers. The form seeks to elicit information about the condition of the property by asking various questions, to which owners may answer "yes," "no," or "no representation." Failure to provide a buyer with this form may allow the buyer to cancel the contract by notifying the seller in writing within three calendar days of contract acceptance.

Note: Licensees in residential real estate transactions have a duty under G.S. 47E-8 to inform their clients of the client's rights and obligations under the statute. The Real Estate Commission also views the Real Estate License Law as imposing on licensees working with sellers and buyers certain additional responsibilities to assure statutory compliance and serve their clients' interests. Licensees are expected to "assist" sellers with completion of the form but should not complete the form for a seller or advise a seller as to what representation (or No Representation) to make. That being said, licensees should be certain to advise sellers that the licensee is obligated by law to disclose all material facts about or relating to the seller's property to prospective buyers regardless of what representation the seller makes on the disclosure form. See the Commission's *North Carolina Real Estate Manual* for a full discussion of the disclosure law and an agent's duties.

Broker's Responsibility for Closing Statements [G.S. 93A-6(a)(14); Rule A.0107(c)]

The cited statute requires a broker, "...at the time a sales transaction is consummated, to deliver to the broker's client a detailed and accurate closing statement showing the receipt and disbursement of all monies relating to the transaction about which the broker knows or reasonably should know." (The rule cited above merely states that this must be done within five days after closing, though as a practical matter it will almost always be done immediately at the settlement meeting.) The statute goes on to provide that if a closing statement is prepared by an attorney or lawful settlement agent, a broker may rely on the delivery of that statement, but *the broker must review the statement for accuracy and notify all parties to the closing of any errors.* Since virtually every residential transaction is closed by an attorney (or lawful settlement agent), it is standard practice for brokers to adopt the attorney's settlement statement to satisfy this License Law requirement.

Commission Guidelines. The Commission recognized that the current HUD-1 Settlement Statement form used in residential closings is fairly complex and has some entries that a broker cannot reasonably be expected to verify. Consequently, the Commission has published in its *North Carolina Real Estate Manual*, 2011-12 edition, the following guidelines for brokers in residential closings where the HUD-1 form is used:

"Each broker involved in the transaction is expected to review the completed HUD-1 statement and to verify its accuracy and completion in accordance with the provisions of the sales contract. The broker is expected to confirm the accuracy of those entries about which he or she has direct knowledge. These would include items from the sales contract like the sales price, earnest money and due diligence fee, if any, as well as items such as the brokerage commission.

With regard to entries on the HUD-1 representing amounts due to or from third parties, the broker may generally assume that the amounts for the charges and credits cited in the settlement statement are correct unless there is some reason that would lead a reasonably prudent broker to believe they are incorrect. However, the broker is expected to assure that:

All relevant charges and credits are appropriately charged or credited (i.e., entered in the proper column) to the borrower-buyer and seller; and

all calculations for prorated items, escrow reserves, interim interest, excise tax and "bottom line" figures (i.e., total settlement charges for borrower-buyer and seller, cash from borrower-buyer and cash to seller) are correct.

The closing attorney should be immediately advised of any noted suspected errors or omissions. The broker must also be especially careful to take appropriate action in the event he or she becomes aware of a misrepresentation of facts on the settlement statement that is potentially harmful to any party with an interest in the transaction." [Note that the cited statute already specifically charges brokers with the duty to notify *all parties* of any errors noted.]

HANDLING TRUST FUNDS

This section addresses those aspects of handling trust funds that are taught in the Real Estate Broker Prelicensing Course and tested on the real estate license examination for entry-level brokers. For a fuller treatment of this subject, including all requirements related to maintaining a broker's trust account, see the Commission's "Trust Account Guidelines" which are contained in the Real Estate License Law and Commission rules booklet and also addressed in the Commission's *Broker-In-Charge Guide*, and are also available on the Commission's website at www.ncrec.gov.

Definition of Trust Money

In the context of real estate transactions, "**trust money**" is most easily defined as *money belonging to others received by a real estate broker who is acting **as an agent** in a real estate transaction.* It is *also any money held by a licensee who acts as the temporary custodian of funds belonging to others.* Such money must be held in trust even if the circumstances are only collateral to the licensee's role as an agent in a real estate related matter, e.g., a listing agent receives monies from his out of town seller for yard maintenance while the property is being marketed. The most common examples of trust money are:

- Earnest money deposits
- Down payments
- Tenant security deposits
- Rents
- Homeowner association dues and assessments, and
- Money received from final settlements

In the case of resort and other short-term rentals, trust money also includes:

- Advance reservation deposits
- State (and local, if applicable) sales taxes on the gross receipts from such rentals

Trust or Escrow Account [G.S. 93A-6(a)(12) & (g); 93A-45(c); Rule A.0107(a), (b), (d) & (i)]

One of the most basic tenets of broker accountability when handling trust money is that it must be deposited into a trust or escrow account as described below. A "trust account" or "escrow account" (the terms are synonymous for

Commission purposes) is simply a bank account into which trust money (and *only* trust money) is deposited. The three primary features of a trust or escrow account are that it is:

1) **separate**, containing only monies belonging to others,
2) **custodial**, meaning *only the broker or the broker's designated employees have access to the account*, but no one who has funds in the account has access, ***and***
3) **available on demand**, that is, the funds may be withdrawn at any time without prior notice.

Type and Location of Trust Account. A broker's trust account or escrow account must be:
1) a demand deposit account
2) in a federally insured depository institution
3) lawfully doing business in North Carolina
4) that agrees to make the account records available for inspection by Commission representatives. [G.S. 93A-6(g)]

Thus, for the purpose of holding *most* trust money, the bank can be located outside North Carolina if the above-stated conditions are met. **Note**, however, that brokers who provide residential property management services should be aware of the potential conflict as of January 1, 2012 between revised G.S. 93A-6(a)(12) discussed above and the provisions of North Carolina residential landlord-tenant law stating that a **residential tenant security deposit** "... shall be deposited in a trust account with a licensed and insured bank or savings institution *located in the State of North Carolina*, or the landlord may, at his option, furnish a bond ...." [G.S. 42-50.]

Generally where two laws conflict, the more restrictive law controls. Thus, it would appear that after January 1, 2012, a broker engaging in residential property management may have his/her trust accounts in any depository institution that otherwise satisfies the four components identified above ***except for*** trust accounts containing residential tenant security deposits from properties located in North Carolina. The latter trust account should be opened in an insured bank or savings and loan physically located in North Carolina to comply with North Carolina residential landlord-tenant law, unless the landlord posts a bond in an amount equivalent to the tenant security deposit.

Designation of Trust Account and FDIC Insurance. The broker-in-charge responsible for the account must ensure that the bank properly designates the account and that the words "trust account" or "escrow account" appear on all signature cards, bank statements, deposit tickets and checks. Even though the escrow account typically is in the name of the company or broker, so long as the broker properly designates the account as a "trust" or "escrow" account and keeps accurate records that identify each owner of the funds and/or depositor (buyer, seller, lessor, lessee, etc.), the depositors are protected from the funds being "frozen" or attached if the broker/trustee becomes insolvent, incapacitated, dies, has tax liens, becomes involved in a lawsuit, etc. Failure to properly designate an account titled in the name of the company/broker as a trust or escrow account may result in attachment of the account by others to collect a judgment or denial of FDIC insurance coverage as to each individual's interest in the account.

So long as the account is properly designated as a trust account, *all deposits are insured by the Federal Deposit Insurance Corporation (FDIC) up to $250,000* **per each individual** *for whom funds are held*. Thus, a broker's trust account may contain $500,000 total, but *all funds are fully insured so long as no one individual's interest in the account exceeds $250,000*. (**Note**, however, that an individual still may be underinsured if the individual maintains accounts in his/her individual name at the same financial institution as the broker's trust/escrow account.)

When a Trust Account Is Required. A broker must open and maintain a trust account when the broker or any affiliated licensee takes possession of trust money. A broker who is inactive or otherwise not using his/her real estate license is not required to open or maintain a trust account. Similarly, if an *active* practicing broker does not collect or otherwise handle the funds of others, no trust account is required.

Number of Trust Accounts. Except for brokers who are managing homeowner or property owner association funds, a broker holding trust money is only required to have one trust account. All earnest money deposits, tenant security deposits, rents, and other trust monies may be deposited into this one common trust account. However, brokers who are active in both sales and property management often find it helpful to use more than one trust account. For example, they may wish to keep a "general sales trust account" for earnest money deposits, settlement proceeds, etc., and a "rental trust account" for tenant security deposits, rents, and related receipts. Although it is not required, many brokers involved in property management and leasing elect to maintain an additional "security deposit trust account" to keep tenant security deposits separate from rents and other related receipts. **Note** the exception for *homeowner association funds*. **Rule A.0107(i)** requires brokers who handle homeowner or property owner association funds to maintain a *separate trust account for each property owner association or homeowner association they manage*. The funds of one homeowner association are not to be commingled with funds from any other association nor with any general trust monies. The broker also must provide the association with periodic written statements not less than once each quarter reporting all monies received, disbursed, and due, but not paid (i.e., delinquent), as well as the balance of funds in the account.

"Commingling" Prohibited. [G.S. 93A-6(a)(12)] The basic statutory provision relating to a licensee's handling of the money or property of others provides that a broker may not "commingle" his or her own money or property with the money or property of others. This means that a broker may not maintain funds belonging to others in the same

North Carolina Real Estate License Law and Commission Rules

bank account that contains his or her personal or business funds. Funds belonging to others must be held in a trust account and, except as described below regarding "bank service charges on trust accounts," a broker may not deposit his or her own funds in that trust account. The prohibition against commingling also means, for example, that a broker acting as a sole proprietor and dealing with his personally owned property is precluded from depositing monies (e.g., earnest money, rent, etc.) related to that property in his brokerage trust account.

Bank Service Charges on Trust Accounts. Trust accounts usually are subject to the same service charges as regular checking accounts. Whenever possible, brokers should arrange for the depository/bank either to bill the broker for these expenses or charge these expenses to the broker's personal or general operating account. However, if such arrangements cannot be made, the Commission will permit a broker to deposit and maintain in his trust account a maximum of $100.00 of his personal funds (or such other amount as may be required) to cover (not avoid) such charges. So, if a broker's monthly service charges and other fees typically are $100, then the broker may deposit up to $200 of his/her own money to *cover* these charges. A broker who deposits any of his/her own money in the trust account to cover bank charges must be careful to properly enter and identify these personal funds in his/her trust account records. While this technically constitutes "commingling," (discussed subsequently) it is permissible commingling to avoid the greater evil of using other people's money to pay these bank charges.

Interest-Bearing Trust Account. [G. S. 93A-6(a)(12) and Rule A.0107(b) provide that when a broker intends to deposit trust money into an interest-bearing trust account, the broker (broker-in-charge) must first obtain from all parties having an interest in the monies being held written authorization for deposit in an interest-bearing account and such authorization must specify how and to whom the interest will be paid. If such authorization is contained in an offer, contract, lease or other transaction instrument, it must be set forth in a conspicuous manner that distinguishes it from other provisions of the instrument. Remember, however, that all trust accounts must be a *demand account*, so investment of trust monies in any type of security, such as a government bond or a fixed term certificate of deposit, is prohibited.

Broker-In-Charge Responsible for Trust Accounts. [Rule A.0107(d) & (f); Rule A.0110(a)(4)] Rule A.0107(d) requires a broker to maintain complete records showing the deposit, maintenance and withdrawal of money belonging to the broker's principals or *held in escrow or in trust for the broker's principals*. Paragraph (f) of that rule also provides that the Commission may inspect trust account records periodically without prior notice and whenever the records are pertinent to investigation of a complaint against a licensee. Rule A.0110(a)(4) refines this requirement by specifying that a **broker-in-charge (BIC)** *is responsible for the proper maintenance of real estate trust accounts and records pertaining thereto.*

Custodian of Trust Account Records Other Than the Broker-In-Charge. While a broker-in-charge may transfer possession of trust money to a bookkeeper, secretary, or some other clerical employee to record and deposit the funds in a trust account and to maintain trust account records, the broker-in-charge nonetheless remains responsible for the care and custody of such funds. Brokers-in-charge should closely and diligently supervise the acts of all persons having access to the trust account, since final accountability for the accuracy and integrity of the account rests with the broker-in-charge. *Access to trust money should be limited and carefully controlled.*

Disbursement of Earnest Money [Rule A.0107(h)] This rule permits a broker-in-charge to transfer an earnest money deposit from his/her trust account to the closing attorney or other settlement agent not more than ten (10) days prior to the anticipated settlement date. Earnest money may **not** be disbursed prior to settlement for any other purpose without the written consent of the parties. Thus, earnest money may not be used by the broker to pay, prior to settlement, for inspection reports or other services on behalf of the buyer without the written consent of the seller, and vice-versa.

Disputed Trust Funds. Rule A.0107(g)'s primary provision on disputed trust funds reads as follows: "In the event of a dispute between the seller and buyer or landlord and tenant over the return or forfeiture of any deposit other than a residential tenant security deposit held by a licensee, the licensee shall retain said deposit in a trust or escrow account until the licensee has obtained a written release from the parties consenting to its disposition or until disbursement is ordered by a court of competent jurisdiction." The rule, as well as G.S. 93A-12, also address procedures for resolution of a dispute that are available to a broker-in-charge when a dispute over trust funds continues for a long period of time and when one party abandons his or her claim to the disputed funds, however, these procedures are beyond the scope of coverage in this document and are more important for brokers-in-charge to know.

Handling of Trust Money [Rule A.0107(a), (h) & (j)]

The **general rule** is that all trust monies received by a licensee must be deposited in a trust account **within three banking days of receipt**. Exception: Earnest money received with offers to purchase and **tenant security deposits** in connection with leases must be deposited in a trust account *not later than three banking days following* **acceptance** *of the offer to purchase or lease agreement* **unless** the deposit is tendered in ***cash*** in which event it must be deposited within ***three banking days following*** receipt, ***even if the contract or lease has not been accepted***. In part, this is because cash is immediately available and may be refunded within a day of deposit, unlike checks which may require a few days to clear.

Note, however, that a broker *may* choose to immediately deposit a check received for an earnest money deposit or tenant security deposit and is *not required* to wait until contract acceptance unless so instructed by the buyer/tenant. Of course, early deposit may cause problems if the offer to purchase or lease is not accepted and the prospective buyer or tenant understandably wants their deposit to be immediately returned. The date of acceptance must be shown in the purchase or lease agreement to determine when the three banking days begins.

Receipt of Trust Money by Provisional Broker. *All trust money received by a **provisional broker** must be delivered immediately to the provisional broker's broker-in-charge.* In other words, provisional brokers may not retain or hold trust money any longer than absolutely necessary to deliver the trust money to his/her broker-in-charge. Similarly, trust monies received by a **nonresident limited commercial broker** are to be delivered immediately to and held by the resident North Carolina broker with whom the nonresident is affiliated. Brokers-in-charge should have written policies that clearly state the procedures to be followed when *any agent* affiliated with the company, whether a provisional or non-provisional broker, receives trust monies.

Handling Option Money and Due Diligence Fee. Rule A.0107(a) provides in part: "A licensee may accept custody of a **check or other negotiable instrument** *made payable to the seller* of real property as payment for **option money** or **option fee** in connection with an option contract or for a non-refundable fee to the seller for a buyer's right to inspect property or determine its suitability for the buyer's needs prior to the closing of a sales transaction, [i.e. "**due diligence fee**"] but only for the purpose of delivering the instrument to the seller. While the instrument is in the custody of the licensee, the licensee shall, according to the instructions of the buyer, either deliver it to the seller or return it to the buyer. The licensee shall safeguard the instrument and shall be responsible to the parties on the instrument for its prompt and safe delivery. In no event shall a licensee retain such an instrument for more than three business days after the acceptance of the option or other sales contract." [Bracketed term and emphasis added.]

The rule quoted above is basically self-explanatory. In the rule, "custody" means possession. Recall that option money or a due diligence fee is paid directly to the seller, to whom the check is written as payee, and so it is not appropriate for a broker to deposit these checks into his/her trust account because the check is not payable to the licensee or real estate company as is the case with earnest money checks. Either the listing agent or buyer's agent may hold the check or negotiable instrument until negotiations are completed and a contract is formed, at which point the check should be delivered to the seller as soon as possible.

If, however, a buyer for some reason gives a licensee *cash for the option money or due diligence fee*, then the licensee must *immediately deposit the cash in his/her trust account* pending contract formation as *cash must **always** be deposited into a trust account within **three banking days of receipt** — **no exceptions**.* If the parties enter into a contract, then the broker would write a check from the trust account payable to the seller, noting in the memo section and trust account records that it is for the option fee or due diligence fee from the buyer.

Safeguarding Trust Money; Improper Use of Trust Money. [Rule A.0107(j)]

This rule places on every licensee the responsibility to safeguard the money or property of others coming into his or her possession according to the requirements of the License Law and Commission rules. In addition, it provides that: "A licensee shall not convert the money or property of others to his or her own use, apply such money or property to a purpose other than that for which it was paid or entrusted to him or her, or permit or assist any other person in the conversion or misapplication of such money or property."

NOTE: The reader is reminded that fuller coverage of Trust Accounts, including detailed record-keeping requirements, may be found in the Commission's "Trust Account Guidelines," which are available on the Commission's website at www.ncrec.gov.

KEY POINT REVIEW

Types of Real Estate Licenses
- **Broker** [93A-4.(a)]
- **Broker on Provisional Status** (Called a PB) [93A-4.(a1)]
- **Firm License** unless acting as a sole proprietor [A.0502]
- **Limited Nonresident Commercial** [A.1800]

Activities Requiring a License [93A-2(a)]
- List, lease, buy, exchange, auction, negotiate, sell for others for compensation

Exceptions to Licensure [93A-2(c)]
- Activities done by business entity property owners
- Acting under a power of attorney
- Attorney
- Person acting under court order
- Acting as a trustee
- Salaried W-2 employee of broker property manager—if they do not negotiate
- For sale/lease by owner
- Housing authority employees

License Status
- **Current:** paid annual renewal fee (currently $45) by June 30; can renew online; must renew even if on inactive status
- **Expired:** did not pay annual renewal by June 30
- **Active:** [A.0504] must be current, plus have completed all required post-licensing and continuing education, plus all provisional brokers and most brokers must be supervised by a BIC
- **Inactive:** [A.0504] must be current, plus at least one of the following situations
  — Provisional broker did not affiliate with supervising BIC
  — Did not complete eight hours of continuing education before June 10
  — Did not complete post-licensing courses by appropriate anniversary dates
  — Chose to remain or be placed on inactive status

Education Requirements
- **Pre-licensing**
  — 75-hour course with end of course exam
  — No residency requirement; at least 18 years of age
  — Prerequisite for state licensing exam
- **Post-licensing** [A.1902]
  — Three 30-hour courses, each with an end of course exam
  — Newly licensed PB must take minimum of one course per year to remain active
  — Must take all three courses by third license anniversary date or license is placed on inactive status
  — Does not count toward Continuing Education requirement

- **Continuing Education (CE) [A.1700]**
  - Must complete eight hours annually to remain active; can take CE while inactive but not required
  - The annual CE hours consists of the current year's four-hour Mandatory Update Course and a NCREC-approved four-hour Elective course
  - Must be completed by midnight on June 10
  - CE is required prior to second license renewal and every active renewal afterwards
  - Must make up CE deficiency before activation; maximum hours required to be made up is 16 hours
  - Credit for one four-hour elective course can be carried over to the next year
  - Nonresident licensee with an active license in their resident jurisdiction is not required to take NC-specific CE to maintain their NC license
  - Nonresident licensee must take CE if they have an address (business or delivery) in North Carolina

Activation of License

- Correct any educational deficiency in either CE or post-licensing
- Affiliate with a supervising BIC
- File a license activation form with the NCREC

Reinstatement of Expired (Revoked or Surrendered) License [A.0505]

- **Expired 6 months or less**
  - Pay $55 reinstatement fee by December 31
  - No license application necessary
  - Correct any educational deficit if wish to be on active status
- **Expired more than 6 months or revoked or surrendered for any period of time**
  - Submit complete license application including criminal record report
  - Pay $55 reinstatement fee
  - Satisfy character requirement
  - Prove current knowledge of and competence in real estate brokerage (See following section)
- **Demonstration of Current Knowledge for former Brokers (Non-Provisional)**
  - **Expired more than 6 months but no more than 2 years (or revoked or surrendered for 2 years or less)**
    - Complete any one of the 30-hour post-licensing courses successfully within 6 months of application; OR
    - Pass current licensing exam; OR
    - Possess an active broker license in another state
  - **More than 2 years but no more than 5 years**
    - Complete all three post-licensing courses successfully within 3 years prior to application; OR
    - Pass current licensing exam; OR
    - Possess an active broker license in another state
  - **More than 5 years**
    - Start over in pre-licensing as if never licensed

- Demonstration of Current Knowledge for former Provisional Brokers and Salespersons
  - **Expired more than 6 months but no more than 5 years (or revoked or surrendered for 5 years or less)**
    - To be reinstated as a Non-Provisional Broker, complete successfully any of the three post-licensing courses not taken within three years prior to filing for reinstatement
  - **More than 5 years**
    - Start over in pre-licensing as if never licensed

Broker-in-Charge [A.0110]

- **General Requirements**
  - A BIC is required in each real estate firm and in each branch office
  - Can be BIC of only one physical location
  - Only one BIC per location
  - Sole proprietor brokers can be BIC of themselves
  - Not a different license—a designation
- **Eligibility Requirements**
  - Full broker
  - At least two years of full-time real estate brokerage experience within the last five years OR equivalent experience.
  - Complete the BIC course within three years prior to or within 120 days after designation as BIC
  - Complete the Broker-in-Charge Annual Review (BICAR) annually as part of the eight-hour CE requirement in conjunction with the Update Course
  - Maintain active status
- **Responsibilities**
  - Retention and display of all current renewal pocket cards of all brokers in the firm
  - Proper notification of NCREC of changes in firm information
  - Proper conduct in all advertisement affiliated with firm
  - Proper maintenance of trust account and associated records
  - Proper retention of all agency and transactional records
  - Proper supervision of all provisional brokers associated with firm
  - Supervision of all licensees associated with firm in regard compliance with agency agreements and disclosures

Trust Accounts [A.0107]

- **General rules**
  - Must be created with an insured bank or savings association legally doing business in North Carolina
  - Checks and deposit slips must be pre-printed with the words "Trust Account" or "Escrow Account"
  - Must be a separate account that only holds trust funds; no illegal commingling
  - Can have up to $100 of firm's money in the trust account to cover payment of bank's service charges—not considered commingling

- Can be interest-bearing if
    - written permission is secured from all parties with funds in the account;
    - how and to whom interest will be dispersed is clearly specified;
    - permission contained in a transactional document must stand out so as to draw attention (i.e., bold, italics, etc.) to the information
- Firms that are entitled to receive the interest from an interest-bearing trust account must remove that earned interest within 30 days to avoid illegal commingling.
- Firms are only required to have one trust account.
- The only requirement to have multiple trust accounts is the requirement for a separate trust account for each property owner association managed.

- **Handling of Trust Money**
    - Earnest money deposit and tenant security deposit paid in the form of a check must be deposited not later than three banking days following acceptance of the offer to purchase or lease.
    - Cash deposits must be deposited not later than three banking days following receipt of such deposits.
    - Rents, settlement proceeds, or other trust money must be deposited not later than three banking days of receipt of the funds.
    - Check or other negotiable instrument made payable to the seller of real property as option money is not required to be deposited in a trust account. Check should be handled according to the instructions of the buyer-optionee. After acceptance of the option contract, the licensee has three business days to deliver the check to the seller. In the event of a dispute between seller-optionor and the buyer-optionee over option money, handle the money according to the buyer's instructions. Option money in the form of cash must be deposited into a trust account within three banking days of receipt; and must be disbursed not later than three business days following the acceptance of the option contract.
    - Provisional brokers must be immediately delivered to their BIC.
    - Trust monies held as part of a sales transaction can be disbursed to the settlement agent not more than 10 days prior to the anticipated closing date.
    - All monies earned by the firm that are in the trust account (i.e., interest earned, earnest money deposit that converted to commission) must be disbursed within 30 days.
    - Licensee must keep **Disputed Funds** in trust account until
        - Obtain written release from the parties agreeing to disposition;
        - Disposition is ordered by a court of competent jurisdiction; or
        - Parties claiming ownership to the funds have been notified by written notice 90 days prior to depositing the funds with the Clerk of Court in the county where the property for the disputed funds are being held is located.

QUESTIONS

1. The North Carolina Real Estate Commission may, after a hearing, take disciplinary action against a North Carolina licensee who has
   I. violated any of the provisions of the North Carolina license law.
   II. been disciplined by the South Carolina Real Estate Commission.
   a. I only
   b. II only
   c. Both I and II
   d. Neither I nor II

2. A person needs an active North Carolina real estate license to rent and manage rental apartments for
   a. himself or herself.
   b. an out-of-state friend for no compensation.
   c. a corporation as part of a salaried corporate job.
   d. a relative that pays $100 per month for the help.

3. A real estate license must be renewed no later than every
   a. June 30.
   b. anniversary of licensure.
   c. June 10.
   d. December 31.

4. A licensee's North Carolina real estate license may be suspended or revoked for
   a. sharing commission with the buyer-client.
   b. advertising properties in multiple counties.
   c. buying a property for personal use that is listed by the licensee's firm.
   d. placing a For Sale sign on a property without a signed listing agreement.

5. All the following people need an active North Carolina real estate license EXCEPT
   a. a court-ordered guardian selling property owned by his charge.
   b. an attorney that serves as a relief agent on Thursdays in a new homes subdivision.
   c. a real estate assistant showing listed property to the buyer-clients of her broker-boss.
   d. an on-site leasing agent that negotiates rental amounts when requested by potential tenants.

6. If a licensee violates any of the provisions of the North Carolina Real Estate License Law, the North Carolina Real Estate Commission may do all the following EXCEPT
   a. revoke the license permanently.
   b. suspend the license for a specified period of time.
   c. allow the license to remain active if a specified fine is paid.
   d. require the licensee to take prescribed education courses before reinstatement of the license.

7. Which statement is TRUE regarding a broker license on provisional status?
   a. The licensee must satisfy a 90-hour postlicensing education requirement in order to remove the provisional license status.
   b. The provisional broker license is converted to a broker-in-charge license upon completion of postlicensing requirements.
   c. The licensee must complete at least one postlicensing course no later than one year from licensure in order to avoid cancellation of license.
   d. The provisional license status may be removed by completing 16 hours of continuing education credits.

8. In North Carolina, all real estate brokers must
   a. maintain a trust account.
   b. belong to the local Board of REALTORS®.
   c. include their firm's name in advertisements of a client's property.
   d. complete continuing education each year in order to keep the license current.

9. An active nonprovisional real estate broker in North Carolina may
   a. prepare deeds for seller-clients.
   b. may interpret protective covenants for a buyer-client.
   c. place an ad today for a listing that she anticipates getting next week.
   d. split the commission with a buyer-client if it is disclosed to the lender and noted on the HUD-1.

10. According to the North Carolina Time Share Act, a certificate of registration for each time-share project must
    I. be obtained from the North Carolina Real Estate Commission.
    II. must be renewed every June.
       a. I only
       b. II only
       c. Both I and II
       d. Neither I nor II

11. According to the North Carolina Time Share Act, all the following are true EXCEPT
    a. a time-share salesperson must have an active real estate broker's license.
    b. a time-share salesperson must provide a public offering statement about the time-share project to a potential buyer prior to showing or sharing project information.
    c. a time-share purchaser must be given a five-day cancellation right after contract formation.
    d. a time-share purchaser that properly exercises the rescission rights under the Act will receive a refund of all monies paid to the developer or his agent.

12. All North Carolina real estate licensees are legally bound by the
    a. REALTORS® Code of Ethics.
    b. North Carolina Real Estate License Law.
    c. Both a and b.
    d. Neither a nor b.

13. An offer to purchase and contract form offered for use by a real estate broker
    I. must not include a disclaimer of liability on the part of the broker.
    II. can include any agent compensation that is being split with the buyer in the contract.
       a. I only
       b. II only
       c. Both I and II
       d. Neither I nor II

14. Appointments to the North Carolina Real Estate Commission are made
    I. by the Governor, the President Pro Tempore of the State Senate, and the Speaker of the State House of Representatives.
    II. for three-year staggered terms.
       a. I only
       b. II only
       c. Both I and II
       d. Neither I nor II

15. The members of the North Carolina Real Estate Commission
    I. must include at least three licensed real estate brokers.
    II. form an arbitration appeal board for licensees dealing with compensation disputes.
       a. I only
       b. II only
       c. Both I and II
       d. Neither I nor II

16. Each time-share developer must deposit all money received from purchasers in
    a. the developer's business account immediately on receipt.
    b. an escrow account for 10 days.
    c. both accounts mentioned in a and b.
    d. neither account mentioned in a nor b.

17. In North Carolina, a real estate licensee's license expires if
    a. continuing education requirements are not met by June 10.
    b. renewal fees are not received by the North Carolina Real Estate Commission by June 30.
    c. postlicensing requirements have not been met by the license anniversary date.
    d. the licensee is no longer supervised by a broker-in-charge.

18. In North Carolina, a written complaint against a licensee should be sent to the
    a. Governor.
    b. Director of Commerce.
    c. Superintendent.
    d. North Carolina Real Estate Commission.

19. A property manager broker must deposit all rents collected for others into a trust account
    a. within three banking days after receipt.
    b. that cannot be an interest-bearing account.
    c. unless directed otherwise by a party to the transaction.
    d. that is reconciled on a quarterly basis.

20. All agency agreements for property owners
    a. may be oral for some period of time.
    b. must have a definite termination date.
    c. can automatically renew.
    d. must only allow exclusive representation.

21. Earnest money deposits other than cash must be deposited into the broker's trust account
    a. within 24 hours of their receipt.
    b. only if the seller authorizes the broker to do so.
    c. no later than three banking days following contract acceptance.
    d. no later than three banking days after their receipt.

22. All written agency agreements are required by license law to
    a. contain a nondiscrimination provision.
    b. describe the agent's duties and list the authorizations given by the client.
    c. include the individual broker's license number.
    d. all the above.

23. Which of the following statements is NOT true?
    a. A broker's trust account must be a separate custodial account.
    b. A property management trust account must provide for withdrawal on demand.
    c. All trust account funds must be located in an insured bank or savings association lawfully doing business in North Carolina.
    d. Brokers responsible for property management accounts, in addition to a trust account, must be bonded as required by Commission Rule.

24. A broker has authorized his bookkeeper to withdraw funds from his trust account. The bookkeeper embezzles an amount equal to less than 10% of the total balance of the trust account. Which of the following statements is TRUE?
    a. Only the bookkeeper is liable for the misuse of the funds, because the broker delegated this responsibility.
    b. The broker is always responsible for the misuse of trust funds for which he maintains or is required to maintain custody.
    c. Only the bookkeeper is liable for the misuse of the funds, because the loss was for less than 10% of the entire balance.
    d. The Commission will issue a letter to the owner of the trust funds, explaining the problem, and relieving the broker of responsibility.

25. A broker-in-charge must have
    a. an active nonprovisional broker's license. ✓
    b. a minimum of three years' full-time real estate brokerage experience.
    c. a bonded bookkeeper.
    d. a trust account for each office he supervises.

26. A broker-in-charge is responsible for all the following EXCEPT
    a. retention and maintenance of all records required by Commission Rule.
    b. all advertising by or on behalf of the firm.
    c. agency compliance by all licensees in the firm.
    d. supervision of all provisional brokers in the principal office and any branch offices. ✓

27. A nonprovisional broker's real estate license has been on inactive status for 12 years. The broker has taken no real estate education courses during that time. In order to activate the license, the broker would have to successfully complete
    a. eight hours of continuing education for each inactive year.
    b. all three postlicensing courses.
    c. 16 hours of continuing education, including the mandatory update course for the current year. ✓
    d. the state license exam because it has been more than 10 years.

28. A broker's trust account must comply with all the following EXCEPT
    a. it can be located in a credit union lawfully doing business in North Carolina. ✓
    b. it can include up to $100 of the broker's money to cover bank charges.
    c. it can be interest-bearing with full disclosure and permission of all parties that have funds in the account.
    d. "trust account" or "escrow account" must be preprinted on the checks and deposit slips.

29. The broker serving as escrow agent may disburse disputed trust funds in all the following situations EXCEPT
    a. the parties have signed a written disbursement plan.
    b. at the direction of the court that heard the lawsuit between the parties.
    c. when contract terms are very clear about who receives the funds. ✓
    d. when the broker sends funds to county clerk of court after appropriate notification of the parties.

30. To retain broker-in-charge eligibility, a broker must
    a. maintain an active license at all times. ✓
    b. take the special continuing education class for brokers-in-charge every other year.
    c. complete the 12-hour broker-in-charge course once every five years.
    d. never have a break in his service as a broker-in-charge.

Appendix D: North Carolina Real Estate Forms

The forms in this appendix are ordered as one might encounter them in a residential sales transaction, followed by property management forms.

Order	NCAR Form	Page
1.	Exclusive Right to Sell Listing Agreement	620
2.	Exclusive Right to Sell Listing Agreement (Vacant Lot/Land)	628
3.	Short Sale Addendum to Exclusive Right to Sell Listing Agreement	635
4.	Internet Advertising Addendum	637
5.	Residential Property and Owners' Association Disclosure Statement	639
6.	Lead-Based Paint or Lead-Based Paint Hazard Addendum	643
7.	Owners' Association Disclosure and Addendum for Properties Exempt from Residential Property Disclosure Statement	645
8.	Professional Services Disclosure and Election	647
9.	Exclusive Buyer Agency Agreement	649
10.	Non-exclusive Buyer Agency Agreement	654
11.	Unrepresented Seller Disclosure and Fee Agreement	657
12.	Confirmation of Compensation	658
13.	Offer to Purchase and Contract (Form 2-T)	659
14.	Offer to Purchase and Contract—Vacant Lot/Land	670
15.	Backup Contract Addendum	679
16.	Contingent Sale Addendum	682
17.	Additional Provisions Addendum	684
18.	Short Sale Addendum	686
19.	Response to Buyer's Offer	689
20.	Due Diligence Request and Agreement	690
21.	Notice to Seller that Buyer Is Exercising Their Right to Terminate the Offer to Purchase and Contract (Form 2-T)	691
22.	Exclusive Property Management Agreement	693
23.	Residential Rental Contract	699

EXCLUSIVE RIGHT TO SELL LISTING AGREEMENT
[Consult "Guidelines" (Form 101G) for guidance in completing this form]

This EXCLUSIVE RIGHT TO SELL LISTING AGREEMENT ("Agreement") is entered into between _____ as Seller(s) ("Seller") of the property described below (the "Property"), and _____ as Listing Firm ("Firm"). The individual agent who signs this Agreement shall, on behalf of the Firm, be primarily responsible for ensuring that the Firm's duties hereunder are fulfilled; however, it is understood and agreed that other agents of the Firm may be assigned to fulfill such duties if deemed appropriate by the Firm. For purposes of this Agreement, the term "Firm," as the context may require, shall be deemed to include the individual agent who signs this Agreement and any other agents of the Firm.

In consideration for Firm's services and efforts to find a buyer for the Property, Firm is hereby granted the exclusive right to sell the Property on the terms and conditions set forth in this Agreement.

Seller represents that as of the Effective Date the Seller is not (or will not be, if the Property is currently listed) a party to a listing agreement with any other real estate firm regarding the Property. Seller also represents that Seller has received a copy of the "WORKING WITH REAL ESTATE AGENTS" brochure and has reviewed it with Firm.

1. **TERM OF AGREEMENT.**
    (a) **Term**. The term of this Agreement ("Term") shall begin on its Effective Date and shall end at midnight on its Expiration Date.
    (b) **Effective Date**. This Agreement shall become effective and the Seller and Firm's respective rights and obligations under this Agreement shall commence ("Effective Date") as follows (*check appropriate box*):
    ❏ The Effective Date shall be the date that this Agreement has been signed by both Seller and Firm
    ❏ The Property is currently listed for sale exclusively with another real estate firm. Seller represents that the current listing agreement expires on _____. The Effective Date of this Agreement shall commence immediately upon the expiration of the current listing agreement. (**NOTE**: According to Article 16 of the REALTORS® Code of Ethics: *"REALTORS® shall not engage in any practice or take any action inconsistent with exclusive representation or exclusive brokerage relationship agreements that other REALTORS® have with clients."*)
    (c) **Expiration Date**. This Agreement shall terminate at midnight on _____ ("Expiration Date").

2. **PROPERTY.** The Property that is the subject of this Agreement shall include all that real estate described below together with all appurtenances thereto including the improvements located thereon and the fixtures and personal property listed in Paragraphs 3 and 4 below.
    Street Address: _____
    City: _____ Zip _____
    County: _____, North Carolina
    (**NOTE**: Governmental authority over taxes, zoning, school districts, utilities and mail delivery may differ from address shown.)
    Legal Description: (Complete *ALL* applicable)

    - Plat Reference: Lot/Unit _____, Block/Section _____, Subdivision/Condominium _____
      _____, as shown on Plat Book/Slide _____ at Page(s) _____
    - The PIN/PID or other identification number of the Property is: _____
    - Other description: _____
    Some or all of the Property may be described in Deed Book _____ at Page _____

3. **FIXTURES.** The following items, if any, are deemed fixtures and are included in the Purchase Price free of liens: range/stove/oven, any built-in appliances, light fixtures, ceiling fans, attached floor coverings, blinds, shades, drapery rods and curtain rods, brackets and all related hardware, window and door screens, storm windows, combination doors, awnings, antennas, satellite dishes and receivers, burglar/fire/smoke/carbon monoxide alarms, pool and spa equipment, solar energy systems, attached fireplace screens, gas logs, fireplace inserts, electric garage door openers with controls, outdoor plants and trees (other than in movable containers), basketball goals, storage sheds, mailboxes, attached wall and/or door mirrors, fuel tank(s) whether attached or buried and including contents, if any, as of Settlement, landscape and/or foundation lighting, invisible fencing including all related equipment, lawn irrigation systems and all related equipment, water softener/conditioner and filter equipment, and any other items attached or affixed to the Property, EXCEPT the following items which are leased or not owned by the Seller or which the Seller does not intend to convey: _____

Seller shall repair any damage caused by removal of any items excepted above.

1 of 8

North Carolina Association of REALTORS®, Inc.

Individual agent initials _____ Seller initials _____ _____

STANDARD FORM 101
Revised 7/2013
© 7/2013

Appendix 1

(**NOTE**: Seller should confirm whether fuel tanks, antennas, satellite dishes and receivers, alarm systems, and other items listed above are leased or not owned by Seller and should be entered in the blank above.)

4. **PERSONAL PROPERTY.** The following personal property shall be transferred to Buyer at no value at Closing:
_____
_____.

5. **HOME WARRANTY.** Seller ❏ agrees ❏ does not agree to obtain and pay for at settlement a one year home warranty for the Property at a cost not to exceed $_____. If Seller agrees to obtain and pay for a home warranty at any time, Firm hereby discloses that a fee of _____ will be offered to Firm by the person or entity through or from which any home warranty is obtained as compensation to Firm for its assistance in obtaining the home warranty, and Seller hereby consents to Firm's receipt of such fee.

6. **LISTING PRICE.** Seller lists the Property at a price of $_____ on the following terms: ❏ Cash ❏ FHA ❏ VA ❏ USDA ❏ Conventional ❏ Loan Assumption ❏ Seller Financing ❏ Other_____.
Seller agrees to sell the Property for the Listing Price or for any other price or on any other terms acceptable to Seller.

7. **FIRM'S COMPENSATION.**
    (a) **Fee**. Seller agrees to pay Firm a total fee of _____ % of the gross sales price of the Property, OR_____ ("Fee"), which shall include the amount of any compensation paid by Firm as set forth in paragraph 8 below to any other real estate firm, including individual agents and sole proprietors ("Cooperating Real Estate Firm").
    (b) **Fee Earned**. The Fee shall be deemed earned under any of the following circumstances:
       (i) If a ready, willing and able buyer is procured by Firm, a Cooperating Real Estate Firm, the Seller, or anyone else during the Term of this Agreement at the price and on the terms set forth herein, or at any price and upon any terms acceptable to the Seller;
       (ii) If the Property is sold, optioned, exchanged, conveyed or transferred, or the Seller agrees, during the Term of this Agreement or any renewal hereof, to sell, option, exchange, convey or transfer the Property at any price and upon any terms whatsoever; or
       (iii) If the circumstances set out in (i) or (ii) above have not occurred, and if, within _____ days after the Expiration Date the ("Protection Period"), Seller either directly or indirectly sells, options, exchanges, conveys or transfers, or agrees to sell, option, exchange, convey or transfer the Property upon any terms whatsoever, to any person with whom Seller, Firm, or any Cooperating Real Estate Firm communicated regarding the Property during the Term of this Agreement or any renewal hereof, provided the names of such persons are delivered or postmarked to the Seller within 15 days after the Expiration Date. HOWEVER, Seller shall NOT be obligated to pay the Fee if a valid listing agreement is entered into between Seller and another real estate broker and the Property is subsequently sold, optioned, exchanged, conveyed or transferred during the Protection Period.
    (c) **Fee Due and Payable**. Once earned as set forth above, the Fee will be due and payable at the earlier of:
       (i) Closing on the Property;
       (ii) The Seller's failure to sell the Property (including but not limited to the Seller's refusal to sign an offer to purchase the Property at the price and terms stated herein or on other terms acceptable to the Seller, the Seller's default on an executed sales contract for the Property, or the Seller's agreement with a buyer to unreasonably modify or cancel an executed sales contract for the Property); or
       (iii) Seller's breach of this Agreement.
    (d) **Transfer of Interest in Business Entity**. If Seller is a partnership, corporation or other business entity, and an interest in the partnership, corporation or other business entity is transferred, whether by merger, outright purchase or otherwise, in lieu of a sale of the Property, and applicable law does not prohibit the payment of a fee or commission in connection with such sale or transfer, the Fee shall be calculated on the fair market value of the Property, rather than the gross sales price, multiplied by the percentage of interest so transferred, and shall be paid by Seller at the time of the transfer.
    (e) **Additional Compensation**. If additional compensation, incentive, bonus, rebate and/or other valuable consideration ("Additional Compensation") is offered to the Firm from any other party or person in connection with a sale of the Property, Seller will permit Firm to receive it in addition to the Fee. Firm shall timely disclose the promise or expectation of receiving any such Additional Compensation and confirm the disclosure in writing before Seller makes or accepts an offer to sell. (**NOTE**: NCAR Form #770 may be used to confirm the disclosure of any such Additional Compensation)
    (f) **Attorney Fees and Costs**. If Firm is the prevailing party in any legal proceeding brought by Firm against Seller to recover any or all of the Fee, Firm shall be entitled to recover from Seller reasonable attorney fees and court costs incurred by Firm in connection with the proceeding.

8. **COOPERATION WITH/COMPENSATION TO OTHER FIRMS.** Firm has advised Seller of Firm's company policies regarding cooperation and the amount(s) of any compensation that will be offered to other brokers, including but not limited to, seller subagents, buyer agents or both, brokers who do or do not participate in a listing service and brokers who are or are not REALTORS®. Seller authorizes Firm to (*Check ALL applicable authorizations*):

Individual agent initials _____ Seller initials _____ _____

Appendix D

❏ Cooperate with subagents representing the Seller and offer them the following compensation:_____% of the gross sales price or $_____; and/or,
❏ Cooperate with buyer agents representing the buyer and offer them the following compensation:_____% of the gross sales price or $_____; and/or,
❏ Cooperate with and compensate other Cooperating Real Estate Firms according to the Firm's attached policy.

Firm will promptly notify Seller if compensation offered to a Cooperating Real Estate Firm is different from that set forth above. Agents with Cooperating Real Estate Firms must orally disclose the nature of their relationship with a buyer (subagent or buyer agent) to Firm at the time of initial contact with Firm, and confirm that relationship in writing no later than the time an offer to purchase is submitted for the Seller's consideration. Seller should be careful about disclosing confidential information because agents representing buyers must disclose all relevant information to their clients.

9. **FIRM'S DUTIES.** Firm agrees to provide Seller the benefit of Firm's knowledge, experience and advice in the marketing and sale of the Property. Seller understands that Firm makes no representation or guarantee as to the sale of the Property, but Firm agrees to use its best efforts in good faith to find a buyer who is ready, willing and able to purchase the property. In accordance with the REALTORS® Code of Ethics, Firm shall, with Seller's approval, in response to inquiries from buyers or Cooperating Real Estate Firms, disclose the existence of offers on the Property. Where Seller authorizes disclosure, Firm shall also disclose whether offers were obtained by the individual agent who signs this Agreement, another agent of the Firm, or by a Cooperating Real Estate Firm. Seller acknowledges that real estate brokers are prohibited by N.C. Real Estate Commission rule from disclosing the price or other material terms contained in a party's offer to purchase, sell, lease, rent or option real property to a competing party without the express authority of the party making the offer.

Seller acknowledges that Firm is required by law to disclose to potential purchasers of the Property all material facts pertaining to the Property about which the Firm knows or reasonably should know, and that REALTORS® have an ethical responsibility to treat all parties to the transaction honestly. Seller further acknowledges that Firm is being retained solely as a real estate professional, and understands that other professional service providers are available to render advice or services to Seller, including but not limited to an attorney, insurance agent, tax advisor, surveyor, structural engineer, home inspector, environmental consultant, architect, or contractor. Although Firm may provide Seller the names of providers who claim to perform such services, Seller understands that Firm cannot guarantee the quality of service or level of expertise of any such provider. Seller agrees to pay the full amount due for all services directly to the service provider whether or not the transaction closes. Seller also agrees to indemnify and hold Firm harmless from and against any and all liability, claim, loss, damage, suit, or expense that Firm may incur either as a result of Seller's selection and use of any such provider or Seller's election not to have one or more of such services performed.

[handwritten: Fair Housing Clause]

THE AGENT (FIRM) SHALL CONDUCT ALL BROKERAGE ACTIVITIES IN REGARD TO THIS AGREEMENT WITHOUT RESPECT TO THE RACE, COLOR, RELIGION, SEX, NATIONAL ORIGIN, HANDICAP OR FAMILIAL STATUS OF ANY PARTY OR PROSPECTIVE PARTY TO THE AGREEMENT. FURTHER, REALTORS® HAVE AN ETHICAL DUTY TO CONDUCT SUCH ACTIVITIES WITHOUT RESPECT TO THE SEXUAL ORIENTATION OF ANY PARTY OR PROSPECTIVE PARTY TO THIS AGREEMENT.

10. **MARKETING.**
(a) **Marketing Date.** Firm's authorization to market the Property as described in subparagraph (b) below shall be effective on: ❏ the Effective Date of this Agreement OR ❏ (insert date) _____ ("Marketing Date"). (**NOTE:** None of the marketing activities authorized in subparagraph (b) below are permitted prior to the Marketing Date)
(b) **Marketing Authorization.** Seller authorizes Firm (*Check ALL applicable sections*):
❏ **Signs**. To place "For Sale," "Under Contract," "Sale Pending," or other similar signs on the Property (where permitted by law and relevant covenants) and to remove other such signs.
❏ **Open Houses**. To conduct open houses of the Property at such times as Seller and Firm may subsequently agree.
❏ **Listing Service**. To submit pertinent information concerning the Property to any listing service of which Firm is a member or in which any of Firm's agents participate and to furnish to such listing service notice of all changes of information concerning the Property authorized in writing by Seller. Seller authorizes Firm, upon execution of a sales contract for the Property, to notify the listing service of the pending sale and the expiration date of any due diligence period, and upon closing of the sale, to disseminate sales information, including sales price, to the listing service, appraisers and real estate brokers.
❏ **Advertising Other Than On The Internet**. To advertise the Property in non-Internet media, and to permit other firms to advertise the Property in non-Internet media to the extent and in such manner as Firm may decide.
❏ **Internet Advertising**. To display information about the Property on the Internet either directly or through a program of any listing service of which the Firm is a member or in which any of Firm's agents participate. Seller further authorizes other firms who belong to any listing service of which the Firm is a member or in which any of Firm's agents participate to display information about the Property on the Internet in accordance with the listing service rules and regulations, and also authorizes any listing service of which the Firm is a member or in which any of Firm's agents participate to use, license or

Individual agent initials _____ Seller initials _____ _____

sell to others information about the Property entered into the listing service. Seller specifically authorizes the display of the address of the Property, automated estimates of the market value of the Property and third-party comments about the Property. If seller desires to limit or prohibit Internet advertising as set forth above, seller must complete an opt-out form in accordance with listing service rules.

(**NOTE**: NCAR Form #105 may be used to limit or prohibit Internet advertising and explains how such limitations may or may not be effective.)

(c) **Lock/Key Boxes**. The Seller ❑ does ❑ does not authorize Firm to place a lock/key box on the Property.

(d) **Seller Acknowledgement**. Seller acknowledges and understands that while the marketing services selected above will facilitate the showing and sale of the Property, there are risks associated with allowing access to and disseminating information about the Property that are not within the reasonable control of the Firm, including but not limited to:
(i) unauthorized use of a lock/key box,
(ii) control of visitors during or after a showing or an open house,
(iii) inappropriate use of information about the Property placed on the Internet or furnished to any listing service in which the Firm participates.

Seller therefore agrees to indemnify and hold harmless Firm from any damages, costs, attorneys' fees and other expenses as a result of any personal injury or property loss or damage to Seller or any other person not caused by Firm's negligence arising directly or indirectly out of any such marketing services.

11. **EARNEST MONEY**. Unless otherwise provided in the sales contract, any initial and additional earnest money deposits and any other earnest monies paid in connection with any transaction shall be held by the Firm, in escrow, until the consummation or termination of the transaction. Any earnest money forfeited by reason of the buyer's default under a sales contract shall be divided equally between the Firm and Seller. In no event shall the sum paid to the Firm because of a buyer's default be in excess of the fee that would have been due if the sale had closed as contemplated in the sales contract. In accordance with NC General Statutes Section 93A-12, if a dispute regarding the return or forfeiture of any earnest money deposit arises between Seller and the buyer, the escrow agent holding the deposit may deposit the disputed monies with the appropriate Clerk of Court following written notice to the parties. In the event of any such dispute, Seller directs Firm to disclose Seller's last known mailing address to the escrow agent upon request to enable the escrow agent to comply with the notice requirement of such law.

12. **SELLER REPRESENTATIONS**.
(a) **Flood Hazard Disclosure/Insurance**. To the best of Seller's knowledge, the Property ❑ is ❑ is not located partly or entirely within a designated Special Flood Hazard Area. The Seller ❑ does ❑ does not currently maintain flood hazard insurance on the Property.
(b) **Synthetic Stucco**. To the best of Seller's knowledge, the Property has not been clad previously (either in whole or in part) with an "exterior insulating and finishing system," commonly known as "EIFS" or "synthetic stucco", unless disclosed as follows: _____.
(c) **Owners' Association**.
(i) Complete ONLY if the Residential Property and Owner's Association Disclosure Statement is required: The name, address and telephone number of the president of the owners' association or the association manager is:_____

Owners' association website address, if any: _____

The name, address and telephone number of the president of the owners' association or the association manager is:_____
_____
Owners' association website address, if any: _____
(ii) Complete ONLY if New Construction or where the Residential Property and Owner's Association Disclosure Statement is NOT required: To the best of Seller's knowledge there ❑ is ❑ is not an owners' association which imposes various mandatory covenants, conditions and restrictions upon the Property. If there is an owners' association, Seller agrees to promptly complete an Owners' Association Disclosure and Addendum For Properties Exempt from Residential Property Disclosure Statement (Standard Form 2A12-T) at Seller's expense and to attach it as an addendum to any contract for the sale of the Property.
(d) **Termite Bond**. To the best of Seller's knowledge there ❑ is ❑ is not a termite bond on the Property. If there is a termite bond, it ❑ is ❑ is not transferable. If transferable, the transfer cost is $ _____, and the bonding company is: _____.
(e) **Ownership**. Seller represents that Seller:
❑ has owned the Property for at least one year;
❑ has owned the Property for less than one year
❑ does not yet own the Property

Page 4 of 8

STANDARD FORM 101
Revised 7/2013
© 7/2013

Individual agent initials _____ Seller initials _____ _____

If Seller does not yet own the Property, Seller agrees to promptly provide Firm information pertaining to Seller's acquisition of the Property, such as a copy of a sales contract or option for the Property, and to keep Firm timely informed of all developments pertaining to Seller's acquisition of the Property.
- (f) **Residence**. Seller represents that the Property ❏ is or ❏ is not the Seller's primary residence
- (g) **Receipt of Sample Forms**.
  - ❏ Seller acknowledges receipt of a sample copy of an Offer to Purchase And Contract (form 2-T) or Offer to Purchase and Contract—New Construction (form 800-T), as may be appropriate for review purposes.
  - ❏ Seller acknowledges receipt of a sample copy of a Professional Services Disclosure and Election form (form #760) for review purposes.
- (h) **Current Liens**. Seller represents to the best of Seller's knowledge:
  - (1) The Property ❏ is ❏ is not encumbered by a deed of trust or mortgage. *Complete any of the following where applicable:*
    - (i) There is a first deed of trust or mortgage on the Property securing a loan held by:
      Lender Name: _____
      Approximate balance: $_____   Lender Phone#: _____
      Lender Address: _____
    - (ii) There is a second deed of trust or mortgage on the Property securing a loan held by:
      Lender Name: _____
      Approximate balance: $_____   Lender Phone#: _____
      Lender Address: _____
    - (iii) There is a deed of trust or mortgage on the Property securing an equity line of credit held by:
      Lender Name: _____
      Approximate balance: $_____   Lender Phone#: _____
      Lender Address: _____
  - (2) Seller is current on all payments for the loans identified in numbered items (i), (ii) and (iii) above except as specified in (7) below.
  - (3) Seller is not in default on any loan identified in numbered items (i), (ii) and (iii) above and has not received any notice(s) from the holder of any loan identified in numbered items (i), (ii) and (iii) above or from any other lien holder of any kind, regarding a default under the loan, threatened foreclosure, notice of foreclosure, or the filing of foreclosure except as specified in (7) below.
  - (4) There are not any liens secured against the Property for Federal, State or local income taxes, unpaid real property taxes, unpaid condominium or homeowners' association fees, mechanics', laborers' or materialmen's liens, or other liens affecting the Property, and Seller has no knowledge of any matter that might result in a lien affecting the Property except as specified in (7) below.
  - (5) There are not any judgments against Seller affecting the Property, and Seller has no knowledge of any matter that might result in a judgment that may potentially affect the Property except as specified in (7) below.
  - (6) There are not any Uniform Commercial Code (UCC) fixture filings affecting the Property, and Seller has no knowledge of any matter that might result in a UCC fixture filing affecting the Property except as specified in (7) below.
  - (7) Specify any information, including approximate balances, required by Seller representations (2) through (6) above (**NOTE**: Outstanding liens may affect Seller's net proceeds): _____
  _____
- (i) **Bankruptcy**. Seller currently:
  - (1) ❏ is ❏ is not under bankruptcy protection under United States law.
  - (2) ❏ is ❏ is not contemplating seeking bankruptcy protection during the term of this Agreement.
- (j) **Access**. Seller represents that the Property has legal access to a public right of way. If access is by private road/easement/other, Seller further represents that there ❏ is ❏ is not an agreement regarding the maintenance of such private road/easement/other means of access. If applicable, Seller agrees to promptly provide Firm information pertaining to any such agreement.
- (k) **Lease(s)**. To the best of Seller's knowledge, the Property ❏ is ❏ is not subject to any lease(s). If applicable, Seller agrees to promptly provide Firm a copy of any such lease(s) or a written statement of the terms of any oral lease(s).
- (l) **VA/FHA Appraisal**. To the best of Seller's knowledge, a VA or FHA appraisal ❏ has ❏ has not been performed on the Property within six months prior to the Effective Date. If applicable, Seller agrees to promptly provide Firm a copy of any such appraisal if available.
- (m) **Special Assessments**. To the best of Seller's knowledge, there are no Proposed or Confirmed Special Assessments (as defined in the sample contract form provided to Seller) regarding the Property except as follows (Insert "none" or the identification of such assessments, if any): _____
- (n) **Manufactured (Mobile) Home**. Complete ONLY if there is a manufactured (mobile) home(s) on the Property that Seller intends to include as a part of the sale of the Property: VIN(s): _____ or ❏ VIN(s) unknown. Other description (*year, model, etc.*): _____

Individual agent initials _____   Seller initials _____ _____

(o) Oil and Gas Rights. (NOTE: Oil and gas rights can be severed from the title to real property by conveyance (deed) of the oil and gas rights from the owner or by reservation of the oil and gas rights by the owner. If oil and gas rights are or will be severed from the property, the owner of those rights may have the perpetual right to drill, mine, explore, and remove any of the subsurface oil or gas resources on or from the property either directly from the surface of the property or from a nearby location.)

With regard to the severance of oil and gas rights, Seller makes the following disclosures:

	Yes	No	No Representation
(1) Oil and gas rights were severed from the Property by a previous owner.	❑	❑	❑
(2) Seller has severed the oil and gas rights from the Property.	❑	❑	
(3) Seller intends to sever the oil and gas rights from the Property prior to transfer of title to a buyer.	❑	❑	

(p) Fuel Tank/Fuel: To the best of Seller's knowledge, there ❑ is ❑ is not a fuel tank(s) located on the Property. *If "yes" complete the following to the best of Seller's knowledge:*

Ownership of tank 1: ❑ owned ❑ leased If leased, the name of tank lessor is: _____
Location of tank 1: ❑ above ground ❑ below ground
Type of fuel: ❑ oil ❑ propane ❑ gasoline and/or diesel ❑ other: _____
Ownership of tank 2: ❑ owned ❑ leased If leased, the name of tank lessor is: _____
Location of tank 2: ❑ above ground ❑ below ground
Type of fuel: ❑ oil ❑ propane ❑ gasoline and/or diesel ❑ other: _____

If, during the term of this Agreement, Seller becomes aware that any of the representations set forth in this paragraph 12 are incorrect or no longer accurate, Seller shall promptly notify Firm and cooperate with Firm in taking appropriate corrective action.

13. **SELLER'S DUTIES.** Seller agrees to cooperate with Firm in the marketing and sale of the Property, including but not limited to:

(a) providing to Firm, in a timely manner, accurate information including but not limited to the Residential Property and Owner's Association Disclosure Statement (unless exempt), and the Lead-Based Paint or Lead-Based Paint Hazard Addendum with respect to any residential dwelling built prior to 1978;

(b) making the Property available for showing (including working, existing utilities) at reasonable times and upon reasonable notice;

(c) providing Firm as soon as reasonably possible after the execution of this Agreement copies of the following documents (where relevant) in the possession of Seller:

(1) restrictive covenants affecting the Property;
(2) bylaws, articles of incorporation, rules and regulations, and other governing documents of the owners' association and/or the subdivision;
(3) title insurance policies, attorney's opinions on title, surveys, covenants, deeds, notes and deeds of trust and easements relating to the Property.

Seller authorizes (1) any attorney presently or previously representing Seller to release and disclose any title insurance policy in such attorney's file to Firm, (2) the Property's title insurer or its agent to release and disclose all materials in the Property's title insurer's (or title insurer's agent's) file to Firm, and (3) the owners' association manager (or other authorized representative) to release and disclose copies of all documents referenced in subparagraphs (c)(1) and (c)(2) above. Seller acknowledges and understands that Firm is under no obligation to acquire any of the information referenced in this subparagraph (c) or to verify the accuracy of any such information that may be provided to Firm.

(d) immediately referring to Firm all inquiries or offers it may receive regarding the Property; showing the Property only by appointment made by or through Firm; and conducting all negotiations through Firm;

(e) executing and delivering at settlement a GENERAL WARRANTY DEED conveying fee simple marketable title to the Property, including legal access to a public right of way, free of all encumbrances except ad valorem taxes for the current year, utility easements, rights-of-way, and unviolated restrictive covenants, if any, and those encumbrances that the buyer agrees to assume in the sales contract.

Seller represents that the Seller has the right to convey the Property, and that there are currently no circumstances that would prohibit the Seller from conveying fee simple marketable title as set forth in the preceding sentence, except as follows *(insert N/A if not applicable)*: _____

(**NOTE**: If any sale of the Property may be a "short sale," consideration should be given to attaching NCAR form 104 as an addendum to this Agreement.)

(f) providing Firm, in a timely manner, any information necessary (including any information omitted under Paragraph 12) to enable Firm to prepare an estimate of Seller's net proceeds at settlement. Seller acknowledges and understands that any such estimate is an approximation only and that Seller should verify the accuracy of the calculations.

(g) if required by N.C.G.S. §44A-11.1, timely designating a Lien Agent, and providing Firm as soon as reasonably possible a copy of the appointment of Lien Agent.

14. **HOME INSPECTION**: Seller is advised to obtain a home inspection for the purpose of evaluating the condition of the Property in order to enhance its marketability and to help reduce concerns of prospective buyers. Seller ❑ agrees ❑ does not agree to obtain and pay for a home inspection by a licensed NC Home Inspector within _____ days after the execution of this agreement.

❑ Seller acknowledges receipt of a copy of *Questions and Answers on: Home Inspections* by the NC Real Estate Commission.

15. **PHOTOGRAPHS AND OTHER MATERIALS:** Firm is specifically authorized to use, for any purposes whatsoever, any and all photographs, drawings, video, advertising copy or other information obtained by or provided to Firm pursuant to this Agreement (including but not limited to any information concerning the price and terms of the sale of the Property, the description of the Property and the length of time the Property is on the market) ("Materials"), both before and after the sale or, in the event there is not a sale, after this Agreement has expired. If Seller provides any Materials to Firm ("Seller Materials"), Seller represents that Seller owns the Seller Materials or otherwise has the legal right to provide the Seller Materials to Firm, and Seller grants to Firm and any listing service in which Firm or its agents participate a non-exclusive, perpetual license to use the Seller Materials, including the rights to display, reproduce, distribute or make derivative works from the Seller Materials. Seller agrees to indemnify and hold Firm and its agents harmless for any and all claims resulting from use of the Seller Materials under the terms of this license.

16. **ADDITIONAL TERMS AND CONDITIONS.** The following additional terms and conditions shall also be a part of this Agreement: _____
_____
_____

17. **DUAL AGENCY.** Seller understands that the potential for dual agency will arise if a buyer who has an agency relationship with Firm becomes interested in viewing the Property. Firm may represent more than one party in the same transaction only with the knowledge and informed consent of all parties for whom Firm acts.

(a) Disclosure of Information. In the event Firm serves as a dual agent, Seller agrees that without permission from the party about whom the information pertains, Firm shall not disclose to the other party the following information:
  (1) that a party may agree to a price, terms, or any conditions of sale other than those offered;
  (2) the motivation of a party for engaging in the transaction, unless disclosure is otherwise required by statute or rule; and
  (3) any information about a party which that party has identified as confidential unless disclosure is otherwise required by statute or rule.
(b) Firm's Role as Dual Agent. If Firm serves as agent for both Seller and a buyer in a transaction involving the Property, Firm shall make every reasonable effort to represent Seller and buyer in a balanced and fair manner. Firm shall also make every reasonable effort to encourage and effect communication and negotiation between Seller and buyer. Seller understands and acknowledges that:
  (1) Prior to the time dual agency occurs, Firm will act as Seller's exclusive agent;
  (2) In its separate representation of Seller and buyer, Firm may obtain information which, if disclosed, could harm the bargaining position of the party providing such information to Firm;
  (3) Firm is required by law to disclose to Seller and buyer any known or reasonably ascertainable material facts.
Seller agrees Firm shall not be liable to Seller for (i) disclosing material facts required by law to be disclosed, and (ii) refusing or failing to disclose other information the law does not require to be disclosed which could harm or compromise one party's bargaining position but could benefit the other party.
(c) Seller's Role. Should Firm become a dual agent, Seller understands and acknowledges that:
  (1) Seller has the responsibility of making Seller's own decisions as to what terms are to be included in any purchase and sale agreement with a buyer client of Firm;
  (2) Seller is fully aware of and understands the implications and consequences of Firm's dual agency role as expressed herein to provide balanced and fair representation of Seller and buyer and to encourage and effect communication between them rather than as an advocate or exclusive agent or representative;
  (3) Seller has determined that the benefits of dual agency outweigh any disadvantages or adverse consequences;
  (4) Seller may seek independent legal counsel to assist Seller with the negotiation and preparation of a purchase and sale agreement or with any matter relating to the transaction which is the subject matter of a purchase and sale agreement.

Should Firm become a dual agent, Seller waives all claims, damages, losses, expenses or liabilities, other than for violations of the North Carolina Real Estate License Law and intentional wrongful acts, arising from Firm's role as a dual agent. Seller shall have a duty to protect Seller's own interests and should read any purchase and sale agreement carefully to ensure that it accurately sets forth the terms which Seller wants included in said agreement.

Individual agent initials _____ Seller initials _____ _____

STANDARD FORM 101
Revised 7/2013
© 7/2013

(d) Authorization *(initial only ONE).*

_____ _____ Seller authorizes the Firm to act as a dual agent, representing both the Seller and the buyer, subject to the terms and conditions set forth in Paragraph 17.

_____ _____ Seller desires exclusive representation at all times during this agreement and does NOT authorize Firm to act in the capacity of dual agent. *If Seller does not authorize Firm to act as a dual agent, the remainder of this paragraph shall not apply.*

(e) Designated Agent Option *(Initial only if applicable).*

_____ _____ Seller hereby authorizes the Firm to designate an individual agent(s) to represent the Seller, to the exclusion of any other individual agents associated with the Firm. The individual designated agent(s) shall represent only the interests of the Seller to the extent permitted by law.

(**NOTE**: When dual agency arises, an individual agent shall not practice designated agency and shall remain a dual agent if the individual agent has actually received confidential information concerning a buyer client of the Firm in connection with the transaction or if designated agency is otherwise prohibited by law.)

18. **MEDIATION.** If a dispute arises out of or related to this Agreement or the breach thereof, and if the dispute cannot be settled through negotiation, the parties agree first to try in good faith to settle the dispute by mediation before resorting to arbitration, litigation, or some other dispute resolution procedure. If the need for mediation arises, the parties will choose a mutually acceptable mediator and will share the cost of mediation equally.

19. **ENTIRE AGREEMENT/CHANGES/TERMINATION.** This Agreement constitutes the entire agreement between Seller and Firm and there are no representations, inducements, or other provisions other than those expressed herein. This Agreement may be signed in multiple originals or counterparts, all of which together constitute one and the same instrument. All changes, additions, or deletions to this Agreement must be in writing and signed by both Seller and Firm. Seller acknowledges and understands that this Agreement constitutes a binding contract between Seller and Firm. Although Seller may at any time withdraw from the fiduciary relationship existing between Seller and Firm, the contract created by this Agreement may not be terminated by Seller or Firm prior to its Expiration Date without legally sufficient cause. Any such termination shall be by mutually-acceptable written agreement signed by both Seller and Firm. **Seller and Firm each acknowledge receipt of a signed copy of this Agreement.**

THE NORTH CAROLINA ASSOCIATION OF REALTORS®, INC. MAKES NO REPRESENTATION AS TO THE LEGAL VALIDITY OR ADEQUACY OF ANY PROVISION OF THIS FORM IN ANY SPECIFIC TRANSACTION.

Seller: _____ _____ _____
          Print Name   Signature   Date

Contact Information: _____ _____ _____ _____
                           Home   Work   Cell   Email

Mailing Address: _____

Seller: _____ _____ _____
          Print Name   Signature   Date

Contact Information: _____ _____ _____ _____
                           Home   Work   Cell   Email

Mailing Address: _____

Firm: _____ Phone: _____
       Print Real Estate Firm Name

By: _____ _____ _____
      Individual Agent Signature   Individual License Number   Date

Office: _____

Address: _____

Office Phone: _____ Fax: _____ E-mail: _____

STANDARD FORM 101
Revised 7/2013
© 7/2013

EXCLUSIVE RIGHT TO SELL LISTING AGREEMENT (VACANT LOT/LAND)

This EXCLUSIVE RIGHT TO SELL LISTING AGREEMENT ("Agreement") is entered into between _____ as Seller(s) ("Seller") of the property described below (the "Property"), and _____ as Listing Firm ("Firm"). The individual agent who signs this Agreement on behalf of the Firm shall, on behalf of the Firm, be primarily responsible for ensuring that the Firm's duties hereunder are fulfilled; however, it is understood and agreed that other agents of the Firm may be assigned to fulfill such duties if deemed appropriate by the Firm. For purposes of this Agreement, the term "Firm," as the context may require, shall be deemed to include the individual agent who signs this Agreement and any other agents of the Firm.

Seller represents that as of the Effective Date the Seller is not (or will not be, if the Property is currently listed) a party to a listing agreement with any other real estate firm regarding the Property. Seller also represents that Seller has received a copy of the "WORKING WITH REAL ESTATE AGENTS" brochure and has reviewed it with Firm.

1. **TERM OF AGREEMENT.**
    (a) **Term:** The term of this Agreement ("Term") shall begin on its Effective Date and shall end at midnight on its Expiration Date.
    (b) **Effective Date.** This Agreement shall become effective and the Seller and Firm's respective rights and obligations under this Agreement shall commence ("Effective Date") as follows (*check appropriate box*):
    ❏ The Effective Date shall be the date that this Agreement has been signed by both Seller and Firm
    ❏ The Property is currently listed for sale exclusively with another real estate firm. Seller represents that the current listing agreement expires on _____. The Effective Date of this Agreement shall commence immediately upon the expiration of the current listing agreement. (**NOTE:** According to Article 16 of the REALTORS® Code of Ethics: *"REALTORS® shall not engage in any practice or take any action inconsistent with exclusive representation or exclusive brokerage relationship agreements that other REALTORS® have with clients."*)
    (c) **Expiration Date.** This Agreement shall terminate at midnight on _____ ("Expiration Date").

2. **PROPERTY.** The Property that is the subject of this Agreement shall include all that real estate described below together with all appurtenances thereto.
    Street Address: _____
    City: _____ Zip _____
    County: _____, North Carolina
    NOTE: Governmental authority over taxes, zoning, school districts, utilities and mail delivery may differ from address shown.)
    Legal Description: (Complete *ALL* applicable)
    - Plat Reference: Lot/Unit _____, Block/Section _____, Subdivision/Condominium _____ _____, as shown on Plat Book/Slide _____ at Page(s) _____
    - The PIN/PID or other identification number of the Property is: _____
    - Other description: _____
    Some or all of the Property may be described in Deed Book _____ at Page _____

3. **LISTING PRICE.** Seller lists the Property at a price of $_____ on the following terms:
❏ Cash ❏ FHA ❏ VA ❏ USDA ❏ Conventional ❏ Loan Assumption ❏ Seller Financing ❏ Other _____.
Seller agrees to sell the Property for the Listing Price or for any other price or on any other terms acceptable to Seller.

4. **FIRM'S COMPENSATION.**
    (a) **Fee.** Seller agrees to pay Firm a total fee of _____ % of the gross sales price of the Property, OR _____ ("Fee"), which shall include the amount of any compensation paid by Firm as set forth in paragraph 5 below to any other real estate firm, including individual agents and sole proprietors ("Cooperating Real Estate Firm").
    (b) **Fee Earned.** The Fee shall be deemed earned under any of the following circumstances:
        (i) If a ready, willing and able buyer is procured by Firm, a Cooperating Real Estate Firm, the Seller, or anyone else during the Term of this Agreement at the price and on the terms set forth herein, or at any price and upon any terms acceptable to the Seller;
        (ii) If the Property is sold, optioned, exchanged, conveyed or transferred, or the Seller agrees, during the Term of this Agreement or any renewal hereof, to sell, option, exchange, convey or transfer the Property at any price and upon any terms whatsoever; or
        (iii) If the circumstances set out in (i) or (ii) above have not occurred, and if, within _____ days after the Expiration Date (the "Protection Period"), Seller either directly or indirectly sells, options, exchanges, conveys or transfers, or agrees to sell, option, exchange, convey or transfer the Property upon any terms whatsoever, to any person with whom Seller, Firm, or any Cooperating Real Estate Firm communicated regarding the Property during the Term of this Agreement or any renewal hereof, provided the names of such persons are delivered or postmarked to the Seller within 15 days after the Expiration Date. HOWEVER, Seller shall NOT be obligated to pay the Fee if a valid listing agreement is entered into between Seller and another real estate broker

North Carolina Association of REALTORS®, Inc.

STANDARD FORM 103
Revised 7/2013
© 7/2013

Individual agent initials _____ Seller initials _____

and the Property is subsequently sold, optioned, exchanged, conveyed or transferred during the Protection Period.

    (c) **Fee Due and Payable.** Once earned as set forth above, the Fee will be due and payable at the earlier of: (i) closing on the Property;

    (ii) The Seller's failure to sell the Property (including but not limited to the Seller's refusal to sign an offer to purchase the Property at the price and terms stated herein or on other terms acceptable to the Seller, the Seller's default on an executed sales contract for the Property, or the Seller's agreement with a buyer to unreasonably modify or cancel an executed sales contract for the Property); or

    (iii) Seller's breach of this Agreement.

    (d) **Transfer of Interest in Business Entity.** If Seller is a partnership, corporation or other business entity, and an interest in the partnership, corporation or other business entity is transferred, whether by merger, outright purchase or otherwise, in lieu of a sale of the Property, and applicable law does not prohibit the payment of a fee or commission in connection with such sale or transfer, the Fee shall be calculated on the fair market value of the Property, rather than the gross sales price, multiplied by the percentage of interest so transferred, and shall be paid by Seller at the time of the transfer.

    (e) **Additional Compensation.** If additional compensation, incentive, bonus, rebate and/or other valuable consideration ("Additional Compensation") is offered to the Firm from any other party or person in connection with a sale of the Property, Seller will permit Firm to receive it in addition to the Fee. Firm shall timely disclose the promise or expectation of receiving any such Additional Compensation and confirm the disclosure in writing before Seller makes or accepts an offer to sell. (**NOTE**: NCAR Form #770 may be used to confirm the disclosure of any such Additional Compensation)

    (f) **Attorney Fees and Costs.** If Firm is the prevailing party in any legal proceeding brought by Firm against Seller to recover any or all of the Fee, Firm shall be entitled to recover from Seller reasonable attorney fees and court costs incurred by Firm in connection with the proceeding.

5. **COOPERATION WITH/COMPENSATION TO OTHER FIRMS.** Firm has advised Seller of Firm's company policies regarding cooperation and the amount(s) of any compensation that will be offered to other brokers, including but not limited to, seller subagents, buyer agents or both, brokers who do or do not participate in a listing service and brokers who are or are not REALTORS®. Seller authorizes Firm to (*Check ALL applicable authorizations*):

- ❑ Cooperate with subagents representing the Seller and offer them the following compensation:_____% of the gross sales price or $_____; and/or,
- ❑ Cooperate with buyer agents representing the buyer and offer them the following compensation:_____ % of the gross sales price or $_____; and/or,
- ❑ Cooperate with and compensate other Cooperating Real Estate Firms according to the Firm's attached policy.

Firm will promptly notify Seller if compensation offered to a Cooperating Real Estate Firm is different from that set forth above. Agents with Cooperating Real Estate Firms must orally disclose the nature of their relationship with a buyer (subagent or buyer agent) to Firm at the time of initial contact with Firm, and confirm that relationship in writing no later than the time an offer to purchase is submitted for the Seller's consideration. Seller should be careful about disclosing confidential information because agents representing buyers must disclose all relevant information to their clients.

6. **FIRM'S DUTIES.** Firm agrees to provide Seller the benefit of Firm's knowledge, experience and advice in the marketing and sale of the Property. Seller understands that Firm makes no representation or guarantee as to the sale of the Property, but Firm agrees to use its best efforts in good faith to find a buyer who is ready, willing and able to purchase the property. In accordance with the REALTORS® Code of Ethics, Firm shall, with Seller's approval, in response to inquiries from buyers or Cooperating Real Estate Firms, disclose the existence of offers on the Property. Where Seller authorizes disclosure, Firm shall also disclose whether offers were obtained by the individual agent who signs this Agreement, another agent of the Firm, or by a Cooperating Real Estate Firm. Seller acknowledges that real estate brokers are prohibited by N.C. Real Estate Commission rule from disclosing the price or other material terms contained in a party's offer to purchase, sell, lease, rent or option real property to a competing party without the express authority of the party making the offer.

Seller acknowledges that Firm is required by law to disclose to potential purchasers of the Property all material facts pertaining to the Property about which the Firm knows or reasonably should know, and that REALTORS® have an ethical responsibility to treat all parties to the transaction honestly. Seller further acknowledges that Firm is being retained solely as a real estate professional, and understands that other professional service providers are available to render advice or services to Seller, including but not limited to an attorney, insurance agent, tax advisor, surveyor, structural engineer, home inspector, environmental consultant, architect, or contractor. Although Firm may provide Seller the names of providers who claim to perform such services, Seller understands that Firm cannot guarantee the quality of service or level of expertise of any such provider. Seller agrees to pay the full amount due for all services directly to the service provider whether or not the transaction closes. Seller also agrees to indemnify and hold Firm harmless from and against any and all liability, claim, loss, damage, suit, or expense that Firm may incur either as a result of Seller's selection and use of any such provider or Seller's election not to have one or more of such services performed.

Individual agent initials _____ Seller initials _____ _____

THE AGENT (FIRM) SHALL CONDUCT ALL BROKERAGE ACTIVITIES IN REGARD TO THIS AGREEMENT WITHOUT RESPECT TO THE RACE, COLOR, RELIGION, SEX, NATIONAL ORIGIN, HANDICAP OR FAMILIAL STATUS OF ANY PARTY OR PROSPECTIVE PARTY TO THE AGREEMENT. FURTHER, REALTORS® HAVE AN ETHICAL DUTY TO CONDUCT SUCH ACTIVITIES WITHOUT RESPECT TO THE SEXUAL ORIENTATION OF ANY PARTY OR PROSPECTIVE PARTY TO THIS AGREEMENT.

7. MARKETING: Seller authorizes Firm (*Check ALL applicable sections*):

(a) **Marketing Date**. Firm's authorization to market the Property as described in subparagraph (b) below shall be effective on: ❑ the Effective Date of this Agreement OR ❑ (insert date) _____ ("Marketing Date"). (NOTE: None of the marketing activities authorized in subparagraph (b) below are permitted prior to the Marketing Date)

(b) **Marketing Authorization**.
- ❑ **Signs**. To place "For Sale," "Under Contract," "Sale Pending," or other similar signs on the Property (where permitted by law and relevant covenants) and to remove other such signs.
- ❑ **Open Houses**. To conduct open houses of the Property at such times as Seller and Firm may subsequently agree.
- ❑ **Listing Service**. To submit pertinent information concerning the Property to any listing service of which Firm is a member or in which any of Firm's agents participate and to furnish to such listing service notice of all changes of information concerning the Property authorized in writing by Seller. Seller authorizes Firm, upon execution of a sales contract for the Property, to notify the listing service of the pending sale and the expiration date of any due diligence period, and upon closing of the sale, to disseminate sales information, including sales price, to the listing service, appraisers and real estate brokers.
- ❑ **Advertising Other Than On The Internet**. To advertise the Property in non-Internet media, and to permit other firms to advertise the Property in non-Internet media to the extent and in such manner as Firm may decide.
- ❑ **Internet Advertising**. To display information about the Property on the Internet either directly or through a program of any listing service of which the Firm is a member or in which any of Firm's agents participate. Seller further authorizes other firms who belong to any listing service of which the Firm is a member or in which any of Firm's agents participate to display information about the Property on the Internet in accordance with the listing service rules and regulations, and also authorizes any listing service of which the Firm is a member or in which any of Firm's agents participate to use, license or sell to others information about the Property entered into the listing service. Seller specifically authorizes the display of the address of the Property, automated estimates of the market value of the Property and third-party comments about the Property. If seller desires to limit or prohibit Internet advertising as set forth above, seller must complete an opt-out form in accordance with listing service rules.

(**NOTE:** NCAR Form #105 may be used to limit or prohibit Internet advertising and explains how such limitations may or may not be effective.)

(c) **Lock/Key Boxes**. The Seller ❑ does ❑ does not authorize Firm to place a lock/key box on the Property.

(d) **Seller Acknowledgement**. Seller acknowledges and understands that while the marketing services selected above will facilitate the showing and sale of the Property, there are risks associated with allowing access to and disseminating information about the Property that are not within the reasonable control of the Firm, including but not limited to:
  (i) unauthorized use of a lock/key box,
  (ii) control of visitors during or after a showing or an open house,
  (iii) inappropriate use of information about the Property placed on the Internet or furnished to any listing service in which the Firm participates.

Seller therefore agrees to indemnify and hold harmless Firm from any damages, costs, attorneys' fees and other expenses as a result of any personal injury or property loss or damage to Seller or any other person not caused by Firm's negligence arising directly or indirectly out of any such marketing services.

8. **EARNEST MONEY.** Unless otherwise provided in the sales contract, any initial and additional earnest money deposits and any other earnest monies paid in connection with any transaction shall be held by the Firm, in escrow, until the consummation or termination of the transaction. Any earnest money forfeited by reason of the buyer's default under a sales contract shall be divided equally between the Firm and Seller. In no event shall the sum paid to the Firm because of a buyer's default be in excess of the fee that would have been due if the sale had closed as contemplated in the sales contract. In accordance with NC General Statutes Section 93A-12, if a dispute regarding the return or forfeiture of any earnest money deposit arises between Seller and the buyer, the escrow agent holding the deposit may deposit the disputed monies with the appropriate Clerk of Court following written notice to the parties. In the event of any such dispute, Seller directs Firm to disclose Seller's last known mailing address to the escrow agent upon request to enable the escrow agent to comply with the notice requirement of such law.

9. **SELLER REPRESENTATIONS.**

(a) **Flood Hazard Disclosure/Insurance**. To the best of Seller's knowledge, the Property ❑ is ❑ is not located partly or entirely within a designated Special Flood Hazard Area.

(b) **Owners' Association.** To the best of Seller's knowledge there ❏ is ❏ is not an owners' association which imposes various mandatory covenants, conditions and restrictions upon the Property. If there is an owners' association, Seller agrees to promptly complete an Owners' Association Disclosure and Addendum For Properties Exempt from Residential Property Disclosure Statement (Standard Form 2A12-T) at Seller's expense and to attach it as an addendum to any contract for the sale of the Property.

(c) **Ownership.** Seller represents that Seller:
   ❏ has owned the Property for at least one year;
   ❏ has owned the Property for less than one year
   ❏ does not yet own the Property

If Seller does not yet own the Property, Seller agrees to promptly provide Firm information pertaining to Seller's acquisition of the Property, such as a copy of a sales contract or option for the Property, and to keep Firm timely informed of all developments pertaining to Seller's acquisition of the Property.

(d) **Receipt Of Sample Forms.**
   ❏ Seller acknowledges receipt of a sample copy of an Offer to Purchase and Contract—New Construction (form #800-T) or Offer to Purchase And Contract—Vacant Lot/Land (form 12-T) as may be appropriate for review purposes.
   ❏ Seller acknowledges receipt of a sample copy of a Professional Services Disclosure and Election form (form #760) for review purposes.

(e) **Access.** Seller represents that the Property has legal access to a public right of way. If access is by private road/easement/other, Seller further represents that there ❏ is ❏ is not an agreement regarding the maintenance of such private road/easement/other means of access. If applicable, Seller agrees to promptly provide Firm information pertaining to any such agreement.

(f) **Current Liens.** Seller represents to the best of Seller's knowledge:
   (1) The Property ❏ is ❏ is not encumbered by a deed of trust or mortgage. *Complete any of the following where applicable:*
      (i) There is a first deed of trust or mortgage on the Property securing a loan held by:
         Lender Name: _____
         Approximate balance: $_____ Lender Phone#:_____
         Lender Address: _____
      (ii) There is a second deed of trust or mortgage on the Property securing a loan held by:
         Lender Name: _____
         Approximate balance: $_____ Lender Phone#:_____
         Lender Address: _____
      (iii) There is a deed of trust or mortgage on the Property securing an equity line of credit held by:
         Lender Name: _____
         Approximate balance: $_____ Lender Phone#:_____
         Lender Address: _____
   (2) Seller is current on all payments for the loans identified in numbered items (i), (ii) and (iii) above except as specified in (7) below.
   (3) Seller is not in default on any loan identified in numbered items (i), (ii) and (iii) above and has not received any notice(s) from the holder of any loan identified in numbered items (i), (ii) and (iii) above or from any other lien holder of any kind, regarding a default under the loan, threatened foreclosure, notice of foreclosure, or the filing of foreclosure except as specified in (7) below.
   (4) There are not any liens secured against the Property for Federal, State or local income taxes, unpaid real property taxes, unpaid condominium or homeowners' association fees, mechanics', laborers' or material men's liens, or other liens affecting the Property, and Seller has no knowledge of any matter that might result in a lien affecting the Property except as specified in (7) below.
   (5) There are not any judgments against Seller affecting the Property, and Seller has no knowledge of any matter that might result in a judgment that may potentially affect the Property except as specified in (7) below.
   (6) There are not any Uniform Commercial Code (UCC) fixture filings affecting the Property, and Seller has no knowledge of any matter that might result in a UCC fixture filing affecting the Property except as specified in (7) below.
   (7) Specify any information, including approximate balances, required by Seller representations (2) through (6) above (**NOTE:** Outstanding liens may affect Seller's net proceeds): _____
   _____
   _____
   _____

(g) **Bankruptcy.** Seller currently:
   (1) ❏ is ❏ is not under bankruptcy protection under United States law.
   (2) ❏ is ❏ is not contemplating seeking bankruptcy protection during the term of this Agreement.

(h) **Lease(s).** To the best of Seller's knowledge, the Property ❏ is ❏ is not subject to any lease(s). If applicable, Seller agrees to promptly provide Firm a copy of any such lease(s) or a written statement of the terms of any oral lease(s).

(i) **Special Assessments**. To the best of Seller's knowledge, there are no Proposed or Confirmed Special Assessments (as defined in the sample contract form provided to Seller) regarding the Property except as follows (Insert "none" or the identification of such assessments, if any): _____
_____

(j) **Manufactured (Mobile) Home**. Complete ONLY if there is a manufactured (mobile) home(s) on the Property that Seller intends to include as a part of the sale of the Property: VIN(s): _____
or ❑ VIN(s) unknown. Other description (*year, model, etc.*): _____
_____

If, during the term of this Agreement, Seller becomes aware that any of the representations set forth in this paragraph 9 are incorrect or no longer accurate, Seller shall promptly notify Firm and cooperate with Firm in taking appropriate corrective action.

10. **SELLER'S DUTIES**. Seller agrees to cooperate with Firm in the marketing and sale of the Property, including but not limited to:

(a) providing to Firm, in a timely manner, accurate information about the Property of which Seller may be aware, including but not limited to presence of or access to any water supply, sewer and/or septic system; problems with drainage, grading or soil stability; environmental hazards; commercial or industrial nuisances (noise, odor, smoke, etc.); utility or other easements, shared driveways, or encroachments from or on adjacent property; lawsuits, foreclosures, bankruptcy, tenancies, judgments, tax liens, proposed assessments, mechanics' liens, materialmens' liens, or notice from any governmental agency; flood hazard; cemetery/grave sites; or abandoned well;

(b) making the Property available for showing (including working, existing utilities) at reasonable times and upon reasonable notice;

(c) providing Firm as soon as reasonably possible after the execution of this Agreement copies of the following documents (where relevant) in the possession of Seller:
   (1) restrictive covenants affecting the Property;
   (2) bylaws, articles of incorporation, rules and regulations, and other governing documents of the owners' association and/or the subdivision;
   (3) title insurance policies, attorney's opinions on title, surveys, covenants, deeds, notes and deeds of trust and easements relating to the Property.

Seller authorizes (1) any attorney presently or previously representing Seller to release and disclose any title insurance policy in such attorney's file to Firm, (2) the Property's title insurer or its agent to release and disclose all materials in the Property's title insurer's (or title insurer's agent's) file to Firm, and (3) the owners' association manager (or other authorized representative) to release and disclose copies of all documents referenced in subparagraphs (c)(1) and (c)(2) above. Seller acknowledges and understands that Firm is under no obligation to acquire any of the information referenced in this subparagraph (c) or to verify the accuracy of any such information that may be provided to Firm.

(d) immediately referring to Firm all inquiries or offers it may receive regarding the Property; showing the Property only by appointment made by or through Firm; and conducting all negotiations through Firm.

(e) executing and delivering at Settlement a GENERAL WARRANTY DEED conveying fee simple marketable title to the Property, including legal access to a public right of way, free of all encumbrances except ad valorem taxes for the current year, utility easements, rights-of-way, and unviolated restrictive covenants, if any, and those encumbrances that the buyer agrees to assume in the sales contract.

Seller represents that the Seller has the right to convey the Property, and that there are currently no circumstances that would prohibit the Seller from conveying fee simple marketable title as set forth in the preceding sentence, except as follows *(insert N/A if not applicable)*: _____

(**NOTE**: If any sale of the Property may be a "short sale," consideration should be given to attaching NCAR form 104 as an addendum to this Agreement.)

(f) providing Firm, in a timely manner, any information necessary (including any information omitted under Paragraph 9) to enable Firm to prepare an estimate of Seller's net proceeds at settlement. Seller acknowledges and understands that any such estimate is an approximation only and that Seller should verify the accuracy of the calculations.

(g) if required by N.C.G.S. §44A-11.1, timely designating a Lien Agent, and providing Firm as soon as reasonably possible a copy of the appointment of Lien Agent.

11. **PHOTOGRAPHS AND OTHER MATERIALS:** Firm is specifically authorized to use, for any purposes whatsoever, any and all photographs, drawings, video, advertising copy or other information obtained by or provided to Firm pursuant to this Agreement (including but not limited to any information concerning the price and terms of the sale of the Property, the description of the Property and the length of time the Property is on the market) ("Materials"), both before and after the sale or, in the event there is not a sale, after this Agreement has expired. If Seller provides any Materials to Firm ("Seller Materials"), Seller represents that Seller owns the Seller Materials or otherwise has the legal right to provide the Seller Materials to Firm, and Seller grants to Firm and any listing

service in which Firm or its agents participate a non-exclusive, perpetual license to use the Seller Materials, including the rights to display, reproduce, distribute or make derivative works from the Seller Materials. Seller agrees to indemnify and hold Firm and its agents harmless for any and all claims resulting from use of the Seller Materials under the terms of this license.

12. **ADDITIONAL TERMS AND CONDITIONS.** The following additional terms and conditions shall also be a part of this Agreement: _____
_____
_____

13. **DUAL AGENCY.** Seller understands that the potential for dual agency will arise if a buyer who has an agency relationship with Firm becomes interested in viewing the Property. Firm may represent more than one party in the same transaction only with the knowledge and informed consent of all parties for whom Firm acts.

(a) **Disclosure of Information**. In the event Firm serves as a dual agent, Seller agrees that without permission from the party about whom the information pertains, Firm shall not disclose to the other party the following information:

(1) that a party may agree to a price, terms, or any conditions of sale other than those offered;

(2) the motivation of a party for engaging in the transaction, unless disclosure is otherwise required by statute or rule; and

(3) any information about a party which that party has identified as confidential unless disclosure is otherwise required by statute or rule.

(b) **Firm's Role as Dual Agent**. If Firm serves as agent for both Seller and a buyer in a transaction involving the Property, Firm shall make every reasonable effort to represent Seller and buyer in a balanced and fair manner. Firm shall also make every reasonable effort to encourage and effect communication and negotiation between Seller and buyer. Seller understands and acknowledges that:

(1) Prior to the time dual agency occurs, Firm will act as Seller's exclusive agent;

(2) In its separate representation of Seller and buyer, Firm may obtain information which, if disclosed, could harm the bargaining position of the party providing such information to Firm;

(3) Firm is required by law to disclose to Seller and buyer any known or reasonably ascertainable material facts. Seller agrees Firm shall not be liable to Seller for (i) disclosing material facts required by law to be disclosed, and (ii) refusing or failing to disclose other information the law does not require to be disclosed which could harm or compromise one party's bargaining position but could benefit the other party.

(c) **Seller's Role**. Should Firm become a dual agent, Seller understands and acknowledges that:

(1) Seller has the responsibility of making Seller's own decisions as to what terms are to be included in any purchase and sale agreement with a buyer client of Firm;

(2) Seller is fully aware of and understands the implications and consequences of Firm's dual agency role as expressed herein to provide balanced and fair representation of Seller and buyer and to encourage and effect communication between them rather than as an advocate or exclusive agent or representative;

(3) Seller has determined that the benefits of dual agency outweigh any disadvantages or adverse consequences;

(4) Seller may seek independent legal counsel to assist Seller with the negotiation and preparation of a purchase and sale agreement or with any matter relating to the transaction which is the subject matter of a purchase and sale agreement.

Should Firm become a dual agent, Seller waives all claims, damages, losses, expenses or liabilities, other than for violations of the North Carolina Real Estate License Law and intentional wrongful acts, arising from Firm's role as a dual agent. Seller shall have a duty to protect Seller's own interests and should read any purchase and sale agreement carefully to ensure that it accurately sets forth the terms which Seller wants included in said agreement.

(d) **Authorization** (initial only ONE).

_____ _____ Seller authorizes the Firm to act as a dual agent, representing both the Seller and the buyer, subject to the terms and conditions set forth in Paragraph 13.

_____ _____ Seller desires exclusive representation at all times during this agreement and does NOT authorize Firm to act in the capacity of dual agent. *If Seller does not authorize Firm to act as a dual agent, the remainder of this paragraph shall not apply.*

(e) **Designated Agent Option** (*Initial only if applicable*).

_____ _____ Seller hereby authorizes the Firm to designate an individual agent(s) to represent the Seller, to the exclusion of any other individual agents associated with the Firm. The individual designated agent(s) shall represent only the interests of the Seller to the extent permitted by law.

(**NOTE**: When dual agency arises, an individual agent shall not practice designated agency and shall remain a dual agent if the individual agent has actually received confidential information concerning a buyer client of the Firm in connection with the transaction or if designated agency is otherwise prohibited by law.)

14. **MEDIATION.** If a dispute arises out of or related to this Agreement or the breach thereof, and if the dispute cannot be settled through negotiation, the parties agree first to try in good faith to settle the dispute by mediation before resorting to arbitration, litigation, or some other dispute resolution procedure. If the need for mediation arises, the parties will choose a mutually acceptable mediator and will share the cost of mediation equally.

Individual agent initials _____ Seller initials _____ _____

15. **ENTIRE AGREEMENT/CHANGES/TERMINATION.** This Agreement constitutes the entire agreement between Seller and Firm and there are no representations, inducements, or other provisions other than those expressed herein. This Agreement may be signed in multiple originals or counterparts, all of which together constitute one and the same instrument. All changes, additions, or deletions to this Agreement must be in writing and signed by both Seller and Firm. Seller acknowledges and understands that this Agreement constitutes a binding contract between Seller and Firm. Although Seller may at any time withdraw from the fiduciary relationship existing between Seller and Firm, the contract created by this Agreement may not be terminated by Seller or Firm prior to its Expiration Date without legally sufficient cause. Any such termination shall be by mutually-acceptable written agreement signed by both Seller and Firm.

Seller and Firm each acknowledge receipt of a signed copy of this Agreement.

THE NORTH CAROLINA ASSOCIATION OF REALTORS®, INC. MAKES NO REPRESENTATION AS TO THE LEGAL VALIDITY OR ADEQUACY OF ANY PROVISION OF THIS FORM IN ANY SPECIFIC TRANSACTION.

Seller: _____   _____   _____
                 Print Name   Signature   Date

Contact Information: _____ _____ _____ _____
                 Home   Work   Cell   Email

Mailing Address: _____

Seller: _____   _____   _____
                 Print Name   Signature   Date

Contact Information: _____ _____ _____ _____
                 Home   Work   Cell   Email

Mailing Address: _____

Firm: _____   Phone: _____
      Print Real Estate Firm Name

By: _____ _____ _____
     Individual Agent Signature   Individual Agent License Number   Date

Office Address: _____

Office Phone: _____ Fax: _____ E-mail: _____

STANDARD FORM 103
Revised 7/2013
© 7/2013

SHORT SALE ADDENDUM TO
EXCLUSIVE RIGHT TO SELL LISTING AGREEMENT
(to be used with NCAR standard form 101 or 103)

Property Address:_____

The additional provisions set forth below are hereby made a part of the Exclusive Right to Sell Listing Agreement for the Property between Seller: _____
and Firm: _____

1. **Short Sale Defined:** For purposes of the Agreement between Seller and Firm, a "Short Sale" is a sale where:
   - The purchase price is or may be insufficient to enable Seller to pay the costs of sale, which include but are not limited to the Seller's closing costs and payment in full of all loans or debts secured by deeds of trust on the Property due and owing to one or more lender(s) and/or other lienholders ("Lienholders")
   - Seller does not or may not have sufficient liquid assets to pay any deficiencies and
   - The Lienholders agree to release or discharge their liens upon payment of an amount less than the amount owed, with or without the Seller being released from any further liability.

2. **Acknowledgement of Short Sale:** Seller acknowledges that any sale of the above Property may or would be a Short Sale. Seller further acknowledges that other options may be available to Seller, including but not limited to negotiating a modification of existing loans or liens, refinancing, bankruptcy, foreclosure, or deed in lieu of foreclosure. Nevertheless, Seller desires to make special arrangements with Firm and any potential Buyer of the Property for a Short Sale. Seller acknowledges that the ability of Firm to successfully market the Property could be limited by any need for a Short Sale

3. **Potential Credit and Tax Consequences:** Seller understands that:
   - A Short Sale may have a negative impact on the credit rating or credit score of Seller
   - A Short Sale may result in taxable income to Seller, even though Seller does not receive any cash proceeds from the sale.

Seller is advised to seek advice from an attorney, a certified public accountant or other professional regarding the credit, legal and tax consequences of a Short Sale.

4. **Lienholders' Conditions:** Seller understands that the Lienholders:
   - Are not obligated to approve a Short Sale
   - Are not obligated to release Seller from further liability even if Lienholders approve a Short Sale
   - May impose conditions prior to consideration or approval of a Short Sale, such as obtaining a current appraisal, requiring Seller to demonstrate financial hardship or provide income tax returns, pay stubs, evidence of financial assets or other financial information

Seller acknowledges that Firm has no control over Lienholders' approval, or any act, omission or decision by any Lienholders in the Short Sale process, and that Firm has not made any promise that a Short Sale of the Property will be successful.

5. **Duties of Seller to Close a Short Sale:** Seller understands that a Short Sale may require Seller to:
   - Deposit with the settlement agent additional funds belonging to Seller to pay obligations of the Seller at closing, and/or
   - Obtain approval of any contract of sale for the Property from the Lienholders, and/or
   - Pay from Seller's other assets at closing or after the sale is completed some or all of the difference between the sales price and the costs of sale

6. **Authorization of Firm:** Seller hereby authorizes Firm to take the following additional actions with regard to the listing and sale of the Property:
   - Market the Property as a Short Sale or "pre-foreclosure" property in the multiple listing services and other advertising or promotional materials
   - Continue to market the Property for sale according to the rules of the multiple listing service until the Short Sale is fully approved and agreed upon by all necessary parties;
   - Disclose or provide any requested information or documentation to the Lienholders (and to the buyer and/or buyer's agent) in order to obtain approval of a Short Sale
   - Contact and communicate directly with the loss mitigation or other similar departments or divisions of Lienholders to obtain loan or lien status, account and payoff-related information and to facilitate a Short Sale

North Carolina Association of REALTORS®, Inc.

Individual agent initials _____ Seller initials _____ _____

STANDARD FORM 104
Revised 7/2012
© 7/2013

- Provide comparable sale information or broker price opinions or other data or information documenting the current fair market value of the Property to the Lienholders
- Provide any and all mortgage and/or other lien account payoff information to settlement agent, prospective buyers and/or buyer's agents
- Coordinate and allow inspection of the Property by authorized representatives of Lienholders;
- Include as a part of any contract of sale that would be a Short Sale a "Short Sale Addendum" (standard form 2A14-T), a copy of which Seller acknowledges has been provided to Seller by Firm

7. **Provision of Information by Seller:** Seller shall be obligated to:
   - Promptly furnish Firm and/or Lienholders with such information or documentation as Lienholders may deem necessary to substantiate and justify the need for a Short Sale, including but not limited to:
     - Providing copies of financial information such as pay stubs, income tax returns, bank statements, proof of Seller's assets and liabilities, homeowner or condominium association lien status letters (when applicable),
     - Composing and providing a hardship letter detailing Seller's financial difficulties.

8. **Lienholder List:** Seller hereby represents to Firm that to the best of Seller's knowledge, the Listing Agreement contains an accurate list of all Lienholders having any lien or encumbrance upon the Property, including the amount now owed by Seller with respect to each such lien or encumbrance.

9. **Potential Foreclosure or Judicial Sale:** Seller understands that:
   - During a Short Sale process a foreclosure or other judicial sale of the Property could occur if Seller is in default of Seller's financial obligations
   - Seller shall remain at all times responsible to be aware of the status of any such sale and to promptly inform Firm of all information possessed by Seller about any sale
   - If a foreclosure or other judicial proceeding is filed with respect to the Property, Firm is required by law to timely disclose it to any prospective buyer
   - Once a foreclosure or other judicial proceeding is filed with the Clerk of Superior Court, Firm may continue to solicit and negotiate offers to purchase between Buyer and Seller. Firm may also contact, communicate with, obtain information from and supply information to Lienholders and to the parties to the foreclosure proceeding.

10. **Limitation of Firm:** While Seller and Seller's attorney may negotiate with Lienholders regarding any foreclosure or the terms of Lienholders' approval of a Short Sale, Firm should avoid negotiating with Lienholders as such conduct may constitute the practice of law.

11. **Disclosure of Offers/Contracts:** Seller understands that in a Short Sale, any offers that may be received by Firm must be presented to Seller according to the Rules of the NC Real Estate Commission, and that the NC Real Estate Commission also requires Firm to inform Lienholders of all offers and contracts of sale on the Property received after a request for a Short Sale has been submitted to any Lienholder.

12. **Firm's Compensation**: Seller understands and acknowledges that Firm's entitlement to the fee set forth in the Listing Agreement shall not be affected by a Short Sale or any other sale of the Property.

IN THE EVENT OF A CONFLICT BETWEEN THIS ADDENDUM AND THE EXCLUSIVE RIGHT TO SELL LISTING AGREEMENT OR THE EXCLUSIVE RIGHT TO SELL LISTING AGREEMENT (VACANT LAND), THIS ADDENDUM SHALL CONTROL.

THE NORTH CAROLINA ASSOCIATION OF REALTORS®, INC. MAKES NO REPRESENTATION AS TO THE LEGAL VALIDITY OR ADEQUACY OF ANY PROVISION OF THIS FORM IN ANY SPECIFIC TRANSACTION.

Date: _____   Date: _____

Seller Signature: _____   Firm: _____

Date: _____   By: _____
                                              Individual Agent Signature
Seller Signature: _____

Date: _____

Seller Signature: _____

STANDARD FORM 104
Revised 7/2012
© 7/2013

INTERNET ADVERTISING ADDENDUM
(**Note**: This form should be used only if a seller has elected to limit or prohibit Internet advertising of their property)

This INTERNET ADVERTISING ADDENDUM hereby modifies the attached: *(Check the appropriate box)*

❑ NCAR Form #101 (Exclusive Right to Sell Listing Agreement) dated _____
❑ NCAR Form #103 (Exclusive Right to Sell Listing Agreement (Vacant Land)) dated _____
❑ NCAR Form #401 (Exclusive Property Management Agreement (Long-Term Rental)) dated _____
❑ NCAR Form #601 (Exclusive Right to Sell Listing Agreement – Auction Sales) dated _____
❑ Other: _____ dated _____

Seller: _____ ("Seller")

Real Estate Firm/Agent/Broker: _____ ("Firm")

Property Address: _____ ("Property")

1. **DEFINITIONS.**
   (a) "**Automated Valuation Model**" or "**AVM**" means a service or computer function that uses statistical calculations to estimate the value of a property based upon data from public records, multiple listing service ("MLS"), and other sources and incorporating certain assumptions. The accuracy of AVMs has sometimes been criticized because they do not take into consideration all relevant factors in valuing a property.
   (b) "**IDX site**" means a web site operated by a broker participating in the MLS on which the broker can advertise the listings of other brokers in MLS, subject to certain MLS rules. The consumer visiting an IDX site is not required to register on the site or to have a brokerage relationship with the broker displaying listings on the site.
   (c) "**Third-party commentary**" means comments and reviews regarding the Property left on a web site by someone other than the operator of the web site.
   (d) "**Virtual office web site**" (**VOW**) means a web site operated by a broker participating in the MLS that delivers brokerage services to consumers over the world wide web. Visitors to a VOW are required to register on the site (with their name and a real email address) and enter a brokerage relationship with the broker operating the VOW. The broker operating the VOW can then show the visiting customer/client nearly all the information available to the broker in MLS. The seller(s) of a listing have the right to opt out of certain kinds of data display under the MLS's VOW policy. The MLS imposes various other rules and restrictions on VOWs.

2. **DISPLAY OF PROPERTY ON THE INTERNET.** (*Seller must choose (a), (b), or (c)*)
   (a) ❑ Seller permits display of information about the Property on the Internet subject to the limitations set forth in paragraphs 3, 4 and/or 5 below.
   (b) ❑ Seller authorizes Firm to display information about the Property on the Internet but does NOT authorize participants of any listing service (MLS) of which the Firm is a member or in which any of Firm's agents participate to display information about the Property on the Internet. **Seller acknowledges and understands that if Seller selects this option, the Property will not be eligible for inclusion in any listing service** (MLS).
   (c) ❑ Seller does NOT authorize the display of information about the Property on the Internet. **Seller acknowledges and understands that consumers who conduct searches for listings on the Internet will not see information about the Property in response to their search.**

If (a) or (b) above is selected, complete paragraphs 3, 4 and 5 below. If (c) above is selected, do not complete paragraphs 3, 4 and 5 below.

3. **DISPLAY OF THE PROPERTY ADDRESS ON INTERNET.** Seller ❑ permits ❑ does not permit display of the Property address (house and unit numbers and street name) in marketing of the Property on the Internet. Seller's election in this section affects all Internet display, including on Firm's web site, IDX and VOW sites, and third-party sites such as Zillow, Trulia and Realtor.com. If Seller does not permit address display on the Internet, brokers participating in MLS can still disclose the address to clients/customers via other means, including email, fax, mail, hand delivery, and orally.

Page 1 of 2

North Carolina Association of REALTORS®, Inc.

Individual agent initials _____ Seller initials _____ _____

STANDARD FORM 105
Revised 11/2010
© 1/2011

4. DISPLAY OF AUTOMATED VALUATIONS ON VOWS/IDX SITES. Seller ❑ permits ❑ does not permit an automated valuation of the Property or a link to an automated valuation of it to be displayed adjacent to the Property on the IDX sites and VOWs of other brokers. Seller's election here affects only the web sites of other real estate brokers, and does not affect display of automated valuations of the Property on third-party web sites such as Zillow, Trulia and Realtor.com.

5. DISPLAY OF THIRD-PARTY COMMENTARY ON VOWS/IDX SITES. Seller ❑ permits ❑ does not permit third-party commentary regarding the Property or a link to third-party commentary regarding it to be displayed adjacent to the property on the IDX sites and VOWs of other brokers. Seller's election here affects only the web sites of other real estate brokers, and does not affect display of third-party commentary regarding the Property on third-party web sites such as Zillow, Trulia and Realtor.com.

THE NORTH CAROLINA ASSOCIATION OF REALTORS®, INC. MAKES NO REPRESENTATION AS TO THE LEGAL VALIDITY OR ADEQUACY OF ANY PROVISION OF THIS FORM IN ANY SPECIFIC TRANSACTION.

Seller: _____ _____
           Print Name   Signature

Contact Information: _____ _____ _____ _____
                      Home   Work   Cell   Email

Seller: _____ _____
           Print Name   Signature

Contact Information: _____ _____ _____ _____
                      Home   Work   Cell   Email

Mailing Address: _____

Firm: _____   Phone: _____
      Print Real Estate Firm Name

By: _____ _____
     Individual Agent Signature   Individual Agent License Number

Office Address: _____

Office Phone: _____ Fax: _____ E-mail: _____

STANDARD FORM 105
Revised 11/2010
© 1/2011

STATE OF NORTH CAROLINA
RESIDENTIAL PROPERTY AND OWNERS' ASSOCIATION DISCLOSURE STATEMENT

Instructions to Property Owners

1. The Residential Property Disclosure Act (G.S. 47E) ("Disclosure Act") requires owners of residential real estate (single-family homes, individual condominiums, townhouses, and the like, and buildings with up to four dwelling units) to furnish purchasers a Residential Property and Owners' Association Disclosure Statement ("Disclosure Statement"). This form is the only one approved for this purpose. A disclosure statement must be furnished in connection with the sale, exchange, option and sale under a lease with option to purchase where the tenant does not occupy or intend to occupy the dwelling. A disclosure statement is not required for some transactions, including the first sale of a dwelling which has never been inhabited and transactions of residential property made pursuant to a lease with option to purchase where the lessee occupies or intends to occupy the dwelling. For a complete list of exemptions, see G.S. 47E-2.

2. You must respond to each of the questions on the following pages of this form by filling in the requested information or by placing a check √ in the appropriate box. In responding to the questions, you are only obligated to disclose information about which you have actual knowledge.

    a. If you check "Yes" for any question, you must explain your answer and either describe any problem or attach a report from an attorney, engineer, contractor, pest control operator or other expert or public agency describing it. If you attach a report, you will not be liable for any inaccurate or incomplete information contained in it so long as you were not grossly negligent in obtaining or transmitting the information.

    b. If you check "No," you are stating that you have no actual knowledge of any problem. If you check "No" and you know there is a problem, you may be liable for making an intentional misstatement. ← Fraud

    c. If you check "No Representation," you are choosing not to disclose the conditions or characteristics of the property, even if you have actual knowledge of them or should have known of them.

    d. If you check "Yes" or "No" and something happens to the property to make your Disclosure Statement incorrect or inaccurate (for example, the roof begins to leak), you must promptly give the purchaser a corrected Disclosure Statement or correct the problem.

3. If you are assisted in the sale of your property by a licensed real estate broker, you are still responsible for completing and delivering the Disclosure Statement to the purchasers; and the broker must disclose any material facts about your property which he or she knows or reasonably should know, regardless of your responses on the Disclosure Statement.

4. You must give the completed Disclosure Statement to the purchaser no later than the time the purchaser makes an offer to purchase your property. If you do not, the purchaser can, under certain conditions, cancel any resulting contract (See **"Note to Purchasers"** below). You should give the purchaser a copy of the Disclosure Statement containing your signature and keep a copy signed by the purchaser for your records.

Note to Purchasers: If the owner does not give you a Residential Property and Owners' Association Disclosure Statement by the time you make your offer to purchase the property, you may under certain conditions cancel any resulting contract without penalty to you as the purchaser. To cancel the contract, you must personally deliver or mail written notice of your decision to cancel to the owner or the owner's agent within three calendar days following your receipt of the Disclosure Statement, or three calendar days following the date of the contract, whichever occurs first. However, in no event does the Disclosure Act permit you to cancel a contract after settlement of the transaction or (in the case of a sale or exchange) after you have occupied the property, whichever occurs first.

---

5. In the space below, type or print in ink the address of the property (sufficient to identify it) and your name. Then sign and date.

Property Address:_____

Owner's Name(s):_____

Owner(s) acknowledge having examined this Disclosure Statement before signing and that all information is true and correct as of the date signed.

Owner Signature:_____ Date_____ , _____

Owner Signature:_____ Date_____ , _____

Purchasers acknowledge receipt of a copy of this Disclosure Statement; that they have examined it before signing; that they understand that this is not a warranty by owners or owners' agents; that it is not a substitute for any inspections they may wish to obtain; and that the representations are made by the owners and not the owners' agents or subagents. Purchasers are strongly encouraged to obtain their own inspections from a licensed home inspector or other professional. As used herein, words in the plural include the singular, as appropriate.

Purchaser Signature:_____ Date_____ , _____

Purchaser Signature:_____ Date_____ , _____

REC 4.22
REV 1/13

640 Appendix D

Property Address/Description:_____

The following questions address the characteristics and condition of the property identified above about which the owner has *actual knowledge*. Where the question refers to "dwelling," it is intended to refer to the dwelling unit, or units if more than one, to be conveyed with the property. The term "dwelling unit" refers to any structure intended for human habitation.

		Yes	No	No Representation

1. In what year was the dwelling constructed?_____.
   Explain if necessary:_____ ☐

2. Is there any problem, malfunction or defect with the dwelling's foundation, slab, fireplaces/chimneys, floors, windows (including storm windows and screens), doors, ceilings, interior and exterior walls, attached garage, patio, deck or other structural components including any modifications to them?............ ☐ ☐ ☐

3. The dwelling's exterior walls are made of what type of material? ☐Brick Veneer ☐Wood ☐Stone ☐Vinyl ☐Synthetic Stucco ☐Composition/Hardboard ☐Concrete ☐Fiber Cement ☐Aluminum ☐Asbestos ☐Other
   _____ (Check all that apply) ☐

4. In what year was the dwelling's roof covering installed?_____ (Approximate if no records are available) Explain if necessary:_____ ☐

5. Is there any leakage or other problem with the dwelling's roof?.. ☐ ☐ ☐

6. Is there any water seepage, leakage, dampness or standing water in the dwelling's basement, crawl space, or slab? ☐ ☐ ☐

7. Is there any problem, malfunction or defect with the dwelling's electrical system (outlets, wiring, panel, switches, fixtures, generator, etc.)?... ☐ ☐ ☐

8. Is there any problem, malfunction or defect with the dwelling's plumbing system (pipes, fixtures, water heater, etc.)? ☐ ☐ ☐

9. Is there any problem, malfunction or defect with the dwelling's heating and/or air conditioning?............ ☐ ☐ ☐

10. What is the dwelling's heat source? ☐Furnace ☐Heat Pump ☐Baseboard ☐Other_____
    _____ (Check all that apply)...
    Age of system:_____ ☐

11. What is the dwelling's cooling source? ☐Central Forced Air ☐Wall/Window Unit(s) ☐Other_____
    _____ (Check all that apply) ....
    Age of system:_____ ☐

12. What are the dwelling's fuel sources? ☐Electricity ☐Natural Gas ☐Propane ☐Oil ☐Other_____
    _____ (Check all that apply) If the fuel source is stored in a tank, identify whether the tank is ☐above ground or ☐below ground, and whether the tank is ☐leased by seller or ☐owned by seller. (Check all that apply).. ☐

13. What is the dwelling's water supply source? ☐City/County ☐Community System ☐Private Well ☐Shared Well ☐Other_____ (Check all that apply).. ☐

14. The dwelling's water pipes are made of what type of material? ☐Copper ☐Galvanized ☐Plastic ☐Polybutylene ☐Other_____ (Check all that apply).. ☐

15. Is there any problem, malfunction or defect with the dwelling's water supply (including water quality, quantity, or water pressure)?... ☐ ☐ ☐

16. What is the dwelling's sewage disposal system? ☐Septic Tank ☐Septic Tank with Pump ☐Community System ☐Connected to City/County System ☐City/County System available ☐Straight pipe (wastewater does not go into a septic or other sewer system [note: use of this type of system violates state law]) ☐Other
    _____ (Check all that apply)... ☐

17. If the dwelling is serviced by a septic system, do you know how many bedrooms are allowed by the septic system permit?
    If your answer is "yes," how many bedrooms are allowed?_____ ☐ ☐ ☐
    ☐No records available

18. Is there any problem, malfunction or defect with the dwelling's sewer and/or septic system?................ ☐ ☐ ☐

19. Is there any problem, malfunction or defect with the dwelling's central vacuum, pool, hot tub, spa, attic fan, exhaust fan, ceiling fans, sump pump, irrigation system, TV cable wiring or satellite dish, garage door openers, gas logs, or other systems?.. ☐ ☐ ☐

20. Is there any problem, malfunction or defect with any appliances that may be included in the conveyance (range/oven, attached microwave, hood/fan, dishwasher, disposal, etc.)?................................... ☐ ☐ ☐

Owner Initials and Date_____ Owner Initials and Date_____
Purchaser Initials and Date_____ Purchaser Initials and Date_____

_____Page 2 of 4

	Yes	No	No Representation

21. Is there any problem with present infestation of the dwelling, or damage from past infestation of wood destroying insects or organisms which has not been repaired?.. ☐ ☐ ☐

22. Is there any problem, malfunction or defect with the drainage, grading or soil stability of the property?.......... ☐ ☐ ☐

23. Are there any structural additions or other structural or mechanical changes to the dwelling(s) to be conveyed with the property?... ☐ ☐ ☐

24. Have you been notified by a governmental agency that the property is in violation of any local zoning ordinances, restrictive covenants, or other land-use restrictions, or building codes (including the failure to obtain proper permits for room additions or other changes/improvements)?.. ☐ ☐ ☐

25. Are there any hazardous or toxic substances, materials, or products (such as asbestos, formaldehyde, radon gas, methane gas, lead-based paint) which exceed government safety standards, any debris (whether buried or covered) or underground storage tanks, or any environmentally hazardous conditions (such as contaminated soil or water, or other environmental contamination) which affect the property?..................................... ☐ ☐ ☐

26. Is there any noise, odor, smoke, etc. from commercial, industrial, or military sources which affects the property? ☐ ☐ ☐

27. Is the property subject to any utility or other easements, shared driveways, party walls or encroachments from or on adjacent property?... ☐ ☐ ☐

28. Is the property the subject of any lawsuits, foreclosures, bankruptcy, leases or rental agreements, judgments, tax liens, proposed assessments, mechanics' liens, materialmens' liens, or notices from any governmental agency that could affect title to the property?... ☐ ☐ ☐

29. Is the property subject to a flood hazard or is the property located in a federally-designated flood hazard area? ☐ ☐ ☐

30. Does the property abut or adjoin any private road(s) or street(s)?.. ☐ ☐ ☐

31. If there is a private road or street adjoining the property, is there in existence any owners' association or maintenance agreements dealing with the maintenance of the road or street?... ☐ ☐ ☐

If you answered "yes" to any of the questions listed above (1-31) please explain (attach additional sheets if necessary):

In lieu of providing a written explanation, you may attach a written report to this Disclosure Statement by a public agency, or by an attorney, engineer, land surveyor, geologist, pest control operator, contractor, home inspector, or other expert, dealing with matters within the scope of that public agency's functions or the expert's license or expertise.

The following questions pertain to the property identified above, including the lot to be conveyed and any dwelling unit(s), sheds, detached garages, or other buildings located thereon.

	Yes	No	No Representation

32. To your knowledge, is the property subject to regulation by one or more owners' association(s) or governing documents which impose various mandatory covenants, conditions, and restrictions upon the lot, including, but not limited to obligations to pay regular assessments or dues and special assessments? If your answer is "yes," please provide the information requested below as to each owners' association to which the property is subject [insert N/A into any blank that does not apply]: ☐ ☐ ☐

• (specify name)_____ whose regular assessments ("dues") are $_____ per _____. The name, address, and telephone number of the president of the owners' association or the association manager are_____

• (specify name)_____ whose regular assessments ("dues") are $_____ per _____. The name, address, and telephone number of the president of the owners' association or the association manager are_____

* If you answered "Yes" to question 32 above, you must complete the remainder of this Disclosure Statement. If you answered "No" or "No Representation" to question 32 above, you do not need to answer the remaining questions on this Disclosure Statement. Skip to the bottom of the last page and initial and date the page.

Owner Initials and Date_____   Owner Initials and Date_____
Purchaser Initials and Date_____   -   Purchaser Initials and Date_____

	Yes	No	No Representation

33. Are any fees charged by the association or by the association's management company in connection with the conveyance or transfer of the lot or property to a new owner? If your answer is "yes," please state the amount of the fees:_____
_____ ☐ ☐ ☐

34. As of the date this Disclosure Statement is signed, are there any dues, fees, or special assessments which have been duly approved as required by the applicable declaration or bylaws, and that are payable to an association to which the lot is subject? If your answer is "yes," please state the nature and amount of the dues, fees, or special assessments to which the property is subject: _____
_____ ☐ ☐ ☐

35. As of the date this Disclosure Statement is signed, are there any unsatisfied judgments against, or pending lawsuits *involving the property or lot to be conveyed*? If your answer is "yes," please state the nature of each pending lawsuit, and the amount of each unsatisfied judgment:_____
_____ ☐ ☐ ☐

36. As of the date this Disclosure Statement is signed, are there any unsatisfied judgments against, or pending lawsuits *involving the planned community or the association to which the property and lot are subject*, with the exception of any action filed by the association for the collection of delinquent assessments on lots other than the property and lot to be conveyed? If your answer is "yes," please state the nature of each pending lawsuit, and the amount of each unsatisfied judgment:_____
_____ ☐ ☐ ☐

37. Which of the following services and amenities are paid for by the owners' association(s) identified above out of the association's regular assessments ("dues")? (Check all that apply).

	Yes	No	No Representation
Management Fees	☐	☐	☐
Exterior Building Maintenance of Property to be Conveyed	☐	☐	☐
Exterior Yard/Landscaping Maintenance of Lot to be Conveyed	☐	☐	☐
Common Areas Maintenance	☐	☐	☐
Trash Removal	☐	☐	☐
Recreational Amenity Maintenance (specify amenities covered)_____ _____	☐	☐	☐
Pest Treatment/Extermination	☐	☐	☐
Street Lights	☐	☐	☐
Water	☐	☐	☐
Sewer	☐	☐	☐
Storm water Management/Drainage/Ponds	☐	☐	☐
Internet Service	☐	☐	☐
Cable	☐	☐	☐
Private Road Maintenance	☐	☐	☐
Parking Area Maintenance	☐	☐	☐
Gate and/or Security	☐	☐	☐

Other: (specify) _____
_____

Owner Initials and Date _____   Owner Initials and Date _____

Purchaser Initials and Date _____   Purchaser Initials and Date _____

LEAD-BASED PAINT OR LEAD-BASED PAINT HAZARD ADDENDUM

Property Address: _____

During the Due Diligence Period, Buyer shall have the right to obtain a risk assessment or inspection of the Property for the presence of lead-based paint and/or lead-based paint hazards* at Buyer's expense. Buyer may waive the right to obtain a risk assessment or inspection of the Property for the presence of lead-based paint and/or lead-based paint hazards at any time without cause.

*Intact lead-based paint that is in good condition is not necessarily a hazard. See EPA pamphlet "Protect Your Family From Lead in Your Home" for more information.

Disclosure of Information on Lead-Based Paint and Lead-Based Paint Hazards

Lead Warning Statement
Every Buyer of any interest in residential real property on which a residential dwelling was built prior to 1978 is notified that such property may present exposure to lead from lead-based paint that may place young children at risk of developing lead poisoning. Lead poisoning in young children may produce permanent neurological damage, including learning disabilities, reduced intelligence quotient, behavioral problems, and impaired memory. Lead poisoning also poses a particular risk to pregnant women. The Seller of any interest in residential real property is required to provide the Buyer with any information on lead-based paint hazards from risk assessments or inspections in the Seller's possession and notify the Buyer of any known lead-based paint hazards. A risk assessment or inspection for possible lead-based hazards is recommended prior to purchase.

Seller's Disclosure (initial)

_____ (a) Presence of lead-based paint and/or lead-based paint hazards (check one below):
❏ Known lead-based paint and/or lead-based paint hazards are present in the housing (explain).
_____

❏ Seller has no knowledge of lead-based paint and/or lead-based paint hazards in the housing.

_____ (b) Records and reports available to the Seller (check one)
❏ Seller has provided the Buyer with all available records and reports pertaining to lead-based paint and/or lead-based paint hazards in the housing (list documents below).
_____

❏ Seller has no reports or records pertaining to lead-based paint and/or lead-based paint hazards in the housing.

Buyer's Acknowledgement (initial)

_____ (c) Buyer has received copies of all information listed above.
_____ (d) Buyer has received the pamphlet *Protect Your Family from Lead in Your Home.*
_____ (e) Buyer has (check one below):
❏ Received the opportunity during the Due Diligence Period to conduct a risk assessment or inspection for the presence of lead-based paint and/or lead-based paint hazards; or
❏ Waived the opportunity to conduct a risk assessment or inspection for the presence of lead-based paint and/or lead-based paint hazards.

Agent's Acknowledgment (initial)

_____ (f) Agent has informed the Seller of the Seller's obligations under 42 U.S.C. 4852d and is aware of his/her responsibility to ensure compliance.

Page 1 of 2

North Carolina Association of REALTORS®, Inc.

Buyer Initials _____ _____   Seller Initials _____ _____

STANDARD FORM 2A9–T
Revised 1/2011
© 1/2011

Source: This form is the property of the North Carolina Association of REALTORS® and the North Carolina Bar Association (NCBA) and is reproduced with the permission of NCAR and NCBA.

644 Appendix D

Certification of Accuracy
The following parties have reviewed the information above and certify, to the best of their knowledge, that the information provided by the signatory is true and accurate.

THE NORTH CAROLINA ASSOCIATION OF REALTORS®, INC. AND THE NORTH CAROLINA BAR ASSOCIATION MAKE NO REPRESENTATION AS TO THE LEGAL VALIDITY OR ADEQUACY OF ANY PROVISION OF THIS FORM IN ANY SPECIFIC TRANSACTION. IF YOU DO NOT UNDERSTAND THIS FORM OR FEEL THAT IT DOES NOT PROVIDE FOR YOUR LEGAL NEEDS, YOU SHOULD CONSULT A NORTH CAROLINA REAL ESTATE ATTORNEY BEFORE YOU SIGN IT.

Buyer:_____(SEAL)   Date_____

Buyer:_____(SEAL)   Date_____

Agent:_____   Date_____

Seller:_____(SEAL)   Date_____

Seller:_____(SEAL)   Date_____

Agent:_____   Date_____

Page 2 of 2

STANDARD FORM 2A9-T
Revised 1/2011
© 1/2011

OWNERS' ASSOCIATION DISCLOSURE AND ADDENDUM FOR PROPERTIES EXEMPT FROM RESIDENTIAL PROPERTY AND OWNER'S ASSOCIATION DISCLOSURE STATEMENT

(For example: New Construction, Vacant Lot/Land)
(If the Property is part of a Development that is a condominium, this form should be used for resale only.)

Property: _____

Buyer: _____

Seller: _____

This Addendum is attached to and made a part of the Offer to Purchase and Contract ("Contract") between Buyer and Seller for the Property.

For the purposes of this Addendum, "Development" means any planned community or condominium project, as defined by North Carolina law, which is subject to regulation and assessment by an owners' association.

Any representations made by Seller in this Addendum are true to the best of Seller's knowledge, and copies of any documents provided by Seller are true copies relating to the Development, to the best of Seller's knowledge. Except with regard to Confirmed Special Assessments, Seller does not warrant the accuracy, completeness, or present applicability of any representation or documents provided by Seller, and Buyer is advised to have all information confirmed and any documents substantiated during the Due Diligence Period.

1. Seller represents to Buyer that the Property is subject to the following owners' association(s) [insert N/A into any blank that does not apply]:
   ❑ (specify name): _____ whose regular assessments ("dues") are $_____ per _____. The name, address and telephone number of the president of the owners' association or the association manager are: _____
   _____.

   Owners' association website address, if any: _____.

   ❑ (specify name): _____ whose regular assessments ("dues") are $_____ per _____. The name, address and telephone number of the president of the owners' association or the association manager are: _____
   _____.

   Owners' association website address, if any: _____.

2. Seller represents to Buyer that the following services and amenities are paid for by the above owners' association(s) from the regular assessments ("dues"): (Check all that apply)

   ❑ Master Insurance Policy Including All Units
   ❑ Real Property Taxes on the Common Areas
   ❑ Casualty/Liability Insurance on Common Areas
   ❑ Management Fees
   ❑ Exterior Building Maintenance
   ❑ Exterior Yard/Landscaping Maintenance
   ❑ Trash Removal
   ❑ Pest Treatment/Extermination
   ❑ Legal/Accounting
   ❑ Recreational Amenities (specify): _____

   ❑ Street Lights
   ❑ Water
   ❑ Sewer
   ❑ Private Road Maintenance
   ❑ Parking Area Maintenance
   ❑ Common Areas Maintenance
   ❑ Cable
   ❑ Internet service
   ❑ Storm Water Management/Drainage/Ponds
   ❑ Gate and/or Security

Page 1 of 2

This form jointly approved by:
North Carolina Bar Association
North Carolina Association of REALTORS®, Inc.

Buyer initials _____ _____   Seller initials _____ _____

STANDARD FORM 2A12-T
Revised 1/2012
© 7/2013

❑ Other (specify)_____

❑ Other (specify) _____

3. As of this date, there are no other dues, fees or Special Assessments, Confirmed or Proposed, payable by the Development's property owners, except: _____
_____.

4. As of this date, there are no unsatisfied judgments against or pending lawsuits involving the Property, the Development and/or the owners' association, except:_____.

5. The fees charged by the owners' association or management company in connection with the transfer of Property to a new owner (including but not limited to document preparation, move in/move out fees, preparation of insurance documents, statement of unpaid assessments, and transfer fees) are as follows: _____
_____
_____

6. Seller agrees, upon Buyer's request, to use best efforts to deliver to Buyer as soon as reasonably possible after the Effective Date, at Seller's expense, copies of any documents relating to the Development in possession of or reasonably available to Seller, including but not limited to:
- the face cover sheet from the Development's master insurance policy showing the total coverage amount and the deductible amount,
- the recorded Declaration and Restrictive Covenants of the Development
- the Rules and Regulations of the Development
- the Articles of Incorporation
- Bylaws of the owners' association
- Rules and Regulations of the owners' association
- the current Financial Statement and budget of the owners' association
- any parking information for the Development
- Architectural Guidelines

The parties have read, understand and accept the terms of this Addendum as a part of the Contract.

IN THE EVENT OF A CONFLICT BETWEEN THIS ADDENDUM AND THE CONTRACT, THIS ADDENDUM SHALL CONTROL, EXCEPT THAT IN THE CASE OF SUCH A CONFLICT AS TO THE DESCRIPTION OF THE PROPERTY OR THE IDENTITY OF THE BUYER OR SELLER, THE CONTRACT SHALL CONTROL.

THE NORTH CAROLINA ASSOCIATION OF REALTORS®, INC. AND THE NORTH CAROLINA BAR ASSOCIATION MAKE NO REPRESENTATION AS TO THE LEGAL VALIDITY OR ADEQUACY OF ANY PROVISION OF THIS FORM IN ANY SPECIFIC TRANSACTION. IF YOU DO NOT UNDERSTAND THIS FORM OR FEEL THAT IT DOES NOT PROVIDE FOR YOUR LEGAL NEEDS, YOU SHOULD CONSULT A NORTH CAROLINA REAL ESTATE ATTORNEY BEFORE YOU SIGN IT.

Date: _____   Date: _____

Buyer _____ (SEAL)   Seller _____ (SEAL)

Date:_____   Date: _____

Buyer _____ (SEAL)   Seller _____ (SEAL)

Date:_____   Date: _____

Buyer _____ (SEAL)   Seller _____ (SEAL)

STANDARD FORM 2A12-T
Revised 1/2012
© 7/2013

PROFESSIONAL SERVICES DISCLOSURE AND ELECTION
[See Guidelines (Form 760G) for instructions on completing this form]

Property Address:_____("Property")
Buyer or Seller:_____
Real Estate Firm: _____("Firm")

1. There are professional services that typically are performed in connection with the purchase and sale of real estate. Buyer or Seller understands that Firm cannot give advice in certain matters that may relate to the purchase or sale of the Property, including but not limited to matters of law, taxation, financing, surveying, wood-destroying insect infestation, structural soundness of engineering.

2. Buyer or Seller acknowledges Firm has recommended that Buyer or Seller consult with a professional for an opinion regarding each service listed below to be performed pursuant to Buyer or Seller's purchase or sale of the Property. Regarding each such service, Buyer or Seller has either selected the service provider listed or elected not to have the service performed. Although Firm may provide Buyer or Seller the names of providers who claim to perform services in one or more of the listed areas, Buyer or Seller understands that Firm cannot guarantee the quality of service or level of expertise of any such provider. Buyer or Seller agrees to pay the full amount due for all services directly to the service provider whether or not the transaction closes.

Service	Selected (initial)	Waived (initial)	Name(s) of Service Providers(s)	Who Orders
Accountant/CPA /Tax Advisor				
Appraisal				
Attorney/Title Exam/Closing				
Home Inspections				
Home Warranty				
Mortgage Loan				
Property Insurance				
Radon Inspection				
Septic Inspection				
Survey* (see note below)				
Title Insurance				
Well/Water Inspection				
Wood Infestation				

North Carolina Association of REALTORS®, Inc.

Individual Agent initials_____   Buyer or Seller initials_____

STANDARD FORM 760
Revised 7/2013
©7/2013

Page 1 of 2

Source: This form is the property of the North Carolina Association of REALTORS® (NCAR) and is reproduced with the permission of NCAR.

3. Buyer or Seller hereby agrees to indemnify and hold Firm harmless from and against any and all liability, claim, loss, damage, suit, or expense that Firm may incue either as a result of Buyer or Seller's selection and use of any of the listed service providers or Buyer or Seller's election not to have one or more of the listed services performed.

*NOTE REGARDING SURVEYS: Situations arise all too often that could have been avoided if the buyer had obtained a new survey from a NC registered surveyor. A survey will normally reveal such things as encroachments on the Property from adjacent properties (fences, driveways, etc.); encroachments from the Property onto adjacent properties; road or utility easements crossing the Property; violations of set-back lines; lack of legal access to a public right-of-way; and indefinite or erroneous legal descriptions in previous deeds to the Property. Although title insurance companies may provide lender coverage without a new survey, the owner's policy contains an exception for easements, set-backs and other matters which would have been shown on a survey. Many such matters are not public record and would not be included in an attorney's title examination. In addition, if the buyer does not obtain their own survey, they would have no claim against a surveyor for inaccuracies in a prior survey.

THE NORTH CAROLINA ASSOCIATION OF REALTORS®, INC. MAKES NO REPRESENTATION AS TO THE LEGAL VALIDITY OR ADEQUACY OF ANY PROVISION OF THIS FORM IN ANY SPECIFIC TRANSACTION.

_____   _____
Buyer or Seller   Signature of individual agent

_____   _____
Buyer or Seller   Real Estate Firm (print name)

Date:_____   Date:_____

STANDARD FORM 760
Revised 7/2013
©7/2013

EXCLUSIVE BUYER AGENCY AGREEMENT

[Consult "Guidelines" (Form 201G) for guidance in completing this form]

This EXCLUSIVE BUYER AGENCY AGREEMENT ("Agreement") is entered into (Date)_____,
between_____ as Buyer(s) ("Buyer"),
and_____ ("Firm")
as the Buyer's exclusive agent to assist the Buyer in the acquisition of real property which may include any purchase, option and/or exchange on terms and conditions acceptable to Buyer. The individual agent who signs this Agreement on behalf of the Firm shall, on behalf of the Firm, be primarily responsible for ensuring that the Firm's duties hereunder are fulfilled; however, it is understood and agreed that other agents of the Firm may be assigned to fulfill such duties if deemed appropriate by the Firm. For purposes of this Agreement, the term "Firm," as the context may require, shall be deemed to include the individual agent who signs this Agreement and any other agents of the Firm.

Buyer represents that, as of the commencement date of this Agreement, the Buyer is not a party to a buyer representation agreement with any other real estate firm. Buyer has received a copy of the "WORKING WITH REAL ESTATE AGENTS" brochure and has reviewed it with Firm. Buyer further represents that Buyer has disclosed to Firm information about any properties of the type described in paragraph 1 below that Buyer has visited at any open houses or that Buyer has been shown by any other real estate firm.

1. **TYPE OF PROPERTY.** ❏ Residential (improved and unimproved)   ❏ Commercial (improved and unimproved)
   ❏ Other _____
   (a) General Location: _____
   (b) Other: _____

2. **EFFECT OF AGREEMENT.** Buyer intends to acquire real property of the type described in paragraph 1. *By employing Firm as Buyer's exclusive agent, Buyer agrees to conduct all negotiations for such property through Firm, and to refer to Firm all inquiries received in any form from other real estate firms, prospective sellers or any other source, during the time this Agreement is in effect.*

3. **DURATION OF AGENCY.** Firm's authority as Buyer's exclusive agent shall begin _____, and subject to paragraph 4, shall expire at midnight, _____, or when Buyer acquires real property of the type described in paragraph 1, whichever occurs sooner.

4. **COMPENSATION OF FIRM.**
   (a) Firm acknowledges receipt of a non-refundable retainer fee in the amount of $_____ which
       ❏ shall ❏ shall not be credited toward any compensation due Firm under this Agreement.
   (b) Buyer agrees that Firm's fee for services hereunder shall be in the amount of _____
       _____ ("Fee")
       (Insert dollar amount, percentage of purchase price, or other method of determining Firm's compensation for each type of property the Buyer may purchase, such as resale, new construction, land/lot and/or unrepresented seller. Do not insert N/A or a zero ($0)).
       (i) Firm shall seek the Fee from a cooperating listing firm (through the listing firm's offer of compensation in MLS or otherwise) or from the seller if there is no listing firm, and Buyer agrees that Firm shall be entitled to receive same in consideration for Firm's services hereunder.
       (ii) If Buyer purchases property where the compensation offered by the listing firm and/or seller is less than the Fee, or where no compensation is offered by either the listing firm or the seller, Buyer and Firm agree that Buyer will pay the difference between the Fee and the compensation offered unless prohibited by law. Firm will timely inform Buyer if the compensation offered is less than expected.
       (iii) If additional compensation, incentive, bonus, rebate and/or other valuable consideration *("Additional Compensation")* is offered through the MLS or otherwise, Buyer will permit the Firm to receive it in addition to the Fee. Firm shall timely disclose the promise or expectation of receiving any such Additional Compensation and confirm the disclosure in writing before Buyer makes or accepts an offer to buy. (Note: NCAR Form #770 may be used to confirm the disclosure of any such Additional Compensation).
   (c) The compensation shall be deemed earned under any of the following circumstances:
       (i) If, during the term of this Agreement, Buyer, any assignee of Buyer or any person/legal entity acting on behalf of Buyer directly or indirectly enters into an agreement to purchase, option, and/or exchange any property of the type described above regardless of the manner in which Buyer was introduced to the property; or

Page 1 of 5

Individual agent initials _____   Buyer initials _____ _____

STANDARD FORM 201
Revised 11/2010
© 1/2011

Source: This form is the property of the North Carolina Association of REALTORS® (NCAR) and is reproduced with the permission of NCAR.

[handwritten left margin: Extender Clause]

    (ii) If, within _____ days after expiration of this Agreement, Buyer enters into a contract to acquire property introduced to Buyer during the term of this Agreement by Firm or any third party, unless Buyer has entered into a valid buyer agency agreement with another real estate firm; or

    (iii) If, having entered into an enforceable contract to acquire property during the term of this Agreement, Buyer defaults under the terms of that contract.

(d) The compensation will be due and payable at closing or upon Buyer's default of any purchase agreement. If Buyer defaults, the total compensation that would have been due the Firm will be due and payable immediately in cash from the Buyer. No assignment of rights in real property obtained for Buyer or any assignee of Buyer or any person/legal entity acting on behalf of Buyer pursuant to this Agreement shall operate to defeat any of Firm rights under this Agreement.

NOTE: Buyer understands and acknowledges that there is the potential for a conflict of interest generated by a percentage of price based fee for representing Buyer. The amount, format or rate of real estate commission is not fixed by law, but is set by each broker individually, and may be negotiable between Buyer and Firm.

5. **OTHER POTENTIAL BUYERS.** Buyer understands that other prospective purchasers represented by Firm may seek property, submit offers, and contract to purchase property through Firm, including the same or similar property as Buyer seeks to purchase. Buyer acknowledges, understands and consents to such representation of other prospective purchasers by Firm through its agents.

6. **FIRM'S DUTIES.** During the term of this Agreement, Firm shall promote the interests of Buyer by: (a) performing the terms of this Agreement; (b) seeking property at a price and terms acceptable to Buyer; (c) presenting in a timely manner all written offers or counteroffers to and from Buyer; (d) disclosing to Buyer all material facts related to the property or concerning the transaction of which Firm has actual knowledge; and (e) accounting for in a timely manner all money and property received in which Buyer has or may have an interest. Unless otherwise provided by law or Buyer consents in writing to the release of the information, Firm shall maintain the confidentiality of all personal and financial information and other matters identified as confidential by Buyer, if that information is received from Buyer during the brokerage relationship. In satisfying these duties, Firm shall exercise ordinary care, comply with all applicable laws and regulations, and treat all prospective sellers honestly and not knowingly give them false information. In addition, Firm may show the same property to other buyers, represent other buyers, represent sellers relative to other properties, or provide assistance to a seller or prospective seller by performing ministerial acts that are not inconsistent with Firm's duties under this Agreement.

Upon closing of any sale of property not entered in a listing service of which Firm is a member, Buyer authorizes Firm to submit pertinent information concerning the property, including sales price, to such listing service.

7. **DISCLOSURE OF BUYER'S NAME/MAILING ADDRESS.**
(a) Unless otherwise stated in Paragraph 13 below, Firm has Buyer's permission to disclose Buyer's name.
(b) In accordance with NC General Statutes Section 93A-12, if a dispute regarding the return or forfeiture of any earnest money deposit arises between Buyer and the seller of any real property Buyer may agree to purchase, the escrow agent holding the deposit may deposit the disputed monies with the appropriate Clerk of Court following written notice to the parties. In the event of any such dispute, Buyer directs Firm to disclose Buyer's last known mailing address to the escrow agent upon request to enable the escrow agent to comply with the notice requirement of such law.

[handwritten left margin: Fair Housing Clause]

8. **NON-DISCRIMINATION. THE AGENT (FIRM) SHALL CONDUCT ALL BROKERAGE ACTIVITIES IN REGARD TO THIS AGREEMENT WITHOUT RESPECT TO THE RACE, COLOR, RELIGION, SEX, NATIONAL ORIGIN, HANDICAP OR FAMILIAL STATUS OF ANY PARTY OR PROSPECTIVE PARTY TO THE AGREEMENT.**

9. **BUYER'S DUTIES.** Buyer shall: (a) work exclusively with Firm during the term of this Agreement; (b) pay Firm, directly or indirectly, the compensation set forth above; (c) comply with the reasonable requests of Firm to supply any pertinent financial or personal data needed to fulfill the terms of this Agreement; (d) be available for reasonable periods of time to examine properties; and (e) pay for all products and/or services required in the examination and evaluation of properties (examples: surveys, water/soil tests, title reports, property inspections, etc.).

10. **OTHER PROFESSIONAL ADVICE.** In addition to the services rendered to Buyer by the Firm under the terms of this Agreement, Buyer is advised to seek other professional advice in matters of law, taxation, financing, insurance, surveying, wood-destroying insect infestation, structural soundness, engineering, and other matters pertaining to any proposed transaction. Although Firm may provide Buyer the names of providers who claim to perform such services, Buyer understands that Firm cannot guarantee the quality of service or level of expertise of any such provider. Buyer agrees to pay the full amount due for all services directly to the service provider whether or not the transaction closes. Buyer also agrees to indemnify and hold Firm harmless from and against any and all liability, claim, loss, damage, suit, or expense that Firm may incur either as a result of Buyer's selection and use of any such provider or Buyer's election not to have one or more of such services performed.

Individual agent initials _____ Buyer initials _____ _____

STANDARD FORM 201
Revised 11/2010
© 1/2011

- ❏ Buyer acknowledges receipt of a sample copy of an Offer to Purchase And Contract for review purposes.
- ❏ Buyer acknowledges receipt of a copy of the brochure *Questions and Answers on: Home Inspections*.
- ❏ Buyer acknowledges receipt of a sample copy of a Professional Services Disclosure and Election form (form #760) for review purposes.

11. HOME WARRANTY. The seller of any property Buyer may be interested in buying may or may not provide a home warranty as a part of any sale. If the seller does not provide a home warranty, Buyer may elect to purchase one. Buyer understands that although Firm will assist Buyer in identifying available home warranty products, Buyer must refer specific questions regarding coverage afforded by any such product to the provider thereof. If Firm assists Buyer in obtaining a home warranty, a fee of _____ will be offered to Firm by the person or entity through or from which any home warranty is obtained as compensation to Firm for its assistance in obtaining the home warranty, and Buyer hereby consents to Firm's receipt of such fee.

12. CONFIDENTIALITY OF OFFERS. Real estate brokers are prohibited by N.C. Real Estate Commission rule from disclosing the price or other material terms contained in a party's offer to purchase, sell, lease, rent or option real property to a competing party without the express authority of the party making the offer. However, sellers may elect not to treat the existence, terms, or conditions of any offers Buyer may make as confidential. Additionally, sellers may elect not to disclose or authorize seller's agent to disclose the existence of any other offer(s).

13. ADDITIONAL PROVISIONS. _____
_____
_____.

14. DUAL AGENCY. Buyer understands that the potential for dual agency will arise if Buyer becomes interested in viewing property listed with Firm. Firm may represent more than one party in the same transaction only with the knowledge and informed consent of all parties for whom Firm acts.

    (a) **Disclosure of Information**. In the event Firm serves as a dual agent, Buyer agrees that without permission from the party about whom the information pertains, Firm shall not disclose to the other party the following information:
      (1) that a party may agree to a price, terms, or any conditions of sale other than those offered;
      (2) the motivation of a party for engaging in the transaction, unless disclosure is otherwise required by statute or rule; and
      (3) any information about a party which that party has identified as confidential unless disclosure is otherwise required by statute or rule.

    (b) **Firm's Role as Dual Agent**. If Firm serves as agent for both Buyer and a seller in a transaction, Firm shall make every reasonable effort to represent Buyer and seller in a balanced and fair manner. Firm shall also make every reasonable effort to encourage and effect communication and negotiation between Buyer and seller. Buyer understands and acknowledges that:
      (1) Prior to the time dual agency occurs, Firm will act as Buyer's exclusive agent;
      (2) In its separate representation of Buyer and seller, Firm may obtain information which, if disclosed, could harm the bargaining position of the party providing such information to Firm;
      (3) Firm is required by law to disclose to Buyer and seller any known or reasonably ascertainable material facts.

Buyer agrees Firm shall not be liable to Buyer for (i) disclosing material facts required by law to be disclosed, and (ii) refusing or failing to disclose other information the law does not require to be disclosed which could harm or compromise one party's bargaining position but could benefit the other party.

    (c) **Buyer's Role**. Should Firm become a dual agent, Buyer understands and acknowledges that:
      (1) Buyer has the responsibility of making Buyer's own decisions as to what terms are to be included in any purchase and sale agreement with a seller client of Firm;
      (2) Buyer is fully aware of and understands the implications and consequences of Firm's dual agency role as expressed herein to provide balanced and fair representation of Buyer and seller and to encourage and effect communication between them rather than as an advocate or exclusive agent or representative;
      (3) Buyer has determined that the benefits of dual agency outweigh any disadvantages or adverse consequences;
      (4) Buyer may seek independent legal counsel to assist Buyer with the negotiation and preparation of a purchase and sale agreement or with any matter relating to the transaction which is the subject matter of a purchase and sale agreement.

Should Firm become a dual agent, Buyer waives all claims, damages, losses, expenses or liabilities, other than for violations of the North Carolina Real Estate License Law and intentional wrongful acts, arising from Firm's role as a dual agent. Buyer shall have a duty to protect Buyer's own interests and should read any purchase and sale agreement carefully to ensure that it accurately sets forth the terms which Buyer wants included in said agreement.

(d) **Authorization** (*initial only ONE*).

_____ _____ Buyer authorizes the Firm to act as a dual agent, representing both the Buyer and the seller, subject to the terms and conditions set forth in this Paragraph 14.

_____ _____ Buyer desires exclusive representation at all times during this agreement and does NOT authorize Firm to act in the capacity of dual agent. *If Buyer does not authorize Firm to act as a dual agent, the remainder of this paragraph shall not apply.*

(e) **Designated Agent Option** (*Initial only if applicable*).

_____ _____ Buyer hereby authorizes the Firm to designate an individual agent(s) to represent the Buyer, to the exclusion of any other individual agents associated with the Firm. The individual designated agent(s) shall represent only the interests of the Buyer to the extent permitted by law.

NOTE: When dual agency arises, an individual agent shall not practice designated agency and shall remain a dual agent if the individual agent has actually received confidential information concerning a seller client of the Firm in connection with the transaction or if designated agency is otherwise prohibited by law.

(f) Dual Agency Compensation. If the Firm acts as a dual agent (including designated agency), the total fee the Firm expects to receive for its services in representing Buyer and the seller shall be _____.
(*Insert dollar amount, percentage of purchase price, or other method of determining Firm's compensation for each type of property such as resale, new construction and/or land/lot the Buyer may purchase.*). THIS WILL IN NO WAY AFFECT OR MODIFY THE AMOUNT OF THE FEE SET FORTH IN PARAGRAPH 4 ABOVE THAT FIRM EXPECTS TO RECEIVE FOR ITS SERVICES IN REPRESENTING BUYER UNDER THIS AGREEMENT. In the event Buyer is interested in purchasing a property where the Firm's total fee is different from that described in this subparagraph (f), the Firm shall timely disclose the fee to Buyer and confirm it in writing before Buyer makes or accepts an offer to buy or sell any such property.

15. **MEDIATION.** If a dispute arises out of or related to this Agreement or the breach thereof, and if the dispute cannot be settled through negotiation, the parties agree first to try in good faith to settle the dispute by mediation before resorting to arbitration, litigation, or some other dispute resolution procedure. If the need for mediation arises, the parties will choose a mutually acceptable mediator and will share the cost of mediation equally.

16. **ENTIRE AGREEMENT/CHANGES/TERMINATION.** This Agreement constitutes the entire agreement between Buyer and Firm relating to the subject thereof, and any prior agreements pertaining thereto, whether oral or written, have been merged and integrated into this Agreement. This Agreement may be signed in multiple originals or counterparts, all of which together constitute one and the same instrument. No modification of any of the terms of this Agreement shall be valid, binding upon the parties, or entitled to enforcement unless such modification has first been reduced to writing and signed by both Buyer and Firm. Buyer acknowledges and understands that this Agreement constitutes a binding contract between Buyer and Firm. Although Buyer may at any time withdraw from the fiduciary relationship existing between Buyer and Firm, the contract created by this Agreement may not be terminated by Buyer or Firm prior to its Expiration Date without legally sufficient cause. Any such termination shall be by mutually-acceptable written agreement signed by both Buyer and Firm.

NOTE: Buyer should consult with Firm before visiting any resale or new homes or contacting any other real estate firm representing sellers, to avoid the possibility of confusion over the brokerage relationship and misunderstandings about liability for compensation.

Page 4 of 5

Individual agent initials _____   Buyer initials _____ _____

STANDARD FORM 201
Revised 11/2010
© 1/2011

Appendix D **653**

Buyer and Firm each hereby acknowledge receipt of a signed copy of this Agreement.

THE NORTH CAROLINA ASSOCIATION OF REALTORS®, INC. MAKES NO REPRESENTATION AS TO THE LEGAL VALIDITY OR ADEQUACY OF ANY PROVISION OF THIS FORM IN ANY SPECIFIC TRANSACTION.

Buyer: _____   _____
              Print Name   Signature

Contact Information: _____ _____ _____ _____
                                         Home   Work   Cell   Email

Mailing Address: _____

Buyer: _____   _____
              Print Name   Signature

Contact Information: _____ _____ _____ _____
                                         Home   Work   Cell   Email

Mailing Address: _____

Firm: _____   Phone: _____
             Print Real Estate Firm Name

By: _____   _____
             Individual Agent Signature   Individual Agent License Number

Office Address: _____

Office Phone: _____ Fax: _____ E-mail: _____

Page 5 of 5

STANDARD FORM 201
Revised 11/2010
© 1/2011

NON-EXCLUSIVE BUYER AGENCY AGREEMENT

This NON-EXCLUSIVE BUYER AGENCY AGREEMENT ("Agreement") is entered into (Date) _____, between_____ as Buyer(s) ("Buyer"), and_____ ("Firm"). The individual agent who signs this Agreement shall, on behalf of the Firm, be primarily responsible for ensuring that the Firm's duties hereunder are fulfilled; however, it is understood and agreed that other agents of the Firm may be assigned to fulfill such duties if deemed appropriate by the Firm. For purposes of this Agreement, the term "Firm," as the context may require, shall be deemed to include the individual agent who signs this Agreement and any other agents of the Firm.

> The purpose of this form is to properly establish a written buyer agency relationship. The various forms of agency relationships are discussed in the "Working with Real Estate Agents" brochure, a copy of which Buyer has received and reviewed with the agent. Buyer's execution of this form confirms that Buyer has read and understands the contents of that brochure, and is making a decision to request buyer agency for the period of time set forth below. Buyer represents that, as of the commencement date of this Agreement, Buyer is not a party to an exclusive buyer representation agreement with any other real estate firm.

1. **PROPERTY.** Firm agrees to act as a non-exclusive buyer's agent representing Buyer in the acquisition of real property by **[Check all that apply]**: ❏ locating suitable real estate ❏ showing the following specific property_____
_____

2. **DURATION OF AGENCY.** Firm's authority as Buyer's non-exclusive agent shall begin _____, and shall expire at midnight, _____.

3. **COMPENSATION OF FIRM.**
   (a) **Fee.** This agreement does not obligate Buyer to pay a brokerage fee or assure the payment of a brokerage fee to Firm. Buyer acknowledges and understands that Firm expects to receive and will seek a fee for Firm's services under an offer of compensation from a cooperating seller/listing firm in the amount of _____
_____ ("Fee")
(Insert dollar amount, percentage of purchase price, or other method of determining Firm's compensation for each type of property the Buyer may purchase, *such as resale, new construction, land/lot and/or unrepresented seller*. Do not insert N/A or a zero ($0)).
   (b) **Modification of Fee.** Provided, however, Firm may inform Buyer that the compensation offered is less than expected and, if Buyer is so informed prior to making an offer to purchase, Firm may seek a reasonable modification of the compensation terms herein and, if unable to reach such a modification, Firm may unilaterally terminate this Agreement.
   (c) **Additional Compensation.** If additional compensation, incentive, bonus, rebate and/or other valuable consideration ("Additional Compensation") is offered through the MLS or otherwise, Buyer will permit the Firm to receive it in addition to the Fee. Firm shall timely disclose the promise or expectation of receiving any such Additional Compensation and confirm the disclosure in writing before Buyer makes or accepts an offer to buy. (Note: NCAR Form #770 may be used to confirm the disclosure of any such Additional Compensation)
   (d) **When Compensation Earned.** The compensation shall be deemed earned if, during the term of this Agreement, Buyer, any assignee of Buyer or any person/legal entity acting on behalf of Buyer directly or indirectly enters into an agreement to purchase, option, and/or exchange property introduced to Buyer by Firm.

NOTE. Buyer understands and acknowledges that there is the potential for a conflict of interest generated by a percentage of price based fee for representing Buyer. The amount, format or rate of real estate commission is not fixed by law, but is set by each broker individually, and may be negotiable between Buyer and Firm.

4. **ACKNOWLEDGMENTS OF RECEIPT.**
   ❏ Buyer acknowledges receipt of a sample copy of an Offer to Purchase And Contract for review purposes.
   ❏ Buyer acknowledges receipt of a copy of the brochure *Questions and Answers on: Home Inspections*.
   ❏ Buyer acknowledges receipt of a sample copy of a Professional Services Disclosure and Election form (form #760) for review purposes.

Page 1 of 3

North Carolina Association of REALTORS®, Inc.

Individual agent initials _____   Buyer initials _____ _____

STANDARD FORM 203
Revised 7/2011
© 7/2011

Source: This form is the property of the North Carolina Association of REALTORS® (NCAR) and is reproduced with the permission of NCAR.

5. **CONFIDENTIALITY OF OFFERS.** Real estate brokers are prohibited by N.C. Real Estate Commission rule from disclosing the price or other material terms contained in a party's offer to purchase, sell, lease, rent or option real property to a competing party without the express authority of the party making the offer. However, sellers may elect not to treat the existence, terms, or conditions of any offers Buyer may make as confidential. Additionally, sellers may elect not to disclose or authorize seller's agent to disclose the existence of any other offer(s).

6. **DISCLOSURE OF BUYER'S NAME/MAILING ADDRESS.**
   (a) **Name.** Unless otherwise stated herein, Firm has Buyer's permission to disclose Buyer's name.
   (b) **Mailing Address.** In accordance with NC General Statutes Section 93A-12, if a dispute regarding the return or forfeiture of any earnest money deposit arises between Buyer and the seller of any real property Buyer may agree to purchase, the escrow agent holding the deposit may deposit the disputed monies with the appropriate Clerk of Court following written notice to the parties. In the event of any such dispute, Buyer directs Firm to disclose Buyer's last known mailing address to the escrow agent upon request to enable the escrow agent to comply with the notice requirement of such law.

7. **DUAL AGENCY.** Buyer understands that the potential for dual agency will arise if Buyer becomes interested in viewing property listed with Firm. Firm may represent more than one party in the same transaction only with the knowledge and informed consent of all parties for whom Firm acts.
   (a) **Disclosure of Information.** In the event Firm serves as a dual agent, Buyer agrees that without permission from the party about whom the information pertains, Firm shall not disclose to the other party the following information:
      (1) that a party may agree to a price, terms, or any conditions of sale other than those offered;
      (2) the motivation of a party for engaging in the transaction, unless disclosure is otherwise required by statute or rule; and
      (3) any information about a party which that party has identified as confidential unless disclosure is otherwise required by statute or rule.
   (b) **Firm's Role as Dual Agent.** If Firm serves as agent for both Buyer and a seller in a transaction, Firm shall make every reasonable effort to represent Buyer and seller in a balanced and fair manner. Firm shall also make every reasonable effort to encourage and effect communication and negotiation between Buyer and seller. Buyer understands and acknowledges that:
      (1) Prior to the time dual agency occurs, Firm will act as Buyer's exclusive agent;
      (2) In its separate representation of Buyer and seller, Firm may obtain information which, if disclosed, could harm the bargaining position of the party providing such information to Firm;
      (3) Firm is required by law to disclose to Buyer and seller any known or reasonably ascertainable material facts.

Buyer agrees Firm shall not be liable to Buyer for (i) disclosing material facts required by law to be disclosed, and (ii) refusing or failing to disclose other information the law does not require to be disclosed which could harm or compromise one party's bargaining position but could benefit the other party.

   (c) **Buyer's Role.** Should Firm become a dual agent, Buyer understands and acknowledges that:
      (1) Buyer has the responsibility of making Buyer's own decisions as to what terms are to be included in any purchase and sale agreement with a seller client of Firm;
      (2) Buyer is fully aware of and understands the implications and consequences of Firm's dual agency role as expressed herein to provide balanced and fair representation of Buyer and seller and to encourage and effect communication between them rather than as an advocate or exclusive agent or representative;
      (3) Buyer has determined that the benefits of dual agency outweigh any disadvantages or adverse consequences;
      (4) Buyer may seek independent legal counsel to assist Buyer with the negotiation and preparation of a purchase and sale agreement or with any matter relating to the transaction which is the subject matter of a purchase and sale agreement.

Should Firm become a dual agent, Buyer waives all claims, damages, losses, expenses or liabilities, other than for violations of the North Carolina Real Estate License Law and intentional wrongful acts, arising from Firm's role as a dual agent. Buyer shall have a duty to protect Buyer's own interests and should read any purchase and sale agreement carefully to ensure that it accurately sets forth the terms which Buyer wants included in said agreement.

   (d) **Authorization** *(initial only ONE).*

   _____ _____ Buyer authorizes the Firm to act as a dual agent, representing both the Buyer and the seller, subject to the terms and conditions set forth in this paragraph.

   _____ _____ Buyer desires exclusive representation at all times during this agreement and does NOT authorize Firm to act in the capacity of dual agent. *If Buyer does not authorize Firm to act as a dual agent, the remainder of this paragraph shall not apply.*

(e) **Designated Agent Option** (*Initial only if applicable*).

_____ _____ Buyer hereby authorizes the Firm to designate an individual agent(s) to represent the Buyer, to the exclusion of any other individual agents associated with the Firm. The individual designated agent(s) shall represent only the interests of the Buyer to the extent permitted by law.

NOTE: When dual agency arises, an individual agent shall not practice designated agency and shall remain a dual agent if the individual agent has actually received confidential information concerning a buyer client of the Firm in connection with the transaction or if designated agency is otherwise prohibited by law.

(f) **Dual Agency Compensation**. If the Firm acts as a dual agent (including designated agency), the total fee the Firm expects to receive for its services in representing Buyer and the seller shall be _____

_____.
(*Insert dollar amount, percentage of purchase price, or other method of determining Firm's compensation for each type of property such as resale, new construction and/or land/lot the Buyer may purchase.*). THIS WILL IN NO WAY AFFECT OR MODIFY THE AMOUNT OF THE FEE SET FORTH IN PARAGRAPH 3 ABOVE THAT FIRM EXPECTS TO RECEIVE FOR ITS SERVICES IN REPRESENTING BUYER UNDER THIS AGREEMENT. In the event Buyer is interested in purchasing a property where the Firm's total fee is different from that described in this subparagraph (f), the Firm shall timely disclose the fee to Buyer and confirm it in writing before Buyer makes or accepts an offer to buy or sell any such property.

8. **NON-DISCRIMINATION. THE AGENT (FIRM) SHALL CONDUCT ALL BROKERAGE ACTIVITIES IN REGARD TO THIS AGREEMENT WITHOUT RESPECT TO THE RACE, COLOR, RELIGION, SEX, NATIONAL ORIGIN, HANDICAP OR FAMILIAL STATUS OF ANY PARTY OR PROSPECTIVE PARTY TO THE AGREEMENT. FURTHER, REALTORS® HAVE AN ETHICAL DUTY TO CONDUCT SUCH ACTIVITIES WITHOUT RESPECT TO THE SEXUAL ORIENTATION OF ANY PARTY OR PROSPECTIVE PARTY TO THIS AGREEMENT.**

9. **EXECUTION.** This Agreement may be signed in multiple originals or counterparts, all of which together constitute one and the same instrument.

THE NORTH CAROLINA ASSOCIATION OF REALTORS®, INC. MAKES NO REPRESENTATION AS TO THE LEGAL VALIDITY OR ADEQUACY OF ANY PROVISION OF THIS FORM IN ANY SPECIFIC TRANSACTION.

Buyer: _____   _____
                Print Name   Signature

Contact Information: _____ _____ _____ _____
                Home   Work   Cell   Email

Mailing Address: _____

Buyer: _____   _____
                Print Name   Signature

Contact Information: _____ _____ _____ _____
                Home   Work   Cell   Email

Mailing Address: _____

Buyer: _____   _____
                Print Name   Signature

Contact Information: _____ _____ _____ _____
                Home   Work   Cell   Email

Mailing Address: _____

Firm: _____   Phone: _____

By: _____   _____
      Print Real Estate Firm Name

      Individual Agent Signature   Individual Agent License Number

Office Address: _____

Office Phone: _____   Fax: _____   E-mail: _____

STANDARD FORM 203
Revised 7/2011
© 7/2011

UNREPRESENTED SELLER DISCLOSURE AND FEE AGREEMENT
(Selling Agent Represents the Buyer)

This Agreement is entered into on (Date) _____, by and between _____ as "Owner(s)",

and _____ ("Firm")

RECITALS:

A. Owner is the owner of property commonly known as _____ (the "Property").

B. Owner is endeavoring to sell the Property without the assistance of a licensed real estate agent; however, Firm has a client, _____ ("Client") who would like to see the Property.

C. If Owner sells the Property to Firm's Client, Owner agrees to pay Firm a fee of _____ ("Fee").

D. **THE AGENT (FIRM) SHALL CONDUCT ALL BROKERAGE ACTIVITIES IN REGARD TO THIS AGREEMENT WITHOUT RESPECT TO THE RACE, COLOR, RELIGION, SEX, NATIONAL ORIGIN, HANDICAP OR FAMILIAL STATUS OF ANY PARTY OR PROSPECTIVE PARTY TO THE AGREEMENT.**

Accordingly, the parties agree as follows:

1. **FEE.** The Fee will be deemed earned if Owner enters into a contract to sell the Property to Firm's Client at any time within _____ days from the date Owner signs this Agreement. Once earned, the Fee will be due and payable at the earlier of closing or Seller's failure to sell the Property as a result of Seller's default on the contract. HOWEVER, if, prior to the expiration of this Agreement and the execution of a contract to sell the Property, Owner enters into a valid listing agreement with another real estate firm, Owner shall NOT be obligated to pay the Fee if the listing firm offers compensation to Firm through a multiple listing service or otherwise.

2. **BUYER AGENCY.** Owner acknowledges that Firm is the agent representing Client with respect to the Property. As the agent of Client, the Firm has the duty to act on behalf of the Client, and will not be acting on behalf of Owner. This duty requires that all information regarding this transaction given to the Firm by Owner be disclosed to Client. For example, if Owner discloses to Firm that Owner is compelled by outside circumstances to sell by a certain date, or that Owner is prepared to lower the price, the Firm would be required to disclose this information to Client. Owner is advised to keep this in mind when communicating with Firm. By signing this Agreement, Owner acknowledges that this Client agency relationship has been previously orally disclosed to Owner when Firm first discussed an appointment to show Property to Client.

DO NOT SIGN THIS FORM UNTIL YOU HAVE RECEIVED AND READ THE "WORKING WITH REAL ESTATE AGENTS" BROCHURE

Owner and Firm each acknowledge receipt of a signed copy of this document.

THE NORTH CAROLINA ASSOCIATION OF REALTORS®, INC. MAKES NO REPRESENTATION AS TO THE LEGAL VALIDITY OR ADEQUACY OF ANY PROVISION OF THIS FORM IN ANY SPECIFIC TRANSACTION.

OWNER(S): _____

_____

Date: _____

FIRM: _____

By: _____

Date: _____

North Carolina Association of REALTORS®, Inc.

STANDARD FORM 150
Revised 1/2011
© 1/2011

Source: This form is the property of the North Carolina Association of REALTORS® (NCAR) and is reproduced with the permission of NCAR.

CONFIRMATION OF COMPENSATION
See Guidelines (Standard Form 770G) on proper use of this form.

Property Address: _____ ("Property")

Buyer or Seller: _____ ("Client")

Real Estate Firm: _____ ("Firm")

1. **Disclosure.** A real estate firm is required by law to timely disclose to their client the receipt of (or promise or expectation of receiving) any compensation, incentive, bonus, rebate and/or other valuable consideration of more than nominal value ("Compensation") from any other party or person in a real estate sales transaction and confirm such disclosure in writing before making or accepting any offer.

2. **Confirmation.** Firm hereby confirms that in connection with the sale or purchase of the Property, Firm expects to receive the following Compensation **(check all applicable boxes)**:

❏ Monetary: $ _____ or _____ percent of sales price of Property received/to be received from _____
_____

❏ Non-monetary: (describe) _____ received/to be
received from _____ estimated value: $ _____

❏ Other: _____
_____
_____

THE NORTH CAROLINA ASSOCIATION OF REALTORS, INC. MAKES NO REPRESENTATION AS TO THE LEGAL VALIDITY OR ADEQUACY OF ANY PROVISION OF THIS FORM IN ANY SPECIFIC TRANSACTION.

Firm _____
    Real Estate Firm Name

By: _____   Date: _____
    Individual agent signature

ACKNOWLEDGEMENT BY CLIENT

Client hereby acknowledges receipt of a completed copy of this form.

Client: _____   Date: _____

Client: _____   Date: _____

Page 1 of 1

North Carolina Association of REALTORS®, Inc.

STANDARD FORM 770
Revised 1/2011
© 1/2011

Source: This form is the property of the North Carolina Association of REALTORS® (NCAR) and is reproduced with the permission of NCAR.

OFFER TO PURCHASE AND CONTRACT

[Consult "Guidelines" (Standard Form 2G) for guidance in completing this form]

For valuable consideration, the receipt and legal sufficiency of which are hereby acknowledged, Buyer offers to purchase and Seller upon acceptance agrees to sell and convey the Property on the terms and conditions of this Offer To Purchase and Contract and any addendum or modification made in accordance with its terms (together the "Contract").

1. **TERMS AND DEFINITIONS**: The terms listed below shall have the respective meaning given them as set forth adjacent to each term.

    (a) "**Seller**": _____

    (b) "**Buyer**": _____

    (c) "**Property**": The Property shall include all that real estate described below together with all appurtenances thereto including the improvements located thereon and the fixtures and personal property listed in Paragraphs 2 and 3 below. **NOTE**: If the Property will include a manufactured (mobile) home(s), Buyer and Seller should consider including the Manufactured (Mobile) Home provision in the Additional Provisions Addendum (Standard Form 2A11-T) with this offer.
Street Address: _____
City: _____ Zip: _____
County: _____, North Carolina
NOTE: Governmental authority over taxes, zoning, school districts, utilities and mail delivery may differ from address shown.

Legal Description: (Complete *ALL* applicable)
Plat Reference: Lot/Unit_____, Block/Section_____, Subdivision/Condominium _____
_____, as shown on Plat Book/Slide _____ at Page(s) _____
The PIN/PID or other identification number of the Property is: _____
Other description: _____
Some or all of the Property may be described in Deed Book _____ at Page _____

    (d) "**Purchase Price**":

$ _____	paid in U.S. Dollars upon the following terms:
$ _____	BY DUE DILIGENCE FEE made payable to Seller by the Effective Date
$ _____	BY INITIAL EARNEST MONEY DEPOSIT made payable to Escrow Agent named in Paragraph 1(f) ☐ with this offer OR ☐ delivered within five (5) days of the Effective Date of this Contract by ☐ cash ☐ personal check ☐ official bank check ☐ wire transfer
$ _____	BY (ADDITIONAL) EARNEST MONEY DEPOSIT made payable to Escrow Agent named in Paragraph 1(f) by cash or immediately available funds such as official bank check or wire transfer to be delivered to Escrow Agent no later than _____, *TIME BEING OF THE ESSENCE* with regard to said date.
$ _____	BY ASSUMPTION of the unpaid principal balance and all obligations of Seller on the existing loan(s) secured by a deed of trust on the Property in accordance with the attached Loan Assumption Addendum (Standard Form 2A6-T).
$ _____	BY SELLER FINANCING in accordance with the attached Seller Financing Addendum (Standard Form 2A5-T).
$ _____	BY BUILDING DEPOSIT in accordance with the attached New Construction Addendum (Standard Form 2A3-T).
$ _____	BALANCE of the Purchase Price in cash at Settlement (some or all of which may be paid with the proceeds of a new loan)

Should Buyer fail to deliver either the Due Diligence Fee or any Initial Earnest Money Deposit by their due dates, or should any check or other funds paid by Buyer be dishonored, for any reason, by the institution upon which the payment is drawn, Buyer shall have one (1) banking day after written notice to deliver cash or immediately available funds to the payee. In the event Buyer

Page 1 of 11

This form jointly approved by:
North Carolina Bar Association
North Carolina Association of REALTORS®, Inc.

STANDARD FORM 2-T
Revised 7/2013
© 7/2013

Buyer initials _____ _____ Seller initials _____ _____

Source: This form is the property of the North Carolina Association of REALTORS® and the North Carolina Bar Association (NCBA) and is reproduced with the permission of NCAR and NCBA.

does not timely deliver cash or immediately available funds, Seller shall have the right to terminate this Contract upon written notice to Buyer.

(e) **"Earnest Money Deposit"**: The Initial Earnest Money Deposit, the Additional Earnest Money Deposit and any other earnest monies paid in connection with this transaction, hereinafter collectively referred to as "Earnest Money Deposit", shall be deposited and held in escrow by Escrow Agent until Closing, at which time it will be credited to Buyer, or until this Contract is otherwise terminated. In the event: (1) this offer is not accepted; or (2) a condition of any resulting contract is not satisfied, then the Earnest Money Deposit shall be refunded to Buyer. In the event of breach of this Contract by Seller, the Earnest Money Deposit shall be refunded to Buyer upon Buyer's request, but such return shall not affect any other remedies available to Buyer for such breach. In the event of breach of this Contract by Buyer, the Earnest Money Deposit shall be paid to Seller upon Seller's request as liquidated damages and as Seller's sole and exclusive remedy for such breach, but without limiting Seller's rights under Paragraphs 4(d) and 4(e) for damage to the Property or Seller's right to retain the Due Diligence Fee. It is acknowledged by the parties that payment of the Earnest Money Deposit to Seller in the event of a breach of this Contract by Buyer is compensatory and not punitive, such amount being a reasonable estimation of the actual loss that Seller would incur as a result of such breach. The payment of the Earnest Money Deposit to Seller shall not constitute a penalty or forfeiture but actual compensation for Seller's anticipated loss, both parties acknowledging the difficulty determining Seller's actual damages for such breach. If legal proceedings are brought by Buyer or Seller against the other to recover the Earnest Money Deposit, the prevailing party in the proceeding shall be entitled to recover from the non-prevailing party reasonable attorney fees and court costs incurred in connection with the proceeding.

(f) **"Escrow Agent"** (insert name): _____
NOTE: In the event of a dispute between Seller and Buyer over the disposition of the Earnest Money Deposit held in escrow, a licensed real estate broker ("Broker") is required by state law (and Escrow Agent, if not a Broker, hereby agrees) to retain the Earnest Money Deposit in the Escrow Agent's trust or escrow account until Escrow Agent has obtained a written release from the parties consenting to its disposition or until disbursement is ordered by a court of competent jurisdiction. Alternatively, if a Broker or an attorney licensed to practice law in North Carolina ("Attorney") is holding the Earnest Money Deposit, the Broker or Attorney may deposit the disputed monies with the appropriate clerk of court in accordance with the provisions of N.C.G.S. §93A-12.

THE PARTIES AGREE THAT A REAL ESTATE BROKERAGE FIRM ACTING AS ESCROW AGENT MAY PLACE THE EARNEST MONEY DEPOSIT IN AN INTEREST BEARING TRUST ACCOUNT AND THAT ANY INTEREST EARNED THEREON SHALL BE DISBURSED TO THE ESCROW AGENT MONTHLY IN CONSIDERATION OF THE EXPENSES INCURRED BY MAINTAINING SUCH ACCOUNT AND RECORDS ASSOCIATED THEREWITH.

(g) **"Effective Date"**: The date that: (1) the last one of Buyer and Seller has signed or initialed this offer or the final counteroffer, if any, and (2) such signing or initialing is communicated to the party making the offer or counteroffer, as the case may be.

(h) **"Due Diligence"**: Buyer's opportunity during the Due Diligence Period to investigate the Property and the transaction contemplated by this Contract, including but not necessarily limited to the matters described in Paragraph 4 below, to decide whether Buyer, in Buyer's sole discretion, will proceed with or terminate the transaction.

(i) **"Due Diligence Fee"**: A negotiated amount, if any, paid by Buyer to Seller with this Contract for Buyer's right to conduct Due Diligence during the Due Diligence Period. It shall be the property of Seller upon the Effective Date and shall be a credit to Buyer at Closing. The Due Diligence Fee shall be non-refundable except in the event of a material breach of this Contract by Seller, or if this Contract is terminated under Paragraph 8(l) or Paragraph 12, or as otherwise provided in any addendum hereto. Buyer and Seller each expressly waive any right that they may have to deny the right to conduct Due Diligence or to assert any defense as to the enforceability of this Contract based on the absence or alleged insufficiency of any Due Diligence Fee, it being the intent of the parties to create a legally binding contract for the purchase and sale of the Property without regard to the existence or amount of any Due Diligence Fee.

(j) **"Due Diligence Period"**: The period beginning on the Effective Date and extending through 5:00 p.m. on _____
_____ **TIME BEING OF THE ESSENCE** with regard to said date.

(k) **"Settlement"**: The proper execution and delivery to the closing attorney of all documents necessary to complete the transaction contemplated by this Contract, including the deed, settlement statement, deed of trust and other loan or conveyance documents, and the closing attorney's receipt of all funds necessary to complete such transaction.

(l) **"Settlement Date"**: The parties agree that Settlement will take place on _____
_____(the "Settlement Date"), unless otherwise agreed in writing, at a time and place designated by Buyer.

Page 2 of 11

STANDARD FORM 2-T
Revised 7/2013
© 7/2013

Buyer initials _____ _____ Seller initials _____ _____

(m) **"Closing"**: The completion of the legal process which results in the transfer of title to the Property from Seller to Buyer, which includes the following steps: (1) the Settlement (defined above); (2) the completion of a satisfactory title update to the Property following the Settlement; (3) the closing attorney's receipt of authorization to disburse all necessary funds; and (4) recordation in the appropriate county registry of the deed(s) and deed(s) of trust, if any, which shall take place as soon as reasonably possible for the closing attorney after Settlement. Upon Closing, the proceeds of sale shall be disbursed by the closing attorney in accordance with the settlement statement and the provisions of Chapter 45A of the North Carolina General Statutes. If the title update should reveal unexpected liens, encumbrances or other title defects, or if the closing attorney is not authorized to disburse all necessary funds, then the Closing shall be suspended and the Settlement deemed delayed under Paragraph 13 (Delay in Settlement/Closing).

WARNING: The North Carolina State Bar has determined that the performance of most acts and services required for a closing constitutes the practice of law and must be performed only by an attorney licensed to practice law in North Carolina. State law prohibits unlicensed individuals or firms from rendering legal services or advice. Although non-attorney settlement agents may perform limited services in connection with a closing, they may not perform all the acts and services required to complete a closing. A closing involves significant legal issues that should be handled by an attorney. Accordingly it is the position of the North Carolina Bar Association and the North Carolina Association of REALTORS® that all buyers should hire an attorney licensed in North Carolina to perform a closing.

(n) **"Special Assessments"**: A charge against the Property by a governmental authority in addition to ad valorem taxes and recurring governmental service fees levied with such taxes, or by an owners' association in addition to any regular assessment (dues), either of which may be a lien against the Property. A Special Assessment may be either proposed or confirmed.

"Proposed Special Assessment": A Special Assessment that is under formal consideration but which has not been approved prior to Settlement.

"Confirmed Special Assessment": A Special Assessment that has been approved prior to Settlement whether or not it is fully payable at time of Settlement.

2. **FIXTURES**: The following items, if any, are deemed fixtures and are included in the Purchase Price free of liens: range/stove/oven, any built-in appliances, light fixtures, ceiling fans, attached floor coverings, blinds, shades, drapery rods and curtain rods, brackets and all related hardware, window and door screens, storm windows, combination doors, awnings, antennas, satellite dishes and receivers, burglar/fire/smoke/carbon monoxide/alarms, pool and spa equipment, solar energy systems, attached fireplace screens, gas logs, fireplace inserts, electric garage door openers with controls, outdoor plants and trees (other than in movable containers), basketball goals, storage sheds, mailboxes, attached wall and/or door mirrors, fuel tank(s) whether attached or buried and including contents, if any, as of Settlement, landscape and/or foundation lighting, invisible fencing including all related equipment, lawn irrigation systems and all related equipment, water softener/conditioner and filter equipment and any other items attached or affixed to the Property, EXCEPT the following items which are leased or not owned by Seller or which Seller does not intend to convey: _____

Seller shall repair any damage caused by removal of any items excepted above.

(**NOTE**: Seller and Buyer should confirm whether fuel tanks, antennas, satellite dishes and receivers, alarm systems, and other items listed above are leased or not owned by Seller and should be entered in the blank above. FUEL TANKS AND ANY FUEL IN THEM WHICH ARE NOT TO CONVEY SHOULD BE NOTED IN THE BLANK ABOVE.)

3. **PERSONAL PROPERTY**: The following personal property shall be transferred to Buyer at no value at Closing:_____
_____.

(**NOTE**: Buyer is advised to consult with Buyer's lender to assure that the Personal Property items listed above can be included in this Contract.)

4. **BUYER'S DUE DILIGENCE PROCESS**:
(a) **Loan**: During the Due Diligence Period, Buyer, at Buyer's expense, shall be entitled to pursue qualification for and approval of the Loan if any.

NOTE: Buyer is advised to consult with Buyer's lender prior to signing this offer to assure that the Due Diligence Period allows sufficient time for the appraisal to be completed and for Buyer's lender to provide Buyer sufficient information to decide whether to proceed with or terminate the transaction since the Loan is not a condition of the Contract.

(b) **Property Investigation**: During the Due Diligence Period, Buyer or Buyer's agents or representatives, at Buyer's expense, shall be entitled to conduct all desired tests, surveys, appraisals, investigations, examinations and inspections of the Property as Buyer deems appropriate, including but NOT limited to the following:

(i) **Inspections**: Inspections to determine the condition of any improvements on the Property, the presence of unusual drainage conditions or evidence of excessive moisture adversely affecting any improvements on the Property, the presence of asbestos or existing environmental contamination, evidence of wood-destroying insects or damage therefrom, and the presence and level of radon gas on the Property.

(ii) **Review of Documents**: Review of the Declaration of Restrictive Covenants, Bylaws, Articles of Incorporation, Rules and Regulations, and other governing documents of any applicable owners' association and/or subdivision. If the Property is subject to regulation by an owners' association, it is recommended that Buyer review the completed Residential Property and Owners' Association Disclosure Statement provided by Seller prior to signing this offer.

(iii) **Insurance**: Investigation of the availability and cost of insurance for the Property.

(iv) **Appraisals**: An appraisal of the Property.

(v) **Survey**: A survey to determine whether the property is suitable for Buyer's intended use and the location of easements, setbacks, property boundaries and other issues which may or may not constitute title defects.

(vi) **Zoning and Governmental Regulation**: Investigation of current or proposed zoning or other governmental regulation that may affect Buyer's intended use of the Property, adjacent land uses, planned or proposed road construction, and school attendance zones.

(vii) **Flood Hazard**: Investigation of potential flood hazards on the Property, and/or any requirement to purchase flood insurance in order to obtain the Loan.

(viii) **Utilities and Access**: Availability, quality, and obligations for maintenance of roads and utilities including water, sewer, electric, gas, communication services, stormwater management, and means of access to the Property and amenities.

(ix) **Fuel Tank**: Inspections to determine the existence, type and ownership of any fuel tank located on the Property.

(**NOTE**: Buyer is advised to consult with the owner of any leased fuel tank regarding the terms under which Buyer may lease the tank and obtain fuel.)

(c) **Repair/Improvement Negotiations/Agreement**: Buyer acknowledges and understands that unless the parties agree otherwise, THE PROPERTY IS BEING SOLD IN ITS CURRENT CONDITION. Buyer and Seller acknowledge and understand that they may, but are not required to, engage in negotiations for repairs/improvements to the Property. Buyer is advised to make any repair/improvement requests in sufficient time to allow repair/improvement negotiations to be concluded prior to the expiration of the Due Diligence Period. Any agreement that the parties may reach with respect to repairs/improvements shall be considered an obligation of the parties and is an addition to this Contract and as such, must be in writing and signed by the parties in accordance with Paragraph 20.

(**NOTE**: See Paragraph 8(b) Access to Property/Walk-Through Inspection and Paragraph 8(k) Negotiated Repairs/Improvements.)

(d) **Buyer's Obligation to Repair Damage**: Buyer shall, at Buyer's expense, promptly repair any damage to the Property resulting from any activities of Buyer and Buyer's agents and contractors, but Buyer shall not be responsible for any damage caused by accepted practices either approved by the N.C. Home Inspector Licensure Board or applicable to any other N.C. licensed professional performing reasonable appraisals, tests, surveys, examinations and inspections of the Property. This repair obligation shall survive any termination of this Contract.

(e) **Indemnity**: Buyer will indemnify and hold Seller harmless from all loss, damage, claims, suits or costs, which shall arise out of any contract, agreement, or injury to any person or property as a result of any activities of Buyer and Buyer's agents and contractors relating to the Property except for any loss, damage, claim, suit or cost arising out of pre-existing conditions of the Property and/or out of Seller's negligence or willful acts or omissions. This indemnity shall survive this Contract and any termination hereof.

(f) **Buyer's Right to Terminate**: Buyer shall have the right to terminate this Contract for any reason or no reason, by delivering to Seller written notice of termination (the "Termination Notice") during the Due Diligence Period (or any agreed-upon written extension of the Due Diligence Period), *TIME BEING OF THE ESSENCE*. If Buyer timely delivers the Termination Notice, this Contract shall be terminated and the Earnest Money Deposit shall be refunded to Buyer.

WARNING: If Buyer is not satisfied with the results or progress of Buyer's Due Diligence, Buyer should terminate this Contract, *prior to the expiration of the Due Diligence Period*, unless Buyer can obtain a written extension from Seller. SELLER IS NOT OBLIGATED TO GRANT AN EXTENSION. Although Buyer may continue to investigate the Property following the expiration

Buyer initials _____ _____   Seller initials _____ _____

STANDARD FORM 2-T
Revised 7/2013
© 7/2013

of the Due Diligence Period, Buyer's failure to deliver a Termination Notice to Seller prior to the expiration of the Due Diligence Period shall constitute a waiver by Buyer of any right to terminate this Contract based on any matter relating to Buyer's Due Diligence. Provided however, following the Due Diligence Period, Buyer may still exercise a right to terminate if Seller fails to materially comply with any of Seller's obligations under Paragraph 8 of this Contract or for any other reason permitted under the terms of this Contract or North Carolina law.

(g) **CLOSING SHALL CONSTITUTE ACCEPTANCE OF THE PROPERTY IN ITS THEN EXISTING CONDITION UNLESS PROVISION IS OTHERWISE MADE IN WRITING.**

5. **BUYER REPRESENTATIONS:**

(a) **Loan**: Buyer ❑ does ❑ does not have to obtain a new loan in order to purchase the Property. If Buyer is obtaining a new loan, Buyer intends to obtain a loan as follows: ❑ FHA ❑ VA (attach FHA/VA Financing Addendum) ❑ Conventional ❑ Other: _____ loan at a ❑ Fixed Rate ❑ Adjustable Rate in the principal amount of _____ plus any financed VA Funding Fee or FHA MIP for a term of _____ year(s), at an initial interest rate not to exceed _____ % per annum (the "Loan").

NOTE: Buyer's obligations under this Contract are not conditioned upon obtaining or closing any loan. If Buyer represents that Buyer does not have to obtain a new loan in order to purchase the Property, Seller is advised, prior to signing this offer, to obtain documentation from Buyer which demonstrates that Buyer will be able to close on the Property without the necessity of obtaining a new loan.

(b) **Other Property**: Buyer ❑ does ❑ does not have to sell or lease other real property in order to qualify for a new loan or to complete purchase.

(**NOTE**: This Contract is not conditioned upon the sale of Buyer's property unless a contingent sale addendum such as Standard Form 2A2-T is made a part of this Contract.)

(c) **Performance of Buyer's Financial Obligations**: To the best of Buyer's knowledge, there are no other circumstances or conditions existing as of the date of this offer that would prohibit Buyer from performing Buyer's financial obligations in accordance with this Contract, except as may be specifically set forth herein.

(d) **Property Disclosure** (*check only one*):
❑ Buyer has received a signed copy of the N.C. Residential Property and Owners' Association Disclosure Statement prior to the signing of this offer.
❑ Buyer has NOT received a signed copy of the N.C. Residential Property and Owners' Association Disclosure Statement prior to the signing of this offer and shall have the right to terminate or withdraw this Contract without penalty (including a refund of any Due Diligence Fee) prior to WHICHEVER OF THE FOLLOWING EVENTS OCCURS FIRST: (1) the end of the third calendar day following receipt of the Disclosure Statement; (2) the end of the third calendar day following the date the Contract was made; or (3) Settlement or occupancy by Buyer in the case of a sale or exchange.
❑ Exempt from N.C. Residential Property and Owners' Association Disclosure Statement because (SEE GUIDELINES):_____
_____.

[Handwritten note: Give at or before the time they make an offer]

6. **BUYER OBLIGATIONS:**

(a) **Owners' Association Fees/Charges**: Buyer shall pay any fees required for confirming account payment information on owners' association dues or assessments for payment or proration and any charge made by the owners' association in connection with the disposition of the Property to Buyer, including any transfer and/or document fee imposed by the owners' association. Buyer shall not be responsible for fees incurred by Seller in completing the Residential Property and Owners' Association Disclosure Statement.

(b) **Responsibility for Proposed Special Assessments**: Buyer shall take title subject to all Proposed Special Assessments.

(c) **Responsibility for Certain Costs**: Buyer shall be responsible for all costs with respect to any loan obtained by Buyer, appraisal, title search, title insurance, recording the deed and for preparation and recording of all instruments required to secure the balance of the Purchase Price unpaid at Settlement.

Buyer initials _____ _____ Seller initials _____ _____

7. **SELLER REPRESENTATIONS**:
   (a) **Ownership**: Seller represents that Seller:
   ❏ has owned the Property for at least one year.
   ❏ has owned the Property for less than one year.
   ❏ does not yet own the Property.

   (b) **Primary Residence**: Seller represents that the Property ❏ is or ❏ is not Seller's primary residence.
   (c) **Lead-Based Paint** (*check if applicable*):
   ❏ The Property is residential and was built prior to 1978 (Attach Lead-Based Paint or Lead-Based Paint Hazards Disclosure Addendum {Standard Form 2A9-T}).

   (d) **Assessments**: To the best of Seller's knowledge there are no Proposed Special Assessments except as follows (Insert "None" or the identification of such assessments, if any):_____.

   Seller warrants that there are no Confirmed Special Assessments except as follows (Insert "None" or the identification of such assessments, if any):_____.

   (e) **Owners' Association(s) and Dues**: Seller authorizes and directs any owners' association, any management company of the owners' association, any insurance company and any attorney who has previously represented the Seller to release to Buyer, Buyer's agents, representative, or lender true and accurate copies of the following items affecting the Property, including any amendments:

   - master insurance policy showing the coverage provided and the deductible amount
   - Declaration and Restrictive Covenants
   - Rules and Regulations
   - Articles of Incorporation
   - Bylaws of the owners' association
   - current financial statement and budget of the owners' association
   - parking restrictions and information
   - architectural guidelines

   The name, address and telephone number of the president of the owners' association or the association manager is:_____
   Owners' association website address, if any: _____

   The name, address and telephone number of the president of the owners' association or the association manager is:_____
   Owners' association website address, if any: _____

   (f) **OIL AND GAS RIGHTS DISCLOSURE:**
   Oil and gas rights can be severed from the title to real property by conveyance (deed) of the oil and gas rights from the owner or by reservation of the oil and gas rights by the owner. If oil and gas rights are or will be severed from the property, the owner of those rights may have the perpetual right to drill, mine, explore, and remove any of the subsurface oil or gas resources on or from the property either directly from the surface of the property or from a nearby location. With regard to the severance of oil and gas rights, Seller makes the following disclosures:

		Yes	No	No Representation
____ ____ **Buyer Initials**	1. Oil and gas rights were severed from the property by a previous owner.	❏	❏	❏
____ ____ **Buyer Initials**	2. Seller has severed the oil and gas rights from the property.	❏	❏	
____ ____ **Buyer Initials**	3. Seller intends to sever the oil and gas rights from the property prior to transfer of title to Buyer.	❏	❏	

STANDARD FORM 2-T
Revised 7/2013
© 7/2013

Buyer initials _____ _____   Seller initials _____ _____

This disclosure does not modify or limit the obligations of Seller under Paragraph 8(f) of this Contract and shall not constitute the assumption or approval by Buyer of any severance of oil and gas rights, except as may be assumed or specifically approved by Buyer in writing.

(**NOTE**: The parties are advised to consult with a NC attorney prior to signing this Contract if severance of oil and gas rights has occurred or is intended.)

8. SELLER OBLIGATIONS:

(a) **Evidence of Title:** Seller agrees to use best efforts to deliver to Buyer as soon as reasonably possible after the Effective Date, copies of all title information in possession of or available to Seller, including but not limited to: title insurance policies, attorney's opinions on title, surveys, covenants, deeds, notes and deeds of trust, leases, and easements relating to the Property. Seller authorizes: (1) any attorney presently or previously representing Seller to release and disclose any title insurance policy in such attorney's file to Buyer and both Buyer's and Seller's agents and attorneys; and (2) the Property's title insurer or its agent to release and disclose all materials in the Property's title insurer's (or title insurer's agent's) file to Buyer and both Buyer's and Seller's agents and attorneys.

(b) **Access to Property/Walk-Through Inspection**: Seller shall provide reasonable access to the Property (including working, existing utilities) through the earlier of Closing or possession by Buyer, including, but not limited to, allowing Buyer an opportunity to conduct a final walk-through inspection of the Property.

(c) **Removal of Seller's Property**: Seller shall remove, by the date possession is made available to Buyer, all personal property which is not a part of the purchase and all garbage and debris from the Property.

(d) **Affidavit and Indemnification Agreement**: Seller shall furnish at Settlement an affidavit(s) and indemnification agreement(s) in form satisfactory to Buyer and Buyer's title insurer, if any, executed by Seller and any person or entity who has performed or furnished labor, services, materials or rental equipment to the Property within 120 days prior to the date of Settlement and who may be entitled to claim a lien against the Property as described in N.C.G.S. §44A-8 verifying that each such person or entity has been paid in full and agreeing to indemnify Buyer, Buyer's lender(s) and Buyer's title insurer against all loss from any cause or claim arising therefrom.

(e) **Designation of Lien Agent, Payment and Satisfaction of Liens**: If required by N.C.G.S. §44A-11.1, Seller shall have designated a Lien Agent, and Seller shall deliver to Buyer as soon as reasonably possible a copy of the appointment of Lien Agent. All deeds of trust, deferred ad valorem taxes, liens and other charges against the Property, not assumed by Buyer, must be paid and satisfied by Seller prior to or at Settlement such that cancellation may be promptly obtained following Closing. Seller shall remain obligated to obtain any such cancellations following Closing.

(f) **Good Title, Legal Access**: Seller shall execute and deliver a **GENERAL WARRANTY DEED** for the Property in recordable form no later than Settlement, which shall convey fee simple marketable and insurable title, without exception for mechanics' liens, and free of any other liens, encumbrances or defects, including those which would be revealed by a current and accurate survey of the Property, except: ad valorem taxes for the current year (prorated through the date of Settlement); utility easements and unviolated covenants, conditions or restrictions that do not materially affect the value of the Property; and such other liens, encumbrances or defects as may be assumed or specifically approved by Buyer in writing. The Property must have legal access to a public right of way.

(**NOTE**: Buyer's failure to terminate this Contract prior to the expiration of the Due Diligence Period as a result of any encumbrance or defect that is or would have been revealed by a title examination of the Property or a current and accurate survey shall not relieve Seller of any obligation under this subparagraph.)

(**NOTE**: If any sale of the Property may be a "short sale," consideration should be given to attaching a Short Sale Addendum (Standard Form 2A14-T) as an addendum to this Contract.)

(g) **Deed, Excise Taxes**: Seller shall pay for preparation of a deed and all other documents necessary to perform Seller's obligations under this Contract, and for state and county excise taxes required by law. The deed is to be made to:_____
_____.

(h) **Agreement to Pay Buyer Expenses**: Seller shall pay at Settlement $_____ toward any of Buyer's expenses associated with the purchase of the Property, including any FHA/VA lender and inspection costs that Buyer is not permitted to pay, less any portion disapproved by Buyer's lender.

NOTE: Examples of Buyer's expenses associated with the purchase of the Property include, but are not limited to, discount points, loan origination fees, appraisal fees, attorney's fees, inspection fees, and "pre-paids" (taxes, insurance, owners' association dues, etc.).

(i) **Payment of Confirmed Special Assessments**: Seller shall pay all Confirmed Special Assessments, if any, provided that the amount thereof can be reasonably determined or estimated.

(j) **Late Listing Penalties**: All property tax late listing penalties, if any, shall be paid by Seller.

(k) **Negotiated Repairs/Improvements**: Negotiated repairs/improvements shall be made in a good and workmanlike manner and Buyer shall have the right to verify same prior to Settlement.

(l) **Seller's Failure to Comply or Breach**: If Seller fails to materially comply with any of Seller's obligations under this Paragraph 8 or Seller materially breaches this Contract, and Buyer elects to terminate this Contract as a result of such failure or breach, then the Earnest Money Deposit and the Due Diligence Fee shall be refunded to Buyer and Seller shall reimburse to Buyer the reasonable costs actually incurred by Buyer in connection with Buyer's Due Diligence without affecting any other remedies. If legal proceedings are brought by Buyer against Seller to recover the Earnest Money Deposit, the Due Diligence Fee and/or the reasonable costs actually incurred by Buyer in connection with Buyer's Due Diligence, the prevailing party in the proceeding shall be entitled to recover from the non-prevailing party reasonable attorney fees and court costs incurred in connection with the proceeding.

9. **PRORATIONS AND ADJUSTMENTS**: Unless otherwise provided, the following items shall be prorated through the date of Settlement and either adjusted between the parties or paid at Settlement:
   (a) **Taxes on Real Property**: Ad valorem taxes and recurring governmental service fees levied with such taxes on real property shall be prorated on a calendar year basis;
   (b) **Taxes on Personal Property**: Ad valorem taxes on personal property for the entire year shall be paid by Seller unless the personal property is conveyed to Buyer, in which case, the personal property taxes shall be prorated on a calendar year basis;
   (c) **Rents**: Rents, if any, for the Property;
   (d) **Dues**: Owners' association regular assessments (dues) and other like charges.

10. **HOME WARRANTY**: Select one of the following:
    ❑ No home warranty is to be provided by Seller.
    ❑ Buyer may obtain a one-year home warranty at a cost not to exceed $_____ and Seller agrees to pay for it at Settlement.
    ❑ Seller has obtained and will provide a one-year home warranty from _____
    at a cost of $ _____ and will pay for it at Settlement.

(**NOTE**: Home warranties typically have limitations on and conditions to coverage. Refer specific questions to the home warranty company.)

11. **CONDITION OF PROPERTY AT CLOSING**: Buyer's obligation to complete the transaction contemplated by this Contract shall be contingent upon the Property being in substantially the same or better condition at Closing as on the date of this offer, reasonable wear and tear excepted.

12. **RISK OF LOSS**: The risk of loss or damage by fire or other casualty prior to Closing shall be upon Seller. If the improvements on the Property are destroyed or materially damaged prior to Closing, Buyer may terminate this Contract by written notice delivered to Seller or Seller's agent and the Earnest Money Deposit and any Due Diligence Fee shall be refunded to Buyer. In the event Buyer does NOT elect to terminate this Contract, Buyer shall be entitled to receive, in addition to the Property, any of Seller's insurance proceeds payable on account of the damage or destruction applicable to the Property being purchased. Seller is advised not to cancel existing insurance on the Property until after confirming recordation of the deed.

13. **DELAY IN SETTLEMENT/CLOSING**: Absent agreement to the contrary in this Contract or any subsequent modification thereto, if a party is unable to complete Settlement by the Settlement Date but intends to complete the transaction and is acting in good faith and with reasonable diligence to proceed to Settlement ("Delaying Party"), and if the other party is ready, willing and able to

complete Settlement on the Settlement Date ("Non-Delaying Party") then the Delaying Party shall give as much notice as possible to the Non-Delaying Party and closing attorney and shall be entitled to a delay in Settlement. If the parties fail to complete Settlement and Closing within fourteen (14) days of the Settlement Date (including any amended Settlement Date agreed to in writing by the parties) or to otherwise extend the Settlement Date by written agreement, then the Delaying Party shall be in breach and the Non-Delaying Party may terminate this Contract and shall be entitled to enforce any remedies available to such party under this Contract for the breach.

14. **POSSESSION**: Possession, including all means of access to the Property (keys, codes, garage door openers, etc.), shall be delivered upon Closing as defined in Paragraph 1(m) unless otherwise provided below:
   - ❑ A Buyer Possession Before Closing Agreement is attached (Standard Form 2A7-T)
   - ❑ A Seller Possession After Closing Agreement is attached (Standard Form 2A8-T)
   - ❑ Possession is subject to rights of tenant(s) (**NOTE**: Consider attaching Additional Provisions Addendum (Form 2A-11-T) or Vacation Rental Addendum (Form 2A13-T))

15. **OTHER PROVISIONS AND CONDITIONS**: CHECK ALL STANDARD ADDENDA THAT MAY BE A PART OF THIS CONTRACT, IF ANY, AND ATTACH HERETO. ITEMIZE ALL OTHER ADDENDA TO THIS CONTRACT, IF ANY, AND ATTACH HERETO. **NOTE**: UNDER NORTH CAROLINA LAW, REAL ESTATE BROKERS ARE NOT PERMITTED TO DRAFT CONDITIONS OR CONTINGENCIES TO THIS CONTRACT.

   - ❑ Additional Provisions Addendum (Form 2A11-T)
   - ❑ Back-Up Contract Addendum (Form 2A1-T)
   - ❑ Contingent Sale Addendum (Form 2A2-T)
   - ❑ FHA/VA Financing Addendum (Form 2A4-T)
   - ❑ Lead-Based Paint Or Lead-Based Paint Hazard Addendum (Form 2A9-T)
   - ❑ Loan Assumption Addendum (Form 2A6-T)
   - ❑ New Construction Addendum (Form 2A3-T)
   - ❑ Seller Financing Addendum (Form 2A5-T)
   - ❑ Short Sale Addendum (Form 2A14-T)
   - ❑ Vacation Rental Addendum (Form 2A13-T)
   - ❑ OTHER: _____

16. **ASSIGNMENTS**: This Contract may not be assigned without the written consent of all parties except in connection with a tax-deferred exchange, but if assigned by agreement, then this Contract shall be binding on the assignee and assignee's heirs and successors.

17. **TAX-DEFERRED EXCHANGE**: In the event Buyer or Seller desires to effect a tax-deferred exchange in connection with the conveyance of the Property, Buyer and Seller agree to cooperate in effecting such exchange; provided, however, that the exchanging party shall be responsible for all additional costs associated with such exchange, and provided further, that a non-exchanging party shall not assume any additional liability with respect to such tax-deferred exchange. Buyer and Seller shall execute such additional documents, including assignment of this Contract in connection therewith, at no cost to the non-exchanging party, as shall be required to give effect to this provision.

18. **PARTIES**: This Contract shall be binding upon and shall inure to the benefit of Buyer and Seller and their respective heirs, successors and assigns. As used herein, words in the singular include the plural and the masculine includes the feminine and neuter genders, as appropriate.

19. **SURVIVAL**: If any provision herein contained which by its nature and effect is required to be observed, kept or performed after the Closing, it shall survive the Closing and remain binding upon and for the benefit of the parties hereto until fully observed, kept or performed.

20. **ENTIRE AGREEMENT**: This Contract contains the entire agreement of the parties and there are no representations, inducements or other provisions other than those expressed herein. All changes, additions or deletions hereto must be in writing and signed by all parties. Nothing contained herein shall alter any agreement between a REALTOR® or broker and Seller or Buyer as contained in any listing agreement, buyer agency agreement, or any other agency agreement between them.

21. **NOTICE**: Any notice or communication to be given to a party herein may be given to the party or to such party's agent. Any written notice or communication in connection with the transaction contemplated by this Contract may be given to a party or a party's agent by sending or transmitting it to any mailing address, e-mail address or fax number set forth in the "Notice Information" section below. Seller and Buyer agree that the "Notice Information" and "Escrow Acknowledgment" sections below shall not constitute

STANDARD FORM 2-T
Revised 7/2013
© 7/2013

Buyer initials _____ _____   Seller initials _____ _____

a material part of this Contract, and that the addition or modification of any information therein shall not constitute a rejection of an offer or the creation of a counteroffer.

22. **EXECUTION**: This Contract may be signed in multiple originals or counterparts, all of which together constitute one and the same instrument, and the parties adopt as their seals the word "SEAL" beside their signatures below.

23. **COMPUTATION OF DAYS**: Unless otherwise provided, for purposes of this Contract, the term "days" shall mean consecutive calendar days, including Saturdays, Sundays, and holidays, whether federal, state, local or religious. For the purposes of calculating days, the count of "days" shall begin on the day following the day upon which any act or notice as provided in this Contract was required to be performed or made.

THE NORTH CAROLINA ASSOCIATION OF REALTORS®, INC. AND THE NORTH CAROLINA BAR ASSOCIATION MAKE NO REPRESENTATION AS TO THE LEGAL VALIDITY OR ADEQUACY OF ANY PROVISION OF THIS FORM IN ANY SPECIFIC TRANSACTION. IF YOU DO NOT UNDERSTAND THIS FORM OR FEEL THAT IT DOES NOT PROVIDE FOR YOUR LEGAL NEEDS, YOU SHOULD CONSULT A NORTH CAROLINA REAL ESTATE ATTORNEY BEFORE YOU SIGN IT.

This offer shall become a binding contract on the Effective Date.

Date: _____ Date: _____

Buyer _____ (SEAL) Seller _____ (SEAL)

Date: _____ Date: _____

Buyer _____ (SEAL) Seller _____ (SEAL)

Date: _____ Date: _____

Buyer _____ (SEAL) Seller _____ (SEAL)

STANDARD FORM 2-T
Revised 7/2013
© 7/2013

NOTICE INFORMATION

NOTE: INSERT THE ADDRESS AND/OR ELECTRONIC DELIVERY ADDRESS EACH PARTY AND AGENT APPROVES FOR THE RECEIPT OF ANY NOTICE CONTEMPLATED BY THIS CONTRACT. INSERT "N/A" FOR ANY WHICH ARE NOT APPROVED.

BUYER NOTICE ADDRESS:

Mailing Address: _____
_____
Buyer Fax#: _____
Buyer E-mail: _____

SELLER NOTICE ADDRESS:

Mailing Address: _____
_____
Seller Fax#: _____
Seller E-mail: _____

SELLING AGENT NOTICE ADDRESS:

Firm Name: _____
Acting as ❑ Buyer's Agent ❑ Seller's (sub)Agent ❑ Dual Agent
Mailing Address: _____
_____
Individual Selling Agent: _____
❑ Acting as a Designated Dual Agent (check only if applicable)
License #: _____
Selling Agent Phone#: _____
Selling Agent Fax#: _____
Selling Agent E-mail: _____

LISTING AGENT NOTICE ADDRESS:

Firm Name: _____
Acting as ❑ Seller's Agent ❑ Dual Agent
Mailing Address: _____
_____
Individual Listing Agent: _____
❑ Acting as a Designated Dual Agent (check only if applicable)
License #: _____
Listing Agent Phone#: _____
Listing Agent Fax#: _____
Listing Agent E-mail: _____

ESCROW ACKNOWLEDGMENT OF INITIAL EARNEST MONEY DEPOSIT

Property: _____

Seller: _____

Buyer: _____

Escrow Agent acknowledges receipt of the Initial Earnest Money Deposit and agrees to hold and disburse the same in accordance with the terms hereof.

Date _____   Firm: _____

By: _____
(Signature)

_____
(Print name)

STANDARD FORM 2-T
Revised 7/2013
© 7/2013

OFFER TO PURCHASE AND CONTRACT - VACANT LOT/LAND
[Consult "Guidelines" (form 12G) for guidance in completing this form]

NOTE: This contract is intended for unimproved real property that Buyer will purchase only for personal use and does not have immediate plans to subdivide. It should not be used to sell property that is being subdivided unless the property has been platted, properly approved and recorded with the register of deeds as of the date of the contract. If Seller is Buyer's builder and the sale involves the construction of a new single family dwelling prior to closing, use the standard Offer to Purchase and Contract—New Construction (Form 800-T) or, if the construction is completed, use the Offer to Purchase and Contract (Form 2-T) with the New Construction Addendum (Form 2A3-T).

For valuable consideration, the receipt and legal sufficiency of which are hereby acknowledged, Buyer offers to purchase and Seller upon acceptance agrees to sell and convey the Property on the terms and conditions of this Offer To Purchase and Contract and any addendum or modification made in accordance with its terms (together the "Contract").

1. **TERMS AND DEFINITIONS**: The terms listed below shall have the respective meaning given them as set forth adjacent to each term.

   (a) "**Seller**": _____

   (b) "**Buyer**": _____

   (c) "**Property**": The Property shall include all that real estate described below together with all appurtenances thereto including the improvements located thereon. **NOTE**: If the Property will include a manufactured (mobile) home(s), Buyer and Seller should consider including the Manufactured (Mobile) Home provision in the Additional Provisions Addendum (Standard Form 2A11-T) with this offer.
   Street Address: _____
   City: _____ Zip: _____
   County: _____, North Carolina
   (**NOTE**: Governmental authority over taxes, zoning, school districts, utilities and mail delivery may differ from address shown.)

   Legal Description: (Complete *ALL* applicable)
   Plat Reference: Lot/Unit_____, Block/Section _____, Subdivision/Condominium _____
   _____, as shown on Plat Book/Slide _____ at Page(s) _____
   The PIN/PID or other identification number of the Property is: _____
   Other description: _____
   Some or all of the Property may be described in Deed Book _____ at Page _____

   (d) "**Purchase Price**":
   $ _____ paid in U.S. Dollars upon the following terms:
   $ _____ BY DUE DILIGENCE FEE made payable to Seller by the Effective Date
   $ _____ BY INITIAL EARNEST MONEY DEPOSIT made payable to Escrow Agent named in Paragraph 1(f) ❑ with this offer OR ❑ delivered within five (5) days of the Effective Date of this Contract by ❑ cash ❑ personal check ❑ official bank check ❑ wire transfer
   $ _____ BY (ADDITIONAL) EARNEST MONEY DEPOSIT made payable to Escrow Agent named in Paragraph 1(f) by cash or immediately available funds such as official bank check or wire transfer to be delivered to Escrow Agent no later than _____, *TIME BEING OF THE ESSENCE* with regard to said date.
   $ _____ BY ASSUMPTION of the unpaid principal balance and all obligations of Seller on the existing loan(s) secured by a deed of trust on the Property in accordance with the attached Loan Assumption Addendum (Standard Form 2A6-T).
   $ _____ BY SELLER FINANCING in accordance with the attached Seller Financing Addendum (Standard Form 2A5-T).
   $ _____ BALANCE of the Purchase Price in cash at Settlement (some or all of which may be paid with the proceeds of a new loan)

   Should Buyer fail to deliver either the Due Diligence Fee or any Initial Earnest Money Deposit by their due dates, or should any check or other funds paid by Buyer be dishonored, for any reason, by the institution upon which the payment is drawn, Buyer shall

Page 1 of 9

This form jointly approved by:
North Carolina Bar Association
North Carolina Association of REALTORS®, Inc.

STANDARD FORM 12-T
Revised 7/2013
© 7/2013

Buyer initials _____ _____ Seller initials _____ _____

have one (1) banking day after written notice to deliver cash or immediately available funds to the payee. In the event Buyer does not timely deliver cash or immediately available funds, Seller shall have the right to terminate this Contract upon written notice to Buyer.

(e) "**Earnest Money Deposit**": The Initial Earnest Money Deposit, the Additional Earnest Money Deposit and any other earnest monies paid in connection with this transaction, hereinafter collectively referred to as "Earnest Money Deposit", shall be deposited and held in escrow by Escrow Agent until Closing, at which time it will be credited to Buyer, or until this Contract is otherwise terminated. In the event: (1) this offer is not accepted; or (2) a condition of any resulting contract is not satisfied, then the Earnest Money Deposit shall be refunded to Buyer. In the event of breach of this Contract by Seller, the Earnest Money Deposit shall be refunded to Buyer upon Buyer's request, but such return shall not affect any other remedies available to Buyer for such breach. In the event of breach of this Contract by Buyer, the Earnest Money Deposit shall be paid to Seller upon Seller's request as liquidated damages and as Seller's sole and exclusive remedy for such breach, but without limiting Seller's rights under Paragraphs 2(c) and 2(d) for damage to the Property or Seller's right to retain the Due Diligence Fee. It is acknowledged by the parties that payment of the Earnest Money Deposit to Seller in the event of a breach of this Contract by Buyer is compensatory and not punitive, such amount being a reasonable estimation of the actual loss that Seller would incur as a result of such breach. The payment of the Earnest Money Deposit to Seller shall not constitute a penalty or forfeiture but actual compensation for Seller's anticipated loss, both parties acknowledging the difficulty determining Seller's actual damages for such breach. If legal proceedings are brought by Buyer or Seller against the other to recover the Earnest Money Deposit, the prevailing party in the proceeding shall be entitled to recover from the non-prevailing party reasonable attorney fees and court costs incurred in connection with the proceeding.

(f) "**Escrow Agent**" (insert name): _____

NOTE: In the event of a dispute between Seller and Buyer over the disposition of the Earnest Money Deposit held in escrow, a licensed real estate broker ("Broker") is required by state law (and Escrow Agent, if not a Broker, hereby agrees) to retain the Earnest Money Deposit in the Escrow Agent's trust or escrow account until Escrow Agent has obtained a written release from the parties consenting to its disposition or until disbursement is ordered by a court of competent jurisdiction. Alternatively, if a Broker or an attorney licensed to practice law in North Carolina ("Attorney") is holding the Earnest Money Deposit, the Broker or Attorney may deposit the disputed monies with the appropriate clerk of court in accordance with the provisions of N.C.G.S. §93A-12.

THE PARTIES AGREE THAT A REAL ESTATE BROKERAGE FIRM ACTING AS ESCROW AGENT MAY PLACE THE EARNEST MONEY DEPOSIT IN AN INTEREST BEARING TRUST ACCOUNT AND THAT ANY INTEREST EARNED THEREON SHALL BE DISBURSED TO THE ESCROW AGENT MONTHLY IN CONSIDERATION OF THE EXPENSES INCURRED BY MAINTAINING SUCH ACCOUNT AND RECORDS ASSOCIATED THEREWITH.

(g) "**Effective Date**": The date that: (1) the last one of Buyer and Seller has signed or initialed this offer or the final counteroffer, if any, and (2) such signing or initialing is communicated to the party making the offer or counteroffer, as the case may be.

(h) "**Due Diligence**": Buyer's opportunity during the Due Diligence Period to investigate the Property and the transaction contemplated by this Contract, including but not necessarily limited to the matters described in Paragraph 2 below, to decide whether Buyer, in Buyer's sole discretion, will proceed with or terminate the transaction.

(i) "**Due Diligence Fee**": A negotiated amount, if any, paid by Buyer to Seller with this Contract for Buyer's right to conduct Due Diligence during the Due Diligence Period. It shall be the property of Seller upon the Effective Date and shall be a credit to Buyer at Closing. The Due Diligence Fee shall be non-refundable except in the event of a material breach of this Contract by Seller, or if this Contract is terminated under Paragraph 6(l) or Paragraph 9, or as otherwise provided in any addendum hereto. Buyer and Seller each expressly waive any right that they may have to deny the right to conduct Due Diligence or to assert any defense as to the enforceability of this Contract based on the absence or alleged insufficiency of any Due Diligence Fee, it being the intent of the parties to create a legally binding contract for the purchase and sale of the Property without regard to the existence or amount of any Due Diligence Fee.

(j) "**Due Diligence Period**": The period beginning on the Effective Date and extending through 5:00 p.m. on _____
_____ ***TIME BEING OF THE ESSENCE*** with regard to said date.

(k) "**Settlement**": The proper execution and delivery to the closing attorney of all documents necessary to complete the transaction contemplated by this Contract, including the deed, settlement statement, deed of trust and other loan or conveyance documents, and the closing attorney's receipt of all funds necessary to complete such transaction.

(l) **"Settlement Date"**: The parties agree that Settlement will take place on _____
_____(the "Settlement Date"), unless otherwise agreed in writing, at a time and place designated by Buyer.

(m) **"Closing"**: The completion of the legal process which results in the transfer of title to the Property from Seller to Buyer, which includes the following steps: (1) the Settlement (defined above); (2) the completion of a satisfactory title update to the Property following the Settlement; (3) the closing attorney's receipt of authorization to disburse all necessary funds; and (4) recordation in the appropriate county registry of the deed(s) and deed(s) of trust, if any, which shall take place as soon as reasonably possible for the closing attorney after Settlement. Upon Closing, the proceeds of sale shall be disbursed by the closing attorney in accordance with the settlement statement and the provisions of Chapter 45A of the North Carolina General Statutes. If the title update should reveal unexpected liens, encumbrances or other title defects, or if the closing attorney is not authorized to disburse all necessary funds, then the Closing shall be suspended and the Settlement deemed delayed under Paragraph 13 (Delay in Settlement/Closing).

WARNING: The North Carolina State Bar has determined that the performance of most acts and services required for a closing constitutes the practice of law and must be performed only by an attorney licensed to practice law in North Carolina. State law prohibits unlicensed individuals or firms from rendering legal services or advice. Although non-attorney settlement agents may perform limited services in connection with a closing, they may not perform all the acts and services required to complete a closing. A closing involves significant legal issues that should be handled by an attorney. Accordingly it is the position of the North Carolina Bar Association and the North Carolina Association of REALTORS® that all buyers should hire an attorney licensed in North Carolina to perform a closing.

(n) **"Special Assessments"**: A charge against the Property by a governmental authority in addition to ad valorem taxes and recurring governmental service fees levied with such taxes, or by an owners' association in addition to any regular assessment (dues), either of which may be a lien against the Property. A Special Assessment may be either proposed or confirmed.

"Proposed Special Assessment": A Special Assessment that is under formal consideration but which has not been approved prior to Settlement.

"Confirmed Special Assessment": A Special Assessment that has been approved prior to Settlement whether or not it is fully payable at time of Settlement.

2. **BUYER'S DUE DILIGENCE PROCESS**:
   (a) **Loan**: During the Due Diligence Period, Buyer, at Buyer's expense, shall be entitled to pursue qualification for and approval of the Loan if any.

   (**NOTE**: Buyer is advised to consult with Buyer's lender prior to signing this offer to assure that the Due Diligence Period allows sufficient time for the appraisal to be completed and for Buyer's lender to provide Buyer sufficient information to decide whether to proceed with or terminate the transaction since the Loan is not a condition of the Contract.)

   (b) **Property Investigation**: During the Due Diligence Period, Buyer or Buyer's agents or representatives, at Buyer's expense, shall be entitled to conduct all desired tests, surveys, appraisals, investigations, examinations and inspections of the Property as Buyer deems appropriate, including but NOT limited to the following:
   - (i) **Soil And Environmental**: Reports to determine whether the soil is suitable for Buyer's intended use and whether there is any environmental contamination, law, rule or regulation that may prohibit, restrict or limit Buyer's intended use.
   - (ii) **Septic/Sewer System**: Any applicable investigation(s) to determine: (1) the condition of an existing sewage system, (2) the costs and expenses to install a sewage system approved by an existing Improvement Permit, (3) the availability and expense to connect to a public or community sewer system, and/or (4) whether an Improvement Permit or written evaluation may be obtained from the County Health Department for a suitable ground absorption sewage system.
   - (iii) **Water**: Any applicable investigation(s) to determine: (1) the condition of an existing private drinking water well, (2) the costs and expenses to install a private drinking water well approved by an existing Construction Permit, (3) the availability, costs and expenses to connect to a public or community water system, or a shared private well, and/or (4) whether a Construction Permit may be obtained from the County Health Department for a private drinking water well.
   - (iv) **Review of Documents**: **Review of Documents**: Review of the Declaration of Restrictive Covenants, Bylaws, Articles of Incorporation, Rules and Regulations, and other governing documents of any applicable owners' association and/or subdivision. If the Property is subject to regulation by an owners' association, it is recommended that Buyer review the completed Owners' Association And Addendum (Standard Form 2A12-T) provided by Seller prior to signing this offer.
   - (v) **Appraisals**: An appraisal of the Property.
   - (vi) **Survey**: A survey to determine whether the property is suitable for Buyer's intended use and the location of easements, setbacks, property boundaries and other issues which may or may not constitute title defects.

Buyer initials _____ _____   Seller initials _____ _____

STANDARD FORM 12-T
Revised 7/2013
© 7/2013

(vii) **Zoning and Governmental Regulation**: Investigation of current or proposed zoning or other governmental regulation that may affect Buyer's intended use of the Property, adjacent land uses, planned or proposed road construction, and school attendance zones.
(viii) **Flood Hazard**: Investigation of potential flood hazards on the Property, and/or any requirement to purchase flood insurance in order to obtain the Loan.
(ix) **Utilities and Access**: Availability, quality, and obligations for maintenance of roads and utilities including electric, gas, communication services, stormwater management, and means of access to the Property and amenities.

(c) **Buyer's Obligation to Repair Damage**: Buyer shall, at Buyer's expense, promptly repair any damage to the Property resulting from any activities of Buyer and Buyer's agents and contractors, but Buyer shall not be responsible for any damage caused by accepted practices applicable to any N.C. licensed professional performing reasonable appraisals, tests, surveys, examinations and inspections of the Property. This repair obligation shall survive any termination of this Contract.

(d) **Indemnity**: Buyer will indemnify and hold Seller harmless from all loss, damage, claims, suits or costs, which shall arise out of any contract, agreement, or injury to any person or property as a result of any activities of Buyer and Buyer's agents and contractors relating to the Property except for any loss, damage, claim, suit or cost arising out of pre-existing conditions of the Property and/or out of Seller's negligence or willful acts or omissions. This indemnity shall survive this Contract and any termination hereof.

(e) **Buyer's Right to Terminate:** Buyer shall have the right to terminate this Contract for any reason or no reason, by delivering to Seller written notice of termination (the "Termination Notice") during the Due Diligence Period (or any agreed-upon written extension of the Due Diligence Period), *TIME BEING OF THE ESSENCE*. If Buyer timely delivers the Termination Notice, this Contract shall be terminated and the Earnest Money Deposit shall be refunded to Buyer.

WARNING: If Buyer is not satisfied with the results or progress of Buyer's Due Diligence, Buyer should terminate this Contract, *prior to the expiration of the Due Diligence Period*, unless Buyer can obtain a written extension from Seller. SELLER IS NOT OBLIGATED TO GRANT AN EXTENSION. Although Buyer may continue to investigate the Property following the expiration of the Due Diligence Period, Buyer's failure to deliver a Termination Notice to Seller prior to the expiration of the Due Diligence Period shall constitute a waiver by Buyer of any right to terminate this Contract based on any matter relating to Buyer's Due Diligence. Provided however, following the Due Diligence Period, Buyer may still exercise a right to terminate if Seller fails to materially comply with any of Seller's obligations under paragraph 6 of this Contract or for any other reason permitted under the terms of this Contract or North Carolina law.

(f) **CLOSING SHALL CONSTITUTE ACCEPTANCE OF THE PROPERTY IN ITS THEN EXISTING CONDITION UNLESS PROVISION IS OTHERWISE MADE IN WRITING.**

3. **BUYER REPRESENTATIONS**:
(a) **Loan**: Buyer ❑ does ❑ does not have to obtain a new loan in order to purchase the Property. If Buyer is obtaining a new loan, Buyer intends to obtain a loan as follows: ❑ Conventional ❑ Other: _____ loan at a ❑ Fixed Rate ❑ Adjustable Rate in the principal amount of _____ for a term of _____ year(s), at an initial interest rate not to exceed _____ % per annum (the "Loan").

(**NOTE**: Buyer's obligations under this Contract are not conditioned upon obtaining or closing any loan. If Buyer represents that Buyer does not have to obtain a new loan in order to purchase the Property, Seller is advised, prior to signing this offer, to obtain documentation from Buyer which demonstrates that Buyer will be able to close on the Property without the necessity of obtaining a new loan.)

(b) **Other Property**: Buyer ❑ does ❑ does not have to sell or lease other real property in order to qualify for a new loan or to complete purchase. (**NOTE**: If Buyer does have to sell, Buyer and Seller should consider including a Contingent Sale Addendum (Standard Form 2A2-T) with this offer.)

(c) **Performance of Buyer's Financial Obligations**: To the best of Buyer's knowledge, there are no other circumstances or conditions existing as of the date of this offer that would prohibit Buyer from performing Buyer's financial obligations in accordance with this Contract, except as may be specifically set forth herein.

4. **BUYER OBLIGATIONS:**
   (a) **Owners' Association Fees/Charges**: Buyer shall pay any fees required for confirming account payment information on owners' association dues or assessments for payment or proration and any charge made by the owners' association in connection with the disposition of the Property to Buyer, including any transfer and/or document fee imposed by the owners' association. Buyer shall not be responsible for fees incurred by Seller in completing the Owners' Association Disclosure and Addendum For Properties Exempt from Residential Property Disclosure Statement (Standard Form 2A12-T).

   (b) **Responsibility for Proposed Special Assessments**: Buyer shall take title subject to all Proposed Special Assessments.

   (c) **Responsibility for Certain Costs**: Buyer shall be responsible for all costs with respect to any loan obtained by Buyer, appraisal, title search, title insurance, recording the deed and for preparation and recording of all instruments required to secure the balance of the Purchase Price unpaid at Settlement.

5. **SELLER REPRESENTATIONS:**
   (a) **Ownership**: Seller represents that Seller:
   ❑ has owned the Property for at least one year.
   ❑ has owned the Property for less than one year.
   ❑ does not yet own the Property.

   (b) **Assessments**: To the best of Seller's knowledge there are no Proposed Special Assessments except as follows (Insert "None" or the identification of such assessments, if any):_____.

   Seller warrants that there are no Confirmed Special Assessments except as follows (Insert "None" or the identification of such assessments, if any):_____.

   (c) **Owners' Association(s) and Dues**: To best of Seller's knowledge, ownership of the Property ❑ subjects ❑ does not subject Buyer to regulation by one or more owners' association(s) and governing documents, which impose various mandatory covenants, conditions and restrictions upon the Property and Buyer's enjoyment thereof, including but not limited to obligations to pay regular assessments (dues) and Special Assessments. If there is an owners' association, then an Owners' Association Disclosure and Addendum For Properties Exempt from Residential Property Disclosure Statement (Standard Form 2A12-T) shall be completed by Seller, at Seller's expense, and must be attached as an addendum to this Contract

   (d) **Sewage System Permit:** (❑ Applicable ❑ Not Applicable) Seller warrants that the sewage system described in the Improvement Permit attached hereto has been installed, which representation survives Closing, but makes no further representations as to the system.

   (e) **Private Drinking Water Well Permit**: (❑ Applicable ❑ Not Applicable) Seller warrants that a private drinking water well has been installed, which representation survives Closing, but makes no further representations as to the well. (If well installed after July 1, 2008, attach Improvement Permit hereto.

6. **SELLER OBLIGATIONS:**
   (a) **Evidence of Title:** Seller agrees to use best efforts to deliver to Buyer as soon as reasonably possible after the Effective Date, copies of all title information in possession of or available to Seller, including but not limited to: title insurance policies, attorney's opinions on title, surveys, covenants, deeds, notes and deeds of trust, leases, and easements relating to the Property. Seller authorizes: (1) any attorney presently or previously representing Seller to release and disclose any title insurance policy in such attorney's file to Buyer and both Buyer's and Seller's agents and attorneys; and (2) the Property's title insurer or its agent to release and disclose all materials in the Property's title insurer's (or title insurer's agent's) file to Buyer and both Buyer's and Seller's agents and attorneys.

   (b) **Access to Property/Walk-Through Inspection**: Seller shall provide reasonable access to the Property (including working, existing utilities) through the earlier of Closing or possession by Buyer, including, but not limited to, allowing the Buyer an opportunity to conduct a final walk-through inspection of the Property. To the extent applicable, Seller shall also be responsible for timely clearing that portion of the Property required by the County to perform tests, inspections and/or evaluations to determine the suitability of the Property for a sewage system and/or private drinking water well.

   (c) **Removal of Seller's Property**: Seller shall remove, by the date possession is made available to Buyer, all personal property which is not a part of the purchase and all garbage and debris from the Property.

(d) **Affidavit And Indemnification Agreement**: Seller shall furnish at Settlement an affidavit(s) and indemnification agreement(s) in form satisfactory to Buyer and Buyer's title insurer, if any, executed by Seller and any person or entity who has performed or furnished labor, services, materials or rental equipment to the Property within 120 days prior to the date of Settlement and who may be entitled to claim a lien against the Property as described in N.C.G.S. §44A-8 verifying that each such person or entity has been paid in full and agreeing to indemnify Buyer, Buyer's lender(s) and Buyer's title insurer against all loss from any cause or claim arising therefrom.

(e) **Designation of Lien Agent, Payment and Satisfaction of Liens**: If required by N.C.G.S. §44A-11.1, Seller shall have designated a Lien Agent, and Seller shall deliver to Buyer as soon as reasonably possible a copy of the appointment of Lien Agent. All deeds of trust, deferred ad valorem taxes, liens and other charges against the Property, not assumed by Buyer, must be paid and satisfied by Seller prior to or at Settlement such that cancellation may be promptly obtained following Closing. Seller shall remain obligated to obtain any such cancellations following Closing.

(f) **Good Title, Legal Access**: Seller shall execute and deliver a GENERAL WARRANTY DEED for the Property in recordable form no later than Settlement, which shall convey fee simple marketable and insurable title, without exception for mechanics' liens, and free of any other liens, encumbrances or defects, including those which would be revealed by a current and accurate survey of the Property, except: ad valorem taxes for the current year (prorated through the date of Settlement); utility easements and unviolated covenants, conditions or restrictions that do not materially affect the value of the Property; and such other liens, encumbrances or defects as may be assumed or specifically approved by Buyer in writing. The Property must have legal access to a public right of way.

(**NOTE**: Buyer's failure to terminate this Contract prior to the expiration of the Due Diligence Period as a result of any encumbrance or defect that is or would have been revealed by a title examination of the Property or a current and accurate survey shall not relieve Seller of any obligation under this subparagraph)

(**NOTE**: If any sale of the Property may be a "short sale," consideration should be given to attaching a Short Sale Addendum (Standard Form 2A14-T) as an addendum to this Contract.)

(g) **Deed, Excise Taxes**: Seller shall pay for preparation of a deed and all other documents necessary to perform Seller's obligations under this Contract, and for state and county excise taxes required by law. The deed is to be made to: _____
_____.

(h) **Agreement to Pay Buyer Expenses**: Seller shall pay at Settlement $_____ toward any of Buyer's expenses associated with the purchase of the Property, less any portion disapproved by Buyer's lender.

NOTE: Examples of Buyer's expenses associated with the purchase of the Property include, but are not limited to, discount points, loan origination fees, appraisal fees, attorney's fees, inspection fees, and "pre-paids" (taxes, insurance, owners' association dues, etc).

(i) **Payment of Confirmed Special Assessments**: Seller shall pay all Confirmed Special Assessments, if any, provided that the amount thereof can be reasonably determined or estimated.

(j) **Late Listing Penalties**: All property tax late listing penalties, if any, shall be paid by Seller.

(k) **Owners' Association Disclosure and Addendum For Properties Exempt from Residential Property Disclosure Statement** (Standard Form 2A12-T): If applicable, Seller shall provide the completed Owners' Association Disclosure and Addendum For Properties Exempt from Residential Property Disclosure Statement to Buyer on or before the Effective Date.

(l) **Seller's Failure to Comply or Breach**: If Seller fails to materially comply with any of Seller's obligations under this Paragraph 6 or Seller materially breaches this Contract, and Buyer elects to terminate this Contract as a result of such failure or breach, then the Earnest Money Deposit and the Due Diligence Fee shall be refunded to Buyer and Seller shall reimburse to Buyer the reasonable costs actually incurred by Buyer in connection with Buyer's Due Diligence without affecting any other remedies. If legal proceedings are brought by Buyer against the Seller to recover the Earnest Money Deposit, the Due Diligence Fee and/or the reasonable costs actually incurred by Buyer in connection with Buyer's Due Diligence, the prevailing party in the proceeding shall be entitled to recover from the non-prevailing party reasonable attorney fees and court costs incurred in connection with the proceeding.

7. **PRORATIONS AND ADJUSTMENTS**: Unless otherwise provided, the following items shall be prorated through the date of Settlement and either adjusted between the parties or paid at Settlement:
   (a) **Taxes on Real Property:** Ad valorem taxes and recurring governmental service fees levied with such taxes on real property shall be prorated on a calendar year basis;
   (b) **Rents**: Rents, if any, for the Property;
   (c) **Dues**: Owners' association regular assessments (dues) and other like charges.

8. **CONDITION OF PROPERTY AT CLOSING**: Buyer's obligation to complete the transaction contemplated by this Contract shall be contingent upon the Property being in substantially the same or better condition at Closing as on the date of this offer, reasonable wear and tear excepted.

9. **RISK OF LOSS**: The risk of loss or damage by fire or other casualty prior to Closing shall be upon Seller. If the improvements on the Property are destroyed or materially damaged prior to Closing, Buyer may terminate this Contract by written notice delivered to Seller or Seller's agent and the Earnest Money Deposit and any Due Diligence Fee shall be refunded to Buyer. In the event Buyer does NOT elect to terminate this Contract, Buyer shall be entitled to receive, in addition to the Property, any of Seller's insurance proceeds payable on account of the damage or destruction applicable to the Property being purchased. Seller is advised not to cancel existing insurance on the Property until after confirming recordation of the deed.

10. **DELAY IN SETTLEMENT/CLOSING**: Absent agreement to the contrary in this Contract or any subsequent modification thereto, if a party is unable to complete Settlement by the Settlement Date but intends to complete the transaction and is acting in good faith and with reasonable diligence to proceed to Settlement ("Delaying Party"), and if the other party is ready, willing and able to complete Settlement on the Settlement Date ("Non-Delaying Party") then the Delaying Party shall give as much notice as possible to the Non-Delaying Party and closing attorney and shall be entitled to a delay in Settlement. If the parties fail to complete Settlement and Closing within fourteen (14) days of the Settlement Date (including any amended Settlement Date agreed to in writing by the parties) or to otherwise extend the Settlement Date by written agreement, then the Delaying Party shall be in breach and the Non-Delaying Party may terminate this Contract and shall be entitled to enforce any remedies available to such party under this Contract for the breach.

11. **POSSESSION**: Unless otherwise provided herein, possession shall be delivered at Closing as defined in Paragraph 1(m). No alterations, excavations, tree or vegetation removal or other such activities may be done before possession is delivered.

12. **OTHER PROVISIONS AND CONDITIONS**: CHECK ALL STANDARD ADDENDA THAT MAY BE A PART OF THIS CONTRACT, IF ANY, AND ATTACH HERETO. ITEMIZE ALL OTHER ADDENDA TO THIS CONTRACT, IF ANY, AND ATTACH HERETO.

(**NOTE**: UNDER NORTH CAROLINA LAW, REAL ESTATE BROKERS ARE NOT PERMITTED TO DRAFT CONDITIONS OR CONTINGENCIES TO THIS CONTRACT.)

❑ Additional Provisions Addendum (Form 2A11-T)
❑ Back-Up Contract Addendum (Form 2A1-T)
❑ Contingent Sale Addendum (Form 2A2-T)

❑ Loan Assumption Addendum (Form 2A6-T)
❑ Owners' Association Disclosure And Addendum For Properties Exempt from Residential Property Disclosure Statement (Form 2A12-T)
❑ Seller Financing Addendum (Form 2A5-T)
❑ Short Sale Addendum (Form 2A14-T)

❑ OTHER: _____
_____
_____

13. **ASSIGNMENTS**: This Contract may not be assigned without the written consent of all parties except in connection with a tax-deferred exchange, but if assigned by agreement, then this Contract shall be binding on the assignee and assignee's heirs and successors.

14. **TAX-DEFERRED EXCHANGE**: In the event Buyer or Seller desires to effect a tax-deferred exchange in connection with the conveyance of the Property, Buyer and Seller agree to cooperate in effecting such exchange; provided, however, that the exchanging party shall be responsible for all additional costs associated with such exchange, and provided further, that a non-exchanging party shall not assume any additional liability with respect to such tax-deferred exchange. Buyer and Seller shall execute such additional

Buyer initials _____ _____   Seller initials _____ _____

STANDARD FORM 12-T
Revised 7/2013
© 7/2013

documents, including assignment of this Contract in connection therewith, at no cost to the non-exchanging party, as shall be required to give effect to this provision.

15. **PARTIES**: This Contract shall be binding upon and shall inure to the benefit of Buyer and Seller and their respective heirs, successors and assigns. As used herein, words in the singular include the plural and the masculine includes the feminine and neuter genders, as appropriate.

16. **SURVIVAL:** If any provision herein contained which by its nature and effect is required to be observed, kept or performed after the Closing, it shall survive the Closing and remain binding upon and for the benefit of the parties hereto until fully observed, kept or performed.

17. **ENTIRE AGREEMENT**: This Contract contains the entire agreement of the parties and there are no representations, inducements or other provisions other than those expressed herein. All changes, additions or deletions hereto must be in writing and signed by all parties. Nothing contained herein shall alter any agreement between a REALTOR® or broker and Seller or Buyer as contained in any listing agreement, buyer agency agreement, or any other agency agreement between them.

18. **NOTICE**: Any notice or communication to be given to a party herein may be given to the party or to such party's agent. Any written notice or communication in connection with the transaction contemplated by this Contract may be given to a party or a party's agent by sending or transmitting it to any mailing address, e-mail address or fax number set forth in the "Notice Information" section below. Seller and Buyer agree that the "Notice Information" and "Escrow Acknowledgment" sections below shall not constitute a material part of this Contract, and that the addition or modification of any information therein shall not constitute a rejection of an offer or the creation of a counteroffer.

19. **EXECUTION**: This Contract may be signed in multiple originals or counterparts, all of which together constitute one and the same instrument, and the parties adopt as their seals the word "SEAL" beside their signatures below.

20. **COMPUTATION OF DAYS**: Unless otherwise provided, for purposes of this Contract, the term "days" shall mean consecutive calendar days, including Saturdays, Sundays, and holidays, whether federal, state, local or religious. For the purposes of calculating days, the count of "days" shall begin on the day following the day upon which any act or notice as provided in this Contract was required to be performed or made.

THE NORTH CAROLINA ASSOCIATION OF REALTORS®, INC. AND THE NORTH CAROLINA BAR ASSOCIATION MAKE NO REPRESENTATION AS TO THE LEGAL VALIDITY OR ADEQUACY OF ANY PROVISION OF THIS FORM IN ANY SPECIFIC TRANSACTION. IF YOU DO NOT UNDERSTAND THIS FORM OR FEEL THAT IT DOES NOT PROVIDE FOR YOUR LEGAL NEEDS, YOU SHOULD CONSULT A NORTH CAROLINA REAL ESTATE ATTORNEY BEFORE YOU SIGN IT.

This offer shall become a binding contract on the Effective Date.

Date: _____ Date: _____

Buyer _____ (SEAL) Seller _____ (SEAL)

Date: _____ Date: _____

Buyer _____ (SEAL) Seller _____ (SEAL)

Date: _____ Date: _____

Buyer _____ (SEAL) Seller _____ (SEAL)

STANDARD FORM 12-T
Revised 7/2013
© 7/2013

NOTICE INFORMATION

(**NOTE**: INSERT THE ADDRESS AND/OR ELECTRONIC DELIVERY ADDRESS EACH PARTY AND AGENT APPROVES FOR THE RECEIPT OF ANY NOTICE CONTEMPLATED BY THIS CONTRACT. INSERT "N/A" FOR ANY WHICH ARE NOT APPROVED.)

BUYER NOTICE ADDRESS:	**SELLER NOTICE ADDRESS:**
Mailing Address: _____	Mailing Address: _____
Buyer Fax#: _____	Seller Fax#: _____
Buyer E-mail: _____	Seller E-mail: _____

SELLING AGENT NOTICE ADDRESS:

Firm Name: _____
Acting as ❑ Buyer's Agent ❑ Seller's (sub)Agent ❑ Dual Agent
Mailing Address: _____

Individual Selling Agent: _____
❑ Acting as a Designated Dual Agent (check only if applicable)
License #: _____
Selling Agent Phone#: _____
Selling Agent Fax#: _____
Selling Agent E-mail: _____

LISTING AGENT NOTICE ADDRESS:

Firm Name: _____
Acting as ❑ Seller's Agent ❑ Dual Agent
Mailing Address: _____

Individual Listing Agent: _____
❑ Acting as a Designated Dual Agent (check only if applicable)
License #: _____
Listing Agent Phone#: _____
Listing Agent Fax#: _____
Listing Agent E-mail: _____

ESCROW ACKNOWLEDGMENT OF INITIAL EARNEST MONEY DEPOSIT

Property: _____

Seller: _____

Buyer: _____

Escrow Agent acknowledges receipt of the Initial Earnest Money Deposit and agrees to hold and disburse the same in accordance with the terms hereof.

Date _____   Firm: _____

By: _____
(Signature)

_____
(Print name)

STANDARD FORM 12-T
Revised 7/2013
© 7/2013

BACK-UP CONTRACT ADDENDUM

NOTE: This Addendum should NOT be used in a short sale transaction. Use ONLY the Short Sale Addendum (form 2A14-T)

Property: _____

Seller: _____

Buyer: _____

This Addendum is attached to and made a part of the Offer to Purchase and Contract ("Back-Up Contract") between Seller and Buyer for the Property.

Buyer and Seller acknowledge that Seller has previously entered into an Offer to Purchase and Contract or an Offer To Purchase and Contract - Vacant Lot/Land (the "Primary Contract") with _____ [insert last name only] (the "Primary Buyer" under the Primary Contract), that the Primary Contract is currently pending, and that this Back-up Contract is accepted in a secondary or back-up position to the Primary Contract under the following terms and conditions:

1. **Condition.** It is a condition of this Back-up Contract that the Primary Contract is terminated as described below before Buyer and Seller shall be obligated to perform under this Back-up Contract.

2. **Termination of Primary Contract.** Termination of the Primary Contract shall be evidenced by:
   (a) written release signed by all parties thereto; or
   (b) written notice of termination from Seller to Primary Buyer that Seller is exercising a right to terminate the Primary Contract; or
   (c) written notice of termination from Primary Buyer to Seller that Primary Buyer is exercising a right to terminate the Primary Contract; or
   (d) final judgment of a court of competent jurisdiction that the Primary Contract is invalid, illegal, unenforceable, or is otherwise terminated.
   NOTE: For example, NCAR Forms 350-T, 351-T, 352-T, 353-T, 390-T or 391-T may be used to evidence the release or notices called for in this paragraph.

3. **Indemnification/Hold Harmless.** Seller shall indemnify Buyer and hold Buyer harmless from any and all claims, damages and costs, including reasonable attorneys' fees, incurred by Buyer as a result of Buyer's reliance upon any wrongful or ineffective termination of the Primary Contract by Seller.

4. **Modification of Primary Contract.** Modification of the terms or conditions of the Primary Contract, including extensions of time, shall not constitute a termination of the Primary Contract and shall not cause this Back-up Contract to move into a primary position.

5. **Access to Primary Contract.** Buyer and Seller agree that Buyer may not examine or otherwise have access to the Primary Contract without written permission from Seller and Primary Buyer. Seller represents that the Primary Contract calls for a settlement date of _____ (date).

6. **Initial Earnest Money Deposit.** Buyer and Seller agree that any Initial Earnest Money Deposit shall be deposited within three (3) banking days following the Effective Date of this Back-up Contract even while this Back-up Contract is in secondary position.

7. **Closing on Primary Contract.** In the event the Primary Contract closes, then this Back-up Contract shall become null and void, and any Earnest Money Deposit shall be refunded to Buyer.

8. **Notification of Termination of Primary Contract.** In the event the Primary Contract is terminated, Seller shall promptly provide Buyer:
   (a) written notice stating that this Back-up Contract has become primary ("Notice of Primary Status"); and
   (b) written evidence that the Primary Contract has been terminated as provided in paragraph 2 above.

Page 1 of 3

This form jointly approved by:
North Carolina Bar Association
North Carolina Association of REALTORS®, Inc.

STANDARD FORM 2A1-T
Revised 7/2012
© 7/2013

Buyer initials _____ _____   Seller initials _____ _____

Source: This form is the property of the North Carolina Association of REALTORS® and the North Carolina Bar Association (NCBA) and is reproduced with the permission of NCAR and NCBA.

9. **Due Diligence/Settlement Dates**.
   (a) Due Diligence Fee. Any Due Diligence Fee provided for in this Contract shall be due and payable within five (5) days after delivery to Buyer of Notice of Primary Status.
   (b) Due Diligence Period. The Due Diligence Period of this Contract shall extend through 5:00 p.m. on the last day of a _____ day period following Seller's delivery to Buyer of Notice of Primary Status.
   (c) Settlement Date. The Settlement Date of this Contract shall be on a date that is _____ days following Seller's delivery to Buyer of Notice of Primary Status.

NOTE: Instead of inserting dates in the "Due Diligence Period" and "Settlement Date" blanks in the Contract, insert "See attached Back-Up Contract Addendum"

10. **Buyer's Right to Terminate**. Buyer may terminate this Back-up Contract before said date without liability by giving written notice of termination to Seller at any time prior to receipt by Buyer of Notice of Primary Status and any Earnest Money Deposit shall be refunded to Buyer.

11. **Automatic Termination**. In any event, Buyer must receive Notice of Primary Status from Seller on or before _____, ***TIME BEING OF THE ESSENCE***, or this Back-up Contract shall become null and void and any Earnest Money Deposit shall be refunded to Buyer.

IN THE EVENT OF A CONFLICT BETWEEN THIS ADDENDUM AND THE BACK-UP CONTRACT THIS ADDENDUM SHALL CONTROL, EXCEPT THAT IN THE CASE OF SUCH A CONFLICT AS TO THE DESCRIPTION OF THE PROPERTY OR THE IDENTITY OF THE BUYER OR SELLER, THE BACK-UP CONTRACT SHALL CONTROL.

THE NORTH CAROLINA ASSOCIATION OF REALTORS®, INC. AND THE NORTH CAROLINA BAR ASSOCIATION MAKE NO REPRESENTATION AS TO THE LEGAL VALIDITY OR ADEQUACY OF ANY PROVISION OF THIS FORM IN ANY SPECIFIC TRANSACTION. IF YOU DO NOT UNDERSTAND THIS FORM OR FEEL THAT IT DOES NOT PROVIDE FOR YOUR LEGAL NEEDS, YOU SHOULD CONSULT A NORTH CAROLINA REAL ESTATE ATTORNEY BEFORE YOU SIGN IT.

Date: _____   Date: _____
Buyer _____(SEAL)   Seller _____(SEAL)
Date: _____   Date: _____
Buyer _____(SEAL)   Seller _____(SEAL)
Date: _____   Date: _____
Buyer _____(SEAL)   Seller _____(SEAL)

STANDARD FORM 2A1-T
Revised 7/2012
© 7/2013

NOTE: The following is a suggested notice that may be copied for the purpose of complying with the notice provision contained in paragraph 8 of the Back-Up Contract Addendum. DO NOT DETACH THE ORIGINAL OF THIS FORM FROM THE BACK-UP CONTRACT.

NOTICE TO BUYER THAT BACK-UP CONTRACT IS NOW IN EFFECT

NOTICE is hereby given to _____(insert name of Buyer) from Seller under the Back-up Contract between them dated _____ that Seller has terminated the Primary Contract with _____(Primary Buyer), as evidenced by the **ATTACHED** (initial any one of the following)**:**

    (a) _____ _____ written release signed by all parties thereto; or
    (b) _____ _____ written notice of termination from Seller to Primary Buyer that Seller is exercising a right to terminate the Primary Contract; or
    (c) _____ _____ written notice of termination from Primary Buyer to Seller that Primary Buyer is exercising a right to terminate the Primary Contract; or
    (d) _____ _____ final judgment of a court of competent jurisdiction that the Primary Contract is invalid, illegal, unenforceable, or is otherwise terminated.

and that the Back-up Contract entered into between Seller and Buyer has become primary and its terms and conditions are now in effect.

Seller: _____ Date: _____

Seller: _____ Date: _____

Seller: _____ Date: _____

STANDARD FORM 2A1-T
Revised 7/2012
© 7/2013

CONTINGENT SALE ADDENDUM

Seller's Property: _____

Seller: _____

Buyer: _____

This Addendum is attached to and made a part of the Offer to Purchase and Contract ("Contract") between Seller and Buyer for the Seller's Property.

1. Closing Contingency for Buyer's Real Property located at: _____
_____ ("Buyer's Property"):

   (a) **Contract For Buyer's Property**: If Buyer's Property is under contract as of the Effective Date of this Contract with Seller OR goes under contract during the Due Diligence Period of this Contract, then Buyer shall deliver a copy of the contract for Buyer's property ("Contract for Buyer's Property") to Seller and it shall be a condition of this Contract that closing on the sale of Buyer's Property occurs on or before the Settlement Date of this Contract. If Buyer fails to deliver to Seller a copy of a Contract for Buyer's Property by the expiration of the Due Diligence Period this Contract shall be null and void and the Earnest Money Deposit shall be refunded to Buyer. In any instance when Buyer is providing to Seller a copy of a Contract for Buyer's Property, Buyer may mark out any confidential information, such as the purchase price and the buyer's identity, prior to providing the copy to Seller.

   (b) **Closing on Contract For Buyer's Property**: If there is a Contract For Buyer's Property, but the closing on the sale of Buyer's Property has not occurred by the Settlement Date of this Contract, then Buyer may terminate this Contract within three days following the Settlement Date of this Contract by written notice to Seller, *TIME BEING OF THE ESSENCE*, and the Earnest Money Deposit shall be refunded to Buyer,

   (WARNING: If Buyer does not terminate this Contract as set out in (b) above, and Buyer fails to timely complete Settlement and Closing as provided in Paragraph 13 of this Contract, Buyer risks the loss of the Earnest Money Deposit).

2. **Termination of Contract for Buyer's Property**. If any Contract for Buyer's Property previously delivered to Seller terminates for any reason, Buyer shall promptly provide Seller written notice and reasonable documentation of such termination. In the event of any such termination, then either party may terminate this Contract by written notice to the other party and the Earnest Money Deposit shall be refunded to Buyer. If Seller elects to terminate the Contract under this paragraph during the Due Diligence Period, Seller also must refund any Due Diligence Fee as a condition of such termination.

3. **Listing of Buyer's Property for Sale.** If Buyer has not entered into a Contract For Buyer's Property as of the Effective Date of this Contract, Buyer's Property (*check only ONE of the following options*):
   ❏ is listed with _____
   ❏ will be listed on or before _____ with _____
   ❏ Buyer is attempting to sell the Buyer's Property without the assistance of a real estate broker.

IN THE EVENT OF A CONFLICT BETWEEN THIS ADDENDUM AND THE CONTRACT, THIS ADDENDUM SHALL CONTROL, EXCEPT THAT IN THE CASE OF SUCH A CONFLICT AS TO THE DESCRIPTION OF THE SELLER'S PROPERTY OR THE IDENTITY OF THE BUYER OR SELLER, THE CONTRACT SHALL CONTROL.

This form jointly approved by:
North Carolina Bar Association
North Carolina Association of REALTORS®, Inc.

STANDARD FORM 2A2–T
Revised 7/2013
© 7/2013

Buyer initials _____ _____   Seller initials _____ _____

Source: This form is the property of the North Carolina Association of REALTORS® and the North Carolina Bar Association (NCBA) and is reproduced with the permission of NCAR and NCBA.

THE NORTH CAROLINA ASSOCIATION OF REALTORS®, INC. AND THE NORTH CAROLINA BAR ASSOCIATION MAKE NO REPRESENTATION AS TO THE LEGAL VALIDITY OR ADEQUACY OF ANY PROVISION OF THIS FORM IN ANY SPECIFIC TRANSACTION. IF YOU DO NOT UNDERSTAND THIS FORM OR FEEL THAT IT DOES NOT PROVIDE FOR YOUR LEGAL NEEDS, YOU SHOULD CONSULT A NORTH CAROLINA REAL ESTATE ATTORNEY BEFORE YOU SIGN IT.

Date _____   Date _____

Buyer:_____(SEAL)   Seller:_____(SEAL)

Date _____   Date _____

Buyer:_____(SEAL)   Seller:_____(SEAL)

Date _____   Date _____

Buyer:_____(SEAL)   Seller:_____(SEAL)

STANDARD FORM 2A2–T
Revised 7/2013
© 7/2013

684 Appendix D

ADDITIONAL PROVISIONS ADDENDUM

Property: _____

Seller: _____

Buyer: _____

This Addendum is attached to and made a part of the Offer to Purchase and Contract ("Contract") between Seller and Buyer for the Property.

NOTE: All of the following provisions which are marked with an "X" shall apply to the attached Offer to Purchase and Contract or Offer to Purchase and Contract – Vacant Lot/Land ("Contract"). Those provisions marked "N/A" shall not apply.

1. _____ **EXPIRATION OF OFFER:** This offer shall expire unless unconditional acceptance is delivered to Buyer on or before _____ ❑ AM ❑ PM, on _____, *TIME BEING OF THE ESSENCE*, or until withdrawn by Buyer, whichever occurs first.

2. _____ (To be used with Offer to Purchase and Contract Form 2-T only) **SEPTIC SYSTEM INSTALLATION/ MODIFICATION:** As a part of the Buyer's Due Diligence, Buyer intends to obtain an Improvement Permit or written evaluation from the County Health Department ("County") for a (check only ONE) ❑ conventional or ❑ other_____ _____ ground absorption sewage system for a _____ bedroom home. Except for the costs for clearing the Property, all costs and expenses of obtaining such Permit or written evaluation shall be borne by Buyer unless otherwise agreed. Seller shall be responsible for clearing that portion of the Property required by the County to perform its tests and/or inspections by no later than _____**(NOTE**: *Insert a date that will allow testing to be completed prior to the end of the Due Diligence Period.)*

3. _____ **RENTAL/INCOME/INVESTMENT PROPERTY:** The Property shall be conveyed subject to existing leases and/or rights of tenants. Seller shall deliver to Buyer on or before_____, true and complete copies of all existing leases, rental agreements, outstanding tenant notices, written statements of all oral tenant agreements, statement of all tenant's deposits, uncured defaults by Seller or tenants, and claims made by or to tenants, if any **(NOTE**: *Insert a date that will allow review to be completed prior to the end of the Due Diligence Period).*
NOTE: DO NOT USE THIS PROVISION FOR PROPERTY SUBJECT TO THE NORTH CAROLINA VACATION RENTAL ACT. A VACATION RENTAL ADDENDUM SHOULD BE USED IN SUCH CASES.

4. _____ **AGREED-UPON REPAIRS AND/OR IMPROVEMENTS:** Seller agrees, prior to Settlement Date and at Seller's expense, to complete the following items:_____
_____
_____
_____
_____
_____
_____
_____.
Buyer shall have the right to verify, prior to Settlement, that the above items have been completed in a good and workmanlike manner.

5. _____ **MANUFACTURED (MOBILE) HOME:** The Property shall include the following manufactured (mobile) home(s) located on the Property: VIN(s): _____ or ❑ VIN(s) unknown Other description (*year, model, etc.*): _____
_____

IN THE EVENT OF A CONFLICT BETWEEN THIS ADDENDUM AND THE CONTRACT, THIS ADDENDUM SHALL CONTROL, EXCEPT THAT IN THE CASE OF SUCH A CONFLICT AS TO THE DESCRIPTION OF THE PROPERTY OR THE IDENTITY OF THE BUYER OR SELLER, THE CONTRACT SHALL CONTROL.

Page 1 of 2

This form jointly approved by:
North Carolina Bar Association
North Carolina Association of REALTORS®, Inc.

Buyer initials _____   _____   Seller initials _____   _____

STANDARD FORM 2A11–T
Revised 7/2012
© 7/2013

THE NORTH CAROLINA ASSOCIATION OF REALTORS®, INC. AND THE NORTH CAROLINA BAR ASSOCIATION MAKE NO REPRESENTATION AS TO THE LEGAL VALIDITY OR ADEQUACY OF ANY PROVISION OF THIS FORM IN ANY SPECIFIC TRANSACTION. IF YOU DO NOT UNDERSTAND THIS FORM OR FEEL THAT IT DOES NOT PROVIDE FOR YOUR LEGAL NEEDS, YOU SHOULD CONSULT A NORTH CAROLINA REAL ESTATE ATTORNEY BEFORE YOU SIGN IT.

Date: _____   Date: _____

Buyer _____ (SEAL)   Seller _____ (SEAL)

Date: _____   Date: _____

Buyer _____ (SEAL)   Seller _____ (SEAL)

Date: _____   Date: _____

Buyer _____ (SEAL)   Seller _____ (SEAL)

STANDARD FORM 2A11–T
Revised 7/2012
© 7/2013

SHORT SALE ADDENDUM

NOTE: The Back-Up Contract Addendum (form 2A1-T) should NOT be used in conjunction with this form when more than one contract of sale is being signed by Seller, as this form manages multiple contracts when necessary

Property: _____

Seller: _____

Buyer: _____

This Addendum is attached to and made a part of the Offer to Purchase and Contract ("Contract") between Seller and Buyer for the Property.

1. **Short Sale Defined**: For purposes of this Contract, a "Short Sale" is a sale where:
   (a) the Purchase Price is or may be insufficient to enable Seller to pay the costs of sale, which include but are not limited to the Seller's closing costs and payment in full of all loans or debts secured by deeds of trust on the Property due and owing to one or more lender(s) and/or other lienholders ("Lienholders");
   (b) Seller does not or may not have sufficient liquid assets to pay the costs of sale; and,
   (c) the Lienholders agree to release or discharge their liens upon payment of an amount less than the amount secured by their liens with or without the Seller being released from any further liability.

2. **Short Sale Approval Risks: Buyer and Seller understand and agree that**:
   - No Lienholder is required or obligated to approve a Short Sale
   - Lienholders may require some terms of the Contract be amended in exchange for approval of a Short Sale, including acceleration of the Due Diligence Period and Settlement Date
   - Buyer and Seller are not obligated to agree to any of Lienholders' proposed terms
   - Seller may not be financially able to make any repairs to the Property that Buyer may request. The Seller's inability to make repairs shall not affect any rights that Buyer may have to terminate the Contract.
   - The costs of Due Diligence and any Due Diligence Fee usually are not refundable to Buyer in the event the Short Sale is not approved.
   - Lienholders' approval may take several weeks or months to obtain, and neither the Seller nor any real estate agent representing Seller or Buyer can guarantee the timeliness of Lienholders' review, approval or rejection.
   - NEITHER THE BUYER, THE SELLER, THE CLOSING ATTORNEY NOR THE BROKERS IN THIS TRANSACTION HAVE ANY CONTROL OVER LIENHOLDERS' APPROVAL, OR ANY ACT, OMISSION OR DECISION BY ANY LIENHOLDERS IN THE SHORT SALE PROCESS.

3. **Contingency**: This Contract is contingent upon Seller obtaining approval for a Short Sale from Lienholders effective through Closing upon terms which are acceptable to Seller and which will enable Seller to close and convey title in accordance with the Contract ("Short Sale Approval").

4. **Notice of Seller's Acceptance of Lienholders' Approval and Parties' Right to Terminate:** Seller agrees to promptly provide Buyer with written notice of Seller's acceptance of Lienholders' approval ("Notice of Approval of Short Sale"). Until Notice of Approval of Short Sale, either party may terminate the Contract by written notice to the other party and the Earnest Money Deposit shall be refunded to Buyer.

5. **Due Diligence/Settlement Date:**
   (a) Buyer and Seller agree that the Due Diligence Period of this Contract shall extend through 5:00 p.m. on the fifteenth (15th) day (or the _____ day, if this blank is completed) following Seller's delivery to Buyer of Notice of Approval of Short Sale, *TIME BEING OF THE ESSENCE*.
   (b) Buyer acknowledges that it could be of substantial benefit to Buyer to conduct any and all Due Diligence soon after the Effective Date. Doing so enables Buyer to inform Seller of defects or other matters that may affect Lienholder approval,

This form jointly approved by:
North Carolina Bar Association
North Carolina Association of REALTORS®, Inc.

STANDARD FORM 2A14-T
Revised 7/2013
© 7/2013

Buyer initials _____ _____   Seller initials _____ _____

Source: This form is the property of the North Carolina Association of REALTORS® and the North Carolina Bar Association (NCBA) and is reproduced with the permission of NCAR and NCBA.

allows Buyer to determine that the Property is suitable and that Buyer can obtain financing, and allows the parties to avoid unnecessary delays.

(c) Buyer and Seller agree that the Settlement Date of this Contract shall be on the thirtieth (30th) day (or the _____ day, if this blank is completed) following Seller's delivery to Buyer of Notice of Approval of Short Sale.

NOTE: Instead of inserting dates in the "Due Diligence Period" and "Settlement Date" blanks in the Contract, insert "See attached Short Sale Addendum".

6. **Other Offers/Additional Contracts:**
   (a) Rules of the NC Real Estate Commission require offers from other buyers received by the Seller's Agent to be presented to the Seller. The NC Real Estate Commission also requires the Seller's Agent to inform Lienholders of all offers and contracts of sale on the Property received after a request for a Short Sale has been submitted to any Lienholder.
   (b) Seller hereby represents to Buyer that there ❑ is ❑ is not an existing contract of sale on the Property ("Existing Sales Contract")
   (c) Offers from other buyers may be accepted by the Seller and become sales contracts ("Additional Sales Contract") Seller or Lienholders may, prior to the Notice of Approval of Short Sale, elect to substitute any Existing or Additional Sales Contract for approval by Lienholders and withdraw this Contract or any Existing or Additional Sales Contract from consideration by Lienholders.
   (d) Unless this Contract has been terminated, Seller shall promptly notify Buyer in writing of the occurrence of any of the following events:
      (i) Seller's acceptance of any Additional Sales Contract; or
      (ii) Seller's or Lienholders' substitution of any Existing or Additional Sales Contract for this Contract for Lienholder approval; or
      (iii) Short Sale Approval of any Additional Sales Contract; or
      (iv) Seller's closing on any Existing or Additional Sales Contract.
   (e) If not sooner terminated by Buyer or Seller hereunder, this Contract shall become null and void upon the completion of closing of any Existing or Additional Sales Contract whether or not Seller notifies Buyer of any such closing, and any Earnest Money Deposit shall be refunded to Buyer.

7. **Foreclosure:** Seller represents that to the best of Seller's knowledge, a foreclosure proceeding ❑ has not ❑ has been filed with respect to the Property. Further, if during the Short Sale process a foreclosure proceeding is filed, the Seller shall disclose such foreclosure filing to the Buyer. Buyer and Seller understand that if Closing does not occur before the completion of a foreclosure of the Property, Seller will lose all rights and interest in the Property. In such event, the Contract shall be void, and the Earnest Money Deposit shall be refunded to Buyer.

8. **Bankruptcy:** Seller represents that Seller ❑ is ❑ is not under bankruptcy protection under United States law. If Seller files a bankruptcy proceeding, Seller shall promptly disclose such filing in writing to Buyer.

9. **Tax Consequences and Advice:** Seller is advised to seek advice from an attorney, a certified public accountant or other professional regarding the credit, legal and tax consequences of a Short Sale.

IN THE EVENT OF A CONFLICT BETWEEN THIS ADDENDUM AND THE CONTRACT, THIS ADDENDUM SHALL CONTROL, EXCEPT THAT IN THE CASE OF SUCH A CONFLICT AS TO THE DESCRIPTION OF THE PROPERTY OR THE IDENTITY OF THE BUYER OR SELLER, THE CONTRACT SHALL CONTROL.

Buyer initials _____ _____   Seller initials _____ _____

STANDARD FORM 2A14-T
Revised 7/2013
© 7/2013

688 Appendix D

THE NORTH CAROLINA ASSOCIATION OF REALTORS®, INC. AND THE NORTH CAROLINA BAR ASSOCIATION MAKE NO REPRESENTATION AS TO THE LEGAL VALIDITY OR ADEQUACY OF ANY PROVISION OF THIS FORM IN ANY SPECIFIC TRANSACTION. IF YOU DO NOT UNDERSTAND THIS FORM OR FEEL THAT IT DOES NOT PROVIDE FOR YOUR LEGAL NEEDS, YOU SHOULD CONSULT A NORTH CAROLINA REAL ESTATE ATTORNEY BEFORE YOU SIGN IT.

Date: _____   Date: _____

Buyer _____ (SEAL)   Seller _____ (SEAL)

Date: _____   Date: _____

Buyer _____ (SEAL)   Seller _____ (SEAL)

Date: _____   Date: _____

Buyer _____ (SEAL)   Seller _____ (SEAL)

STANDARD FORM 2A14-T
Revised 7/2013
© 7/2013

Appendix D **689**

RESPONSE TO BUYER'S OFFER

TO:_____

RE: OFFER TO PURCHASE_____
                                  Property Address

_____

Dated:_____

Thank you for your offer to purchase the above property (the "Property"). I/we cannot accept the offer as written and hereby reject it. However, while this is not a counter offer, I/we would favorably consider the following changes:

_____
_____
_____
_____
_____
_____
_____

If the above changes are acceptable to you, please submit another offer with the noted changes.

It is further understood that until an offer has been accepted, I/we are free to consider and may accept any other offers to purchase presented that contain terms and conditions satisfactory to me/us in my/our sole discretion.

THE NORTH CAROLINA ASSOCIATION OF REALTORS®, INC. MAKES NO REPRESENTATION AS TO THE LEGAL VALIDITY OR ADEQUACY OF ANY PROVISION OF THIS FORM IN ANY SPECIFIC TRANSACTION.

_____   _____   _____
Seller   Date   Time

_____   _____   _____
Seller   Date   Time

Page 1 of 1

North Carolina Association of REALTORS®, Inc.

STANDARD FORM 340-T
Revised 7/2008
© 1/2011

Source: This form is the property of the North Carolina Association of REALTORS® (NCAR) and is reproduced with the permission of NCAR.

690 Appendix D

DUE DILIGENCE REQUEST AND AGREEMENT
[See Guidelines for completing this form (Standard form # 310G)]

NOTE: The parties may also use the Agreement to Amend Contract (Form 330-T) to memorialize any change to the Contract, including but not limited to, an adjustment to the Purchase Price and/or Seller payment of Buyer's expenses in lieu of or in addition to any agreement regarding any due diligence request from Buyer.

_____, as Buyer,

and _____, as Seller,

have entered into an Offer to Purchase and Contract ("Contract") regarding the purchase and sale of the following property (insert property address): _____

_____ ("Property").

1. Based upon Buyer's Due Diligence, the Buyer requests and the Seller agrees to the following: _____

_____
_____
_____
_____
_____
_____
_____

In the event the parties have agreed to any adjustment in the condition of the Property, then such adjustment shall be completed prior to Settlement in a good and workmanlike manner. Seller shall notify Buyer upon completion of the above and provide Buyer with documentation thereof. Buyer shall have the right to verify that the items above have been completed in a good and workmanlike manner. Unless otherwise indicated in the Contract or this Agreement, such verification shall be at Buyer's expense.

NOTE: Unless otherwise agreed, Buyer retains the right agreed to in Paragraph 1(j), Due Diligence Period, of the Offer to Purchase and Contract. Buyer is advised to consult with Buyer's lender regarding this Agreement and/or any Agreement to Amend Contract prior to the expiration of the Due Diligence Period.

2. **Release of Inspection Reports**: Buyer ❏ does ❏ does not agree to release any inspection reports to Seller.

3. **Agreement**: This agreement shall become effective on the date it has been signed by both parties. All changes, additions or deletions hereto must be in writing and signed by all parties.

THE NORTH CAROLINA ASSOCIATION OF REALTORS®, INC. MAKES NO REPRESENTATION AS TO THE LEGAL VALIDITY OR ADEQUACY OF ANY PROVISION OF THIS FORM IN ANY SPECIFIC TRANSACTION.

Buyer: _____	Date _____	Seller: _____	Date _____
Buyer: _____	Date _____	Seller: _____	Date _____
Buyer: _____	Date _____	Seller: _____	Date _____
Buyer: _____	Date _____	Seller: _____	Date _____

North Carolina Association of REALTORS®, Inc.

STANDARD FORM 310-T
Revised 1/2011
© 1/2011

Source: This form is the property of the North Carolina Association of REALTORS® (NCAR) and is reproduced with the permission of NCAR.

NOTICE TO SELLER THAT BUYER IS EXERCISING THEIR RIGHT TO TERMINATE THE OFFER TO PURCHASE AND CONTRACT (FORM 2-T)

Buyer: _____ ("Buyer")

Seller: _____ ("Seller")

Property Address: _____ ("Property")

1. **Contract**. Buyer and Seller entered into a contract for the purchase and sale of the Property on the Offer to Purchase and Contract (form 2-T) ("Contract"). The Effective Date of the Contract is _____.

2. **Termination by Buyer**. Buyer hereby terminates the Contract for the following reason(s) (check all applicable boxes):

    ❑ Non-receipt of a signed copy of the N.C. Residential Property Disclosure Statement prior to the signing of the Contract (see Paragraph 5(d) of Contract)

    ❑ Exercise by Buyer of right to terminate during the Due Diligence Period (see paragraph 4(f) of the Contract)

    ❑ Improvements on the Property have been destroyed or materially damaged by fire or other casualty (See Paragraph 12 of the Contract)

    ❑ Seller's delay in Settlement and Closing for more than fourteen (14) days from the Settlement Date or any extension of the Settlement Date agreed upon in writing (see Paragraph 13 of the Contract)

    ❑ Exercise by Buyer of right to terminate under Paragraph 8 of Back-Up Contract Addendum (form 2A1-T) prior to receipt by Buyer of written notice from Seller that Back-Up Contract has become primary

    ❑ Exercise by Buyer of right to terminate under Paragraph 1 of Contingent Sale Addendum (form 2A2-T) because Buyer has not closed on the sale of Buyer's Property by the Settlement Date

    ❑ Exercise by Buyer of right to terminate under Paragraph 2 of Contingent Sale Addendum (form 2A2-T) because the Contract For Buyer's Property has terminated (**NOTE**: Notice must be accompanied by reasonable documentation of termination of Contract For Buyer's Property)

    ❑ Exercise by Buyer of right to terminate under Paragraph 4 of Short Sale Addendum (form 2A14-T) at any time prior to receipt of Notice of Approval of Short Sale

    ❑ Exercise by Buyer of right to terminate as provided in the FHA/VA Financing Addendum (Form 2A4-T)

THE NORTH CAROLINA ASSOCIATION OF REALTORS®, INC. MAKES NO REPRESENTATION AS TO THE LEGAL VALIDITY OR ADEQUACY OF ANY PROVISION OF THIS FORM IN ANY SPECIFIC TRANSACTION.

_____   _____   _____
Buyer   Date   Time

_____   _____   _____
Buyer   Date   Time

Mailing Address: _____

Page 1 of 2

North Carolina Association of REALTORS®, Inc.

STANDARD FORM 350-T
Revised 7/2012
© 7/2013

Source: This form is the property of the North Carolina Association of REALTORS® (NCAR) and is reproduced with the permission of NCAR.

RELEASE OF EARNEST MONEY DEPOSIT BY SELLER*

Property Address:_____

Seller acknowledges that Buyer is entitled to a refund of the Earnest Money Deposit received in connection with the Contract as a result of Buyer's termination of the Contract for the reason(s) set forth above, and hereby agrees that Escrow Agent may disburse the Earnest Money Deposit to Buyer.

_____   _____
Seller   Date

_____   _____
Seller   Date

Mailing Address: _____

*As set forth in Paragraph 1(f) of the Contract, in the event of a dispute between Seller and Buyer over the return or forfeiture of the Earnest Money Deposit held in escrow by a broker, the broker is required by state law (and Escrow Agent, if not a broker, has agreed) to retain said Earnest Money Deposit in the Escrow Agent's trust or escrow account until a written release from the parties consenting to its disposition has been obtained or until disbursement is ordered by a court of competent jurisdiction. Alternatively, if the broker or an attorney licensed to practice law in North Carolina ("Attorney") is holding the Earnest Money Deposit, the broker or Attorney may deposit the disputed monies with the appropriate clerk of court in accordance with the provisions of N.C.G.S. §93A-12.

STANDARD FORM 350-T
Revised 7/2012
© 7/2013

EXCLUSIVE PROPERTY MANAGEMENT AGREEMENT
Long-term Rental Property

This Exclusive Property Management Agreement is entered into by and between _____
_____ ("Owner")
and _____ ("Agent").

IN CONSIDERATION of the mutual covenants and promises set forth herein, Owner hereby contracts with Agent, and Agent hereby contracts with Owner, to lease and manage the property described below, as well as any other property Owner and Agent may from time to time agree in writing will be subject to this Agreement (the "Property"), in accordance with all applicable laws and regulations, upon the terms and conditions contained herein.

1. Property. City:_____ County:_____, NC
Street Address:_____
Other Description:_____

2. Duration of Agreement. This Agreement shall be binding when it has been signed and dated below by Owner and Agent. It shall become effective on _____, _____, and shall be for an initial term of _____.
NOT LESS THAN _____ DAYS PRIOR TO THE CONCLUSION OF THE INITIAL TERM, EITHER PARTY MAY NOTIFY THE OTHER PARTY IN WRITING OF ITS DESIRE TO TERMINATE THIS AGREEMENT, IN WHICH CASE IT SHALL TERMINATE AT THE CONCLUSION OF THE INITIAL TERM. IF NOT SO TERMINATED, THIS AGREEMENT SHALL AUTOMATICALLY RENEW FOR SUCCESSIVE TERMS OF _____ EACH UNLESS EITHER PARTY GIVES THE OTHER PARTY WRITTEN NOTICE OF ITS DESIRE TO TERMINATE THIS AGREEMENT AT LEAST _____ DAYS PRIOR TO THE CONCLUSION OF ANY SUCH RENEWAL TERM, IN WHICH CASE THIS AGREEMENT SHALL TERMINATE AT THE CONCLUSION OF SUCH TERM. If Owner terminates this Agreement within _____ days of its effective date, Owner shall pay Agent a termination fee of _____
_____.

3. Agent's Fee. For services performed hereunder, Owner shall compensate Agent in the following manner:
- ❑ A fee equal to _____ percent (____%) of gross rental income received on all rental agreements, or $_____ per month, whichever is greater.
- ❑ Other *(describe method of compensation)*:_____
_____.

Agent may deduct Agent's Fee from gross receipts and collections received before remitting the balance of the receipts and collections to Owner. *Note:* No fees may be deducted from any tenant security deposit until the termination of the tenancy. Thereafter, any fees due Agent from Owner may be deducted from any portion of the security deposit due to Owner.

4. Other Fees: Agent may charge tenants reasonable administrative fees permitted by law and retain any such fees, including but not limited to, fees to cover the costs of processing tenant rental applications. If, in Agent's discretion, tenant leases provide for late payment fees and/or returned check fees, such fees, when collected by Agent, shall belong to _____
_____(Owner or Agent). Fees for purposes covered under the Tenant Security Deposit Act will be collected, held and disbursed in accordance with paragraphs 7 and 8 of this Agreement.

5. Authority and Responsibilities of Agent: During the time this Agreement is in effect, Agent shall:
(a) Manage the Property to the best of Agent's ability, devoting thereto such time and attention as may be necessary;
(b) OFFER THE PROPERTY TO THE PUBLIC FOR LEASING IN COMPLIANCE WITH ALL STATE AND FEDERAL HOUSING LAWS, INCLUDING BUT NOT LIMITED TO, ANY STATE AND FEDERAL LAWS PROHIBITING DISCRIMINATION ON THE BASIS OF RACE, COLOR, RELIGION, SEX, NATIONAL ORIGIN, HANDICAP OR FAMILIAL STATUS;
(c) Use Agent's best efforts to solicit, secure and maintain tenants, including the authority to negotiate, execute, extend and renew leases in Owner's name for terms not in excess of _____;
(d) Collect all rentals and other charges and amounts due under tenant leases and give receipts for amounts so collected;
(e) Deliver to Owner within 45 days following the date of execution of any rental agreement an accounting which sets forth the name of the tenant, the rental rate and rents collected, and promptly provide a copy of any rental agreement to Owner upon reasonable request;

Owner Initials _____ _____   Agent Initials _____

North Carolina Association of REALTORS®, Inc.

STANDARD FORM 401
Revised 1/2009
© 1/2011

(f) Provide Owner monthly statements of all monies received and disbursed in connection with Agent's management of the Property, and remit to Owner rental proceeds collected, less any deductions authorized hereunder; provided: (1) this shall not constitute a guarantee by Agent for rental payments that Agent is unable to collect in the exercise of reasonable diligence; and (2) if, pursuant to this Agreement or required by law, Agent either has refunded or will refund in whole or in part any rental payments made by a tenant and previously remitted to Owner, Owner agrees to return same to Agent promptly upon Agent's demand;

(g) Make or cause to be made any repairs which, in Agent's opinion, may be necessary to preserve, maintain and protect the Property; provided, Agent may not make any repairs that exceed $_____ without prior approval of Owner, except that in the case of an emergency, Agent may, without prior approval, make whatever expenditures on behalf of Owner that are reasonably necessary to preserve the Property or prevent further damage from occurring;

(h) Answer tenant requests and complaints and perform the duties imposed upon Owner by tenant leases or any local, state or federal law or regulations, including the authority to purchase such supplies and hire such labor as may be necessary in Agent's opinion to accomplish any necessary repairs;

(i) Retain such amounts from Owner's rental proceeds as may be necessary from time to time to establish and maintain a fund on behalf of Owner in the amount of $_____, from which Agent may pay expenses associated with the management and operation of the Property for which Owner is responsible hereunder;

(j) Negotiate partial refunds with tenants if, in Agent's reasonable opinion, the tenant's use and enjoyment of the Property has been or will be materially and adversely affected as a result of a defect in the condition of the Property (such as a repair to the electrical, plumbing, sanitary, heating or ventilating facilities or a major appliance that cannot be made reasonably and promptly);

(k) Institute and prosecute such proceedings in small claims court as may be necessary and advisable, in Agent's opinion, to recover rents and other sums due the Owner from tenants or to evict tenants and regain possession, including the authority, in Agent's discretion, to settle, compromise and release any and all such small claims proceedings; and

(l) _____
_____
_____
_____

6. Cooperation With/Compensation To Other Agents: Agent has advised Owner of Agent's company policies regarding cooperation and the amount(s) of any compensation, if any, that will be offered to subagents, tenant agents or both. Owner authorizes Agent to (*Check ALL applicable authorizations*):

❏ Cooperate with subagents representing only the Owner and offer them the following compensation: _____
_____

❏ Cooperate with tenant agents representing only the tenant and offer them the following compensation: _____
_____

❏ Cooperate with and compensate agents from other firms according to the attached company policy.

Agent will promptly notify Owner if Agent offers compensation to a cooperating agent(s) that is different from that set forth above.

7. Marketing. Owner authorizes Agent to advertise the Property in such manner as may be appropriate in Agent's opinion, including the authority to: (*Check ALL applicable sections*)

❏ place "For Rent" signs on the Property (where permitted by law and relevant covenants) and to remove other such signs.

❏ submit pertinent information concerning the Property to any listing service of which Agent is a member or in which any of Agent's associates participates and to furnish to such listing service notice of all changes of information concerning the Property authorized in writing by Owner. Owner authorizes Agent, upon execution of a rental contract for the Property, to notify the listing service of the rental, and to disseminate rental information, including rental price, to the listing service, appraisers and real estate brokers.

❏ advertise the Property in non-Internet media, and to permit other firms to advertise the Property in non-Internet media to the extent and in such manner as Agent may decide.

❏ display information about the Property on the Internet either directly or through a program of any listing service of which the Agent is a member or in which any of Agent's associates participates, and to authorize other firms who belong to any listing service of which the Agent is a member or in which any of Agent's associates participates to display information about the Property on the Internet in accordance with the listing service rules and regulations. *If Owner does not authorize Internet advertising as set forth above, Owner MUST complete an opt-out form in accordance with listing service rules. (NOTE: NCAR Form #105 may be used for this purpose.)*

If Owner authorizes Internet Advertising as set forth above, Owner further authorizes the display of (*Check ALL applicable sections*):
- ❏ The address of the Property
- ❏ Automated estimates of the market value of the Property
- ❏ Third-party comments about the Property

8. **Responsibilities of Owner:** During the time this Agreement is in effect, Owner shall:
   (a) Be responsible for all costs and expenses associated with the maintenance and operation of the Property in accordance with the requirements of tenant leases or any local, state or federal law or regulations, including but not limited to NC General Statutes Section 42-42, and advance to Agent such sums as may be necessary from time to time to pay such costs and expenses;
   (b) Provide funds to Agent promptly upon Agent's request for any cost or expense for which Owner is responsible that Agent, in Agent's discretion, incurs on Owner's behalf, including but not limited to, the costs of advertising, emergency maintenance and repairs, utilities, property taxes, owners' association dues and assessments, court costs and attorney's fees; and further, pay interest at the rate of _____ percent (%) per month on the amount of any outstanding balance thereof not paid to Agent within _____ days of Agent's written request therefore;
   (c) NOT TAKE ANY ACTION OR ADOPT ANY POLICY THE EFFECT OF WHICH WOULD BE TO PREVENT AGENT FROM OFFERING THE PROPERTY FOR RENT IN COMPLIANCE WITH ALL APPLICABLE FEDERAL AND STATE LAWS AND REGULATIONS, INCLUDING BUT NOT LIMITED TO, THOSE LAWS AND REGULATIONS PROHIBITING DISCRIMINATION ON THE BASIS OF RACE, COLOR, RELIGION, SEX, NATIONAL ORIGIN, HANDICAP OR FAMILIAL STATUS IN THE LEASING OF THE PROPERTY;
   (d) Carry, at Owner's expense, commercial general liability insurance (including products and completed operations coverage) against any and all claims or demands whatever arising out of, or in any way connected with, the operation, leasing and maintenance of the Property, which policies shall be written to the extent allowable so as to protect Agent in the same manner as Owner and which shall be in the minimum amounts of $_____ for each injury or death of one person in each accident or occurrence, and $_____ for property damage in each accident or occurrence; and provide at least annually a copy of such insurance policy or policies to Agent upon Agent's request; (Name of insurance agent:_____; telephone no.:_____)
   (e) Indemnify and hold Agent harmless to the extent allowable by law from any and all costs, expenses, attorneys' fees, suits, liabilities, damages or claims for damages, including but not limited to, those arising out of any injury or death to any person or loss or damage to any property of any kind whatsoever and to whomsoever belonging, including Owner, in any way relating to the management of the Property by Agent or the performance or exercise of any duty, obligation or authority set forth herein or hereafter granted to Agent, except to the extent that such may be the result of gross negligence or willful or intentional misconduct by Agent; and
   (f) _____
   _____
   _____
   _____
   _____
   _____
   _____

9. **Tenant Security Deposits.** Agent may, in Agent's discretion, require tenants to make security deposits in an amount permitted by law to secure tenants' lease obligations (such security deposits shall hereinafter be referred to as "Tenant Security Deposits"). If the Agent requires Tenant Security Deposits, they shall be placed in a trust account in Agent's name in a North Carolina bank or savings and loan association. Upon the commencement of this Agreement, Owner shall deliver to Agent a list of any current tenants who previously made Tenant Security Deposits under existing leases and the amounts thereof. Simultaneously therewith, any such Tenant Security Deposits shall be placed in a trust account in Agent's name in a North Carolina bank or savings and loan association, and shall thereafter be administered in accordance with this Agreement.

10. **Trust Account Interest.** Agent may, in Agent's discretion, place gross receipts and collections, including **Tenant Security Deposits**, in an interest bearing trust account in the name of Agent in an insured bank or savings and loan association in North Carolina. Interest on any such amounts shall belong to _____(Owner or Agent), except that with respect to any Tenant Security Deposits, tenant leases shall specify, in Agent's discretion, whether such interest shall be payable to Owner or to the tenant. If the lease provides that such interest is payable to the tenant, Agent shall account for the interest in the manner set forth in such lease. If the lease provides that such interest is payable to Owner or as Owner directs, then such interest shall be paid to Owner or Agent as set forth above. Agent may remove any interest payable to Agent from the account at all times and with such frequency as is permitted under the terms of the account and as the law may require.

11. **Entry by Owner.** Owner agrees that neither Owner nor any third party acting at Owner's direction, shall enter the Property for any purpose whatsoever during any time that it is occupied by a tenant in the absence of reasonable notice to Agent or tenant and scheduling by Agent or tenant of an appropriate time for any such entry.

12. **Lead-Based Paint/Hazard Disclosure**. If the Property was built prior to 1978, Landlord understands that Landlord is required under 42 U.S.C. 4852(d) to disclose information about lead-based paint and lead-based paint hazards, and that Agent is required to ensure Landlord's compliance with said law. Landlord agrees to complete and sign a "Disclosure Of Information On Lead-Based Paint And Lead-Based Paint Hazards" form (NCAR form #430-T), photocopies of which will be provided by Agent to prospective tenants. In the alternative, Landlord authorizes Agent, in Agent's discretion, to fulfill Landlord's disclosure obligations by completing and signing said form on Landlord's behalf based on information provided by Landlord to Agent.

13. **Duties on Termination.** Upon termination of this Agreement by either party, each shall take such steps as are necessary to settle all accounts between them, including, but not limited to, the following:
    (a) Agent shall promptly render to Owner all rents then on hand after having deducted therefrom any Agent's fees then due and amounts sufficient to cover all other outstanding expenditures of Agent incurred in connection with operating the Property;
    (b) Agent shall transfer any security deposits held by Agent to Owner or such other person or entity as Owner may designate in writing; provided, Owner understands and acknowledges that the Tenant Security Deposit Act requires Owner to either deposit any such deposits in a trust account with a licensed and insured bank or savings institution located in North Carolina, or furnish a bond from an insurance company licensed to do business in North Carolina;
    (c) Owner shall promptly pay to Agent any fees or amounts due the Agent under the Agreement and shall reimburse Agent for any expenditures made and outstanding at the time of termination;
    (d) Agent shall deliver to Owner copies of all tenant leases and other instruments entered into on behalf of Owner (Agent may retain copies of such leases and instruments for Agent's records); and
    (e) Owner shall notify all current tenants of the termination of this Agreement and transfer of any advance rents and security deposits to Owner.

14. **Sale of Property.** In the event Owner desires to sell the Property through Owner's own efforts or those of a firm other than Agent, Owner shall: (a) promptly notify Agent that the Property is for sale and, if applicable, disclose to Agent the name of the listing firm; and (b) promptly notify Agent if the Property goes under contract and disclose to Agent the agreed-upon closing date.

15. **Entire Agreement; Modification.** This Agreement contains the entire agreement of the parties and supersedes all prior written and oral proposals, understandings, agreements and representations, all of which are merged herein. No amendment or modification to this Agreement shall be effective unless it is in writing and executed by all parties hereto.

16. **Non-Waiver of Default.** The failure of either party to insist, in any one or more instances, on the performance of any term or condition of this Agreement shall not be construed as a waiver or relinquishment of any rights granted hereunder or of the future performance of any such term or condition, and the obligations of the non-performing party with respect thereto shall continue in full force and effect.

17. **Governing Law; Venue.** The parties agree that this Agreement shall be governed by and construed in accordance with the laws of the State of North Carolina, and that in the event of a dispute, any legal action may only be instituted in the county where the Property is located.

18. **Relationship of Parties.** Although Owner and Agent agree that they will actively and materially participate with each other on a regular basis in fulfilling their respective obligations hereunder, the parties intend for their relationship to be that of independent contractors, and nothing contained in this Agreement shall be construed to create a partnership or joint venture of any kind.

19. Exclusivity. Owner agrees that Agent shall be the exclusive rental agent for the Property, and that no other party, including Owner, shall offer the Property for rent during the time this Agreement is in effect. Any rent nevertheless received by Owner or any third party will be transferred to Agent and thereafter accounted for as if originally received by Agent, including the deduction therefrom of any fee due Agent hereunder.

20. Default. If either party defaults in the performance of any of its obligations hereunder, in addition to any other remedies provided herein or by applicable law, the non-defaulting party shall have the right to terminate this Agreement if, within thirty days after providing the defaulting party with written notice of the default and the intent to terminate, the default remains uncured.

21. Costs in Event of Default. If legal proceedings are brought by a party to enforce the terms, conditions or provisions of this Agreement, the prevailing party shall be entitled to recover all expenses (including, but not limited to, reasonable attorney fees, legal expenses and reasonable costs of collection) paid or incurred by such prevailing party in endeavoring to enforce the terms, conditions, or provisions of this Agreement and/or collect any amount owing in accordance with this Agreement.

22. Authority to Enter into Agreement; Principal Contact. Owner represents and warrants to Agent that Owner has full authority to enter into this Agreement, and that there is no other party with an interest in the Property whose joinder in this Agreement is necessary. Either _____ or _____ shall serve as Owner's principal contact for purposes of making all decisions and receiving all notices and rental payments contemplated by this Agreement, and all persons signing this Agreement as Owner hereby appoint either of said persons as Owner's agent and attorney-in-fact for the purposes set forth in this section.

23. Notices. Any notices required or permitted to be given hereunder shall be in writing and mailed by certified mail to the appropriate party at the party's address set forth below.

24. Binding Nature of Agreement. This Agreement shall be binding upon and inure to the benefit of the heirs, legal and personal representatives, successors and permitted assigns of the parties.

25. Assignments by Agent; Change of Ownership. Owner agrees that at any time during the term of this Agreement, Agent may either assign Agent's rights and responsibilities hereunder to another real estate agency, or transfer to another person or entity all or part of the ownership of Agent's real estate agency, and that in the event of any such assignment or transfer, this Agreement shall continue in full force and effect; provided, that any assignee or transferee must be licensed to engage in the business of real estate brokerage in the State of North Carolina. In the event of any such assignment or transfer, Owner may, in addition to all other termination rights hereunder, terminate this Agreement without cause on sixty (60) days' prior written notice to the assignee or transferee of Owner's intent to terminate this Agreement.

26. Other Professional Services. Owner acknowledges that Agent is being retained solely as a real estate professional, and understands that other professional service providers are available to render advice or services to Owner at Owner's expense, including but not limited to an attorney, insurance agent, tax advisor, engineer, home inspector, environmental consultant, architect, or contractor. If Agent procures any such services at the request of Owner, Owner agrees that Agent shall incur no liability or responsibility in connection therewith.

27. Addenda. Any addenda to this Agreement are described in the following space and attached hereto:_____
_____
_____
_____.

The parties agree that any such addenda shall constitute an integral part of this Agreement. In the event of a conflict between this Agreement and any such addenda, the terms of such addenda shall control.

THE AGENT SHALL CONDUCT ALL BROKERAGE ACTIVITIES IN REGARD TO THIS AGREEMENT WITHOUT RESPECT TO THE RACE, COLOR, RELIGION, SEX, NATIONAL ORIGIN, HANDICAP OR FAMILIAL STATUS OF ANY PARTY OR PROSPECTIVE PARTY TO THE AGREEMENT.

698 Appendix D

THE NORTH CAROLINA ASSOCIATION OF REALTORS®, INC. MAKES NO REPRESENTATION AS TO THE LEGAL VALIDITY OR ADEQUACY OF ANY PROVISION OF THIS FORM IN ANY SPECIFIC TRANSACTION.

OWNER:

_____(SEAL)   DATE:_____

_____(SEAL)   DATE:_____

_____(SEAL)   DATE:_____

_____(SEAL)   DATE:_____

AGENT: _____
       [Name of real estate firm]

BY:_____ Individual license #_____ DATE:_____
   [Authorized Representative]

Real Estate Agency:_____

Address:_____

Telephone: _____ Fax:_____ E-mail:_____

Owner:_____

Address:_____

Telephone: _____ Fax:_____ E-mail:_____

Social Security/Tax ID#:_____

Owner:_____

Address:_____

Telephone: _____ Fax:_____ E-mail:_____

Social Security/Tax ID#:_____

Owner:_____

Address:_____

Telephone: _____ Fax:_____ E-mail:_____

Social Security/Tax ID#:_____

Owner:_____

Address:_____

Telephone: _____ Fax:_____ E-mail:_____

Social Security/Tax ID#:_____

STANDARD FORM 401
Revised 1/2009
© 1/2011

RESIDENTIAL RENTAL CONTRACT

RESIDENT: _____ ("Tenant")

OWNER: _____ ("Landlord")

REAL ESTATE MANAGEMENT FIRM: _____ ("Agent")

PREMISES: City: _____ County: _____ State of North Carolina
    ❑ Street Address: _____
    ❑ Apartment Complex: _____ Apartment No. _____
    ❑ Other Description (Room, portion of above address, etc.): _____
_____

INITIAL TERM: Beginning Date of Lease: _____ Ending Date of Lease: _____

RENT: $ _____ PAYMENT PERIOD: ❑ monthly ❑ weekly ❑ yearly ❑ other: _____

LATE PAYMENT FEE: $ _____ OR _____ % of rental payment, whichever is greater
(State law provides that the late fee may not exceed $15.00 or five percent (5%) of the rental payment, whichever is greater.)
RETURNED CHECK FEE: $ _____ *(The maximum processing fee allowed under State law is $25.00.)*
SECURITY DEPOSIT: $ _____ to be deposited with: (check one) ❑ Landlord ❑ Agent
LOCATION OF DEPOSIT: (insert name of bank): _____
BANK ADDRESS: _____

FEES FOR COMPLAINT FOR SUMMARY EJECTMENT AND/OR MONEY OWED (See paragraph 16) (NOTE: Landlord may charge and retain only one of the following fees in addition to any court costs):
- COMPLAINT-FILING FEE: $ _____ OR _____ % of rental payment, whichever is greater *(Fee may not exceed $15.00 or five percent (5%) of the rental payment, whichever is greater.)*
- COURT APPEARANCE FEE: _____ % of rental payment *(Fee may not exceed ten percent (10%) of the rental payment.)*
- SECOND TRIAL FEE: _____ % of rental payment *(Fee may not exceed twelve percent (12%) of the rental payment.)*

PETS: ❑ PETS NOT ALLOWED ❑ PETS ALLOWED   NONREFUNDABLE PET FEE (if pets allowed): $ _____
TYPE OF PET PERMITTED (if pets allowed): _____

PERMITTED OCCUPANTS (in addition to Tenant): _____
_____

    IN CONSIDERATION of the promises contained in this Agreement, Landlord, by and through Agent, hereby agrees to lease the Premises to Tenant on the following terms and conditions:

    1. **Termination and Renewal:** EITHER LANDLORD OR TENANT MAY TERMINATE THE TENANCY AT THE EXPIRATION OF THE INITIAL TERM BY GIVING WRITTEN NOTICE TO THE OTHER AT LEAST _____ DAYS PRIOR TO THE EXPIRATION DATE OF THE INITIAL TERM. IN THE EVENT SUCH WRITTEN NOTICE IS NOT GIVEN OR IF THE TENANT HOLDS OVER BEYOND THE INITIAL TERM, THE TENANCY SHALL AUTOMATICALLY BECOME A _____ (PERIOD) TO _____ (PERIOD) TENANCY UPON THE SAME TERMS AND CONDITIONS CONTAINED HEREIN AND MAY THEREAFTER BE TERMINATED BY EITHER LANDLORD OR TENANT GIVING THE OTHER _____ DAYS WRITTEN NOTICE PRIOR TO THE LAST DAY OF THE THEN CURRENT PERIOD OF THE TENANCY.

    2. **Rent:** Tenant shall pay the Rent, without notice, demand or deduction, to Landlord or as Landlord directs. The first Rent payment, which shall be prorated if the Initial Term commences on a day other than the first day of the Payment Period, shall be due on _____ (date). Thereafter, all rentals shall be paid in advance on or before the **FIRST** day of each subsequent Payment Period for the duration of the tenancy.

North Carolina Association of REALTORS®, Inc.

Tenant Initials _____ _____

STANDARD FORM 410 – T
Revised 10/2009
© 1/2011

3. **Late Payment Fees and Returned Check Fees:** Tenant shall pay the Late Payment Fee if any rental payment is not received by midnight on the fifth (5th) day after it is due. *This late payment fee shall be due immediately without demand therefor and shall be added to and paid with the late rental payment.* Tenant also agrees to pay the Returned Check Fee for each check of Tenant that is returned by the financial institution because of insufficient funds or because the Tenant did not have an account at the financial institution.

4. **Tenant Security Deposit:** The Security Deposit shall be administered in accordance with the North Carolina Tenant Security Deposit Act (N.C.G.S. § 42-50 et. seq.). IT MAY, IN THE DISCRETION OF EITHER THE LANDLORD OR THE AGENT, BE DEPOSITED IN AN INTEREST-BEARING ACCOUNT WITH THE BANK OR SAVINGS INSTITUTION NAMED ABOVE. ANY INTEREST EARNED UPON THE TENANT SECURITY DEPOSIT SHALL ACCRUE FOR THE BENEFIT OF, AND SHALL BE PAID TO, THE LANDLORD, OR AS THE LANDLORD DIRECTS. SUCH INTEREST, IF ANY, MAY BE WITHDRAWN BY LANDLORD OR AGENT FROM SUCH ACCOUNT AS IT ACCRUES AS OFTEN AS IS PERMITTED BY THE TERMS OF THE ACCOUNT.

Upon any termination of the tenancy herein created, the Landlord may deduct from the Tenant Security Deposit amounts sufficient to pay: (1) any damages sustained by the Landlord as a result of the Tenant's nonpayment of rent or nonfulfillment of the Initial Term or any renewal periods, including the Tenant's failure to enter into possession; (2) any damages to the Premises for which the Tenant is responsible; (3) any unpaid bills which become a lien against the Premises due to the Tenant's occupancy; (4) any costs of re-renting the Premises after a breach of this lease by the Tenant; (5) any court costs incurred by the Landlord in connection with terminating the tenancy; and (6) any other damages of the Landlord which may then be a permitted use of the Tenant Security Deposit under the laws of this State. No fees may be deducted from the Tenant Security Deposit until the termination of the tenancy. After having deducted the above amounts, the Landlord shall, if the Tenant's address is known to him, refund to the Tenant, within thirty (30) days after the termination of the tenancy and delivery of possession, the balance of the Tenant Security Deposit along with an itemized statement of any deductions. If the extent of Landlord's claim against the security deposit cannot be determined within 30 days, Landlord shall provide Tenant with an interim accounting no later than 30 days after termination of the tenancy and delivery of possession of the Premises to Landlord and shall provide a final accounting within 60 days after termination of the tenancy and delivery of possession of the Premises to Landlord. If there is more than one person listed above as Tenant, Agent may, in Agent's discretion, pay said balance to any such person, and the other person(s) agree to hold Agent harmless for such action. If the Tenant's address is unknown to the Landlord, the Landlord may deduct the above amounts and shall then hold the balance of the Tenant Security Deposit for the Tenant's collection for a six-month period beginning upon the termination of the tenancy and delivery of possession by the Tenant. If the Tenant fails to make demand for the balance of the Tenant Security Deposit within the six-month period, the Landlord shall not thereafter be liable to the Tenant for a refund of the Tenant Security Deposit or any part thereof.

If the Landlord removes Agent or Agent resigns, the Tenant agrees that Agent may transfer any Tenant Security Deposit held by Agent hereunder to the Landlord or the Landlord's designee and thereafter notify the Tenant by mail of such transfer and of the transferee's name and address. The Tenant agrees that such action by Agent shall relieve Agent of further liability with respect to the Tenant Security Deposit. If Landlord's interest in the Premises terminates (whether by sale, assignment, death, appointment of receiver or otherwise), Agent shall transfer the Tenant Security Deposit in accordance with the provisions of North Carolina General Statutes § 42-54.

5. **Tenant's Obligations:** Unless otherwise agreed upon, the Tenant shall:
(a) use the Premises for residential purposes only and in a manner so as not to disturb the other tenants;
(b) not use the Premises for any unlawful or immoral purposes or occupy them in such a way as to constitute a nuisance;
(c) keep the Premises, including but not limited to all plumbing fixtures, facilities and appliances, in a clean and safe condition;
(d) cause no unsafe or unsanitary condition in the common areas and remainder of the Premises used by him;
(e) comply with any and all obligations imposed upon tenants by applicable building and housing codes;
(f) dispose of all ashes, rubbish, garbage, and other waste in a clean and safe manner and comply with all applicable ordinances concerning garbage collection, waste and other refuse;
(g) use in a proper and reasonable manner all electrical, plumbing, sanitary, heating, ventilating, air conditioning, and other facilities and appliances, if any, furnished as a part of the Premises;
(h) not deliberately or negligently destroy, deface, damage or remove any part of the Premises (including all facilities, appliances and fixtures) or permit any person, known or unknown to the Tenant, to do so;
(i) pay the costs of all utility services to the Premises which are billed directly to the Tenant and not included as a part of the rentals, including, but not limited to, water, electric, telephone, and gas services;
(j) conduct himself and require all other persons on the Premises with his consent to conduct themselves in a reasonable manner and so as not to disturb other tenants' peaceful enjoyment of the Premises; and
(k) not abandon or vacate the Premises during the Initial Term or any renewals or extensions thereof. Tenant shall be deemed to have abandoned or vacated the Premises if Tenant removes substantially all of his possessions from the Premises.

Tenant Initials _____ _____

STANDARD FORM 410 – T
Revised 10/2009
© 1/2011

(l) _____

_____

6. Landlord's Obligations: Unless otherwise agreed upon, the Landlord shall:

(a) comply with the applicable building and housing codes to the extent required by such building and housing codes;

(b) make all repairs to the Premises as may be necessary to keep the Premises in a fit and habitable condition; provided, however, in accordance with paragraph 10, the Tenant shall be liable to the Landlord for any repairs necessitated by the Tenant's intentional or negligent misuse of the Premises;

(c) keep all common areas, if any, used in conjunction with the Premises in a clean and safe condition;

(d) promptly repair all facilities and appliances, if any, as may be furnished by the Landlord as part of the Premises, including electrical, plumbing, sanitary, heating, ventilating, and air conditioning systems, provided that the Landlord, except in emergency situations, actually receives notification from the Tenant in writing of the needed repairs; and

(e) within a reasonable period of time based upon the severity of the condition, repair or remedy any imminently dangerous condition on the Premises after acquiring actual knowledge or receiving notice of the condition. Notwithstanding Landlord's repair or remedy of any imminently dangerous condition, Landlord may recover from Tenant the actual and reasonable costs of repairs that are the fault of Tenant.

7. Smoke and Carbon Monoxide Detectors: Pursuant to North Carolina General Statutes § 42-42 and 42-43, the Landlord shall provide and install operable smoke detectors, either battery-operated or electrical, having an Underwriters' Laboratories, Inc., listing or other equivalent national testing laboratory approval. Effective January 1, 2010, if the Premises has a fossil-fuel burning heater or appliance, fireplace, or an attached garage, the Landlord shall provide and install a minimum of one operable carbon monoxide detector per level in the Premises, either battery operated or electrical, that is listed by a national, OSHA-approved testing laboratory. The Tenant shall notify the Landlord, in writing, of the need for replacement of or repairs to a smoke or carbon monoxide detector. The Landlord shall replace or repair the smoke or carbon monoxide detector within 15 days of receipt of notification if the Landlord is notified of needed replacement or repairs in writing by the Tenant. The Landlord shall ensure that a smoke or carbon monoxide detector is operable and in good repair at the beginning of the Initial Term of the Tenancy. The Landlord shall place new batteries in any battery-operated smoke or carbon monoxide detectors at the beginning of the Initial Term of the tenancy; **the Tenant shall replace the batteries as needed during the tenancy.**

8. Rules and Regulations: The Tenant, his family, servants, guests and agents shall comply with and abide by all the Landlord's existing rules and regulations and such future reasonable rules and regulations as the Landlord may, at Landlord's discretion, from time to time, adopt governing the use and occupancy of the Premises and any common areas used in connection with them (the "Rules and Regulations"). Landlord reserves the right to make changes to the existing Rules and Regulations and to adopt additional reasonable rules and regulations from time to time; provided however, such changes and additions shall not alter the essential terms of this lease or any substantive rights granted hereunder and shall not become effective until thirty (30) days' written notice thereof shall have been furnished to Tenant. Tenant also agrees to abide by any applicable homeowners' association regulations as they now exist or may be amended. A copy of the existing Rules and Regulations, and any applicable homeowners' association regulations, are attached hereto and the Tenant acknowledges that he has read them. The Rules and Regulations shall be deemed to be a part of this lease giving to the Landlord all the rights and remedies herein provided.

9. Right of Entry: Landlord hereby reserves the right to enter the Premises during reasonable hours for the purpose of (1) inspecting the Premises and the Tenant's compliance with the terms of this lease; (2) making such repairs, alterations, improvements or additions thereto as the Landlord may deem appropriate; and (3) showing the Premises to prospective purchasers or tenants. Landlord shall also have the right to display "For Sale" or "For Rent" signs in a reasonable manner upon the Premises.

10. Damages: Tenant shall be responsible for and liable to the Landlord for all damage to, defacement of, or removal of property from the Premises whatever the cause, except such damage, defacement or removal caused by ordinary wear and tear, acts of the Landlord, his agent, or of third parties not invitees of the Tenant, and natural forces. Tenant agrees to pay Landlord for the cost of repairing any damage for which Tenant is responsible upon receipt of Landlord's demand therefor, and to pay the Rent during the period the Premises may not be habitable as a result of any such damage.

11. Pets: If pets are not allowed, Tenant agrees not to keep or allow anywhere on or about the Property any animals or pets of any kind, including but not limited to, dogs, cats, birds, rodents, reptiles or marine animals. If pets are allowed, Tenant acknowledges that the amount of the Pet Fee is reasonable and agrees that the Landlord shall not be required to refund the Pet Fee in whole or in part. If pets are allowed, Tenant agrees to reimburse Landlord for any primary or secondary damages caused thereby whether the damage is to the Premises or to any common areas used in conjunction with them, and to indemnify Landlord from any liability to third parties which may result from Tenant's keeping of such pet or pets.

The Tenant shall remove any pet previously permitted within _____ hours of written notification from the Landlord that the pet, in the Landlord's sole judgment, creates a nuisance or disturbance or is, in the Landlord's opinion, undesirable. If the pet is caused to be removed pursuant to this paragraph, the Landlord shall not be required to refund the Pet Fee; however, the Tenant shall be entitled to acquire and keep another pet of the type previously authorized.

Tenant Initials _____ _____

STANDARD FORM 410 – T
Revised 10/2009
© 1/2011

12. **Alterations**: The Tenant shall not paint, mark, drive nails or screws into, or otherwise deface or alter walls, ceilings, floors, windows, cabinets, woodwork, stone, ironwork or any other part of the Premises or decorate the Premises or make any alterations, additions, or improvements in or to the Premises without the Landlord's prior written consent and then only in a workmanlike manner using materials and contractors approved by the Landlord. All such work shall be done at the Tenant's expense and at such times and in such manner as the Landlord may approve. All alterations, additions, and improvements upon the Premises, made by either the Landlord or Tenant, shall become the property of the Landlord and shall remain upon and become a part of the Premises at the end of the tenancy hereby created.

13. **Occupants:** The Tenant shall not allow or permit the Premises to be occupied or used as a residence by any person other than Tenant and the Permitted Occupants.

14. **Rental Application:** In the event the Tenant has submitted a Rental Application in connection with this lease, Tenant acknowledges that the Landlord has relied upon the Application as an inducement for entering into this Lease and Tenant warrants to Landlord that the facts stated in the Application are true to the best of Tenant's knowledge. If any facts stated in the Rental Application prove to be untrue, the Landlord shall have the right to terminate the tenancy and to collect from Tenant any damages resulting therefrom.

15. **Tenant's Duties Upon Termination:** Upon any termination of the Tenancy created hereby, whether by the Landlord or the Tenant and whether for breach or otherwise, the Tenant shall: (1) pay all utility bills due for services to the Premises for which he is responsible and have all such utility services discontinued; (2) vacate the Premises removing therefrom all Tenant's personal property of whatever nature; (3) properly sweep and clean the Premises, including plumbing fixtures, refrigerators, stoves and sinks, removing therefrom all rubbish, trash, garbage and refuse; (4) make such repairs and perform such other acts as are necessary to return the Premises, and any appliances or fixtures furnished in connection therewith, in the same condition as when Tenant took possession of the Premises; provided, however, Tenant shall not be responsible for ordinary wear and tear or for repairs required by law or by paragraph 6 above to be performed by Landlord; (5) fasten and lock all doors and windows; (6) return to the Landlord all keys to the Premises; and (7) notify the Landlord of the address to which the balance of the Security Deposit may be returned. If the Tenant fails to sweep out and clean the Premises, appliances and fixtures as herein provided, Tenant shall become liable, without notice or demand, to the Landlord for the actual costs of cleaning (over and above ordinary wear and tear), which may be deducted from the Security Deposit as provided in paragraph 4 above.

16. **Tenant's Default:** In the event the Tenant shall fail to:
    (a) pay the rentals herein reserved as and when they shall become due hereunder; or
    (b) perform any other promise, duty or obligation herein agreed to by him or imposed upon him by law and such failure shall continue for a period of five (5) days from the date the Landlord provides Tenant with written notice of such failure,

then in either of such events and as often as either of them may occur, the Landlord, in addition to all other rights and remedies provided by law, may, at its option and with or without notice to Tenant, either (i) terminate this lease or (ii) terminate the Tenant's right to possession of the Premises without terminating this lease. Regardless of whether Landlord terminates this lease or only terminates the Tenant's right of possession without terminating this lease, Landlord shall be immediately entitled to possession of the Premises and the Tenant shall peacefully surrender possession of the Premises to Landlord immediately upon Landlord's demand. In the event Tenant shall fail or refuse to surrender possession of the Premises, Landlord shall, in compliance with Article 2A of Chapter 42 of the General Statutes of North Carolina, reenter and retake possession of the Premises only through a summary ejectment proceeding. If a summary ejectment proceeding is instituted against Tenant, in addition to any court costs and past-due rent that may be awarded, Tenant shall be responsible for paying Landlord the relevant Complaint-Filing Fee, Court Appearance Fee or Second Trial Fee, only one of which Landlord is entitled to charge and retain. The Complaint-Filing Fee may be charged if: (i) Tenant was in default of this lease, (ii) the Landlord filed and served a complaint for summary ejectment and/or money owed, (iii) Tenant cured the default or claim, and (iv) Landlord dismissed the complaint prior to judgment. The Court Appearance Fee may be charged if: (i) Tenant was in default of the lease, Landlord filed, served, and prosecuted successfully a complaint for summary ejectment and/or monies owed in small claims court, and (iv) neither party appealed the judgment of the magistrate. The Second Trial Fee may be charged for a new trial following an appeal from the judgment of a magistrate, provided Landlord proves: (i) that Tenant was in default of the lease and (ii) Landlord prevailed. (NOTE: If the rent is subsidized by HUD, the US Department of Agriculture, a State Agency, a public housing authority, or a local government, any fee charged pursuant to this paragraph 16 shall be calculated on Tenant's share of the rent only.) In the event Landlord terminates this lease, all further rights and duties hereunder shall terminate and Landlord shall be entitled to collect from Tenant all accrued but unpaid rents and any damages resulting from the Tenant's breach. In the event Landlord terminates the Tenant's right of possession without terminating this lease, Tenant shall remain liable for the full performance of all the covenants hereof, and Landlord shall use reasonable efforts to re-let the Premises on Tenant's behalf. Any such rentals reserved from such re-letting shall be applied first to the costs of re-letting the Premises and then to the rentals due hereunder. In the event the rentals from such re-letting are insufficient to pay the rentals due hereunder in full, Tenant shall be liable to the Landlord for any deficiency. In the event Landlord institutes a legal action against the Tenant to enforce the lease or to recover any sums due hereunder, Tenant agrees to pay Landlord reasonable attorney's fees in addition to all other damages. No fees may be deducted from the Tenant Security Deposit until the termination of the tenancy.

Tenant Initials _____ _____

STANDARD FORM 410 – T
Revised 10/2009
© 1/2011

17. **Landlord's Default; Limitation of Remedies and Damages**: Until the Tenant notifies the Landlord in writing of an alleged default and affords the Landlord a reasonable time within which to cure, no default by the Landlord in the performance of any of the promises or obligations herein agreed to by him or imposed upon him by law shall constitute a material breach of this lease and the Tenant shall have no right to terminate this lease for any such default or suspend his performance hereunder. In no event and regardless of their duration shall any defective condition of or failure to repair, maintain, or provide any area, fixture or facility used in connection with recreation or recreational activities, including but not limited to swimming pools, club houses, and tennis courts, constitute a material breach of this lease and the Tenant shall have no right to terminate this lease or to suspend his performance hereunder. In any legal action instituted by the Tenant against the Landlord, the Tenant's damages shall be limited to the difference, if any, between the rent reserved in this lease and the reasonable rental value of the Premises, taking into account the Landlord's breach or breaches, and in no event, except in the case of the Landlord's willful or wanton negligence, shall the Tenant collect any consequential or secondary damages resulting from the breach or breaches, including but not limited to the following items: damage or destruction of furniture or other personal property of any kind located in or about the Premises, moving expenses, storage expenses, alternative interim housing expenses, and expenses of locating and procuring alternative housing.

18. **Removal, Storage and Disposition of Tenant's Personal Property**:

(a) Ten days after being placed in lawful possession by execution of a writ of possession, the Landlord may throw away, dispose of, or sell all items of personal property remaining on the Premises. During the 10-day period after being placed in lawful possession by execution of a writ of possession, the Landlord may move for storage purposes, but shall not throw away, dispose of, or sell any items of personal property remaining on the Premises unless otherwise provided for in Chapter 42 of the North Carolina General Statutes. Upon the Tenant's request prior to the expiration of the 10-day period, the Landlord shall release possession of the property to the Tenant during regular business hours or at a time agreed upon. If the Landlord elects to sell the property at public or private sale, the Landlord shall give written notice to the Tenant by first-class mail to the Tenant's last known address at least seven days prior to the day of the sale. The seven-day notice of sale may run concurrently with the 10-day period which allows the Tenant to request possession of the property. The written notice shall state the date, time, and place of the sale, and that any surplus of proceeds from the sale, after payment of unpaid rents, damages, storage fees, and sale costs, shall be disbursed to the Tenant, upon request, within 10 days after the sale, and will thereafter be delivered to the government of the county in which the rental property is located. Upon the Tenant's request prior to the day of sale, the Landlord shall release possession of the property to the Tenant during regular business hours or at a time agreed upon. The Landlord may apply the proceeds of the sale to the unpaid rents, damages, storage fees, and sale costs. Any surplus from the sale shall be disbursed to the Tenant, upon request, within 10 days of the sale and shall thereafter be delivered to the government of the county in which the rental property is located.

(b) If the total value of all property remaining on the Premises at the time of execution of a writ of possession in an action for summary ejectment is less than one hundred dollars ($100.00), then the property shall be deemed abandoned five days after the time of execution, and the Landlord may throw away or dispose of the property. Upon the Tenant's request prior to the expiration of the five-day period, the Landlord shall release possession of the property to the Tenant during regular business hours or at a time agreed upon.

19. **Bankruptcy**: If any bankruptcy or insolvency proceedings are filed by or against the Tenant or if the Tenant makes any assignment for the benefit of creditors, the Landlord may, at his option, immediately terminate this Tenancy, and reenter and repossess the Premises, subject to the provisions of the Bankruptcy Code (11 USC Section 101, et. seq.) and the order of any court having jurisdiction thereunder.

20. **Tenant's Insurance; Release and Indemnity Provisions**: The Tenant shall be solely responsible for insuring any of his personal property located or stored upon the Premises upon the risks of damage, destruction, or loss resulting from theft, fire, storm and all other hazards and casualties. Regardless of whether the Tenant secures such insurance, the Landlord and his agents shall not be liable for any damage to, or destruction or loss of, any of the Tenant's personal property located or stored upon the Premises regardless of the cause or causes of such damage, destruction, or loss, unless such loss or destruction is attributable to the intentional acts or willful or wanton negligence of the Landlord. The Tenant agrees to release and indemnify the Landlord and his agents from and against liability for injury to the person of the Tenant or to any members of his household resulting from any cause whatsoever except only such personal injury caused by the negligent, or intentional acts of the Landlord or his agents.

21. **Agent**: The Landlord and the Tenant acknowledge that the Landlord may, from time to time in his discretion, engage a third party ("the Agent") to manage, supervise and operate the Premises or the complex, if any, of which they are a part. If such an Agent is managing, supervising and operating the Premises at the time this lease is executed, his name will be shown as "Agent" on the first page hereof. With respect to any Agent engaged pursuant to this paragraph, the Landlord and the Tenant hereby agree that: (1) Agent acts for and represents Landlord in this transaction; (2) Agent shall have only such authority as provided in the management contract existing between the Landlord and Agent; (3) Agent may perform without objection from the Tenant, any obligation or exercise any right of the Landlord imposed or given herein or by law and such performance shall be valid and binding, if authorized by the Landlord, as if performed by the Landlord; (4) the Tenant shall pay all rentals to the Agent if directed to do so by the Landlord; (5) except as otherwise provided by law, the Agent shall not be liable to the Tenant for the nonperformance of the obligations or promises of the Landlord contained herein; (6) nothing contained herein shall modify the management contract existing between the

Tenant Initials _____ _____

STANDARD FORM 410 – T
Revised 10/2009
© 1/2011

Landlord and the Agent; however, the Landlord and the Agent may from time to time modify the management agreement in any manner which they deem appropriate; (7) the Landlord, may, in his discretion and in accordance with any management agreement, remove without replacing or remove and replace any agent engaged to manage, supervise and operate the Premises.

22. **Form**: The Landlord and Tenant hereby acknowledge that their agreement is evidenced by this form contract which may contain some minor inaccuracies when applied to the particular factual setting of the parties. The Landlord and Tenant agree that the courts shall liberally and broadly interpret this lease, ignoring minor inconsistencies and inaccuracies, and that the courts shall apply the lease to determine all disputes between the parties in the manner which most effectuates their intent as expressed herein. The following rules of construction shall apply: (1) handwritten and typed additions or alterations shall control over the preprinted language when there is an inconsistency between them; (2) the lease shall not be strictly construed against either the Landlord or the Tenant; (3) paragraph headings are used only for convenience of reference and shall not be considered as a substantive part of this lease; (4) words in the singular shall include the plural and the masculine shall include the feminine and neuter genders, as appropriate; and (5) the invalidity of one or more provisions of this lease shall not affect the validity of any other provisions hereof and this lease shall be construed and enforced as if such invalid provision(s) were not included.

23. **Amendment of Laws**: In the event that subsequent to the execution of this lease any state statute regulating or affecting any duty or obligation imposed upon the Landlord pursuant to this lease is enacted, amended, or repealed, the Landlord may, at his option, elect to perform in accordance with such statute, amendment, or act of repeal in lieu of complying with the analogous provision of this lease.

24. **Eminent Domain and Casualties**: The Landlord shall have the option to terminate this lease if the Premises, or any part thereof, are condemned or sold in lieu of condemnation or damaged by fire or other casualty.

25. **Assignment**: The Tenant shall not assign this lease or sublet the Premises in whole or part.

26. **Waiver**: No waiver of any breach of any obligation or promise contained herein shall be regarded as a waiver of any future breach of the same or any other obligation or promise.

27. **Other Terms and Conditions:**
   (a) ❑ (Check if applicable) The Premises were built prior to 1978. (Attach Standard Form # 430 - T, "Disclosure of Information on Lead-Based Paint and Lead-Based Paint Hazards.")
   (b) If there is an Agent involved in this transaction, Agent hereby discloses to Tenant that Agent is acting for and represents Landlord.
   (c) The following additional terms and conditions shall also be a part of this lease: _____
   _____
   (d) Itemize all addenda to this Contract and attach hereto: _____
   _____

28. **Inspection of Premises:** Within _____ days of occupying the Premises, Tenant has the right to inspect the Premises and complete a Move-in Inspection Form.

29. **Notice**: Any notices required or authorized to be given hereunder or pursuant to applicable law shall be mailed or hand delivered to the following addresses:
   Tenant: the address of the Premises
   Landlord: the address to which rental payments are sent.

30. **Execution; Counterparts:** When Tenant signs this lease, he acknowledges he has read and agrees to the provisions of this lease. This lease is executed in_____ (number) counterparts with an executed counterpart being retained by each party.

31. **Entire Agreement:** This Agreement contains the entire agreement of the parties and there are no representations, inducements or other provisions other than those expressed in writing. All changes, additions or deletions hereto must be in writing and signed by all parties.

THE NORTH CAROLINA ASSOCIATION OF REALTORS®, INC. MAKES NO REPRESENTATION AS TO THE LEGAL VALIDITY OR ADEQUACY OF ANY PROVISION OF THIS FORM IN ANY SPECIFIC TRANSACTION.

TENANT:
_____(SEAL)
_____(SEAL)
Date: _____

LANDLORD:
_____(SEAL)
_____(SEAL)
By:_____, AGENT
_____(SEAL)
Date: _____

STANDARD FORM 410 – T
Revised 10/2009
© 1/2011

MATH FAQs

Answers to Your Most Frequently
Asked Real Estate Math Questions

MATH FAQS CONTENTS

Math FAQs Introduction   709
Using This Math Review   709
Special Features   710

SECTION 1   Introduction to Calculators   711

What Kind of Calculator Do I Need?   711
What Are the Specific Real Estate Functions I Should Look for?   711
How Do I Use the Percent Key?   712

SECTION 2   Measurement Problems   713

What Are Linear Measurements?   713
What Does the Term *Front Foot* Refer to?   713
How Do I Convert One Kind of Linear Measurement to Another?   713
How Do I Solve for Area Measurement?   714
How Do I Convert One Kind of Area Measurement to Another?   715
How Do I Determine the Area of a Square or Rectangle?   715
How Do I Determine the Area of a Triangle?   716
How Do I Solve for Volume?   716
How Do I Convert from One Kind of Volume Measurement to Another?   717
How Do I Determine the Volume of a Room?   717
How Do I Determine the Volume of a Triangular Prism?   717

SECTION 3   Fractions, Decimals, and Percentages   719

What Are the Parts of a Fraction?   719
What Is Meant by a *Proper* and an *Improper* Fraction?   719
What Is a Mixed Number?   719
How Do I Multiply Fractions?   719
How Do I Divide by Fractions?   720
How Do I Convert Fractions to Decimals?   721
How Do I Add or Subtract Decimals?   721
How Do I Multiply Decimals?   721
How Do I Divide Decimals?   722
What Is a Percentage?   722
How Can I Convert a Percentage to a Decimal?   722
How Can I Convert a Decimal to a Percentage?   723
How Do I Multiply by Percentages?   723
How Do I Divide by Percentages?   723
Is There Any Easy Way to Remember How to Solve Percentage Problems?   723

What Is the T-Bar Method? 723

How Do I Use the T-Bar? 724

Word Problems Can Be Tricky. How Should I Deal with Them? 725

SECTION 4 Percentage Problems 727

How Do I Work Commission Problems? 727

What Is Meant by Seller's Dollars After Commission? 729

How Do I Determine Interest? 730

How Much Interim Interest Will Be Due at Closing? 731

How Do I Determine Monthly Principal and Interest Payments? 731

How Do I Work Problems About Points? 732

How Do I Determine Profit? 732

What Is The Difference Between Appreciation and Depreciation? 734

How Do I Solve Appreciation Problems? 734

How Do I Solve Depreciation Problems? 735

How Do I Estimate Value for Income-Producing Properties? 736

How Do I Solve Problems Involving Percentage Leases? 737

SECTION 5 Proration Problems 740

What Are The Different Calendars Used for Prorating? 740

What Is the Difference Between Prorating Through and Prorating to the Day of Closing? 741

How Do I Calculate Proration Problems? 741

What Is the Difference Between Debit and Credit in a Proration Problem? 741

How Do I Calculate Interest in a Proration Problem? 742

How Do I Prorate Taxes? 743

Is Insurance Always Prorated? 745

If Insurance Is Prorated, How Do I Calculate It? 745

How Do I Prorate Rent? 747

Real Estate Math Practice Problems 749

Answer Key for Real Estate Math Practice Problems 755

MATH FAQS INTRODUCTION

Math is an integral part of the real estate profession. The amount and complexity of the math you encounter will vary, depending on your chosen area of real estate. Calculators and computers are great time-savers, but licensees still need a solid, basic knowledge of math. It is a matter of taking the math concepts and adapting them to the real estate profession.

People react differently to the word *math*. Some people like math. Some people are comfortable with math. Some people, though, are uncomfortable with math and become anxious and stressed when they encounter numbers. If you're that kind of person, you will find the approach taken here to be helpful. Even if you're someone who's comfortable working with numbers, this clear and simple review will reinforce what you know—and maybe teach you a few tricks and shortcuts, too.

This review covers the basics of real estate math to prepare you for the real-world situations you will encounter, as well as the math problems you will most likely find on your real estate licensing examination.

Study, review, and practice will help you overcome stress and anxiety so you can become comfortable with math. With practice and review, your confidence and ability in real estate math will grow.

■ USING THIS MATH REVIEW

This math review is designed to provide you with a quick check of your math knowledge and to help reinforce what you already know. It's organized in a way that makes it easy to look up just the information you need. The subject matter is presented in a straightforward manner with a minimum of wordy explanations and a maximum of quick tips, examples, formulas, memory aids, and shortcuts to help you become confident in real estate math.

Divided into sections, this review is organized into the following five general subject areas:

1. Calculators
2. Measurement
3. Fractions
4. Percentages
5. Proration

Within each general subject heading are a series of frequently asked questions (FAQs) and brief, clear explanations. If you read Math FAQs through from start to finish, you'll get a good, general review of real estate math principles. You also can use Math FAQs for a last-minute review of difficult issues or even as a reference in your daily real estate practice. Check the Math FAQs contents to see if your question is listed. If your question is more complicated or fact-specific, you may need to look at several different items to find your answer.

■ SPECIAL FEATURES

Throughout the text you will find **Math Tips** that offer insight into the trickier aspects of real estate math in general and the real estate exam's math content in particular. The **For Example** feature applies formulas and concepts to practical situations to show how the concept works in the real world. A generous collection of practice problems at the end of the review provides the opportunity to apply your understanding in an exam-style context. The **T-Bar method** is offered as a shortcut that's easy to understand and easy to apply.

SECTION 1

Introduction to Calculators

Basic calculators are permitted when taking most state licensing examinations. The rules usually require that the calculator be silent, handheld, battery-operated, and nonprinting. Many states will not allow test takers to use a real estate or financial calculator while taking the real estate exam. Check with your state regarding the appropriate calculator for your exam.

■ WHAT KIND OF CALCULATOR DO I NEED?

A calculator that will add (+), subtract (−), multiply (×), and divide (÷) is all that is needed for licensing examinations. A calculator with a battery only or solar power with a battery backup is recommended over solar-powered only. Choose a calculator that is most comfortable for you; allow yourself time to learn to use it correctly and to become comfortable with it before you take the licensing examination.

■ WHAT ARE THE SPECIFIC REAL ESTATE FUNCTIONS I SHOULD LOOK FOR?

Many business or financial calculators have additional functions that are very beneficial to the real estate professional. Some of the keys you would want are "N" (number of interest compounding periods/number of payments), "I" (interest rate per period), "PV" (present value of money/loan), "PMT" (amount of payment), and "FV" (future value of money). Business or financial calculators vary according to brand and/or model; therefore, the user's manual should always be followed to use the calculator properly. For example, some have "TERM" instead of "N"; therefore, you enter the number of years of the term instead of the number of payments or compounding periods. Some have "LOAN" instead of "PV." Some instruct you to enter the interest rate as an annual rate instead of a monthly rate. You may wish to purchase a business or financial calculator that contains these extra functions. Check with your state real estate commission to see if you will be permitted to use them during the exam.

MATH TIP Be careful! Business or financial calculators are often set at the factory to round to two decimals. Follow the user's manual and set the decimal to float or to a minimum of five decimals. This will enable you to arrive at an answer with enough decimals to match multiple-choice answers on exams. No matter which calculator you choose, *read the user's manual.*

■ HOW DO I USE THE PERCENT KEY?

If you use the "%" key on calculators to solve percentage problems, read the user's manual for the key's proper use. Some calculators require the use of the "%" key or the "=" key *but never both in the same calculation*. Other calculators require the use of *both* the "%" key and the "=" key to get a correct answer. No matter which calculator you choose, *read the user's manual*.

■ **FOR EXAMPLE** If a property sold for $100,000 and a 7% commission was paid to the broker, how much was the broker paid?

This question may be worked two ways, as illustrated below.

Convert 7% to the decimal 0.07. (How to convert percents to decimals is shown in Section 3.) Touch $100,000 into your calculator, then the × or multiplication key, then 0.07, then the = key to read $7,000.

Or, touch in $100,000, then the × or multiplication key, then 7, then the % key. If your calculator now reads $7,000, you've finished the question. If when you touch the % key, it reads 0.07, then you must touch the = key to complete the calculation.

The use of the % key allows the calculator to convert to the proper decimal place, and there's no question about the placement of the decimal. The choice is yours: you can convert the percent to a decimal or use the % key for the conversion.

FIGURE 1.1

Calculator Functions to Look For

SECTION 2

Measurement Problems

■ WHAT ARE LINEAR MEASUREMENTS?

Linear measures are used for length or distance (e.g., length of a wall). Linear measures include feet, yards, inches, and miles. Linear feet are sometimes called running feet and are used to measure **frontage** (front feet) on a road or lake. **Linear measurement** is line measurement. When the terms

- *foot,*
- *linear foot,*
- *running foot,* or
- *front foot*

are used, you are being asked to determine the *total length* of the object, whether measured in a straight line, crooked line, or curved line. The abbreviation for feet is '. Thus, 12 feet can be written as 12'. The abbreviation for inches is ". Thus, 12 inches can be written as 12".

■ WHAT DOES THE TERM *FRONT FOOT* REFER TO?

When the term *front foot* is used, you are dealing with the number of units on the **frontage** of a lot. The frontage is usually the street frontage, but it might be the water frontage if the lot is on a river, lake, or ocean. If two dimensions are given for a tract of land and they are not labeled, the first dimension is the frontage. The word *width* also means frontage; the length is called the *depth*.

■ HOW DO I CONVERT ONE KIND OF LINEAR MEASUREMENT TO ANOTHER?

12 inches = 1 foot
    Inches ÷ 12 = Feet (144 inches ÷ 12 = 12 feet)
    Feet × 12 = Inches (12 feet × 12 = 144 inches)

36 inches = 1 yard
    Inches ÷ 36 = Yards (144 inches ÷ 36 = 4 yards)
    Yards × 36 = Inches (4 yards × 36 = 144 inches)

3 feet = 1 yard
    Feet ÷ 3 = Yards (12 feet ÷ 3 = 4 yards)
    Yards × 3 = Feet (4 yards × 3 = 12 feet)

5,280 feet = 1 mile
    Feet ÷ 5,280 = Miles (10,560 feet ÷ 5,280 = 2 miles)
    Miles × 5,280 = Feet (2 miles × 5,280 = 10,560 feet)

16½ feet = 1 rod
    Feet ÷ 16.5 = Rods (82.5 feet ÷ 16.5 = 5 rods)
    Rods × 16.5 = Feet (5 rods × 16.5 = 82.5 feet)

320 rods = 1 mile
    Rods ÷ 320 = Miles (640 rods ÷ 320 = 2 miles)
    Miles × 320 = Rods (2 miles × 320 = 640 rods)

■ **FOR EXAMPLE** A rectangular lot is 50 feet by 150 feet. The cost to fence this lot is priced per linear/running foot. How many linear/running feet will be used to calculate the price of the fence?

```
                      150'
        ┌─────────────────────────────┐
    50' │                             │ 50'
        └─────────────────────────────┘
                      150'
```

50 feet + 150 feet + 50 feet + 150 feet = 400 linear/running feet

400 linear/running feet is the answer.

■ **FOR EXAMPLE** A parcel of land that fronts on Interstate 45 in Houston, Texas, is for sale at $5,000 per front foot. What will it cost to purchase this parcel of land if the dimensions are 150 feet by 100 feet?

150 is the frontage because it is the first dimension given.

150 front feet × $5,000 = $750,000 cost

$750,000 is the answer.

■ HOW DO I SOLVE FOR AREA MEASUREMENT?

Area is the two-dimensional surface of an object. Area is quoted in *square units* or in *acres*. A linear measure multiplied by another linear measure always equals a square measure: feet times feet equals square feet; miles times miles equals square miles, yards times yards equals square yards, et cetera. We will look at calculating the area of squares, rectangles, and triangles. Squares and rectangles are four-sided objects. All four sides of a square are the same. Opposite sides of a rectangle are the same. A triangle is a three-sided object. The three sides of a triangle can be the same dimension or three different dimensions.

MATH TIP When two dimensions are given, assume it to be a rectangle unless told otherwise.

■ HOW DO I CONVERT ONE KIND OF AREA MEASUREMENT TO ANOTHER?

144 square inches = 1 square foot
Square inches ÷ 144 = Square feet (14,400 square inches ÷ 144 = 100 square feet)
Square feet × 144 = Square inches ÷ (100 square feet × 144 = 14,400 square inches)

1,296 square inches = 1 square yard
Square inches ÷ 1,296 = Square yards (12,960 ÷ 1,296 = 10 square yards)
Square yards × 1,296 = Square inches (10 square yards × 1,296 = 12,960 square yards)

9 square feet = 1 square yard
Square feet ÷ 9 = Square yards (90 square feet ÷ 9 = 10 square yards)
Square yards × 9 = Square feet (10 square yards × 9 = 90 square feet)

43,560 square feet = 1 acre
Square feet ÷ 43,560 = Acres (87,120 ÷ 43,560 = 2 acres)
Acres × 43,560 = Square feet (2 acres × 43,560 = 87,120 square feet)

640 acres = 1 section = 1 square mile
Acres ÷ 640 = Sections (square miles) (1,280 acres ÷ 640 = 2 sections)
Sections (square miles) × 640 = Acres (2 sections × 640 = 1,280 acres)

■ HOW DO I DETERMINE THE AREA OF A SQUARE OR RECTANGLE?

Length × Width = **Area of a square or rectangle**

■ **FOR EXAMPLE** How many square feet are in a room 15'6" × 30'9"? Remember, we must use like dimensions, so the inches must be converted to feet.

6" ÷ 12 = 0.5' + 15' = 15.5' wide

9" ÷ 12 = 0.75' + 30' = 30.75' long

30.75' × 15.5' = 476.625 square feet

476.625 square feet is the answer.

■ **FOR EXAMPLE** If carpet costs $63 per square yard to install, what would it cost to carpet the room in the previous example?

476.625 square feet ÷ 9 = 52.958333 square yards × $63 per square yard = $3,336.375, or $3,336.38 rounded

$3,336.38 is the answer.

> ■ **FOR EXAMPLE** How many acres are there in a parcel of land that measures 450' × 484'?
>
> 484' × 450' = 217,800 square feet ÷ 43,560 = 5 acres of land
>
> **5 acres** is the answer.

■ HOW DO I DETERMINE THE AREA OF A TRIANGLE?

½ Base × Height = **Area of a triangle**

or

Base × Height ÷ 2 = **Area of a triangle**

> ■ **FOR EXAMPLE** How many square feet are contained in a triangular parcel of land that is 400 feet on the base and 200 feet high?
>
> 400' × 200' ÷ 2 = 40,000 square feet
>
> **40,000 square feet** is the answer.
>
> ■ **FOR EXAMPLE** How many acres are in a three-sided tract of land that is 300' on the base and 400' high?
>
> 300' × 400' ÷ 2 = 60,000 square feet ÷ 43,560 = 1.377 acres
>
> **1.377 acres** is the answer.

■ HOW DO I SOLVE FOR VOLUME?

Volume is the space inside a three-dimensional object. Volume is measured in *cubic units*. We will look at calculating the volume of boxes and triangular prisms because there are three measures (length, width, and height). Multiplying three measures results in cubic units; for example, feet times feet times feet equals cubic feet.

■ HOW DO I CONVERT FROM ONE KIND OF VOLUME MEASUREMENT TO ANOTHER?

1,728 cubic inches = 1 cubic foot
Cubic inches ÷ 1,728 = Cubic feet
(17,280 cubic inches ÷ 1,728 = 10 cubic feet)

Cubic feet × 1,728 = Cubic inches
(10 cubic feet × 1,728 = 17,280 cubic inches)

46,656 cubic inches = 1 cubic yard
Cubic inches ÷ 46,656 = Cubic yards
(93,312 cubic inches ÷ 46,656 = 2 cubic yards)

Cubic yards × 46,656 = Cubic inches
(2 cubic yards × 46,656 = 93,312 cubic inches)

27 cubic feet = 1 cubic yard
Cubic feet ÷ 27 = Cubic yards (270 cubic feet ÷ 27 = 10 cubic yards)
Cubic yards × 27 = Cubic feet (10 cubic yards × 27 = 270 cubic feet)

■ HOW DO I DETERMINE THE VOLUME OF A ROOM?

For purposes of determining volume, think of a room as if it were a box.
Length × Width × Height = **Volume of a box**

■ **FOR EXAMPLE** A building is 500 feet long, 400 feet wide, and 25 feet high. How many cubic feet of space are in this building?

500' × 400' × 25' = 5,000,000 cubic feet

5,000,000 cubic feet is the answer.

■ **FOR EXAMPLE** How many cubic yards of concrete would it take to build a sidewalk measuring 120 feet long; 2 feet, 6 inches wide; and 3 inches thick?

6" ÷ 12' = 0.5' + 2' = 2.5' wide

3" ÷ 12' = 0.25' thick

120' × 2.5' × 0.25' = 75 cubic feet ÷ 27 = 2.778 cubic yards (rounded)

2.778 cubic yards is the answer.

■ HOW DO I DETERMINE THE VOLUME OF A TRIANGULAR PRISM?

The terms *A-frame*, *A-shaped*, or *gable roof* on an exam describe a triangular prism.

½ Base × Height × Width = **Volume of a triangular prism**
or
Base × Height × Width ÷ 2 = **Volume of a triangular prism**

■ **FOR EXAMPLE** An A-frame cabin in the mountains is 50 feet long and 30 feet wide. The cabin is 25 feet high from the base to the highest point. How many cubic feet of space does this A-frame cabin contain?

50' × 30' × 25' ÷ 2 = 18,750 cubic feet

18,750 cubic feet is the answer.

■ **FOR EXAMPLE** A building is 40 feet by 25 feet with a 10-foot-high ceiling. The building has a gable roof that is 8 feet high at the tallest point. How many cubic feet are in this structure, including the roof?

40' × 25' × 10' = 10,000 cubic feet in the building

40' × 25' × 8' ÷ 2 = 4,000 cubic feet in the gable roof

10,000 cubic feet + 4,000 cubic feet = 14,000 cubic feet

14,000 cubic feet is the answer.

SECTION 3

Fractions, Decimals, and Percentages

■ WHAT ARE THE PARTS OF A FRACTION?

The **denominator** shows the number of equal parts in the whole or total. The **numerator** shows the number of those parts with which you are working. In the example below, the whole or total has been divided into eight equal parts, and you have seven of those equal parts.

$$\frac{7}{8} \quad \frac{\text{Numerator}}{\text{Denominator}} \quad \frac{\text{(Top number)}}{\text{(Bottom number)}}$$

■ WHAT IS MEANT BY A *PROPER* AND AN *IMPROPER* FRACTION?

The value of a proper fraction is always less than one whole. ⅞ is an example of a **proper fraction**. ⅞ represents 7 parts out of 8 parts needed to make one whole. All proper fractions have a numerator smaller than the denominator. For example, ⅝ < ¾ < 1.

$$\frac{11}{8} \quad \frac{\text{Numerator}}{\text{Denominator}}$$

This is an example of an **improper fraction.** The value of an improper fraction is always equal to or greater than one whole. The improper fraction ¹¹⁄₈ states you have 11 parts but only need 8 parts to make one whole. All improper fractions have a numerator larger than the denominator. For example, ¹¹⁄₈ > ⁵⁄₄ > 1.

■ WHAT IS A MIXED NUMBER?

11½ is a **mixed number.** You have a whole number plus a fraction. A mixed number is greater than the whole or greater than 1.

■ HOW DO I MULTIPLY FRACTIONS?

When multiplying fractions, numerator is multiplied by numerator, and denominator by denominator. Let's start with an easy question. What is ½ × ¾?

First multiply the numerators (top numbers), 1 × 3 = 3; then the denominators (bottom numbers), 2 × 4 = 8. Thus, ½ × ¾ = ⅜.

What is 4⅔ × 10⅝? The first step is to convert the whole number 4 into thirds. This is done by multiplying 4 × 3 = 12. (Multiply the whole number 4 by the denominator of the fraction, 3.) Thus, the whole number 4 is equal to $^{12}/_3$.

4⅔ is equal to $^{12}/_3$ + ⅔ = $^{14}/_3$.

The next step is to convert the whole number 10 into eighths. This is done by multiplying 10 × 8 = 80. (Multiply the whole number 10 by the denominator of the fraction, 8.) Thus, the whole number 10 is equal to $^{80}/_8$. $^{80}/_8$ + ⅝ = $^{85}/_8$.

So, what is $^{14}/_3$ × $^{85}/_8$? First multiply 14 × 85 = 1,190. Then, 3 × 8 = 24. $^{1,190}/_{24}$ = 49.58. (That is, 1,190 ÷ 24 = 49.58.)

An easier way to work the question is to convert the fractions to decimals.

⅔ is equal to 2 ÷ 3 or 0.67.

⅝ is equal to 5 ÷ 8 or 0.625.

4.67 × 10.625 = 49.62.

When working with fractions or decimal equivalents, you will find that the answers will be close but not exact.

■ HOW DO I DIVIDE BY FRACTIONS?

Dividing by fractions is a two-step process. What is ¾ ÷ ¼?

First, invert the ¼ to $^4/_1$. Then, multiply ¾ × $^4/_1$ = $^{12}/_4$. Finally, 12 ÷ 4 = 3.

You may also convert ¾ to the decimal 0.75 and ¼ to the decimal 0.25.
    0.75 ÷ 0.25 = 3. (There are three 0.25 in 0.75.)

What is 100⅞ ÷ ¾?
    100 × 8 = 800.
    800 + 7 = 80⅞.

¾ is inverted to $^4/_3$.
    80⅞ × $^4/_3$ = 807 × 4 = 3,228; 8 × 3 = 24. $^{3,228}/_{24}$ = 3,228 ÷ 24 = 134.5.
    Or, 7 ÷ 8 = 0.875 and 3 ÷ 4 = 0.75.
    100.875 ÷ 0.75 = 134.50.

■ HOW DO I CONVERT FRACTIONS TO DECIMALS?

Fractions will sometimes be used in real estate math problems. Because calculators may be used on most licensing examinations, it is best to convert fractions to decimals.

MATH TIP To convert a fraction to a decimal, the top number, called the numerator, is divided by the bottom number, the denominator.

For example:

$7/8 = 7 \div 8 = \mathbf{0.875}$
$11/8 = 11 \div 8 = \mathbf{1.375}$
$11\frac{1}{2} = 1 \div 2 = 0.5 + 11 = \mathbf{11.5}$

Once fractions have been converted to decimals, other calculations can be easily completed using the calculator. Note that many calculators automatically display the zero before the decimal point.

■ HOW DO I ADD OR SUBTRACT DECIMALS?

Line up the decimals, add or subtract, and bring the decimal down in the answer. You may add zeros if necessary as placeholders. For example, 0.5 is the same as 0.50, or .5.

```
   0.50         8.20
 +3.25        - 0.75
 = 3.75       = 7.45
```

MATH TIP When you use a calculator, the decimal will be in the correct place in the answer (0.5 + 3.25 = 3.75, and 8.2 − 0.75 = 7.45).

■ HOW DO I MULTIPLY DECIMALS?

Multiply the numbers, then count the number of decimal places in each number. Next, start with the last number on the right and move the decimal the total number of decimal places to the left in the answer.

Multiply as you normally would to get the 1,500, then count the four decimal places in the numbers (.20 and .75). In the 1,500, start at the last zero on the right and count four decimal places to the left. The decimal is placed to the left of the **1**.

```
    0.20
  × 0.75
    100
    140
  0.1500 or 0.15
```

MATH TIP When you use a calculator, the decimal will be in the correct place in the answer (0.2 × 0.75 = 0.15).

■ HOW DO I DIVIDE DECIMALS?

Divide the **dividend** (the number being divided) by the **divisor** (the number you are dividing by) and bring the decimal in the dividend straight up in the **quotient** (answer). If the divisor has a decimal, move the decimal to the right of the divisor and move the decimal the same number of places to the right in the dividend. Now divide as stated above.

$$
\begin{array}{r} = 0.75 \\ 2\overline{)1.5} \\ 1.4 \\ 10 \\ 10 \\ 0 \end{array}
\qquad
0.5\overline{)15.5} =
\begin{array}{r} 1 = 31. \\ 5\overline{)155.} \\ 15 \\ 05 \\ 5 \\ 0 \end{array}
$$

MATH TIP When you use a calculator, you can have a decimal in the divisor and the decimal will be in the correct place in the answer (1.5 ÷ 2 = 0.75, and 15.5 ÷ 0.5 = 31).

■ WHAT IS A PERCENTAGE?

Percent (%) means *per hundred* or *per hundred parts*. The whole or total always represents 100%.

5% = 5 parts of 100 parts, or 5 ÷ 100 = 0.05 or 1/20
75% = 75 parts of 100 parts, or 75 ÷ 100 = 0.75 or 3/4
120% = 120 parts of 100 parts, or 120 ÷ 100 = 1.2 or 1 1/5

■ HOW CAN I CONVERT A PERCENTAGE TO A DECIMAL?

Move the decimal *two places* to the *left* and *drop* the % sign.

20% = 2 ÷ 100 = 0.20 or **0.2**
1% = 1 ÷ 100 = **0.01**
12 1/4 = 12.25%, 12.25 ÷ 100 = **0.1225**

See Figure 3.1.

FIGURE 3.1

Converting Decimal to Percentage and Percentage to Decimal

Decimal to Percentage

.10 ⟹ 10%

Move decimal two places right to find the percentage

Percentage to Decimal

.10 ⟸ 10%

Move percentage two places left to find the decimal

■ HOW CAN I CONVERT A DECIMAL TO A PERCENTAGE?

Move the decimal *two places* to the *right* and *add* the % sign.

$$0.25 = 25\%$$
$$0.9 = 90\%$$
$$0.0875 = 8.75\% \text{ or } 8\tfrac{3}{4}\%$$

See Figure 3.1.

■ HOW DO I MULTIPLY BY PERCENTAGES?

$$500 \times 25\% = 500 \times \tfrac{25}{100} = \tfrac{12{,}500}{100} = 125$$
or
$$500 \times 25\% = 125, \text{ or } 500 \times 0.25 = 125$$

■ HOW DO I DIVIDE BY PERCENTAGES?

$$100 \div 5\% = 100 \div \tfrac{5}{100} = 100 \times \tfrac{100}{5} = \tfrac{10{,}000}{5} = 2{,}000$$
or
$$100 \div 5\% = 2{,}000, \text{ or } 100 \div 0.05 = 2{,}000$$

■ IS THERE ANY EASY WAY TO REMEMBER HOW TO SOLVE PERCENTAGE PROBLEMS?

The following three formulas are important for solving all percentage problems:

Total × Rate = Part
Part ÷ Rate = Total
Part ÷ Total = Rate

There is a simple way to remember how to use these formulas:

■ **Multiply** when **Part** is **unknown**.
■ **Divide** when **Part** is **known**.
■ When you divide, always enter **Part** into the calculator first.

■ WHAT IS THE T-BAR METHOD?

The T-Bar is another tool to use to solve percentage problems. For some people, the "three-formula method" is more difficult to remember than the visual image of a T.

```
              ÷ Part ÷
   ─────────────────────────
       Total    │    Rate
                │
                ×
```

■ HOW DO I USE THE T-BAR?

The procedure for using the T-Bar is as follows:

1. Enter the two *known* items in the correct places.
2. If the line between the two items is *vertical*, you *multiply* to equal the missing item.
3. If the line between the two items is *horizontal*, you *divide* to equal the missing item. When you divide, the top (**Part**) always goes into the calculator first and is divided by the bottom (**Total** or **Rate**).

See Figure 3.2.

FIGURE 3.2

Using the T-Bar

The following examples show how the T-Bar can be used to solve percentage problems. These examples deal with discounts because everyone can relate to buying an item that is on sale. Later, we will see how the T-Bar can be used for many types of real estate problems.

■ **FOR EXAMPLE** John purchased a new suit that was marked $500. How much did John save if it was on sale for 20% off?

= ? ($100)	
$500	20%
total price	0.2

$100 Saved

$500 × 20% (0.20) = $100

How much did John pay for the suit?

$500 total price − $100 discount = **$400 paid**

or

100% total price − 20% discount = 80% paid

= ? ($400)	
$500	80%
total price	0.8

$400 paid

$500 × 80% (0.80) = $400

■ **FOR EXAMPLE** Susie paid $112.50 for a dress that was reduced 25%. How much was it originally marked?

100% original price − 25% discount = 75% paid

$112.50 ÷	
= ? ($150)	75%
	0.75

$150 original price

$112.50 ÷ 75% (0.75) = $150

■ **FOR EXAMPLE** Chris paid $127.50 for a coat that was marked down from the original price of $150. What percent of discount did Chris receive?

$150 original price − $127.50 discount price = $22.50 discount

÷ 22.50 discount	
($150) = ? original price	**(0.15 = 15%) 15%** 0.85

15% discount

$22.50 ÷ $150 = 0.15, or 15%

or

÷ $127.50 paid	
$150 original price	= (0.85 = 85%) 0.15

85% of original price paid

$127.50 ÷ $150 = 0.85, or 85%

85% was the percent paid; therefore

100% original price − 85% paid = **15% discount**

■ WORD PROBLEMS CAN BE TRICKY. HOW SHOULD I DEAL WITH THEM?

There are five important steps that must be taken to solve word problems.

1. **Read** the problem carefully and completely. Never touch the calculator until you have read the entire problem.
2. **Analyze** the problem to determine what is being asked, what facts are given that *will* be needed to solve for the answer, and what facts are given that *will not* be needed to solve for the answer. Eliminate any information and/or numbers given that are not needed to solve the problem. Take the remaining information and/or numbers and determine which will be needed first, second, et cetera, depending on the number of steps it will take to solve the problem.
3. **Choose** the proper formula(s) and steps it will take to solve the problem.
4. **Insert** the known elements and calculate the answer.

5. **Check** your answer to be sure you keyed in the numbers and functions properly on your calculator. Be sure you finished the problem. For example, when the problem asks for the salesperson's share of the commission, do not stop at the broker's share of the commission and mark that answer just because it is one of the choices.

SECTION 4: Percentage Problems

■ HOW DO I WORK COMMISSION PROBLEMS?

The full **commission** is a percentage of the sales price, unless it is stated differently in the problem. Remember that full commission rates, commission splits between brokers, and commission splits between the brokerage firm and brokers are always negotiable. Always read a problem carefully to determine the correct rate(s).

```
            ÷ Full commission ÷
Sales price  |  Full commission rate
             ×
```

Sales price × Full commission rate = **Full commission**
Full commission ÷ Full commission rate = **Sales price**
Full commission ÷ Sales price = **Full commission rate**

```
              ÷ Firm's share of the commission ÷
Full commission  |  % of full commission to
                 |          the firm
                 ×
```

| Full commission | × | % of full commission to the firm | = | **Firm's share of the commission** |

| Firm's share of the commission | ÷ | % of full commission to the broker | = | **Full commission** |

| Firm's share of the commission | ÷ | Full commission | = | **% of full commission to the firm** |

```
              ÷ Broker's share of the commission ÷
Firm's share of  |  Broker's % of the
the commission   |     firm's share
                 ×
```

Firm's share of the commission	×	Broker's % of the firm's share	=	**Broker's share of the commission**
Broker's share of the commission	÷	Broker's % of the firm's share	=	**Firm's share of the commission**
Broker's share of the commission	÷	Firm's share of the commission	=	**Broker's % of the firm's share**

■ **FOR EXAMPLE** A seller listed a home for $200,000 and agreed to pay a full commission rate of 5%. The home sold 4 weeks later for 90% of the list price. The listing firm agreed to give the selling firm 50% of the commission. The listing firm paid the listing broker 50% of her share of the commission, and the selling firm paid the selling broker 60% of his share of the commission. How much commission did the selling broker receive?

```
              = $180,000 sales price
$200,000         |                 90%
list price       |                 or 0.9
                 ×
```

$200,000 × 90% (0.90) = $180,000

```
              = $90,000 full commission
$180,000         |                 5%
sales price      |                 or 0.05
                 ×
```

$180,000 × 5% (0.05) = $9,000

```
              = $4,500 firm's share of the commission
$9,000           |                 50%
full commission  |                 or 0.5
                 ×
```

$9,000 × 50% (0.50) = $4,500

```
              = $2,700 broker's commission
$4,500 broker's share  |           60%
of commission          |           or 0.6
                       ×
```

$4,500 × 60% (0.60) = $2,700

$2,700 selling broker's commission is the answer.

Section 4   Percentage Problems   **729**

■ WHAT IS MEANT BY SELLER'S DOLLARS AFTER COMMISSION?

The first deduction from the sales price is the real estate commission. For example, if a house sold for $100,000 and a 7% commission was paid, that means $7,000 was paid in commissions. The seller still has 93%, or $93,000. The seller's dollars after commission will be used to pay the seller's other expenses and hopefully will leave some money for the seller.

÷ Seller's dollars after commission ÷	
Sales price	Percentage after commission
×	

Remember, the sales price is 100%. Thus, 100% − Commission % = Percent after commission.

Sales price × Percentage after commission = **Seller's dollars after commission**

Seller's dollars after commission ÷ Percentage after commission = **Sales price**

Seller's dollars after commission ÷ Sales price = **Percentage after commission**

■ **FOR EXAMPLE**   After deducting $5,850 in closing costs and a 5% brokerage commission, the sellers received their original cost of $175,000 plus a $4,400 profit. What was the sales price of the property?

$5,850 closing costs + $175,000 original cost + $4,400 profit = $185,250 seller's dollars after commission

100% sales price − 5% commission = 95% after commission

$185,250 seller's dollars after commission ÷	
= $195,000 sales price	95% or 0.95

$185,250 ÷ 95% (0.95) = $195,000

$195,000 sales price is the answer.

HOW DO I DETERMINE INTEREST?

Interest is the cost of using money. The amount of interest paid is determined by the agreed annual interest rate, the amount of money borrowed (loan amount) or the amount of money still owed (loan balance), and the period of time the money is held. When a lender grants a loan for real estate, the loan-to-value ratio (LTV) is the percentage of the sales price or appraised value, whichever is less, that the lender is willing to lend.

÷ Loan amount ÷	
Sales price or appraised value (whichever is less)	Loan-to-value ratio (LTV)

×

| Sales price or appraised value (whichever is less) | × | Loan-to-value ratio (LTV) | = | **Loan amount** |

| Loan amount | ÷ | Loan-to-value ratio (LTV) | = | **Sales price** or **appraised value** (whichever is less) |

| Loan amount | ÷ | Sales price or appraised value (whichever is less) | = | **Loan-to-value ratio (LTV)** |

÷ Annual interest ÷	
Loan amount (principal)	Annual interest rate

×

| Loan amount | × | Annual interest rate | = | **Annual interest** |

| Annual interest | × | Annual interest rate | = | **Loan amount** |

| Annual interest | × | Loan amount | = | **Annual interest rate** |

■ **FOR EXAMPLE** A parcel of real estate sold for $335,200. The lender granted a 90% loan at 7.5% for 30 years. The appraised value on this parcel was $335,500. How much interest is paid to the lender in the first monthly payment?

= $301,680 loan amount ÷	
$335,200 sales price	90% or 0.9

×

$335,200 × 90% (0.90) = $301,680 Loan

= $22,626 annual interest
| $301,680 | 7.5% |
| loan amount | or 0.075 |
×

$301,680 × 7.5% (0.075) = $22,626

$22,626 annual interest ÷ 12 months = $1,885.50 monthly interest

$1,885.50 interest in the first monthly payment is the answer.

■ HOW MUCH INTERIM INTEREST WILL BE DUE AT CLOSING?

Interim interest is charged by a lender when a borrower obtains a new loan. This interest is called *interim* because it is for the interim period of time from the day of closing through the end of the closing month. Most real estate loan interest is paid in arrears, but interim interest is an example of interest paid in advance.

If a borrower closes on a loan on June 12, then the borrower will owe interim interest for 19 days. The first full payment (PI) will be due August 1; this payment will include interest for July. If the closing is September 21, interim interest for 10 days will be paid at closing, and the first full payment will be due November 1 (paying interest for October).

■ **FOR EXAMPLE** A borrower is closing on a $114,300 loan with an interest rate of 6.75% on November 18. How much interim interest will be due at closing? The first full payment is due January 1.

30 days in November − 18 (days until closing) = 12 days + 1 (day of closing) = 13 days

$114,300 × 6.75% = 7,715.25 annual interest

$7,715.25 ÷ 360 = $21.43125 interest per day

$21.43125 × 13 days = $278.61 (rounded) interim interest due at closing

$278.61 interim interest due at closing is the answer.

■ HOW DO I DETERMINE MONTHLY PRINCIPAL AND INTEREST PAYMENTS?

A **loan payment factor** can be used to calculate the monthly principal and interest payment on a loan. The factor represents the monthly principal and interest payment to amortize a $1,000 loan and is based on the annual interest rate and the term of the loan.

Loan amount ÷ $1,000 × Loan payment factor = **Monthly PI payment**
Monthly PI payment × Loan payment factor = **Loan amount**

■ **FOR EXAMPLE** If the lender in the previous example uses a loan payment factor of $6.99 per $1,000 of loan amount, what will be the monthly PI (principal and interest) payment?

$301,680 loan amount ÷ $1,000 × $6.99 = $2,108.74 monthly PI payment

$2,108.74 monthly PI payment is the answer.

■ HOW DO I WORK PROBLEMS ABOUT POINTS?

The word *point* means percent. One **point** equals 1% of the loan amount.

Two points mean 2%, or ½ point means ½%. A loan point is a percentage of the loan amount.

```
            ÷ Amount for points ÷
Loan amount   |   Points converted
              |   to a percentage
              ×
```

Loan amount × Points converted to a percentage = **Amount for points**

Amount for points ÷ Points converted to a percentage = **Loan amount**

Amount for points ÷ Loan amount = **Points converted to a percentage**

■ **FOR EXAMPLE** The lender will charge 3½ loan discount points on an $80,000 loan. What will be the total amount due?

```
              ÷ Amount for points ÷
$80,000       |                3.5%
loan amount   |            or 0.035
              ×
```

$80,000 × 3.5% (0.035) = $2,800

$2,800 for points is the answer.

■ HOW DO I DETERMINE PROFIT?

A **profit** is made when we sell something for more than we paid for it. If we sell something for less than we paid, we have suffered a **loss**.

Sales price − Cost = Profit

When setting the T-Bar, the whole is the original investment or cost (i.e., the amount paid years ago). The original cost must be the whole thing (the 100%)

because percentages of profit or loss are percentages of the money invested. A 20% loss is 20% of the original investment.

	÷ Profit ÷
Cost	Percentage of profit
×	

Cost	×	Percentage of profit	=	**Profit**
Profit	÷	Percentage of profit	=	**Cost**
Profit	÷	Cost	=	**Percentage of profit**

The cost plus the profit equals the sales price. The cost minus the loss equals the sales price.

	÷ Sales price ÷
Cost	Percentage sold of cost
×	

(100% Cost + % Profit = % Sales price)

Cost	×	Percentage sold of cost	=	**Sales price**
Sales price	÷	Percentage sold of cost	=	**Cost**
Sales price	÷	Cost	=	**Percentage sold of cost**

■ **FOR EXAMPLE** Your home listed for $285,000 and sold for $275,000, which gave you a 10% profit over the original cost. What was the original cost?

100% original cost + 10% profit = 110% sales price

	÷ $275,000 sales price ÷
Original cost	110% or 1.1
×	

$275,000 ÷ 110% (1.1) = $250,000

$250,000 original cost is the answer.

■ **FOR EXAMPLE** You invested in a mountain cabin a few years ago. You just sold the cabin for $80,640 losing 16% of your investment. What was the original cost of the cabin? The $80,640 is today's value after suffering a 16% loss.

100% original investment − 16% loss = 84% today's value

```
            ÷ $80,640 sales price ÷
─────────────────────────────────────────
Original investment      │         84%
                         │       or 0.84
                         ×
```

$80,640 ÷ 0.84 = $96,000

$96,000 original investment is the answer.

■ WHAT IS THE DIFFERENCE BETWEEN APPRECIATION AND DEPRECIATION?

Appreciation is increase in value. **Depreciation** is decrease in value. Both are based on the original cost. We will only cover the **straight-line method,** which is what should be used in math problems, unless you are told differently. The straight-line method means that the value is increasing (appreciating) or decreasing (depreciating) the same amount each year. The amount of appreciation or depreciation is based on the original cost.

However, to calculate more than one year's worth of appreciation or depreciation while using an "average annual rate," lump them together. For example, 4% for 5 years = 20%. An "over previous year's value" means year by year. If depreciation is 2 percent for 3 years, then divide today's value by 98% three times. If the appreciation is 6% for two years, then divide today's value by 106% twice.

■ HOW DO I SOLVE APPRECIATION PROBLEMS?

```
            ÷ Annual appreciation ÷
─────────────────────────────────────────
Cost                     │ Annual appreciation rate
                         ×
```

Cost × Annual appreciation rate = **Annual appreciation**

Annual appreciation ÷ Annual appreciation rate = **Cost**

Annual appreciation ÷ Cost = **Annual appreciation rate**

Annual appreciation rate × Number of years = **Total appreciation rate**
100% Cost + Total appreciation rate = **Today's value as a percentage**

```
         ÷ Today's value (appreciated value) ÷
─────────────────────────────────────────────────
Cost                     │ Today's value as a percentage
                         ×
```

| Cost | × | Today's value as a percentage | = | **Today's value (appreciated value)** |

| Today's value (appreciated value) | ÷ | Today's value as a percentage | = | **Cost** |

| Today's value (appreciated value) | ÷ | Cost | = | **Today's value as a percentage** |

■ **FOR EXAMPLE** Seven years ago you purchased a piece of real estate for $93,700, including the original cost of the land, which was $6,700. What is the total value of the land today using an appreciation rate of 8% per year?

8% appreciation per year × 7 years = 56% total appreciation rate

100% cost + 56% appreciation = 156% today's value

Today's value	
$6,700 original cost	156% or 1.56
×	

$6,700 × 156% (1.56) = $10,452

$10,452 today's value is the answer.

■ HOW DO I SOLVE DEPRECIATION PROBLEMS?

	÷ Annual depreciation ÷	
Cost		Annual depreciation rate
	×	

| Cost | × | Annual depreciation rate | = | **Annual depreciation** |

| Annual depreciation | ÷ | Annual depreciation rate | = | **Cost** |

| Annual depreciation | ÷ | Cost | = | **Annual depreciation rate** |

Annual depreciation rate × Number of years = **Total depreciation rate**

100% Cost − Total depreciation rate = **Today's value as a percentage**

$$\frac{\div \text{ Today's value (depreciated value) } \div}{\text{Cost} \quad | \quad \text{Today's value as a percentage}}$$
$$\times$$

Cost × Today's value as a percentage = **Today's value (depreciated value)**

Today's value (depreciated value) ÷ Today's value as a percentage = **Cost**

Today's value (depreciated value) ÷ Cost = **Today's value as a percentage**

■ **FOR EXAMPLE** The value of a house without the lot at the end of four years is $132,300. What was the original cost of the house if the yearly rate of depreciation was 2.5%?

2.5% depreciation per year × 4 years = 10% total depreciation rate

100% cost − 10% depreciation = 90% today's value

$$\frac{\$132{,}300 \text{ today's value } \div}{\text{Original cost} \quad | \quad 90\% \text{ or } 0.9}$$
$$\times$$

$132,300 ÷ 90% (0.90) = $147,000

$147,000 original cost is the answer.

■ HOW DO I ESTIMATE VALUE FOR INCOME-PRODUCING PROPERTIES?

When appraising income-producing property, the value is estimated by using the annual net operating income (NOI) and the current market rate of return or capitalization rate. Annual scheduled gross income is adjusted for vacancies and credit losses to arrive at the annual effective gross income. The annual operating expenses are deducted from the annual effective gross income to arrive at the annual NOI.

Vacancy/credit loss is usually expressed as a percentage of the scheduled gross.

Scheduled gross income − Vacancies and credit losses = **Effective gross income**

Effective gross income − Annual operating expenses = **NOI**

Section 4   Percentage Problems   **737**

```
                    ÷ NOI ÷
Value          |        Annual rate of return
               ×         (capitalization rate)
```

NOI   ÷   Rate of return   =   **Value**

Value   ×   Rate of return   =   **NOI**

NOI   ÷   Value   =   **Rate of return**

■ **FOR EXAMPLE**   An office building produces $132,600 annual gross income. If the annual expenses are $30,600 and the appraiser estimates the value using an 8.5% rate of return, what is the estimated value?

$132,600 annual gross income − $30,600 annual expenses = $102,000 NOI

```
               $102,000 NOI
Value     |         8.5% rate
          |         of return
          |         or 0.085
          ×
```

$102,000 ÷ 8.5% = $1,200,000

$1,200,000 value is the answer.

The above formulas also can be used to calculate either the return on investment (ROI) for real estate investing or the monthly NOI. The total becomes *original cost* or *investment* instead of value.

■ **FOR EXAMPLE**   You invest $335,000 in a property that should produce a 9% rate of return. What monthly NOI will you receive?

```
                     NOI
$335,000        |              9%
investment      |              or 0.09
                ×
```

$335,000 × 9% (0.09) = $30,150

$30,150 NOI ÷ 12 months = $2,512.50

$2,512.50 monthly NOI is the answer.

■ HOW DO I SOLVE PROBLEMS INVOLVING PERCENTAGE LEASES?

When establishing the rent to be charged in a lease for retail space, the lease may be a percentage lease instead of a lease based on dollars per square foot. In a **percentage lease**, there is normally a base or minimum monthly rent plus a percentage of the gross sales in excess of an amount set in the lease. The percentage lease also can be set up as a percentage of the total gross sales or of the base/minimum rent, whichever is larger. We will look at the minimum plus percentage lease only.

Gross sales − Gross sales not subject to the percentage = **Gross sales subject to the percentage**

Gross sales subject to the percentage × % in the lease = Percentage rent

Percentage rent ÷ % in the lease = Gross sales subject to the percentage

Percentage rent ÷ Gross sales subject to the percentage = % in the lease

Add the percentage rent and the base/minimum rent to find the total rent. Compute the total rent by combining the percentage rent and the base/minimum rent. Together they equal the total rent.

■ **FOR EXAMPLE** A lease calls for monthly minimum rent of $900 plus 3% of annual gross sales in excess of $270,000. What was the annual rent in a year when the annual gross sales were $350,600?

$900 monthly minimum rent × 12 months = $10,800 annual minimum rent

$350,600 annual gross sales − $270,000 annual gross sales not subject to the percentage = $80,600 annual gross sales subject to the percentage

$80,600 annual gross subject to the percentage × 3% or 0.03 = $2,418 annual percentage rent

$80,600 × 3% = $2,418 annual percentage rent

$10,800 annual minimum rent + $2,418 annual percentage rent = $13,218 total annual rent

$13,218 total annual rent is the answer.

SECTION 5

Proration Problems

Prorate means to divide proportionately. Some expenses and income may be prorated for the closing of a real estate transaction. We will look at prorating interest on a loan, ad valorem taxes on a property, homeowners' insurance on a property, and rent on income-producing property.

■ WHAT ARE THE DIFFERENT CALENDARS USED FOR PRORATING?

When we prorate, we calculate the number of days owed for the expense or the rental income. The days may be calculated using a *banker's year*, *statutory year*, or *calendar year*. The **banker's year** and **statutory year** are the same because they both contain 12 months with 30 days in each month. The total number of days in both a banker's year and a statutory year is 360 days. The **calendar year** contains 12 months with 28 to 31 days in each month. The total number of days in a calendar year is 365. The total number of days in a calendar *leap* year is 366. The following chart shows the days in each month.

FIGURE 5.1

Days in Each Month

	Banker's or Statutory Year	Calendar Year	Calendar Leap Year
January	30	31	31
February	30	28	29
March	30	31	31
April	30	30	30
May	30	31	31
June	30	30	30
July	30	31	31
August	30	31	31
September	30	30	30
October	30	31	31
November	30	30	30
December	30	31	31
Total days in a year	360	365	366

WHAT IS THE DIFFERENCE BETWEEN PRORATING THROUGH AND PRORATING TO THE DAY OF CLOSING?

In a proration problem, we will be told whether to prorate *through* the day of closing or *to* the day of closing. **This is very important when calculating the days owed. When we prorate *through* the day of closing, the *seller* is responsible for the day of closing. When we prorate *to* the day of closing, the *buyer* is responsible for the day of closing.**

HOW DO I CALCULATE PRORATION PROBLEMS?

Once we know the number of days owed, we then need to know the amount of the expense or income per day. We take either the annual amount divided by the total days in the year to get the daily amount or the monthly amount divided by the total days in the month to get the daily amount.

MATH TIP Be sure you use the correct type of year (banker's or statutory year of 360 days, calendar year of 365 days, or calendar leap year of 366 days) when computing the daily amount.

The final step is to multiply the amount per day by the number of days owed to get the prorated amount.

WHAT IS THE DIFFERENCE BETWEEN DEBIT AND CREDIT IN A PRORATION PROBLEM?

To calculate a proration problem, you need to know how expenses and income are posted on the closing statement. **Debit** takes money from a person. **Credit** gives money to a person. (See Figure 5.2.) When the prorated amount involves both the buyer and the seller, there will always be a double entry (i.e., it appears twice, once as a debit to one party and once as a credit to the other party). If the seller owes the buyer, the prorated amount will be debited to the seller and credited to the buyer. If the buyer owes the seller, the prorated amount will be debited to the buyer and credited to the seller. When the prorated amount involves the buyer and someone other than the seller, there will be only a single entry. When the prorated amount involves the seller and someone other than the buyer, there will be only a single entry. We will discuss debits and credits as we learn to prorate each expense.

FIGURE 5.2

The Debit/Credit Flow

		Buyer	Seller
	Sales Price	DEBIT	CREDIT
	Tenants' Security Deposits	CREDIT	DEBIT
	Fuel Oil (in tank)	DEBIT	CREDIT
	Prorated Accrued Water Bill	CREDIT	DEBIT
	Unearned Rents	CREDIT	DEBIT
	Tax Reserve Account	DEBIT	CREDIT

Different items are treated differently as credits or debits to the buyer or seller on a closing statement.

The five questions to ask when prorating are as follows:

1. What calendar do we use?
2. Is the expense paid in arrears or in advance?
3. Who has or will pay the expense?
4. Who has earned or received income?
5. When will the expense be paid?

■ HOW DO I CALCULATE INTEREST IN A PRORATION PROBLEM?

When a loan is assumed or paid off, the accrued interest for the month of closing must be prorated. Interest is paid in arrears; therefore, the monthly payment made on the first day of the month pays interest for the entire previous month. The payment includes interest *up to but not including* the day of the payment unless specified otherwise. Not all payments are due on the first day of the month; therefore, pay attention when you are told what day the interest has been paid through. The sellers owe unpaid interest (also called accrued, earned, or current interest) from the date of the last payment to or through the closing date.

If the prorations are to be calculated *through* the day of closing, the seller will owe payments *including* the day of closing. If the prorations are to be calculated *to* the day of closing, the seller will *owe up to but not including* the day of closing. Remember to use the correct type of year. A banker's or statutory year has 360 days. A calendar year has 365 days. A calendar leap year has 366 days. When a loan is paid off, unpaid interest is calculated and added to the outstanding loan balance and is a **debit** *to the seller only*. Loan payoff is the sum of the principal balance and the accrued interest. On an assumption of the loan, the interest proration is a **debit** to the *seller* and a **credit** to the *buyer*.

■ **FOR EXAMPLE** A home was purchased on April 4, 2010, for $110,000, and the closing was set for May 8, 2010. The buyer assumed the balance of the seller's $93,600 loan with 11.5% interest and monthly payments of $990.29 due on the first day of each month. How much will the interest proration be, using a banker's year and prorating through the day of closing? Who will be debited and who will be credited?

Banker's Year/Statutory Year

Step 1. Find the exact number of days of earned or accrued interest.

Seller owes 8 days (May 1 *through* May 8).

Note: It would be 7 days (8 days minus 1 day) if the problem had said prorate *to* the day of closing.

Step 2. Find the daily interest charge. Outstanding loan balance × Annual interest rate = Annual interest ÷ 360 days per year = Daily interest.

$93,600 × 11.5% (0.115) = $10,764 annual interest ÷ 360 days = $29.90 daily interest

Step 3. Compute the total amount of accrued interest. Daily interest × Days owed = Interest proration.

$29.90 daily interest × 8 days = $239.20

$239.20 debit seller, credit buyer is the answer.

Calendar Year (if the problem had said to use a calendar year)

Step 1. Find the exact number of days of earned or accrued interest.

Seller owes 8 days (May 1 *through* May 8).

Note: It would be 7 days (8 days minus 1 day) if the problem had said prorate *to* the day of closing.

Step 2. Find the daily interest charge. Outstanding loan balance × Annual interest rate = Annual interest ÷ 365 days per year = Daily interest.

$93,600 × 11.5% (0.115) = $10,764 annual interest ÷ 365 days = $29.49041096 daily interest

Step 3. Compute the total amount of accrued interest. Daily interest × Days owed = Interest proration.

$29.49041096 daily interest × 8 days = $235.92 rounded

$235.92 debit seller, credit buyer is the answer.

■ HOW DO I PRORATE TAXES?

Real estate taxes are normally assessed from January 1 through December 31. The tax rate is *always* applied *to the assessed value of the property* instead of the market value. Taxes are usually paid in arrears; therefore, the seller will owe the buyer for accrued taxes from January 1 *through* the day of closing or *to* the day of closing. The most recent tax bill is used to compute the proration, and this is usually the past year's tax bill. Remember to use the correct type of year. A banker's or statutory year has 360 days. A calendar year has 365 days. A calendar leap year has 366 days.

If the taxes are paid in arrears, the tax proration will be a **debit** to the *seller* and a **credit** to the *buyer*. If the taxes are paid in advance, the tax proration will be a **debit** to the *buyer* and a **credit** to the *seller*.

■ **FOR EXAMPLE** The market value of a home is $115,000. For tax purposes, the home is assessed at 90% of the market value. The annual tax rate is $2.50 per $100 of assessed value. If the closing is on March 13, 2010, what is the prorated amount? Prorations are calculated through the day of closing and using a statutory year.

Banker's Year/Statutory Year

Step 1. Find the exact number of days of accrued taxes from the beginning of the tax period (January 1, 2010) up to and including the day of closing (March 13, 2010).

2 months (January and February) × 30 days per month = 60 days + 13 days in March = 73 days

Note: It would be 72 days (73 days minus 1 day) if the problem had said prorate *to* the day of closing.

Step 2. Calculate the annual taxes. Market value × Assessment ratio = Assessed value ÷ $100 × Tax rate per hundred = Annual taxes.

$115,000 × 90% = $103,500 ÷ $100 × $2.50 = $2,587.50 annual taxes

Step 3. Find the tax amount per day. Annual taxes ÷ 360 days per year = Daily taxes.

$2,587.50 ÷ 360 days = $7.1875 daily taxes

Step 4. Compute the prorated tax amount. Daily taxes × Days owed = Tax proration.

$7.1875 per day × 73 days = $524.69 rounded

$524.69 debit seller, credit buyer is the answer.

Calendar Year (if the problem had said to use a calendar year)

Step 1. Find the exact number of days of accrued taxes from the beginning of the tax period (January 1, 2010) up to and including the day of closing (March 13, 2010).

31 days in January + 28 days in February + 13 days in March = 72 days

Note: It would be 71 days (72 days minus 1 day) if the problem had said prorate *to* the day of closing.

Step 2. Calculate the annual taxes. Market value × Assessment ratio = Assessed value ÷ $100 × Tax rate per hundred = Annual taxes.

$115,000 × 90% = $103,500 ÷ $100 × $2.50 = $2,587.50 annual taxes

Step 3. Find the tax amount per day. Annual taxes ÷ 365 days per year = Daily taxes.

$2,587.50 ÷ 365 days = $7.089041096 daily taxes

Step 4. Compute the prorated tax amount. Daily taxes × Days owed = Tax proration.

$7.089041096 per day × 72 days = $510.41 rounded

$510.41 debit seller, credit buyer is the answer.

■ IS INSURANCE ALWAYS PRORATED?

When buying a home, insurance coverage must be provided by the owners if they have a loan. The buyers normally purchase their own insurance policy. There will *not* be a proration if the buyers purchase a new policy because the sellers will cancel their existing policy effective the day of closing and the buyer's new policy will become effective the day of closing.

■ IF INSURANCE IS PRORATED, HOW DO I CALCULATE IT?

If the insurance company will allow a policy to be assumed and the buyers choose to do so, an insurance proration is necessary. Today, insurance policies are written for one year. The premiums are payable in advance; therefore, the sellers have paid the entire yearly premium. If the policy is transferred to the buyers, the buyers owe the sellers for the unused portion of the policy. If you are to prorate *through* the day of closing, the buyers owe the sellers from the day after closing until the expiration of the policy. If you are to prorate *to* the day of closing, the buyers owe the sellers starting with the day of closing until the expiration of the policy. Insurance policies become effective at 12:01 am and expire exactly one year later at 12:01 am; therefore, no coverage is counted on the day of expiration of the insurance policy. Remember to use the correct type of year. A banker's or statutory year has 360 days. A calendar year has 365 days. A calendar leap year has 366 days. The insurance proration will be a **debit** to the *buyer* and a **credit** to the *seller*.

■ **FOR EXAMPLE** A one-year fire insurance policy expires on August 20, 2010. The total premium for this policy was $800 and was paid in full in 2009. The house was sold, and the closing date was set for January 25, 2010. The proration is to be calculated through the day of closing using a banker's year. What will be the total credit to the seller to transfer the insurance policy to the buyer?

Banker's Year/Statutory Year

Step 1. Compute the number of days of insurance coverage that the buyer assumed.

	30	days in January
−	25	day of closing
	5	days left in January
+	180	days (6 months × 30 days per month/February–July)
+	19	days coverage in August
	204	days left on the policy

Note: It would be 205 days (204 days plus 1 day) if the problem had said prorate *to* the day of closing.

Step 2. Compute the amount of the policy cost per day. Annual insurance premium ÷ 360 days per year = Daily insurance.

$800 insurance premium ÷ 360 days = $2.2222222 daily insurance

Step 3. Calculate what the buyer owes. Daily insurance × Days left on the policy = Insurance proration.

$2.2222222 daily insurance × 204 days = $453.33 rounded

$453.33 credit seller, debit buyer is the answer.

Calendar Year (if the problem had said to use a calendar year)

Step 1. Compute the number of days of insurance coverage that the buyer assumed.

	31	days in January
−	25	day of closing
	6	days left in January
+	28	days in February
+	31	days in March
+	30	days in April
+	31	days in May
+	30	days in June
+	31	days in July
+	19	days coverage in August
	206	days left on the policy

Note: It would be 207 days (206 days plus 1 day) if the problem had said prorate *to* the day of closing.

Step 2. Compute the amount of the policy cost per day. Annual insurance premium ÷ 365 days per year = Daily insurance.

$800 Insurance premium ÷ 365 days = $2.1917808 daily insurance

Step 3. Calculate what the buyer owes. Daily insurance × Days left on the policy = Insurance proration.

$2.1917808 daily insurance × 206 days = $451.51 rounded

$451.51 credit seller, debit buyer is the answer.

■ HOW DO I PRORATE RENT?

When prorating rents, the amount of rent collected for the month of closing is the only amount prorated. The seller owes the buyer for the unearned rent starting with the day after closing through the end of the month if you are prorating *through* the day of closing. The seller owes the buyer for the unearned rent starting with the day of closing through the end of the month if you are prorating *to* the day of closing. If security deposits are being held by the seller, they are not prorated; therefore, the entire amount of the security deposits are transferred to the buyer. Always use the actual number of days in the month of closing for rent prorations, unless you are told differently. Both the rent proration and the security deposit amount will be a **debit** to the *seller* and a **credit** to the *buyer*.

■ **FOR EXAMPLE** A man is purchasing an apartment complex that contains 15 units that rent for $450 per month. A $450 security deposit is being held on each unit. The sale is to close on March 14, and the March rent has been received for all 15 units. Compute the rent proration by prorating through the day of closing. Compute the security deposit.

Calendar Days (remember to use actual days in the month unless specified differently)

Step 1. Compute the unearned days of rent for the month of closing.

```
  31   days in March
- 14   day of closing
  17   days of unearned rent
```

Note: It would be 18 days (17 days plus 1 day) if the problem had said prorate *to* the day of closing.

Step 2. Compute the daily rent. Monthly rent × Number of units paid = Total rent collected ÷ Number of actual days in the month of closing = Daily rent.

$450 × 15 units = $6,750 monthly rent collected ÷ 31 days in March = $217.7419355 daily rent

Step 3. Compute the prorated rent amount. Daily rent × Days of unearned rent

$217.7419355 daily rent × 17 days = $3,701.61 rounded

Step 4. Compute the security deposit.

$450 per unit × 15 units = $6,750

$3,701.61 rent proration and **$6,750 security deposit** are the answers. They are both **debit seller** and **credit buyer.**

Real Estate Math Practice Problems

1. The value of your house, not including the lot, is $91,000 today. What was the original cost if it has depreciated 5% per year for the past seven years?
   a. $67,407.41
   b. $95,789.47
   c. $122,850.00
   d. $140,000.00

2. What was the price per front foot for a 100' × 125' lot that sold for $125,000?
   a. $1,250
   b. $1,000
   c. $556
   d. $10

3. If the savings and loan gives you a 90% loan on a house valued at $88,500, how much additional cash must you produce as a down payment if you have already paid $4,500 in earnest money?
   a. $3,500
   b. $4,000
   c. $4,350
   d. $8,850

4. What did the owners originally pay for their home if they sold it for $98,672, which gave them a 12% profit over their original cost?
   a. $86,830
   b. $88,100
   c. $89,700
   d. $110,510

5. What would you pay for a building producing $11,250 annual net income and showing a minimum rate of return of 9%?
   a. $125,000
   b. $123,626
   c. $101,250
   d. $122,625

6. The sale of a home is to close on September 28. Included in the sale is a garage apartment that is rented to the tenant for $350 per month. The tenant has paid the September rent. What is the rent proration, using actual days and prorating through the day of closing?
   a. $325.67
   b. $23.33
   c. $350.00
   d. $175.00

7. What is the total cost of a driveway 15' wide, 40' long, and 4" thick if the concrete costs $60.00 per cubic yard and the labor costs $1.25 per square foot?
   a. $527.25
   b. $693.75
   c. $1,194.00
   d. $1,581.75

8. An owner agrees to list his property on the condition that he will receive at least $47,300 after paying a 5% broker's commission and paying $1,150 in closing costs. At what price must it sell?
   a. $48,450
   b. $50,815
   c. $50,875
   d. $51,000

9. A gift shop pays rent of $600 per month plus 2.5% of gross annual sales in excess of $50,000. What was the average monthly rent last year if gross annual sales were $75,000?
   a. $1,125.00
   b. $756.25
   c. $600.00
   d. $652.08

10. Your monthly rent is $525. What is your rent as a percentage of an annual income of $21,000?
    a. 25%
    b. 30%
    c. 33%
    d. 40%

11. Two brokers split the 6% commission on a $73,000 home. The selling salesperson was paid 70% of his broker's share. The listing salesperson was paid 30 of her broker's share. How much did the listing salesperson receive?
    a. $657
    b. $4,380
    c. $1,533
    d. $1,314

12. Find the number of square feet in a lot with a frontage of 75 feet 6 inches and a depth of 140 feet 9 inches.
    a. 10,626.63
    b. 10,652.04
    c. 216.25
    d. 25,510.81

13. You attempt to appraise a 28-unit apartment house, employing the income approach. You discover that each unit rents for $775 a month, an amount that seems consistent with like rental units in the vicinity. For the past five years, the annual expenses of operation have averaged $82,460. The complex has maintained a consistent vacancy rate of 5%. A potential investor is only interested if the return is 9.5 percent. What value would you arrive at using these variables?
    a. $2,741,100
    b. $868,000
    c. $1,736,000
    d. $1,873,100

14. How much interest will the seller owe the buyer for a closing date of August 10 if the outstanding loan balance is $43,580? The interest rate on this assumable loan is 10.5%, and the last payment was paid on August 1. Prorations are to be done through the day of closing, using a statutory year.
    a. $127.11
    b. $254.22
    c. $125.37
    d. $381.33

15. The buyer has agreed to pay $175,000 in sales price, 2.5 loan discount points, and a 1% origination fee. If the buyer receives a 90% loan-to-value ratio, how much will the buyer owe at closing for points and the origination fee?
    a. $1,575.00
    b. $3,937.50
    c. $5,512.50
    d. $6,125.00

16. Calculate eight months' interest on a $5,000 interest-only loan at 9.5%.
    a. $475.00
    b. $316.67
    c. $237.50
    d. $39.58

17. A 100-acre farm is divided into lots for homes. The streets require one-eighth of the whole farm, and there are 140 lots. How many square feet are in each lot?
    a. 43,560
    b. 35,004
    c. 31,114
    d. 27,225

18. The 2004 tax bill on a home was $1,282 and was paid in December 2009. The home sold and will close on April 23, 2010. How much will the tax proration be, using a calendar year and prorating to the day of closing?
    a. $393.38
    b. $402.41
    c. $396.89
    d. $427.33

19. What is the monthly net income on an investment of $115,000 if the rate of return is 12.5%?
    a. $1,150.00
    b. $1,197.92
    c. $7,666.67
    d. $14,375.00

20. A salesperson sells a property for $58,500. The contract he has with his broker is 40% of the full commission earned. The commission due the broker is 6%. What is the salesperson's share of the commission?
    a. $2,106
    b. $1,404
    c. $3,510
    d. $2,340

21. A woman buys 348,480 square feet of land at $0.75 per square foot. She divides the land into half-acre lots. If she keeps three lots for herself and sells the others for $24,125 each, what percentage of profit does she realize?
    a. 47.4%
    b. 32.2%
    c. 20%
    d. 16.7%

22. A homeowners' insurance premium of $437 was paid in full in 2009 for a one-year policy that expires June 6, 2010. The house is sold and scheduled to close on February 16, 2010. The buyers are assuming the sellers' insurance policy. What is the amount of the insurance proration if a banker's year is used and all prorations are done through the day of closing?
    a. $132.31
    b. $134.74
    c. $302.26
    d. $304.69

23. What is the interest rate on a $10,000 loan with semiannual interest of $450?
    a. 7%
    b. 9%
    c. 11%
    d. 13.5%

24. A warehouse is 80 feet wide and 120 feet long with ceilings 14 feet high. If 1,200 square feet of floor surface has been partitioned off, floor to ceiling, for an office, how many cubic feet of space will be left in the warehouse?
    a. 151,200
    b. 134,400
    c. 133,200
    d. 117,600

25. An office building produces $68,580 annual net operating income. What price would you pay for this property to show a minimum return of 12% on your investment?
    a. $489,857
    b. $571,500
    c. $685,800
    d. $768,096

26. A buyer is assuming the balance of a seller's loan. The interest rate is 8% and the last monthly payment of $578.16 was paid on April 1, leaving an outstanding balance of $18,450. Using a banker's year, compute the interest to be paid by the seller if the sale is to close on April 19. Prorate through the day of closing.
    a. $110.83
    b. $82.00
    c. $77.90
    d. $123.00

27. The lot you purchased five years ago for $15,000 has appreciated 3.5% per year. What is it worth today?
    a. $12,375
    b. $15,525
    c. $17,250
    d. $17,625

28. A lot has a frontage of 100 feet and a depth of 150 feet. If the building line regulations call for a setback of 25 feet at the front and 6 feet on the two sides, how many square feet of usable space are left for the building?
    a. 10,350
    b. 11,000
    c. 11,750
    d. 15,000

29. A lease calls for $1,000 per month minimum plus 2% of annual sales in excess of $100,000. What is the annual rent if the annual sales were $150,000?
    a. $12,000
    b. $13,000
    c. $14,000
    d. $15,000

30. In the year 2009, taxes on a home were paid in full and amounted to $1,468. The home was later sold, and the sale closed on August 29, 2010. What was the prorated tax amount using a calendar year if the proration was calculated to the day of closing?
    a. $965.26
    b. $502.74
    c. $970.51
    d. $497.49

31. A tract of land measures 1.25 acres. The lot is 150 feet deep. How much will the lot sell for at $65 per front foot?
    a. $9,750
    b. $8,125
    c. $23,595
    d. $25,420

32. If the broker received a 6.5% commission that was $5,200, what was the sales price of the house?
    a. $80,400
    b. $80,000
    c. $77,200
    d. $86,600

33. A man earns $20,000 per year and can qualify for a monthly PITI payment equal to 25% of his monthly salary. If the annual tax and insurance is $678.24, what loan amount will he will qualify for if the monthly PI payment factor is $10.29 per $1,000 of loan amount?
    a. $66,000
    b. $43,000
    c. $40,500
    d. $35,000

34. Find the cost of building a house 29' × 34' × 17' with a gable roof 8' high at the highest point. The cost of construction is $2.25 per cubic foot.
    a. $55,462.50
    b. $46,588.50
    c. $37,714.50
    d. $27,731.25

35. You invest $50,000 at a rate of return of 12%. What is the net operating income?
    a. $6,000
    b. $5,600
    c. $5,000
    d. $4,167

36. You pay $65.53 monthly interest on a loan bearing 9.25% annual interest. What is the loan amount rounded to the nearest hundred dollars?
    a. $1,400
    b. $2,800
    c. $6,300
    d. $8,500

37. What percentage of profit would you make if you paid $10,500 for a lot, built a home on the lot that cost $93,000, and then sold the lot and house together for $134,550?
    a. 13%
    b. 23%
    c. 30%
    d. 45%

38. You are purchasing a fourplex and closing on November 4. Each apartment rents for $575 per month. On November 1, one apartment is vacant and the other tenants paid their November rent. Compute the rent proration through the day of closing.
    a. $230.00
    b. $306.67
    c. $1,495.00
    d. $1,993.33

39. An income-producing property has $62,500 annual gross income and monthly expenses of $1,530. What is the appraised value if the appraiser uses a 10% capitalization rate?
    a. $441,400
    b. $625,000
    c. $183,600
    d. $609,700

40. A new house and lot cost the buyer $65,000. Of this total price, the lot was estimated to be worth $13,000. The buyer held the property for eight years. Using the straight-line method and assuming an annual depreciation of 1% on the house and an annual increase of 8% on the lot, what would be the total value of the property at the end of eight years?
    a. $47,840
    b. $69,160
    c. $81,120
    d. $101,400

41. The seller received a $121,600 check at closing after paying a 7% commission, $31,000 in other closing costs, and the $135,700 loan payoff. What was the total sales price?
    a. $288,300
    b. $306,300
    c. $308,500
    d. $310,000

42. A fence is being built to enclose a lot 125 feet by 350 feet. If there will be one 10-foot gate, how many running feet of fence will it take?
    a. 465
    b. 600
    c. 940
    d. 960

43. A buyer pays $2,500 each for four parcels of land. He subdivides them into six parcels and sells each of the six parcels for $1,950. What was the buyer's percentage of profit?
    a. 14.5%
    b. 17%
    c. 52%
    d. 78%

44. A property sells for $96,000. If it has appreciated 4% per year straight line for the past five years, what did the owner pay for the property five years ago?
    a. $76,800
    b. $80,000
    c. $92,300
    d. $115,200

45. A woman earns an annual income of $60,000, and her husband earns $2,400 per month. How much can the couple pay monthly for their mortgage payment if the lender uses a 28% qualifying ratio?
    a. $2,072
    b. $1,400
    c. $2,352
    d. $672

46. If a buyer borrows $4,400, agreeing to pay back principal and interest in 18 months, what annual interest rate is the buyer paying if the total payback is $5,588?
    a. 15%
    b. 18%
    c. 21.3%
    d. 27%

47. If you purchase a lot that is 125' × 150' for $6,468.75, what price did you pay per front foot?
    a. $23.52
    b. $43.13
    c. $51.75
    d. $64.69

48. A buyer is granted a 90% loan on a $340,500 home purchase. How much will her monthly principal and interest payment be, using a loan payment factor of $7.16 per $1,000 of loan?
    a. $2,194.18
    b. $4,755.59
    c. $2,437.98
    d. $3,064.50

49. Calculate the amount of commission earned by a broker on a property selling for $61,000 if 6 percent is paid on the first $50,000 and 3 percent on the remaining balance.
    a. $3,330
    b. $3,830
    c. $3,600
    d. $3,930

50. A 50' × 100' lot has a 2,400-square-foot house on it that contains four bedrooms and three bathrooms. What percentage of the lot is not taken up by the house?
    a. 21%
    b. 48%
    c. 50%
    d. 52%

Answer Key for Real Estate Math Practice Problems

1. **d** $140,000.00 original cost

    5% depreciation per year × 7 years = 35% total depreciation
    100% original cost − 35% total depreciation = 65% today's value

$91,000 today's value ÷	
= $140,000 original cost	65% or 0.65

    $91,000 ÷ 65% (0.65) = **$140,000 original cost**

2. **a** $1,250 per front foot

    $125,000 sales price ÷ 100 front feet = **$1,250 per front foot**

3. **c** $4,350 due at closing

    100% value − 90% LTV = 10% down payment

= $8,850 down payment	
$88,500 value ×	10% or 0.1

    $88,500 × 10% (0.10) = $8,850
    $8,850 down payment − $4,500 earnest money = **$4,350 due at closing**

4. **b** $88,100 original cost

    100% original cost + 12% profit = 112% sales price

$98,672 sales price ÷	
= $88,100 original cost	112% or 1.12

    $98,672 ÷ 112% (1.12) = **$88,100 original cost**

5. **a** $125,000 price

$11,250 annual net income ÷	
= $125,000 price	9% or 0.09

    $11,250 ÷ 9% (0.09) = **$125,000 price**

6. **b** $23.33 rent proration

    30 days in September − 28 day of closing = 2 days due
    $350 monthly rent ÷ 30 days = $11.666667 per day × 2 days = **$23.33 rent proration**

755

7. **c $1,194.00 total cost**

   4" ÷ 12 = 0.333'

   Concrete: 40' × 15' × 0.333' = 199.8 cubic feet ÷ 27 = 7.4 cubic yards × $60 per cubic yard = $444

   Labor: 40' × 15' = 600 square feet × $1.25 per square foot = $750

   $444 concrete + $750 labor = **$1,194.00 total cost**

8. **d $51,000 sales price**

   $47,300 net to seller + $1,150 closing costs = $48,450 seller's dollars after commission

   100% sales price – 5% commission = 95% seller's percentage after commission

= $51,000 sales price	$48,450 seller's dollars after commission ÷	95% or 0.95

   $48,450 ÷ 95% (0.95) = **$51,000 sales price**

9. **d $652.08 average monthly rent**

   $75,000 gross annual sales – $50,000 = $25,000 gross annual sales subject to 2.5%

= $625 annual percentage rate		
$25,000 value gross annual sales	×	2.5% or 0.025

   $25,000 × 2.5% (0.025) = $625

   $625 annual percentage rent ÷ 12 months = $52.08 monthly percentage rent

   $600 monthly minimum rent + $52.08 monthly percentage rent = **$652.08 average monthly rent**

10. **b 30%**

    $525 monthly rent × 12 months = $6,300 annual rent

÷ $6,300 annual rent	
$21,000 annual income	= 0.3 or 30%

    $6,300 ÷ $21,000 = 0.30 or **30%**

11. **a $657 commission to Janice**

= $4,380 full commission		
$73,000 sales price	×	6% or 0.06

    $73,000 × 6% (0.06) = $4,380

    $4,380 full commission ÷ 2 brokers = $2,190 broker's share of the commission

= $657 Janice's commission		
$2,190 broker's share of the commission	×	30% 0.3

    $2,190 × 30% (0.30) = **$657 commission**

12. a 10,626.63 square feet

    6" ÷ 12 = 0.5' + 75' = 75.5' frontage

    9" ÷ 12 = 0.75' + 140' = 140.75' depth

    140.75' × 75.5' = **10,626.63 square feet**

13. c $1,736,000 value

    $775 monthly rent × 28 units × 12 months = $260,400 annual scheduled gross income

    $260,400 annual scheduled gross income − 5% vacancy rate = $247,380 annual effective gross income

    $247,380 annual effective gross income − $82,460 annual expenses = $164,920 annual net operating income

÷ $164,920 annual net operating income ÷	
= **$1,736,000 value**	9.5% or 0.095

    $164,920 ÷ 9.5% (0.095) = **$1,736,000 value**

14. a $127.11 interest due

    Seller owes buyer 10 days (August 1 through August 10)

= $4,575.90 annual interest	
$43,580 loan balance ×	10.5% 0.105

    $43,580 × 10.5% (0.105) = $4,575.90

    $4,575.90 annual interest ÷ 360 days = $12.71083 per day × 10 days = **$127.11 interest due**

15. c $5,512.50 for points and origination fee

    2.5 points loan discount + 1 point origination fee = 3.5 points

= $157,500 loan	
$175,000 sales price ×	90% or 0.9

    $175,000 × 90% or (0.90) = $157,500

= $5,512.50 for points and origination fee	
$157,500 loan ×	3.5% or 0.035

    $157,500 × 3.5% (0.035) = **$5,512.50 for points and origination fee**

16. b $316.67 interest

= $475 annual interest	
$5,000 loan ×	9.5% or 0.095

    $5,000 × 9.5% (0.095) = $475

    $475 annual interest ÷ 12 months × 8 months = **$316.67 interest**

17. d   **27,225 square feet per lot**

   1/8 = 1 ÷ 8 = 0.125 for streets

   100 acres × 0.125 = 12.5 acres for streets

   100 acres − 12.5 acres for streets = 87.5 acres for lots × 43,560 = 3,811,500 square feet ÷ 140 lots = **27,225 square feet per lot**

18. a   **$393.38 tax proration**

   Seller owes the buyer January 1 to April 23

     31 January

   + 28 February

   + 31 March

   + 22 April

    112 days due

   $1,282 annual tax ÷ 365 days = $3.51233 per day × 112 days = **$393.38 tax proration**

19. b   **$1,197.92 monthly net operating income**

   $$\frac{= \$14{,}375 \text{ annual net operating income}}{\$115{,}000 \text{ investment} \quad \times \quad 12.5\% \text{ or } 0.125}$$

   $115,000 × 12.5% (0.125) = $14,375

   $14,375 annual net operating income ÷ 12 months = **$1,197.92 monthly net operating income**

20. b   **$1,404 salesperson's commission**

   $$\frac{= \$3{,}510 \text{ full commission}}{\$58{,}500 \text{ sales price} \quad \times \quad 6\% \text{ or } 0.06}$$

   $58,500 × 6% (0.06) = $3,510

   $$\frac{= \$1{,}404 \text{ salesperson's commission}}{\$3{,}510 \text{ full commission} \quad \times \quad 40\% \text{ or } 0.4}$$

   $3,510 × 40% (0.40) = **$1,404 salesperson's commission**

21. **c   20% profit**

348,480 square feet × $0.75 per square foot = $261,360 cost

348,480 square feet ÷ 43,560 = 8 acres × 2 lots per acre = 16 lots − 3 lots = 13 lots sold × $24,125 each = $313,625 total sales price

$313,625 sales price − $261,360 cost = $52,265 profit

÷ $52,265 profit	
$231,360 cost	= 0.199973 or 20% profit

$52,265 ÷ $261,360 = 0.199973 or **20% profit**

22. **a $132.31 insurance proration**

    30 February
− 16 closing date
    14 days left in February
+ 30 March
+ 30 April
+ 30 May
+ 5 June
 109 days due

$437 annual premium ÷ 360 days = $1.21389 per day × 109 days due = **$132.31 insurance proration**

23. **b   9% annual interest rate**

$450 × 2 = $900 annual interest

÷ $900 annual interest	
$10,000 loan	= 0.09 or 9%

$900 ÷ $10,000 = **0.09 or 9% interest rate**

24. **d   117,600 cubic feet**

120' × 80' = 9,600 square feet in building − 1,200 square feet for office = 8,400 square feet left in warehouse × 14-foot ceiling = **117,600 cubic feet left in warehouse**

25. **b $571,500 price**

$68,580 annual net operating income ÷	
= $571,500 price	12% or 0.12

$68,580 ÷ 12% (0.12) = **$571,500 price**

26. c **$77.90 interest proration**

   Seller owes buyer 19 days (April 1 *through* April 19)

   $$\frac{}{\$18,450 \text{ loan balance} \quad \times \quad 8\% \text{ or } 0.08} = \$1,476 \text{ annual interest}$$

   $18,450 × 8% (0.08) = $1,476

   $1,476 annual interest ÷ 360 days = $4.10 per day × 19 days = **$77.90 interest proration**

27. d **$17,625 today's value**

   3.5% appreciation per year × 5 years = 17.5% total appreciation

   100% cost + 17.5% total appreciation = 117.5% today's value

   $$\frac{}{\$15,000 \text{ original cost} \quad \times \quad 117.5\% \text{ or } 1.175} = \$17,625 \text{ today's value}$$

   $15,000 × 117.5% (1.175) = **$17,625 today's value**

28. b **11,000 square feet left**

   150' depth − 25' setback = 125' left

   100' frontage − 6' on one side − 6' on one side = 88' left

   125' × 88' = **11,000 square feet left**

29. b **$13,000 annual rent**

   $1,000 monthly minimum rent × 12 months = $12,000 annual minimum rent

   $150,000 annual sales − $100,000 = $50,000 annual sales subject to 2%

   $$\frac{}{\$50,000 \text{ annual sales} \quad \times \quad 2\% \text{ or } 0.02} = \$1,000 \text{ annual percentage rent}$$

   $50,000 × 2% (0.02) = $1,000

   $12,000 annual minimum rent + $1,000 annual percentage rent = **$13,000 annual rent**

30. a **$965.26 tax proration**

   Seller owes buyer January 1 to August 29

   ```
     31   January
   + 28   February
   + 31   March
   + 30   April
   + 31   May
   + 30   June
   + 31   July
   + 28   August
    240   days due
   ```

$1,468 annual tax ÷ 365 days = $4.02192 per day × 240 days = **$965.26 tax proration**

31. c $23,595 sales price

    1.25 acres × 43,560 = 54,450 square feet ÷ 150' deep = 363' frontage × $65 per front foot = **$23,595 sales price**

32. b $80,000 sales price

    $$\frac{\$5,200 \text{ Full commission} \div}{= \$80,000 \text{ sales price} \quad | \quad 6.5\% \text{ or } 0.065}$$

    $5,200 ÷ 6.5% (0.065) = **$80,000 sales price**

33. d $35,000 loan

    $20,000 annual salary ÷ 12 months = $1,666.67 monthly salary

    $$\frac{= \$416.67 \text{ monthly PTI payment}}{\$1,666.67 \text{ monthly salary} \quad | \quad 25\% \text{ or } 0.25} \times$$

    $1,666.67 × 25% = $416.67

    $678.24 annual taxes and insurance ÷ 12 months = $56.52 monthly taxes and insurance

    $416.67 monthly PITI payment − $56.52 monthly TI = $360.15 monthly PI payment

    $360.15 monthly PI payment ÷ $10.29 × $1,000 = **$35,000 loan**

34. b $46,588.50 cost

    29' × 34' × 17' = 16,762 cubic feet in house

    29' × 34' × 8' ÷ 2 = 3,944 cubic feet in roof

    16,762 cubic feet + 3,944 cubic feet = 20,706 cubic feet total × $2.25 per cubic foot = **$46,588.50 cost**

35. a $6,000 annual net operating income

    $$\frac{= \$6,000 \text{ annual net operating income}}{\$50,000 \text{ investment} \quad | \quad 12\% \text{ or } 0.12} \times$$

    $50,000 × 12% (0.12) = **$6,000 annual net operating income**

36. d $8,500 loan

    $65.53 monthly interest × 12 months = $786.36 annual interest

    $$\frac{\$786.36 \text{ annual interest} \div}{= \$8,501.19 \text{ or } \$8,500 \text{ loan} \quad | \quad 9.25\% \text{ or } 0.0925}$$

    $786.36 ÷ 9.25% (0.0925) = **$8501.19 loan**

37. c 30%

$10,500 cost of lot + $93,000 cost of home = $103,500 total cost

$134,550 sales price − $103,500 total cost = $31,050 profit

$$\frac{\$31,050 \text{ profit}}{\$103,500 \text{ total cost}} = 0.3 \text{ or } 30\%$$

$31,050 ÷ $103,500 = **0.3 or 30%**

38. c **$1,495.00 rent proration**

    30 November
    − 4 day of closing
    26 days due

$575 monthly rent × 3 units = $1,725 monthly rent ÷ 30 days = $57.50 per day × 26 days = **$1,495 rent proration**

39. a **$441,400 value**

$1,530 monthly expenses × 12 months = $18,360 annual expenses

$62,500 annual gross income − $18,360 annual expenses = $44,140 annual net operating income

$$\frac{\$44,140 \text{ annual net operating income}}{10\% \text{ or } 0.1} = \$441,400 \text{ value}$$

$44,140 ÷ 10% (0.10) = **$441,400 value**

40. b **$69,160 property value**

$65,000 cost of house and lot − $13,000 cost of lot = $52,000 cost of house

Lot:

8% annual appreciation × 8 years = 64% total appreciation

100% cost + 64% total appreciation = 164% today's value

$$\$13,000 \text{ cost of lot} \times 164\% \text{ or } 1.64 = \$21,320 \text{ today's value of lot}$$

$13,000 × 164% (1.64) = $21,320

House:

1% annual depreciation × 8 years = 8% total depreciation

100% cost − 8% total depreciation = 92% today's value

$$\$52,000 \text{ cost of house} \times 92\% \text{ or } 0.92 = \$47,840 \text{ today's value of house}$$

$52,000 × 92% (0.92) = $47,840

$21,320 lot + $47,840 house = **$69,160 property value**

41. **d $310,000 sales price**

$121,600 seller's net + $31,000 closing costs + $135,700 loan payoff = $288,300 seller's dollars after commission

100% sales price − 7% commission = 93% seller's dollars after commission

$288,300 seller's dollars after commission ÷	
= **$310,000 sales price**	93% or 0.93

$288,300 ÷ 93% (0.93) = **$310,000 sales price**

42. **c   940 running feet**

125' + 350' + 125' + 350' − 10' gate = **940 running feet**

43. **b   17% profit**

$2,500 cost × 4 parcels = $10,000 total cost
$1,950 sales price × 6 parcels = $11,700 sales price
$11,700 sales price − $10,000 cost = $1,700 profit

÷ $1,700 profit	
$10,000 cost	= 0.17 or **17% profit**

$1,700 ÷ $10,000 cost = 0.17 or **17% profit**

44. **b $80,000 original cost**

4% annual appreciation × 5 years = 20% total appreciation
100% cost + 20% total appreciation = 120% today's value

$96,000 today's value ÷	
= **$80,000 original cost**	120% 1.2

$96,000 ÷ 120% (1.20) = **$80,000 original cost**

45. **a $2,072 monthly payment**

$60,000 annual salary ÷ 12 Months = $5,000 wife's monthly salary + $2,400 husband's monthly salary = $7,400 total monthly salary

= **$2,072 monthly payment**	
$7,400 total monthly salary ×	28% or 0.28

$7,400 × 28% (0.28) = **$2,072 monthly payment**

46. **b 18% annual interest rate**

$5,588 payback (principal + interest) − $4,400 loan (principal) = $1,188 interest for 18 months ÷ 18 months = $66 monthly interest × 12 months = $792 annual interest

÷ $792 annual interest	
$4,400 loan	= 0.18 or **18% annual interest rate**

$792 ÷ $4,400 = 0.18 or **18% annual interest rate**

47. **c $51.75 per front foot**

$6,468.75 price ÷ 125 front feet = **$51.75 per front foot**

48. **a $2,194.18 monthly principal and interest payment**

$340,500 sales price × 90% LTV = $306,450 loan ÷ $1,000 × $7.16 = **$2,194.18 monthly principal and interest payment**

49. **a $3,330 total commission**

= $3,000 commission	
$50,000 sales price ×	6% or 0.06

$50,000 × 6% (0.06) = $3,000

$61,000 total sales price − $50,000 sales price at 6% = $11,000 sales price at 3%

= $330 commission	
$11,000 sales price ×	3% or 0.03

$11,000 × 3% (0.03) = $330

$3,000 commission + $330 commission = **$3,330 total commission**

50. **d 52% not taken up by house**

50' × 100' = 5,000 square feet of lot − 2,400 square feet of house = 2,600 square feet not taken up by house

÷ 2,600 square feet	
5,000 square feet total	= 0.52 or 52% **not taken up by house**

2,600 ÷ 5,000 = 0.52 or **52% not taken up by house**

Glossary

abstract of title The condensed history of a title to a particular parcel of real estate, consisting of a summary of the original grant and all subsequent conveyances and encumbrances affecting the property and a certification by the abstractor that the history is complete and accurate.

acceleration clause The clause in a mortgage or deed of trust that can be enforced to make the entire debt due immediately if the borrower defaults on an installment payment or another covenant.

acceptance Expression of intent by the offeree to be bound by the terms of the offer; must be in writing if the contract pertains to real property. Acceptance must be communicated to the opposite party to create a contract.

accession Acquiring title to additions or improvements to real property as a result of the annexation of fixtures or the accretion of alluvial deposits along the banks of streams.

accretion The increase or addition of land by the deposit of sand or soil washed up naturally from a river, lake, or sea.

accrued items On a closing statement, items of expense that are incurred but not yet payable, such as interest on a mortgage loan or taxes on real property.

acre A measure of land equal to 43,560 square feet, 4,840 square yards, 4,047 square meters, 160 square rods, or 0.4047 hectare.

actual eviction The legal process that results in the tenant's being physically removed from the leased premises; summary ejectment.

adjustable rate mortgage (ARM) A loan characterized by a fluctuating interest rate, usually one tied to a published index. Caps for adjustments on periodic interest, lifetime interest, and payment amounts are normal.

adjusted basis *See* basis.

ad valorem tax A tax levied according to value, generally used to refer to real estate tax.

adverse possession The open, continuous, exclusive, adverse, notorious, (OCEAN) possession of another's land under a claim of title. Possession for a statutory period of 20 years in North Carolina may be a means of acquiring title.

aesthetic zoning Zoning ordinances that regulate the appearance of real property, such as exterior color, exterior construction material, required screening and fencing.

age-life method A method of depreciation computed by dividing the replacement cost of a property by the number of years of remaining useful life; also called the straight-line method.

agency The relationship between a principal and an agent wherein the agent is authorized to represent the principal in certain transactions.

agent One who acts or has the power to act for another. A fiduciary relationship is created under the law of agency when a property owner, as the principal, executes a listing agreement or management contract authorizing a licensed real estate broker to be the property owner's agent. *See* LOADS.

agricultural fixture In North Carolina, a fixture attached to leased property by a tenant farmer is considered the landowner's real property rather than the tenant's personal property.

air rights The right to use the open space above a property, usually allowing the surface to be used for another purpose.

alienation The act of transferring property to another. Alienation may be voluntary, such as by gift or sale, or involuntary, as through eminent domain or adverse possession.

alienation clause This clause prevents the borrower from letting someone else assume the debt without the lender's approval. *See* due-on-sale clause.

Americans with Disabilities Act (ADA) Federal act implementing regulations that protect citizens with mental or physical disabilities. Does not apply to residential housing but to commercial facilities and places of public accommodation.

American Land Title Association (ALTA) policy A title insurance policy that protects the interest in a collateral property of a mortgage lender that originates a new real estate loan.

amortized loan A loan in which principal as well as interest is payable in periodic installments over the term of the loan.

annual percentage rate (APR) The relationship of the total finance charges associated with a loan. This must be disclosed to borrowers by lenders under the Truth in Lending Act.

anticipation The appraisal principle that value can increase or decrease based on the expectation of some future benefit or detriment affecting the property.

antitrust laws Laws designed to preserve the free enterprise of the open marketplace by making illegal certain private conspiracies and combinations formed to minimize competition. Most violations of antitrust laws in the real estate business involve either price fixing (brokers conspiring to set fixed compensation rates) or allocation of customers or markets (brokers agreeing to limit their areas of trade or dealing to certain areas or properties).

appraisal An estimate of the quantity, quality, or value of something. The process through which conclusions of property value are obtained; also refers to the report that sets forth the process of estimation and conclusion of value.

appreciation An increase in the worth or value of a property due to economic or related causes, which may prove to be either temporary or permanent; opposite of depreciation.

appurtenance A right, a privilege, or an improvement belonging to, and passing with, the land.

arm's-length transaction A transaction where the parties are dealing from equal bargaining positions.

asbestos A fire-resistant mineral fiber used in a wide variety of building supplies prior to 1978; environmental health hazard, when friable, that can cause respiratory diseases and cancer.

assessment (1) The imposition of a tax, charge, or levy, usually according to established rates. (2) Official valuation of property for the purpose of establishing assessed value for tax purposes.

assignment The transfer to another party in writing of rights or interest in a bond, a mortgage, a lease, or another instrument.

assumption of mortgage Acquiring title to property on which there is an existing mortgage and agreeing to be personally liable for the terms and conditions of the mortgage, including payments.

auction A form of selling property where oral bids are taken and the property is sold to the highest bidder.

avulsion The sudden tearing away of land, as by earthquake, flood, volcanic action, or the sudden change in the course of a stream. The loss of land may not result in loss of title to the property.

backup offer An offer submitted to the property owner with knowledge that the owner is already under contract; a secondary offer.

balloon payment A final payment of a mortgage loan that is larger than the required periodic payments because the loan amount was not fully amortized.

bargain and sale deed A deed that carries with it no warranties against liens or other encumbrances but that does imply that the grantor has the right to convey title. The grantor may add warranties to the deed at his discretion.

baseboard A board around the bottom of a wall perpendicular to the floor. Sometimes called wains, baseboards cover the gap between the floor and the wall, protecting the wall from scuffs and providing a decorative accent.

base line The main imaginary line running east and west and crossing a principal meridian at a definite point; used by surveyors for reference in locating and describing land under the rectangular (government) survey system of legal description.

basement Story-high space below the first floor that is totally or partially below the exterior grade; floor is usually concrete slab.

basis The financial interest that the IRS attributes to an owner of an investment property for the purpose of determining annual depreciation and gain or loss on the sale of the asset. If a property was acquired by purchase, the owner's basis is the cost of the property plus allowable closing costs plus the value of any capital expenditures for improvements to the property, minus any depreciation allowable or actually taken. This new basis is called the *adjusted basis*.

before-tax cash flow The money left after debt service has been subtracted from the net operating income and before income tax is paid; also called cash throw-off or cash flow after debt service.

benchmarks Permanent reference marks or points established for use by surveyors in measuring differences in elevation.

beneficiary (1) The person for whom a trust operates or in whose behalf the income from a trust estate is drawn. (2) A lender in a deed of trust loan transaction. (3) The recipient of personal property (a bequest or legacy) in a will.

bilateral contract *See* contract.

blanket loan A mortgage covering more than one parcel of real estate, providing for each parcel's partial release from the mortgage lien upon repayment of a definite portion of the debt.

blockbusting The illegal practice of inducing homeowners to sell their properties by making representations regarding the entry or prospective entry of persons of a particular protected class into the neighborhood.

blue-sky laws Common name for state and federal laws that regulate the registration and sale of investment securities.

boot Money or property given to make up any difference in value or equity between two properties in a 1031 exchange.

branch office A secondary place of business apart from the principal or main office from which real estate business is conducted. A branch office usually must be run by a broker-in-charge working on behalf of the broker.

breach of contract The violation of any terms or conditions in a contract without legal excuse; for example, failure to make a payment when it is due.

broad form (HO-2) An insurance policy covering buildings and personal property against loss or damage from fire, lightning, removal, windstorm, hail, explosion, riot, smoke, vandalism, and theft. This form also covers falling objects; weight of snow, ice, or sleet; collapse of buildings; malfunctioning heating systems; accidental discharge of water or steam; and electrical currents that are artificially generated.

broker (1) One who acts as an intermediary on behalf of others for a fee or commission. (2) One who is licensed to list, lease, buy, exchange, auction, negotiate or sell interest in real estate for others for a fee.

brokerage The bringing together of buyers and sellers in the marketplace.

broker-in-charge (BIC) Required for each brokerage firm and each branch office, the full broker responsible for displaying all licenses properly, notifying the North Carolina Real Estate Commission of any change of business address or trade name, ensuring that all advertising and agency compliance is done properly, maintaining the trust account and trust account records properly, retaining and maintaining all real estate transaction records properly, and supervising all provisional brokers associated with the firm or office.

broker price opinion (BPO) *See* comparative market analysis.

BTU (British Thermal Unit) A measure of heat used in rating the capacity of heating and cooling systems.

budget comparison statement Compares actual results with the original budget, often giving either percentages or a numerical variance of actual versus projected income and expenses.

buffer zone A strip of land, usually used as a park or designated for a similar use, separating and screening land dedicated to one use from land dedicated to another use (e.g., residential from commercial).

building code An ordinance that specifies minimum standards of construction for buildings to protect public safety and health.

building permit Written governmental permission for the construction, alteration, or demolition of an improvement, showing compliance with building codes and zoning ordinances. *See* certificate of occupancy.

bulk transfer *See* Uniform Commercial Code.

bundle of legal rights The concept of land ownership that includes ownership of all legal rights to the land—i.e. disposition, exclusion, enjoyment, possession and control.

business cycle The upward and downward fluctuations in business activities generally characterized by four stages: expansion, recession, depression, and revival.

buydown A financing technique used to reduce the monthly payments for the first few years of a loan. Funds in the form of discount points are given to the lender to buy down or lower the effective interest rate paid by the buyer, thus reducing the monthly payments for a set time.

buyer-agency agreement A principal-agent relationship in which the broker is the agent for the buyer, with fiduciary responsibilities to the buyer. The broker represents the buyer under the law of agency.

call In surveying, a reference to a course, distance, or monument when a describing a boundary.

capital gain The taxable profit earned from the sale of a capital asset such as real property. Profits from assets owned for 12 months or less are treated as short-term capital gain, which is taxable as ordinary income. Profits from assets owned longer than 12 months are treated as long-term capital gain that is usually taxed at a much lower rate than ordinary income.

capital loss A loss derived from the sale of a capital asset such as real property that may be deductible from ordinary taxable income.

capitalization A mathematical process for estimating the value of a property using a proper rate of return on the investment and the annual net operating income expected to be produced by the property. The formula is Income ÷ Rate = Value.

capitalization rate The rate of return a property will produce on the owner's investment.

carbon monoxide A colorless, odorless gas produced as a byproduct of inefficient burning of fuel such as gas, oil or wood; poor ventilation can lead to deadly concentration of gas.

cash flow The net spendable income from an investment, determined by deducting all operating and fixed expenses from the gross income. When expenses exceed income, a negative cash flow results.

cash flow after debt service *See* before tax cash flow.

cash-on-cash rate of return Derived by dividing the before-tax cash flow by the owner's cash investment; equity dividend rate.

cash throwoff See before tax cash flow.

casualty insurance See property insurance.

caveat emptor A Latin phrase meaning "Let the buyer beware." In a caveat emptor state, sellers do not have to disclose any facts about their property when selling.

ceiling joist Attached to the top plate of a wall, these joists carry the weight of the roof.

certificate of occupancy (CO) A certificate issued by a government authority stating that a building is fit for occupancy and there are no building code violations; the end result of a successful building permit.

certificate of reasonable value (CRV) A form indicating the appraised value of a property being financed with a VA loan.

certificate of title A statement of attorney's opinion on the status of the title to a parcel of real property based on a title search of specified public records.

chain of title The succession of title conveyances, from some accepted starting point, whereby the present holder of real property derives title.

change The appraisal principle that no physical or economic condition remains constant.

channeling See steering.

chattel See personal property.

Civil Rights Act of 1866 A federal act that prohibits racial discrimination in the sale and rental of all real and personal property.

client See principal.

closing The consummation of a real estate transaction; seller delivers clear title and buyer delivers payment of the purchase price; occurs at the recordation of the deed per the standard residential sales contract.

closing agent A third party that conducts the closing of the transaction, usually an attorney in North Carolina.

closing statement A detailed cash accounting of a real estate transaction showing all cash received, all charges and credits made, and all cash paid out in the transaction.

cloud on the title Any document, claim, unreleased lien, or encumbrance that may impair the title to real property or make the title doubtful; usually revealed by a title search and removed by either a quitclaim deed or suit to quiet title.

clustering The grouping of homesites within a subdivision on smaller lots than normal, with the remaining land used as common area.

code of ethics A written system of standards for ethical conduct.

codicil A supplement or an addition to a will, executed with the same formalities as a will, that normally does not revoke the entire will.

coinsurance clause A clause in insurance policies covering real property that requires that the policyholder maintain fire insurance coverage generally equal to at least 80% of the property's actual replacement cost.

commingling The illegal act by a real estate broker of placing consumer funds with personal funds. By law, brokers are required to maintain a separate trust or escrow account for other parties' funds held temporarily by the broker.

commission Payment to a broker for services rendered, as in the sale or purchase of real property; traditionally, a percentage of the gross sales price of the property but can be a flat fee or some other calculation.

common elements Parts of a property that are necessary or convenient to the existence, maintenance, and safety of a condominium or are normally in common use by all of the condominium residents. Each condominium owner has an undivided ownership interest in the common elements.

common law The body of law based on custom, usage, and court decisions.

comparable Property used in an appraisal report that is substantially equivalent to the subject property.

comparative market analysis (CMA) A comparison of the prices of recently sold homes that are similar to a listing seller's home in terms of location, style, and amenities; an estimate of market value; also called a broker price opinion.

compensatory damages Money damages awarded to the injured party to compensate them for the breach of contract, but not to punish the breaching party.

competition The appraisal principle that states that excess profits generate competition.

comprehensive plan See master plan.

concrete slab See slab.

condemnation A judicial or an administrative proceeding to exercise the power of eminent domain, through which a government agency takes private property for public use and justly compensates the owner.

condition It limits coverage of a specified property in an insurance policy.

conditional-use permit Written governmental permission allowing a use inconsistent with zoning but in the public interest, such as locating an emergency medical facility in a predominantly residential area: special-use permit.

condition subsequent A defeasible fee simple estate that dictates some action or activity that the new owner must not perform. The former owner retains a right of reentry, so if the condition is broken, the former owner can take repossession of the property.

condominium The absolute ownership of a unit in a multiunit building based on a legal description of the airspace the unit actually occupies, plus an undivided interest in the ownership of the common elements, which are owned jointly with the other condominium unit owners.

conforming loan A standardized conventional loan that meets Fannie Mae's or Freddie Mac's purchase requirements.

conformity The appraisal principle that holds that the greater the similarity among properties in an area, the better they will hold their value.

Conner Act A North Carolina law that requires many types of real estate documents to be recorded for protection against claims from third parties. These documents include deeds, mortgages, purchase contracts, installment land contracts, assignments, options, leases exceeding three years, easements, and restrictive covenants; a pure race statute.

consequential damages Award of special damages if the breaching party entered the contract with plans to breach; injured party may sue for lost profits.

consideration (1) That received by the grantor in exchange for a deed. (2) Something of value that induces a person to enter into a legally enforceable contract.

construction loan *See* interim financing.

constructive eviction The actions of a landlord that so materially disturb or impair a tenant's enjoyment of the leased premises that the tenant is effectively forced to move out and terminate the lease without liability for any further rent.

constructive notice The notice given to the world by recorded documents. All people are charged with knowledge of such documents and their contents, whether or not they have actually examined them. Possession of property is also considered constructive notice that the person in possession has an interest in the property.

Consumer Financial Protection Bureau (CFPB) A federal agency created by the Dodd-Frank Act in 2010 to oversee consumer protection via financial regulations within seven federal agencies.

contingency A provision in a contract that requires a certain act to be done or a certain event to occur before the contract becomes binding; a condition of the contract.

contract A legally enforceable promise or set of promises between legally competent parties that must be performed for consideration. If a breach of the promise occurs, the law provides a remedy. A contract may be either unilateral, by which only one party is bound to act, or bilateral, by which all parties to the instrument are legally bound to act as prescribed.

contribution The appraisal principle that states that the value of any component of a property is what it gives to the value of the whole or what its absence detracts from that value.

conventional loan A loan from private investors that requires no government insurance nor guarantee.

conveyance A term used to refer to any document that transfers title to real property. The term is also used in describing the act of transferring.

cooperating broker/firm *See* listing broker.

cooperative ownership A residential multiunit building whose title is held by a trust or corporation that is owned by and operated for the benefit of persons living within the building, who are the beneficial owners of the trust or stockholders of the corporation, each possessing a proprietary lease to a specific apartment in the building.

co-ownership Title ownership held by two or more persons or entities.

corporation An entity or organization, created by operation of law, whose rights of doing business are essentially the same as those of an individual. The entity has continuous existence until it is dissolved according to legal procedures.

cost approach The process of estimating the value of a property by adding the appraiser's estimate of the reproduction or replacement cost of the building, less depreciation to the estimated land value.

cost recovery An Internal Revenue Service term for *depreciation.*

counteroffer A new offer made in response to an offer received. It has the effect of rejecting the original offer.

covenant A written agreement between two or more parties in which a party or parties pledge to perform or not perform specified acts with regard to property; usually found in such real estate documents as deeds, mortgages, leases, and contracts for deed.

covenant of quiet enjoyment The covenant implied by law by which a landlord guarantees that a tenant may take possession of leased premises and that the landlord will not interfere in the tenant's possession or use of the property.

crawl space The space between the ground surface and the first floor; frequently found in houses without basements that are not built on a slab foundation.

credit On a closing statement, an amount entered in a person's favor—an amount the party has paid or an amount received from another party.

customer A third party to whom is owed honesty and fairness; not a fiduciary relationship.

datum A horizontal plane from which heights and depths are measured.

debit On a closing statement, an amount charged; an amount the party must pay at settlement.

debt service The principle and interest payment on a loan.

decedent A person who has died.

declaration of restrictive covenants A statement of all covenant, conditions and restrictions (CC&Rs) affecting a parcel of land; sometimes noted on the plat map or in a separate document. Restrictions are appurtenant and aim to protect property values.

dedication The voluntary transfer of private property by its owner to the public for some public use, such as for streets or schools.

deductible Loss not covered by the insurer.

deed A written instrument that, when executed and delivered, conveys title to or interest in real estate; evidence of title.

deed in lieu of foreclosure A deed given by the mortgagor to the mortgagee when the mortgagor is in default under the terms of the mortgage. This avoids foreclosure but does not remove liens from the property; "friendly foreclosure."

deed of trust An instrument used to create a mortgage lien by which the borrower conveys title to a trustee, who holds it as security for the benefit of the note holder (the lender); also called a trust deed.

deed restriction Clause placed in a deed by the owner to control the future uses of the property. *See* restrictive covenants.

default The nonperformance of a duty, whether arising under a contract or otherwise; failure to meet an obligation when due.

defeasance clause A clause used in leases and mortgages that cancels a specified right upon the occurrence of a certain condition, such as cancellation of a mortgage upon repayment of the mortgage loan.

defeasible fee estate An estate in which the holder has a fee simple title that may be terminated upon the occurrence or nonoccurrence of a specified event. Two categories of defeasible fee estates exist: fee simple determinable and fee simple on condition subsequent.

deficiency judgment A personal judgment levied against the borrower when a foreclosure sale does not produce sufficient funds to pay the mortgage debt in full; a general lien.

delivery and acceptance The actual delivery of a deed by a grantor and the actual or implied acceptance of the deed by the grantee; recordation of the deed is viewed as acceptance.

demand The amount of goods people are willing and able to buy at a given price; often coupled with supply.

Department of Housing and Urban Development (HUD) A federal cabinet department active in national housing programs. Among its many programs are urban renewal, public housing, model cities, rehabilitation loans, FHA subsidies, fair housing enforcement, and water and sewer grants.

depreciation (1) In appraisal, a loss of value in property due to any cause, including physical deterioration, functional obsolescence, and external obsolescence. (2) In real estate investment, an expense deduction for tax purposes taken over the period of ownership of income property.

descent The acquisition of an estate by inheritance in which an heir succeeds to the property by intestate succession.

designated dual agency An agency option under dual agency that allows the firm, with both clients' permission, to appoint one or more licensees to exclusively represent the seller-client and one or more licensees to exclusively represent the buyer-client; also called designated agency.

developer A person or company that attempts to put land to its most profitable use through the construction of improvements.

devise A gift of real property by will. The donor is the devisor, and the recipient is the devisee.

direct reduction loan A mortgage loan that requires a fixed amount of principal payment in each period; the total debt service payment starts higher than with a level payment loan since interest portion will reduce with each payment.

discount point Interest paid in advance; one point equals 1% of the loan amount for the borrower and increases the yield for the investor approximately 1/8%.

dominant tenement A property that includes in its ownership the appurtenant right to use an easement over another person's adjacent property (called the servient tenement) for a specific purpose; ownership of the easement runs with the land.

dormer A projection built out from the slope of a roof, used to house windows on the upper floor and to provide additional headroom. Common types of dormers are the gable dormer and the shed dormer.

dual agency Representing both parties to a transaction; must be consensual and reduced to writing prior to presentation of first offer.

due diligence (1) a buyer's investigative process of having experts inspect the property, examine title, and review any leases to determine if the property meets the buyer's needs and if buyer wishes to proceed with the purchase. During the "due diligence period," the buyer can terminate the purchase contract for any reason or no reason. (2) a licensee's affirmative duty to discover and disclose any material facts about the property in question.

due-on-sale clause A provision in a mortgage that states that the entire balance of the note is immediately due and payable if the mortgagor transfers (sells) the property. *See* alienation clause.

duress The unlawful constraint or action exercised on a person whereby the person is forced to perform an act against that person's will. A contract entered into under duress is voidable.

earnest money Money deposited by a buyer under the terms of a contract, to be forfeited if the buyer defaults but applied to the purchase price if the sale is closed.

easement A right to limited use and enjoyment of the land of another for a specific purpose without ownership; a nonpossessory interest in real estate. Two types of easements are easement appurtenant and easement in gross.

easement appurtenant An easement that runs with the land; the easement is part of both the dominant and the servient tracts and conveys with the title to either tenement.

easement by necessity An easement allowed by law as necessary for the full enjoyment of a parcel of real estate; i.e., to allow a landlocked owner a right of ingress and egress over a grantor's land.

easement by prescription An easement acquired through adverse use of another's property for a period of 20 or more years in North Carolina.

easement in gross An easement that is not created for the benefit of any land owned by the owner of the easement but that attaches personally to the easement owner. There is no dominant tract; the easement attaches to the servient tract. Personal easement in gross is not assignable; a commercial easement in gross is assignable.

eave The overhang of a sloping roof that extends beyond the walls of the house.

economic life The number of years during which an improvement will add value to the land.

economic obsolescence *See* obsolescence.

effective age The apparent age of a building based on observed condition rather than chronological age.

effective gross income (EGI) The anticipated income from a rental property resulting from potential gross income minus an allowance for vacancy and bad debts.

electromagnetic fields (EMFs) Naturally occurring energy fields near power lines and electrical appliance thought to be linked with adverse health effect but research is inconclusive.

emblements Growing crops, such as grapes and corn, that are produced annually through labor and industry; also called fructus industriales. Usually considered to be personal property.

eminent domain The right of a government or municipal quasi-public body to acquire property for public use through a court action called condemnation, in which the court decides that the use is a public use and determines fair compensation to be paid to the owner.

employee Someone who works as a direct employee of an employer and has employee status. The employer is obligated to withhold income taxes and Social Security taxes from the compensation of the employee.

employment contract A document evidencing formal employment between employer and employee or between principal and agent. In real estate, this is generally a listing agreement, a buyer agency agreement or a management agreement.

enabling acts State legislation that confers zoning powers on municipal governments.

encapsulation Sealing off environmental hazards instead of removal.

encroachment An unauthorized intrusion of an improvement, or any part of an improvement, on the real property of another party; can make title to both parcels unmarketable. Best discovered by survey.

encumbrance Any charge, claim, lien, or liability held by someone other than the owner of property that may diminish the value or use and enjoyment of a property. May not prevent the transfer of title.

endorsement In an insurance policy, coverage added to the general policy; a rider.

Equal Credit Opportunity Act (ECOA) The federal law that prohibits discrimination in the extension of credit because of race, color, religion, national origin, sex, age, or marital status.

equitable title (1) The interest held by the grantor in a deed of trust that allows possession and use of the pledged property. (2) The interest held by a vendee under a contract for deed or an installment contract; the equitable right to obtain absolute ownership to property when legal title is held in another's name.

equity The interest or value that an owner has in property over and above any indebtedness.

equity buildup That portion of the loan payment directed toward the principal rather than the interest, plus any gain in the property value due to appreciation.

equity dividend rate *See* cash on cash rate of return.

equity of redemption The right of a borrower in default on a mortgage loan to reclaim the forfeited property prior to the foreclosure sale through payment in full of all debt and associated costs.

erosion The gradual wearing away of land by water, wind, or other natural forces; the diminishing of property by the elements may cause loss of ownership.

escheat The reversion of property to the state, as provided by state law, in cases where a decedent dies intestate without heirs capable of inheriting or when the property is abandoned.

escrow The closing of a transaction through a third party called an escrow agent who receives certain funds and documents to be delivered upon the performance of certain conditions outlined in the escrow instructions.

escrow account The trust account established by a broker under the provisions of the license law for the purpose of holding funds on behalf of the broker's principal or some other person until the consummation or termination of a transaction.

estate taxes Federal taxes on a decedent's real and personal property.

estate (tenancy) at sufferance The tenancy of a lessee who lawfully comes into possession of a landlord's real estate but who continues to occupy the premises after the lease has expired against the landlord's wishes.

estate (tenancy) at will An estate that gives the lessee the right to possession until the estate is terminated by either party; the term of this estate is indefinite and no prior notice to terminate is needed.

estate (tenancy) for years A possessory interest in property for a definite period of time leased for a specified consideration.

estate (tenancy) from period to period A possessory interest in leased property that automatically renews from period to period—week to week, month to month, or year to year; notice is necessary to terminate. Also called periodic tenancy.

estoppel A method of creating an agency relationship in which a person states incorrectly that a second person is the first person's agent and a third person relies on that representation.

estover A necessity allowed by law; for example, the right of a life tenant to use some of the property's resources to provide for needed repairs.

ethics The system of moral principles and rules that becomes the standard for conduct.

eviction A legal process to oust a person from possession of real estate.

evidence of title Proof of ownership of property; commonly a certificate of title, an abstract of title with lawyer's opinion, or a Torrens registration certificate.

excise tax Deed transfer tax paid by the seller and required to be noted on a deed by state law; the rate is $1 per $500 of sales price.

exchange A transaction in which all or part of the consideration is the transfer of like-kind property (such as investment real estate for investment real estate).

exclusion Something that is not covered for loss in an insurance policy.

exclusive-agency listing A listing contract under which the owner appoints a real estate broker as the exclusive agent for a designated period of time to sell the property, on the owner's stated terms, for a commission. The owner reserves the right to sell without paying anyone a commission if the owner sells to a prospect who has not been introduced or claimed by the broker.

exclusive right-to-sell listing A listing contract under which the owner appoints a real estate broker as the exclusive agent for a designated period of time to sell the property, on the owner's stated terms, and agrees to pay the broker a commission when the property is sold, regardless of who sells the property.

executed contract A contract in which all parties have fulfilled their promises in the contract.

execution The signing and delivery of an instrument. Also, a legal order directing an official to enforce a judgment against the property of a debtor.

executory contract A contract under which something remains to be done by one or more of the parties.

express agreement/contract An oral or written contract in which the parties state the contract's terms and express their intentions in words.

extender clause A carry-over or protection clause in a listing contract that says the listing broker is entitled to commission for a time period after expiration of the listing term if the property is transferred to a prospect that the broker introduced to the property during the listing term; override clause. This clause is void if the property is listed with another broker.

external depreciation The reduction in a property's value caused by outside factors (those that are off the property).

external obsolescence *See* obsolescence.

extra-territorial jurisdictions (ETJs) A municipality's right to regulate development in areas adjacent to but not part of the city's corporate limits. Population determines if the power extends for 1 to 3 miles from the corporate limits.

Fannie Mae (FNMA) A quasi-government agency established to purchase any kind of mortgage loans in the secondary mortgage market from the primary lenders.

fascia board A flat strip of wood or metal that encloses the ends of the rafters; gutters are usually attached to the fascia board.

Federal Emergency Management Agency (FEMA) A federal agency responsible for disaster preparedness, response and recovery. Now under Department of Homeland Security.

Federal Fair Housing Act The federal law that prohibits discrimination in housing based on race, color, religion, sex, handicap, familial status, or national origin.

Federal Reserve System The country's central banking system, which controls the nation's monetary policy by regulating the supply of money and interest rates.

fee-for-service Arrangement where consumer asks licensee to perform specific real estate services for a set fee; unbundling of services; limited service firms.

fee simple absolute The maximum possible estate in real property; most complete and absolute ownership; indefinite in duration, freely transferable and inheritable.

fee simple defeasible *See* defeasible fee estate.

fee simple determinable An estate in real estate that continues "so long as" a prescribed land use continues. Estate ends automatically upon the termination of the prescribed use; no lawsuit is necessary for reversion.

fee simple subject to a condition subsequent An estate in real estate that prohibits a specific condition on the property. Grantor has the right to re-enter the property and reclaim ownership through legal proceedings.

FHA loan A loan insured by the Federal Housing Administration and made by an approved private lender in accordance with the FHA's regulations.

fiduciary One in whom trust and confidence are placed; a reference to a principal-agent relationship.

financing statement *See* Uniform Commercial Code.

first substantial contact A flexible moment in time when conversation between a licensee and a consumer begins to address confidential needs, desires and abilities; latest moment to legally disclose agency choices to a consumer.

fixed rental lease *See* gross lease.

fixture An item of personal property that has been converted to real property by being permanently affixed to the realty.

flood hazard area Property identified by flood certification to be in a flood-prone area with a likelihood that a flood may occur once every 100 years therefore usually requiring flood insurance if federally related financing is involved.

floor joist A horizontal board laid on edge, resting on the beams that provide the main support for the floor. The subflooring is nailed directly to the joists.

footing A concrete support under a foundation, chimney, or column that usually rests on solid ground and is wider than the structure being supported. Footings are designed to distribute the weight of the structure over the ground.

foreclosure A legal procedure whereby property used as security for a debt is sold to satisfy the debt in the event of default in payment of the mortgage note or default of other terms in the mortgage document. The foreclosure procedure brings the rights of all parties to a conclusion and passes the title in the mortgaged property to either the holder of the mortgage or a third party who may purchase the realty at the foreclosure sale, free of all liens affecting the property subsequent to the mortgage.

foreshore Land at the coast between average high tide and average low tide this is owned by the state of North Carolina.

foundation wall The masonry or concrete wall below ground level that serves as the main support for the frame structure. Foundation walls form the side walls of the basement or crawlspace.

frame The wooden skeleton of the house consisting of the floors, walls, ceilings, and roof.

fraud An intentional misrepresentation of material fact so as to harm or take advantage of another person.

Freddie Mac A corporation established to purchase primarily conventional mortgage loans in the secondary mortgage market.

freehold estate An estate in land in which ownership is for an indeterminate length of time, in contrast to a leasehold estate.

frieze board A wooden board fastened at the top of the exterior wall under the eave soffit to prevent penetration of weather elements; frequently the base for additional exterior decorative trim.

front footage The measurement of a parcel of land by the number of feet of street or road frontage, or water frontage.

frontage The length of property along the street or waterfront.

fructus industriales *See* emblements.

fructus naturales Plants that do not require annual cultivation and are considered real property.

full broker *See* nonprovisional broker.

functional obsolescence A loss of value to an improvement to real estate arising from functional problems, often caused by age or poor design.

future interest A person's present right to an interest in real property that will not result in possession or enjoyment until sometime in the future, such as a reversion or right of reentry.

gable The triangular portion of an end wall rising from the level top wall under the inverted V of a sloping roof that aids water drainage. A gable can be made of weatherboard, tile, or masonry and can extend above the rafters.

gambrel A curb roof, having a steep slope and a flatter one above, as seen in Dutch colonial architecture.

gap A defect in the chain of title of a particular parcel of real estate; a missing document or conveyance that raises doubt as to the present ownership of the land.

general agent One who is authorized to represent the principal in a broad range of matters related to a specific business or activity; a property manager might have this power.

general lien The right of a creditor to have all of a debtor's current and future property for the next 10 years—both real and personal—sold to satisfy a debt; i.e. judgment lien.

general partnership *See* partnership.

general warranty deed A deed in which the grantor fully warrants good clear title to the premises through four covenants in the deed. Used in most real estate deed transfers, a general warranty deed offers the greatest protection to the grantee of any deed.

Ginnie Mae A government agency under HUD that plays an important role in the secondary mortgage market. It sells mortgage-backed securities that are backed by pools of FHA and VA loans.

girder A heavy wooden or steel beam supporting the floor joists and providing the main horizontal support for the floor.

graduated lease A commercial lease that contracts for pre-set rental increases over the lease period.

graduated payment mortgage (GPM) A loan in which the monthly principal and interest payments increase by a set amount each year for a certain number of years and then level off for the remaining loan term; probable negative amortization in early years.

grantee A person who receives a conveyance of real property from a grantor.

granting clause Words in a deed of conveyance that state the grantor's intention to convey the property at the present time. This clause is generally worded as convey and warrant, grant, bargain and sell, or the like.

grantor (1) The property owner that is transferring title to or an interest in real property to a grantee. (2) A borrower in a deed of trust loan transaction; also called trustor.

gross income multiplier (GIM) A figure used as a multiplier of the gross annual income of a property to produce an estimate of the property's value.

gross lease A lease of property under which a landlord pays all property charges regularly incurred through ownership, such as repairs, taxes, insurance, and operating expenses. Most residential leases are gross leases; also called flat or fixed rental lease.

gross rent multiplier (GRM) The figure used as a multiplier of the gross monthly income of a property to produce an estimate of the property's value.

ground lease A lease of land only, on which the tenant usually is required to build as specified in the lease. Such leases are usually long-term net leases.

groundwater Water under the surface of the earth.

growing-equity mortgage (GEM) A loan in which the monthly payments increase annually, with the increased amount being used to reduce directly the principal balance outstanding and thus shorten the overall term of the loan.

header The extra thick framing over doors and windows to bear the weight of the building above the opening.

heir One who might inherit or succeed to an interest in land under the state law of descent when the owner dies without leaving a valid will.

highest and best use The possible use of a property that would produce the greatest net income and thereby develop the highest value.

hip roof A pitched roof with sloping sides and ends.

historic preservation zoning Zoning to preserve the historic nature of a particular property or neighborhood. Change will require a certificate of appropriateness from the necessary regulatory power.

holdover tenant A person who retains possession of leased property after the lease has expired; the landlord may continue to accept rent or make start eviction procedures.

home equity loan A loan (sometimes called a line of credit) under which a property owners use their residence as collateral and can then draw funds up to a prearranged amount against the property.

homeowners' insurance policy A standardized package insurance policy that covers a residential real estate owner against financial loss from fire, theft, public liability, and other common risks.

homestead Land that is owned and occupied as the family home. In many states, a portion of the area or value of this land is protected for exempt from judgments for debts.

Housing and Community Development Act of 1974 An act that added gender as a protected class under the Federal Fair Housing Act.

HUD *See* Department of Housing and Urban Development

HUD-1 *See* Uniform Settlement Statement

HVAC An acronym for heating, ventilation, and air-conditioning.

hypothecation The pledging of property as security for an obligation or a loan without losing possession of it.

implied agreement/contract A contract under which the agreement of the parties is demonstrated by their conduct.

implied warranty of habitability A theory in landlord/tenant law in which the landlord renting residential property implies that the property is habitable and fit for its intended use.

improvement (1) Any structure, usually privately owned, erected on a site to enhance the value of the property—for example, a fence or a driveway. (2) A publicly owned structure added to or benefiting land, such as a curb, sidewalk, street, or sewer.

income capitalization approach The process of estimating the value of an income-producing property through capitalization of the annual net income expected to be produced by the property during its remaining useful life.

independent contractor Someone who is retained to perform a certain act but who is subject to the control and direction of another only as to the end result and not as to the way in which the act is performed. Unlike an employee, an independent contractor pays all expenses and Social Security and income taxes and receives no employee benefits. Most real estate licensees are independent contractors.

index lease A commercial lease that allows the periodic adjustment of rent based on a named index such as Consumer Price Index (CPI).

inflation The gradual reduction of the purchasing power of the dollar, usually related directly to the increases in the money supply by the federal government.

inheritance taxes State-imposed taxes on a decedent's real and personal property.

in-house sale A real estate transaction where the listing firm actually produces the buyer for their listing, as opposed to a co-brokered or cross sale that involves two firms.

installment land contract A contract for the sale of real estate financed by the seller whereby the purchase price is paid in periodic installments by the purchaser, who is in possession of the property even though legal title is retained by the seller until a future date, which may not be until final payment. Also called a contract for deed or land contract.

insulation Pieces of plasterboard, asbestos sheeting, compressed wood-wool, fiberboard, or other material placed between inner and outer surfaces, such as walls and ceilings, to protect the interior from heat loss. Insulation works by breaking up and dissipating air currents.

interest A charge made by a lender for the use of money.

interim financing A short-term loan usually made during the construction phase of a building project (in this case, often referred to as a construction loan).

Interstate Land Sales Full Disclosure Act A federal law regulating the interstate advertising and sale or lease of lots in subdivisions with 25 or more lots. Developer must be provide a property report and register the subdivision with HUD.

intestate The condition of a property owner who dies without leaving a valid will. Title to the property will pass to the decedent's heirs as provided in the state law of descent.

intrinsic value An appraisal term referring to the value created by a person's personal preferences for a particular type of property.

investment Money directed toward the purchase, improvement, and development of an asset in expectation of income or profits.

involuntary lien A lien placed on property without the consent of the property owner; such as a judgment lien.

joint tenancy A concurrent form of ownership of real estate between two or more parties who have been named in one conveyance as joint tenants. Ownership interest may be unequal. Right of survivorship is not automatic in North Carolina but can be added by an attorney.

joint venture The joining of two or more people to conduct a specific business enterprise. A joint venture is similar to a partnership in that it must be created by agreement between the parties to share in the losses and profits of the venture. It is unlike a partnership in that the venture is for one specific project only, rather than for a continuing business relationship.

judgment The formal decision of a court upon the respective rights and claims of the parties to an action or a suit. After a judgment has been entered and recorded with the county recorder, it becomes a general involuntary lien on the current and future real and personal property of the debtor in the county where recorded for the next 10 years.

judicial foreclosure The form of foreclosure used in lien theory states. *See* foreclosure.

jumbo loan A residential mortgage loan in excess of acceptable loan amounts for purchase by Fannie Mae or Freddie Mac; also called nonconforming loans.

junior mortgage A mortgage that is subordinate in right or lien priority to an existing lien on the same realty.

laches A legal doctrine to bar a legal claim or prevent the assertion of a right because of undue delay or failure to assert the claim or right.

land The earth's surface, extending downward to the center of the earth and upward infinitely into space, including things permanently attached by nature, such as trees and water.

land contract *See* installment land contract.

landfill An enormous burial hole for various types of waste disposal.

lateral support The support a parcel of land receives from adjacent land; a neighbor's duty to support adjoining land in its natural state.

law of negligence If a tenant or guest is injured on the landlord's rental property, the landlord, and his/her agent, may be held liable due to their responsibility to maintain common areas and comply with the Residential Rental Agreement Act.

Lead-Based Paint Hazard Reduction Act A federal law that requires sellers/landlords to disclose the known presence of lead-based paint in residential property to potential buyers/tenants via a required disclosure addendum to sales contracts or leases; delivery of a mandatory EPA pamphlet about lead poisoning is also required. Buyer/tenant is allowed a 10-day assessment period.

lease A written or an oral contract between a landlord (the lessor) and a tenant (the lessee) that transfers the right to exclusive possession and use of the landlord's real property to the lessee for a specified period of time and for a stated consideration (rent).

leasehold estate A tenant's right to occupy real estate during the term of a lease, generally considered a personal property interest; nonfreehold estate.

lease option A lease under which the tenant has the right to purchase the property either during the lease term or at its end.

lease purchase The purchase of real property, the consummation of which is preceded by a lease, usually longterm; typically done for tax or financing purposes.

legal description A description of a specific parcel of real estate complete enough for an independent surveyor to locate and identify it.

legality of object The purpose of a legally enforceable contract cannot be for illegal actions or acts against public policy.

legally competent parties People who are recognized by law as being able to contract with others; those of legal age and sound mind; a requirement of a legally enforceable contract.

lessee/lessor *See* lease.

leverage The use of borrowed money to finance an investment.

levy To assess; to seize or collect. To levy a tax is to assess a property and set the rate of taxation. To levy an execution is to officially seize the property of a person to satisfy an obligation.

liability insurance Insurance providing protection of the property owner against financial claims of others.

license (1) A privilege or right granted to a person by a state to operate as a real estate broker. (2) The personal revocable nontransferable right to a temporary use of another's land—a personal right that cannot be sold.

lien A right given by law to certain creditors to have their debts paid out of the property of a defaulting debtor, usually by means of a court sale. An encumbrance on real property that can be general or specific.

lien agent A title insurance entity that is designated under the North Carolina Mechanic's Lien Law by a real property owner to receive notifications of possible mechanics' liens from construction project vendors.

lien theory Some states interpret a mortgage as being purely a lien on real property. The mortgagee thus has no right of possession but must foreclose the lien and sell the property if the mortgagor defaults.

life estate An interest in real or personal property that is limited in duration to the lifetime of its owner or some other designated person or persons.

life tenant A person in possession of a life estate.

limited common elements Common elements of a condominium project reserved for the exclusive use of one or more units, such as parking spaces or storage areas.

limited liability company (LLC) A hybrid business entity with combined characteristics and benefits of a limited partnership and an S corporation.

limited partnership *See* partnership.

liquidated damages An amount predetermined by the parties to a contract as compensation to an injured party if the other party breaches the contract.

liquidity The ability to sell an asset and convert it into cash, at a price close to its true value, in a short period of time.

lis pendens A recorded legal document giving constructive notice that an action potentially affecting title to a particular property has been filed in either a state or a federal court; title is effectively unmarketable during the litigation.

listing agreement An employment contract between a property owner (as principal) and a real estate firm/broker (as agent) by which the broker is employed to find a ready, willing and able buyer for the owner's real estate on the owner's terms, for which service the owner agrees to pay a commission.

listing broker The broker/firm in a multiple-listing situation representing the seller, as opposed to the cooperating broker/firm, that brings the buyer to the transaction. The listing broker and the cooperating broker may be the same person/firm.

littoral rights (1) A landowner's claim to use water in large navigable lakes and oceans adjacent to the property. (2) The ownership rights to land bordering these bodies of water up to the average high-water mark.

LOADS A mneumonic to remember the fiduciary duties of an agent to the principal: Loyalty, Obedience, Accountability, Disclosure of information, Skill, care and diligence.

loan origination fee An administrative fee charged to the borrower by the lender for making a mortgage loan; usually computed as a percentage of the loan amount.

loan-to-value (LTV) ratio The relationship between the amount of the mortgage loan and the value of the real estate being pledged as collateral.

lot-and-block (recorded plat) system A method of describing real property that identifies a parcel of land by reference to lot and block numbers within a subdivision, as specified on a recorded subdivision plat.

Machinery Act The North Carolina General Statutes that govern the ad valorem taxation of property.

mailbox rule A rule of law stating that once written acceptance is placed in control of the mailing service, and out of the control of the offeree, it is considered accepted—not when the acceptance is actually received by the offeror.

mansard roof An architectural style in which the top floor or floors of a structure are designed to appear to be the roof. Such a roof has two slopes on each of the four sides of the building, with the upper slope less steeply inclined.

manufactured home A dwelling, also known as a mobile home or house trailer; built under HUD regulations with a permanent chassis. It is considered personal property until the moving hitch, wheels and axles are removed, the unit is attached to a permanent foundation on land owned by the owner of the manufactured home, and an affidavit attesting to these actions has been filed with the Dept. of Motor Vehicles.

market A place where goods can be bought and sold and value established.

marketable title A good or clear title, reasonably free from the risk of litigation over possible defects.

Marketable Title Act The act is designed to eliminate obsolete defects in a chain of title. If a chain of title can be traced back for 30 years without a problem, it becomes a marketable title.

market value The most probable price property will bring in an arm's-length transaction under normal conditions on the open market.

mass appraisal A valuation technique sometimes used for tax assessment purposes that applies a standard percentage increase or decrease to all property in a given location; sometimes referred to as horizontal adjustments.

master plan A comprehensive plan to guide the long-term physical development of a particular area.

material fact Any fact that is important or relevant to the issue at hand; mandatory disclosure by all agents in a transaction to all parties of the transaction.

mechanic's lien A specific, involuntary lien secured by interest in real property to give security to contractors, laborers, and materialmen who have performed work or furnished materials in the erection or repair of a building.

"meeting of the minds" See mutual assent.

metes-and-bounds description A legal description of a parcel of land that begins at a well-marked point and follows the boundaries, using directions and distances around the tract, back to the place of beginning.

mill One-tenth of one cent. Some states use a mill rate to compute real estate taxes; for example, a rate of 52 mills would be $0.052 tax for each dollar of assessed valuation of a property.

minor Someone who has not reached the age of majority and therefore does not have legal capacity to transfer title to real property; under 18 years of age in North Carolina.

mitigation Systems to limit the source of environmental hazards and reduce their effect on humans and the surrounding environment.

modular home A dwelling consisting of a series of rooms or units built off site according to the NC State Building Code; is considered real property as soon as it is assembled on the land. May be multi-storied.

monetary policy Governmental regulation of the amount of money in circulation through such institutions as the Federal Reserve Board.

monument A fixed natural or artificial object used to establish real estate boundaries for a metes-and-bounds description.

mortgage A conditional transfer or pledge of real estate as security for the payment of a debt. Also, the document creating a mortgage lien in a lien theory state.

mortgage banker A mortgage loan company that originates, services, and sells loans to investors.

mortgage broker An agent of a lender who brings the lender and borrower together for a fee. A broker may represent several lenders.

mortgagee/mortgagor A mortgagee is the lender in a mortgage loan transaction; a mortgagor is the borrower in a mortgage loan transaction.

mortgage lien A lien or charge on the property of a mortgagor that secures the underlying debt obligations.

multiperil policy An insurance policy that offers protection from a range of potential perils, such as those of fire, hazard, public liability, and casualty.

multiple listing service (MLS) A marketing organization composed of member brokers who agree to share their listing agreements with one another in the hope of procuring ready, willing, and able buyers for their properties more quickly than they could on their own. Most MLSs accept only exclusive right-to-sell or exclusive-agency listings from their member brokers.

mutual assent A deliberate agreement between parties; offer and acceptance; "meeting of the minds." A requirement of a legally enforceable contract.

National Do Not Call Registry A national registry, managed by the Federal Trade Commission, that lists the phone numbers of consumers who prefer to limit the telemarketing calls they receive.

negative amortization When the debt service payment on a loan is not large enough to pay the interest due; the principal balance actually grows with each payment.

negligent misrepresentation Unintentionally misinforming any party involved in a transaction about a material fact.

negligent omission Unintentionally failing to disclose a material fact to any party involved in a transaction.

negotiable instrument A written promise or order to pay a specific sum of money that may be transferred by endorsement or delivery. The transferee then has the original payee's right to payment.

net lease A lease requiring that the tenant pay rent plus some or all of the property charges, such as taxes, insurance, utilities, and repairs.

net listing A listing based on the net price the seller will receive if the property is sold. Under a net listing, the broker can offer the property for sale at the highest price obtainable to increase the commission. While this type of listing is illegal in many states, it is legal but not encouraged in North Carolina.

net operating income (NOI) The income projected for an income-producing property after deducting losses for vacancy and collection and operating expenses.

nonconforming use An existing use of property that is permitted to continue after a zoning ordinance prohibiting it has been established for the area; a grandfathered use. Illegal nonconforming use occurs when zoning in place before the prohibited use.

nonfreehold estate *See* leasehold estate.

nonhomogeneity A lack of uniformity; dissimilarity; heterogeneity. Because no two parcels of land are exactly alike, real estate is said to be nonhomogeneic.

nonprovisional broker A North Carolina real estate licensee that has completed the 90-hour postlicensing education to remove the provisional license status; also called a full broker.

North Carolina Condominium Act of 1986 Specifies that a condominium is created and established when the developer of the property executes and records a declaration of its creation in the county where the property is located. The declaration must include any covenants, conditions, or restrictions on the use of the property. Other requirements include disclosure and other consumer protection measures in connection with new residential condominium unit sales.

North Carolina Fair Housing Act of 1983 State fair housing law containing similar prohibitions to those of the federal fair housing law. Unlike the federal law, however, the North Carolina law does not exempt owners who are selling their own property, and it does exempt the rental of a unit in a one-unit to four-unit residential building if the owner or one of the owner's family members lives in one of the units.

North Carolina Human Relations Council The state agency responsible for enforcing the North Carolina Fair Housing Act.

North Carolina Intestate Succession Act The state law of descent that dictates distribution of the real and personal property of the deceased that died without a will (intestate).

North Carolina Real Estate Commission The state governmental agency whose primary duties include making rules and regulations to protect the general public involved in real estate transactions, granting licenses to real estate brokers, and suspending or revoking licenses for cause.

North Carolina Residential Property Disclosure Act The state law that requires sellers to provide a prescribed property disclosure statement to any prospective buyer prior to presentation of first offer on the property. Exemptions include new construction, foreclosed properties and lease purchases but not for sale by owner transactions.

North Carolina Time Share Act The portion of North Carolina real estate law that defines time-shares and regulates their development and sales.

note *See* promissory note.

novation Substituting a new contract for an old one or substituting new parties to an existing contract.

obsolescence The loss of value due to factors that are outmoded or less useful. Obsolescence may be functional or economic.

occupancy permit A permit issued by the appropriate local governing body to establish that the property is suitable for habitation by meeting certain safety and health standards.

octennial reappraisal In North Carolina, the statutory reappraisal of all real property in every county every eight years for tax purposes.

offer The promise by one party to act or perform in a certain manner if the other party agrees to act or perform as requested; shows an intention to enter into a contract.

offer and acceptance Two essential components of a valid contract; *See* mutual assent and acceptance.

offeror/offeree The person who makes the offer is the offeror. The person receiving the offer is the offeree.

Office of Equal Opportunity (OEO) The federal agency under the direction of the secretary of the Department of Housing and Urban Development, which is in charge of administering the Federal Fair Housing Act.

Office of Thrift Supervision (OTS) Monitors and regulates the savings and loan industry. OTS was created by the Financial Institutions Reform, Recovery, and Enforcement Act (FIRREA).

open-end loan A mortgage loan that is expandable by increments up to a maximum dollar amount, the full loan being secured by the same original mortgage; an equity line mortgage.

open listing A listing agreement under which the broker's commission is contingent on the broker personally producing a ready, willing, and able buyer before the property is sold by the seller or another broker.

operating expenses Periodic and necessary expenses essential to the continuous operation and maintenance of an income property.

operating statement A detailed statement prepared on a periodic basis showing the financial picture of a business through the revenues and expenses; profit and loss statement.

opinion of title An abstract of title that a lawyer has examined and has certified to be, in the lawyer's opinion, an accurate statement of the facts concerning the property ownership.

option An agreement between the property owner (optionor) and the possible buyer (optionee), secured by the payment of an option fee, to buy or not buy property within a specific time period at terms that have been negotiated in the underlying contract; also called option to purchase or option contract.

oral buyer agency A non-exclusive verbal agency agreement between a firm and a buyer-client. There can be no time limit on oral agency, but it must be reduced to writing prior to presentation of first offer.

override clause *See* extender clause.

package insurance An insurance policy that combines the coverage of property insurance and liability insurance.

package loan A real estate loan used to finance the purchase of both real property and personal property, such as in the purchase of a furnished home that includes window coverings and major appliances.

panic peddling *See* blockbusting.

parol evidence rule A rule of evidence providing that a written agreement is the final expression of the agreement of the parties, not to be varied or contradicted by prior or contemporaneous oral or written negotiations.

partition The division of cotenants' interests in real property when all parties do not voluntarily agree to terminate the co-ownership; takes place through court procedures.

partnership An association of two or more individuals who carry on a continuing business for profit as co-owners. Under the law, a partnership is regarded as a group of individuals rather than as a single entity. A general partnership is a typical form of joint venture in which each general partner shares in the administration, profits, and losses of the operation. A limited partnership is a business arrangement whereby the operation is administered by one or more general partners and funded, by and large, by limited or silent partners, who are by law responsible for losses only to the extent of their investments.

party wall A wall that is located on or at a boundary line between two adjoining parcels of land and is used or is intended to be used by the owners of both properties; walls shared between town houses.

payment cap The limit on the amount the monthly payment can be increased on an adjustable-rate mortgage when the interest rate is adjusted.

percentage lease A commercial lease, commonly used for retail tenants; rent is based on the tenant's gross sales at the premises. There is usually a small base monthly rental plus a percentage of any gross sales above a certain amount.

percolation test A test of the soil to determine whether it will absorb and drain water adequately to use a septic system for sewage disposal; a soil evaluation test.

periodic estate (tenancy) *See* estate (tenancy) from period to period.

personal property Items, called chattels or personalty, that do not fit into the definition of real property; movable objects. Examples would include furniture, clothing, jewelry, money, vehicles, etc.

physical deterioration A reduction in a property's value resulting from a decline in physical condition; can be caused by action of the elements or by ordinary wear and tear.

pier A column, usually of masonry block or steel-reinforced concrete. Piers are evenly spaced under a structure to support the weight. May also refer to the part of the wall between the windows or other openings that bears the wall weight.

pitch The slope of a roof measured as the vertical distance in inches (rise) divided by the horizontal distance in feet (run).

planned unit development (PUD) A planned combination of diverse land uses, such as housing, recreation, and shopping, in one contained development or subdivision.

plat map A map of a subdivision indicating the location and boundaries of individual properties. Generally shows lots, blocks, easements, streets, floodplains, etc. Usually requires official approval before recordation.

point of beginning (POB) In a metes-and-bounds legal description, the starting point of the survey, situated at one corner of the parcel. All metes-and-bounds descriptions must follow the boundaries of the parcel back to the point of beginning.

police power The government's right to impose laws, statutes, and ordinances, including zoning ordinances and building codes, to protect the public health, safety, and welfare.

potential gross income The amount of rental income the property could produce with 100% occupancy and with all tenants paying full rent; also called scheduled gross income.

power of attorney A written instrument authorizing a person, the attorney-in-fact, to act as agent for another person to the extent indicated in the instrument.

power of sale foreclosure The form of foreclosure used in a title theory state, such as North Carolina; also called nonjudicial foreclosure.

predatory lending Unscrupulous, sometimes fraudulent, lending practices usually intending to make repayment impossible; designed to take advantage of unwary borrowers that are frequently the low-income, uninformed, elderly, or non-English-speaking.

preemptive right A provision giving a person the first right to purchase real property; most often found in commercial leases.

premium The consideration for an insurance policy.

prepaid item On a closing statement, (1) expenses paid before they are due, such as hazard insurance or rent; also called prepaids; (2) a lump-sum payment to set up a reserve account, such as deposits of taxes and insurance to set up the borrower's mortgage loan escrow account.

prepayment penalty A charge imposed on a borrower who pays off the loan principal early. This penalty compensates the lender for interest and other charges that would otherwise be lost due to payments made ahead of schedule.

price fixing *See* antitrust laws.

primary mortgage insurance (PMI) Insurance coverage used for obtaining conventional loans with loan-to-value ratios exceeding 80%.

primary mortgage market The mortgage market in which loans are originated, consisting of lenders such as commercial banks, savings associations, and mortgage brokers.

principal (1) A sum loaned or employed as a fund or an investment, as distinguished from its income or profits. (2) The original amount (as in a loan) of the total balance due and payable at a certain date. (3) A main party to a transaction—the person for whom the agent works; the client.

principal meridian The main imaginary line running north and south and crossing a base line at a definite point; used by surveyors for reference in locating and describing land under the rectangular (government) survey system of legal description.

priority The order of position or time. The priority of liens is generally determined by the chronological order in which the lien documents are recorded. Property tax and assessment liens have priority even over previously recorded liens.

private mortgage insurance (PMI) Insurance provided by a private carrier that protects a lender against a loss in the event of a foreclosure and deficiency.

probate A legal process by which a court determines who will inherit a decedent's property and what the estate's assets are.

procuring cause The effort that began a chain of events that brings about the desired result. Under an open listing, the broker who is the procuring cause of the sale receives the commission.

profit and loss statement *See* operating statement.

promissory note A financing instrument that states the terms of the underlying obligation, is signed by its maker, and is negotiable (transferable to a third party); a personal IOU.

property insurance A policy that provides property owner coverage for the basic structure on that property.

property management agreement An agency contract between the owner of income property and a management firm or an individual property manager that outlines the scope of the manager's authority.

property manager Broker who for compensation preserves the value of an investment property while generating income as an agent for the owner. Duties include collecting rents, maintaining the property, and keeping up all accounting.

property report The mandatory federal and/or state documents compiled by developers to provide potential purchasers with material facts about a property prior to its purchase.

proprietary lease A lease given by the corporation that owns a cooperative apartment building to the shareholder for the shareholder's right as a tenant to an individual apartment.

prorations Shared expenses, either prepaid or paid in arrears, that are divided equitably between buyer and seller at settlement.

protected class Any group of people designated as such by statute in consideration of federal and state civil rights and lending legislation; currently includes familial status, marital status, age, race, gender, handicapping condition, color, religion, source of income, and national origin.

protection agreement An agreement between an unlisted property owner and a broker to secure payment for the broker if the property is sold to the particular buyer named in the agreement; it does not create a general listing, and may not create agency at all—only compensation for a buyer's agent. Sometimes called a "one-shot" listing.

provisional broker A real estate licensee who performs real estate activities under the supervision of a licensed real estate broker-in-charge. Must complete postlicensing courses to remove the provisional license status.

public offering statement The document all prospective time-share purchasers must receive before signing a sales contract. The statement must disclose all material facts about the property, as required by the state.

puffing Exaggerated or superlative comments or opinions: e.g. "This house has the best view in town!".

pur autre vie For the life of another. A life estate pur autre vie is a life estate that is measured by the life of a person other than the grantee.

purchase money mortgage A note secured by a mortgage or deed of trust given by a buyer, as borrower, to a seller, as lender, as part of the purchase price of the real estate.

quantity-survey method The appraisal method of estimating building costs by calculating the cost of all of the physical components in the improvements, adding the cost to assemble them, and then including the indirect costs associated with such construction.

quiet title A court action to remove a cloud on the title.

quitclaim deed A conveyance by which the grantor transfers interest in the real estate, if any, without warranties or obligations; frequently used to remove clouds on the title.

radon A colorless, odorless radioactive gas that naturally occurs in all areas of the state from the decay of radioactive minerals in the ground; EPA suggests that a reading of 4.0 picocuries or higher is cause for a mitigation system. Considered to be one of the leading causes of lung cancer.

rafter One of a series of sloping beams that extends from the center ridge board to an exterior wall and provides the main support for the roof.

range A strip of land six miles wide, extending north and south and numbered east and west according to its distance from the principal meridian in the rectangular (government) survey system of legal description.

rate cap The limit on the amount the interest rate can be increased at each adjustment period in an adjustable rate loan. The cap may also set the maximum interest rate that can be charged during the life of the loan.

ratification A method of creating an agency relationship in which the principal accepts/confirms the conduct of someone who acted without prior authorization as the principal's agent.

ready, willing, and able buyer One who is prepared to buy property on the seller's terms and is ready to take positive steps to consummate the transaction; one of the agent's requirements for entitlement to commission.

real estate Land; a portion of the earth's surface extending downward to the center of the earth and upward infinitely into space, including all things permanently attached to it, whether naturally or artificially.

real estate investment syndicate See syndicate.

real estate investment trust (REIT) Trust ownership of real estate by a group of individuals who purchase certificates of ownership in the trust, which in turn invests the money in real property and distributes the profits back to the investors free of corporate income tax.

real estate license law The state law enacted to protect the public from fraud, dishonesty, and incompetence when dealing with real estate licensees in the purchase and sale of real estate.

real estate mortgage investment conduit (REMIC) A tax entity that issues multiple classes of investor interests (securities) backed by a pool of mortgages.

real estate recovery fund A fund established in some states from real estate license revenues to cover claims of aggrieved parties who have suffered monetary damage through the actions of a real estate licensee.

Real Estate Settlement Procedures Act (RESPA) Federal law that ensures that residential buyers and sellers receive full disclosure of all settlement charges when a 1–4 family unit residence is financed by federally-related first mortgage loans. The Act mandates a HUD booklet about closing costs, a good-faith estimate of closing costs, and a standardized HUD-1 closing statement. The Act, known as Regulation X, also prohibits kickbacks from lenders.

reality of consent If misrepresentation, fraud, mistake of fact, undue influence or duress are absent in contract formation, good contract is formed.

real property The land plus permanent improvements and the interests, benefits, and rights inherent in real estate ownership.

REALTOR® A registered trademark term reserved for the sole use of active members of local REALTORS® boards affiliated with the National Association of REALTORS®.

reconciliation The final step in the appraisal process, in which the appraiser combines the estimates of value received from the sales comparison, cost, and income capitalization approaches to arrive at a final estimate of market value for the subject property.

recording The act of entering or recording documents into the public record at the recorder's office established in each county. Until recorded, a deed or mortgage ordinarily is not effective against third parties, such as subsequent purchasers or mortgagees.

rectangular (government) survey system A system established in 1785 by the federal government, providing for surveying and describing land by reference to principal meridians and base lines; used mainly west of the Mississippi River.

redemption period A 10-day period of time after a foreclosure auction during which a property owner in default has the right to redeem the pledged real estate by paying the loan balance plus interest, and costs; also called the upset bid period.

redlining The illegal practice of a lending institution denying loans or restricting their number for certain areas of a community.

reduction certificate (payoff statement) The document signed by a lender indicating the amount required to pay a loan balance in full and satisfy the debt; used in the settlement process to protect both the seller's and the buyer's interests.

reference to recorded plat See lot-and-block (recorded plat) system.

registration certificate The document that developers of time-shares in North Carolina must obtain from the North Carolina Real Estate Commission before they can offer a project's time-shares for sale to the public.

regression An appraisal principle that states that between dissimilar properties, the value of the better quality property is affected adversely by the presence of the lesser quality property.

Regulation Z Implements the Truth in Lending Act requiring credit institutions to inform borrowers of the true cost of obtaining credit.

reliction Gradual recession of water which uncovers land that usually belongs to the riparian owner.

remainder interest A future interest in real estate created by the grantor for some third party that will be enjoyed after the termination of a prior estate, such as when an owner conveys a life estate to one party and the remainder to another.

remainderman One entitled to receive a remainder interest in some estate sometime in the future.

rent A fixed, periodic payment made by a tenant of a property to the owner for possession and use, usually by prior agreement of the parties.

rental schedule A statement of proposed rental rates, determined by the owner, or the property manager, or both, based on a building's estimated expenses, market supply and demand, and the owner's long-range goals for the property.

replacement cost The construction cost at current prices of a property that is not necessarily an exact duplicate of the subject property but serves the same purpose or function as the original.

reproduction cost The construction cost at current prices of an exact duplicate of the subject property.

rescission The legal remedy of canceling, terminating, or annulling a contract and restoring the parties to their original positions. Contracts may be rescinded due to mistake, fraud, or misrepresentation. There is no need to show any money damage.

reserves A portion of earnings set aside to cover possible future losses.

Residential Rental Agreement Act The state law that mandates delivery of habitable residential rental units; obligations of the landlord and the tenant are mutually dependent. Provides tenant with rights and remedies such as the Retaliatory Eviction Doctrine.

Resolution Trust Corporation The organization created by the Financial Institutions Reform, Recovery, and Enforcement Act (FIRREA) to liquidate the assets of failed savings and loan associations.

restrictive covenant Private agreements usually imposed by the owner when property is sold that limits the way the real estate ownership may be used; frequently used by owner/developer to maintain specific standards in a subdivision. The covenants are appurtenant. Also called protective covenants.

retainer fee A small fee paid by the client upon creation of a buyer agency relationship as an advance partial compensation for services; it may be non-refundable or applied to final compensation due depending on the agency agreement.

retaliatory eviction Illegal eviction of a tenant that has exercised protected rights under the law.

return on investment (ROI) An annual percentage derived from dividing cash invested into net after-tax income.

revenue stamps *See* excise tax.

reverse mortgage A loan under which the homeowner receives monthly payments based on the homeowner's accumulated equity rather than a lump sum. The loan must be repaid at a prearranged date, upon the death of the owner, or the sale of the property.

reversionary interest A future estate that the grantor holds while granting a life estate to another person.

ridge board A heavy horizontal board, set on edge at the apex of the roof, to which the rafters are attached.

right of first opportunity to purchase The right of a party to have the first opportunity to purchase or lease real estate for a designated price, if the owner ever decides to sell or lease; if the holder of the right does not opt to purchase, the owner may sell to a third party within a specified time. If sale to third party does not occur, the right is still valid and process restarts.

right of first refusal The right of a person to have the first opportunity to either purchase or lease real property, if the owner ever decides to sell or lease; no terms are negotiated.

right of survivorship *See* tenancy by the entirety.

right-of-way The right given by a landowner to another to use the land as a pathway, without actually transferring ownership.

riparian rights An owner's rights in land that borders on or includes a stream, river, or lake. These rights include access to and use of the water.

roofing felt Sheets of flat or other close-woven, heavy material placed on top of the roof boards to insulate and waterproof the roof.

roofing shingle Thin, small sheet of wood, asbestos, fiberglass, slate, metal, clay, or other material used as the outer covering for a roof. Shingles are laid in overlapping rows to completely cover the roof surface. Shingles are sometimes used as an outer covering for exterior walls.

rules and regulations Real estate licensing authority orders that govern licensees' activities. They usually have the same force and effect as statutory law.

R-value The insulation value of materials. The higher the R-value, the more resistant the material is to the transfer of heat.

sale and leaseback A transaction in which an owner sells improved property and, as part of the same transaction, signs a long-term lease to remain in possession of the premises.

sales comparison approach The process of estimating the value of a property by examining and comparing actual sales of comparable properties.

satisfaction of mortgage A document acknowledging the full repayment of a mortgage debt.

scheduled gross income (SGI) The amount of rental income the property could produce with 100% occupancy and all tenants paying full rent; also called potential gross income.

secondary mortgage market A market for the purchase and sale of existing mortgages, designed to provide greater liquidity for mortgages; also called the secondary money market. Mortgages are first originated in the primary mortgage market.

section A portion of township under the rectangular (government) survey system. A township is divided into 36 sections, numbered 1 through 36. A section is a square with mile-long sides and an area of one square mile, or 640 acres.

security agreement *See* Uniform Commercial Code.

security deposit A payment by a tenant, held by the landlord during the lease term and kept (wholly or partially) on default or destruction of the premises by the tenant.

self-help eviction Illegal eviction practices used by landlords instead of lawful use of summary ejectment.

servient tenement Land on which an easement exists in favor of an adjacent property (called the dominant tenement); also called a servient estate or tract. Easement runs with the land.

setback The amount of space local zoning regulations require between a lot line and a building line.

settlement The process of adjusting and prorating credits, debits, and closing expenses to conclude a real estate transaction; referred to as closing.

severalty The ownership of real property by only one person or entity; also called sole ownership.

severance Changing an item of real estate to personal property by detaching it from the land; for example, cutting down a tree.

sharecropping In an agricultural lease, the agreement between the landowner and the tenant farmer to split the crop or the profit from its sale, actually sharing the crop.

shared-appreciation mortgage (SAM) A mortgage loan in which the lender, in exchange for a loan with a lower interest rate, participates in the profits (if any) the borrower receives when the property is eventually sold.

sheathing Insulating material that is applied to the wall framing; siding is applied on top of the sheathing.

shingles Exterior roofing material frequently made of fiberglass, asphalt, or wood.

short sale When a lender allows a borrower in default on mortgage loan payments to sell the mortgaged property for less money than necessary to satisfy the loan to avoid the delay and expense of a foreclosure sale; lender usually "forgives" the balance owed after the sale, although the IRS will frequently consider the forgiven amount to be taxable income for the borrower.

siding Boards nailed horizontally to the vertical studs, with or without intervening sheathing, to form the exposed surface of the outside walls of the building. Siding may be made of wood, metal, or masonry sheets.

sill The lowest horizontal member of the house frame, which rests atop the foundation wall and forms a base for the studs. The term can also refer to the lowest horizontal member in the frame for a window or door.

situs The personal preference of people for one location over another, not necessarily based on objective facts and knowledge.

slab A flat, horizontal reinforced concrete area, usually the interior floor of a building but also an exterior or a roof area.

soffit The external underside of the eave; usually contains ventilation for the attic and/or roof.

soil suitability test An engineer's test to determine the ability of the ground to absorb and drain water; used to determine suitability and location of septic system; also called a percolation or perk test.

sole plate The bottom of the wall frame that connects the studs to the flooring.

special agent One who is authorized by a principal to perform a single act or transaction. A real estate broker is usually a special agent of the seller authorized to find a ready, willing, and able buyer for a particular property, or a special agent of the buyer to find a specific type of property to purchase. Special agent has limited authority and cannot bind his principal.

special assessment A tax or levy customarily imposed against only those specific parcels of real estate that will benefit from a proposed public improvement like a street or sewer.

special warranty deed A deed in which the grantor only warrants, or guarantees, the title against defects arising during the period of the grantor's tenure and ownership of the property and not against defects existing before that time, generally using the language *by, through or under the grantor but not otherwise.*

specific lien A lien affecting or attaching only to a specific parcel of land or piece of real property; i.e. mortgage lien.

specific performance A legal action to compel a party to carry out the terms of a contract.

split-level Usually a house in which two or more floors are located directly above one another, and one or more additional floors, adjacent to them, are placed at a different level; a tri-level.

spot zoning Zoning that illegally singles out property for either special or more restrictive treatment than is usual under the area zoning ordinance.

square-foot method The appraisal method of estimating building costs by multiplying the number of square feet in the improvements being appraised by the cost per square foot for recently constructed similar improvements.

statute of frauds A state law that requires that certain instruments that convey interest in real estate be in writing to be legally enforceable, such as deeds, real estate sales contracts, and certain leases.

statute of limitations That law pertaining to the period of time within which certain actions must be brought to court or be lost.

statutory right of redemption The right of a defaulted property owner to recover the property after its sale by paying the appropriate fees and charges.

steering The illegal practice of channeling home seekers to particular areas, either to maintain the homogeneity of an area or to change the character of an area, which limits their choices of where they can live.

stigmatized property Property regarded as undesirable because of events that occurred there; also called psychologically impacted property. Some conditions that typically stigmatize a property are murder, gang-related activity, proximity to a nuclear plant, and even the alleged presence of ghosts.

straight-line method A method of calculating depreciation for tax purposes, computed by dividing the adjusted basis of a property by the estimated number of years of remaining useful life.

stud The vertical members in the wall framing; usually placed 16–24 inches apart and serve as main support for the roof and/or the story above.

subagent One who is employed by a person already acting as an agent; typically a reference to a provisional broker licensed under a broker (agent) who is employed under the terms of a listing agreement. A subagent has the same duties to the client as the agent.

subdivision A tract of land divided into two or more parcels by the owner, known as the subdivider, for the purpose of sale or development (either now or in the future); all land division involving the dedication of a new street or a change in an existing street.

subdivision and development ordinances Municipal ordinances that establish requirements for subdivisions and development.

subdivision plat *See* plat map.

subflooring Boards or plywood sheets nailed directly to the floor joists, serving as a base for the finish flooring. Subflooring is usually made of rough boards, although some houses have concrete subflooring.

subjacent support The support of the surface of land by the land's subsurface; duty of the owner of subsurface rights to support the surface of the land.

sublease/sublet The leasing of premises by a tenant to a third party for part of the lessee's remaining term. *See* assignment.

subordination Relegation to a lesser position, usually in respect to a right or security.

subordination agreement A written agreement between holders of liens on a property that changes the priority of mortgage, judgment, and other liens under certain circumstances.

subprime loan A loan made to a borrower with a credit rating below what is required for regular loans creating greater risk liability for the lender that is countered by higher interest rates and fees; called B, C, or D paper.

subrogation clause Any rights the insured had to sue the person who caused the damage are assigned to the insurance company that has already paid the insured for the damages.

substitution An appraisal principle that states that the maximum value of a property tends to be set by the cost of purchasing an equally desirable and valuable substitute property, assuming that no costly delay is encountered in making the substitution.

subsurface rights Ownership rights in a parcel of real estate to the water, minerals, gas, oil, and so forth that lie beneath the surface of the property.

success fee Compensation that is due and payable upon the creation of a valid sales contract for property located by the buyer's agent.

suit to quiet title A court action intended to establish or settle the title to a particular property, especially when a cloud on the title exists.

summary ejectment Legal eviction procedure heard before a magistrate for removal of a tenant that has breached the lease terms.

supply The amount of goods available in the market to be sold at a given price. The term is often coupled with demand.

supply and demand The appraisal principle that follows the interrelationship of the supply of and demand for real estate. As appraising is based on economic concepts, this principle recognizes that real property is subject to the influences of the marketplace, as is any other commodity.

surety bond An agreement by an insurance or a bonding company to be responsible for certain possible defaults, debts, or obligations contracted for by an insured party; in essence, a policy insuring one's personal or financial integrity. In the real estate business, a surety bond is generally used to ensure that a particular project will be completed at a certain date or that a contract will be performed as stated.

surface rights Ownership rights in a parcel of real estate that are limited to the surface of the property and do not include the air above it (air rights) or the minerals below the surface (subsurface rights).

survey The process by which boundaries are measured and land areas are determined; the on-site measurement of lot lines, dimensions, and position of a house on a lot, including the determination of any existing encroachments or easements.

syndicate A combination of people or firms formed to accomplish a business venture of mutual interest by pooling resources. In a real estate investment syndicate, the parties own and/or develop property, with the main profit generally arising from the sale of the property.

tacking Adding or combining successive periods of continuous occupation of real property by adverse possessors. This concept enables someone who has not been in possession for the entire statutory period to establish a claim of adverse possession.

taxation The process by which a government or municipal quasi-public body raises monies to fund its operation.

tax credit An amount by which tax owed is reduced directly.

tax deed An instrument, similar to a certificate of sale, given to a purchaser at a tax sale. *See also* certificate of sale.

tax lien A statutory lien against real property for nonpayment of taxes. Real and personal property tax liens and assessments take priority over all other liens. Real property tax and assessment liens are specific liens; personal property tax liens are general liens.

tax sale A court-ordered sale of real property to raise money to cover delinquent taxes.

tenancy by the entirety A concurrent form of ownership reserved for property owned by husband and wife. Right of survivorship is mandatory; making the surviving spouse owner in severalty immediately upon the death of a spouse.

tenancy in common A concurrent form of ownership in which each owner holds an undivided interest in the real property. Ownership interests can be unequal and the right of survivorship is not allowed.

Tenant Security Deposit Act The state act that regulates the amount and use of money that can be required as a security deposit and how the landlord holds that deposit. The maximum amount of the deposit depends on the term of the tenancy.

term loan A loan in which only interest is paid during the term of the loan, with the entire principal due with the final interest payment; also called a straight loan.

testate Having made and left a valid will.

tier (township strip) A strip of land six miles wide, extending east and west and numbered north and south according to its distance from the base line in the government rectangular survey system of legal description.

"time is of the essence" A phrase in a contract that requires the performance of a certain act no later than a stated time or the noncompliant party is in breach and the contract may be voidable by the opposite party.

time-share Any right to occupy a unit of real property during five or more separated time periods over a period of at least five years.

title (1) The right to or ownership of land. (2) The evidence of ownership of land.

title insurance A policy insuring the owner and/or mortgagee against loss by reason of defects in the title to a parcel of real estate, other than encumbrances, defects, and matters specifically excluded by the policy.

title search The search of public records to determine the current state of ownership of real estate; examining chain of title.

title theory Describing those states like North Carolina that interpret a mortgage to mean that the lender is the owner of mortgaged land who vests the legal title with the trustee while borrower holds equitable title. Borrower regains legal title upon full payment of the mortgage debt.

top plate The top part of the wall framing that connects the stud to the ceiling framing.

topographic survey A survey that measures the features of the earth's surfaces such as hills and valleys plus the location of roads.

Torrens system A method of evidencing title by registration with the proper public authority, generally called the registrar, named for its founder, Sir Robert Torrens.

tort A wrongful act, injury or violation of legal right to the person or property of another.

town house A hybrid form of ownership where the owner holds fee title to their unit and the ground beneath; horizontal ownership. Frequent use of party walls; row houses. Common areas are usually owned and maintained with other unit owners through a homeowners' association.

township The principal unit of the rectangular (government) survey system. A township is a square with six-mile sides and an area of 36 square miles.

township lines All the lines in a rectangular survey system that run east an west, parallel to the base line six miles apart.

trade fixture An article installed by a tenant under the terms of a lease and removable by the tenant before the lease expires.

transfer tax Tax stamps required to be affixed to a deed by state or local law; excise tax, formerly know as revenue stamps.

trust A fiduciary arrangement whereby property is conveyed to a person or an institution, called a trustee, to be held and administered on behalf of another person, called a beneficiary. The one who conveys the trust is called the trustor.

trustee The holder of bare, legal title in a deed of trust loan transaction on behalf of a beneficiary.

trustee's deed A deed executed by a trustee conveying land held in a trust.

trust funds Those monies received on behalf of others by a real estate licensee while acting as an agent in a real estate transaction. Generally, trust funds include earnest money deposits, down payments, tenant security deposits, rents, and monies received from final settlements and must be deposited into a trust account in accordance with NC Real Estate Commission Rules.

Truth in Lending Act *See* Regulation Z.

underground storage tank (UST) A tank and any underground piping connected to the tank that has at least 10% of its combined volume underground; federal UST regulations apply to only those storing either petroleum or certain hazardous substances.

undivided interest *See* tenancy in common.

unenforceable contract A contract that has all the elements of a valid contract, yet neither party can sue the other to force performance of it. For example, a verbal contract is generally unenforceable.

Uniform Commercial Code A codification of commercial law, adopted in most states, that attempts to make uniform all laws relating to commercial transactions, including chattel mortgages and bulk transfers. When chattels are purchased on credit, security interests are created by an instrument known as a security agreement. To give notice of the security interest, a financing statement must be recorded. Article 6 of the code regulates bulk transfers—the sale of a business as a whole, including all fixtures, chattels, and merchandise.

Uniform Electronic Transactions Act (UETA) North Carolina version of the federal E-sign legislation that validates electronic contracts, documents and signatures.

Uniform Settlement Statement The standard HUD-1 closing statement form required to be given to the borrower, lender, and seller at or before settlement by the closing agent in a transaction covered under the Real Estate Settlement Procedures Act.

unilateral contract A one-sided contract wherein one party makes a promise to induce a second party to do something. The second party is not legally bound to perform; however, if the second party does comply, the first party is obligated to keep the promise.

unit-in-place method The appraisal method of estimating building costs by calculating the costs of all of the physical components in the structure, with the cost of each item including its proper installation, connection, etc.; also called the segregated cost method.

universal agent Person empowered to do anything the principal could do personally; unlimited authority; unusual in real estate.

urea-formaldehyde foam insulation (UFFI) A 1970s foam insulation that released gases that can cause respiratory problems such as skin irritations or asthma attacks.

usury Charging interest at a higher rate than the maximum rate established by state law.

vacancy and collection losses The amount of income lost due to empty units or tenants not paying full rent.

vacancy rate The percentage of the total space that is unoccupied.

valid contract A contract that complies with all the essentials of a contract and is binding and enforceable on all parties to it.

VA-guaranteed loan A mortgage loan on approved property made to a qualified veteran by an authorized lender and guaranteed by the Department of Veterans Affairs to limit the lender's possible loss.

value The power of a good or service to command other goods in exchange for the present worth of future rights to its income or amenities.

variance Permission obtained from zoning authorities to build a structure or conduct a use that is expressly prohibited by the current zoning laws; an exemption from ordinances due to unique hardship not created by the property owner.

vendee/vendor Vendee is a buyer, usually under the terms of a land contract; vendor is a seller, usually in a land contract.

vicarious liability Liability for the actions of another party due to the legal relationship between them. Principals and agents can be held responsible for the actions of subagents.

voidable contract A contract that seems to be valid on the surface but may be rejected or disaffirmed by one or both of the parties.

void contract A contract that has no legal force or effect because it does not meet the essential elements of a contract.

voluntary lien A lien placed on property with the knowledge and consent of the property owner; such as a mortgage lien.

walk-through The final inspection of the property by the buyer prior to closing to assure that the seller has vacated, made required repairs satisfactorily, and delivered the property in the condition it was in at contract.

waste An improper use or abuse of a property by a possessor who holds less than fee ownership, such as a tenant, life tenant, mortgagor, or vendee. Such waste ordinarily impairs the value of the land or the interest of the person holding the title or the reversionary rights.

water table Natural water level whether it is above or below ground level.

wetlands Areas periodically inundated or saturated to the extent that they can or do support vegetation adapted to aquatic conditions.

will A written document, properly witnessed, providing for the transfer of title to property owned by the deceased.

willful misrepresentation Intentionally misinforming any party involved in a transaction about a material fact.

willful omission Intentionally failing to disclose a material fact to any party involved in a transaction.

Working with Real Estate Agents A mandatory agency information brochure that a licensee must give to and review with consumers in all real estate sales transactions no later than first substantial contact; it does not create agency.

wraparound loan A method of refinancing in which the new mortgage is placed in a secondary, or subordinate, position. The new mortgage includes both the unpaid principal balance of the first mortgage and whatever additional sums are advanced by the lender. In essence, it is an additional mortgage in which another lender refinances a borrower by lending an amount exceeding the existing first mortgage amount without disturbing the existence of the first mortgage.

writ of attachment At the request of a creditor, the court retains custody of the unsecured property during the lawsuit to ensure that the property remains available to satisfy a judgment ordered as resolution of the suit by the court. A recorded writ is an encumbrance on the property.

writ of execution A court order directing the county sheriff to sell a defendant's property as required by judgment or court decree.

yield The return on investment; amount of profit.

yield spread premium A fee, usually expressed as a percentage of the loan amount, paid by a lender to a mortgage broker for making a loan at an above-market interest rate with little or no origination fee. The lender will receive an increased yield due to the higher interest rate, thus allowing the compensation of the mortgage broker without an origination fee.

zoning ordinance An exercise of police power by a municipality to regulate and control the character and use of property. Zoning is local in nature.

Answer Key

CHAPTER 1
Basic Real Estate Concepts

1. c (2)
2. b (3–4)
3. b (4)
4. c (4)
5. a (4–5)
6. d (5)
7. b (10)
8. c (12–13)
9. b (9)
10. a (13)
11. d (11–12)
12. c (6–7)
13. b (10)
14. d (10)
15. d (12–13)
16. d (11)
17. a (5)
18. b (11–12)
19. b (4)
20. a (8)

CHAPTER 2
Property Ownership and Interests

1. b (19)
2. b (21)
3. d (21)
4. c (23)
5. b (24)
6. c (24)
7. d (24)
8. a (24)
9. a (28)
10. b (28)
11. b (28)
12. c (28–29)
13. d (27)
14. c (31)
15. b (33)
16. a (35–36)
17. d (33)
18. b (33–34)
19. a (37)
20. c (36, 38)

CHAPTER 3
Encumbrances on Real Property

1. b (47)
2. d (48–49)
3. d (48)
4. c (49)
5. b (49)
6. d (47–48)
7. a (50)
8. a (50–52)
9. b (50–53)
10. c (55)
11. a (54–55)
12. a (56) $0.80 + 0.50 = $1.30 city + county tax rate ÷ 100 = 0.013; $1,600 annual taxes ÷ 0.013 = $123,076.92 assessed value
13. b (56) $133,000 assessed value × 0.01678 tax rate = $2,231.74 annual taxes ÷ 12 months = $185.97833 = $185.98 monthly tax liability
14. b (56) $2,000 annual taxes ÷ $183,500 assessed value = 0.010899 × $100 = $1.0899 = $1.09 per $100 of assessed value
15. b (56) $129,000 appraised value × 75% = $96,750 assessed value
16. c (56) $389,000 appraised value × 85% = $330,650 assessed value × $0.011 tax rate = $3,637.15 annual tax liability
17. a (56) $295,000 market value × 80% = $236,000 assessed value × $0.0063 county tax rate = $1,486.80 annual tax bill ÷ 12 months = $123.90 monthly tax bill
18. a (56) $7,248,000 annual budget ÷ $1,135,500,000 ÷ 100 = $0.64 per $100 assessed value
19. d (55) $47,250 assessed value × 1.25 equalization factor = $59,062.50 × 0.025 mill rate = $1,476.56 annual tax rounds up to $1,477

20. a (56) $75,000 lot + $250,000 house = $325,000 new assessed value × 0.01678 rate = $5,453.50 ÷ 12 months = $454.46 monthly tax
21. a (48)
22. c (48)

CHAPTER 4
Property Description

1. c (64)
2. b (65)
3. b (64–65)
4. c (70)
5. a (71)
6. c (77)
7. c (77)
8. d (77)
9. a (72) 21,780 square feet ÷ 43,560 number of sq. ft. in acre = 0.5 acre × $25,000 per acre = $12,500
10. b (72) 350 acres × 43,560 (sq. ft./acre) = 15,246,000 sq. ft. ÷ 1,300' = 11,727.692' depth; 11,727.692 × 6,000' frontage = 70,366,152 sq. ft. ÷ divided by 43,560 = 1,615.4 acres rounded
11. c (72) 660' × 660' = 435,600 sq. ft. ÷ 43,560 = 10 acres ÷ 2 = 5 acres in each lot
12. b (710–712) 29' × 34' × 17' = 16,762 cubic feet in house; 29' × 34' × 8' ÷ 2 = 3,944 cubic feet in roof; 16,762 cubic feet + 3,944 cubic feet = 20,706 cubic feet total × $2.25 per cubic foot = $46,588.50 cost
13. c (707) $6,468.75 price ÷ 125 front feet = $51.75 per front foot
14. b (68–69)
15. d (65–66)
16. d (67–69)
17. b (64)
18. c (67)
19. c (67)
20. a (67)
21. a (67)
22. a (68–69)
23. b (72)
24. a (67–69) 2640' × 2640' = 6,969,600 sq. ft. ÷ 43,560' per acre = 160 acres ÷ 2 = 80 acres

CHAPTER 5
Transfer of Title to Real Property

1. c (92)
2. d (90) $75,000 sales price ÷ 500 = 150 × $1 = $150
3. d (90) $185,900 sales price ÷ 500 = 371.80 × $1 = $371.80; round up to $372.00
4. c (79)
5. b (81–94)
6. c (80, 93)
7. d (89)
8. d (81)
9. c (96)
10. a (96)
11. a (96, 100)
12. d (96)
13. c (99)
14. c (91)
15. b (90–92)
16. b (99–100)
17. d (96–97)
18. a (93)
19. b (84)

CHAPTER 6
Land-Use Controls

1. a (119–120)
2. d (110–111)
3. b (108)
4. a (109)
5. b (111)
6. b (111–112)
7. c (109)
8. b (117–118)
9. a (113–114)
10. b (119)
11. a (111)
12. d (111)
13. b (119)
14. a (120)
15. b (111)
16. a (112)
17. c (116)
18. b (116–117)
19. d (120)
20. b (111–112)
21. d (111)
22. d (112, 115–116)

23. b (116)
24. a (110)
25. c (115–116)

CHAPTER 7
Real Estate Brokerage and the Law of Agency

1. a (145)
2. b (128, 145)
3. b (129, 154)
4. b (130)
5. a (132)
6. d (154–155)
7. a (133)
8. c (153–154)
9. c (153–154)
10. b (127)
11. d (145–147)
12. b (132)
13. d (143)
14. c (140, 601)
15. b (145–147)
16. c (145–146)
17. d (146)
18. c (146, 153)
19. c (134–139)
20. b (138)
21. d (148–149)
22. c (138–139)
23. d (148–149, 152)
24. c (154)
25. c (139–140)

CHAPTER 8
Basic Contract Law

1. b (166–167)
2. b (171–172)
3. b (171)
4. b (166)
5. d (164–165)
6. b (165)
7. a (169)
8. c (166)
9. b (164)
10. d (171)
11. d (167)
12. c (167)
13. c (169)
14. b (165)

15. d (171)
16. d (167)
17. a (169–170)
18. c (168)
19. d (167–168)
20. b (167)

CHAPTER 9
Agency Contracts

1. d (179)
2. c (184–185)
3. c (189)
4. b (178–179)
5. a (179)
6. d (191–192)
7. c (182)
8. a (179, 185)
9. a (192)
10. d (183, 191)
11. d (185)
12. a (197–198)
13. b (197–198)
14. b (181) $125,000 sales price × 6% commission rate = $7,500 commission × 60% (100% − 40% other firm's split) = $4500 ABC's share
15. a (181) $4287.50 commission portion ÷ 70% = $6125 Listing firm split ÷ 50% = $12,250 total commission ÷ 5% commission rate = $245,000
16. a (181) $73,000 sales price × 0.06 = $4,380 gross commission ÷ 2 = $2,190 listing firm's share × 0.30 listing licensee's share = $657
17. d (181) $135,000 SP × 0.065 = $8,775 gross commission × 0.55 selling broker's share = $4,826.25 × 0.60 your share = $2,895.75
18. b (196) 2% + 5% + 3% = 10% total commission rate; $2,000 total comm. ÷ 0.10 comm. rate = $20,000 sales price
    Listing agent: $20,000 × 0.02 = $400
    Firm: $20,000 × 0.05 = $1,000
    Selling agent: $20,000 × 0.03 = $600
19. d (196) $120,000 + $1000 + $50,000 = $171,000 net amount seller needs ÷ 95% (100% − 5% comm. rate) = $180,000
20. d (196) $85,000 seller desired net + $1,000 closing costs + $65,000 loan payoff = $151,000 net amount seller needs ÷ 0.93 (100% − 7% comm. rate) = $162,365.59 sales price (rounded up to $162,366.00)
21. b (197)

CHAPTER 10
Sales Contracts and Practices

1. b (224)
2. b (228–229)
3. d (224–225)
4. b (224)
5. d (215, 220–221)
6. a (215–216)
7. d (217–218)
8. b (216)
9. a (218)
10. c (226–228)
11. d (226)
12. b (215)
13. b (228)
14. a (216)
15. c (225)
16. d (229)
17. c (212)
18. d (218)
19. a (220)
20. a (219–220)

CHAPTER 11
Landlord and Tenant

1. b (243)
2. a (236–237)
3. c (238)
4. b (243)
5. c (243)
6. b (242)
7. d (247)
8. a (250)
9. d (245–246)
10. c (245–246)
11. c (239–240)
12. b (244)
13. c (248)
14. c (247)
15. b (245–246)
16. b (236)
17. c (238)
18. d (237)
19. b (245–246)
20. a (248–249)
21. b (236)
22. a (242)
23. a (243–244)
24. b (240)
25. c (239) $900 monthly rent × 12 months = $10,800 base rent; $275,000 gross sales – $150,000 = $125,000 sales subject to percentage rent × 4% = $5,000 percentage rent + $10,800 base rent = $15,800 total annual rent

CHAPTER 12
Property Management

1. a (264)
2. c (262)
3. c (264)
4. c (264)
5. b (267)
6. d (261, 265, 268)
7. c (265) $750 monthly rent × 12 months × 20 units = $180,000 total rent × 8% = $14,400 commission
8. b (259–260)
9. c (265)
10. c (262, 266–267)
11. c (263) 2–4BR × $1,000/mo. = $2,000 × 12 mos. = $24,000 rent received; 25–3BR × $850/mo. = $21,250 × 12 mos. = $255,000 × 0.95 (5% vacancy) = $242,250 rent received; 10–2BR × $750/mo. = $7,500 × 12 mos. = $90,000 × 0.95 (5% vacancy) = $85,500 rent received; 11–1BR × $650/mo. = $7,150 × 12 mos. = $85,800 × 0.90 (10% vacancy) = $77,220; Total rent received = $428,970 × 0.12 mgmt. fee = $51,476
12. c (263)
13. a (258)
14. b (259)
15. c (269–270)
16. d (268–269)
17. b (263)
18. c (263)
19. c (270)
20. d (268)

CHAPTER 13
Real Estate Financing: Principles

1. b (276)
2. a (279)
3. b (277–278)
4. b (283) $120,000 loan × 0.03 (3 discount points) = $3,600

5. b (277–278)
6. c (286–287)
7. b (282)
8. b (283) $2,700 points ÷ $90,000 loan = 0.03 = 3 points
9. a (294)
10. d (279)
11. c (277, 293)
12. a (277)
13. b (282–283)
14. c (279)
15. d (294)
16. b (295)
17. c (295)
18. b (297–298)
19. a (286)
20. c (288)
21. b (285)
22. b (295)
23. b (288)
24. a (278)
25. b (276)
26. b (297)
27. d (283) $185,500 SP × 0.80 = $148,400 loan × 0.01 = 15. $1,484 origination fee; $148,400 × 0.02 = $2,968 discount points; $1,484 + $2,968 = $4,452 loan fees
28. c (283–285) $180,000 SP × 0.85 = $153,000 loan amount ÷ 12. 1,000 = 153 × 6.65 factor = $1,017.45 PI; Taxes: $996 ÷ 12 months = $83. Insurance: $480 ÷ 12 months = $40; $1,017.45 PI + $83 T + $40 I = $1,140.45 monthly PITI
29. b (284–285) $1,017.45 monthly PI × 360 payments = 13. $366,282 PI – $153,000 original P = $213,282 total interest
30. b (285) $153,000 LV × 0.07 = $10,710 I ÷ 12 months 14. = $892.50 I; $1,017.45 PI – $892.50 I = $124.95 P; $153,000 P – $124.95 P = $152,875.05 new LV

CHAPTER 14
Real Estate Financing: Practices

1. a (308)
2. a (318)
3. c (312)
4. b (319)
5. b (327–328)
6. d (316–317)
7. c (320)
8. b (319)
9. a (317–318)
10. b (319)
11. c (313)
12. b (327)
13. d (308)
14. b (321)
15. c (323, 325) Housing Expense = $750 ÷ 0.28 = $2,678.57, rounded up to $2,679 for income ratio; Recurring Obligations $750 + $500 = $1,250 ÷ 0.36 = $3,472.222 rounded to $3,472 for debt ratio = higher income need
16. a (328)
17. c (314)
18. d (308–309)
19. d (307–308)
20. c (319–320)
21. a (327–328)
22. c (316)
23. c (226, 318)
24. d (320)
25. d (328)
26. b (311) $114,500 appraised value × 0.80 = $91,600 loan amount
27. c (311)
28. c (323) $847 PITI + $745 recurring obligations = $1,592 ÷ 0.36 = $4,422.22 × 12 months = $53,066.66 annual income; rounds to $53,067
29. a (323) $60,000 annual income ÷ 12 months = $5,000 monthly income × 0.36 = $1,800 maximum PITI and Recurring obligations; $1,800 – ($160 taxes + $700 recurring debts) = $940 maximum PI ÷ 6.67 loan factor = $140.92953 × $1,000 = $140,929.53
30. a (323) $42,000 annual gross income ÷ 12 months = $3,500 × 0.36 = $1,260 – $500 = $760
31. a (323) $40,800 ÷ 12 months = $3,400 monthly gross income; Housing: $895 ÷ $3,400 = 0.26 = 26%: Yes; Recurring Obligations: $895 housing + $425 debt = $1,320 ÷ $3,400 = 0.39 = 39%: No
32. c (323) $719.32 PI + $135 TI + $500 debt = $1,354.32 total debt ÷ 0.36 = $3,762 monthly income × 12 months = $45,144

33. b (323) $53,000 ÷ 12 = $4,416.67 monthly income; 20. $4,416.67 × 0.36 = $1,590 maximum recurring obligations; $1,590 − $150 TI − $650 recurring obligations = $790 maximum PI; $790 ÷ 8.0462 = $98.182993 × 1,000 = $98,182.99
34. b (311) $123,000 sales price × 0.05 down payment = $6,150 down payment amt.
35. b (311) $356,000 loan amt. ÷ $1,200,000 value = 0.2966666 = 29.67% LTV

CHAPTER 15
Closing the Real Estate Transaction

1. b (354, 356)
2. d (341)
3. c (352)
4. d (357) $1,800 annual taxes ÷ 360 days = $5.00 per day; Jan 1–Sep 15 = 255 days × $5 = $1,275 seller's liability; Seller prepaid $1,800 − $1,275 = $525 credit seller/debit buyer
5. b (357–358) $450 rent ÷ 30 days = $15 × 23 days = $345 seller's portion; $450 − $345 = $105 debit seller/credit buyer
6. c (357) $150,000 sales price × 0.90 = $135,000 (loan amount) × 0.03 = $4,050 (loan fees) + $15,000 (down payment) = $19,050
7. d (359)
8. a (359)
9. a (359)
10. b (359)
11. c (358)
12. d (345)
13. b (346–347)
14. b (359)
15. d (359)
16. a (348)
17. b (355)
18. c (353, 359)
19. d (358) $575 × 3 = $1,725 ÷ 30 = $57.50/day Nov 1 to Nov 14 = 14 days × $57.50 = $805 seller retains $1,725 − $805 = $920 credit buyer/debit seller
20. a (356, 359) $82,000 × 0.07 = $5,740 annual interest ÷ 360 days = $15.944/daily interest; Aug 1 to Aug 11 = 11 days × $15.944 = $175.38 seller's interest portion
21. b (358–359, 364–365) $1,260 ÷ 360 days = $3.50/day; Jan 1 to Nov 15 = 315 days × $3.50 = $1,102.50 seller's share of taxes; $1,260 total tax − $1,102.50 seller's share = $157.50 credit seller/debit buyer for buyer's share
22. b (358–359, 364–365, 799–801)
23. c (358–359, 364–365, 799–801)
24. c (358–359, 364–365, 799–801)
25. a (358–359, 364–365, 799–801)

CHAPTER 16
Basic Residential Construction

1. a (384)
2. b (377)
3. d (378)
4. c (376)
5. c (383)
6. a (377)
7. c (385)
8. a (378)
9. c (378)
10. c (378)

CHAPTER 17
Real Property Valuation

1. c (408)
2. b (401–402)
3. a (405–406) Net operating income (NOI) of $24,000 ÷ $300,000 value = 0.08 = 8%
4. c (405–407)
5. b (392)
6. c (405)
7. b (405)
8. c (403)
9. b (403–404)
10. d (404)
11. c (405)
12. a (390)
13. b (392)
14. b (405–406)
15. a (404)
16. c (400)
17. b (405)
18. b (405)
19. b (404)
20. a (407)
21. a (401–402)
22. b (405–406)

23. d (404)
24. a (392)
25. c (405–406) Gross income of $6,000 – $1,000 mgt. ex. – $300 taxes – $1,100 repairs = $3,600 (Debt service is not an operating expense.)
26. d (399–400)
27. c (399–400)

Subject	Comparable		Sold for **$140,000**
2,100 SF	1,900 SF (200 × $72)	=	+ 14,400
4BR	3 BR (1 × $2,000)	=	+ 2,000
2 CG	1 CG (1 × $1,500)	=	+ 1,500
No patio	Patio (1 × $2,000)	=	– 2,000
No pool	Pool (1 × $14,000)	=	– 14,000
2.5 baths	2 baths (½ = $800)	=	+ 800
1 acre	1.5 acres (½ = $15,000)	=	– 15,000
Subject Property		=	$127,700

28. c (399–400)

Comp A	Comp B	Comp C	Comp D
$73,000	$74,000	$62,000	$71,000
–$3,000	–$2,000	+$3,500	–$5,000
$70,000	$72,000	$65,500	$66,000
Range = $65,500 low to $72,000 high			

29. b (401)
30. b (399–400) Comps #1 and #2 are the same except for square footage: $110,000 – $100,000 = $10,000 ÷ 200 sq ft (3,000 – 2,800) = $50 per sq ft

Comp #2 and Comp #3:

$110,000 – $86,000	=	$24,000
3,000 sq ft – 2,600 sq ft	=	
400 sq ft × $50		– 20,000
Value of garage:		$ 4,000

	Comp #1	Comp #2	Comp #3
	$100,000	$110,000	$ 86,000
Sq ft	+ 10,000	-0-	+$20,000
Garage	– 4,000	– 4,000	-0-
	$106,000	$106,000	$106,000

CHAPTER 18
Property Insurance

1. d (417, 421)
2. b (419–420)
3. a (420–421)
4. a (420)
5. d (270)
6. c (416)
7. b (419–420) ($175,00 × 50% bought coverage) ÷ ($175,000 × 80% required coverage) × $82,000 claim = $51,250
8. b (270)
9. c (270)
10. b (419)

CHAPTER 19
Federal Income Taxation of Real Property Ownership

1. c (428–429)
2. a (427)
3. c (427)
4. b (428–429)
5. d (426–427)
6. b (427–429)
7. a (428–429)
8. a (428–429)
9. a (427–428) $127,500 sales price less selling expenses of $750 = $126,750 amount realized – $75,000 original cost = $51,750
10. c (428–429)
11. b (427) $72,000 basis + $15,000 addition + $3,000 deck = $90,000. Repairs and painting would be considered ordinary repairs or maintenance and would not increase the adjusted basis.
12. d (431)
13. c (430–431)
14. b (427) $120,000 SP + $2,600 CC = $122,600 basis
15. c (427) $120,000 + $2,600 + $16,000 = $138,600
16. d (428) $165,000 SP × 0.93 – $1,300 = $152,150
17. a (428) $152,150 amount realized – $138,600 adjusted 33. basis = $13,550 gain
18. b (432–433) $5,000 profit ÷ $20,000 original price = 25% profit

19. c (432–433) $20,000 × 5 lots = $100,000 original value; $17,000 × 9 lots = $153,000 present value − $100,000 = $53,000 profit ÷ $100,000 original value = 0.53 = 53% profit
20. c (432–433) $105,000 × 0.90 = $94,500 original debt; $105,000 − $94,500 = $10,500 original equity; $105,000 × 1.20 = $126,000 new value; $94,500 × 0.92 (100% − 8%) = $86,940 new debt; $126,000 − $86,940 = $39,060 new equity; $39,060 − $10,500 = $28,560 increase in equity; $28,560 ÷ $10,500 = 2.72 = 272%

CHAPTER 20
Fair Housing and Ethical Practices

1. c (440–441)
2. d (447)
3. d (440)
4. b (451)
5. c (452)
6. a (453)
7. b (445)
8. c (445)
9. d (452–453)
10. b (440–441)
11. a (440, 442)
12. b (440)
13. c (440, 442)
14. b (448–449)
15. b (448)
16. b (448–450)
17. d (440–442)
18. b (451–452)
19. b (447)
20. a (440)

CHAPTER 21
Environmental Issues and the Real Estate Transaction

1. b (463–464)
2. c (464)
3. c (464)
4. a (463–464)
5. b (469)
6. c (468)
7. b (470–471)
8. d (473–474)
9. c (468)
10. d (466–467)
11. b (464–465)
12. c (466)
13. c (466)
14. d (464–465)
15. b (467)

CHAPTER 22
Basic Real Estate Investment

1. a (485, 488) $50,000 income − $10,000 expenses − $35,000 debt service = $5,000 cash flow
2. b (485)
3. b (488) $104,500 EGI − $36,500 operating expenses = $68,000 NOI − $54,000 debt service = $14,000 cash flow ÷ $100,000 investment equity = 0.14 = 14% EDR
4. c (488) $18,000 NOI − $13,500 debt service = $4,500 cash flow ÷ $30,000 investment equity = 0.15 = 15% EDR
5. b (489)
6. b (484–485)
7. d (483)
8. a (489)
9. c (484)
10. d (485)

APPENDIX A
Practice Exam

1. b (64)
2. c (57)
3. c (64–65)
4. d (79–80)
5. d (27)
6. b (84)
7. d (22–23)
8. b (100)
9. a (81)
10. a (29–30)
11. b (236–237)
12. a (111)
13. d (244)
14. b (108)
15. a (84)
16. b (47)
17. c (111)
18. d (21)
19. b (237)
20. a (342–343)

21. d (216)
22. b (170)
23. c (166–167)
24. c (191–192)
25. d (218–219)
26. d (215)
27. a (165–166)
28. a (354)
29. d (184)
30. a (220)
31. c (185)
32. c (168)
33. d (359)
34. c (143)
35. d (259–260)
36. b (215–216)
37. a (25, 219)
38. b (52)
39. d (113, 116)
40. d (139–140)
41. b (191)
42. a (200–201)
43. a (427–429)
44. b (428–429)
45. a (451–452)
46. c (440–441, 447)
47. a (451)
48. d (378)
49. a (464–466)
50. d (197–198)
51. b (464–465)
52. a (93A–6)
53. d (93A–2)
54. a (A.0105)
55. a (A.0108)
56. a (A.0107)
57. b (A.0110)
58. a (A.0101, A.0503)
59. a (A.0110)
60. c (A.0503)
61. d (A.1902)
62. d (A.1902)
63. a (A.1902)
64. a (93A Article 4)
65. c (288)
66. a (276)
67. b (276)
68. c (279)
69. c (286–287)
70. c (285)
71. d (276)
72. a (289)
73. d (282–283)
74. b (279)
75. b (279)
76. c (295)
77. d (286)
78. b (319)
79. a (327)
80. b (327–328)
81. b (403)
82. a (390)
83. b (398–399)
84. d (405–406)
85. d (405)
86. c (392)
87. c (401–402)
88. d (390)
89. c (392)
90. a (398)
91. b (404)
92. d (408)
93. a (405)
94. c (284–285, 724) $98,763 loan balance × 5.75% annual interest rate ÷ 360 days × 30 days = $473.24 monthly interest; $584 monthly PI – $473.24 monthly I = $110.76 monthly P; $98,763 loan balance – $110.76 P = $98,652.24 new loan balance
95. d (90) $143,900 sales price ÷ 500 = $287.80 rounds up to $288.00
96. b (705, 707) 150' × 375' = 56,250 square feet ÷ 43,560 = 1.2913 acres × $50,000 price per acre = $64,565 sales price ÷ 150 front feet = $430.43 per front foot
97. c (284, 724) $412.50 monthly interest × 12 months = $4,950 annual interest ÷ $60,000 loan amount = 0.0825 = 8.25%
98. c (181, 719–720) $2,593.50 × 2 = $5,187 gross commission ÷ 0.065 (6.5%) = $79,800 SP
99. d (196, 721) $65,000 seller net ÷ 0.94 (100% – 6%) = $69,148.936 rounded to $69,149
100. b (181, 719–720) Sales price of $50,000 × 0.0775 (7¾%) = $3,875 commission
101. b (283, 724) $107,000 sales price × 0.80 (80%) = $85,600 loan × 0.025 = $2,140 points

797

102. a (56, 355–356) $64,000 assessed value × 0.0072 tax rate ÷ 360 days × 118 days that seller is responsible for tax = $151.04 seller debit/buyer credit
103. a (181, 719–720) $84,500 sales price × 0.07 (7%) = $5,915 gross commission × 0.40 (40% to listing broker) = $2,366 × 0.50 (50% of the 40%)= $1,183 to listing licensee
104. c (281, 358) $138,000 loan amount × 6.5% interest rate = $8970 annual interest ÷ 360 days × 4 days = $99.67 interim interest
105. c (400–401) $166,200 comp's sales price – $2750 (50 extra square feet × $55) – $1000 (extra ½ bath) + $2500 (short 1-car garage) + $1662 ($166,200 × 6% annual appreciation ÷ 12 months × 2 months) = $166,612 indication of value
106. c (196, 721) Seller net of $72,000 ÷ 0.94 (100% – 6%) = $76,595.744 rounded to $76,596
107. a (358–359) $84,500 purchase price less $67,600 loan, less $2,000 deposit, less $183.53 prorated taxes, plus $1,250 closing costs = $15,966.47 rounded to $15,966; proration of taxes: $880.96 ÷ 360 days = $2.447 per day × 75 days (Jan 1–Mar 15) = $183.25 credit buyer/debit seller
108. c (725–727) $105,000 sales price (present value) ÷ 1.25 (100% + 25%) = $84,000
109. b (323) $1386 housing expense ÷ 28% income ratio = $4,950 minimum income; $1,386 + $725 debt = $2,111 long term recurring debt ÷ 36% debt ratio = $5,864 minimum income; chose larger income amount because must qualify on both ratios
110. b (284–285) $2364 payment × 360 total # of payments = $851,040 total P&I – $394,000 original principal amount = $457,040 total interest paid

APPENDIX C
Real Estate License Law*

1. c (93A-6)(A.0113)
2. d (93A-2)
3. a (A.0503)
4. d (93A-6)(A.0105)
5. a (93A-2)
6. c (93A-6)
7. a (A.1902)
8. c (A.0105)
9. d (A.0109)
10. c (93A-40)(58B.0103)
11. b (93A-40 & 45)
12. b (93A-8)
13. a (A.0112)
14. c (93A-45)
15. a (93A-3)
16. b (A.0107)
17. b (A.0503)
18. d (A.0601)
19. a (A.0107)
20. b (A.0104)
21. c (A.0107)
22. d (A.0104)
23. d (A.0107)
24. b (A.0107)
25. a (93A-4.2)
26. d (A.0110)
27. c (A.1703)
28. a (A.0107)
29. c (A.0107)
30. a (A.0110)

* Answers to these and all license law questions can be found in Appendix C: Real Estate License Law and Commission Rules.

Answer key to closing statement worksheet from Chapter 15, questions 22 through 25

NORTH CAROLINA REAL ESTATE COMMISSION

Closing Exercise Worksheet - Part A

Settlement Charges	Paid from Borrower's Funds at Settlement *Charges to Borrower*	Paid from Seller's Funds at Settlement *Charges to Seller*
Real Estate Broker Fees		
Commission paid at settlement		6600.00
Items Payable in Connection with Loan		
Loan origination fee/charge	880.00	
Loan discount points for specific interest rate chosen	1320.00	
Appraisal fee	150.00	
Credit report fee	50.00	
Items Required by Lender to be Paid in Advance		
Daily interest charges from 10/15 to 10/30 @ $24.444 per day	391.10	
Mortgage insurance premium for ____ months		
Homeowner's insurance premium for _1_ years	345.00	
Reserves Deposited with Lender (for Escrow Account)		
Homeowner's insurance ____months @ $_____per month		
Mortgage insurance ____months @ $_____per month		
Property taxes ____months @ $_____per month		
Escrow Account Deposit	500.00	
Title Charges		
Closing attorney's fee	500.00	
Title insurance premium (lender's and/or owner's policy)	250.00	
Deed preparation fee		50.00
Government Recording and Transfer Charges		
Recording fees: Deed $7 Mortgage $7	14.00	
Excise tax (state tax stamps)		220.00
Additional Settlement Charges		
Survey	200.00	
Pest Inspection	75.00	
Courier Fees		
Homeowner's Warranty		
Other: Seller property tax portion 1/1 to 10/15		870.96
Buyer property tax portion 10/16 to 12/30	229.04	
Total Settlement Charges *(Enter here and on the lines where indicated on **Part B** of the Worksheet)*	4,904.14	7,740.96

12/02/09

NORTH CAROLINA REAL ESTATE COMMISSION

Closing Exercise Worksheet - Part B

Summary of Borrower's Transaction

Charges to Borrower

Gross Amount Due From Borrower	
Contract sales price	110,000.00
Personal property	
Settlement charges to borrower *(from bottom line of borrower's column on Part A of Worksheet)*	4,904.14
Adjustments for items paid by seller in advance	
Real property taxes	
Assessments	
Gross Amount Due from Borrower *(Total Charges to Borrower)*	114,904.14

Credits to Borrower

Amounts Paid By or In Behalf of Borrower	
Deposit or earnest money	5,000.00
Principal amount of new mortgage loan(s)	88,000.00
Due Diligence Fee	50.00
Adjustments for items unpaid by seller	
Real property taxes	
Assessments	
Total Paid By/For Borrower *(Total Credits to Borrower)*	93,050.00

Summary of Seller's Transaction

Credits to Seller

Gross Amount Due to Seller	
Contract sales price	110,000.00
Personal property	
Adjustments for items paid by seller in advance	
Real property taxes	
Assessments	
Gross Amount Due to Seller *(Total Credits to Seller)*	110,000.00

Charges to Seller

Reductions in Amount Due to Seller	
Settlement charges to seller *(from bottom line of seller's column on Part A of Worksheet)*	7,740.96
Payoff of seller's mortgage loan(s)	82,750.00
Due Diligence Fee	50.00
Accrued mortgage interest	344.79
Adjustments for items unpaid by seller	
Real property taxes	
Assessments	
Total Reduction In Amount Due to Seller *(Total Charges to Seller)*	90,885.75

Cash at Settlement
(Reconciliation of Total Charges and Credits)

Cash At Settlement From/To Borrower

Gross amount due from borrower *(Total Charges to Borrower)*	114,904.14
Less amounts paid by/for Borrower *(Total Credits to Borrower)*	93,050.00
Cash X From ☐ To Borrower	21,854.14

Cash at Settlement To/From Seller

Gross amount due to seller *(Total Credits to Seller)*	110,000.00
Less reductions in amount due to seller *(Total Charges to Seller)*	90,885.75
Cash X To ☐ From Seller	19,114.25

12/02/09

Computation of figures on settlement statement:

Principal amount of new loan:	$110,000 sales price × 80% loan = $88,000 loan
Buyer's interim interest:	$88,000 loan amount × 10% = $8,800 annual interest $8,800 annual interest ÷ 360 days = $24.444 daily interest $24.444 daily interest × 16 days (Oct 15 to Oct 30) = $391.10 interest
Seller's accrued interest:	$82,750 loan balance × 10% = $8,275 annual interest $8,275 annual interest ÷ 360 days = $22.986 daily interest $22.986 daily interest × 15 days (Oct 1 to Oct 15) = $344.79 interest
Property taxes:	$1,100 ÷ 360 days = $3.056 daily taxes January 1 to October 15 = 285 days 285 × $3.056 = $870.96 (seller's taxes) $1,100.00 − $870.96 = $229.04 (buyer's taxes)
Revenue stamps:	$110,000 ÷ $500 = 220 × $1 = $220
Broker's commission:	$110,000 × 6% = $6,600
Loan origination fee:	$88,000 × 1% = $880
Discount points:	$88,000 × 1.5% = $1,320
Buyer's statement:	Buyer's debits $114,904.14 − Buyer's credits $93,050.00 $21,854.14 balance (cash) due from buyer
Seller's statement:	Seller's credits $110,000.00 − Seller's debits $90,885.75 $19,114.25 balance (cash) due to seller

Index

SYMBOLS

360-day year/30-day month method, 354
365-day year/actual-days-in-the-month method, 355

A

Abstract of title, 97, 102
Acceleration clause, 279
Acceptance, 215, 216
Accession, 25
Accounting, 147, 157
Accretion, 22
Accrued items, 354, 355
Action to quiet title, 93
Adaptation test, 24
Addenda, 221, 222
Adjustable-rate mortgage (ARM), 286, 287
Adjusted basis, 427, 430
Adjusted cost basis, 434
Adjustment, 220
Adjustment period, 287
Administrative law judge (ALJ), 446
Ad valorem tax, 54, 59
Adverse possession, 92, 102
Advertising, 328, 452
Aesthetic zoning, 112
Affidavit of lien waiver, 343
After-tax cash flow, 487
Age-life method, 404
Agency
    creation, 130, 156
    definition, 128, 156
    disclosure, 139, 190
    law of, 127
    relationship, 130, 132, 139
    termination, 132, 156
Agent
    breach of duty, 153
    definition, 128, 156
    due diligence, 194, 206
    principal's duties to, 153
    responsibilities, 145, 198
    third party responsibilities, 148, 157
Agricultural fixture, 26, 40
Agricultural property, 10, 15
Air rights, 20, 39
Alienation, 79
Alienation clause, 279, 299
ALTA (American Land Title Association) policy, 98
Americans with Disabilities Act Accessibility Guidelines (ADAAG), 450
Americans with Disabilities Act (ADA)
    commercial lease provisions, 252
    exempt properties, 457
    Federal Fair Housing Act and, 451
    new construction requirements, 444

property management issues, 268, 272
    purpose, 119
Amortization, 284, 285
Amortized loans, 280
Annexation, 24
Annual percentage rate (APR), 327
Anticipation, 392
Anticyclical efforts, 13
Antitrust laws, 183, 206
Appraisal
    definition, 8, 14, 57, 389, 409
    due diligence, 340
    fair housing practices, 452
    fees, 353
    methods, 398
    process, 393
    profession, 408
Appraiser, 409
Appreciation, 484
Appropriation, 55
Approved attorney state, 98
Appurtenance, 19, 39
Architectural styles, 376
Area preference, 4
Arm's-length transaction, 398
Asbestos, 463, 477
Assessed value, 54
Assessment, 54, 57, 59
Assignment
    of contract, 169, 174
    of lease, 242
    of mortgage, 289
Assumption
    fees, 285
    rules, 314, 316
Attorney's fees, 351
Auction, 172
Automated underwriting, 323
Avulsion, 22

B

Backup contract addendum, 223
Backup offer, 223
Balloon framing, 378
Balloon payment, 281, 288
Banker's year/banker's month method, 354
Bargain and sale deed, 84, 102
Baseboards, 384
Base line, 66, 73
Basement, 377
Basis, 427
Before-tax cash flow, 487
Beneficiary, 93, 276, 299
Bequest, 93, 102
Bilateral agreement, 236
Bilateral contract, 164, 173
Blanket loan, 332
Blanket mortgage, 319

Blockbusting, 451
Bona fide lease, 248
Bonding, 270
Boot, 431
Breach of contract, 170
Breakdown method, 404
Broad form (HO-2), 417
Broker, 7
    authority, 130
    commission, 181, 205
    compensation, 350
    definition, 14, 129
    documentation preparation, 171
    fair housing implications, 448
    responsibilities, 120
    role, 7
    settlement statement, 349
Brokerage
    business, 154
    definition, 7, 14, 129
    fee, 191
    services, 193
Broker-in-charge (BIC)
    agency policy, 128
    licensed associate relationship, 154
Broker price opinion (BPO), 196, 390, 409
BTU, 385
Budget comparison statement, 263
Buffer zones, 110
Building codes, 12, 117, 122, 385, 386
Building permit, 117
Bundle of legal rights, 19, 39
Business cycles, 13
Buydown, 320, 332
Buyer
    agency, 133
    agency agreement, 199, 202
    due diligence, 219, 339, 370
    loan, 339
    obligations, 220
    possession, 222
    prequalifying, 322
    respresentations, 220
    right of rescission, 198
    working with, 199
Buyer's agent
    responsibilities, 201
    switching from seller subagent, 200
    working with buyers, 200, 207
    working with sellers, 202

C

Caissons, 20
Calls, 64
CAN-SPAM Act (Controlling the Assault of Non-Solicited Pornography and Marketing Act), 181
Capacity to contract, 241

802

Capital expenditures, 262
Capital gain, 427, 434
Capitalization rate, 405, 410
Capital loss, 427, 434
Capping, 471
Carbon monoxide, 467, 478
Cash flow
    definition, 485
    formula, 263
    report, 263
Cash-on-cash rate of return, 488
Cash reserve fund, 262
Cash throw-off, 487
Casualty insurance, 270, 416
Caveat emptor, 127
Ceiling joists, 378
Certificate of eligibility, 316
Certificate of occupancy (CO), 117, 122, 385, 386
Certificate of reasonable value (CRV), 316
Certified general appraiser, 389
Certified residential appraiser, 389
Chain of title, 96, 102
Change, 393
Channeling, 452
Chattel, 2, 40
Civil Rights Act of 1866, 440, 455
Clean Air Act Amendments, 478
Client
    definition, 128, 156
    solicitation, 179
Closing
    definition, 338, 370
    delay, 221
    documents, 341
    finalizing, 344
    IRS requirement, 344
    procedures, 343
Closing exercise worksheet, 364, 365
Cloud on title, 84, 102
Cluster zoning, 110
Code of ethics, 454
Coinsurance clause, 419, 422
Color of title, 92
Commercial banks, 307
Commercial lease, 242
Commercial property, 10, 15
Commingling, 147
Commission
    brokerage, 129
    calculation, 196
    entitlement, 181, 206
    sharing, 181
Common elements, 36, 42
Common interest community ownership, 36
Comparables, 399, 410
Comparative market analysis (CMA)
    comparable selection, 401
    definition of, 389, 409
    listing price and, 195
Compensatory damages, 170, 174
Competition, 393
Comprehensive Environmental Response, Compensation, and Liability Act (CERCLA), 473, 479
Comprehensive Loss Underwriting Exchange (CLUE), 422

Computerized loan origination (CLO), 323, 346
Conciliation, 446
Concrete slab, 377
Concurrent ownership, 32, 36, 41
Condemnation, 90
Condition, 418, 421
Conditional-use permit, 111
Condominium, 36
Condominium laws, 41
Condominium ownership, 36
Confidentiality, 145, 157, 203
Confirmation of compensation form, 191
Conforming loan, 311, 312, 331
Conformity, 392
Conner Act, 100, 103, 244
Consequential damages, 171, 174
Consequential loss insurance, 270
Consideration, 167, 240
Construction
    costs, 11
    elements of, 378
    loan, 319, 332
    property management, 267
Constructive eviction, 245, 251
Constructive notice, 99, 103
Consumer Financial Protection Bureau (CFPB), 305
Consumer protection, 37
Contents and personal property insurance, 270
Contingencies, 212
Contingent sale addendum, 224
Contract
    definition, 164
    discharge of, 170, 173
    law, 164
    legal effects, 165
    performance, 169
    period, 260
    preprinted forms, 172
    rate, 286
    written requirements, 214
Contractor licensing, 386
Contribution, 392
Controlled business arrangement (CBA), 346
Conventional life estate, 29
Conventional loan, 311, 325, 331
Conversion option, 287
Conveyance, 79
Cooperating broker, 129, 192
Cooperative, 38, 42
Corporation, 489
Correction deed, 89
Corrective maintenance, 267
Cost approach, 401, 402, 410
Cost basis, 427
Cost-benefit analysis, 265
Counseling, 8, 15
Counteroffer
    contract law, 167, 173
    sales contract, 215, 224
Counterparts, 225
Covenant, 81, 102
Covenant of quiet enjoyment, 243, 252
Covenants, conditions, and restrictions (CC&R), 50, 58
Crawl space, 377
Creation of a condominium, 37

Credit
    application, 321
    history, 322
    score, 321, 332
    settlement statement accounting, 350, 351, 371
Credit union, 307
Customer
    allocation, 184
    definition, 128, 156
    solicitation, 179

D

Data sheet, 188
Debit, 350, 351, 371
Debt
    collateral, 276
    liquidation, 284
    ratio, 325
    service, 280
Debt service, 280
Deceased person, 93
Declaration of restrictive covenants, 119
Declaration page, 418
Deductibles, 418
Deed
    definition, 79, 80
    elements, 79
    executed pursuant to court order, 89
    in lieu of foreclosure, 295, 299
    nonessential elements, 80, 101
    reference, 71, 73
    restriction, 50, 58, 116
    transfer tax, 352
    types, 81, 101
Deed of trust
    definition, 299
    document, 288
    explanation, 277
    lien, 47
    sample, 290, 291, 292
Default, 170, 243, 276
Deficiency judgment, 295, 299, 300
Deliberate agreement, 166
Delivery and acceptance, 80
Demand, 10, 12, 15
Demographics, 12, 15
Department of Housing and Urban Development (HUD)
    advertising guidelines, 453
    fair housing, 441
    FHA, 313
    minimum standards, 385
Depository Institutions Deregulation and Monetary Control Act, 282
Depreciation, 403, 431, 435
Descent and distribution statute, 93
Designated agency, 138
Designated agent, 135, 157, 194
Designated dual agency, 138
Devise, 93, 102
Devisee, 93
Direct public ownership, 121
Direct reduction loans, 280
Direct Single Family Housing Loan, 318
Disclosed dual agency, 135

Disclosure
    loan servicing requirements, 348
    RESPA requirements, 346
Discount points
    calculation, 285
    explanation, 282, 300
    investor yield, 283
Discount rate, 11, 306
Dominant tenement, 50
Dual agency
    authorization, 194, 203
    definition, 134, 203
Dual agent
    definition, 134
    working as, 203
Due diligence
    buyer's process, 219, 370
    by agent, 194
    fee, 218, 353
    period, 218, 339
Due-on-sale clause, 279, 299

E

Earnest money
    as damages, 171
    handling of, 193
    sales contract provisions, 217
Easement, 52
    appurtenant, 50
    by appurtenant, 58
    by necessity, 52, 58
    by prescription, 52, 58
    creation, 52
    definition, 50, 58
    in gross, 52, 58
    termination, 52, 59
Eave, 378
Economic characteristics, 4
Economic forces, 391
Economic life, 404
Economic obsolescence, 404
Education, 8, 15
Effective age, 404
Effective date, 218
Effective gross income (EGI), 263, 487
EIFS. See Exterior insulating finishing system
Electromagnetic field (EMF), 468, 478
Emblements, 23, 40
Eminent domain, 90, 102
Employee, 154, 158
Employment, 13, 15
Employment contract, 179, 204
Enabling acts, 109, 121
Encapsulation, 464
Encroachment, 53, 59
Encumbrance, 46, 58
End loan, 319
Endorsement, 418, 421
Endowment fund, 307
Entitlement, 317
Environmental hazards, 463, 476, 479
Environmental issues, 241, 268, 462
Environmental protection legislation, 118
Equal Credit Opportunity Act (ECOA), 328, 333, 447, 456
Equal housing opportunity poster, 442
Equitable right of redemption, 299

Equitable title, 276
Equity, 288
Equity buildup, 486
Equity dividend rate, 488
Equity of redemption, 294
Erosion, 22
Escheat, 90, 102
Escrow account, 347, 352
Escrow agent, 217, 371
Escrow type settlement, 343
Estate
    at sufferance, 238, 252
    at will, 237, 252
    definition, 26
    for years, 236, 252
    from period to period, 237, 252
    in land, 26
    of inheritance, 27
Estovers, 31
Ethics, 454
Eviction, 247
Excise tax, 89, 102, 352
Exclusion, 19, 418, 421
Exclusive-agency listing, 184, 205
Exclusive buyer-agency agreement, 201
Exclusive right-to-sell listing, 185, 205
Executed contract, 165, 173
Executory contract, 165, 173
Expense, 349, 353
Express agreement, 131
Express contract, 164, 173
Extender clause, 192
Exterior doors, 381
Exterior walls, 380, 381
Extra-territorial jurisdiction (ETJ), 110, 122

F

Face-to-face closing, 343
Fair and Accurate Credit Transaction Act (FACT Act), 328
Fair Credit Reporting Act, 328
Fair housing
    prohibited practices, 451
Fair Housing Amendments Act, 455
Familial status, 441, 456
Fannie Mae, 12, 308, 309, 331
Farm Service Agency (FSA), 317
Fascia board, 378
Federal Emergency Management Agency (FEMA), 118, 420
Federal Fair Housing Act
    enforcement, 446
    exemptions, 445, 456
    prohibitions under, 455
    protected classes under, 440
    restrictions, 443
Federal Housing Administration (FHA)
    minimum standards, 113, 116
    purpose, 313
Federal Housing Finance Agency, 309
Federally related loan, 345
Federal Open Market Committee, 305
Federal Reserve Board, 11
Federal Reserve System, 305, 330
Fee for services, 129
Fee-for-services agreement, 185, 186, 206

Fee simple, 40
    absolute, 28
    defeasible, 28, 40
    determinable, 28, 40
    estate, 28
    subject to a condition subsequent, 28, 40
FHA-insured loan
    definition, 313
    explanation, 313
    financing addendum, 222
    mortgage insurance premium, 332
    programs, 314
    qualifying ratios, 326
    VA program comparisons, 315
Fiduciary, 128, 145
Fiduciary lenders, 307
Final value estimate, 394
Financial Institutions Reform, Recovery and Enforcement Act (FIRREA), 389
Financial policies, 11
Financing
    calculations, 284
    definition, 8, 15
    legislation, 327
Fire and hazard insurance, 270
First substantial contact, 140
Fixed lease, 238, 252
Fixed rate-level payment mortgage, 285
Fixture, 24
    definition, 40
    example, 24
    lease provisions, 241
    legal tests, 24
    sales contract provisions, 219
Floating slab, 377
Flood hazard area, 118
Flood insurance, 118
Flood insurance program, 420
Floor joist, 378
Footings, 376, 386
Foreclosure, 293
Foreign broker, 183
Foreshore, 21
Foundation, 376
Foundation walls, 377, 386
Frame, 378, 386
Fraud, 148, 158
Freddie Mac, 12, 309, 331
Freehold estate, 27, 40
Friendly foreclosure, 295
Frieze board, 378
Frontage, 188
Fructus industriales, 23, 39
Fructus naturales, 23, 39
Full-service lease, 240
Fully amortized fixed-rate mortgage, 280, 299
Functional obsolescence, 403
Future interest, 29, 30

G

Gain, 427
General agent, 130, 156, 259
General data, 393
General lien, 48, 58
General partnership, 489, 491
General plan, 109
General tax, 54

General warranty deed
   definition, 81, 101
   sample, 82, 83
Gift deed, 89
Ginnie Mae, 12, 308, 309, 331
Girder, 378
Good faith estimate (GFE)
   disclosure requirements, 346
   RESPA requirements, 371
Good Funds Settlement Act, 344
Government controls, 11, 15
Government financial policies, 15
Government ownership, 121
Government survey system, 65, 73
Graduated lease, 239, 252
Graduated payment mortgage (GPM), 287
Grantee, 79, 80, 101
Granting clause, 80, 101
Grantor, 79, 101, 276, 299
Gratuitous agency, 132
Gross income multiplier (GIM), 407
Gross lease, 238, 252
Gross profit, 433
Gross rent multiplier (GRM), 407
Ground lease, 240, 252
Groundwater, 468, 478
Group boycotting, 184
Growing-equity mortgage (GEM), 288, 332
Guaranteed Single Family Housing Loan, 318

H

Habendum clause, 101
Handicapping condition, 444, 456
Hazardous substances, 462
Header, 378
Heated living area, 195
Heterogeneity, 4
Highest and best use, 5, 392, 393
Highway access restrictions, 118
Historic preservation zoning, 112
HO-3 policy, 418, 421
Holdover tenant, 238, 252
Home construction, 382
Home equity loan, 320, 332
Home Mortgage Disclosure Act, 453
Home office, 429
Homeowners association, 36
Homeowners' insurance policy, 416, 417, 421
Homeowners Protection Act, 312
Homestead, 31
   exemption, 31
Home warranty, 220
Horizontal adjustment, 57
Horizontal property acts, 36
Housing, 443
Housing and Community Development Act, 455
Housing and Economic Recovery Act, 311
Housing for Older Persons Act, 445, 456
HVAC, 384, 386
Hypothecation, 277, 298

I

Identification survey, 72
Imminently dangerous condition, 245
Immobility, 4

Implied agreement, 131
Implied contract, 164, 173
Implied warranty of habitability, 245, 251
Impossibility of performance, 170
Impound account, 352
Improvement, 4
Income capitalization approach, 405
Income ratio, 325
Independent contractor, 154, 158
Indestructibility, 4
Index, 286
Index lease, 239, 252
Indirect misrepresentation, 149
Industrial lease, 241
Industrial property, 10, 15
Inflation, 484
Informal description, 64
Informal reference, 71, 73
Information disclosure, 146, 157
Informed consent, 135
In-house sale, 138
Innocent landowner immunity, 474
Inspection, 341
Installment land contract, 226, 231
Installment sale, 430, 435
Insulation, 383
Insurability issues, 420
Insurable interest, 418
Insurance
   claims, 271
   companies, 307
   coverage types, 270
   due diligence, 339
   reserves, 352
Intent, 454
Intention, 24
Interest, 280, 284
Interest-only balloon payment loan, 288
Interest-only mortgage, 286
Interest rate
   calculation, 281
   cap, 286
   FHA-insured loan, 314
Interim interest, 358
Interior finishes, 384
Internal Revenue Service (IRS)
   employee/independent contractor distinction, 155
   qualified agent under, 155
   reporting requirement, 344, 371
   tax lien, 49
Internet, 185
Internet Advertising Addendum, 193
Interstate Land Sales Full Disclosure Act, 116, 122
Intestate, 90
Intestate succession, 93
Investment
   decisions, 6
   permanence, 5
Investment group financing, 307
Involuntary alienation, 90, 102
Involuntary lien, 47

J

Joint tenancy, 33, 36, 41
Judgment, 48
Judicial foreclosure, 276, 293, 298
Jumbo loan, 312
Junk Fax Prevention Act, 180

K

Kelo v. City of New London, 91
Kickbacks, 345, 348

L

Labor force, 11
Laches, 120
Land
   acquisition costs, 72
   definition, 2, 14
   economic characteristics, 4
   physical characteristics, 4
   value, 393
Landfill, 470, 478
Landlord
   duties, 266
   obligations, 245, 251
   right to enter, 243
   statutory duties, 245
Land-use
   concepts, 5
   controls, 6, 12
   private controls, 119, 122
   public controls, 108, 121
Lateral support, 22
Law of negligence, 246, 251
Lead, 477
Lead-based paint, 464
Lead-based paint addendum, 222
Lead-Based Paint Hazard Reduction Act, 193, 266, 477
Lead-Based Paint Poisoning Act, 465
Lead poisoning, 464
Leaking Petroleum Underground Storage Tank Cleanup Act, 474
Lease
   characteristics, 238
   default, 243
   definition, 236, 251
   environmental issues, 241
   provisions, 240, 252
   renewal, 242
   term, 242
   termination, 243
   types, 238
Leased fee estate plus reversionary right, 236
Leasehold estate, 27, 236, 252
Legacy, 93, 102
Legal description
   deed provisions, 80
   definition, 64, 73
Legality of object, 167
Legal life estate, 31
Legally competent parties, 166
Legal objectives, 241
Lender
   closing role, 344
   rights, 289
Lessee, 236, 251

Lessor, 236, 251
Level-payment amortized loan, 281
Leverage, 483, 485, 490
Liability insurance, 270, 416
License, 53
Lien, 47
    agent, 48
    definition, 47, 58
    effects, 49
    foreclosure, 92
    priority, 49, 58
    theory, 276
    types, 47
Lien theory, 276, 298
Life cycle, 393
Life estate, 29, 41
Life tenant, 29, 31
Like-kind property, 431
Limited common element, 37
Limited liability company (LLC), 489, 490
Limited partnership, 489, 491
Limited service broker, 202
Limited-service listing agreement, 187, 206
Limited warranty deed, 84
Liquidated damages, 171, 174
Liquidity, 483, 490
Lis pendens, 50, 58
Listing agreement
    definition, 179, 204
    form, 189
    purpose, 179
    term, 190
    termination, 189
    types, 184
Listing price, 191
Littoral rights, 21, 40
Livery of seisin, 19
Loan
    expense, 426
    fees, 352
    fraud legislation, 329
    origination fee, 283, 285, 352
    servicing, 348
Loan-to-value ratio (LTV), 311, 331
Location, 4
Locational obsolescence, 404
Long-term capital gain, 427, 434
Loss, 432
Lot-and-block, 70, 73
Loyalty, 145, 157

M

Machinery Act, 54, 55, 59
Mailbox rule, 216, 231
Management fee, 260
Management plan, 262
Manufactured home, 22, 23, 40
Margin, 286
Market
    allocation, 184
    definition, 10
    price, 391
    supply and demand, 15
Marketable title, 96, 103
Marketable Title Act, 97, 103

Market value
    cost versus, 391
    definition, 390, 409
    explanation, 196
    market price versus, 391
Mass appraisal, 57
Master plan, 108, 121
Material facts, 148, 149, 194
Mechanic's lien, 48
Meeting of the minds, 166
Merger, 53
Metes-and-bounds description, 64, 65, 73
Mill, 55, 59
Mineral deed, 89
Minimum standards, 385
Mitigation, 466
Modular home, 23, 40
Mold, 471, 478
Money judgment, 48
Monolithic slab, 377
Monument, 65, 73
Mortgage, 277
    assumption, 297
    debt reduction, 285
    definition, 298
    instrument, 276, 288
    interest, 357
    loan types, 311
    location survey, 72
    priority, 321
    repayment plans, 285, 300
Mortgage-backed securities, 308
Mortgage banking companies, 307
Mortgage brokers, 308
Mortgage Debt Relief Act, 296
Mortgagee, 276, 298
Mortgage insurance premium (MIP), 332
Mortgagor, 276, 277, 298
Mountain Ridge Protection Act, 475
Multi-peril policies, 270
Multiple listing service (MLS)
    creation, 127
    explanation, 187
    information needed, 188
Multiple-use zoning, 110
Mutual agreement, 170, 240
Mutual assent, 166

N

National Association of REALTORS® (NAR), 9
National Do Not Call Registry, 180, 205
National Flood Insurance Act, 420, 422
National Flood Insurance Program (NFIP), 118
National Flood Insurance Reform Act, 299
Navigable waters, 21
Negative amortization, 286
Negligent misrepresentation, 149, 158
Negligent omission, 149, 151, 158
Negotiable instrument, 278
Neighborhood life cycle, 393
Neighborhood market analysis, 262
Net lease, 239, 252
Net listing, 192, 205
Net operating income (NOI), 263, 405, 410
Net profit, 433
No documentation loan, 310

Nonconforming loan, 312
Nonconforming use, 111
Nonexclusive buyer-agency agreement, 200
Nonfreehold estate, 27, 236
Nonhomogeneity, 4
Nonjudicial foreclosure, 293
Nonverbal harassment, 448
Non-warranty deed
    definition, 84
    sample, 87, 88
North Carolina Appraisers Act, 389
North Carolina Association of REALTORS® (NCAR), 9
North Carolina Coastal Area Management Act (CAMA), 474
North Carolina Commercial Real Estate Broker Lien, 48, 58
North Carolina Condominium Act of 1986, 37, 42
North Carolina Department of Insurance (NCDI), 117
North Carolina Department of Transportation (DOT), 115
North Carolina Dredge and Fill Act, 475
North Carolina Fair Housing Act, 447, 457
North Carolina Human Relations Commission, 448
North Carolina Intestate Succession Act, 93
North Carolina Leaking Petroleum Underground Storage Tank Cleanup Act, 474
North Carolina Real Estate Commission (NCREC), 9
    commission arrangements, 184
    material facts, 149
    oral agency agreement, 179
    preprinted forms, 212
    residential square footage guidelines, 195
    trust account, 266
    written agreement requirements, 168
North Carolina Real Estate Licensing Law, 149
North Carolina Residential Property Disclosure Act, 194, 197, 206, 223
North Carolina Sediment Pollution Control Act, 475
North Carolina Time Share Act, 38, 42
North Carolina Uniform Commercial Code (UCC), 26
North Carolina Vacation Rental Act, 250, 252
Note rate, 286
Novation, 169, 170, 242

O

Obedience, 145, 157
Octennial reappraisal, 55, 59
Offer
    communication, 215, 231
    contract requirements, 214
    copies of, 225
    modification, 224
    response, 225
    revocation, 167, 173
    submission, 224
    termination, 231
Offer and acceptance, 166
Offeree, 214
Offeror, 214

Offer to Purchase and Contract, 193
Office of Fair Housing and Equal Opportunity (OFHEO), 446
Oil and mineral lease, 240
OLD CAR, 145, 157
Open-end loan, 332
Open-end mortgage, 319
Open listing, 184, 205
Open market operation, 305
Operating budget, 262
Operating expenses, 263, 487
Operating statement, 487, 488
Operation of law, 170
Option
    definition, 228
    requirements, 229
    to purchase, 231, 243
Optionee, 228, 231
Optionor, 228, 231
Oral agency agreement, 179
Oral buyer agency, 143, 200
Overlay district, 112
Override
    clause, 192
Oversupply, 10
Owners' association disclosure, 223
Ownership
    in severalty, 32, 41
    rights of, 19
Owner's title insurance policy, 99

P

Package insurance, 416
Package loan, 319, 332
Paid outside of closing (POC), 347, 352
Panic peddling, 451
Parcel, 2
Parol evidence rule, 168, 173
Partial estate, 29
Partially amortized fixed-rate mortgage, 281
Partially amortized loan, 288
Partial performance, 170
Partial release clause, 319
Partnership, 489, 491
Party wall, 52
Payment cap, 286
Pension fund, 307
Percentage lease, 238, 239, 252
Percolation test, 340
Periodic tenancy, 237, 252
Personal property
    definition, 2, 22, 40
    listing agreement provision, 191
    real property versus, 22
    sales contract provisions, 219
    tax lien, 49
Personalty, 2, 40
Physical characteristics, 3
Physical deterioration, 403
Physical forces, 391
Physical harassment, 448
Physical survey, 72
Piers, 377, 386
Piggyback loan, 312
Pitch, 383, 386
Planned unit development (PUD), 39
Planning commissions, 114
Plants, 23
Platform framing, 378
Plat map, 70, 114
Point of beginning (POB), 64, 73
Point of equilibrium, 10
Points
    FHA-insured loan, 314
    VA-guaranteed loan, 317
Police power, 108, 121
Political forces, 391
Population, 12, 15
Possession, 19, 221
Potential gross income, 263
Potentially responsible parties (PRP), 473
Power of sale foreclosure, 276, 293
Preclosing procedures, 338
Predatory Lending Act, 329
Preemptive right, 229, 231
Premium, 416
Prepaid items, 354, 356
Prepayment
    FHA-insured loan, 314
    promissory note, 279
    VA-guaranteed loan, 317
Preventive maintenance, 267
Price fixing, 183
Primary mortgage market, 306, 330
Prime rate, 306
Principal, 280
    agent's responsibilities, 145, 157
    definition, 128
    duties, 153
Principal and interest payment (P&I), 280
Principal, interest, taxes, insurance (PITI), 284
Principal meridian, 66, 73
Principal residence, 428
Principle of contribution, 262
Priority, 49, 58
Private mortgage insurance (PMI), 312, 332
Procuring cause, 182, 206
Professional advice, 203
Professional designations, 9
Professional ethics, 454
Professional organizations, 9
Professional Services Disclosure and Election, 193
Profile sheet, 188
Profitability, 486
Profit and loss statement, 263
Promissory note, 276, 278, 299
Property
    analysis, 262
    charges, 238
    condition, 220
    condition checklist, 266
    damages, 249
    description, 191, 259
    development, 8, 15
    disclosure statement, 197
    insurance, 416
    investigation, 339
    maintenance, 266
    price, 195
    report, 117
    type, 203
    value, 391
Property management
    agreement, 139, 259, 271
    definition, 8, 15
    duties, 260
    fee, 261
Property manager
    accountability, 266
    authority, 260
    definition, 15, 259, 271
    duties, 272
    environmental concerns, 268
    functions, 259
    licensing requirements, 258
    responsibilities, 260
    risk management, 269
Property tax
    categories, 53
    formulas, 56
    lien, 57
Property tax rate, 55
Proprietary lease, 38, 42
Proration
    accrued item calculation, 355
    assumed loan interest, 358
    calculation, 354, 369
    items, 358
    new loan interest, 358
    prepaid item calculation, 356
    rent calculation, 357
    rules, 356
    sales contract provisions, 220
Protected classes, 440
Protecting Tenants at Foreclosure Act of 2009, 247
Protection agreement, 185, 205
Protection period clause, 192
Protective covenant, 119
Provisional broker, 8, 14, 129, 154
Public housing, 250
Public liability insurance, 270
Public offering statement, 37
Public use, 92
Puffing, 148, 158, 188
Pur autre vie, 30, 41
Purchase money mortgage, 318, 332
Purchase price, 217
Pure race statute, 100
Pure race system, 49

Q

Qualified fee estate, 28
Qualified real estate agent, 155
Qualifying ratios, 322
Qualifying standards, 322
Quantity-survey method, 403
Quitclaim deed
    definition, 84, 102
    sample, 87, 88

R

Race, 455
Radon, 466, 477
Rafters, 378
Ranch-style homes, 376
Range, 66
Range lines, 73

Rapid-payoff mortgage, 332
Rate of return, 486
Ratification, 131
Ready, willing, and able buyer, 181, 182
Real estate
    business, 7
    characteristics, 2, 3, 4, 14
    cycle, 13
    definition, 2, 14
    economic characteristics, 5
    specializations, 7
Real estate investment
    advantages, 6, 482, 490
    concepts, 5
    disadvantages, 6, 483, 490
    ownership forms, 488
    tax benefits, 430
    value, 7
Real estate investment trust (REIT), 489, 491
Real Estate Settlement Procedures Act (RESPA)
    consumer protection, 345
    controlled business arrangement, 346
    disclosure requirements, 346
    escrow restrictions, 347
    mortgage loan requirements, 345
    penalties, 348
    purpose, 371
    requirements, 329, 371
Reality of consent, 167
Real property, 2
    characteristics, 3
    definition, 2, 3, 14, 22
    encumbrance, 46
    estates, 26
    ownership, 32
    personal property versus, 22
    tax lien, 47
    types, 15
    uses, 10
REALTOR-ASSOCIATES®, 9
REALTORS®, 9
Realty, 2
Reasonable accommodations, 450
Reasonable skill and care, 147, 157
Reconciliation, 408, 410
Recorded plat, 73
Recorded plat system, 70
Recording, 99, 352
Recordkeeping, 266
Rectangular survey system, 65, 66, 68, 73
Redemption, 294
Redlining, 453
Reference, 64
Reference to a recorded plat, 70
Referral fee, 183, 348
Regional market analysis, 262
Regulation X, 345
Regulation Z, 327, 333
Relationship test, 24
Release deed, 89
Reliction, 22
Remainder interest, 30
Remainderman, 29, 30
Renewal clause, 243
Renovation, 267

Rent
    collection, 266
    proration, 357
    rates, 264
    schedule, 264
    withholding, 246
Rental commissions, 265
Repair, 242, 267, 340
Repair loans/grants, 318
Replacement cost, 402
Reporting, 260
Reproduction cost, 402
Resale unit, 37
Rescission, 171, 174
Reserve requirements, 305
Residential Lead-Based Paint Hazard Reduction Act, 222, 465
Residential Mortgage Fraud Act, 329
Residential property, 10, 15
Residential Property and Owners' Association Disclosure Statement, 193, 197
Residential Rental Agreement Act
    landlord negligence under, 246
    purpose, 244
    withholding rent provisions, 246
Residual-income method, 326
Resource Conservation and Recovery Act, 470
Response to Buyer's Offer, 225, 231
Restrictive covenants
    declaration of, 119
    definition, 119
    subdivision regulations, 116
Retainer fee, 182
Retaliatory eviction, 247, 251
Return on investment (ROI), 488, 490
Revenue stamp, 89
Reverse mortgage, 320
Reversionary interest, 29, 30
Reversionary right, 28
Ridge boards, 378, 386
Right of defeasance, 289
Right of first opportunity to purchase, 229
Right of first refusal, 229, 243
Right of survivorship, 33, 35, 41
Right to terminate, 340
Riparian rights, 21, 40
Risk management, 269, 272
Roof designs, 383
Roof framing, 378
Roof framing systems, 379
Roofing felt, 381
Roofing materials, 381
Routine maintenance, 267
Row house, 38
Rural Economic and Community Development Services (USDA), 317
Rural Housing Service Agency, 318
R-value, 384, 386

S

Safe Drinking Water Act (SDWA), 468, 478
Sale-and-leaseback, 319
Sales comparison approach, 398, 410
Sales contract
    addenda, 221, 222
    provisions, 216, 230
    purpose, 211
    Rule A.0112, 213

Sales price, 196
Sandwich lease, 242
Satisfaction of mortgage, 289
Savings associations, 307
Scarcity, 4
Scheduled gross income (SGI), 487
School section, 67
Secondary mortgage market, 308, 331
Section, 67, 68
Security, 276
Security deposit, 248, 358
Sedimentation, 475
Self-help eviction, 247, 251
Seller
    closing issues, 341
    nets to, 196
    obligations, 193, 220
    offer submission, 224
    possession, 222
    representations, 220
Septic system, 340
Servient tenement, 50
Setback, 109
Settlement
    agent, 344, 371
    date, 219
    definition, 219, 338, 370
    delay, 221
    meeting, 343
Settlement agent, 344
Settlement statement (HUD-1)
    broker's responsibility, 349
    completed form, 366, 367, 368
    completion, 350
    explanation, 370, 371
    preparation, 348
Severalty, 32, 36, 41
Severance, 23
Sex offender disclosure, 152
Sexual harassment, 448
Sexual harassment statutes, 251
Sheathing, 381
Sheriff's deed, 293
Sherman Antitrust Act, 184
Shingles, 381
Short sale, 295
Short sale addendum, 193, 223
Short-term capital gain, 427, 434
Siding, 381
Sill, 378, 386
Single agency, 133, 157
Single agent, 133
Situs, 4
Social forces, 391
Soffit, 378
Soil suitability test, 340
Sole plate, 378
Sole proprietorship, 490
Special agent, 130, 156, 259
Special assessment, 57, 59, 219, 357
Special assessment lien, 47
Special information booklet, 346
Specializations, 7
Special-purpose deed, 89
Special-purpose property, 10, 15, 404
Special-use permit, 111

Special warranty deed
    definition, 84, 102
    sample, 85, 86
Specific data, 393
Specific lien, 47, 58
Specific performance, 4, 171, 174
Split-level home, 376
Spot zoning, 112
Square footage, 195, 206
Square-foot method, 403
Standards of practice, 455
Stated income loan, 310
Statute of fraud
    lease recording, 244
    mineral lease provisions, 240
    written requirements, 168
Statute of limitations, 171
Statutory method, 354
Statutory redemption period, 294
Statutory right of redemption, 294
Steering, 452
Stigmatized properties, 152, 158
Straight-line method, 404
Straight loan, 332
Strict foreclosure, 293
Studs, 378, 386
Subagency, 134
    definition, 128
Subagent, 157
    definition, 128
    of seller, 200, 207
Subdivision
    definition, 113
    plan, 122
    PLAT, 116
    plat map, 70
    process, 114
    regulations, 113, 114
    street disclosure, 115
Subfloor, 378
Subjacent support, 22
Subject to mortgage, 297, 300
Sublease, 242
Subordination agreement, 58, 321
Subprime loan, 312
Subprime mortgage, 309
Subrogation clause, 420
Substantial performance, 170, 173
Substitution, 392
Subsurface rights, 20, 39
Success fee, 182
Suit to quiet title, 97
Summary ejection, 244, 247, 251
Sun rights, 20
Superfund Amendments and Reauthorization Act, 474
Superior lien, 49
Supply, 10, 11, 15
Supply and demand, 392
Surety bonds, 270
Surface rights, 20, 39
Survey, 71, 73, 340
Survey fees, 353
Survey sketch, 72
Syndicate, 489, 491

T

Take-out loan, 319
Takings Clause, 92
Tandem plan, 308
Tax
    basic concepts, 427
    effects, 12
    home office, 429
    homeowner benefits, 426
    incentives, 12
    levy, 55
    lien, 47, 49
    loss deduction, 432
    proration, 356
    real estate investment, 430
    reserves, 352
    sale benefits, 426
    sale of principal residence, 428
    timetable, 55, 57
Tax-deferred exchange, 431, 435
Telephone Consumer Protection Act, 180
Tenancy at sufferance, 238
Tenancy at will, 237
Tenancy by the entirety, 35, 36, 41
Tenancy for years, 236
Tenancy in common, 33, 41
Tenant
    damages, 249
    early termination, 248
    foreclosure protection, 247
    obligations, 245, 251
    public housing, 250
    selection, 265
    statutory duties, 246
    use of premises, 241
Tenant Security Deposit Act, 248, 251, 266
Tenants in common, 36
Termite protection, 377
Term loan, 286, 288, 332
Third party
    agent's responsibilities, 148, 157
    principal's duties to, 153
Threats, 454
Thrifts, 307
Tiers, 73
Timber deed, 89
Time is of the essence, 169
Time-share, 38
Time-share ownership, 38, 42
Title
    assurance, 96
    closing procedures, 342
    commitment, 99
    definition, 78, 101
    expense, 352
    insurance, 103
    lien effects, 49
    recordation, 99
    search, 96, 103
    theory, 276, 299
Title to airspace, 36
Topographic survey, 72
Top plate, 378
Torrens System, 100
Tort, 154
Total Circumstances Test, 24, 40
Town house, 38
Town house ownership, 38, 42
Township, 67, 69
Township line, 66, 73
Township square, 66
Township tier, 66
Trade fixture, 25, 40, 241
Trade organizations, 9
Trigger terms, 328
Tri-level home, 376
Truss framing, 378
Trustee, 276
Trustee's deed, 89, 293
Trustor, 276, 299
Truth in Lending Act, 327, 333
Two-story home, 376

U

UFFI. *See* Urea-formaldehyde foam insulation
Unbundling services, 186
Underground storage tank (UST), 469, 478
Underwriting guidelines, 322
Undisclosed dual agency, 135
Unenforceable contract, 166
Uniform Commercial Code (UCC), 40
Uniform Electronic Transactions Act (UETA), 214, 230
Uniform Residential Appraisal Report, 394, 395, 396, 397
Uniform Settlement Statement (HUD-1), 347
Unilateral contract, 165, 173
Unilateral subagency, 127
Unimproved land, 484
Uniqueness, 4
Unit-in-place method, 403
Universal agent, 130, 156
Unoccupied building exclusion, 419
Unrepresented seller, 202
Unrepresented Seller Disclosure and Fee Agreement, 185
Upfit allowance, 242
Up-fits, 25
Upset bid period, 294
Urea-formaldehyde foam insulation (UFFI), 467
Usury, 282, 300

V

Vacancy and collection loss, 263
Vacation home, 430
Vacation rental addendum, 223
Vacation rentals, 250
VA-guaranteed loan
    definition, 315, 316
    explanation, 332
    FHA program comparisons, 315
    financing addendum, 222
    qualifying ratios, 326
Valid contract, 165, 166
Value
    approaches to, 398
    characteristics, 390
    definition, 390
    principles, 391, 409
Variance, 111
Vendee, 226
Vendor, 226
Verbal harassment, 448

Vicarious liability, 134
Violent acts, 454
Voidable contract, 166, 173
Void contract, 165, 173
Voluntary alienation, 79, 101
Voluntary lien, 47

W

Wage levels, 13, 15
Walk-through, 341
Warranty deed, 81
Waste, 31
Waste disposal sites, 470, 478
Water rights, 20, 40
Water table, 468
Websites
    agency contracts, 204
    brokerage, 155
    construction, 386
    environmental issues, 477
    fair housing, 455
    financing, 298, 330
    insurance, 421
    investment, 489
    landlord/tenant issues, 251
    land-use, 121
    property description, 73
    property management, 271
    property ownership, 39
    property valuation, 409
    real estate concepts, 13
    sales contracts, 230
    settlement statement, 370
    taxation, 434
    title transfer, 101
Wetlands, 475
Will
    definition, 93
    title transfer by, 102
Willful misrepresentation, 149
Willful omission, 149, 151
Windows, 381
Working with Real Estate Agents brochure, 139, 141, 142, 157, 190
Workout arrangement, 296
Writ of attachment, 50
Writ of execution, 50

Y

Yield, 282, 283, 300
Yield spread premium, 347

Z

Zoning
    definition, 109
    disclosures, 113
    variations, 111
Zoning ordinance
    definition, 109, 121
    due-process, 110

Notes

Notes

Notes

Notes

Notes

Notes

Notes

Notes

Notes

Notes